A CONCORDANCE TO THE SHORT FICTION OF
D. H. LAWRENCE

A Concordance to the Short Fiction of

D. H. LAWRENCE

Edited by

Reloy Garcia and James Karabatsos

UNIVERSITY OF NEBRASKA PRESS • LINCOLN

Copyright © 1972 by the University of Nebraska Press
International Standard Book Number 0–8032–0807–3
Library of Congress Catalog Card Number 72–77195
Manufactured in the United States of America

CONTENTS

ACKNOWLEDGMENTS

The Complete Short Stories of D. H. Lawrence and *Four Short Novels of D. H. Lawrence* are reprinted by kind permission of The Viking Press. Stories from *The Woman Who Rode Away*, copyright 1927, copyrights renewed 1955 by Frieda Lawrence Ravagli, are reprinted by permission of Alfred A. Knopf. Grateful acknowledgment is also extended to Alfred A. Knopf, Inc., for permission to use *St. Mawr* and *The Man Who Died*, and to Alfred A. Knopf and Lawrence Pollinger, Ltd., for *The Virgin and the Gipsy*.

We should also like to thank Father Edward Sharp, S.J., who programmed our entire project and who made available to us the resources of the Creighton University Computer Center; Father Clement Schneider, S.J., Academic Vice-President of Creighton University, who once again provided necessary funds to complete the project; Dr. Lloyd J. Hubenka, colleague and friend, for his unhesitating support and encouragement; Kathy Hotovy, Jo Ann Leichliter, and Theresa Heise, who key-punched the short fiction, and Mary Lynn Strecker for typing other related parts of the concordance; and, especially, Lucy Karabatsos, who typed the final copy of the concordance.

INTRODUCTION

A Concordance to the Short Fiction of D. H. Lawrence consists of two major parts: a word index to the complete short stories and a word index to the short novels. A table of symbols, discussed below, immediately follows this introduction, and codes of abbreviation precede each major part of the concordance.

Since there is no standard collection of the short fiction of D. H. Lawrence, selection of the texts used was based on practical rather than textual considerations. Most of all, we hoped to make this concordance as widely usable as possible; thus, we chose those texts which promise to be in general circulation. Part One is based on the three-volume Compass edition of *The Complete Short Stories of D. H. Lawrence,* first issued by the Viking Press in 1961. The plates for that collection have an interesting history indeed, having first been used in the preparation of the Phoenix edition of *The Complete Short Stories of D. H. Lawrence in Three Volumes,* published by William Heinemann, Ltd., in 1955, with subsequent reprintings in 1958, 1960, 1963, 1965, and 1968. The original plates contained numerous errors, some of which were eliminated during the later Phoenix reprintings. However, the original Compass edition and its later reprintings were made from the original uncorrected plates. We chose the Compass set for several reasons: first, the Compass edition is more widely distributed in this country, and our concordance can be used with any of the Phoenix or Compass reprintings; secondly, the corrected Phoenix plates have not had all the errors eliminated (see errata sheet) ; lastly, we felt that it might be of some interest to Lawrentian scholars to trace the evolution of the plates. Part Two is based on the Compass edition of *Four Short Novels of D. H. Lawrence,* first issued by Viking Press in 1965, a collection selected, again, for its easy accessibility in this country, and on the single-volume Vintage edition of *St. Mawr* and *The Man Who Died,* published by Alfred A. Knopf, Inc., a book also in general circulation. Unfortunately, we found no acceptable paperbound edition of *The Virgin and the Gipsy,* and chose not to use the Bantam edition of this work because we did not feel that it would enjoy lasting circulation. Instead, we returned to the Phoenix edition in *The Short Novels of D. H. Lawrence,* volume 2, first published by William Heinemann, Ltd., in 1956.

In general, we followed the procedures outlined in our earlier *A Concordance to the Poetry of D. H. Lawrence.* We first key-punched the short fiction on our 1130 computer, one line per card, coding each entry by story (as abbreviated in our code of abbreviations), page, and line. Then each of us proofread the first IBM copy, omitting the words listed below. Next we corrected our own typographical errors, uncovering in the process a number of errors in the parent texts. The governing principle in compiling our deletion list was to omit only those common words for whose retention we saw no obvious or compelling reason and whose inclusion would have doubled the length of the index. On the other hand, where words, concepts, or images are of obvious or even limited interest to the student of Lawrence, we retained them despite their sometimes high frequencies. This index, then, excludes only the following words, which are listed together with their frequencies:

DELETION LIST

	I	II		I	II		I	II
A	7864	4778	AS	2146	1386	CANNOT	17	12
ABOUT	508	301	ASIDE	65	57	CAN'T	170	133
ABOVE	94	69	ASKED	404	260	COME	574	320
ACROSS	145	97	AT	2444	1354	COMES	27	24
AFTER	358	216	AWAY	546	363	COMING	144	102
AGAIN	637	399	B	3		COULD	837	430
AGAINST	224	99	BACK	472	323	DID	740	439
AH	98	99	BE	1110	818	DIDN'T	188	118
ALL	1255	911	BECAUSE	215	141	DO	741	567
ALMOST	341	175	BEEN	443	312	DOES	91	67
ALONG	112	52	BEFORE	261	156	DOESN'T	70	48
ALSO	117	77	BEGAN	194	80	DON'T	560	535
ALWAYS	313	227	BEHIND	143	80	DOWN	784	453
AM	163	213	BELOW	88	63	E	1	
AMONG	169	71	BETWEEN	233	109	EACH	110	34
AN	705	397	BEYOND	119	86	EVEN	356	276
AND	10362	6727	BOTH	93	50	EVER	187	117
ANOTHER	256	166	BUT	2263	1437	EVERY	95	64
ANY	275	232	BY	575	390	EVERYTHING	129	105
ARE	460	440	CAME	694	355	FAR	126	102
AROUND	45	28	CAN	263	210	FINE	127	72

	I	II		I	II		I	II
FOR	1872	1157	M	3	2	SAT	412	170
FORTH	30	17	MADE	392	254	SAW	330	240
FROM	1120	781	MAKE	200	171	SAY	283	256
GAVE	180	109	MAKES	25	46	SAYING	91	48
GET	315	188	MAKING	82	49	SAYS	39	15
GIVE	136	102	MANY	123	78	SEE	475	311
GO	621	396	MAY	75	85	SEEM	30	29
GOES	26	30	ME	1105	823	SEEMED	447	295
GOING	322	189	MIGHT	157	118	SEEN	89	56
GONE	219	139	MINE	55	28	SET	121	59
GOT	348	187	MOMENT	187	97	SHALL	187	185
GREAT	278	214	MORE	507	361	SHE	6994	3940
HAD	2546	1468	MOST	116	84	SHE'D	20	4
HAS	166	153	MUCH	282	230	SHE'LL	13	12
HAVE	802	697	MUST	307	171	SHE'S	64	40
HAVING	123	56	MY	677	482	SHOULD	270	198
HE	7788	3917	MYSELF	119	87	SINCE	68	47
HER	5946	3489	N	3		SIT	73	55
HERE	247	184	NEAR	165	110	SMALL	187	113
HERSELF	381	206	NEVER	501	362	SO	1217	1010
HE'S	146	113	NO	1013	765	SOME	454	295
HIM	2732	1362	NOR	83	66	SOMETHING	346	226
HIMSELF	507	235	NOT	1961	1210	SOON	94	55
HIS	4467	2315	NOW	573	387	SORT	201	160
HOW	373	272	O	4	9	STILL	475	293
HOWEVER	82	36	OF	7345	4635	STOOD	424	293
I	3406	2710	OFF	355	192	SUCH	118	145
IF	1151	785	OH	322	309	SUDDENLY	230	129
I'M	293	233	ON	2151	1290	SURE	156	102
IN	5584	3496	ONE	673	537	TAKE	205	130
INSIDE	105	73	ONLY	533	345	TAKEN	55	36
INTO	750	443	OR	550	441	TAKES	11	9
IS	997	951	OTHER	309	179	TAKING	58	35
ISN'T	82	92	OUR	123	74	TELL	122	113
IT	3692	2447	OUT	992	515	THAN	310	216
ITS	246	177	OVER	552	337	THAT	2179	1705
IT'S	326	214	OWN	396	265	THAT'S	226	94
ITSELF	54	53	P	1		THE	16784	11366
JUST	337	264	PERHAPS	143	110	THEIR	542	341
KEEP	92	68	PUT	329	180	THEM	617	401
KEPT	106	56	QUITE	288	241	THEN	1170	650
LEAVE	82	69	R	1		THERE	1211	765
LEFT	194	126	RATHER	346	246	THERE'S	78	58
LET	235	185	REALLY	251	243	THESE	107	99
LIKE	1184	867	REPLIED	233	107	THEY	1471	892
LITTLE	983	674	ROOM	226	112	THEY'RE	30	35
LONG	352	207	ROOMS	22	15	THEY'VE	9	13
LOOK	368	266	ROUND	366	285	THING	199	166
LOOKED	746	446	SAID	2598	1706	THINGS	208	136
LOOKING	312	189	SAME	152	153	THIS	825	524

	I	II		I	II		I	II
THOSE	99	81	WANT	305	267	WHOM	70	20
THOUGH	133	77	WANTED	259	184	WHOSE	57	40
THROUGH	313	174	WAS	6454	3461	WHY	427	321
TILL	167	93	WASN'T	65	42	WILL	396	337
TO	7013	4578	WATCHED	173	107	WITH	3335	2002
TOLD	70	44	WATCHING	107	69	WITHOUT	208	93
TOO	336	252	WAY	301	226	WON'T	91	115
TOOK	250	97	WE	489	309	WOULD	886	575
TOWARDS	163	103	WELL	464	287	YES	347	347
TURN	54	42	WENT	722	327	YET	337	196
TURNED	323	157	WERE	1267	692	YOU	2981	2430
TURNING	72	46	WHAT	933	705	YOU'D	64	33
UNDER	283	227	WHEN	823	514	YOU'LL	72	34
UP	1045	648	WHERE	323	217	YOUR	394	348
UPON	134	82	WHICH	570	359	YOU'RE	144	73
US	180	106	WHILE	186	112	YOU'VE	89	52
VERY	717	417	WHO	454	369			

As we have indicated, the Compass editions contain a number of errors, listed below by page and line. Where an error is clearly typographical we have noted it, corrected it in the index and marked that indexed entry with an asterisk, and indicated below that the error was corrected parenthetically (corr. *I, I* standing for Index) ; further, we have noted whether or not the error was corrected in a later Phoenix edition, by corr. *P, P* standing for Phoenix, or uncorr. *P*. Where we felt that there was a probable but not certain error we noted it but did not correct it. Because our computer concordance did not list punctuation, errors in punctuation are not listed in the following errata:

ERRATA

PART I: The Complete Short Stories

VOLUME I

Page-Line

8.10 for "YOUR'RE" read "YOU'RE" (corr. *I,* uncorr. *P*)

40.09 for "WEIGH" probably "WAY" (uncorr. *I,* uncorr. *P*)

42.24 for "AUT" read "OUT" (corr. and deleted *I,* corr. *P*)

46.36 for "SAUVELY" read "SUAVELY" (corr. *I,* corr. *P*)

47.13 for "SAM COURTS" read "SAM COUTTS" (corr. *I,* uncorr. *P*)

62.14 for "WAN'T" read "WANT" (corr. and deleted *I*, uncorr. *P*)

63.21 for "OFF" read "OF" (corr. *I*, corr. *P*)

78.2 for "RESERVATION" read "RESERVATIONS" (corr. *I*, uncorr. *P*)

106.37 for "KIT" read "KITS" (corr. *I*, uncorr. *P*)

109.5 for "AT" read "A" (corr. and deleted *I*, corr. *P*)

109.40 for "IT" probably "HE" (uncorr. *I*, uncorr. *P*)

113.11 insert "A" between "WITH" and "PIECE" (corr. and deleted *I*, uncorr. *P*)

124.2 probably insert "AN" between "WAS" and "ACCIDENT" (uncorr. *I*, uncorr. *P*)

130.10 for "IN" read "IT" (corr. *I*, uncorr. *P*)

140.26 for "HABERDANSHERY" read "HABERDASHERY" (corr. *I*, corr. *P*)

146.34 for "TENENTS" probably "TENETS" (uncorr. *I*, uncorr. *P*)

147.25 insert "A" between "LIKE" and "SICKLY" (corr. and deleted *I*, uncorr. *P*)

155.10 for "HIS" read "HER" (corr. and deleted *I*, corr. *P*)

157.32 for "THEY" read "THE" (corr. and deleted *I*, corr. *P*)

170.14 for "DOWNSTAIR" read "DOWNSTAIRS" (corr. *I*, uncorr. *P*)

174.10 for "HESELF" read "HERSELF" (corr. and deleted *I*, uncorr. *P*)

179.42 for "GOT" read "GET" (corr. *I*, corr. *P*)

186.17 for "LOOK" read "TOOK" (corr. and deleted *I*, uncorr. *P*)

190.01 for "DARE" probably "DARED" (uncorr. *I*, uncorr. *P*)

195.32 for "CRID" read "CRIED" (corr. *I*, corr. *P*)

201.07 for "ANSWERERED" read "ANSWERED" (corr. *I*, uncorr. *P*)

250.14 for "GIDDLY" read "GIDDY" (corr. *I*, uncorr. *P*)

257.29 for "NECESITY" read "NECESSITY" (corr. *I*, uncorr. *P*)

264.07 for "BLACK" probably "BACK" (uncorr. *I*, uncorr. *P*)

VOLUME II

286.38 for "GRATEFULLY" probably "GRACEFULLY" (uncorr. *I*, uncorr. *P*)

297.31 for "BUSINES" read "BUSINESS" (corr. *I*, corr. *P*)

xiii

306.98 for "SOUTHENERNER" read "SOUTHERNER" (corr. *I,* corr. *P*)

307.15 for "SHIRT-SLEVES" read "SHIRT-SLEEVES" (corr. *I,* uncorr. *P*)

311.13 for "LILES" read "LILIES" (corr. *I,* corr. *P*)

311.24 for "UNSUCCESFULLY" read "UNSUCCESSFULLY" (corr. *I,* uncorr. *P*)

316.38 for "HIMSELF" read "HERSELF" (corr. and deleted *I,* uncorr. *P*)

334.12 for "SEEMS" read "SEEM" (corr. *I,* uncorr. *P*)

338.21 for "ANNE" probably "ANNIE" (uncorr. *I,* uncorr. *P*)

354.30-31 probably delete second "OUT" (uncorr. *I,* uncorr. *P*)

359.04 for "STRANGNESS" read "STRANGENESS" (corr. **I,** uncorr. *P*)

377.24 for "NEED" read "HEED" (corr. *I,* uncorr. *P*)

380.27 for "NO" read "NOT" (corr. and deleted *I,* uncorr. *P*)

394.21 for "LIKE" probably "LIKED" (uncorr. and deleted *I,* uncorr. *P*)

394.24 for "IT" read "ITS" (corr. and deleted *I,* corr. *P*)

422.18 for "PRISIONER" read "PRISONER" (corr. *I,* uncorr. *P*)

445.33 note variant spellings of "FERGUSSON" and "FERGUSON" see also 444.7, 445.22, 445.24, 445.33, 448.11, 451.24 (uncorr. *I,* uncorr. *P*)

465.28 for "INAPPROPIATE" read "INAPPROPRIATE" (corr. *I,* uncorr. *P*)

475.07 for "WHERE" read "WERE" (corr. and deleted *I,* corr. *P*)

476.07 for "OTHER" probably "OTHERS" (uncorr. and deleted *I,* uncorr. *P*)

480.33 for "HIS" read "HER" (corr. and deleted *I,* uncorr. *P*)

482.30 for "MEANINGLESS" read "MEANINGLESSNESS" (corr. *I,* uncorr. *P*)

486.23 for "THESE" read "THERE" (corr. and deleted *I,* uncorr. *P*)

488.17 for "ARANGE" read "ARRANGE" (corr. *I,* uncorr. *P*)

490.16 for "MISSS" read "MISS" (corr. *I,* uncorr. *P*)

494.7 for "FAIRLY-LIKE" read "FAIRY-LIKE" (corr. *I,* uncorr. *P*)

497.19 for "GOVERMENT" probably "GOVERNMENT" (uncorr. *I,* uncorr. *P*)

501.18 for "AMONGS" read "AMONG" (corr. *I,* uncorr. *P*)

506.20 "BLUE-AND-BLUFF" probably "BLUE-AND-BUFF" (CF. 499.04, without hyphens; uncorr. *I*, uncorr. *P*)

509.04 delete "A" between "WITH" and "AGONY" (corr. and deleted *I*, uncorr. *P*)

522.25 delete the second "AND" (corr. and deleted *I*, uncorr. *P*)

533.3 for "ALTOGTHER" read "ALTOGETHER" (corr. *I*, uncorr. *P*)

544.01 for "CAME" read "COME" (corr. and deleted *I*, uncorr. *P*)

557.35 for "LOOK" read "LOOKED" (corr. and deleted *I*, uncorr. *P*)

566.31 for "LANGUROUS" read "LANGUOROUS" (corr. *I*, corr. *P*)

567.25 for "CHANGE" probably "CHANGED" (uncorr. *I*, uncorr. *P*)

569.11 for "RYTHMICALLY" read "RHYTHMICALLY" (corr. *I*, uncorr. *P*)

574.27 for "THERE" read "THEIR" (corr. and deleted *I*, uncorr. *P*)

576.01 for "GITTER" read "GLITTER" (corr. *I*, corr. *P*)

579.18 for "AGAIN" read "AGAINST" (corr. and deleted *I*, uncorr. *P*)

580.30 for "ESCTASY" read "ECSTASY" (corr. *I*, uncorr. *P*)

Volume III

606.39 for "SIMPLE" read "SIMPLY" (corr. *I*, corr. *P*)

607.03 insert "A" between "WAS" and "FASCINATING" (corr. and deleted *I*, uncorr. *P*)

607.38 for "MRS. PENNEGAR" read "MRS. PINNEGAR" (corr. *I*, uncorr. *P*)

608.19 for "BREATHS" read "BREATHES" (corr. *I*, uncorr. *P*)

610.31 for "UNINHABITATED" probably "UNINHABITED" (uncorr. *I*, corr. *P*)

610.42 for "MR. FIRTH" read "MR. FRITH" (corr. *I*, corr. *P*)

617.08 for "SLIPPER" probably "SLIPPERS" (uncorr. *I*, uncorr. *P*)

634.04 for "IT" read "HE" (corr. and deleted *I*, uncorr. *P*)

634.12 for "CAREFUL" read "CAREFULLY" (corr. *I*, corr. *P*)

641.04 for "SAD-FATED" probably "SAD-FACED" (uncorr. *I*, uncorr. *P*)

655.19 for "STRUCK" probably "STUCK" (uncorr. *I*, uncorr. *P*)

664.01 for "TIME" read "TIMES" (corr. *I*, corr. *P*)

665.07 insert "AT" between "UP" and "ME" (corr. and deleted *I*, uncorr. *P*)

671.31 for "OFF" read "OF" (corr. and deleted *I*, uncorr. *P*)

672.18 for "KNEW" probably "KNOW" (uncorr. *I*, uncorr. *P*)

679.24 for "OT" read "TO" (corr. and deleted *I*, corr. *P*)

699.23 for "CONSCIOUSNES" read "CONSCIOUSNESS" (corr. *I*, uncorr. *P*)

704.31 for "PADRON" probably "PATRON" (uncorr. *I*, uncorr. *P*)

712.26 capitalize "IT" (deleted *I*, uncorr. *P*)

715.01 for "IT" read "IS" (corr. and deleted *I*, uncorr. *P*)

716.40 for "STRANGLY" read "STRANGELY" (corr. *I*, corr. *P*)

718.37 for "FUROUS" read "FURIOUS" (corr. *I*, corr. *P*)

725.19 for "PEAECFUL" read "PEACEFUL" (corr. *I*, corr. *P*)

738.39 for "THEN" read "THEM" (corr. and deleted *I*, uncorr. *P*)

754.25 for "ASCENT" read "SCENT" (corr. *I*, corr. *P*)

779.19 for "ONY" probably "ONLY" (uncorr. *I*, uncorr. *P*)

790.32 for "COMES" read "COME" (corr. and deleted *I*, corr. *P*)

816.11 for "OFF" read "OF" (corr. and deleted *I*, uncorr. *P*)

822.30 for "SANG-FOID" read "SANG-FROID" (corr. *I*, uncorr. *P*)

830.42-831.42 lines were transposed here. Lines 831.41-831.42 should be 831.1-831.2 (uncorr. and not asterisked *I*, corr. *P*)

831.34 for "LITLE" read "LITTLE" (corr. and deleted *I*, uncorr. *P*)

PART TWO: THE SHORT NOVELS

St. Mawr 65.36 for "ENJOYNG" read "ENJOYING" (corr. *I*)

St. Mawr 85.28 for "HERELF" read "HERSELF" (corr. and deleted *I*)

Love Among the Haystacks 30.21 for "SO" read "TO" (corr. and deleted *I*)

The Virgin and the Gipsy 17.9 for "TRE" read "TREE" (corr. *I*)

The Virgin and the Gipsy 30.29 for "AS" read "IF" (corr. and deleted *I*)

The Virgin and the Gipsy 38.10 for "MAUSTACHE" read MOUSTACHE" (corr. *I*)

The Virgin and the Gipsy 74.15 for "SIGH" read "SIGN" (corr. *I*)

Because of the limited storing capacity of the 1130 computer, it was not feasible to indicate capitalization or diacritical marks in this index. As in our earlier poetry concordance, we have linked foreign expressions, concepts, and names which Lawrence clearly intended to stand as units. These units are alphabetized by the lead word in the unit; for easy reference, we have cross-referenced names.

Lastly, we hope that this concordance will be of use to students of Lawrence's short fiction, and that Lawrence has not suffered at our hands. We also wish to communicate to Lawrentians at large that the IBM cards for both the poetry and the short fiction are in storage at Creighton University, Omaha, Nebraska, and that we hope eventually to find a more suitable storing place—perhaps a university library with Lawrence holdings—which would allow scholars easy access to these materials for further studies.

R. G.

J. K.

Creighton University

SYMBOLS

+ indicates that a unit is not reproduced in its entirety.

* indicates that the reader should consult the errata regarding the asterisked entry.

PART ONE
THE SHORT STORIES

CODE OF ABBREVIATIONS

VOLUME I

MO: A Modern Lover
OA: The Old Adam
HT: Her Turn
SP: Strike-Pay
WM: The Witch à la Mode
EA: New Eve and Old Adam
PO: The Prussian Officer
TF: The Thorn in the Flesh
DV: Daughters of the Vicar
FG: A Fragment of Stained
    Glass
SS: The Shades of Spring
SB: Second Best
SG: The Shadow in the Rose
    Garden
GF: Goose Fair
WS: The White Stocking
SC: A Sick Collier
CH: The Christening

VOLUME II

OC: Odour of
    Chrysanthemums
EE: England, My England
TP: Tickets, Please
BL: The Blind Man
MN: Monkey Nuts
WP: Wintry Peacock
YT: You Touched Me

SD: Samson and Delilah
PP: The Primrose Path
HD: The Horse-Dealer's
    Daughter
FA: Fanny and Annie
PR: The Princess
TB: Two Blue Birds
SU: Sun
WR: The Woman Who Rode
    Away
SM: Smile

VOLUME III

BO: The Border Line
JD: Jimmy and the
    Desperate Woman
LA: The Last Laugh
IL: In Love
GG: Glad Ghosts
NT: None of That
ML: The Man Who Loved
    Islands
OV: The Overtone
LL: The Lovely Lady
RR: Rawdon's Roof
RH: The Rocking-Horse
    Winner
MD: Mother and Daughter
BM: The Blue Moccasins
TH: Things

A' SP 50.7 52.18 WS 243.9
  CH 276.29 OC 285.38 PP 435.33

'A WP 389.7

'A' SC 269.29 269.31 CH 277.21
  OC 285.29

ABACK SS 200.11 GG 664.11

ABANDON WS 244.12 259.37
  EE 332.9

ABANDONED MO 1.11 OA 26.13
  SS 200.6 OC 283.18 ML 737.35

ABANDONING TH 846.18

ABANDONMENT MO 7.16

ABASHED OA 28.19 DV 174.2
  TP 334.24 BL 350.2

ABATED YT 404.28

ABBEY FG 187.6 187.9 SS 202.36

ABBREVIATION TP 336.26 IL 655.5

ABDOMEN DV 162.36 PP 433.14
  HD 450.17

A-BEGGING SD 426.15

ABET EE 311.28

ABHORRENT EE 329.7

ABIDE TF 131.39

ABIDING DV 171.33 WR 570.11

ABJECT GF 243.26 GG 685.34
  NT 718.32

ABJECTLY GG 684.13

ABLAZE YT 398.7

ABLE MO 10.11 EA 90.10 94.8
  TF 132.17 SG 227.13 SC 267.32
  269.39 OC 294.30 294.33
  301.20 EE 305.9 314.10
  FA 468.2 PR 497.28 498.8
  506.5 509.12 BO 589.29 597.21
  JD 624.13 627.28 GG 687.38
  NT 716.13 ML 745.12 RH 790.36

ABNEGATION EE 315.16

ABNORMAL WM 66.39 SD 415.14
  IL 652.22 652.24

ABOARD TP 335.40 336.6 336.16
  336.34 336.36

ABOMINABLE GG 685.36 690.29

ABORTION DV 145.13 153.38

ABORTIONS OV 754.29

ABOVE-GROUND SP 49.17

ABRAHAM ML 722.15

ABROAD DV 165.20 GF 235.16
  YT 409.37

ABRUPT CH 279.2

ABRUPTLY WM 58.31 WP 380.13
  FA 472.9 JD 626.5 LA 643.29
  GG 670.6 675.36 693.30

ABSENCE MO 4.16 GG 674.38
  RR 785.35

ABSENT OA 34.18 SG 229.23
  EE 313.5 HD 443.27 PR 474.1
  477.16 GG 686.15 RH 799.33
  MD 825.40

ABSENTLY GG 675.25

ABSENT-MINDED NT 713.21
  LL 769.16

ABSENT-MINDEDLY NT 713.25

ABSOLUTE TF 133.7 133.11
  DV 151.24 PR 476.14 480.7
  WR 566.11 580.16 581.25
  JD 610.35 611.37 618.34
  625.12 MD 823.37 BM 832.34

ABSOLUTELY EA 73.13 88.33 93.19
  TF 131.32 OC 294.37 PR 508.12
  511.9 TB 518.7 523.9
  WR 550.38 JD 607.19 611.40
  613.17 615.12 615.13 616.2
  624.19 628.27 LA 640.37
  641.36 IL 650.36 656.42
  GG 661.20 685.30 695.33
  NT 710.22 ML 743.1 RR 784.32
  RH 797.30 798.4 804.28
  MD 812.41 BM 828.22 831.21
  840.3

ABSORB PR 503.20

ABSORBED EA 71.26 86.31
  TF 132.31 DV 158.37 GF 240.26
  MN 367.32 367.35 HD 450.34
  PR 474.13 TB 521.37 SU 536.24
  537.33 WR 569.4 569.32 577.8
  577.10 JD 616.16 NT 711.24
  719.36 ML 726.15 RH 792.40
  MD 819.8

ABSORBEDLY MO 9.42 EA 72.27
  72.31 TF 124.8 DV 159.37
  SS 210.36

ABSORBING MO 9.27 MN 367.29
  ML 736.8

ABSORBS LL 768.34

ABSORPTION EA 88.3 BL 350.3
  SU 536.9

ABSTAIN EE 315.22 315.25

ABSTRACT MO 16.25 OA 37.18
  EA 90.27 PO 99.31 TF 134.25
  DV 145.21 146.35 151.8 151.23
  153.2 EE 314.26 PR 480.28
  481.41 WR 546.28 581.23
  BO 593.21 JD 618.19 GG 663.7

ABSTRACTED EA 88.7 SG 221.35
  WP 384.32 386.1 SD 412.29
  PP 438.32 FA 462.29 WR 566.9
  BO 604.15 JD 625.27 GG 677.17
  NT 702.34

ABSTRACTEDLY EA 71.28 87.38
  DV 171.19 WS 245.21 YT 408.1
  JD 617.39 618.6 623.42
  LA 643.27 RR 785.10

ABSTRACTEDNESS WP 390.30

ABSTRACTING DV 171.36

ABSTRACTION OA 32.1 SG 225.34
  WP 389.41 PR 480.27
  WR 567.26

ABSTRUSE BL 350.31

ABSURD CH 274.11 YT 397.10
  TB 520.33 JD 624.15
  LA 640.38 642.14 642.18
  642.21 642.37 IL 652.7

ABSURDITY DV 145.41

ABSURDLY PP 430.16

ABUSED FG 191.25

ABUSIVE DV 144.10

ACCELERATORS IL 649.38

ACCENT MO 5.17 SG 222.26
  TP 345.4 BL 357.1 SD 412.24
  415.41 PP 429.38 HD 444.33
  FA 468.2 JD 610.4 RH 796.8
  TH 849.35

ACCENTING SP 53.17

ACCENTUATING MO 6.3

ACCEPT DV 137.6 OC 299.15
  NT 718.25 MD 817.28
  BM 830.21 TH 852.42 853.4

ACCEPTANCE SS 202.31

ACCEPTED HT 44.20 SP 50.12
  EA 89.7 PO 96.35 109.16
  TF 131.35 131.42 DV 146.34
  152.27 154.17 SC 267.15
  EE 328.28 328.29 BL 349.25
  SD 412.24 417.8 PR 512.6
  GG 661.5 676.30 679.16
  OV 747.35 BM 830.17

ACCEPTING EA 79.1 DV 151.3
  BO 591.11 IL 647.17

ACCEPTS OV 747.16 MD 820.8

ACCESS YT 406.42

ACCESSORY EE 310.25 ML 725.21

ACCIDENT SP 50.41 TF 124.2
  DV 168.5 SC 269.19
  OC 294.20 EE 317.18
  PR 512.13 512.22 BO 591.20
  591.21 GG 667.13

ACCIDENTALLY OA 35.20 BL 363.33

ACCIDENTS WR 546.11

ACCOMMODATE SD 418.16

ACCOMPANIED MO 5.37 DV 146.40
  WS 251.12 WR 562.35

ACCOMPANIMENT WM 59.8 TF 129.16
  JD 610.28 LA 645.14 RR 783.15

ACCOMPANYING GG 697.9

ACCOMPLICE MD 807.9

ACCOMPLISH WR 581.27 NT 706.41

ACCOMPLISHED EE 307.39 WR 546.12
  546.14

ACCOMPLISHING EA 83.7

ACCOMPLISHMENTS YT 395.8

ACCORDING WM 63.33 DV 153.42
  EE 326.35 326.36 PR 504.17
  GG 663.13 698.13

ACCOSTED SS 197.4

ACCOSTING TP 339.34

ACCOUNT DV 184.1 CH 279.41
  EE 309.2 BL 350.18 LA 644.30
  GG 699.18 NT 708.9

ACCOUNTING WR 546.13

ACCOUNTS DV 146.25 ML 731.41
  732.4 732.9 MD 808.33

ACCUMULATED WM 54.14 PO 108.22
  ML 745.20

ACCUMULATING EA 81.39

ACCURACY EA 83.28 GF 235.22

ACCURATE MO 5.16 16.18

ACCURATELY GF 235.36 PP 435.40
  WR 576.36

ACCUSATION FG 187.26 EE 317.11
  LL 763.14

ACCUSATIONS EA 80.27 89.37
  LL 763.9

ACCUSED EA 89.8 GF 240.2
  LL 768.17

ACCUSING GG 692.17 ML 731.2
  LL 775.8

ACCUSTOMED DV 136.33 SB 212.3
  GG 682.5 ML 741.4

ACH TF 124.9

ACHE WM 69.27 PO 104.11 113.19
  115.24 115.25 FG 190.4 190.5
  190.7 ML 736.21

ACHED OA 36.41 WM 69.39
  YT 402.21 HD 453.37 GG 692.29
  NT 711.1 OV 749.36 751.20
  LL 761.13

ACHIEVE WR 581.28 ML 737.33
  737.34

ACHIEVED OV 749.32

ACHING ML 739.16 739.27

ACID PO 102.13 MD 815.41

ACIDLY IL 658.24 LL 777.25

ACKNOWLEDGE PO 99.35 DV 160.29

ACKNOWLEDGED MO 5.36 PO 100.21
  DV 137.14 EE 324.31 325.12
  MN 368.4

ACKNOWLEDGMENT MO 22.8 WM 64.26
  65.29 TF 130.19 PP 433.1

ACQUAINTANCE OA 38.37 EA 75.19
  TP 339.7 MD 819.22

ACQUAINTANCES WM 67.35 JD 606.16
  NT 709.7 MD 812.3

ACQUAINTED WM 58.4 JD 619.9
  GG 691.41

ACQUIESCE OV 749.18

ACQUIESCED OV 750.11 BM 832.21

ACQUIESCENT DV 185.2

ACQUIESCING DV 153.12

ACQUIRED ML 722.11 722.22

ACQUIRES TB 517.25

ACQUIT OA 28.30

ACRES TF 123.8 WP 382.5
  IL 648.22 ML 738.18

ACRID PO 106.29 EE 313.28
  313.29 314.21 FA 463.42
  OV 753.9

ACROBATIC EA 90.6

ACROSS-STREAM PR 494.24

ACT PO 108.7 DV 155.22 184.30
  OC 288.28 YT 408.26 PR 507.40
  508.5 BO 604.38 GG 663.1
  663.13 NT 718.16 718.35
  718.36 718.40 718.41 ML 738.4
  OV 747.18 RR 788.24 788.29
  MD 817.16 BM 837.16 838.10
  839.12 839.14 840.16 840.28

ACTED WM 68.8 PO 97.6 TF 126.13
  BL 347.12 NT 708.20 718.17
  BM 836.26 838.29

ACTING PP 429.12 JD 628.13
  NT 717.36 718.18 LL 769.9

ACTION HT 39.20 WM 64.30
  EA 72.12 DV 177.1 EE 329.31
  329.41 330.33 331.31
  BL 360.28 WP 391.15
  SD 419.37 419.38 419.40
  424.40

ACTIONS SD 425.3

ACTIVE PO 99.36 112.16
  EE 325.5 TP 334.28
  BL 360.26 NT 710.9

ACTIVELY BL 353.24 ML 724.20

ACTIVITIES DV 137.16 176.31
  177.2 BL 350.4 TB 525.19
  BM 827.36

ACTIVITY TF 132.34 DV 153.25
  WS 254.38 EE 331.1 331.5
  BL 360.22 HD 449.37
  SU 536.15 ML 735.26
  OV 748.11 748.42

ACT ONE BM 836.30 836.42

ACTOR RR 783.26

ACTORS BM 838.29

ACTRESS LL 768.22

ACTS DV 146.37 GG 664.30
  NT 718.35 718.36 BM 839.33

ACT TWO BM 836.42 837.3

ACTUAL DV 171.41 PR 474.31
  485.41 WR 565.41 JD 614.8
  ML 734.6 MD 816.36

ACTUALLY EA 85.4 DV 165.23
  SS 205.26 TP 335.5 337.31
  343.15 BL 363.22 364.23
  TB 513.18 518.1 518.26
  519.23 WR 546.14 572.16
  BO 588.35 588.37 JD 614.17
  614.18 629.10 LA 640.35
  NT 716.31 721.4 ML 722.11
  RR 788.3 RH 804.2

ACUTE MO 5.13 DV 174.19
  BL 349.13

ACUTELY WP 390.21 LL 775.38

ACUTENESS WR 572.12

'AD OC 291.19 292.21 295.39

ADAM MD 814.26

ADAMS WS 255.37 255.40
  256.6 256.8 256.15 256.17
  257.12 257.19 257.25
  257.34 257.40 258.6 258.36

ADAMS'S WS 250.20 259.32

ADD MO 13.24 GF 240.39
  EE 319.15 PR 473.13
  MD 820.29 BM 831.3

ADDED MO 5.28 10.21 12.8 12.36
  12.40 15.18 20.3 EA 75.8
  77.2 PO 108.13 DV 150.24
  SS 199.22 209.16 SB 218.22
  218.41 SG 227.31 233.1
  GF 236.2 WS 258.41 EE 309.40
  TP 342.10 BL 358.28 359.15
  360.16 363.27 MN 373.4 376.1
  SD 412.13 FA 472.11 488.41
  491.27 TB 523.30 SU 533.28
  WR 571.33 LA 633.21 IL 658.19
  ML 729.41 LL 773.26 RH 798.26
  MD 819.32 BM 828.36 828.41
  TH 844.6

ADDERS EE 316.24

ADDING WM 57.20 61.38 SB 213.35
  RR 787.16 BM 834.1

ADDIOS WM 68.2

ADDLE FA 471.30

ADDLED SP 46.31 46.39

ADDRESS MO 5.33 EA 82.9 88.42
  SS 201.23 SC 271.10 YT 395.38
  HD 445.6 FA 466.4 GG 667.25
  MD 826.8

ADDRESSED WS 265.35 TP 336.25
  MN 374.18 WP 380.32 YT 409.30
  WR 559.27 BO 594.31 GG 681.36

ADDRESSES WS 245.23

ADDRESSING HD 444.26 JD 614.7
  625.27

ADDY SS 201.5 201.22 201.35
  209.15

ADELA PP 428.8

A DEUX TB 515.40

ADHERED DV 163.33

ADHERING WS 256.15

AD INFINITUM MO 14.38 TH 849.4

ADIOS PR 495.40 WR 553.20
  553.22

ADJOINING SC 267.20

ADJOURNED WM 58.33

ADJUNCT EE 310.25

ADJUST MO 10.39

ADJUSTED TF 118.28

ADJUSTER BO 592.17

ADJUSTING MO 18.10 NT 702.26

ADJUSTMENT MO 18.21

AD MAIOREM GLORIAM DEI GG 700.5

ADMINISTERED GF 239.12

ADMIRABLE DV 146.17 PR 483.17
  GG 661.25

ADMIRATION MO 15.18 WM 59.27
  DV 146.41 TB 526.8 SU 540.16
  541.22 WR 547.19 ML 729.12

ADMIRE SD 425.40

ADMIRED PO 96.12 DV 166.1
  SS 202.28 BL 359.40 MN 371.18
  WP 379.10 WR 547.26 JD 607.36
  LL 770.6 771.12

ADMIRER TB 513.17

ADMIRERS TF 127.7

ADMIRING FA 460.39 JD 606.15

ADMIRINGLY HT 44.16 ML 727.2

ADMIT OA 24.28 WM 68.13
  PO 100.12 WS 252.40 SU 533.13
  544.11 BO 602.22 GG 699.42
  TH 849.31

ADMITTED MO 21.3 TF 131.34
  DV 147.31 172.18 PR 479.27
  TB 518.4 523.25 NT 702.5
  RR 781.5 TH 847.1

ADMONISHED WM 63.40

ADMONITORY SB 218.31

ADO PR 512.6 WR 555.9

ADOBE PR 489.4 WR 546.19 547.6
  547.39 548.11 561.17

ADOBE-WORK WR 576.22

ADOPT DV 147.22

ADOPTED BL 349.21 YT 395.26
  PP 430.11

ADORABLE EA 86.40 86.41
  EE 316.17 IL 654.29 TH 849.39

ADORABLY TB 514.31 MD 813.23

ADORATION WS 260.9

ADORE EE 309.24 TB 513.34 515.5
  JD 628.18

ADORED EE 309.4 310.26 315.9
  316.2 316.14 324.8 326.1
  BL 349.6 359.24 PP 430.1
  TB 513.23 513.24 513.32
  519.34 BO 589.11 JD 606.19
  ML 739.17 RR 781.5 MD 813.22
  813.30

ADORES RH 790.15

ADORING TB 513.27 ML 739.22

ADORNED DV 178.20 WR 578.15

ADORNS FG 187.30

ADRIAN MD 813.40 814.3 814.7

ADRIAN'S MD 813.29

ADULATION ML 727.24

ADULTERY TB 513.30

ADVANCE WM 54.29 SB 217.17

ADVANCED MO 3.23 FG 191.18
  SB 217.40 OC 284.29
  BL 357.32 SD 416.7
  SU 539.32 RH 799.37

ADVANCING WM 62.23 WS 264.10
  OC 283.8 EE 331.9 BL 355.34
  YT 401.35

ADVANTAGE WS 255.41 FA 461.12

ADVANTAGES RH 790.2

ADVENTURE MO 19.24 TF 133.5
  DV 166.21 TP 334.15 334.27
  PR 493.32 WR 546.2 546.9
  554.35 JD 615.40 624.19
  OV 747.36 LL 766.24

ADVENTUROUS JD 627.39

ADVERSARY OA 35.37

ADVERTISE ML 733.28

ADVERTISEMENTS RH 799.19
  799.23

ADVICE EE 320.16 TB 514.21
  IL 647.13 BM 830.17

ADVISED BM 830.20

A'EF OC 292.24

AESTHETIC EA 84.28 NT 706.14
  MD 810.40

AFAR SU 530.3 JD 623.18
  GG 694.29

AFFABLE OA 32.13

AFFAIR EA 77.29 PO 103.25
  DV 155.26 184.25 EE 310.3
  MN 367.16 WP 385.9
  PR 512.16 515.8 NT 721.11
  LL 771.32 RR 779.12 779.13
  780.11 780.12 782.30

AFFAIRE EA 85.20

AFFAIRS EA 82.5 DV 146.24
  SG 227.20 BL 350.8 FA 459.12
  TB 513.14 514.14 515.3
  515.23 516.9 522.12
  IL 653.14 NT 708.32
  MD 820.42

AFFECT MN 371.18 PP 437.15
  GG 688.40

AFFECTATION GF 242.9

AFFECTED MO 12.7 OA 31.9
  EA 84.36 DV 163.31 SB 217.32
  HD 443.20

AGONY OA 36.9 EA 93.11
  PO 100.27 103.15 105.15
  115.21 TF 120.12 132.6 133.7
  DV 173.34 174.36 180.21
  180.24 WS 257.37 OC 301.19
  EE 322.2 322.5 322.6 331.33
  331.35 332.13 332.14 332.22
  332.31 332.41 TP 345.8
  HD 454.12 455.12 PR 492.6
  509.4 510.24 WR 570.2 570.3
  SM 582.13 LA 646.18 646.20
  RR 787.25 RH 800.24

AGREE MO 13.1 13.14 DV 155.12
  EE 321.14 BL 361.9 IL 657.39
  GG 693.18

AGREEABLE HT 39.10 DV 137.21
  MN 368.33 BM 830.19

AGREED DV 144.22 SS 205.7
  YT 394.20 PP 436.19 RH 804.7
  BM 832.22

AGREEING MO 13.8 ML 729.1

AGREEMENT RH 800.6

AGREES GG 680.16

AGRICULTURE SB 213.42 BL 350.5

AHA LA 638.17

AH'D OC 293.1

AHEAD MO 1.34 HT 40.37 PO 95.19
  95.35 DV 167.16 CH 274.15
  EE 332.41 MN 371.41 PP 431.27
  435.40 436.2 PR 489.29 490.34
  493.22 WR 551.26 553.17
  553.28 555.41 558.31 578.11
  JD 620.3 NT 714.41 TH 847.28

AH'VE OC 293.1 WP 389.21

AID EE 311.28

AILED EA 86.22

AILMENT LA 641.6

AIM EE 330.7 331.27 MN 366.13
  PR 510.23

AIMED PP 436.1

AIMLESS SB 217.14 BL 356.40

AIMLESSLY HD 444.8

AIN'T GF 242.4 MN 377.38
  PR 508.25 510.20

AIR MO 11.24 OA 34.2 EA 83.29
  PO 95.31 106.26 106.27 107.11
  114.21 TF 118.25 121.29
  DV 138.27 140.21 143.5 145.27
  160.28 162.31 166.23
  FG 193.39 SS 200.7 201.39
  210.6 210.22 SG 221.19 226.4
  228.22 228.31 GF 238.23
  WS 247.22 249.23 260.12
  SC 268.30 OC 296.18 296.30

AIR (CONT.) EE 323.26 323.33
  324.1 324.2 329.24 329.40
  330.11 330.20 BL 351.28
  MN 371.39 376.16 376.37
  376.39 377.10 WP 379.2 381.6
  HD 441.13 442.36 450.30
  FA 466.10 PR 480.5 497.26
  498.17 505.4 511.5 511.6
  TB 517.23 522.35 523.24 527.7
  SU 530.13 543.6 WR 556.16
  558.5 563.17 563.22 565.39
  566.1 568.12 570.18 572.25
  572.27 574.3 574.5 578.36
  BO 592.31 592.32 599.31
  599.34 602.9 JD 608.16 608.21
  610.10 610.15 LA 638.6 638.10
  638.11 638.16 638.20 640.34
  641.32 646.33 IL 651.1 651.2
  652.32 654.33 656.10
  GG 669.23 670.41 674.5 684.1
  686.5 688.34 690.14 694.23
  695.12 ML 723.27 724.26
  730.36 734.16 741.40 742.7
  743.42 744.6 744.25 744.29
  744.42 OV 748.25 751.17
  755.29 757.1 758.20 LL 766.32
  MD 811.1 821.2 822.20
  TH 845.5 845.40

AIRED OC 302.1 RR 787.33

AIRILY WR 554.10 554.32

AIRING RR 785.41

AIRLESS TF 118.20

AIRS DV 137.25 PR 478.9

AIRY OC 285.13

AISLE FA 468.20

AITCHES FA 464.13

AKIN YT 396.5

ALABASTER WM 58.40

A LA MADEMOISELLE DE MAUPIN SM 110.6

ALAN BO 588.26 588.30 589.5
  589.11 589.21 589.32 589.36
  589.39 589.42 590.8 590.9
  590.14 590.19 591.24 592.9
  592.28 592.34 592.39 593.7
  596.15 596.23 602.23 603.7
  603.12 603.19 603.25 603.31
  604.17 604.30 604.32 604.39

ALAN ANSTRUTHER BO 588.25

ALAN'S BO 590.32 602.5

ALARM TF 119.3

ALARMED OC 292.35 OV 755.37

ALARMING TF 119.6 ML 734.7

ALAS EE 310.37 324.20 IL 649.18
  ML 727.37 MD 812.9 813.17
  816.39 TH 844.11 845.2 850.3
  851.10

ALBERT MN 366.2 366.4 366.10

ALBERT (CONT.) 366.12 366.19
  366.23 367.8 367.13 367.21
  367.32 368.5 368.8 368.9
  368.17 368.24 368.28
  368.37 368.41 369.5 369.9
  369.12 369.16 369.20
  369.24 369.29 369.37
  370.3 370.10 370.16 370.23
  370.27 370.37 370.41 371.3
  371.5 371.6 371.28 371.33
  372.1 372.3 372.6 372.8
  372.12 372.15 372.20
  372.29 372.34 373.2 373.10
  373.13 373.30 373.35
  373.37 373.40 374.6 374.8
  374.13 374.16 374.18
  374.28 374.34 374.41
  375.10 375.22 375.28
  375.36 375.42 376.3 376.9
  376.14 376.17 376.25
  378.10 378.19 378.26

ALBERTS MN 367.34

ALBERT'S MN 378.15

ALCOHOL PO 103.36 PR 480.16
  GG 675.41

ALCOVES WR 576.29

ALDECROSS DV 136.1 136.11
  136.29 138.38 144.30 147.5

ALDER SS 210.3

ALDERS OC 283.18 EE 303.12
  LL 762.26

ALE SD 412.10 412.11 414.18

ALEC RR 780.37 781.34 786.33
  786.36

ALEC DRUMMOND RR 780.31
  780.39

ALERT MO 8.19 OA 29.9 30.9
  DV 172.32 SB 218.40
  SG 221.12 221.14 228.32
  TP 342.33 YT 402.41
  SD 413.38 HD 442.32
  PR 483.13 510.37 SU 536.14
  538.7 539.25 541.17 544.32
  LA 630.18 631.39 634.22
  GG 675.18 LL 768.2 769.17
  MD 809.27 BM 840.42

ALERTNESS SD 417.9 LA 631.7

'ALF OC 291.20

ALFRED DV 141.18 141.26
  142.6 143.8 150.8 150.34
  160.34 162.39 162.40
  163.35 164.11 170.17
  171.29 174.12 174.33
  175.23 175.26 176.29
  177.12 177.15 WP 380.34
  381.10 381.19 381.20 383.4
  383.30 383.32 384.12
  384.13 384.24 388.8 388.25
  389.5 389.6 389.22 389.23
  390.8 390.40 391.34 392.14

ALFRED (CONT.) SD 420.38

ALFRED DURANT DV 149.38 163.32
  172.23

ALFREDS WP 381.29

ALFRED'S DV 162.3 170.5

ALGEBRA MO 10.11

ALI BM 835.39 836.1 837.19

ALICE SD 413.2 BM 831.26 835.38
  836.6 836.37 837.4 837.6
  837.42 838.8 838.15 840.3
  840.39 841.4 841.26 842.15

ALICE HOWELLS BM 831.25 832.7
  834.8 835.23 835.33 836.6
  836.15 839.6 839.7 841.23
  841.37 842.1 843.7

ALICE'S BM 836.22

ALIEN OC 300.26 HD 449.8
  ML 741.35

ALIENS MD 819.12

ALIGHT WM 54.25 TF 131.30
  PR 500.22

ALIGHTED WM 54.1 ML 734.40

ALIKE MO 14.10 DV 142.26
  PP 427.16 WR 549.22 576.13
  NT 713.37 ML 742.21 MD 812.30

ALIVE MO 19.28 PO 116.12
  DV 161.14 182.22 SC 271.16
  EE 314.41 328.6 TP 337.35
  WP 384.9 YT 403.1 404.17
  SD 419.19 HD 449.25 PR 483.4
  483.27 493.23 503.18
  SU 530.29 WR 571.5 BO 602.18
  603.10 JD 618.5 LA 637.13
  GG 679.29 680.5 683.21 689.17
  689.23 689.31 689.41 696.26
  698.3 ML 724.7 724.19 735.21
  741.21 744.12 745.15
  OV 756.40

ALLCOCK (SEE MR. ALLCOCK)

ALLCOCK'S HT 42.39

ALL-CONCEALING GG 695.38

ALLEGIANCE OA 30.39 30.40
  BM 842.38

ALLEVIATING ML 744.41

ALLEYS PP 436.6

ALLIANCE TF 126.36 127.3

ALLIANCES MD 807.10

ALL-IN-ALL GG 695.39

ALLOTMENT-GARDENS PP 436.5

ALLOTTED DV 150.32

ALLOW OA 37.7 PO 96.27 98.15
  DV 149.27 GF 239.14 EE 315.42
  PR 478.22 TB 515.6 MD 807.20

ALLOWANCE EE 308.40 PP 430.18

ALLOWANCES OC 295.15 295.16

ALLOWED MO 18.4 DV 141.26
  WS 249.39 EE 321.12 BL 350.12
  MN 372.24 SD 419.40 WR 550.22
  JD 608.10 LA 634.17 GG 674.12
  NT 710.36 720.39

ALLOWS OV 747.17

ALL-ROUND TP 339.14

ALL'S HD 446.20

ALLSOP (SEE MRS. ALLSOP)

ALLUS SS 201.39

ALLUSION DV 142.9

ALMANAC DV 142.28 161.15

ALMANACS DV 138.39 142.38

ALMOND WM 63.19 SU 535.31
  542.29 LA 640.8 643.6 646.33

ALMOND-BLOSSOM RH 800.14

ALOFT BO 595.34

ALONE MO 16.21 OA 24.16 30.41
  EA 77.11 PO 98.2 98.27 99.38
  103.10 113.31 115.31 TF 129.7
  129.24 DV 156.15 166.19
  176.11 176.26 178.11 178.35
  FG 192.28 SS 210.27 SG 227.38
  229.27 230.9 GF 236.27 238.42
  241.11 WS 255.7 255.9
  SC 271.36 CH 281.17 OC 298.42
  EE 304.6 305.4 306.13 318.33
  323.29 323.30 329.20 330.35
  331.2 332.30 TP 337.11
  BL 347.14 357.14 359.3 361.10
  363.9 MN 374.4 WP 381.17
  387.9 YT 404.26 408.32
  SD 411.7 420.19 PP 430.42
  431.1 436.22 HD 441.15 445.17
  PR 476.4 476.6 477.20 485.19
  487.37 493.12 493.32 495.5
  496.1 496.5 507.15 509.10
  TB 518.16 SU 532.41 536.11
  537.5 543.3 WR 546.12 549.9
  550.23 550.37 550.39 550.40
  551.1 551.3 BO 588.2 596.16
  602.17 JD 605.10 608.9
  LA 630.33 638.42 640.23
  IL 648.11 649.10 650.8
  GG 664.28 665.27 666.22
  690.21 690.26 694.7 NT 716.20
  718.42 719.9 719.11 719.15
  719.25 719.29 719.30 ML 722.4
  743.2 743.2 OV 748.31 759.30
  LL 765.34 770.38 772.41
  774.34 RH 800.28 MD 814.28
  815.2 817.12 818.42 820.10
  822.42 825.15 BM 829.39
  830.15 834.20 836.33 839.32

ALONENESS BM 834.21

ALONGSIDE HT 41.29 WR 555.10
  MD 805.23

ALOOF EA 89.33 93.25
  TF 127.23 EE 313.7 313.8
  313.12 331.2 YT 402.28
  PR 483.17 BO 596.34
  LA 634.15 OV 747.15 754.22
  MD 822.41 BM 834.6

ALOUD MO 9.35 11.10 15.1
  EA 74.32 DV 149.12 FG 193.8
  193.22 WS 266.3 OC 293.21
  295.6 296.8 EE 306.40
  WP 392.5 PR 511.15
  LA 642.37 IL 651.17
  LL 769.12 769.20 RH 791.7
  791.25 MD 825.4

ALP PR 494.26

ALREADY WM 69.32 EA 90.14
  PO 110.10 114.39 TF 122.24
  125.27 125.41 DV 136.20
  138.19 139.40 139.41
  148.18 151.36 163.14 167.5
  183.13 FG 191.8 OC 283.14
  283.18 EE 306.19 311.16
  321.19 329.32 MN 378.9
  YT 394.28 SD 411.3 PP 438.9
  PR 483.39 487.26 489.1
  489.12 490.41 491.2 493.20
  501.31 505.13 507.4 511.16
  TB 522.13 SU 536.3 544.18
  WR 551.30 552.34 552.35
  579.2 JD 616.13 GG 664.1
  664.16 669.34 685.19 690.1
  695.16 NT 701.21 705.13
  710.42 ML 730.23 732.29
  733.25 742.29 LL 765.15
  MD 805.4 806.2 814.3 818.9
  BM 827.26

ALSATIAN BO 594.32 594.41
  595.13 598.35

ALSATIANS BO 595.20

ALTAR TF 122.9 WR 573.31
  573.33 573.37 581.1
  ML 724.41

ALTAR-CLOTH LA 639.41

ALTARS SS 205.5

ALTER EE 304.11 306.1
  YT 405.39 SD 417.25
  FA 464.21 BO 591.1 591.2
  LA 642.3

ALTERED MO 8.34 WM 55.25
  DV 158.28 YT 398.23
  SD 419.24 422.18 HD 455.19
  BO 587.13 LA 642.5

ALTER EGO MD 816.29 816.38
  817.6

ALTERING EA 75.34

ALTHOUGH OA 26.21 26.22
  31.22 SP 47.24 DV 146.21

ALTHOUGH (CONT.) WS 250.29
  SC 267.13 HD 447.36 WR 551.32
  BO 587.15 RH 790.21 TH 846.32

ALTITUDE WR 553.11 561.9

ALTOGETHER SU 533.3*

ALTOS FA 466.34

ALUMINIUM PR 505.28

ALYSSUM WM 55.15

AMASSED GG 699.10

AMATEUR EE 307.18 307.19
  RR 781.42 BM 834.6 835.16
  835.17 838.29

AMATEURISH EE 307.32 308.22

A-MATTER WS 259.12 259.16
  259.17

AMAZED FG 193.35 WS 259.26
  259.29 HD 453.11 PR 474.14
  SU 531.33 IL 658.29

AMAZEDLY GG 692.4

AMAZEMENT WR 547.11 IL 656.17
  656.27 656.30 GG 668.24
  674.18 680.40 RH 803.10

AMAZING PO 96.12 99.37 TB 517.9
  BO 589.42 JD 621.17 LA 633.4
  643.15 IL 653.8 GG 667.8
  NT 708.27 ML 726.31 726.32
  732.37 RR 789.11 797.17

AMAZINGLY BL 360.1 TB 517.19
  MD 814.18 821.25

AMAZON SD 418.22

AMBER WM 63.31

AMBITION DV 138.13 EE 308.15
  FA 462.21

AMBITIOUS FA 459.10 GG 661.22

AMBULANCE SC 269.26

AMELIORATE DV 185.20

AMERICA TF 131.16 132.39 135.10
  SD 411.27 415.10 419.18
  PR 474.42 WR 546.5 GG 667.13
  NT 716.29 TH 844.15 846.9
  847.37 849.27 849.34 850.28
  852.2 852.15 852.27 852.34
  853.27 853.29

AMERICAN OC 291.40 SD 417.39
  420.6 423.26 PR 473.5 476.39
  505.39 WR 553.22 BO 587.31
  JD 605.14 606.36 NT 701.15
  703.38 705.3 705.4 705.10
  705.21 705.35 705.37 707.6
  707.28 708.28 709.8 711.2
  714.15 715.23 716.38
  MD 812.33 814.8 TH 849.33

AMERICAN (CONT.) 850.20 853.26

AMERICAN GOVERNMENT NT 708.3

AMERICANS PR 505.37 NT 714.39

AMETHYST WS 260.26 263.38
  263.41 264.39

AMIABLE WM 66.27 BO 589.3
  BM 840.14

AMIABLY MO 9.1 HT 41.33
  PO 109.17 SB 217.25 OV 756.29

AMICABLY OA 32.4 DV 186.15
  LL 769.31

AMID EA 72.26 PO 114.19
  DV 176.23 SS 210.24 EE 303.14
  303.27 303.29 LA 638.4
  GG 676.33

AMISS EE 311.7 FA 469.26
  RR 779.17

AMITY MN 377.39

AMMONIA BL 353.3

AMOLE WR 576.40

A-MONDAY SP 46.30

AMONGST EA 82.12 SD 422.25

AMORPHOUS DV 154.33

AMOUNT SP 50.17 SS 205.34
  EE 314.14 ML 739.23 RR 782.20
  BM 835.22 TH 844.16

AMOUNTED EE 314.14 HD 441.12
  JD 607.16

AMOUNTING TB 519.12

AMOURETTE WS 252.6

AMPHITHEATRE WR 579.23 580.7

AMPLE SS 206.36

AMUCK PP 428.36

AMUSE SS 198.23 GG 682.15
  NT 704.28 BM 840.21

AMUSED WM 54.35 65.15 PO 114.5
  DV 164.7 WS 249.10 EE 319.14
  BL 351.26 WP 393.10 407.26
  BO 587.25 JD 627.14 627.27
  LA 633.27 634.34 638.33
  LL 771.15 MD 816.9 816.10
  825.22

AMUSEMENT MO 19.38 OA 24.29
  EA 82.25 SB 213.34 RH 795.34
  MD 822.33

AMUSES BM 834.2

AMUSING WM 56.29 LA 642.25
  642.27 MD 821.27 BM 828.9

AN' HT 41.40 41.41 43.2
  43.13 SP 47.20 48.17
  48.23 48.28 49.38 49.40
  50.4 50.9 51.32 51.35
  52.22 52.25 52.30 52.32
  DV 157.26 169.10 SS 201.39
  210.25 SB 213.24 218.13
  GF 242.41 243.5 243.6
  243.8 243.14 WS 248.33
  258.41 SC 267.26 268.12
  268.34 269.30 269.36
  270.23 270.33 271.34
  273.8 CH 277.39 279.12
  279.13 279.17 279.19
  279.20 281.10 281.13 282.4
  OC 285.29 287.11 291.19
  291.30 291.33 292.22
  292.23 292.24 292.25
  292.34 294.18 294.20
  294.22 294.24 295.13
  295.14 295.39 296.2 297.19
  297.33 297.39 WP 388.38
  389.5 389.7 389.21 389.27
  392.17 SD 419.21 424.13
  PP 428.12 431.13 431.36
  432.6 432.19 433.8 433.9
  436.15 439.5 440.4
  FA 463.30 463.33 464.18
  469.13 469.28 470.32

ANACONDA NT 717.30

ANALYSE JD 627.39

ANATHEMA TH 849.28

ANCHORED BO 595.5

ANCHOVY ML 729.18

ANCHUSAS EE 329.22

ANCIENT MO 12.42 EE 304.10
  SU 529.15 533.6 WR 550.7
  550.15 570.10 BO 595.38
  595.40 600.16 LA 637.19
  ML 728.6 734.10 BM 835.41
  TH 847.41 848.12 848.23
  849.1 849.20

ANCIENT OF DAYS BM 835.35

ANCIENTS WM 67.32

'AND CH 276.30

ANEMONES WM 63.36 TB 520.32
  SU 535.33

ANGEL SS 209.32 WS 256.11
  SU 534.14 IL 647.36 657.12
  NT 717.15

ANGELIC MO 20.22

ANGELS FG 194.23 PR 493.31
  BO 602.2 GG 692.17

ANGER OA 37.15 HT 44.6
  WM 60.12 PO 97.24 TF 127.26
  127.36 DV 138.1 152.33
  160.2 164.29 178.18
  SG 229.9 229.11 229.28
  231.31 GF 242.16 242.27

ANGER (CONT.) WS 248.14 248.29
249.29 262.19 262.33 265.23
CH 276.6 278.7 279.38 279.40
280.24 280.27 281.24 OC 288.5
289.29 289.31 290.20 290.26
EE 310.38 321.1 TP 342.31
YT 409.17 SD 414.30 414.41
424.20 424.32 HD 455.39
FA 463.36 468.15 PR 492.23
493.15 506.11 507.6 TB 526.30
SU 529.20 532.13 WR 555.26
555.38 556.2 JD 611.3 622.18
622.23 623.40 LA 637.39
IL 654.24 658.21 GG 691.37
NT 720.27 ML 743.33 OV 759.1
BM 841.21 841.29 841.30
841.33

ANGERED FG 191.15 191.24 192.15
SB 219.15 WS 261.5 RH 792.37

ANGLE EE 304.14 PP 436.27

ANGRIER WR 575.17

ANGRILY EE 307.4 FA 465.32
WR 555.16 LA 638.31 ML 738.30

ANGRY MO 17.26 21.30 21.35
OA 33.19 HT 41.19 SP 51.26
WM 59.12 60.36 67.29 PO 99.4
DV 141.35 141.38 144.23
155.13 159.20 159.30 185.1
FG 193.26 SG 224.5 228.38
WS 260.7 261.39 MN 371.27
374.8 YT 395.25 400.34 405.41
408.31 409.21 SD 425.7
PP 436.9 FA 467.7 PR 493.12
WR 555.15 571.29 571.32
572.28 572.29 575.5 575.17
SM 584.37 585.3 BO 590.20
592.11 JD 605.15 IL 651.39
654.18 655.22 655.32 656.33
657.22 LL 773.37 RH 804.6

ANGUISH OA 37.12 WM 69.41
PO 104.9 115.37 TF 122.27
130.11 131.27 DV 154.27
166.23 173.19 176.24 179.38
180.12 SG 226.39 232.42
WS 259.4 259.22 266.1 266.5
OC 301.35 EE 317.37 325.25
PR 509.7 SU 531.13 RH 802.14

ANGUISHED LL 767.23

ANIMA SM 586.11

ANIMAL OA 36.6 37.16 HT 40.10
PO 97.26 TF 123.24 SS 198.13
SB 215.5 216.23 WS 254.18
SC 268.39 TP 343.29 343.35
BL 353.9 354.34 SD 422.22
HD 442.17 442.33 442.34
447.14 453.11 PR 492.2 501.22
504.13 504.14 SU 536.24
537.33 542.25 543.28 544.9
WR 578.3 BO 596.35 LA 633.3
633.28 638.32 646.1 646.17
GG 683.11 688.30 NT 703.1
703.2 703.3 703.36 715.14
715.15 716.8 716.17 717.31
720.18 720.24 ML 729.14
742.19 742.40 RH 802.2

ANIMALISM MO 13.23

ANIMALS SP 49.17 PO 98.23
SS 206.27 PR 486.20 486.23
486.27 488.1 500.14 WR 557.7
579.22 GG 680.25 NT 703.5
712.35 ML 742.20

ANIMAL'S WM 65.21 SS 206.31
WR 557.9

ANIMATED WS 253.21

ANIMATEDLY EA 86.7 DV 167.24
WS 244.4

ANKLE-DEEP MO 19.15

ANNA PP 427.37 428.10 428.19

ANNABEL EE 310.9 316.32 317.24
317.40 326.1

ANNE SB 212.3 212.7 212.17
212.24 212.31 212.32 213.7
214.7 214.21 214.28 214.32
215.1 215.4 215.10 215.18
215.20 215.29 216.5 216.12
216.18 216.29 216.38 216.42
218.10 218.12 218.14 218.30
219.20 TP 338.21*

ANNE, QUEEN (SEE QUEEN ANNE)

ANNE'S SB 212.16

ANNIE OC 287.38 288.42 289.2
289.37 290.9 TP 335.30 335.41
336.2 336.17 336.18 336.37
337.6 337.9 338.39 339.1
339.3 339.8 339.19 339.34
339.37 339.42 340.8 340.13
340.18 340.33 342.1 342.5
342.9 342.26 342.37 343.4
343.26 343.32 343.38 343.42
344.5 344.8 344.13 344.20
344.39 344.40 344.42 345.1
345.4 345.13 345.21 345.37
346.3 YT 406.1 FA 469.20

ANNIE, (SEE MISS ANNIE)

ANNIE NIXON FA 470.32

ANNIE'S TP 342.29 345.36

ANNIHILATE PR 504.14 MD 819.34

ANNIHILATED BL 364.4 MD 812.19

ANNIVERSARY WS 260.24 PR 474.37

ANNOUNCED WM 65.13 DV 160.11
YT 396.21 LA 632.8 RH 793.37
MD 815.26

ANNOUNCEMENT SP 46.22

ANNOUNCING TP 338.16 FA 468.20

ANNOYED FA 470.25 PR 476.35

ANNUL EE 326.14

ANNULLED EE 325.38

ANNULLING EE 325.23

ANONYMOUS ML 731.2

ANSTRUTHER, ALAN (SEE ALAN)

ANSTRUTHER, KATHERINE (SEE
KATHERINE)

ANSWER MO 9.20 11.14 15.15
21.37 OA 31.36 31.40
37.15 SP 51.39 52.21
WM 55.5 57.16 58.6 58.19
65.37 EA 72.40 74.29
79.13 87.42 88.37 90.20
91.14 PO 100.42 101.5
TF 125.6 133.35 DV 162.27
171.20 172.11 176.9
178.38 179.26 FG 192.14
SG 226.37 231.40 232.3
232.12 GF 239.30 WS 254.4
256.35 258.25 CH 277.22
OC 284.14 284.20 284.26
EE 311.10 320.26 325.22
328.2 BL 354.3 364.4
364.20 364.21 MN 369.31
369.34 373.12 375.9
375.13 376.10 YT 408.2
SD 422.21 425.9 425.25
PP 439.14 HD 441.3 442.41
443.34 443.41 447.20
SU 531.38 544.25 545.1
WR 552.14 562.39 581.12
BO 602.28 JD 628.36
GG 664.40 681.42 694.6
698.19 698.22 NT 714.29
719.29 LL 771.35 RH 802.3
803.36 BM 839.37 842.24

ANSWERED MO 5.34 7.30 7.36
8.3 11.37 12.19 12.27
13.18 15.37 19.9 20.7
20.30 21.19 OA 29.42 31.6
31.8 31.41 38.3 SP 51.30
52.12 52.18 WM 57.25
58.29 59.28 61.2 63.26
66.22 67.16 67.18 67.36
68.27 70.21 EA 74.17
76.31 77.26 77.37 78.7
78.40 79.6 79.30 88.31
89.1 93.6 93.10 94.4
PO 99.1 101.16 TF 128.19
129.31 DV 146.11 159.42
163.26 168.7 169.38
177.41 178.37 179.31
183.25 FG 191.36 192.25
192.31 193.18 195.16
195.40 196.6 196.8
SS 198.34 200.16
201.7* 203.34
209.3 210.42 211.14
SB 219.9 GF 236.35 237.4
237.8 WS 249.18 256.25
259.24 SC 270.23 CH 275.12
OC 298.36 TP 345.19
BL 352.32 353.31 353.34
355.3 355.5 355.8 355.9
355.15 356.19 359.13
MN 377.13 WP 380.18 385.22
388.3 388.12 391.26
YT 402.5 408.12 409.30
SD 414.24 PP 437.31

ANSWERED (CONT.) HD 451.26 452.1
 452.8 456.31 457.7 FA 459.32
 460.15 463.34 470.9 PR 474.30
 474.31 508.32 510.13
 TB 517.39 WR 554.16 567.24
 573.6 BO 590.22 590.26
 LA 634.4 634.37 644.8
 GG 684.4 698.17 698.28
 NT 721.3 ML 727.2 OV 755.2
 756.11 756.16 756.22
 BM 833.42

ANSWERING MO 3.1 OA 28.41
 WM 57.2 EA 93.14 PO 101.21
 101.30 DV 152.17 171.37
 SS 205.3 SG 228.29 WS 253.27
 265.30 CH 275.4 OC 292.27
 301.39 EE 324.42 SD 414.35
 424.36 WR 559.28 566.15
 569.15 IL 651.40 654.8
 GG 698.17 ML 729.8 RR 785.18

ANSWERS OA 33.12 MN 368.7
 BO 598.11 GG 698.14

ANT WR 558.2

ANTAGONISM WS 257.17 TP 337.4
 344.2 PP 432.2 HD 446.6

ANTAGONIST OA 33.11

ANTAGONISTIC DV 150.39

ANTHEM FA 466.26

ANTICIPATED PR 483.18

ANTICIPATING WM 59.1

ANTICIPATION TF 133.2 WS 251.24
 253.10 YT 404.32

ANTI-LIFE PR 496.42 TH 850.36

ANTIPATHIES PR 477.18

ANTIPATHY PP 428.31 PR 477.21
 492.13

ANTIPHONY TP 335.24

ANTIQUE SS 202.39

ANTIQUE-DEALER'S MD 820.28

ANTIQUES LL 778.37

ANTITHESIS WM 61.14

AN'T SP 50.1

ANTS TB 516.13

ANXIETY PO 97.41 TF 118.26
 120.31 125.28 132.23
 DV 146.27 157.19 176.1
 SB 214.29 EE 318.5 BL 348.26
 MN 377.39 SU 532.4 WR 557.16
 GG 691.15 RH 790.21 802.13
 802.17 802.38 803.7 MD 815.24
 815.38

ANXIOUS MO 16.41 OA 35.3

ANXIOUS (CONT.) DV 165.8
 GF 237.21 WS 250.18
 OC 293.40 EE 320.8 TP 346.7
 WP 384.19 387.24 YT 401.26
 PR 488.36 488.39 SU 531.15
 532.33 WR 581.16 581.19
 581.20 JD 621.28 628.21
 LA 635.7 637.11 OV 753.32
 RH 790.11 793.33 799.10
 BM 838.36 TH 846.34

ANXIOUSLY OA 34.37 DV 148.25
 154.13 170.6 GF 236.1
 BL 355.14 358.37 364.38
 MN 368.17 WP 387.11 PP 438.1
 438.5 PR 491.5 511.28
 LA 635.7 646.12 IL 653.31
 654.6 GG 665.8 ML 740.28
 LL 772.12 RH 800.37 BM 838.25
 841.28

ANYBODY MO 20.32 EA 75.1 82.42
 87.32 94.8 PO 104.35 105.23
 DV 140.20 185.9 SB 215.27
 SG 223.15 229.1 SC 270.23
 273.6 OC 285.23 294.23
 YT 399.31 HD 447.20 FA 468.21
 470.8 471.28 471.37 PR 475.31
 478.22 508.33 TB 513.7 518.36
 519.32 WR 549.5 JD 608.4
 621.22 LA 642.25 IL 652.20
 652.21 GG 672.1 675.1 689.21
 NT 702.41 703.17 717.8
 LL 767.8 769.14 778.11
 RH 790.13 MD 805.19 815.31
 BM 842.10

ANYBODY'D SP 52.36

ANYBODY'S PR 508.35

ANYHOW EE 314.3 WP 392.29
 SD 419.36 FA 471.27 PR 493.40
 TB 526.9 WR 567.18 SM 583.1
 JD 626.2 LA 641.28 642.27
 IL 655.24 658.16 659.8
 GG 662.28 663.38 671.18
 NT 714.35 721.12 LL 762.8
 765.37 RR 779.18 779.31
 RH 792.26 793.22 MD 818.10
 BM 840.23

ANYONE WM 68.15 EA 86.25
 PO 111.23 TF 117.31 DV 146.20
 150.37 154.41 160.9 SB 217.1
 WS 245.21 OC 302.3 BO 587.7
 LA 636.3 GG 664.33 ML 727.34
 OV 753.38 RH 790.20

ANYTHING MO 9.10 12.39 20.8
 22.21 22.27 OA 28.11 31.7
 37.8 HT 41.1 SP 52.27
 WM 55.25 62.14 EA 76.21 77.30
 78.21 80.5 80.24 82.8 88.9
 PO 100.14 111.29 114.12
 TF 128.18 129.30 133.41
 DV 141.18 155.38 160.3 162.38
 165.22 165.39 168.35 173.1
 181.29 181.36 183.8 SS 205.31
 SG 223.9 232.3 WS 249.16
 258.22 260.28 262.30 263.9
 263.29 263.37 265.5 SC 273.10
 CH 275.6 276.42 OC 287.6 291.5
 295.34 EE 307.26 307.27

ANYTHING (CONT.) 309.42
 310.41 318.25 321.16
 BL 348.7 348.12 355.11
 361.28 WP 382.11 385.17
 391.5 392.2 392.32
 YT 398.38 399.31 401.1
 401.5 405.21 405.25 408.18
 409.1 SD 419.11 424.42
 PP 429.37 430.14 435.26
 435.31 438.36 HD 441.5
 444.38 PR 473.21 473.22
 480.19 483.25 487.9
 487.22 492.1 493.34 495.14
 500.10 503.34 510.1
 TB 513.28 514.42 515.25
 516.39 517.6 518.12 518.33
 519.18 526.38 SU 529.21
 535.35 541.37 542.6
 WR 547.37 548.30 565.13
 BO 591.19 592.35 593.40
 JD 612.23 613.36 615.36
 616.4 616.19 617.12 619.35
 620.14 620.37 628.23
 IL 649.15 649.32 GG 675.8
 677.3 680.26 682.1 688.19
 689.26 693.41 NT 705.9
 711.10 711.15 712.9 712.27
 715.20 716.21 717.7
 717.12 718.13 ML 728.13
 731.11 734.38 735.16
 737.29 OV 751.36 751.38
 753.4 LL 763.4 767.39
 772.23 773.13 RR 780.26
 780.37 RH 790.32 791.1
 794.18 794.26 797.4 799.30
 MD 809.34 809.41 814.37
 814.38 815.12 815.42
 816.42 817.4 817.22 818.19
 819.21 819.36 820.20
 824.16 BM 831.4 833.24
 836.11 842.10 TH 846.24

ANYTHINK OC 291.30

ANYWAY HD 446.17 PR 488.41
 JD 628.12 LA 644.12
 IL 653.19 655.19 659.27
 NT 715.6 TH 851.23

ANYWHERE EA 81.24 83.25
 TF 132.20 DV 155.39
 EE 324.6 BL 353.1 SD 416.34
 PP 429.35 436.13 PR 473.21
 WR 561.30 JD 612.19 619.36
 GG 666.20 NT 702.38
 LL 769.16

APART MO 21.23 22.12
 WM 61.40 EA 80.9 82.32
 94.6 PO 115.38 116.1
 TF 118.29 DV 138.6 146.7
 146.17 151.16 156.10
 SS 210.21 SG 221.33
 WS 252.41 OC 299.40 300.26
 300.34 301.4 301.8 301.32
 302.6 EE 308.25 BL 365.2
 SD 423.22 423.28 424.35
 PP 438.31 FA 463.40
 PR 502.2 TB 513.11 519.16
 WR 570.32 SM 585.16
 JD 617.25 622.2 NT 715.25
 OV 750.13 754.3 759.26
 LL 778.9 RH 793.38 MD 807.7
 807.28

APARTMENT   EA 81.10   PO 97.19
   SS 206.29   206.34   SG 222.15
   GG 671.1   671.10   NT 710.3
   721.13   MD 807.33   810.23
   811.16   811.27   814.2   815.14
   817.15   817.21   817.35   817.38
   821.13   821.16   823.35   824.23
   824.33   825.38   TH 844.23
   847.41   848.41   849.15   849.16
   849.42   850.38   851.32

APATHETIC   PO 107.20   PP 433.19
   SU 537.7

APATHY   JD 613.21   614.22

APIECE   GF 243.6

APLOMB   DV 140.24   SD 413.34
   TB 517.23   GG 688.27

APOLLO'S   EA 92.36

APOLOGETIC   JD 624.12

APOLOGISE   DV 185.32

APOLOGISED   OC 291.36

APOLOGISING   CH 274.26

APOLOGY   OC 291.37

APPALLED   EA 78.22   DV 165.21

APPARATUS   SU 536.18

APPARENT   GG 675.4   LL 776.27

APPARENTLY   WM 58.26   SS 199.27
   206.40   SG 221.28   WS 245.31
   EE 321.13   321.20   SD 411.15
   PR 511.24   512.17   TB 517.32
   WR 567.30   JD 610.20   610.33
   610.35   614.30   LA 634.4
   GG 672.19   672.21   687.21
   NT 721.9   ML 738.25   RR 781.13
   783.1   MD 806.38

APPARITION   ML 723.16

APPEAL   WM 68.1   EA 79.22   90.25
   93.12   SS 204.37   SU 542.12
   BO 601.38

APPEALED   MO 5.28   WS 255.13
   PP 434.21   RR 786.27

APPEALING   OA 36.39   DV 169.6
   WS 250.4   MD 809.5   809.7

APPEALINGLY   OA 38.35

APPEAR   TP 335.5   OV 753.20
   LL 775.27   MD 815.39

APPEARANCE   SB 217.22   SG 225.8
   226.18   GF 235.26   WS 250.24
   CH 275.21   MN 366.22   374.22
   HD 456.13   PR 483.14   484.33
   484.37   488.30   SM 586.21
   MD 809.24   BM 832.1

APPEARANCES   EA 91.25

APPEARED   OA 28.39   PO 103.28
   TF 134.21   SG 224.26   WS 246.17
   254.9   CH 276.23   278.18
   OC 283.3   EE 320.10   330.39
   MN 366.36   PP 436.34   PR 511.11
   TB 516.20   522.3   524.15
   SU 538.4   WR 562.22   SM 583.12
   JD 615.5   IL 649.11   GG 661.13
   672.23   ML 730.4   739.7   744.2
   LL 766.3   766.4   777.4
   RR 783.23   784.9   RH 799.35

APPEARING   OC 292.35

APPEARS   DV 143.8

'APPEN   HT 42.2   SB 213.28   215.30
   OC 292.18   294.19   294.20
   294.25   300.18

APPENWEIER   BO 599.41

APPLAUDING   NT 714.10

APPLAUSE   OA 32.23

APPLE   DV 136.14   139.6   160.31
   SS 204.2   204.5   SG 221.22
   221.23   OC 283.35   MN 366.9
   YT 398.7   PR 481.27   OV 759.38

APPLE-BLOSSOM   PR 476.29   479.36

APPLE-CART   EE 311.30

APPLE-PIE   DV 163.6

APPLES   MO 18.28   18.33   SG 222.31
   FA 465.3

APPLICATION   DV 164.38

APPLIED   DV 174.6   EE 314.7
   HD 449.18

APPLY   ML 729.6

APPLYING   WP 381.38

APPOINTED   BO 594.34

APPOINTMENT   WM 63.29   MN 369.29
   369.32   NT 721.5

APPOINTMENTS   MD 823.35

APPRAISE   MD 820.28

APPRECIATE   MO 5.25   BO 588.34
   JD 607.16   GG 665.25

APPRECIATED   EE 309.27   TP 339.6
   SU 533.32

APPRECIATION   SG 221.15   BL 351.8

APPRECIATIVELY   WS 244.16
   OC 285.30

APPREHENSION   TF 131.28   DV 151.31
   154.41   168.38   SU 528.15
   IL 647.24   ML 737.16

APPREHENSIVELY   GG 667.6

APPROACH   WM 68.7   DV 160.9
   164.42   172.40   173.18
   178.25   SG 228.33   BL 359.32
   ML 738.24   740.30   742.33
   BM 836.3

APPROACHED   HT 42.29   PO 108.32
   SB 214.31   217.28   SG 228.3
   GF 240.17   242.2   BL 347.33
   MN 373.19   376.26   WP 388.4
   388.29   YT 409.30   WR 562.37
   ML 740.31

APPROACHING   OA 27.2   WM 54.8
   54.30   PO 107.26   TF 134.19
   GF 241.42   BL 361.18
   MN 376.23   PP 432.26
   HD 447.28   PR 507.23

APPROPRIATE   LL 764.16

APPROVAL   SB 218.4

APPROVED   DV 146.36

APRON   OA 23.9   TF 129.33
   130.3   DV 159.2   SS 203.41
   SC 268.7   CH 277.26   OC 284.6
   288.32   WP 379.22

APRON-BAND   OC 284.41   289.1

APRON-STRINGS   GG 678.26

APROPOS   HD 443.14

APT   MO 6.33

AQUILA NERA   EA 88.42

ARABLE   MO 1.8   FG 187.5

ARC   WM 54.24   60.34

ARCADE   BO 596.28

ARCADY   SS 205.2

ARCH   SG 225.11   EE 306.6
   WP 379.15   LA 635.7   635.21
   GG 688.16   LL 761.14   776.25

ARCHAEOLOGIST   FG 187.33

ARCHAIC   SM 584.9

ARCHANGELS   NT 719.27

ARCHED   MO 9.13   13.16
   DV 167.3   EE 304.26
   BL 351.21   351.24   WP 388.21
   FA 460.41   PR 479.36
   BO 588.39   JD 606.23
   LA 631.12   GG 670.33
   LL 761.25   MD 809.3

ARCHER   EE 304.22

ARCHES   LL 761.26

ARCHIE   SG 231.6

ARCHING   LA 632.24   MD 809.20

ARCHITECT   SP 45.7

ARCHITECTURE TB 521.7 521.8

ARCHLY WP 379.9

ARC-LAMP LA 640.17

'ARD CH 279.16

ARDENT BO 587.29

A'READY SP 48.32 SS 209.14

ARENA SC 270.42

AREN'T MO 8.29 9.2 12.41
  SP 52.37 WM 59.37 59.38 59.41
  EA 75.39 77.18 DV 140.42
  179.29 SS 207.10 SB 212.5
  215.23 SG 228.35 GF 236.1
  WS 253.1 255.35 SC 268.18
  CH 279.14 EE 319.39 BL 355.14
  357.38 358.37 364.26
  MN 372.15 372.35 WP 382.21
  383.26 384.23 389.21
  SD 417.20 PP 439.7 439.12
  TB 522.24 WR 570.30 571.19
  BO 600.32 JD 608.10 620.6
  IL 653.27 659.8 GG 666.40
  NT 718.12 LL 776.12 RR 788.33
  788.35 RH 792.16 792.18
  793.29 MD 813.35 BM 833.16
  839.34 839.42 842.16

ARGUMENT OA 30.29 33.10 33.31
  WR 549.32

ARID WR 562.2

ARISTOCRAT PO 96.23 GG 661.36

ARISTOCRATIC MD 809.3

ARITHMETIC MO 10.13

ARIZONA BM 827.19

ARK OF THE COVENANT TH 848.25

ARM MO 20.42 22.6 OA 24.26
  HT 44.7 WM 59.12 65.27 70.9
  EA 91.26 PO 100.1 116.11
  TF 121.25 DV 138.38 158.33
  180.38 FG 191.21 191.29
  193.26 194.40 196.4 SS 210.39
  211.2 211.5 211.7 211.13
  SB 218.34 219.40 SG 222.16
  222.19 222.25 GF 236.17
  236.28 237.30 WS 244.18
  245.34 252.1 254.19 254.26
  255.15 257.15 257.21 259.11
  OC 288.30 298.30 TP 337.39
  338.23 338.30 344.1 BL 354.13
  364.1 MN 373.9 373.13 373.27
  376.7 WP 386.32 386.33
  SD 415.35 HD 454.20 455.16
  455.25 455.29 455.36
  PR 487.15 497.21 507.35
  507.38 WR 563.32 SM 583.5
  584.17 586.27 BO 596.24
  596.26 597.26 603.37
  JD 618.14 LA 633.16 634.12
  IL 650.17 652.37 654.9 655.26
  GG 681.27 683.1 687.33 689.36
  RR 784.2 784.5 MD 822.13
  BM 828.29 829.28 838.21

ARM-CHAIR MO 12.31 OA 27.25
  DV 140.16 178.17 SC 268.14
  269.5 WP 387.13 JD 617.5
  618.27 623.21 625.4 IL 654.12
  RR 784.34

ARM-CHAIRS WM 63.31

ARMENIAN MD 818.11 818.15
  818.22 819.28 826.16

ARMFUL PR 501.34 RR 785.39

ARMISTICE MN 378.37 YT 396.37

ARMOUR MO 5.35 LL 777.42

ARM-PITS TF 127.31

ARMS MO 2.20 5.2 5.42 13.41
  17.14 19.32 21.11 OA 25.16
  30.34 36.20 WM 58.15 58.18
  67.2 67.3 67.4 67.5 67.6
  68.32 68.35 68.36 69.9 69.20
  70.12 EA 72.1 73.21 75.41
  79.31 89.9 91.15 91.33 93.14
  TF 123.7 130.1 130.9 130.16
  DV 148.23 149.39 169.25
  170.37 171.1 178.22 179.34
  180.40 181.6 181.7 FG 191.31
  191.37 192.38 195.11 196.16
  SS 201.19 203.7 SB 212.25
  WS 247.14 251.34 253.10
  259.14 259.21 259.22 266.6
  SC 268.26 268.41 CH 280.7
  EE 317.13 317.14 330.20
  TP 343.18 BL 360.4 360.10
  WP 381.9 383.15 YT 397.13
  399.7 SD 420.9 420.36 421.11
  421.19 421.22 423.4 424.36
  425.32 425.33 PP 432.38
  433.12 437.9 HD 452.40 454.10
  457.2 PR 504.10 506.21 511.5
  SU 531.16 540.10 540.34
  540.39 540.40 WR 552.40
  563.39 568.26 569.1 580.35
  BO 604.26 JD 605.14 IL 653.29
  658.39 GG 669.34 671.33 673.2
  679.27 679.28 679.32 687.36
  689.34 696.20 NT 709.28 713.2
  713.3 713.6 713.8 713.9 713.6
  719.8 719.26 ML 732.32
  LL 763.23 773.35 RR 784.25
  785.8 RH 796.7 MD 818.3
  BM 835.42 837.20 837.29

ARM'S TP 336.38 337.6

ARMY PO 96.26 99.35 101.2
  SG 231.12 232.27 EE 327.31
  SD 415.9 WR 551.10 NT 704.32

ARNAULT MD 818.12 818.17 821.25
  822.14 822.15 822.16 822.22
  824.1 824.6 824.24 824.28
  824.38 825.6

ARNAULT, MONSIEUR (SEE MONSIEUR)

ARNO TH 847.39 849.15 851.32

ARNOLD ML 726.1 MD 818.12

AROSE OC 299.10

AROUSE ML 739.24

AROUSED TP 339.18 PR 482.36
  511.21 WR 547.10

ARRANGE TF 132.2 SG 223.37
  SD 419.29 PR 488.17*

ARRANGED EA 85.32 TF 131.11
  DV 143.16 GF 235.23
  TP 340.20 340.27 HD 447.41
  FA 464.4 PR 493.9 JD 627.31
  IL 655.18

ARRANGEMENT EA 78.19 DV 137.6
  PP 430.23 TB 516.5

ARRANGEMENTS YT 407.1
  JD 624.30 GG 668.27

ARRANGING WM 63.38 EA 92.32
  DV 176.13 SG 223.40
  SC 267.35

ARRAY HT 43.37 WR 546.34
  MD 810.38

ARRAYED TH 853.22

ARREST BL 356.3 PR 496.40

ARRESTED SG 225.35 WS 264.15
  OC 299.11 BL 354.39
  WP 387.21 PR 508.17
  WR 547.34 572.26 579.26
  580.13 BO 592.10 599.24
  LL 768.1 RR 788.24 RH 802.7
  802.41

ARRIVAL PO 114.18 YT 395.33
  397.7 400.37 FA 459.40

ARRIVALS BO 601.25

ARRIVE DV 176.12 GF 240.6
  EE 315.4 BL 356.16 WR 555.6
  JD 628.38 ML 744.3
  LL 775.29

ARRIVED MO 1.35 SP 51.13
  WM 58.3 DV 145.9 154.21
  154.37 158.1 182.29
  WS 260.25 SC 268.3
  YT 395.28 FA 460.19 460.25
  PR 481.20 SU 543.37
  JD 610.2 GG 669.2 NT 708.36
  ML 737.41 TH 849.39

ARRIVES HT 39.26

ARRIVING EA 72.22 PR 473.21

ARROGANCE MO 7.7 SS 204.3
  LL 774.3

ARROW WR 574.3 JD 606.32

ARROWS WR 549.14 JD 606.37

ARROW-STRING WR 568.17 574.4

ART MO 16.24 HT 41.34
  WS 246.11 248.25 SC 271.12
  CH 280.37 280.38 281.6
  281.37 FA 468.7 GG 661.2

ART (CONT.) 661.3 661.28 669.9
  NT 701.4 BM 827.14 TH 844.32
  844.33

ARTFUL MN 369.42

ARTHUR SS 209.5 209.8 209.16
  FA 460.1

ARTHUR PILBEAM SS 199.2

ARTICHOKE GG 689.14

ARTICLE BL 349.35 TB 521.6
  523.40

ARTICLES JD 607.22

ARTICULATED GF 235.36

ARTICULATING CH 276.11

ARTIFICIAL TP 337.16 BO 594.13
  LL 775.8

ARTIFICIALLY BO 594.15

ARTILLERY EE 328.15 IL 648.13
  653.16

ARTIST GG 662.27 RH 799.17
  799.19

ARTISTIC PR 479.14

ARTISTS PR 481.38 MD 811.22

ARTS EE 308.36 TP 338.34

'AS SC 262.9

ASCENDING WR 566.1 574.6 574.22

ASCENT WR 580.5 OV 754.25

ASCOT RH 794.5

ASH EA 77.5 SG 230.22 GF 241.35
  TP 334.9 HD 449.1 WR 573.32
  BO 593.29 598.12

ASHAMED HT 42.1 TF 125.30 134.3
  DV 147.30 165.1 165.9 169.15
  GF 236.34 239.25 OC 301.9
  301.29 302.2 BL 359.31
  PP 440.9 WR 564.15 LL 765.28

ASHES GF 239.23 WS 245.11
  WR 557.1

ASH-GREY PR 496.14

ASHORE SU 528.29 528.31

ASHTAROTH EE 326.13

ASH-TRAY RR 785.5

ASH-TWIGS WP 379.5

ASHY OC 283.20 BO 593.32 596.1
  597.21 598.14

ASIATIC EA 77.5

ASK MO 9.8 9.16 19.36 OA 26.37
  37.9 SP 51.24 52.10 52.42
  EA 77.7 87.2 87.41 88.18
  DV 159.37 182.33 SS 198.24
  SB 215.36 SG 224.41 GF 237.25
  WS 260.33 CH 280.32 OC 291.30
  294.21 EE 314.13 332.21
  BL 350.21 350.22 WP 391.16
  YT 404.19 404.21 405.8 406.19
  406.21 SD 414.1 416.4
  PP 437.21 HD 443.35 PR 510.5
  TB 517.1 524.22 WR 575.33
  BO 598.9 598.15 JD 607.41
  609.2 610.16 615.31 616.1
  616.6 622.8 622.40 622.41
  623.1 LA 633.39 GG 663.3
  667.4 NT 714.17 715.12
  OV 751.7 751.36 LL 771.33
  773.10 773.18 RR 782.15
  RH 797.13 801.7 MD 819.16
  823.12 823.13 824.36 BM 832.7
  832.9 839.26 839.28 839.29

ASKEW WR 561.36

ASKING WM 67.27 PO 98.40
  DV 178.26 183.13 185.32
  SG 228.10 232.7 BL 350.16
  PP 433.30 TB 513.20 JD 610.18
  RR 787.35 RH 794.20 799.36

ASKS MO 9.15 WR 560.6 571.12
  RH 794.15

ASLEEP MO 16.20 DV 174.37
  174.40 OC 298.21 298.22
  YT 401.35 401.37 PR 503.15
  504.35 SU 536.42 GG 690.16
  ML 723.37 BM 832.4

AS'LL BM 841.3

'ASNA OC 292.14

'ASN'T OC 291.19

ASPECT HT 38.18

ASPECTS MN 370.11

ASPEN PR 490.33 493.19 499.33
  500.39 WR 552.39 553.14
  559.15 579.18

ASPENS PR 486.10 487.26 489.15
  493.20 494.4 494.8 494.25
  499.31 WR 556.5 559.9

ASPETTATO COME L'AGONIZZANTE
  ASPETTA LA + LL 774.19

ASPHODEL MD 812.36

ASPHODELS SU 535.34 MD 812.35

ASPIC MD 818.20

ASS MO 20.23 EE 312.38 312.40
  SU 536.1 543.37

ASSAILED PR 504.19 JD 606.37

ASSEMBLE MD 811.39

ASSEMBLED MO 5.10 ML 730.1

ASSEMBLY EA 72.20

ASSENTED MO 20.14 WM 68.41
  SS 207.18 YT 394.19
  SD 412.13 · TB 522.38

ASSERT DV 181.41

ASSERTED OA 27.40 EE 327.15
  BO 589.12 591.17 GG 693.15
  RH 792.30

ASSERTING DV 152.32

ASSERTION DV 145.23 145.24
  RH 792.37

ASSERTIVE OC 285.25 ML 740.18
  MD 817.17

ASSERTS BO 590.23

ASSET JD 625.10

ASSETS ML 731.41

ASSIDUOUSLY DV 146.23

ASSISTANT HD 448.12 BO 592.36

ASSISTING DV 159.19

ASSOCIATE EE 332.1

ASSOCIATES HD 447.4

ASSOCIATION TF 118.9

ASSORTED GF 235.19 CH 274.27

ASS'S NT 718.26

ASSUME BO 587.36 588.36
  MD 823.34

ASSUMED PO 103.28 SS 201.26
  YT 403.26 LL 766.26

ASSUMING SS 201.22 EE 315.22
  316.11

ASSUMPTION CH 278.32 BO 588.35

ASSURANCE MO 20.30 DV 181.9
  SS 204.40 205.30 EE 320.38
  HD 453.27 FA 466.7 466.8
  WR 554.19 554.36 BO 591.16
  MD 822.33 BM 840.4

ASSURE MO 7.21 OC 295.5
  BO 604.7 GG 695.2 MD 822.35
  BM 829.6

ASSURED DV 157.41 CH 277.24
  PP 437.15 FA 472.13 PR 476.37
  477.23 WR 553.22 MD 809.27
  BM 838.9

ASTERS FA 464.31 465.3

ASTONISHED OA 30.32 PO 112.6
  DV 162.9 SS 199.13 205.16
  LL 776.6 776.18

ASTONISHING MD 811.35

ASTON VILLA   SP 47.26

ASTOUNDED   GG 674.23   LL 776.6

ASTRIDE   TP 338.5   PR 478.40
  WR 551.6

ASTRONOMY   BO 589.14   590.31

ATE   MO 5.20   5.30   WM 67.33
  PO 109.30   TF 124.40   SG 222.42
  WS 255.25   SC 268.26   CH 278.41
  OC 288.4   EE 318.33   SD 414.8
  PP 437.19   439.15   PR 494.23
  502.19   WR 552.25   JD 618.39
  618.40   625.22   GG 674.32
  674.37   688.26   689.18
  ML 738.39   739.7   743.22   743.37
  744.24   MD 806.32   816.5

ATLANTIC   SU 529.7

ATLANTIC OCEAN   SD 411.26

ATMOSPHERE   MO 5.25   17.15
  OA 23.27   WM 69.8   EA 81.23
  84.37   89.32   89.35   PO 95.9
  107.37   108.30   DV 166.21
  173.24   SS 202.25   GF 234.27
  235.8   WS 254.31   EE 320.19
  323.27   PP 436.28   HD 447.31
  BO 601.37   GG 688.37   689.1
  ML 735.18   BM 831.9

ATMOSPHERIC   MD 811.6

ATOP   OC 295.40

ATROCIOUS   LL 773.23

ATROCITIES   EE 327.20   NT 711.7

ATTACHED   TF 126.30   TB 513.3
  LA 632.16   TH 845.2

ATTACHMENT   TF 126.36   SS 208.14
  LL 768.23   TH 845.3

ATTACK   PO 111.11   FA 467.20
  TB 520.3   WR 557.18

ATTACKS   YT 408.19

ATTAINMENT   BO 597.10

ATTEMPT   WM 55.35   PP 437.4
  GG 675.27   BM 835.40

ATTEMPTED   FG 188.34

ATTEMPTING   HD 441.7

ATTEMPTS   SB 215.4   ML 725.10

ATTENBOROUGH, PAULINE   (SEE
  PAULINE)

ATTEND   DV 156.25   SG 227.20
  EE 307.12   BL 360.10   HD 448.13
  451.12   451.32   PR 500.18
  MD 817.27   826.9

ATTENDANCE   PO 97.10   WR 578.22
  LL 770.7

ATTENDANT   EA 81.6

ATTENDED   SP 53.25   EA 86.26
  DV 146.23   163.27   164.13
  177.12   SS 208.40   SG 226.42
  WS 251.11   BL 347.22   WP 389.33
  HD 447.6   JD 617.12   GG 674.36

ATTENDING   DV 143.11   BL 353.35
  356.15   MN 367.20   WP 389.36
  PR 499.26   ML 729.12   MD 815.14
  815.17   815.21   TH 848.41

ATTENTION   OA 29.12   WM 58.35
  PO 98.42   100.36   102.6
  TF 122.16   134.28   134.29
  DV 157.42   170.9   172.32   184.41
  SG 221.9   WS 265.39   BL 348.30
  MN 368.9   WP 381.2   YT 403.16
  SD 414.21   PP 427.4   438.30
  PR 509.16   IL 656.36   GG 663.41
  NT 709.17   ML 726.19   LL 764.10
  RR 785.21   RH 792.37   792.38
  BM 827.15

ATTENTIONS   TB 516.21   BM 827.10

ATTENTIVE   MO 5.14   DV 179.18
  HD 449.25   449.32   GG 663.25

ATTENTIVELY   LL 771.26

ATTENTIVENESS   SB 218.40

ATTEST   GG 699.16

ATTIC   PP 429.32

ATTITUDE   MO 11.18   WM 59.1
  EA 84.34   DV 147.23   GF 236.20
  BL 349.21   MN 377.11   TB 523.36
  BO 591.22   BM 830.40

ATTITUDES   MN 367.35

ATTRACT   OA 23.14

ATTRACTED   DV 173.6   MN 367.39
  PR 480.26   WR 576.4   JD 608.30
  GG 682.5   NT 709.1   MD 813.36

ATTRACTING   OA 29.12   PR 509.16

ATTRACTION   DV 160.19   165.11
  WS 250.31   252.25   257.35
  FA 465.34   PR 480.25   SU 543.8
  GG 683.14

ATTRACTIONS   EE 305.14   FA 462.20

ATTRACTIVE   SG 224.29   EE 323.4
  TP 336.31   MN 374.22   SD 413.34
  413.35   PP 438.27   FA 465.18
  PR 473.13   TB 513.4   BO 587.2
  LL 771.23   RR 782.23   MD 813.25
  814.6

ATTRIBUTED   MD 812.26

ATTRIBUTES   EA 89.10

AUBURN   SG 221.32

AUBUSSON   MD 810.35   810.41
  817.17   818.4   821.15

AUCTION   ML 738.15   738.16

AUDIBLE   BO 600.14   LL 772.34

AUDIENCE   MO 12.42   EA 85.42
  FA 467.26   468.17   GG 664.33
  LL 763.39   BM 835.21   835.33
  836.25   837.12   837.24   838.2
  838.16   841.18   843.6

AUDITORIUM   GG 665.29

AUGUST   PR 481.21   GG 663.35
  ML 740.2

AUNT   PP 430.11   FA 460.26
  460.30   460.33   460.38
  461.9   461.10   461.13   461.19
  461.27   461.28   461.30
  461.32   463.7   463.8   463.11
  GG 667.14   LL 762.12   763.37
  764.2   766.18   768.39   775.41
  776.4   777.41

AUNT BELL'S   BL 358.21

AUNTIE LOUISA   DV 159.15

AUNT KATE   FA 463.39

AUNT LIZZIE   FA 463.15

AUNT MAUD   PP 430.39   432.3
  437.36   PR 476.33

AUNT PAULINE   LL 762.11   762.18
  762.24   762.37   763.36
  765.37   766.3   768.2   768.3
  768.36   768.38   769.11
  769.22   769.28   775.20
  775.27   778.26

AUNT PAULINE'S   LL 762.17
  768.37

AUNTS   PR 473.1

AUNT'S   FA 460.25   470.12
  LL 770.29   772.38   772.42

AURA   PR 480.3   BO 596.39
  JD 629.11

AUSTERITY   OA 31.21

AUSTRALIA   PP 427.27   430.20
  431.6   432.13

AUSTRIAN   MD 810.25

AUTHOR   RR 786.11

AUTHORESS   JD 609.27

AUTHORISE   GG 689.8

AUTHORITIES   SC 271.26
  TP 335.17

AUTHORITY   PO 99.31   TF 122.24
  132.25   EE 314.38   315.2
  315.4   315.11   315.30   315.32
  315.41   316.6   316.7
  TP 343.2   PR 478.12   488.17
  WR 554.14   BO 596.25

BABBLED   WM 56.18

BABIES   DV 177.27   EE 311.14
   WR 568.26

BABY   OA 24.28   24.37   25.11
   25.30   25.36   25.39   25.41
   26.24   26.32   26.42   27.3   27.9
   27.15   34.11   DV 141.26   154.23
   154.26   155.3   156.18   156.26
   156.33   157.5   157.10   157.12
   158.13   158.20   158.37   159.14
   159.25   159.36   164.17   186.2
   CH 275.34   275.39   276.38   277.6
   278.8   279.2   279.25   280.13
   280.16   281.20   281.29   281.38
   282.4   282.8   282.16   OC 300.11
   EE 326.2   BL 348.22   WP 381.3
   381.12   381.23   383.13   383.30
   383.32   391.33   391.39
   SD 419.17   420.8   HD 443.4
   PR 474.10   474.14   474.21
   TB 520.14   SU 530.24   541.29
   GG 667.12   667.17   ML 739.12

BABY'S   OA 25.32   28.40   DV 159.5
   159.18

BACCHAE   WM 67.4

BACCHANAL   OA 25.11   26.8

BACCHANTE   LL 762.2

BACCHUS   GG 677.27   677.29

BACHELOR   FG 187.13   WS 250.22
   BL 359.20   FA 468.4   WR 547.20
   547.21   BM 827.27   830.21

BACHELOR'S   WR 547.23

BACHELOR'S BUTTONS   TB 520.33

BACHMANN   TF 117.16   118.19
   119.26   119.31   119.40   121.31
   121.42   123.13   123.40   124.24
   124.32   125.6   125.22   126.5
   127.40   128.4   128.19   128.28
   128.32   129.7   129.13   131.9
   131.13   131.16   131.20   132.2
   132.36   133.34   134.11   134.24
   134.35   134.41

BACHMANN'S   TF 120.1

BACK-CLOTH   BM 835.17

BACKED   SP 50.24   DV 155.26
   OC 297.14   SU 544.5   RR 784.7
   MD 806.29   807.3

BACKERS   SP 50.20

BACKFIRE   WS 261.39

BACK-FIRE   WS 262.6

BACKGROUND   EA 86.27   PO 99.34
   WP 388.4   WR 579.32   SM 585.19
   JD 621.19   MD 806.14

BACKING   OC 297.3   SU 544.4
   MD 818.41

BACKS   MO 5.1   SP 49.20   PO 95.28
   WS 261.8   PR 498.3   SU 531.1
   WR 578.16   NT 707.13   707.39
   ML 741.10

BACKWARD   PO 110.5   DV 170.41

BACKWARDS   OA 35.22   EA 83.3
   PO 110.1   TF 121.28   EE 332.42
   BL 360.19   SD 422.1   SM 585.11
   MD 816.28

BACK-WASH   TB 517.33

BACK-YARD   DV 161.1   JD 610.38

BACON   FG 190.31   190.32
   CH 274.19   YT 398.18   HD 442.25
   PR 495.23   495.30   ML 745.17

BACON-RIND   HD 442.20

BAD   MO 1.3   SP 45.23   WM 67.13
   EA 81.12   PO 105.26   TF 128.26
   128.28   DV 142.4   143.38   143.40
   152.22   169.37   SS 200.31
   GF 235.8   238.36   240.38
   WS 262.28   262.30   SC 269.36
   OC 288.21   291.42   292.33
   294.16   295.26   EE 321.3   326.32
   326.35   BL 363.18   MN 374.31
   374.34   YT 398.32   408.19
   SD 419.20   PP 431.10   431.13
   435.7   435.11   437.38   438.6
   HD 444.29   444.35   446.42
   FA 463.35   468.38   471.28
   PR 491.14   491.17   TB 517.20
   517.28   519.39   519.42   520.5
   IL 648.2   652.36   GG 667.4
   683.29   683.33   NT 704.35
   706.29   711.15   711.18
   LL 768.31   RH 801.4   804.34
   MD 808.34   815.32   819.2

BADE   HT 41.6   SP 50.39   DV 157.28
   WS 253.9   OC 298.30   MN 373.14

BADEN-BADEN   BO 588.4   600.27

BADGE   YT 396.17

BADGER   PR 497.12

BADINAGE   MO 5.11

BADISCH   BO 600.5

BADLY   MO 6.32   13.2   13.7
   DV 144.18   169.9   YT 402.24
   406.32   HD 447.13   PR 482.5
   492.5   WR 555.25   IL 649.40
   ML 743.9   MD 815.41

BAFFLED   SB 219.18   EE 311.42
   324.4   324.9   SD 416.37
   JD 611.18   LA 632.1   640.41
   RR 786.17   MD 822.28   TH 852.41

BAFORE   OC 285.35

BAG   DV 174.1   SB 216.16   CH 275.8
   275.16   275.21   275.38   281.27
   281.31   WP 387.26   387.31
   387.37   HD 447.29   FA 460.36
   JD 625.32   RR 783.6

BAGGALEY, MURIEL   (SEE MURIEL)

BAGGING   PO 108.17

BAGGY   TF 119.23

BAGPIPES   FG 189.21

BAGS   FA 458.15   458.25   458.35
   459.33   460.9   PR 495.34
   BO 587.4   587.24   600.36
   GG 669.41

BAH   BO 589.36

BAILIFF   ML 725.17   726.11
   726.40   727.2   727.4   727.16
   728.23   728.30   729.1   729.7
   729.11   730.1   730.4   730.16
   732.17

BAIN'T   MN 372.40

BAITED   TB 525.29

BAITING   SG 232.23

BAKE   CH 281.40

BAKER   WS 250.7

BAKERS   CH 274.18

BAKER'S   CH 281.29   281.39
   MN 372.31   JD 616.1

BAKER STREET   EE 321.25

BALAAM'S ASS   FA 466.13

BALANCE   MO 15.14   18.21
   OA 27.16   29.9   PO 112.7
   TF 127.6   DV 176.35
   WS 265.2   HD 450.27
   SU 536.23   BO 592.21
   JD 617.4   GG 683.38
   RR 780.18

BALANCED   OA 28.2   29.3
   SP 48.9   DV 145.21   SS 198.14
   SG 225.25   WS 247.15
   BL 354.18   FA 465.7
   OV 755.7   LL 770.14

BALANCING   WS 251.31   SU 534.2
   ML 732.9

BALCONY   SU 542.27   542.35
   543.38

BALD   MO 10.13   JD 613.20
   614.41   LA 631.9   GG 670.24
   673.15   692.38

BALDNESS   WS 250.24   GG 694.18

BALES   SD 420.14

BALKING   WM 62.32

BALL   MO 15.2   WS 248.36
   GG 686.6   686.13

BALLAD   SS 203.21

BALLET-DANCER'S WS 261.35 262.4

BALLROOM BO 594.17

BALLS SS 204.6 TB 515.34

BALSAM PR 478.42 WR 556.33

BALUSTRADED LL 765.10

BALZAC MO 6.29 MD 805.3

BALZACIAN MD 805.36

BANAL BM 836.29

BAND WS 252.19 WR 558.25
  LA 632.17 637.5

BANDAGED EE 319.23

BANDED TF 123.25 LA 632.36

BANG PR 510.30 IL 652.30

BANGED OC 295.19

BANISTERS PO 101.34

BANK DV 167.11 FG 195.2
  SS 210.7 MN 371.14 374.26
  YT 401.11 PP 436.28 HD 449.38
  450.7 450.38 450.39 451.5
  PR 499.30 BO 599.35 ML 729.33
  730.26 OV 748.29 748.32
  752.31 BM 827.37 830.16 834.9

BANK-CLERKS YT 394.37

BANK-MANAGER BM 832.1

BANKRUPT ML 732.14

BANKS WM 55.19 SG 225.24
  EE 330.25 MN 376.20

BANNISTER OA 35.23

BANNISTERS OA 36.15

BANNS DV 185.36

BANTER MO 15.8

BANTLE OC 292.26

BAPTIZE CH 280.12

BAPTIZING CH 279.13

BAR HT 39.27 SP 47.11 FG 191.13
  TP 338.8 SD 412.1 415.21
  416.24 417.36 418.13 419.7
  419.10 420.16 423.15
  PP 432.24 432.37 433.12
  433.33 WR 569.2 BO 589.22

BARB JD 620.25

BARBARA EE 316.19 326.2

BARBARIAN EE 305.30

BARBARIC SS 206.41 EE 309.37
  WR 550.11 580.30 BO 599.32
  600.12 JD 618.41 LL 764.22

BAR-COUNTER SD 423.19 PP 433.21

BARE MO 6.2 19.31 OA 34.31
  PO 113.6 114.38 TF 117.9
  125.34 125.37 DV 139.6 139.12
  173.4 180.23 FG 189.10
  SS 197.27 201.20 206.16
  206.19 206.24 211.13 WS 255.8
  SC 268.26 268.27 EE 303.5
  304.33 TP 344.1 WP 386.2
  386.5 YT 400.31 408.15
  PP 432.18 HD 453.10 453.32
  455.16 455.25 PR 493.18
  493.20 496.7 498.23 SU 533.37
  WR 549.18 556.9 558.6 562.2
  569.11 578.27 LA 641.31
  GG 661.29 669.34 674.10
  NT 720.11 ML 740.18 OV 749.42
  751.18 LL 763.24 BM 829.27
  841.7

BARE-ARMED BM 831.16

BARED SM 585.4 585.13 OV 753.30

BAREFOOT DV 155.17 WR 564.26
  BM 836.33 837.19

BARE-FOOT PO 106.14

BARE-FOOTED TF 134.22

BAREHEADED EE 321.40 BO 604.30
  604.32 LA 630.10 OV 751.17

BARE-HEADED MN 367.13 PR 510.36
  WR 562.23

BARELY PR 498.18 ML 742.37
  MD 818.13

BARENESS SS 202.6

BARFORD DV 186.23

BARGAIN DV 154.3 155.8
  FA 463.35 OV 758.16 758.18

BARGAINED DV 155.7 FA 461.30
  IL 652.20

BARGAINING OV 758.8 758.10

BARK PO 114.7 FG 190.6 193.11
  WP 379.34 SU 538.15 538.21
  WR 570.8

BARKED TF 119.24 CH 277.26
  BL 362.12 MN 372.39 375.41
  SD 418.5 418.34 PP 430.40
  HD 444.16 GG 674.17

BARKING MO 10.29 TF 118.17
  121.23 FG 191.3 GG 685.12

BARLEY SB 214.1 214.6 217.4

BARLOW (SEE PERCY; MR. BARLOW;
  MRS. BARLOW)

BARMAN PP 432.25

BARN MO 1.25 10.31 17.30 17.41
  18.3 18.8 18.37 SP 45.4
  EE 304.34 BL 362.14 ML 729.40

BARN-PLACE BL 362.24

BARON TF 127.17 128.37
  129.11 133.21 133.31
  133.36 133.42 134.9
  134.10 134.14 134.39
  135.3 135.7 135.12
  BO 587.14

BARONESS TF 126.30 127.14
  127.16 128.37 129.11

BARONET BO 588.28

BARON'S TF 123.11 133.38

BAROQUE TH 844.17

BAR-PARLOUR HT 39.24

BARRACKS PO 112.20 TF 117.8
  122.28 122.34 123.13
  124.20 132.15 135.2

BARRANCA WR 559.7

BARRASS, JIMMY (SEE JIMMY)

BARRED YT 406.20

BARREL MO 14.34

BARRELS GF 241.16 PP 432.21

BARREN MO 4.39 5.33 SP 45.12
  EA 80.10 82.6 DV 142.41
  WS 265.3 PR 478.9 478.11
  OV 755.14

BARRENLY PO 99.24

BARRENNESS TH 845.24

BARRIER PO 95.20 NT 713.23
  OV 750.22

BARRING SS 198.2 SD 422.38

BARRISTER BL 349.4 349.30
  358.33 359.36 LL 762.30

BARROWS PP 433.8

BARS PO 114.25 SS 197.12
  SD 423.34 WR 564.31 577.16

BAR-STIFF FG 190.17

BASE PO 103.21 107.5 110.8
  BO 601.35

BASES PO 108.42

BASHFUL TF 123.35

BASHFULNESS TF 128.23

BASIC EA 82.36 EE 313.5

BASILISK'S WR 573.23

BASIN YT 399.8

BASINS SU 533.37

BASIS   WS 250.13   LL 769.39

BASK   LL 766.31

BASKET   FG 188.16   OC 283.7
  WP 387.2   NT 707.10

BASKET-TRAY   WR 565.1

BASKING   SU 536.42

BASLE   BO 593.35

BASSETT   RH 794.7   794.9   794.14
  794.16   794.23   795.3   795.26
  795.27   795.33   796.14   796.19
  796.22   796.23   796.25   796.28
  796.30   796.40   797.1   797.7
  797.8   797.10   797.19   797.22
  797.27   797.32   797.38   798.1
  800.22   801.7   801.18   803.26
  803.37   804.4   804.8   804.23
  804.25

BASTA   EE 314.17

BAT   IL 651.31

BATES   (SEE ELIZABETH; MRS. BATES)

BATH   EA 81.20   81.21   88.34
  DV 158.20   158.27   158.30
  158.35   158.42   159.2   159.5
  GG 672.28   672.33   MD 815.20

BATH-CHAIR   MD 808.16

BATH-CLOSET   EA 81.21   81.27

BATHE   MO 2.42   OA 37.34   EA 82.3
  FA 471.15   471.19   SU 535.38

BATHED   OA 36.32   DV 165.28
  SU 537.36   ML 723.24   OV 752.23

BATHERS   PR 481.17

BATHING   WM 54.30   JD 618.5
  NT 701.10   702.31   703.38

BATHING-SUIT   NT 703.38   703.39

BATHOS   SM 582.25

BATH ROAD   MN 368.31

BATHROOM   BL 355.23

BATMAN   RH 794.11

BATS   FG 193.19

BATTERED   WP 386.28   387.17
  WR 546.29

BATTER-PUDDING   OC 286.36

BATTERY   SU 529.5

BATTLE   OA 33.25   SP 48.37   51.11
  EA 71.16   72.16   EE 315.42
  BL 352.41   JD 624.36   GG 687.14

BATTLE-AXE   MD 817.8

BATTLED   EA 71.26

BATTLEFIELD   WM 66.14

BATTLES   OA 29.34

BAWLED   SP 53.17   SC 271.9   271.12

BAY   PO 96.3   SG 224.19   225.12
  OC 283.26   284.42   290.33
  TP 342.34   YT 402.28   GG 678.34
  ML 725.22   739.36   742.31

BAZAAR   MD 823.4

BEACH   ML 725.2   739.31

BEAD   FA 458.33   PR 506.21
  BM 827.22

BEADS   YT 399.11   SM 584.21
  585.20   586.11   NT 713.34
  BM 833.13

BEADY   TH 852.39

BEAK   PO 113.3   WP 382.23   386.42
  387.30   387.39   NT 719.8
  ML 741.35

BEAM   MO 6.16   17.42   18.1   18.3
  SD 423.7   PR 484.29   485.25

BEAM-ENDS   WR 561.37

BEAMS   ML 729.42   OV 753.27

BEAN-POLE   TH 847.29

BEANS   MN 377.38

BEANSTALK   TH 846.38

BEAR   MO 21.22   OA 31.30   WM 61.18
  EA 80.25   82.15   82.35
  PO 103.36   108.17   110.39
  111.23   TF 122.15   122.23
  124.26   125.2   127.26   129.29
  135.15   DV 148.29   153.26   155.4
  156.7   170.8   176.7   179.41
  180.24   181.19   FG 189.28
  SB 218.16   SG 227.39   GF 239.7
  WS 260.7   SC 269.37   EE 320.24
  323.1   323.2   324.28   326.35
  TP 343.13   345.40   BL 347.34
  348.11   350.12   357.37   359.1
  365.13   YT 402.32   SD 424.24
  PP 434.40   HD 451.28   453.42
  454.9   FA 458.29   460.7
  PR 473.6   486.21   486.26   486.32
  491.42   492.39   497.40   505.1
  507.21   509.12   TB 517.36
  521.13   SU 544.15   544.24
  544.41   WR 571.25   571.26
  BO 604.23   604.25   604.26
  JD 622.25   624.11   IL 656.33
  ML 739.12   742.14   OV 752.11
  752.27   752.28   752.42
  LL 777.36   RH 799.9   MD 819.17
  BM 836.41   837.30   TH 849.32

BEARD   SP 45.25   PO 110.10
  DV 139.24   140.7   147.40   149.28
  OC 285.4   EE 321.37   PR 490.7
  WR 553.39   554.3   LA 630.10

BEARD (CONT.)   630.12

BEARDLESS   WR 554.2

BEARERS   WR 561.13

BEARING   OA 23.19   37.38
  38.38   WM 54.14   TF 125.20
  SS 202.18   202.28   EE 305.26
  313.36   BL 350.40   354.35
  359.9   MN 369.41   WP 388.1
  388.33   389.39   SD 413.37
  PP 439.28   HD 441.35
  FA 466.30   PR 479.38   483.13
  SM 586.22   GG 685.28
  LL 771.2   MD 809.27   818.37

BEARISHLY   TF 133.28

BEARS   NT 712.33

BEAR-SKIN   SS 202.3

BEAST   SB 214.29   OC 285.42
  WR 556.14   BO 595.41   602.27
  NT 714.24   714.25   715.4

BEASTLY   MO 13.1   WS 249.31
  263.33   WP 384.18   384.34
  IL 658.33   GG 661.15   665.27
  MD 814.35   817.17

BEASTS   EE 306.26   TB 522.24

BEAST'S   HT 42.35

BEAT   OA 29.24   29.33
  WM 60.23   69.28   EA 71.20
  89.37   PO 105.6   112.14
  112.19   112.20   TF 129.32
  129.40   131.14   FG 188.21
  190.6   191.30   BL 349.12
  356.1   358.1   SD 411.6
  425.11   425.21   FA 467.21
  PR 503.23   503.32   503.41
  503.42   TB 521.23   WR 568.37
  JD 608.13   MD 825.4
  BM 842.42

BEATEN   MO 11.25   DV 137.38
  GF 235.13   WS 264.37
  MD 816.24   824.9

BEATING   MO 3.1   OA 30.19
  EA 89.32   DV 175.7   175.24
  EE 332.34   TP 343.10
  FA 460.4   TB 521.28
  WR 568.34   569.11   BO 603.9
  JD 608.11   LL 774.37

BEATRICE   SS 209.36

BEATS   GG 691.18

BEAU MONDE   GG 662.15

BEAUTE MALE   PR 477.32

BEAUTIES   SP 48.14   ML 729.37
  OV 755.10

BEAUTIFUL   MO 10.26   12.24
  16.32   18.7   18.15   18.41
  20.30   OA 26.8   26.27
  SP 49.11   WM 58.16   61.1

BEAUTIFUL (CONT.) 64.35 EA 71.22
  71.33 72.33 '77.5 78.31 85.38
  86.11 PO 107.35 110.42
  TF 122.7 122.11 126.21
  DV 143.3 147.2 150.14 160.17
  171.9 SS 199.36 200.6 200.17
  202.30 211.28 SB 212.12
  216.24 SC 268.7 CH 275.28
  OC 287.29 289.6 300.13 300.16
  EE 304.17 304.27 309.6 310.27
  322.35 TP 339.32 BL 351.3
  351.22 359.21 359.28
  MN 370.14 WP 381.20 383.21
  383.25 383.26 YT 399.9 403.3
  PP 427.34 429.27 429.35
  431.35 434.27 437.13
  HD 453.35 FA 460.40 465.13
  465.27 466.27 467.33
  PR 473.13 477.28 482.41
  487.24 494.16 494.30 510.37
  TB 524.9 SU 533.22 533.27
  533.30 533.31 538.12 538.34
  WR 555.19 566.31 569.6
  SM 583.36 JD 606.24 LA 631.14
  GG 663.22 666.24 691.31
  692.40 695.18 697.14 699.22
  NT 703.36 704.15 712.23
  ML 730.22 730.40 OV 747.8
  748.8 749.20 LL 763.24 763.25
  769.35 777.42 778.21
  RR 780.22 782.5 RH 790.1
  BM 830.1 TH 844.13 845.1
  845.3 845.36 848.1 849.27
  850.22 850.33 851.32 852.14

BEAUTIFULLY DV 171.3 WS 261.22
  CH 279.39 TB 516.5 GG 663.25
  LL 770.14 774.10 RR 780.29
  TH 848.13

BEAUTIFULLY-SHAPED BM 832.2

BEAUTY MO 16.27 18.11 21.2
  OA 23.5 PO 116.8 TF 123.9
  SS 203.7 SB 212.10 GF 243.14
  EE 329.28 BL 354.33 SD 424.22
  PP 429.35 PR 474.5 478.11
  483.14 WR 572.15 JD 607.14
  GG 661.10 666.12 666.31
  NT 712.40 OV 753.39 755.22
  LL 763.27 TH 844.10 844.16
  844.17 844.19 845.38 847.8
  847.37 848.9 849.5

BEAUVALE FG 187.1 187.13 188.5
  188.30

BEAUVALE ABBEY FG 188.31

BEAVER PR 479.35

BECAME MO 5.14 5.19 13.19
  OA 30.24 36.34 SP 46.39
  WM 65.9 69.30 EA 74.39
  PO 99.14 TF 118.30 122.27
  122.30 128.13 DV 138.1 140.19
  154.36 167.17 177.6 179.18
  FG 190.6 SB 216.30 SG 225.6
  228.38 229.25 232.33
  GF 238.23 243.15 WS 244.21
  247.34 248.9 252.26 259.20
  CH 280.6 OC 287.8 EE 306.29
  310.13 310.37 317.15 331.20
  TP 339.23 343.22 BL 348.20
  MN 370.21 374.2 374.37 376.36

BECAME (CONT.) WP 389.30 390.37
  YT 403.15 405.34 PP 439.21
  HD 449.25 451.34 452.26
  PR 474.5 486.39 489.41 507.25
  TB 516.10 WR 572.13 BO 592.1
  604.5 JD 614.23 623.20
  623.40 LA 638.9 IL 650.36
  657.4 GG 666.13 679.14
  679.23 693.33 699.6 NT 706.10
  719.36 ML 725.2 728.25 731.33
  732.4 RR 785.20 RH 797.40
  799.27 800.25 BM 829.14
  836.27 TH 844.24 849.2 850.31

BECK SG 225.17

BECKONED SC 272.9 OC 298.38

BECOME MO 12.17 OA 30.16
  SP 46.10 WM 66.39 69.8
  EA 73.38 PO 97.7 97.11
  TF 129.22 DV 139.42 141.2
  141.15 141.17 150.38 152.2
  152.6 153.8 154.33 163.39
  SS 201.27 207.31 SB 217.34
  CH 277.23 280.29 OC 301.36
  EE 315.4 327.5 329.1 329.14
  BL 365.1 MN 367.32 HD 445.4
  446.28 451.24 454.17 455.3
  455.17 FA 460.12 SU 543.35
  WR 547.35 BO 587.15 594.19
  JD 619.30 624.12 LA 641.33
  GG 678.14 688.34 690.5 693.4
  NT 703.4 707.16 707.37 710.36
  ML 736.34 737.5 744.16
  RR 781.40 MD 805.11 821.37
  TH 847.16 848.4

BECOMES TP 334.30 JD 609.11
  NT 711.17

BECOMING MO 11.12 OA 29.11
  DV 143.20 WS 257.29 259.24
  TP 339.14 PP 429.41 PR 479.18
  480.22 TB 517.24 519.41
  SU 536.14 ML 724.8 740.36
  LL 763.36 773.38 RH 800.42
  BM 837.4 837.5

BED MO 16.20 OA 26.19 26.24
  27.23 33.36 34.6 37.20 37.40
  38.2 38.17 HT 41.9 42.7
  SP 46.21 EA 81.12 81.19 88.12
  88.34 PO 104.7 104.31 106.42
  114.39 TF 125.36 126.23
  129.27 129.37 130.28 131.26
  134.13 DV 147.39 148.41
  149.15 149.21 149.24 160.5
  161.5 161.23 162.18 162.23
  168.9 170.2 174.30 174.33
  174.36 174.40 175.2 175.12
  184.27 FG 195.6 SG 222.9
  228.17 229.12 230.5 231.9
  233.11 GF 237.25 239.21
  WS 244.2 244.23 265.38 265.40
  SC 269.25 269.29 270.5 272.20
  OC 290.8 293.6 294.18
  EE 317.14 317.22 318.9 319.21
  319.24 319.28 319.32 321.35
  322.4 322.17 323.31 BL 358.8
  361.37 MN 369.13 369.16
  369.24 369.38 370.2 373.39
  375.3 375.4 377.36 YT 397.5
  398.5 400.41 401.34 401.36
  401.38 402.1 402.4 402.12

BED (CONT.) 407.13 SD 415.5
  415.19 418.15 420.20
  423.36 PP 434.4 434.11
  434.13 434.25 HD 451.16
  FA 463.16 PR 478.42 502.27
  502.29 503.7 503.30 505.9
  512.10 TB 518.6 518.19
  SU 528.6 529.37 WR 562.33
  563.4 564.2 SM 582.3
  583.26 584.23 586.1
  BO 603.22 603.26 604.13
  604.21 604.33 604.39
  JD 616.2 616.12 IL 647.35
  GG 687.38 688.31 NT 709.10
  ML 739.33 741.12 744.38
  746.23 OV 753.22 LL 770.35
  778.32 RR 788.2 788.11
  788.24 788.31 789.10
  789.13 RH 802.27

BED-BUNK PR 500.8

BED-CHAMBER PP 433.28

BEDCLOTHES DV 175.16
  OC 298.19 EE 318.20
  RR 788.13 788.25

BEDDING PR 501.30 502.4
  503.13

BED-HEAD SM 583.33

BEDIZENED BM 840.40

BEDROOM EA 80.4 81.2 81.9
  TF 126.2 133.18 DV 148.34
  162.19 168.22 SG 221.26
  229.26 GF 237.10 237.33
  239.15 WS 244.5 251.2
  OC 298.9 298.18 MN 368.38
  SD 417.33 PP 434.3 435.7
  TB 515.15 LA 640.28
  NT 721.6 LL 765.33 769.14
  RR 788.9 788.21 788.32
  788.39 RH 801.40 802.8
  MD 810.41

BEDS TF 117.15 WR 556.33

BEDSIDE MN 369.30 PP 434.15
  WR 564.8 SM 582.6 RH 804.12

BED-SLIPPERS BM 842.29

BEDTIME DV 176.41

BED-TIME OA 25.35 OC 291.20

BEE SS 210.38 210.42 211.4
  OV 754.31 758.26 LL 770.35

BEECH PO 107.6 107.35 109.2
  FG 190.25

BEECHES PO 106.30 112.12

BEECH-MAST PO 113.14

BEE-CLUSTERS WR 578.20

BEE-HIVE OV 755.10

BEELEY MN 376.18

BEER   MO 14.38   OA 31.25   31.35
    PO 103.35   109.15   DV 140.6
    140.11   142.17   SD 412.19
    PP 433.21   440.24   ML 728.24
    RR 785.30   785.33

BEER-POT   PO 111.20

BEES   PO 106.29   SS 210.30

BEETLES   MN 374.26

BEFORE-DAWN   GG 692.41

BEFRIEND   SS 208.16

BEG   DV 155.17   JD 628.25
    GG 675.14

BEGGAR   OV 754.17

BEGGED   MO 4.33   BM 830.19

BEGGING   JD 615.9

BEGIN   MO 7.20   9.39   20.7
    SP 45.3   EA 91.17   GF 242.34
    OC 286.20   PP 426.2   HD 450.42
    FA 460.14   465.24   PR 488.39
    494.32   WR 568.15   570.38
    JD 620.3   627.34   628.21
    GG 669.38   697.15   ML 725.10
    728.16   730.40   LL 773.23
    RH 790.30   BM 835.16

BEGINNING   MO 6.26   OA 32.6   35.19
    WM 56.16   56.34   TF 120.39
    133.9   DV 136.2   SS 203.10
    WS 246.29   257.24   OC 294.36
    295.18   PP 435.19   PR 481.21
    486.16   493.17   SU 530.41
    WR 547.12   573.38   GG 696.36
    NT 704.16   ML 743.39   OV 755.33
    LL 770.20   771.37   BM 826.12
    833.15   TH 852.6

BEGINS   BL 359.13   ML 724.14

BEGOD   PP 431.20

BEGRUDGE   TB 527.9

BEGUILED   SP 47.37

BEGUN   MO 13.32   OA 30.31
    SP 48.17   EA 71.18   81.31
    DV 155.10   178.8   OC 289.21
    BL 350.38   YT 395.1   HD 451.31
    TB 522.14   WR 552.35   NT 717.40
    MD 811.38

BEHALF   EE 325.12   TB 527.18
    NT 711.16   MD 818.23

BEHAVE   DV 185.17   GF 240.1
    OC 301.40   TP 336.35   WR 549.22

BEHAVED   RR 781.2   MD 811.2

BEHAVIOUR   DV 153.41   WS 250.11
    262.10   EE 316.13   RR 782.37

BEHINT   OC 292.25

BEHOVED   TF 122.18

BEING   MO 18.5   20.27   20.33
    OA 30.26   35.19   37.42   38.19
    HT 39.7   SP 49.17   53.2
    WM 64.37   66.5   66.32   EA 82.18
    82.20   82.34   82.39   83.7   83.17
    87.8   87.13   89.22   90.10   93.18
    PO 98.12   104.16   107.4   109.29
    111.29   TF 118.27   121.2   126.30
    128.4   129.2   130.32   132.30
    133.8   DV 136.33   139.41   143.17
    146.22   146.31   147.31   150.7
    150.31   153.6   154.33   155.22
    157.4   166.5   166.8   170.30
    171.13   171.15   177.1   FG 191.16
    192.2   SS 205.19   207.40   211.28
    SB 217.23   217.29   217.33
    SG 226.15   228.23   229.14
    229.16   229.23   GF 239.36
    WS 255.27   256.31   259.38
    262.21   SC 267.7   269.27
    CH 275.26   277.30   282.23
    OC 283.24   301.21   EE 306.9
    308.42   316.8   319.4   329.33
    332.21   TP 339.28   BL 347.36
    349.13   350.5   MN 366.9   370.21
    WP 380.23   382.9   388.22
    YT 395.34   SD 423.2   PP 427.18
    430.14   HD 441.24   448.11
    448.27   FA 462.37   465.13
    471.12   PR 473.22   476.2   482.6
    488.24   509.8   TB 514.29   514.34
    519.14   519.17   520.1   520.28
    522.3   522.36   524.13   525.29
    526.32   527.12   SU 533.15   536.6
    WR 548.25   548.40   550.25
    559.42   560.4   561.30   BO 590.16
    592.14   JD 606.19   611.31
    616.22   627.2   LA 641.6   642.1
    642.2   642.35   642.36   IL 647.14
    648.12   650.7   652.12   655.36
    657.8   657.14   657.35   GG 661.10
    661.16   661.36   674.5   681.29
    682.5   696.18   NT 701.4   703.40
    709.8   ML 724.33   726.17   727.7
    727.23   729.36   730.37   733.12
    742.42   OV 748.20   748.23   749.4
    752.28   755.17   759.7   LL 761.31
    764.37   RR 781.33   783.35
    784.10   785.17   RH 802.23
    MD 805.32   806.29   811.14
    814.12   819.30   819.33   820.23
    821.24   BM 827.16   828.3   828.18
    829.12   829.19   830.14   830.15
    833.30   TH 846.26   851.7   851.15

BEING-IN-LOVE   LA 642.31

BEINGS   DV 157.20   OC 300.34
    EE 312.19   SU 533.3   JD 624.10
    NT 703.3   MD 819.30   TH 844.37
    845.10

BELBURY STATION   MN 368.14   368.34
    369.1

BELGIAN   WP 381.2   385.8   391.33
    392.24

BELIEF   EA 94.1   DV 164.32
    WS 259.30   EE 313.20   TP 335.32
    RH 791.2

BELIEVE   MO 14.28   15.16   16.37
    SP 49.33   WM 57.11   57.26   64.7
    67.33   EA 75.15   75.16   75.18

BELIEVE (CONT.)   77.29   89.21
    90.2   PO 112.23   112.24
    112.30   DV 141.16   173.37
    SS 208.21   GF 243.23
    CH 276.41   EE 313.26   316.7
    BL 352.16   360.15   MN 371.29
    WP 383.18   392.36   YT 405.16
    SD 413.12   416.25   417.1
    418.41   PP 438.7   HD 450.3
    TB 519.32   WR 577.28
    JD 622.38   623.24   LA 631.21
    643.4   644.11   IL 657.34
    GG 679.3   NT 709.33
    ML 724.31   732.2   LL 767.26
    768.34   771.24   RR 783.7
    RH 792.36   BM 833.29

BELIEVED   MO 16.27   17.16
    17.18   EA 91.8   93.30
    TF 118.2   CH 280.30   YT 399.2
    SD 424.4   PP 429.19
    SU 534.17   IL 650.12
    GG 693.25   LL 765.13
    769.22   777.11   RH 802.19
    TH 852.14

BELIEVING   EE 313.13   YT 405.18

BELL   WM 59.36   60.1   SG 229.16
    EE 331.42   BL 356.17
    PP 434.20   SM 583.11
    ML 725.18   734.6   RR 785.11
    785.19   785.22   786.8

BELL-BUTTON   RR 785.13

BELL-LIKE   FA 467.33   GG 684.34

BELLOWED   PP 431.12

BELLOWING   EE 307.1

BELL-PULL   WM 56.12

BELLS   SU 542.15   WR 572.19
    ML 732.24

BELL'S   (SEE AUNT BELL'S)

BELL-SHAPED   BL 351.7

BELLY   SP 53.9   EA 71.19
    PO 106.3   109.5   TF 120.15
    120.16   130.4   130.8
    SB 214.25   SU 530.32
    GG 695.38

BELONG   EA 92.20   EE 306.32

BELONGED   EA 89.15   PO 111.36
    GF 243.30   WS 256.14   OC 301.22
    EE 304.5   310.28   322.25
    322.26   WP 391.39   YT 396.27
    FA 464.10   WR 574.21
    GG 662.7   662.13   ML 723.8
    726.37   733.8   MD 820.7

BELONGING   DV 136.34   IL 651.9

BELONGINGS   WR 557.5
    MD 825.39

BELONGS   PR 475.32   487.2
    SU 543.7   BO 596.40

BELOVED SP 49.30 SS 211.11
  SB 212.4 YT 398.6 FA 468.5

BELT PO 100.17 TF 126.16
  SS 202.25 WS 244.24 TP 343.6
  MN 372.21 PR 484.40 WR 569.5

BELTED EA 72.26 WR 564.24

BELTS TF 127.27 WR 565.41

BEN SP 45.28 46.8

BENCH TF 117.17 SS 206.24
  SG 226.25 BL 354.22 SD 414.19
  BM 841.23

BENCHES SP 50.14

BEND MO 22.31 PO 97.21 FG 192.4
  OC 299.6 EE 307.22 SU 529.4
  539.22 GG 670.38

BENDING WM 59.14 69.9 FG 189.38
  OC 288.42 EE 317.25 SU 544.1
  WR 569.3 577.14 BO 604.25
  GG 670.8 695.9 ML 732.23
  RH 791.17 BM 838.2

BENEATH MO 18.13 WM 54.12
  PO 109.27 TF 119.33 122.16
  DV 149.26 161.6 165.33 173.26
  FG 194.30 195.3 SG 225.20
  GF 239.12 WP 385.31 SD 421.28
  PP 434.20 HD 450.10 451.2
  PR 497.3 WR 569.14 BO 599.12
  LA 637.38 GG 671.29 682.8
  LL 761.14 BM 832.17 834.10
  839.8

BENEDICTINE WS 249.20

BENEFIT EA 85.19

BENEVOLENT TP 341.34 PR 476.16
  TB 523.12

BENEVOLENT-SEEMING WR 566.15

BENISSIMO GG 672.22

BENJAMIN MO 5.4 12.2

BENT MO 1.10 3.28 12.29 18.9
  21.13 22.8 OA 25.21 25.38
  27.3 30.10 36.9 HT 44.12
  WM 64.9 66.17 69.33 EA 91.11
  PO 109.10 109.15 TF 117.22
  124.15 DV 143.16 146.42 148.4
  148.24 153.37 158.14 170.25
  SB 214.38 218.28 WS 246.2
  247.25 255.7 261.40 262.4
  CH 276.10 276.38 277.5 277.9
  280.5 280.15 OC 298.37
  EE 317.6 317.11 317.27 319.5
  319.6 BL 351.41 354.26 358.35
  WP 383.23 389.39 SD 411.18
  PP 435.14 439.14 HD 454.40
  456.37 FA 468.12 468.14
  PR 484.9 491.15 491.33 508.40
  511.30 TB 521.25 WR 567.30
  581.8 JD 618.40 LA 636.28
  GG 673.16 OV 749.10 LL 774.32

BEN TOWNSEND SP 45.23 47.6

BENT-SHOULDERED DV 147.25

BE'OLD FA 464.15

BE-OUT SP 46.32

BERKELEY WR 547.28 547.32

BERKSHIRE ML 726.12

BERNARD COUTTS WM 54.1

BERRIES EE 331.15

BERRY PP 427.6 427.12 427.15
  428.23 428.30 428.38 429.14
  430.29 430.34 432.9 432.16
  433.21 436.16 436.19 436.24
  436.31 437.17 437.25 438.7
  438.10 438.23 440.9 440.24

BERRY (SEE DAN; MR. BERRY)

BERRYMAN (SEE JOHN; MR. BERRYMAN)

BERRYMAN'S CH 274.18 281.30

BERTHA CH 276.32 277.2 277.16
  277.25 278.35 279.1 281.20

BERTICE BL 358.31

BERTIE BL 349.3 349.4 349.14
  349.21 349.29 350.16 350.22
  350.34 354.9 356.18 357.19
  357.24 357.31 357.33 357.40
  358.3 358.6 358.11 358.25
  358.27 358.28 358.33 358.38
  358.40 359.2 359.8 359.19
  360.8 360.15 360.21 360.27
  360.33 360.40 360.42 361.1
  361.5 361.12 361.16 361.22
  362.1 362.8 362.20 362.22
  362.30 362.36 363.4 363.10
  363.16 363.22 363.28 364.8
  364.14 364.20 364.25 364.28
  364.35 364.39 365.3 365.11

BERTIE REID BL 348.37 357.11

BERTIE REID'S BL 363.36

BERTIE'S BL 357.1 363.33

BERTRAM REID BL 349.30

BESANT (SEE MRS. BESANT)

BESEECHING MO 10.35 GG 684.5

BESEECHINGLY GG 685.35

BESIDE MO 7.6 11.4 OA 23.13
  23.17 26.31 27.41 SP 51.37
  WM 60.23 63.32 65.10 PO 107.6
  108.36 TF 134.12 135.1
  DV 136.7 147.5 147.10 175.27
  FG 193.28 SS 202.13 204.23
  SB 212.7 212.36 215.17
  SG 226.25 227.15 232.22
  WS 251.16 256.4 256.18
  CH 281.9 OC 283.13 283.27
  284.1 EE 321.6 322.17 325.21
  BL 350.42 357.5 MN 370.4
  WP 383.12 387.20 PP 429.10

BESIDE (CONT.) 429.14 430.24
  434.10 FA 459.34 460.1
  460.5 PR 476.22 499.17
  WR 552.10 563.4 576.34
  SM 583.27 BO 593.21 603.5
  JD 618.28 LA 631.27 634.24
  IL 650.14 NT 719.27
  ML 730.16 MD 824.2
  BM 837.31 840.39 842.18

BESIDES MO 10.41 WM 67.12
  DV 142.15 158.30 SS 209.29
  SG 222.38 WS 263.36
  SC 270.25 TP 337.7 337.40
  340.19 FA 471.6 JD 608.4
  IL 648.13 653.31 NT 709.34
  711.35 ML 722.3 RR 779.17
  RH 801.3 MD 812.2

BESIEGED NT 704.19

BEST MO 16.34 18.29 OA 36.26
  SP 46.21 EA 92.3 PO 96.11
  DV 143.27 144.7 185.34
  SS 200.30 SB 217.38 217.40
  EE 314.8 315.38 321.10
  321.15 321.29 328.12
  WP 387.8 391.37 YT 397.30
  SD 420.9 PP 428.6 428.9
  431.32 HD 452.21 456.28
  FA 462.8 472.12 TB 514.38
  516.40 517.2 JD 606.29
  623.26 623.29 626.19
  626.31 626.36 GG 663.20
  677.32 677.34 683.24
  NT 702.6 717.22 ML 739.20
  741.2 LL 761.9 RR 789.13
  RH 804.35 MD 814.4 853.25

BESTWOOD SP 48.33 50.23
  TP 337.8

BET SG 223.27 WS 246.28
  248.17 WP 383.16 385.14
  385.16 FA 470.32

BETHOUGHT MO 15.31 SD 417.28

BETIMES HT 42.33

BETOKENS PR 485.11

BETRAY EE 326.12 327.35
  PR 498.21

BETRAYAL TF 119.41 IL 659.33

BETRAYING WM 65.5

BETROTHED WM 55.6 64.37

BETS FA 470.33

BETTER MO 14.40 16.2 20.29
  OA 34.21 37.13 HT 41.32
  SP 46.7 WM 62.39 67.36
  EA 77.31 78.26 TF 121.33
  124.20 DV 141.22 143.33
  144.19 145.8 158.20
  158.31 158.35 164.6
  169.14 171.35 172.1 185.4
  185.29 FG 192.26 SB 219.25
  SG 222.37 223.38 224.2
  GF 236.25 WS 253.5 253.42
  255.42 265.38 CH 281.5

BETTER (CONT.) EE 317.20 317.33
  318.16 318.41 320.29 328.9
  332.41 332.42 BL 348.41
  MN 366.10 366.21 WP 382.7
  382.12 384.2 YT 394.17 394.21
  404.21 405.10 406.11
  SD 419.27 PP 427.34 431.20
  431.23 437.33 HD 443.37
  445.12 FA 463.9 PR 485.18
  492.41 505.21 TB 518.35
  523.10 525.6 SM 585.25
  BO 602.5 604.2 JD 615.24
  615.25 615.28 615.29 615.32
  620.2 625.31 626.4 LA 630.35
  636.27 637.25 642.28 645.24
  645.41 IL 647.29 655.25
  657.19 GG 670.29 674.7 684.22
  687.12 691.41 693.42 696.36
  NT 705.32 719.10 719.12
  720.41 ML 722.6 744.14
  LL 767.36 771.19 777.7
  RR 787.17 788.40 RH 791.2
  792.5 800.35 800.36 MD 817.38
  818.1 BM 841.17 842.35
  TH 849.33 851.21 852.27
  852.42 853.3

BETTERS OA 38.41

BETTING SP 50.18 PP 428.41
  RH 795.20 798.2

BETTS (SEE MRS. BETTS)

BETWIXT OV 748.42 749.36

BEWARE OA 35.8

BEWILDERED MO 13.3 OA 30.8
  EA 84.29 PO 102.4 104.18
  TF 129.3 DV 175.28 CH 279.24
  YT 403.24 404.34 405.17
  SD 419.24 HD 453.11 FA 468.15
  JD 611.18 LA 637.11 RR 783.24
  BM 829.22 829.23

BEWILDERING DV 176.22

BEWILDERMENT SM 585.26 GG 691.37
  RR 789.5

BEWITCHED SD 420.33 WR 573.2

BEYONDS TP 334.21

BHO TH 846.20 846.23

BIARRITZ MD 806.14

BIBLE DV 151.27 FG 188.2 188.3
  LA 644.38 GG 690.11

BIBLICAL CH 280.9

BICEPS IL 650.18

BICYCLE MO 17.25 18.18 TF 131.3
  131.12 132.2 CH 277.30
  EE 318.6 320.37 324.6
  MN 372.1

BICYCLE-BELL MO 10.32

BICYCLE-LAMP MO 18.9

BICYCLES TF 131.6

BID MO 15.2 OC 289.34 WP 383.3

BIDDING TF 135.13 DV 141.33 157.14
  SC 270.17 CH 275.17

BIG MO 4.3 6.37 8.2 9.20
  HT 39.5 40.21 42.30 SP 45.4
  45.25 51.19 53.2 WM 62.23
  63.31 EA 71.19 80.22 84.10
  84.13 86.35 91.29 PO 112.14
  113.28 113.30 TF 117.12
  DV 139.16 139.24 139.33
  140.27 157.9 161.2 162.35
  167.19 167.28 168.36 174.2
  SB 212.33 216.3 SG 221.6
  224.39 225.24 GF 238.37
  WS 250.33 252.14 263.22 264.1
  SC 271.18 271.23 CH 276.20
  280.7 282.17 OC 292.10 299.28
  299.33 EE 303.7 306.24 321.35
  329.22 BL 349.10 357.25
  360.35 MN 366.29 WP 381.20
  382.5 384.13 384.24 386.11
  386.15 387.17 392.6 YT 399.29
  SD 412.22 414.12 421.9
  PP 427.7 427.37 433.39 434.1
  436.17 437.29 438.20
  HD 446.24 446.36 PR 475.33
  476.22 489.34 502.36 511.36
  TB 526.40 SU 532.12 543.14
  WR 552.23 559.9 561.16 562.8
  562.20 564.33 566.6 566.29
  568.24 568.25 568.28 568.34
  568.41 569.13 569.14 571.24
  576.20 577.37 577.38 578.38
  SM 585.5 BO 595.7 603.27
  604.35 JD 608.15 616.9 616.24
  617.15 618.13 624.17
  LA 634.14 634.25 636.5 639.35
  640.26 GG 671.3 677.17
  NT 704.29 ML 722.6 724.25
  724.27 725.40 739.31 740.25
  741.25 741.27 743.26
  OV 752.38 LL 761.11 762.13
  769.22 771.8 RR 784.11
  RH 791.18 793.2 793.10 793.29
  793.31 795.12 798.27 800.32
  801.41 802.16 MD 810.41 811.3
  811.4 811.5 811.7 817.18
  824.8 BM 829.38 830.35 833.11

BIG-BONED CH 277.31

BIG-BUILT BM 829.34

BIGGER MO 20.28 OA 30.12
  EA 91.37 DV 183.22 SD 424.4
  PR 486.23 WR 558.39 561.34
  561.35 561.39 GG 696.22
  ML 723.3 733.13 RR 786.33
  RH 795.33 MD 808.21

BIGGEST WP 384.39 386.12
  ML 735.11 TH 853.16

BIG-LEAVED DV 136.17

BIGNESS EA 87.16

BIKE MN 372.30 372.36

BILIOUS NT 705.37

BILL PR 511.23 TB 520.17
  MD 806.42

BILL BOWER'S FA 470.37

BILLETED MN 366.3

BILL HEATHER FA 462.4

BILLOW MO 2.3

BILLS DV 137.27 142.10
  ML 728.8 728.18 731.40

BILLY GF 243.2 243.7

BIN SP 51.27 OC 292.21
  MN 369.22 369.25 WP 388.10
  388.32 389.4 389.15 389.16

BINDING SD 420.14

BINGHAM EE 320.30

BI-OUT SP 48.23

BIRD OA 24.34 24.38 PO 113.1
  113.2 113.3 113.8
  FG 194.33 GF 234.16
  SC 267.6 EE 330.36
  331.34 MN 368.6 WP 382.22
  382.27 382.30 382.36
  386.11 386.15 386.16
  386.22 390.6 SD 416.8
  PP 434.20 435.21 FA 465.39
  PR 481.40 499.3 499.5
  TB 521.36 521.40 522.1
  522.3 524.30 526.39
  SM 583.18 LA 630.18 631.41
  639.39 GG 661.17 670.19
  ML 726.41 741.32 741.38
  RH 800.1

BIRD-ERECT WR 569.28

BIRDILY SU 540.26

BIRD-LIKE SU 531.13 534.22
  536.27

BIRD-LIME JD 623.10

BIRDS MO 1.16 PO 113.16
  SS 200.8 202.2 202.16
  204.28 204.35 GF 234.6
  234.11 242.38 243.5
  243.9 OC 283.12 WP 379.8
  382.17 386.12 PP 428.42
  TB 520.28 522.5 522.8
  523.33 527.26 WR 551.35
  572.23 SM 585.17 585.38
  IL 653.20 NT 709.25
  ML 723.18 734.42 741.16
  741.20 741.22 744.2
  744.8 OV 755.28

BIRD'S PR 499.9

BIRD-SINGING SS 202.7

BIRD-TRAILS SU 538.23

BIRDY TB 524.40 SU 535.1

BIRKIN, POLLY (SEE POLLY)

BIR-RRD WP 382.31

BIRTHDAY PO 101.23 PR 480.34
  RH 799.2 799.4 799.7 799.10
  799.24 799.30 TH 850.23

BIRTHRIGHT DV 156.3

BISHOP'S TH 853.21

BIT MO 4.23 7.5 14.11 16.35
  OA 32.29 HT 40.18 40.27
  SP 45.33 47.20 47.22 49.40
  WM 61.4 64.42 EA 79.2 80.41
  91.21 91.25 92.28 92.29
  93.11 PO 102.13 104.15 111.42
  DV 142.30 148.20 157.37
  158.24 164.18 169.12 171.35
  182.3 FG 189.5 SS 201.25
  SB 212.28 215.40 216.8 218.12
  GF 236.11 236.13 236.22
  WS 253.9 255.36 259.9
  SC 267.13 268.16 269.37
  272.38 CH 276.13 277.39
  OC 287.4 288.22 296.28
  EE 303.15 305.6 313.38 313.40
  314.5 322.42 323.20 332.10
  TP 341.5 341.7 BL 352.28
  362.37 363.8 MN 374.18
  WP 380.35 381.41 384.8 388.11
  389.3 389.8 390.16 YT 403.37
  SD 413.40 419.19 419.29
  419.31 419.35 426.17
  PP 436.15 436.40 HD 442.40
  FA 460.14 461.12 461.16 469.7
  471.1 PR 473.3 473.6 474.9
  482.11 482.38 488.24 492.7
  492.31 496.29 TB 514.30 515.9
  515.30 515.33 WR 547.25 563.4
  BO 587.28 598.39 604.1
  JD 610.6 616.34 618.32 622.2
  624.40 625.38 626.42
  LA 639.42 640.19 644.1
  IL 648.29 649.8 650.31 652.1
  654.41 GG 661.17 662.11
  663.28 664.11 666.25 667.35
  667.36 675.20 676.14 677.27
  681.10 685.14 688.16 696.8
  NT 702.41 703.9 703.20 707.42
  712.6 ML 724.39 729.22 729.26
  730.22 738.21 740.15 741.32
  743.17 OV 755.38 LL 761.11
  764.13 RR 789.10 RH 794.30 797.5
  801.20 MD 807.40 807.41
  826.29 BM 828.18 829.20 831.1
  832.37 833.38 840.16 840.23
  842.9 TH 850.26

BITCH WS 262.41 HD 446.1

BITE EA 89.30 SG 221.24
  MN 374.40 SD 424.39 PR 484.19
  SU 536.40 537.21 ML 745.7

BITES OA 26.18 WR 571.31

BITING WM 67.20 EA 89.24
  DV 174.16 FG 193.14 GF 243.20
  WS 262.9 MN 374.11 PP 436.1

BITINGLY EA 74.30

BITS PO 108.37 OC 284.5

BITS (CONT.) EE 312.20 323.36
  TP 344.38 BL 359.1 SD 424.41
  HD 446.8 WR 547.3 565.2
  578.19 MD 812.42 814.34

BITTEN TH 850.7

BITTEN-OFF SG 230.20

BITTER OA 37.6 WM 66.22
  EA 87.20 TF 120.1 DV 137.37
  152.33 169.8 175.22 175.31
  SG 232.36 GF 243.18 243.35
  OC 289.15 EE 312.4 317.11
  322.1 322.3 TP 345.4 345.14
  HD 456.41 WR 550.10 572.6
  IL 652.19 OV 753.29 754.26
  757.40 LL 767.21 RH 792.32
  MD 815.1 BM 828.27 TH 847.30
  852.19

BITTER-CONTEMPTUOUS EA 73.41

BITTER-LOOKING WP 380.25

BITTERLY MO 4.27 7.36 OA 28.28
  37.36 WM 66.42 EA 86.34
  DV 138.12 164.26 SS 200.19
  207.19 207.28 SB 213.11
  GF 243.3 SC 272.41 CH 279.27
  280.26 OC 285.33 285.39
  287.13 291.27 EE 317.34
  FA 460.40 461.31 462.21
  466.17 PR 492.11 TB 526.25
  SU 528.18 OV 747.34 757.13
  757.16 757.31 LL 771.37
  778.20 RH 791.35 792.9

BITTERNESS MO 7.30 11.6 11.10
  OA 38.36 EA 78.8 SG 232.29
  WS 249.29 EE 314.11 316.15
  322.28 TP 345.6 FA 461.32
  TB 514.10 JD 624.1 GG 671.30
  OV 755.18 LL 766.33

BIZ GF 236.7

BLACK MO 3.30 15.16 OA 23.7
  25.4 36.13 HT 41.10 SP 47.41
  48.9 WM 54.14 55.30 55.37
  63.31 64.12 EA 78.32 78.35
  84.28 87.11 PO 95.6 96.2
  97.2 99.11 99.26 100.33
  102.32 106.32 112.29 112.30
  114.27 114.31 115.11 116.7
  116.11 116.12 TF 123.24
  DV 138.16 138.37 139.15
  139.28 147.3 149.25 159.1
  160.25 166.12 166.13 166.30
  167.5 167.16 169.24 169.26
  170.38 170.40 176.37 178.21
  179.11 180.31 181.24 182.1
  FG 195.37 195.39 SS 198.8
  202.30 207.24 207.25
  SB 212.13 216.16 SG 224.21
  225.13 226.19 226.22 227.25
  GF 239.1 240.14 241.28 241.32
  242.1 242.15 243.13 WS 244.7
  245.3 258.30 258.39 263.18
  264.1 264.7* SC 268.5 268.11
  268.24 268.27 268.31 CH 274.9
  274.16 280.20 280.23
  OC 283.10 283.22 284.8 290.20
  291.39 293.30 299.33
  EE 303.35 304.12 305.1 306.24

BLACK (CONT.) 306.36 333.1
  333.8 TP 334.2 334.26
  335.7 335.10 337.23
  338.36 BL 347.37 348.2
  348.10 348.35 352.2
  MN 366.28 371.19 373.36
  WP 379.30 380.8 380.17
  380.25 385.20 385.31
  385.34 386.4 386.8 390.2
  SD 412.3 415.32 417.36
  417.37 423.40 424.37
  PP 427.2 428.39 429.25
  430.30 434.10 434.16
  436.31 HD 441.32 442.3
  448.41 449.22 449.28
  449.40 450.10 456.28
  FA 459.1 459.34 462.2
  463.42 467.8 PR 473.11
  473.26 482.25 482.37
  483.8 483.15 483.42 484.6
  484.7 484.39 484.40 486.14
  487.17 489.17 489.18
  489.30 490.13 490.34
  490.36 492.16 493.10
  494.2 494.33 494.39 496.36
  497.22 503.6 506.11 506.27
  510.36 TB 525.3 SU 528.7
  529.1 536.33 537.17 537.18
  537.20 537.22 538.4 542.24
  WR 551.9 552.29 553.32
  553.33 553.37 553.38
  553.39 554.1 554.18 554.34
  555.17 555.20 555.31
  556.12 559.20 559.23
  559.37 560.28 561.11
  563.3 563.7 563.13 564.25
  565.9 565.26 566.9 567.31
  567.34 567.35 568.32
  568.33 568.42 569.2 569.9
  569.21 569.29 570.23
  573.16 573.21 573.35
  574.37 575.29 575.32
  576.29 576.39 577.1 578.5
  578.11 578.16 578.19
  578.34 581.9 581.10 581.11
  581.20 581.22 SM 582.8
  582.12 583.23 583.30
  583.33 584.21 585.21
  585.28 BO 589.23 595.22
  595.35 600.20 600.21
  JD 606.24 606.26 610.8
  610.15 610.27 610.28
  610.30 610.32 614.41
  615.8 618.26 624.6 624.23
  624.24 626.14 LA 631.11
  632.25 633.33 634.25
  635.31 636.29 636.35
  639.31 639.40 GG 663.21
  668.35 668.39 670.7 670.23
  673.4 675.11 675.18 681.31
  683.9 683.23 699.35
  NT 701.7 702.21 709.24
  711.22 ML 735.8 741.29
  742.31 742.35 744.22
  745.24 745.34 OV 747.10
  748.42 LL 763.35 773.32
  775.41 RR 784.13 784.14
  MD 808.39 809.19 815.39
  BM 839.9 TH 848.14 853.13

BLACK-AND-GREY SU 540.42

BLACK-AND-TAN TB 523.22

BLACK-AND-WHITE WS 250.33

BLACK-AVISED SM 585.21

BLACK BESS TP 338.5 338.8

BLACKBIRD OV 759.41

BLACKBIRDS ML 723.14

BLACK-BROWED CH 276.30 MN 375.1
  YT 408.16 GG 677.2 681.1

BLACK-CLAD SU 544.21

BLACKEN EE 312.21

BLACKENED SG 229.29 CH 280.22
  HD 447.32 BM 840.24

BLACKER GF 235.6

BLACK-FACED GG 690.38

BLACK FOREST TF 126.4 BO 600.18

BLACK-GREY SU 542.22

BLACK-HAIRED HT 40.21 SP 47.30

BLACKIE'S SS 204.26

BLACKISH OA 23.18 PO 106.18
  SB 213.3 214.5 WR 567.36
  JD 616.31 624.24 GG 673.3
  ML 745.6

BLACKNESS OA 28.32 WM 60.31
  PO 112.31 TP 334.37 PR 483.11
  SU 528.8 JD 615.38 NT 702.3
  ML 745.32

BLACK-RIMMED JD 616.24

BLACK-SILK GG 670.17

BLACKSMITH SS 197.2

BLACKTHORN ML 722.32 723.12
  723.15 724.39 736.7

BLADDER SC 269.20

BLADDER CAMPION ML 736.11

BLADE WM 55.1 PP 435.17
  RH 794.12

BLADES IL 648.34

BLAME MO 17.37 LL 775.7

BLAMED MN 369.5 369.12
  ML 731.37

BLANCHED SS 203.30 SG 226.21

BLAND MN 373.11

BLANDLY IL 653.10

BLANK SP 49.19 PO 97.33 103.16
  TF 119.39 DV 136.6 156.15
  SG 228.14 PR 480.28 486.14
  499.9 506.10 TB 523.2 527.11
  WR 548.34 562.5 SM 584.33
  JD 616.25 623.35 623.41 624.1

BLANK (CONT.) 625.34 625.42
  626.1 LA 632.38 640.27
  GG 677.39 RR 783.24 MD 823.17
  BM 839.10 842.23

BLANKET DV 162.24 HD 455.36
  455.41 456.2 456.4 PR 478.42
  510.8 511.37 WR 551.11 552.18
  556.9 561.6 562.36 564.40
  573.30 577.38

BLANKETS HD 451.16 451.19
  452.27 PR 488.11 488.21
  494.35 495.1 501.2 502.5
  502.17 502.33 503.22 505.13
  506.32 507.5 509.18 509.21
  WR 553.18 559.25 568.33
  570.20 577.41

BLANKLY MN 367.32 JD 617.40
  GG 692.1 692.3 692.7
  BM 839.16 842.18

BLANKNESS TF 134.29 PR 481.7
  RR 783.27

BLASPHEMOUS PR 477.36

BLAST TF 120.20 EE 331.21
  PR 505.3 JD 616.30 BM 840.17

BLASTED SP 53.16 TP 343.1
  WP 391.25 393.14 FA 459.2

BLATANTLY RR 781.15

BLAZE WM 70.13 PO 99.27
  WS 251.29 PR 500.20 500.27
  SU 533.10 WR 558.33 578.42
  JD 621.26 ML 729.38 RH 803.13

BLAZED HT 44.8 SP 48.8 PO 107.28
  EE 303.26 PR 496.13 498.7
  498.27 500.6 RH 803.19
  BM 841.30 842.3

BLAZES MN 369.22

BLAZES' GG 681.13

BLAZING TF 133.42 134.14
  FG 189.24 GF 238.18 PR 500.39
  502.37 WR 555.28 ML 729.35
  RH 796.10 800.32

BLEACHED SB 217.6

BLEAK GF 240.6

BLEAKLY GG 693.40

BLEARED ML 746.23

BLEAT GG 699.36

BLEATING SU 529.15 ML 738.28

BLED OA 36.28 EE 322.25

BLEED WS 264.18 EE 318.19
  LL 767.36

BLEEDING OA 36.33 WS 264.17
  264.26 EE 317.31 317.41
  322.19 322.20 TP 343.25

BLEEDING (CONT.) 344.12
  345.10 PR 491.25
  WR 572.15

BLEMISH GG 698.40

BLENCH OA 29.37

BLENCHED GG 681.21

BLENCHING TF 122.32

BLENDING ML 736.4

BLESS OC 300.3 300.4 300.11
  RR 781.26

BLESSED WM 67.24 DV 183.6
  SB 212.6 215.33 CH 279.13
  OC 294.23

BLESSED BLOOD FG 188.25

BLESSING FG 195.17

BLEST TB 522.1 522.2 522.6

BLEW FG 194.31 BL 352.40
  353.9 361.13 WP 392.30
  392.31 PP 430.28 PR 496.23
  498.30 503.13 BO 594.39
  LA 639.2 644.35 644.38
  NT 713.1 ML 728.22 728.26

B'LIEVE SC 270.27

BLIGHT GG 686.4

BLIGHTED MD 815.42

BLIND MO 13.27 20.11
  OA 30.40 35.42 WM 62.41
  EA 80.7 83.3 84.2
  PO 97.25 101.30 108.18
  TF 119.32 120.13 121.7
  DV 154.35 157.9 163.36
  164.21 164.29 165.40
  SB 215.6 215.8 216.3
  216.9 SG 228.15 OC 291.15
  EE 313.29 314.23 BL 347.9
  347.23 350.31 354.27
  357.33 358.11 358.34
  358.41 360.23 360.34
  362.22 363.32 363.42
  364.9 365.14 WP 383.18
  PR 493.13 498.42 JD 615.6
  615.8 615.9 GG 693.42
  NT 717.41 LL 765.26
  TH 851.14

BLINDED FG 191.32 WS 264.7
  EE 316.23 BL 347.7

BLINDFOLD ML 745.41

BLINDFOLDED BO 592.21 592.24
  592.25

BLINDING HT 44.6

BLINDLY MO 20.6 20.8
  WM 70.24 EA 80.18 82.22
  83.19 91.8 PO 104.4
  108.9 TF 120.9 122.27
  DV 154.15 180.41 FG 193.3

BLINDLY (CONT.) SG 228.12
  GF 242.29 PP 435.33 HD 457.7

BLINDNESS SB 214.24 BL 348.17
  350.9 354.31 SU 531.10
  OV 753.33

BLINDS OA 29.11 29.14 29.29
  WM 63.34 WP 387.4

BLINK TB 515.33

BLINKED DV 159.10 WP 380.10
  TB 515.31 515.32 LA 638.25

BLINKING MO 5.42 DV 156.33
  WP 386.30 WR 573.22 GG 678.40
  ML 744.37

BLISS TF 130.11 DV 181.16
  BM 830.14 830.15

BLISSFUL BM 837.23

BLITHE EE 316.26 LA 637.20

BLITHENESS BO 592.42

BLITHERING IL 650.25

BLOBS TB 520.35

BLOCK PO 114.28 IL 654.26

BLOCKS SS 197.29

BLOND WM 63.30 TF 127.42 130.32
  132.17 OC 299.28 300.1
  FA 465.17 SU 534.10 534.40
  BO 594.31

BLONDE WM 58.13 59.15 SB 217.5
  EE 309.3 309.5 310.8 316.27
  318.31 324.25 MN 367.23
  YT 399.10 WR 580.22 NT 705.24
  705.32 707.22 709.30 709.37
  715.9 719.7 RH 803.14

BLONDE BESTIE NT 715.6

BLONDE-HEADED SB 213.39

BLONDNESS YT 408.17 FA 462.35

BLOOD OA 23.5 36.6 37.22
  WM 60.23 67.22 69.11 69.17
  EA 76.4 80.23 82.14 82.22
  83.15 83.16 90.37 91.1 93.4
  PO 97.24 99.6 100.19 100.30
  110.12 110.26 110.34 111.1
  113.16 113.25 115.22
  TF 127.11 129.21 DV 152.41
  FG 188.27 192.16 195.21
  195.26 196.7 196.9 196.11
  SS 203.10 SB 216.26 216.28
  220.1 SG 228.24 WS 249.24
  250.26 254.7 CH 277.12
  OC 292.41 293.20 EE 305.32
  306.1 306.33 314.10 317.4
  323.37 328.42 329.8 331.20
  331.21 332.16 332.19 332.20
  332.30 332.31 332.32 332.34
  TP 343.10 BL 349.12 354.30
  356.2 SD 418.17 FA 465.37

BLOOD (CONT.) 466.20 PR 473.4
  473.7 476.3 490.42 491.7
  511.16 TB 521.13 SU 543.24
  544.42 WR 574.37 BO 587.18
  595.35 595.40 596.4
  JD 606.34 606.39 LA 633.30
  GG 688.20 688.22 689.23
  689.27 689.31 690.8 690.13
  690.3 699.29 NT 707.25
  712.25 712.34 ML 731.23
  731.25 OV 753.12 753.17
  MD 825.24

BLOOD-ALLEY SC 271.1

BLOOD-AUTHORITY EE 316.9

BLOOD-CONTACT BL 355.30

BLOOD-CREATURE BO 596.2

BLOOD-DESIRE EE 306.21

BLOOD-DISFIGURED PO 112.33

BLOOD-DUSKY BO 596.6 596.9

BLOOD-MARK WS 265.12

BLOOD-POWER EE 316.1

BLOOD-PRESCIENCE BL 355.28

BLOOD-RED WM 69.3 PR 490.27

BLOOD-SACRIFICES EE 323.41

BLOODSHOT NT 705.31

BLOOD-SOAKED EE 317.26

BLOOD-STAINED ML 724.42

BLOODSTONE FG 196.6

BLOODY SP 53.13 53.17

BLOOM NT 706.1 MD 825.30
  TH 844.18

BLOOMERS BM 839.38

BLOOMIN' GF 243.8 MN 372.36

BLOOMING WR 562.26

BLOOMSBURY MD 810.23

BLORTIN' CH 281.25

BLOSSOM MO 18.41 TF 117.17
  DV 161.9 SS 200.35 202.14
  210.8 SG 226.9 PR 478.11
  SU 535.32 LA 640.8 643.6
  646.33 GG 694.23 699.28
  ML 732.22 OV 753.21 MD 821.37

BLOSSOMED PR 479.39 ML 728.6

BLOSSOMING EE 303.15 304.18
  RH 800.12

BLOSSOM-LIKE ML 725.8

BLOSSOMS EE 311.12 GG 682.36
  OV 753.18

BLOSSOM-ON-A-BENDING-STALK
  MD 809.1

BLOT SG 226.6 SU 538.41

BLOTCH MO 22.23

BLOTCHED BL 351.6

BLOTTING BO 596.6 GG 685.27
  RR 784.15

BLOTTING-PAPER SU 539.26

BLOUSE DV 149.6 179.4 182.10
  SC 268.6 SD 414.14 WR 551.9
  BO 598.38

BLOW MO 19.11 OA 35.37
  WM 62.39 70.3 TF 121.27
  DV 176.2 FG 189.6 SB 216.14
  218.35 GF 243.24 WS 247.25
  247.28 264.10 TP 343.7
  MN 368.16 371.27 YT 398.1
  405.32 SD 422.12 PR 505.32
  WR 555.12 BO 590.37
  ML 731.1 LL 769.24
  MD 817.37

BLOWING TF 120.21 FG 193.41
  WS 247.11 SD 411.4 TB 523.7
  SU 535.14 BO 595.8
  LA 639.17 ML 723.38 727.6

BLOWN MO 2.30 TF 118.24
  WP 385.28 LA 639.30

BLOWS OA 35.29 CH 278.28
  TP 343.21 BL 354.6

BLUE MO 12.24 OA 33.21
  HT 40.22 SP 49.11 51.20
  WM 54.19 55.10 58.11
  58.16 65.20 65.36 66.17
  70.8 EA 85.38 PO 95.8
  97.21 97.38 99.21 102.21
  102.28 106.40 107.29
  108.37 114.30 115.29
  TF 117.2 117.5 117.21
  117.33 119.5 119.23
  119.25 119.28 123.6 123.26
  125.24 126.22 DV 148.7
  149.6 167.14 167.27
  FG 187.8 192.35 194.10
  194.16 SS 198.7 200.2
  200.17 202.5 204.35
  210.6 SG 224.18 225.12
  225.14 WS 246.17 246.20
  249.15 250.36 250.37
  251.15 258.19 CH 279.8
  OC 287.9 292.11 292.13
  293.31 EE 303.9 306.7
  312.24 312.31 326.33
  329.22 TP 335.20 338.15
  342.31 BL 351.7 MN 367.2
  367.24 368.14 368.19
  368.21 376.19 376.36
  WP 379.1 379.6 386.23
  386.26 388.17 388.19
  390.5 390.20 390.34 391.3
  391.4 YT 400.19 400.20

BLUE (CONT.) 402.36 407.30
  PP 427.8 429.12 431.2
  435.22 437.13 437.37 HD 446.5
  PR 473.10 473.27 474.14
  474.17 475.10 476.24 479.39
  484.26 489.7 489.13 489.20
  489.36 490.6 490.25 493.28
  493.30 494.26 497.37 499.4
  499.18 506.27 506.35 507.8
  508.2 TB 520.34 521.36 521.38
  521.39 521.40 522.1 522.3
  522.5 522.8 523.33 525.8
  525.29 525.36 526.39 527.26
  SU 530.8 530.17 530.28 530.29
  530.31 534.13 534.16 534.35
  534.38 535.34 536.36 538.4
  542.19 543.14 545.1 WR 551.39
  554.21 564.22 565.4 569.21
  573.30 573.31 574.17 574.18
  574.20 574.30 574.38 574.42
  575.3 575.11 575.31 576.39
  577.31 577.38 578.27 578.38
  578.42 SM 583.31 BO 588.31
  588.39 590.41 595.11
  JD 611.12 611.37 613.30
  614.23 616.31 617.42 621.26
  625.14 627.27 LA 630.8 640.27
  641.36 GG 669.39 670.13
  670.32 672.39 672.42 674.34
  675.10 677.39 679.36 680.8
  694.16 696.6 699.36 NT 705.26
  707.35 ML 723.16 723.17
  728.25 728.32 740.3 740.19
  743.29 OV 748.11 758.30
  LL 767.24 775.25 777.4
  RH 793.31 793.37 795.12 796.5
  798.27 800.32 800.39 804.1
  BM 827.21 827.31 828.35
  829.18 832.42 833.9 833.16
  833.17 833.21 833.25 835.25
  835.26 835.28 835.31 835.32
  835.42 836.31 836.36 837.1
  837.18 838.4 838.7 838.17
  838.21 840.5 840.18 841.4

BLUE-AND-BLUFF PR 506.20*

BLUE-AND-BROWN PR 495.27

BLUE-AND-WHITE EE 304.36
  GG 692.5

BLUEBELLS SS 197.17 199.34
  199.38 199.41 MN 373.18
  ML 732.22

BLUE-BLACK PR 489.15 WR 561.13

BLUE-CLAD TB 524.40

BLUED PR 473.7

BLUE-EYED PP 428.22 WR 547.12
  ML 726.30

BLUE-GREY SU 530.6

BLUE-MOLTEN SU 532.36

BLUENESS PR 489.16 OV 753.16

BLUE SISTERS SM 582.31

BLUEST SU 529.8

BLUE-TIT TB 521.38 522.4 522.5

BLUE-TITS TB 523.6

BLUE-TIT'S SS 204.1

BLUE-TOPPED PR 499.5

BLUE-WHITE SU 532.11

BLUEY PO 97.30 WP 385.34

BLUFF SU 530.4

BLUISH WM 70.5 PO 95.21
  DV 167.22 YT 395.31 WR 554.20
  LA 640.27 LL 761.12

BLUNDER MO 21.20

BLUNDERED OV 747.20

BLUNDERING FG 190.18 OV 747.36

BLUNTLY YT 408.11

BLUNTNESS BM 839.2

BLURTED EA 93.8 SS 199.10
  MN 370.39 TH 853.8

BLUSH WM 58.20

BLUSHED WS 252.7 YT 397.15

BLUSH OF DAWN RH 796.34

BLUSTER PP 432.26

BLUSTERING PP 429.36 438.20

BOA-CONSTRICTOR IL 658.28

BOADICEA, QUEEN (SEE QUEEN
  BOADICEA)

BOAR EE 326.34

BOARD OA 32.25 SP 52.8 52.26
  WS 253.33 TP 336.14 341.42
  SU 528.7 OV 754.18

BOARD OF TRADE MD 818.23 818.31

BOARDS OC 298.9 TP 338.16

BOAT SU 528.34 BO 592.33
  ML 739.32 740.1 741.3 742.5
  743.12 745.9 745.12 745.27
  746.11

BOATLOAD ML 725.24

BOATS WP 379.10 379.12

BOAT-SHAPED MN 366.34

BOB SP 46.6 46.30 46.32 50.10
  FA 467.22 469.24 471.29
  471.41

BOBBED YT 397.9 397.39 HD 442.9
  PR 479.35 512.20 SU 533.24
  LA 632.36 LL 763.35

BOBBIN' SP 48.31

BOBBING PO 113.9

BOB-CAT PR 501.17

BOB OSBORNE GF 242.30

BOBS YT 397.10

BOB'S FA 471.13 471.18

BOB-TAIL PR 501.26

BOCHE BO 587.12 587.35

BOD WP 388.28 388.39 389.5

BODICES GF 241.18

BODIES MO 5.4 PO 108.41
  116.17 TF 118.22 132.22
  FG 190.17 EE 306.18
  WP 379.9 SU 534.6 WR 568.42
  576.23 GG 690.29 ML 724.28
  OV 753.27 TH 851.9 851.12
  851.13

BODILESS PR 478.40 LL 767.10
  767.29

BODILY MO 22.5 JD 629.10
  GG 689.18 689.19 694.5
  694.36 BM 833.2

BODOIN (SEE RACHEL, ROBERT,
  VIRGINIA; MRS. BODOIN)

BODY MO 18.21 WM 68.9 68.39
  69.26 69.29 69.39 EA 72.9
  76.5 78.12 80.12 81.31
  81.34 82.1 83.26 91.6
  91.34 PO 97.11 104.17
  106.8 107.22 108.15 108.20
  108.34 109.27 110.15
  110.20 110.29 110.39
  113.38 115.40 TF 118.5
  118.28 118.31 120.26
  121.19 132.8 132.16
  132.18 133.16 134.29
  135.7 DV 145.19 151.32
  153.17 153.18 153.21
  154.6 154.22 156.8 165.11
  165.28 171.9 179.40 180.25
  SS 198.12 SB 212.7 215.8
  SG 221.20 WS 252.22 254.34
  254.37 255.1 255.2 256.13
  257.34 266.1 SC 267.6
  CH 279.39 OC 292.41 297.15
  298.39 299.20 299.36
  299.42 301.6 301.8 301.9
  302.4 EE 306.5 312.6
  322.26 322.37 325.29
  325.31 327.32 329.29
  BL 350.41 SD 418.18 420.41
  422.2 HD 442.13 449.13
  450.17 452.24 FA 467.3
  469.1 471.26 PR 473.13
  482.27 509.31 511.30
  SU 531.27 531.29 532.32
  533.38 533.42 534.10
  535.25 536.3 537.1 537.10
  538.1 544.5 544.11
  WR 547.26 564.10 564.19

BODY (CONT.) 577.2 577.6 577.9
  SM 584.17 BO 587.15 589.26
  597.22 604.36 JD 617.16
  617.35 618.2 618.4 LA 635.2
  637.41 640.16 GG 661.32
  661.33 662.1 662.30 662.31
  667.10 670.16 671.33 671.35
  671.36 671.37 680.7 681.30
  683.8 683.20 686.26 689.37
  690.7 690.19 690.22 691.27
  691.40 692.3 692.7 692.9
  692.13 692.14 692.15 692.30
  692.31 692.34 692.38 693.12
  693.29 693.38 695.27 696.24
  696.26 696.32 696.33 696.34
  697.3 697.28 697.35 697.40
  698.10 NT 702.42 703.41
  707.31 710.3 710.15 710.21
  710.31 710.38 712.26 713.5
  713.9 713.42 714.2 717.13
  717.17 717.22 718.8 718.11
  718.13 718.14 718.17 718.18
  718.30 718.32 720.41
  ML 744.17 OV 752.17 754.9
  754.37 755.40 758.23 LL 763.4
  766.38 771.2 777.15 777.31
  MD 816.19 822.11 BM 831.24
  832.3 832.5 837.21 839.39
  TH 852.26

BODY'S GF 240.7

BOG PO 107.9 SS 210.3 EE 305.3

BOGGY EE 305.7

BOILED JD 618.25

BOILER MO 6.4 JD 617.4

BOILING JD 616.12 IL 650.14
  NT 706.42

BOISTEROUS WS 251.34 254.9

BOISTEROUSLY MO 7.10 WS 254.12
  WP 392.18 HD 444.34

BOLD JD 625.18 LL 763.1
  BM 836.8 837.3

BOLDLY TP 334.2 BM 836.7

BOLOGNA TH 849.29 850.38 853.20

BOLSTER JD 604.13

BOLT MN 368.14 SM 585.19
  MD 807.3

BOLTED OA 28.37

BOMB BM 835.28 835.36

BOMBS MO 15.2

BONAMY IL 653.15 655.16

BONAMY'S IL 654.28 655.7 659.14
  660.1

BOND PO 116.2 SG 230.37
  LL 765.21 765.22

BONDAGE CH 280.27 EE 308.21

BONDAGE (CONT.) BM 836.32 836.38
  837.18

BONDS SD 423.4 LL 765.21

BOND STREET ML 735.40

BONE WM 67.22 FA 471.25
  TB 518.25 518.31 WR 557.25
  JD 623.34 LL 761.7 MD 817.26

BONES OC 292.10 EE 319.26
  TP 339.5 MN 373.28 PP 434.8
  SU 530.38 544.5 WR 577.24
  JD 622.20 GG 690.12 700.10
  TH 848.20

BONNET DV 139.29 OC 293.30
  294.22 299.33 WP 379.24
  FA 462.2 467.8 JD 626.13

BONNY OA 24.14 WM 57.39
  DV 154.22 SB 214.37 CH 277.5
  282.16 SU 534.12 GG 666.40
  RH 790.3

BONY WM 65.16 CH 278.36
  OC 283.32 292.11 BO 588.32
  588.39 592.27 JD 622.24 625.3

BOOK OA 31.33 32.41 34.23
  DV 139.38 152.13 FG 188.9
  188.39 PR 483.30 SM 586.15
  IL 656.37 ML 728.1 729.5
  735.1 735.41 736.3 740.20
  741.17 743.15 LL 766.17
  769.10

BOOKCASE TH 848.19 848.30

BOOK-KEEPING TB 526.36

BOOK OF JOB LA 644.39

BOOKS MO 21.33 DV 164.6 165.30
  SS 200.10 200.21 202.41
  BL 347.16 YT 396.17 TB 525.33
  525.41 526.11 JD 609.31
  LA 639.37 ML 733.19 733.24
  739.34 RR 784.8 TH 846.2
  848.20 848.31

BOOKSHELVES LL 775.37

BOOK-SHELVES TH 853.20

BOOK-STALLS TH 844.29

BOOM WR 574.3 ML 722.24

BOOMING WR 568.18

BOOR OA 33.3

BOORS FG 187.22

BOOT SB 214.36

BOOTLEG PR 501.37

BOOTS OA 37.23 SP 50.2
  PO 108.18 TF 126.15 DV 148.41
  167.35 168.12 168.16
  SS 197.12 WS 250.38 251.18
  SC 268.8 OC 299.7 TP 335.35

BOOTS (CONT.) BL 354.26
  PP 433.39 PR 483.42
  484.41 485.1 506.24
  506.27 WR 563.3 563.41
  JD 611.8 617.8

BOOT-SOLE SB 214.39

BORDER EA 84.12 BO 590.25
  593.28

BORDERING BL 355.32 HD 448.6
  TH 852.35

BORDERLAND PP 436.30

BORDER-LINE BO 595.18 599.25

BORDERS TB 520.32 MD 810.37

BORE OA 25.29 WM 65.2 70.11
  DV 162.27 WS 254.42
  EE 324.29 PR 474.3
  LL 770.40

BORED EE 308.37 WR 579.37
  GG 662.17 662.18 NT 708.4
  OV 748.14 756.28 RR 783.11

BOREDOM NT 709.36 TH 845.4

BORN PO 115.24 DV 137.40
  150.18 154.39 156.26
  185.11 WS 252.6 CH 279.33
  OC 289.9 EE 306.2 307.19
  309.21 315.34 326.3 327.40
  BL 348.23 WP 381.4 383.14
  391.33 PP 430.5 PR 474.10
  482.42 SU 541.29 BO 588.35
  592.15 GG 664.9 690.10
  693.25 693.28 NT 705.21
  ML 722.1 739.5 739.11
  OV 755.21 756.42 LL 764.8
  769.30 769.36 RH 792.5
  BM 840.23 TH 851.1

BORNE WM 69.6 EA 71.23
  WS 257.16 EE 323.12
  YT 402.35 SU 531.38
  WR 561.1

BOSOM OA 37.28 FG 195.6
  195.36 TP 335.41 SD 415.12
  SU 530.14 SM 583.31
  JD 605.9 605.24 605.27
  GG 694.37 695.16 OV 747.7
  MD 812.20

BOSS MO 14.21 YT 406.23
  TB 514.40 WR 547.24
  ML 726.29

BOSSES SS 210.4

BOSSY BM 831.26

BOSTON PR 473.1 474.39
  NT 705.23

BOTELL SS 208.15

BOTELL'S SS 208.13

BOTHER DV 185.35 GF 238.5
  CH 276.8 EE 311.31

BRACES (CONT.) 419.9 421.21
  421.36 422.29

BRACKEN FG 189.25 189.33 189.37
  SS 206.36 EE 303.4

BRACKET WM 54.20

BRADLEY (SEE MR. BRADLEY)

BRAGGART MO 12.3

BRAGGIN' OC 285.34

BRAHMS WM 59.6 EA 75.34

BRAID WR 564.24 578.5

BRAIDED EA 86.10 WR 558.17
  559.22 559.35 562.23 578.5

BRAID-HAIR PR 495.30

BRAIDS WR 559.34

BRAIN PO 114.10 114.20 115.19
  115.26 TF 126.13 DV 157.15
  181.1 SS 209.37 WS 248.35
  264.24 EE 332.18 PP 435.38
  PR 485.38 498.11 GG 697.8
  NT 708.6 717.12 LL 768.24
  MD 819.6

BRAINED MD 813.5

BRAIN-FEVER RH 803.24

BRAINLESS MD 814.6

BRAINS RH 790.31 BM 832.3

BRAITHWAITE (SEE MRS. BRAITHWAITE)

BRAKES OC 293.19 295.9 295.10

BRAMBLE SS 210.31 SB 213.40

BRAN-BAG DV 162.34 169.32

BRANCH MN 372.22 BM 830.17

BRANCHED HD 442.2

BRANCHES MO 1.33 FG 189.34
  TB 517.12 OV 750.30

BRANCH-LINE FA 458.14

BRAND SU 544.37 ML 727.39

BRAND, FRANZ (SEE FRANZ)

BRANDED SU 544.37

BRANDY DV 140.37 162.6
  GF 239.12 WP 387.8 YT 399.16
  PP 434.1 435.10

BRASS WM 63.33 TF 125.24
  GF 234.26 241.19 CH 274.23
  TP 338.8 PP 427.4 TB 513.30
  JD 617.4 ML 743.16

BRAVADO IL 659.16

BRAVE FG 194.6 EE 322.8
  YT 403.6 GG 693.36

BRAVELY MO 12.15

BRAVING FA 467.30

BRAVO NT 713.12 713.12

BRAVO SI MOLTO + LL 774.4

BRAY FG 188.20 HD 446.8

BRAZEN BM 836.37

BRAZENING RH 792.30

BREACH EA 80.38 SG 233.10

BREAD MO 3.21 14.11 SP 50.27
  PO 109.25 109.29 109.31
  TF 135.4 FG 190.31 190.32
  195.28 SG 223.6 WS 248.2
  CH 274.19 275.35 277.5 277.16
  279.21 281.28 OC 285.26
  285.29 287.26 291.40
  EE 312.41 TP 341.5 341.8
  PR 488.12 495.24 502.19
  SU 542.38 JD 611.20 619.17
  ML 743.5 OV 758.27

BREAD-AND-BUTTER MO 3.28 5.23
  OA 26.18 32.29

BREAD-KNIFE IL 651.12

BREADTH PO 110.11 PP 435.40
  ML 724.34

BREAK MO 1.15 OA 29.21
  DV 149.39 158.10 176.19
  WS 263.3 263.30 263.32 264.18
  EE 307.24 333.4 333.6 333.9
  TP 342.19 SD 422.4 HD 453.19
  FA 471.25 PR 509.8 SU 534.26
  WR 550.20 575.33 BO 597.37
  JD 613.8 621.38 626.40
  GG 678.13 682.40 686.29
  LL 767.36 RH 793.18

BREAKABLE EA 84.16

BREAKDOWN GG 678.2

BREAKFAST EA 83.28 SG 222.5
  222.35 GF 241.20 WS 244.33
  247.33 SC 267.26 PR 505.16
  JD 625.22 LA 641.25 644.6
  644.7 RH 799.24

BREAKFAST-CUPS HT 43.1

BREAKFASTS MO 19.2 TF 133.20

BREAKFAST-SERVICE HT 42.19

BREAKFAST-TABLE HD 441.7 443.12

BREAKING WM 60.5 PO 98.19
  103.14 DV 174.26 185.25
  WP 386.19 YT 401.26 PR 489.8
  GG 691.22

BREAKIN' CH 279.17 OC 293.2

BREAKS JD 626.40

BREAST MO 5.4 OA 24.4 25.24
  26.32 30.35 36.36 WM 68.7
  68.34 69.21 EA 79.23
  90.42 PO 102.23 111.5
  114.7 TF 127.32 DV 149.5
  179.42 FG 191.30 194.12
  195.30 195.34 SS 210.13
  210.16 WS 245.4 249.4
  251.17 SC 268.40 CH 278.3
  278.9 EE 317.37 317.40
  322.8 322.18 322.19
  TP 343.31 MN 367.15
  WP 384.13 SD 412.34 421.3
  421.26 PP 439.18 439.30
  440.1 HD 450.1 454.8
  454.13 455.1 456.36
  PR 490.22 511.17 WR 558.12
  BO 595.29 602.26 604.34
  JD 617.34 618.2 LA 637.36
  GG 689.42 690.36 694.9
  694.10 694.12 694.37
  695.14 695.17 695.18
  695.37 696.10 NT 709.30
  ML 730.29 745.4 OV 751.29
  758.13 759.41 LL 769.13
  772.9 775.31 775.35
  778.29 MD 822.12 822.18
  BM 835.37

BREAST-FEATHER TB 522.26

BREASTING BO 595.24

BREASTS MO 1.27 OA 27.2
  WM 67.5 EA 92.7 92.13
  TF 123.27 127.31 SB 212.27
  SD 419.33 425.15 426.11
  426.14 HD 452.41 455.17
  SU 530.18 530.21 530.24
  530.31 536.7 536.14
  537.26 539.24 541.17
  544.32 WR 564.10 LA 637.38
  GG 684.6 690.17 698.29

BREATH MO 2.30 OA 36.36
  WM 64.42 EA 93.28 PO 95.25
  106.26 TF 121.23 DV 149.13
  FG 188.17 190.5 SB 219.39
  GF 242.5 WS 264.27
  SC 272.41 CH 280.11
  TP 338.25 343.24 SD 418.18
  PP 428.6 SU 529.24
  WR 568.40 IL 656.10
  GG 672.25 687.13 NT 713.1
  ML 746.37 OV 751.17 RH 791.27
  BM 837.28

BREATHE MO 17.14 OA 30.11
  WM 63.5 EA 77.28 90.16
  90.26 PO 102.15 DV 176.23
  YT 408.20 PR 496.22
  BO 592.31 TH 845.40

BREATHED MO 2.31 11.24
  EA 73.20 PO 95.32 108.2
  DV 160.26 WS 257.24 260.12
  SD 425.12 WR 556.16
  JD 610.14 GG 690.37 694.12

BREATHES JD 608.19* GG 695.17

BREATHING MO 1.30 OA 36.29
  36.34 EA 89.4 90.30 91.7

BREATHING (CONT.) DV 175.35
  WS 255.6 HD 450.7 450.42
  451.1 451.12 PR 503.31
  JD 608.14 RH 791.27

BREATHLESS PO 107.9 TP 334.18
  SU 533.29 IL 656.21 ML 728.10
  BM 843.1

BREATHLESSLY MO 9.6 9.34
  SB 216.18

BREATHS SD 421.32

BRED PO 99.17 EE 306.22 327.40

BREECHES SP 50.1 WP 388.35
  390.11 390.39 393.11
  PR 495.27 499.3 500.27 506.19
  506.27 WR 551.8 GG 665.32
  667.31 MD 823.3

BREED ML 728.42

BREEDING TF 128.12 DV 157.2
  EE 306.2 314.4 YT 403.20
  ML 722.17 MD 820.3

BREEDS ML 727.39

BREEZE MO 19.11 SU 531.7 535.33
  536.12 541.18

BREEZINESS BM 841.13

BRENT SC 269.12

BREVIARY SM 583.28

BREVITY JD 607.36

BREW GG 688.7 688.25

BREWER'S PP 432.21

BRIAR-ENTANGLED EE 304.7

BRICK MO 17.30 SP 50.14
  DV 136.19 161.13 161.17
  YT 394.1 JD 624.24

BRICKED OC 283.33 HD 446.23

BRICK-RED SS 206.16

BRICKS WR 561.17 562.10
  ML 729.23

BRIDE EE 304.9 MD 811.14

BRIDEGROOM GG 694.17

BRIDGE PO 111.10 TF 121.41
  SB 216.39 EE 303.3 303.12
  316.37 TP 334.31 WR 558.38
  561.29 570.14 BO 597.32
  599.13 LL 765.10 773.7

BRIDGED LL 761.10

BRIDGE-HEAD BO 597.25

BRIDGES WR 561.23

BRIDLE PO 112.8 PR 493.10

BRIDLE (CONT.) WR 555.28 556.28

BRIDLED WM 68.17

BRIDLING WS 246.6

BRIDLINGTON SG 222.37

BRIEF MO 17.22 TF 134.23
  DV 156.20 SS 202.27 OC 285.18
  286.9 BL 353.17 MN 368.7
  SD 415.27 BO 601.17 JD 607.33
  LA 637.26 NT 720.12 OV 758.13
  BM 827.29 836.42 TH 852.19

BRIEFLY WS 245.25 HD 455.39
  WR 554.14 JD 628.11 GG 665.40

BRIGHT MO 5.2 OA 26.12 WM 54.23
  54.29 59.27 EA 76.1 78.32
  91.22 PO 106.6 106.16 107.18
  108.39 112.2 112.23 113.28
  113.30 114.33 115.4 TF 119.5
  119.29 124.40 DV 136.4 139.16
  161.14 173.11 175.15
  FG 194.20 196.21 SS 197.7
  203.6 203.30 206.19 210.24
  210.39 SG 222.23 226.1 226.19
  GF 240.8 241.31 OC 291.3
  TP 335.13 344.11 WP 387.40
  389.4 YT 397.37 407.13 407.15
  SD 412.12 412.28 414.30
  416.17 417.17 422.22 423.31
  425.21 425.25 PP 439.35
  FA 458.36 459.1 460.6 463.15
  464.18 PR 487.42 491.28 494.9
  498.29 500.31 502.25
  SU 537.11 WR 553.37 555.17
  555.20 555.30 559.12 561.28
  565.37 BO 601.2 JD 617.4
  LA 634.22 637.37 IL 655.40
  GG 671.5 692.20 ML 728.37
  737.23 LL 761.14 761.16
  761.36 764.26 RR 786.2
  RH 794.34 795.8 795.22 796.21
  796.25

BRIGHT-COLOURED PR 499.13

BRIGHT-EYED LA 632.37 RR 786.28

BRIGHTLY MO 10.21 19.12 EA 79.8
  PO 113.10 DV 166.28 SB 218.26
  SD 424.1 FA 463.1 466.35
  468.35 TB 522.18 JD 616.10
  ML 731.19

BRIGHTNESS MO 5.28 DV 173.26
  SS 200.8 210.33 SC 267.14
  EE 304.25 WR 572.18 ML 738.33

BRIGHTON ROAD WM 60.34

BRILLIANCE TP 337.17 SU 530.29
  LA 635.1

BRILLIANCY LL 763.41

BRILLIANT MO 5.24 PO 108.36
  109.2 TF 123.7 123.9
  SS 199.24 204.15 SB 216.33
  BL 359.8 359.36 360.7
  WP 387.24 389.10 SD 423.7
  FA 459.10 465.31 465.32
  PR 507.13 510.34 WR 559.21

BRILLIANT (CONT.) 568.28
  LA 634.39 637.35 NT 709.25
  ML 729.5 LL 769.23
  MD 812.21 BM 828.35

BRILLIANTLY TF 117.10
  SS 201.8 WS 250.7 251.28
  FA 461.7 464.35 TH 850.17

BRIM SP 48.9 DV 161.8
  PR 493.36

BRIMMED PO 110.26

BRIMMING SB 212.8

BRINDLED DV 161.24 WR 552.34

BRINE TB 514.28

BRING MO 1.12 7.37 OA 33.38
  EA 81.30 DV 137.36 154.8
  158.25 FG 187.26 190.30
  191.40 192.19 192.28
  192.31 GF 239.13 WS 265.19
  CH 280.39 OC 289.16 290.11
  EE 312.38 314.1 318.42
  321.41 WP 381.19 388.2
  YT 406.6 HD 452.34
  FA 471.33 PR 500.35
  TB 524.22 SU 531.33 531.34
  538.35 538.36 WR 560.13
  560.40 563.18 568.9
  575.2 575.30 JD 622.4
  622.42 GG 695.14 NT 707.10
  711.32 714.42 715.2 715.6
  715.14 ML 729.17 743.3
  RR 783.40 786.6 MD 804.8
  823.35

BRINGING OC 296.14 296.34
  MN 366.27 PP 439.3 FA 466.31
  466.34 467.12 PR 488.31
  WR 550.10 557.12 GG 695.42
  NT 715.1

BRINGIN' OC 295.23

BRINGS SG 222.17 JD 619.4
  623.28 OV 753.25

BRINK MO 2.5 OA 34.30

BRINSLEY COLLIERY OC 283.22

BRISK SB 214.19 BL 356.38
  SD 421.15

BRISKLY WS 244.2 246.22
  MN 376.17

BRISKNESS GG 669.3

BRISTLED TF 117.5 OC 290.6
  298.1 PP 427.9 WR 556.6

BRISTLES PR 496.9 TB 517.38

BRISTLING PO 110.25 SC 272.1
  SD 420.11 PP 433.5
  PR 484.3 494.2 494.28
  496.8 496.36 BO 600.11
  602.30 603.10

BRISTLY PO 96.17 SS 200.26

BRISTLY (CONT.) ML 734.14

BRITISH EE 327.19 PR 505.39
  TB 528.38 GG 662.41

BRITISH GOVERNMENT MD 818.27
  818.28

BRITISH SCHOOL CH 274.1

BRITTLE TF 134.42 DV 158.9

BRITTLENESS BO 596.4

BROACH MO 14.34 SS 209.41

BROAD MO 2.1 4.11 SP 51.30
  WM 55.14 PO 105.27 106.42
  107.5 SB 218.16 OC 291.2
  MN 367.33 WP 388.30 HD 441.31
  FA 458.32 462.16 465.11 468.3
  PR 473.12 485.10 TB 521.15
  SU 542.18 542.37 543.9 543.15
  WR 567.33 576.17 GG 662.18
  671.28 685.22 NT 702.12
  ML 726.39 727.11 LL 762.39
  763.35 MD 808.22

BROAD-BRIMMED PR 511.12

BROADEST WR 561.25

BROADLY MO 7.7 15.17 WS 245.16

BROCADE GG 691.6 696.12
  NT 705.42 706.13 LL 763.30
  MD 811.3 811.12 815.15

BROCADES NT 705.41

BROKE MO 12.3 20.27 WM 63.21
  70.17 EA 85.18 85.41
  TF 117.27 DV 181.20 FG 188.17
  191.12 193.12 SB 218.10
  SG 221.23 GF 236.35 238.34
  240.40 240.42 WS 263.27
  SC 272.38 CH 281.35 OC 284.37
  288.7 EE 326.18 326.22
  WP 392.3 SD 423.3 HD 456.41
  PR 473.32 487.22 506.29
  509.20 TB 519.15 BO 591.14
  LA 635.25 GG 688.29 689.28
  ML 730.31 OV 754.34 754.42
  LL 775.27 MD 817.26 BM 827.25

BROKEN MO 18.33 OA 28.33
  SP 45.12 51.3 EA 91.41
  PO 107.11 109.29 110.31
  110.39 TF 117.2 132.2
  DV 137.42 154.32 176.23
  180.32 FG 188.24 189.28
  191.27 194.27 CH 278.33
  OC 297.24 TP 344.34 345.21
  BL 365.14 365.15 SD 417.42
  PP 434.42 436.27 436.31
  HD 454.12 455.8 PR 491.14
  TB 526.22 BO 591.15 LA 641.34
  GG 684.14 690.19 690.33
  690.34 NT 711.9 ML 740.34
  OV 755.10 MD 807.25 TH 844.27

BROKENLY GG 678.14

BRONZE FG 187.31 PR 473.15
  WR 559.33 TH 853.22

BRONZES TH 848.31

BROOCH GF 240.15 WS 260.26
  260.29 263.38 263.41 264.39

BROOCHES SS 202.5

BROOD BL 363.4 WP 380.9

BROODED EE 331.32

BROODING MO 7.23 WM 65.28
  EA 87.42 DV 151.9 151.10
  160.16 EE 330.34 330.35
  PR 476.42 WR 566.17 GG 664.12
  NT 719.37

BROOK MO 22.17 SS 210.2
  SB 213.41 216.37 OC 283.35
  284.11 284.19 284.24 286.28
  EE 303.2 316.24 316.34
  WR 553.9

BROOK-COURSE SB 213.5

BROOKS OV 755.27

BROOM ML 730.22 736.11

BROTHER MO 5.10 GF 240.30
  241.41 242.11 242.28
  CH 280.20 280.26 BL 348.41
  WP 383.15 383.37 391.40
  PP 429.16 HD 442.31 446.1
  FA 463.13 IL 653.21 653.30
  653.39 LL 762.16 768.18
  RH 803.33 BM 827.26 829.11

BROTHER-IN-LAW'S EA 78.25 81.4

BROTHERS MO 3.36 17.8 TF 128.6
  DV 170.19 BL 348.41 HD 441.6
  441.17 441.19 446.42
  FA 470.17

BROTHER'S MN 377.4 RH 804.32

BROUGHT OA 35.31 35.39 HT 41.29
  WM 69.30 70.12 TF 126.28
  DV 139.40 140.24 140.32
  142.28 182.6 FG 189.10 190.26
  192.9 SS 200.36 SG 223.22
  233.12 GF 239.5 WS 245.35
  265.28 SC 270.25 OC 285.29
  289.10 294.15 294.40 298.16
  299.25 EE 307.25 309.14
  314.31 315.3 324.23 332.39
  BL 348.39 352.39 YT 408.27
  HD 448.2 455.21 PR 481.16
  501.1 TB 516.1 524.14
  SU 532.2 535.11 WR 548.15
  564.29 565.3 568.13 573.29
  BO 588.24 JD 606.9 606.15
  608.26 617.19 624.38
  IL 652.16 GG 667.23 673.30
  NT 712.41 ML 725.14 725.41
  735.12 738.38 739.32 742.12
  746.15 OV 754.16 LL 765.40
  RR 783.22 788.41 RH 796.11
  MD 816.41 822.10 825.26

BROW MO 1.35 15.23 OA 26.26
  WM 64.35 EA 84.29 85.37
  PO 96.20 96.31 107.16
  DV 143.4 160.16 168.38 170.10

BROW (CONT.) SS 197.19
  199.34 207.25 WS 248.12
  261.8 OC 297.30 EE 318.31
  323.5 325.26 332.15
  TP 343.25 BL 347.8 358.13
  364.17 MN 373.35 374.2
  WP 380.12 YT 401.40 402.2
  SD 412.7 414.10 414.31
  414.42 PP 433.23 434.26
  FA 469.37 PR 473.12
  SU 534.11 534.32 539.4
  543.17 SM 585.3 JD 612.21
  615.40 GG 662.25 MD 809.17
  817.10

BROWN MO 3.24 4.3 8.2
  19.39 OA 31.19 33.7 33.16
  35.27 36.38 37.14 HT 39.34
  40.21 42.25 SP 49.2 49.10
  WM 59.27 PO 97.22 98.38
  107.35 108.34 113.36
  DV 149.26 168.13 169.27
  172.31 SS 206.16 206.22
  210.4 210.9 211.12
  SB 212.14 213.1 213.2
  213.10 214.1 217.21
  SG 221.11 228.38 GF 235.32
  WS 250.23 250.37 251.39
  SC 268.11 OC 286.41 289.11
  290.18 EE 306.41 TP 336.15
  BL 354.27 WP 379.7
  YT 397.19 SD 412.31 414.11
  PP 437.11 HD 442.37 443.27
  454.23 FA 460.42 PR 475.10
  481.6 483.20 484.1 484.16
  497.21 504.37 504.40
  505.18 511.26 SU 539.25
  543.15 543.16 WR 546.4
  558.41 559.16 574.36
  JD 612.29 618.24 LA 631.24
  640.40 646.28 IL 648.18
  648.20 654.17 658.20
  GG 668.39 669.25 684.20
  NT 719.33 ML 728.34 729.8
  733.32 736.21 737.23
  739.27 OV 753.15 753.36
  LL 763.20 763.22 771.11
  RH 804.9 804.10 MD 807.37
  818.36 819.39 820.3
  820.38

BROWN-EYED WR 547.13
  MD 813.27

BROWN-HUSKED SB 213.40

BROWNING PP 430.17

BROWNISH EE 306.36 YT 395.31
  400.30 PR 479.34

BROWN-PAPER PO 102.36

BROWN-RED SG 221.23 PP 433.16

BROWN-ROSY SU 544.39

BROWN-SKINNED PO 108.41

BROWS MO 9.13 15.2 OA 26.27
  26.33 WM 66.17 69.1
  EA 79.22 PO 97.39 99.12
  SB 214.37 GF 241.18
  EE 303.6 TP 337.24
  BL 363.40 MN 374.6 WP 380.8

BROWS (CONT.) 391.3 SD 413.29
  424.23 PP 429.27 433.18
  434.34 TB 522.31 JD 606.25
  611.22 615.8 629.2 LA 631.12
  632.25 633.34 GG 673.4
  ML 736.24 MD 812.38 822.26
  BM 828.11

BROWT WP 388.32

BRUISE NT 721.7

BRUISED HT 38.24 WM 64.6
  EA 91.3 OC 297.34 TP 343.25
  SD 423.4

BRUISES PO 95.27 95.28 104.33
  104.34 116.15 NT 721.8

BRUSH MO 18.13 MD 818.35 820.1
  820.5 BM 829.26

BRUSHED EA 84.28 PO 111.3
  SS 207.24 SG 226.19 230.22
  OC 284.5 PR 473.12 JD 618.27
  MD 809.17

BRUSHES PO 104.4

BRUSHING MO 10.32 FG 191.38
  OC 299.28 299.34 LL 768.9
  BM 829.25 829.29

BRUSSEL-SPROUT DV 161.34

BRUSSEL-SPROUTS DV 162.4

BRUTAL MO 10.24 OA 27.37
  PO 96.17 98.37 TF 118.17
  121.16 121.27 GF 234.9
  WS 249.6 261.11 CH 275.35
  278.20 HD 446.39 PR 477.20
  477.34 478.12 JD 617.19
  NT 703.15

BRUTALITY GG 683.30 TH 851.10

BRUTALLY MO 7.31 17.7 WM 62.29
  TF 122.25 DV 155.32 SG 231.29
  232.32 BL 359.34 HD 447.2
  PR 483.8 JD 617.31 617.35
  ML 745.34

BRUTE OA 35.42 DV 165.36
  SB 214.23 214.34 WP 393.1
  SD 420.20 420.31 GG 687.29
  NT 702.2 702.5 702.6 718.29
  ML 745.19 OV 747.29 BM 842.5
  TH 851.11 851.14

BRUTES HT 38.29 TF 127.21

BRYAN HT 39.16 SP 45.9

BUBBLE OA 27.10 TP 337.32

BUBBLES PO 107.10

BUBBLING OA 25.40 WR 552.16

BUCK GG 677.8

BUCKET MO 3.18 TB 516.31
  ML 725.26

BUCKLE TP 343.8

BUCKLES PR 484.42

BUCKSKIN PR 490.16 490.37
  490.40 491.3 491.11 491.25
  492.4 492.17 492.26 493.8

BUCKSKIN'S PR 493.10

BUD SS 206.18 SU 535.34
  OV 755.23 755.26

BUDDHA TH 845.42

BUDDHA'S TH 846.4

BUDDHISM TH 846.13

BUDDHISTIC TH 846.1

BUDDING SP 48.7 SB 212.26

BUDS MO 4.29 OA 24.30 WM 63.20
  DV 139.11 SS 202.25 204.5
  WR 565.5

BUFF PR 490.41 491.8 494.18
  499.4

BUFFERS NT 708.34

BUGLE PO 104.11 TF 131.21
  132.15 132.23

BUILD SP 51.23 WM 58.12 59.14
  PO 113.11 SB 217.20 SC 267.3
  CH 275.32 JD 617.2 TH 847.12

BUILDING EA 81.25 82.16
  DV 136.12 FA 459.34 WR 566.37
  LA 639.35 ML 738.20

BUILDINGS WM 54.14 DV 167.21
  SS 201.41 BL 362.13 FA 471.14
  WR 558.39 561.34 561.39
  ML 735.34 LL 766.23

BUILT SP 45.5 EA 89.8 PO 97.1
  TF 118.12 DV 136.11 SC 267.18
  CH 275.31 278.26 EE 304.39
  SD 416.30 425.18 PR 487.3
  SU 529.34 BO 595.26 IL 648.18
  GG 691.2 700.12 ML 725.38
  739.31 746.18 RR 786.11

BULBS OV 754.27

BULGARIA MD 818.26 818.34
  818.42

BULGE SC 268.41

BULGING WS 251.18 FA 462.29

BULK WM 54.14 PO 115.10
  EE 308.3 PR 487.25 489.11
  495.16 ML 728.15 TH 849.40

BULKED OC 290.34

BULKING WR 569.23

BULL OA 35.26 NT 702.9 702.26
  702.27 702.29 703.32 703.33

BULL (CONT.) 712.11 712.16
  712.25 712.39 712.41
  713.6 713.9 713.22 713.26
  713.27 713.30 713.33

BULLDOG FA 471.36

BULL-DOG HD 441.18

BULLET SC 268.23 IL 652.11

BULLET-HEADED SC 270.13

BULL-FIGHT NT 709.27 711.40
  712.2 714.38

BULL-FIGHTER NT 701.13 702.2
  711.38

BULL-FIGHTS NT 714.12

BULLIED PO 98.30 110.32
  SS 208.5 PP 438.10
  MD 817.16 817.19

BULLOCK-WAGON TF 123.5

BULL-RING NT 702.25 703.26
  704.24 711.42 712.7
  714.28 716.29 721.7

BULLS NT 712.29 712.38
  714.8

BULLY WS 265.20 SD 420.5
  PP 429.19 PR 477.34

BULLYING EA 74.38 PO 99.15
  PP 429.41 NT 719.2
  MD 817.16

BULWELL SP 48.40 49.28
  50.13

BUMPER ML 729.39

BUMPING SD 421.14 FA 459.29

BUNBURY WM 57.14

BUNCH MO 6.16 MN 367.7
  PP 428.6 WR 548.31
  IL 651.18 TH 853.24

BUNCHES WM 62.22 DV 160.30
  WS 251.26 FA 465.1
  JD 610.9

BUNCHY WR 564.5

BUNDLE MO 9.39 TP 345.33
  PR 502.4 JD 618.11

BUNDLED JD 626.13

BUNDLES DV 161.18 PR 501.2
  501.30

BUNGALOW IL 648.18 649.10
  651.4 651.23 652.29
  652.35 652.40 653.18
  OV 748.29 748.31 750.24
  752.2

BUNGLED EA 76.24

BUNGLING   MO 17.4

BUNK   PR 502.5   502.8   502.13
   503.12   504.26   510.34   511.3

BUNS   JD 611.20

BUNTINGS   SS 204.23

BUOYED   WR 552.15

BURDEN   MO 3.34   HT 43.23
   TF 128.36   DV 162.27   165.25
   FG 194.14   BL 347.32   348.29
   WP 384.12   HD 451.6   LA 634.9

BURDENED   OV 747.37

BURDENS   EE 305.26

BURGUNDY   GG 674.30   675.9   675.12
   675.40

BURIAL   PR 474.25

BURIED   OA 31.33   WM 70.7
   TF 130.3   DV 136.18   175.14
   EE 308.2   PR 503.18   GG 678.31
   ML 745.14

BURLY   MO 19.6   PP 427.7   434.1

BURN   MO 16.35   PO 95.16   SB 218.2
   GF 238.25   WS 246.15   WP 385.18
   HD 453.32   454.7   PR 501.40
   OV 749.7

BURNED   WM 68.22   TF 126.8   131.18
   DV 144.18   169.16   SS 201.11
   SB 217.21   GF 238.23   241.34
   WS 249.40   BL 361.16   PR 503.27
   JD 617.34   ML 744.33   TH 852.31

BURNETT   LL 764.30

BURNING   MO 6.23   SP 51.18
   PO 112.15   114.20   TF 122.15
   DV 167.31   CH 281.27   OC 290.36
   300.26   EE 314.29   317.15
   SD 412.2   423.21   424.28
   PP 440.2   HD 451.11   454.12
   FA 467.20   PR 509.7   509.9
   WR 565.33   576.20   580.24
   SM 583.26   JD 608.15   608.17
   610.22   616.9   IL 658.20
   GG 671.5

BURNING BUSH   OV 752.40

BURNING-RED   WM 70.23

BURNISHED   PO 95.12   114.26

BURNT   CH 276.19   276.30
   EE 306.18   WP 391.12   391.25
   392.35   392.36   SU 536.21
   537.11   544.42

BURROW   FG 194.42

BURST   EA 71.8   PO 107.11   114.1
   TF 121.21   DV 176.21   183.1
   SB 213.34   SG 230.2   CH 281.32
   OC 290.20   EE 332.17   TP 343.15
   345.29   WP 393.8   PP 438.20

BURST (CONT.)   WR 568.38   569.15
   578.13   LA 639.33   643.37
   644.18   GG 681.14   RH 795.23
   BM 828.27   841.41

BURSTING   SP 48.10   WM 69.11
   69.29   GF 238.17   OC 301.17
   SD 412.31   FA 460.31   LA 633.3
   NT 708.29

BURSTS   DV 176.16   LA 640.2

BURYING   ML 730.26   RR 788.25

BUSH   EA 84.6   FG 189.22
   SS 204.16   OC 290.18   EE 304.19
   331.25   MN 373.20   ML 736.9
   RH 800.1

BUSH-BLOSSOMS   EE 326.33

BUSH-COVERED   OC 283.34

BUSHEL   RR 780.41

BUSHES   MO 1.7   DV 139.12   158.40
   161.7   161.22   161.24   167.30
   167.34   FG 194.10   SS 197.10
   197.18   200.3   210.8   210.28
   SG 225.24   225.26   OC 284.3
   284.18   EE 313.36   330.17
   331.23   HD 441.22   PR 499.17
   TB 520.31   SU 544.6   WR 552.11
   579.17   579.22   579.32   580.8
   BO 600.11   LA 634.5   634.28
   634.40   635.1   635.13   637.35
   642.22   642.34   GG 683.14
   ML 722.32   723.17   733.14
   734.14   736.7   740.18   OV 748.33
   750.39

BUSHY   PO 96.21   EE 330.1
   SU 544.8

BUSILY   PO 110.41   TF 132.36
   DV 139.3   YT 397.10   TB 518.18

BUSINESS   MO 18.27   OA 32.27
   WM 66.27   EA 78.17   80.21   82.4
   83.27   84.35   DV 142.39   172.4
   176.14   SG 227.20   GF 238.4
   CH 280.26   OC 294.38   297.31*
   EE 308.18   308.30   311.29   314.2
   WP 382.37   TB 515.39   519.27
   SU 539.9   540.19   541.39
   WR 548.5   549.39   554.33
   BO 590.26   594.7   LA 642.32
   642.36   IL 648.13   652.23
   657.1   GG 680.27   688.36   690.20
   OV 756.6   758.15   758.16
   MD 811.15   819.7   819.8   819.10
   821.1   821.13   821.28   824.17
   825.42   BM 835.40   836.22

BUSINESS-LIKE   EA 81.28

BUSTLE   MO 6.5   OA 34.40
   GF 237.19   BO 600.1

BUSTLED   SD 413.20   PP 437.25

BUSY   PO 108.6   112.16   TF 133.19
   DV 169.39   FG 191.17   WS 260.2
   OC 288.3   294.29   BL 353.35
   YT 400.40   TB 522.41   524.12

BUSY (CONT.)   524.13   526.15
   ML 725.41   RR 786.21
   BM 831.31

BUTCHER'S   PR 508.22

BUTLER   ML 725.16   726.2
   729.16   729.17   729.28
   730.13   731.7   732.14
   732.15   732.16

BUTT   SS 198.14   GG 687.28

BUTTE CITY   SD 424.10

BUTTED   TP 342.32   343.20

BUTT-END   EE 303.13   RR 788.39

BUTTER   CH 275.35   277.17
   OC 285.26   285.29   EE 312.42
   PR 502.19   JD 611.20

BUTTERFLIES   DV 178.20

BUTTERFLY   SG 225.40   OV 749.40

BUTTERING   GG 661.7

BUTTER-MUSLIN   BM 838.39
   839.38

BUTTIES   OC 295.39

BUTTON   TP 343.15   SD 418.25
   MD 811.37

BUTTONED   TF 123.27   DV 147.1
   WS 249.37   TP 337.23   345.33

BUTTONED-UP   DV 145.14

BUTTON-HOLE   WS 250.34
   OC 289.11

BUTTONING   EA 79.7

BUTTONS   SP 49.41   EA 86.9
   TF 125.24   SB 212.11
   WP 390.22   PP 427.4   433.36

BUTTRESS   MO 1.25

BUTTRESSES   ML 725.38

BUTTY   OC 293.11

BUXOM   SB 212.8   MN 367.1
   SD 412.2   412.30   ML 725.14
   726.6

BUXTON AND CO.'S   GF 238.28

BUY   SP 52.10   WM 64.4   64.16
   DV 140.27   GF 243.5
   NT 709.23   MD 806.37
   TH 848.8

BUYING   WS 261.28   HD 447.24
   LL 769.40

BUZZ   FG 190.41

BUZZARDS   WP 386.16

BUZZED WM 60.1

BUZZING BM 835.1

BYGONE EE 306.19 306.21 307.30
  ML 723.41 724.19 TH 848.28

BY-GONE SD 411.10

BY-ROAD MN 376.19

BYRON, LORD (SEE LORD BYRON)

CAB OA 33.41 EA 80.2 OC 285.5
  PP 427.10 428.36 429.10
  FA 459.24

CABBAGE DV 162.3 163.5 168.29

CABBAGES DV 161.29 168.40
  OC 284.1

CABBAGE-STALKS JD 624.29

CABIN PR 487.20 487.41 499.41
  500.4 500.7 500.21 501.31
  502.24 503.2 506.33 506.38
  507.19 507.31 510.35 511.8
  511.35 ML 729.29 741.27
  741.34 742.9 743.18 TH 850.37

CABINET MD 818.5 823.32

CABINETS MD 811.3 811.12

CABLE TH 853.3

CABLEGRAM TH 853.7

CABMAN PR 477.25 478.10

CABMEN PR 477.18

CACHE PR 501.1

CACHET MD 821.14

CACIQUE WR 567.14 573.15 573.22
  576.13 578.5 578.12 581.11

CACIQUES WR 566.34

CACTUS SU 530.5 530.6 530.7
  530.13 532.24 534.29 536.20

CACTUSES-IN-A-POT GG 661.25
  693.21

CACTUS-IN-A-POT GG 661.15

CAGE HT 42.27 DV 167.2
  TH 853.11 853.32

CAGED EA 89.38 ML 729.14

CAJOLE HT 39.18

CAJOLED WP 380.23

CAKE EA 74.21 74.25 CH 281.40
  OC 291.40 WR 552.26

CAKES MO 14.11 FG 190.32
  CH 274.19 274.27 275.7 275.38
  278.38 FA 471.6

CALAMITIES MO 21.20

CALAMITY EA 75.17

CALCULATE MO 11.17

CALCULATED DV 145.26 146.33
  OC 296.24

CALCULATING TF 126.33 YT 406.34
  ML 728.36 MD 822.10

CALCULATION DV 155.30

CALF SD 421.42 ML 723.7

CALF-SKIN SS 206.37

CALIBAN PR 477.29

CALIFORNIA PR 478.31 WR 550.26
  552.41 TH 850.42

CALIFORNIAN WR 547.28 TH 850.42
  851.18 851.24

CALIPH BM 835.39 835.41

CALL MO 7.9 WM 57.15 62.6
  EA 93.22 TF 117.16 132.26
  132.33 DV 178.15 FG 190.29
  SS 201.32 SB 214.21 SG 227.32
  WS 254.18 255.13 SC 267.4
  269.8 OC 291.21 EE 324.38
  TP 335.1 BL 353.29 MN 370.31
  372.17 378.14 378.24
  WP 383.32 384.18 384.34
  391.34 YT 403.34 SD 424.31
  424.40 424.42 PP 432.16
  FA 461.23 461.34 TB 513.30
  516.13 519.17 527.12 527.14
  WR 548.42 556.13 572.26
  572.27 575.22 575.32 BO 590.1
  590.4 604.5 LA 630.31 641.8
  641.9 642.2 644.29 IL 650.35
  652.40 657.1 659.17 GG 662.31
  667.8 690.28 698.27 NT 705.22
  715.17 716.19 718.10 720.7
  720.12 ML 724.18 725.19
  734.32 743.20 OV 749.30
  LL 770.11 RR 788.15 RH 801.25
  804.20 MD 806.25 820.19

CALLED MO 6.20 8.17 OA 25.25
  25.27 35.6 HT 41.2 42.26
  SP 50.13 WM 59.32 EA 80.1
  87.2 PO 108.7 TF 132.24
  DV 141.41 148.16 150.23
  161.16 161.19 177.32
  FG 190.31 196.10 SS 201.6
  204.1 GF 242.34 242.35
  WS 244.27 251.15 SC 270.16
  OC 284.13 287.18 290.5
  EE 308.31 309.9 310.32
  TP 336.23 BL 353.6 MN 374.16
  378.4 WP 382.17 388.25
  YT 396.4 396.6 HD 441.19
  451.10 456.25 FA 458.18
  PR 474.15 474.16 475.7 482.13
  485.11 488.6 491.1 508.25
  510.40 TB 520.34 526.37
  SU 530.6 534.14 534.18 540.8
  WR 568.13 BO 588.20 LA 635.42
  643.42 IL 656.28 GG 661.7
  685.14 686.6 690.28 698.27

CALLED (CONT.) 699.35
  NT 710.11 713.35 717.31
  720.29 OV 748.5 755.36
  LL 762.12 775.20 RH 794.3
  MD 805.33 812.34 812.35
  818.12 818.15 818.30
  823.3 BM 839.22 839.25
  TH 849.22

CALLER OV 754.15

CALLERS MD 815.18

CALLING MO 18.38 SP 45.21
  45.26 SC 270.39 271.19
  OC 298.2 EE 303.16
  329.12 330.7 331.14
  BL 356.17 WP 385.21
  SD 420.37 425.1 PR 495.40
  511.21 SU 531.13 538.5
  WR 564.35 572.24 BO 587.22
  604.18 LA 638.14 638.15
  639.22 643.39 IL 651.37
  652.4 656.24 GG 698.17
  698.18 699.33 NT 716.12
  ML 723.14 OV 752.14

CALLOUS DV 137.28 137.30
  151.21 WP 381.1 HD 441.26
  450.6

CALLOUSLY DV 137.7 SG 231.25

CALLS OA 24.40 SP 45.24
  PR 475.5 GG 698.13 698.16
  NT 720.26 ML 723.15

CALM OA 37.32 DV 147.2
  152.16 152.20 168.20
  176.3 176.17 SS 202.31
  SB 212.14 216.30 216.35
  GF 236.40 OC 284.11
  BL 350.40 351.21 YT 402.17
  402.34 WR 554.19 BO 595.36
  GG 691.31 NT 703.30
  ML 735.10 740.6 OV 748.38
  MD 808.27 809.27 812.7
  814.42 822.40

CALMED DV 149.23 GF 239.18

CALMER SC 273.4 LL 768.13

CALMLY OA 27.40 32.28
  EA 78.39 DV 151.15 175.34
  WS 244.16 BL 354.11
  WP 390.4 LA 639.11
  644.16 GG 661.6 MD 806.17
  825.2 BM 834.6 836.14
  838.13

CALVARY GG 690.30

CALVES WS 261.29

CAMARADERIE DV 166.18

CAMBRE MD 809.2

CAMBRIDGE DV 136.25 146.28
  SS 208.16

CAMBRIDGESHIRE DV 136.26
  145.2

CAMERON TB 527.1

CAMP DV 151.7 EE 325.18 328.24
  328.27 328.34 329.2 329.6
  329.15 329.17 PR 495.1 495.26
  495.34 501.3 501.30 WR 555.7
  556.26 IL 653.14 655.20

CAMPED WR 552.10

CAMP-FIRE EE 325.21 PR 478.37
  483.20 495.29 WR 552.14

CAMPING PR 485.16

CAMPS JD 610.9

CAMP-STOVE PR 501.3 505.17

CANAAN'S FA 467.38

CANADA DV 178.2 179.17 186.10
  186.11 YT 396.26 396.31
  399.18 399.38 401.14 408.22
  409.14

CANAILLE EE 327.38

CANAL TP 334.31

CANALS TP 334.4 BO 599.6

CANARIES LA 640.32 641.1 643.38
  645.13

CANARY FA 466.18

CANCELLED BL 357.17

CANCER PP 428.17 JD 608.6

CANDID EA 92.28 PR 475.11
  JD 606.14 GG 696.13

CANDIED TB 515.2

CANDLE OA 34.8 34.27 34.40
  WM 60.20 62.39 DV 167.31
  167.38 173.9 174.42 175.1
  175.11 OC 296.17 296.19
  296.37 297.11 299.6 MN 368.42
  WP 387.11 SU 530.9 SM 583.40
  586.13 LL 766.7

CANDLE-GLOW SM 585.3

CANDLELIGHT OC 296.20

CANDLE-LIGHT WM 64.22 LL 763.26

CANDLES WM 62.36 62.38 62.40
  DV 173.21 SM 583.26 583.27
  585.11 586.12 LL 763.27

CANDOUR MO 10.24 WR 567.16
  GG 692.20 696.6 OV 749.33
  751.23 LL 773.29

CANE MN 376.20

CANE, ETHEL (SEE ETHEL CANE)

CANES DV 161.22 MN 371.37

CANKER DV 165.32

CANKERING PP 427.31

CANNA SC 269.40 270.31
  CH 277.13 OC 288.15 288.20
  FA 462.13

CANNON EE 330.4

CANNON-SHOT GG 672.34

CANNON-SHOTS ML 728.26

CANNY PR 477.12

CANOE PR 478.36

CANOPY WR 576.22

CANS DV 139.16

CANTEEN WR 551.10

CANTER OC 283.5

CANTERED PO 106.3 111.28

CANTERING PO 112.8

CANVAS RR 783.8

CANVASES BM 830.1

CANYON PR 483.29 483.38 484.3
  488.3 489.16 489.38 490.1
  490.20 490.30 493.7 493.28
  494.6 496.16 496.19

CANYONS PR 486.12

CAP OA 23.9 HT 41.17 DV 139.16
  139.28 149.25 SS 207.23
  WS 250.33 SC 271.18 EE 328.40
  TP 336.13 337.24 342.27
  345.27 MN 377.12 377.28
  377.35 WP 388.34 YT 396.17
  397.17 400.5 SD 412.6 417.36
  422.28 423.6 423.25 PP 433.4
  433.22 433.34 435.34
  HD 444.20 448.21 FA 458.11
  BO 595.11 597.27 603.33
  LA 637.8 RH 804.11

CAPABLE DV 140.9 PP 429.37
  430.22 PR 488.41 SM 582.28
  MD 825.11

CAPACITY DV 172.19 PR 485.22
  BO 587.32 JD 607.5 RR 783.22

CAPE SG 225.28 BO 595.11

CAPES PR 476.27

CAPITAL WR 547.23 BO 588.12
  ML 728.11 732.12 732.28
  TH 851.25 851.37

CAPITALS MD 805.6

CAPRICE NT 717.36

CAPS SP 50.19 OC 298.39
  TP 335.21

CAPTAIN PO 95.35 96.9 96.15

CAPTAIN (CONT.) 96.26 98.4
  98.25 99.9 100.3 100.6
  100.42 101.2 102.40
  104.25 104.37 105.5
  105.7 105.11 105.30
  105.39 106.3 106.7 106.8
  107.14 107.27 107.29
  107.34 107.36 108.6
  108.28 108.38 109.3 109.7
  109.11 109.15 109.24
  110.37 112.33 112.35
  113.23 115.23 BO 588.29
  BM 829.14

CAPTAIN'S PO 95.33 98.1
  98.38 102.2 102.18 102.42
  104.22 105.1 108.11 109.21

CAPTIVE TF 128.29

CAPTIVITY SU 542.26

CAPTOR TP 343.30

CAPTURED OA 36.10 BM 835.39

CAR WM 54.18 54.33 55.8
  55.11 59.24 59.30 60.2
  63.14 EE 321.23 TP 334.20
  334.35 335.7 336.3 336.14
  336.17 336.20 336.34
  339.26 340.21 340.22
  340.33 PP 428.35 429.13
  431.3 431.27 435.36 435.41
  435.42 436.2 436.8 436.20
  436.24 WR 546.29 IL 649.40
  649.41 650.3 653.7 653.23
  654.2 654.20 654.38
  658.14 GG 662.7 669.5
  NT 715.19 719.32 LL 765.1
  RH 791.30 794.25 794.32
  BM 834.17 834.28 834.39
  839.24 839.27 840.9

CARA CARA MIA BELLISSIMA TI
  HO + LL 774.18

CARAVANS MN 371.11

CARD WM 55.21 PO 101.23
  TF 117.19 117.21 117.22
  117.29 118.6 131.22
  133.34 WS 252.2 252.15
  257.11 BO 587.24

CARDBOARD WS 245.27

CARDED MO 9.38

CARDING MO 9.36

CARD-PARTY SD 412.29

CARD-PLAYERS SD 412.22

CARD-PLAYING SD 414.42

CARD-ROOM WS 253.20

CARDS GF 238.25 WS 253.40
  254.1 254.2 254.4 SD 412.3
  412.32 412.37 GG 665.39

CARE MO 14.4 WM 66.23 67.22
  EA 82.4 88.19 88.21 88.27

CARE (CONT.) 88.29 88.30 88.36
89.16 90.9 DV 140.19 144.12
153.15 153.39 155.27 156.3
172.13 SB 216.42 217.1 217.37
218.19 SG 232.24 WS 265.8
OC 287.13 288.10 291.29
EE 310.40 321.15 324.31
324.41 BL 350.28 WP 381.18
YT 398.39 399.8 SD 424.33
PP 429.37 HD 441.5 FA 462.24
462.25 PR 475.21 475.25
475.31 475.33 475.39 481.36
506.9 512.17 TB 517.4
SU 529.19 WR 551.26 553.1
556.39 BO 598.36 604.1
JD 609.27 615.24 IL 659.16
659.17 GG 661.30 661.31 670.4
680.11 691.16 NT 707.4 707.42
711.23 711.41 ML 727.29
737.36 LL 767.39 RH 801.4
801.15 MD 810.24 815.20
819.21 BM 832.8 TH 846.16
846.17 852.42

CARED DV 140.37 WS 260.22
HD 449.7 WR 576.14 577.36
BO 590.24 ML 733.9 MD 822.6
BM 841.35

CARED-FOR SU 543.4

CAREER LA 639.17 TH 850.16
850.19

CAREERED RH 793.4

CAREERING SP 49.21 TP 336.6
337.32

CAREERS ML 724.12

CAREFUL TF 134.33 DV 137.35
SG 221.9 SC 271.26 BL 354.17
MN 366.21 PR 510.23 BO 597.36
601.18 601.20 LA 633.19
GG 671.27 ML 727.35 728.38
RH 796.40 797.33

CAREFULLY MO 1.4 18.6 18.17
20.21 WM 64.39 EA 76.19
TF 119.31 SS 204.19 SG 231.9
GF 235.25 WS 247.18 OC 299.28
EE 318.17 318.20 319.5
BL 356.12 358.33 MN 375.4
YT 399.9 407.8 PP 433.39
HD 447.41 448.2 450.34
PR 484.39 490.15 491.11
502.23 SU 537.24 539.9 539.17
540.38 WR 557.14 576.41
LA 634.12* IL 649.40 650.18
GG 669.13 ML 746.18 LL 770.10
775.30 RR 785.5

CAREFULLY-COOKED MD 816.4

CARELESS TF 131.23 DV 150.1
WS 244.12 EE 322.11 MN 377.11
GG 680.10

CARELESSLY EA 77.4 79.20
FA 466.39

CARELESSNESS OC 289.15 LA 644.5

CARES IL 647.10

CARESS MO 13.37 WS 252.21
BL 363.6 YT 402.29 MD 822.18

CARESSED WM 61.28 SB 214.25
WS 259.18 BL 362.27 BO 591.39
MD 807.38 822.6 825.20 825.25
825.34

CARESSES EA 76.6 PP 430.2

CARESSING MO 12.21 13.36
WM 63.16 EA 73.16 76.17
MD 821.33 822.23 BM 828.12
841.6

CARESSINGLY EA 79.35 WP 386.29

CARESSIVE SG 223.30 WP 382.21
389.20 LL 774.7

CARESSIVELY WP 379.31

CARESSIVENESS LL 774.2

CARICATURE LL 777.17

CARING FA 462.27

CARLIN (SEE MRS. CARLIN)

CARLOTTA GG 661.5 661.8 663.24
663.27 664.5 664.19 666.10
666.15 666.28 666.38 667.1
667.15 667.20 667.24 668.42
669.11 669.33 670.3 670.9
670.29 670.37 671.23 672.9
672.24 672.28 672.29 672.37
673.17 673.29 675.1 675.3
675.7 675.24 675.31 675.36
676.5 676.13 676.31 676.37
677.12 681.24 682.28 682.30
683.27 683.31 683.36 684.19
685.21 685.35 686.2 686.7
686.20 687.11 687.20 687.34
687.36 690.3 690.8 690.15
690.31 690.40 691.15 692.40
693.8 693.20 693.30 696.39
697.25 699.26 699.34

CARLOTTA FELL GG 661.1

CARLOTTA'S GG 664.29 671.22
674.13 687.41 690.1

CARLYLE MO 6.27

CARNAL OA 27.37 SU 533.1

CARNATION WS 250.34

CARO CARO TU L'HAI VISTO
LL 773.41

CARPENTER ML 725.32 726.15
727.28 729.41 730.17 733.9
733.22 734.27

CARPENTER'S SS 206.24 ML 734.22

CARPET EA 84.11 OC 296.29
BL 351.5 LA 646.25 GG 669.39
671.4 671.7 MD 810.35 810.42
817.17 818.4 821.15

CARPETS ML 725.12 MD 811.11

CARPETS (CONT.) 819.22

CARRANZA NT 706.11

CARRANZISTA NT 701.20

CARRIAGE HT 40.26 TF 129.1
DV 157.8 157.11 SG 222.2
BL 356.22 FA 458.14 458.25
459.40 WR 560.40 560.41
BO 588.1 593.5 593.10
593.16 594.11 598.37

CARRIAGE-APPROACH FA 459.42

CARRIED OA 23.12 27.23
WM 60.14 60.21 TF 123.7
DV 159.32 162.25 168.16
173.33 174.24 FG 195.4
SB 220.3 SG 226.3 WS 252.28
252.38 254.21 260.9
264.19 SC 269.28 CH 275.21
EE 314.13 317.13 BL 347.21
354.25 355.27 MN 369.7
YT 400.21 PP 439.31
HD 442.35 PR 493.15
501.30 506.40 SU 528.3
WR 561.5 GG 681.26 NT 708.1
LL 764.29

CARRIERS OC 297.6 297.13

CARRIER'S DV 140.26

CARRIES BO 597.8

CARRIN' WP 388.39

CARRION WR 551.35 551.36

CARRY OA 26.24 30.41
PO 99.39 TF 120.5 SC 269.38
OC 287.34 292.32 WP 387.16
YT 406.2 SD 422.14 422.25
FA 459.15 460.13 460.16
SU 536.16 541.39 BO 600.36
LA 634.7 MD 811.18 TH 850.35

CARRYING MO 6.5 DV 139.31
180.8 SG 232.8 232.10
232.13 WS 255.22 SC 272.33
OC 297.10 EE 303.2 317.23
BL 347.17 WP 379.22
PR 507.24 511.13 WR 558.24
BO 587.4 587.24 LA 637.27

CARS TP 334.24 334.27 335.13
335.40 340.28

CAR'S TP 335.1 BM 841.11

CART HT 43.31 TF 123.7
DV 140.27 162.13 SD 421.42
FA 459.22 460.37 461.36

CARTE BLANCHE WS 252.3

CARTER HT 43.11 43.15 43.20
43.24 43.29 43.36

CARTING SP 51.1

CARTOON WS 245.25 247.7

CART-RUTS MO 1.26

CECILIA (CONT.) 774.6 774.11
774.24 774.32 774.36 775.3
775.14 775.23 775.26 775.29
775.34 775.36 776.4 776.17
776.32 776.39 777.40 778.8
778.10

CECILIA'S LL 764.6

CEDAR PR 489.33 WR 565.33

CEILING OC 288.25 MN 375.15
WR 576.28 RR 779.31 787.13
MD 823.30 823.39

CEILINGS RR 779.29 779.31
779.32 779.35

CELANDINE ML 736.12

CELEBRATED LL 777.38

CELERY GG 676.24

CELL ML 744.42

CELLARS ML 725.14

CELLS EA 81.26

CELT BO 588.25

CELTIC SD 411.13 413.30
PR 473.16 474.12 ML 723.13
734.1

CEMENT ML 739.30

CEMETERY PP 430.26

CENSERS OV 754.7

CENSORIOUS FA 469.15 LA 641.26

CENSORIOUSLY LA 641.21

CENSURE OC 285.18

CENTRAL SP 50.15 SU 530.27
WR 561.31 562.2 IL 659.36
659.37

CENTRAL-HEATED GG 670.2

CENTRAL-HEATING EA 81.25

CENTRALISED DV 176.32

CENTRE PO 108.26 DV 171.8
SS 199.39 SG 225.39 CH 275.25
EE 309.24 331.2 BL 351.39
359.33 359.38 MN 371.15
HD 449.41 PR 483.9 SU 534.17
534.18 WR 552.21 552.22
GG 664.12 666.30 698.11
RR 785.23 RH 790.9 790.12
MD 819.6

CENTRES WM 64.12 EE 315.5

CENTURIES WR 561.26 ML 724.17

CENTURY FG 188.30 BO 593.26
593.27 MD 809.11 809.21
810.31

'CEPT SD 424.18

CEREMONIAL DV 159.19 WR 573.29
578.15

CEREMONY WR 576.31 MD 806.13

CERTAIN MO 7.37 17.15 HT 40.26
44.5 SP 51.22 WM 56.1
EA 75.28 83.28 85.15 PO 98.23
DV 141.28 145.12 153.13
156.32 174.8 174.31 SS 204.3
206.33 SB 214.10 216.31
WS 262.29 OC 292.28 EE 304.20
306.30 314.9 314.21 314.22
314.27 322.28 326.39 326.40
326.41 328.2 TP 335.40
BL 347.29 355.32 MN 376.21
WP 391.3 YT 396.1 396.5
PP 429.4 431.14 431.16
HD 441.36 FA 464.20 466.14
466.15 466.19 466.22
PR 480.37 481.7 482.3 483.13
483.14 484.15 484.36 484.41
502.20 TB 513.12 515.21
520.37 SU 528.16 530.15 533.3
WR 553.33 560.37 570.3 573.24
BO 587.36 591.26 593.41
598.42 600.38 JD 611.24
619.26 619.27 628.28
LA 634.17 635.1 IL 650.17
GG 664.13 669.40 685.20
693.22 699.7 NT 704.41 706.22
706.23 709.2 718.1 LL 772.5
RR 780.25 782.20 RH 800.10
MD 805.2 808.11 811.1 815.16
818.38 BM 835.22 TH 844.16
845.4 845.5

CERTAINLY HT 38.8 DV 144.21
EE 320.34 320.35 320.41
MN 370.29 YT 394.22 TB 518.41
520.10 520.11 SU 538.35
JD 609.29 615.24 619.36
626.36 LA 641.23 641.37
641.40 642.1 645.9 IL 648.39
652.20 GG 668.10 676.4
NT 708.11 709.4 721.12
LL 768.36 771.32 RR 780.29
780.31 MD 821.39

CERTAINTY MO 20.4 SS 203.23
MN 367.21 HD 453.1 WR 571.3
GG 699.3

CERTIFICATES JD 608.7

CERTIFIED PR 474.33

C'EST CA SU 528.35

CHAFF MO 6.23 SC 269.1
MN 374.31

CHAFFED GF 234.24 MN 371.33

CHAFFINCHES SS 204.22

CHAFFING MO 8.14 MN 375.6

CHAGRIN DV 163.40 WS 250.25
EE 324.36 HD 445.22 TB 526.30
LL 769.25

CHAGRINED MO 4.18

CHAIN DV 167.3 EE 309.40
YT 401.10 401.13 401.20
401.22 SU 545.5

CHAIR MO 6.20 6.37 8.21
9.22 10.8 11.3 12.33
13.20 13.40 13.41 OA 27.41
29.15 30.19 HT 41.28
WM 56.7 56.15 65.22 67.37
68.5 69.19 EA 78.10 85.9
85.23 89.9 90.31
TF 126.12 DV 140.40 159.23
168.12 179.15 179.34
180.36 SS 203.15 GF 239.10
239.17 WS 247.4 263.24
264.23 SC 271.11 272.28
CH 276.21 282.17 OC 290.28
295.30 296.31 298.29
BL 352.5 357.42 SD 413.10
423.21 424.6 424.35 425.34
425.38 PP 440.24 HD 443.16
FA 465.14 TB 525.13 525.24
JD 608.19 613.28 620.23
620.34 627.8 IL 657.3
GG 671.25 677.9 682.27
696.3 NT 706.3 706.5
715.25 OV 747.15 753.2
LL 763.29 769.15 770.23
RR 786.23 BM 835.7 835.10
835.11 837.14 853.21

CHAIRMAN OA 32.17 32.22

CHAIRMAN (SEE MR. CHAIRMAN)

CHAIRS EA 84.14 SS 202.37
CH 280.15 OC 296.26
EE 311.22 TP 340.26
BL 352.1 359.5 PP 437.2
HD 441.21 GG 682.26
NT 706.14 706.17 ML 727.17
739.33 RR 786.3 MD 811.3
811.12 815.15 824.5
TH 848.32 850.39

CHAISE-LONGUE LL 770.18

CHALICE OV 755.27 755.30

CHALK BM 841.12

CHALLENGE MO 9.7 12.13
OA 23.6 EA 74.40 DV 185.37
SB 212.21 PR 479.40
WR 554.14 560.2 JD 612.31
612.39 GG 678.7 NT 713.16

CHALLENGED SS 200.21

CHALLENGING TF 123.23
SS 198.4 MN 370.5 SD 420.32
PP 427.11 SU 534.38 542.7
JD 612.30

CHAMBER WR 576.20 576.24
577.37

CHAMBERS LL 762.29 763.5

CHAMPAGNE LL 763.33

CHAMPED ML 745.6

CHAMPING RH 791.18

CHAMPION SP 50.24

CHANCE DV 144.29 FG 189.7
  WS 253.19 PP 430.14 HD 444.32
  PR 487.6 SU 534.4 JD 606.2
  615.14 IL 655.36 659.10
  OV 758.34

CHANCEL FG 187.10 SS 210.18

CHANCES JD 606.19

CHANDELIERS WS 251.30

CHANGE MO 8.32 10.15 14.41
  15.35 OA 27.1 HT 43.35
  WM 61.31 EA 83.12 PO 96.41
  111.17 DV 155.15 156.37
  SS 203.10 208.26 WS 257.1
  SC 268.34 EE 330.14 TP 335.9
  BL 354.42 MN 377.1 YT 399.5
  HD 455.34 PR 479.16 TB 523.17
  527.8 SU 532.3 WR 567.25*
  BO 600.27 JD 611.30 625.13
  625.23 IL 647.4 GG 693.4
  696.17 NT 708.24 708.31
  708.35 ML 744.7 RR 782.40
  782.41 RH 803.40 BM 831.13
  834.2

CHANGED MO 10.18 10.19 WM 68.1
  PO 97.16 TF 125.28 132.27
  135.16 DV 165.35 GF 237.17
  EE 306.33 322.3 BL 354.35
  MN 369.30 WP 391.23 PP 439.19
  PR 475.1 483.36 486.12
  TB 524.16 SM 584.2 GG 683.20
  NT 713.18 719.17 ML 729.9
  746.7 OV 748.5 LL 772.21
  RR 785.19 BM 831.7 836.27
  839.5 840.37 TH 853.10

CHANGELESS WR 569.32 SM 582.24
  BO 591.7 596.33 JD 611.34
  LL 761.35 772.1

CHANGELING PR 476.22 477.16
  484.2

CHANGES MO 6.21 WM 65.18
  PR 475.25 484.15 BM 827.1

CHANGING EA 89.33 DV 165.25
  SG 228.27 EE 316.32 BL 356.30
  GG 691.15

CHANNEL BO 592.33 592.38

CHANNELS OC 301.23

CHANT PR 474.12 WR 578.36

CHANTED FG 188.11

CHANTING CH 280.13

CHAOS EA 83.4 PO 103.16
  DV 173.33 176.20 180.21
  BL 356.2 356.3 PP 430.13
  PR 493.37 SU 528.12 BO 591.12
  591.13

CHAP WS 256.2 MN 375.40
  PP 431.15 GG 680.40

CHAPEL SP 45.17 DV 137.9
  FG 188.18 FA 464.40 465.15
  468.18 468.30 469.2 472.7

CHAPEL OF LYONESSE SS 210.15

CHAPELS FA 464.23

CHAPERON NT 715.24

CHAPLET OA 26.9

CHAPS GF 243.10 EE 303.35
  SD 424.13 FA 471.31 472.1

CHAP'S FA 469.16

CHAPTER EE 308.4

CHARACTER DV 137.17 TP 339.16
  FA 467.23 PR 476.17 TB 521.30
  JD 628.13 NT 706.39 LL 771.14

CHARACTERISED SU 543.20

CHARACTERISTIC EE 311.4
  PR 482.30 487.38 TB 523.36
  WR 554.4 GG 694.34

CHARACTERS BM 833.39

CHARADES MO 7.11

CHARGE MO 19.18 DV 136.23
  GF 235.1 OC 292.27 EE 315.36
  HD 443.19 TB 516.29 OV 752.33
  LL 762.19 MD 821.42 BM 835.9
  TH 852.17

CHARGED SS 200.15 YT 400.11

CHARGING CH 279.10 NT 702.27
  RH 793.2

CHARIOTS ML 724.16

CHARITABLE EA 87.14

CHARITY EA 87.25 DV 153.25
  YT 402.27 403.7 407.16

CHARITY-BOX YT 400.10

CHARITY-BOY YT 396.15

CHARITY HOME YT 395.30

CHARITY INSTITUTION YT 395.27
  397.19

CHARLES ML 726.1

CHARLOTTE CUMMINS PR 480.10

CHARM TF 133.24 EE 329.28
  FA 462.35 SU 537.14 543.9
  NT 712.31 LL 761.6 761.28
  774.7 RR 780.3 MD 808.18
  BM 832.2 TH 847.23

CHARMED MO 12.34 PR 476.35

CHARMING EE 310.18 PR 473.34
  481.33 JD 605.5 GG 664.41
  666.18 NT 712.7 RR 780.22

CHARMING (CONT.) 780.23
  780.24 781.21 781.25
  TH 847.23

CHARMS PR 473.15

CHARRED GF 241.31

CHARRING OV 747.28

CHARTRES TH 848.17 850.39
  853.21

CHARYBDISES JD 610.26

CHASE WM 67.17 OV 759.2

CHASED LA 642.36

CHASING SP 49.26 PO 113.41
  LA 642.36 643.16 643.17

CHASM WR 558.35 GG 673.25

CHASMS TF 122.2

CHASTE OA 30.26 DV 164.36

CHAT TP 336.21 336.22
  LL 764.25 RR 781.3

CHATELAINE FA 458.33 459.19

CHATS TP 336.4

CHATTED GF 241.38 BL 358.40

CHATTER PO 106.39 FA 471.7
  GG 674.7 BM 830.11

CHATTER-CHATTER PR 475.18
  475.27

CHATTERED WM 55.27 56.19
  DV 143.5 GF 242.29
  WS 253.26 BL 361.14
  MD 820.16

CHATTERING PO 113.42 SC 269.5
  PR 509.34 LA 646.31
  BM 838.30

CHATTING SB 217.25 GF 234.19
  BL 360.33 WP 390.1 YT 399.17

CHATTY PR 483.22

CHAUFFEUR WP 382.13

CHEAP HD 448.32 FA 464.22
  TB 527.10 527.13 527.15
  NT 701.19 TH 852.22 852.29

CHEAPER DV 165.3

CHEAPEST HD 447.24

CHEAPLY MO 7.32 NT 701.6

CHEAT OV 758.34 758.35

CHEATED OV 758.19

CHEATING OV 758.15

CHECK MO 12.3 OA 33.26 SB 213.9
WS 250.33 EE 304.36

CHECKED BL 355.41 YT 397.31
PR 492.23 IL 647.29

CHECK-PATTERN SB 214.4

CHECK-WEIGHMAN SC 272.12

CHEEK OA 27.4 38.24 EA 72.14
73.26 TF 123.32 DV 175.30
FG 187.16 195.35 SS 201.11
205.30 SB 216.25 WS 249.39
CH 277.7 282.2 OC 299.21
EE 332.20 TP 340.1 BL 355.6
PP 433.15 434.10 FA 462.30
PR 484.26 LA 638.27 IL 650.14
650.15 653.3 653.8 GG 693.31
LL 772.7

CHEEK-BONES GG 679.8 681.22

CHEEKS MO 18.12 PO 96.18
TF 124.41 SS 203.28 BL 355.17
MN 377.27 PP 434.31 PR 484.21
498.30 499.18 500.32 502.32
SU 534.11 536.22 WR 554.2
577.8 BO 597.33 JD 606.23
617.34 617.41 624.32
LA 637.13 IL 647.23 GG 669.21
683.22 NT 705.28 MD 809.4

CHEER BM 836.10

CHEERFUL DV 166.8 FA 458.20
GG 669.22 675.3 RR 785.29
BM 831.31 841.21

CHEERFULLY DV 137.11 BL 353.34
PP 435.21 FA 459.3

CHEERFULNESS DV 165.34 BL 348.4
FA 460.6

CHEERING GG 668.41 ML 730.7
BM 838.15

CHEERY SG 228.29 OC 285.6
285.13 SD 415.6 ML 739.9

CHEESE HT 41.22 41.29 SP 50.27
SS 202.21 WP 392.17

CHEESE-MAKING ML 726.32

CHENILLE HD 445.42

CHEQUE JD 623.35 623.41 625.34
625.42 626.1 MD 806.36

CHEQUE-BOOK ML 739.23

CHEQUERED TF 122.11 134.40

CHEQUERING SB 213.42

CHEQUER-SQUARES WR 578.29

CHERISH MO 5.3 GG 671.33

CHERISHED PR 477.2 SU 529.42
OV 750.4 TH 851.15

CHERISHINGLY WR 566.30

CHER PETIT BEBE WP 392.14

CHERRIES TF 123.29 123.41 124.3
124.18 124.40 DV 178.20

CHERRY MN 373.18

CHERRY-STONES TF 124.7

CHERUB SU 535.2

CHEST MO 18.34 OA 30.33
EA 90.25 90.42 91.3 PO 95.30
100.4 104.11 108.1 108.26
110.5 110.18 TF 125.38
DV 149.6 173.31 173.36
FG 192.1 SS 198.11 WS 259.30
SC 267.5 PP 433.13 435.11
440.7 HD 450.23 PR 484.30
SU 538.34 WR 555.4 BO 600.42
GG 694.25 695.23 697.14

CHESTNUTS GG 674.29 674.40

CHETIF DV 145.9 BO 601.3

CHEWED FG 190.33 SB 213.26
SU 542.37

CHEWING PO 109.31 BL 352.15
WR 556.42 ML 722.35

CHIAROSCURO LL 763.28

CHIC LL 761.3

CHICAGO PR 488.41 WR 566.38

CHICKEN PR 502.11 502.18 502.19
GG 676.28

CHICKEN-RUNS IL 648.21

CHICKENS WS 250.14 MN 366.30
IL 649.6

CHICORY-BLUE TB 524.16 524.35

CHID OC 287.1

CHIDING MO 6.12

CHIEF TF 120.32 DV 160.18
TP 336.12 TB 514.40 WR 559.32
560.36 561.5 561.11 563.13
RH 799.17

CHIEFLY SP 49.2 CH 279.2
YT 400.35 LA 646.18 RR 781.21

CHIFFONIER OC 296.25

CHIHUAHUA WR 547.30 549.10
NT 701.20

CHIHUAHUA STATE WR 550.2

CHILBLAINS MO 17.38 17.39

CHILCHUI WR 550.9 560.14 560.17
560.20 560.24 563.19

CHILCHUI INDIANS WR 554.16
554.39

CHILCHUIS WR 550.3

CHILD MO 15.38 19.12
OA 24.12 25.14 25.18 25.28
25.33 25.36 25.39 26.1
26.7 26.29 27.16 27.20
27.22 36.35 HT 39.14
SP 51.16 WM 59.25 EA 72.8
91.22 TF 125.26 DV 139.35
139.37 143.11 150.16
150.17 154.19 154.21
154.31 154.32 154.36
154.42 155.6 157.3 158.18
159.3 159.27 159.32
SS 208.17 208.27 SB 212.10
SG 225.33 GF 237.25
CH 276.32 277.3 277.9
278.42 279.33 279.39
280.6 280.24 281.21 282.1
OC 284.20 287.8 287.29
288.1 288.32 288.38 289.4
293.39 294.8 294.23
298.15 298.17 298.25
298.34 299.40 300.14
300.35 EE 309.4 309.9
309.13 309.21 309.24
309.27 309.33 309.34
309.41 310.8 311.8 315.1
315.23 315.24 315.29
316.41 317.2 317.5 317.13
317.17 317.22 317.24
317.29 317.38 317.39
318.10 318.24 318.30 319.6
319.10 319.14 319.31
319.34 320.3 320.20 320.22
320.41 321.13 321.20 322.1
322.2 322.5 322.13 322.17
322.32 322.42 323.11
324.24 324.41 325.4 325.17
325.18 BL 348.27 348.29
348.32 350.12 356.39
357.6 359.10 361.26
WP 381.6 381.8 381.13
381.15 381.18 381.19
384.42 389.36 YT 410.10
PP 434.36 435.17 438.6
FA 460.28 461.9 461.15
463.6 PR 474.26 474.34
474.36 474.42 475.4 475.7
476.16 476.19 486.28
TB 525.35 526.5 526.7
526.31 SU 528.3 528.6
529.21 529.25 531.12
531.16 531.21 531.37
532.4 534.20 535.1 535.15
535.36 536.2 536.5 536.8
536.19 537.15 537.23
537.25 537.33 537.37
538.33 538.34 540.10
540.26 540.32 541.2 541.36
542.12 543.33 544.15
544.24 544.41 545.4
WR 551.4 566.23 SM 584.26
JD 607.42 611.17 611.18
612.23 612.26 613.24
613.27 613.29 613.34
616.12 621.24 621.37
621.40 622.42 623.28
624.31 625.30 627.34
628.32 628.42 IL 648.10
GG 666.17 679.3 679.27
NT 711.18 712.8 718.19
ML 727.18 738.11 738.37
739.2 739.5 LL 769.29
RH 792.23 795.32 796.1

CHILD (CONT.) 796.4 796.10
800.32 800.39 801.15 803.28
804.13 MD 811.14 815.2 820.37
822.5 BM 834.2 TH 848.22
849.40 851.27 851.37

CHILDER OC 291.33

CHILDHOOD GG 682.35 683.41

CHILDISH EA 91.10 DV 138.18
138.19 WS 263.22 264.1
OC 291.38 EE 303.17 324.27
324.35 BL 356.37 357.6
PP 434.22 PR 475.13 WR 567.16
NT 704.1 705.27 RH 792.39
BM 836.4 TH 848.25

CHILDISHNESS BL 356.42

CHILDLIKE SM 584.32 JD 625.9
625.11

CHILD-LIKE WM 60.9 SG 232.40
EE 305.30 BL 359.42 PR 474.18
BO 593.41

CHILDREN MO 13.24 13.30
SP 45.14 45.22 46.3 53.8
53.11 TF 125.4 128.36
DV 137.40 138.3 138.12 138.24
138.25 143.4 143.16 145.16
157.19 158.9 158.12 CH 278.20
280.38 280.40 280.41 281.8
281.11 OC 289.12 289.23
289.29 289.34 289.36 290.15
290.21 293.6 294.37 295.33
296.11 298.19 298.37 298.41
301.7 301.22 301.24 301.29
301.31 302.11 EE 308.32 309.3
311.1 311.9 311.12 313.9
314.15 314.24 314.27 314.30
315.2 315.3 315.7 315.22
315.33 315.35 316.10 316.14
316.23 321.25 322.24 323.13
324.19 326.1 328.3 329.11
329.12 332.38 332.40
BL 349.39 MN 366.30 YT 395.21
PP 430.7 430.9 430.12
HD 447.1 FA 470.17 471.13
471.26 PR 475.28 SU 543.1
WR 547.9 548.4 548.13 554.27
567.22 567.23 570.36
SM 584.39 584.40 BO 588.26
JD 610.36 GG 666.38 666.40
678.23 682.37 690.9 692.12
NT 718.21 ML 726.12 727.19
731.14 731.15 731.16
OV 747.27 747.28 752.20
754.11 759.18 RR 780.23
780.24 781.6 781.22 781.38
782.3 RH 790.3 790.8 790.11
790.15 790.33 791.6 791.11
802.24 TH 847.11

CHILDREN'S TF 133.20 DV 144.12
EE 303.16 323.25 RR 781.22
781.38 RH 802.22

CHILD'S OA 25.38 TF 125.24
CH 276.41 OC 284.17 286.22
EE 321.32 323.8 JD 619.21
BM 839.35

CHILDT CH 279.12 279.13 280.33
280.34 280.38 281.9 FA 469.12

CHILL FG 190.12 GF 240.10
WS 246.5 EE 330.20 330.28
MN 376.17 PR 490.9 SM 582.21
IL 652.33 GG 684.29

CHILLED DV 144.31 171.42
SU 531.3 BO 598.22 GG 684.9
ML 746.34

CHILLY DV 158.23 TP 334.17
PR 509.40 LL 773.34

CHIMED HD 443.10

CHIMING GF 241.14

CHIMNEY DV 160.38 OC 286.13
EE 304.12 BL 359.8 PR 500.23

CHIMNEY-PIECE WM 58.34 MD 810.31

CHIMNEY-PLACE EE 306.24

CHIMNEYS OC 283.21 YT 394.7
ML 725.20 LL 767.7

CHIN MO 7.17 OA 31.17 31.37
EA 87.42 PO 101.29 105.33
110.5 110.8 110.9 110.17
DV 147.1 WS 249.37 CH 281.38
TP 337.24 BL 363.42 MN 376.37
WP 390.18 YT 403.4 PP 433.13
SU 539.18 WR 553.39 554.3
563.10 567.37 SM 584.13
JD 606.23 LA 631.34 IL 647.35
GG 671.24 680.10

CHINA EA 84.13 88.37 TF 124.23
CH 280.1 BL 351.5 MD 818.4
823.31 BM 827.18

CHINA-BLUE SG 222.23

CHINAMAN NT 715.28

CHINESE NT 715.30 ML 737.4
MD 811.4 811.5

CHINK PO 111.5 SG 222.34
BL 353.16 PR 503.28

CHINKS PR 503.3 504.40
WR 558.28

CHINTZ DV 161.14 GG 682.26

CHINTZ-COVERED EA 84.14

CHIP TB 522.37

CHIPMUNKS PR 486.20 488.35

CHIPPED PR 498.10

CHIPPING GG 675.29

CHIPS PO 108.41 111.16

CHIRP SU 535.1 535.15

CHIRPED SU 536.39

CHIRPING TB 518.21 SU 540.26

CHIRRUP WS 263.36

CHISELLING GF 234.8

CHIVALROUS GG 663.32

CHIVALROUSLY BL 359.25

CHOCOLATE WS 249.28

CHOCOLATES EE 305.36

CHOICE EE 327.14 327.15
327.16 327.28 328.23
MN 372.40 ML 745.10
LL 770.19 TH 848.19

CHOIR DV 143.35 164.12
FA 464.9 466.8 466.13
467.1 467.4 467.26 469.2
BM 830.20 831.31 832.16

CHOIR-MASTER SP 46.16

CHOIR-MISTRESS BM 831.26

CHOKED MO 2.35 21.24
OA 36.23 GF 235.5
MN 374.31

CHOKING OA 36.7 36.18

CHOOSE MO 20.2 PO 97.15
TP 342.37 343.3 344.18
344.30 344.33 344.39
345.13 GG 670.29 686.23
NT 711.3 ML 722.16 739.25
MD 819.19

CHOOSES TB 516.40

CHOP GF 240.17 240.22

CHOPIN WM 59.7

CHOPPED EE 304.13

CHOPPING PR 501.33 509.37

CHORDS WR 574.23

CHORES PR 507.7 TH 850.31
851.8

CHORUS TP 344.42 RH 800.9

CHORUS-GIRL TB 520.38

CHOSE EE 327.20 TP 338.40
PR 479.13

CHOSEN TF 128.9 WS 254.26
EE 328.28 TP 342.10
342.39 342.41 344.42
345.12 WR 556.30 SM 582.32
OV 750.42

CHRIS SP 48.3 48.18 48.22
49.34 49.35 49.38 50.4
50.7 50.10 50.21 50.24
50.38

CLANG PO 109.23 EE 322.39
  FA 459.37 JD 619.27 BM 836.28
  840.1 841.21

CLANGED PO 106.13 EE 332.3

CLANGING EE 331.39 331.42 332.7
  332.17 SU 542.16

CLANK DV 139.10

CLANKING OC 283.1

CLAP CH 282.27 WP 393.9

CLAPPED SP 47.35

CLAPPING LA 638.38 BM 843.6

CLARET-COLOURED SS 202.37

CLARISSA JD 605.16 605.20
  606.35 606.41 615.13 621.19
  628.8

CLARISSA'S JD 605.13

CLARITY BO 601.5

CLASH NT 708.33

CLASP WM 70.12 TF 130.19
  WS 252.30 BL 355.36 MN 372.25
  PR 504.24

CLASPED MO 21.15 EA 91.34
  TF 132.10 FG 191.31 195.28
  195.29 CH 279.39 HD 450.12
  GG 691.8 691.13 692.18

CLASPING MO 3.1 OA 25.31
  WM 69.21 SS 202.5

CLASS DV 151.15 174.11
  MN 366.21 SU 543.7 GG 662.13
  662.20 663.14 MD 819.30
  819.31 TH 852.20

CLASSED OV 748.10

CLASSES DV 137.1 138.6
  YT 400.13

CLASSIC FG 187.30

CLASSICAL ML 728.3

CLASSICS FA 464.16

CLASSIFYING MO 13.22

CLASS-ROOM BM 838.28 838.37
  840.39

CLAT-FARTIN' SC 273.9

CLATTER MO 10.31 PO 100.39
  CH 281.21 PR 490.36

CLATTERING PO 106.30

CLAUDIA LL 766.41 767.16

CLAVEL'S NT 714.14

CLAW OC 283.32 RR 783.8

CLAWEY PO 114.6

CLAWING WS 264.12 264.17
  BL 362.33

CLAWINGS MO 3.2

CLAWS PO 106.16 BL 362.33
  TH 844.37

CLAY SS 205.22 YT 394.24
  HD 450.12 450.13 450.38
  WR 562.6 BO 593.20 593.31

CLAY-COLOURED YT 394.14

CLAYEY HD 451.29

CLEAN MO 1.11 WM 58.41 59.2
  EA 83.26 PO 116.8 TF 126.21
  DV 138.8 171.29 182.19
  SS 207.25 SG 221.24 GF 237.23
  242.25 SC 267.33 272.15
  OC 296.30 297.33 297.38
  300.13 TP 337.42 SD 422.4
  423.30 PP 431.35 FA 471.35
  SU 543.4 JD 606.20 606.22
  616.41 618.13 618.26 LA 630.3
  631.29 638.12 638.31 640.34
  GG 665.24 ML 726.12 OV 749.35
  750.18 751.21 RR 785.41
  RH 804.15 MD 809.17 TH 850.29
  850.35

CLEANED GF 240.32 EE 323.30

CLEANING SC 272.10 JD 617.36

CLEAN-LIMBED HD 442.32

CLEANLINESS SC 268.7

CLEANLY GF 235.24

CLEANNESS DV 179.6 OV 749.38

CLEAN-SHAVEN EA 84.27 MN 366.12
  PR 483.7 SU 539.8 SM 582.11
  LA 633.6 637.16 NT 702.35
  LL 762.40

CLEAR OA 26.27 28.40 WM 54.28
  63.33 EA 73.7 83.27 PO 103.4
  TF 119.11 121.33 125.10
  126.26 128.1 DV 138.18 171.9
  176.17 183.16 SS 207.26
  211.17 SB 216.2 WS 257.7
  CH 276.10 277.36 OC 289.22
  300.11 300.13 TP 334.31
  334.32 MN 374.17 378.14
  WP 379.2 387.15 YT 403.5
  405.10 406.29 406.39 410.2
  SD 413.41 414.23 414.29 423.7
  424.11 PP 429.27 431.20
  434.34 438.25 PR 476.17 481.6
  490.24 TB 518.37 SU 533.37
  WR 574.13 574.15 IL 655.25
  GG 665.35 684.24 NT 705.28
  ML 725.12 725.13 727.13
  744.27 746.12 OV 749.35
  749.37 749.42 750.17 751.21
  LL 768.28 RR 784.1 788.36
  MD 825.42 BM 836.27 837.33

CLEAR-CUT WS 249.5 TB 513.18
  514.33

CLEARED SP 52.23 EE 312.30
  SD 415.4 PP 431.18 PR 504.1
  RH 798.5

CLEARING MO 18.42 EA 83.25
  PO 101.24 108.35 108.39
  WS 249.7 HD 445.31

CLEARLY MO 10.9 19.2
  DV 185.6 185.13 185.37
  SG 227.14 OC 300.37
  PP 440.19 TB 525.26

CLEAVED OC 283.15

CLEAVING TF 119.34

CLEFT WM 60.33 EE 323.6
  325.26 SU 529.12 GG 668.36

CLENCH BL 356.7

CLENCHED HT 44.7 PO 109.22
  109.32 109.35 TF 118.29
  DV 176.36 177.28 TP 343.18
  SD 421.1

CLENCHING OA 24.3 24.4
  HD 446.5 SM 586.12

CLERGYMAN DV 139.13 139.20
  140.8 140.13 140.31 140.42
  141.3 141.16 141.38 142.3
  142.9 142.21 142.31 144.34
  144.37 147.32 147.37
  149.19 151.36 157.8 158.19
  158.36 CH 277.30 278.18
  278.31 279.10 279.31 280.3
  280.7 280.13 280.16 280.25
  YT 408.29

CLERGYMEN YT 394.38

CLERICAL DV 145.14

CLERK BM 827.37

CLERKING MD 813.18

CLEVELAND TH 853.12

CLEVELAND (SEE MR. CLEVELAND)

CLEVELAND UNIVERSITY TH 852.38
  853.19

CLEVER MO 13.20 SP 49.25
  EA 93.38 SB 212.10
  CH 278.21 EE 306.3 318.40
  319.16 BL 354.17 YT 408.4
  FA 464.33 TB 514.22 514.30
  526.6 526.16 SM 584.32
  BO 588.8 588.36 589.9
  589.24 JD 605.5 606.18
  GG 661.23 679.41 NT 703.13
  703.14 703.18 707.40
  709.12 709.14 709.16
  709.34 709.41 711.25
  OV 747.24 LL 771.16
  776.23 MD 808.39 809.33
  812.8 813.19 816.36
  TH 845.21 845.23

CLEVERER BO 592.18 TH 845.21

CLEVERLY ML 729.11 MD 810.3

CLEVERNESS GG 679.40 NT 709.14
  MD 813.19 813.24 820.42 821.1
  821.25

CLICK HT 42.17 WM 69.18
  PO 103.5 SB 213.25 SD 412.17

CLICKED SP 47.12 DV 149.1

CLIENTS BM 834.9

CLIFF WR 579.36 ML 730.20
  OV 750.34 750.38

CLIFF-EDGE SU 533.34

CLIFFS SG 224.5 SD 411.6 423.8
  SU 532.24 ML 733.31

CLIFFS' ML 723.2

CLIMAX MO 15.27 BM 837.17

CLIMB MO 21.10 OA 37.32
  WM 60.14 TF 120.9 131.28
  FG 194.14 PR 493.17 WR 568.23
  570.12 LL 766.23 TH 845.8
  845.12

CLIMBED MO 21.31 22.14 WM 63.15
  EA 72.26 73.5 TF 117.10
  FG 188.34 195.2 SS 197.11
  210.7 TP 338.16 PP 433.38
  HD 448.40 PR 489.42 491.6
  496.13 WR 551.38 BO 597.33
  IL 651.27 ML 736.41 746.27
  OV 752.31 LL 766.27 RH 793.8
  TH 846.39

CLIMBERS WR 546.20 GG 662.19

CLIMBING TF 119.27 DV 141.32
  174.14 WP 387.20 PP 436.8
  HD 450.35 WR 553.17 558.5
  558.7 579.36 579.40 LA 631.36
  IL 653.25 654.1 OV 750.25
  RR 788.24 TH 848.5

CLING OV 747.13 758.38

CLINGING MO 1.19 PO 114.7
  TF 120.36 WS 247.19 SU 528.16
  WR 558.20 BO 601.38

CLINK WR 557.24

CLINKED PR 489.33

CLINKING DV 139.14 PR 490.18

CLIPPED WM 69.31 HD 447.41

CLIPT SP 48.10

CLIQUES SC 271.22

CLOAK FG 192.42 193.2 194.14
  195.22 195.25 SS 206.39
  GF 237.34 PR 500.36 501.10
  502.7 505.11 505.12 506.33
  507.8 508.2 ML 727.16

CLOAK (CONT.) RH 802.35

CLOAKED SS 207.22

CLOAK-LIKE EE 304.4

CLOAK-ROOM WS 251.25

CLOAKS PR 476.27 ML 726.39

CLOCK OA 24.8 EA 88.37
  DV 178.20 SG 221.6 CH 277.14
  OC 286.26 289.14 290.27
  TP 334.14 BL 352.27 361.35
  SD 415.18 415.22 421.39
  HD 443.10 456.22 TB 518.1
  JD 612.2 624.2 LA 630.1
  IL 659.25 659.26 LL 765.4
  766.25

CLOCK'S CH 277.15

CLOG PO 115.40

CLOMMAXED SC 268.8

CLOSE MO 3.31 20.42 OA 26.1
  38.38 HT 41.5 SP 52.36
  WM 69.35 EA 82.35 92.30
  PO 101.15 TF 121.21 125.7
  129.10 130.1 130.18 132.13
  DV 149.26 157.13 168.13 179.1
  179.5 181.8 182.21 182.35
  WS 252.24 254.27 BL 353.11
  354.14 359.30 363.38 MN 372.9
  373.20 WP 390.20 SD 411.30
  424.37 PP 429.38 436.8 439.30
  440.7 HD 454.18 454.20
  FA 467.1 468.34 PR 483.41
  486.30 504.29 511.11
  WR 551.26 LA 636.13 ML 723.13
  OV 751.29 RH 795.13 MD 810.9

CLOSE-CUT OA 26.35

CLOSED MO 4.18 7.16 OA 24.4
  24.30 34.9 WM 55.7 67.37
  68.4 EA 74.29 75.38 77.40
  91.11 91.32 PO 101.37 112.13
  112.31 TF 130.7 DV 138.18
  152.20 169.28 170.13 181.26
  FG 188.7 SS 206.26 209.39
  SG 225.22 230.5 GF 237.37
  238.32 WS 245.22 OC 284.4
  284.12 286.28 301.34
  EE 321.36 322.30 332.28
  TP 340.42 345.22 345.42
  BL 354.9 356.22 358.32 361.15
  363.40 MN 375.4 YT 394.10
  402.14 SD 415.33 423.18
  423.37 PP 432.15 440.21
  HD 455.25 PR 482.25 489.41
  497.42 TB 526.10 WR 547.5
  561.22 562.6 577.18 SM 582.22
  BO 596.11 596.32 LA 637.3
  IL 656.29 GG 675.33 677.19
  691.11 697.24 ML 741.30
  RR 784.16 BM 838.10 838.19
  841.25

CLOSE-FITTING WS 251.14

CLOSELY OA 30.7 WM 58.1
  PO 107.30 TF 123.25 126.7
  DV 177.22 181.10 SS 199.21

CLOSELY (CONT.) GF 237.7
  MN 367.40 373.28 WP 386.10
  YT 410.6 WR 551.23 571.17
  RH 794.28 MD 823.31

CLOSENESS WS 257.25

CLOSER EA 91.15 91.34
  TF 132.11 DV 181.27 182.28
  GF 239.27 240.31 WS 255.2
  WR 553.26 GG 684.6
  BM 837.25

CLOSES FA 471.21

CLOSE-SET RH 793.31

CLOSING PO 109.23 TF 125.32
  DV 158.22 WS 257.20
  BL 347.5 363.36 363.38
  WP 386.27 SD 415.37
  GG 687.34

CLOSURE WM 68.33

CLOTH WM 55.15 56.25
  PO 97.21 111.3 114.28
  DV 140.5 SS 202.19
  SG 223.24 SC 267.30
  OC 284.30 286.15 291.40
  296.28 EE 329.8 BL 351.1
  351.4 SD 423.26 PP 438.35
  HD 445.42 PR 494.22
  TB 524.16 SU 538.4 540.36
  542.30 544.20 JD 616.14
  GG 683.21

CLOTHE OC 302.4 GG 690.11

CLOTHED SU 534.6 539.35

CLOTHES HT 43.28 SP 45.19
  PO 115.28 TF 134.24
  DV 147.3 SG 226.29
  WS 244.9 OC 284.32
  EE 329.28 TP 345.10
  SD 423.5 HD 452.15 456.9
  456.18 456.20 456.30
  FA 471.20 PR 478.28
  483.16 503.14 506.18
  509.19 TB 516.4 SU 529.27
  530.13 530.26 531.23
  543.4 544.28 WR 563.34
  576.38 BO 595.7 NT 704.4
  709.11 ML 726.39 742.7
  LL 770.9 MD 806.38 807.1
  808.20 811.32

CLOTHES-BASKET HT 42.40

CLOTHES-LINE MN 366.32

CLOTHES-LINES SP 45.20

CLOTHES-'OSSES SC 268.34

CLOTHING PP 437.24 HD 450.10
  450.25 450.32 451.18
  451.28 452.11 452.30
  453.8 PR 506.24 506.30
  WR 563.31 563.42 564.21
  573.14

CLOTHS TF 123.6 SC 267.31
  OC 284.2 297.20 WP 386.39

CLOTHS (CONT.)

CLOTHS (CONT.) 387.3 WR 576.41

CLOTS SU 530.41

CLOUD WS 253.20 EE 310.19
SU 532.9 532.15 533.25 538.8
WR 577.26 577.27 LA 638.3
OV 750.22 753.31 753.34
BM 831.40

CLOUDED MN 369.15 SU 532.18

CLOUDS MO 1.9 OA 27.24
PO 115.10 115.15 TF 117.3
EE 312.20 312.26 BL 359.7
360.7 PR 509.24 WR 574.9
575.33

CLOUDY SU 535.14 WR 572.22

CLOVE-PINK-HALF-OPENED RR 780.24

CLOVER PO 106.29 107.8 SB 217.8

CLOWN MO 7.6 EA 75.40 MN 371.21
371.26 372.15

CLOWNISH LL 774.12

CLUB PO 96.30 ML 735.39

CLUBBED LA 646.1

CLUCK PO 110.13

CLUCKING DV 158.13 SS 206.21

CLUE EE 333.6 BL 349.19
IL 654.7 RH 792.40 MD 821.5

CLUMP EE 330.13

CLUMSILY PO 104.4 DV 180.40
SB 215.16 GF 234.11 SD 422.27
BM 835.22

CLUMSINESS LL 774.12

CLUMSY WM 70.22 PO 97.25
TF 119.22 119.25 SB 215.9
218.29 CH 278.18 OC 283.22
FA 466.27 ML 742.7 742.10
LL 774.11 MD 820.22 BM 832.28
834.39

CLUNG MO 20.20 OA 24.42 25.12
25.30 25.37 25.40 EA 79.27
PO 101.33 101.35 105.7
TF 119.34 120.11 120.17
DV 148.22 151.11 FG 193.6
193.42 WS 247.15 256.19
259.21 SD 421.19

CLUSTER DV 157.36 WR 552.30
561.21 570.13

CLUSTERED SP 45.17 49.2
PO 105.29 TF 117.6 SB 214.14
HD 449.1 WR 580.9

CLUSTERS WP 387.21 WR 558.36

CLUTCH HD 454.20 GG 686.41
687.1 TH 845.7 845.12

CLUTCHED WM 60.6 70.9 PO 104.31
TF 127.32 FG 189.41 OC 283.32
GG 696.10

CLUTCHES FG 188.14 HD 450.37

CLUTCHING EA 91.15 PO 115.35
TF 121.29 HD 452.42 PR 511.8
SU 531.19 SM 584.21 GG 681.21
694.38 695.23 TH 845.10 848.7

COACH-HOUSE LL 764.42 765.1

COAL DV 139.40 166.12 CH 277.39
OC 288.12 TP 344.41 MN 366.28
HD 456.14 JD 608.21 608.25
609.23 610.10 618.1 621.11
ML 739.34 746.17

COAL-BLACKENED JD 616.32

COAL-CARTS DV 139.10 MN 366.27
PP 435.42

COAL-DUST MO 3.37 DV 169.26
OC 292.12 297.36 JD 609.22
616.40

COAL-MINE MO 2.8 JD 610.5

COAL-MINE'S JD 610.29

COALS WS 247.11 CH 275.42 276.3
OC 286.12 JD 618.1

COAL-SHED ML 743.20

COARSE TF 126.23 127.30
DV 169.27 YT 408.15 PP 429.19
429.39 HD 442.37 446.39 447.3
PR 477.29 477.35 478.4
WR 551.7 JD 617.10 NT 714.14
715.38 716.24 ML 725.2 734.15

COARSELY SS 201.19

COARSENESS EE 305.32

COAST PR 481.17 WR 548.36
ML 729.27 TH 850.42 851.9
851.10 851.24

COASTGUARDS' ML 722.28

COAST-PLAIN SU 529.10

COAT MO 6.1 HT 41.16 SP 49.35
49.36 49.38 EA 73.22 83.9
84.10 TF 125.24 DV 145.14
168.1 168.7 179.2 180.26
180.28 SS 210.35 211.30
SG 226.14 226.29 228.9
WS 250.32 SC 268.13 OC 297.14
TP 345.32 BL 364.33 SD 420.19
420.30 421.28 422.19
PP 433.12 438.21 439.12
439.17 439.18 439.23 439.32
439.34 439.36 HD 451.27
FA 458.31 SU 540.35 540.37
JD 626.13 626.14 LA 630.8
637.10 IL 655.26 656.25
ML 743.27 LL 765.9 RR 779.33

COAT-CUFFS TH 852.36

COATES (SEE MRS. COATES)

COATS DV 138.16 SS 206.27
PR 476.27

COAX OA 24.24 PR 507.3

COAXED SG 225.1 SD 420.29

COAXING MO 21.8 OA 24.20
SD 420.32

COAXINGLY SG 224.37 OC 285.19
PP 439.32

COBBLE-STONES GF 234.5 241.22

COBRAS TH 848.24

COCK TB 517.25 OV 755.3
LL 773.8

COCKED JD 606.26 615.8
BM 839.10

COCKNEY YT 395.32

COCK-OF-THE-WALK TP 337.2

COCKSURE YT 398.31

COCKTAIL TB 513.15

COCKTAILS TB 515.32 NT 715.21

COCKY YT 398.27

COCONUT TP 337.15

COCONUTS TP 337.15

COCOON OV 758.21

CODDLED HT 38.19

CODDY TP 336.24 344.33
346.2

COEVALS MD 808.35

COFFEE PO 95.33 103.28
104.23 104.25 105.9
TF 123.22 124.14 SG 223.20
223.25 GF 240.25 WS 249.20
255.22 YT 402.38 PP 431.24
PR 495.36 495.37 502.20
506.3 SU 542.27 WR 557.29
557.31 ML 745.17 OV 748.34
LL 764.18 765.40 770.33
776.33 MD 822.41

COFFEE'S GG 681.25

COFFEE-TRAY LL 764.30

COFFIN GG 675.2

COGITATINGLY LA 633.23

COIF SM 583.28

COIF-BANDS SM 583.42

COIFED SM 586.5

COIFS SM 585.12

COIL SS 202.17

COILED DV 159.1 175.16
  GF 237.33 EE 306.36 WP 390.19
  ML 723.35

COILING WP 390.5 BM 831.16

COILS SU 536.42 BO 599.10

COIN SP 50.3

COLBRAN (SEE MR. COLBRAN)

COLD MO 3.10 4.9 22.7 OA 36.31
  37.18 37.32 37.38 SP 51.20
  53.19 WM 58.26 63.29 67.36
  PO 95.17 95.25 96.22 96.37
  TF 127.25 127.37 134.6
  DV 143.1 144.32 145.24 146.7
  146.41 149.35 152.1 152.7
  152.11 152.16 152.24 152.31
  154.1 154.15 158.15 158.20
  158.24 158.28 159.36 159.40
  169.40 174.39 183.10 FG 193.4
  194.20 194.26 194.36 195.9
  195.23 195.28 SS 201.23 209.4
  SB 213.32 SG 227.6 230.41
  GF 237.29 239.23 243.25
  WS 244.5 244.21 245.37 249.14
  249.26 252.38 255.21
  CH 276.25 OC 291.41 296.18
  296.22 300.37 EE 312.28
  315.13 320.22 322.8 330.5
  TP 334.6 334.10 335.7 343.34
  MN 376.5 376.15 377.41
  WP 379.2 390.34 YT 405.16
  SD 411.4 412.11 414.6 420.29
  422.31 422.32 423.12 423.38
  PP 429.31 429.36 429.40
  430.14 HD 444.28 444.35
  446.16 450.12 450.13 450.16
  450.18 450.22 FA 471.16
  PR 477.15 479.8 486.41 487.33
  488.5 488.34 492.26 495.18
  495.19 496.32 497.32 498.11
  499.10 501.11 501.19 501.20
  501.22 501.27 501.28 502.30
  502.40 503.22 503.31 503.40
  504.3 504.26 505.3 505.10
  507.26 508.22 509.17 509.33
  510.39 SU 529.34 530.40
  532.32 534.24 536.17
  WR 549.17 552.8 552.17 552.24
  556.16 556.20 557.21 557.22
  560.33 568.20 570.18 572.6
  572.22 579.18 SM 583.21
  586.10 586.19 BO 591.10
  592.37 594.36 595.7 596.34
  598.21 598.29 599.11 600.34
  601.18 602.9 602.31 602.41
  604.14 JD 610.19 610.32
  622.18 LA 632.19 640.20
  640.33 IL 652.32 GG 665.40
  668.36 669.15 670.19 674.5
  681.25 684.33 685.3 685.18
  685.28 686.4 686.16 686.18
  686.20 686.39 687.4 687.6
  687.11 691.18 NT 707.12
  717.42 ML 741.6 741.32 743.32
  743.42 744.2 744.4 744.5
  744.7 744.21 745.2 745.22
  OV 749.17 LL 776.41 RH 798.28

COLD (CONT.) 799.27 799.32
  BM 839.15 TH 845.23 848.26
  849.1 849.9 851.28 851.29

COLD-BLOODED EE 323.40

COLDER DV 144.6 PR 498.17
  503.18 507.25 WR 568.19
  BO 604.12 GG 684.3 684.10

COLD-FLOORED TH 849.20

COLDISH PR 489.13

COLDLY OA 37.26 38.7 WM 67.28
  EA 75.15 87.4 SB 219.3 219.26
  SG 232.9 GF 243.22 WS 263.2
  263.6 SC 272.37 YT 397.2
  405.10 407.23 409.27
  PR 492.39 JD 611.3 614.35
  615.22 621.23 621.39
  IL 658.23 GG 675.31 686.40
  RH 790.5

COLDLY-COAXING SD 420.18

COLDNESS MO 22.10 EA 86.13
  OC 285.19 HD 448.38 PR 476.38
  BO 602.25 JD 622.24 ML 734.16

COLD-PERFUMED WR 572.31

COLIN URQUHART PR 473.3 473.28
  474.24

COLIN URQUHART'S PR 481.11

COLLAPSE OA 36.24 HD 441.27
  GG 678.4 678.14 NT 720.31

COLLAPSED SC 272.27 LL 767.33
  778.1

COLLAPSES EE 313.40

COLLAR OA 35.39 35.41 37.24
  SP 46.17 WS 247.26 TP 343.14
  SD 417.40 FA 458.12 GG 672.31
  OV 751.10 751.14 BM 841.9

COLLAR-BONE SD 417.42

COLLARLESS YT 400.31

COLLARS PR 476.24

COLLAR-STUD BM 831.15

COLLECT DV 180.22 MD 810.4

COLLECTED WR 574.11 TH 852.11

COLLECTING PO 102.1 EE 305.16
  SU 536.22 BO 588.4 LL 769.40

COLLECTION TF 117.9 LL 763.8
  769.36 769.39

COLLECTIVE DV 156.35

COLLECTOR LL 769.34

COLLECTORS LL 769.41

COLLECTORS' LL 764.20

COLLEGE OA 35.32 CH 278.22
  PR 481.38 482.7 TH 853.2
  853.19

COLLEGE-TRAINED CH 278.27

COLLIER SP 46.6 DV 137.5
  138.25 165.37 184.6
  SC 269.21 CH 278.20
  278.25 281.38 OC 297.3
  JD 617.31 619.25 620.12
  621.18 621.21 622.31
  623.13 623.30 625.4 626.15
  626.23 626.30 627.24

COLLIERIES FG 187.5 TP 334.8
  JD 624.25

COLLIER-INHABITANTS DV 136.10

COLLIERS HT 39.4 SP 45.5
  45.27 46.14 47.25 48.25
  50.5 50.16 50.30 DV 136.33
  SC 269.7 OC 297.41
  TP 335.23 YT 394.32 395.20
  HD 449.10

COLLIER'S DV 184.36 SC 267.24
  JD 617.23 622.17 624.23

COLLIERS' DV 138.33

COLLIERY DV 160.26 161.25
  OC 283.27 TP 334.26
  JD 610.31

COLMENARES NT 702.3 711.22
  711.30

COLMENARES' NT 702.21 702.34
  704.41 720.40

COLMENARES, LUIS (SEE LUIS
  COLMENARES)

COLONEL SP 48.13 48.15
  SG 231.12 MN 376.39
  GG 672.38 673.16 673.41
  674.29 674.40 675.27
  675.34 676.8 677.8 677.36
  680.38 681.6 681.9 681.21
  682.22 682.26 682.27
  684.1 684.7 684.13 684.17
  684.31 684.38 685.15
  685.16 685.22 685.24
  687.38 689.24 691.6 691.10
  691.12 691.13 691.28
  691.35 692.1 692.12 692.22
  692.37 693.10 693.35 694.6
  694.25 694.36 695.4 695.6
  695.22 696.4 697.11 699.40

COLONEL HALE GG 670.25 673.11
  688.12 694.39

COLONEL'S GG 682.10 685.29
  691.27 695.14 695.18

COLONEL THAT BO 588.37 588.38

COLONIES YT 396.22

COLONNADE BL 347.33

COLOSSAL EE 333.11 BO 591.19

COLOSSUS BL 365.2

COLOUR OA 23.26 29.28 WM 54.26
  64.2 EA 84.12 86.8 TF 124.40
  DV 142.30 183.18 FG 194.17
  SG 225.11 226.6 WS 250.32
  SC 267.4 CH 282.2 WP 389.14
  YT 398.9 PR 479.35 484.21
  485.9 489.8 494.19 499.18
  500.32 501.7 506.28 TB 524.37
  SU 530.34 532.9 WR 574.31
  574.33 574.34 JD 617.34
  617.41 NT 702.13 709.26
  LL 769.38 775.41 MD 811.6
  819.39 BM 833.13 833.16 837.1

COLOURED MO 8.1 PO 107.13
  TF 122.10 FG 195.36 SS 200.36
  210.17 SB 218.27 SG 224.9
  GF 242.1 TP 334.12 SD 412.27
  PP 434.19 FA 460.41 TB 520.32
  521.20 SU 543.5 WR 559.35
  574.14 576.39 GG 698.35
  MD 809.26 811.38

COLOURING WM 55.1 63.29
  PP 427.16

COLOURINGS MO 6.15

COLOURLESS ML 741.5 BM 829.18

COLOURS SP 49.1 FG 194.3 194.5
  TB 522.33 WR 566.8 570.21
  OV 749.20 LL 770.22 778.4

COLT OC 283.4

COLTS HT 42.24

COLUMBINE EE 313.1

COLUMBINES EE 303.13 303.34
  LL 775.31

COLUMN EE 312.35 WR 580.13
  581.26

COLUMNS DV 160.27 JD 609.6

COM' DA 24.23 SC 271.20 271.40

COMA DV 170.2 BM 832.4

COMB SP 47.32 WR 564.4
  LA 635.34 OV 754.33 754.34
  LL 763.19 763.22

COMBATED SB 215.18

COMBATIVE EE 327.8

COMBINATION CH 274.20 MD 818.38

COMBINATIONS MD 809.24

COMBING MO 9.36

COMBUSTION SB 213.1

COME-AND-GO HD 446.30

COMED WP 389.7

COME-DOWN FA 460.5 IL 649.22

COMELINESS OA 23.5

COMELY TP 336.33

COMFORT SB 212.26 CH 279.33
  OC 290.22 EE 322.20 WP 384.12
  PP 440.8 HD 457.1 TB 517.20
  517.32 518.3 GG 694.4
  BM 828.31

COMFORTABLE MO 6.9 EA 81.9
  81.22 DV 171.18 WS 254.5
  EE 319.23 MN 370.22 TB 517.18
  517.40 IL 649.12 LL 770.18
  RR 789.2 789.3 MD 825.28

COMFORTABLENESS TB 518.5

COMFORTABLY HT 41.6 EA 85.32
  SG 223.5 IL 649.34

COMFORTED WP 381.6 GG 697.12

COMFORTING SG 223.32 TP 338.24

COMFORTINGLY CH 277.37

COMIC GF 242.9 WS 247.6
  MD 822.26 822.27

COMICAL DV 170.34 TP 342.21

COMICALNESS LA 640.37

COMIN' HT 41.26 SP 47.13 48.18
  SC 268.12 CH 277.13 277.21
  OC 292.23

COMMAND OA 32.26 PO 107.31
  108.9 TF 118.12 119.25 121.5
  121.15 132.17 132.33 134.4
  134.23 DV 150.35 EE 315.38
  316.13 RH 793.11 MD 820.18
  BM 838.11

COMMANDED MO 19.17 OA 36.26
  FG 196.12 CH 276.35 277.27
  OC 298.6

COMMANDING DV 162.11 MN 375.6

COMMANDS PO 98.6 108.12
  DV 151.2 EE 316.26

COMMENT DV 169.39 OC 297.42

COMMENTATOR JD 607.34 607.35
  608.27 609.26 619.13 619.30

COMMERCE OV 758.32

COMMINGLE EE 333.6

COMMIN' SC 270.27 272.6
  CH 277.40

COMMISSION PO 108.23 PP 432.10

COMMISSIONED EE 327.39

COMMIT EE 327.34 NT 711.13

COMMITTED EE 327.21 NT 705.11

COMMITTEE OA 32.8

COMMODIOUS EE 304.32

COMMON MO 13.34 WM 66.19
  PO 107.32 TF 127.12 127.15
  127.21 127.25 127.40
  134.10 DV 137.3 137.20
  170.31 170.37 SB 212.8
  212.35 213.5 213.39
  GF 235.29 WS 263.33
  CH 278.24 279.28 EE 303.1
  303.4 304.6 305.7 305.42
  314.18 316.34 323.26
  323.35 325.17 328.35
  TP 334.35 YT 394.30 399.32
  PP 429.38 FA 458.10 461.19
  461.39 462.32 462.33
  463.19 466.8 466.24
  TB 515.35 515.37 519.37
  521.41 IL 652.9 GG 662.29
  LL 763.10 RH 802.20

COMMONER TB 519.41

COMMONERS PR 476.9

COMMONNESS FA 466.9 BM 840.31

COMMONPLACE YT 403.18
  FA 462.22 WR 573.41
  GG 662.32 689.33 ML 733.19

COMMON-ROOM EA 86.36

COMMONS EE 303.28 303.29
  304.1 308.2

COMMOTION TP 337.14 FA 465.31
  468.25

COMMUNICATED FA 469.1
  MD 825.40

COMMUNICATION GF 239.35
  WR 560.3

COMMUNICATIVE GG 669.22
  NT 701.31

COMMUNING ML 734.13

COMMUNION NT 719.24 ML 737.10

COM'N SP 48.16 OC 292.22
  292.24

COMPACT WM 65.24 PO 108.23
  113.11 SG 227.9 SC 267.7

COMPAGNONS VOYEZ VOUS BIEN +
  GG 676.18

COMPANION SG 231.5 FA 463.12
  PR 479.27 WR 554.28 555.32

COMPANIONS DV 165.19 TP 336.6
  WR 553.42 554.12

COMPANIONSHIP DV 142.4

COMPANY HT 41.7 PO 96.7
  106.12 TF 118.18 DV 147.31
  167.25 SS 199.14 TP 341.39
  BL 362.39 MN 367.27 370.32
  HD 447.3 449.7 WR 562.41
  IL 654.42 ML 723.10 733.1

COMPANY (CONT.) 733.27 740.8
LL 770.39 771.17 771.23
RH 802.4 802.5 MD 817.13
819.19

COMPANY'S PO 107.37 108.30

COMPARATIVE EA 89.7 TB 519.28

COMPARATIVELY ML 743.40
OV 748.29 RH 794.40

COMPARE FA 459.40

COMPARED TB 514.39 524.36
JD 623.37

COMPARISON DV 158.39 TB 515.2
GG 689.32 699.5 LL 774.13

COMPARTMENT SM 582.4

COMPASSION WS 265.23 WR 573.24
GG 694.14 694.22

COMPASSIONATE SM 583.42
GG 694.20 695.30

COMPASSIONATELY SM 585.39

COMPEL BL 356.8 NT 707.31
RH 792.38

COMPELLED OA 32.17 DV 140.21
180.15 CH 282.22

COMPENSATION SC 273.11 273.13

COMPENSATIONS BL 360.13 360.15

COMPETENT TB 513.23 515.35
525.31 526.7 BO 587.30 594.34
IL 649.35

COMPILING FG 188.2 ML 728.1

COMPLACENCY SG 228.31 BL 357.3

COMPLACENT WP 389.31 GG 663.41
BM 836.5

COMPLACENTLY SB 213.26 WR 554.25

COMPLAIN EE 310.3

COMPLAINED PP 439.7 PR 486.19
TH 847.2

COMPLAINING WM 62.3 DV 139.21
140.13 GF 234.16 OC 288.19
EE 305.26

COMPLAININGLY OC 287.37

COMPLAISANT TP 338.4

COMPLETE EA 89.12 PO 115.17
TF 130.23 130.33 133.16
FG 187.21 GF 243.26 MN 374.9
HD 455.7 TB 526.21 SU 531.27
BO 603.34 603.40 GG 674.38
676.30 677.30 683.37 683.40
691.3 698.30 698.34 RR 780.17
TH 852.23

COMPLETED TF 130.18

COMPLETELY DV 154.25 SC 272.7
PR 473.34 481.41 501.14
SU 542.26 WR 547.34 JD 613.24
617.30 621.18 GG 663.40
674.34 ML 729.40 LL 764.4
765.30

COMPLETENESS PO 97.34 DV 173.6
OV 751.24

COMPLETING PO 113.38

COMPLEX EE 314.40 WR 568.15

COMPLEXION OA 23.7 26.27
WM 55.29 SB 212.13 CH 275.33
PR 476.28 BO 587.16 GG 671.27

COMPLICATED EA 90.14 SU 541.15
542.11 IL 649.37

COMPLICATION LA 631.16

COMPLIED YT 395.39

COMPLIMENT OA 32.3

COMPLIMENTS WP 389.32

COMPOSED TF 122.34 BL 350.40
IL 647.35

COMPOSING GF 236.36

COMPOSURE OA 30.16 DV 147.16
SM 583.36 BM 838.8

COMPOUNDED BO 593.19 OV 751.2

COMPREHENDING PR 500.32

COMPRESSED PO 95.24

COMPROMISE JD 624.12

COMPULSIVE MD 822.24

COMPUNCTION BL 349.34

COMRADE PR 511.21

COMRADES OA 34.18 SP 50.27
50.33 TF 118.7 129.14
MN 371.15

COMRADES' TF 118.22

CONCAVE WM 65.25 PR 493.42
496.11 498.18 498.25

CONCAVES PR 496.38 497.9

CONCEIT SS 206.6 CH 280.37
BO 602.20 MD 818.38 820.14

CONCEITED MO 15.19 20.26
EA 84.36 GG 664.3

CONCEIVE DV 146.19 170.39
WR 568.15

CONCEIVED OV 754.28

CONCENTRATE RR 780.20
MD 814.20 814.23

CONCENTRATED OA 36.1 36.2
PO 107.18 108.23 WS 245.42
254.36 SD 417.26 IL 650.40
GG 677.17 ML 725.5 BM 830.4
837.10

CONCENTRATEDLY OC 295.7

CONCENTRATION TF 129.22
WR 581.22 BO 591.9
JD 622.18 625.15 GG 691.26
MD 814.30

CONCEPTION EE 326.24 TH 845.37

CONCERN DV 144.13 161.28
162.12

CONCERNED CH 279.2 279.4
BL 364.27 MN 378.34
HD 444.40 FA 471.7
SU 529.25 BO 589.14
JD 623.41 GG 668.1
ML 722.14 MD 821.19
BM 829.2

CONCERNING GF 239.30

CONCERNS ML 735.8

CONCERTINA TF 129.15

CONCERTS FA 464.22

CONCESSION BO 594.42

CONCESSIONS WM 54.11

CONCILIATED OC 284.23

CONCILIATORY OA 33.37
MD 820.24

CONCLAVE HD 442.30 443.13

CONCLUDED MO 11.37 17.9
WP 387.13 388.11

CONCLUSIONS WM 64.25

CONDEMN LL 775.12 775.13

CONDEMNATION GF 243.25
LL 777.41

CONDEMNED TF 119.40 PP 434.14
HD 444.14 GG 693.40

CONDENSING SS 210.23

CONDESCENDING EE 309.1 319.14

CONDESCENSION PR 476.38
477.27

CONDITION SP 49.23 TF 120.4
DV 165.27 GF 243.27
HD 441.15 452.27 PR 478.15
SM 582.2

CONDITIONAL YT 407.1

CONDITIONS DV 154.10 185.14
  PR 478.17 ML 722.18

CONDUCT CH 278.23

CONDUCTED TP 335.17

CONDUCTING MN 377.14

CONDUCTOR WM 59.32 59.36 60.1
  60.3 TP 335.1

CONDUCTORS TP 336.27

CONE WR 546.21

CONES FA 459.1

CONEY GREY MO 1.3 1.22

CONFAB YT 399.33

CONFESS FA 459.6 BO 587.25
  LL 778.10

CONFESSED MO 10.34 WM 54.16
  57.36 MN 376.2 376.13

CONFESSION GG 682.10

CONFIDED YT 405.28 SU 539.10
  ML 731.11 BM 828.4

CONFIDENCE TF 134.6 DV 165.35
  MN 368.26 374.9 WR 554.22
  RR 789.12

CONFIDENT SG 221.20 222.25
  HD 446.40 453.5 TB 513.21

CONFIDENTIAL WM 56.17 WS 250.16

CONFIDENTIALLY SG 227.31
  MN 371.1 WP 391.24

CONFIDING BM 828.4

CONFINE EE 315.20

CONFINED DV 137.16

CONFIRM WM 64.25

CONFIRMATION EE 331.8

CONFLAGRATION EE 331.35

CONFLICT EA 71.21 SD 411.29
  WR 566.41

CONFLICTING BL 356.5 PR 502.32
  508.18 JD 612.38 RR 784.23

CONFORM DV 149.30

CONFRONTING EE 325.31

CONFUSE PO 114.35 DV 173.2

CONFUSED MO 12.29 PO 97.31
  TF 132.4 SS 201.18 EE 311.10
  HD 441.20 PR 477.11 WR 572.9
  LA 630.5 637.2 LL 763.38
  764.5 764.9

CONFUSEDLY MO 5.29 12.34
  BO 592.23 LA 630.7 639.22

CONFUSION SP 45.28 DV 148.41
  177.42 SG 225.16 MN 368.19
  WP 392.22 HD 455.41 SU 541.23
  JD 611.4 LA 639.8 LL 764.6
  765.31

CONFUSIONS MO 10.6

CONGEALING EE 332.20

CONGRATULATE WM 66.30 SS 207.2

CONGRATULATION OA 32.18

CONGREGATE EE 312.28

CONGREGATION FA 466.20 467.3
  467.10 468.27

CONGREGATIONAL LL 762.15 762.17

CONGREGATIONAL CHAPEL FA 464.7

CONICAL PO 106.36 DV 160.26
  BO 602.31

CONNECTED EA 82.42 PO 96.4
  TF 131.5 WS 254.33 LA 632.20
  LL 761.19 MD 819.5

CONNECTICUT PR 479.12 479.21
  TH 844.4

CONNECTING PR 481.41 BO 600.37

CONNECTION EA 91.37 PO 112.9
  115.42 TF 126.35 127.9
  DV 151.6 173.17 OC 299.22
  BL 348.15 HD 448.8 PR 473.30
  SU 535.21 LL 764.37 MD 812.21

CONNECTIONS TH 851.41

CONNIE WM 64.33

CONNIE'S WM 54.5

CONNOISSEUR'S MD 820.27

CONNUBIAL BL 349.40 350.3

CONQUER FA 468.2 PR 508.15
  508.16 508.41 ML 745.19

CONQUERED TF 120.40 WS 262.36
  BO 595.9 595.17 597.6

CONQUERORS GG 661.6

CONQUESTS EE 327.13

CONSCIENCE WM 54.12 WS 253.18
  PP 427.14 NT 706.29

CONSCIENCE-KEEPER GF 243.31

CONSCIENCELESS PR 501.23

CONSCIENTIOUS ML 728.8

CONSCIOUS OA 30.24 30.32 30.38
  WM 68.4 69.25 EA 72.14 90.22

CONSCIOUS (CONT.) 95.29
  PO 103.24 114.4 114.18
  TF 120.25 120.37 DV 137.14
  154.40 173.31 178.33
  SB 217.34 WS 256.10 256.12
  257.10 BL 359.3 PP 438.37
  HD 451.13 451.14 451.24
  PR 498.19 SU 531.7 535.23
  WR 547.33 556.19 GG 681.30
  698.33 698.41 ML 742.37
  RR 779.19 MD 815.24

CONSCIOUSLY CH 276.6
  LL 761.21

CONSCIOUSNESS SP 48.37
  WM 69.31 EA 82.1 82.12
  82.21 82.32 83.22 83.35
  90.38 PO 100.16 103.17
  106.2 106.20 112.13 112.25
  113.15 116.4 TF 117.30
  118.1 118.10 118.30 120.34
  130.11 DV 167.8 173.38
  174.25 180.41 WS 256.28
  256.42 257.23 EE 324.27
  330.23 331.21 331.38
  331.42 332.8 332.9 332.13
  332.14 BL 355.31 355.38
  358.10 YT 402.31 402.36
  402.41 HD 448.22 455.20
  PR 478.40 497.42 498.8
  499.25 SU 535.21 544.10
  WR 569.38 572.14 573.41
  574.24 574.26 577.25
  BO 590.42 593.18 604.10
  JD 614.7 614.33 618.10
  618.20 620.25 GG 676.1
  676.10 696.32 698.15
  698.16 698.35 699.4
  699.23* LL 763.42 764.12
  764.14 764.17 768.25
  RR 784.16 RH 804.1 804.8
  MD 820.11 BM 837.15

CONSENT DV 151.38 TP 336.32
  YT 407.2

CONSENTED WP 387.16 YT 408.24
  PR 488.26

CONSEQUENCE DV 146.38
  BM 828.7

CONSEQUENCES FA 467.15

CONSEQUENTLY YT 394.37

CONSERVATORY OA 24.10

CONSIDER HT 40.8 40.18
  PO 101.13 DV 163.10
  SB 219.1 SG 230.12 WS 260.7
  CH 277.23 OC 294.37
  EE 311.5 311.13 TP 339.8
  MN 372.36 WP 380.40
  BO 590.27 591.19 JD 612.25
  LA 642.42 IL 659.27
  MD 811.16 819.26 BM 833.41
  842.26

CONSIDERABLE HT 39.7
  EE 305.14 TP 336.26
  PR 478.14 ML 733.1
  TH 845.28

CONSIDERABLY HT 38.15

CONSIDERATE DV 154.14 WR 576.12

CONSIDERATION DV 142.11 153.22
  184.30

CONSIDERED HT 39.15 DV 136.34
  153.19 154.14 165.31 170.16
  SS 206.11 WS 248.4 SC 267.15
  WP 391.21 YT 403.40 404.20
  BO 591.26

CONSIDERING WM 64.31 EE 311.16
  TB 517.42 JD 613.37 IL 659.28
  RH 796.37 TH 851.41

CONSIST TB 518.6

CONSISTED DV 146.35 BO 588.10

CONSISTENTLY JD 607.1

CONSISTING WR 560.41

CONSOLATION EE 311.38 311.39
  BO 591.17 591.32

CONSOLE BL 355.9

CONSOLIDATE RR 780.20

CONSOLING BL 355.8

CONSOLINGLY EA 92.31 93.10

CONSPICUOUS WS 260.33

CONSPIRACY JD 627.29

CONSPIRATOR GG 676.35

CONSPIRATORS LL 776.32

CONSTANCE WM 55.6 57.8

CONSTANCY BL 359.28

CONSTANT DV 163.42 FG 187.16
  WS 251.34 BL 359.25 HD 449.9
  NT 709.20

CONSTANT-AND-TRUE WS 251.3

CONSTANTLY PR 499.1

CONSTERNATION TF 128.25 WR 555.1
  JD 628.3 LL 776.30 BM 835.4
  835.5

CONSTITUTIONALLY MO 7.23

CONSTRAINED SS 202.11 WS 257.25

CONSTRAINT PO 98.1

CONSTRUED TF 128.23

CONSUL LL 769.34

CONSULTATION HD 441.7 441.12

CONSULTATIONS EE 321.7

CONSUME HD 455.9 MD 815.38

CONSUMED OA 33.34

CONSUMING MO 16.32 HT 40.2
  BL 355.40

CONSUMMATION WR 573.9

CONSUMPTION PP 432.6 434.39

CONTACT MO 17.2 EA 82.33 82.38
  87.32 PO 95.16 99.32 100.2
  111.23 TF 122.20 125.7 126.32
  DV 146.15 146.22 171.7 178.9
  SG 231.30 233.12 WS 254.28
  257.20 TP 345.31 BL 347.24
  354.18 355.36 359.30
  WP 390.31 HD 448.5 449.17
  BO 588.38 JD 606.10 LA 634.16
  GG 663.8 695.39 698.7 698.39
  ML 742.14 743.3 MD 816.27
  819.33 BM 827.36 TH 848.22

CONTADINA PR 475.1

CONTAIN OA 30.5 GF 238.33
  EE 315.28 323.15 PR 500.11
  NT 701.35

CONTAINED TF 129.8 SS 201.15
  WS 245.30 255.26 CH 282.24

CONTAINING HT 42.40 DV 142.37
  WR 565.1 581.12 GG 674.5

CONTEMPLATED SG 221.20

CONTEMPLATING TH 846.24

CONTEMPT MO 7.25 WM 67.36
  EA 89.3 PO 99.15 100.11
  TF 127.15 DV 137.12 SB 219.8
  GF 242.16 243.35 WS 249.29
  265.22 TP 345.19 BL 359.41
  WP 383.7 YT 398.38 399.35
  403.19 404.10 SU 533.3
  SM 582.25 BO 588.40 589.10
  589.37 LA 633.40 634.4
  NT 703.36 MD 807.18 812.10
  816.17 816.18 826.19 BM 842.7

CONTEMPTUOUS OA 28.40 EA 87.22
  DV 137.11 164.18 YT 396.14
  SD 424.31 SM 584.37 BO 603.17
  NT 712.5

CONTEMPTUOUSLY OA 31.6

CONTENT SC 269.9 BL 361.31
  363.1 GG 678.25 697.13
  ML 730.10 OV 758.14 RR 788.33
  MD 822.17 822.33 825.28

CONTENTED ML 731.13

CONTENTMENT WR 567.42 BO 596.42
  597.3 597.8 597.15 597.24

CONTENTS WP 391.15

CONTEST WP 392.6

CONTINENT ML 722.6 738.7
  TH 852.28

CONTINENTS TH 852.10

CONTINUAL GF 241.21 EE 303.23
  MN 366.26 YT 395.20

CONTINUALLY MO 12.13 WM 59.18
  PP 440.17 PR 474.41
  WR 576.26 ML 729.1

CONTINUATION EE 303.3
  MD 816.37

CONTINUE SG 221.35 EE 319.31
  BL 348.5 PR 510.1

CONTINUED MO 4.5 8.24 9.27
  9.35 10.24 11.38 20.20
  20.34 OA 32.11 HT 40.19
  WM 66.24 EA 73.19 83.7
  PO 101.20 105.26 TF 121.19
  131.35 DV 137.41 149.29
  180.7 GF 240.21 243.4
  SC 270.8 270.25 CH 276.40
  277.16 281.26 OC 289.16
  291.8 295.6 EE 330.15
  330.42 BL 358.40 363.6
  MN 375.24 WP 383.13 389.14
  391.28 391.30 392.32
  YT 407.33 SD 426.14 PP 439.27
  HD 445.41 452.5 PR 498.41
  WR 571.5 IL 647.27
  GG 669.15 672.14 678.12
  678.20 ML 744.5 OV 747.23
  758.4 LL 772.28

CONTINUING OA 32.1 WS 245.22
  OC 296.36 EE 315.5
  WR 579.31

CONTINUITY SU 545.5

CONTINUOUSLY EA 71.16
  DV 166.31

CONTORTED SU 530.13

CONTORTIONIST EA 90.7

CONTOUR MO 2.27

CONTOURS MO 13.25 GF 234.9

CONTRACTED WM 69.26 SG 231.41
  ML 740.27

CONTRACTING ML 744.9 744.10

CONTRACTION EA 71.24
  ML 740.14

CONTRADICT TB 518.7

CONTRADICTED MO 16.28 OA 33.4

CONTRARIES MD 826.24

CONTRARY DV 141.30 BL 356.33
  GG 669.6 TH 851.24

CONTRASTED MO 5.18

CONTRASTING WM 56.3 EE 324.40
  RR 780.19

CONTRIVANCES EE 307.28

CONTRIVE OV 759.3

CONTRIVED   SC 269.16

CONTROL   TF 120.6   120.22   122.26
129.3   129.5   DV 140.22   146.25
148.26   WS 257.31   CH 282.21
EE 327.32   327.34   BL 356.5
YT 402.39   403.20   PR 499.25
WR 565.29   568.3   NT 718.13
718.15   RR 782.37   RH 799.13
MD 816.2

CONTROLLED   TF 128.3   DV 180.11
HD 442.34   LL 774.10

CONTROLS   HD 442.34

CONTROVERT   DV 152.38

CONTUSIONS   SD 423.3

CONUNDRUM   HT 40.9   WM 57.2

CONUNDRUMS   HT 40.3

CONVENIENCE   DV 136.10

CONVENT   EE 322.40   WR 550.27
550.31   550.32

CONVENTION   EE 325.23   BO 587.35

CONVENTIONAL   WM 55.34   PO 100.15
PR 485.42   GG 662.38   663.1
663.2   664.29

CONVENTIONALLY   OA 29.13

CONVENTIONS   GG 663.13

CONVERGING   OC 290.37

CONVERSATION   MO 5.11   HT 39.33
EA 85.1   DV 145.21   145.28
151.30   CH 279.5   MN 369.7
PP 432.12   437.4   MD 823.1

CONVERSED   WR 554.11   556.24

CONVERSING   EA 85.41   SG 226.2

CONVERTED   FA 471.12

CONVEY   MD 816.16

CONVEYANCE   BM 839.24

CONVEYED   WS 256.35   LA 632.29
LL 768.8

CONVICTION   DV 145.23   PR 512.3
TB 522.38   SU 532.42   BO 588.26
589.1

CONVINCED   EA 85.20   WS 262.36

CONVOLVULUS   WR 551.39

CONVULSE   BO 604.36

CONVULSED   OA 32.36   LL 765.15

CONVULSION   PR 503.21

CONVULSIONS   PO 110.15   115.20

CONVULSIVE   WM 70.9   SD 421.10
HD 452.42

CONVULSIVELY   GG 689.42

COOED   SS 200.7

COOING   HT 42.28   DV 158.16

COOK   SC 267.10   PR 475.22   481.27
483.19   TB 516.6   MD 810.25
TH 850.34

COOKED   EE 323.29   NT 719.10
ML 745.18   OV 748.33

COOK-HOUSEKEEPER   TB 516.3

COOKING   PR 501.2   508.24   508.40
IL 649.1   TH 851.5

COOK-MOTHER   TB 516.32

COOL   PO 101.42   112.3   115.30
116.8   PP 430.7   430.13
PR 483.39   489.41   509.10
509.11   SU 533.35   537.32
BO 589.29   JD 623.19   LA 631.17
IL 650.42   NT 702.15   703.35
MD 811.33

COOL-BLADED   IL 651.27

COOLER   WS 255.28

COOLLY   OA 33.3   TP 341.23
MN 367.10   367.23   WP 385.22
PR 511.29   SU 538.12   WR 553.28
LA 633.24   IL 653.6   BM 836.14

COOLNESS   FA 471.1

CO-OOP   SP 49.15   49.15

COOPERATIVE WHOLESALE SOCIETY'S
TP 334.14

COPIES   FG 187.30   TB 518.28

COPING-STONE   HD 448.3

COPPER   HT 44.2   WM 54.25
OC 288.29   WR 579.12

COPPER-DARK   WR 579.7

COPPER-PALE   WR 579.8

COPPERS   SP 50.20

COPPER-TOP   HD 456.20

COPPICE   DV 167.18   OC 283.11

COPSE   EE 304.41

COPY   YT 400.39

COPYING   PO 101.23

COQUETRY   MD 808.5

COQUETTISH   LL 777.15

COQUETTISHLY   YT 397.14

CORAL   WR 575.11

CORD   MO 3.13   SD 423.1

CORDIAL   WM 55.41   ML 729.9
TH 853.26

CORDIALITY   FA 463.42
ML 728.38

CORDIALLY   MO 11.32

CORDS   FG 195.4

CORDY LANE   SS 198.38

CORE   MO 18.7   EA 87.15
PO 108.22   TF 120.31
DV 165.17   EE 333.4
PR 497.2   SU 533.8   534.6
BO 591.16   GG 698.5
LL 766.34

CORK   PO 109.14

CORKER   HT 43.22   JD 628.18

CORKS   SP 48.32

CORN   OA 24.16   PO 95.5   107.8
107.15   114.29   SB 217.5
TP 335.32   FA 465.1   467.37
WR 561.8   575.32   BO 591.28

CORNCRAKE   OV 749.30   749.39

CORNEMUSE   RR 783.11

CORNER   MO 6.7   HT 42.21
EA 91.30   TF 123.17
DV 157.12   157.24   157.35
162.30   168.36   183.38
186.1   FG 187.15   SG 224.25
225.19   OC 283.3   TP 334.32
345.27   BL 362.18   WP 382.15
PP 432.17   432.38   435.9
436.11   HD 442.5   FA 460.22
470.11   WR 576.21   JD 611.35
613.24   614.24   LA 630.33
IL 651.29   ML 736.14
LL 766.29   769.3   770.21
770.25   775.19   RR 788.7

CORNERED   PR 502.14   502.21
TH 853.5

CORNERS   DV 136.14   BL 351.5
SD 423.42   FA 465.2
SM 586.6   LL 761.14   BM 839.8

CORNFLOWER   SU 535.34

CORNICES   BO 588.23

CORNISH   SD 411.20   412.27
412.28   414.23

CORNISHMAN   SD 416.30

CORNISH-YANKEE   SD 412.24
415.40

CORN-MUSH   WR 565.2

CORN-PLAITED   FA 465.1

CORNWALL ML 726.11

CORONET GG 662.25

CORPORAL MN 366.2 366.12 366.21
  367.3 367.5 367.8 367.9
  367.17 367.26 368.19 368.20
  368.39 370.18 374.1 374.25
  375.3 375.14 375.16 375.18
  376.12 377.21 378.30 SD 413.9

CORPSE SB 219.32 PR 496.14
  BO 593.30

CORPSE-LIKE PR 496.11 ML 744.24

CORPSES PR 496.27 BO 593.27
  GG 689.13 696.31

CORRAL PR 488.32

CORRECT EA 81.15 FA 463.23
  GG 672.31 MD 823.2 823.34

CORRECTED DV 183.28 MD 805.34

CORRECTLY EA 81.14

CORRECTNESS EA 83.29 PR 484.37

CORRESPONDENCE SS 209.20 209.34
  WP 380.39 JD 607.39 RR 779.9

CORRESPONDENT JD 607.25

CORRESPONDING TB 520.39

CORRIDOR TF 125.30 134.9
  BL 355.22 356.15 SM 583.21
  586.16 GG 669.38 670.38
  RH 802.40

CORRIDORS BL 362.25

CORRIDOR'S SM 586.20

CORROBORATED WM 57.23

CORRODING PO 100.31

CORRUGATED TF 117.9 ML 739.32

CORRUPT EA 93.29

CORRUPTION SC 271.10

CORSETS MO 20.35 WM 59.13

CORUSCATE GG 661.22

'COS OC 287.11

COSIER SD 413.24

COSINESS LL 764.24

COSMIC SU 533.1 WR 574.25

COSMOPOLITAN NT 708.25

COSMOS WR 566.2 572.19
  GG 699.15

COSSED SP 53.16

COSSETING DV 169.12

COST SP 52.19 SG 233.5
  EE 321.31 321.32 321.33
  BL 348.5 348.13 HD 454.36
  ML 732.41 TH 850.25

COSTING TH 850.40

COSTUME EA 78.30

COSY TP 338.22 338.24 340.25
  WP 388.41 390.17 SD 411.33
  PR 483.22 IL 650.9 ML 722.30
  LL 764.24

COTS GG 666.36

COTTAGE DV 139.6 139.8 147.31
  160.35 184.36 SG 221.2
  CH 275.31 OC 283.31 293.9
  EE 303.14 304.4 304.35 304.39
  305.4 306.18 307.29 308.27
  323.15 323.25 323.30 324.5
  329.18 MN 366.3 FA 464.38
  PR 481.26 JD 607.17 GG 666.16
  ML 725.27 725.31 725.36 740.7
  TH 850.42 851.3

COTTAGES DV 136.1 136.8 136.14
  137.16 SD 411.11 ML 722.28
  725.22 733.21

COTTAGEY IL 654.30

COTTON TF 123.26 GF 234.19
  WS 245.31 OC 302.1 MN 369.42
  WP 379.23 PR 494.35 WR 559.16
  564.21 BM 829.33 TH 845.15

COTTON, JOHN (SEE JOHN COTTON)

COTTONWOOD PR 490.2 WR 553.10
  553.12 558.40 561.30 578.26

COTTON-WOOD PR 483.38

COTTONWOODS PR 483.39 486.11
  489.6

COUCH EA 81.14 DV 138.2 143.1
  152.20 160.2 162.6 184.8
  SS 206.35 OC 296.25 WR 562.33
  562.37 564.39 565.32 576.42
  LA 640.26 NT 709.22 MD 816.7
  825.20

COUGH SU 539.30

COUGHED SU 539.40

COUGHING MO 17.35 PR 501.39

COULDNA OC 292.15

COULDN'T MO 10.16 12.40 21.22
  OA 30.5 SP 51.28 EA 75.1
  75.19 75.35 79.1 DV 179.12
  SS 208.5 208.14 SB 219.35
  SG 222.8 OC 295.38 EE 312.40
  313.4 314.3 BL 352.10 355.3
  356.21 360.31 361.8 MN 367.12
  WP 382.7 YT 401.5 PP 431.13
  FA 463.8 463.21 PR 491.37
  491.38 491.39 491.42 492.31

COULDN'T (CONT.) 492.32
  TB 514.8 517.36 520.14
  526.9 SU 541.30 JD 606.40
  610.15 615.1 LA 637.1
  641.27 645.34 IL 647.23
  647.26 649.23 651.20
  657.8 657.11 GG 679.1
  679.29 690.25 NT 709.39
  709.42 710.38 710.39
  711.32 714.26 714.38
  714.39 719.1 ML 732.2
  732.13 LL 762.15 762.31
  765.38 RR 782.13 787.8
  RH 800.29 800.40 800.41
  803.5 MD 805.18 805.19
  805.25 807.7 825.5
  BM 831.18 832.10 835.7
  835.12 842.11 TH 852.25

COUNCIL CHAMBER OA 32.23

COUNCILLOR JARNDYCE OA 32.8
  32.11

COUNT MO 10.12 11.15 15.28
  DV 151.17 185.19 EE 319.15
  TP 339.21 BL 349.37
  PP 439.27 JD 606.34 606.40

COUNTED SP 52.13 OC 294.31
  JD 606.33

COUNTENANCE WM 56.1 PO 101.11
  FG 187.18 FA 458.3

COUNTER HT 42.17 DV 139.35
  161.18 CH 274.23 SD 412.6
  412.17 420.12

COUNTERACTED EA 75.27

COUNTERACTING WS 257.27

COUNTERACTION PO 103.13

COUNTERMANDED OC 299.13

COUNTESS MO 6.20 PO 96.24

COUNTESS'S SS 203.15 203.22

COUNTING SP 46.3 OC 292.5

COUNTLESS GG 698.10

COUNTRIES LL 764.22

COUNTRY MO 5.19 PO 107.5
  113.29 TF 125.40 126.35
  DV 136.3 136.9 141.23
  142.20 157.10 177.9
  SS 197.15 200.6 211.31
  SB 212.35 GF 234.6
  EE 304.27 308.16 308.34
  318.36 329.39 TP 334.11
  BL 349.7 WP 388.12
  PP 427.32 430.27 436.21
  HD 447.40 448.42 FA 464.7
  468.30 PR 473.23 SU 530.2
  WR 550.23 551.33 SM 582.27
  BO 587.19 593.28 594.28
  599.5 600.23 602.10
  JD 610.21 624.7 GG 662.6
  662.34 666.19 667.26
  OV 748.37 750.36 RH 794.32

COUNTRY (CONT.) 802.21 BM 827.28
827.35 828.3 834.37

COUNTRYSIDE OV 751.33

COUNTRY-SIDE TP 334.3 HD 448.12

COUNTS HD 443.23 SU 528.23

COUNTY DV 137.2 TP 334.2
YT 396.12 GG 669.15 669.17
OV 754.25

COUPLE SP 49.20 SG 222.24
222.35 EE 304.27 307.21 308.1
308.33 SD 420.22 PP 427.28
PR 477.5 477.6 TB 522.5
GG 679.28 ML 725.32 733.9
739.10 OV 754.24 MD 805.12
809.29 BM 840.36 TH 846.21
848.27 848.28

COUPLES SM 585.17

COURAGE PO 108.7 TF 122.32
GF 242.17 OC 290.10 EE 305.26
314.21 324.29 TP 342.19
YT 407.36 407.39 PP 435.23
437.7 FA 461.4 SU 544.31
544.34 SM 583.6 GG 671.35
NT 702.17 702.42 703.9 703.20
714.1

COURSE MO 9.15 12.37 16.1
WM 55.33 61.39 PO 98.7
DV 149.34 151.25 152.4
SS 205.26 209.35 SB 212.30
216.37 GF 240.37 OC 283.35
284.11 EE 305.18 307.18
308.17 309.3 316.1 319.40
320.28 321.12 328.7 TP 336.29
338.4 338.7 338.18 BL 349.26
350.2 359.19 WP 383.34 390.40
FA 458.16 458.17 464.1
PR 480.35 TB 513.23 515.11
516.12 516.18 517.33 519.11
519.36 519.42 520.4 520.8
525.38 525.40 526.34 WR 558.9
SM 582.6 582.16 BO 587.34
592.8 JD 606.7 607.6 607.27
613.32 614.1 614.16 615.10
621.7 LA 642.5 642.39
IL 648.23 652.7 652.28 655.42
GG 668.22 669.19 669.38
672.14 682.18 688.1 NT 703.26
704.8 706.36 707.21 709.13
709.21 711.6 713.10 720.4
ML 726.25 734.23 737.28
LL 761.3 762.5 762.33 776.22
RR 781.9 783.3 783.13
RH 797.16 798.12 MD 805.11
808.14 809.30 811.16 811.20
812.1 812.28 812.35 813.14
813.32 815.3 821.24 824.19
BM 827.24 835.24 835.34
TH 844.14 848.7 849.9 849.17
850.11 852.7

COURT SS 198.39 SG 224.17
FA 470.40

COURTED SB 217.24

COURTEOUS OA 32.13 HT 39.5
PR 473.35 479.29

COURTEOUSLY OC 293.8 PR 474.27

COURTESY MO 12.35 HT 39.8
LL 764.4

COURTIN' SS 199.10

COURTING OA 32.38 HT 40.14
SG 231.42 WS 251.1 SC 267.2

COURTLY WM 58.5

COURTSHIP OA 32.6 BL 359.24

COURTYARD TF 123.14 125.40
134.38 SG 224.20 228.14
LL 764.41 BM 835.18

COUSIN EA 85.31 BL 348.38
YT 395.38 398.1 FA 459.10
464.29 464.33 IL 653.24
LL 762.12 763.37 764.2 770.37

COUSIN EMMIE YT 395.39 396.5
397.9 397.36 398.24

COUSIN FLORA YT 395.38

COUSIN HENRY LL 771.3

COUSIN MATILDA YT 395.38 396.4
396.12 397.11 397.15 397.21
397.25 397.29 397.35 403.32
407.28

COUSINS LL 777.11 777.13

COUSIN'S LL 771.8

COUTTS SP 47.23 WM 55.13 55.36
56.20 56.24 56.32 57.6 57.9
57.12 57.16 57.23 57.39 58.3
58.5 58.17 59.8 59.27 59.32
59.35 60.8 63.3 65.8 67.4

COUTTS' WM 58.35

COUTTS (SEE FRED; MR. COUTTS)

COVE ML 723.23 734.21

COVEITOUS (SIC.) FG 188.13

COVER EA 93.38 94.4 94.5
WS 264.13 OC 300.24 BL 358.9
MN 373.21 YT 397.37 PR 478.28
510.30 510.32 TB 520.28
WR 566.19 GG 690.13 OV 759.14
RH 790.6 790.7

COVERED MO 6.24 OA 29.32
WM 55.38 63.42 PO 104.20
111.2 DV 148.41 FG 195.7
SG 221.22 OC 297.15 298.19
302.9 BL 363.39 364.11
WP 383.24 SD 423.26 PP 430.29
437.11 HD 443.25 FA 468.24
PR 509.22 SU 532.28 WR 546.32
559.23 562.34 570.41 580.36
SM 584.16 GG 694.37 NT 709.22
OV 753.31 LL 764.4 775.30

COVERING SS 202.4 203.41
SG 225.17 WP 385.29 OV 750.22

COVERINGS OV 759.16

COVERS SG 222.13

COVETED NT 706.1

COVETOUS WR 560.28

COW MO 3.17 17.35 ML 723.7
730.19

COWARD MO 21.25 TF 131.35

COWARDICE DV 151.14

COWARDLY NT 708.15

COWBOY PR 484.41

COWED PO 105.35 SD 425.31
425.34 SU 533.11 LA 639.27

COWERED DV 175.17 SU 533.10
ML 723.34

COWERING SU 544.37

COWS MO 17.38 BL 347.21
WP 379.3 385.6 IL 648.22
ML 722.35 725.18 726.32

COW-SHED MO 3.17

COWSHEDS WP 379.4

COW-SHEDS MO 5.10

COWSLIP EE 309.13

COWSLIPS ML 723.5 723.21

COY JD 625.9 625.18

COYOTE WR 570.7

COYOTES PR 503.1

CRAB-APPLE SB 214.13

CRAB-APPLES SB 216.33

CRAB-LIKE LL 776.31

CRACK SB 213.10 MN 375.15
PR 493.29 WR 558.13 558.15
LA 643.23 TH 846.36

CRACKED OA 33.6 33.33
EA 79.18

CRACKING LL 775.34

CRACKLE EE 330.3

CRACKLED LA 641.35 ML 746.22

CRACKLING PO 102.38 FG 188.11
189.24 PP 434.38 434.42
PR 502.40 507.16

CRACKS OA 29.29

CRADLE WR 578.33 OV 747.25

CRAG WR 579.38

CRAMP PR 507.25

CRAMPED DV 152.13 GF 239.26
  FA 460.36 PR 507.20

CRAMPING DV 164.29 171.39

CRANED HD 444.12

CRANE'S-BILL PR 490.8

CRANING FA 468.28

CRANKING IL 650.1

CRANNIES ML 733.30

CRASH OA 35.40 PO 110.1
  TF 121.30 WS 264.7 264.11
  PR 494.15 511.7 WR 552.21
  552.22 LA 639.33 GG 685.24
  RH 803.21 TH 846.37

CRASHED OA 35.21 EE 331.32
  SD 421.13 421.21

CRASHING GF 238.17 241.22

CRATES YT 394.11

CRAVATS WS 251.31

CRAVEN DV 153.40

CRAVING MO 2.39 SG 226.38
  HD 449.11 PR 477.1 WR 581.10
  NT 709.20

CRAWL PP 431.14 OV 759.3

CRAWLED PO 103.38 SS 210.42
  PR 488.35 MD 817.23

CRAWLING SP 52.24 YT 406.24
  WR 558.20

CRAZY PR 512.21 WR 550.20
  LA 639.39 IL 656.40 GG 688.17
  NT 717.16 LL 769.19 776.29

CREAK FG 189.35 189.36
  GG 684.33

CREAKED FG 189.33 WS 244.26

CREAM WM 64.6 DV 179.4
  SS 202.21 207.26

CREAM-COLOURED EA 84.5 OC 289.26
  TP 334.24 TB 521.16 LA 632.2

CREAMY EA 79.19 TP 334.12
  LA 633.17 ML 726.39 LL 762.40
  771.38 772.1 BM 829.17

CREAMY-DUSKY SM 583.30 585.30

CREAMY-SMOOTH ML 726.3

CREAMY-WHITE ML 726.41

CREAMY-YELLOW BL 351.6 NT 703.42

CREASED PR 485.28

CREASES GG 672.39

CREATE TB 516.22 ML 726.5

CREATED EA 87.19 PR 474.34
  ML 726.3

CREATING SD 422.19 MD 811.29

CREATION ML 742.19

CREATURE EA 81.37 DV 180.37
  SS 196.2 SB 212.19 214.26
  214.31 215.16 216.5 216.9
  219.30 WS 250.10 CH 274.11
  EE 312.11 TP 337.35 345.16
  WP 381.22 SD 413.42 420.25
  HD 442.23 FA 464.9 PR 475.21
  498.40 501.25 504.24
  SU 532.12 536.8 537.6
  BO 599.2 602.21 GG 693.2
  693.4 ML 730.23 BM 835.32

CREATURES MO 7.38 17.3 EA 87.6
  TP 343.12 WR 548.1 570.5
  BO 602.31

CREDIT ML 739.24

CREDITOR TB 516.10

CREED DV 154.17

CREEP TP 335.19 LL 765.36
  RR 784.26 MD 813.9

CREEPER WR 551.40 LL 770.26

CREEPING MO 21.39 PO 105.37
  113.1 113.5 113.6 113.16
  113.17 GF 239.24 PP 428.33
  SU 537.17 WR 581.3 ML 734.17

CREEPY LL 767.29

CREME DE LA CREME GG 699.42

CREPE SU 542.17

CREPT PO 113.12 FG 190.37
  191.14 OC 283.14 290.1
  WR 556.38 BO 599.1 JD 610.13
  ML 745.17 746.15

CRESCENTS MD 809.20

CREST EE 330.40 WP 386.28
  PP 436.9 PR 496.33 510.9
  SU 531.6 WR 551.42 GG 670.12
  670.34 677.16 694.35

CRESTED TF 119.2 WP 386.34
  387.6

CRESTS WP 379.8

CRESSWELL, OSCAR (SEE OSCAR
  CRESSWELL)

CREVICE SU 534.25 WR 558.15

CREW PP 428.33

CRIBBAGE WS 253.21 253.25
  255.33

CRIBBAGE-BOARD WS 253.29

CRICKET DV 164.15 165.29

CRIED MO 10.14 16.4 22.7
  OA 24.20 25.11 25.28
  25.33 36.11 SP 45.33
  46.25 48.18 48.29 WM 59.37
  59.41 60.4 66.7 68.31
  70.15 EA 71.9 74.4 74.25
  75.21 76.41 77.16 86.3
  86.40 87.31 88.26
  TF 127.37 128.25 DV 141.6
  141.24 141.35 142.7
  149.9 149.11 155.31 157.22
  157.27 157.34 158.24
  161.32 162.26 175.23
  184.6 184.9 184.23 184.39
  185.16 FG 189.19 189.20
  190.5 193.6 193.22 193.35
  194.21 195.32* 195.33 196.1
  196.5 SS 199.36 206.8
  208.26 SB 214.7 216.8
  216.38 218.30 SG 230.18
  232.22 232.32 GF 242.12
  WS 244.17 244.35 245.8
  245.13 246.26 246.29
  247.2 247.21 249.31 253.7
  254.3 254.12 258.28 259.3
  259.25 262.20 262.29
  265.39 266.5 SC 269.40
  270.20 272.3 272.20 272.24
  CH 276.16 276.18 276.22
  280.32 OC 288.21 289.2
  293.35 295.21 295.41
  EE 317.2 317.35 320.6
  TP 341.18 342.1 342.23
  343.3 344.30 345.1 345.18
  346.3 MN 374.36 WP 382.41
  383.15 383.18 383.34 384.3
  384.8 384.17 384.40 385.11
  387.36 YT 407.24 407.32
  SD 413.11 416.3 416.10
  416.22 417.11 419.42
  420.36 421.8 422.11 422.11
  425.13 PP 433.9 438.8
  HD 445.39 457.5 FA 463.15
  PR 491.5 491.7 491.19
  491.22 492.3 493.1 509.20 509.27
  TB 515.38 526.19 526.29
  526.31 527.3 527.23 527.29
  SU 538.14 538.18 WR 551.4
  555.16 555.29 580.23
  SM 585.40 BO 601.20 601.28
  JD 614.16 620.33 621.7
  622.26 625.21 LA 630.12
  630.14 630.22 632.9 632.12
  632.31 632.39 634.31 635.9
  635.22 641.14 644.19
  644.40 645.11 645.21
  IL 647.33 648.5 648.32
  649.29 653.8 653.38 654.15
  655.29 655.34 656.24
  656.27 657.13 658.33
  658.35 658.40 659.28
  GG 689.38 NT 717.27 718.37
  OV 749.39 757.35 LL 776.4
  RH 796.12 803.16 803.28
  MD 817.41 BM 834.10 843.7

CRIER SP 45.2

CRIES TF 127.35 DV 155.5

CRIES (CONT.) 161.31 ML 741.1
 741.40

CRIME EE 327.22 IL 655.19

CRIMINAL EA 87.9 EE 327.21
 NT 715.2

CRIMINALS PP 428.32

CRIMSON SG 225.11 225.31
 TP 334.24 FA 464.39 SU 532.13
 OV 753.8 LL 772.15 MD 811.42

CRINGED TP 343.21

CRINGING TF 119.34

CRIPPLED HT 39.23 TF 122.26
 SS 198.34 CH 278.13 EE 322.42
 324.35 328.38 TP 335.18
 ML 730.32

CRIPPLES TP 334.29

CRISES OA 37.5

CRISIS OA 30.17 EA 78.15
 SS 209.10 TB 516.11 OV 748.26
 TH 846.14

CRISP HT 41.19 DV 167.20 168.14
 OC 288.3 BL 354.27 MN 367.23
 WP 379.1 FA 466.20 BO 603.1

CRISPED PO 110.40 FA 466.20

CRISPING PO 115.35

CRISS-CROSS ML 725.25

CRITIC PP 428.42

CRITICAL HD 441.26 SM 582.2
 582.26 JD 606.18 RH 803.39

CRITICISE WM 59.9 EE 307.33
 314.35

CRITICISES OA 28.8

CRITICISM DV 177.37 EE 314.37
 TB 526.42

CROAKING HD 444.35

CROCHETY PR 477.5

CROCKERY HT 42.41 43.3 43.37
 PO 101.38

CROCKHAM EE 306.33 307.5 311.20
 316.21 321.39 328.31 329.20

CROCKHAM COTTAGE EE 306.12
 307.38 308.2

CROCUS GG 695.33 695.36 697.19
 699.27

CROCUSES SP 48.8 48.9 WM 55.18
 SU 532.20 OV 758.26

CROCUS-FLAME ML 738.3

CROCUS-LIKE GG 697.40

CRONES BM 835.41

CRONIES YT 399.17 400.35

CROOK PO 106.32

CROOKED SG 221.22

CROOKEDLY MD 824.24

CROONED WM 68.26

CROP SB 217.8 ML 729.39

CROP-HEADED SD 415.19

CROPPED SS 198.8 PP 433.24
 SU 543.15 WR 552.6 BO 603.18

CROPPING PR 492.20 500.40

CROPS FA 465.26 ML 728.40
 731.41

CROQUET BM 831.25

CROSS WM 55.22 61.33 61.35
 EA 71.2 DV 159.4 FG 188.12
 193.29 SB 218.39 WS 248.16
 WP 389.13 HD 447.42 WR 557.17
 SM 582.12 BO 596.7 598.35
 LA 631.15 GG 662.13 690.21
 690.29 OV 758.7 758.14 758.42
 759.6 759.8

CROSSED MO 1.4 3.7 6.36
 TF 121.42 DV 136.3 161.15
 180.34 SG 226.12 GF 234.34
 237.15 MN 376.18 SD 419.8
 HD 455.2 PR 490.19 490.27
 490.32 WR 552.12 561.28
 BO 595.4 RR 786.37

CROSS-EXAMINED GF 239.36

CROSS-EXAMINING OA 31.38

CROSSING PO 114.36 DV 160.30
 160.36 FG 193.24 195.19
 GF 235.35 OC 286.5 290.37
 PP 432.15 432.23 435.37
 PR 490.21 BO 592.33 595.13

CROSSLEIGH BANK MO 8.25

CROSSLY WP 389.12 YT 397.40

CROSS-PURPOSES GG 680.29

CROSS-ROAD MN 372.27

CROUCHED MO 18.19 OA 27.23
 EA 73.14 75.41 PO 107.6
 DV 136.12 139.9 WS 247.11
 247.14 264.16 OC 287.25
 EE 303.14 317.5 WP 382.20
 388.15 390.4 HD 450.21
 PR 501.10 501.18 506.2 508.24
 SU 540.25 GG 684.39 ML 736.15

CROUCHING EA 73.3 89.28
 PO 101.31 TF 129.37 DV 158.17
 EE 305.4 MN 378.9 WP 387.3 390.9

CROUCHING (CONT.) PR 483.19
 501.17 502.37 505.17
 510.35 WR 557.25 IL 651.26
 GG 688.30

CROW OV 755.3

CROWD SP 46.18 46.26
 PO 107.42 DV 176.13
 SG 226.2 GF 237.38 238.1
 238.19 238.31 TP 337.42
 MN 371.11 FA 458.7 458.17
 PR 480.21 481.21 SU 528.34
 528.35 WR 568.35 573.39
 GG 674.10 674.25 NT 712.7
 ML 724.18

CROWDED SP 45.27 47.25
 CH 274.30 FA 465.6 PR 490.1
 496.39

CROWDING HT 43.38 PR 499.31
 BO 602.31

CROWING OA 36.29

CROWN HT 43.35 SP 50.26
 SS 202.17 JD 614.41

CROWN HILL WM 54.14

CROWNING EA 93.1 GG 667.17

CROYDON WM 59.22

CROZZLED OC 288.9

CRUCIFIED GG 690.20 690.22
 690.26

CRUCIFIX TF 125.35 126.3
 EE 330.37 ML 724.29
 OV 758.6 758.37 759.4
 759.6

CRUCIFIXES ML 725.1

CRUCIFIXION EE 322.2
 GG 690.20

CRUDE SS 204.13 EE 304.20
 WR 550.24 BO 595.20
 GG 664.17 683.14 683.30
 NT 716.41

CRUDELY DV 147.30

CRUEL WM 66.18 DV 154.31
 170.9 180.28 WS 255.10
 259.25 MN 372.8 PR 492.6
 492.29 494.30 505.32
 TB 526.1 526.34 WR 576.18
 BO 602.26 GG 684.24
 NT 710.15 712.27 ML 732.21
 740.31 744.12

CRUELLEST OV 754.13

CRUELLY WM 61.17 PO 99.14
 DV 138.6 180.40 SG 226.12
 OC 301.20 GG 690.23
 ML 743.30

CRUELTY SU 530.16 GG 680.25
 NT 712.33 712.34 ML 731.24

CURIOUS (CONT.) 601.4 JD 612.11
  614.31 618.13 623.6 623.39
  624.7 LA 632.1 635.25 636.1
  643.2 643.6 644.5 646.18
  IL 654.40 GG 662.29 663.7
  664.21 669.41 670.13 680.22
  681.3 NT 702.23 706.25 712.31
  ML 726.3 728.32 738.35 741.35
  744.19 OV 756.33 RR 781.23
  785.16 785.32 785.35 788.13
  RH 800.8 801.15 MD 809.42
  816.41 820.1 823.18 BM 829.37
  832.20 833.31

CURIOUSLY MO 12.24 OA 29.6
  WM 64.10 64.14 EA 71.24
  PO 110.23 113.4 TF 132.27
  132.31 DV 138.8 146.3 151.24
  SS 197.34 207.7 GF 243.30
  WS 245.42 261.3 TP 345.17
  BL 363.14 MN 374.38 375.26
  YT 403.3 SD 413.38 PP 429.1
  429.14 430.2 435.7 436.24
  437.26 PR 485.4 494.39 496.2
  WR 551.32 561.6 565.22 570.25
  575.42 BO 603.2 604.28
  JD 623.17 LA 644.27 646.1
  646.4 IL 654.36 GG 669.20
  673.14 683.20 684.42 685.41
  695.41 ML 737.23 744.22
  745.29 LL 775.36 RH 796.10
  800.37 MD 808.31 820.1

CURL GF 243.29 243.35 SM 586.6
  RR 781.19 MD 813.39 816.20

CURLED EE 324.9 BL 361.19
  SU 533.24 SM 584.8

CURLING GF 236.3 SU 533.19
  WR 563.9 JD 606.28 NT 712.40

CURLS WS 251.26 254.6 260.41
  OC 286.41 290.19 EE 304.24
  MD 807.40 813.27

CURLY PP 429.18 JD 614.41
  LA 631.10 RH 803.40

CURRANT DV 139.12 161.7
  EE 313.36 PR 502.18 GG 674.36
  ML 736.9

CURRENT SP 48.27 SS 200.1
  GG 685.18

CURRENTS MO 2.24 TB 527.8

CURSE FG 191.4 191.6 CH 281.12
  282.20

CURSED EA 79.40 FG 189.21
  MN 371.6 TH 852.15

CURSES WS 250.15

CURSING MN 377.34

CURTAIN SS 206.34 WR 579.41
  BM 836.42

CURTAINLESS SG 225.8

CURTAINS WM 55.37 EA 77.38
  91.29 GF 237.11 239.24

CURTAINS (CONT.) SC 273.7
  EE 304.36 307.11 ML 725.13
  BM 835.16 838.14 838.15
  838.19 TH 848.11 848.12
  848.16 848.31 850.39 853.21

CURTLY IL 647.6 LL 778.18

CURVE WM 61.22 YT 396.14
  WR 558.32 LA 630.11 631.9
  OV 749.12 LL 761.10

CURVED CH 280.21 OC 283.11
  WR 558.32 567.34 LA 630.34
  631.28 GG 695.28 ML 741.35
  LL 761.26

CURVES EA 92.33 SU 537.2
  LA 633.18 GG 681.30

CURVING PO 106.16 WR 565.10
  RR 787.38

CUSHION DV 157.30 HD 452.20

CUSHIONS MO 6.39 WM 63.31 67.6
  EA 84.13 DV 161.14 EE 307.11
  RH 800.15

CUSTARD WS 255.25

CUSTOM LA 644.7 LL 761.36
  RR 781.40

CUSTOMER JD 620.32

CUSTOMS EE 305.18 308.29
  WR 549.13 BO 599.16

CUT MO 1.4 OA 34.22 SP 46.17
  50.38 PO 96.17 FG 189.9 195.5
  195.28 GF 235.24 WS 248.2
  249.30 253.42 261.4 CH 277.5
  277.16 280.41 OC 284.32
  EE 303.4 317.31 318.3 319.7
  319.8 319.21 319.27 320.18
  BL 358.42 WP 387.23 YT 403.25
  403.26 408.35 SD 421.18
  PR 491.4 WR 556.31 567.1
  BO 600.21 JD 619.17 NT 717.36
  718.10 ML 741.39 OV 757.5
  LL 773.7 MD 809.17 818.35

CUTS FG 190.35

CUTTING MO 3.28 TF 135.3 DV 174.17
  CH 275.35 EE 317.10 318.40
  BO 591.36 ML 732.19

CUTTING-SHORT WM 69.41

CUTTLEFISH SD 421.11 NT 719.6
  719.7 719.9

CYCLE MO 13.33 TF 125.19
  EE 320.30

CYCLING EE 318.5

CYNICALLY SS 200.16 SU 538.13

CYNICISM MO 15.1 WS 256.16
  TH 845.39

CYPRESS SU 530.7 530.12 531.6

CYPRESS (CONT.) 532.23
  532.30 534.28 534.35
  535.12 535.13 535.16
  536.13 537.23

CYRIL MO 4.4 6.9 12.26

CYRIL MERSHAM MO 1.12 10.30

CYRIL MERSHAM'S MO 12.10

DAB CH 282.7

DABBED OA 37.22 JD 618.36

DABBING SB 215.4

DAD DV 149.2 GF 243.20

DADDA SB 215.14 GF 238.3
  240.34

DADDY EE 316.2 316.3 316.41
  316.42 317.3 318.27
  SU 540.24 540.31 540.32
  540.35 540.37 541.3

DAD'S GF 236.19

DAEMONS PR 486.2

DAFFODIL PR 493.22 RH 794.36
  794.38 794.39 794.40
  795.14 795.28 795.40
  795.41 796.3 796.9
  797.2 797.4 797.9 797.31
  797.35

DAFFODILS MO 16.13 16.15
  HT 42.24 WM 55.18 SS 201.15
  202.1 202.42 PR 490.24
  493.23 LA 641.1

DAHLIAS FA 464.39 465.4

DAILY MO 4.12 EE 323.11
  HD 448.30 TB 516.17
  JD 617.40 ML 725.5
  RR 782.22

DAILY MIRROR MN 373.32

DAILY NEWS MO 6.7

DAILY SKETCH MN 373.32

DAINTILY PR 484.11

DAINTILY-SLIPPERED LL 777.14

DAINTY EE 309.7 PR 475.9
  476.21 478.34 479.4
  481.1 TB 523.33

DAIRY MO 3.21 BL 351.32
  351.34 WP 389.2

DAIS WR 576.21

DAISIES EA 86.9 91.17
  TF 118.40 119.12 CH 282.27
  TB 520.32 521.19

DAISY SC 268.21 MD 815.22

DAISY-LIKE WR 559.9

DAISY-SPIRIT EE 309.8

DALE TP 334.3 LL 762.22

DALLIED BM 827.17

DAMAGE SB 215.13 219.14
  OC 293.26 EE 313.7 YT 406.16
  NT 711.11 RH 801.6 801.7

DAMAGED EE 319.26 IL 652.38

DAME DE COMPAGNIE MD 811.17

DAMN HD 444.39 445.1 TB 519.9
  JD 628.3 IL 652.35 NT 718.41

DAMNABLY RR 782.34

DAMNATION TH 846.18

DAMNED PO 96.6 EE 325.34
  BL 361.24 PP 427.24 427.28
  428.8 428.21 428.35 GG 680.22
  681.3 RH 795.4 BM 841.39
  841.40

DAMP SC 268.30 OC 296.18
  TP 338.34 HD 454.22 456.29
  SU 534.24 IL 652.33 ML 736.14
  743.4 RR 788.2

DAMPER SP 50.40

DAMPNESS GF 240.11 ML 723.33
  738.29

DAMSEL WP 381.2

DAMSELS TP 341.12

DAMSONS FA 465.3

DAN PP 432.33 437.38 439.17
  439.32 440.20

DAN BERRY PP 432.35

DANCE TF 127.33 WS 252.4 253.3
  253.5 253.11 254.23 254.36
  255.1 256.10 256.17 257.12
  257.14 257.19 257.32 258.3
  258.6 261.34 261.41 WR 568.25
  569.4 569.13 569.16 569.28
  572.21 573.40 578.17 578.33
  579.5 579.13 579.31 580.15
  GG 682.15 682.17 682.22 683.3
  683.4 684.8 685.17 685.23
  686.13 687.26 NT 707.2 707.5
  707.41 RH 802.21 BM 832.10
  836.32

DANCED WS 251.27 256.15 257.8
  257.15 262.8 WR 576.26 578.24
  LA 635.27 GG 682.28 683.42
  686.15 686.28 687.7 687.31
  NT 707.15 BM 836.32

DANCER DV 140.1 WS 252.24

DANCERS WR 568.40 579.20 579.30

DANCER'S WR 569.7

DANCES MO 7.10 WS 252.3 257.10
  EE 308.29 312.2 LL 771.13

DANCE-STEP WR 578.24

DANCE-TREAD WR 579.8

DANCING PO 101.25 102.21 108.34
  TF 127.25 127.28 WS 254.10
  254.27 255.35 255.38 EE 309.7
  SU 543.33 WR 568.25 570.17
  570.18 578.23 579.7 580.8
  GG 682.30 685.19 685.41
  686.23 688.21 NT 714.41
  ML 730.17 BM 831.32

DANCING-GREEN OV 750.34 750.38

DANCING-ROOM WS 253.19 256.6

DANDIACAL SP 46.15

DANE OV 748.10

DANE'S OV 755.40

DANGER TF 131.36 EE 321.20
  321.32 BL 359.24 SD 424.21
  ML 724.8 OV 752.26 BM 836.2

DANGEREUSE GG 664.34

DANGEROUS MO 14.30 OA 27.6
  SP 51.25 TF 133.1 DV 143.28
  155.14 166.19 SS 209.10
  GF 238.27 WS 249.25 262.1
  OC 285.19 TP 335.16 YT 407.16
  SD 414.16 416.8 HD 445.34
  PR 478.1 TB 516.10 LA 637.14
  GG 699.37 NT 706.15 720.31
  RR 786.36

DANGEROUSLY HT 43.42 SP 51.33
  TP 345.17 MN 374.6 SD 414.12

DANGLED WS 246.3 SM 585.20
  IL 654.33

DANGLING WS 254.6 260.41 261.30
  TP 338.40 FA 459.8 465.1
  PR 495.31 TB 521.29 GG 687.36

DANIEL BERRY PP 427.23

DANIEL SUTTON PP 427.13

DANISH-LOOKING WP 388.30

DANK HD 446.25

DANSE MACABRE PP 428.32

DANS LA PREMIERE AUBERGE +
  GG 677.20

DAN'S PP 438.3

DANTE SS 209.36

DAPPER NT 705.36

DAPPLED PP 430.31 PR 490.24
  494.29 SU 538.2

DARE WM 66.20 66.21 PO 99.35

DARE (CONT.) FG 190.1*
  SD 417.12 PR 478.27
  TB 517.8 SU 544.35
  IL 651.30

DARED MO 7.22 OA 37.4
  TF 122.18 DV 137.14 149.18
  181.32 181.41 182.8 184.4
  FG 191.19 EE 322.10
  YT 403.23 SU 533.11
  WR 558.18 OV 751.2 752.40
  753.41 LL 771.33 778.10
  RH 793.5

DARE-DEVIL TP 334.25 NT 706.25

DARE-DEVILRY TF 118.4

DAREN'T GG 679.31 679.34
  BM 832.8 832.9

DARES SP 53.15

DARINGLY OA 26.10

DARK MO 3.8 3.29 4.5 9.17
  9.24 9.27 17.6 17.42 18.3
  19.14 19.21 19.29 21.40
  22.5 22.31 OA 23.27 24.7
  25.4 25.8 26.25 26.34
  27.24 27.27 29.30 SP 51.14
  WM 54.13 54.26 55.17
  55.37 63.18 65.20 65.36
  66.17 68.33 EA 77.23
  82.13 82.19 82.20 82.24
  82.28 PO 96.3 97.4 99.12
  99.19 100.8 100.10 102.9
  102.16 102.20 105.32
  106.23 107.2 107.30 111.37
  112.3 114.19 114.25 114.39
  115.10 115.14 TF 118.25
  119.13 122.3 123.32 127.10
  131.21 135.7 135.15
  DV 143.3 156.29 161.24
  166.14 167.15 167.17
  168.36 176.3 176.4 178.32
  FG 187.32 192.22 SS 198.7
  198.16 199.13 202.17 205.3
  206.34 211.12 SB 212.20
  214.3 214.18 214.28 217.9
  SG 224.16 224.28 225.8
  226.29 228.14 GF 234.21
  238.25 WS 251.22 251.38
  258.26 261.40 SC 267.4
  CH 275.33 276.38 OC 284.27
  286.35 287.2 287.4 290.33
  291.13 296.21 299.34
  300.42 301.1 EE 306.20
  306.23 306.25 306.26
  306.40 313.27 315.41 316.5
  316.9 322.1 323.25 323.27
  323.35 324.2 330.17 330.35
  330.36 330.38 331.2 331.33
  332.26 332.27 332.34
  TP 334.37 336.28 338.34
  341.13 341.20 BL 347.28
  348.17 351.36 352.36
  353.12 354.4 354.11 355.25
  357.8 357.24 359.41 361.17
  MN 368.19 371.6 371.32
  371.40 372.21 373.20 374.37
  WP 385.32 386.17 388.16
  389.34 389.38 YT 400.19
  401.33 407.30 SD 412.28

DARK (CONT.) 412.30 413.28
   414.14 414.23 415.39 416.17
   417.39 419.37 421.33 422.22
   PP 427.2 429.31 432.30 432.38
   433.18 433.26 433.34 433.38
   434.6 435.32 436.10 436.30
   436.41 437.12 437.28
   HD 441.22 447.31 448.41 450.9
   451.4 451.33 451.35 455.18
   455.21 456.8 456.15 FA 458.2
   465.29 PR 475.9 482.28 482.29
   483.3 483.7 484.8 484.22
   484.29 485.25 485.28 485.31
   489.11 489.33 489.41 490.24
   490.38 491.18 493.26 493.29
   494.27 494.29 494.39 495.21
   496.33 497.10 497.21 497.32
   499.18 499.36 500.2 501.10
   501.31 503.26 504.5 506.16
   506.25 507.17 507.21 511.12
   TB 513.17 515.31 521.25
   524.42 SU 530.39 530.40
   533.19 534.2 535.25 538.39
   539.5 540.18 542.32 WR 553.18
   553.26 553.30 553.38 553.40
   554.3 556.6 556.9 556.16
   557.1 557.7 557.8 557.17
   559.33 560.42 562.28 562.33
   563.9 563.12 563.17 563.29
   563.31 564.15 564.40 565.7
   565.10 566.17 566.30 567.25
   567.39 570.18 572.21 576.16
   576.20 577.4 577.6 577.8
   577.15 577.23 577.33 577.41
   578.18 579.16 579.19 579.34
   579.37 580.1 580.27 580.36
   SM 582.11 583.27 584.7 584.20
   586.17 BO 589.25 589.26
   589.31 594.27 595.27 596.15
   596.22 597.40 602.29 602.38
   JD 607.29 610.2 610.35 610.37
   611.21 618.8 621.26 624.23
   LA 630.4 630.6 630.8 630.17
   631.10 631.30 631.33 634.39
   635.33 635.34 636.5 636.14
   636.15 637.2 637.34 638.26
   639.38 IL 647.22 647.33
   649.34 654.3 GG 663.21 664.11
   664.22 666.34 668.33 668.34
   668.36 669.17 669.28 673.1
   681.26 683.8 683.21 683.31
   685.18 690.35 691.8 691.14
   692.19 694.26 696.23 696.38
   696.40 698.3 ML 723.32 723.34
   723.40 724.2 724.6 724.15
   724.38 725.3 733.26 738.28
   741.14 742.27 743.30 743.31
   744.22 745.36 746.1 OV 747.5
   749.10 753.11 755.29 758.30
   LL 763.20 765.35 766.15 773.6
   RR 785.2 RH 793.4 803.8
   MD 821.28 822.8 822.26 823.22
   BM 828.10 828.11 833.8 835.20
   841.28 842.42

DARK-AVISED SM 585.42

DARK-BEARDED ML 725.42

DARK-BLANKETED WR 577.40

DARK-BLUE OA 26.27 EA 73.8
   84.32 MN 367.41 WP 379.8
   382.19 PR 490.26 JD 624.32
   LA 634.21 637.9 BM 841.32

DARK-BROWED CH 276.15

DARK-BROWN WR 577.41 BM 839.38

DARK-COMPLEXIONED LL 762.13

DARKENED PO 113.31 EE 304.26
   TP 344.24 MN 374.23 WP 385.28
   HD 444.5 PR 484.27 WR 577.7
   ML 744.28 746.34 LL 775.26
   BM 835.19 842.41

DARKENING EE 324.26 MD 809.25

DARKER PO 104.32 MN 374.2
   PR 487.27 499.19 WR 552.32

DARK-FACED SU 542.38 WR 553.29
   580.19 SM 586.14 GG 666.37
   694.28

DARK-GREEN PO 95.5 95.12
   PR 506.23 507.9 BM 833.14
   834.31 835.27

DARK-GREY PP 429.27 JD 606.24
   625.12 ML 738.27

DARK-HEADED PR 495.28

DARKISH HT 40.22 PO 107.9
   DV 170.38 EE 309.11 YT 402.35

DARKLY MO 10.23 WM 68.42
   EA 83.4 DV 139.9 SS 200.14
   BL 355.34 WP 380.22 HD 447.22
   447.33 SU 543.34 WR 567.38
   BO 597.27 598.3 602.32
   LA 634.31 GG 698.26

DARKLY-STRETCHED EA 72.22

DARKLY-VISIBLE WR 562.40

DARKNESS MO 1.19 3.19 18.8
   22.26 22.32 OA 28.2 WM 60.32
   61.20 70.19 EA 83.17
   PO 104.20 115.11 115.13
   115.16 TF 123.9 DV 156.30
   167.21 181.4 182.21 182.27
   FG 188.42 190.37 191.18
   194.36 SG 225.17 GF 236.8
   WS 259.1 OC 286.6 286.28
   287.19 287.24 288.3 288.14
   295.27 EE 331.32 331.36
   331.37 332.2 332.29 332.31
   333.5 TP 338.18 338.36 340.31
   BL 347.25 350.35 352.30
   352.38 353.2 353.8 353.24
   353.26 353.36 354.19 355.20
   355.23 361.40 YT 401.38 402.8
   SD 411.6 411.9 411.11 411.26
   423.15 FA 458.6 459.36 461.39
   462.1 PR 503.27 SU 530.10
   WR 568.31 576.36 BO 595.23
   595.25 595.32 JD 609.9 609.23
   610.3 610.11 624.6 LA 632.19
   IL 651.1 651.33 GG 678.41
   698.31 ML 723.39 OV 748.41
   749.5 750.5 750.17 753.24
   759.22 LL 772.40 BM 834.25

DARKNESSES PO 114.17

DARK-PANELLED GG 669.38

DARK-PURPLE PP 436.6 OV 753.7

DARK-RED WP 379.33 TH 847.42

DARK-SCENTED OV 759.30

DARK-YELLOW TB 522.10

DARLING SB 212.17 WS 252.16
   255.11 OC 300.12 EE 303.21
   309.27 317.1 317.36 320.20
   321.18 321.28 WP 383.15
   383.30 PP 428.39 PR 475.38
   476.2 476.4 476.9
   SU 534.42 536.35 536.40
   LL 766.41 767.13

DARN SD 425.18 425.37 426.3
   426.4 426.5 TH 852.27

DARNED SD 425.39

DARNING MD 815.14

DART SB 216.11 WS 249.13

DARTED OA 24.36 27.16
   SP 51.32 WM 60.6 WP 379.25
   SD 415.11 421.6 LL 776.31

DARTING PO 113.17 EE 323.40
   WP 387.33 FA 464.1
   BM 843.7

DARTS NT 713.10

DARWIN MO 6.28

DASH MO 12.3 TP 336.34
   IL 651.8 ML 724.17

DASHED EA 83.36

DASHING WM 67.25 TB 521.36

DATA LL 763.42

DATE SU 542.5 GG 669.9

DATED LL 764.6

DATES WM 60.41

DAUBED BM 835.18

DAUGHTER HT 40.13 SP 52.12
   WM 56.14 56.34 TF 126.34
   DV 136.26 138.35 144.17
   158.11 183.32 FG 190.23
   191.25 SS 201.29 SC 272.12
   CH 278.34 OC 285.12 288.31
   EE 304.35 304.40 309.3
   YT 404.26 404.29 405.41
   406.8 SD 417.6 PP 438.1
   438.14 FA 463.20 PR 478.30
   478.33 TB 516.33 WR 550.27
   BO 587.13 LA 633.9
   GG 699.35 ML 725.40 731.6
   733.10 733.23 734.24
   734.27 734.30 735.2 736.17
   739.11 LL 762.15 769.37
   MD 805.10 805.12 805.34
   806.40 807.18 807.21
   807.26 807.31 810.26
   811.41 811.42 812.14

DEADENED HD 448.37 GG 667.37

DEADENING HD 448.39 GG 686.16

DEAD-GREY PR 493.42

DEADLOCK WM 67.10 PR 492.14

DEAD-LOOKING PR 509.41

DEADLY MO 6.34 EA 88.24
  OC 300.31 TP 344.8 FA 459.4
  460.8 SU 540.16 JD 609.18
  MD 816.21

DEADNESS EA 91.5 WR 547.1 547.2

DEAD-SEEMING GG 669.32

DEAD-WHITE MO 13.42 NT 713.16
  BM 833.14

DEAF BL 360.14 MN 377.26
  LA 630.24 632.37 633.8 634.28

DEAFNESS LA 631.25 638.14

DEAL OA 37.36 HT 40.24 SP 50.16
  DV 154.12 155.10 SS 205.35
  SB 212.34 219.24 EE 321.31
  TP 339.2 BL 347.18 347.19
  360.25 WP 384.38 YT 397.33
  SD 412.3 PP 437.17 PR 481.37
  TB 514.6 525.33 525.41
  SU 543.3 543.27 WR 567.20
  BO 589.41 JD 626.25 NT 709.4
  ML 728.7 732.27 741.12
  OV 758.10 758.42 759.7
  LL 761.4 778.8 RR 781.21
  MD 807.12 818.22 BM 829.40
  TH 845.28 845.34 846.7 847.20

DEALER HD 446.29

DEALERS HD 446.31 447.3

DEALING FA 467.14 LL 764.21

DEALINGS TF 127.7

DEALT WS 254.1 ML 726.8

DEAR OA 27.8 HT 39.25 WM 68.31
  EA 83.33 TF 117.24 DV 159.13
  FG 188.19 SS 211.24 GF 237.25
  WS 259.17 OC 300.4 300.20
  EE 311.5 311.21 318.14 319.7
  320.15 320.21 320.24 321.10
  321.14 BL 350.32 353.37
  354.13 355.12 358.29 360.38
  365.10 WP 381.3 381.8 381.12
  381.23 382.20 383.4 383.13
  383.27 384.1 384.3 FA 468.5
  PR 476.19 491.40 TB 522.12
  526.5 526.7 526.26 526.31
  527.25 JD 628.23 IL 647.1
  647.8 648.5 650.11 650.28
  654.10 659.5 GG 690.31 696.29
  696.35 697.3 LL 766.40 767.14
  767.19 767.37 774.14 774.17
  RR 780.36 781.18 RH 792.31
  MD 806.34 821.36 822.13
  822.14 822.15 826.29
  BM 828.31 828.36 TH 847.7
  847.18 852.42

DEAR EMILY JD 628.22

DEAREST BL 347.3 LL 775.7

DEARLY EA 79.24 91.31 92.34
  EE 317.17 PP 429.17 MD 822.14
  TH 849.6

DEAR MRS. PINNEGAR JD 628.21

DEARS SD 413.16 415.25
  TH 849.14

DEATH SP 51.10 WM 54.5 69.41
  EA 91.37 TF 129.26 133.17
  DV 149.35 154.8 163.29 174.24
  181.3 181.29 FG 190.37
  SB 220.9 WS 251.4 OC 299.11
  299.36 301.15 302.14
  EE 313.22 315.39 322.25
  326.24 329.41 331.39 331.40
  332.32 332.33 333.1 333.4
  333.8 BL 356.28 357.22
  WP 386.1 YT 407.13 409.26
  SD 412.35 421.2 PP 431.29
  439.30 HD 448.10 454.2
  PR 474.38 483.1 485.5 485.6
  485.7 506.37 509.42 SU 533.10
  WR 552.22 564.12 569.30
  574.33 BO 594.26 597.19
  598.14 604.27 604.36
  JD 616.28 GG 674.13 674.14
  678.30 691.33 NT 702.9 703.29
  703.30 703.34 703.37 712.16
  712.21 713.34 719.2 720.38
  ML 724.10 737.7 OV 756.3
  757.36 LL 769.24

DEATH-AGONY EE 332.38

DEATH-GOD JD 609.17

DEATH-HORROR PP 439.29

DEATHLY PO 106.27 SS 208.8
  OC 296.22 WR 557.21 GG 678.1
  ML 744.5 RR 783.32

DEATH-MADNESS EE 332.18

DEATH-MASK JD 616.26

DEATH'S-HEAD FA 468.27

DEATH-WORSHIP PR 482.40

DEBATED PR 474.33 507.3
  GG 667.23

DEBAUCHED DV 164.40

DEBONAIR WP 388.22 SU 540.36
  GG 688.16

DEBRIS GF 241.30 PR 490.9
  MD 811.13 TH 853.19

DEBT MO 20.41 HD 446.34 447.12
  TB 516.19 520.16 RH 799.38
  MD 809.30

DEBTS PO 96.25 DV 145.5
  SC 269.15 TB 516.12 519.26
  RR 780.33

DECAMERON PR 477.13

DECANTERS BL 359.6 MD 824.2

DECAY PR 490.10 GG 680.11

DECAYED LA 645.19

DECEIVE DV 163.23 168.10
  BO 590.13

DECEIVED DV 166.7 NT 707.23
  707.24

DECEMBER WR 573.12

DECENT HT 39.26 PO 111.3
  DV 145.16 145.38 SC 267.8
  EE 308.15 MN 366.16
  YT 409.1 409.6 BO 602.37
  LA 637.18 637.33 IL 649.15
  657.40 GG 690.4 LL 777.8
  RR 779.34

DECENTLY TH 851.31

DECIDE DV 172.2 EE 327.19
  WP 379.37 TB 518.35
  JD 628.25 MD 818.7

DECIDED SP 48.5 WP 387.16
  PR 478.6 502.7 SM 582.1
  BO 593.15 604.20 JD 609.26
  IL 659.41 ML 728.40 741.3
  741.19 MD 808.41 809.6
  809.13 818.9 BM 834.23
  TH 849.32

DECIDEDLY DV 185.38 IL 649.21

DECIPHERED LL 764.33

DECISION TF 121.34 DV 151.26
  184.24 SB 216.13 TP 344.19
  BL 352.21 TB 520.21
  WR 577.20 IL 659.13

DECISIVE GF 239.12 PR 473.29
  488.16

DECISIVELY EA 75.2 SB 218.39
  PR 505.25 JD 625.40
  LA 637.22 IL 656.25
  GG 677.8

DECLAIMED YT 400.12

DECLAIMING WR 578.2

DECLARATION YT 396.23
  FA 471.3

DECLARE TP 335.17 SD 418.18
  418.30 FA 470.42 GG 662.35

DECLARED SP 47.31 50.22
  SC 271.30 271.33 TP 337.16
  LA 637.40 GG 663.16 666.4

DECLARING CH 282.26

DECLINE TP 337.17

DECLINED HD 446.32

DECLIVITY ML 730.21

DECOMPOSING PO 115.22 GG 691.23

DECORATED PR 485.1 WR 555.3

DECORATIONS WR 556.11

DECORATORS MD 811.35

DECREE EE 309.16

DEED GG 690.24

DEEDS EE 326.40 326.41

DEEMED ML 737.4

DEEP MO 13.12 20.30 HT 40.22
  SP 51.2 WM 58.38 59.3 63.31
  66.22 66.28 68.4 69.17
  EA 82.29 84.14 91.3 92.4
  PO 95.9 95.27 96.19 98.35
  100.20 101.1 103.12 111.40
  112.34 TF 118.20 120.31 121.7
  122.14 132.11 135.15
  DV 139.25 143.20 145.8 153.40
  155.13 155.34 164.1 164.41
  FG 193.30 SS 201.11 205.29
  205.38 210.16 GF 236.23
  WS 262.19 262.42 CH 281.24
  EE 308.2 309.28 317.31 319.7
  330.26 331.4 331.6 BL 351.6
  WP 385.28 385.36 YT 397.15
  398.1 SD 421.32 HD 449.21
  450.11 453.26 PR 474.23
  489.16 500.37 501.7 502.38
  506.23 507.11 TB 519.34
  SU 528.24 529.11 531.33
  533.34 533.37 534.31 535.19
  535.25 536.35 540.4 540.21
  543.42 WR 546.19 552.11 555.4
  563.16 564.16 568.38 569.27
  572.35 581.5 581.24 SM 582.8
  BO 599.33 LA 631.26 642.39
  643.34 GG 663.8 668.35 675.35
  681.2 684.27 694.7 694.13
  698.5 698.12 698.13 698.14
  698.16 698.18 698.19 698.22
  698.23 698.27 NT 709.18
  717.35 721.8 ML 734.3 744.18
  744.26 746.6 LL 762.30 763.22
  767.34 774.33 774.42 775.2
  775.8 RH 790.32 MD 826.18
  BM 828.12

DEEP-BLONDE DV 160.19

DEEPEN GG 684.30

DEEPENED BL 349.23 SM 584.30
  NT 716.34

DEEPENING WM 54.26 FA 459.36
  BM 831.12

DEEPER OA 36.30 EA 82.33
  PO 97.32 114.18 TF 130.8
  DV 147.27 150.7 EE 306.9
  309.29 331.7 BL 352.38
  HD 449.42 450.15 450.23
  TB 515.31 SU 528.10 528.21
  535.20 JD 608.17 GG 665.12
  683.41 ML 737.33 OV 753.24

DEEPEST MO 4.15 EA 82.35
  EE 327.1 328.23

DEEPLY MO 4.18 11.1 20.33
  OA 32.31 PO 99.40 TF 120.39
  132.9 DV 171.24 WS 249.40
  261.5 OC 293.42 BL 358.39
  MN 371.18 YT 402.23 HD 450.18
  PR 503.34 SU 541.29 WR 559.33
  573.38 GG 696.2 NT 701.34
  OV 751.27 LL 773.19 TH 847.3

DEEPLY-MOVING MO 22.2

DEEPS GG 698.28 699.23

DEEP-SET SU 528.25

DEEP-SOILED EE 307.13

DEEP-TONED MD 807.38

DEER FG 193.32 EE 316.37
  PR 486.21 486.25 486.33 487.8
  494.11 495.15 495.17 507.24
  508.21 OV 759.39

DEER-MEAT PR 507.27

DEE-URR WP 382.34 383.27 386.29

DEFEAT GG 682.39 MD 820.8
  825.11

DEFEATED TP 343.29 BO 600.31
  MD 820.5 820.7 820.10

DEFECT TF 131.42

DEFENCELESS MO 7.24 WM 65.7

DEFEND DV 146.10 FG 188.20
  191.41 GF 242.9

DEFENDED DV 144.17 164.42

DEFENSIVE MO 21.25 PP 427.18

DEFERENCE OC 292.15 TB 516.21
  ML 727.23 728.38 729.9

DEFERENTIAL MO 16.30 OA 34.20
  DV 172.27 172.34 GG 663.25
  OV 752.12

DEFIANCE SS 199.12 WS 261.36
  CH 275.16 TP 344.25 PP 427.9
  BO 602.2 GG 678.10 678.12

DEFIANT OA 25.11 29.5 EA 90.25
  PP 438.27 FA 466.19 467.30
  468.20 BO 602.2 GG 683.26

DEFIANTLY SB 219.17 OC 284.22
  PP 427.14 431.31

DEFICIENT EA 90.2 90.3
  BL 361.22

DEFINE BL 361.6

DEFINITE PO 99.33 TF 117.28
  DV 145.20 174.9 OC 284.8
  PR 485.39 SU 544.10 JD 614.3
  GG 699.7 NT 718.2 LL 777.41

DEFINITELY PO 115.26 DV 138.5
  SG 230.14 PP 433.41
  PR 473.22 474.10 BO 598.1
  JD 612.27 BM 829.9
  TH 851.29

DEFT PR 483.20

DEFTLY WR 564.4

DEFY EE 326.30

DEGENERATING PR 482.34

DEGRADATION EE 328.30
  BO 591.41 592.7

DEGRADED DV 156.7 WS 249.5
  EE 328.28 BO 592.7

DEGRADING ML 741.10

DEGREE PO 97.27 TF 127.10
  TB 516.9

DEJECTED SG 221.18

DEJECTEDLY WR 553.4 IL 658.11
  658.15 BM 839.23

DEJECTION PR 491.26 GG 674.40

DELAY WM 57.11 CH 274.26
  EE 321.19 RR 785.3

DELEGATION WR 549.10

DELIBERATE CH 274.11
  JD 625.39

DELIBERATELY SP 53.18
  DV 157.33 WP 388.14
  HD 449.41 FA 466.9
  GG 694.8 MD 811.32 TH 846.2

DELICACY OA 30.28 YT 403.13
  SM 583.34 GG 663.28
  ML 737.9 RR 782.6

DELICATE OA 24.9 HT 40.38
  WM 59.6 DV 159.24 SB 217.29
  EE 305.28 TP 335.19
  BL 354.37 358.12 358.42
  364.30 WP 382.18 388.19
  YT 401.40 PP 437.11
  HD 453.22 454.30 PR 476.24
  485.35 485.36 489.18
  494.7 494.9 494.26 508.8
  SU 534.12 GG 663.23 683.37
  ML 726.24 734.30 737.42
  738.1 LL 770.18 770.22
  774.9 RR 782.1 MD 809.24
  BM 827.31

DELICATE-COMPLEXIONED PR 482.2

DELICATELY SG 223.3 BL 355.17
  MN 373.9 WP 388.21
  YT 401.39 FA 460.41
  WR 564.9 SM 586.9 GG 685.20
  ML 737.17 BM 827.33

DELICATELY-WILD GG 693.8

DELICATE-STEMMED PR 494.8

DELICIOUS OA 33.22 TF 132.33
  133.4 SS 203.11 SB 217.30
  WS 252.23 253.14 254.35
  257.20

DELICIOUSLY EA 91.40 WS 252.31
  252.36 WR 572.13

DELIGHT TF 122.14 EE 305.30
  328.35 SD 418.37 LA 635.25
  638.28 OV 753.19

DELIGHTED MO 19.18 SP 46.27
  50.31 WM 55.33 56.36
  SB 214.24 WS 254.22 255.12
  EE 305.11 MN 371.17 WP 383.37
  LA 639.9 IL 650.13 RH 794.8

DELIGHTFUL MO 15.6 19.23
  DV 166.18 SG 222.22 WS 244.9
  245.5 249.12 250.10 EE 305.31
  306.3 308.16 TH 844.24

DELINQUENT MD 812.27

DELIRIOUS YT 405.18 JD 614.29

DELIRIUM PO 112.17 112.36
  115.18

DELIVER PR 478.15 JD 628.34

DELIVERED EA 72.30 GF 243.24
  HD 448.29 JD 628.35

DELIVERING TF 118.3 DV 138.39
  142.38 WR 564.37

DELIVERY SP 46.37 47.6

DELPHINIUMS BM 833.21

DELUDED BO 592.38

DEMAND EA 76.33 PO 115.39

DEMANDED OA 25.14 DV 184.11
  SD 424.16 PR 476.34 BO 598.11
  IL 653.11 653.19

DEMANDING NT 706.34

DE MAUPASSANT, GUY (SEE GUY
  DE MAUPASSANT)

DEMEAN HD 447.23

DEMEANOUR WR 566.9

DEMOCRATIC EE 327.30 YT 399.39
  JD 626.20 BM 839.26 840.14

DEMOLISHED MD 812.41

DEMON YT 405.29 PR 475.21
  475.24 475.25 475.29 475.30
  483.34 483.35 497.23
  NT 714.40 715.30

DEMONISH PR 475.34 501.23
  501.27 506.37 WR 559.38
  BO 595.36 JD 610.10 ML 745.35

DEMONISH-HEATHEN BO 595.39

DEMON-LIKE PR 490.39

DEMONS FG 194.1 PR 475.32
  475.33 475.40 506.36 TB 523.7
  JD 610.9

DEMURE TH 844.4

DEMURELY SM 583.14

DEMURRED SC 267.30

DEN EE 306.22

DENIAL PO 103.31 DV 154.8

DENIED EA 73.24 PO 103.30
  OC 299.39 301.9 301.12 301.34
  OV 753.35

DENLEY'S EE 321.23

DENOTES SC 267.6

DENOUNCING FA 467.9

DENSE DV 173.10 173.11 182.20
  PR 494.2 495.41 499.30
  WR 568.35

DENSER WS 254.29 EE 315.28

DENSITY SM 585.16

DENUDED MD 826.2

DENY EA 73.26 73.31 DV 144.2
  150.25 156.1 SD 426.18
  FA 470.34 OV 758.38

DENYING GG 693.38 MD 808.42

DEPART EA 79.9 WP 392.31
  PP 435.23 TB 522.40 GG 682.42
  MD 826.3 BM 832.15

DEPARTED TF 125.32 129.11
  131.20 DV 176.12 SS 211.30
  211.32 SB 219.19 YT 396.25
  SD 418.4 FA 460.37 468.28
  PR 512.16 SU 529.32 WR 550.19
  IL 649.5 GG 685.15 TH 851.17

DEPARTING PR 501.13 TB 524.17
  WR 549.38 JD 606.35

DEPARTMENT MD 805.1 814.31

DEPARTURE WM 59.31 TF 130.28
  DV 142.36 TB 520.22 WR 549.40
  BO 590.32 ML 731.39 MD 807.5

DEPARTURES ML 731.36

DEPEND OC 287.14 BL 357.10
  MN 368.11

DEPENDED DV 137.18 164.12
  EE 308.13 TB 513.35 GG 663.3
  ML 730.8 RR 780.3

DEPENDENCE BL 357.10 BO 601.38

DEPENDENT EE 310.41 328.3
  LL 762.10

DEPENDENTS ML 734.39

DEPENDING HD 447.9

DEPENDS FA 461.23 WR 549.4

DEPLORABLE NT 718.22

DEPLORED OA 26.22 OC 292.33

DE POICTIERS, DIANE (SEE
  DIANE DE POICTIERS)

DEPOSED EA 92.26

DEPOSIT SP 51.2 RH 797.25

DEPOSITED HT 43.12 RH 798.40
  BM 834.40

DEPOT TP 335.12 336.29
  340.21 340.24

DEPRAVITY ML 743.15

DEPRECATING OA 38.32
  SS 201.36 SD 414.31
  JD 615.23

DEPRECATINGLY TB 523.1
  BO 601.27

DEPRESSED DV 156.27 WS 261.1
  YT 409.21 GG 666.18 685.34
  ML 739.12

DEPRESSING MN 376.17
  GG 686.27 689.1

DEPRESSION BL 347.35 347.36
  HD 450.6 GG 677.14 685.34

DEPRIVATION BL 360.41

DEPRIVE JD 622.8

DEPTH MO 8.28 EA 83.18
  TF 120.38 DV 160.38
  WR 572.36 GG 698.24
  TH 845.25

DEPTHS SP 50.11 WS 259.38
  SU 537.32 WR 566.18 573.23
  580.25 SM 583.38 GG 698.13
  698.22

DEPUTY SC 269.23 269.30
  269.39 OC 293.22

DERAILED NT 708.34

DERANGED SG 226.31 228.5

DERBY RH 800.4 800.31 800.32
  800.40 801.2 801.12 801.23
  802.9 802.16 803.36

DERBYSHIRE MO 2.10 SP 51.31
  GG 664.8 664.9 666.16
  667.22 668.29 668.33
  669.15

DERIDING JD 617.27

DERISION TP 335.14 WR 555.32

DERISION (CONT.) 557.33 557.37
570.33 BO 602.27 LA 633.27

DERISIVE YT 400.12 JD 617.27
LA 633.18 633.21

DERISIVELY LA 631.19

DERIVED DV 153.4 ML 742.42
TH 847.40

DESCEND PR 487.41 498.12
IL 655.16

DESCENDANTS WP 382.33 PR 482.21
WR 550.5

DESCENDED DV 139.7 160.39
OC 293.19 WR 562.20 576.25
ML 725.20 LL 770.11 RR 786.1

DESCENDING DV 160.24 OC 297.40
WR 566.1 574.8 574.22
RR 785.38

DESCENT PR 498.41 WR 559.6

DESCRIBE LA 633.39

DESCRIBED GG 679.12

DESCRIPTIONS EA 86.7

DESERT EE 325.22 PR 481.22
482.20 489.1 493.29 496.16
496.17 497.36 WR 548.36
BO 595.9

DESERTED TF 117.14 WS 259.1
OC 287.20 MN 376.38 YT 395.22
PP 436.33 437.27 WR 548.30
551.18 ML 741.40

DESERTING OC 292.27 SD 419.38

DESERTION JD 610.36

DESERTS BM 827.18 835.30

DESERVE YT 408.10 NT 720.3

DESERVEDLY MD 817.3

DESIGNED SP 45.5

DESIGNS GF 241.26

DESIRABLE MO 20.1 EE 310.18
310.27 323.4

DESIRE MO 22.1 EA 82.37
TF 123.33 127.22 129.20 130.3
133.12 DV 147.26 166.23
181.31 181.35 SB 219.39
WS 257.2 257.12 260.21 264.29
EE 306.19 308.22 308.23 313.5
313.6 322.25 323.39 326.23
326.30 BL 365.12 YT 407.6
HD 452.12 FA 466.17 PR 474.21
493.36 504.15 506.37 509.3
510.5 SU 529.41 529.42 544.17
544.32 WR 557.29 568.20
JD 629.6 IL 659.36 659.37
GG 676.11 697.32 697.35
697.38 ML 735.14 735.15

DESIRE (CONT.) 737.10 737.37
738.1 738.3 738.5 738.35
739.1 741.22 OV 751.20 752.35
BM 830.29 832.30 833.2 837.20

DESIRED MO 4.34 15.27 EA 80.12
EE 312.10 TB 516.7

DESIRELESS ML 737.41

DESIRELESSNESS ML 737.8

DESIRES OA 37.11 WM 54.11
YT 406.36 PR 497.1 ML 731.30

DESIROUS DV 146.39 NT 717.42

DESIST OA 24.35

DESISTED MN 368.41

DESK DV 151.27 BM 840.38

DESOLATE EE 305.3 YT 394.5
SD 411.12 411.31 HD 441.6
446.23

DESOLATION MO 1.7 TP 339.24
BL 356.38 356.41

DESPAIR MO 10.37 SP 50.11
WM 62.9 69.40 DV 175.9 175.22
175.31 TP 339.25 FA 465.33
PR 483.11 490.11 505.3 506.12
506.32 507.5 OV 755.33
LL 771.1

DESPAIRING PR 502.13

DESPAIRINGLY WM 68.31

DESPERATE TF 120.25 SB 212.12
BL 353.36 HD 450.26 TB 527.29
SU 544.31 SM 586.27 JD 608.31
609.25 627.38 IL 650.5

DESPERATELY TF 120.17 TP 335.9
JD 612.40 627.41 IL 647.11
650.35 TH 844.32

DESPERATION SG 230.18 EE 324.33
IL 648.5

DESPICABLE DV 165.34 GF 243.26
BM 832.6

DESPISE MO 6.33 DV 166.5
EE 310.17 TB 515.6

DESPISED DV 150.30 EE 327.20
BL 359.39 MN 370.9 YT 409.21
FA 466.12 GG 692.25 NT 710.40
717.34 LL 768.22

DESPISES TH 845.12

DESPISING BO 589.30

DESPITE MD 814.41

DESSAY SD 424.27

DESSERT GG 676.30

DESTINATION WR 552.37 BO 600.27

DESTINY EE 311.6 WR 549.36
BO 590.42 591.10 591.11
MD 822.20 822.21 825.35

DESTROY WM 68.12 EA 76.30
WS 264.19 264.30 EE 322.14
BL 364.23 JD 607.35

DESTROYED TF 125.13
BL 348.36 WR 569.39
BO 597.2 OV 759.11

DESTROYING MO 16.33

DESTRUCTION MO 2.37 DV 154.9
GF 238.27 BO 591.11 591.13

DESTRUCTIVE SG 230.39
BO 593.12

DESULTORILY BL 361.13
LL 764.22 TH 848.40

DESULTORY HT 42.23 EE 323.4
HD 441.7 FA 458.7

DETACHED EA 73.12 TF 122.38
DV 149.23 SB 213.17 217.16
WS 256.23 256.36 258.10
263.6 OC 300.37 SD 424.20

DETACHMENT PR 479.8 SU 533.2

DETAIL GG 679.13

DE-TAIL OA 31.37

DETAILS OA 32.16 JD 627.31
NT 721.10 BM 834.7

DETAINED WS 256.17

DETAINING WS 258.29 MN 378.16

DETAININGLY BO 596.24

DETECT LL 772.33

DETECTED HD 449.22 WR 565.36

DETERIORATING TB 518.3

DETERMINATION OA 25.37
SD 421.1 PR 498.28
LA 642.19 GG 663.2
RR 779.14

DETERMINED OA 32.12 34.3
HT 41.33 SP 50.35 EA 79.37
PO 95.23 DV 175.17
TP 339.28 MN 375.1
WP 379.35 379.36 384.21
SU 534.28 JD 612.41
LA 642.17 642.18 IL 655.41
RH 795.35 799.27 MD 812.8
BM 836.12

DETERMINEDLY SG 230.7
OC 288.5

DETERRENT EE 327.29

DETERRING MN 369.37

DETESTED BL 359.27

DIGNITY (CONT.) DV 149.1
   SB 217.16 GF 240.1 CH 278.32
   OC 299.10 MN 370.23 PR 474.18
   492.27 ML 732.23 MD 809.8
   814.4 BM 834.10 834.11 838.20
   TH 849.21

DILAPIDATED PP 436.26 PR 500.22
   500.26

DILATED MO 9.29 16.14 OA 26.34
   30.15 EA 90.22 90.28 PP 434.6
   434.16 PR 511.26 NT 702.21

DILIGENTLY MO 11.17 TB 521.26
   GG 661.4

DIM MO 5.8 EA 91.30 91.35
   92.38 PO 103.25 SS 207.24
   CH 278.10 OC 291.14 299.5
   BL 351.1 352.27 SD 413.36
   PP 436.28 HD 451.4 SU 531.11
   WR 563.23 570.13 SM 582.20
   BO 595.6 595.38 597.14
   LA 639.32 IL 651.1 ML 742.39
   744.30 LL 768.30 MD 810.41
   811.5

DIMINISHED EA 73.8 SD 415.24
   WR 578.28 GG 681.9

DIMINISHING GG 669.40

DIM-LIT ML 735.17

DIMLY MO 13.3 WM 68.10 EA 91.21
   TF 129.13 DV 166.11 SG 225.13
   GF 241.33 BL 354.8 368.18
   HD 452.3 455.17 BO 592.23
   593.4 595.31 596.1 597.12
   GG 669.39 MD 825.3

DIMMED DV 161.23 WR 547.15
   RR 788.23

DIMNESS MO 18.19 DV 161.1
   FG 190.34 BO 597.23 LA 636.4
   IL 651.2 OV 751.33

DIMPLES WM 65.28

DINE EA 90.17 SS 202.22

DINED FG 187.28

DINERS GG 673.31

DINGY DV 155.9 158.41

DINING-ROOM OA 24.6 DV 146.6
   183.37 GF 236.39 WS 255.18
   255.21 BL 351.1 357.14
   PP 437.8 438.21 HD 441.9
   451.20 RR 783.35

DINNER HT 42.37 SP 52.23 53.23
   EA 87.41 88.5 88.20 91.23
   91.27 91.39 DV 162.3 163.3
   169.10 169.13 169.20 169.33
   170.19 178.6 FG 187.36
   SS 201.12 201.29 SG 223.39
   229.14 229.19 GF 236.2 236.41
   237.9 SC 268.4 268.16 268.20
   268.23 CH 277.1 OC 286.25
   288.9 288.11 291.19 EE 305.35

DINNER (CONT.) 318.27 BL 358.4
   PP 436.15 438.41 440.3 440.16
   PR 475.6 481.28 TB 516.34
   BO 594.37 JD 617.13 618.23
   620.31 625.20 628.1 IL 648.40
   GG 666.22 666.32 NT 706.24
   720.13 720.14 OV 748.5
   754.16 LL 775.31 RR 779.2
   781.12 783.12 MD 815.22
   815.26 816.4 818.11 818.17
   818.18 820.14 822.40

DINNER-DRESS RR 784.14

DINNER-JACKET GG 670.24 MD 823.2

DINNER-PARTY GG 674.42

DINNERS MO 5.8 5.21 CH 274.4
   GG 689.13 MD 812.3

DINNER'S WM 61.39

DINNER-TABLE SS 201.19

DINNER-TIME GG 679.6 689.12
   MD 815.38

DIONYSUS OV 758.25

DIP EE 303.2 HD 448.42 449.3

DIPLOMAT RR 780.18

DIPLOMATIC RR 780.15

DIPPED WM 54.27 SS 210.18
   GF 234.4 PR 490.32

DIPPING MN 376.5

DIRECT EA 82.33 PO 97.5 97.17
   TF 125.9 DV 165.41 PP 434.6
   HD 449.18 449.35 PR 473.18
   TB 522.33 JD 606.4 NT 719.14
   ML 737.24

DIRECTED JD 610.12

DIRECTING BM 843.5

DIRECTION OA 30.40 EA 77.4
   TF 122.28 122.33 DV 153.24
   GF 236.12 EE 312.37 313.13
   315.25 330.3 331.1 MN 372.16
   376.22 WP 392.33 SD 418.3
   PP 432.16 FA 462.42 467.16
   470.28 SU 541.31 BO 596.13
   596.18 JD 612.26 ML 732.32
   LL 763.12

DIRECTIONS EA 72.22 GF 238.19
   EE 330.9 GG 689.17

DIRECTLY MO 7.22 8.37 20.39
   OA 36.34 WM 67.42 FG 193.33
   SG 228.16 WS 253.2 OC 285.9
   286.38 287.33 LA 633.19
   GG 679.21 688.41

DIRECTNESS DV 155.33 OC 294.6

DIRT DV 180.14 CH 279.3 280.20
   JD 616.41 TH 851.6

DIRT-EATING TH 852.28

DIRTY MO 17.5 DV 142.23
   155.22 178.22 182.10
   OC 289.20 EE 329.9 330.21
   BL 352.19 SD 418.1 418.31
   419.37 419.38 419.39
   WR 549.23 557.9
   GG 661.27 ML 744.23
   OV 747.29 MD 810.28 819.39

DIRTY-LOOKING GG 683.7

DISABLED LL 767.16

DISADVANTAGE DV 151.39
   YT 397.32 MD 820.7

DISAFFECTED DV 136.32

DISAGREE MO 13.11

DISAGREEABLE PP 439.8
   BO 587.33

DISAGREEABLY OA 31.4

DISAGREED GG 663.4 663.5

DISAPPEAR EE 310.22 MN 377.33
   SU 534.32 GG 698.42

DISAPPEARED CH 280.23
   BL 364.35 WP 389.23
   SD 413.27 FA 470.29
   PR 506.30 507.7 SU 532.33
   LA 637.6 GG 672.36 699.2
   699.8 ML 743.19 745.36
   BM 840.13

DISAPPEARING WR 558.31
   LA 643.16 GG 687.13

DISAPPOINTED MO 11.19
   SS 205.37 GF 236.9
   CH 274.34 LL 774.27
   TH 845.27 845.29 846.42
   847.3 847.19

DISAPPOINTMENT MO 4.7 17.22
   WM 60.5 DV 145.6 171.27
   GF 236.23 FA 461.6
   PR 492.23

DISAPPROVAL MO 19.10
   OC 292.4 OV 757.8

DISAPPROVE SS 207.30 207.31

DISAPPROVING DV 177.21
   LA 641.7 OV 757.4

DISARMED ML 726.5

DISARMING ML 726.3

DISASTER PO 101.39 OC 292.28
   HD 441.28 GG 667.17

DISASTROUSLY MD 805.20

DISBELIEF WS 255.21

DISCARDED MO 13.5

DISCERN WR 576.30

DISCERNMENT BL 358.12

DISCHARGE WP 381.42

DISCHARGED DV 170.14

DISCIPLE EA 86.16 86.18

DISCIPLINE PO 98.13 99.14
TF 118.2 DV 143.32 148.13
150.39 164.28 184.4

DISC-LIKE PR 499.32

DISCLOSED SS 206.29

DISCLOSING BM 835.16

DISCOLOURED ML 745.42

DISCOMFITED MN 371.5

DISCOMFORT MO 6.12 CH 278.41
WP 379.14

DISCONCERTED SB 212.22

DISCONCERTING PR 482.4 GG 677.10

DISCONNECTED CH 280.31 PR 488.14

DISCONSOLATE SG 228.28 GF 234.6
LL 773.8

DISCONSOLATION WR 572.35

DISCONTENT GF 234.28 GG 662.17

DISCONTENTED GG 662.37

DISCONTINUE BL 349.29

DISCONTINUED PR 474.24

DISCORD MO 5.13 6.13 WM 60.13
62.32 CH 276.37 OV 755.12

DISCORDANCE LL 777.32

DISCORDANT PR 493.40

DISCOURSE CH 279.23 279.36

DISCOVER FG 191.14 SB 214.23
SG 227.36

DISCOVERED SS 210.9 NT 706.32
OV 755.26 RH 799.14

DISCOVERING EA 86.21

DISCOVERY BM 829.13

DISCREET TP 337.40 RR 783.29
RH 790.19

DISCREETLY TP 338.7 LL 775.20
RR 788.27

DISCRIMINATION ML 741.24

DISCS PR 493.21

DISCUSS WM 56.38 BL 347.18

DISCUSSED TF 131.8 FA 464.5
ML 729.21 735.41 LL 764.34

DISCUSSING MO 12.41 ML 728.24
OV 747.33

DISEASE CH 274.13 YT 395.16
BO 592.1 JD 608.6 ML 730.33
LL 768.23

DISEASED WM 66.8

DISEMBARKED ML 729.30

DISEMBODIED GG 694.2 ML 742.35

DISEMBODIMENT GG 690.10 693.33

DISEMBOWELLED PO 105.36

DISENGAGE EA 82.40

DISENGAGED DV 181.31

DISFIGURE WR 561.27

DISFIGURED PO 103.38 TF 117.22
GF 243.27 BL 363.15 364.12

DISFIGUREMENT BL 363.16

DISFIGURING BL 347.7

DISGRACE DV 143.25

DISGRACEFUL YT 405.5 BO 591.20

DISGUISING BM 833.39

DISGUST MO 3.10 EA 75.14
DV 138.1 GF 242.6 TP 345.6
PP 427.30 MD 805.33 819.33

DISGUSTED OA 32.36 NT 712.5

DISGUSTING YT 405.8 NT 703.15
MD 817.4

DISH HT 41.29 TF 125.34
SS 203.6 GG 673.42 ML 743.21

DISHEARTENED WR 552.38 BO 599.1

DISHEARTENING BO 599.11

DISHED SC 268.4

DISHES PO 100.39 101.27 101.32
102.1 SS 202.35 CH 275.8
HD 445.5 PR 502.22 SU 528.36
IL 648.42 TH 850.35

DISHEVELLED GF 241.32 243.26
OC 284.2 SD 422.36 MD 807.40

DISHONESTY OA 33.32

DISHONOUR DV 141.34 141.35

DISHONOURED CH 278.3

DISILLUSION EE 303.23 314.19

DISILLUSIONED TH 847.3

DISILLUSIONMENT MO 11.26
OC 284.12

DISINTEGRATED PO 105.11
BO 599.5

DISINTEGRATING BO 593.14
JD 621.18

DISINTERESTED MD 820.41

DISLIKE MO 14.5 YT 402.23
PR 508.34 LA 643.19
ML 736.38 740.41 LL 776.2

DISLIKED DV 147.26 150.30
155.25 SG 229.13 EE 326.39
326.40 BL 354.3 357.1
357.2 357.3 YT 394.27
GG 662.20 692.34 ML 740.38
741.7 MD 815.7 BM 828.5

DISLIKES ML 727.35

DISLIKING NT 709.8

DISMAL GF 234.28 WP 386.9
PP 437.3 BO 593.22 598.34
JD 610.24 GG 673.18

DISMALLY HD 442.27 FA 458.28
459.24

DISMAY EE 313.16 MN 377.26
PR 511.27 GG 691.37

DISMAYED PR 501.4 LA 632.27

DISMISSED OA 37.26 DV 151.11

DISMISSING MD 825.12

DISMOUNT TP 335.6

DISMOUNTED PR 498.20 510.10
511.30

DISOBEDIENCE EE 316.27

DISORDER SD 411.12 WR 563.6

DISORDERED GF 239.21

DISORDERLY WR 563.11

DISOWN MD 813.5

DISPASSIONATE DV 148.31
149.32 PR 479.4 OV 749.31

DISPATCH-CASE LA 630.9 631.24

DISPERSED PO 106.38

DISPLACE TF 126.10

DISPLAY TB 520.30

DISPLAYED WS 245.29 CH 274.18
OC 288.26 BM 832.28

DISPLAYING IL 654.12

DISPLEASED WS 246.31

DISPLEASURE WM 62.36 66.22

DISPOSAL MD 825.1

DISPOSE ML 732.37

DISPOSED OA 38.41

DISPOSES EA 92.9 GF 236.7

DISPOSING DV 154.7

DISREGARDED MO 5.34

DISREPUTABLE CH 274.16

DISSATISFIED PR 486.24 486.28
  RH 799.21

DISSIPATE EE 326.19

DISSOLUTION CH 282.22 EE 332.41
  333.2 ML 742.28

DISSOLVE EA 76.5 SU 530.41
  531.1

DISSOLVED HD 442.31 TB 522.34
  LL 766.34

DISSOLVING EE 333.1 ML 742.28

DISTANCE WM 55.14 TF 117.5
  129.34 DV 138.27 173.18
  SB 213.3 214.3 GF 237.14
  238.32 SC 267.12 OC 302.7
  EE 323.26 330.15 TP 335.27
  336.25 338.40 345.17 BL 349.8
  351.38 352.26 353.16 YT 409.9
  PP 438.12 HD 448.42 PR 480.38
  482.8 484.18 485.23 487.16
  487.18 489.20 497.22 507.11
  507.22 TB 518.15 518.20
  SU 537.33 542.36 543.26
  543.36 WR 551.11 551.36
  558.42 574.17 574.35
  SM 586.19 BO 599.2 600.22
  JD 618.38 IL 652.18 660.3
  GG 669.41 672.41 685.24
  ML 723.42 RR 780.16 MD 823.18

DISTANT OA 28.36 TF 118.24
  129.9 DV 174.15 177.14
  SS 202.18 202.28 BL 358.1
  MN 369.41 YT 408.16 PR 511.21
  WR 551.34 JD 609.3 612.11
  614.24 LA 643.7 IL 658.10
  GG 700.9 MD 812.7

DISTASTE WR 553.33 GG 675.15

DISTASTEFUL HD 453.16 MD 808.32

DISTENDED CH 278.9

DISTILLING DV 171.27

DISTINCT WM 56.14 56.23 58.41
  61.24 69.31 PO 95.14 102.9
  105.33 TF 119.28 123.7
  DV 150.36 179.10 SS 210.24
  211.17 SB 214.6 WS 256.19
  WP 383.3 HD 448.22 ML 741.30

DISTINCT (CONT.) LL 764.16
  MD 824.18

DISTINCTION TF 126.37 EE 326.31
  326.32 ML 739.4

DISTINCTLY MO 11.34 TF 119.15
  123.3 DV 149.41 184.25
  SS 207.23 CH 277.36 OC 284.15
  291.4 298.10 EE 319.10
  TP 342.36 HD 449.4 PR 492.39
  WR 565.34 LA 633.9 633.13
  RR 783.6 BM 828.10 832.17

DISTINCTNESS DV 170.32

DISTINGUISH WM 55.14 SS 211.16
  WR 565.40 JD 616.27

DISTINGUISHED DV 138.25 146.13
  SS 208.25 FA 458.31 GG 661.24
  LL 777.19 777.20 BM 834.33

DISTORTED PO 115.24 TF 121.21
  LA 646.17 646.26

DISTRACTED SB 218.7 WS 257.8
  PP 436.16

DISTRACTION WS 256.14 EE 322.29
  HD 456.39

DISTRAUGHT NT 719.36

DISTRESS DV 186.18 GF 239.6
  WS 259.3 OC 290.21 BM 842.1

DISTRESSED EA 87.35 PO 110.29
  DV 185.27 HD 455.29 LA 645.35
  IL 655.40

DISTRESSING FA 469.32

DISTRIBUTING MD 807.5

DISTRICT DV 137.20 YT 394.29
  SD 415.10

DISTRUST HD 443.28

DISTRUSTED DV 155.22

DISTURB SG 226.27 GG 669.4
  BM 841.20

DISTURBANCE SP 47.1 SD 422.20

DISTURBED PO 112.10 WS 252.35
  BL 358.39 PP 434.29 TB 522.8
  IL 654.6

DISTURBING HT 40.24 WS 251.39
  254.13 MN 369.8

DITCH TP 334.34 PR 488.35
  WR 561.20 ML 727.6

DITCHES ML 725.37 729.36

DITCHING ML 726.33

DITHER MO 17.32

DITTO OV 756.17

DIVE WM 61.22 HD 452.7

DIVERGED TF 118.33

DIVERGING OC 283.30

DIVERT BO 591.5

DIVESTING HD 451.27

DIVIDED PO 111.30 115.41
  WS 257.18 RR 785.21

DIVIDING BL 354.33

DIVINE EE 316.7 IL 653.15
  655.15

DIVORCE PP 431.42 JD 606.36
  606.37 607.9 613.11
  626.29 626.32 626.34
  627.35 ML 732.40 RR 782.36

DIVORCED JD 605.5 606.41
  626.28 NT 706.9

DIVULGED RH 801.18

DIZZY FG 194.39 WS 264.25

DOCILE EE 324.23

DOCTOR TF 126.35 DV 162.7
  162.10 163.11 163.13
  163.19 168.27 SC 269.20
  270.29 OC 295.28 297.37
  EE 317.33 317.42 318.36
  319.23 319.29 320.1
  321.6 YT 400.26 HD 444.34
  444.37 445.1 445.5 445.8
  445.16 445.27 445.29
  446.3 446.10 446.13 453.13
  455.11 SU 529.26 533.16
  BO 603.23 LA 646.8
  GG 679.25 NT 718.10
  ML 739.7 LL 776.38 777.32

DOCTOR JACKSON EE 321.24

DOCTOR OF CHEMISTRY SB 215.37

DOCTORS PO 116.15 SC 270.6
  SU 528.1 NT 721.8

DOCTOR'S EE 320.28 HD 448.11
  449.22

DOCTOR WAYNE EE 320.31 320.36
  320.40 321.1

DOCTOR WING EE 318.11 319.38
  319.41 320.14 321.20

DOCTOR WYER WS 247.27

DOCUMENT LL 763.14 763.42

DOCUMENTS LL 763.8

DODGE NT 711.19 ML 724.9

DODGED OA 33.28 SP 45.22
  45.28 WS 244.32 IL 656.6
  656.13

DOOR (CONT.) 415.31 416.7
  417.33 422.39 423.16
  PP 432.22 432.38 434.1
  438.20 440.17 440.21
  HD 444.17 446.22 451.9 453.38
  FA 458.14 461.37 462.39
  468.30 468.42 469.31 470.6
  PR 500.8 503.4 505.4 506.22
  511.8 WR 561.22 562.4 563.24
  563.26 563.27 563.38 572.17
  576.24 SM 583.22 583.25
  585.27 586.15 BO 604.29
  JD 624.28 624.31 627.13 LA 630.6
  630.32 635.29 635.35 635.38
  637.3 640.29 IL 652.29 654.1
  654.11 654.13 654.38 655.27
  656.25 656.28 656.29 658.4
  658.10 660.2 GG 666.10 669.29
  670.8 670.39 677.19 678.17
  681.15 681.20 691.5 691.11
  694.32 694.35 697.24
  ML 727.13 741.13 741.26
  742.31 744.21 745.3 746.2
  OV 747.3 747.20 LL 772.37
  775.37 775.38 775.40 777.3
  777.4 RR 783.20 784.1 784.17
  784.27 785.26 785.38 788.7
  788.17 RH 802.41 MD 815.33
  BM 829.37 837.26 838.22
  839.23 841.2 841.14 841.25
  843.7

DOOR-BELL FA 460.26

DOOR-HANDLE IL 657.2 RH 803.7

DOOR-KNOB DV 159.6

DOOR-LATCH BL 353.21

DOORS MO 6.6 EA 81.20 GF 234.26
  235.3 WS 263.14 BL 354.5
  354.7 354.10 YT 394.10
  PP 435.35 PR 476.28 502.30
  TB 523.14 WR 546.24 548.28
  561.17 562.4 562.5 568.30
  LA 639.15 644.36 RR 787.28
  TH 849.16 849.19

DOORSTEPS GF 234.19

DOORWAY MO 3.21 19.3 OA 24.17
  25.8 WM 58.9 TF 133.28 134.21
  134.39 FG 192.4 196.2
  SS 201.17 207.22 208.37
  SG 224.15 224.17 CH 282.25
  OC 296.39 EE 303.11 BL 351.37
  WP 388.42 390.10 SD 422.32
  423.19 PP 433.34 FA 461.38
  PR 507.9 507.19 507.37 510.7
  LA 637.2 644.3 GG 672.23
  672.31 OV 749.13 LL 775.42
  RR 783.24 784.9 788.18
  RH 803.15 BM 842.42

DOORWAYS OC 297.16 PP 427.6
  WR 568.26

DORMANT NT 717.39

DOROTHY HALE GG 699.34

DOST HT 43.25 HD 443.23

DOSTOEVSKY PR 477.10

DOT GG 670.14

DOTED WR 547.19

DOTS PO 107.6 GF 242.40
  TB 520.34 ML 741.30

DOTTED MN 366.8 PR 489.32

DOUBLE WR 571.18 GG 672.6
  MD 812.22

DOUBLE-BARRELLED IL 649.31

DOUBLED OA 33.28 WP 383.23

DOUBLE-ENTRANCE TB 526.36

DOUBLY OA 35.17

DOUBT MO 9.24 11.26 EE 308.12
  BL 350.37 MN 372.8 WP 391.18
  HD 453.41 454.34 PR 481.15
  TB 519.39 JD 616.16 628.13
  LA 643.34 643.35 RR 779.28
  RH 794.37 MD 806.37

DOUBTED FA 458.28 PR 487.36

DOUBTFUL HD 456.36 SU 535.3
  LA 631.15 GG 671.34 ML 727.30
  727.31

DOUBTLESS FA 466.31 466.33

DOUBTS DV 137.4

DOVE-GREY DV 184.8 SU 532.25

DOVES HT 42.27

DOVE-TAILED WM 61.10

DOWAGER GG 670.11 674.3 682.23
  688.14

DOWAGER'S GG 681.15

DOWNCAST CH 275.36 EE 325.31

DOWNED WR 547.38

DOWNFALL HD 441.37

DOWNHILL WM 59.29 PO 106.15
  107.3 108.2 108.16 SS 197.34
  SC 270.32 TP 334.16 LA 630.34
  634.30

DOWNLAND ML 723.5

DOWNRIGHT MN 372.17 SD 417.12
  BM 828.7

DOWNS EE 308.3

DOWN-SITTING PR 496.35

DOWNSLOPE SS 199.37

DOWNSTAIRS OA 37.29 38.11
  WM 65.11 EA 78.29 PO 101.37
  TF 132.27 DV 160.11 169.4
  169.17 170.3 170.14* 172.38
  SG 229.12 GF 240.16 WS 244.24

DOWNSTAIRS (CONT.) 265.28
  SC 268.2 273.4 OC 291.34
  298.22 EE 318.33 TP 335.24
  BL 357.14 YT 397.5 402.7
  402.32 FA 468.25 LA 644.20
  645.8 645.23 GG 682.17
  LL 776.14 RR 788.27
  RH 802.21 802.37

DOWN-STREAM TB 524.11

DOWN-TOWN WS 260.40

DOWN-TRODDEN PP 437.41

DOWNWARD HD 443.16 PR 498.14

DOWNWARDS MO 1.35 TF 119.35
  FG 194.28 SS 197.16
  PR 490.12 WR 558.30
  JD 620.15 LA 630.11
  GG 688.30 RR 785.8

DOWNY EE 329.23 WP 384.38

DOZED LL 769.15

DOZEN DV 167.2 GF 234.6
  TP 336.27 FA 459.8 TB 514.8
  SM 584.38 BO 590.29
  NT 721.6 ML 740.8 LL 765.17
  TH 848.19

DOZENS HT 43.30 DV 166.29
  NT 719.38

DRAFTED EE 328.15

DRAG OA 30.38 FA 460.33
  466.24 JD 625.33

DRAGGED HT 43.21 TF 121.3
  DV 137.23 GF 234.23
  SC 268.14 CH 276.17
  BL 352.5 FA 462.4 465.19
  465.39 PR 509.21 TB 520.21
  MD 826.11

DRAGGING DV 168.41 168.42
  OC 286.40 PP 435.29
  PR 499.10 509.24 JD 610.4

DRAGON TP 337.31

DRAGONS TP 337.29 338.3

DRAGS FG 187.15

DRAIN SB 216.40 OC 286.29
  ML 727.7

DRAINAGE SP 50.42 ML 729.22
  729.36

DRAINED GG 671.31

DRAMA MN 371.22

DRAMATIC TB 517.41 IL 655.38
  NT 706.12

DRAMATICALLY DV 157.37

DRANK EA 71.14 PO 103.19
  103.35 109.38 DV 142.17

DRANK (CONT.) SG 223.25
   OC 288.4 YT 395.19 PP 433.2
   440.24 HD 451.21 PR 499.26
   TB 513.15 525.8 WR 556.35
   JD 611.33 GG 675.9 ML 730.6
   OV 748.34 LL 763.32 RR 786.30

DRAPERS RH 799.17

DRAPERY SM 586.17 GG 684.38
   RH 799.23

DRASTIC TB 520.18 520.19

DRAUGHT MO 16.35 DV 159.12
   WP 379.14

DRAUGHT-HORSES HD 441.38

DRAUGHTS MO 6.6 DV 157.11
   FG 193.39

DRAUGHTY DV 157.18

DRAW MO 4.13 WM 63.6 EA 77.38
   80.17 DV 164.41 171.6
   FG 190.11 193.26 WS 252.24
   256.3 OC 300.8 TP 334.22
   BL 352.31 GG 677.9 NT 703.27
   709.31 709.40 OV 758.21
   LL 765.22 MD 814.27 822.4

DRAWER DV 162.21 WS 250.1
   261.12 265.25 OC 296.30

DRAWERS TF 125.38 PP 435.11

DRAWING OA 32.30 32.35 SP 49.28
   EA 73.22 PO 116.1 TF 127.31
   130.2 DV 179.28 181.10
   SG 227.40 227.42 228.30
   WS 259.2 OC 295.36 TP 345.5
   MN 366.36 371.40 YT 400.38
   HD 450.33 453.1 453.28 453.30
   TB 517.42 GG 698.33 698.34
   NT 708.42 ML 742.24 744.9
   RH 802.9

DRAWING-ROOM WM 58.33 63.28
   70.17 EA 75.24 84.9 86.41
   YT 397.12 PP 437.2 GG 670.6
   681.23 LL 764.19 765.7 765.12
   772.36 772.39 775.32 776.41
   RR 783.36 MD 808.2 810.42
   815.19 815.27 815.33 825.22
   825.23 826.4

DRAWINGS PR 478.34

DRAWL MO 13.20 TB 523.31
   IL 654.40 MD 823.6 823.14

DRAWLED MO 11.1 14.19 14.23
   OA 27.37 SD 425.33 JD 623.27
   IL 654.36 MD 826.22

DRAWLING GF 236.4

DRAWN WM 60.24 EA 72.31 73.11
   82.36 PO 110.35 TF 123.14
   123.22 127.41 133.9 DV 157.9
   181.18 WS 246.13 261.8 264.10
   EE 311.1 WP 387.4 YT 394.13
   406.42 SD 418.21 420.32
   424.23 PP 439.22 LA 646.17

DRAWN (CONT.) IL 647.22 GG 667.33
   ML 725.23 OV 758.23 LL 764.10
   BM 835.16 842.39

DRAWS WR 571.13

DRAY FA 462.5

DRAYS YT 394.13

DREAD DV 150.7 174.32 FG 188.23
   WS 257.12 OC 289.25 299.37
   300.9 300.31 302.5 BL 348.1
   356.3 PR 501.29 505.24 507.26
   GG 681.32 LL 767.2 767.33
   MD 822.8

DREADED DV 178.24 SS 204.9
   PR 504.24 504.25 507.26

DREADFUL MO 6.34 7.31 DV 147.42
   GF 239.38 PR 474.5 JD 607.29
   LL 777.17 777.26 MD 820.32
   BM 831.24

DREAM MO 2.16 PO 106.18 115.37
   FG 190.4 SS 202.8 TB 517.7
   GG 699.16 NT 713.29 714.28
   ML 735.23 MD 806.21 BM 831.40
   837.35

DREAMED FG 192.40 PR 503.16
   WR 550.25 TH 846.6 849.42
   850.37

DREAMILY SS 204.38

DREAM-PEOPLE PO 106.17

DREAMS MO 2.34 WM 66.2
   ML 731.26 MD 826.24

DREAMY ML 728.25 OV 748.15

DREARILY MO 22.10 WM 67.7

DREARINESS MO 4.8 SU 528.33

DREARY MO 1.6 SP 49.18
   PO 104.13 SB 216.32 GF 239.38
   WS 265.8 OC 283.16 286.10
   YT 394.23 SD 411.23 HD 441.9
   PR 509.42 WR 552.30 BO 599.15
   GG 669.40

DREE GG 685.17 203.34

DRENCHED MO 21.12

DRESDEN EA 84.13

DRESS MO 20.36 SP 47.40 WM 70.9
   EA 70.13 71.27 78.9 86.8 92.8
   TF 123.26 134.23 SB 212.11
   SG 222.3 224.7 226.10 231.9
   GF 237.18 240.15 WS 251.15
   CH 274.9 278.29 TP 345.26
   MN 376.24 YT 399.11 HD 456.12
   456.28 FA 465.13 TB 524.16
   524.33 524.36 GG 669.35
   671.29 683.10 OV 747.7 747.13
   749.11 LL 763.25 763.36
   775.41 RH 799.15 803.14
   MD 815.20 BM 831.7 834.31
   834.36

DRESSED OA 24.14 WM 55.31 58.14

DRESSED (CONT.) PO 104.39
   DV 183.3 SB 217.15 217.32
   SG 226.28 GF 235.22 237.33
   239.9 241.18 WS 244.8
   250.22 250.31 252.10
   OC 284.30 EE 319.23
   TP 337.10 BL 356.42
   YT 398.4 398.39 399.8
   SD 412.23 PP 438.15
   PR 476.23 505.1 TB 521.21
   SU 531.5 WR 564.26
   GG 669.34 NT 715.19
   ML 735.39 742.9 OV 747.8
   LL 775.18 775.30 775.33
   MD 807.40 815.41 BM 829.25
   831.15 834.31 835.19

DRESSER DV 162.21 SC 268.13
   OC 296.29 JD 618.11 618.21

DRESSES TB 525.9

DRESSING PR 488.31

DRESSING-GOWN HT 38.16
   EA 80.41 GF 237.21 GG 691.6
   694.9

DRESSING-JACKET GF 237.18
   WS 245.3

DRESSING-ROOM BM 838.29

DRESSING-TABLE GF 237.15
   WS 244.12

DRESSMAKING BM 831.32

DREW MO 21.23 OA 25.36 25.40
   WM 69.19 69.31 EA 74.13
   91.29 PO 95.13 98.42
   111.24 TF 118.29 125.2
   126.1 129.38 133.39
   DV 140.15 147.9 148.37
   156.27 180.28 180.36
   181.12 FG 194.33 SS 209.7
   GF 235.29 237.11 243.24
   WS 249.30 261.19 CH 275.28
   OC 283.6 284.5 293.36
   EE 308.4 331.20 TP 337.39
   338.21 BL 353.10 359.5
   MN 373.16 373.27 WP 380.31
   386.20 387.25 SD 412.19
   414.13 414.19 417.19
   424.15 PP 430.6 432.13
   436.5 439.37 HD 454.25
   PR 484.13 508.1 SU 529.24
   537.7 WR 563.42 564.11
   BO 593.36 596.19 597.25
   599.27 604.39 JD 627.40
   IL 651.23 GG 666.37 686.11
   NT 709.13 ML 727.27 742.27
   RH 799.17 MD 822.7 BM 841.5

DR. FERGUSSON HD 451.25

DRIBBLES SU 528.9

DRIBBLING EA 71.12

DRIED FG 192.35 195.25
   GF 238.14 WS 264.35
   BL 356.31 YT 397.25
   PR 502.22 WR 546.25 576.41
   579.15 JD 617.37 IL 648.42

DRIED (CONT.) ML 743.37

DRIFT SS 204.35 BL 350.13
  PR 481.22 ML 746.5 746.11
  OV 750.3 752.29

DRIFTED MO 15.30 FG 194.36
  SG 225.40 WS 257.9 WP 385.36
  OV 748.2 748.16

DRIFTING WS 256.3 FA 458.3
  WR 573.9

DRILL TF 117.16 117.26

DRILLING PO 116.2

DRILLING-YARD TF 117.13

DRINK MO 14.38 SP 48.5 52.32
  PO 103.19 105.29 105.38
  114.10 TF 118.16 DV 140.6
  142.4 144.17 164.20 165.7
  WS 249.19 SC 267.12 OC 286.25
  294.34 300.1 EE 312.39 319.17
  MN 368.32 SD 414.15 PP 432.11
  432.19 FA 471.41 PR 487.8
  501.36 WR 551.20 552.8 565.2
  565.20 568.10 572.10 576.34
  580.16 GG 675.12 675.24
  RR 784.36 786.26

DRINK-BLEARED GF 241.24

DRINKERS DV 142.5

DRINKING SP 50.16 50.17 52.39
  PO 109.21 DV 140.11 OC 291.6
  PP 428.41 SU 542.23 WR 557.1
  568.11 BM 838.29

DRINKING-GLASS OA 31.27

DRINKING-HOUSE DV 165.3

DRINKING-WATER SS 201.15

DRINKS SP 49.29 50.27 SD 413.20

DRIPPED WS 249.35

DRIPPIN' TP 341.5

DRIPPING PR 490.8 WR 579.25
  579.27

DRIVE WM 66.38 BL 347.2 347.4
  354.9 356.21 356.23 WP 385.37
  FA 459.42 PR 496.10 NT 706.24
  OV 760.4 LL 776.20 RR 787.23
  787.29 BM 834.37 835.6 838.41
  838.42 839.28

DRIVEN WM 68.17 EA 93.34
  TF 131.14 FG 193.31 193.32
  SG 229.5 WS 252.39 OC 299.23
  TP 335.18 MN 368.7 FA 469.24
  471.29 WR 575.4 ML 737.13
  LL 778.9

DRIVER TP 335.1 336.4 PP 427.17
  427.22 428.5 428.24 429.10
  431.26 436.3

DRIVERS TP 334.28 336.5

DRIVER'S PP 433.4 IL 653.20

DRIVING SP 49.21 DV 162.14
  FG 191.25 WS 253.17 WP 382.13
  385.6 WR 559.16 ML 745.5
  BM 834.38

DRIZZLE JD 616.11

DRIZZLING TP 337.10 338.36
  JD 624.23

DROLL MO 14.24

DRONE TF 129.15

DROOP CH 275.23 WP 386.35

DROOPED HD 455.5 455.14
  GG 690.33

DROOPING MO 22.24 SS 204.6
  PR 492.16 BO 603.11 GG 691.1

DROP WM 68.36 DV 140.12 144.30
  162.26 SS 209.19 210.25 211.6
  SB 216.28 TP 334.18 340.4
  340.9 SD 415.27 418.17
  OV 747.7 RR 783.29

DROPPED MO 6.20 OA 29.33
  HT 44.9 WM 67.5 EA 82.13 85.9
  PO 116.13 TF 124.25 124.33
  DV 160.37 180.24 FG 189.32
  SB 212.2 216.9 SG 226.9
  227.26 GF 238.22 WS 245.25
  258.8 263.23 CH 277.39
  OC 283.12 284.34 288.12
  295.29 EE 318.6 TP 340.3
  340.29 345.42 BL 351.4 363.13
  MN 373.12 WP 384.32 389.41
  YT 400.20 SD 423.25 423.31
  HD 454.9 455.28 FA 459.30
  470.26 471.11 PR 489.37
  498.40 510.27 TB 521.23
  SU 531.30 JD 617.5 GG 678.19
  678.31 690.16 694.7 NT 721.11
  ML 735.42 746.20 LL 777.27
  BM 842.15

DROPPIN' SC 268.32

DROPPING TF 123.29 123.38
  SS 204.41 CH 275.7 OC 290.27
  299.1 MN 374.5 FA 465.5
  PR 494.8 498.34 499.21
  WR 570.19 BO 588.22 GG 690.2
  ML 746.21 OV 571.18 LL 763.23
  MD 826.18

DROPPINGS PR 500.14 BO 588.22

DROPS OA 32.30 PO 95.25
  DV 166.30 WS 246.4 260.40
  OC 299.19 JD 606.33 606.39
  OV 754.38

DROPSY YT 396.36

DROSS TF 124.34

DROVE SP 48.15 EA 80.7 SB 220.3
  GF 234.6 234.17 242.9
  YT 409.42 BO 589.33 GG 662.6
  ML 730.33 737.33 746.2

DROVE (CONT.) OV 752.22
  RH 797.22 802.34 BM 834.16

DROWNED FG 196.21 FA 465.31
  OV 759.40

DROWSE MO 15.5

DROWSED SU 531.14 536.13

DROWSY ML 735.28

DRUDGERY HD 449.9

DRUG MO 2.33 EA 87.33
  HD 448.28 FA 458.5

DRUGGED TF 126.17 BL 349.11
  YT 402.36 407.30 WR 569.26
  574.26 578.39

DRUGS HD 448.33 NT 717.17
  LL 777.33

DRUM WR 564.34 568.34 568.37
  569.17 570.5 570.13 573.38
  578.1 IL 651.5

DRUMMING WS 244.30 WR 569.26
  IL 651.23

DRUMMOND RR 781.1 781.37

DRUMMOND (SEE JACK, ALEC; MRS.
  DRUMMOND)

DRUMMONDS RR 789.20

DRUMS WR 570.4 578.13 578.21
  578.35 579.21 JD 609.3
  609.13 609.18

DRUM-SOUND BL 361.14

DRUNK HT 41.16 SP 50.17
  DV 165.19 FG 190.33 191.23
  OC 289.10 298.20 EE 328.42
  YT 405.18 HD 448.27
  SU 529.14 JD 614.40
  LA 633.25 633.26 633.27
  MD 811.29

DRUNKARD DV 144.16

DRUNKEN DV 143.20 143.22
  FA 467.21 472.4 JD 614.4
  614.5 623.4 OV 747.29

DRUNKENNESS PO 103.26
  JD 614.19

DRY MO 14.11 EA 82.7
  PO 102.29 102.35 102.36
  103.3 112.15 112.18
  TF 117.9 DV 183.25
  FG 195.3 195.6 SS 210.9
  GF 243.3 SC 268.33 268.35
  EE 332.20 HD 451.28 452.6
  WR 579.15 ML 741.9
  OV 755.29 LL 778.29

DRY-FRETTED FG 195.3

DRYING MO 4.42 WS 245.9
  OC 299.33

DRYING-GROUND SP 45.14

DRYISH EE 303.5

DRYNESS PO 104.12

DRY-ROTTEN TH 846.35

DU BIST WIE EINE BLUME MO 16.6
  16.17

DUCHY MD 811.40

DUCK SB 212.24 TP 341.18

DUCKED OA 31.34 DV 170.33
  TP 343.21 WP 380.2 380.16
  PP 440.12

DUCKING LA 635.27 GG 681.20
  BM 829.36

DUE DV 142.11 SS 204.13 204.14

DUEL PO 98.18

DUET BM 838.10 838.14

DUETS BM 836.29

DUG OA 35.40

DUG-OUT GG 678.32

DULL WM 58.34 68.37 69.17
  EA 78.13 78.20 PO 95.6 104.42
  DV 140.4 142.38 146.2 148.7
  148.10 158.38 FG 192.7
  GF 234.27 241.28 WS 248.27
  263.1 263.3 OC 289.27
  ML 744.5 745.25 LL 767.38
  MD 820.2 820.3

DULLED PO 103.37 DV 171.31
  WS 257.6

DULL-GOLD OA 26.8 PR 489.15

DULLY CH 277.1

DULY ML 739.24

DUMB WM 62.15 PO 107.34
  TF 134.1 WS 264.14 OV 755.11

DUMB-BELL NT 717.12

DUMB-BELLS DV 165.28

DUMBFOUNDED YT 404.40 BM 828.40

DUMBLY ML 746.25 OV 750.11

DUMPLING HT 41.10 SP 46.20

DUPLICITY WR 566.40

DURANT (SEE ALFRED, GEORGE, JOHN,
  WALTER; MR. DURANT; MRS. DURANT)

DURANTS DV 143.7

DURANT'S DV 183.25

DURANTS' DV 142.5

DURING ML 745.37 OV 753.16
  RR 783.22 MD 816.23 818.25
  822.40 BM 829.41 836.41

DUSK OV 751.19

DUSK-BLUE OA 24.7

DUSKILY BO 596.30

DUSKINESS GG 683.7

DUSKY LL 772.1

DUSKY-AND-SCARLET SB 212.13

DUST OV 755.15 755.19 755.29
  RH 790.3

DUST-BIN TB 520.14

DUSTERS DV 162.21

DUST-PAN CH 275.42 OC 288.18

DWARFED WP 386.9

DWELLING HD 449.9 SM 585.32

DWELLING-HOUSE ML 722.25 725.11

DWELLING-HOUSES PP 436.7

DWELLINGS SP 45.11 DV 136.6
  136.15 SS 197.30 OC 291.10
  SD 411.24 WR 548.32 JD 610.34

DWINDLED PR 475.40 GG 678.39
  ML 724.4

DWINDLING TH 851.37

DYEING MD 808.40

DYING RH 804.13

DYKE-BANK EE 305.2

'E CH 277.13 OC 291.19 291.30
  292.14 292.23 292.25 292.34
  294.18 295.28 295.39 296.1
  296.2 296.6 WP 388.10 389.5
  389.7

EAGER WM 55.11 EA 83.36 85.35
  86.22 PO 100.38 101.25
  SG 225.6 BO 587.8 OV 754.2
  MD 810.8

EAGERLY BO 587.9 587.22
  RR 787.1

EAGERNESS WR 581.10 LL 764.34
  TH 846.5

EAGLE PR 493.27 497.26
  WR 574.12 574.15 575.14
  LL 761.30

EAR MO 16.18 OA 35.30 WM 69.15
  PO 101.19 101.22 101.26
  102.14 BO 591.28 600.17
  LA 632.3 646.15 OV 755.16
  LL 766.39 774.38

EARLIER YT 397.42 SU 539.39

EARLY SP 45.2 52.20 WM 63.20
  EA 88.12 DV 148.20
  FG 187.14 SS 201.30 204.29
  GF 237.10 240.20 WS 244.23
  SC 270.11 EE 328.31
  TP 340.29 BL 352.30
  YT 404.26 PR 476.13 478.6
  483.38 487.25 SU 543.10
  SM 582.21 BO 596.25
  JD 628.23 GG 661.1
  NT 719.31 ML 723.11
  MD 809.21 BM 832.27

EARN DV 184.13 OC 294.31
  EE 310.41 311.18 TB 526.38
  MD 806.4 806.6 814.19
  TH 852.15

EARNED HT 39.8 SP 46.31
  DV 144.30 SC 267.7
  EE 305.15 309.17 310.40
  PR 477.18 TB 524.38
  LL 762.31 769.33 RH 799.19
  MD 805.3

EARNEST MO 7.23 EA 87.35
  88.24 89.20 89.21
  PO 110.3 EE 325.2 IL 655.12

EARNESTLY GF 236.18 236.23
  WS 245.38 245.41 248.10

EARNESTNESS MO 5.35 17.16
  EA 75.3 GG 665.11
  OV 751.20

EARNING EE 328.8 MD 806.2

EAR-RINGS WS 245.39 246.3
  246.14 246.30 247.10
  247.32 249.42 250.6 260.32
  260.38 261.18 263.38
  263.41 264.39 LL 763.23

EARS PO 114.6 DV 136.14
  158.6 171.10 171.12
  FG 189.24 WS 245.41 246.1
  246.3 250.3 254.6
  OC 289.31 EE 331.11
  BL 353.4 PP 437.12
  HD 442.19 FA 468.23 470.18
  PR 501.21 WR 561.8
  LA 632.18 633.4 634.24
  LL 763.23 RR 779.31 783.10
  BM 841.10

EARSHOT PO 98.31

EAR-SHOT IL 651.6

EARTH MO 1.19 1.21 14.26
  SP 49.3 PO 95.20 112.15
  116.6 TF 125.37 FG 189.42
  192.2 SS 197.9 SG 225.26
  CH 282.27 EE 303.14 303.26
  306.25 307.21 321.16
  331.23 331.25 333.14
  BL 348.12 354.18 354.20
  354.25 WP 379.32 PP 436.30
  FA 465.39 PR 489.5 511.8
  TB 518.30 518.39 SU 529.12
  530.10 542.1 WR 548.40

EFFECT MO 14.24 19.11 WM 63.21
  SB 213.6 WS 251.38 BL 349.30
  351.3 355.18 362.10 MN 371.17
  HD 451.22 PR 481.10 WR 567.17
  LA 640.34 GG 675.25 675.26
  675.28 675.30 675.31 675.37
  675.41 682.11 RH 799.10

EFFECTIVE MN 368.12 FA 466.38

EFFICIENT NT 708.7

EFFICIENTLY SU 539.10

EFFLUENCE GG 685.4 OV 750.19
  750.20

EFFORT EA 78.22 PO 102.23
  112.21 TF 119.8 120.32
  DV 142.40 164.8 SS 202.33
  205.32 SG 229.10 EE 313.21
  325.5 325.12 332.2 332.24
  332.38 332.42 BL 348.5 361.34
  362.7 SD 421.11 422.42
  PP 434.5 HD 450.26 454.36
  PR 498.8 LA 641.1 642.19
  GG 682.6 OV 750.24 750.28
  MD 823.1 825.35 825.36
  BM 841.13

EFFORTLESS RR 782.4

EFFORTS OA 33.29 SB 215.18
  BO 597.16 597.17

EFFRONTERY GG 676.23

EFFULGENCE EE 314.35 WR 556.7

EFFUSE GF 235.36

EFFUSIONS WP 381.1

EGBERT EE 304.8 305.10 305.38
  306.2 307.7 307.35 307.39
  308.8 308.11 308.14 308.32
  308.35 308.41 308.42 309.19
  309.42 310.10 310.16 311.2
  311.35 312.33 312.39 313.4
  313.15 314.1 314.6 314.19
  315.31 315.39 316.9 316.17
  317.6 317.27 317.33 317.39
  317.42 318.12 318.19 318.22
  319.6 319.35 320.7 320.30
  320.33 320.37 321.23 321.39
  322.32 323.13 324.34 326.8
  326.37 327.7 327.18 328.10
  328.14 328.34 328.39

EGBERT'S EE 315.16 318.10

EGG YT 398.18 PR 494.23 499.9
  TB 515.23 522.37 ML 722.20

EGGED MD 805.24

EGG-LIKE PR 493.29

EGGS SS 202.20 PR 505.18 506.2
  ML 741.41 RH 797.3

EGOISM ML 727.40

EGOISTIC LL 774.8

EGYPT ML 731.10

EH MO 14.35 OA 27.39 28.31
  WM 56.36 57.5 62.38 SB 213.12
  214.7 214.27 218.30 GF 240.22
  OC 289.16 289.19 291.42
  293.34 294.8 294.23 297.29
  300.20 EE 319.12 319.18
  WP 384.8 SD 416.32 425.35
  HD 446.18 FA 461.30 OV 756.5
  RH 794.5 794.39 795.15
  MD 822.22 BM 837.39

EIDERDOWN PP 434.4

EIGHT OA 24.6 30.8 SS 197.7
  SG 221.3 GF 241.14 WS 253.34
  OC 290.27 EE 328.36 FA 459.27
  JD 607.42 621.12 NT 720.15
  LL 764.23 MD 813.22

EIGHTEEN HT 39.16 PP 429.26
  GG 661.12

EIGHTEENTH MD 809.11 809.21
  810.31

EIGHTEENTH-CENTURY PR 476.28
  MD 812.7

EIGHTY-ODD RH 804.33

EIGHTY THOUSAND RH 804.17

EIGHTY THOUSAND POUNDS RH 804.20
  804.21

EITHER MO 1.8 16.38 SP 50.19
  EA 79.40 PO 95.4 95.11 111.1
  DV 157.2 167.13 FG 194.36
  WS 251.27 263.16 EE 312.14
  327.4 330.17 TP 341.39
  WP 379.35 YT 407.21 PP 430.28
  PR 482.36 497.35 WR 561.35
  563.12 579.30 JD 620.38
  628.22 IL 647.4 647.28
  GG 661.21 661.30 662.5 678.3
  NT 718.33 718.37 718.41
  ML 736.40 OV 756.3 LL 767.9
  768.6 777.36 RR 781.30 784.22
  RH 792.16 MD 818.15 TH 846.28
  848.36 852.29

EJACULATED SD 412.38 GG 665.5

EJACULATION TP 341.26

EKING NT 701.3

ELABORATE TB 516.21 WR 559.26
  569.8 577.29

ELABORATED EE 313.21 313.22

ELAINE PP 437.20 438.3 438.8
  438.17

ELASTIC MO 18.21

ELATE JD 624.9

ELATED SP 48.20 SS 197.34
  WS 250.9 PR 485.32 489.31
  JD 624.16 624.20 GG 663.30

ELATION SP 48.35 BL 364.39

ELATION (CONT.) TB 524.12
  WR 552.9 552.16 JD 624.7

ELBOW WM 65.28 PO 116.5
  DV 136.19 MN 367.14
  TB 524.25 WR 562.41 563.5
  RR 785.10

ELBOWED GF 238.30

ELBOWS MO 7.17 SS 201.20
  GF 241.6

ELDER OA 34.18 34.36 35.26
  PO 97.19 97.24 99.3 99.8
  99.23 100.10 109.37
  TF 121.11 DV 138.24 183.35
  SS 206.18 SB 212.31
  OC 293.38 EE 321.33
  YT 404.20 PP 430.32 430.36
  431.6 432.12 435.37 437.25
  440.14 WR 555.1 557.35
  564.15 SM 583.13 IL 653.39
  ML 736.9 LL 764.38 768.18
  RH 793.20 MD 814.42 816.19
  BM 836.39

ELDERBERRIES SB 214.12

ELDERLY DV 139.15 139.24
  141.6 176.26 OC 293.29
  EE 320.9 320.17 327.15
  328.10 WP 388.18 388.36
  YT 396.9 403.9 PP 436.33
  436.39 437.1 PR 512.26
  WR 566.6 SM 582.15
  GG 672.31 672.35 694.15
  BM 838.1

ELDERS WR 559.24 559.27
  560.35

ELDEST MO 5.9 5.22 DV 138.20
  145.9 SS 201.32 CH 282.13
  EE 316.18 HD 441.31
  WR 547.9

ELECTED DV 153.13 EE 325.37

ELECTRIC MO 11.36 SP 48.27
  DV 166.31 EE 321.29
  TP 337.20 345.32 SD 415.12
  424.2 PR 501.19 BO 595.6
  JD 610.30 LL 775.40
  TH 851.5

ELECTRICALLY TP 338.29

ELECTRICIAN MO 11.38
  SG 229.32

ELECTRICIANS YT 399.22

ELECTRICITY TP 337.21
  YT 396.31 PR 502.40

ELECTRIFIED MN 371.23
  FA 467.7

ELEGANCE PR 484.42 MD 807.41

ELEGANT TF 122.10 BL 351.1
  WP 382.19 YT 399.12
  PR 485.2 TB 521.23 522.20
  GG 700.1 ML 726.40 729.29

ELEGANT (CONT.) LL 764.25
   RR 779.21 MD 808.3 808.17

ELEGANTLY ML 735.39 MD 808.4

ELEMENT SP 49.24 GF 236.14
   WS 254.29 EE 315.28 HD 448.16
   450.18 453.15 JD 624.8
   MD 810.19 811.25

ELEMENTAL EA 72.16 82.14 83.3
   83.6 83.14

ELEMENTARY YT 396.3

ELEMENTS BL 356.5 ML 745.11
   746.24 746.25

ELEVATION ML 740.21

ELEVEN OA 30.42 HT 39.17 41.8
   42.9 SP 47.24 51.17 52.23
   WM 67.42 GF 234.17 235.9
   MN 371.31 FA 467.36 TB 515.25
   JD 625.26 NT 720.23 RR 781.11

ELEVEN-FORTY HD 445.9

ELFIN PR 479.8 ML 723.16

ELIGIBLE DV 144.29

ELIMINATE TH 846.3

ELIMINATED TH 846.8 846.12
   846.16 846.29

ELIMINATING TH 846.16 846.30

ELIOT, GEORGE (SEE GEORGE ELIOT)

ELISE WP 381.25 383.8 384.30
   392.9 393.3

ELIZA WP 381.31 381.32 383.6

ELIZABETH OC 293.36 293.40
   294.3 294.11 294.16 294.17
   294.41 295.4 295.7 295.11
   295.22 295.29 295.32 295.36
   296.4 296.9 296.13 296.23
   296.33 296.36 297.1 297.10
   297.23 298.4 298.42 299.13
   299.20 299.27 299.33 300.6
   300.14 300.23 301.39

ELIZABETH, QUEEN (SEE QUEEN
   ELIZABETH)

ELIZABETH BATES OC 286.9 291.27
   291.35 291.42 292.9 292.28
   292.36 292.39 293.15

ELIZABETH'S OC 294.6 294.29
   295.23

ELIZA'S WP 383.5

'E'LL CH 277.24 OC 293.11

ELM MO 1.33

ELMS MO 1.20 BL 352.37
   LA 634.26 LL 767.9

ELM-TOPS LL 766.28

'ELP SC 269.40

EL PASO WR 548.8

ELSA LASKELL OV 747.34 748.15
   753.2 760.5

ELSE MO 10.27 14.35 EA 75.1
   84.39 89.18 92.34 94.8
   PO 113.23 DV 137.8 142.14
   146.3 154.35 154.41 180.4
   SS 205.27 SB 215.27 SG 232.32
   WS 247.17 253.17 255.38
   263.34 CH 275.1 EE 305.14
   307.27 311.30 324.11
   TP 339.27 BL 349.39 355.11
   361.3 WP 392.2 YT 401.5
   SD 418.31 PP 429.20 438.36
   440.27 HD 442.42 444.3
   PR 486.31 493.13 500.10
   502.23 508.30 TB 513.8 515.25
   SU 529.25 WR 552.22 565.15
   566.23 JD 607.38 608.30 614.1
   615.36 621.23 LA 632.41
   644.40 IL 659.3 GG 661.20
   671.20 678.39 680.6 NT 702.38
   705.23 706.4 711.34 716.25
   718.33 718.37 ML 724.35 731.3
   738.22 LL 767.19 768.7 778.16
   RR 780.40 781.20 786.38
   RH 790.14 791.30 800.4
   MD 817.14 BM 832.11 833.41
   834.30 836.35 837.23 TH 845.4
   846.29 852.9

ELSE'LL SD 425.9

ELSE'S FA 470.8 IL 651.22

ELSEWHERE OC 294.29 SD 413.36
   424.10 TB 522.12 ML 726.15
   MD 807.10

ELSIE WS 246.37 250.28 250.39
   251.11 252.21 253.41 254.12
   255.23 255.38 256.3 256.8
   256.15 256.17 257.31 259.16

ELUSIVE WR 551.34 RR 782.11

ELVERY ML 729.16

ELVISH MD 806.16 806.32 807.36

'EM MO 14.32 HT 43.2 43.40
   SP 49.5 SB 218.37 GF 238.37
   239.3 WS 262.3 262.12 265.6
   SC 268.34 CH 280.42 281.5
   281.8 WP 389.8 SD 413.18
   PP 428.1 428.6 428.7 428.10
   428.26 428.29 428.34 428.35
   428.36 FA 470.38 WR 549.9

EMACIATED FA 465.8

EMANATE EE 314.23

EMANATING LL 764.26

EMANCIPATED RH 801.38

EMBANKMENT OA 25.4

EMBARRASSED DV 152.29
   NT 719.20

EMBARRASSMENT JD 615.20
   NT 715.38 720.27

EMBARRASSMENTS OV 750.17

EMBEDDED GG 661.32

EMBERS MO 2.29 2.32

EMBITTERED ML 732.18

EMBRACE MO 21.23 TF 130.16
   WS 253.14 MD 820.33

EMBRACED TF 130.17 OC 299.20

EMBRACES TF 127.36

EMBRACING HD 453.17

EMBROIDERED DV 179.4
   PR 484.41 485.1 WR 564.23
   NT 709.26 LL 763.20

EMBROIDERY WM 55.38 WS 246.36
   WR 569.2 LL 763.21

EMERALDS GG 665.28

EMERGE SU 533.11 LA 638.22
   643.26 TH 846.13

EMERGED MO 19.31 PO 112.32
   DV 161.22 OC 290.39
   EE 332.14 PR 490.34 490.36
   493.18 493.41 494.33
   495.42 496.7 496.33 497.33
   499.12 499.40 WR 558.23
   561.7 561.31 579.2
   LA 630.7 GG 670.35 ML 732.8
   LL 763.30

EMERGENCIES SU 536.24

EMERGENCY BO 601.40

EMETIC WR 568.10

EMIGRATING DV 186.9
   PP 430.19

EMIGRATION DV 177.9 177.10

EMILE TF 123.21 123.32

EMILIA JD 607.32 624.15

EMILIE TF 123.11 123.39
   124.9 124.14 124.22 124.29
   124.32 124.42 125.6 125.7
   125.9 125.20 125.22 125.25
   125.30 126.18 126.36 127.4
   127.8 127.41 128.12 128.21
   128.22 128.29 130.33 131.5
   131.9 131.16 131.19 131.23
   131.39 132.1 132.4 133.8
   133.19 133.29 133.33
   133.35 133.37 134.7 134.34
   135.3 135.13

EMILIE'S TF 124.4 134.11

EMILY JD 624.14 624.15 627.32
  628.11 628.39

EMILY PINNEGAR JD 616.33

EMINENCE EE 330.39

EMITTING JD 610.5

EMMA CH 275.14 275.39 276.17
  276.24 276.27 276.34 277.1
  277.9 277.22 282.14 TP 341.19
  344.5 JD 628.10

EMMA HOUSELAY TP 341.17

EMMA ROWBOTHAM CH 276.5

EMMIE YT 394.28 395.6 395.27
  396.1 396.29 397.4 398.1
  398.18 398.26 398.30 398.35
  398.38 399.1 399.33 399.35
  399.38 400.1 400.8 400.14
  400.40 401.7 401.19 401.23
  404.23 405.24 405.28 405.35
  406.20 407.12 407.24 407.32
  407.40 408.4 408.9 408.16
  408.26 409.37

EMMIE, COUSIN (SEE COUSIN EMMIE)

EMMIE ROCKLEY YT 394.19

EMMIE'S YT 395.4 404.15

EMOTION MO 16.14 OA 30.40
  WM 60.22 61.28 DV 148.30
  SS 203.34 CH 279.40 EE 316.12
  FA 468.16 SU 528.19 530.40
  WR 564.16 SM 584.18 584.20
  BO 602.10 JD 623.23 623.32
  TH 846.1

EMOTIONAL OA 31.20 CH 280.26
  BL 350.6 PP 430.8 HD 449.15
  FA 468.4 JD 605.30

EMOTIONLESS SD 416.33 WR 564.36

EMOTIONS DV 168.38 SS 200.35
  OC 299.37 BL 349.15 419.24
  PR 508.17 SU 528.20 530.39
  BO 594.18 GG 673.27 674.10

EMPHASIS DV 144.8 OC 292.37
  SD 417.23 425.6 WR 550.41
  JD 615.11 623.4 IL 652.39
  657.10 ML 728.29

EMPHATIC GF 237.27 WS 246.35

EMPHATICALLY MO 14.30 EA 85.3
  DV 185.41 MN 369.13 RR 779.26
  779.27 MD 809.7

EMPIRE MD 810.33

EMPLOYED TP 336.9 YT 406.33

EMPLOYER WS 250.21 255.27
  YT 406.32

EMPLOYERS YT 399.24

EMPTIED MO 22.1 DV 155.3

EMPTIED (CONT.) SD 412.16
  HD 456.17

EMPTINESS FG 192.2 BO 599.39
  600.24 GG 666.26 666.28

EMPTY EA 73.5 76.34 76.36
  83.26 PO 105.36 106.9
  DV 178.12 SS 206.21 OC 290.24
  EE 316.15 323.17 323.18
  PP 432.25 439.16 HD 446.27
  448.1 451.10 PR 480.13 480.14
  496.36 SU 529.16 WR 562.32
  581.22 BO 594.39 599.38
  599.42 600.33 LA 639.4
  GG 686.16 OV 754.22 755.10
  RR 785.29 785.33

EMPTYING SP 51.1

EMPYREAN EE 312.29

ENAMEL PR 502.18 ML 728.33

EN BLOC EE 326.38

ENCHANT NT 704.24

ENCHANTED NT 703.21

ENCHANTMENT NT 703.21 703.25

ENCLOSED YT 304.2 MD 806.36

ENCLOSING SP 45.12 JD 607.21

ENCLOSURE TF 118.21 118.26
  766.15 770.17

ENCLOSURES WR 558.42

ENCOMPASSED MD 812.15 812.28

ENCOUNTERS PR 477.37

ENCOURAGE GG 680.27

ENCOURAGED PR 498.39 NT 721.12

ENCROACH BL 359.26

ENCUMBRANCE DV 139.42

END MO 9.38 14.33 16.10 20.34
  OA 30.21 34.26 38.37 HT 40.31
  42.25 43.20 SP 49.22 50.22
  50.26 EA 73.7 PO 98.31 100.17
  100.26 111.1 TF 119.4 124.19
  DV 141.7 FG 189.38 190.24
  GF 236.27 240.18 243.1
  CH 278.33 279.6 OC 287.23
  293.42 295.18 296.39 297.4
  EE 304.7 306.17 313.33 329.31
  330.23 330.35 TP 335.27 343.8
  345.23 BL 351.32 MN 373.6
  WP 379.19 381.24 382.35
  384.26 385.9 387.33 YT 407.3
  407.37 408.20 SD 414.8 418.12
  421.8 PP 430.16 HD 447.16
  447.21 447.25 FA 464.2
  PR 474.3 477.2 481.21 486.9
  486.15 493.7 499.14 SU 535.31
  WR 561.35 562.9 562.33 565.5
  568.27 571.5 571.6 581.2
  SM 586.20 JD 617.32 617.42

END (CONT.) 618.13 626.24
  LA 635.29 GG 668.29 670.40
  675.3 675.35 684.8 700.11
  NT 704.16 712.24 717.35
  718.30 ML 725.27 730.3
  731.35 732.11 LL 766.24
  766.39 RR 787.28 788.37
  RH 793.7 MD 806.29 815.6
  BM 836.30 TH 845.24

ENDEARING NT 713.2 713.3

ENDED MO 2.1 WM 56.28 58.24
  PO 111.7 TF 132.21
  GF 241.1 PR 494.1 SU 541.21
  WR 548.10 ML 723.32
  RR 788.40 BM 841.21

ENDERBY (SEE REV. ENDERBY;
  MR. ENDERBY)

ENDING WM 65.41 JD 609.22

ENDLESS SC 270.39 EE 325.3
  WR 562.3 569.27 LA 639.24
  ML 740.14

ENDLESSLY TH 845.23

ENDS DV 138.12 SD 423.34
  WR 558.40 GG 674.26
  MD 812.22 TH 845.5

ENDURANCE SG 221.7 ML 735.37

ENDURE MO 14.1 DV 176.6
  177.4 SG 229.20 EE 313.12
  YT 402.16

ENDURED TF 131.34 DV 176.16
  HD 447.19 BO 589.38
  IL 650.17

ENDURING DV 176.37 SS 198.1
  WS 255.30 256.20 EE 307.29
  322.22 BO 597.7

ENEMIES HT 39.9 DV 138.23
  TP 342.8

ENEMY OA 31.28 EA 93.38
  PO 111.11 FG 189.6
  GF 235.2 EE 329.38 330.41
  SD 415.24 WR 571.17
  GG 662.33 662.34 ML 732.24

ENEMY'S EE 330.13

ENERGETIC SB 217.20 PR 501.4
  JD 617.1 NT 707.36
  MD 808.34 815.22

ENERGETICALLY BM 827.17

ENERGIC EE 304.24

ENERGIES PR 482.34

ENERGY MO 22.26 23.12
  EA 78.20 PO 104.5 108.22
  108.30 112.19 DV 174.38
  OC 289.28 EE 304.18 304.28
  YT 400.11 SD 412.32
  PR 492.25 TB 520.22
  SU 543.8 WR 546.11 547.15

ENERGY (CONT.) 551.4 JD 618.5
    NT 705.35 706.38 706.42
    707.7 707.27 707.31 707.41
    708.27 708.41 ML 745.16
    MD 808.25 808.30 808.38
    815.18 816.18 817.22

ENFORCED OA 23.7

ENGAGED WM 57.8 EA 83.23
    PO 100.7 DV 147.21 SB 215.24
    215.25 215.26 215.34 215.37
    215.41 SG 231.26 EE 329.42
    HD 442.14 IL 647.3 NT 720.15
    720.22

ENGAGEMENT WM 61.37 DV 155.11
    IL 648.16

ENGINE OC 283.1 283.8 283.15
    283.23 283.26 284.28 285.2
    285.28 286.4 286.8 295.10
    JD 608.22 618.7

ENGINE-CAB OC 285.25

ENGINE-DRIVER OC 285.4 285.13

ENGINEER'S WR 548.21

ENGINES SU 528.27

ENGLAND WM 65.13 EA 86.2
    FG 187.1 EE 303.28 304.5
    304.20 307.30 308.29 313.2
    326.30 327.26 TP 335.16
    WP 381.15 381.18 383.40 384.7
    384.27 YT 396.22 399.20
    399.21 TB 513.12 BO 587.15
    LA 641.5 GG 666.22 667.23
    MD 825.7

ENGLISH MO 5.16 11.35 EA 85.14
    86.1 FG 188.2 SS 202.42
    EE 304.22 305.40 305.41
    314.25 326.31 327.12
    BL 349.23 WP 380.37 381.7
    383.21 383.25 386.16
    FA 463.23 PR 484.34 WR 566.39
    SM 583.10 BO 587.27 LA 634.26
    641.6 LL 763.13 MD 815.12
    819.2 819.11 820.21 820.22
    820.32 821.4 821.6 821.7
    821.20 TH 849.35

ENGLISHMAN EE 326.26 BO 587.12

ENGLISHMEN EE 327.9 BO 587.13

ENGLISHNESS EE 326.20 326.28

ENGLISHWOMAN BO 587.31

ENGLISHWOMEN SM 582.15

ENGROSSED CH 277.22

ENHANCED SB 217.22

ENIGMATIC TB 514.22 514.30
    WR 567.26

ENIGMATICAL TB 524.25

ENJOY SP 52.38 TF 129.12

ENJOY (CONT.) SG 223.4 WS 252.41
    253.4 253.5 253.8 TB 515.19
    519.7 526.34 BO 590.29 592.5
    BM 840.25

ENJOYED MO 18.4 OA 33.15
    TF 132.7 DV 140.25 GF 243.25
    FA 464.11 TB 519.10 519.13
    519.14 LA 640.38 IL 649.12
    MD 815.21

ENJOYING PO 113.40 WS 256.22
    TP 339.28 LA 634.35

ENJOYMENT TB 519.8

ENLIVENED FG 190.4

ENMITY SU 541.35

ENNUI BL 347.32 MN 366.18
    ML 735.14

ENORMITY GG 661.12

ENORMOUS OA 28.1 EA 81.26
    EE 310.11 PR 480.14 BO 596.9

ENORMOUSLY PR 497.34 BO 591.23
    NT 701.23 MD 809.37

ENOUGH MO 2.38 2.40 OA 23.4
    30.2 31.33 HT 40.16 43.40
    SP 46.38 48.24 51.37 WM 58.14
    69.33 EA 74.5 75.22 76.7
    89.19 TF 119.42 131.40
    DV 150.18 164.3 164.6 166.2
    166.17 176.14 184.13 184.21
    185.19 SS 203.25 SB 215.36
    SG 222.4 GF 238.5 243.30
    WS 244.34 256.30 OC 285.17
    287.36 294.1 295.4 EE 306.1
    329.37 BL 350.33 MN 368.24
    370.38 WP 382.42 383.19
    383.34 384.42 389.27
    YT 397.20 404.38 405.9 405.23
    406.15 409.11 SD 413.14
    416.39 417.6 418.5 418.35
    420.21 PP 429.31 431.41
    HD 441.30 447.20 449.32
    FA 459.24 459.38 461.17
    461.26 PR 483.27 501.28
    TB 519.33 524.32 SU 536.17
    WR 547.22 549.2 549.24
    BO 588.13 JD 626.34 LA 632.30
    IL 648.39 GG 675.30 678.25
    NT 703.14 708.6 708.18 713.35
    713.36 718.5 ML 722.6 735.11
    OV 748.6 748.7 754.1
    LL 761.31 768.31 768.32 769.7
    RR 780.17 780.28 780.38
    RH 790.22 790.24 797.22
    MD 808.31 812.24 815.32
    BM 827.34 835.14 839.33
    TH 845.16 846.22 851.16

ENQUIRINGLY FA 470.36

ENRAGE PR 477.31

ENRAGED TF 121.14 BL 357.11

ENRAPTURED BM 837.19

ENRICH OA 23.5

ENSUED MO 2.34

ENTER DV 142.24 EE 322.27
    BL 357.15 359.30 PR 485.39
    BM 838.39

ENTERED MO 3.19 4.12 7.14
    11.31 17.41 HT 40.9
    WM 58.7 64.19 EA 74.27
    75.37 PO 100.32 102.2
    TF 123.15 125.30 129.24
    129.29 DV 139.23 139.36
    148.34 171.19 SS 203.6
    208.36 208.38 SB 217.4
    SG 222.21 228.31 230.4
    GF 236.39 WS 251.32
    CH 275.38 275.41 277.31
    279.34 OC 286.40 291.10
    292.9 EE 308.18 TP 341.17
    BL 353.10 362.23 WP 379.4
    390.8 YT 396.31 397.34
    401.32 SD 412.1 418.11
    423.17 423.23 PP 432.29
    436.41 439.3 HD 444.19
    FA 470.15 PR 490.9 499.36
    WR 562.27 579.6 579.9
    JD 610.18 616.30 624.35
    LA 637.2 640.12 GG 669.30
    670.6 672.8 681.16 694.34
    ML 739.24 RR 785.31
    MD 823.40 TH 845.42 846.9

ENTERING OA 23.16 DV 139.31
    BL 353.22 SD 411.30
    WR 565.1

ENTERTAIN MD 811.42 812.2

ENTERTAINED PR 481.29

ENTERTAINING ML 733.27

ENTHUSIASM WR 549.33 ML 729.8
    730.6

ENTHUSIASMS NT 706.7

ENTHUSIAST BL 350.6

ENTICE SC 269.2

ENTIRE SS 204.13

ENTIRELY SP 48.2 DV 160.20
    172.41 184.30 FG 189.2
    SS 206.35 WS 250.30
    SC 269.21 EE 312.22
    TP 335.17 BL 347.14 348.9
    PR 512.18 TB 515.17 SU 544.34
    BO 588.10 JD 617.22
    LA 644.23 GG 693.4 MD 811.9
    811.18 816.4 821.1 821.2
    821.19 822.41 BM 838.40
    TH 848.9 849.34

ENTITLED RR 780.18

ENTITY SG 228.19

ENTRAILS SG 228.24

ENTRANCE PO 108.32 BL 364.38
    SD 413.8 LA 640.13

ENTRANCED YT 401.26 401.27

ENTRANCED (CONT.) 401.42

ENTREAT HT 39.18

ENTRENCHED FA 466.9

ENTRY HT 43.11 43.16 43.29
  SP 51.18 OC 292.39 293.2
  JD 616.29

ENUNCIATION EA 85.15 LL 774.42

ENVELOP BO 604.17 BM 837.22

ENVELOPE DV 142.32 142.36
  WS 245.24 245.30 ML 742.15

ENVELOPED EE 306.31 SU 530.31
  BO 593.2 597.37

ENVELOPES WS 245.19

ENVELOPING BL 355.34

ENVIED DV 165.39

ENVIOUS ML 731.33

ENVY DV 165.10 PR 476.2
  TH 849.10

EPHRAIM SP 47.13 48.12 49.7
  49.13 49.20 49.25 49.29
  49.36 50.1 50.11 50.25 50.35
  51.9 51.18

EPHRAIM'S SP 47.27

EPHRAIM WHARMBY SP 47.3 52.28

EPICUREAN EE 308.28 314.4

EPISODE OC 301.33 WP 385.27

EPISTOLARY RR 779.10

EPOCH-MAKING NT 706.36 706.38

EQUAL SG 222.28

EQUALLY YT 401.7 SU 543.25

EQUIPMENT ML 728.4 MD 806.9

EQUIPPED TH 851.4

EQUIVALENT DV 152.18 GG 671.1
  671.10

EQUIVOCATOR BO 592.17

ER WP 383.29 383.35 384.27
  SU 540.1 540.2 541.7 541.9
  541.12 541.39 542.4 542.9
  544.29

'ER SC 272.4 272.22 272.23
  272.26 OC 287.41 294.20
  294.25 MN 375.41 WP 389.15
  389.16 389.25 389.28
  FA 463.29 469.13 470.27

ERASMUS TH 848.38 848.40 849.4
  849.19 850.3 850.11 850.15
  850.22 851.29 851.30 851.34

ERASMUS (CONT.) 851.38 852.11
  852.13 852.14 852.24 852.33
  852.34 853.24 853.27

ERASMUS MELVILLE TH 851.22

ERASMUS'S TH 851.42

ERE FA 465.24

'ERE SC 271.1 CH 277.21

ERECT SP 47.29 51.19 51.25
  TF 127.42 133.29 133.35
  DV 174.19 184.3 SS 198.12
  SG 222.22 OC 284.5 EE 325.30
  BL 354.15 357.15 358.1 358.10
  YT 405.12 PP 427.4 HD 442.31
  FA 460.40 PR 476.21 SU 533.18
  538.10 539.23 WR 558.17
  558.18 561.10 569.9 BO 596.4
  JD 623.20 LA 630.8 630.18
  631.1 631.26 632.35 634.41
  IL 651.32 GG 675.18 681.30
  690.38 MD 824.39 BM 827.29
  836.13 836.21

ERECTED EE 313.35 WR 556.32
  ML 725.38

ERECTIONS EE 329.24

ERECTNESS EE 325.29 BM 834.35

ERMINE GG 674.4 674.16 674.32
  675.6

EROS GG 677.28 677.29

ERRAND EE 320.38 OV 748.40

ERRANDS GF 238.38 ML 724.3

ERRATIC PO 113.13

'ERS CH 279.18 WP 389.4 389.14

'ER'S SP 46.8 WP 389.16
  FA 463.28

ERUPT NT 717.40

'E'S CH 276.30 OC 291.20 292.16
  292.18 292.30 WP 389.24
  FA 463.30

ESCAPE EA 81.24 TF 121.37
  123.33 131.7 133.6 DV 157.16
  173.32 176.42 GF 240.12
  WS 255.20 EE 306.42 TP 342.12
  BL 348.7 359.35 364.28 365.12
  WP 386.5 FA 465.35 TB 521.3
  BO 593.33 599.11 ML 725.4
  737.6 739.6 MD 813.42
  BM 827.20

ESCAPED TF 124.39 130.28
  DV 176.40 WS 253.19 SC 272.8

ESCAPING OA 27.10 PR 501.25
  TB 521.4 BO 592.37 GG 661.2

ESCORT BO 587.37

ESCORTED DV 147.19

ESCORTING MN 370.29 BO 594.32

ESPECIALLY MO 14.28 SP 50.31
  TP 338.35 341.13 MN 374.22
  PR 477.19 482.7 TB 526.17
  SU 531.20 BO 591.38
  JD 607.9 LA 640.39 642.16
  IL 648.36 GG 669.16 671.17
  671.23 NT 705.29 706.7
  706.15 710.18 LL 774.6
  MD 814.31 BM 840.12
  TH 845.11

ESPIED TP 345.27

ESSENCE OV 749.22

ESSENTIAL HT 38.29 WS 254.29
  LL 778.23

ESSENTIALLY WR 547.20
  OV 752.21

ESTABLISHED OA 29.19
  PP 430.18 HD 447.2
  MD 821.8

ESTABLISHMENT EA 89.14
  EE 313.35 313.40 TB 516.2

ESTATE EE 305.9 314.15
  HD 442.15

ESTATES SU 543.42

ESTEEM TB 514.13

ESTEEMED NT 719.11

ESTIMATION EE 314.20
  JD 605.18

ESTRADA, DON MIGUEL (SEE DON
  MIGUEL ESTRADA)

ESTRANGED PR 479.21

ETC. FG 188.19 CH 281.28

ETC. ETC. JD 606.12

ETCETERA MO 8.40

ETERNAL EA 76.33 82.21
  TF 130.14 132.18 134.30
  DV 157.15 179.37 181.15
  SS 197.13 GF 240.12
  HD 454.41 FA 458.5
  PR 479.40 SU 533.35
  WR 548.12 548.28 557.23
  BO 596.3 JD 625.16
  LA 646.14 ML 743.12
  MD 813.35

ETERNALLY SG 230.40 OC 301.32
  TB 513.6 SU 538.23
  SM 585.22 GG 680.10

ETERNITIES HD 454.17
  MD 824.31

ETERNITY DV 156.20 GF 241.36
  EE 331.35 HD 450.29
  FA 467.24 WR 563.23 563.30
  BO 598.24 GG 664.6

ETERNITY (CONT.) ML 735.34
  744.40 MD 819.4 819.39

ETHEL SC 272.15 272.20 272.33
  273.5 273.7 273.14 NT 707.12
  712.30 712.35 713.12 713.34
  715.20 715.37 716.35 717.4
  717.35 718.9 719.3 720.32
  721.12

ETHEL CANE NT 705.14

ETHEL MELLOR SC 272.12

ETHEL'S SC 272.28

ETHER GG 661.28

ETHEREAL PR 497.38 ML 742.40

ETON RH 800.11

ETRUSCAN SM 584.10 LL 761.6

EURIPIDES' WM 67.4

EUROPE YT 396.34 PR 481.13
  NT 701.21 707.32 716.29
  MD 805.7 TH 844.14 847.17
  847.21 847.22 847.31 847.34
  848.34 848.35 849.14 849.33
  849.37 849.40 850.7 850.18
  852.16 852.18 852.23 852.26
  853.1 853.20

EUROPEAN TH 847.34 847.35 848.6
  853.25

EUROPEANS TH 847.22 847.27

EUROPE'S TH 853.29

EVADE TP 335.26 SU 536.18
  BM 835.41

EVADED HD 450.25 FA 470.41

EVADING MO 9.8

EVANESCENCE ML 735.32

EVANGELICAL DV 140.35

EVAPORATE WM 65.34 PR 480.16
  497.42

EVAPORATED PR 480.2

EVAPORATING SU 531.4

EVASION WS 255.34 WR 554.6

EVASIVE FA 471.40 WR 570.25

EVASIVELY WR 576.10

EVE IL 655.23 MD 814.28

EVENIN' SD 413.31

EVENING MO 2.2 16.19 OA 23.18
  23.30 24.7 27.32 SP 47.40
  50.38 WM 54.13 54.29 55.31
  57.21 58.36 59.17 61.2
  EA 82.25 84.17 92.25

EVENING (CONT.) PO 100.28 101.9
  101.13 103.34 TF 127.34
  128.35 133.34 DV 149.37
  152.27 170.19 173.21 177.18
  177.25 177.31 183.3 FG 187.28
  189.26 190.10 SB 219.29
  GF 234.1 WS 252.16 SC 269.4
  EE 320.36 325.20 BL 350.34
  358.5 361.35 MN 368.31
  368.33 374.3 374.42 376.15
  WP 388.3 YT 400.38 406.41
  409.22 SD 412.8 412.10 415.1
  PR 481.28 WR 554.18 565.37
  565.40 570.4 BO 594.17 602.37
  604.16 JD 609.1 619.12 628.35
  IL 650.5 650.8 652.6
  GG 678.33 683.21 NT 714.22
  715.18 719.13 719.31 720.15
  720.22 ML 725.20 727.10
  OV 748.33 752.13 LL 764.33
  770.31 773.1 776.40 777.2
  778.12 RR 781.13 783.6
  RH 800.9 804.4 MD 808.29
  815.23 816.6 817.13 818.11
  BM 830.18 831.12 833.35

EVENINGS MO 4.14 7.29 WM 57.20
  PO 100.7 101.14 DV 176.30
  178.5 GG 681.34 LL 761.32
  763.17 MD 812.4 TH 844.30
  849.1

EVENING-SUNNY YT 400.42

EVENLY PO 107.15 FG 194.31

EVENT PO 96.31 103.29 OC 288.33
  GG 685.13 698.26

EVENTS TF 131.27 RH 794.13
  796.31 801.25

EVER-DEEPENING GG 699.14

EVEREST GG 674.3

EVER-GRATEFUL WP 384.30

EVERLASTING PO 116.3 EE 309.39
  SM 585.29 BO 595.18 ML 722.14
  OV 755.17 LL 761.29 772.27
  TH 847.35

EVER-RECURRING EE 310.7

EVERYBODY EA 86.36 DV 151.21
  152.24 152.34 156.5 159.19
  SG 224.37 GF 235.11 243.23
  WS 257.34 SC 267.1 CH 278.15
  EE 309.4 TP 335.29 336.9
  BL 349.39 SD 413.33 425.9
  PP 438.11 FA 460.1 460.20
  460.23 463.39 467.7 PR 475.20
  475.24 SU 529.25 WR 547.3
  549.31 568.25 578.23
  BO 587.34 IL 655.35 GG 672.24
  673.32 675.26 684.30 693.17
  NT 703.26 703.27 703.28 709.7
  710.25 711.20 ML 726.16
  726.25 730.40 732.6 732.38
  737.35 LL 763.7 RH 790.14
  MD 816.33 BM 831.34 831.38
  836.4 836.34 TH 850.5 852.2

EVERYBODY'S BL 356.28 TB 527.20

EVERYDAY WM 64.30 66.19
  EA 82.30 PO 111.37
  DV 146.5

EVERYONE SS 198.21 201.18
  HD 447.37 GG 672.20
  NT 711.40 ML 726.21
  BM 830.23

EVERYWHERE MO 19.27 HT 42.11
  SP 49.12 OC 291.39
  BL 362.11 WP 385.36
  PP 432.22 SU 537.25
  WR 549.8 NT 719.32
  RH 791.25

EVIDENCE TP 336.9 BO 588.5
  588.6 GG 699.7 699.8
  699.12

EVIDENT MO 5.25 OA 33.32
  EA 85.41 GF 237.13
  WS 250.24 OC 288.6
  WR 552.27 NT 701.32
  ML 732.4 732.13

EVIDENTLY MO 14.24 EA 85.18
  86.32 DV 155.19 155.30
  CH 274.33 275.4 OC 284.32
  292.19 WP 391.17 392.5
  YT 398.31 PP 430.36 432.29
  432.39 433.20 437.5 437.9
  437.14 437.19 437.41
  438.14 HD 444.26 WR 554.30
  JD 613.6 620.24 TH 853.33

EVIL OC 288.1 YT 405.34
  PR 509.25 ML 730.38
  LL 777.35 TH 853.34

EVILS EE 327.15

EVIL-SMELLING ML 742.20

EVOKED EE 326.15

EWELL WM 59.23

EXACT TP 344.31

EXACTLY MO 7.28 WM 67.20
  SG 227.21 OC 284.9
  BL 360.27 WP 391.8 392.19
  YT 403.21 PR 476.31
  WR 546.2 JD 605.20 LA 636.3
  636.8 642.2 GG 671.19
  677.34 689.3 ML 736.25
  MD 809.15 BM 830.38

EXAGGERATED GF 236.5

EXAGGERATING PO 110.24

EXALT EE 326.30 BO 596.7

EXALTED EA 92.40 ML 728.37

EXAMINATION DV 163.11
  EE 321.2 BO 599.16

EXAMINE DV 177.22 EE 317.6

EXAMINED SP 49.36 SS 203.19
  206.26 WS 250.1 EE 320.1
  ML 733.33

EXAMINING   DV 146.3   SS 198.16
   SB 219.33   SG 222.12   PR 491.4
   SU 537.24

EXAMPLE   DV 140.11   BO 588.18
   IL 650.24   ML 735.35   TH 844.16

EXAMS   TH 850.16

EXASPERATED   DV 159.40   SG 229.3
   WS 257.27   258.23   JD 620.9
   ML 737.31   BM 831.34

EXASPERATEDLY   IL 658.3

EXASPERATING   PO 100.22

EXASPERATION   EA 79.5   TF 133.38
   BL 356.11   HD 443.40   446.7
   IL 656.32   ML 737.30   737.33
   LL 776.2   776.11

EXCEEDINGLY   MO 3.9   DV 144.26
   147.26   156.24   CH 279.6
   PP 434.18   PR 479.38   JD 612.1

EXCELLENT   WS 252.24   PR 481.27
   TB 516.5   ML 728.4   RH 792.34
   MD 817.19

EXCEPT   MO 14.41   EA 86.37   91.14
   94.9   PO 96.39   104.40
   DV 138.14   148.10   158.42   172.6
   174.10   SG 229.8   WS 248.23
   EE 307.27   TP 336.1   336.24
   345.21   PP 429.2   429.35
   FA 471.35   PR 481.32   486.20
   501.42   TB 524.12   WR 548.20
   549.17   553.31   JD 612.24
   LA 636.3   GG 669.26   672.24
   675.1   680.14   NT 708.2   719.18
   LL 766.1   769.17   RH 795.16
   MD 806.6   TH 851.6

EXCEPTION   HT 39.3

EXCEPTIONAL   NT 714.30

EXCESS   PR 509.3   LL 776.13

EXCESSIVE   OA 32.35   PR 473.20

EXCESSIVELY   GG 688.8

EXCHANGE   JD 613.31

EXCHANGED   BL 358.22

EXCHANGING   OC 300.33

EXCITABLE   WM 59.26   59.37

EXCITE   DV 174.29

EXCITED   SP 46.14   TF 121.33
   132.5   SC 271.21   TP 337.36
   338.13   YT 404.24   SD 411.28
   411.35   412.32   421.30   421.36
   HD 449.14   449.17   WR 558.31
   BO 593.4   600.1   JD 612.28
   612.40   NT 710.15   712.12

EXCITEDLY   FA 468.18

EXCITEMENT   SP 49.16   DV 143.14

EXCITEMENT (CONT.)   SS 203.35
   SG 226.4   MN 371.39   PR 498.28
   TB 526.31   SU 536.4   WR 550.14
   GG 685.21   RH 796.7   BM 835.1

EXCITING   EA 81.30   DV 169.21
   WS 253.25   260.19   EE 331.1
   TP 337.30   338.31

EXCITINGLY   WS 249.13

EXCLAIM   ML 727.12

EXCLAIMED   MO 21.27   21.32
   OA 27.27   HT 43.7   SP 47.2
   WM 55.21   59.18   TF 124.9
   134.19   DV 141.21   168.6
   FG 188.36   SS 198.35   200.5
   201.5   204.17   205.16   208.11
   210.34   SB 212.1   GF 236.16
   241.39   242.4   242.6   243.3
   WS 260.6   CH 277.2   OC 288.27
   288.34   TP 342.11   BL 352.4
   352.24   WP 392.4   YT 397.21
   397.40   399.1   SD 413.13   418.13
   425.5   PP 436.39   437.39   439.39
   HD 444.7   444.9   444.24   445.16
   445.22   450.3   SM 585.15
   GG 668.24   678.16   680.22
   693.31   BM 833.15   840.20

EXCLAMATION   MO 8.28   TF 124.4
   DV 145.13   145.22

EXCLAMATIONS   FG 188.3   TP 340.38
   RH 792.35

EXCLUDED   DV 171.26   EE 310.1
   BL 356.40   JD 617.31

EXCLUSIVELY   TB 515.15   BM 827.10

EXCRUCIATED   NT 711.33

EXCRUCIATINGLY   MD 808.8

EXCULPATE   PP 438.19

EXCURSION   DV 167.4

EXCUSE   MO 9.9   BL 361.37
   WP 391.1   JD 626.10   RR 785.18
   RH 797.19   MD 825.1

EXCUSED   BO 587.21   MD 824.15

EXECUTED   PO 108.23

EXED   SP 51.34

EXERCISE   HD 441.24

EXERCISED   SD 425.17

EXERTING   WS 257.35

EXHAUSTED   MO 4.36   PO 113.15
   DV 168.15   174.37   177.5
   SB 214.14   SC 268.30   270.1
   YT 400.26   WR 550.9   ML 745.16

EXHAUSTION   PO 113.19

EXHILARATED   SG 226.3

EXILE   PR 478.24   NT 701.2

EXIST   OA 31.31   PO 105.7
   DV 156.2   SG 229.4   229.7
   OC 300.38   WP 390.29
   GG 677.15

EXISTED   EA 89.15   89.16
   PO 113.31   DV 163.33
   SS 209.37   WS 255.24
   OC 300.39   PR 509.14
   BO 592.39   JD 617.23
   LA 640.35

EXISTENCE   EA 93.18   PO 105.3
   DV 147.27   SG 226.7
   HD 445.4   PR 474.31
   SU 531.39   NT 701.4
   ML 743.10   RR 784.16
   MD 816.19   817.31

EXISTING   DV 140.3   RR 784.33

EXISTS   FG 187.22   BO 589.34

EXIT   DV 160.13   FA 468.25

EXONERATED   GF 243.34

EXOTIC   OV 748.18   LL 769.35

EXPAND   ML 724.14

EXPANDED   MO 11.26

EXPANDS   ML 735.18

EXPANSE   SB 217.7

EXPANSION   MO 12.28   EA 93.17
   DV 174.23   ML 740.14

EXPATRIATED   TH 851.28

EXPECT   MO 7.35   WM 58.21
   DV 147.36   176.2   SB 212.30
   GF 236.1   238.35   238.36
   OC 285.12   291.26   292.30
   294.26   BL 359.35   MN 377.17
   WP 381.37   389.29   YT 397.22
   PR 494.11   TB 525.10   525.32
   527.26   WR 560.3   JD 620.33
   620.35   LA 642.41   IL 654.27
   GG 661.26   682.6   RH 795.29
   796.14   BM 834.15   839.33

EXPECTANCY   OC 290.24
   OV 753.19

EXPECTATION   DV 151.21   151.33

EXPECTATIONS   YT 394.29
   TB 519.27

EXPECTED   WM 55.21   55.24
   EA 84.22   DV 144.38   145.7
   147.30   154.3   SB 216.10
   WS 255.8   OC 301.40
   EE 315.10   TP 337.11
   WP 386.37   SD 412.14
   425.19   BO 587.34   589.12
   602.23   IL 658.26   658.31
   GG 663.20   669.2   NT 707.16
   707.37   ML 733.17   TH 847.21
   853.5

EYE (CONT.)

EYE (CONT.) 523.27 WR 555.31
SM 585.28 BO 588.31 588.39
JD 613.16 614.31 IL 649.33
659.30 GG 666.11 694.16 700.3
NT 711.6 ML 726.29 728.38
OV 749.5 749.6 749.27 750.16
751.17 757.29 RR 789.6 RH 793.10
MD 820.3 820.28

EYE-BATTLE GG 688.15

EYEBROWS MO 18.14 HT 40.35
PO 96.21 97.4 99.23 100.33
102.9 DV 169.27 SS 202.29
OC 284.8 BL 351.24 MN 377.12
WP 389.37 YT 401.40 SD 412.28
PP 434.27 FA 458.10 465.17
SU 543.16 WR 563.13 567.34
SM 582.13 JD 606.26 622.34
GG 670.33 NT 705.32 LL 761.26
MD 808.39 809.19 820.29
BM 839.10

EYED TP 345.17 WP 391.19
TB 517.21 SU 538.11 GG 699.37

EYELASH MD 820.5

EYELESS GG 698.9

EYELIDS MO 12.12 13.16 13.40
14.13 DV 181.26 GF 234.10
WS 263.1 BL 351.25 FA 466.12
SM 582.22 LL 761.25

EYES MO 3.24 4.1 4.5 5.23 8.2
8.25 9.9 9.24 9.25 9.27
10.34 12.24 15.12 16.13 17.6
19.9 OA 23.6 26.9 26.27
26.34 26.39 27.1 27.5 28.18
29.40 30.14 31.20 33.7 33.16
33.21 35.27 36.9 36.10 36.38
37.14 38.3 38.25 38.27
HT 39.34 40.22 41.11 44.8
44.15 SP 47.35 51.20 WM 55.7
55.34 57.37 58.11 58.16
59.27 61.24 64.26 65.18
65.36 66.11 66.17 67.37
67.41 68.4 68.34 68.35 69.33
69.35 70.1 EA 71.24 71.32
72.33 73.2 73.29 73.32 74.38
75.42 76.7 81.12 84.23 84.32
85.11 85.38 90.22 90.28
91.11 92.28 PO 96.22 96.32
97.4 97.30 97.39 99.11 99.12
99.18 99.19 99.22 99.26
100.9 100.19 101.24 102.16
102.18 102.20 102.28 102.33
104.13 105.14 105.32 106.23
107.14 109.37 110.23 110.28
110.33 111.24 112.13 112.31
112.39 113.25 114.14 114.35
115.21 116.7 TF 117.33 118.15
121.14 121.16 121.22 123.24
123.25 123.35 124.29 125.9
132.10 133.42 134.13 134.15
134.21 135.8 135.15 DV 138.19
139.19 143.4 148.10 148.39
149.42 156.6 158.6 160.17
163.14 168.3 169.27 170.13
170.26 172.30 172.31 175.13
175.18 176.3 176.6 178.29
178.32 179.10 180.21 180.23
180.30 180.34 181.13 181.23

EYES (CONT.) 184.3 FG 187.18
187.24 188.7 189.24 191.32
192.22 192.35 193.37 195.11
195.35 196.20 SS 198.7
198.16 198.40 199.12 199.26
202.29 203.8 203.31 204.7
207.25 208.32 208.33
SB 212.20 214.16 218.4 219.17
SG 221.12 222.23 226.22
226.23 227.25 227.34 227.39
228.38 230.32 230.41 231.41
GF 238.13 WS 246.17 246.19
249.5 249.15 249.32 252.32
252.35 253.14 254.16 255.29
258.19 262.2 262.24 263.22
263.40 264.1 264.3 264.9
264.13 264.17 264.31 265.42
SC 268.11 268.24 CH 279.8
282.17 OC 286.41 287.9 289.12
289.30 293.31 294.2 294.5
294.7 294.35 298.32 300.24
EE 303.9 304.24 306.7 314.34
325.33 332.7 332.23 332.29
TP 336.14 336.42 340.17
340.18 342.31 343.27 344.7
344.12 344.24 344.27
BL 351.26 351.30 353.34
357.25 358.23 359.41 361.17
363.40 364.6 364.10 364.40
365.4 MN 367.2 367.24 368.19
368.21 369.10 369.14 370.12
374.11 375.15 375.32 375.33
376.36 WP 379.31 380.10
380.17 380.22 381.6 383.21
383.25 383.26 384.33 387.39
388.19 389.31 391.3 391.4
391.35 393.7 YT 395.31 398.10
398.28 398.31 399.27 400.19
401.3 401.16 402.31 402.36
402.37 403.29 404.7 404.11
407.13 407.31 409.33 410.6
SD 412.28 412.31 413.29
413.41 413.42 414.11 414.12
414.24 414.29 414.38 415.11
415.39 416.1 416.17 416.21
417.1 417.17 417.26 417.31
418.21 418.30 418.33 419.41
420.24 420.40 422.22 423.42
424.1 424.12 425.22 425.26
PP 427.8 427.37 429.12 429.27
431.2 432.30 432.39 433.18
433.26 433.28 434.5 434.6
434.16 434.29 434.35 435.32
435.38 437.13 437.37 438.37
439.19 439.21 439.28 439.30
439.35 440.1 HD 441.33 441.36
442.12 442.23 444.23 444.39
445.34 446.6 448.19 448.25
448.26 450.8 451.13 451.33
451.37 452.32 453.3 453.40
454.5 454.6 454.26 454.28
454.32 455.4 455.22 456.36
FA 460.42 465.16 468.18
PR 473.28 474.14 474.18
475.10 477.9 478.8 478.23
479.39 481.6 482.4 482.9
482.26 482.37 483.2 483.8
484.20 484.21 484.26 487.18
488.36 491.28 493.3 494.39
496.3 497.3 497.21 497.42
499.18 499.34 500.31 501.15
501.16 501.19 504.37 505.19
505.22 506.13 506.15 506.35
506.39 507.33 511.26 511.36

EYES (CONT.) 512.20 TB 513.16
522.19 522.21 524.40
524.41 526.30 SU 528.22
528.23 530.3 530.34
530.36 533.19 533.23
534.16 534.18 534.20
534.38 536.36 538.26
538.29 542.2 542.7 542.25
543.15 544.4 544.25 544.31
545.1 WR 546.4 550.38
553.37 554.17 554.21
554.23 554.34 555.17
555.18 555.28 555.30
555.38 557.33 557.37
559.29 559.36 559.39
559.41 560.9 560.28 563.13
565.7 565.9 565.26 566.17
566.30 566.40 567.2 567.25
567.35 567.40 570.25
570.34 573.1 573.15 573.21
574.38 576.1 576.8 576.16
577.8 577.17 577.33 578.8
578.39 581.9 581.10 581.13
581.20 SM 582.19 583.13
583.42 584.1 585.12 585.21
BO 589.25 590.41 591.7
596.32 600.39 603.27 604.8
604.23 JD 606.24 606.27
611.12 611.18 611.22
611.24 611.38 612.12
612.30 613.17 613.30
613.40 614.5 614.18 614.23
615.6 616.32 616.36 617.42
618.8 620.37 620.39 621.27
622.26 624.32 624.35
624.40 625.9 625.12 625.14
625.17 625.38 627.14
627.27 628.41 629.1
LA 632.26 633.12 634.28
634.32 634.34 634.39
636.5 636.15 637.34 637.35
638.33 640.27 643.15 644.4
644.14 645.30 646.10
646.19 646.28 IL 647.22
647.33 654.17 655.39
656.32 658.20 659.35
GG 661.14 663.21 664.11
664.23 664.39 665.41
666.25 666.29 668.4 668.39
669.25 670.13 670.25
670.32 672.11 672.35
672.39 672.42 673.4 673.9
673.14 674.34 675.11
677.13 677.39 678.19
679.37 680.8 681.16 681.29
683.16 683.21 684.39
687.9 687.41 690.1 691.21
692.1 692.20 694.21 695.8
696.6 NT 701.7 702.13
702.21 702.33 702.38
702.40 703.6 703.35 704.2
705.26 705.28 705.29
707.26 707.35 711.22
713.16 713.39 715.11
715.29 719.6 719.8 719.16
720.25 ML 727.9 728.25
728.34 729.8 729.12 735.8
736.21 737.23 738.34
739.17 739.23 739.27
741.5 743.30 OV 748.11
753.40 758.3 758.29
LL 761.11 761.14 761.15
761.21 761.25 762.42
763.38 765.27 769.2 771.8

FACES (CONT.)   TF 127.29 130.24
   DV 138.18 FG 194.24 GF 238.1
   OC 287.24 290.15 290.22
   TP 337.19 337.32 343.27
   343.30 346.8 BL 351.40 351.42
   MN 367.37 371.14 YT 394.15
   SD 412.4 PP 430.29 FA 458.2
   PR 482.34 TB 515.31 WR 559.29
   562.30 573.35 573.39 577.6
   577.14 577.22 577.33 580.28
   SM 584.3 584.4 586.23
   IL 658.11 GG 664.42 665.31
   681.25 ML 727.26

FACETS GG 665.31

FACILE WP 380.40 MD 814.18

FACILITY MD 810.1 814.18

FACING MN 377.8 FA 468.20
   PR 498.23 SU 542.34 WR 561.36
   563.26 579.23 580.12 580.24
   SM 584.3 OV 756.25

FACINGS PO 96.1

FACT OA 34.42 WM 56.20
   PO 101.13 DV 140.38 164.32
   165.16 GF 236.10 242.13
   OC 300.31 EE 314.2 TP 340.12
   BL 349.34 YT 408.2 SD 417.8
   PP 428.10 HD 447.36 449.17
   PR 473.8 479.26 480.9
   TB 514.7 523.5 523.13 523.40
   BO 601.6 JD 619.12 IL 652.9
   652.11 NT 718.25 ML 727.37
   LL 771.11 771.20 RH 791.27
   MD 815.7 816.27 816.40
   BM 832.1 TH 845.29 849.7
   849.38

FACTORIES TP 334.22 BO 595.2
   JD 610.25

FACTORY GF 235.3 237.5 239.32
   241.28 242.3 243.19 WS 250.20
   251.8 PP 429.28

FACTORY-LIKE YT 394.6

FACTS PR 480.30 JD 619.37
   LL 768.25

FACULTIES HD 448.39

FACULTY SU 544.9 MD 812.32

FADE BL 349.39 WR 577.27
   LL 766.5

FADED WR 556.15 SM 585.10
   585.21 LA 641.1 GG 671.2
   671.5 671.6 LL 767.22
   MD 807.4 811.41 TH 848.13

FADED-RED OV 747.10

FADING FG 189.36 ML 723.26

FAERY FG 193.36 194.8

FAGGED IL 648.29

FAGGOTS PR 501.34

FAILED MO 5.24 YT 395.1
   PR 482.8

FAILING HD 449.29 PR 485.12

FAILURE EA 82.3 89.7 DV 180.7
   PR 482.19 IL 658.4 OV 748.27
   LL 773.17 RH 790.32 TH 852.23

FAINT OA 23.34 30.16 WM 60.36
   61.30 68.26 EA 89.28
   PO 103.41 104.34 104.35
   106.29 109.23 115.12
   TF 122.36 132.19 DV 161.39
   170.4 FG 189.32 WS 258.3
   GF 237.15 241.33 WS 258.3
   SC 268.29 OC 292.4 300.5
   EE 319.3 330.11 331.8 331.19
   TP 336.15 WP 386.6 YT 400.20
   401.31 409.25 SD 421.25
   HD 442.21 442.23 454.30
   PR 500.16 WR 554.19 557.33
   563.12 570.25 572.31 578.19
   SM 582.27 586.6 BO 588.40
   595.34 596.26 JD 623.10
   LA 646.33 GG 683.8 687.3
   698.35 ML 744.34 RH 802.40
   MD 813.42 820.38 BM 836.25
   843.1

FAINTED NT 713.7

FAINTER WM 60.30

FAINTEST EA 73.10 74.37
   WS 260.27 EE 326.23 MN 368.35
   368.36 FA 469.38 JD 613.1
   IL 647.16 651.40 655.13
   LL 772.33 BM 828.14

FAINTING TF 131.29 FA 467.9

FAINTLY WM 65.37 EA 73.35
   DV 175.23 GF 240.28 241.7
   OC 298.20 EE 331.37 BL 354.37
   MN 369.19 373.23 373.26
   YT 401.33 PP 430.31 HD 442.27
   443.24 446.10 456.16
   FA 467.29 PR 497.28 WR 554.35
   572.22 573.36 BO 604.22
   604.32 JD 622.37 LA 634.40
   ML 723.22 740.35 744.42
   745.42 OV 748.41 TH 847.3

FAIR OA 30.1 SP 51.21 WM 70.5
   EA 71.22 78.32 PO 96.21
   TF 117.20 117.34 SS 203.28
   GF 234.2 234.7 234.24 235.9
   235.16 235.37 236.13 237.1
   237.13 241.15 243.7 WS 245.10
   246.11 248.25 SC 267.10 268.7
   CH 280.21 OC 287.32 EE 304.26
   304.30 TP 337.8 338.2 341.41
   BL 359.23 363.13 MN 368.29
   YT 395.3 SD 412.36 412.38
   412.40 FA 462.15 464.18
   467.37 SU 533.24 538.8
   WR 564.5 JD 611.11 611.36
   616.30 617.32 617.41 618.27
   624.31 ML 725.30 730.39
   732.22 OV 748.10 RR 780.31

FAIR-COMPLEXIONED WR 550.40

FAIRER WS 246.11 248.25

FAIRER (CONT.) SC 268.28

FAIR-FACED FA 460.38

FAIR-GROUND TP 337.11

FAIR-HAIRED FA 462.15
   JD 608.16 LA 645.29

FAIRIES MO 20.13 PR 475.32
   475.34 479.16

FAIRLY GF 242.40 EE 319.30
   TP 336.16 337.40 YT 396.30
   HD 446.29 FA 463.22
   PR 490.29 NT 716.19
   ML 731.17 OV 758.42 759.7
   RH 802.30 MD 819.2
   BM 833.35

FAIR-SKINNED SB 217.21

FAIRY PR 475.35 478.2
   TB 516.13

FAIRYLAND MD 811.39

FAIRY-LAND PR 494.27

FAIRY-LIKE DV 158.39
   PR 494.7* 498.31

FAIRY-TALES MO 19.28

FAITH WM 57.4 DV 152.34
   EE 313.28 313.29 313.30
   313.33 326.14 BL 349.35

FAITHFUL TF 128.33 BL 359.22
   PR 479.12 TB 513.14 516.24
   BO 594.34 IL 647.21
   GG 666.37 ML 725.32 733.8

FAITHFULLY TB 514.41 MD 814.9
   814.10 814.11 814.12

FAITHFULNESS ML 734.27

FAKIR OV 757.5

FALL MO 14.8 SP 45.6
   WM 65.27 EA 83.16 84.29
   PO 116.3 TF 119.33 120.23
   DV 176.28 FG 187.7 195.33
   SB 216.29 GF 234.34
   EE 331.15 TP 345.9 MN 368.1
   378.26 WP 384.20 384.21
   HD 455.15 FA 468.5
   SU 535.8 WR 552.36 570.39
   572.26 BO 602.21 JD 605.9
   629.14 IL 652.7 652.8
   GG 690.16 NT 708.21 718.24
   ML 730.23 731.1 735.36
   MD 812.17 812.25 813.14

FALLEN SP 51.13 DV 140.18
   180.42 FG 190.28 193.24
   SS 197.23 204.8 211.12
   SG 226.10 GF 234.32
   OC 300.23 PR 490.14 490.33
   496.14 SU 537.38 540.4
   544.40 544.42 WR 569.36
   JD 613.25 IL 657.41
   GG 671.35 674.13 NT 718.24
   718.28 718.31 ML 730.19

FALLEN (CONT.) 736.37 737.42
  OV 747.10 753.14

FALLING EA 75.28 PO 105.9
  DV 161.13 181.2 FG 192.6
  SS 200.35 210.23 HD 448.37
  449.33 PR 503.16 SU 535.32
  WR 557.7 565.37 576.19
  BO 602.29 LA 631.6 IL 649.19
  652.21 NT 709.31 ML 744.38
  745.31 TH 848.16

FALLOW MO 1.15 SP 48.41 PO 95.5
  111.34 SB 214.2 ML 726.42

FALLS TP 338.18 BL 352.30
  SU 532.34

FALSE MO 6.24 12.1 WM 69.42
  EA 87.33 88.2 DV 158.4
  WS 263.31 YT 402.20 BO 590.15
  BM 841.15

FALSEHOOD FA 465.25

FALSE-INNOCENT NT 705.29 705.30

FALSELY OC 301.7 LA 636.21
  IL 656.8 BM 841.21

FALTERED EA 83.35 SG 228.32
  SC 272.35 OC 291.7 MN 367.42
  376.26 WR 571.39 OV 749.21

FALTERING DV 149.3 HD 454.35

FAME EE 305.28 FA 464.12
  SU 536.2 NT 701.33

FAMED FA 464.32

FAMILIAR DV 169.29 CH 277.41
  280.28 OC 301.4 TP 339.26
  BL 354.35 355.24 FA 459.5
  LL 767.31 767.35

FAMILIARITIES EA 86.11

FAMILIARITY FA 460.8 ML 726.7
  742.7

FAMILIARLY WM 54.18

FAMILIES DV 137.2 ML 731.17

FAMILY MO 5.32 11.32 13.30
  TF 128.6 DV 138.14 138.26
  140.18 144.26 145.2 150.32
  184.31 185.19 SS 201.17
  SB 212.11 CH 278.19 278.23
  279.22 279.28 EE 304.27
  305.38 308.15 309.1 309.6
  309.16 309.34 309.37 313.12
  314.8 321.41 329.13 BL 349.3
  349.8 358.26 WP 381.9 384.7
  391.41 PP 428.19 428.39
  HD 441.8 442.30 443.5 446.28
  447.15 FA 470.16 471.7 472.10
  PR 473.4 482.17 482.21
  TB 516.15 516.20 517.14
  519.22 520.3 520.13 WR 554.26
  IL 649.13 659.26 GG 661.10
  661.23 665.42 666.8 671.15
  671.18 672.7 672.8 695.41
  699.32 699.38 ML 731.39

FAMILY (CONT.) RH 791.32 798.40
  801.4 801.5 MD 805.23 813.17
  819.1 819.9 819.10 820.9
  821.8 BM 827.28 829.10

FAMOUS EA 86.16 FA 464.40
  IL 647.20 GG 661.3 NT 711.7
  LL 764.35 MD 822.40

FANCIED HD 448.36

FANCIES RH 794.18

FANCY EA 87.19 YT 397.25 398.37
  GG 689.33 RH 795.38

FANG WR 579.42

FANGED WR 579.33

FANG-LIKE WR 579.25

FANGS WR 578.28

FANNY FA 459.24 460.30 460.38
  460.40 461.4 461.10 461.11
  461.14 461.16 461.23 461.27
  461.30 461.35 462.1 462.8
  462.11 462.14 462.20 462.37
  463.2 463.11 463.17 463.26
  463.38 464.4 464.8 464.26
  464.27 465.12 465.27 466.4
  466.20 467.16 467.18 467.23
  468.12 468.19 468.22 468.29
  468.35 468.38 468.42 469.6
  469.8 469.14 469.19 469.26
  469.30 469.41 470.6 470.12
  470.25 470.26 470.28 470.41
  472.8 472.9

FANNY'S FA 460.30 460.33 463.13
  463.37 463.39

FANTASTIC LA 642.24 642.25
  GG 696.12 RR 779.7 783.22

FAR-AWAY WR 564.36 574.39

FAR-AWAYNESS SD 413.36

FAR-DISTANT GG 670.19

FARE JD 628.33

FAREWELL SP 50.39 WR 551.14
  572.24 573.19 573.26
  BO 597.29

FAR-GONE ML 724.24

FARING PR 499.2

FARM MO 1.3 1.23 2.15 7.8
  PO 107.5 114.30 DV 136.33
  SS 200.32 BL 347.18 351.32
  361.41 MN 366.26 377.32
  WP 382.5 385.7 BO 593.21
  IL 648.12 651.10 653.17
  ML 728.24 728.28 732.17
  732.18 732.27

FARM-BELL PO 106.13

FARM-BOY ML 730.19

FARMER SS 201.18 201.22
  WP 390.40 391.42

FARMERS BL 347.12 WP 379.2

FARMER'S SS 201.6

FARM-HAND ML 726.11 726.13
  731.39

FARM-HANDS ML 725.17 727.3
  727.17

FARM-HAND'S ML 731.11

FARMHOUSE PO 95.35 105.27
  EE 304.32 ML 722.26 725.17

FARMING TF 128.2 128.6
  DV 179.23 WP 382.12
  IL 649.35 GG 699.41

FARM-KITCHEN BL 351.33

FARM-LAND DV 136.3

FARM-LANDS OV 756.40

FARM-MEN MN 366.35

FARM-PEOPLE BL 351.38

FARMS MO 2.7 SS 202.4
  WP 386.2

FARMSTEAD BL 347.11

FARM-WIFE ML 727.11 727.17

FARM-WORK MO 5.40

FARMYARD BL 351.33

FAR-OFF MO 2.8 SB 217.18
  EE 330.4 WR 563.7 565.35
  570.8 573.16 SM 583.22
  NT 715.41 ML 734.5 743.29
  744.29

FAROUCHE SU 543.25

FARQUHAR (SEE ELLEN, KATHERINE,
  PHILIP)

FARQUHAR'S BO 590.22

FAR-REACHING GG 665.3

FARTHER MO 2.17 OA 28.1
  EA 81.7 89.7 PO 110.5
  114.17 114.41 116.1
  DV 174.26 GF 243.32 WS 259.9
  OC 291.2 MN 372.39
  PR 484.7 498.38 499.28
  TB 526.6 SU 530.39
  WR 558.10 574.36 581.4
  SM 585.21 BO 603.15
  LA 632.1 IL 653.17
  TH 851.2

FARTHEST SG 225.13

FASCINATE DV 173.22

FASCINATED HT 41.18 WM 65.2

FAUN   JD 606.21   607.1   623.16
   LA 631.14   631.15   OV 757.29
   758.3   758.7   758.12   758.32
   758.36   759.4   759.9

FAUNS   OV 757.6   757.14   757.18

FAUN'S   JD 606.21

FAVOUR   OA 26.4   SP 50.22
   YT 398.31   BM 838.11

FAVOURED   SS 198.7

FAVOURING   WS 250.10

FAVOURITE   EA 86.16   EE 316.18
   TP 340.37   IL 650.38   651.5
   RR 783.13

FAWN   FG 193.28   WS 250.32

FAWNING   BO 592.24

FAWNS   PR 494.11

FEAR   MO 2.36   21.28   22.22
   OA 25.23   WM 65.8   EA 76.19
   PO 112.28   112.37   114.3   114.24
   TF 119.42   120.14   120.18
   120.21   120.22   120.40   122.22
   122.27   123.33   131.29
   DV 137.37   137.38   144.31
   149.22   150.1   153.40   164.35
   179.39   180.15   181.14   181.30
   FG 190.36   190.37   190.41
   191.21   192.13   193.25   194.24
   195.12   195.42   SS 203.35
   203.36   211.26   GF 238.14
   240.30   WS 259.22   263.23
   SC 269.22   270.15   272.13
   CH 281.34   OC 289.24   290.26
   290.39   299.11   299.30   300.5
   300.28   300.41   301.6   302.15
   EE 321.1   323.9   TP 335.28
   342.32   344.2   344.32   BL 348.37
   360.1   364.22   MN 369.7   371.41
   WP 385.18   YT 405.16   409.39
   PP 428.1   430.8   431.28   432.27
   437.40   438.4   439.23   440.1
   HD 452.30   453.41   PR 501.28
   507.20   SU 533.9   533.10   534.6
   534.17   534.18   WR 557.16
   560.32   566.25   571.3   SM 584.1
   584.24   BO 587.7   595.38   600.39
   JD 624.8   624.9   LA 637.19
   640.20   640.21   640.27
   IL 647.26   649.16   GG 664.12
   665.41   666.30   667.10   669.26
   679.35   680.8   684.38   690.42
   691.15   691.36   NT 708.2
   ML 724.10   737.16   738.33
   740.27   743.42   OV 752.8   753.34
   754.41   757.9   LL 772.5
   RH 803.7   803.10   MD 821.35

FEARED   SP 51.42   PO 96.34
   BL 363.11   HD 454.33   OV 754.10
   BM 828.6

FEARFUL   OA 35.8   SS 208.32
   WS 261.36   PR 501.9   NT 710.22

FEARFULLY   TF 125.29   WS 252.36
   OV 756.37   757.33   LL 767.30

FEARING   TF 119.36

FEARLESS   TP 335.20

FEARLESSNESS   PR 501.20

FEARS   TP 335.29   SU 534.19
   GG 699.38

FEARSOME   MD 815.11

FEAST   FG 191.11   JD 626.34

FEAT   SP 49.25   EA 90.7

FEATHER   TB 522.28   523.8
   WR 559.21   559.35

FEATHERED   WR 578.23

FEATHERS   SS 197.9   WP 379.13
   382.29   PR 494.28   496.36
   TB 522.9   522.27   527.27
   WR 556.11   568.32   569.1   569.8
   569.10   573.31   578.15   580.4
   ML 741.30

FEATHERY   ML 734.2

FEATS   MN 371.20

FEATURES   WM 65.17   PO 108.25
   GF 234.8   PP 427.16   PR 481.7
   TB 513.19   GG 694.15   ML 743.33
   BM 828.8

FEBRUARY   SU 535.31   JD 610.1
   610.20

FED   TF 128.37   FG 191.21
   CH 277.4   EE 308.6   WP 382.3
   385.15   PR 501.33   WR 551.19
   ML 743.23   RR 778.21   TH 849.6

FEEBLE   DV 151.26   SU 540.8
   BO 604.31   LL 775.22

FEEBLENESS   PR 498.21

FEEBLY   DV 148.8   WR 547.3

FEED   MO 2.27   DV 159.27
   FG 191.26   SB 217.13   PR 503.9
   BO 588.7   LL 778.20

FEEDING   MN 374.32   PR 507.12
   GG 674.33

FEEDING-TIME   DV 155.6   BL 351.42

FEEL   MO 2.36   7.21   18.1   18.32
   20.26   OA 30.4   30.5   35.38
   37.13   HT 42.7   WM 63.22
   EA 76.37   80.17   89.32   92.34
   93.1   PO 97.42   109.28   110.18
   110.19   DV 140.41   144.5   144.22
   152.31   153.5   153.11   153.12
   167.12   171.34   180.27   183.23
   FG 193.40   194.38   194.39
   SS 203.2   SB 215.40   218.42
   SG 223.12   228.19   GF 236.10
   241.35   WS 253.28   SC 267.32
   270.31   CH 274.34   EE 317.19
   319.38   323.33   329.5   332.16
   BL 348.31   353.22   354.17   355.3

FEEL (CONT.)   361.25   361.27
   361.32   362.11   363.12
   363.21   WP 384.11   391.9
   YT 402.31   403.21   PP 428.35
   429.3   435.20   HD 446.19
   450.22   450.42   451.2   457.6
   FA 462.36   PR 475.22   504.31
   510.38   TB 517.13   526.4
   526.5   SU 529.21   530.38
   530.42   WR 564.13   566.29
   BO 592.3   592.7   592.11
   592.34   593.1   593.8   602.15
   603.7   603.11   604.4
   JD 607.6   607.10   607.12
   608.4   629.8   LA 634.20
   IL 652.22   GG 661.32   661.33
   661.35   663.39   674.13
   676.14   678.30   678.35
   678.36   679.9   690.11   691.26
   691.31   694.30   695.13
   696.5   700.12   NT 709.13
   716.3   717.16   ML 723.34
   730.41   731.14   731.15
   735.23   735.24   736.1   736.32
   740.22   740.29   OV 749.5
   749.31   749.35   749.41
   LL 767.16   770.34   773.11
   773.13   RR 782.6   784.17
   RH 790.13   794.21   802.4
   802.13   MD 810.1   810.7
   811.29   812.38   BM 829.35
   833.40   TH 851.9   851.13
   851.14

FEELER   SG 223.3

FEELING   MO 4.8   5.13   12.28
   OA 25.37   28.4   35.13   35.14
   SP 49.17   EA 76.36   77.8
   79.23   80.10   89.15   91.12
   91.35   91.41   PO 97.36   98.26
   100.13   103.36   104.12
   105.10   105.38   107.31
   109.40   TF 120.10   122.38
   125.39   126.12   129.2
   DV 137.33   152.14   153.9
   154.36   154.37   163.42
   165.12   165.13   173.35
   175.34   179.6   182.21   182.28
   183.3   183.7   FG 191.22
   195.33   SS 197.34   198.12
   SB 217.34   SG 226.7   228.35
   229.13   GF 241.5   WS 246.21
   250.9   251.10   256.14   257.6
   257.27   257.28   SC 270.20
   CH 278.15   279.26   OC 301.5
   EE 318.1   326.42   327.3
   TP 336.5   342.3   BL 348.28
   353.9   354.7   358.7   361.20
   WP 392.5   YT 402.20   409.6
   SD 419.16   425.33   PP 428.30
   434.21   HD 447.9   448.19
   448.20   448.28   FA 459.1
   460.39   461.35   PR 481.2
   485.4   491.11   501.11   505.3
   TB 514.10   524.8   SU 533.2
   537.12   WR 552.19   555.23
   566.16   567.38   568.1   572.7
   572.12   SM 582.28   583.1
   BO 589.25   589.29   592.13
   592.38   596.38   596.41   602.9
   JD 607.28   614.3   615.39
   616.14   627.40   IL 647.24
   647.26   649.7   649.9   652.36
   GG 662.40   666.1   689.8

FELT (CONT.) 643.26 IL 649.24
  649.42 650.5 651.8 651.10
  652.19 659.40 GG 661.7 663.9
  664.5 664.17 666.27 674.23
  675.8 679.1 679.2 679.24
  679.29 680.3 683.14 683.30
  685.5 685.18 685.27 686.3
  686.25 690.31 695.12
  NT 702.15 702.18 704.11 710.8
  ML 723.38 727.37 731.20
  731.29 736.38 737.21 737.37
  737.38 739.12 739.14 742.28
  744.12 745.4 746.37 OV 747.12
  749.14 749.34 750.15 750.25
  753.13 757.38 LL 764.8 764.40
  775.14 RR 781.7 781.32 781.34
  RH 790.4 790.6 790.9 790.20
  790.21 803.4 MD 806.12 806.21
  807.12 807.30 811.1 812.12
  813.8 813.9 813.30 814.12
  816.34 817.9 817.15 817.16
  817.18 818.42 819.9 822.20
  BM 830.22 831.2 832.15 832.29
  834.18 836.18 836.19 841.34
  TH 845.17 845.25 845.41
  846.15 846.32 848.38 851.23

FELT-COVERED OC 284.3

FEMALE EA 87.19 TF 127.31
  TP 339.18 PP 438.26 438.40
  FA 467.3 467.7 WR 554.22
  558.2 568.13 BO 591.28 592.19
  594.8 JD 628.14 GG 672.31
  RR 779.15 MD 805.26 805.29
  810.19 816.26 BM 833.12

FEMININE EA 76.35 EE 315.13
  SM 583.33 BO 587.2 JD 605.3
  611.26 LL 761.6 RR 788.22
  788.39

FENCE MO 1.7 22.14 22.24
  TF 117.13 DV 160.31 167.28
  SS 197.11 WS 263.16 WP 390.41
  PP 436.31 PR 493.31 WR 561.40
  IL 648.21 651.19

FENCES WR 578.29 GG 668.34
  ML 725.38

FENCING ML 726.33 OV 752.26

FENDER DV 159.26 OC 286.14
  287.25 288.7 SD 412.26 423.22
  423.28 HD 442.22 JD 617.10
  617.18 GG 671.26

FERGUSON* HD 445.22 445.24

FERGUSON, JACK (SEE JACK FERGUSON)

FERGUSSON* HD 445.33 448.11

FERGUSSON (SEE DR. FERGUSSON)

FERMENT NT 701.34

FERN SS 206.19

FEROCIOUS WR 566.18

FEROCITY MN 375.41 WR 570.11
  581.17 581.18 MD 811.35
  BM 839.15

FERRET'S GG 670.32

FERRY-BOATS SU 528.36

FERTILE OC 289.24

FERTILIZERS ML 728.41

FERVENT SS 208.13 WS 256.23

FERVENTLY DV 140.35 SS 203.4

FERVOUR WM 54.20 67.25

FESTOON PR 490.7

FET SD 426.2

FETCH SP 46.11 PO 108.12
  TF 131.13 DV 172.1 OC 291.7
  EE 307.12 BL 347.6 FA 459.22
  459.27 WR 556.14 OV 756.15
  BM 834.29

FETCHED OA 35.29 EA 87.24
  DV 162.29 FG 189.6 SS 203.18
  WS 247.7 OC 296.27 TP 342.26
  343.7 344.23 PR 506.41 510.14
  BO 602.19 GG 676.27 LL 776.17

FETTERS SU 544.36

FEVER PO 105.22 115.18 DV 183.1
  OC 292.31 MN 373.31 ML 730.32
  745.16

FEVERISH EA 71.20 EE 320.3

FEW MO 4.10 5.12 13.29 OA 24.3
  27.34 33.10 37.29 HT 39.32
  42.14 SP 52.3 WM 56.2 58.1
  69.12 EA 74.18 75.23
  PO 107.39 111.6 114.25
  TF 118.29 DV 138.30 149.4
  150.33 157.16 162.9 166.10
  180.23 FG 187.4 188.31 190.22
  191.2 SS 197.17 198.2 199.35
  207.9 SG 228.41 GF 239.2
  240.21 WS 254.23 258.38
  259.36 265.41 CH 277.25
  OC 283.33 284.9 290.35 293.17
  299.12 EE 318.26 324.7 330.17
  TP 334.13 337.21 341.16
  BL 348.22 350.24 357.23
  359.24 MN 372.25 YT 404.40
  SD 422.6 HD 442.4 450.29
  PR 474.6 479.24 491.12 499.25
  502.26 511.10 SU 536.19
  538.10 WR 549.23 550.31
  559.27 559.33 560.5 563.9
  563.16 564.1 578.8 BO 593.22
  594.40 595.5 598.34 598.40
  600.11 JD 606.3 615.1 625.32
  626.11 LA 631.30 637.17
  IL 652.28 GG 667.17 670.11
  694.26 NT 707.1 720.29 721.8
  ML 722.26 727.1 734.14 734.39
  738.18 739.34 744.32
  LL 763.24 768.25 771.30
  772.26 MD 811.20 815.20
  BM 834.31 838.20

FEWER OC 286.33 286.34

FEZ MD 819.28 823.3 BM 835.27

FIANCEE WM 57.13 58.27

FIASCO MD 817.35

FIBBER MO 10.7

FIBRE WM 69.15 TF 126.25
  EE 306.10 312.17 313.23
  BL 364.13 GG 662.41

FICHU GG 670.15

FICO NT 713.9

FIDDLER ML 730.17

FIDDLES BM 837.29

FIDELITY TB 513.13

FIDGET SB 214.9 IL 651.40

FIDGETED WM 56.24 RH 798.18

FIDGETING SD 415.21

FIELD MO 1.14 HT 42.24
  SP 49.2 49.4 49.10 49.22
  50.6 PO 108.4 TF 123.4
  SS 197.5 197.9 210.29
  SB 217.4 217.7 CH 275.22
  275.30 OC 286.32 EE 322.35
  330.40 MN 366.8 HD 449.23
  449.37 WR 569.31 BO 599.29
  600.21 IL 648.22 651.9
  651.18 ML 723.22 RR 780.19

FIELD-GATE SS 197.2

FIELD-MOUSE OA 24.15

FIELD-PATH TF 123.1

FIELD-PATHS DV 176.38

FIELDS MO 2.7 19.20 SP 48.40
  49.1 PO 115.9 TF 117.4
  117.8 118.24 123.12 132.20
  DV 136.14 136.19 174.15
  182.27 SS 197.26 204.38
  210.12 WS 259.11 SC 267.21
  OC 283.16 286.27 EE 330.38
  TP 338.34 HD 446.25 447.31
  448.41 449.21 450.5 451.5
  BO 593.19 599.39 ML 722.27
  722.35 RR 787.37

FIEND FG 188.15 188.20
  188.26 189.9

FIEND'S LL 768.7

FIERCE MO 19.40 OA 37.12
  EA 71.23 91.35 PO 105.32
  106.33 TF 121.12 134.4
  DV 151.10 174.17 176.16
  FG 190.6 SB 220.4 WS 259.37
  EE 303.27 MN 375.35
  PP 428.22 431.2 PR 494.30
  499.37 WR 570.10 581.16
  BO 603.20 JD 616.31
  LA 637.42 LL 773.38
  TH 848.3 848.4

FIERCELY MO 11.22 TF 127.11

FIERCELY (CONT.) CH 280.10
 TP 346.3 YT 403.26 407.24
 PP 429.6 430.32 433.4 439.42
 WR 555.39 JD 621.39 LA 639.2
 IL 658.5 ML 743.30 RH 793.37

FIERCER MO 2.35

FIERCEST PP 440.2

FIERY DV 180.12 SD 425.11
 425.21 ML 728.32

FIESTA NT 709.28

FIFTEEN SP 46.4 EA 75.37
 SS 199.25 SC 269.18 270.36
 YT 396.21 SD 424.9 425.23
 BO 587.12 RH 796.15 796.19
 797.14

FIFTEEN HUNDRED POUNDS RH 797.23

FIFTEENTH FG 188.30

FIFTH ML 732.42

FIFTH AVENUE TH 850.1

FIFTIETH BM 829.16

FIFTY EE 304.38 PR 473.20
 NT 704.37 RH 795.30 MD 808.32
 BM 831.23 TH 850.8

FIFTY DOLLARS TH 850.40

FIFTY-FIVE PP 428.13 428.14

FIFTY-FOUR HD 447.10

FIFTY-ONE OV 747.11

FIFTY POUNDS RH 800.25

FIFTY-SEVEN BM 832.18 832.40

FIFTY-THREE WR 547.14

FIFTY-TWO OV 747.12 748.12

FIGET CH 277.16

FIGHT OA 35.35 38.34 SP 51.12
 EA 71.17 SS 205.1 SG 231.35
 GF 243.14 259.35 EE 308.24
 YT 407.12 SD 426.5 426.17
 TB 522.5 522.11 GG 663.32
 663.35 682.1 686.11 686.33
 697.29 MD 814.26

FIGHTER YT 407.12 BO 592.15

FIGHTING MO 2.37 WM 67.9
 WS 257.35 OC 300.38 EE 305.30
 PP 434.34 TB 522.8 BO 588.25
 590.35 592.32 JD 619.28
 ML 732.26 MD 814.25 820.6
 BM 835.4

FIGHTS PO 96.21

FIGURATIVELY YT 409.35

FIGURE OA 29.2 WM 59.13 65.25

FIGURE (CONT.) EA 84.34
 PO 95.34 96.1 96.4 96.10
 100.33 105.34 107.14 107.17
 107.40 109.7 109.10 TF 119.22
 119.25 119.27 119.33 119.37
 126.5 DV 138.36 146.42 150.3
 158.11 158.14 FG 188.23
 SG 221.13 221.27 226.12
 227.10 228.32 WS 255.30
 256.19 263.21 SC 268.5
 CH 274.8 OC 288.26 EE 317.39
 320.11 BL 358.11 360.3 360.18
 360.35 MN 371.41 374.21
 378.4 WP 390.37 393.13
 YT 400.9 400.11 SD 417.40
 421.40 PP 438.34 440.21
 HD 449.22 449.28 449.40
 FA 460.5 PR 482.5 483.41
 489.30 510.37 511.10 511.14
 TB 518.17 522.20 SM 586.19
 BO 587.17 600.31 JD 625.4
 LA 634.19 IL 651.32 GG 691.2
 NT 707.26 ML 726.41 728.35
 LL 762.32 775.24 MD 808.41
 809.1 820.26 BM 830.4

FIGURED WP 385.34

FIGURES MO 3.15 OA 24.36 25.9
 35.2 WM 58.40 PO 108.37
 TF 134.39 DV 167.16 EE 333.10
 SD 411.20 PR 494.32 495.42
 510.9 510.10 WR 579.35
 SM 586.23 LA 631.30 637.2
 LL 769.42 RH 799.17 BM 838.39

FIGURE-TOI COMME JE SUIS DESOLEE
 WP 392.21

FILAMENT SU 531.6

FILBERT MN 376.39

FILE SP 48.41 TF 118.20 118.33
 134.37 DV 174.3 SB 217.10
 PR 489.17 RR 787.36

FILED FA 468.27 BO 593.22

FILES WR 578.17

FILIGREE WP 379.9

FILL SP 53.9 69.7 SG 225.42
 OC 293.2 EE 304.9 307.14
 312.21 312.29 TB 525.34
 BO 602.38 ML 722.9 MD 811.4

FILLED OA 36.19 PO 105.16
 110.26 TF 125.16 133.16
 DV 136.8 154.37 155.2 156.32
 176.30 183.6 FG 188.17 190.40
 SG 226.33 227.10 229.29
 231.14 WS 261.25 CH 280.24
 TP 344.3 BL 364.23 PP 434.32
 HD 454.5 455.4 PR 502.21
 SU 537.13 WR 568.11 SM 582.9
 GG 675.23 678.41 686.5 693.3
 ML 725.7 733.24 737.7
 OV 754.26 RH 791.8 MD 807.18
 812.1 BM 830.5

FILLET EA 71.31

FILLING SP 47.39 PO 114.39

FILLING (CONT.) FG 196.19
 SG 227.15 229.9 PP 439.13
 HD 448.32 WR 580.42
 OV 754.32 TH 851.9

FILLS JD 608.16

FILM MO 2.15 EE 330.11
 PR 489.20

FILMED WS 255.20

FILTERED PP 427.6

FILTHY RH 791.42 792.1

FINAL OA 33.9 WM 66.28
 EE 307.10 311.34 HD 441.8
 FA 467.2 SM 584.27
 JD 620.29 LA 646.21
 GG 698.3 MD 817.29 817.37
 TH 848.26

FINALITY JD 620.39 GG 665.25
 667.41 675.33 ML 739.2

FINALLY OA 33.29 EA 75.6
 FG 187.5 EE 331.32 YT 397.5
 PR 474.27 TB 514.1
 WR 573.10 JD 628.25
 LA 640.14 GG 662.13 681.8
 MD 821.6 821.17 823.40

FINANCIAL TB 516.11

FIND MO 9.20 13.38 20.10
 22.12 HT 39.30 WM 62.10
 EA 90.9 PO 111.24 DV 142.2
 151.29 163.5 171.32
 174.39 SS 204.36 SB 218.11
 GF 238.40 WS 254.12 255.41
 257.4 EE 313.22 TP 337.11
 338.41 BL 363.8 MN 374.41
 WP 382.21 383.41 384.3
 YT 394.30 399.15 SD 423.17
 426.5 426.9 PP 433.6
 433.8 HD 444.3 451.27
 452.6 FA 471.22 PR 476.11
 486.41 490.35 TB 516.40
 BO 590.35 594.6 598.4
 603.41 JD 605.27 621.29
 GG 662.36 663.20 700.13
 NT 708.21 715.3 715.4
 ML 732.15 OV 749.16 758.4
 RH 790.31 794.8 804.36
 MD 806.6 806.36 BM 833.24
 839.24

FINDING SP 50.39 PO 104.4
 TF 119.8 FG 191.27
 YT 395.25 JD 615.29
 RH 790.5 TH 845.8 851.3

FINDS FG 192.10 ML 724.16

FINE-FLESHED EE 306.15

FINE-HEARTED EA 86.20

FINELY TF 133.23 DV 168.13
 FA 460.41 LA 631.34
 LL 761.10

FINELY-CUT EA 84.32

FINELY-KNIT   PO 96.10

FINELY-KNITTED   TH 848.13

FINELY-WORKED   SM 476.25

FINENESS   OA 33.13

FINER   EE 312.1   312.11   315.11
  ML 739.4

FINEST   MD 813.24

FINE-TEMPERED   EE 324.32

FINE-WORKED   BO 586.9

FINGER   MO 7.18   9.25   10.37
  WM 62.11   DV 157.36   SS 204.19
  SB 216.7   216.18   SG 226.30
  WS 246.35   SC 269.42   CH 277.7
  HD 441.33   TB 522.28   BO 599.3
  LA 630.23   NT 718.10   OV 758.22
  RR 785.13   MD 820.11   BM 832.26
  833.4

FINGER-BOWL   GG 677.7

FINGERED   WS 246.1   PP 437.20
  GG 677.36   OV 747.6

FINGER-ENDS   TB 525.32

FINGERING   WM 65.11   SS 202.14
  SM 586.11   IL 650.40

FINGER-NAIL   EA 89.24

FINGER-NAILS   EA 89.30

FINGERS   MO 10.12   18.31   OA 31.27
  34.22   35.36   EA 85.36   90.40
  92.32   PO 104.34   110.40   111.24
  SS 203.22   203.24   SB 219.33
  SG 227.16   GF 234.20   WS 245.9
  245.34   254.38   CH 276.13
  279.29   279.39   TP 341.19
  BL 355.18   358.32   358.33   363.7
  364.10   364.11   MN 372.23
  372.25   YT 401.39   402.2   403.7
  SD 424.42   HD 450.26   TB 526.23
  SU 530.27   WR 557.1   GG 677.36
  695.42   OV 749.28   749.29   753.7
  753.11   LL 773.32   RR 784.25
  785.7

FINGER-TIP   SG 223.24   TB 523.8

FINGERTIPS   MD 807.39

FINGER-TIPS   EA 92.35   WR 564.9
  564.11   573.14   GG 677.7   696.1
  OV 750.4   BM 836.17

FINISH   MO 20.32   SP 50.30
  WM 66.8   PO 101.24   DV 174.38
  SC 270.33   YT 398.22   HD 445.31
  BM 839.18

FINISHED   OA 31.13   37.35
  HT 42.37   EA 79.7   DV 142.17
  154.25   178.1   178.6   FG 187.25
  SS 201.35   WS 255.33   OC 293.16
  299.42   301.35   302.9   WP 392.22
  SD 415.4   HD 446.2   448.31

FINISHED (CONT.)   456.13
  PR 476.17   482.21   JD 615.12
  615.14   GG 668.1   677.5
  688.10   LL 770.12   MD 817.10
  817.25   BM 838.14   TH 853.1

FINISHIN'   OC 292.21   295.39

FINISHING   DV 178.37   SS 201.12
  GG 676.24

FIR   PO 112.29   SS 204.25
  BL 351.11   BO 602.31

FIR-CONE   MO 4.19

FIRE   MO 3.15   6.1   6.36   7.19
  9.33   12.33   15.25   16.34   16.36
  16.38   17.10   OA 23.28   WM 55.10
  63.33   65.3   68.6   68.23
  EA 72.9   73.23   73.33   77.5
  85.33   87.36   87.37   89.24
  PO 96.22   97.30   99.28   107.24
  108.1   TF 131.15   131.33
  DV 139.27   139.40   140.16
  140.37   142.18   159.37   162.24
  162.28   163.25   163.27   169.23
  178.36   180.19   FG 188.15
  189.14   189.23   189.24   189.25
  195.18   195.31   196.20   SG 221.5
  GF 234.30   237.10   237.39
  238.13   238.15   238.19   238.26
  239.1   239.23   239.32   241.7
  243.23   WS 245.2   246.15   247.11
  247.25   247.28   248.37   261.17
  261.21   264.25   265.39
  SC 267.27   267.33   268.6   268.14
  CH 276.3   276.9   276.15   277.11
  OC 286.15   286.35   287.26
  287.29   287.35   287.39   288.13
  296.18   296.30   296.36
  EE 306.16   308.5   321.1   323.29
  329.26   330.9   331.29   TP 335.2
  340.25   340.30   341.1   341.19
  BL 350.12   356.15   359.5   359.7
  360.6   361.19   MN 373.31   377.23
  WP 386.39   389.40   SD 412.20
  412.27   413.21   413.37   415.32
  419.6   419.22   420.13   423.21
  423.24   423.29   424.27   424.36
  424.42   426.1   426.8   426.14
  PP 437.29   HD 443.18   451.11
  451.17   456.12   456.14   FA 458.4
  458.6   458.25   464.20   PR 477.16
  494.23   494.42   495.25   495.40
  500.17   500.19   500.21   500.28
  500.39   501.33   503.26   504.36
  504.39   505.7   505.14   508.9
  509.15   509.33   509.36   509.38
  SU 530.30   530.31   532.11
  532.37   545.2   WR 552.25   556.34
  556.41   557.4   557.14   557.26
  557.28   568.31   570.15   570.19
  570.28   573.37   574.14   576.20
  576.26   576.32   576.33   580.24
  580.29   581.1   BO 602.40
  JD 608.17   616.9   616.12   616.21
  617.15   617.33   617.40   618.6
  618.16   625.5   LA 640.24   640.26
  IL 649.8   650.9   654.13   654.32
  658.20   GG 671.5   671.25   682.8
  691.3   696.23   697.19   ML 744.4
  746.17   746.19   OV 748.36   749.7
  LL 776.41   777.5   777.14
  RR 783.35   784.7   785.42   786.3
  RH 796.5   798.28

FIRE-BACK   WS 261.13   262.3

FIREBRAND   EE 310.38

FIRED   TF 135.11   SG 230.26
  GF 243.10   EE 330.12
  PR 496.10

FIRE-DARKENED   GF 239.16

FIRE-ENGINE   GF 237.32

FIREGLOW   DV 158.18   158.42

FIRE-GLOW   WM 68.9   FA 462.28
  WR 570.15   570.18   576.22

FIRE-GRATE   PR 500.26

FIRELESS   DV 183.9

FIRELIGHT   EA 71.27   76.24
  DV 161.13   OC 286.12
  SD 423.30

FIRE-LIGHT   MO 5.1   5.3

FIREPLACE   OC 296.19   PR 500.10

FIRE-PLACE   DV 162.28
  GG 671.5

FIRE-REDDENED   GF 237.39

FIRES   MO 2.30   2.35   DV 179.1
  FG 194.6   GF 240.39   FA 459.2
  JD 610.22

FIRE'S   GF 239.3   WS 247.16

FIREWOOD   WR 562.6

FIRING   EE 330.15   MN 378.36
  PR 511.42   RR 786.32   786.39

FIRM   MO 1.11   WM 61.24
  PO 108.27   TF 120.10   120.19
  DV 148.19   149.27   182.26
  SB 219.14   WS 250.17
  CH 278.9   EE 310.20
  BL 363.37   SM 586.13   BO 603.6
  LA 631.28   BM 830.16

FIRMER   PO 106.9   106.11

FIRMLY   MO 11.13   PO 97.4
  DV 183.20   CH 274.15
  PP 435.39

FIRST   MO 14.11   16.10
  OA 34.15   34.21   HT 39.2
  SP 45.6   47.37   52.11
  WM 57.17   65.13   68.13   69.24
  EA 74.20   79.27   80.5   81.33
  84.3   PO 95.24   95.29   96.37
  TF 126.5   DV 136.1   137.25
  145.11   145.14   145.15
  152.8   153.11   154.19   155.5
  155.17   167.33   182.23
  SS 204.26   207.5   SG 231.17
  231.19   231.20   231.36
  232.14   GF 235.8   238.18
  WS 244.28   254.23   256.27
  260.9   260.24   263.3
  SC 268.18   CH 280.36

FIRST (CONT.) OC 289.10 292.31
  294.40 297.2 EE 306.12 307.7
  307.37 309.5 309.22 309.23
  309.38 332.11 TP 335.37
  337.22 339.20 342.1 BL 348.23
  349.17 352.36 MN 366.1 366.35
  366.36 373.18 WP 382.1
  SD 411.6 413.19 415.9 423.33
  PP 431.36 436.34 HD 453.3
  455.15 455.21 FA 462.9 464.8
  465.35 471.11 PR 474.4 474.6
  476.13 488.11 489.17 490.24
  493.12 493.35 496.3 502.16
  511.29 TB 520.20 522.4
  WR 546.33 547.28 552.24
  555.17 559.7 562.11 562.17
  568.29 574.6 SM 586.5 BO 587.5
  588.24 591.13 591.37 595.15
  598.38 601.4 601.13 606.20
  609.31 613.38 614.2 614.29
  615.29 624.1 IL 659.18 659.36
  GG 678.18 681.7 683.17 683.25
  693.23 698.40 700.2 NT 704.18
  705.25 705.27 707.21 712.5
  ML 723.14 725.42 728.7 736.10
  736.31 OV 754.10 LL 769.42
  777.40 RH 795.6 795.7 796.9
  798.2 799.22 804.15 MD 810.27
  811.8 818.28 820.36 BM 828.1
  834.13 TH 845.15 845.20
  848.33

FIRST-BORN EE 317.17 BO 588.35
  LL 769.23 RH 802.18

FIRST-CLASS DV 157.8 SM 582.4
  BO 588.1 598.36

FIRST-LOVE FA 459.7 459.13

FIRTH (SEE MR. FIRTH)

FIR-TRUNK BO 603.9

FISH CH 276.14 EE 315.27
  PR 481.40 JD 623.5 623.8
  GG 673.30 673.39 673.42 698.3
  ML 725.30 735.19 OV 756.24
  LL 774.29 MD 807.19

FISH-BAG WP 387.17

FISHED DV 170.40

FISHERMAN PR 484.5

FISHERMEN SG 224.10 ML 742.11
  742.21

FISHES TB 516.17 LA 631.31

FISHING PR 483.29 484.7 485.23
  ML 725.29 735.9 740.37
  LL 774.30

FISHING-BOAT ML 743.32

FISHING-NET ML 725.24

FISHY SU 533.42 GG 680.8

FIST HT 44.7 44.9 PO 109.32
  WS 264.10 CH 281.32 BM 830.2
  TH 851.13

FISTICUFFING MD 811.7

FISTICUFFS OA 35.36

FISTS OA 24.4 35.34 PO 109.22
  DV 176.36 177.27 BL 356.7
  MD 824.40

FIT DV 165.29 WS 262.14
  TP 338.23 BL 356.24 357.35
  MN 370.40 YT 406.25 SU 529.28
  BO 601.11 JD 616.38 IL 648.39
  GG 693.29 693.32 ML 738.8
  RR 784.22

FITFULLY MN 373.32

FITS BL 347.35 PR 479.22 479.30

FITTED SS 203.22 TP 338.27
  ML 735.5 MD 810.23

FITTING DV 179.5 BO 601.13
  NT 706.37

FITZPATRICK MD 811.13 811.14

FIVE SP 46.3 47.36 51.23 52.16
  52.25 DV 150.17 155.7
  FG 190.16 SS 204.21 SB 217.18
  SG 222.8 WS 253.34 SC 267.27
  268.1 CH 274.4 OC 284.21
  287.6 294.26 BL 350.9
  YT 397.2 SD 415.23 PR 491.21
  491.22 491.36 495.12
  TB 514.16 WR 550.28 GG 661.11
  NT 716.19 LL 762.19 763.41
  764.7 RR 780.14 RH 795.7
  795.38 796.33 799.2 799.5
  799.37 800.7 MD 807.24 808.6
  823.33 825.42 826.2

FIVE-AND-SIXPENCE SP 52.5

FIVE-AND-TWENTY SS 198.6

FIVE HUNDRED RH 798.1

FIVE-POUND RH 796.11

FIVER RH 795.41 796.1

FIVE THOUSAND POUNDS RH 798.39
  798.41

FIX PR 508.26 508.28 RR 784.39

FIXED MO 11.13 EA 89.13
  PO 97.12 102.20 TF 119.30
  DV 156.16 163.31 164.10
  165.30 170.29 171.32 180.34
  SG 227.42 230.32 230.39
  GF 239.29 WS 263.40 264.32
  CH 279.8 MN 368.8 SD 414.11
  414.20 420.24 424.1 425.36
  425.37 PP 429.12 HD 451.38
  PR 483.31 493.35 511.1
  TB 516.39 525.24 SU 542.22
  WR 577.17 581.11 581.13
  581.21 SM 584.27 JD 611.28
  614.24 LA 646.19 IL 655.10
  GG 670.13 689.10 NT 702.21
  LL 765.27 RR 785.2

FIXEDLY DV 149.3 151.28

FIXEDLY (CONT.) SG 226.24
  WS 264.16 WP 392.3
  SD 425.22 PP 431.27 435.40
  HD 452.5 PR 486.14 491.25
  JD 623.21 GG 665.29 670.18
  674.6 674.34 694.6
  ML 744.39 LL 778.13
  RH 793.9 MD 823.23

FIXING HD 446.6 PR 483.31
  WR 578.8 MD 811.15

FIXITY SD 417.10 HD 441.18
  WR 577.20 JD 622.20 622.25
  GG 666.29 669.42

FIXTURE TF 119.20

FIZZ RR 786.7 786.18
  MD 824.4

FLAG MO 12.13 12.14

FLAGGED BL 351.35

FLAGS OA 27.32

FLAG-SIGNALS PO 107.16

FLAGSTAFF ML 740.6

FLAGSTONES SG 224.9

FLAKED WR 579.12

FLAKES PO 105.24 DV 157.9
  PR 494.8 OV 747.9

FLAME MO 4.13 16.39 SP 48.11
  WM 70.5 70.8 70.18 EA 76.38
  90.30 90.37 91.1 PO 97.10
  99.6 100.36 102.30 108.8
  109.18 109.26 109.41
  TF 117.2 129.26 130.4
  130.6 130.10 DV 149.40
  175.2 175.11 FG 189.15
  SS 210.9 WS 254.8 OC 288.29
  EE 304.1 304.17 306.18
  306.31 308.6 314.42 329.22
  PP 434.8 440.2 HD 453.22
  453.32 FA 458.27 PR 485.31
  506.16 SU 530.10 530.34
  544.4 545.1 WR 561.11
  571.42 LA 637.41 638.4
  638.28 GG 671.33 677.35

FLAME-COLOURED SG 225.35

FLAMED PO 115.27 TF 127.11
  TP 342.31 PR 478.23

FLAMELETS RR 782.4

FLAME-LIKE EE 310.9

FLAME-LIT FA 458.1 458.5

FLAME-LURID FA 458.1

FLAMES WM 70.16 EA 73.23
  GF 238.14 OC 283.20
  TP 335.5 340.14 BL 361.16
  FA 458.12 466.21 BM 833.14
  837.37

FLAMEY LA 638.4

FLAMING FG 188.15 GF 238.21
EE 331.33 HD 445.1 PR 489.12
499.18

FLAMINGO CH 275.27

FLAMY EE 303.27 303.36 325.13

FLAN GG 676.29 676.31

FLANDERS EE 329.31 BL 347.7
MN 366.11

FLANK WS 257.14 PR 499.8

FLANNEL OA 24.32 DV 159.18
170.41 SC 267.34 OC 289.27
290.15 299.25 299.29
MN 367.13 PR 511.12 JD 617.20
OV 751.14

FLANNELETTE SD 414.14 JD 618.26

FLANNELLED DV 159.25

FLANNELS OA 23.12 DV 158.25
158.33 159.4 162.21 162.33
169.31

FLAP PP 433.33

FLAPPED OA 28.2

FLAPPING SP 45.22 WP 386.10
387.37 OV 748.19

FLAPPINGS WP 387.17

FLARE MO 4.14 13.16 OA 29.30
PO 99.27 114.25 GF 234.1

FLARED OA 35.27 PO 107.22
GF 235.16 SD 416.21 HD 455.15
FA 459.36 WR 556.5 RH 793.40

FLARES TP 337.20

FLARING WM 65.21 SB 212.20
MN 371.17 HD 453.2 RH 793.38

FLASH OA 25.9 28.32 29.38
30.12 PO 97.23 101.5 106.7
106.10 107.22 107.28 108.14
109.5 109.26 113.6 DV 149.22
167.10 SS 207.11 210.6
SB 216.11 WS 245.39 266.1
EE 312.16 312.17 SD 411.5
415.15 421.20 PR 501.25
LA 633.29 NT 713.38 ML 741.39
744.30 OV 750.4 750.6 750.12

FLASHED OA 24.18 26.14 27.5
WM 70.2 EA 76.23 88.1 90.8
SC 268.11 EE 312.24 324.33
WP 384.33 389.31 SD 422.31
IL 647.34 653.29 653.33
LL 762.25 762.26 RR 789.11
MD 826.27

FLASHES OA 30.20 MN 373.21
ML 744.37

FLASHING MO 2.18 OA 34.26

FLASHING (CONT.) WM 57.29
PO 96.22 MN 373.24 LA 634.32
OV 748.42 749.3

FLASHLIGHT RR 787.30 787.35
787.38 787.40

FLAT SP 53.15 EA 72.18 84.1
PO 114.39 TF 122.1 124.15
FG 190.1 195.5 SS 206.18
206.27 SB 214.15 214.18
214.41 GF 234.32 EE 306.41
307.2 308.33 323.14 MN 370.31
PP 437.23 PR 487.27 489.4
494.3 SU 528.17 541.26
WR 558.36 558.38 561.33
561.38 578.32 580.33
BO 593.18 599.29 GG 665.1
665.11 NT 715.29 715.39
716.24 719.17 ML 739.36
LL 761.9 764.41 766.22
MD 817.23

FLAT-BOTTOMED WP 379.10

FLAT-LEAVED SU 530.5

FLATS BO 599.5

FLATTENED GF 239.17 BL 363.7

FLATTERED WM 66.33 SG 223.28
FA 463.36 472.12 TB 526.2
JD 605.4 GG 661.24 663.23
682.5 NT 709.12

FLAUNTING SC 267.5

FLAVOUR TB 514.27 WR 565.24
NT 706.23

FLAW BL 357.9

FLAWED DV 156.10

FLAWLESS PR 508.42

FLAY PR 508.21

FLAYED RH 796.7

FLEAS GG 674.8

FLECKED PO 112.1 ML 745.25

FLECKS SU 538.1 JD 612.30

FLED MO 2.11 FG 190.15 193.11
194.37 RR 780.32

FLEE OV 758.36 758.37

FLEECE MO 9.37 PR 493.22
ML 741.9

FLEECY WS 244.7 PR 489.35
493.23 494.18 506.19

FLEEING FG 194.38

FLEET OA 24.38 SU 539.25

FLEETING RR 783.34 MD 822.19

FLEET-LOOKING SU 540.14

FLESH WM 55.31 EA 93.9 93.13
PO 104.33 TF 122.15 122.23
126.8 126.21 DV 153.30
154.23 154.28 154.29
WS 245.7 254.39 SC 270.8
OC 300.8 300.29 EE 306.6
319.27 322.12 322.14
323.32 323.34 326.4 330.21
BL 362.34 SD 424.4 425.20
PP 434.28 435.18 FA 466.16
PR 474.7 474.8 TB 521.12
SU 531.31 WR 577.24 579.18
BO 592.3 595.27 JD 620.27
623.33 GG 688.20 688.22
689.23 689.27 689.31
690.7 690.11 691.22 699.29
LL 761.9

FLEW MO 12.14 OA 24.33
29.33 WM 60.35 PO 98.29
113.40 114.2 TF 117.2
FG 194.18 WS 247.10
TP 342.29 BL 357.17
YT 409.37 PP 430.27
TB 516.10 SU 529.29 544.4
WR 555.38 573.4 SM 585.16
585.37 LA 635.21 IL 653.5
656.41 BM 837.19

FLEXIBLE OA 34.23 SD 417.3
TB 514.31 SU 530.8 531.6
ML 729.10 LL 774.7 774.10

FLICKED ML 728.29

FLICKER MO 5.36 WM 68.24
PO 108.11 BL 351.25
ML 741.18

FLICKERED MO 1.16 9.25 14.13
EA 73.35 OC 283.4 EE 324.41
SU 536.32

FLICKERING HT 38.4 PO 108.34
SS 207.27 EE 325.26
WP 386.13 PR 489.18 499.32
WR 580.25 LA 634.11
ML 731.19 MD 822.32

FLICKERS OV 749.7

FLICKING WS 244.8

FLIES WM 63.1 WR 551.35

FLIGHT OA 23.15 36.4
DV 178.11 PR 485.37
JD 606.38 ML 741.42

FLIGHTS WS 250.14

FLIGHTY TF 127.6

FLIMSY EA 81.1 DV 145.28

FLING SP 53.9 EA 74.8
DV 151.32 SG 232.27

FLINGING OA 24.31 FG 190.9
TP 338.10 IL 655.36
NT 709.36 BM 837.19

FLINT MO 9.31 9.32 9.33
SP 50.31 FG 195.14 195.15
WR 557.24 578.20 580.32

FLIP DV 153.3

FLIPPANCY SB 218.36 EE 325.1
  HD 441.2 GG 665.41

FLIPPANT EA 79.10

FLIPPANTLY WM 66.37 EA 74.37
  86.29 WS 261.12

FLIPPED OA 33.9 DV 152.39

FLIRT TF 126.34

FLIRTED TP 336.42 GG 662.7

FLIRTING BM 831.32 836.10

FLIRTS TP 336.27 336.30

FLITCHES CH 274.19

FLITTING RR 780.2

FLOAT TB 522.9 WR 568.12

FLOATED PR 502.41 JD 605.13
  LL 761.26

FLOATING WM 60.32 DV 136.8
  WS 251.31 252.1 OC 288.37
  FA 458.4 IL 653.7

FLOCK MO 3.5 PO 106.32
  DV 137.15 GF 234.31 CH 274.31
  TP 340.17 WR 572.23 ML 734.40

FLOCKED SM 583.32

FLOCKS PR 482.19

FLOGGED FG 189.11 189.13

FLOOD MO 2.20 2.42 DV 176.22
  SS 200.3 WS 252.28 BL 355.28
  BO 597.8 597.15 598.7 599.29

FLOODED WR 556.4 BO 599.7
  ML 728.8 BM 836.16

FLOODING RH 803.22

FLOODS ML 731.23

FLOOR MO 13.30 OA 34.9 SP 50.14
  WM 55.10 63.30 70.5 EA 85.13
  PO 101.41 108.42 112.23
  113.37 DV 145.28 149.1 161.13
  162.29 168.21 SS 197.21
  206.37 SB 216.9 SG 228.27
  GF 238.18 WS 245.26 257.39
  263.23 OC 288.37 289.18
  290.13 291.39 292.6 296.25
  298.9 299.1 299.7 300.6
  TP 345.10 HD 452.20 FA 471.17
  PR 500.8 502.29 502.34
  WR 572.20 BO 594.11 LA 646.25
  GG 669.39 ML 725.13 LL 770.20
  MD 810.39 TH 847.38

FLOORING GF 238.21

FLOORS TH 847.42 850.35

FLOPPED WP 387.37 BO 603.7

FLOPPED (CONT.) ML 741.9

FLORA YT 395.41 WR 568.13
  ML 738.10 738.32 738.41 739.6
  739.14

FLORA, COUSIN (SEE COUSIN FLORA)

FLORENCE PR 474.26 BM 831.42
  TH 850.38

FLORENTINE EA 81.11 PR 479.37
  NT 705.25 TH 848.40

FLORID WS 250.22 250.37 254.9
  254.16 GG 683.26 MD 810.37

FLORIDITY MD 811.1

FLORIN SP 46.40 47.28

FLOSS EE 322.42

FLOTSAM WM 68.28

FLOUNCE SD 414.41

FLOUNDERING PR 477.30 490.33

FLOUR CH 274.19

FLOURISH EA 82.12

FLOURISHED SG 221.21 FA 466.35

FLOUR-SCOOP CH 275.10

FLOURY OV 758.26

FLOUTINGLY HD 442.3

FLOW WM 63.7 WS 254.31
  OC 286.10 TP 339.4 BL 355.41
  TB 515.41 520.11 524.11
  SU 535.25 BO 591.2 591.3
  591.5 591.9 591.12 597.3
  604.17 GG 683.40 MD 812.14

FLOWED TF 132.34 OC 299.20
  301.24 PR 473.5 SU 535.22

FLOWER MO 3.32 WM 69.6
  FG 194.11 SS 203.29 OC 284.40
  288.32 EE 310.23 311.15
  311.17 322.9 322.35 PR 477.24
  478.9 479.34 479.38 490.8
  SU 532.34 534.3 GG 682.32
  NT 703.30 ML 728.5 731.1
  736.23 OV 748.9 751.26
  LL 764.11 766.6 774.16 774.21
  MD 815.23 BM 831.11

FLOWER-BED EE 306.38 306.41

FLOWER-BORDER OA 24.13

FLOWERED EE 306.1 WR 546.21
  GG 694.21

FLOWERING OA 24.37 WM 60.28
  MN 366.9 WR 561.24

FLOWERLESS SS 205.21

FLOWER-LIKE GG 693.24

FLOWER-PETAL ML 725.13

FLOWERS MO 20.10 WM 55.15
  64.1 64.8 64.16 EA 71.31
  72.34 79.20 PO 107.9
  TF 117.18 119.1 122.9
  DV 161.10 SS 200.3 204.36
  206.18 210.5 210.31
  SG 225.16 225.18 225.21
  225.23 225.26 OC 284.38
  289.1 296.23 297.25
  EE 303.12 303.14 303.34
  304.1 304.9 307.14 311.22
  313.1 330.18 BL 358.29
  MN 376.19 YT 400.4
  PR 489.35 TB 520.30 520.32
  520.34 520.38 SU 537.38
  538.22 WR 547.7 549.16
  551.40 556.11 559.9 559.10
  559.12 561.19 561.21
  561.41 562.25 564.23
  564.32 565.4 565.36 565.40
  575.13 SM 584.5 GG 695.30
  NT 709.25 715.20 ML 726.33
  728.2 736.8 736.10
  OV 753.18 753.35 754.28
  754.30 LL 775.35 RH 800.12
  MD 811.4 811.7 815.16
  817.18 822.16 BM 830.1
  833.20

FLOWER-STALK EA 72.5

FLOWER-STALLS TH 844.29

FLOWERY TF 118.37 WR 547.7

FLOWING EA 91.5 WS 252.26
  EE 313.10 332.19 SU 535.29
  BO 599.8 ML 730.40

FLOWN MD 816.28

FLUENT MD 809.37 819.2

FLUFFED PR 479.35

FLUFFY WP 379.33 PR 483.42

FLUID OV 755.19 BM 836.19

FLUMMERY TB 525.11

FLUNG OA 27.25 29.14 34.35
  35.22 35.38 WM 55.13
  EA 75.5 PO 99.25 TF 134.11
  DV 175.16 FG 194.14
  SS 210.39 SB 215.6
  GF 241.21 WS 244.12 248.36
  264.7 OC 289.36 EE 316.36
  SD 420.36 HD 442.21
  SU 529.5 IL 654.12 658.39
  GG 670.39 MD 825.10

FLUSH TF 123.32 131.29
  DV 152.38 SS 198.18 201.11
  205.29 WS 248.27 OC 294.13
  MN 368.1 HD 454.31
  PR 477.16 BO 594.9 595.23
  595.26 IL 659.39 GG 700.2

FLUSHED MO 2.18 10.23
  OA 26.21 31.15 WM 58.17
  58.19 EA 76.4 PO 98.31
  TF 124.40 DV 143.2 185.8

FLUSHED (CONT.) SS 199.13 200.14
  SG 226.3 WS 247.12 249.32
  258.19 261.40 262.42 CH 278.2
  TP 343.27 345.25 BL 349.10
  MN 371.5 376.27 WP 387.39
  388.16 389.9 391.31 YT 404.17
  405.11 409.16 SD 418.21
  421.33 PP 439.35 HD 441.32
  PR 484.26 SU 544.3 544.42
  WR 577.26 JD 617.41 624.32
  LL 772.15 RR 786.1 786.28
  RH 796.10 MD 825.24

FLUSHING OA 23.32 DV 184.41
  CH 275.6 275.20 YT 407.29
  SD 419.37 NT 715.37 720.26
  BM 828.37

FLUSTERED OA 35.10 FA 458.21
  BM 835.8

FLUSTERING BM 835.8

FLUTE BM 837.29

FLUTTER PO 115.12 CH 281.18
  YT 397.4 TB 526.39 527.27
  JD 621.19 627.39

FLUTTERED OA 29.24 29.31
  WM 54.24 PO 115.7 TF 130.7
  DV 162.12 CH 274.29 279.5
  YT 396.40 400.7 PP 430.3
  PR 499.13 SM 583.24 583.32
  BO 591.1

FLUTTERING OA 36.37 WM 55.17
  TF 118.23 BL 350.19 PR 493.20
  499.2 506.30 TB 521.40 523.33
  SM 586.7

FLUX EE 330.36

FLY MO 9.32 DV 157.22 SG 226.9
  YT 395.23 PR 474.17 483.31
  TB 515.28 522.27 WR 572.23
  JD 623.22 OV 759.11

FLYED WP 388.9 388.32 389.5

FLYING MO 2.25 WM 63.3 EA 85.2
  PO 110.2 FG 193.34 WS 247.24
  CH 275.27 EE 331.34 TP 342.27
  BL 351.13 SM 585.38 JD 606.38
  ML 744.8

FOAM ML 728.27 744.23

FOBBED LA 645.17

FOCUSED IL 656.36

FOCUSSED PR 487.18 SU 532.38
  532.40

FODDER SP 49.4 SB 217.13

FOG WM 62.35 62.37 67.25
  GF 235.15 237.13 237.37
  238.23 240.4 240.6 ML 734.17

FOG-DRIPPING GF 237.35

FOGGY WM 62.34

FOG-HORN ML 723.27

FOGS GF 234.2

FOIL MD 812.8

FOILED SG 229.31

FOILS OV 752.26

FOLD PO 95.19 95.20 106.41
  GF 237.11

FOLDED MO 3.5 DV 142.27 173.12
  FG 192.38 SS 202.19 SB 212.25
  WS 245.32 OC 295.30 BL 360.4
  360.11 YT 399.9 PP 432.38
  433.12 HD 445.42 455.6
  PR 478.41 502.33 SM 585.31
  ML 741.29 LL 770.23 MD 808.27

FOLDED-UP PR 495.17

FOLDING OA 23.8 SG 231.9

FOLDS SG 221.33 GG 679.32
  OV 751.18 LL 772.1

FOLIAGE MO 9.23 PO 107.7 112.2
  TF 118.35 SB 213.3 MN 376.16
  SM 585.38 IL 651.27 TH 846.37

FOLK MO 2.34 5.18 WM 62.6
  EA 78.19 DV 136.3 FG 189.16
  CH 278.25 279.28 PP 428.25
  JD 619.39

FOLK-DANCES EE 305.17

FOLK'LL BM 834.9

FOLK-MUSIC EE 305.16

FOLKS CH 280.30 MN 374.33
  ML 731.5

FOLKS'LL SC 271.39 272.5

FOLK-SONGS EE 305.17 312.2
  329.27

FOLLOW MO 19.17 EA 80.16
  DV 161.20 SS 197.33 BL 361.12
  HD 447.17 PR 486.31 493.13
  LL 774.2 RR 789.18

FOLLOWED MO 21.31 HT 43.16
  43.19 43.29 PO 96.5 109.36
  115.23 TF 130.30 134.10
  DV 159.32 161.27 FG 193.3
  193.32 SS 201.16 GF 238.31
  SC 267.11 CH 275.4 EE 322.1
  MN 373.23 375.3 376.19
  WP 380.35 387.42 388.42
  SD 418.10 422.37 PP 433.36
  433.39 438.38 HD 445.14 448.9
  449.35 FA 459.20 469.21 470.6
  PR 490.15 498.1 500.36 506.11
  SU 540.13 WR 560.18 560.27
  561.13 562.19 573.29
  JD 607.39 617.9 LA 634.18
  637.19 639.33 640.33
  ML 723.21 736.29 739.27
  OV 750.27 LL 776.32 MD 818.32
  BM 838.36

FOLLOWERS TH 844.26

FOLLOWING OA 35.7 WM 63.26
  EA 77.11 TF 125.22
  FG 194.41 MN 370.26
  YT 403.16 SD 422.28
  HD 448.41 PR 481.15 489.27
  498.36 507.32 SU 538.20
  WR 553.5 559.7 561.5
  561.25 579.14 LA 637.29
  IL 647.12 GG 670.30 699.24
  ML 736.32 737.21 RH 800.11

FOLLY SS 200.28

FOMENTATIONS OA 37.35

FOND MO 11.11 12.38
  DV 147.18 151.17 164.9
  SB 216.42 SG 231.15
  SC 272.25 BL 359.26
  PR 477.2 SU 541.2 IL 648.1
  GG 678.27 LL 772.2
  RR 781.18 MD 807.5 809.8
  BM 842.2 842.3 842.5
  842.10

FONDLED PP 437.25 438.29

FONDLES SG 225.32

FONDNESS WS 248.7 250.27

FOOD MO 5.9 PO 109.11
  DV 165.6 169.23 FG 189.30
  190.26 192.6 193.1 195.20
  EE 323.29 BL 351.40 358.41
  WP 386.41 387.3 387.6
  387.11 HD 447.24 FA 462.33
  PR 495.22 495.33 506.4
  TB 518.6 WR 551.2 551.9
  565.1 BO 602.34 JD 618.37
  ML 739.35 LL 768.32 776.28
  MD 817.19

FOOL MO 11.9 18.15 WM 62.14
  70.22 EA 71.10 73.42 75.4
  86.28 86.30 TF 135.17
  DV 145.29 184.6 184.23
  SS 200.27 209.33 WS 248.33
  261.31 261.33 261.38
  CH 281.25 281.37 OC 289.19
  291.4 EE 303.20 314.6
  YT 405.14 FA 463.30
  TB 520.24 526.4 526.5
  BO 590.12 JD 628.3 628.12
  LA 646.22 IL 649.8 650.2
  653.33 658.12 NT 711.36
  711.37 717.26 720.4
  ML 730.23 MD 813.10
  BM 840.23 840.26 842.13

FOOLED BO 590.11 BM 842.16

FOOLHARDY MO 3.32 WR 560.15

FOOLING MO 17.27

FOOLISH MO 17.8 SS 202.13
  HD 441.2 442.19 442.24
  452.17 452.19 FA 468.9
  WR 549.35 NT 704.7
  OV 759.36 RH 791.21 791.22

FOOLISHLY MN 369.18

FOOLISHNESS YT 405.15

FOOLS MO 17.5 WS 247.9
    WP 384.39 FA 468.3

FOOT MO 1.29 18.18 SP 47.26
    WM 70.3 PO 102.19 102.37
    106.42 TF 118.38 119.18
    119.21 119.32 120.20 128.27
    DV 180.10 FG 187.7 SB 213.5
    214.32 SG 231.32 OC 284.41
    297.33 298.4 EE 303.30
    BL 354.39 WP 385.39 393.11
    SD 412.26 417.21 PP 433.30
    HD 456.10 456.24 FA 471.11
    PR 481.23 496.7 SU 532.24
    532.30 WR 556.30 562.13
    JD 607.30 LA 645.38 646.1
    IL 655.24 GG 691.33 ML 744.26
    LL 777.14 RH 794.10 BM 841.6
    841.7 841.8

FOOTBALL DV 164.15 165.29
    SC 271.37

FOOTBALLER OA 35.30

FOOTBALL-GROUND SP 50.42

FOOTBOARD WM 59.38 60.1

FOOT-BOARD TP 336.21 340.1

FOOT-HILLS PR 489.32

FOOTHOLD ML 724.36

FOOTHOLDS WR 579.40

FOOTING OA 23.23 BL 352.39
    HD 450.30 PR 490.35 ML 743.2
    MD 811.2

FOOTMARKS LA 635.40

FOOT-PASSENGERS BO 594.40

FOOTPLATE OC 283.8 285.27

FOOT-SOLES EA 92.7

FOOTSTEP GF 235.28 LL 766.19

FOOTSTEPS DV 148.15 161.20
    SG 228.28 GF 236.36 CH 280.18
    OC 289.33 289.35 293.28
    296.41 BL 347.3 364.37

FOOT-WARMER GG 669.14

FOOTWAYS ML 724.18

FOOTWEAR BM 833.11

FORAGED SP 49.38

FORBADE DV 160.9 OV 758.11

FORBEARANCE MD 814.42

FORBIDDEN EE 325.15

FORBIDDING WR 553.4

FORBORE WM 64.36

FORCE EA 80.20 PO 104.29 110.11
    TF 120.14 DV 146.38 176.34
    177.4 EE 312.41 SD 419.39
    PR 501.4 NT 702.23 ML 737.25
    745.19 LL 767.39 TH 851.11
    851.14

FORCED WM 61.13 EA 81.25 90.12
    PO 98.9 103.42 104.39 106.2
    TF 121.16 DV 137.41 170.30
    SC 268.22 EE 331.40 BL 348.4
    WP 383.25 PR 482.4 LL 767.26
    RH 793.15 MD 819.33

FORCEDLY RR 781.20

FORCES EA 72.16 WS 257.9
    MN 368.11 SD 417.29

FORCIBLE BM 829.29

FORCING OA 36.3 EA 88.41
    WS 256.42 TP 343.37 PR 496.26
    RH 793.35

FORD FG 193.12 WR 546.29

FORE SP 45.30

FOREARM TF 121.26

FOREARMS SS 203.29

FOREFEET PR 498.37 498.40

FOREFINGER SB 216.6 216.25

FOREHEAD MO 17.42 EA 76.35
    PO 95.25 102.9 SG 221.33
    GF 240.18 WS 253.24 BL 349.10
    357.25 YT 397.10 397.39
    401.39 WR 558.26 JD 611.12
    GG 668.40 670.34 683.23
    NT 715.28 LL 761.27 BM 828.27

FOREIGN WM 55.37 TF 120.34
    126.2 126.23 DV 160.21 169.25
    PP 434.32 PR 484.34 502.40
    ML 746.30

FOREIGNERS SP 52.36 DV 171.31
    EE 326.24

FOREMOST MD 820.36

FOREST FG 190.19 193.30
    PR 481.40 496.30 497.9 500.13
    502.40 511.25 SU 530.13
    WR 568.39 579.14 BO 600.15
    600.20 603.1 603.25 603.32

FORESTALL WM 61.39

FORESTER TF 127.2

FORESTS PR 490.11 BO 600.10
    TH 853.13

FOREST SERVICE PR 496.13 497.17
    511.11 511.18

FORETASTE DV 149.35

FORETHOUGHT FG 191.9

FOREVER WR 570.18

FOREWARNED FA 465.10

FORFEIT SD 424.24

FORFEITURE TH 844.16

FORGE SS 197.2

FORGET MO 10.18 WM 65.35
    GF 238.16 EE 333.3 333.4
    WP 383.33 383.39 384.7
    390.1 YT 409.2 409.3
    PP 438.17 PR 476.6
    LA 641.39 GG 696.28
    NT 717.21 717.25 718.33
    ML 746.13 RH 801.9
    MD 814.34

FORGETFUL WM 65.29 DV 178.10
    SB 217.16

FORGETFULNESS EA 73.3

FORGET-ME-NOT BM 840.18

FORGET-ME-NOTS SS 204.34
    207.11 207.16 TB 520.33

FORGETS DV 177.3

FORGETTING WM 60.19 EA 92.33
    FG 190.42 SG 225.5 EE 333.4
    WP 381.5 390.2 TB 521.34
    JD 621.18 GG 688.22
    NT 713.20

FORGIVE EA 93.33 WS 249.41
    YT 402.22 GG 689.24
    LL 778.24 RR 784.33

FORGIVING GF 243.32

FORGOT WM 56.11 EA 86.25
    92.24 PO 102.20 FG 193.40
    SB 213.35 WS 245.17
    OC 299.35 EE 314.37
    WP 382.36 390.30 GG 689.23
    ML 743.37 OV 756.31
    BM 838.13

FORGOTTEN WM 55.13 TF 130.5
    SS 198.33 GF 240.26
    WS 253.13 EE 304.5
    WR 546.30 BO 596.38
    LA 641.15 ML 743.41

FORK DV 169.34 BL 358.8

FORKED SU 536.32 BM 833.14

FORLORN OA 33.23 WM 54.5
    EA 92.29 WS 265.42
    TP 335.12 WR 572.3
    SM 586.18 BO 598.34 GG 697.12
    BM 831.27 834.18

FORLORNLY OA 37.22

FORLORNNESS BM 834.26

FORM MO 16.32 19.6 22.31
    SP 45.6 47.34 WM 56.4
    69.38 70.12 EA 73.8

FORM (CONT.) PO 106.19 TF 128.8
  DV 137.36 139.42 145.42
  148.21 152.19 SS 201.22
  206.24 SB 212.25 WS 252.26
  252.31 256.20 258.25
  SC 268.1 269.38 271.10
  OC 292.15 MN 367.39 368.42
  SD 415.15 PP 439.38 FA 463.22
  PR 501.17 WR 557.25 561.10
  LA 633.6 638.22 ML 727.40
  OV 755.17 LL 768.11 769.38
  778.37 MD 805.28 816.3
  BM 837.21

FORMAL OA 38.40 WM 64.32
  PR 475.5 WR 549.10 JD 618.32

FORMALITY MO 11.33 WM 55.35
  PP 437.6

FORMALLY OA 37.41

FORMATION WR 573.40 GG 698.11

FORMED OA 30.37 SS 200.33
  PR 506.25 WR 562.18 578.16
  579.30 GG 698.10

FORMER WM 59.22 EA 86.26
  LL 762.4

FORMING MO 5.26

FORMLESS SD 411.31 OV 755.21

FORMS SP 45.13 TF 128.16
  WR 557.17

FORSAKEN MO 1.2 SS 197.28
  OC 283.16 EE 308.26

FORTHCOMING DV 144.28 PR 483.21
  MD 812.27

FORTIFICATIONS TF 117.27 118.42
  124.1 124.5

FORTITUDE GF 236.24

FORTNIGHT EE 319.25 320.4
  GG 666.4 NT 717.25 MD 809.37
  824.41

FORTNIGHT'S FA 464.6 PR 512.17

FORTNUM AND MASON'S GG 677.33

FORTUNATE OA 32.19 SU 532.17

FORTUNATELY EE 319.26

FORTUNE EE 307.42 YT 394.36
  HD 445.38 PR 478.14 GG 671.15
  671.16 NT 720.37 LL 769.39
  770.3

FORTUNES SS 209.1 209.3
  HD 441.9 446.33 GG 671.18

FORTY OA 31.16 HT 39.23 SP 45.9
  WM 59.26 PO 96.9 TF 118.13
  WS 250.22 MN 366.13 PR 473.24
  TB 513.4 520.25 520.26
  SU 539.8 WR 547.22 BO 587.1
  NT 704.15 708.40 RH 797.15

FORTY (CONT.) BM 827.5 TH 850.23
  851.37 852.41

FORTY-FIVE BM 827.26

FORTY-SEVEN BM 828.25

FORTY-TWO FG 187.13

FOR'T SC 271.2

FORWARD MO 12.3 19.22 OA 25.21
  26.42 31.17 35.38 36.3 36.10
  SP 47.4 50.31 WM 58.10 58.42
  59.4 59.11 59.31 60.2 60.6
  64.9 69.9 EA 71.28 76.41
  PO 101.29 101.32 109.3 109.5
  109.8 TF 118.13 118.18
  DV 165.38 179.34 180.20
  FG 190.42 193.11 194.3
  SS 198.11 199.35 SG 224.23
  225.5 225.33 226.16 228.15
  230.20 GF 235.24 WS 251.33
  251.37 256.8 257.31 262.4
  264.3 OC 288.39 291.13 295.36
  EE 306.35 317.27 333.1
  TP 335.19 342.26 343.6
  BL 351.37 352.5 354.7 359.17
  WP 380.1 382.17 382.22 387.34
  387.35 YT 395.1 397.26 410.13
  SD 423.34 426.10 PP 429.11
  432.37 433.15 433.35 438.32
  439.14 HD 450.1 452.40 454.40
  FA 458.19 460.27 468.12
  468.14 PR 484.9 492.4 495.30
  501.21 TB 522.22 525.2
  SU 536.28 WR 555.13 555.35
  555.41 559.18 561.12 563.2
  563.8 563.39 567.30 569.3
  579.20 LA 639.14 646.24
  GG 665.29 669.7 670.11 670.16
  671.26 671.29 677.16 681.20
  NT 712.37 713.14 716.1 720.9
  MD 823.23 BM 829.19 830.33
  837.11 838.3 838.31 839.26

FORWARDS MO 1.21 EA 83.4
  EE 333.7 SD 411.16 425.38

FOSTER SS 208.13

FOSTERED TB 518.11

FOUGHT OA 29.35 35.42 WM 66.15
  PO 103.21 DV 164.27 FG 190.9
  OC 301.1 301.2 BO 597.13
  GG 671.35 697.31 RH 802.19
  MD 820.6

FOUL HD 450.28 FA 471.35
  ML 742.21

FOULED HD 450.14

FOUL-MINDED WS 262.21 262.22

FOUL-MOUTHED HD 446.41 FA 471.9

FOUL-SMELLING LA 631.37

FOUND MO 7.24 11.29 16.11
  17.22 17.23 19.26 SP 51.5
  WM 59.14 66.6 PO 116.10 TF 118.2
  127.41 DV 137.5 137.29 144.34
  153.41 154.19 156.1 160.24

FOUND (CONT.) 161.30 162.21
  168.10 FG 187.36 188.4
  189.30 194.4 SS 197.15
  202.41 203.16 207.13
  207.36 SB 212.19 219.27
  SG 221.10 GF 239.9 240.16
  WS 253.20 256.17 260.4
  260.14 265.27 OC 298.42
  EE 313.15 320.31 BL 357.2
  MN 376.41 378.33 WP 385.27
  388.7 389.19 389.21
  YT 398.31 399.14 PP 440.5
  HD 448.21 456.17 FA 471.24
  PR 479.24 480.20 480.23
  482.39 487.22 TB 514.6
  SU 530.4 538.21 WR 549.34
  BO 598.31 GG 679.25 679.26
  683.4 688.7 NT 706.18
  706.23 707.12 708.14 709.7
  714.2 718.6 ML 732.37
  736.6 736.17 736.19 741.10
  742.6 LL 775.28 776.8
  776.23 778.32 MD 810.40
  821.27 BM 832.40 TH 845.36
  850.5 851.41 852.23 852.25
  852.38

FOUNDATION TB 517.32

FOUNDLING TF 126.28

FOUNDRIES HD 447.32

FOUNDRY FA 459.2 459.7
  459.34 459.37

FOUNDRY-HAND FA 462.17

FOUNT ML 726.26 726.34

FOUNTAIN SS 198.14 HD 454.7
  GG 690.12

FOUNTAIN-HEAD TH 844.14

FOUNTAIN-PEN EA 80.22

FOUNTAINS OC 294.5

FOUR SP 46.11 50.5 50.32
  52.19 EA 72.22 TF 118.20
  134.39 DV 159.26 163.1
  SS 198.6 201.18 WS 253.33
  SC 268.3 271.2 CH 274.5
  277.16 OC 284.38 286.19
  297.33 EE 317.42 BL 359.20
  WP 382.42 386.6 YT 395.24
  SD 413.8 422.26 HD 442.1
  FA 463.19 PR 480.40 481.23
  498.15 TB 514.9 WR 563.25
  578.10 580.25 580.34
  IL 655.14 GG 679.15 682.18
  688.33 ML 722.30 RH 796.11
  MD 805.15 818.8 BM 831.8
  TH 847.38

FOUR-FOOTED PR 499.15

FOUR HUNDRED AND FIFTY MD 806.3

FOUR-LANE TP 334.31

FOURTEEN TF 126.31 SB 212.8
  YT 395.27 HD 447.7
  RH 803.38

FOURTEENTH-CENTURY RR 783.15

FOURTH EA 72.18 SS 200.33
  PR 510.7 NT 712.39 ML 732.35

FOWL OV 760.3

FOWL-HOUSE OC 283.19 284.3

FOWLS DV 164.14 SS 197.8 202.16
  OC 283.17

FOX FG 190.29 WR 570.8
  OV 750.37 MD 825.17

FOX-FUR WR 569.5 569.6

FOXGLOVES ML 723.23 732.23

FOXSKIN PR 493.23

FOX-SKINS WR 569.19

FOX-TAILED WR 569.28

FOX-TERRIERS PP 437.30

FRAGILE PO 107.19 DV 156.24
  186.4 YT 402.28 BO 597.39

FRAGMENT MO 2.27 PO 107.11
  FG 187.4 188.4 SD 415.9
  OV 759.40

FRAGMENTARY DV 154.34 GG 683.39

FRAGMENTS MO 1.6 EA 79.19
  EE 331.25 LL 777.28

FRAGRANT BL 358.20 ML 723.22
  OV 753.19 753.23

'FRAID IL 653.30 653.39

FRAIL WM 59.25 59.37 60.9
  EA 76.31 PO 106.24 DV 149.19
  SS 207.4 SB 220.4 CH 274.10
  EE 322.8 322.9 332.38
  WP 379.12 YT 396.41 408.16
  PR 474.14 477.28 478.37
  490.33 493.19 499.8 GG 662.10
  ML 737.10 738.3 LL 761.26
  RH 802.11 MD 808.23 809.1
  815.2

FRAILER ML 727.23

FRAILTIES TB 521.33

FRAME PO 110.20 GF 235.5
  CH 277.34 278.33 278.36
  GG 691.2 LL 761.4 MD 808.23

FRAMED PR 476.32 SM 586.23

FRAMES OA 24.8 GF 234.21
  SM 585.12

FRAMEWORK EA 72.21 GF 238.23

FRAN SB 214.27

FRANCE OA 35.32 SP 48.18
  TF 124.27 131.13 133.1
  BL 348.24 349.27 WP 380.32

FRANCE (CONT.) 382.14 SM 582.5
  BO 590.33 GG 664.30 TH 845.26
  845.31 845.33 845.37

FRANCES SB 212.1 212.4 212.9
  212.20 212.21 212.25 212.31
  212.33 213.10 213.14 213.17
  213.22 213.27 213.32 213.34
  213.38 214.10 214.20 214.29
  214.33 214.39 215.3 215.12
  215.21 215.28 215.32 215.38
  216.10 216.14 216.18 216.26
  216.29 216.39 217.10 217.15
  217.23 217.29 217.35 218.18
  218.19 218.27 218.35 219.23
  219.26

FRANCO-PRUSSIAN TF 133.24

FRANCS NT 705.9

FRANK WM 65.4 SG 223.9
  PP 437.13

FRANKLY DV 155.27

FRANKNESS MO 10.5 12.34
  YT 396.7 IL 650.20

FRANTIC SB 214.41 215.8
  WS 259.23 PR 490.37

FRANTICALLY SB 216.2 SD 421.4

FRANZ TF 127.1 132.1

FRANZ BRAND TF 126.39

FRANZ BRAND'S TF 131.19

FRAUGHT TB 514.32

FRAULEIN HESSE TF 124.5 124.10
  124.17 124.28 125.5 125.8
  125.18 127.40 128.19 130.30
  130.35

FRAYED SD 423.2 MD 814.34
  TH 852.37

FREAKISH BL 349.26

FREAKISHNESS BL 358.26

FRECKLED TF 123.30 OV 759.39

FRED DV 179.32

FRED COUTTS FA 471.25

FREDDY HD 445.27 WR 550.33

FREDDY MANSELL GF 242.30

FREDERICK PINNOCK'S HT 40.13

FRED HENRY HD 442.31 442.42
  443.30 443.35 443.39 444.25
  444.27 445.17 445.30 445.39
  446.5

FREE WM 61.36 EA 79.25 79.28
  82.35 82.41 PO 97.12 98.23
  99.7 99.13 104.24 109.40
  TF 118.25 122.12 127.20

FREE (CONT.) 128.30 133.10
  DV 140.30 153.15 153.21
  154.12 164.23 165.36
  170.26 184.30 SS 205.36
  SB 217.26 SG 223.12 230.3
  230.35 GF 236.33 243.14
  WS 256.38 256.40 260.16
  CH 276.2 EE 311.26 325.8
  327.40 SD 421.11 422.35
  HD 443.17 WR 550.1 550.25
  574.10 BO 600.8 JD 622.28
  LA 637.12 GG 662.28 682.40
  685.28 NT 720.23 ML 731.30
  OV 754.16 758.12 MD 811.7
  TH 844.7 844.8 845.1 846.5
  849.26 851.8

FREED SD 423.3

FREEDOM SP 49.8 WM 64.29
  TF 125.28 133.6 133.7
  133.11 DV 153.14 153.17
  153.18 164.31 EE 325.5
  HD 441.29 MD 805.9 TH 844.8
  845.10 847.7 850.21 852.13

FREEHOLD ML 722.12

FREELY OA 30.11 EA 84.15
  TF 128.11 WR 551.19 566.27
  BM 838.30

FREESIAS WM 64.4

FREE WILL WM 56.38 56.41

FREEZE PR 502.42

FREEZES BO 600.41

FREEZING FG 189.17 ML 744.3
  745.22

FRENCH OA 27.26 27.34
  EA 85.21 TF 122.1 123.13
  WP 380.13 380.24 380.40
  382.13 383.6 384.37 391.5
  FA 464.35 SM 582.35
  BO 587.3 587.18 593.39
  593.42 594.42 595.11
  595.13 598.38 599.15
  599.22 599.36 NT 707.28
  715.19 715.22 715.34
  RH 796.8 MD 818.12 819.2
  820.16 820.18 820.22
  821.27 821.38 822.7
  TH 845.17 845.19 845.21
  845.23 845.39 849.35
  852.38

FRENCH-GREY NT 719.33

FRENCHMAN RH 796.6

FRENCHMAN'S BO 587.32

FRENCHMEN GF 235.11 BO 587.9
  587.10 587.30 592.42
  594.35 595.19 TH 845.21

FRENCH-SPEAKING WP 380.36

FRENCHWOMAN NT 704.34

FRENZIED FA 467.15

FRENZY OA 36.11   TP 343.16
   ML 745.9   LL 776.11   RH 793.3

FREQUENTLY TP 336.30   MN 371.34

FRESH MO 15.3   HT 39.9   WM 56.9
   DV 176.28   SS 201.39   SG 223.1
   WS 249.15   MN 367.39   YT 401.41
   402.21   SD 413.28   PP 434.22
   HD 443.5   PR 497.13   TB 516.40
   WR 565.3   BO 587.16   LA 634.11
   634.33   638.32   IL 656.10
   GG 681.25   690.36   692.19
   ML 725.30   737.9   737.13   742.22
   OV 753.23   LL 766.5   MD 815.22

FRESH-COLOURED LL 771.10

FRESH-COMFORT EA 84.16

FRESH-COMPLEXIONED WR 554.19

FRESHEN GG 677.28

FRESH-FACED LA 633.11   637.16
   RR 783.23

FRESHLY IL 651.2

FRESHNESS PR 482.1   GG 692.41
   694.15

FRET DV 140.28   168.25   SB 213.37
   BL 356.32   IL 553.28

FRETFUL EA 72.8   BL 357.5
   HD 451.40

FRETFULLY GG 662.37

FRETTED WM 57.40   EA 79.37
   OC 292.31   HD 448.29   ML 735.29

FRETTIN' OC 293.10

FRETTING OV 748.26

FRIDAY WM 57.20   57.21

FRIDAYS SG 224.34

FRIED PR 502.11   502.18

FRIEND HT 38.22   EA 80.3
   DV 144.35   SS 201.33   SG 228.11
   EE 324.12   BL 347.3   348.38
   348.40   351.20   WP 391.40
   HD 446.14   BO 589.21   589.22
   590.21   590.22   590.27
   GG 679.10   679.13   NT 716.37
   720.32   ML 729.28   LL 770.8
   RR 781.4   781.18   781.25
   RH 799.16   MD 819.24   TH 850.41

FRIENDLY OA 31.23   34.16
   DV 163.30   BL 350.40   WR 549.3
   JD 605.3   GG 697.16   OV 754.24
   LL 764.27   RR 780.42   MD 807.30

FRIENDS MO 2.28   20.12   OA 38.38
   HT 39.11   EA 75.5   PO 99.36
   SS 209.40   SG 231.6   EE 308.35
   323.16   329.20   329.26   TP 337.5
   BL 348.14   349.34   349.41   350.1
   358.22   359.22   359.23   360.39

FRIENDS (CONT.)   365.1   365.3
   YT 395.18   PR 485.16   TB 514.3
   JD 606.30   606.42   607.3
   LA 642.9   642.10   IL 649.13
   649.14   649.22   GG 661.29
   662.21   662.24   NT 709.3
   OV 754.23   RR 779.2   783.3
   MD 810.6   819.26

FRIENDSHIP BL 349.29   350.17
   364.24   364.25   364.30   365.12
   BO 589.38   RR 781.26   MD 818.31

FRIEZE WR 560.42   569.1

FRIGHTEN OA 34.6   YT 408.28
   SU 537.21   537.22

FRIGHTENED OA 24.42   HT 44.8
   WM 58.11   59.42   EA 92.18
   PO 99.40   DV 137.34   144.19
   146.29   149.21   150.38
   FG 188.32   189.17   189.23
   SB 219.40   SG 232.21   GF 240.29
   WS 248.15   262.39   262.40   263.5
   263.7   263.9   OC 294.14   298.25
   EE 317.1   317.38   WP 381.17
   YT 404.35   SD 419.23   420.28
   PP 428.15   HD 441.27   455.24
   455.37   457.8   FA 471.27
   PR 496.41   497.6   507.15   507.16
   507.33   SU 531.26   531.32
   541.29   WR 559.5   565.8
   JD 612.27   622.17   LA 638.33
   638.34   640.18   GG 677.4   678.42
   NT 712.6   ML 736.22   744.4
   OV 757.42   LL 769.4   RH 800.20
   MD 813.1   824.19   BM 828.28
   829.22   842.17

FRIGHTENEDEST FA 472.2

FRIGHTENED-LOOKING PP 439.21

FRIGHTENING PO 110.15   SD 415.14
   416.2   417.31   HD 453.21
   WR 551.32   JD 624.10

FRIGHTENS WM 62.16

FRIGHTFUL SD 421.5   JD 611.7

FRIGHTFULLY BO 600.34   602.13
   IL 652.9   655.16   GG 665.37
   676.35   688.21   RR 780.27
   TH 845.14

FRIJOLES PR 488.3   488.28

FRILLS WS 261.30   TB 520.35

FRINGE DV 161.7   SS 206.17
   HD 449.2   PR 480.20   WR 557.7
   573.30   577.39   JD 611.11
   611.12   LA 636.36   NT 709.29
   ML 738.18

FRINGED WR 580.4

FRINGES DV 161.6   WR 568.34

FRISKILY PO 113.40

FRISKY GF 236.13   WP 379.35

FRITTER DV 174.24

FRIVOLOUS SM 582.4

FRIZZY SP 51.21

FRO MO 2.17   GF 237.20
   RH 803.9

FROCK EE 317.22   TB 521.25

FROCKS DV 138.16   OC 291.37

FROG OC 290.1   EE 306.42
   307.3

FROGS RH 800.9

FRONT MO 1.22   1.34   4.3
   12.33   19.26   21.9   WM 60.29
   62.24   68.39   PO 95.7   115.29
   TF 118.38   121.14   DV 150.36
   161.17   FG 192.5   SS 198.2
   GF 237.14   WS 252.18   260.41
   EE 305.4   332.6   BL 347.13
   351.35   362.25   WP 388.34
   390.11   390.15   390.21
   390.39   391.2   393.12
   YT 397.39   407.9   SD 422.27
   423.20   423.21   PP 432.18
   439.25   FA 465.7   465.15
   466.6   466.14   471.2
   PR 489.14   496.34   500.26
   SU 538.10   WR 558.11   558.16
   561.7   561.15   563.33   568.29
   578.7   579.24   580.14
   SM 583.24   BO 603.29
   JD 617.15   617.16   618.15
   LA 631.28   637.34   IL 653.21
   654.32   GG 664.4   664.32
   669.29   672.28   NT 714.4
   ML 741.26   741.33   LL 769.1
   RR 786.8   787.36   787.38
   787.39   RH 793.8   796.6
   MD 810.1   BM 828.29   835.11
   835.36   836.33

FRONTED SD 420.17

FRONTIER TF 125.17   SM 582.18

FRONTING TF 134.13   DV 151.6
   GF 234.16   CH 274.15

FROST FG 189.33   189.39
   190.11   190.42   WS 251.22
   GG 675.33   684.1   684.19
   ML 723.33   OV 757.7   757.8
   757.9   757.14

FROST-BITTEN BO 602.11

FROSTED FG 195.23

FROWARD FA 468.9

FROWN SB 214.38   WS 248.12
   253.24   OC 295.32   EE 323.5
   WP 380.8   380.12   PP 439.42
   440.12   SU 534.16   SM 585.3
   BO 604.30   GG 665.18

FROWNED MO 10.10   SB 214.29
   MN 375.28   ML 740.36

FROWNING WP 380.26   GG 665.17

FROZE WP 388.10 LA 640.20

FROZEN DV 168.41 176.27
  FG 189.26 189.41 194.19
  SG 227.2 WS 258.42 WP 387.15
  PR 506.23 507.5 507.10
  WR 578.36 BO 595.17 599.7
  599.30 599.33 601.24 604.16
  LA 637.42 638.1 GG 675.8
  ML 744.7 744.9 744.29 746.5
  RH 803.7

FROZENNESS WR 579.16

FRUGALITY ML 728.19

FRUIT PO 95.11 SG 221.23 221.25
  EE 313.37 313.39 WP 381.5
  PP 436.6 436.27 WR 561.19
  NT 710.21

FRUITS MO 4.30 SG 221.36
  CH 278.37 SU 530.20

FRUSTRATED DV 158.5 WS 256.32
  EE 316.22 BO 593.27

FRUSTRATION EE 323.19 SU 529.20
  LL 771.9 TH 852.35

FRYING-PAN EA 87.36 87.37
  YT 398.26 398.29 PR 505.28
  505.31

FUEL MO 16.36 BO 602.34

FULFILLED WS 260.1 PR 497.1
  TB 513.22

FULFILLING PR 479.1

FULFILMENT BL 364.30 HD 447.27

FULFILMENTS GG 697.38

FULL MO 2.6 4.19 4.30 6.5
  7.42 8.42 16.13 18.13 19.38
  19.39 OA 24.37 32.8 33.7
  37.6 37.19 HT 40.33 SP 50.16
  WM 61.23 63.23 65.20 65.33
  66.7 69.22 EA 87.15 PO 96.17
  98.21 100.35 101.27 110.24
  114.29 DV 145.18 154.40
  180.19 182.22 FG 191.16
  191.22 SS 199.20 199.37
  199.38 200.7 202.41 205.11
  210.22 SB 212.19 SG 225.41
  231.10 GF 239.26 WS 251.30
  SC 271.21 CH 274.10 275.26
  275.42 277.35 278.1 280.13
  OC 283.2 286.12 287.31 295.1
  EE 311.15 312.6 316.23 328.11
  TP 344.40 BL 347.23 353.3
  363.40 MN 366.14 368.2 368.6
  369.9 370.24 371.39 373.18
  374.13 WP 380.18 382.19
  YT 394.31 400.19 401.16
  SD 423.21 426.11 PP 435.10
  438.4 439.13 HD 446.29 446.31
  450.36 451.22 451.33 452.32
  FA 460.23 PR 489.16 489.39
  498.24 501.4 502.32 TB 520.30
  SU 528.15 529.11 536.14
  WR 547.15 549.34 553.20
  553.39 554.18 558.33 561.19

FULL (CONT.) 565.31 575.34
  577.19 577.33 581.5 BO 587.2
  587.17 595.1 596.42 597.14
  599.11 604.10 JD 605.36
  606.23 610.3 LA 637.13 637.36
  638.6 639.22 IL 648.34
  GG 664.35 678.9 680.9 682.38
  699.19 NT 705.30 707.35 708.40
  712.40 737.39 741.39
  OV 748.23 749.6 753.28
  754.27 754.28 754.38 754.40
  LL 765.28 766.30 770.34
  RH 793.32 MD 809.2 809.4
  809.18 809.20 815.23 821.42
  823.3 BM 828.12 835.34
  836.27 840.17 TH 844.13 845.1
  845.2 845.38 849.26 850.21
  852.14

FULL-BLOODED OA 36.4 EE 322.37

FULL-BOSOMED OA 26.25

FULLER EA 84.17 SU 528.11

FULL-FLESHED OC 300.1

FULL-LIT SU 538.3

FULLNESS BO 597.1 TH 847.8

FULL-SKIRTED PO 114.27 WS 251.14
  251.19

FULL-TILT WM 55.8

FULLY SG 230.11 WS 245.29
  EE 328.22 TP 339.6 LL 766.36
  MD 817.2 823.40

FUMBLE HT 40.42

FUMBLED WM 70.21 SB 216.10
  BL 356.41 PR 512.1

FUMBLING MO 5.20 WM 56.11
  PO 104.4 SB 215.29 IL 652.15
  RR 787.30

FUMBLINGLY SB 214.32

FUME WM 55.9 55.12

FUMED WS 263.17 ML 746.8

FUMES MO 2.32 JD 608.15

FUMIGATED WR 573.33 580.30
  580.33

FUN MO 7.13 DV 174.29 GF 242.41
  WS 249.26 260.37 TP 337.28
  338.31 342.30 MN 366.14 368.6
  374.7 374.10 374.13 WP 388.10
  TB 514.6 MD 826.20

FUN-AND-NONSENSE MN 369.2

FUNCTION CH 279.5

FUNCTIONS BO 596.13

FUND DV 142.32 SC 269.10

FUNDAMENTAL SD 417.9 WR 577.19

FUNERAL DV 177.11 ML 745.6
  MD 817.27

FUNK OA 34.40

FUNNEL PR 496.16 496.18

FUNNEL-SHAPED WR 581.2

FUNNILY LA 642.16

FUNNY EA 94.4 DV 146.1
  170.35 BL 357.26 MN 377.25
  FA 464.21 WR 549.15
  JD 623.5 LA 642.12 642.15
  GG 697.6 LL 772.14
  MD 806.15 816.10 BM 835.23

FUR DV 160.13 SS 206.40
  SB 216.24 PR 479.35
  WR 559.22 559.35 578.19
  LA 630.8 632.35 637.8
  RH 802.35

FUR-CLOAKED SS 208.37

FUR-COVERED WR 563.4

FURIOUS EA 76.16 87.28
  TF 130.6 134.3 134.14
  DV 160.10 CH 282.12
  SD 415.25 PR 506.35
  NT 718.37* RH 793.16 793.25
  MD 807.18

FURIOUSLY EA 75.25 SB 218.27
  CH 277.26

FUR-LIKE WR 567.35

FURLING PO 113.39

FURNACE FA 458.2 458.6
  458.26

FURNACES FA 458.30 TH 853.12

FURNISHED SC 267.18 PP 437.1
  437.3 437.28 MD 810.24
  810.32 TH 848.10

FURNISHER-AND-UPHOLSTERER'S
  HT 42.13

FURNISHERS MD 811.35

FURNISHINGS RH 800.10

FURNITURE HT 42.16 SC 269.14
  BL 351.2 SD 421.14
  HD 441.10 GG 671.4 685.14
  685.23 NT 705.41 764.19
  764.21 MD 823.31 TH 848.1
  848.23 848.28 849.2 852.3
  852.8

FURROWED WP 386.30

FURROWS BO 599.30 599.32

FURRY PR 489.21

FURS EA 78.30 78.32 DV 147.4
  SS 206.38 WR 562.34 573.27
  RH 799.15 799.18

FURTHER MO 6.3 PO 99.2 113.19
   EE 320.16 BL 348.3 348.15
   HD 443.22 TB 514.26 SU 539.32
   543.30 GG 667.20 675.33
   682.38 NT 719.12 OV 749.38
   RH 795.2 795.10 795.35
   TH 846.40 851.23

FURTIVE BL 365.4 WP 379.25
   LL 776.17

FURTIVELY SP 52.9 EA 72.32
   TP 345.17 SD 418.2 SU 541.22
   542.24 LA 643.32 GG 676.27

FURY SP 53.17 EA 77.20
   SG 229.25 232.26 WS 258.26
   258.39 TP 336.25 339.23
   342.32 343.16 YT 406.20
   SD 417.27 IL 647.34 656.41
   BM 836.39 TH 852.41

FURZE SD 423.20 424.28

FUSE WS 254.41 255.3 PP 434.9

FUSED PO 114.31 WS 255.31

FUSING EA 91.36

FUSION TF 120.27 WS 254.40
   255.24 255.26

FUSS PO 96.38 DV 154.11
   OC 298.16 PR 490.16

FUSSES PR 475.28

FUSSING SB 216.15

FUTILE HD 445.39

FUTILITY DV 169.3 EE 323.19
   323.21 HD 443.41

FUTURE MO 8.39 EE 312.3
   WP 384.29 PP 430.23 TB 523.41
   JD 627.12 GG 662.10 ML 724.7
   MD 824.16 824.22

FUTURITY EE 333.8 RR 779.28

GA-ARD SD 425.32 425.36

GABLES BO 595.22 GG 668.30

GABRIEL GG 699.33

GABRIELLE GG 699.35

GAFFER SP 48.28 SC 267.23

GAIETY DV 174.31 LL 764.27

GAILY SB 218.28 WS 253.37

GAIN FG 193.29

'GAIN WP 388.6

GAINED SG 224.25 ML 736.36

GAIT SG 226.21

GAITERS BL 354.26 MN 367.1

GALA SP 52.37

GALE JD 628.16 RR 780.32

GALL EE 314.11 JD 605.7 605.19

GALLANT SB 218.25 WS 252.1
   TP 337.28 BL 351.7 TB 513.14
   514.14 515.3 515.8 515.22
   515.30 BM 836.1

GALLANTLY TP 341.38

GALLANTRY WM 56.11 RR 779.11

GALLED JD 605.4

GALLERIES GG 697.41

GALLERY FA 465.7 465.15 466.8
   466.13 468.24 468.42

GALLIPOLI BM 829.14

GALLIVANT SP 53.5

GALLIVANTIN' FA 463.32

GALLOP PR 510.29 RH 793.36

GALLOPING MN 371.20

GAMBLE JD 612.39

GAMBLER JD 612.37 612.39

GAMBLING PO 96.25 RH 801.5

GAME MO 19.30 SP 52.20 WM 65.6
   OC 289.38 EE 305.31 SD 412.5
   412.32 WR 548.41 BO 590.30
   JD 605.7 IL 655.2 655.10
   659.32 OV 754.3 MD 816.24

GAMES MO 7.11

GAMIN MD 808.11

GANDER GF 242.35 RR 780.1

GANG OA 28.1 SP 47.24 47.27
   SC 270.35 271.6 PP 429.22
   IL 654.23 NT 721.7

GANG-LAD DV 166.14

GANGS HT 42.11 SP 47.9

GANGWAY NT 713.23

GAP PO 106.6 106.20 TF 126.10
   FG 190.39 194.22 SS 197.11
   WS 245.9 OC 302.8 PR 493.28
   LA 639.32

GAPED SB 215.8

GAPING TH 853.24

GAPS GG 669.25

GARABAY, GENERAL (SEE GENERAL
   GARABAY)

GARAGE PP 436.24 BM 834.27

GARAGE (CONT.) 839.28

GARDEN MO 4.39 OA 24.11
   24.25 24.34 24.36 25.3
   HT 42.25 44.11 WM 55.15
   63.19 TF 117.11 123.12
   127.34 133.22 DV 160.33
   160.36 161.4 161.8 161.21
   161.23 164.13 167.26
   168.7 176.41 179.29
   SG 221.18 221.27 222.16
   224.24 224.29 224.36
   225.10 225.15 225.18
   225.22 228.4 228.13 229.15
   229.27 WS 263.16 OC 283.34
   284.4 286.27 EE 303.2
   303.3 303.11 303.33 303.36
   304.40 306.34 307.13
   307.21 308.27 310.23
   311.21 312.2 313.37 316.39
   323.17 323.23 328.35
   329.21 TP 334.26 BL 358.19
   YT 394.8 398.7 400.4
   400.17 400.22 400.42
   406.9 PP 436.26 FA 464.2
   464.3 TB 515.16 520.27
   520.29 521.1 524.15
   SU 529.9 529.11 537.28
   WR 546.19 561.19 561.40
   562.20 562.25 564.27
   564.32 565.18 566.4
   JD 624.29 LA 630.6 635.29
   635.32 636.35 OV 754.27
   755.5 755.33 LL 762.25
   765.32 772.10 772.37 773.3
   773.6 RH 790.19

GARDEN-END OA 26.6

GARDENER SG 224.26 225.5
   RH 794.9 804.9

GARDEN-HOUSE RH 797.23

GARDENING HT 42.23 ML 726.33

GARDENS TF 122.6 EE 305.6
   FA 464.38 WR 561.19 561.24
   578.29 MD 810.28

GARE DE L'EST BO 587.34

GARLAND WM 60.34 WR 565.4
   565.5

GARMENT DV 179.5 OC 301.42
   WR 557.10 OV 747.13 755.11
   757.21 MD 811.31

GARMENTS OA 29.1 37.22
   SS 202.5 OC 284.31
   HD 456.11

GARRULOUS GF 238.33

GARRY FA 471.18

GAS HD 456.16 FA 462.9

GASH FG 189.8

GASPED OA 36.29 DV 162.1
   TP 343.32 343.38 HD 450.31
   BO 592.26 IL 650.42

GASPING   OA 36.19   DV 161.36
   EE 315.28   ML 734.8

GASPS   MO 3.3   OA 36.35

GASSIN'   PP 429.8

GAS-WORKS   TP 334.21

GATE   MO 18.37   WM 63.18   DV 139.4
   167.26   167.28   174.16   182.29
   186.17   SS 197.8   198.30   209.39
   210.1   210.29   211.31   SB 217.12
   219.29   SG 225.11   CH 274.2
   274.31   OC 285.3   289.36   293.9
   295.19   MN 366.29   377.32
   HD 444.12   449.23   FA 463.32
   WR 575.9   575.10   575.20   575.39
   LA 630.32   635.33   636.13
   636.26   636.28   640.12   IL 653.2
   653.9   653.41   654.23   655.22
   OV 756.25   RR 787.26   BM 834.40

GATE-DOOR   WR 564.30   564.32

GATE-POSTS   WP 385.38

GATES   WS 251.20   OC 290.38
   EE 322.38   MN 378.1   PP 432.14

GATEWAY   WR 551.13   LA 630.10
   630.27

GATHER   MO 22.26   28.42   TF 126.9
   DV 161.10   SD 417.29   JD 618.31
   NT 710.20   LL 761.27   RH 803.22

GATHERED   MO 13.4   WM 70.11
   PO 105.4   110.41   FG 188.27
   195.2   SS 202.17   210.9
   GF 235.15   CH 281.31   MN 371.12
   378.23   WP 381.2   387.38
   PP 437.7   HD 456.10   456.19
   FA 465.23   TB 524.17   SU 540.34
   WR 562.24   563.28   IL 655.26
   GG 674.2   690.1   NT 705.33
   LL 777.27   BM 838.21

GATHERING   MO 18.10   EA 89.23
   DV 173.27   174.23   BL 363.37
   WP 386.31   PP 435.23   SU 537.38
   OV 754.31

GAUL   ML 724.25

GAUNT   GF 241.30   SU 538.25
   WR 550.9

GAUZE   BM 835.25   840.39

GAUZY   FA 465.13

GAY   OA 24.18   EA 91.39   DV 174.28
   SG 225.42   SU 543.33   LA 639.42
   640.2   NT 712.19   712.22
   ML 730.1   LL 761.16   BM 831.31

GAZE   MO 9.42   SS 197.26   198.5
   MN 367.41   YT 407.33   SD 426.14
   FA 471.2   PR 492.29   GG 678.12
   RR 784.26

GAZED   HT 44.15   WM 59.26
   PO 115.5   SS 199.26   207.8
   BL 364.20   SD 426.1   HD 452.35

GAZED (CONT.)   PR 501.15   SM 583.5
   584.29   JD 626.6   IL 654.29
   GG 666.39   677.5   677.39   682.23
   692.1   694.25   696.39   RR 785.9
   RH 795.12   801.17   803.9
   MD 823.23   824.7   BM 840.38
   842.41

GAZING   SG 221.28   221.34   225.36
   SC 270.13   CH 274.5   HD 452.19
   TB 522.18   SU 543.14   SM 583.1
   BO 589.14   JD 617.39   LA 643.27
   646.4   GG 665.29   666.36   669.26
   678.10   681.28   694.6   ML 736.42
   743.29   743.30   RR 784.26
   787.21   RH 801.14   BM 829.30
   837.42

GEE   (SEE MR. GEE; MRS. GEE)

GEESE   FG 190.22   GF 234.3   235.10
   235.17   242.32   242.33   242.39
   243.8   WP 386.16

GEL   FA 469.25   472.12

GELSIE   WS 246.38

GENERAL   TF 127.15   DV 137.28
   154.9   OC 292.4   MN 367.30
   WP 389.30   FA 465.31   471.7
   JD 620.2   NT 703.14   ML 727.35
   727.37   727.39   MD 825.2
   BM 832.32

GENERAL ISIDOR GARABAY   NT 707.15

GENERALLY   MO 14.26   17.5   18.36
   SB 218.24   BL 355.39

GENERALS   NT 701.20   707.21

GENERAL THIS   BO 588.36   588.38

GENERATIONS   TF 128.2   EE 306.23
   306.28   313.34   WR 562.3

GENEROSITY   EA 87.15   FG 187.22
   TB 514.13   SU 543.23   543.24

GENEROUS   MO 12.24   WS 251.9
   EE 305.21   311.36   BO 587.29
   OV 752.11

GENEROUSLY   BO 602.22

GENIAL   DV 186.6

GENIE   MD 820.34

GENIUS   WM 67.21   SD 421.20
   ML 728.29   LL 769.38   MD 812.40

GENOA   DV 165.2

GENTEEL   DV 138.5   138.9

GENTILITY   DV 138.13   138.27

GENTLE   MO 12.21   OA 33.24   37.19
   PO 115.33   DV 147.17   CH 276.38
   PP 437.11   HD 454.4   FA 468.4
   PR 489.26   TB 520.19   SU 541.27
   WR 565.7   567.29   575.42   576.4
   576.12   BO 590.40   596.34

GENTLE (CONT.)   GG 663.28
   664.10   ML 738.34   RR 779.6
   RH 790.10   MD 810.32

GENTLEMAN   MO 8.8   WM 55.39
   56.18   58.5   66.27   EA 86.33
   PO 98.14   TF 127.18   127.19
   128.10   DV 145.32   163.41
   SS 197.4   SB 218.20
   SG 228.9   YT 396.13
   PR 483.34   485.40   WR 548.23
   JD 616.33   LL 764.3
   MD 819.16   824.11   824.35

GENTLEMANLY   WM 64.33
   SG 226.26

GENTLEMEN   TF 134.26   SD 415.24
   PR 473.19   TB 522.12
   WR 548.21   548.26

GENTLENESS   OA 38.38   CH 277.35
   OC 298.13   PR 485.22   494.7
   WR 566.22   GG 694.14   694.17

GENTLY   MO 2.30   8.14   10.7
   16.5   20.21   21.19   OA 29.41
   WM 68.3   PO 95.8   DV 144.1
   163.4   WS 245.30   266.2
   SC 272.37   CH 278.4
   OC 284.27   MN 375.31   375.33
   WP 386.39   YT 401.37   402.1
   402.21   SD 414.2   PP 439.36
   HD 454.41   456.20   456.38
   PR 476.8   489.10   494.6
   498.39   507.34   SU 531.21
   BO 590.38   ML 734.35
   OV 751.28   753.9   LL 772.7
   MD 806.23   TH 845.26

GENTRY   ML 726.8

GENUINE   DV 147.11   155.23
   GF 243.35   JD 606.4   606.5
   606.11   GG 661.20   662.28
   689.8   LL 764.36

GENUINELY   WM 69.24

GEOGRAPHICALLY   TB 513.11

GEOGRAPHY   BL 358.9

GEORGE   GF 240.40   TP 335.4
   PP 432.34   432.35

GEORGE, KING   (SEE KING GEORGE)

GEORGE DURANT   DV 144.17

GEORGE ELIOT   MO 6.25

GEORGE MOORE   MO 13.28

GEORGIAN   LA 630.6

GERMAN   WM 58.3   59.6   59.25
   EA 84.27   85.19   85.22   85.30
   85.36   86.4   86.16   86.26
   86.32   88.1   SS 202.42
   EE 326.31   327.12   327.19
   SD 420.20   420.31   FA 464.35
   BO 587.14   587.16   591.21
   594.32   594.33   594.41
   594.42   598.40   599.14

GIRLS' DV 144.31 TP 340.34

GIRT YT 394.1

GIST ML 729.5

GIVEN MO 21.32 OA 37.1 SP 46.9
    46.35 WM 60.8 69.24 EA 81.33
    83.12 TF 130.22 DV 146.33
    165.39 180.37 SS 202.22
    SG 229.33 WS 254.36 CH 278.40
    OC 299.38 EE 305.26 314.31
    BL 359.34 SD 425.32 HD 441.8
    PR 476.27 504.15 504.16
    505.32 SU 535.20 WR 576.9
    580.15 580.16 OV 753.37
    RR 779.32 BM 833.37 TH 846.39
    847.20

GIVES HT 39.32 CH 279.33
    OC 285.39 TP 334.15 336.34
    BL 358.5 PP 428.34 TB 515.17
    525.33 527.3 527.4 GG 669.12
    RR 780.6 TH 845.24

GIVING MO 14.23 17.4 OA 25.41
    EA 73.10 76.19 80.32
    PO 105.12 116.11 TF 119.6
    DV 138.32 167.11 SB 215.21
    218.30 SG 221.9 225.7 231.32
    231.34 WS 251.10 252.20
    SC 270.23 EE 327.29 330.7
    331.29 TP 344.16 YT 409.32
    TB 527.2 WR 555.34 564.41
    BO 587.23 590.5 594.8
    GG 665.6 NT 719.19 RH 794.22

GLACIER-RIVER PO 105.20

GLACIERS GG 674.8

GLAD MO 8.29 9.2 SP 52.35
    WM 59.28 EA 74.1 87.29 91.22
    PO 99.8 TF 123.23 DV 142.11
    142.14 151.25 152.41 153.2
    153.3 153.22 167.23 169.17
    172.18 172.42 177.42 181.32
    181.34 185.35 SS 197.14
    197.16 205.12 208.6 209.19
    SB 216.20 WS 247.32 CH 279.34
    OC 292.37 EE 329.16 TP 337.27
    BL 350.25 354.32 357.35
    359.10 359.13 359.14 362.37
    365.6 YT 410.5 PR 474.12
    TB 516.26 WR 549.11 BO 602.13
    JD 629.5 LA 639.11 GG 667.26
    668.41 675.15 683.28 683.36
    689.34 696.15 ML 736.2 740.17
    743.6 743.19 OV 760.6
    RR 787.32 RH 801.33 BM 833.3
    841.18 TH 851.19

GLADE ML 723.18

GLADES ML 722.33 723.12

GLADLY TB 513.22 WR 576.35

GLADNESS MO 4.31 20.14

GLAMOROUS MO 1.31 TF 123.9

GLAMOUR MO 21.41 DV 166.20
    SS 203.2 EE 325.14 BL 347.30
    YT 403.8 PR 473.31 TB 519.37

GLAMOUR (CONT.) WR 556.7
    GG 663.32 LL 762.8

GLANCE OA 29.10 38.26 SS 201.1
    202.30 GF 235.25 235.30
    BL 357.28 MN 372.16 PP 432.31
    PR 490.21 SU 539.12 539.26
    544.32 WR 567.39 BO 603.9
    IL 656.33 657.33 NT 702.28
    ML 726.9 728.37 RR 783.34
    MD 820.25 BM 829.31 841.34

GLANCED MO 8.13 8.17 15.21
    OA 30.13 33.20 35.10 36.14
    37.38 WM 56.17 59.14 61.4
    EA 72.3 73.7 77.5 85.31
    PO 109.24 DV 178.36 SS 201.17
    207.32 208.36 SB 218.18
    SG 221.37 GF 239.16 242.16
    243.18 WS 256.37 257.11
    CH 274.6 OC 286.26 289.37
    290.2 TP 343.30 BL 351.19
    357.36 MN 370.8 377.26
    WP 380.26 380.30 390.5 391.22
    YT 397.30 398.10 SD 423.41
    PP 430.32 433.25 437.18
    437.27 437.33 437.42 440.11
    HD 442.38 FA 469.31 PR 484.10
    504.40 TB 524.27 524.31
    525.36 SU 538.19 539.28
    541.21 542.1 542.24 542.35
    WR 553.37 576.7 BO 596.29
    JD 612.2 618.36 623.17 624.37
    625.3 LA 630.26 634.32 634.33
    637.28 GG 666.38 673.11 695.3
    697.4 NT 703.35 ML 728.35
    RR 784.11 MD 823.1 823.22
    823.40 BM 841.32 842.18

GLANCES MO 13.10 SU 539.32
    LL 776.17

GLANCING MO 14.27 OA 24.34
    27.29 WM 56.31 63.41 68.6
    EA 85.24 DV 159.15 162.13
    178.19 SG 221.23 224.20 225.6
    GF 236.27 236.38 CH 280.19
    OC 292.7 YT 397.23 PP 438.36
    HD 448.14 PR 495.6 WR 555.2
    JD 612.8 612.23 624.28
    LA 636.29 637.26 GG 675.7
    NT 711.30 OV 753.17 LL 771.7

GLARE OA 29.31 PO 95.3 114.29
    SB 213.41 GF 237.13 237.36
    EE 314.30 333.14 PP 439.20
    WR 558.6 JD 618.1 LA 631.37
    633.11 640.34 ML 723.26
    RH 793.5 793.31

GLARED PO 99.11 SB 217.7
    PP 427.8 427.17 431.2
    SM 585.13 LA 633.10 RH 793.21

GLARING PO 106.21 114.27
    PP 428.22 435.40 BO 588.31
    JD 611.1 622.27 NT 713.16

GLASS OA 24.12 HT 39.26
    PO 101.40 106.24 DV 140.37
    142.7 165.4 SG 222.13
    WS 245.42 255.39 OC 288.35
    294.18 YT 399.16 SD 412.10
    412.11 412.16 412.20 414.19
    PP 427.3 433.10 PR 501.8

GLASS (CONT.) WR 563.9 580.36
    BO 598.30 LA 632.20
    GG 675.10 675.23 677.36
    678.20 LL 777.27 RR 779.2
    786.27 788.28

GLASSE FG 188.14

GLASSES PP 432.36 432.37
    SU 542.31 GG 676.15
    LL 763.33 RR 785.30 785.33

GLASS-LIKE WR 573.21

GLASSY WR 563.12

GLASSY-BRIGHT RH 793.10

GLASSY-DARK WR 564.8

GLAUCOUS WS 257.13

GLAZE PR 483.5 GG 665.41

GLAZED OC 300.25 BL 365.5
    HD 441.36 442.12 GG 677.39
    678.10 678.12 680.8
    MD 818.36 819.40 821.29
    823.22 BM 840.38

GLEAM FG 193.33 WS 252.33
    253.15 MN 374.17 SU 539.33
    544.31 WR 576.8 577.18
    577.27 JD 606.27 616.37
    LA 630.5 633.2 633.18
    644.15 OV 751.16 LL 761.25
    BM 837.10

GLEAMED MO 3.15 DV 160.20
    SG 227.40 WS 254.11

GLEAMING PO 95.8 96.2 115.1
    115.4 116.5 FG 193.38
    WS 252.35 EE 326.15
    TP 344.6 PR 489.12 493.27
    497.39 498.15 LA 632.25
    632.39 634.33 NT 702.22
    OV 750.11

GLEAMS MO 1.16 PO 104.9

GLEAMY SP 47.15

GLEANING JD 605.35

GLEE OA 27.9 DV 157.27

GLEE, JOE (SEE JOE GLEE)

GLEEFULLY WM 59.25 MD 805.30

GLIB WS 249.21 BL 357.4

GLIBLY TH 845.18

GLIMMER DV 167.11 174.15
    GF 243.16 JD 610.33
    LA 637.14

GLIMMERED TF 118.40

GLIMMERING DV 167.13

GLIMMERS MO 1.28

GLIMPSE   DV 148.40   HD 456.2

GLIMPSED   GG 683.14

GLINT   PR 483.5   496.3   RR 781.28
781.29   MD 820.4   820.25   821.28

GLINTED   OA 24.8   OC 286.15
PR 489.4

GLINTING   WR 568.31   MD 822.8
822.26

GLISSADED   OA 35.21

GLISTEN   WM 55.30   WR 578.40

GLISTENED   WM 54.25   58.41   63.20
TF 117.34   DV 173.11   173.21
FG 190.21   BL 351.4   OV 750.3

GLISTENING   OA 26.10   WM 55.38
PO 95.7   108.40   109.12   114.29
TF 123.41   DV 160.19   SG 227.24
WS 249.9   WP 385.32   SU 539.23
WR 561.14   567.31   576.42
577.15   NT 707.36   709.28
719.33   MD 825.6   BM 834.35
TH 847.42

GLISTENS   GG 698.14

GLITTER   EA 73.10   SB 216.33
WR 557.38   565.9   572.2   576.1*
576.16

GLITTERED   PO 95.4   SG 224.19
OC 296.20   MN 374.11   WR 559.4
560.29   577.8   578.31   NT 709.25

GLITTERING   EA 72.5   PO 111.16
TF 124.23   WS 262.24   CH 274.23
TP 343.28   PP 433.37   WR 560.31
561.21   577.33   581.9   581.14
GG 664.6   669.35   RH 804.12

GLITTERINGS   PO 114.16

GLOATING   GG 679.36   680.8
ML 736.33

GLOBE   PO 107.9   BM 827.15

GLOOM   OA 27.30   EA 82.21
DV 148.28   158.41   GF 234.1
SD 419.10   420.15   PR 483.2
500.5   506.37   SU 530.11
WR 562.30   SM 582.9   583.19
GG 669.40   684.29   686.16
ML 723.36   OV 750.30

GLOOMILY   EA 71.33   GF 242.2
PP 433.19

GLOOMY   DV 137.39   156.28
SS 205.21   209.26   WS 245.10
252.40   253.24   261.11   261.16
SC 270.38   TP 334.11   336.12
WP 379.30   WR 564.16   GG 668.31
NT 701.12   ML 722.25   732.3

GLORIED   BL 349.34

GLORIFICATION   HD 447.27

GLORIFIED   HD 447.28

GLORIOUS   MO 16.34   18.23

GLORY   SG 221.4   TH 848.28

GLOSSED   FG 188.38

GLOSSY   EA 86.8   SS 207.24
WR 558.12

GLOUCESTER   FA 459.40

GLOVE   EA 79.7   PO 99.25
OV 749.41

GLOVED   LA 630.23

GLOVES   MO 11.3   OV 749.34   749.36

GLOW   MO 2.31   3.39   4.11   WM 59.4
EA 81.36   81.37   TF 130.24
DV 161.12   WS 244.13   250.9
252.22   253.16   OC 287.28
EE 306.30   307.40   314.38
315.12   WP 386.6   TB 515.32
WR 556.17   565.11   577.23
SM 583.40   BO 596.22   598.30
JD 618.6   618.16   624.38
GG 661.27   695.29   TH 848.15
849.5   849.6   849.8   849.13

GLOWED   SG 224.19   EE 329.29
BL 351.3   PR 500.28   WR 556.7

GLOWER   FG 188.16

GLOWERED   DV 160.3   TH 853.5

GLOWERING   WS 261.21   262.33
CH 279.38   MN 375.32   SD 426.8

GLOWING   TF 123.8   DV 181.24
WS 264.31   OC 286.13   HD 454.31
PR 493.22   499.19   500.32
WR 556.9   576.22   BO 603.27
LL 764.32

GLUM   CH 275.5   PP 431.26

GLUTTED   BO 595.1

GNATS   WM 60.32   ⁓

GNAW   TH 851.12

GNAWED   TH 851.15

GNAWING   EA 89.27   EE 303.23
MD 815.24

GNOMES   TH 853.14

GOAD   SU 532.1

GOADING   WS 261.9

GOAL   DV 171.8

GOALS   SP 50.29   50.33

GO-AS-YOU-PLEASE   DV 166.17

GOAT   SU 529.15   WR 575.13
ML 733.35   735.8

GOAT-LIKE   LA 632.26

GOATS   WR 558.42

GOATY   JD 606.27

GOBBLED   IL 657.39

GO-BETWEEN   WR 574.21

GOD   WM 64.35   DV 142.20
145.16   154.20   FG 188.5
195.17   SS 205.19   GF 242.6
242.25   CH 280.39   281.10
EE 315.1   BL 364.18
WP 393.10   PP 428.1   428.19
428.20   428.24   429.20
TB 518.16   521.1   521.8
527.12   527.15   527.17
WR 560.13   560.16   560.21
560.22   563.18   JD 624.18
624.41   628.6   GG 664.24
668.7   680.39   685.38   689.34
698.18   NT 715.30   719.26
ML 742.20   OV 752.36
LL 769.8   774.22   RH 792.15
792.30   804.33   BM 842.13

GODDESS   WM 67.34

GODFATHERS   CH 280.5

GOD-FORSAKEN   MO 4.22   SS 200.28
PP 428.33

GODFREY MARSHALL   EE 307.37
313.22   315.6   321.5   327.11

GODHEAD   EE 314.29

GOD-LIKE   TF 128.31

GODMOTHER   CH 280.4

GODS   WM 67.32   EA 87.7
SS 205.6   EE 323.39   326.11
WR 554.40   560.20   560.24
570.6   570.38   570.39   571.1
ML 726.37

GOD'S   TP 346.3   FA 467.6
467.11   468.3   471.10
SU 529.31   NT 717.35
RR 784.3   RH 803.3   BM 842.13

GOEST   EE 331.17

GOETH   FA 466.30

GOIN'   SP 53.13   53.16
SS 199.6   SC 268.18   271.12
271.17   271.27   271.29
271.33   271.37   CH 279.14
WP 389.21   PP 432.28
HD 443.22   445.10   FA 463.31
469.12

GOLD   WM 61.20   64.6   EA 72.6
PO 107.10   114.25   114.27
114.32   114.42   TF 118.40
DV 173.13   179.4   FG 188.27
SS 197.21   200.25   210.5
OC 286.41   PR 475.9   487.3
487.22   487.26   489.35
490.4   493.26   494.29   497.11

GOLD (CONT.) 499.34 499.35
  SU 530.37 532.9 532.15
  533.39 534.12 534.13 536.21
  WR 574.7 JD 612.30 ML 741.34
  OV 759.39 TH 848.14

GOLD-AND-BLACK WM 61.21

GOLD-BRONZE WR 569.19

GOLD-BROWN SU 536.21 537.1

GOLD-DUSKY SU 534.41

GOLDEN WM 55.10 60.35 PO 114.16
  114.42 115.3 DV 172.31 173.11
  SD 421.33 FA 467.37 PR 493.23
  SU 534.40 WR 574.5 GG 699.42
  ML 723.30 724.29 OV 747.2

GOLDEN-BRONZE WR 568.42

GOLDEN-BROWN EA 84.4 DV 149.42

GOLDEN-GREEN PO 114.16

GOLDEN HORN HT 39.22

GOLDEN-LIGHTED OA 25.6

GOLDEN-RED WR 578.14

GOLDEN-ROSE SU 539.35

GOLDEN SAXIFRAGE ML 736.14
  736.19

GOLDEN-SKINNED SD 419.22

GOLDEN-SWEET TH 844.19

GOLDERS GREEN IL 648.17
  ML 739.10

GOLD-FLECKED JD 612.32 624.39

GOLD-GREEN PO 108.36

GOLD-GREY SU 542.25 MD 810.38
  BM 837.36

GOLD-MINES WR 546.6

GOLD-SCARLET OA 28.2

GOLD-SPARKLING PR 490.30

GOLIATH'S MD 817.7

GOO SP 51.36

GOOD MO 9.30 10.36 11.11 11.35
  13.23 14.20 14.24 15.5 15.7
  18.30 18.31 18.33 20.18 21.1
  OA 28.14 31.18 37.36 38.13
  HT 39.8 39.11 40.24 40.39
  SP 47.2 49.22 50.29 50.37
  52.19 WM 57.4 66.26 66.28
  66.34 68.18 EA 73.28 73.29
  73.31 75.31 80.37 90.4
  PO 99.37 TF 117.35 123.31
  124.32 DV 137.8 143.10 145.4
  147.22 150.21 153.13 156.37
  156.38 163.25 163.27 165.8
  167.38 169.13 171.37 177.8

GOOD (CONT.) 177.19 177.34
  184.21 186.12 FG 190.31
  SS 200.24 206.3 208.29
  SB 212.34 213.17 217.22
  218.37 219.24 SG 222.23
  231.26 GF 236.33 236.34
  239.13 WS 246.24 248.3
  248.4 250.25 250.35 254.3
  255.11 256.2 259.25 259.27
  SC 267.1 267.7 267.8 269.16
  CH 275.17 277.2 282.14
  OC 288.21 293.21 294.40
  298.17 EE 305.23 305.36
  311.14 326.32 326.35 TP 336.5
  336.22 338.35 339.2 339.6
  341.33 341.40 342.4 BL 347.18
  347.19 348.16 349.7 352.28
  356.36 359.24 360.25 361.29
  MN 366.10 366.15 367.24
  367.36 373.14 WP 380.18
  381.16 382.6 382.11 383.38
  384.13 384.24 384.28 387.19
  389.26 391.36 392.4 YT 395.5
  397.33 403.37 407.2 SD 411.21
  412.8 412.10 415.7 415.25
  415.27 416.16 421.34 424.26
  425.1 426.5 PP 428.19 429.21
  430.10 431.35 432.7 435.15
  435.16 435.19 437.17
  FA 458.28 460.3 460.11 461.17
  461.21 461.24 461.26 463.4
  464.19 470.4 470.5 PR 473.22
  481.37 481.39 484.19 485.8
  502.19 502.25 506.1 508.10
  512.4 TB 515.7 516.42 517.24
  517.34 517.40 518.6 519.11
  519.33 521.1 521.4 521.7
  523.22 523.24 525.33 525.41
  SU 528.13 528.14 529.30
  529.31 539.12 543.27
  WR 547.18 555.6 555.8 555.9
  559.42 567.20 JD 606.20
  607.36 615.18 619.14 619.19
  624.36 626.21 626.34 628.6
  IL 649.2 654.30 655.25 656.16
  GG 666.11 667.8 669.12 672.7
  672.32 672.35 673.17 673.19
  674.5 674.30 675.9 675.12
  675.17 676.35 680.41 686.38
  688.21 691.38 691.39 691.40
  692.9 692.10 692.14 693.14
  693.15 695.27 695.32 697.2
  697.23 700.5 NT 701.30 702.8
  708.17 715.1 717.36 719.9
  720.36 ML 722.14 722.25
  728.17 731.41 732.27 735.29
  739.30 OV 752.22 752.38
  754.23 756.10 LL 764.29 769.8
  771.16 771.23 773.36 776.33
  778.8 RR 781.21 783.25 787.24
  788.6 789.1 RH 790.14 790.26
  795.18 796.2 802.5 802.32
  804.34 MD 805.1 805.16 807.1
  807.10 807.12 808.6 810.25
  813.17 818.22 819.23 820.15
  823.25 823.38 825.32
  BM 827.34 829.40 831.28 832.1
  836.9 839.27 842.8 842.22
  TH 849.11 849.12 851.16
  853.30

GOODALL FA 467.12

GOODALL (SEE HARRY, JACK; MR.
  GOODALL; MRS. GOODALL)

GOODALLS FA 464.3

GOOD-BYE MO 8.37 17.24 22.28
  22.29 22.32 WM 69.4
  EA 79.9 80.1 YT 396.27
  BO 590.38 JD 627.25 627.26
  LA 630.28 630.31 IL 656.24
  GG 699.21 NT 714.18 720.35
  OV 747.30 MD 826.7 826.9
  BM 828.25 841.19 841.20

GOOD-BYE'S MO 8.31

GOOD GOD GG 679.1

GOOD-HEARTED BM 842.13

GOOD-HUMOUR WS 247.35

GOOD-HUMOURED DV 137.9
  SD 415.2

GOOD-LOOKING MO 7.5 OA 29.17
  31.16 TF 117.20 DV 138.7
  140.20 183.30 SS 198.10
  205.2 SG 221.31 TP 336.12
  MN 367.36 374.17 PP 432.29
  HD 441.17 TB 513.24
  JD 606.28 LL 768.21
  MD 813.17 BM 828.10 830.34

GOODLY WS 247.13

GOOD-NATURE BM 831.37

GOOD-NATURED TF 126.33
  TB 513.21 IL 658.29
  LL 771.15 BM 833.6 842.13

GOOD-NATUREDLY LL 762.3
  BM 833.27

GOODNESS DV 147.11 150.23
  150.24 153.2 OC 288.34
  PR 491.7 JD 610.15
  LA 642.32 643.17 645.11
  645.18 GG 674.6 TH 843.7

GOOD-NIGHT MO 18.39 HT 38.13
  41.7 TP 342.12

GOODS HT 43.38 SP 46.38
  DV 140.28 161.18 BO 595.1
  NT 707.11 TH 853.34

GOOD-SIZED GG 671.2

GOODS-YARD MN 366.25

GOODWILL ML 727.35 727.37

GOOD-WILL ML 727.40

GOOSE GF 243.6 RR 780.1

GOOSEBERRIES SS 202.21
  SG 224.28 224.39 YT 408.34

GOOSE-GRASS SB 212.11

GORD MN 377.38

GORE PR 487.28 SU 528.21

GORGE DV 158.32

GORGEOUS   EE 311.21   WR 573.34
   NT 712.12   MD 810.38

GORGEOUSNESS   EE 312.25   WR 580.4

GORPING   SC 273.9

GORSE   SS 210.8   SB 213.40
   OC 283.4   EE 303.29   323.35
   330.17   330.25   ML 722.31   723.1
   725.18   734.14

GOSSAMER   ML 735.29   735.30
   735.31   OV 747.11   750.31

GOSSAMY   ML 735.32   735.42

GOSSIP   BL 360.34   MN 368.30

GOTTEN   WP 388.25

GOULD, NAT   (SEE NAT GOULD)

GOURD   SU 530.36   WR 557.2

GOVERMENT (SIC.)   PR 497.19*

GOVERNED   DV 149.32

GOVERNESS   TF 123.28   123.38
   124.35   124.41   125.1   125.21
   126.33   127.7   DV 138.30
   PP 430.7   RH 802.32

GOVERNESSES   EE 329.13

GOVERNMENT   WR 549.7   549.8
   549.11   JD 626.21   MD 805.2
   815.8

GOWN   WM 55.32   58.14   DV 184.8
   CH 275.34   GG 692.5   696.12
   OV 747.9

GOYTE   (SEE LANCE-CORPORAL GOYTE;
   MR. GOYTE; MRS. GOYTE)

GRACE   OA 37.10   TF 117.35
   DV 143.15   EE 304.18   309.10
   313.26   325.8   SU 538.41
   GG 699.32

GRACEFUL   OA 23.11   YT 395.3
   PR 483.16   LL 777.16

GRACEFULLY   OA 25.41

GRACIOUS   CH 277.2   282.14
   OC 288.21   293.21   PR 473.35
   ML 725.8   MD 812.6

GRACIOUSNESS   WP 389.34

GRADATIONS   OA 30.30

GRADE   TF 126.37

GRADUALLY   MO 4.36   6.23   EA 78.12
   81.32   82.30   PO 95.13   96.41
   97.7   106.22   108.21   110.26
   112.26   TF 126.35   129.22
   129.38   DV 137.42   138.10   149.8
   170.1   171.4   181.1   SS 203.39
   WS 260.10   264.27   EE 310.1
   312.31   313.39   332.14

GRADUALLY (CONT.)   MN 375.32
   HD 449.42   SU 543.35   WR 548.7
   BO 591.41   NT 717.4   OV 752.16
   LL 775.26   RR 785.21   MD 807.11
   807.29   816.41   TH 849.13

GRAFT   EE 305.42

GRAFTED   EE 305.41

GRAIN   MO 6.24   DV 155.39
   WS 255.16   HD 441.4

GRAINS   FG 193.34   JD 611.22
   611.25   LA 638.1

GRAMMAR SCHOOL   SS 208.12

GRAMOPHONE   MD 816.8   816.13
   817.14

GRAMOPHONES   PR 474.29

GRAN'   SG 222.31

GRAND   WM 59.18   EE 304.37
   SD 426.9   FA 464.26   MD 811.1
   817.16

GRANDCHILD   PR 476.42

GRANDCHILDREN   MD 818.34

GRANDDAUGHTER   SG 222.29
   LL 765.42

GRANDEUR   PR 481.9

GRANDFATHER   EE 309.17   309.18
   321.36   323.12   PR 476.33
   476.40   477.4   478.13

GRANDFATHER'S   OC 284.28

GRANDLY   WS 251.21

GRANDMOTHER   WS 260.39   OC 293.41
   294.5   298.28   PR 476.33   477.3
   MD 810.11

GRAND NATIONAL   RH 800.3   800.22

GRANDPAPA   MD 826.16

GRANDPARENTS   TH 851.27

GRANDSON   WR 566.33   LL 769.36

GRANDSONS   MD 821.9

GRANGE   TF 123.13   BL 347.10
   349.8   362.35

GRANITE   ML 723.24

GRANTED   PO 98.6   DV 153.24
   SS 201.26   GG 678.27   678.29
   679.42

GRAPES   FA 465.1   SU 530.24
   OV 754.38

GRAPE-VINE   OA 24.11

GRAPH   MO 6.27

GRASP   OA 31.27   SP 48.1
   WM 69.3   EA 93.19   PO 97.23
   TF 128.16   DV 181.39
   WS 249.12   BL 363.37
   363.38   364.2   HD 450.26
   PR 507.35   WR 577.13
   GG 673.14

GRASPED   OA 38.36   TF 121.1
   124.3   FG 194.25   BL 364.1
   HD 450.32   453.32   453.33

GRASPING   OA 24.32   PO 103.17
   TF 124.18   OC 302.1   ML 729.5

GRASS   MO 1.2   1.5   OA 24.13
   WM 60.26   EA 73.9   PO 106.14
   115.36   TF 118.36   118.39
   118.41   119.2   119.12   119.29
   121.5   122.8   SS 197.18
   OC 283.15   EE 305.1   317.10
   317.17   330.25   SD 420.14
   423.2   PP 436.32   HD 447.41
   PR 489.40   494.3   494.7
   494.10   494.18   497.20
   498.24   498.35   499.22
   500.40   510.27   SU 538.22
   WR 559.14   561.26   OV 755.5
   LL 773.4

GRASSED   EE 304.33

GRASSES   MO 1.10   SU 539.3

GRASSHOPPER   TB 518.21

GRASSLAND   MO 1.8

GRASSLANDS   WR 575.23

GRASSY   WM 55.19   SS 199.33
   EE 304.7   MN 371.14
   PR 507.22   510.9   510.26
   ML 733.30

GRATE   GF 239.23   HD 451.11
   PR 500.18   IL 654.34
   ML 744.4

GRATEFUL   MO 17.6   OC 301.14
   BO 598.16   GG 672.18   682.33
   688.34   ML 734.32

GRATEFULLY   MO 18.2   OC 286.38*

GRATIFICATION   PO 103.12
   TP 338.37   WR 565.24

GRATIFIED   WS 253.15   EE 307.40
   HD 449.14   WR 565.27

GRATIFYING   WS 253.11

GRATING   OA 34.33   EE 320.18

GRATISSIMA   GG 672.20

GRATITUDE   TF 130.14   130.15
   DV 181.35   ML 742.38

GRAVE   EA 88.17   DV 163.12
   GF 242.19   EE 320.40
   MN 366.16   HD 447.41   448.2
   448.15   WR 555.1   566.9
   LL 778.34

GREY-WHISKERED OC 285.42

GRID MN 372.38

GRIEF MO 16.38 22.22 OA 36.20
 DV 174.12 174.15 174.18
 176.15 176.17 181.29 182.38
 SB 216.32 WS 264.28 OC 301.17
 LL 767.37 BM 830.40

GRIEF-STRICKEN OA 36.42

GRIEG WM 59.7

GRIEVE WM 62.7 WP 384.10

GRIEVED WS 259.26 EE 324.8
 FA 461.32 GG 671.31

GRIFF LOW WP 388.32

GRILLING BO 594.11

GRIM GF 241.27 TB 513.13
 BO 595.7 JD 613.1

GRIMACE FG 187.16 WS 246.13
 263.33 CH 274.7 281.29
 WP 380.17 392.12 YT 398.25
 399.1 408.5 HD 446.6
 GG 687.11 NT 715.32 RR 784.19
 BM 842.7

GRIMACED TP 342.21 WP 381.32

GRIMED OC 297.36

GRIMLY CH 282.8 FA 461.14
 461.27 470.19 TB 521.34
 JD 622.37 GG 675.6 MD 826.16
 TH 849.24

GRIMNESS WR 577.19 577.20
 JD 612.28

GRIM-TOOTHED TP 337.29

GRIMY DV 166.9 CH 282.5
 TP 334.6 PP 430.27 FA 458.14

GRIN SS 203.4 WS 246.13 262.37
 MN 369.11 WP 391.35 YT 396.15
 HD 442.23 BO 604.36 604.38
 JD 618.35 623.10 627.5 627.14
 629.3 LA 632.1 646.18 646.21
 GG 663.38 LL 776.24 MD 806.16
 808.17 813.10 822.29
 BM 836.25 842.3 842.21

GRINDING TP 337.13 BL 362.14
 RH 790.27

GRINNED OA 31.34 SP 47.1
 SS 200.30 CH 280.22 281.29
 281.33 282.5 WP 391.28
 HD 444.1 456.12

GRINNING OA 32.2 SP 46.34
 CH 280.20 MN 369.14 376.32
 WP 391.35 392.3 JD 607.1
 LA 630.27 GG 675.39

GRIP OA 25.38 WM 69.12
 TF 120.11 DV 150.31 173.38
 174.35 PP 433.40 HD 455.29

GRIP (CONT.) SM 586.13 MD 814.23

GRIPPED MO 19.23 WM 69.2
 EA 89.9 90.31 TF 118.31 120.6
 DV 173.35 174.22 181.1
 SB 219.19 CH 276.1 OC 302.5
 YT 405.16 WR 563.39 RR 784.5
 RH 802.18

GRIPPING SS 210.34

GRIPS EE 307.26 308.14 310.29
 312.34

GRISLY LL 776.24

GRIT EE 329.10 TB 515.9 515.30
 515.33

GRITTY EE 328.25 328.39 329.9

GRIZZLE PP 438.24

GRIZZLY WR 571.25 571.26

GROAN FG 188.20 EE 312.12
 HD 454.3

GROANED MO 19.14 FG 195.10
 OC 286.5 FA 458.24 458.28
 465.38

GROCER BM 835.10

GROCER'S DV 162.13

GROOBY, JOSEPH (SEE JOSEPH
 GROOBY)

GROOM HD 442.7

GROOMED PR 484.39

GROOMING FG 189.5

GROOMS HD 446.31

GROOVE PR 490.30 498.36

GROOVES BM 830.21

GROPE TF 120.42

GROPED TF 120.24 DV 170.40
 171.40 SG 227.27

GROPING TF 119.22 119.32 119.35
 SB 216.12

GROSS TF 127.29 SG 232.5
 FA 462.31 ML 740.40

GROSSLY TF 118.8 127.33

GROSSNESS BL 354.34

GROTESQUE PR 477.26 485.30
 LA 640.39

GROUND SP 45.12 WM 58.15
 PO 111.17 TF 117.9 117.18
 121.2 DV 141.3 145.36 155.37
 168.41 FG 194.42 SS 198.15
 210.36 SB 217.6 218.33 219.15
 SG 227.27 WS 260.11 SC 271.29

GROUND (CONT.) TP 337.18
 MN 373.7 WP 379.1 380.7
 386.20 YT 394.4 SD 411.22
 417.28 422.33 422.37
 422.40 PR 494.14 494.17
 SU 541.34 541.36 542.31
 WR 557.8 559.30 561.2
 562.14 577.41 LA 630.1
 IL 651.22 GG 686.34
 NT 712.42 ML 737.11 744.26
 RH 803.21 TH 845.9

GROUNDS YT 394.2 LL 762.23

GROUP SP 45.27 TF 118.7
 119.4 119.38 WP 386.9
 388.26 SU 543.32 WR 551.37
 568.29 GG 662.14 NT 707.1

GROUPED TP 345.3

GROUPING WR 572.20

GROUPS WM 60.31 SC 270.37
 271.22 OC 283.29 286.8
 MN 368.31 WR 550.1 578.13

GROVE PO 114.38 WP 386.1
 PR 499.30 499.40 SU 532.24
 537.32 WR 559.17 561.5
 LA 635.22 639.1 639.6
 ML 724.39

GROVELLING TF 121.4

GROVES PR 494.8 SU 529.11

GROW PO 105.5 DV 147.8
 178.12 178.33 SS 206.13
 CH 281.7 EE 311.14 323.10
 PP 429.19 SU 531.35
 WR 547.12 556.16 558.31
 575.32 BO 604.18 GG 696.22
 RH 801.6

GROWING OA 26.15 HT 41.19
 SP 49.11 EA 80.38
 PO 114.18 TF 120.26 135.2
 SG 226.18 228.29 GF 238.20
 WS 250.22 255.28 EE 311.14
 PR 487.27 503.18 SU 537.30
 541.22 SM 584.5 BO 594.15
 594.27 JD 623.2 624.2
 LL 766.22 768.13 RH 790.33
 793.23 793.29 MD 818.34
 821.9

GROWING-UP DV 158.8

GROWLED DV 140.7 PP 438.28·

GROWN MO 1.2 11.27 OA 31.16
 EA 77.23 DV 163.36 SS 201.3
 CH 280.42 EE 310.11 311.16
 324.21 PP 439.35 PR 475.11
 TB 516.1 SU 538.22
 SM 584.36 584.37 GG 662.26
 OV 757.21

GROWN-UP HT 39.13 SB 216.30
 FA 467.23 BO 588.26
 JD 613.27

GROWTH EE 313.30

GRUBBINESS WM 65.15

GRUDGE SS 200.30 WS 253.12
   TP 345.40 SU 544.23 OV 752.12

GRUDGING WS 252.42

GRUDGINGLY DV 146.11 SG 222.14
   NT 702.5

GRUESOME PR 482.38 497.2
   JD 610.1 610.6 GG 678.6
   678.12 686.3

GRUESOMENESS PR 497.3

GRUFF ML 726.15

GRUMBLE WP 383.2

GRUMBLED HT 43.8 OC 287.41
   288.15 HD 449.16

GRUMBLERS ML 731.20

GRUNT OA 38.32 HT 43.12 SM 583.38

GRUNTED DV 139.25 FG 191.13
   191.28 CH 275.16 MN 373.38

GRUNTING FG 191.23

GUADALUPE ROAD NT 716.14 720.20

GUARD MO 2.12 OA 35.34
   WR 559.41 BO 594.33 600.2
   600.22 ML 740.15 LL 766.17
   BM 835.3

GUARDED BL 359.21 YT 402.42
   WR 547.29

GUARDIAN WS 256.11 PR 474.33
   479.19 SU 530.9 IL 657.12

GUARDING FG 191.21 BO 600.19

GUARDS GG 663.18

GUARD'S FA 459.17

GUARDSMAN'S GG 683.24

GUERILLA EE 316.26

GUESS MO 17.38 WM 64.26
   WS 248.22 248.28 WP 384.38
   SD 425.8 PR 492.18 511.18
   SU 540.12

GUESSED MO 7.1 DV 176.7
   WP 383.5 GG 664.35 LL 774.25

GUEST WM 56.19 EA 85.28
   ML 725.42 MD 813.8

GUEST-CHAMBER RR 788.3 788.6

GUEST-HOUSE PR 481.29

GUEST-ROOM ML 738.41

GUESTS HT 40.20 PR 481.31
   WR 548.22 ML 726.27 730.4
   733.28 RR 788.4 MD 812.12

GUFFAW MO 15.22

GUIDE MO 18.4 PR 483.18 483.29
   512.23 BM 827.22

GUIDES PR 482.12

GIULIETTA, SIGNORA (SEE SIGNORA
   GIULIETTA)

GUILT EE 317.16 GG 684.32 687.3
   691.37

GUILTILY MO 10.34 WS 246.16

GUILTINESS SG 223.28

GUILTY GF 239.34 240.3
   WS 249.18 EE 317.19 JD 613.30
   ML 738.32 LL 769.11 BM 842.17

GUINEAS MD 808.6

GULF GF 238.18 238.26 TP 335.10
   HD 455.2

GULFING JD 615.38

GULL ML 741.25 741.33

GULLIES SU 535.38

GULLS PO 105.23 SD 419.4
   ML 741.1 741.14

GULLY SU 533.34 537.36 542.28
   543.42

GULP HD 451.21 JD 619.8
   GG 676.31

GULPED PO 101.41

GUM GF 243.13

GUN SS 198.14 EE 330.10 331.4
   PR 506.39 507.7 507.24 510.14
   511.13

GUNFIRE EE 316.26

GUNS EE 330.1 330.12 330.33
   331.1 PR 494.35 NT 708.15

GURGLING WR 554.29 OV 760.3

GURRL WP 385.15

GUSH TF 120.13 131.33 SU 545.2

GUSHED PO 97.29 TF 129.26

GUSHING TH 853.14

GUST TF 122.37 WP 379.11

GUSTS ML 723.38

GUTTED GF 234.29 240.32

GUTTER GF 234.12 LL 769.4
   MD 820.37

GUTTERING EE 332.34

GUTTERSNIPE YT 406.29 407.25

GUTTURAL MD 819.2

GUY DE MAUPASSANT MO 6.29

GUZZLE SP 53.4

HA EA 73.42 74.10 78.5
   87.22 88.23 TF 134.19
   FG 193.6 WS 247.21 263.11
   BO 590.17 GG 678.13

HA' SP 46.32 46.35 SG 222.27
   223.1 WS 246.21 261.38
   SC 269.30 270.25 CH 281.4
   281.5 OC 297.31 300.17
   MN 369.22 FA 463.29

HABERDASHERY DV 139.32
   140.26*

HABIT MO 5.19 WM 63.34
   64.22 PO 111.13 DV 145.39
   169.19 170.40 SB 214.20
   FA 464.9 SU 528.24
   BO 589.40

HABITABLE ML 739.30

HABITS SU 528.25

HABITUAL PP 437.10 LL 763.2

HACENDADO NT 704.31

HACIENDA NT 701.19 704.29

HADES SM 583.19 583.22
   GG 674.27

HADNA HT 41.42

HADN'T DV 158.35 CH 281.3
   OC 294.21 300.19 YT 404.21
   FA 462.23 TB 520.40
   IL 650.34 655.13 GG 696.36
   ML 737.14 MD 806.1 814.25
   BM 831.28 TH 846.22 847.20

HADRIAN YT 395.29 395.36
   395.42 396.9 396.23 396.30
   396.33 396.38 396.41 397.1
   397.21 397.23 397.28
   397.30 397.34 397.42
   398.12 398.16 398.20 399.2
   399.6 399.14 399.17 399.21
   399.25 399.31 400.29
   400.39 401.10 401.21 402.7
   402.9 402.22 402.24 403.38
   404.1 404.3 404.11 404.13
   404.19 404.22 404.25
   404.33 404.38 405.24
   405.31 406.9 406.13 407.2
   407.4 407.9 407.15 407.21
   407.27 407.29 407.35
   407.37 408.2 408.14 408.21
   408.30 409.29 409.38
   409.42 410.3 410.4

HADRIAN ROCKLEY YT 396.4

HADRIAN'S YT 398.30 400.37
   402.5

HALF-PAST (CONT.)

HALF-PAST (CONT.) 177.25 178.6
  SS 201.30 SG 221.3 GF 241.14
  SC 268.1 CH 277.15 OC 286.19
  295.17 EE 318.11 TP 340.21
  MN 371.9 SD 411.3 FA 459.27
  462.39 BO 594.29 IL 648.40
  LL 764.23 BM 834.42

HALF-PERVERSE EA 78.31 90.21

HALF-PLEADING WM 61.7

HALF-PORTENTOUS ML 726.36

HALF-REAL ML 726.37

HALF-REVEALED PO 115.12

HALF-REVERENTIAL BO 590.8

HALF-SAD WR 567.41

HALF-SEEING SU 531.9

HALF-SHADE PO 108.33

HALF-SHUT EA 76.27

HALF-SMILE EA 71.32 JD 623.15
  NT 716.33

HALF-SOVEREIGN HT 44.17 SP 46.24
  49.30 50.2

HALF-SOVEREIGNS SP 47.11
  SC 271.8

HALF-STUBBORN WM 61.7

HALF-SUNK WM 69.35

HALF-THING OV 759.40

HALF-TIME SP 50.30

HALF-TRUTH MD 816.39

HALF-WAY HT 42.27 PO 114.3
  114.6 DV 169.33 OC 284.4
  MN 371.23 SD 419.8 PR 507.13
  WR 579.37

HALF-WICKED EE 324.4 324.9

HALF-WILD BL 362.21 GG 683.11

HALF-WISTFUL EA 78.31 FA 466.35

HALF-WITTED ML 739.15

HALL OA 24.2 31.12 WM 58.6
  EA 84.5 TF 125.23 134.7
  134.34 DV 173.39 GF 235.31
  WS 244.27 245.14 BL 347.3
  351.31 YT 397.36 LA 643.39

HALL-MARK SU 544.38

HALLO RH 793.27

HALLOOING LA 638.16

HALLS BO 597.19

HALLUCINATION GG 699.16

HALO TB 516.31 TH 849.2

HALT PO 106.36 TP 334.36
  WP 391.2 PP 433.20 FA 472.10

HALTED MO 21.9 OC 295.24 297.6

HALTING BL 352.2 PR 496.21

HALTINGLY MO 5.11

HALTS TP 334.19

HAM CH 278.38 ML 729.18

HAMLET DV 136.2 EE 304.32
  FA 464.6 RR 788.29

HAMLETISH TB 524.26

HAMLETS EE 304.5

HAMMER PO 113.4 NT 707.19
  MD 812.42 813.7 816.25 816.31
  816.35 816.42 817.3 817.7
  817.10 817.37

HAMMER-LIKE MD 813.4

HAMMOCK TB 521.20 521.23 524.25
  WR 560.42 561.2

HAMPERED CH 281.7 BL 360.36

HAMPSHIRE EE 303.14 304.31
  314.15 JD 607.18 RH 794.33

HAMPSTEAD EA 85.34 LA 630.2

HAMPSTEAD TUBE STATION LA 631.37

HAMS CH 274.20 WR 556.42

HAND MO 3.23 4.4 5.22 12.23
  12.27 18.1 19.19 OA 28.21
  29.23 30.6 36.37 37.1 38.39
  HT 42.30 43.15 SP 46.40
  WM 55.41 56.3 60.4 62.21
  62.22 EA 77.9 84.20 84.31
  89.31 90.36 90.41 PO 95.4
  95.33 97.23 98.38 105.8
  109.35 TF 117.23 123.34 124.7
  125.25 133.24 133.38 134.15
  DV 137.26 139.5 148.38 149.2
  151.22 151.26 154.8 157.31
  158.22 161.38 167.13 170.23
  175.1 175.11 180.37 182.18
  182.35 FG 189.2 191.29 192.17
  193.20 193.23 194.16 194.18
  194.19 195.24 SS 209.2 209.17
  SB 212.14 219.40 SG 225.33
  226.36 227.12 GF 235.3 236.17
  WS 245.36 254.1 254.5 256.20
  257.37 264.6 265.28 SC 271.35
  CH 275.2 275.31 276.16 276.32
  277.37 277.40 278.6 OC 284.39
  286.4 289.3 293.20 296.10
  297.40 298.30 299.16
  EE 324.14 324.16 330.17 332.3
  TP 337.42 BL 355.35 357.33
  358.31 358.32 359.7 363.33
  363.36 363.42 364.1 364.9
  364.11 364.16 365.8 MN 372.23
  375.23 378.10 378.15 378.18
  WP 383.22 383.24 385.13

HAND (CONT.) YT 397.22 397.26
  397.38 401.38 401.40
  402.15 402.20 402.26
  402.37 403.13 403.24
  407.14 408.40 SD 419.7
  423.39 426.10 426.13
  PP 433.11 435.34 439.20
  HD 453.31 453.32 453.39
  455.25 455.29 FA 460.36
  469.5 469.36 470.42
  PR 484.16 497.10 497.21
  498.6 505.11 TB 521.23
  521.29 SU 536.30 WR 549.16
  558.26 563.2 569.10 573.24
  575.30 578.7 SM 583.4
  583.15 583.20 BO 591.29
  591.35 592.21 596.24
  597.26 597.28 604.37
  JD 611.5 614.17 616.35
  618.12 618.13 629.1 629.3
  LA 631.21 632.35 634.12
  634.14 634.18 636.25
  IL 654.8 GG 669.37 670.12
  671.27 672.11 682.34
  683.5 683.28 684.6 685.22
  686.12 687.24 689.36
  689.42 690.35 691.8 692.18
  694.37 695.23 696.10
  697.1 NT 703.33 710.1
  711.28 713.23 ML 726.31
  729.37 730.30 OV 750.13
  751.9 753.6 LL 771.38
  772.9 773.35 RR 784.41
  786.16 RH 800.1 800.24
  MD 816.35 817.11 820.41
  821.32 822.4 822.5 822.11
  822.13 825.14 BM 837.33
  837.40 838.4 838.22 840.6
  840.29 841.6

HAND-BREADTHS ML 733.30

HANDED HT 44.17 DV 170.41
  WS 252.15 CH 275.16
  OC 286.2 WP 380.32
  YT 398.28 PR 483.32 502.16
  JD 618.11 LA 631.24 632.15
  GG 683.31 NT 721.6 721.14
  RH 798.39

HANDFUL FG 195.24 SB 213.8
  OC 295.1 PR 500.17
  RR 780.31

HANDFULS SS 202.9 OC 284.34

HANDICAPPED JD 606.9

HANDING EA 74.30 WS 245.16
  FA 460.18

HAND-IN-HAND MO 19.19

HANDKERCHIEF HT 42.21
  SB 215.16 216.6 WS 245.27
  245.31 246.23 257.33
  257.36 257.38 258.2 258.9
  265.11 SC 270.21 270.24
  CH 279.8 EE 317.12 317.27
  SD 419.17 TB 522.11
  WR 567.5

HANDLE OA 34.22 PO 109.35
  OC 302.2 BL 356.12 362.16
  FA 460.36 PR 484.4

HANDLE (CONT.) IL 649.39
  NT 717.10

HANDLED MO 7.31 FA 464.13
  PR 504.19 IL 649.40 ML 727.24

HANDLES TP 341.3 FA 459.28

HANDLING TH 850.33

HANDS MO 5.32 7.17 13.41 17.5
  19.23 OA 25.32 30.3 31.26
  34.24 35.40 36.8 36.14 36.18
  36.41 38.36 SP 48.1 WM 58.10
  63.10 64.28 64.31 65.13
  65.16 69.1 69.10 70.24
  EA 72.4 76.24 87.42 91.2
  91.36 PO 98.15 100.29 100.35
  101.27 104.41 107.24 109.12
  109.28 110.10 110.17 114.7
  115.35 TF 121.4 121.29 122.24
  123.38 124.37 126.27 127.30
  130.7 130.9 132.7 DV 154.23
  158.22 168.8 172.17 174.35
  177.17 178.22 180.27 181.9
  181.35 181.41 184.42 FG 190.6
  SS 197.16 201.24 209.18 211.3
  SB 214.34 214.41 216.4
  SG 226.30 226.32 227.16
  227.24 229.3 231.1 232.4
  232.5 GF 237.6 WS 251.8
  251.37 261.8 264.12 264.17
  266.2 SC 268.27 CH 276.4
  278.11 279.5 282.27 OC 290.15
  295.30 299.18 302.3 EE 313.41
  TP 343.19 BL 348.29 351.40
  354.27 358.12 364.6 WP 388.34
  390.10 390.38 393.11
  YT 397.26 400.4 400.17 403.18
  SD 413.21 415.18 422.42
  425.33 PP 427.25 429.12
  437.13 438.35 439.33
  HD 441.26 443.25 445.13
  450.21 450.24 451.2 452.24
  453.28 453.30 455.6 FA 458.34
  465.11 468.12 471.1 PR 474.35
  476.25 478.14 483.20 495.35
  500.27 511.7 SU 530.23 531.19
  540.25 540.29 WR 558.14
  573.31 577.4 577.8 577.24
  578.41 SM 583.17 583.30
  585.16 585.30 585.37 586.23
  BO 598.5 604.28 604.31 604.33
  JD 616.38 617.39 627.24
  LA 631.26 632.21 634.10
  637.32 637.39 643.31
  IL 648.19 654.31 654.33
  GG 690.2 691.13 695.37 695.42
  NT 715.26 718.38 ML 726.38
  728.29 744.3 746.13 OV 748.13
  749.24 749.40 754.21 754.42
  755.7 755.8 758.20 RR 788.12
  RH 799.1 MD 807.19 808.27
  809.29 820.2 821.32 BM 828.6

HAND'S JD 616.38

HANDSOME MO 7.42 12.22 13.23
  OA 23.2 26.35 SP 50.33
  WM 64.17 EA 72.19 PO 96.1
  96.10 96.19 99.13 TF 127.42
  DV 147.2 150.5 SS 202.38
  SG 227.34 OC 284.7 299.42
  EE 306.5 311.15 BL 347.13
  351.5 MN 370.16 372.15 374.23

HANDSOME (CONT.) WP 387.39
  389.10 393.12 YT 398.11
  SD 412.27 417.8 419.22 425.19
  425.20 425.23 HD 441.31
  FA 461.7 465.13 465.29
  PR 473.10 476.22 479.29
  482.27 TB 513.4 513.19 514.33
  517.22 SU 534.39 543.1
  SM 582.11 583.2 583.4 583.21
  BO 587.1 588.30 JD 606.16
  611.21 612.29 613.2 617.26
  623.16 624.35 LA 630.15
  GG 663.19 671.7 691.6
  ML 726.24 728.24 741.25
  LL 769.23 771.10 771.23
  RR 779.30 782.18 785.8
  RH 790.35 794.28 MD 807.14
  810.22 820.26 825.23 BM 831.1
  835.19 836.7

HANDSOMELY WS 251.17 OC 288.29
  SD 416.30

HANDSOMENESS YT 407.15

HANDY WS 244.34 TP 337.25
  ML 733.3 BM 840.10

HANG MO 17.20 TF 129.22
  FG 190.17 SS 200.18 JD 621.25
  IL 647.33 649.29 652.39

HANG-DOG MN 374.4 GG 670.41
  684.32

HANGED FG 190.16 BM 829.3

HANGELS FA 464.18

HANGING MO 3.14 13.41 OA 36.13
  HT 43.17 EA 84.10 93.23
  PO 106.15 115.15 TF 121.16
  126.6 DV 139.12 139.29 159.6
  161.8 167.39 FG 192.5
  SS 206.38 SG 225.24 CH 274.9
  EE 311.29 328.32 PP 432.18
  432.34 433.13 PR 500.25
  SU 534.35 539.36 WR 562.39
  579.34 JD 618.18 628.16
  NT 710.17 713.15 OV 748.13
  756.26 TH 849.24

HANGINGS WM 55.38

HANG-OVER TB 519.6

HANGS DV 163.15 WR 579.41

HAN'KERCHER SC 270.18

HANKIN (SEE MRS. HANKIN)

HANKY SU 528.33 IL 652.16

HANNAH PRESCOTT PR 473.25 474.20

HANNAH'S PR 474.25

HANOVER'S WS 244.3

HA'P'NY HT 41.42

HAPPEN OA 30.39 DV 150.27
  FG 193.39 MN 369.25 YT 401.15
  PR 475.26 492.36 504.17

HAPPEN (CONT.) 504.18 504.21
  LA 636.12 643.5 645.31
  GG 686.21 BM 842.33

HAPPENED PO 104.14 DV 141.18
  144.25 144.35 156.23
  168.14 172.13 GF 240.30
  OC 291.5 TP 337.9 340.15
  340.21 YT 402.33 PR 504.21
  WR 556.21 556.39 576.37
  JD 609.28 612.33 615.10
  615.16 LA 645.33 646.11
  IL 655.39 GG 663.18 667.12
  NT 711.12 ML 724.22 728.37
  738.15 OV 759.5 LL 773.1
  RH 800.8 MD 807.23 812.13

HAPPENING DV 173.32 SG 231.8
  EE 309.42 SU 531.3
  WR 580.39 LA 638.9
  GG 678.8 687.12 BM 828.29

HAPPENINGS GG 666.12

HAPPENS DV 155.29 YT 401.1
  PP 435.31 PR 508.31

HAPPIER BL 365.10

HAPPILY FG 196.24 MD 814.5

HAPPINESS TF 130.25 FG 196.18
  WS 260.11 BL 357.4
  WP 384.15 384.29 HD 448.7
  TB 517.32 522.1 522.5
  523.33 527.26 ML 726.26
  730.9 730.41 735.22
  RR 780.29

HAPPY OA 25.26 EA 86.6
  TF 130.29 132.4 132.31
  DV 166.8 SG 222.32 WS 250.5
  260.9 SC 268.42 OC 294.42
  TP 337.36 338.12 BL 347.10
  347.27 348.32 349.41
  349.42 355.30 355.39
  356.34 WP 379.35 381.24
  383.30 384.1 389.36
  YT 395.10 FA 462.27
  PR 489.23 TB 517.17 526.28
  526.29 526.32 526.33
  WR 571.7 BO 593.4 JD 613.6
  GG 665.4 665.13 665.14
  697.12 ML 726.25 727.33
  735.24 736.29 OV 753.16
  LL 765.12 RR 780.27
  MD 825.16 826.10 BM 829.12
  829.22 830.6 830.7 831.25
  TH 844.36 845.14

HAPPY ISLE ML 725.6

HARASSED WR 550.21

HARBINGER GG 695.34

HARBOUR OC 283.28

HARD MO 22.11 OA 25.15 36.35
  SP 46.8 WM 65.19 68.40
  69.14 EA 73.13 73.17 73.20
  73.33 75.14 76.11 77.6
  77.14 77.19 78.37 79.23
  81.3 90.42 91.6 PO 98.20
  100.12 108.26 110.10

HARD (CONT.) 110.19 112.18
   TF 117.13 DV 145.24 150.2
   152.7 163.34 168.10 168.24
   168.29 172.27 FG 187.19
   SS 204.7 SG 226.6 228.26
   231.2 GF 241.17 WS 258.19
   CH 276.23 276.31 279.31
   279.32 OC 284.31 302.4
   EE 303.23 305.11 305.22
   305.24 306.31 307.19 307.42
   314.33 322.35 BL 361.6
   WP 384.10 PP 428.12 430.15
   434.39 435.24 436.18
   HD 447.11 FA 461.16 PR 486.29
   488.13 496.3 497.30 504.23
   507.5 507.6 508.42 510.39
   TB 515.29 SU 530.15 WR 553.28
   575.35 577.34 SM 584.12
   BO 589.9 592.27 593.12 598.29
   JD 610.14 620.7 620.23 620.28
   620.36 620.39 623.34
   LA 643.27 GG 673.15 NT 703.23
   ML 729.24 745.22 745.31
   OV 751.29 753.42 LL 766.33
   773.23 RH 790.9 790.13
   MD 806.6 814.19 817.32
   819.19 BM 828.18

HARD-DRIVEN JD 622.24

HARDEN DV 170.34 JD 620.26

HARDENED MO 4.39 WM 66.11
   TF 121.17 DV 144.31 168.31
   SG 230.32 231.25 EE 324.36
   325.40 PR 504.40 GG 666.25
   RH 799.26

HARDENING OA 23.32

HARDENS JD 620.26

HARDER MO 21.17 DV 159.9
   SB 218.41 SG 229.39 RH 799.6

HARDEST SG 230.38 TB 515.32

HARD-FACED FA 467.15

HARD-HEADED SD 415.35

HARDLY DV 179.16 SC 270.8 271.5
   OC 287.4 EE 309.22 329.33
   TP 337.38 PP 431.14 HD 443.8
   451.32 454.38 FA 460.12
   PR 496.19 500.11 501.41
   509.14 TB 516.15 SU 530.19
   536.10 WR 567.25 577.36
   BO 596.21 599.23 602.14
   JD 616.15 616.27 IL 646.31
   656.33 GG 669.1 670.32 672.18
   682.31 686.2 687.30 688.10
   693.35 NT 703.42 712.37
   ML 728.13 728.31 739.22
   744.17 RR 779.20 RH 802.10
   802.18 MD 807.6 816.5
   BM 830.8 839.12 TH 848.15

HARDNESS WM 60.40 SS 204.3
   GG 666.26

HARD-SEEMING BO 587.30

HARD-USED PP 437.41

HARDY DV 145.30

HARE OV 749.2

HAREBELLS SB 216.29 ML 733.31

HAREM MD 826.17 826.25

HARK MO 17.33 SP 52.42

HARK-YE SP 52.42

HARM OA 35.24 DV 169.2
   SD 424.26 WR 575.23

HARMFUL SU 537.19

HARMLESS EE 324.15 GG 688.8
   BM 830.23

HARMONY OA 37.10 WR 572.13
   572.16 OV 747.9 748.23 750.6

HARNESS WM 68.17 EE 312.36
   HD 442.17

HARP WR 566.2 JD 628.16

HARRISON (SEE MRS. HARRISON)

HARROW IL 648.17

HARROWED TB 526.12

HARROWING PO 111.33

HARRY FA 458.16 458.18 458.34
   459.15 460.11 460.23 460.34
   461.11 461.19 462.4 462.7
   462.10 462.14 463.37 463.41
   464.8 464.25 464.30 465.15
   465.28 466.26 467.27 468.1
   468.13 468.19 468.23 469.4
   469.7 469.10 469.16 469.29
   469.31 469.34 469.37 469.41
   470.5 470.6 470.11 470.13
   470.20 470.23 470.27 470.30
   470.33 470.38 472.1

HARRY GOODALL FA 467.16

HARRY'S FA 461.34 464.16 466.39
   470.17

HARSH PO 97.39 99.14 BL 351.6
   BO 594.41 595.12 JD 619.26
   619.28 620.12

HARSHLY EA 75.21 DV 184.7
   WS 261.13

HARVARD PR 486.7

HARVEST MO 6.22 FA 468.6
   SU 529.5 ML 729.39 OV 758.28

HARVEST FESTIVAL FA 464.24
   464.29 464.36

HARVEST-HOME FA 465.22 ML 729.39

HASN'T TF 128.25 SB 213.33
   216.24 SG 229.6 GF 240.28
   WS 248.35 OC 282.15 285.33
   287.11 290.9 291.17 TP 339.42

HASN'T (CONT.) BL 352.9
   MN 377.16 WP 384.36
   LA 641.16 IL 657.23
   GG 687.38 TH 845.30

HAST HT 42.42 SP 48.16

HASTE OC 287.38 HD 448.33
   SU 543.19 SM 583.24

HASTENED SG 222.22 GF 237.37
   WS 250.17 OC 292.28
   HD 450.4 BO 598.32
   LL 770.10 770.17 775.26

HASTENING FG 188.19 SG 228.3
   228.15 CH 274.3 HD 449.9
   PR 491.2 496.20 LA 636.32

HASTILY MO 5.21 TF 133.31
   DV 159.22 159.24 178.31
   185.27 SG 226.5 WS 245.36
   254.1 YT 409.28 PP 439.15
   HD 448.32 448.40 PR 491.6
   500.17 SU 542.15 WR 552.25
   BO 597.33 LA 637.4
   IL 653.41 659.26 RR 784.7
   MD 820.22 BM 828.41 841.7

HASTY WS 255.33 JD 619.8

HAT MO 19.13 WM 60.6
   EA 79.17 79.20 DV 160.13
   179.3 180.4 180.7
   SB 218.7 218.23 SG 224.4
   224.6 228.17 WS 249.36
   250.38 CH 274.9 OC 286.42
   293.15 EE 321.37 TP 338.12
   338.30 341.2 BL 352.35
   363.34 MN 367.20 367.34
   371.25 376.24 WP 379.24
   FA 458.32 465.13 469.4
   470.23 470.24 PR 483.15
   484.1 484.8 491.25 511.12
   511.39 SU 538.38 540.18
   540.41 543.5 543.14
   WR 551.9 556.10 558.26
   559.16 562.36 563.3 567.4
   SM 586.26 JD 615.40 626.14
   LA 630.26 630.30 631.1
   631.7 631.9 631.13 632.35
   633.10 633.26 633.33
   634.23 634.29 635.5
   635.10 635.20 635.36
   636.34 643.33 NT 719.33
   ML 727.11 727.17 RR 780.36
   787.25 MD 826.5

HATCHET FG 189.9 EE 323.6

HATE MO 13.29 OA 33.7 34.14
   WM 60.16 60.23 61.11
   61.26 EA 73.34 73.35 73.37
   76.4 77.20 79.5 81.3
   81.31 PO 97.24 99.33
   115.23 DV 138.29 155.35
   SG 230.18 232.19 232.22
   WS 262.37 263.32 EE 326.38
   WP 393.1 PP 440.25
   PR 478.22 509.13 TB 515.6

HATE (CONT.) SU 543.29 WR 571.39
    571.40 572.1 576.2 576.3
    GG 676.7 691.25 691.27
    NT 710.22 715.12 715.33
    718.40 720.11 ML 731.17
    737.27 OV 752.14 754.10
    LL 777.6 RH 798.16 MD 815.9

HATED MO 6.18 SP 51.39 WM 60.19
    61.18 63.10 63.13 65.7 67.31
    EA 75.29 75.35 79.10 81.9
    86.10 87.30 91.7 92.27 93.27
    PO 99.11 110.36 112.34
    TF 127.13 127.31 DV 150.9
    150.39 151.13 153.35 154.26
    154.27 155.34 164.26
    SG 230.27 230.38 233.14
    CH 277.10 280.25 280.26
    281.21 TP 339.17 BL 357.11
    WP 387.37 PP 430.12 HD 449.16
    FA 463.23 465.34 PR 478.7
    488.24 TB 515.24 WR 548.1
    548.2 576.5 JD 623.7 627.1
    627.3 627.16 627.22 IL 647.25
    GG 662.14 662.19 NT 710.7
    712.28 712.34 712.35 718.39
    ML 730.34 732.6 737.4
    OV 752.9 752.13 754.9
    LL 774.8 MD 815.8 TH 849.5
    849.30 852.26

HATEFUL MO 6.19 SB 218.36
    GF 242.20 CH 276.37 OC 294.34
    EE 312.28 GG 687.17 ML 739.3

HATES GG 680.25 691.20
    NT 719.23

HATING DV 137.34 NT 710.9
    TH 852.37

HAT-PIN EA 79.32

HAT-PINS TP 338.15

HATRED DV 137.14 137.15 150.7
    SG 230.3 WS 262.19 BL 349.24
    357.12 PR 477.40 478.5
    WR 576.5 NT 704.41

HATS EA 83.12 PR 476.28
    WR 549.15 553.30 555.3 557.6
    ML 726.38 726.40 727.1

HAT-SHOP EA 83.11

HAUGHTILY OA 23.35 DV 185.33
    WS 263.2 MN 369.39 TB 527.10
    TH 851.31

HAUGHTINESS DV 158.9 WP 391.3
    LL 772.6

HAUGHTY PO 96.23 DV 158.8
    BO 589.5 589.19 LA 644.5

HAUL TP 334.34 ML 730.25

HAULAGE MO 11.36

HAULED OA 33.12 SP 51.6 51.7
    TF 121.2 121.10

HAUNCH WR 555.13

HAUNCHES HD 442.4 442.10 442.28
    PR 496.21 WR 557.35

HAUNT EE 325.27

HAUNTED MO 9.24 EE 306.19
    FA 462.28 RH 791.4

HAUNTING MO 22.19 PR 474.5
    482.37

HAUNTS WR 549.36 GG 692.33

HAUPTMANN, HERR (SEE HERR
    HAUPTMANN)

HAVEN TP 335.7 ML 734.32

HAVEN'T SP 44.1 52.20 WM 67.35
    EA 74.37 79.16 TF 128.22
    FG 188.2 SG 226.41 WS 246.33
    249.16 252.3 CH 273.10
    EE 318.27 MN 366.22 YT 401.12
    SD 412.39 412.41 418.6
    PP 438.28 HD 445.11 TB 525.25
    SU 538.17 JD 620.11 LA 645.18
    646.13 GG 689.26 690.3 692.27
    695.12 NT 717.14 RR 787.10
    789.16 RH 797.32 MD 818.8
    BM 835.1 839.36

HAVIN' WS 262.26

HAVOC SD 420.7

HAWK WP 386.15 SU 534.34
    GG 670.20 RR 784.18

HAWKEN RR 783.21 783.22 783.34
    784.16 785.16 785.17 785.22
    785.24 785.38 786.1 786.20
    786.25 786.28 787.4 787.23
    787.28 787.35 787.37 788.39
    789.18

HAWKEN'S RR 788.21 788.39

HAWKS WP 386.12

HAWKSE SC 269.30

HAWTHORN EE 304.21 305.41

HAWTHORNS FG 190.20

HAY TF 123.5 123.7 MN 366.1
    366.27 366.35 378.34
    ML 723.22 LL 773.7 773.26

HAY-LOADING MN 374.19

HAZE TF 132.21 SB 214.5
    IL 651.3 ML 723.22 OV 750.40

HAZEL OA 26.9 DV 148.38
    SS 197.16 SB 213.8 SM 583.13
    LL 763.38 771.26

HAZEL-BUSHES EE 328.33

HAZEL-GREEN GG 677.13

HAZY ML 738.25 740.23

HEAD MO 3.29 4.40 5.5 5.30
    6.38 8.7 8.27 10.17 12.29
    21.4 21.13 OA 25.29 25.33
    25.38 28.18 29.5 35.18
    35.23 36.3 36.40 37.28
    HT 40.7 42.31 42.35 44.12
    SP 47.41 52.1 WM 54.33
    60.21 60.23 65.24 67.2
    68.16 EA 71.30 73.15 73.28
    74.18 74.35 76.36 76.42
    77.28 79.32 84.24 85.9
    90.42 91.2 91.4 91.8
    PO 106.22 106.25 107.23
    107.30 108.25 109.10
    109.15 110.12 110.14 112.4
    113.4 113.7 113.9 113.17
    113.20 114.28 TF 118.13
    121.14 121.20 123.40
    124.25 124.33 125.14
    129.21 130.8 DV 147.39
    149.24 154.4 164.7 168.12
    170.22 170.25 175.15
    179.10 180.10 180.24
    180.30 181.19 FG 189.9
    190.34 191.37 194.19
    195.13 195.33 SS 202.18
    203.14 203.41 207.23
    207.34 211.11 SB 213.11
    215.6 216.3 218.7 218.28
    SG 223.36 225.27 227.9
    230.23 230.28 230.34
    231.23 232.6 232.11
    GF 234.14 235.30 235.33
    236.12 237.22 238.31
    239.26 WS 245.18 246.2
    246.4 246.6 246.29 247.22
    249.37 253.23 260.30
    260.35 261.40 262.1 263.28
    264.31 265.14 SC 267.5
    268.24 269.20 269.21 272.1
    CH 280.5 280.10 OC 286.1
    288.6 289.34 290.20 290.25
    292.2 292.16 293.39 294.27
    297.6 299.34 EE 305.22
    305.24 307.2 309.4 314.37
    321.36 332.8 332.11 332.15
    TP 339.27 340.34 342.25
    342.27 343.7 345.28 345.42
    BL 354.25 357.15 358.35
    363.7 363.36 364.5 364.29
    MN 366.37 367.38 369.17
    369.24 369.40 373.12 374.5
    375.33 376.3 377.35 378.7
    WP 380.1 380.16 384.32
    385.21 386.34 387.6 387.17
    387.33 389.34 389.41
    390.15 391.22 392.33 393.4
    393.12 YT 397.13 397.32
    398.11 398.28 399.7 400.5
    400.21 SD 416.29 418.3
    418.39 421.4 422.1 423.31
    423.35 424.23 424.37 425.8
    PP 429.18 432.16 433.35
    434.18 435.27 438.31 439.14
    440.12 440.15 HD 441.38
    442.7 444.15 444.21 445.41
    449.38 452.20 454.10
    454.19 455.28 FA 462.41
    468.13 469.33 470.28
    471.34 PR 477.41 484.8
    488.19 491.13 495.27
    499.4 499.5 499.19 509.19
    TB 516.31 521.26 524.5
    SU 538.5 542.19 543.22

HEAD (CONT.) WR 551.9 553.11
  555.10 556.8 557.33 559.6
  561.12 566.41 567.3 567.5
  567.30 SM 585.18 JD 612.25
  613.16 613.23 613.32 614.16
  614.40 617.16 617.18 618.17
  618.40 623.3 625.3 626.8
  627.7 628.6 629.9 629.13
  LA 630.18 632.17 632.21
  632.35 634.24 634.41 635.27
  638.40 642.11 642.13 643.32
  IL 651.33 653.23 GG 673.15
  675.13 678.17 678.19 690.15
  691.17 692.37 692.39 693.10
  694.7 694.8 696.42 NT 709.37
  711.6 713.1 713.23 718.26
  719.34 ML 728.39 OV 749.10
  LL 767.6 767.10 RR 779.20
  779.23 779.24 RH 791.18
  MD 805.1 811.28 813.5 813.8
  813.11 814.31 816.27 816.28
  816.32 816.34 817.3 819.42
  820.9 822.25 824.3 826.12
  BM 829.38 831.17 832.2 839.19
  841.9 841.37 842.15

HEAD-DRESS PO 114.28 WR 569.8

HEAD-DRESSES WR 559.21 559.25
  568.32 578.12

HEAD-FIRST CH 276.8

HEADGEAR PR 483.15

HEADLAND SG 225.13

HEADLIGHTS IL 653.2 654.38

HEADLONG OV 759.16

HEADS MO 22.6 TF 123.6
  DV 143.16 149.31 OC 297.41
  TP 335.22 336.10 BL 351.41
  WR 557.6 569.32 575.24 575.27
  SM 586.5 JD 616.4 LA 643.38
  GG 674.10 NT 707.6 ML 741.42
  742.31 742.35 742.36
  MD 809.38 820.9

HEADSTOCKS SS 197.31 OC 283.22

HEADSTONE HD 448.3

HEADSTRONG DV 163.36

HEAD-WATERS WR 579.16

HEADWAY JD 612.1

HEALING EE 319.31 319.33 319.36
  SU 536.2

HEALTH HT 39.8 EA 77.1
  EE 305.20 YT 396.42 HD 451.29
  TB 517.31 JD 624.37 NT 707.36
  ML 730.5 730.6 MD 806.9

HEALTHY MO 13.19 13.23 HT 41.15
  WM 56.29 66.4 TF 118.27
  DV 138.3 154.22 165.33
  SG 221.32 227.18 EE 312.6
  313.24 322.36 329.1 BL 357.16
  SD 412.30 414.11 PP 433.16
  PR 482.31 SU 534.13 IL 648.26

HEALTHY (CONT.) GG 678.3
  NT 708.40 710.2 MD 813.16

HEAP MO 1.24 TF 123.29
  DV 157.35 157.39 FG 192.40
  195.10 SG 225.38 EE 307.24
  333.14 HD 449.1 456.19 456.20
  PR 497.12 500.41 506.28
  OV 753.36

HEAPED MO 1.24 WM 55.10
  TF 121.42 122.7 SG 221.33
  BL 362.18 BO 600.19

HEAPING SU 538.33 ML 746.7

HEAPS MO 19.37 SB 213.40
  GF 241.32 PR 500.1

HEAR MO 4.23 12.19 OA 24.11
  32.26 32.26 EA 86.5 88.1
  PO 102.28 111.14 TF 122.36
  129.32 DV 142.11 148.6 159.9
  159.41 169.4 171.37 181.19
  FG 193.18 SS 204.18 209.6
  GF 239.7 WS 263.17 SC 270.39
  271.39 272.5 OC 285.31 287.20
  298.8 298.10 298.18 300.21
  EE 319.21 TP 342.2 344.20
  344.22 344.26 BL 352.24 353.4
  353.22 364.32 MN 375.10
  375.11 WP 380.20 384.25
  384.27 389.33 YT 404.36
  407.27 SD 421.39 PP 428.7
  435.1 HD 443.23 PR 489.27
  498.29 502.9 502.39 503.30
  WR 557.20 568.16 572.16
  572.22 574.2 JD 609.16
  LA 631.36 632.4 632.8 632.12
  632.13 632.28 632.31 633.13
  633.25 635.23 638.8 638.14
  638.37 639.23 639.26 640.5
  640.6 641.24 644.9 644.26
  644.31 644.34 646.31
  IL 650.30 652.3 659.11
  GG 672.24 673.7 674.39 674.42
  679.5 NT 705.5 705.10 705.15
  ML 731.8 740.32 740.42 745.38
  746.21 OV 760.1 LL 765.7 765.37
  766.19 768.39 775.20
  RR 782.21 782.24 783.10 786.8
  RH 791.6 791.19 800.29
  MD 815.32 816.9 823.26
  TH 849.18 851.8

HEARD MO 3.16 3.26 10.30 10.31
  21.15 22.19 OA 25.10 31.1
  32.23 35.7 37.29 SP 45.17
  48.16 WM 58.5 58.6 68.36
  69.17 EA 75.21 75.24 76.13
  80.2 85.4 PO 101.42 103.3
  108.8 109.3 109.21 111.8
  TF 119.14 121.11 127.34
  129.14 133.14 133.20
  DV 139.13 139.31 140.39
  146.27 148.15 149.13 152.3
  156.39 167.34 170.2 FG 190.40
  191.4 191.6 193.21 SS 201.2
  211.23 211.25 SG 227.23
  228.26 228.28 229.17 229.37
  231.36 GF 235.28 237.20
  237.31 WS 244.25 244.30
  245.12 246.16 259.8 SC 269.27
  273.10 CH 280.18 OC 285.15
  291.4 292.39 295.8 295.9

HEARD (CONT.) 296.4 296.38
  297.1 298.2 298.24
  EE 306.38 316.34 316.36
  331.3 331.10 331.11 331.13
  331.24 333.13 TP 341.16
  343.40 BL 353.15 355.23
  356.14 356.16 356.37
  356.38 357.19 357.29
  362.14 MN 378.36 WP 385.21
  387.10 YT 399.29 401.33
  SD 417.32 417.33 419.20
  419.21 422.38 424.10
  424.13 424.16 424.18
  424.25 PP 432.26 438.16
  HD 443.8 444.15 456.9
  456.27 FA 461.38 464.22
  PR 501.32 502.10 504.6
  TB 518.15 520.41 SU 536.26
  WR 552.13 552.20 559.19
  564.34 565.34 568.14
  570.3 JD 609.11 616.20
  617.11 LA 632.29 633.15
  633.20 633.35 639.8 642.6
  643.7 646.3 646.14
  IL 649.31 652.29 652.42
  658.14 GG 667.11 667.20
  669.33 NT 704.33 705.17
  706.11 713.13 713.37
  ML 742.26 OV 748.1 753.6
  754.13 755.3 756.42
  LL 767.34 770.11 770.29
  772.30 772.42 774.6 775.38
  RR 783.7 785.37 788.14
  RH 791.7 791.13 791.14
  791.18 791.23 802.10
  802.36 803.9 804.32
  MD 815.28 816.14 824.25
  824.42 BM 843.5

HEARING OA 33.2 WM 68.13
  EA 75.33 TF 124.4 131.21
  DV 146.4 149.22 SS 204.28
  SC 272.13 CH 281.16
  TP 338.15 BL 356.13
  WR 568.12 GG 698.7 ML 731.7
  OV 755.31 LL 768.37

HEARS FA 463.30 463.32
  LA 633.25

HEART MO 4.18 4.40 16.10
  20.13 OA 24.35 25.26 30.17
  30.20 36.19 HT 44.13 SP 49.31
  WM 54.17 54.33 60.17 60.22
  69.26 69.27 69.40 70.2
  EA 73.31 75.32 76.5 78.8
  78.37 81.3 86.35 86.37
  87.11 87.16 87.20 88.2
  89.11 89.31 89.37 90.8
  90.12 90.30 91.38
  PO 101.30 101.40 102.3
  102.15 103.1 103.40 105.6
  106.11 108.1 108.14 109.18
  110.6 110.36 112.19 112.20
  112.28 TF 120.21 120.28
  121.20 121.37 122.30
  129.32 129.39 133.14
  DV 147.8 148.32 149.37
  151.10 151.18 152.7 154.22
  155.14 155.34 163.31
  163.32 169.4 171.8 171.14
  171.20 171.28 174.13 175.7
  175.9 175.21 175.24 179.38
  179.41 181.13 181.21
  181.32 183.2 FG 189.35

HEART (CONT.) 191.30 192.26
  195.10 SS 203.35 SB 218.4
  SG 227.6 229.18 229.29 229.38
  229.40 230.27 230.32 231.30
  232.41 GF 239.11 239.33 240.2
  WS 249.40 250.17 253.18 257.4
  259.28 263.8 SC 269.11
  CH 274.13 280.25 281.18
  281.26 OC 290.20 292.42
  294.12 295.23 301.17 302.12
  EE 303.23 309.31 312.3 317.15
  317.20 317.28 318.5 318.10
  320.8 321.1 322.7 322.12
  322.13 322.15 322.16 322.18
  322.24 322.38 323.19 323.20
  323.38 324.36 328.10
  TP 334.37 335.33 BL 350.6
  353.14 354.40 358.1 361.20
  MN 368.16 370.19 371.6 371.41
  WP 381.1 YT 396.36 401.25
  SD 415.17 425.11 425.21
  PP 427.19 435.28 HD 454.3
  454.7 454.11 454.21 454.38
  454.42 455.15 FA 460.3 460.39
  466.17 PR 479.24 481.3 484.30
  485.25 487.40 490.10 490.22
  503.23 503.32 503.41 503.42
  510.39 TB 516.9 SU 531.3
  531.14 531.28 532.33 536.29
  544.40 WR 546.15 549.34
  563.18 571.4 581.24 BO 592.10
  596.19 597.31 597.40 603.9
  JD 608.13 612.32 IL 647.25
  659.39 GG 683.37 685.23 686.2
  691.18 694.2 694.3 695.36
  697.13 697.42 698.6 698.7
  ML 728.18 729.12 730.11
  740.27 OV 747.38 748.2 753.5
  753.18 753.28 753.31 753.36
  754.19 LL 762.26 766.33
  766.38 767.36 771.35 773.30
  774.36 778.28 778.33
  RR 782.15 RH 790.9 790.12
  800.37 802.18 802.38 803.1
  804.2 MD 816.11 BM 828.19
  839.19 842.42 TH 852.30

HEART-BEATING TP 343.39

HEART-BEATS OV 753.14

HEART-BREAKING BM 832.24

HEART-BROKEN HD 456.41

HEART-BROKENLY SD 419.32

HEART-CHAMBERS EA 93.5

HEART-FELT MD 806.27

HEART-FROZEN RH 803.30

HEARTH MO 6.22 OA 29.2 33.6
  EA 84.21 DV 159.1 159.18
  CH 276.5 OC 285.21 286.14
  288.19 EE 304.14 WP 390.20
  SD 418.34 JD 618.12 GG 691.3
  RR 786.16

HEARTH-RUG MO 4.41 19.10
  EA 73.14 DV 158.17 170.17
  SG 222.13 SC 268.36 PP 438.31
  439.10 440.12 HD 443.11
  451.10 455.8 JD 617.26

HEARTIEST OC 300.21

HEARTILY WM 56.3 WS 255.37
  BM 840.8

HEARTINESS BM 841.15

HEARTLESS PR 507.17 ML 732.12

HEARTS SP 47.39 48.38 TF 130.24
  131.14 DV 138.29 144.31
  FG 188.3 188.16 CH 279.35
  PP 433.6 433.8 MD 806.24

HEART'S MO 18.32 HD 456.38

HEART-SEARCHING LL 765.8

HEARTY OC 285.6 300.20 GG 700.4

HEAT EA 81.23 PO 95.4 95.13
  106.39 112.16 116.11
  TF 118.21 DV 169.32 171.10
  FG 189.18 SB 213.1 214.5
  216.16 219.28 OC 300.30
  PR 502.25 509.9 WR 552.5
  556.34 574.15 BO 594.9 602.40

HEATED OA 37.34 PR 509.17

HEATH LA 631.36

HEATHEN WR 549.27

HEATHER SS 206.35 FA 462.10
  ML 734.15 740.15

HEATHER'S FA 459.22 459.26
  460.37

HEATING PR 502.10 TH 851.5

HEAT-WAVES WR 574.18

HEAVE EA 83.34 DV 149.6 174.25
  SU 528.12 ML 724.14

HEAVED EA 82.22 83.18 TP 338.9
  SD 420.41 421.9 421.12 421.26
  421.33 HD 442.1 PR 506.29

HEAVE-HALF-A-BRICK-AT-HIM
  JD 610.17

HEAVEN MO 14.26 PO 95.20 116.6
  FG 188.19 EE 313.25 313.27
  314.9 MN 366.11 YT 396.19
  PR 490.23 499.23 TB 520.41
  520.42 SU 530.17 531.8 532.11
  532.31 532.36 534.14
  WR 546.23 558.8 569.21 572.17
  572.20 572.31 579.27
  BO 595.31 LA 641.36 IL 650.3
  651.24 GG 665.30 ML 730.14
  OV 755.25 RR 781.26 RH 797.2
  797.38 MD 820.30 BM 837.2

HEAVENS DV 174.13 GF 238.25
  EE 312.21 312.27 TP 337.33
  PR 498.15 WR 565.41 BO 592.31
  595.35 596.6 OV 755.22
  LL 766.27

HEAVEN'S GG 672.30

HEAVES MO 4.7

HEAVIER WS 252.39 ML 745.41

HEAVILY MO 8.1 15.14 19.15
  OA 31.25 37.21 SP 50.24
  WM 66.32 68.36 70.11
  EA 89.5 90.23 91.7
  PO 101.35 102.31 103.1
  103.9 112.19 112.20
  TF 129.32 DV 137.32 168.11
  175.7 178.39 SB 214.33
  SG 230.27 GF 234.15
  WS 257.24 263.23 264.23
  OC 283.8 EE 328.9 TP 343.31
  BL 354.23 WP 385.38
  SD 421.12 421.16 425.12
  PP 438.16 HD 450.8
  PR 497.41 WR 574.27
  SM 583.41 JD 617.5 618.28
  622.10 LA 637.42 GG 664.39
  677.15 677.37 690.37 695.3
  696.3 ML 743.11 MD 822.10
  BM 841.14

HEAVILY-BUILT GF 234.7

HEAVILY-SOUNDED MO 5.17

HEAVINESS PR 482.35 OV 748.18

HEAVING EA 83.14 PO 102.23
  104.28 DV 149.12 SB 214.40
  SD 421.31 425.15 FA 464.17
  GG 690.17

HEAVY MO 1.1 3.11 5.2
  OA 25.39 26.28 26.33 27.1
  34.29 35.1 35.29 36.20
  HT 44.13 WM 58.15 58.16
  65.36 66.1 66.17 69.38
  69.39 EA 73.19 73.25
  78.20 84.5 PO 97.1 99.25
  105.2 107.24 108.16 109.7
  110.14 110.37 112.29
  114.21 TF 118.12 119.40
  126.13 126.14 126.16
  DV 144.2 152.19 156.13
  158.40 160.16 160.19
  166.30 167.35 168.14
  171.20 173.11 175.35
  179.35 FG 187.17 SB 215.8
  SG 224.25 225.31 GF 237.11
  239.34 WS 257.6 257.23
  258.4 SC 268.8 CH 275.35
  280.18 OC 295.20 299.7
  302.4 302.6 302.12
  EE 309.10 309.11 322.37
  324.40 325.6 330.15 331.22
  BL 349.10 351.4 351.25
  354.24 WP 385.33 386.37
  387.13 389.15 390.8
  YT 395.16 SD 415.15 421.1
  PP 432.30 432.32 440.12
  HD 441.10 448.26 448.38
  451.6 FA 460.13 PR 482.25
  482.29 482.30 483.3 483.7
  483.8 486.18 487.31 488.14
  494.30 497.3 501.11 503.22
  505.36 510.5 TB 513.17
  524.40 SU 528.8 531.11
  WR 558.27 561.11 564.34
  567.36 568.11 568.38 569.2
  569.28 573.10 573.37
  573.38 574.11 574.13

HEAVY (CONT.) 574.15 BO 600.5
600.24 JD 610.4 610.11 620.12
626.14 LA 638.11 GG 670.12
670.17 670.31 683.13 685.24
685.28 690.17 696.39
NT 703.34 709.37 ML 730.36
739.22 OV 747.7 749.24 753.32
LL 761.13 773.2 RR 784.31
784.39 785.2 RH 800.38 800.42
802.42 MD 818.36 819.40
BM 836.23 841.13

HEAVY-FOOTED MD 820.20

HEAVY-FOOTEDNESS ML 742.10

HEAVY-HEARTED DV 148.12

HEAVY-SHOD JD 616.29

HEAVY-SITTING PR 487.24

HECATE JD 610.24

HECTIC SB 212.20 PR 500.32

HE'D MO 19.40 SB 213.15 213.19
213.33 215.26 215.37
SG 231.37 232.18 GF 238.38
CH 277.21 OC 287.13 289.10
297.31 300.18 BL 350.25
WP 382.2 384.22 385.18
TB 512.4 IL 657.19 GG 675.30
675.34 RH 793.19 794.21

HEDGE MO 2.14 22.17 WM 70.5
TF 127.35 127.38 DV 160.35
SS 204.2 210.30 SB 214.14
OC 283.7 283.11 YT 394.3
394.5 394.6 394.7 TB 520.41
521.5 521.14 521.18

HEDGE-BOTTOM SB 212.2 214.15

HEDGEROW SS 202.1

HEDGES DV 167.14 EE 304.2
MN 371.38 PP 430.30 436.7
HD 442.11 450.5 JD 616.7
624.24 LL 766.15

HEED SG 226.42 TP 345.30
MN 377.24* WP 387.7 LA 646.4
RH 792.40

HEEDED OA 32.16 FG 194.2
BO 599.22

HEEDING SS 198.17 HD 447.33
450.15

HEEL PO 106.2 MN 377.20 377.34
WP 390.12

HEELED WM 60.32 WP 379.12

HEELS MO 18.19 SP 47.10
DV 166.10 SS 205.21 SC 269.7
PP 437.26 TB 524.18 SU 531.2
WR 569.7 JD 617.16 617.25
NT 707.39 RR 785.28

HEERD OC 285.34

HEFTY BO 594.31 594.40

HEIDELBERG BO 600.29

HEIGHT HT 41.10 WM 55.29 58.11
EA 72.23 72.32 PO 97.1
TF 131.32 SS 198.11 SG 222.27
EE 329.34 SD 411.18 PP 427.19
HD 444.22 PR 490.3 497.25
498.10 JD 617.1

HEIGHTENED MO 14.6 PR 484.21
WR 572.11 574.1

HEIGHTS TF 131.36 PR 486.10
487.28 490.23 490.31 500.6
500.38 WR 556.20

HEIN MD 825.31

HEIR PR 482.23 GG 699.26

HELD MO 12.23 22.1 OA 36.28
HT 39.2 42.30 WM 63.10 64.42
68.35 70.24 EA 72.10 72.12
73.13 84.19 90.42 92.30 93.4
93.24 PO 97.30 97.36 99.8
100.4 103.10 103.17 111.10
112.34 TF 117.28 118.10
119.22 127.23 130.17
DV 148.38 149.39 151.18 161.9
174.16 180.31 180.34 181.1
181.7 181.8 181.35 181.41
182.26 183.20 FG 192.19 196.4
196.15 SS 209.17 SG 224.27
229.28 WS 252.34 254.32
259.11 259.22 259.28 264.2
CH 276.20 282.21 OC 283.7
284.38 290.4 296.21 300.9
EE 307.21 313.11 TP 338.24
BL 358.16 358.31 358.38 365.9
MN 368.26 368.39 WP 386.33
386.34 YT 397.26 407.2 409.39
SD 412.33 PP 435.39 HD 442.7
442.10 FA 458.32 463.28
PR 480.12 489.29 489.35
TB 514.13 SU 534.23 535.27
540.25 WR 581.8 SM 583.15
BO 602.14 JD 605.6 616.34
629.3 LA 632.16 634.15
GG 681.20 691.8 NT 703.40
713.5 OV 749.23 750.20 751.29
752.12 752.30 752.32 755.7
755.22 LL 773.34 777.14
RR 784.41 MD 805.2 812.6
TH 846.37 850.14

HELIOTROPE WS 245.29 246.35

HELL SS 210.13 WS 258.39
PP 427.32 433.3 HD 445.29
PR 508.9 NT 704.14 RR 782.28

HELLISH HD 449.16

HELLO MO 12.16 SS 201.22
TP 335.30 336.18 BL 353.34
356.20 WP 382.17 PP 434.12
438.22 HD 444.24 PR 511.38
SU 539.30 539.36 540.8 540.9
540.23 540.31 JD 624.33
IL 653.6

HELLOA GF 236.38

HE'LL MO 17.20 DV 141.36 142.2
163.2 163.27 170.5 171.18

HE'LL (CONT.) SB 215.40
GF 238.5 238.41 OC 287.34
289.16 289.17 290.13
292.32 EE 318.11 TP 340.3
BL 362.2 MN 377.6 WP 381.41
YT 398.42 408.1 PP 436.36
PR 491.26 491.40 LA 642.5
GG 665.3 665.15 665.19
RH 795.29 BM 839.27

HELMET PO 96.2 105.31 105.39
111.2 LA 637.16

HELMETS PO 95.15 105.29

HELP OA 36.22 37.20 38.9
HT 41.32 WM 57.5 EA 77.2
87.34 TF 131.31 131.32
DV 146.22 146.26 150.2
172.6 176.42 183.31
SS 208.6 WS 246.8 258.5
260.21 261.9 CH 275.40
277.6 278.13 OC 299.8
301.20 EE 307.18 314.3
318.1 326.24 BL 348.28
MN 378.27 WP 384.20 YT 401.11
SD 418.19 418.20 PR 485.22
498.20 503.41 TB 514.34
516.14 SU 541.30 WR 556.27
580.5 BO 587.33 590.16
LA 634.13 IL 647.24 648.23
GG 664.25 668.5 668.8
680.20 688.20 690.40
691.10 ML 725.37 730.14
733.11 LL 775.7 RR 781.10
MD 805.25 806.20 821.3
TH 846.10

HELPED HT 43.31 EA 86.26
DV 162.2 SG 223.20
GF 239.13 BL 359.1
MN 366.31 WP 384.22
PP 430.8 TB 516.19
GG 696.15 LL 763.36
MD 806.19 809.37

HELPING OA 33.39 38.6
DV 146.31 YT 401.12
SD 421.16 PR 484.18 484.24
IL 648.40 ML 734.24

HELPLESS OA 30.6 30.7
SP 51.42 PO 104.31
TF 126.6 130.7 132.8
134.17 134.18 DV 181.9
184.7 SG 226.28 OC 301.19
BL 356.41 MN 373.27
HD 442.29 PR 489.31 509.22
SU 541.35 BO 587.28
JD 629.7 GG 683.11
LL 767.33 773.2 MD 805.22
821.35 821.39

HELPLESSLY DV 174.24 180.33
WS 254.21 256.3 TP 344.4
BL 359.33 WP 386.41
HD 451.34 PR 503.17
SM 584.3 IL 657.26
GG 666.38 ML 746.12

HELPLESSNESS OA 30.16 EA 80.7
WS 256.15 SD 425.13
HD 441.36 PR 510.24
IL 655.9 GG 687.24
NT 707.25

HELPS TB 523.18 GG 680.29
  680.31 LL 761.4

HEM SG 231.10 231.13

HEMMING WR 553.13

HEN SS 206.21

HENCE EE 311.41 BL 359.36
  BO 599.36 GG 662.31

HENCEFORTH DV 153.23 MD 817.30

HENCEFORWARD OA 37.10 PO 97.37
  DV 153.21

HENRIETTA IL 647.1 647.14
  647.23 647.34 647.35 648.10
  653.4 653.21 653.31 653.33
  653.34 654.1 654.6 654.8
  654.10 654.15 654.20 654.28
  654.33 655.5 655.6 655.9
  655.12 655.29 655.32 655.34
  655.39 656.1 656.3 656.20
  656.24 656.27 657.2 657.6
  657.12 657.26 657.32 657.35
  657.37 658.1 658.3 658.15
  658.24 658.33 658.36 658.40
  658.41 659.12 659.41 660.1

HENRIETTA, MARY (SEE MARY
  HENRIETTA)

HENRIETTA'S IL 647.32 653.6
  653.10 656.35 657.16

HENRY LL 766.40 768.17 768.18
  768.27 769.21 769.26 769.29
  769.36 774.31 775.2 775.6
  775.12 778.22 MD 805.17
  805.21 805.24 805.31 806.1
  806.4 806.11 806.17 806.29
  806.37 807.1 807.10 810.16
  812.27

HENRY (SEE COUSIN, FRED)

HENRY LUBBOCK MD 805.16 807.22

HENS TB 517.26 IL 648.33

HERB WR 572.10

HERBAGE PR 492.21 SU 539.21

HERBS WR 561.19 565.22

HERCULES'S OV 757.21

HERD SP 49.22 PR 496.40

HERDING DV 170.31

HERE'S SP 52.22 WM 56.9
  SB 214.7 GF 238.4 240.22
  HD 444.7 JD 628.17 IL 654.15

HERMES ML 726.30

HERMIT EE 308.28

HERO PR 473.16 TB 521.34
  JD 628.7 BM 836.34

HEROES WP 384.23 NT 708.37

HEROINE YT 399.12 TB 521.35
  BM 835.23

HEROINES NT 708.37

HEROISM DV 155.19

HERR BARON TF 124.21 133.37

HERR HAUPTMANN PO 99.1

HERS OA 24.39 WM 64.40 69.9
  EA 80.13 91.11 TF 131.24
  DV 181.26 182.35 SS 208.3
  SG 228.1 WS 248.14 260.29
  OC 301.12 EE 305.7 MN 365.8
  PP 429.16 PR 479.9 TB 515.34
  517.37 522.23 524.9 SU 528.27
  BO 589.4 IL 649.13 OV 747.25
  750.20 LL 762.2 763.1
  RR 780.34 783.2

HESITATE DV 160.23 BL 357.28

HESITATED MO 3.19 EA 80.1
  PO 101.20 110.27 TF 123.19
  DV 151.3 168.7 SS 199.32
  GF 235.30 WS 256.6 OC 284.39
  TP 342.42 SD 423.16 PP 427.12
  428.14 HD 452.10 FA 469.41
  470.12 TB 524.20 SU 539.28
  541.9 541.15 WR 555.5
  SM 586.18 BO 596.17 JD 608.28
  GG 671.19 675.23 LL 771.33

HESITATING MO 7.15 HT 44.13
  WM 58.9 EA 73.11 79.2 90.37
  SG 228.15 SC 269.26 CH 278.13
  280.16

HESITATINGLY OA 28.34

HESITATION PO 101.10 DV 175.5
  GF 236.5 SD 412.21 PR 484.35
  MD 822.1 BM 838.20

HESPERIDES ML 725.7

HESSE (SEE FRAULEIN, IDA)

HESTER IL 647.6 647.8 647.11
  647.18 647.20 647.23 647.30
  647.33 648.1 648.3 648.5
  648.9 648.11 648.14 648.15
  648.24 648.29 648.32 649.3
  649.6 649.7 649.10 649.27
  649.36 649.42 651.4 651.10
  651.37 651.38 651.39 653.6
  653.8 653.11 653.19 653.25
  653.28 653.29 653.31 653.33
  653.34 653.35 653.38 653.40
  654.7 654.9 654.15 654.23
  654.25 654.36 654.40 655.6
  655.8 655.19 655.21 655.28
  655.29 655.34 655.42 656.8
  656.18 656.20 656.26 656.30
  656.31 656.36 657.13 657.17
  657.23 657.31 657.42 658.12
  658.17 658.23 658.32 658.35
  658.36 658.39 659.6 659.15
  659.16 659.20 659.41 659.42
  660.3 660.4 MD 804.33

HESTER'S IL 656.32 656.40

HEVER FA 464.18

HEWED ML 725.39

HEY SB 215.41 TP 339.34

HID MO 5.37 10.23 10.42
  OA 36.13 WM 58.8 EA 73.3
  74.13 DV 137.37 181.8
  FG 193.2 CH 279.37 280.16
  OC 290.21 FA 471.21 471.22
  PR 505.3 SU 541.16
  ML 742.15 RH 799.28
  MD 812.31 813.3 822.36

HIDDEN MO 2.7 DV 153.28
  SS 197.11 204.4 SG 224.8
  OC 286.18 287.24 300.15
  TP 337.41 PR 510.33
  SU 529.12 530.3 532.26
  534.23 544.8 WR 554.29
  LA 630.5 GG 662.30
  ML 725.2 737.20 741.14
  LL 765.24 MD 813.7

HIDE PO 110.40 TF 124.30
  125.1 DV 136.17 166.4
  SB 219.33 GF 239.35 239.37
  IL 647.5 RR 780.40 781.24
  RH 792.24 MD 808.26

HIDEOUS PO 106.31 110.33
  WS 245.24 EE 328.25 328.40
  329.8 YT 405.34 HD 450.18
  FA 460.4 PR 477.35
  SU 530.13 ML 740.40
  LL 777.35 MD 819.29
  TH 850.34 851.10

HIDEOUSLY EA 81.24

HIDING MO 3.30 3.38 WM 68.32
  CH 278.7 PP 440.13
  PR 486.17 RR 781.24 784.34

HIGH MO 18.8 OA 24.12 25.4
  25.5 26.4 SP 47.7 WM 56.14
  56.40 58.40 EA 72.23
  PO 95.12 105.28 106.38
  TF 118.33 119.12 120.32
  121.36 127.10 DV 136.7
  136.15 137.26 138.22
  155.23 160.26 174.29
  SS 202.40 SB 214.14
  SG 224.14 GF 234.21 238.31
  WS 254.13 262.8 CH 278.16
  278.22 OC 285.5 286.30
  EE 303.17 330.7 330.24
  TP 334.5 335.35 BL 351.10
  354.25 358.4 359.37 362.24
  MN 371.16 373.11 WP 385.39
  386.13 YT 394.14 400.21
  PP 429.13 430.30 HD 442.24
  443.20 FA 463.41 PR 487.26
  488.32 490.23 490.25
  490.29 493.17 493.24
  TB 524.18 SU 534.34 538.3
  538.22 WR 550.4 552.35
  561.9 568.37 570.12 572.5
  576.21 578.35 579.27
  BO 587.5 595.22 595.29
  LA 646.23 GG 668.31 670.33

HIGH (CONT.) NT 712.3 ML 723.27
  730.21 743.7 745.4 745.29
  746.5 OV 750.35 LL 763.19
  763.22 763.29 RH 795.29
  804.24

HIGH-BRED YT 403.5 403.6
  LL 763.26

HIGH-BROW JD 606.13

HIGH-CLASS JD 606.13

HIGHER MO 18.34 PO 107.39
  TF 119.25 120.24 DV 149.30
  153.6 153.14 153.18 FG 194.18
  194.19 EE 306.9 312.1
  HD 450.35 FA 462.37 WR 552.4
  553.14 572.15 GG 676.6 680.38
  ML 723.30 727.23 LL 767.11
  BM 836.14

HIGHEST DV 183.23 BO 597.9
  597.15 BM 830.14

HIGH-HEELED LA 636.31

HIGHLAND BO 588.29

HIGHLANDER BO 589.23

HIGHLY OA 30.27 SC 267.17
  BM 834.25

HIGHLY-BRED WR 569.38

HIGHLY-COLOURED HT 39.34

HIGH-MINDED DV 153.25

HIGH-PITCHED EE 304.38 ML 729.42

HIGH-RIDGED EA 72.19

HIGHROAD EE 330.24

HIGH-ROAD SP 48.7 SS 210.1
  PP 436.25 HD 441.23 442.2

HIGH SCHOOL YT 396.11

HIGH-UP WM 60.25

HIGH-WAISTED OA 26.17

HIGHWAY MO 22.14 DV 139.8
  160.35 OC 291.9

HILDA SS 202.11 206.22 206.26
  206.38 209.20 210.28 210.41
  211.16 CH 275.38 278.18
  278.20 278.26 278.35

HILDA MILLERSHIP SS 198.39
  199.10

HILDA ROWBOTHAM CH 274.12 274.21

HILL MO 1.35 16.15 WM 60.10
  60.14 60.31 PO 106.12 107.16
  TF 117.7 DV 160.24 182.20
  182.23 FG 192.40 SS 199.35
  SC 267.19 OC 286.31 TP 334.3
  WP 390.35 392.33 393.15
  YT 394.13 PP 436.8 HD 448.40

HILL (CONT.) FA 459.33 460.4
  460.20 JD 610.13 LA 630.10
  637.27 638.42 ML 746.27
  OV 750.7 750.23 750.28 750.33
  752.9

HILLOCK EE 330.1

HILLS MO 2.9 DV 160.28 167.13
  FG 187.4 SS 202.3 202.19
  SB 214.4 WP 390.40 PR 502.42
  WR 546.26 548.12 548.29
  548.34 548.35 548.37 550.26
  552.4 BO 600.18 600.20
  GG 668.33 668.34 669.16
  ML 722.34 746.7 746.8
  OV 758.25

HILLSIDE MO 19.31

HILL-SIDE PO 106.21 106.38
  107.30 SB 212.36

HILL-TOP SS 197.26 TP 334.17

HILLY SD 411.11

HIM'S SD 419.20

HIND EE 306.42

HINDQUARTERS BL 353.12

HINT SB 218.29 TB 525.34
  GG 670.23 RR 780.37 MD 813.28

HINTED PR 482.7

HINTERLANDS BM 827.17

HINTING ML 731.3

HINTS TB 525.42 526.14

HIPS FG 189.31 OC 283.13
  SD 411.17 411.19 422.3
  PP 437.23 PR 495.1 SU 540.15
  GG 670.12 670.17 670.31
  677.17 697.7 BM 829.34 829.38

HIRED SP 45.7 HD 448.12

HISS DV 149.13 WS 264.28
  EE 306.37 SU 536.33

HISSED FG 195.3 EE 323.40
  BO 599.24

HISSING TF 124.13 GF 235.18
  OC 285.28 EE 306.37 PR 502.11
  JD 610.29 618.24

HISTORY BO 591.2 591.3 591.5
  GG 666.19 NT 708.9 708.24
  708.36 709.15 716.28

HISTRIONIC TB 514.33 517.22

HISTRIONICALLY SD 418.12

HIT TF 121.27 WS 265.21
  EE 332.11 332.15 TP 335.37
  LA 638.1 ML 741.9 LL 778.34
  MD 816.28

HITCH TF 120.10

HITCHED SB 217.27

HITCHING BM 829.33

HITHER MO 2.39 SB 214.18
  EE 323.3 LL 766.16

HITHERTO DV 155.16

HITTING NT 707.19 MD 817.6
  BM 828.18

HM HT 43.4 SD 418.8
  PP 431.25

H'M WM 56.5 56.6 PR 511.18
  512.5

HM-HM OA 32.1 32.5 32.14

HO MN 372.34 SD 413.31

HOARDING WS 261.14 261.15

HOARSE OA 25.7 PO 114.1
  OC 290.5 PR 481.11
  ML 734.8 740.39 745.33
  BM 836.27 841.26 841.36
  841.41

HOARSELY PO 111.21 YT 410.3
  ML 738.28 OV 755.32

HOARSENESS EE 331.13 SD 416.8
  BM 828.13

HOB OC 286.36

HOBBLED DV 139.4 WR 557.20

HOBBY FG 187.34

HOBNOB GG 661.21

HOES ML 727.4

HOG WS 258.41 PR 496.9

HOG-BACKED PR 496.39

HOGGER SG 232.30

HOG-PROOF IL 648.21

HOGS WR 548.1 GG 700.1

HOLD MO 22.11 OA 25.38 HT 43.20
  SP 45.33 WM 67.23 70.6
  EA 75.21 83.2 PO 99.6
  100.13 104.31 112.36
  TF 120.11 120.19 DV 138.10
  148.23 154.4 157.12 165.30
  181.29 184.30 SG 225.35
  229.35 GF 243.2 243.5
  WS 257.1 258.28 259.29
  SC 271.3 272.1 CH 276.20
  EE 307.20 307.31 313.7
  313.8 TP 335.38 343.14
  WP 384.13 PP 439.17 439.36
  HD 447.18 448.27 452.12
  PR 487.39 509.5 SM 581.29
  585.30 BO 604.18 604.26
  604.27 OV 750.12 MD 807.10

HOLD (CONT.) 814.39 BM 839.12

HOLDING OA 26.31 34.38 36.37
  SP 50.19 WM 60.4 EA 93.7
  PO 95.31 99.21 106.32
  TF 123.2 125.25 127.30
  DV 149.11 159.3 159.18 176.36
  FG 194.40 GF 237.11 243.6
  WS 251.16 253.13 264.9 266.6
  OC 297.4 EE 317.24 329.38
  TP 338.8 338.22 338.36 338.36
  339.22 341.19 BL 351.40
  353.11 362.15 362.16 364.17
  YT 402.15 SD 415.31 PP 433.36
  HD 457.2 PR 499.14 505.28
  507.37 508.2 WR 556.28 563.32
  569.10 573.31 580.34 580.36
  BO 587.24 604.18 JD 611.23
  611.34 628.42 LA 631.20
  GG 694.37 ML 723.34 741.34
  BM 837.27 838.38

HOLDS FG 187.3 NT 720.35
  ML 722.20

HOLE MO 4.22 DV 145.28 160.37
  FG 188.25 WS 253.39 OC 289.20
  HD 449.16 PR 497.12 500.7
  500.10 502.24 ML 728.11
  728.13 732.12 732.27 732.28
  LL 769.2 769.3 769.6 769.8
  770.28 MD 807.42 BM 840.16
  TH 851.25 852.4

HOLES WR 574.19 JD 621.4
  ML 732.29

HOLIDAY HT 42.34 SP 52.31
  TB 514.5

HOLIDAYS SU 541.40 RR 780.3

HOLIES TH 848.21

HOLING DV 166.20

HOLLAND WR 546.5

HOLLOW WM 54.13 EA 74.24
  SG 224.10 EE 303.37 TP 334.8
  WP 385.34 385.41 386.3
  PP 434.10 HD 449.20 449.28
  PR 485.10 498.26 499.8
  WR 552.15 563.16 578.9 579.24
  579.27 579.36 580.7 580.31
  581.6 BO 600.31 603.5
  IL 648.9 657.6 GG 664.13
  664.22 668.36 669.25 669.26
  686.3 ML 736.21 745.40

HOLLOW-EYED ML 732.8

HOLLOWLY FG 189.41 SS 211.20

HOLLOWNESS MD 808.42

HOLLOWS HD 454.15 GG 695.36
  ML 723.35

HOLLOW STONE GF 234.23

HOLLY MO 6.17 7.2 SS 197.10
  EE 305.40 331.15 HD 441.22
  456.16 LA 634.25 634.39
  635.13 637.35 642.22 642.34

HOLY TF 125.35 WP 381.9
  FA 467.6 467.11 471.10
  SM 586.15 OV 752.35 MD 820.30
  820.35 BM 841.40 TH 848.20

HOLY-HOLY-HOLY BM 841.40

HOLY WOUNDS FG 188.25

HOMAGE TF 130.28 BL 359.25
  BO 588.40 589.4 592.20

HOME MO 3.36 5.18 OA 31.1
  HT 39.13 41.8 42.16 42.24
  SP 50.35 50.39 51.9 51.13
  53.2 53.6 WM 55.11 EA 71.2
  78.24 81.7 84.3 88.4 89.14
  PO 112.21 TF 133.10 DV 138.4
  141.25 142.1 142.41 144.14
  155.9 156.31 160.12 160.34
  164.33 165.25 167.16 167.26
  172.19 175.34 182.37 182.38
  185.11 FG 188.4 SS 202.6
  211.24 SB 215.14 SG 222.38
  GF 238.5 238.6 238.9 238.11
  239.6 240.27 242.26 WS 244.28
  250.15 259.3 259.4 259.7
  261.1 262.42 SC 267.8 268.3
  268.10 272.16 CH 274.3 275.30
  OC 283.30 284.42 286.8 286.24
  286.33 287.2 287.35 288.8
  289.10 291.17 292.32 294.21
  294.42 296.14 EE 305.23
  305.27 305.32 305.33 308.16
  313.14 313.18 318.5 321.11
  321.25 321.29 322.3 323.11
  323.13 324.8 325.20 325.24
  325.35 331.34 TP 340.20
  340.30 341.9 341.13 341.20
  341.24 342.3 BL 347.9
  MN 371.8 371.36 372.29 373.30
  WP 381.36 381.37 381.38 382.4
  382.11 382.33 383.36
  YT 395.28 395.33 395.42
  396.23 396.38 400.30 408.27
  409.42 SD 419.35 PP 432.12
  438.22 HD 446.37 FA 460.3
  462.24 462.42 463.42 464.26
  470.15 PR 492.26 492.31
  492.35 492.37 TB 515.8 516.20
  SU 531.9 WR 551.12 553.7
  557.13 581.27 SM 582.31
  BO 593.6 603.21 603.41
  JD 621.3 621.29 621.35 621.40
  622.6 622.15 627.38 628.20
  LA 640.14 644.25 646.9
  IL 648.15 GG 663.10 666.17
  678.32 678.40 680.42 695.14
  695.19 697.17 700.9 NT 707.11
  ML 722.23 723.26 725.29
  729.33 737.15 738.32 739.26
  744.34 OV 754.16 758.26
  LL 761.22 761.34 764.24
  776.20 RR 779.5 780.21 780.32
  781.12 783.11 783.17 786.33
  787.18 787.20 RH 797.22
  802.30 MD 810.34 811.9 811.13
  811.30 812.33 814.35 816.41
  826.5 BM 827.25 827.28 828.21
  829.8 829.10 829.15 830.18
  830.25 831.13 834.16 835.6
  838.41 838.42 839.12 839.24
  839.28 841.19 TH 847.36 848.5
  848.9 852.2 852.7

HOME-BREWED MO 14.38

HOME-COMING OC 289.25
  FA 458.4

HOMELESS GG 696.8 BM 828.8
  TH 851.36

HOME-LIKE ML 722.30

HOMELINESS SD 411.13
  ML 742.10

HOMELY ML 742.7 LL 764.24

HOMES PP 437.3 HD 449.12
  PR 479.13

HOMESPUN OV 748.4

HOMEWARD TB 515.28

HON. GG 661.8

HONEST MO 20.31 20.32
  DV 174.5 BO 592.27
  IL 659.35 RR 781.28

HONESTLY EA 93.33 TB 526.14

HONEST-TO-GOD BM 827.34

HONESTY OV 758.40 759.15

HONEY PO 106.29 WR 565.3
  565.23 OV 754.31 754.32

HONEYMOON BM 829.11

HONEYMOON-AND-GOLF ML 733.3
  733.5

HONEYMOON-GOLFERS ML 733.28

HONEYSUCKLE MO 3.14 SS 207.5
  EE 329.24 ML 731.19
  OV 747.19 747.35 748.19
  748.25 748.32 750.31
  LL 770.41

HONOUR MO 7.3 DV 143.33
  146.37 147.11 EE 314.26
  326.12 HD 453.16 GG 670.42
  674.15 674.18 674.21
  RH 794.34 795.8 795.22
  796.20 796.22 796.24
  MD 823.15 823.20

HONOURABLE EE 325.12

HONOURABLY EE 325.18 OV 758.9

HONOUR AND ARMS MO 16.3

HONOURED DV 146.29 GG 674.19
  674.24

HONOURING GG 692.32

HOOD SS 206.40 WR 576.21
  LL 770.25

HOOF WR 561.27

HOOFS HD 442.2 PR 489.27

HOOFS (CONT.) ML 741.8

HOOK WS 245.41

HOOKAH MD 823.5 823.7

HOOKED FA 468.29 LA 631.12
  631.35 MD 807.19

HOOTED LL 772.41

HOOTER IL 653.1

HOP GG 674.8

HOPE OA 28.24 37.7 HT 43.41
  EA 94.2 94.5 TF 120.8 122.30
  DV 141.10 163.14 164.32
  183.29 184.17 185.23
  SG 222.18 223.7 GF 237.28
  237.32 239.3 241.36 SC 273.10
  OC 294.16 295.2 295.3
  EE 320.24 BL 359.34 362.35
  PP 435.25 HD 444.39 445.2
  PR 477.2 482.37 496.5 507.19
  TB 514.18 SU 528.16 WR 573.3
  573.5 JD 609.20 621.30 627.6
  IL 647.30 655.16 GG 669.4
  681.25 697.20 ML 730.41
  732.26 RR 786.4 RH 792.31
  799.5 MD 819.16 825.18 826.10
  TH 851.2

HOPED TP 345.20 JD 614.26
  IL 654.7 GG 672.2 NT 716.13
  ML 730.10 LL 778.9 MD 816.35

HOPEFUL MD 813.18

HOPELESS MO 7.30 DV 169.5
  OC 297.41 301.36 HD 442.12
  WR 546.32 560.3 572.3

HOPELESSLY HD 447.12 FA 464.13
  JD 629.12

HOPELESSNESS TP 345.14 PR 483.9
  510.24 BO 598.42 OV 751.39

HOPENED FA 464.14

HOPES MO 4.30 WP 384.18
  LA 636.9 MD 813.16 TH 852.10

HOPING YT 399.2 399.3 TB 516.28
  SU 542.12 LA 636.9 RH 793.16

HOPPED WP 379.13 SD 422.30
  PR 498.36

HOPPING SD 421.13 WR 557.20

HOPS TP 336.3

HORIZON EE 312.27 PR 493.31
  497.38 GG 698.34 ML 740.3
  740.27

HORIZON-BLUE BO 593.40

HORIZONS ML 745.25

HORIZONTAL OA 27.11 GG 667.33

HORIZONTALLY SU 537.17 TH 848.3

HORIZONTALLY (CONT.) 848.7

HORN IL 656.27 NT 713.24

HORNBEAM ML 724.42

HORNY HT 44.12 JD 618.13

HORRIBLE EA 80.10 82.19
  PO 103.14 111.1 113.20
  DV 144.32 FG 190.14 EE 323.21
  331.21 BL 363.21 PP 437.39
  HD 453.17 453.18 453.34
  456.39 456.42 457.6 FA 459.37
  PR 479.23 509.25 JD 610.25
  615.39 LA 646.20 GG 692.28
  LL 768.36 777.28

HORRIBLY EA 90.16 SG 230.37
  EE 324.34 324.35 SD 421.2
  HD 450.27 SU 529.22 GG 689.1
  MD 805.21

HORRID OA 36.7 EA 73.16
  HD 454.24 BO 593.29 IL 647.24
  ML 722.18 MD 817.1 TH 850.25

HORRIFIED WS 264.21 HD 453.29
  IL 658.32 BM 837.37

HORRIFYING PO 110.16 TP 342.35

HORROR OA 36.16 PO 110.35
  112.34 113.16 115.27 116.13
  TF 120.22 120.29 121.26 124.6
  DV 154.20 SG 226.33 227.11
  227.26 228.1 SC 270.28
  OC 297.18 298.1 301.18 302.7
  EE 331.33 BL 363.23 PP 434.15
  434.32 434.36 436.18 440.1
  HD 450.38 453.37 457.9
  PR 508.18 WR 568.4 BO 593.25
  593.32 597.21 GG 693.7
  ML 742.17 742.33 743.3
  OV 757.26 LL 767.25 768.12
  RH 789.15 TH 850.35

HORRORS PP 428.34

HORSE SP 49.26 51.2 51.4 51.7
  PO 96.4 104.22 106.3 107.21
  107.35 107.40 108.33 111.25
  112.6 112.7 FG 189.5 191.3
  191.34 EE 333.11 TP 338.5 338.6
  BL 353.5 MN 371.20 HD 442.9
  442.35 446.29 PR 485.24
  489.17 489.24 490.14 490.27
  491.8 491.22 492.20 493.7
  493.10 493.17 494.15 495.33
  497.16 497.22 498.32 498.36
  498.38 498.40 499.38 510.28
  510.31 511.25 512.14 512.23
  WR 550.25 550.35 551.7 551.21
  552.1 552.6 552.18 552.25
  553.3 553.8 553.18 555.12
  555.13 555.24 555.27 555.29
  555.34 555.39 555.42 556.13
  557.19 558.10 561.27 572.38
  575.2 IL 648.22 651.8
  GG 696.30 NT 709.36 RH 791.17
  793.4 793.13 793.14 793.18
  793.35 794.18 794.27 794.40
  795.38 797.42 798.1 801.37
  802.1 802.7 803.14 803.20
  804.23 804.27

HORSEBACK PO 95.35 96.5
  105.12 105.30 107.26
  TF 121.40 PR 478.39
  485.15 489.23 494.33
  494.34 WR 550.17 550.22

HORSE-CHESTNUT TF 122.8
  DV 182.30 EE 330.13
  PP 432.18 TB 521.21

HORSE-HAIR MO 6.37

HORSEMAN PO 105.35

HORSEMAN'S PO 107.17

HORSEMEN PO 96.11 EE 330.39
  PR 510.8

HORSEPOOL SC 267.11

HORSEPOOL (SEE MR. HORSEPOOL;
  MRS. HORSEPOOL)

HORSE-RACES RH 794.7

HORSE-RACING RH 801.25

HORSES SP 49.14 49.16 49.22
  PO 96.29 FG 190.26 190.32
  EE 331.14 TP 338.3
  BL 347.22 353.2 353.9
  353.13 353.19 353.23
  353.25 353.35 MN 366.37
  367.5 367.20 371.2
  YT 394.13 PP 432.22
  HD 441.23 441.25 441.36
  442.12 442.18 442.32
  446.29 446.30 PR 483.30
  488.32 489.33 489.40
  489.42 490.4 490.18 490.32
  494.42 495.39 496.20
  496.27 496.29 498.13
  498.16 498.22 499.27
  500.18 500.40 503.1 503.5
  503.9 507.12 510.25
  IL 651.18 GG 687.23
  LL 764.42 MD 813.22 813.23
  BM 834.39

HORSE'S PR 491.33 WR 555.10
  555.41 556.8 556.28
  RH 793.42

HORSES' HD 441.20

HORSE-SERFS FG 189.12

HORSE-SHOE OA 32.24

HORSE-SOLDIER WP 391.23

HORSE-TROUGH DV 166.16

HORSEWOMAN PR 485.8

HORSEY HD 443.17 443.29

HOSE GF 234.20

HOSIERY GF 234.21

HOSPITABLE GG 669.30

HOSPITAL PO 116.14 TF 128.27

HOSPITAL (CONT.) SC 269.20
   269.22 OC 294.32 TH 846.10

HOSPITALITY DV 147.19

HOST WM 56.21 EA 85.16
   SG 225.21 WS 253.13 ML 742.2
   OV 748.16

HOSTESS WM 58.31 EA 85.38
   GG 675.3 675.5 OV 748.8
   748.16 755.31 756.26 756.36
   756.41 RR 780.3

HOSTESSES PR 476.19

HOSTILE OA 28.41 31.24 37.38
   PO 96.32 DV 183.10 SG 221.9
   230.41 TP 344.27 WP 388.1
   PR 483.4 507.33 SU 528.26
   BO 595.16 JD 610.14 611.19
   618.29 GG 686.32

HOSTILITY OA 29.4 EA 74.4
   DV 164.19 183.34 SG 231.10
   PR 506.14 SU 541.28 BO 592.11
   GG 662.32

HOSTS EA 72.21 JD 606.15

HOT MO 2.36 WM 56.39 63.33
   EA 73.31 76.4 90.8 PO 95.2
   95.6 95.30 99.6 101.30
   102.15 103.41 106.6 106.7
   107.37 108.29 109.5 109.8
   109.17 114.11 TF 120.26
   131.14 DV 139.23 139.40 147.9
   148.32 158.35 162.33 163.6
   166.9 171.8 179.38 179.42
   SB 214.25 GF 240.22 241.31
   WS 255.20 257.4 CH 276.16
   OC 299.17 EE 306.21 332.19
   TP 344.41 BL 353.9 361.16
   364.24 MN 370.13 SD 425.11
   425.21 HD 441.32 454.13
   454.15 455.15 FA 465.6 465.32
   PR 501.38 502.32 509.14
   SU 530.25 535.31 537.31
   543.19 543.41 544.41 WR 558.6
   BO 599.24 600.35 602.39
   JD 611.37 613.29 614.23 617.3
   617.9 617.42 624.32 IL 649.3
   659.39 GG 672.33 672.34
   684.11 688.25 NT 707.26
   717.42 ML 744.35 746.18
   746.28 LL 770.22 773.38
   774.35 RH 795.12

HOT-CHEEKED JD 614.23

HOTEL EA 81.4 81.10 90.17
   PR 488.6 BO 594.33 597.33
   598.32 601.26 ML 733.1 733.27
   RR 787.3 MD 807.31 807.32
   817.20 821.30 825.37

HOTEL-LIKE EA 81.24

HOTEL ROMANO NT 701.10

HOTELS ML 729.30 RR 780.4

HOT-HOUSE PR 480.3 480.4

HOTLY BM 828.42

HOTTER PO 95.14 WS 263.8
   MN 366.29

HOT-WATER BO 602.39

HOUND LA 636.32

HOUR HT 38.8 EA 82.8 84.22
   PO 103.15 TF 133.13 DV 163.2
   GF 236.22 240.7 240.13
   WS 256.27 OC 289.23 291.20
   293.23 EE 306.20 325.20
   TP 335.11 WP 379.3 PP 427.25
   PR 493.16 495.38 496.20
   496.25 SU 544.15 544.17
   WR 566.13 567.27 570.14
   570.17 BO 604.19 IL 650.4
   658.9 GG 683.39 697.29
   NT 719.31 OV 755.1 755.13
   758.35 LL 765.34 766.7
   RR 779.11 RH 802.13 TH 850.25
   851.7 852.19

HOURI BM 835.24

HOURS MO 18.24 SP 53.3 EA 81.13
   83.7 PO 116.10 DV 138.11
   154.13 178.11 FG 189.25
   GF 242.1 SC 269.34 CH 277.3
   OC 295.28 EE 332.21 TP 334.20
   336.8 YT 405.27 PR 491.20
   491.22 491.36 492.30 509.27
   510.35 TB 515.25 515.39 518.1
   518.2 518.18 SU 528.5 537.31
   WR 552.5 556.23 558.14 569.25
   GG 679.28 NT 713.30 ML 728.1
   735.26 736.42 OV 757.25
   LL 761.22 RR 781.3 RH 800.21
   BM 834.16 TH 848.42

HOURS' TB 519.28 JD 621.12
   LL 765.42

HOUSE MO 3.12 6.1 11.30 16.20
   17.29 18.42 OA 23.17 37.33
   38.2 HT 42.15 43.38 SP 52.42
   WM 55.14 63.18 64.32 65.3
   EA 72.19 85.8 TF 123.11
   DV 138.31 139.23 141.9 145.7
   146.6 153.36 154.12 160.38
   167.34 170.21 173.3 173.19
   173.25 174.2 175.36 176.13
   178.12 179.14 179.29 180.6
   184.18 185.11 FG 188.28
   189.15 191.25 193.11
   SS 198.20 198.22 200.34 202.1
   SG 221.24 224.20 224.25 225.8
   228.13 228.16 GF 234.21
   237.20 237.34 WS 244.28 250.6
   251.7 259.2 SC 267.17 267.23
   CH 275.31 278.25 278.28
   282.22 OC 283.32 284.33 285.2
   285.25 288.35 292.1 293.7
   293.15 296.40 298.40
   EE 304.10 304.28 304.32
   304.38 305.6 306.23 307.10
   310.22 317.14 318.6 320.18
   321.41 323.18 BL 347.33
   MN 377.23 WP 379.19 385.28
   386.18 386.38 387.4 387.33
   YT 394.1 394.3 397.1 401.2
   401.8 403.22 SD 416.11 416.27
   417.12 417.20 418.14 418.16
   422.25 423.30 PP 429.31
   431.31 436.22 436.26 436.41

HOUSE (CONT.) HD 446.22
   446.36 447.3 448.11 449.4
   451.7 451.9 451.10 456.8
   456.14 FA 464.2 467.6
   467.11 471.10 471.16
   471.37 PR 479.11 479.12
   479.21 486.41 486.42 488.6
   510.6 511.11 TB 517.6
   519.21 SU 529.8 529.34
   529.36 530.1 539.19 541.33
   542.20 WR 546.19 547.6
   547.39 548.11 560.12
   561.22 561.36 562.9 562.18
   562.20 562.26 564.27
   564.31 564.32 564.33 566.3
   566.6 568.24 568.28 568.41
   569.13 569.14 570.1 571.10
   571.11 571.34 572.29
   573.32 573.33 576.20
   577.38 JD 608.1 610.37
   611.7 614.37 616.29 620.31
   621.36 622.2 622.4 624.10
   624.23 627.33 LA 630.6
   636.30 638.42 640.23
   640.31 641.3 IL 648.35
   650.41 651.29 652.18
   653.42 654.4 656.6 656.9
   656.12 GG 666.32 668.29
   668.30 669.28 669.32
   669.42 672.24 677.25
   681.29 686.3 686.16 686.27
   697.16 700.6 700.12
   NT 714.14 716.14 720.19
   720.20 721.4 721.9
   ML 725.40 726.1 730.35
   733.10 733.19 734.23
   738.41 738.42 739.36
   744.27 744.42 746.15
   OV 760.5 LL 762.21 770.13
   775.25 775.30 RR 779.17
   780.6 786.10 787.37 789.13
   789.18 RH 790.19 790.22
   791.4 791.9 791.23 798.16
   798.23 799.7 800.8 800.14
   801.13 801.16 801.40
   802.34 MD 811.28 811.31
   815.25 815.31 815.36
   819.20 825.4 BM 829.11
   829.39 830.9 830.18 839.36
   TH 853.2 853.18

HOUSED FG 191.2

HOUSE-GARDEN EE 304.42

HOUSEHOLD YT 395.17 395.26

HOUSEHOLDERS MN 369.8

HOUSE-HUNTED TH 850.3

HOUSEKEEPER WM 64.19 70.16
   DV 176.26 176.33 178.18
   PP 436.34 PR 479.13
   LA 641.4 641.11 641.21
   641.26 ML 725.14 726.6
   731.36 732.5 RR 779.6
   787.7

HOUSEKEEPING YT 395.6
   MD 815.17

HOUSELAY, EMMA (SEE EMMA
   HOUSELAY)

HOUSELESS GG 696.9

HOUSE OF LORDS MD 813.18

HOUSE-PASSAGE BL 354.21

HOUSE-PLACE CH 274.25 FA 470.15

HOUSE-PROPERTY YT 394.35

HOUSE-ROOF EA 72.25

HOUSES SP 45.11 WM 54.28 60.27
  EA 72.42 TF 117.6 122.1
  DV 136.19 140.31 FG 187.3
  SC 270.35 OC 291.2 291.9
  TP 334.4 MN 366.8 SD 411.30
  HD 449.2 FA 459.32 PR 487.1
  WR 552.29 554.39 558.37
  558.39 559.3 561.33 561.41
  562.2 562.5 578.30 BO 593.23
  595.22 JD 610.35 624.24
  LA 631.31 639.2 640.12
  RR 781.32

HOUSE-SERVANT WR 550.30

HOUSE-SIDE GF 238.37

HOUSE-SLIPPERS OA 35.14

HOUSE-TOP WR 564.35 578.2

HOUSEWIFE MN 368.25 JD 622.9

HOUSE-YARD HD 446.23 451.8

HOVERED DV 167.19 WR 577.26
  SM 585.11 585.26 MD 813.8

HOVERING MO 2.24 FG 195.19
  WR 551.35 559.13 574.8
  LA 639.12 ML 740.24

HOW'D TB 525.7

HOW-DE-DO SD 426.17

HOWELLS (SEE ALICE; MRS. HOWELLS)

HOWL TP 335.14 GG 684.28 685.12
  NT 704.13 ML 735.35 735.37

HOWLED SM 585.33 MD 807.15

HOWLING FG 189.21 TP 335.23
  MN 373.23 PR 502.42 WR 549.27
  570.5 570.9

HOWLINGLY TP 335.7

HOW'RE PP 430.34

HOW'S SP 47.18 WS 243.20
  CH 275.9 BL 354.2 356.29
  YT 399.22 SD 413.31 PP 427.35
  IL 653.7 653.10 654.16

HUB CH 277.40

HUBBUB NT 708.32 721.11

HUBER, SERGEANT (SEE SERGEANT
  HUBER)

HUDDLE PO 106.33

HUDDLED WP 387.5 PR 507.8 510.7
  GG 684.31 RR 787.29

HUDSON SU 528.8 529.1 529.3

HUE PR 493.26

HUFFY EE 309.2 TP 338.41

HUGE TF 123.29 EE 333.11 333.12
  BL 351.11 PR 496.31 496.35
  SU 530.9 542.31 WR 546.21
  556.17 569.23 BO 596.9
  RH 803.2 TH 849.40

HUGELY SP 50.31 TH 847.32

HUGGED PR 510.8

HUGGING OA 26.1 PP 439.40
  PR 506.32

HULKED WP 390.2 390.7

HULKING CH 278.36 WP 389.39

HULLO PR 511.23

HUM BO 600.15 IL 652.3

HUMAN MO 17.2 EA 81.27 86.20
  87.20 TF 119.39 126.6
  DV 145.18 146.4 146.31 153.36
  154.35 170.39 171.15
  OC 299.40 EE 309.35 309.38
  312.19 PP 438.34 PR 477.17
  TB 521.33 522.7 SU 533.3
  541.28 WR 546.13 550.7 555.18
  559.42 560.3 561.26 561.29
  565.11 570.10 BO 591.9 591.11
  591.31 JD 622.20 623.34
  624.10 NT 702.39 703.3 705.40
  717.15 ML 730.29 734.9 740.30
  742.33 743.3 LL 767.3 767.35
  MD 819.30 BM 830.14 TH 844.37
  845.10 851.6

HUMANITY BO 591.31 595.42

HUMANLY DV 146.9

HUMANNESS BO 595.25

HUMBLE OA 34.8 DV 137.2 147.28
  GF 243.20 CH 275.36 OC 302.3
  WP 389.35 HD 453.3 FA 461.20
  BO 598.16 JD 605.35 LA 640.18
  NT 704.20 716.14 OV 750.14
  LL 764.11 MD 818.37 819.11
  819.12 820.13 820.14 820.15
  820.24 823.10

HUMBLED DV 174.2 CH 277.23

HUMBLY EA 92.9 PO 108.21
  DV 186.19 WS 247.38 PP 438.13
  LA 640.19 OV 750.14

HUMILIATED SS 200.11 BO 601.6
  ML 738.5 LL 765.28 MD 816.1
  818.40 BM 832.15 833.40

HUMILIATING PR 480.22 BO 601.5
  LA 642.32 IL 657.30 NT 710.37
  MD 815.12

HUMILIATION MO 20.24 OA 33.35
  DV 164.30 SS 200.18
  FA 461.6 ML 739.5 MD 817.29
  BM 832.16

HUMILITY DV 164.35 SS 204.4
  WP 379.32 380.22 GG 674.1
  675.5 MD 822.1

HUMMED IL 647.15

HUMMING-BIRD WR 564.33
  LL 774.16 774.21

HUMOROUS SM 584.13 585.22
  JD 627.5 RR 779.10
  MD 812.32 816.8

HUMOROUSLY LL 768.22
  MD 816.33

HUMOUR DV 145.42 146.2
  166.25 SB 217.22 218.8
  PR 508.10 TB 517.24
  SM 584.9 MD 812.31 812.39
  812.41 813.4 815.41 816.26
  816.31

HUMP ML 733.12

HUMPED DV 136.12 ML 734.18

HUMPED-UP BO 599.2

HUMPS ML 722.34

HUNCHBACKS TP 334.29

HUNDRED TF 128.4 DV 136.30
  145.33 SS 200.32 YT 401.10
  401.13 GG 661.11 NT 705.9
  LL 762.31 778.36 RH 795.30
  796.15 796.19 797.14

HUNDRED AND FIFTY POUNDS
  EE 305.13

HUNDRED POUNDS RH 800.23

HUNDREDS MN 367.34 JD 620.16
  NT 702.31 ML 731.42
  RH 799.21

HUNG MO 5.30 6.16 OA 25.21
  WM 55.2 55.15 65.41 69.38
  PO 104.1 107.11 115.9
  TF 118.15 125.23 DV 158.40
  161.15 168.8 180.20
  FG 188.12 191.31 194.32
  SS 206.17 211.12 SB 215.9
  216.28 SG 221.4 221.8
  224.7 227.19 GF 234.9
  235.34 236.34 WS 247.14
  247.22 251.28 264.15
  OC 284.1 284.2 286.39
  288.24 TP 343.12 343.26
  345.31 WP 386.13 SD 420.37
  PP 437.22 438.33 FA 470.23
  PR 506.18 508.20 TB 524.4
  SU 532.21 533.35 WR 553.40
  557.13 558.25 559.35
  569.5 579.24 579.41
  GG 675.6 686.8 692.37
  ML 729.41 733.31 OV 747.6
  748.38 750.11 MD 818.36

HUNG (CONT.) BM 833.9 833.18
   833.26 841.37 842.25 TH 849.3

HUNGER FG 189.28 191.20 192.3
   EE 315.14 315.16 WR 550.10
   ML 737.20

HUNGERED TF 128.14

HUNGRILY DV 143.26

HUNGRY CH 276.41 BL 357.39
   PR 495.19 495.22 502.17
   WR 550.12

HUNT FG 189.30 191.5 SB 219.27
   WR 557.13

HUNTED OA 24.41 SC 270.14
   MN 375.32 BM 833.23

HUNTER NT 716.9

HUNTERS TH 848.4

HUNTING PR 495.11

HUNTING-KNIFE FG 192.42

HURL WR 558.21

HURRAY TP 334.30

HURRIED WM 59.31 GF 235.1
   237.35 238.1 239.5 241.18
   SC 272.15 CH 277.25 OC 290.36
   292.2 298.4 WP 390.34
   HD 448.13 FA 458.19 PR 496.31
   TB 524.31 BO 597.32 LA 636.30
   636.31 GG 662.22 664.37
   696.42 697.4

HURRIEDLY SS 201.16 OC 286.9
   TP 346.8 GG 695.7 ML 727.12
   RH 790.6

HURRY WM 62.16 EA 71.2 73.37
   PO 100.40 101.4 MN 367.27
   377.31 TB 523.12 BO 600.3

HURRYING MO 2.17 DV 167.11
   GF 237.20 WS 256.8 TP 340.30
   LA 643.33 ML 727.10

HURT MO 8.39 OA 35.18 37.2
   SP 46.12 WM 57.12 58.20 69.30
   70.15 70.22 EA 81.2 84.2
   90.38 91.3 91.16 93.4
   PO 111.26 TF 133.26 DV 154.22
   157.5 169.30 170.29 172.7
   173.2 181.32 185.26 FG 190.6
   190.9 191.33 192.15 194.39
   196.6 SS 200.6 202.26
   SG 231.30 WS 249.40 SC 272.29
   CH 277.37 279.38 OC 294.31
   EE 316.38 317.18 318.2 318.15
   318.42 319.34 320.21
   TP 344.31 YT 402.15 SD 423.4
   PR 475.18 491.5 492.2 492.11
   492.12 SU 529.32 WR 563.36
   LA 631.17 646.6 IL 659.20
   RR 784.5 MD 808.8 BM 840.21
   840.26

HURTFUL ML 730.37

HURTING EA 91.18 92.38
   DV 181.30 BL 351.9 HD 454.21
   WR 563.40

HURTLING ML 724.27

HURTS EA 90.39 PR 491.32 491.34
   491.42

HUSBAND MO 14.25 14.31 15.5
   15.7 OA 31.2 31.12 32.34
   34.1 37.27 37.30 HT 39.19
   39.23 42.23 42.42 43.26
   43.34 WM 55.28 66.26 EA 72.37
   73.12 74.34 77.39 85.18
   85.26 85.27 86.10 86.24
   86.40 87.4 DV 137.34 139.39
   140.5 140.15 140.19 142.16
   153.20 153.27 153.31 156.33
   159.3 159.32 186.4 SG 221.34
   228.26 231.13 231.16 231.24
   231.29 231.39 233.7 WS 244.16
   250.13 260.10 260.15 261.20
   SC 269.16 OC 286.10 286.23
   297.23 299.21 300.38 301.27
   301.37 EE 309.29 309.35 315.9
   328.17 BL 347.6 347.13 348.4
   348.8 348.23 348.26 348.28
   349.36 349.38 350.8 353.22
   357.29 359.16 360.3 WP 380.28
   381.36 YT 410.14 SD 418.28
   418.30 419.12 PP 430.6 433.38
   434.14 434.33 FA 467.22
   469.24 470.17 TB 513.1 513.2
   513.19 514.38 514.39 514.42
   515.4 515.11 515.34 516.18
   527.1 SU 528.6 528.13 538.13
   538.14 538.17 540.13 540.42
   542.21 542.33 WR 546.29
   547.13 547.18 547.35 547.40
   548.15 549.39 549.41 550.19
   550.21 551.30 553.7 553.31
   554.27 554.31 BO 588.4 588.24
   590.39 590.41 592.39 592.40
   593.8 596.42 603.40 604.4
   604.40 JD 616.16 622.38 623.2
   623.20 625.14 625.34 629.11
   629.15 GG 663.17 664.30 667.6
   673.12 683.4 684.21 693.2
   NT 706.9 706.34 706.36 706.37
   OV 754.14 759.20 LL 762.17
   769.29 769.31 770.4 RR 780.15
   780.17 RH 792.17 802.36
   MD 805.8 824.16 824.22 824.30
   825.14 BM 830.39 TH 849.22
   851.36

HUSBAND-CARE BO 591.7

HUSBAND-FAMILIARITY JD 623.6
   623.7

HUSBANDS EE 316.16 YT 394.30
   NT 710.42 711.2

HUSBAND'S OA 33.18 33.31 35.7
   EA 84.23 87.39 DV 145.5
   SG 229.15 BL 347.2 349.28
   350.18 PR 473.32 475.27
   SU 544.24 WR 547.5 BO 599.22
   JD 617.12 617.24 625.14
   OV 756.33 RR 781.37 RH 792.34

HUSBANDS' CH 274.4

HUSH DV 184.9 FG 193.10
   OC 289.34 295.32 GG 697.34
   RR 781.35 782.11

HUSHED FG 193.7 GF 234.22
   PP 428.14 432.27 PR 473.14
   473.18 473.35 481.10
   482.2 512.16 NT 720.33
   RH 803.2

HUSHEDNESS PR 481.11

HUSK PP 438.34

HUSKILY MO 10.4 HD 444.32

HUSKY HT 40.24 SS 203.9
   GG 666.25 LL 767.40

HUSSIES TP 335.20

HUSTLE ML 742.17

HUT MO 22.25 TF 131.12
   SS 206.20 206.22 207.32
   PR 511.38 ML 739.32
   OV 749.11 749.23

HUTS TF 117.9 117.14
   WR 551.37 561.34 561.35

HUXLEY MO 6.28

HYACINTH SS 197.22

HYACINTHS WM 55.17 FG 187.8
   ML 723.16

HYMN FA 465.25 465.28
   467.35 467.36 467.39

HYMN NUMBER NINE SP 46.19

HYMNS TP 335.24

HYMN-SHEET FA 467.35 467.36

HYPNOTIC WR 577.4 MD 812.15
   812.28

HYPNOTISE MD 806.22 806.27

HYPNOTISED BL 364.9 PR 501.16
   MD 806.23 806.27

HYPNOTISING BL 355.18

HYPOCRITICAL IL 650.9

HYSTERIA GG 685.39 LL 768.1

HYSTERIC TP 345.29

HYSTERICAL PR 485.13 BO 604.6
   JD 615.18

HYSTERICS PR 492.3 509.22
   NT 718.3
I' HT 44.2 SP 48.6 48.16 48.18
   OC 292.25 295.28 LH 38.10

IBSEN MO 6.29

ICE FG 189.28 189.38 190.21
   190.23 193.13 193.30
   194.30 SG 225.39 OC 300.28
   300.36 PR 488.34 506.25

IMAGINATION (CONT.) 716.31
  717.12 718.8 718.11 718.13
  718.15 718.17 718.19 718.25
  718.28 720.41

IMAGINATIONS ML 731.24

IMAGINATIVE NT 718.16 718.33
  718.35 718.37 718.40 719.1

IMAGINATIVELY NT 718.29

IMAGINE MO 13.30 20.21
  SC 270.30 OC 291.5 EE 314.18
  319.39 SD 419.30 TB 514.41
  LA 643.16 GG 687.11 NT 712.28
  ML 746.31 MD 813.26 813.29

IMAGINED OA 31.9 TF 132.29
  SS 210.32 MN 368.12 YT 394.22
  TB 518.17 520.12 WR 557.32
  566.6 JD 605.31 IL 649.24
  GG 662.1 687.42 OV 757.25

IMAGINES SU 528.10

IMAGINING EA 85.26 DV 165.13
  183.4

IMBECILE DV 150.13 150.15
  BL 362.11

IMITATE MD 805.3 812.32 812.39

IMITATION MD 812.32

IMMACULATE ML 728.35 RR 788.31

IMMATERIAL WR 574.1

IMMATURE SD 413.29

IMMEDIACY BL 355.29

IMMEDIATE WM 66.12 TF 121.34
  125.28 OC 302.14 BL 347.24
  361.7 WP 380.3 HD 448.5
  452.27 WR 573.42 MD 825.39

IMMEDIATELY MO 4.2 7.9 10.35
  SP 50.21 WM 65.5 PO 112.12
  SG 222.1 CH 275.41 EE 328.14
  TP 343.8 BL 361.39 WP 380.25
  390.30 HD 456.27 PR 486.39
  506.11 TB 524.15 SU 531.29
  WR 567.40 BO 596.14 JD 611.3
  623.40 LA 642.4 IL 652.3
  652.15 652.28 NT 707.16
  710.40 ML 736.32 BM 828.2

IMMENSE WM 58.37 PO 114.25
  DV 176.22 179.1 SB 213.42
  PP 438.21 PR 496.18 TB 518.21
  WR 553.4 553.9 568.17 569.41
  577.19 MD 821.3 BM 838.15

IMMENSELY PR 480.41 GG 668.42
  BM 828.15

IMMENSITY PR 497.39

IMMERSION TB 514.26

IMMINENT OC 285.1

IMMOBILE PR 502.32 TB 523.35
  MD 819.5

IMMOVABLE DV 179.37 WS 261.21
  YT 407.19 SM 584.22

IMMUNE HD 447.39

IMMUTABLE WS 257.6 HD 444.6

IMPAIRED MD 815.41

IMPARTED ML 726.35

IMPASSIVE WM 58.12 TF 124.24
  DV 142.16 177.12 179.36
  BL 360.3 HD 442.38 445.7
  446.2 PR 487.18 492.34
  WR 563.27 LL 771.27

IMPATIENCE MO 12.8 DV 141.38
  SG 222.34 228.34 CH 276.33
  SU 541.18 GG 686.35 NT 709.36
  719.20 MD 812.2 813.42

IMPATIENT MO 3.17 OA 31.32
  37.17 WM 65.14 WS 260.7
  OC 285.18 BL 348.20 LA 633.16
  BM 843.6

IMPATIENTLY WM 60.1 TF 134.19
  DV 185.16 EE 321.34

IMPECUNIOUS MD 811.21

IMPEDIMENTS OA 34.28

IMPENDING BO 599.40

IMPENETRABLE SD 417.17 BO 596.34
  OV 753.31

IMPERATIVE BO 604.5

IMPERCEPTIBLE PP 435.27 PR 483.17

IMPERCEPTIBLY PR 479.15

IMPERFECTIONS SM 585.9 585.32

IMPERIAL ENGLAND EE 326.25

IMPERIOUS TF 133.7 OC 284.7

IMPERIOUSLY LA 634.36 643.40

IMPERSONAL EA 72.16 73.17 73.38
  80.14 PO 96.33 TF 122.38
  DV 165.11 171.10 SS 198.5
  SG 232.33 233.14 WS 254.11
  PP 438.40 WR 565.12 566.21
  566.22 569.40 576.2 577.10
  MD 821.2

IMPERSONALITY WS 255.12

IMPERSONALLY DV 151.7 171.35
  172.41 WS 256.12 WR 576.5

IMPERTINENCE MO 13.35 WM 61.15
  PR 477.22 477.36 478.9

IMPERTINENT BL 348.19 PR 482.11

IMPERTINENTLY TB 521.20

IMPERTURBABLY NT 719.21

IMPERTURBED SD 418.38

IMPERVIOUS PO 98.33 DV 152.1
  CH 281.19 PR 476.18
  NT 720.18

IMPETUOUS PP 429.36

IMPLACABILITY PR 477.40

IMPLACABLE EE 321.38
  BO 595.37 596.3 596.5
  599.9 ML 732.24

IMPLICATE PO 98.8

IMPLICATED TF 128.29
  ML 729.15

IMPLICITLY MO 17.16 DV 172.28

IMPLIED PR 480.29

IMPLORINGLY GG 695.26

IMPORT DV 146.12

IMPORTANCE WS 260.42 CH 278.39
  EE 310.12 314.16 TB 519.31
  ML 741.36

IMPORTANT OA 32.21 EE 310.13
  318.8 321.4 BL 349.36
  FA 462.34 IL 649.9
  GG 678.38 680.17 689.27
  MD 805.7 BM 835.42
  TH 847.33

IMPORTANTLY PO 108.6
  ML 735.27

IMPORTED ML 728.42

IMPOSE DV 137.22

IMPOSED PR 480.27 MD 825.5

IMPOSING GG 697.31

IMPOSSIBILITY PR 476.14
  NT 710.1 MD 812.29

IMPOSSIBLE PO 104.24
  DV 165.16 178.24 WP 380.3
  YT 405.32 TB 517.6
  WR 550.39 IL 650.36
  NT 710.30 718.38 OV 747.12
  LL 769.9 RR 781.38
  MD 812.18 815.4 BM 831.4

IMPOTENCE BO 600.6

IMPOTENT DV 165.23 SS 199.19
  ML 745.7

IMPOVERISHED DV 158.10

IMPRECATION ML 725.3

IMPREGNABLE OC 299.23

IMPRESS WS 250.34 YT 399.6

INDEPENDENT MO 11.24 OA 29.9
  WM 59.13 PO 99.42 TF 128.9
  DV 164.16 MD 809.6 BM 827.4
  827.6 827.9 827.16

INDESCRIBABLE SC 268.29

INDESCRIBABLY SC 268.5

INDESTRUCTIBLE MD 820.10 820.13

INDIA PR 475.2 TB 526.9

INDIAN WM 55.38 55.39 PR 481.24
  483.5 495.3 495.12 WR 553.20
  554.12 554.24 554.28 554.38
  555.10 555.33 555.40 556.8
  556.14 558.16 558.24 558.27
  559.18 559.27 560.5 560.11
  560.40 562.15 562.35 563.1
  563.2 563.19 563.21 563.32
  564.4 564.7 564.17 564.27
  564.42 566.12 566.27 568.35
  570.22 571.21 571.33 571.35
  573.1 574.29 575.5 575.10
  575.12 575.14 575.18 575.19
  575.21 576.32 NT 703.41 707.6
  715.26 715.36 BM 827.22
  TH 844.10 846.32 846.38 847.1
  848.6

INDIAN-LOOKING PR 483.8

INDIANS PR 494.34 495.29 495.32
  495.36 495.39 495.41
  WR 548.41 549.33 549.37
  549.41 550.5 553.34 554.4
  558.30 560.26 561.2 568.4
  571.19 572.35 574.26 575.9
  575.28 NT 704.21 716.28
  BM 833.12

INDICATED DV 157.32 PP 433.28

INDICATING MO 8.24 12.30

INDICATION HT 38.26

INDICATIONS DV 169.29

INDIFFERENCE MO 12.7 WM 65.15
  SB 216.32 216.35 217.3
  WS 262.9 OC 286.22 BL 350.11
  YT 396.5 FA 467.28 SU 531.27
  531.34 533.14 WR 568.8

INDIFFERENT MO 1.10 OA 32.28
  33.1 34.41 HT 39.34 40.29
  PO 96.37 DV 137.30 BL 361.26
  WP 379.16 379.17 PP 427.20
  FA 462.26 466.11 BO 587.20
  589.40 590.20 BM 832.41

INDIFFERENTLY OA 31.39 SB 217.40
  PP 434.35 TB 517.39

INDIGNANT DV 178.3 178.4
  FA 471.2 TB 524.9 526.30
  RR 789.15 BM 841.29

INDIGNATION OA 36.12 EA 85.25
  DV 137.13 GF 238.16 WS 248.31
  TP 339.23 BO 589.7 BM 836.36
  836.41 841.22

INDIRECTLY GG 688.41

INDISCERNIBLE GG 673.2

INDISCRIMINATELY HD 453.8
  GG 661.21

INDISCRIMINATING BM 832.30

INDISPENSABLE BL 347.4 HD 454.17

INDISPUTABLE BO 589.1

INDISPUTABLY DV 137.1

INDISTINCTLY OC 283.5

INDIVIDUAL TP 339.15 WR 569.34
  569.36 RR 779.24 MD 807.22

INDIVIDUALS EE 326.39 SU 543.7
  NT 706.40 707.1

INDOLENCE HT 40.26 SU 531.27

INDOLENTLY MO 9.22 12.23

INDOMITABLE YT 407.16 407.36
  BO 588.34 595.40

INDOMITABLENESS JD 619.27

INDOORS OA 26.7 31.2 HT 43.36
  44.15 DV 137.30 158.40 162.5
  174.28 SS 202.20 SG 222.2
  229.17 229.37 GF 236.37
  WS 259.1 263.21 OC 286.10
  286.35 EE 321.9 WP 385.37
  388.40 SD 422.30 422.37
  SU 541.1 IL 652.5 652.30
  ML 745.17 LL 773.36 RR 787.42

INDUCE WR 576.35

INDUCED TH 852.8

INDULGE MO 14.1 MN 368.8

INDULGENCE DV 165.15 EE 316.5

INDULGENT MO 12.38 13.12 16.30
  DV 177.36 SS 211.21 SG 222.14
  OC 291.24 PR 486.34

INDULGENTLY MO 13.18 CH 278.1

INDULGING MO 15.37

INDUSTRIAL TP 334.3 YT 394.29
  394.30 FA 458.7 TH 849.28

INDUSTRIALISM EE 327.13 327.14
  327.20

INDUSTRY SS 197.28 TP 334.10
  MD 809.38

INEFFABLE TF 127.16 ML 725.1

INEFFECTUAL DV 171.39 EE 308.35
  HD 443.12 446.37 IL 651.34

INEFFECTUALITY HD 441.13

INEFFECTUALLY DV 159.8

INERT SP 49.8 WM 67.6
  EA 85.1 PO 103.38 104.7
  104.17 104.27 110.30
  TF 120.30 126.19 126.22
  DV 140.2 148.7 149.14
  149.21 SB 216.16 OC 302.5
  302.6 PR 492.34 WR 556.39
  BO 604.37 LA 637.12
  GG 662.32 671.31 677.36
  683.6 684.29 686.25
  OV 748.13 LL 767.33 768.13
  768.42 775.17 BM 832.5

INERTIA PO 104.29 PR 482.19
  MD 817.25 817.41

INESTIMABLY OA 32.19

INEVITABILITY MN 376.25

INEVITABLE PO 96.6 96.36
  104.23 104.26 OC 283.9
  HD 452.33 PR 481.10
  BO 591.22

INEVITABLY EE 312.25 312.26
  327.2

INEXORABLE DV 149.35

INEXORABLY DV 149.32
  GG 690.22

INEXPENSIVE EE 304.30

INEXPERIENCED DV 164.34

INEXPLICABLE YT 404.11
  TB 524.42 JD 629.10

INEXPLICABLY WP 387.2

INEXPRESSIBLE BO 591.32
  GG 683.36

INEXTINGUISHABLE PR 484.41

INFANT DV 154.40 158.16
  159.28 CH 279.3 279.37
  BL 348.23 SU 536.21 540.28
  540.40

INFANTILE SC 269.4

INFANTRY PO 96.26

INFANTS' BM 841.23

INFATUATED MD 813.23

INFERIOR DV 138.28 151.4
  151.8 151.12 151.16
  EE 314.36 327.5 327.21
  327.33 327.34

INFERIORITY DV 164.30

INFERIORS EE 327.36

INFERNO SM 582.14

INFINITE OC 302.8 WP 380.22
  FA 467.34 IL 651.8 651.9
  GG 690.31 ML 723.39 723.40
  723.42 724.11 746.21

INFINITE (CONT.) LL 774.2

INFINITELY MO 6.25 SG 222.38
    WR 565.38 SM 584.9 585.5
    JD 627.9 IL 650.27 GG 671.12
    ML 734.31 MD 813.25

INFINITY ML 724.21

INFLAMED EA 71.20 78.11
    PO 114.11 EE 320.5 FA 465.33

INFLAMMATION EE 320.2

INFLATED CH 281.32

INFLATING MO 18.19

INFLECTION SS 209.8

INFLECTIONS GG 663.23

INFLUENCE EA 82.34 PO 98.12
    DV 170.40 EE 315.21 NT 709.39

INFLUENCES EE 306.21 WP 386.5
    WR 574.5 ML 724.24

INFLUENCING EE 315.22 315.25

INFLUENTIAL SS 208.15

INFLUX TH 851.23

INFORM RH 798.40

INFORMATION MO 7.13 FA 469.3
    MD 810.4

INFORMED DV 175.37

INFRA DIG LA 642.35 642.37
    BM 833.38

INFREQUENT IL 655.5

INFURIATED OA 35.26 PO 99.12
    BL 357.8 YT 406.13 PR 476.38

INFUSED BO 588.40

INFUSION WR 576.40

INGRATIATING WS 245.20 SD 412.8
    JD 624.38

INHABIT MD 824.30

INHABITANTS WR 577.42

INHABITED SG 225.9

INHERIT MD 806.8 821.11

INHERITANCE OA 23.3

INHERITED WS 260.38 HD 448.10
    MD 811.40

INHUMAN PO 103.3 DV 145.12
    150.7 180.39 PR 496.41 496.42
    WR 554.18 555.20 557.37
    569.16

INHUMANLY PR 496.32

INIMICAL WR 555.22

INITIAL WS 245.28 246.34

INITIALS WS 252.5

INITIATIVE FA 462.25

INJURED DV 144.11 155.33
    OC 301.20 YT 402.22 GG 667.10

INJURY SG 229.34

INK EA 80.23 SU 538.41 539.26

INKLING TF 130.13 WS 256.28
    GG 662.29

INK-STAND EA 81.15

INLAY PR 485.1

IN-LOVE IL 652.22

INMATES GG 700.6

INN PO 108.12 SD 411.33 422.27
    423.14 PP 432.11 432.17
    432.22

INNATE PO 98.16 BO 588.26 589.1

INNER TF 118.20 121.31 131.2
    DV 164.31 SS 208.37 TP 338.6
    BL 353.21 HD 441.29 PR 493.37
    497.9 497.32 WR 546.19
    BO 600.17 600.19 LA 630.32
    NT 710.31 710.38 TH 847.25

INNERLY SU 533.11

INNERMOST EA 93.23 DV 165.1
    HD 449.13 WR 581.6 GG 699.14

INNOCENCE BO 593.42 IL 654.21
    655.12 GG 676.39 BM 839.19

INNOCENT WM 59.26 WP 384.37
    NT 707.22 707.24 711.17
    711.20 BM 839.39 839.40

INNOCENTLY OA 32.33 IL 654.29

INNS LL 762.29

INNUMERABLE MO 1.27 OA 32.15

INORDINATE BL 348.8

INORDINATELY BL 357.26

INQUEST NT 721.8

INQUIRE MD 822.39

INQUIRED SP 51.24 SS 198.20
    GF 242.20 MN 373.10

INQUIRING OC 299.22 LA 641.7

INQUIRINGLY DV 172.23 SB 212.17
    IL 655.29 RR 786.27

INQUIRY TF 128.18

INQUISITIVE SD 413.38

INQUISITIVELY WS 245.20
    LA 631.40

INQUISITIVENESS LA 631.40

INSANE PO 99.40 DV 176.16
    BL 365.14 NT 717.6 718.1

INSANITY WM 66.39 LL 777.32
    TH 852.35

INSCRUTABILITY WR 555.31

INSCRUTABLE MO 3.38 DV 181.15
    BL 358.10 WP 387.25 388.20
    SD 414.23 HD 442.39
    FA 468.14 468.26 ML 727.9

INSCRUTABLY YT 404.8

INSECT EA 85.1 TF 119.35
    TB 518.20

INSECTS MD 819.31

IN SEINEM AUG DIE MUTTER SEH
    TF 129.18

INSENTIENT CH 280.30

INSEPARABLE PR 475.4

INSIDER TH 848.35

INSIDIOUS HT 43.9 EE 325.30
    PR 484.25 WR 566.25 568.5
    576.15 BO 589.24 589.31
    LL 774.3

INSIGNIFICANCE DV 165.20
    BL 349.40

INSIGNIFICANT EA 92.14
    IL 651.34 MD 807.13

INSIGNIFICANTLY OC 283.10

INSINUATED SD 426.13

INSINUATING YT 408.36
    PP 429.13

INSINUATINGLY MO 14.5

INSIST SD 411.22

INSISTED EA 78.15 DV 163.38
    EE 320.7 YT 395.37
    FA 460.16 SU 534.9
    WR 568.21 SM 585.32
    BO 594.32 IL 655.39
    RH 797.42 801.35

INSISTENCE WR 554.9 569.17
    570.10

INSISTENT GG 679.14

INSISTING JD 608.18 LA 635.10

INSOLENCE OA 28.9 ML 741.5

INSOLENT OA 23.3 WM 65.20

INSOLENT (CONT.) MD 809.20

INSOLENTLY EA 76.27 WP 391.4

INSPECTING TP 336.20

INSPECTORS TP 336.8 336.11

INSPECTOR'S TP 336.23

INSPIRATION WS 261.18 RH 803.29

INSPIRED EE 327.28 TB 517.9
  MD 816.34

INSTALL JD 627.33

INSTANCE MO 18.28 FA 462.33
  JD 606.35

INSTANT OA 36.32 WM 70.23
  SB 212.2 214.32 WS 251.33
  257.40 264.10 EE 331.34
  PP 435.42 PR 510.25 SU 532.26
  BO 591.14 LA 635.20

INSTANTANEOUS HD 451.22

INSTANTLY OA 35.33 35.40
  WM 70.5 DV 174.41 TP 337.28
  YT 402.5 PR 483.33 483.35
  SU 543.23 SM 583.37 GG 684.29
  691.26

INSTEAD OA 23.16 27.3 EA 81.4
  PO 95.17 101.30 DV 145.9
  SS 210.1 GF 239.20 WS 257.38
  CH 274.2 OC 284.40 EE 310.29
  TP 335.2 340.30 PR 476.27
  483.15 TB 515.42 JD 609.13
  LA 634.42 IL 651.15 LL 766.40
  RR 781.30 RH 800.36 BM 841.3
  TH 851.11 852.21

INSTINCT OA 35.16 35.36
  WM 62.41 66.41 EA 80.14 82.2
  PO 97.6 99.32 103.11 109.39
  TF 126.26 130.15 DV 177.6
  EE 326.22 327.1 327.17 328.1
  YT 395.35

INSTINCTIVE PO 97.25 TF 121.34
  DV 165.11

INSTINCTIVELY MO 19.4 PO 99.30
  TF 130.15 WS 250.35 EE 324.15
  BL 349.2 363.30 YT 397.38
  SD 421.31 PR 480.38 SU 544.13
  RR 788.16 BM 830.27

INSTINCTS WM 66.42 EA 82.15
  PO 103.23 EE 327.10

INSTITUTION EA 87.14 EE 322.22
  YT 396.26

INSTRUCTION TF 119.6

INSTRUCTIONS MD 824.35

INSTRUMENT SP 47.30 47.34 48.1
  EA 80.21 DV 164.8 JD 626.39
  626.40 NT 706.37 MD 810.2

INSUBORDINATE PO 103.32

INSUFFERABLE LL 768.40

INSUFFICIENCY DV 146.11

INSUFFICIENT DV 154.2

INSULATION ML 722.19

INSULT OA 31.30 EA 79.10 93.32
  DV 153.30 WS 262.42 ML 727.38

INSULTED OA 37.42 GF 240.24
  TB 524.10 NT 710.40

INSULTING GF 235.16 IL 652.14

INSULTINGLY OA 32.38

INSUPPORTABLE TF 129.2

INTACT PO 99.30 OC 300.30
  PR 479.5 503.35 509.10 509.11
  512.19

INTANGIBLE BO 597.7 GG 697.37

INTEGUMENT LA 641.33

INTELLECT TF 128.11 DV 145.20

INTELLECTUAL MO 8.18 OA 33.31
  BL 349.5 GG 679.41

INTELLIGENCE MO 13.16 13.23
  14.19 OA 36.1 PO 98.32
  TF 118.32 SG 227.40 SC 267.14
  PR 483.18

INTELLIGENT TF 122.18 DV 172.24
  TP 339.9 339.10 339.15 339.17
  BL 354.28 YT 395.12 PR 480.39
  NT 709.13 BM 832.1

INTEND WM 66.10 66.25 PO 97.39
  YT 408.18 TB 514.1 BM 839.14

INTENDED EA 88.8 TP 339.13
  HD 453.24 455.1 BO 588.19
  IL 659.25 NT 717.2 LL 765.13
  BM 840.35

INTENDING HD 451.27 NT 710.4

INTENSE OA 33.25 WM 60.11 65.9
  65.10 69.16 EA 90.34 93.7
  PO 103.12 TF 118.41 119.7
  130.4 130.10 SB 217.6
  GF 240.7 WS 263.29 EE 323.41
  331.1 TP 343.22 PP 428.24
  PR 500.2 502.39 WR 557.37
  576.32 JD 629.6 RH 800.21

INTENSELY MO 17.2 22.20
  TF 129.25 DV 178.2 SB 212.35
  SC 268.39 BL 353.15 357.4
  PR 501.21 503.25 TB 521.35
  SU 543.29 WR 569.34 581.23
  LA 634.15 634.30 IL 647.36
  ML 732.36 RR 783.24 MD 820.21

INTENSEST BO 594.25

INTENSIFIED PO 99.38 LA 637.10

INTENSIFY BM 834.21

INTENSITY MO 9.23 WM 69.12
  69.40 EA 91.35 TF 133.13
  DV 184.9 SB 215.3 EE 306.28
  BL 347.31 PP 440.13 HD 445.40
  PR 499.7 BO 594.16 LL 774.8
  MD 811.34 BM 839.17
  TH 852.37

INTENT OA 24.15 PO 100.40
  SG 227.42 WS 246.1 246.17
  SC 268.38 OC 289.24
  HD 448.15 449.35 PR 501.27
  WR 560.29 573.21

INTENTION PO 105.16 WS 260.28
  EE 308.14 MN 368.35 368.36
  SD 417.10 420.26 HD 453.29
  453.33 IL 647.11 647.16
  651.40 GG 674.21 MD 824.30
  BM 828.15

INTENTLY HD 443.25 LL 768.10
  774.1

INTENTNESS SD 420.33
  PR 501.19 WR 563.7 573.16

INTERCEPT WP 390.38

INTERCHANGE PO 98.9

INTERCOURSE TB 515.40

INTEREST MO 12.2 12.9 15.35
  HT 39.9 EA 85.35 SG 221.12
  EE 309.24 TP 339.9 339.16
  339.17 BL 347.17 350.5
  PR 480.25 WR 557.11
  GG 669.12 NT 709.18
  ML 739.24 740.20 741.24
  BM 840.38 TH 848.35

INTERESTED EA 74.34 WS 245.19
  265.31 SD 414.9 FA 460.24
  468.18 PR 480.26 TB 525.14
  SU 532.4 WR 557.5 JD 612.10
  625.10 LA 634.14 NT 709.21
  711.34 LL 763.6 MD 815.42

INTERESTEDLY HD 446.3

INTERESTING MO 13.15 15.10
  WM 63.8 DV 143.18 FG 188.29
  PR 479.14 481.36 BO 589.26
  JD 619.35 NT 702.1
  MD 809.34

INTERESTS HT 39.33 NT 704.8

INTERFERE DV 172.4 SG 229.21
  TB 517.8 GG 697.37 NT 718.7

INTERFERING FA 470.22
  GG 697.39 NT 707.15

INTERIM MO 9.12 TB 527.29

INTERIOR JD 613.14 TH 848.38

INTERLOCUTOR PR 479.8

INTERLOPER RR 784.12

INTERMEDIATE BL 362.14

INTERMINABLE FA 460.4 SU 529.3

INTERMINGLED BL 353.24

INTERMISSION WR 579.31

INTERMITTENT GG 683.9

INTERMITTENTLY EE 307.15

INTERNAL DV 147.14 168.19

INTERPOLATED HD 443.1

INTERPRETED PP 435.3

INTERPRETER EA 83.10 NT 716.24
716.34 716.37

INTER-RECOGNITION PR 485.35
485.36 486.5

INTERRUPT BL 352.6

INTERRUPTED DV 184.28 OC 294.3
SD 413.7 FA 461.33 GG 670.26
674.31 NT 711.19 TH 851.40

INTERRUPTING TB 523.4

INTERRUPTION OC 298.33 RR 785.14

INTERRUPTIONS OA 36.37 NT 711.23

INTERSPACED DV 178.29

INTERTWINING OC 290.19

INTERVAL SB 215.17 MN 373.22
YT 409.29 FA 459.38 IL 659.3
GG 666.10 BM 838.19

INTERVALS EA 71.29 WR 557.3
MD 807.28

INTERVENE JD 609.4

INTERVENED SD 414.35

INTERVENING MO 15.11 WS 257.29

INTERVENTION DV 180.13 BL 355.31

INTERVIEW YT 408.28 RH 799.36

INTESTINAL PR 497.5

INTESTINES WM 67.33

INTIMACIES MO 7.32

INTIMACY WM 64.29 EA 82.29
82.36 TF 127.3 DV 170.30
SS 203.10 SB 218.2 SG 225.37
EE 328.27 TP 339.8 BL 347.16
350.10 365.12 WP 380.3
PR 476.14 484.32 486.5
TB 514.3 IL 648.7 659.33
GG 663.7 693.7 NT 706.26
LL 764.32 BM 836.30 840.1

INTIMATE MO 20.12 DV 171.12
SS 201.33 204.41 WS 254.18
PP 438.29 HD 448.8 SU 543.35
WR 547.25 MD 822.38 BM 831.30

INTIMATE (CONT.) 840.41

INTIMATELY DV 179.9 SG 226.35
WS 256.12 PR 480.36 TB 513.7

INTOLERABLE WM 69.27 PO 112.4
TF 128.35 CH 276.37 PR 478.9
BO 589.11 JD 622.1

INTOLERABLY WR 578.31

INTONATION SS 198.37 203.37
GF 236.5 EE 306.4 SD 411.23
HD 457.8 WR 564.36 MD 813.39

INTONED FA 466.33 SM 585.19
ML 728.30

INTOXICATE MO 2.40

INTOXICATED WM 59.10 PO 102.1
WS 254.10

INTOXICATION PO 103.19 103.25
WS 254.23 255.4

INTRICATE PR 496.35 GG 697.41

INTRIGUED PR 482.12 GG 675.20
BM 831.33

INTRIGUING MD 821.28

INTRINSIC EA 82.34 GG 663.11

INTRINSICALLY DV 165.24

INTRODUCE EA 77.31 77.34
SS 209.13 GG 662.4 666.14
NT 711.39

INTRODUCED GG 673.7 MD 811.21
811.27

INTRODUCING SP 47.38

INTRODUCTION HD 453.15 SM 583.14

INTRUDE EE 305.27

INTRUDED WM 61.13 RH 802.31

INTRUDER MO 11.15 SS 198.8
199.11 199.16 RR 784.12

INTRUDING MO 12.36 IL 654.27
LL 764.30

INTRUSION TF 125.3 ML 742.9
RH 804.7

INTUITION OA 30.27 BL 359.42
GG 682.40 683.13 MD 814.21

INTUITIVELY TF 120.3

INTURNED JD 615.6

INVALID DV 138.1 143.10 144.13
185.31 SS 201.36

INVARIABLY MO 5.34 YT 396.3
SD 411.21 GG 671.15

INVENT WS 248.13 248.35

INVENTED SS 204.31 EE 314.41
ML 742.20

INVENTION EE 307.5

INVENTIVE SS 206.32

INVERTED WR 579.33 NT 702.24

INVESTIGATE DV 146.28

INVESTIGATED DV 146.23

INVESTMENT MD 806.35 821.12

INVIDIOUS GF 235.2

INVINCIBILITY OA 33.12

INVINCIBLE WR 547.38

INVIOLABLE OC 299.14

INVISIBLE OC 288.15 BL 347.26
353.20 353.26 354.1 361.16
PP 434.8 PR 489.5 496.12
498.5 510.27 SU 529.33
532.28 WR 562.30 570.6
572.24 574.6 574.21
ML 724.41 725.3 730.29
732.31 LL 761.19 RR 788.26

INVISIBLY TF 130.1 BL 353.23

INVITE PP 437.7 IL 654.25

INVITED SS 201.25 WS 251.8
BL 348.14 ML 729.29

INVITIN' SP 51.35

INVITING EA 91.10 JD 625.11
625.19

INVITINGLY JD 623.17

INVOCATION WM 68.34

INVOKE MD 820.35

INVOLUNTARILY TF 121.25
123.20 SG 233.4 SD 416.7
425.27

INVOLUNTARY OA 30.34 WM 70.3
DV 161.30 CH 282.19
SD 415.16 SM 584.3

INVOLVED HD 441.28 PR 497.41
GG 668.8 RR 782.16

INVULNERABLE JD 622.22

INWARD HD 454.3 PR 476.38
JD 614.5 MD 808.25

INWARDLY DV 175.33 FA 461.1
PR 483.25 508.11 509.9
GG 664.20 RH 792.41
BM 830.35 831.27

INWARDS PR 498.3 WR 580.24
JD 613.17 613.40 622.27
625.38 OV 753.36

IRASCIBLY TF 133.32

IRELAND MD 811.13

IRIDESCENCE EA 82.24 OV 748.17

IRIDESCENT WR 580.12 RH 800.15

IRIS OA 27.37 27.42

IRISH DV 146.2 WS 250.26
  MD 812.33

IRISHWOMAN MD 815.13

IRKED EA 79.22 SG 221.34
  WS 253.9

IRKSOME GF 240.31

IRON SP 51.1 TF 117.10
  DV 157.15 173.35 FG 188.14
  GF 241.31 WS 262.35 EE 324.20
  330.6 WP 389.18 FA 459.2
  459.38 SU 528.20 528.24
  WR 558.29 BO 594.11 599.13
  JD 610.14 LA 634.25 IL 653.2
  653.9 GG 662.26 698.1
  NT 719.23 ML 739.32 RR 787.28
  MD 823.39

IRON-BLUE JD 618.8

IRON-GREY MD 808.38 809.25

IRONIC OA 23.19 WM 57.38
  DV 146.8 SS 202.34 SB 213.18
  LL 764.27

IRONICAL MO 11.12 FG 187.21
  SS 201.33 WS 259.34 CH 275.15
  BL 349.5 349.21 SM 586.6

IRONICALLY WM 56.24 62.26
  EA 91.25 GF 236.4 242.17
  TP 339.37 MN 375.17 TB 523.29
  525.35 LA 630.13

IRON-MEN MO 11.36

IRONS EE 328.37 TP 337.17

IRON-WORKERS HD 449.10

IRONY MO 4.28 5.27 5.36 8.3
  14.24 OA 23.34 28.27 33.21
  38.4 WM 61.30 68.16 SG 232.36
  GF 236.8 WS 252.37 EE 311.4
  324.39 324.42 BL 349.22
  PR 486.40 JD 613.42 MD 825.19
  BM 842.4

IRREGULAR OA 36.34 BL 359.1

IRREGULARLY GG 694.13

IRREPLACEABLE TH 849.39

IRREPROACHABLE WS 250.38

IRRESISTIBLY WS 255.13

IRRESOLUTELY SG 224.22

IRRESPECTIVE WS 253.12

IRRESPONSIBLE MO 16.29

IRREVERENT OV 756.6

IRREVOCABLY MO 5.26

IRRIGATION PR 488.35

IRRITABILITY GF 238.33 LL 776.1
  776.16 776.21

IRRITABLE PO 96.20 96.32 99.9
  DV 142.41 GF 238.30 239.30
  CH 275.28 MN 374.8 BM 831.20
  TH 853.10

IRRITABLY OA 35.10 WM 67.15
  PO 99.40 DV 152.19 OC 288.21
  289.1 EE 317.7 SD 422.24
  HD 442.38

IRRITANT SG 229.8

IRRITATE WS 247.35

IRRITATED MO 6.2 PO 97.14 97.22
  97.27 98.24 SS 200.25
  BL 348.20 SU 529.21 GG 663.28
  ML 740.34 RR 782.21 TH 852.26

IRRITATING MO 13.33 DV 145.39
  CH 275.37 OC 295.7 RR 781.8

IRRITATION MO 5.37 15.24
  PO 100.6 100.27 WS 256.31
  261.7 BL 351.16 HD 444.1
  GG 662.17 662.18 TH 851.16

'IS SP 46.32 CH 276.30
  OC 291.19 WP 389.24

ISAAC EE 315.1

ISABEL BL 347.12 347.32 348.38
  349.2 349.17 349.25 349.34
  350.3 350.10 350.24 350.31
  350.35 351.7 352.6 352.11
  352.18 352.21 352.25 352.30
  352.33 353.31 353.40 354.11
  354.32 356.20 356.26 357.4
  357.14 357.28 357.30 357.36
  358.19 358.26 358.27 358.36
  358.39 358.40 359.1 359.2
  359.7 359.10 359.20 359.28
  359.39 360.8 360.14 360.33
  360.38 361.17 361.23 361.35
  362.30 362.37 364.34 364.37
  365.3 365.8

ISABEL PERVIN BL 347.1

ISABEL'S BL 350.4 356.17 357.2
  358.1 358.23 362.39

ISHMAEL EE 325.19 325.21 325.28

ISLAND ML 722.3 722.6 722.7
  722.11 722.14 722.16 722.19
  722.22 722.31 723.4 723.6
  723.7 723.11 723.19 723.28
  723.33 723.34 723.39 723.40
  724.1 724.4 724.13 724.25
  725.5 725.28 725.30 726.22
  728.7 728.11 728.14 728.16
  728.26 729.25 730.1 730.8

ISLAND (CONT.) 730.11 730.12
  730.13 730.28 730.37
  731.3 731.9 731.18 731.22
  731.25 731.28 731.42
  732.20 732.29 732.37
  732.38 733.3 733.4 733.5
  733.7 733.12 733.18 733.27
  733.36 734.9 734.19 734.37
  735.4 735.7 735.11 736.2
  736.5 736.13 737.35 737.40
  738.17 738.31 738.38 739.2
  739.25 739.29 740.8 740.19
  740.21 740.25 741.15
  741.38 743.2 743.13 743.26
  744.3 746.6 746.28 746.30

ISLANDER ML 722.21 722.22
  723.8 723.11 724.8 724.22
  724.31 725.4 725.35 725.41
  726.21 727.42 733.6 733.18
  734.25 734.26 734.38 735.6
  735.16 735.22 741.31 742.5

ISLANDERS ML 725.16 731.13

ISLANDER'S ML 726.18

ISLANDS ML 722.1 722.10
  723.9 738.16

ISLE ML 725.6

ISLES ML 738.19 740.5

ISLET ML 724.11 733.15
  734.17 736.8 738.6

ISNA WP 388.13

ISOLATE ML 724.13

ISOLATED WM 59.16 TF 119.21
  DV 137.30 138.7 138.9
  153.28 156.5 CH 278.16
  OC 300.34 RR 787.40

ISOLATION EA 87.23 SB 217.2
  OC 299.39 TB 519.28
  WR 546.16 GG 694.13

ISSUE WM 62.32 GF 240.8
  OC 301.24 HD 452.4
  GG 662.37

ISSUING MO 1.19 HT 42.31
  PO 106.27 FG 194.6
  SS 197.21 SU 529.13

ITALIAN EA 83.8 DV 165.10
  PR 477.14 SM 584.18
  NT 709.29 LL 762.41
  774.4 774.6 774.26
  777.13 TH 849.35 852.39

ITALIAN RENAISSANCE FG 187.31

ITALIANS TH 849.14

ITALY EA 78.17 79.12 88.39
  92.1 93.16 PR 475.1
  SM 582.27 NT 701.6
  TH 845.35 845.36 845.40
  845.41 847.7 847.18 849.14
  852.36

ITEM   TB 516.19   NT 708.34

IT'LL   DV 166.36   SB 215.33
  WS 248.38   SC 273.16   OC 287.33
  SD 412.35

IVORY   WM 70.2   LL 770.1   775.41
  BM 827.30

IVORY-COLOURED   WM 63.29   63.30

IVORY-INLAID   MD 818.5   823.32

IVORY-WHITE   BM 829.27

IVY   MO 3.13   DV 136.17   FG 187.10
  SS 202.25   SG 228.20   PP 434.20
  434.23   435.22

JAB   HT 40.28

JABBING   JD 606.38

JACK   DV 157.17   157.30   159.8
  159.9   159.13   159.21   GF 237.32
  242.4   242.7   242.12   243.4
  OC 291.24   291.30   PP 439.5
  HD 444.24   444.25   445.12
  445.28

JACK   (SEE MR. JACK)

JACK AND JILL   TH 846.39

JACKET   SP 51.37   DV 160.14
  SS 210.35   SG 221.18   227.12
  GG 694.10   ML 730.4

JACK FERGUSON   HD 444.7

JACK GOODALL   FA 471.30

JACK RIGLEY   OC 294.17

JACK'S   GF 240.27   OC 291.19

JACKSON   BM 835.2   838.24   838.31
  838.36   839.22

JACKSON   (SEE DOCTOR JACKSON;
  MR. JACKSON)

JADED   DV 142.39

JAGGED   GF 241.29

JAGUAR   NT 717.29

JAM   MO 14.11   JD 611.20

JAMES   LA 632.3   635.9   643.41

JAMES, WILLIAM   (SEE WILLIAM
  JAMES)

JAMMED   WS 249.36

JAMMING   LA 631.13

JAM-TARTS   HT 41.28

JANE   JD 611.16   611.17   612.7
  613.24   614.27   615.17   615.20
  624.33   626.13   628.38

JANE EYRE   MO 6.25

JANET   RR 780.35   781.4   781.9
  781.13   781.31   782.11   782.29
  782.42   784.19   784.35   785.23
  786.15

JANET DRUMMOND   RR 781.18   782.39

JANET'S   RR 785.20

JANGLE   EA 75.29

JANGLED   IL 647.24   ML 736.42

JANGLING   ML 736.37

JANUARY   EE 313.1   NT 712.41

JANUS   JD 619.38

JAPANESE   FA 465.4

JAR   MO 4.6   SS 207.4   HD 448.1
  WR 564.29   565.6

JARNDYCE, COUNCILLOR   (SEE
  COUNCILLOR JARNDYCE)

JARRED   SB 218.20

JARRING   BL 353.21

JAUNT   SP 52.19

JAUNTING   SP 51.29

JAUNTY   TP 334.25   HD 443.5
  ML 725.21

J'AVONS BIEN BU ET NOUS BOIRONS +
  GG 676.16

JAW   OA 31.18   35.30   EA 76.11
  77.19   PO 104.6   109.38   110.10
  TF 118.14   DV 144.2   156.13
  160.16   GF 243.1   WS 249.2
  WP 392.37   PP 434.9   HD 443.24
  WR 576.17   SM 585.4   GG 671.24

JAWING   SB 219.21

JAZZ   GG 685.12

JEALOUS   EA 87.5   TF 130.36
  WS 246.33   OC 299.31   TB 527.30
  WR 547.30   GG 680.1   NT 711.32

JEALOUSY   HT 40.35   40.36
  SU 543.29   GG 680.1   NT 711.33
  711.35

JEER   WS 261.4   HD 455.11

JEERED   EA 75.16   SG 232.16
  NT 710.25

JEERING   EA 71.8   74.39   TF 127.13
  SS 201.7   WS 261.35   263.12
  CH 282.5   MN 378.22   YT 395.36
  408.4   BO 598.40   JD 619.26
  IL 658.31   ML 731.33   LL 778.8

JEERINGLY   MN 370.39

JELLY   PR 502.18   GG 674.36
  NT 719.8

JENNY   SS 204.16

JEOPARDISING   IL 647.16

JEOPARDY   OA 30.9

JERK   OA 27.9   BL 351.29
  HD 443.17   PR 498.41
  SU 538.30   LA 633.16

JERKED   PO 109.28   109.40
  112.8   DV 180.25   GF 236.12
  OC 292.16   297.41   WP 393.4
  SD 421.35   PP 427.4   434.18
  440.14   WR 555.24   555.41
  JD 612.25   613.23   GG 678.17

JERKILY   PO 112.8

JERKING   PO 109.39   110.20
  WP 392.32   SD 418.3
  PP 432.16   HD 442.8
  FA 462.41   470.28   LA 632.39

JERKS   OA 25.42

JERKY   OA 36.35   PR 502.13

JERSEY   YT 400.30   408.15
  TB 521.16   ML 725.18
  726.32

JERUSALEM   GG 689.14

JESSDALE   HD 446.15

JESUIT   LL 774.28   774.29

JESUS   EE 311.13   322.21
  FA 468.5   468.7   GG 689.39
  690.25   OV 758.12

JESUS, LORD   (SEE LORD JESUS)

JET   DV 150.4   SS 198.13
  GF 240.15

JETSAM   WM 68.27

J'EUS B'EN BU +   GG 677.21

JEWELLERY   WS 265.6   NT 709.29

JEWEL-LIKE   SD 415.39

JEWELS   MO 19.26   WS 265.32
  GG 698.2   MD 809.26
  BM 834.32

JEWESS   LA 636.18

JEWISH   OA 23.5   LA 636.17

JEWISH-LOOKING   LA 643.9
  643.17

JEWS   PR 481.35   481.37   483.23
  MD 818.39

J. F.   JD 628.32

JIGGED   BO 594.3

JIGGERED GF 242.4

JILTED FA 459.11

JIM OC 297.2 297.13

JIMMY SB 215.19 215.30 217.18
217.37 217.38 218.20 219.25
JD 605.8 605.17 605.29 606.9
606.29 606.36 606.37 607.28
607.35 612.27 613.12 613.32
615.38 616.14 616.22 616.34
616.40 617.28 618.29 618.34
618.39 618.42 619.6 619.10
619.11 619.20 619.23 619.28
619.34 619.41 620.9 620.13
620.20 620.33 620.39 621.7
621.14 621.17 621.26 622.11
622.17 622.23 622.32 622.40
623.3 623.11 623.15 623.26
623.31 624.2 624.37 625.37
626.15 626.19 626.25 626.36
626.37 626.42 627.4 627.7
627.15 627.16 627.22 627.23
627.27 627.32 627.37 628.5
628.9 628.11 628.19 628.40

JIMMY BARRASS SB 215.25

JIMMY'S JD 605.15 605.18 620.37
629.13

JIM STOKES BM 843.5

JINNY FA 464.1 464.2 470.16
470.22 470.31 470.34 470.40
471.9 471.27 471.34 471.42
472.3

JINNY'S FA 470.16

JINTY'S SS 204.17

JOAN RH 793.20 794.7

JOB HT 38.9 39.11 SS 198.19
CH 279.16 OC 297.29 297.37
MN 366.1 367.17 WP 389.24
PP 430.10 HD 442.16 JD 620.2
ML 731.5 LL 766.26 RH 794.11
MD 805.1 809.38 814.9 815.8
TH 850.11 850.15 851.30
852.41

JOBS HT 40.29 EE 311.20 311.21
BL 362.31 JD 608.9 IL 648.41
ML 725.33

JOCKEY SP 52.37 RH 793.27

JOE OA 34.1 SP 45.31 45.33
46.2 46.3 MN 366.1 366.4
366.16 366.19 366.24 367.7
367.13 367.30 368.4 368.6
368.9 368.13 368.18 368.23
368.25 368.34 368.39 369.3
369.4 369.9 369.14 369.17
369.23 369.27 369.31 369.36
369.39 370.6 370.18 370.20
370.22 370.31 370.35 370.39
370.42 371.5 371.23 371.33
371.34 372.9 372.33 372.34
372.37 372.39 373.7 373.12
373.25 373.34 373.38 373.40
373.42 374.3 374.13 374.19

JOE (CONT.) 374.25 374.27
374.42 375.8 375.11 375.14
375.18 375.20 375.23 375.26
375.38 375.41 376.2 376.8
376.13 376.42 377.10 377.37
378.4 378.8 378.13 378.14
378.15 378.21 378.22 378.30
378.35 HD 441.2 441.30
442.12 442.29 442.33 443.1
443.14 443.28 444.3 444.9
444.16 444.24 444.34 445.2
445.10 445.14 IL 647.22
647.28 648.11 648.18 648.22
648.25 648.38 649.6 649.8
649.22 650.2 650.9 650.11
650.27 651.15 652.2 652.4
652.25 652.40 652.41 653.17
653.30 654.12 654.24 654.26
654.32 655.1 655.10 655.12
655.30 656.1 656.3 656.13
656.17 656.33 656.39 657.21
657.33 658.12 658.16 658.30
659.42 660.3 660.5 RR 787.10
787.18 788.15 789.7

JOE'D IL 654.5

JOE GLEE RH 797.24

JOES MN 367.36

JOE'S MN 367.38 371.41 372.23
373.16 374.1 374.9 374.11
374.37 375.33 IL 650.9 650.35
651.12 651.19 651.24 653.2
653.5 653.9 653.16 653.21
657.4

JOEY WP 382.17 382.20 382.27
382.28 382.34 383.27 384.8
386.22 386.24 386.29 387.23
387.36 388.7 390.29 392.41
393.14

JOHN SP 46.17 46.20 DV 148.6
OC 284.14 287.18 287.23
288.15 290.1 SD 420.39
ML 727.12

JOHN ADDERLEY SYSON SS 198.38

JOHN BERRYMAN CH 281.28

JOHN COTTON SG 227.3

JOHN DURANT DV 140.3

JOHN MERFIN SP 46.13

JOHN MILTON DV 140.38

JOHNNY SU 540.8 540.9 540.23
540.30

JOHN THOMAS RAYNOR TP 336.23

JOHN THOMAS TP 336.24 336.26
336.38 337.23 337.33 337.37
338.3 338.7 338.21 338.32
338.39 339.1 339.3 339.13
339.30 339.34 340.16 340.22
340.27 340.33 340.37 340.40
341.22 341.24 341.28 341.36
342.1 342.11 342.37

JOHN WESLEY DV 140.38

JOHN WHARMBY SP 47.29 48.4
48.20 48.31 50.8 50.21
50.24 50.36

JOIE DE VIVRE SB 214.20

JOIN TF 118.7 131.17
DV 143.9 FG 193.31
EE 327.24 327.42

JOINED DV 141.21 142.11
EE 328.14 TP 344.5
WP 382.1 YT 396.33
FA 464.2

JOINED-TOGETHER ML 733.21

JOINT EE 317.32

JOINTS TF 120.15 120.16
OV 752.18

JOKE SB 212.31 EE 326.25
PR 482.32 BO 587.9
NT 714.20 OV 756.5
LL 776.7 RH 795.18

JOKES MO 17.31 MN 368.10

JOKY SUTTON PP 429.25

JOLLY WM 57.39 DV 168.14
OC 295.4 PP 435.22
LA 639.11 IL 647.27
649.29 GG 678.3 LL 771.15
BM 829.6

JOLT BO 593.17

JOLTED SS 197.23

JOLTING OC 283.10 PP 435.36

JOSEPH GROOBY SP 45.31

JOSEPH PERVIN HD 446.27

JOSEPH WILLIAM CH 280.11
280.12

JOT WS 260.22

JOURNALISM BO 589.22

JOURNALIST BO 591.30 602.6

JOURNEY EA 83.8 SB 212.16
SG 222.7 WR 574.2 BO 604.41
JD 627.37 RH 793.7

JOURNEYS RR 780.36

JOVE PP 431.10 OV 756.1
RR 779.23

JOVIAL SU 532.31

JOY MO 16.39 17.22 OA 24.16
33.4 37.12 EA 90.38
TF 123.34 130.26 132.9
DV 159.5 173.1 182.11
FG 188.27 SG 225.15
CH 282.26 BL 347.28 348.5

JOY (CONT.)

JOY (CONT.) 348.9 348.16 348.24
   348.29 PP 430.3 HD 454.32
   FA 466.29 466.37 PR 504.31
   SU 532.10 538.32 NT 712.34
   ML 730.29 730.31 739.15
   OV 753.23 753.37 754.40
   757.16 757.40 758.23 759.17
   759.18 LL 777.21 TH 851.1

JOYCE EE 309.9 310.9 316.18
   316.32 316.38 317.7 317.35
   318.8 318.13 318.14 318.25
   318.30 319.3 319.10 319.12
   319.13 319.19 319.28 320.13
   320.20 321.10 321.26 321.35
   322.8 322.9 324.19 325.7
   325.10 328.34 329.14

JOYCE'S EE 319.36

JOYCEY EE 317.41

JOYFUL SU 539.18

JUAN WR 550.36

JUBILANT LA 638.18

JUDGE GF 241.13 FA 468.6 468.7

JUDGED SM 582.26 MD 823.25

JUDGEST FA 468.10

JUDGMENT DV 153.1 WS 256.11
   BO 588.27 592.19 OV 759.1
   BM 835.35

JUDGMENT DAY OV 752.34

JUDICIOUS SD 419.13 422.8

JUDICIOUSLY DV 158.22

JUG DV 139.36 139.39 140.8

JUGS GF 241.19

JUICY TB 521.39

JULIA PP 428.18

JULIE SU 539.30 541.7

JULIET SU 529.26 529.29 529.37
   530.12 533.27 533.30 535.24
   535.35 537.23 538.6 538.14
   538.18 538.26 538.36 540.12
   540.20 540.41 542.33 543.1
   543.10 543.35 544.14 544.23

JULIET'S SU 533.24 538.29

JULY LL 774.35

JUMBLE TF 122.2 OC 296.40

JUMP OA 24.18 FG 188.5
   WS 253.35 EE 329.34 TP 334.31
   MN 378.9 WR 555.14 GG 684.28
   ML 745.40 MD 807.3

JUMPED PO 109.40 TF 123.16
   DV 157.26 WR 553.18 ML 724.5
   741.8

JUMPER PR 506.19 BM 831.10

JUMPING DV 157.27

JUMPING-OFF ML 724.4

JUMPS ML 741.8

JUNCTURE SP 48.38 DV 186.1
   SB 216.1

JUNE OA 24.7

JUNGLE EE 313.32 JD 610.32
   NT 716.2

JUNIOR PR 480.41

JUSTICE EA 90.12 DV 147.27
   149.36

JUSTIFIED MO 11.5 HT 41.27
   PO 100.15

JUSTIFY NT 711.15

JUSTIFYING MO 10.14

JUSTLY DV 141.16 OV 752.11

JUTTED PR 494.27 494.35

JUTTING DV 166.12 SG 225.13
   SU 539.23 WR 579.18

KALEIDOSCOPE OV 755.10

KANGAROO PR 510.31

KATE OA 23.22 23.29 28.7 28.13
   28.26 28.39 28.42 29.5 34.5
   34.12 36.9 36.31 37.31 38.41

KATE, AUNT (SEE AUNT KATE)

KATE'S OA 28.6 33.40 34.28

KATHERINE BO 587.29 588.5
   588.24 588.27 588.34 588.42
   589.29 590.1 590.17 591.39
   593.4 599.42 600.6 601.28
   601.34 602.5 602.35 603.24
   604.23 604.36

KATHERINE ANSTRUTHER BO 601.12

KATHERINE FARQUHAR BO 587.1
   588.1 599.21 601.7 601.14

KATHERINE'S BO 600.17 604.31

KATHERINE VON TODTNAU BO 601.11

KATHY BO 602.13 603.15

KEEN WM 55.2 61.34 62.9 65.3
   EA 90.38 PO 104.32 114.5
   FG 191.34 191.39 SB 214.26
   GF 242.7 CH 278.38 EE 303.9
   MN 368.21 372.39 WP 380.12
   392.30 YT 402.40 PP 433.18
   FA 463.7 463.8 PR 484.14
   WR 563.42 LA 637.39 GG 667.28
   ML 743.29 OV 747.34 RR 784.18
   RH 796.32 TH 846.26

KEEN-EARED LL 766.19

KEEN-EYED TH 844.3

KEENLY MO 6.12 13.14
   DV 144.37 172.30 SS 209.6
   GF 236.9 MN 373.35
   SU 533.24 WR 565.36
   OV 757.17 RR 782.16

KEEPER SS 198.1 198.18
   198.20 198.25 198.34
   198.36 199.7 199.13
   199.19 199.26 199.32
   199.39 200.10 200.14
   200.21 205.27 208.35
   209.6 209.11 209.14 209.17
   209.39 210.33 211.2 211.10
   SG 228.5 MN 377.4

KEEPER'S SS 197.12 206.20
   211.25

KEEPIN' SP 47.20

KEEPING MO 2.12 13.13 15.8
   OA 28.20 HT 42.20 PO 100.15
   111.27 DV 151.28 152.16
   172.42 SS 199.14 GF 242.38
   CH 274.13 278.22 EE 317.27
   TP 336.18 WP 380.18
   PP 427.5 HD 446.37
   PR 497.31 WR 559.29
   BO 594.33 596.32 GG 684.1
   ML 734.41 LL 761.13
   RR 785.2 MD 810.33
   TH 853.23

KEEPS OC 287.41 EE 313.33
   PP 428.26 FA 471.36
   RH 795.26 795.33 802.4
   802.5

KEHL BO 599.14

KEN WS 255.24

KENDAL (SEE MR. KENDAL)

KENILWORTH TB 516.23

KENT ML 726.14

KERB PP 427.3 436.1
   MD 808.10

KERBSTONE HD 444.4

KERCHIEF PR 495.28 499.4
   499.19 506.20

KERNEL SB 213.13 213.26

KERNELS SS 203.30

KERNEL-WHITE SS 203.7

KETTLE WS 244.31 247.24
   OC 299.3 PR 500.34

KEY OA 28.13 SS 206.23
   TP 345.36 ML 738.8
   MD 815.28

KEYS HD 447.18 RR 780.6

KITTENS NT 712.18 712.32

KNACK RH 799.15

KNAPSACK PO 105.13

KNAPSACKS PO 95.15

KNEADING BL 358.8

KNEE OA 26.17 EA 73.15 73.27
  PO 110.4 DV 159.15 SG 226.9
  WS 256.21 EE 317.5 317.6
  317.12 317.26 317.31 318.2
  318.16 318.40 319.6 319.21
  319.24 319.30 319.36 320.1
  320.5 320.21 320.26 320.40
  321.3 321.12 322.5 323.8
  PR 491.4 491.11 491.23 491.25
  491.33 492.32 GG 692.5

KNEE-BREECHES WP 388.29

KNEEL DV 157.30

KNEELED OA 36.14 DV 149.20
  159.2 CH 281.19 OC 299.32
  HD 451.12 PR 510.23 JD 617.25
  MD 814.11

KNEELING MO 4.2 OA 36.18
  DV 161.32 170.17 SC 268.36
  TP 343.23 345.1 PR 497.41
  BO 595.6 GG 679.26

KNEES MO 5.42 7.17 EA 75.41
  90.41 PO 110.19 TF 121.4
  DV 151.37 FG 190.36 195.29
  SB 213.8 GF 241.6 WS 254.42
  256.19 261.23 TP 335.21
  BL 349.5 354.29 360.5
  SD 421.19 421.38 423.22
  423.28 424.36 HD 443.16
  443.28 452.40 452.42 453.7
  453.8 453.17 454.10 PR 473.17
  490.41 491.15 510.15
  SU 530.32 WR 558.14 564.22
  BO 603.34 JD 617.25 617.39
  628.20 GG 685.26 696.25
  NT 715.25 MD 810.30 813.30
  824.40 TH 848.16

KNELT MO 4.41 CH 280.14 281.15
  OC 299.4 TP 343.26 PR 510.36
  GG 679.28

KNEW MO 3.8 4.28 18.2 OA 27.1
  38.4 HT 40.29 SP 50.36 52.2
  WM 54.1 58.7 58.35 62.29
  65.1 69.37 EA 73.31 76.6
  76.7 79.39 79.41 80.28 80.29
  82.18 88.7 89.5 89.39 90.12
  92.29 92.40 93.15 PO 96.38
  98.4 98.19 99.7 104.13
  104.14 104.26 104.33 107.38
  111.15 112.27 112.35 TF 120.3
  120.12 120.17 120.18 120.19
  120.31 122.19 124.31 128.8
  134.36 DV 137.35 144.2 147.8
  150.27 150.28 151.34 152.33
  154.5 160.14 161.19 162.20
  164.11 165.6 165.9 169.10
  177.5 177.30 177.39 180.6
  181.40 183.13 184.21
  FG 189.38 190.12 190.40 191.7

KNEW (CONT.) 191.30 193.13
  194.36 194.41 SS 203.23
  203.38 208.2 210.19 SB 217.27
  217.35 217.39 SG 223.12
  225.19 226.30 230.26 231.17
  231.19 231.20 231.27 232.25
  GF 235.12 239.31 240.2 240.3
  242.42 WS 248.14 249.1 254.25
  260.20 261.7 262.17 263.12
  265.17 SC 270.7 271.5 273.2
  OC 290.32 291.28 292.37
  297.31 297.32 300.27 300.41
  301.15 301.25 301.31 302.13
  EE 310.41 311.10 311.41
  314.19 315.29 326.10 326.40
  327.33 327.37 332.1 TP 337.4
  337.26 338.1 338.26 339.17
  340.27 BL 348.6 353.8 357.12
  359.28 359.39 361.3 364.21
  365.11 MN 368.15 368.29
  370.11 371.30 WP 382.13
  386.19 390.31 YT 395.35
  396.23 400.40 401.17 403.8
  406.33 408.2 SD 411.31 415.2
  417.22 425.4 PP 428.18 428.38
  428.40 430.24 434.26 434.38
  435.39 436.16 HD 450.31
  452.21 452.27 455.11 456.1
  456.37 FA 459.4 460.7 460.12
  462.37 463.39 465.40 466.1
  467.20 469.2 469.27 PR 476.31
  477.26 479.13 480.30 480.36
  483.34 484.4 484.18 484.24
  485.34 488.25 500.15 501.28
  507.4 507.36 509.1 TB 513.7
  514.1 514.29 516.9 517.20
  517.35 517.37 519.2 519.26
  SU 532.31 532.36 533.1 534.5
  534.7 536.17 542.36 543.36
  544.25 WR 551.30 556.2 557.26
  559.40 560.2 566.26 567.37
  573.28 577.27 577.28 578.40
  580.11 580.39 SM 584.30
  BO 588.13 591.21 593.11
  596.14 596.36 597.11 597.18
  597.26 597.38 598.13 598.23
  600.23 603.34 JD 605.19 610.7
  619.25 627.19 627.27 LA 635.3
  640.20 641.12 646.23
  IL 659.30 GG 661.1 662.10
  663.14 665.17 665.31 668.28
  672.18* 673.26 678.30 679.2
  679.5 679.13 682.34 682.41
  683.13 689.5 691.34 693.1
  693.5 693.23 693.41 694.30
  696.7 698.8 699.9 NT 701.28
  703.23 704.19 705.20 705.32
  705.39 706.8 706.18 710.30
  710.42 715.8 715.17 715.39
  716.12 718.42 719.12 720.16
  ML 726.20 726.32 728.10 729.4
  729.7 731.30 731.32 736.15
  737.35 740.36 743.34 746.26
  746.32 746.36 OV 748.6 750.33
  755.4 758.2 LL 761.37 762.1
  763.18 763.28 764.1 764.5
  768.16 768.25 771.27 773.30
  774.24 RR 781.32 782.15
  784.13 785.34 RH 790.8 790.12
  790.16 793.14 793.17 799.25
  801.16 803.4 804.19 804.22
  MD 805.12 805.31 816.11
  820.41 823.11 825.17
  BM 827.18 828.28 833.5 836.36
  838.10 839.20 839.40

KNEW (CONT.) TH 844.34 847.4
  851.20

KNICKERS WS 261.30

KNIFE MO 5.32 WM 55.3
  FG 191.40 192.19 192.28
  192.31 194.22 CH 274.22
  276.36 OC 286.17 BL 358.8
  WR 580.36 580.38 NT 704.26

KNIFE-POINT BL 358.42

KNIGHT WM 64.34 SS 210.15
  TB 516.22

KNIPE, SIR (SEE SIR KNIPE)

KNIT SD 414.10

KNITS HT 39.32

KNITTED MO 15.2 EA 79.22
  DV 168.39 WS 253.24
  TB 521.25 RR 784.24
  BM 831.10

KNITTING HT 39.25 SB 214.37

KNIVES WR 563.42 580.32
  ML 724.29

KNOB DV 159.9 BM 834.35
  836.21

KNOBS SB 217.9 YT 397.38

KNOCK EA 74.27 DV 139.13
  TP 340.1 LA 635.35

KNOCKED HT 42.37 TF 124.1
  124.5 DV 161.3 161.12
  GF 242.42 OC 297.21
  EE 330.37 BL 352.14 359.7
  363.33 PP 436.33 JD 610.38
  624.28 LA 635.38 635.41
  636.8 636.22 IL 650.19
  GG 685.33 MD 813.11 816.26
  816.32 817.3 BM 830.5

KNOCKIN' SB 218.37

KNOCKING MO 3.20 PO 112.21
  112.25 112.29 112.32
  112.36 PR 509.37 WR 562.27
  MD 816.33

KNOCK-OUT WP 393.10 HD 444.34

KNOCKS SB 218.32 EE 305.23

KNOLL PO 106.38 107.9
  SU 530.6 532.24

KNOT TF 117.30 SD 422.35
  PR 496.35 497.5

KNOTCH SS 206.28

KNOTS WR 565.4

KNOTTED OC 299.5 BL 351.22
  FA 458.11

KNOW MO 8.7 10.25 10.26

LAMP-GLASS OC 288.29

LAMPLIGHT OA 30.13 WM 63.24
  IL 652.34

LAMP-LIGHT OA 29.37 FA 460.10

LAMP-LIT IL 654.12

LAMP-POST FA 460.9

LAMPS WM 54.24 58.41 60.28
  60.34 63.17 DV 166.12 166.29
  182.23 WS 251.29 OC 286.30
  290.35 BL 355.22 356.14
  MN 371.13 FA 462.2 LA 630.3
  630.4 631.29 OV 747.2
  TH 853.22

LAMP'S OC 287.4

LAMP-SHADE OA 29.18

LAMP-STAND WM 70.4

LANCE-CORPORAL GOYTE WP 380.32

LANCELOT RH 796.6 796.8 796.9

LAND MO 1.13 OA 37.6 SP 53.2
  PO 95.19 106.41 113.35 115.14
  TF 125.41 131.17 132.29
  FG 187.5 SS 197.24 EE 304.30
  329.35 329.41 TP 336.7
  SD 411.24 PP 430.32 HD 450.33
  FA 467.38 PR 482.17 SU 543.21
  BO 600.9 IL 653.17 NT 708.7
  ML 729.22 740.24 744.24
  OV 751.15 752.10

LANDED TF 119.37 121.4
  PR 484.19 ML 738.25 739.36
  TH 848.34

LAND-GIRL MN 367.10 372.1

LAND-GIRLS BL 351.41 MN 366.36

LANDING OA 34.5 34.9 35.20
  35.22 35.35 38.5 DV 148.21
  148.28

LANDING-BAY ML 722.27

LANDING-PLACE ML 722.25 733.20

LANDLADIES MO 14.8 14.17

LANDLADY MO 14.3 14.25 OA 37.41
  HT 39.31 40.4 40.11 40.19
  41.3 DV 162.9 162.12
  SG 222.26 229.42 SD 412.8
  412.11 412.15 414.9 415.11
  415.21 415.28 415.34 415.39
  416.1 418.10 418.39 419.14
  419.26 419.32 419.41 JD 616.7
  616.8

LANDLORD OA 33.4 33.37 35.4
  36.18 36.27 MN 370.1
  PP 435.30

LANDLORD'S OA 35.18 36.3 36.33

LAND'S SU 538.3

LANDSCAPE EE 310.20 HD 449.21
  PR 482.42 483.17 489.19
  BO 593.17 593.18

LANE DV 138.15 FG 194.37
  SG 224.13 EE 304.7 321.5
  MN 373.6 376.38 377.8
  HD 442.1 442.5 442.9
  JD 610.18 610.28 IL 653.1
  654.39 656.23 658.14

LANES DV 136.3 PP 430.30
  GG 699.4 BM 830.8

LANGUAGE PO 114.33 DV 157.1
  SS 204.31 SB 218.14 CH 281.16
  PP 429.39 FA 471.17 PR 484.34
  WR 564.36 566.11 BO 599.23
  NT 704.22 ML 728.20 LL 773.42
  MD 809.40

LANGUAGES MD 809.36

LANGUID EA 73.17 PP 438.39

LANGUIDLY MO 12.30 13.13

LANGUOR WR 565.30 565.31 568.11
  GG 662.17

LANGUOROUS WR 566.31*

LANK GG 668.39

LANKY FA 467.22

LANTERN MO 18.8 BL 352.40 362.8
  362.15 364.35 PR 501.32
  503.13

LANTERNS ML 729.41

LANTHORN FG 192.5 192.19 192.34
  193.2

LAOCOON FG 187.30 SD 421.5

LAP OA 30.3 TF 123.39 SB 213.8
  WS 252.22 CH 276.40 279.1
  EE 317.6 WP 388.17 HD 455.6
  PR 493.41 494.2 SU 537.11
  GG 690.2 BM 838.7 838.18

LA POMPADOUR MD 809.14

LAPPED MO 5.35 OV 755.23

LAPPING BL 355.33

LAPSE PO 116.3 SG 226.7
  CH 279.14 EE 332.2 332.4
  332.30 333.5 WR 547.15

LAPSED PO 113.15 WS 252.27
  EE 332.8 BL 348.21 360.33
  WR 551.40 JD 626.25 RR 787.13
  BM 833.34

LAPSES GF 241.39 OC 295.12
  WR 570.11

LAPSING WM 55.34 DV 177.28
  TP 339.37

LARCH FG 195.18 MN 376.18

LARCHES SS 203.42

LARCHWOOD FG 195.3

LARD CH 274.20

LARGE MO 1.8 2.7 2.18 2.22
  3.13 4.5 4.42 13.21 19.9
  OA 25.3 34.10 HT 39.7
  39.22 SP 48.32 51.21
  51.23 WM 58.33 63.31
  EA 72.19 72.42 TF 121.4
  125.23 DV 139.39 139.42
  142.27 170.18 FG 187.3
  193.33 SS 206.35 WS 250.23
  250.37 251.16 254.37
  255.25 SC 271.18 CH 274.22
  275.42 278.17 OC 283.32
  287.9 292.10 EE 321.22
  332.3 TP 338.14 BL 351.7
  352.2 352.34 354.28
  357.25 358.12 358.32
  362.21 MN 367.2 367.24
  376.35 WP 385.29 386.12
  388.5 390.10 YT 395.4
  403.4 SD 414.11 419.33
  422.4 423.39 424.1
  HD 446.22 446.29 448.24
  FA 460.42 463.18 PR 481.29
  SU 530.5 542.38 WR 547.12
  550.40 551.10 553.37
  554.19 554.20 555.17 578.1
  578.5 580.33 BO 603.29
  JD 618.5 619.18 LA 633.6
  634.17 GG 696.6 NT 709.22
  ML 725.28 OV 747.20
  RR 785.24

LARGE-FEATURED SM 584.11

LARGELY GF 239.13 BL 352.15
  PR 480.10 SM 584.40
  IL 648.18

LARGE-NOSED YT 397.31

LARGER DV 145.10

LARGEST FG 187.1 WP 386.16

LARK GF 242.30

LARKED YT 394.16

LARKS SS 210.22 210.33

LARYNX GG 675.2

LASHED FG 189.7 ML 728.22
  728.26

LASHES WM 69.35 SS 202.29
  PP 437.12 SU 542.24
  WR 565.10 567.35 JD 606.24
  625.12 MD 818.37 821.29
  822.9

LASKELL, ELSA (SEE ELSA
  LASKELL)

LASS HT 40.15 TP 337.1
  WP 388.27

LASSES TP 335.25 WP 392.25
  YT 394.26

LASSITUDE BL 351.16   MD 808.33

LAST   MO 7.27   8.22   16.35   17.23
  OA 23.31   28.1   28.6   28.16
  29.41   30.3   33.26   33.33   36.35
  38.2   HT 43.27   SP 45.7   51.16
  WM 55.23   55.26   55.33   60.25
  60.37   67.41   69.20   EA 71.15
  76.6   76.22   76.29   79.5   80.15
  82.8   88.10   88.33   93.32
  PO 98.38   100.17   100.32   104.7
  104.15   104.28   106.36   107.21
  108.14   112.9   114.38   TF 119.22
  119.36   126.25   133.34
  DV 137.13   140.29   141.26
  141.40   142.41   143.17   155.36
  163.41   168.26   181.12   181.23
  181.31   185.26   FG 187.7   191.21
  191.23   191.30   SS 199.25   202.8
  204.8   211.30   211.32   SG 222.34
  224.41   225.41   229.24   232.36
  233.9   GF 234.5   238.33   238.40
  239.3   239.4   239.8   239.35
  239.36   240.14   240.27
  WS 247.36   248.38   251.12
  259.14   259.31   261.27   263.27
  264.39   SC 270.1   CH 274.24
  278.18   280.6   OC 286.2   289.21
  289.37   298.35   299.7   299.42
  302.9   EE 313.22   314.31   315.18
  331.29   TP 334.10   334.21
  340.22   341.16   343.23   343.28
  BL 350.9   351.10   352.42   354.7
  358.37   362.13   364.3   MN 369.12
  371.36   373.6   373.25   373.34
  376.41   WP 381.35   386.29
  388.42   389.15   YT 396.25
  396.33   401.28   402.13   404.25
  405.27   407.11   408.33   409.9
  SD 415.22   415.30   422.36
  PP 428.5   432.14   432.28
  HD 441.25   442.9   443.32   450.29
  451.7   FA 464.34   464.39   467.35
  467.36   468.28   469.4   PR 474.11
  475.36   475.37   476.6   479.20
  480.11   482.16   482.20   482.21
  487.7   489.23   491.12   492.18
  496.29   499.16   505.29   506.7
  508.39   509.32   509.38   TB 514.8
  514.9   SU 528.16   529.4   529.8
  529.32   530.24   538.27
  WR 547.24   552.28   556.4   558.23
  558.33   563.16   569.29   577.24
  577.37   579.9   579.20   580.12
  SM 583.16   BO 589.30   596.3
  598.7   599.27   600.8   600.36
  603.28   JD 605.6   610.33   613.34
  618.17   619.20   627.6   627.23
  LA 631.42   641.23   641.40
  641.41   641.42   643.8   643.36
  645.31   IL 651.16   GG 666.21
  667.25   683.38   688.35   695.20
  697.14   698.35   699.21
  NT 701.12   702.16   703.9   712.11
  713.29   713.31   713.32   714.42
  ML 725.6   729.24   733.10   733.24
  733.31   734.18   735.16   735.36
  737.41   739.11   742.23   744.42
  745.42   OV 754.9   LL 762.19
  768.1   769.6   772.38   773.35
  774.38   775.4   776.36   778.14
  RR 783.38   785.42   788.29
  RH 790.29   793.17   793.35   794.4
  MD 807.33   814.40   816.28
  817.16   817.37   821.22   826.4

LAST (CONT.)   826.11   BM 828.24
  828.33   829.31   830.6   840.28
  841.42   TH 847.38   848.35
  849.31   853.33

LASTED   DV 174.36   GG 691.4
  ML 740.10   MD 807.24

LASTS   SU 544.17   OV 748.9

LATCH   MO 10.31   WM 70.21
  SS 208.35   OC 286.39   MD 815.28

LATCH-GATE   DV 174.12

LATCH-KEY   WM 63.27

LATE   MO 13.36   OA 31.33   38.15
  WM 61.40   FG 192.23   GF 234.7
  237.19   WS 244.23   251.24
  251.36   SC 269.32   OC 285.22
  287.1   287.15   BL 352.25   352.30
  358.20   MN 374.4   YT 401.25
  405.27   PP 427.25   HD 446.32
  FA 465.14   470.7   PR 488.26
  WR 547.36   550.20   564.42
  JD 615.30   624.2   628.22
  GG 667.15   693.39   NT 708.37
  720.26   ML 733.27   737.15
  745.15   LL 771.40   773.8
  RR 783.16   MD 810.31   BM 833.8

LATE-AT-NIGHT   YT 402.6

LATE-FLOWERING   ML 730.22

LATELY   WM 65.31   EA 80.37
  PO 108.35   PR 497.14   WR 553.41
  IL 647.20   LL 768.26   RR 782.23
  RH 799.8

LATENT   PR 485.33

LATER   MO 6.34   WM 59.21   64.39
  EA 77.34   93.7   93.16   PO 116.10
  DV 178.8   FG 192.4   CH 277.25
  BL 358.3   361.24   YT 401.19
  PP 430.5   PR 477.10   508.13
  512.26   WR 577.31   BO 590.19
  597.2   JD 626.24   GG 664.26
  666.4   666.15   667.17   NT 704.18
  708.22   716.41   720.29
  ML 742.37   OV 752.13   RR 778.32
  RH 799.6   MD 807.1   814.7
  TH 844.20

LATEST   ML 735.39

LATHER   WM 64.31   DV 170.22
  YT 397.12   397.22   399.8

LATHKILL   GG 667.18   668.23
  700.12

LATHKILL   (SEE LADY, LORD
  LATHKILL)

LATIN   OA 26.20   FA 464.34
  BO 593.28   ML 728.2   RH 800.20

LATIN AMERICA   NT 701.33

LATINS   BO 593.1

LATTER   MO 12.23   18.2   WM 59.22

LATTER (CONT.)   PO 99.31
  TF 121.27   133.21   134.14
  134.21   DV 148.29   171.19
  SS 209.17   SG 228.10
  GF 234.15   EE 327.16
  PR 477.11   TB 522.41
  WR 555.5   RR 780.31   788.8

LATTICE   OA 29.14   29.24

LAUGH   MO 2.41   8.6   19.38
  OA 27.6   38.32   SP 47.16
  48.25   WM 55.35   56.34
  57.19   57.29   68.26   EA 71.1
  73.27   73.41   85.17   85.22
  85.36   90.34   92.37
  DV 146.10   150.25   168.3
  182.32   182.36   SB 213.34
  219.38   220.1   SG 222.19
  GF 242.37   243.8   WS 251.35
  257.41   CH 275.1   OC 289.7
  300.20   300.21   TP 344.4
  344.16   345.29   MN 368.10
  WP 381.26   381.33   382.26
  383.25   392.3   YT 402.11
  FA 461.8   PR 482.32   495.13
  495.21   SU 533.20   533.23
  533.29   538.15   538.21
  538.32   540.5   WR 575.39
  JD 615.18   LA 630.25   632.24
  633.2   635.25   637.26   638.34
  640.42   641.2   641.40   641.41
  641.42   643.7   643.13   643.21
  643.23   643.36   643.38
  644.39   646.14   646.24
  IL 648.9   656.40   GG 673.23
  673.38   681.14   689.5   689.29
  LL 761.17   762.2   765.8
  773.22   RH 792.27   792.31
  BM 840.25

LAUGHED   MO 7.33   8.6   8.28
  9.13   9.18   11.10   13.17
  14.22   14.27   15.1   15.22
  17.1   17.40   19.33   19.38
  20.3   20.9   20.20   20.24
  20.37   OA 24.1   24.24   25.1
  25.35   25.37   26.5   27.7
  27.22   27.39   28.27   29.42
  34.29   35.5   35.9   HT 43.19
  SP 46.12   WM 56.39   57.6
  57.15   57.30   61.34   62.4
  62.8   62.18   62.27   63.12
  65.14   65.40   65.42   66.4
  66.5   66.42   67.12   67.32
  68.19   68.20   68.30
  EA 74.31   75.37   78.5   85.6
  85.26   85.39   87.22   91.25
  PO 99.28   TF 127.1   DV 167.1
  179.9   182.2   182.11   182.17
  182.32   FG 189.22   SS 199.24
  201.39   203.26   206.10
  206.41   207.15   207.19
  207.29   208.34   211.20
  SB 212.26   213.37   215.1
  215.38   218.1   218.6   218.28
  219.6   219.10   219.23   219.38
  SG 223.5   223.22   GF 234.32
  243.4   WS 248.5   252.7
  254.18   260.39   263.31
  CH 275.1   OC 285.39   288.16
  TP 341.27   341.35   BL 352.11
  358.25   MN 371.21   371.33
  WP 380.16   383.6   385.13
  385.16   385.25   390.17   392.5

LAUGHED (CONT.) 392.18 393.2
YT 398.25 407.33 408.6
SD 412.33 HD 441.35 FA 461.14
461.30 PR 495.20 SU 534.8
534.15 BO 601.29 601.33
LA 637.25 637.30 638.33
640.42 IL 656.8 GG 663.27
672.13 672.37 NT 712.26
OV 756.9 LL 775.15 RH 795.13
795.31 802.4 BM 840.24

LAUGHING MO 14.4 14.40 OA 25.22
25.29 25.41 26.31 26.33
27.17 28.33 35.24 35.26
SP 47.9 WM 55.27 56.23
EA 75.37 91.10 91.22 TF 118.8
DV 144.4 158.13 SS 203.21
211.7 SG 223.32 226.2
WS 246.8 247.23 247.30
TP 338.11 342.7 BL 355.7
MN 371.26 WP 390.1 SD 411.36
414.42 SU 534.3 538.28
WR 576.10 BO 601.22 JD 606.21
LA 632.4 632.5 632.14 633.3
633.14 633.15 635.23 636.7
636.8 636.19 638.26 639.23
640.5 640.31 642.22 642.39
643.4 643.15 643.30 644.31
NT 703.30 709.7 RH 795.25
797.29 798.23

LAUGHINGLY OA 26.38

LAUGHS LA 641.39

LAUGHTER MO 2.19 2.41 3.2 8.42
OA 25.40 25.42 26.11 27.10
SP 47.7 WM 56.28 56.31 62.8
63.13 68.1 EA 71.8 75.8
WS 263.37 WP 383.23 393.8
393.15 SD 412.34 413.7
SM 583.37 BO 601.23 JD 613.5
619.41 620.14 LA 633.20
633.28 633.30 635.27 639.25
639.34 639.36 640.3 641.39
642.23 644.18 644.26 645.7
645.13 646.4 GG 665.6 667.5
668.25 676.38 684.28
NT 712.27 RH 795.23

LAUNDRESS TB 516.7

LAUNDRY TB 516.4 RR 785.41

LAURA WM 56.9 56.23 56.39 57.6
57.15 57.17 57.36 57.39 58.1
59.6 59.17 TP 341.29 341.41
342.10 344.6 344.19 345.18
345.35 346.1

LAURA SHARP TP 340.36 341.14
341.20

LAURA'S WM 59.8 61.14

LAURELS GG 661.8

LAURESTINUS GG 674.11 674.26

LAURIE ROWBOTHAM CH 281.31

LAURIERS EA 85.12

LAVA SU 529.7

LAVISH MD 806.32

LAVISHLY FG 193.42 LL 762.35

LAW OA 31.11 32.21 EE 308.18
325.37 SD 419.40 419.42
NT 707.34 LL 763.5 763.10
771.24

LAWLESS WR 550.23

LAWLESSNESS TP 340.31

LAWN DV 158.39 SG 221.21 224.19
225.7 225.10 YT 394.8
HD 441.22 TB 521.19 524.35
SM 583.35 ML 728.32 OV 749.12
LL 765.6

LAWNS EE 304.41

LAWS EA 75.36 EE 314.25 325.39
GG 662.32

LAW-SUITS SG 227.5

LAWYER BL 363.30 364.4
YT 406.41 RH 798.40 799.36
MD 824.34

LAWYER'S OA 33.12 RH 799.26

LAY MO 5.41 6.37 8.19 9.22
13.19 OA 26.14 27.26 35.42
38.17 WM 53.15 61.36 68.5
68.9 69.20 EA 72.11 86.12
93.7 PO 103.32 104.27 107.19
108.40 111.4 112.37 113.15
115.37 116.17 TF 117.3 120.29
120.36 125.36 126.16 126.23
130.12 DV 143.1 148.10 149.14
159.31 162.16 171.21 174.36
184.7 FG 189.22 189.28 190.2
190.3 190.39 191.6 191.23
192.1 192.38 195.8 SS 197.23
200.3 210.15 SB 216.16
SG 224.17 225.12 WS 244.6
244.23 245.27 254.26 257.39
265.29 266.3 SC 267.22
CH 274.22 OC 289.29 296.14
296.24 296.26 297.19 299.3
299.14 302.3 EE 307.6 315.16
317.22 322.41 TP 343.28 344.1
344.11 BL 347.36 362.17
WP 386.5 386.29 388.16 390.20
YT 404.28 406.7 SD 421.23
421.27 422.21 422.32
PP 432.21 HD 442.21 442.28
449.5 449.21 452.19 PR 478.42
481.22 488.36 489.5 490.11
493.27 494.17 496.37 502.8
503.14 504.18 507.10 509.18
509.29 512.10 SU 529.37
530.26 530.27 530.34 530.36
531.2 531.5 532.8 532.9
532.29 532.38 534.34 WR 546.9
552.17 556.39 557.3 562.6
562.31 564.39 565.32 570.26
577.23 SM 584.25 BO 591.6
598.5 IL 646.25 646.26 651.2
GG 661.32 NT 706.41 ML 722.35
724.38 741.11 744.39 744.40
745.14 746.23 OV 747.1 748.12
752.29 753.9 LL 766.29 768.12
768.42 770.17 772.29 773.37

LAY (CONT.) 773.42 774.36
775.3 775.16 775.17
MD 804.32 809.29 816.31
817.23 820.11 822.12
BM 833.4 837.41

LAYING MO 4.37 19.1 OA 30.3
EA 72.1 73.15 DV 149.2
159.5 GF 236.16 OC 284.40
EE 318.1 TB 522.17
SU 536.22 WR 562.37

LAYS FA 469.13

LAZARUS IL 658.18

LAZILY MO 12.40

LAZY MO 13.20 HT 40.27
40.30 SC 267.13

LEAD SP 49.32 WM 62.40
FG 193.30 GF 239.34
EE 315.23 315.24 PR 486.6
491.37 492.26 492.35
493.8 498.22 BO 601.35
LL 769.3

LEADEN ML 744.22

LEADER DV 138.20

LEADING SB 214.3 217.11
GF 243.7 MN 371.4 HD 442.8
PR 492.4 492.31 499.14
499.27 WR 555.42 JD 609.6
RH 799.17 BM 835.10

LEAD-MINES GG 666.19

LEADS LL 767.7

LEAF MO 3.13 LA 644.38
ML 740.12

LEAFY SB 213.9

LEAN TF 126.4 GF 234.30
PR 483.20 SU 536.27
JD 609.14 622.19 625.3
LA 634.13 NT 716.6 ML 731.9

LEANED MO 2.31 5.4 16.30
19.22 OA 26.42 36.12
WM 58.42 59.4 63.19
DV 160.31 161.2 161.38
FG 194.32 SG 222.19 225.33
GF 235.24 237.16 OC 285.5
291.13 TP 337.33 338.25
BL 360.19 361.18 YT 402.1
SD 411.16 413.10 423.33
425.38 PP 432.37 433.11
436.27 SU 528.9 530.8
WR 562.41 SM 583.8 583.34
586.2 586.5 IL 651.25
653.9 GG 666.36 671.29
NT 712.36 OV 746.17 756.9
LL 774.40 RR 785.10
MD 822.18 823.18 BM 828.26
837.11

LEANING OA 32.41 34.26 37.21
EA 71.25 71.28 PO 101.42
115.5 DV 179.34 SS 207.20
SG 224.23 GF 241.6

LEANING (CONT.)

LEANING (CONT.) WS 263.16
  SC 272.20 OC 299.1 BL 360.4
  WP 387.5 SD 423.10 PR 484.17
  495.30 TB 525.1 WR 563.5
  563.8 577.6 SM 583.5 LA 631.1
  632.3 IL 648.36 GG 664.32
  665.29 669.10 670.11 670.16
  671.26 NT 713.14 ML 727.3
  OV 755.35 MD 821.34 823.23
  823.29 BM 841.5

LEAP PO 115.13 TF 133.15
  WR 575.19 575.27 581.18

LEAPED OA 29.38 WM 54.25 54.33
  70.4 70.6 PP 430.3 PR 510.31
  511.5 511.6 WR 555.35
  SM 583.37 GG 684.28

LEAPING PR 501.25 SU 535.7

LEAPS TP 334.33

LEAPT HT 44.7 PO 108.8 108.14
  TF 121.20 130.7 SB 218.4
  TP 334.31 MN 371.19 LL 765.32

LEARN TP 346.1 WP 380.15
  YT 408.18 NT 708.9

LEARNED WM 67.36 DV 137.31
  156.24 SG 233.9 OC 295.15
  EE 314.34 YT 405.33 PR 476.13
  478.1 SU 543.2 GG 667.15
  MD 814.39 815.1 TH 845.17

LEARNING DV 144.15 FA 464.34

LEARNS NT 708.10

LEASE ML 722.13 MD 817.40

LEAST WM 58.13 58.24 67.33
  DV 144.20 182.25 SS 197.6
  SG 231.27 WS 246.34 EE 311.11
  311.13 311.27 318.42 328.8
  BL 351.17 MN 371.28 SD 416.13
  PR 486.6 487.37 508.34
  TB 514.18 521.38 524.38
  525.40 SU 541.10 WR 548.9
  BO 600.16 602.36 JD 605.23
  628.27 IL 655.35 GG 661.21
  664.36 666.11 677.33 683.40
  NT 706.23 718.21 LL 772.27
  RR 779.12 780.37 782.19
  782.39 788.1 MD 813.15
  BM 828.9 829.1 834.16
  TH 845.4 846.24 848.28 852.27

LEASTWISE WP 388.31

LEATHER PO 107.38 OC 299.5
  BL 351.33 FA 458.33 459.19
  PR 484.40 WR 558.17 LA 637.7
  RR 784.34

LEAVES MO 4.25 4.26 PO 108.34
  111.3 111.16 FG 190.25
  SB 213.2 214.15 CH 274.30
  OC 283.12 299.19 TP 334.2
  PP 434.20 434.23 435.22
  FA 467.32 PR 475.26 483.39
  487.26 490.27 493.21 494.16
  499.33 TB 520.38 SU 530.35
  532.34 533.38 WR 549.8 561.26

LEAVES (CONT.) BO 598.8 JD 627.6
  LA 639.37 IL 648.35 648.37
  651.31 ML 746.29 OV 747.13
  753.36 755.9 759.17 LL 770.26
  RR 780.6 786.39 TH 845.23
  845.29

LEAVE-TAKING EA 79.10 TF 131.20
  SC 268.2

LEAVIN' CH 279.17

LEAVING MO 7.8 OA 29.7 WM 69.32
  EA 77.11 TF 121.37 DV 175.27
  176.26 SS 206.16 WS 261.17
  OC 286.29 293.6 296.29
  EE 303.4 310.24 313.25 314.9
  320.38 BL 363.25 MN 373.14
  YT 395.2 405.23 SD 421.29
  FA 470.13 PR 478.13 501.13
  508.13 509.24 WR 560.33
  560.36 568.8 572.8 JD 624.4
  LA 641.35 GG 666.22 682.42
  NT 714.16 714.35 BM 834.22
  840.15 TH 852.17

LECTURE JD 609.29 609.30

LECTURED JD 621.17

LECTURES JD 612.9

LED OA 34.8 PO 111.30 DV 139.8
  183.36 SS 205.3 GF 238.28
  238.32 WS 251.37 255.15
  OC 283.17 290.39 EE 329.7
  SD 420.6 PP 436.25 HD 442.5
  PR 507.36 SU 539.2 WR 551.16
  551.28 558.30 562.11 563.2
  564.7 577.39 BO 603.36
  OV 755.35 BM 838.28 TH 851.34

LEDERMAN WR 548.35 550.13

LEDGE TF 119.18 122.9 SS 204.26
  ML 730.21 736.42 OV 750.33

LEDGED TF 119.12

LEE WP 379.15 PR 497.8 497.32
  ML 745.28

LEE-SHORE MO 2.13

LEG TF 120.36 EE 306.42 317.41
  321.13 321.21 321.32 323.8
  323.9 324.21 328.37 TP 338.10
  BL 362.21 362.32 WP 381.40
  386.19 389.18 HD 456.3
  PR 491.8 491.35 IL 654.1
  ML 730.31 RR 788.22

LEGACY YT 399.3

LEGAL SG 227.20 LL 763.8

LEGALLY SS 205.26

LEGATION MD 814.9

LEGER RH 797.40

LEGS OA 24.32 WM 67.37
  PO 113.10 116.15 TF 126.22
  127.32 FG 188.17 WS 261.24

LEGS (CONT.) 261.36 262.16
  262.18 262.22 SC 269.31
  OC 293.3 EE 304.23 329.7
  333.11 BL 354.17 354.24
  357.27 359.40 MN 371.19
  378.17 WP 382.18 SD 419.7
  421.37 422.30 HD 444.31
  445.15 450.13 450.36
  452.41 453.9 FA 459.29
  PR 499.3 TB 521.16 522.23
  WR 549.18 556.9 557.8
  563.29 569.20 580.35
  BO 603.7 LA 631.28 637.28
  637.36 639.28 643.33
  NT 719.7 ML 740.9 RH 793.38

LEICESTERSHIRE MO 2.9

LEILA BM 836.1 836.22 836.30
  837.17 837.36

LEISURELY OA 23.16 MN 367.25
  BO 596.27

LE MARQUIS, MONSIEUR (SEE
  MONSIEUR LE MARQUIS)

LEMON SU 529.11 533.38
  534.3 537.32 539.4 540.22
  540.28

LEMONADE BM 838.30

LEMONS SU 533.35 534.2
  537.37 537.38 538.33
  540.4 540.10 540.26
  540.27 540.30

LENA SC 273.8

LEND SD 420.22 TB 515.32

LENGTH MO 13.40 OA 27.33
  27.37 SP 51.7 WM 61.12
  65.38 67.22 68.11 EA 86.39
  PO 110.42 TF 132.1
  DV 148.5 SS 205.5 SB 215.30
  SG 223.2 224.15 229.5
  232.7 232.20 GF 236.32
  WS 259.12 259.20 264.31
  CH 275.19 TP 336.38 337.7
  343.32 343.38 BL 360.23
  360.35 360.40 362.32
  MN 376.21 YT 405.12
  SD 414.24 PR 493.41 496.22
  496.23 SU 537.6 WR 559.14
  559.30 563.31 572.13
  580.6 BO 594.4 JD 607.39
  623.14 626.27 ML 722.34
  724.34 LL 766.31 MD 807.7

LENGTHEN ML 743.39

LENGTHY IL 659.12

LENT EE 323.16 RH 795.7

LEONARD BM 839.29

LEONARDO LL 761.17

LEOPARD NT 712.18 712.24
  712.32

LEOPARD-LIKE WR 579.35

LEOPARD-SKIN WR 559.23

LEOPARD-SPOTTED WR 561.6

LEPER DV 165.13

LESS PO 108.31 TF 119.39
  DV 157.17 165.2 166.5
  SS 200.32 SG 222.28 CH 274.12
  274.37 EE 308.23 310.13
  312.31 TP 337.18 MN 369.15
  WP 380.14 386.33 YT 402.28
  PP 438.15 HD 448.9 PR 476.7
  481.19 TB 514.23 522.7
  WR 546.7 549.22 549.28 552.37
  JD 621.13 NT 702.20 704.37
  715.5 ML 746.1 OV 752.15
  LL 774.31 RR 780.11 TH 852.21
  853.10

LESSENING MO 1.20 SU 541.22

LESSER TF 130.33 DV 138.24

LESSON PR 476.13 476.15
  NT 708.9 708.10

LESSON-BOOKS SS 202.41

LESSONS DV 138.32 138.34
  LL 765.42

LEST DV 165.8 FG 189.27 192.2
  GF 241.11 SC 269.28 OC 302.11
  FA 323.9 BL 364.22 HD 457.9
  GG 681.33 ML 740.27

LETHARGY SB 214.21 BL 350.11
  350.38 BM 832.4

LETS SG 224.34 FA 471.37
  BO 590.9

LET'S SP 49.5 49.13 SC 268.16
  OC 287.17 TP 342.2 WP 388.39
  YT 410.7 SD 412.18 413.19 413.24
  LA 634.7 GG 687.5 MD 805.30

LETTER TF 117.25 BL 350.20
  WP 380.24 380.28 380.31
  380.33 380.36 381.3 381.34
  382.38 389.24 391.5 391.6
  391.16 392.20 392.24 392.29
  392.35 PP 437.38 HD 443.30
  FA 463.34 JD 607.25 613.39
  628.21 628.34 628.36
  GG 699.25 ML 738.10 RH 799.10
  799.26 799.28 MD 806.15
  806.17 825.41

LETTERING ML 743.17

LETTERS SG 223.42 GF 238.21
  WS 245.23 EE 305.29 BL 349.4
  WP 385.9 385.13 385.16 385.18
  SU 537.29 JD 607.21 ML 742.12
  742.16 743.15 RH 799.25
  MD 815.20

LETTIN' CH 279.13

LETTING MO 21.1 SS 204.33
  GF 243.32 TP 339.26 PR 494.15
  WR 550.21 NT 708.15 ML 735.27
  BM 828.17

LETTUCES TF 117.12

LEVANTINE MD 819.28 825.4

LEVEL EA 81.23 PO 107.15 109.1
  114.26 115.9 TF 117.3 129.33
  DV 160.38 163.39 167.32
  SS 197.26 OC 283.30 EE 307.13
  WP 386.13 YT 399.40 SD 424.23
  PP 435.37 436.26 PR 489.3
  SU 532.15 WR 567.34 GG 673.4
  NT 712.10 ML 733.31 744.1
  OV 748.37 MD 810.30 BM 839.42
  840.3

LEVEL-BROWED SM 584.8

LEVEL-CROSSING DV 139.2
  FA 459.29

LEVEL-HEADED JD 605.2 605.7

LEVELS SS 199.41 ML 737.41

LEVEL-SAWN PO 109.11

LEVER OC 286.4

LIAISON GG 664.34

LIAR EA 88.28 YT 407.32
  SD 418.33 IL 658.22

LIBERALLY ML 726.28

LIBERATED TF 130.29 SS 203.12

LIBERATOR JD 619.38

LIBERTIES OC 292.35

LIBERTY TF 122.14 131.2
  WS 249.12 260.14 EE 314.31
  315.26 315.27 316.1 325.7
  327.13 SU 529.5

LIBRARY TB 515.35 517.42
  ML 728.1 728.23 732.4

LICENSED DV 165.20

LICK OA 27.17

LICKED OA 27.4 WM 70.8
  IL 657.38

LICKING OC 283.20

LID PO 109.34 SG 221.10
  EE 312.32 LA 632.16 LL 772.27
  MD 813.40

LIDO NT 701.11 702.32 703.38

LIDS YT 400.20 SU 530.35
  LL 761.12 MD 818.36 819.40

LIE OA 32.36 WM 68.28 EA 74.7
  92.10 94.7 PO 104.19 112.10
  DV 184.27 FG 187.6 WS 247.38
  248.11 SC 269.33 OC 289.18
  299.38 YT 406.7 PR 502.6
  504.23 SU 529.26 537.26
  537.31 WR 556.36 BO 603.26
  IL 658.35 NT 709.22 720.17

LIE (CONT. OV 755.27
  LL 767.32 MD 816.7

LIED OV 752.14

LIES DV 151.26 OC 300.40
  TP 343.29 SD 424.16 424.18
  BO 590.5

LIEUTENANT PO 107.38 108.5
  108.38 109.4 111.8 111.12
  111.14 111.21 TF 133.39
  134.6 134.10 134.20 134.32
  134.42 EE 330.6 BM 829.10

LIFE MO 2.20 2.27 2.37
  2.39 5.3 6.24 8.37 9.31
  9.36 9.37 14.21 16.31
  16.32 16.34 16.37 16.39
  16.40 17.10 17.23 21.42
  OA 37.5 37.8 HT 39.9
  39.25 40.33 SP 49.18
  49.19 49.40 WM 61.32
  65.34 EA 77.1 80.17 80.35
  81.30 81.33 81.39 82.30
  82.37 83.3 83.21 83.22
  86.19 87.33 89.8 89.13
  91.5 91.37 93.24 94.1
  PO 96.21 97.5 97.15 106.9
  108.23 111.7 111.37 112.5
  113.21 113.27 113.28
  116.19 TF 125.41 126.5
  128.8 129.4 133.17 134.8
  DV 137.36 138.10 140.18
  140.22 143.28 150.4 153.27
  154.42 155.29 156.22
  164.35 167.23 170.30
  171.15 171.26 173.5 176.20
  176.30 176.35 177.16
  179.21 180.32 FG 187.14
  SS 198.13 211.18 SG 229.21
  GF 237.26 239.38 241.26
  241.27 SC 267.7 267.24
  269.41 273.8 CH 280.9
  282.23 282.26 OC 285.20
  286.13 297.31 297.32
  300.10 300.25 301.14
  301.22 301.24 301.33
  301.34 302.13 EE 304.17
  306.11 308.8 308.14 308.27
  309.39 310.6 310.20 310.24
  310.26 310.30 310.32
  311.16 312.7 312.8 312.34
  313.14 315.14 315.39
  318.42 320.42 321.8 321.33
  324.30 325.17 325.31
  325.39 327.32 329.2 329.6
  329.32 329.33 331.7 331.10
  331.35 332.9 332.37 332.39
  333.3 333.5 TP 336.34
  338.42 339.16 BL 347.22
  347.37 348.40 350.7 350.9
  353.9 353.27 355.33 357.7
  MN 366.10 366.14 366.25
  377.2 WP 382.2 384.10
  384.25 384.27 385.41
  388.9 392.13 YT 403.34
  SD 411.15 412.31 416.31
  420.6 420.8 PP 428.12
  428.19 428.42 431.29
  438.18 439.29 HD 441.17
  442.17 442.37 448.8 448.29
  449.13 451.35 452.24
  454.21 FA 465.40 PR 479.20
  480.18 482.28 496.36

LIFE (CONT.) 509.20 TB 519.26
   520.6 524.2 SU 532.7 533.11
   536.16 537.34 539.24 544.16
   WR 548.3 550.21 551.3 553.39
   562.7 569.31 580.12 580.27
   SM 582.10 BO 592.1 594.12
   594.38 599.19 JD 607.4 614.28
   616.28 620.4 627.35 LA 634.15
   634.33 642.13 642.16 642.17
   643.12 643.13 IL 652.27
   GG 661.27 661.32 662.30
   662.31 662.34 663.20 663.32
   671.30 671.36 677.35 678.30
   679.11 682.41 683.25 686.18
   687.16 689.20 691.33 694.27
   695.30 697.15 698.7 NT 703.12
   708.17 708.18 708.19 709.15
   709.32 710.11 710.23 711.4
   711.11 712.35 712.40 ML 730.5
   741.16 744.9 OV 748.27 749.7
   750.6 751.27 755.19 755.21
   757.35 LL 762.24 771.32
   771.36 778.21 778.23
   MD 804.35 807.11 808.14
   810.12 810.14 810.26 811.8
   811.37 816.6 816.30 821.26
   822.4 822.16 825.36 BM 827.4
   827.8 830.22 831.28 831.30
   834.19 842.10 TH 844.8 844.13
   845.2 845.3 847.30 847.34
   849.27 850.22 850.30 851.34
   851.35 852.14

LIFE-AND-DEATH EE 315.1

LIFE-DAY BO 594.17

LIFE-FLOW GG 686.25

LIFE-GUARDSMAN YT 398.14

LIFE-HOME BO 587.15

LIFE-IDOL EE 326.16

LIFELESS PR 496.37 WR 546.16
   ML 745.14 745.24 746.30

LIFE-LONG SU 528.24 LL 765.31

LIFE-MYSTERIES ML 737.5

LIFE OF JOHN WESLEY DV 140.35

LIFE'S MO 9.30 16.36 WM 62.1
   OV 756.2 756.10 758.15

LIFE-STONE FG 196.13

LIFT MO 1.14 12.12 EA 81.5
   83.16 84.1 92.34 DV 154.8
   CH 279.29 281.7 281.13
   OC 289.34 FA 468.7 ML 745.5
   OV 758.30 LL 771.30

LIFTED MO 2.20 10.17 17.13
   19.4 OA 26.41 34.39 WM 64.26
   67.5 68.32 68.34 69.1
   EA 74.18 91.33 92.36
   PO 102.19 TF 125.9 130.1
   DV 180.29 FG 192.34 194.24
   195.32 SS 197.2 209.2
   SB 218.7 SG 223.35 225.27
   230.28 230.34 231.23 232.11
   GF 235.32 WS 245.39 247.19

LIFTED (CONT.) 253.23 253.33
   258.14 262.1 263.19 263.28
   264.31 265.41 CH 274.15
   279.36 280.10 EE 317.13
   BL 354.16 356.17 362.33
   364.9 364.29 MN 368.18
   373.7 375.15 376.36 377.12
   WP 384.33 SD 412.4 412.16
   416.1 416.21 423.35 425.11
   425.14 PP 428.23 HD 448.19
   448.21 448.23 450.37 451.4
   454.40 PR 487.15 490.29
   497.21 504.10 SU 529.35
   539.17 541.17 544.3 WR 578.7
   SM 583.35 BO 604.31 JD 615.6
   615.16 LA 630.23 632.23
   632.38 633.10 633.17 633.33
   IL 647.35 651.32 GG 684.23
   687.24 692.40 NT 713.38
   ML 728.24 742.1 742.24
   OV 753.6 753.10 753.39
   LL 767.6 770.23 778.16
   RR 783.34 RH 800.39 MD 822.25
   BM 837.35

LIFTING WM 67.5 69.5 DV 149.9
   159.23 FG 194.33 195.41
   196.16 GF 234.3 WS 251.33
   TP 345.15 MN 377.34 378.7
   SD 417.31 425.8 PR 498.6
   500.41 SU 539.24 540.14
   544.32 GG 690.17 693.10 694.8
   ML 733.25 BM 835.34

LIGATURES EE 319.26

LIGHT MO 3.15 5.35 12.6 18.7
   18.10 18.14 18.20 OA 23.13
   27.28 28.37 29.17 29.19
   34.38 37.40 38.1 SP 51.18
   WM 55.9 60.29 63.20 67.24
   EA 73.29 77.39 82.11 82.25
   84.17 90.11 91.29 92.34
   PO 105.32 106.2 107.18 107.29
   108.42 113.30 114.16 115.10
   TF 119.5 128.38 DV 162.28
   166.11 167.26 167.30 167.38
   173.10 175.2 175.11 181.13
   FG 189.3 192.7 194.4 194.11
   195.37 196.21 SS 202.23
   202.31 SG 224.16 GF 235.32
   238.16 WS 244.5 244.20 245.2
   245.9 251.32 254.11 CH 279.4
   282.27 OC 283.21 288.24
   288.41 290.34 291.14
   EE 309.13 314.33 314.36
   315.13 319.24 328.15 332.7
   332.33 332.34 333.10 TP 338.9
   338.29 BL 351.3 351.36 353.1
   354.26 MN 373.16 373.21
   WP 379.10 379.16 386.6
   YT 400.21 401.31 402.14
   SD 423.15 PP 434.3 435.8
   HD 453.21 453.23 453.41
   456.15 FA 458.2 462.9
   PR 477.15 489.13 493.27
   497.26 499.34 503.2 503.26
   504.40 SU 528.9 530.10 538.1
   WR 552.24 552.32 553.11
   554.18 556.4 556.10 571.41
   578.13 BO 594.13 594.14 595.7
   598.28 JD 610.9 610.38 611.1
   619.3 LA 630.6 635.31 637.6
   637.27 639.32 639.34 640.17
   644.4 GG 678.33 678.39 683.22

LIGHT (CONT.) 697.5 NT 705.30
   707.36 711.3 712.15 712.20
   715.19 721.10 ML 725.12
   734.22 734.28 738.24
   740.1 745.1 OV 747.2
   747.21 749.10 749.40
   757.15 759.22 759.37
   759.40 LL 766.10 766.14
   772.38 775.40 776.13
   RR 787.39 788.9 788.10
   788.18 RH 803.11 803.13
   MD 808.29 BM 840.42
   TH 844.27

LIGHT-BLUE PO 96.22 107.14
   MN 367.41

LIGHT-BOMB EE 333.14

LIGHTED MO 5.41 TF 122.9
   DV 162.30 174.42 SG 222.20
   GF 235.31 236.15 WS 251.28
   262.1 OC 287.5 296.17
   TP 337.19 340.18 BL 350.42
   MN 371.13 SD 423.19
   WR 563.23 BO 596.28 602.38
   LA 637.2 LL 765.11

LIGHTENED WM 70.6 LA 638.30

LIGHTER PO 114.20

LIGHTEST MO 4.15

LIGHTHOUSE SD 411.5 423.8

LIGHTING OA 33.21 BL 356.14
   358.23 FA 458.7 RR 785.3

LIGHTLY OA 26.26 EA 86.29
   PO 95.32 TF 120.1 120.2
   DV 184.38 SG 222.5
   MN 373.13 PP 430.26
   PR 490.15 IL 647.15
   GG 663.36

LIGHTNESS WM 66.12

LIGHTNING OA 28.16 28.25
   29.23 29.26 29.30 29.37
   30.22 PO 115.7 DV 180.9
   WS 264.6 EE 312.16 312.23
   312.30 LA 638.19 638.21
   638.25 646.27 ML 744.30
   744.37 745.41 746.23

LIGHTNING-LIKE EE 330.31

LIGHTNING-RAPID EE 331.29

LIGHTS MO 22.3 WM 55.12
   60.31 62.23 DV 153.42
   166.31 167.20 167.21
   WS 263.17 OC 291.1
   TP 337.20 MN 371.17
   SD 411.10 411.24 411.25
   411.33 FA 459.36 SU 528.36
   529.5 LA 632.19 639.3
   GG 697.9 ML 733.26 734.20
   LL 765.32 772.38 RR 787.40
   BM 835.15

LIGURIAN SM 584.7

LIKED HT 39.5 WM 62.33

LIKED (CONT.) EA 88.2 92.17
  TF 124.38 DV 137.23 140.11
  140.17 146.14 154.11 155.28
  163.41 164.6 164.7 164.12
  166.2 166.35 167.4 167.7
  167.24 167.25 167.33 167.38
  SB 218.8 218.28 GF 239.33
  WS 249.9 252.23 EE 308.39
  310.34 316.3 318.34 318.35
  326.20 326.39 TP 336.39 339.1
  339.3 340.19 BL 352.40 356.23
  MN 368.2 371.29 WP 382.12
  FA 462.17 PR 484.33 TB 513.17
  WR 576.3 BO 587.25 JD 606.17
  IL 648.36 649.32 650.7 658.35
  658.37 658.38 GG 675.30
  679.42 NT 702.7 704.23 710.34
  712.29 713.33 715.34 716.11
  ML 727.30 727.32 740.21
  743.11 OV 752.24 LL 771.15
  MD 809.9 809.39 811.4 812.23
  821.13 821.24 BM 828.2
  TH 853.35

LIKELY MO 17.1 HT 40.8
  DV 179.16 185.31 SB 212.5
  OC 285.39 BL 352.8 TB 513.26

LIKES HT 39.28 SC 267.28
  TP 340.41 YT 403.32 SU 537.5
  JD 621.5 625.35 ML 727.35
  RH 797.13

LIKING MN 370.32

LILAC TF 122.7 TB 520.31

LILIES EA 84.7 EE 311.5 311.11
  311.12 311.13* MD 810.38 811.5
  821.14

LILT SS 203.18

LIMB EE 325.4 BO 602.11

LIMBER TF 117.20 118.4
  MN 374.21

LIMBS MO 13.21 OA 26.14 27.29
  WM 68.39 EA 72.11 89.25
  PO 97.1 99.13 104.6 111.2
  DV 179.39 FG 190.8 WS 244.9
  254.34 255.2 257.20 257.21
  CH 279.1 OC 300.2 EE 309.6
  309.11 BL 349.10 354.24
  SD 421.41 PP 435.29 HD 452.28
  WR 565.31 568.11 577.3 577.24
  LA 637.12 637.30 638.4
  IL 651.14 GG 683.11 687.8
  696.24 699.4 699.16 OV 748.11
  757.21 LL 766.36 774.1
  BM 829.38 836.15 840.42

LIME TF 117.8 117.16 117.18
  123.17 125.26 134.41

LIMITED BM 842.11

LIMITEDNESS FA 462.38

LIMITLESS MO 4.37

LIMP MO 6.38 PO 95.23 SB 214.15
  PR 492.7 MD 808.42

LIMPED PR 492.5

LIMPIDLY EA 83.27

LIMPING EE 324.34 324.35

LIMPLY MO 13.20

LIMPS WP 381.41 PR 492.8

LINA BM 840.14

LINA M'LEOD BM 827.2

LINCOLN RH 794.31 795.36 797.3
  800.24 800.25

LINCOLNSHIRE RH 800.4

LINDLEY DV 136.1

LINDLEY (SEE REVEREND LINDLEY;
  MR. LINDLEY; MR. AND MRS.
  LINDLEY)

LINDLEYS DV 145.9 177.14

LINE MO 16.16 WM 60.27 63.35
  66.11 DV 139.3 OC 283.6
  284.28 290.5 291.9 294.19
  BL 351.22 MN 366.7 378.26
  WP 391.15 SD 419.19 PR 483.31
  483.32 484.4 484.13 484.14
  WR 554.1 567.36 569.13 569.16
  BO 599.41 GG 679.1 679.42
  ML 728.42 MD 809.14 809.15

LINED OA 24.10 29.18 DV 167.2
  WR 559.33 577.16 LA 635.28

LINEN OA 35.41 TF 133.22
  SG 226.14 226.29 228.9
  MN 367.1 PR 476.25 506.19
  506.27 TB 521.22 WR 551.7
  551.8 563.3 RR 786.3 786.6

LINES OA 27.34 SP 49.3 49.9
  EA 72.22 PO 96.19 DV 167.15
  OC 283.27 284.42 286.32
  287.19 290.33 290.38 WR 554.3
  554.20 568.40 577.7 578.18
  579.30 JD 606.20 606.22
  616.13 LA 631.14 633.19
  IL 647.22 GG 667.34 RH 790.32
  792.24 MD 815.39

LINGER MO 5.39

LINGERED OA 33.37 GF 235.27
  PR 495.38 LA 644.15

LINGERERS FA 468.28

LINGERING SG 225.29 CH 279.31
  EE 303.31 PR 484.36 WR 565.23

LINGERINGLY BO 590.38

LINGERS EE 303.28

LINGUIST MD 820.20

LINK EE 309.33 309.40 313.4
  PR 493.39

LINKED WM 68.11

LINNET OV 760.3

LINNETS SS 204.22

LINOLEUM HT 42.19 43.6
  43.37

LINTEL OC 297.6

LION SC 272.2 PR 486.22
  502.38 BO 602.6 NT 703.7

LIONESS BO 602.5

LION'S NT 703.6

LIP WM 64.42 PO 109.34
  SS 203.28 GF 236.3 242.21
  243.29 243.35 WS 245.37
  249.32 249.40 EE 328.41
  YT 396.15 HD 442.38
  TB 514.32 WR 579.34
  OV 750.33

LIPS MO 7.18 9.25 10.38
  18.13 21.14 22.8 WM 63.7
  69.24 69.31 EA 73.17
  76.27 85.6 90.28 91.11
  PO 101.16 110.24 DV 181.18
  FG 192.17 SG 226.21 230.21
  GF 237.37 238.32 WS 255.8
  263.22 263.42 264.26
  SC 268.25 272.38 CH 274.29
  OC 289.5 289.12 299.21
  EE 318.18 TP 338.26 338.28
  WP 387.39 SD 412.16
  HD 446.5 452.36 PR 512.1
  WR 563.10 567.36 577.18
  BO 604.35 JD 615.12 623.35
  LA 632.31 GG 678.9 680.9
  685.29 ML 729.9 736.24
  OV 754.20 754.34 RR 779.4
  782.25 783.32 783.39
  MD 822.4

LIQUID DV 139.17 WS 255.4
  PR 501.39 BM 836.19

LIQUOR WR 565.22

LIRE EA 83.10

LISA, MONA (SEE MONA LISA)

LISPED OA 26.20

LIST SP 45.29 GF 240.39
  ML 736.8

LISTEN EA 74.19 FG 193.16
  GF 235.28 235.38 238.29
  OC 289.31 EE 323.24
  MN 374.32 SU 539.25
  WR 570.13 JD 609.15
  GG 687.34 OV 755.16
  LL 767.41 RH 791.12

LISTENED MO 8.34 10.31
  OA 29.22 WM 54.18 59.9
  EA 84.35 86.6 TF 119.8
  127.1 DV 141.13 146.3
  170.6 SG 222.33 231.7

LISTENED (CONT.) GF 236.35
  CH 280.27 BL 353.4 353.15
  WP 392.22 YT 401.32 SD 411.35
  FA 466.21 TB 521.5 WR 555.33
  559.28 564.37 571.17
  LA 634.29 639.21 IL 650.33
  GG 693.35 NT 709.17 ML 726.38
  727.3 739.22 LL 768.10 772.32
  775.16

LISTENER PO 101.6

LISTENING MO 4.38 10.28 12.12
  OA 26.21 32.8 EA 72.11 86.27
  PO 111.13 GF 235.25 SC 269.5
  272.14 OC 289.29 290.29
  291.29 293.23 296.39 299.21
  BL 347.1 354.39 354.40 362.16
  362.19 364.29 364.32
  SD 417.32 HD 441.3 WR 552.18
  559.30 565.32 568.12
  LA 631.25 631.35 632.21
  632.38 634.8 634.24 639.28
  ML 728.31 741.12 OV 747.15
  LL 767.23 774.1 774.37 775.33
  775.38 RR 783.12 784.18
  RH 802.41

LISTS DV 146.25

LIT WM 63.34 EA 75.29 76.25
  PO 102.30 FG 192.34 OC 286.30
  YT 410.1 HD 456.16 FA 458.8
  PR 501.31 BO 594.15 GG 669.29
  ML 728.38 734.23 LL 775.32
  776.41 RH 803.13 803.14

LITERAL LL 772.29

LITERALLY YT 409.35 LL 778.5

LITERARY EA 84.38 87.6 87.7
  87.33 EE 305.25 306.4
  BL 350.4 PR 479.14 TB 525.19

LITERATURE EA 84.37 86.19
  EE 305.15 308.36 329.13
  GG 669.9 TH 848.41 852.39

LITERATURE-BEWILDERED EA 86.31

LITHE OA 24.38 29.8 LA 637.30
  BM 837.21

LITTER WM 63.42 PO 112.22
  OC 291.39 292.8 WR 560.41
  578.3 578.4 578.7 578.10
  578.12 578.22 578.38 579.9
  JD 607.24

LITTERATEUR BL 359.37

LITTER-BEARER WR 580.5

LITTER-BEARERS WR 562.13 578.24
  579.39

LITTERED SP 45.12 PO 108.41

LITTERING SS 197.8

LITTLER DV 140.26 WS 252.10

LIVE MO 9.30 9.31 14.9 17.2
  EA 82.41 86.21 PO 98.21 105.8

LIVE (CONT.) TF 128.36 DV 136.29
  147.30 153.14 154.25 154.28
  154.30 184.18 185.3 185.25
  SS 198.38 199.3 201.39 208.14
  SG 223.10 231.2 SC 267.16
  EE 308.29 310.34 312.15
  312.19 313.34 314.7 323.15
  325.38 BL 348.13 364.27
  WP 381.12 YT 403.30 406.25
  PP 429.28 430.20 431.21
  431.27 HD 451.2 FA 469.25
  PR 474.21 477.3 TB 513.2
  513.3 513.10 514.8 514.15
  514.17 SU 541.32 WR 549.12
  554.8 BO 589.17 602.5
  JD 608.9 609.23 612.36
  613.3 613.9 613.10 614.27
  621.32 621.37 622.3 622.41
  625.29 626.33 GG 667.38 668.2
  668.7 679.33 680.7 680.36
  686.23 697.15 NT 701.6 708.19
  711.4 LL 768.33 775.9 778.3
  778.5 RR 782.38 MD 806.10
  813.35 814.4 817.33 817.38
  821.10 826.3 BM 830.41
  TH 844.8 844.13 847.12 848.27
  851.31

LIVED SP 51.14 WM 58.27
  EA 82.21 TF 128.9 DV 138.7
  145.19 153.28 156.12 164.4
  174.8 FG 196.24 CH 282.23
  OC 301.5 EE 306.34 308.20 310.15
  328.20 BL 347.12 359.21
  YT 395.17 396.35 403.22
  PP 429.26 429.33 HD 447.6
  FA 464.2 465.37 470.11 471.14
  PR 473.31 474.40 480.3
  SU 528.12 543.27 WR 547.6
  549.30 550.6 572.7 BO 587.19
  599.37 JD 609.32 LA 638.41
  GG 680.37 691.32 NT 704.20
  711.11 ML 723.41 725.27
  725.31 726.2 733.22 733.23
  743.20 OV 752.22 LL 762.16
  762.20 765.18 RR 780.14
  781.14 RH 790.18 790.21
  794.12 794.13 MD 805.6 805.14
  806.11 BM 829.40 TH 847.34
  848.38

LIVELY WM 63.23 PO 106.40
  BL 362.39 SD 422.5 TB 524.2
  LA 642.26

LIVELY SPARK RH 797.41 798.2

LIVER GG 672.40 674.41

LIVERPOOL SB 212.6 215.20 218.1

LIVES MO 4.13 8.26 OA 38.42
  EA 85.33 DV 137.7 144.33
  171.31 172.5 172.19 SG 224.40
  YT 394.23 394.27 PP 431.37
  HD 441.27 449.15 TB 519.22
  519.23 519.24 SU 528.26
  WR 548.38 549.31 571.6
  JD 608.1 608.21 611.19
  GG 696.31 NT 703.9 LL 778.20
  TH 847.6 847.9 847.12 847.13
  848.2

LIVESTOCK GF 235.19

LIVID PO 115.9 PR 496.23

LIVING MO 9.40 OA 37.10
  EA 87.32 89.11 PO 106.5
  TF 128.16 133.13 DV 153.25
  160.34 164.35 164.38
  171.7 173.21 184.36
  SB 213.16 OC 300.8 300.29
  300.30 300.40 301.5
  EE 308.4 309.20 313.41
  315.17 325.31 325.32
  TP 334.36 BL 347.4
  WP 382.3 SD 414.32 419.12
  PP 430.38 PR 473.33 474.7
  474.41 477.6 WR 550.3
  558.11 577.17 JD 622.21
  624.26 GG 667.21 667.40
  668.1 671.37 689.34 692.34
  697.16 NT 701.2 704.32
  ML 741.41 OV 748.25 751.16
  758.30 MD 816.31 818.1
  821.26 BM 827.7 836.19
  TH 845.1 847.22 847.33
  848.39 849.21 849.26
  850.30 852.4 852.15

LIVING-ROOM EE 306.39
  WP 388.41 IL 649.8 654.12

'LIZABETH OC 301.38

LIZARD GG 678.33 678.39

LIZZIE OC 293.34 294.22
  294.25 294.27 295.13
  295.21 300.16 300.17
  300.18 300.21 HD 446.18

LIZZIE, AUNT (SEE AUNT LIZZIE)

'LL OC 293.2

LOAD HT 38.12 DV 148.12
  EE 331.38 MN 366.36 378.27
  YT 394.14 TH 853.10

LOADING DV 166.20 MN 366.1
  366.28

LOAF MO 3.21 PO 97.23
  CH 276.35 277.8

LOATHE IL 652.24 652.27
  657.31 659.8 659.10
  ML 742.18 LL 776.33
  MD 817.15

LOATHED EA 81.27 87.13
  OC 289.38 IL 650.15 659.5
  LL 767.27 MD 817.21

LOATHING GG 662.18 662.19

LOAVES GF 241.20 TB 516.17

LOBES WS 246.1

LOBSTER TH 853.30 853.35

LOCAL SS 204.18 FA 464.12
  BM 830.16

LOCALITY PR 482.31

LOCK SG 230.2 EE 312.7

LOCKED   OA 28.36 37.33 38.2
 DV 167.29 FG 193.16 SG 221.10
 229.26 229.39 GF 239.16
 EE 323.8 TP 342.33 345.34
 YT 405.26 BO 599.10 GG 682.8
 683.11 RR 785.7 787.26
 RH 797.12

LOCKING   OC 290.29 SD 422.38

LOCKS   WR 563.11

LOCOMOTIVE   OC 283.1

LOCOMOTIVE-ENGINE   NT 708.28

LOCOMOTOR ATAXY   CH 277.34

LODESTONE   CH 282.20

LODGE   OA 26.2

LODGED   LA 639.40

LODGER   MO 14.20 14.24 15.10

LODGIN'   SS 199.4

LODGING   TF 131.19

LODGINGS   MO 14.15 14.20
 HD 444.3

LOFT   LL 766.23 770.10 775.23

LOFTILY   SP 46.24

LOFTY   OA 37.18 EA 73.2 DV 156.8
 FG 187.11 SM 583.26 585.36
 TH 847.41

LOG   SS 206.20 OC 290.12
 EE 303.12 PR 488.6 WR 561.29
 562.31 562.32 563.26

LOG-ENDS   PR 501.38

LOGICAL   JD 622.24 626.19 626.20

LOGICALLY   DV 154.16

LOG-LENGTHS   PR 500.9

LOGS   PO 111.1 111.6 BL 359.7
 361.15 PR 500.42

LOIN-CLOTH   WR 557.10 559.16
 562.24 563.28 570.16

LOINS   WM 59.5 PO 96.12
 TF 124.15 130.10 WS 244.24
 WP 388.30 SD 421.29 HD 450.16
 SU 531.1 JD 617.21 BM 837.11
 838.3

LOIS   GF 236.6 236.10 237.4
 237.10 237.27 237.30 237.32
 238.31 239.5 239.8 239.12
 239.16 239.25 240.4 240.13
 240.20 240.24 240.28 240.29
 240.42 241.5 241.9 241.23
 241.33 241.41 242.1 242.4
 242.7 242.27 243.16 243.24

LOIS'   GF 238.13 239.33

LOITER   MN 370.2

LOITERING   SS 210.29 SM 586.19

LOLLING   WM 67.6

LOMAS, TOM   (SEE TOM LOMAS)

LONDON   MO 12.10 OA 25.3 WM 54.4
 60.29 62.23 EE 306.32 307.41
 308.31 321.11 323.14 328.36
 329.19 YT 395.26 FA 464.34
 PR 479.11 WR 549.30 549.31
 JD 612.10 613.9 614.11 618.42
 624.5 627.40 LA 630.11 638.11
 641.34 GG 667.25 673.17
 RR 789.17 MD 807.31 811.6
 814.10 821.10

LONELINESS   EE 325.28 WR 552.8

LONELY   EA 72.32 EE 306.27
 TP 341.36 SD 411.13 PR 488.5
 WR 552.7 573.16 BO 595.12
 598.34 GG 663.39 678.30
 NT 701.3 710.33 ML 733.32
 OV 750.36 757.25 RR 782.23
 MD 821.22

LONELY-O   TP 341.25

LONESOME   PR 487.23 487.33
 NT 710.33 710.34 TH 846.27

LONG-ABANDONED   WR 552.30

LONG-CONTINUED   EE 323.10

LONG-DRAWN   TP 344.16

LONGED   BL 348.8 354.14
 YT 396.13 PR 478.11 MD 814.36
 817.19 BM 832.7

LONGER   MO 11.21 21.24 OA 37.7
 PO 111.36 114.15 TF 128.30
 128.33 DV 155.23 FG 189.29
 195.26 195.27 SS 203.3
 SG 233.14 WP 379.22 384.11
 390.16 SD 425.3 425.4
 HD 451.1 PR 479.7 496.26
 SU 532.3 536.11 BO 587.2
 LA 638.11 GG 699.9 NT 704.13
 706.17 ML 726.21 734.25
 734.37 734.38 735.29 740.20
 741.41 742.1 742.40 743.14
 744.7 744.23 RR 783.17 785.23
 RH 793.30 MD 811.30 BM 843.4
 TH 847.15 853.1

LONGEST   LA 641.39

LONG-FRINGED   LA 635.31

LONG-HAIRED   WR 561.1

LONGING   GF 240.7 NT 713.8
 MD 817.36

LONG-LEGGED   DV 138.15 RR 780.23

LONG-LIMBED   PP 438.38

LONG-SHANKED   SS 203.19

LONGSHIPS LIGHTHOUSE   SD 411.26

LOOKING-GLASS   WM 67.24
 WS 265.25

LOOK-OUT   TF 128.28 EE 310.35

LOOKS   HT 39.28 TF 117.31
 117.35 DV 170.35 SB 212.22
 BL 357.21 MN 370.16
 YT 398.35 SD 413.5 415.11
 HD 444.35 FA 463.22 463.31
 463.33 PR 511.29 SU 540.20
 WR 548.39 555.2 559.42
 JD 606.20 616.3 618.30
 LA 636.38 GG 670.20 700.2
 NT 703.8 LL 774.15 776.19
 MD 819.28

LOOM   BO 598.28

LOOMED   WS 251.21 OC 283.19
 285.2 SD 411.9 LA 633.6
 RR 785.24 BM 831.24

LOOMING   PO 115.15 TF 129.36
 SS 197.31 EE 310.19 316.6
 HD 447.38 BO 595.34 596.9
 BM 841.26

LOOMS   TP 334.21 BO 596.6

LOOP   PO 106.12 WP 390.35

LOOPED   OA 23.7 SB 212.12
 OV 747.5

LOOP-HOLE   IL 656.39

LOOPS   SS 203.22 TP 334.17
 334.19

LOOSE   MO 9.24 OA 25.36
 26.9 HT 42.22 43.18
 SP 51.20 WM 65.27 EA 76.2
 84.30 92.33 DV 176.29
 184.8 FG 190.28 SG 227.7
 228.24 GF 236.26 WS 251.26
 CH 279.9 279.37 279.41
 BL 361.19 MN 367.35 376.24
 PR 484.6 495.2 498.13
 TB 522.9 SU 536.30
 WR 551.29 553.39 565.31
 GG 683.23 OV 748.11 755.39
 756.34 BM 830.25 836.14
 TH 845.5

LOOSE-ALL   DV 166.27 OC 292.21

LOOSELY   CH 276.11 BL 351.22
 JD 613.16

LOOSEN   OA 25.38 FG 193.26
 SD 422.34

LOOSENED   DV 181.6 182.25
 FG 190.11 BO 604.33
 RR 785.21

LOOSENING   PO 101.16

LOOSER   PP 428.41

LOOTED   WR 548.25

LORD MO 10.36 13.15 EA 92.9
92.14 92.26 FG 188.12
CH 279.32 279.35 280.32
280.35 280.37 280.38 280.41
281.1 281.3 281.4 281.6
281.14 OC 294.17 WP 379.32
PP 432.7 FA 468.5 468.8
468.12 TB 512.4 BO 588.35
GG 674.27

LORD BYRON IL 650.23

LORD JESUS FA 468.10

LORD LATHKILL GG 663.15 663.39
666.15 667.21 667.42 668.14
668.38 669.15 670.37 671.8
672.14 672.25 674.37 675.21
676.33 677.23 677.26 677.29
677.34 680.22 680.35 680.39
681.3 681.14 682.10 682.28
683.16 684.12 684.15 684.42
685.5 685.11 685.19 685.31
685.41 686.6 687.19 687.32
688.1 688.35 692.17 695.1
695.11 696.20 699.25

LORD LATHKILL'S GG 667.29 668.28

LORDLIEST EA 92.16

LORDLINESS BO 589.2

LORD'LL OC 295.2

LORDLY OA 32.39 BO 588.41
602.23

LORD NELSON OC 285.34

LORD'S CH 279.18

LORD STAINES GG 662.24

LORENZO LA 630.14 630.21 630.29

LORRY LA 634.30 634.31

LOS ANGELES WR 566.37

LOSE MO 7.38 OA 30.16 EA 76.20
SC 270.7 EE 315.8 321.13
HD 449.34 PR 477.41 JD 612.40
IL 651.16 GG 687.16 ML 728.28
RH 792.6 MD 826.12

LOSING MO 19.42 DV 173.14
WS 253.32 253.41 SC 269.21
EE 321.21 SD 425.12 HD 443.26
449.8 PR 487.26 GG 666.31
BM 837.15

LOSS SP 51.10 EA 84.39
DV 156.39 172.11 185.24
SS 209.22 GF 240.34 WS 258.4
CH 279.26 BL 347.28 350.18
360.9 PR 502.26 SU 538.39
540.16 WR 554.30 IL 651.34
ML 733.1

LOSSES WP 384.11 ML 732.18

LOST MO 22.11 OA 31.42 36.5
SP 49.33 51.40 EA 81.32
PO 104.30 112.5 116.9

LOST (CONT.) TF 125.28 130.11
DV 138.10 158.36 170.31
171.40 173.16 176.4 176.21
180.41 SB 216.35 GF 241.35
WS 257.8 257.31 CH 278.10
OC 287.24 EE 304.6 311.24
323.39 323.41 324.2 331.21
MN 370.2 WP 389.21 PP 434.32
HD 449.6 450.27 FA 463.3
WR 564.14 568.1 571.21
572.37 BO 586.23 LA 645.18
GG 686.9 NT 701.5 705.14
718.3 ML 725.34 731.42
732.27 737.40 739.3 OV 755.25
756.39 LL 767.20 RH 795.7
796.33 796.34 800.23 800.25
MD 807.12 807.15 820.6 820.37
821.42 BM 829.41 830.39
837.13 TH 850.38

LOT OA 34.28 HT 43.13 DV 140.18
144.27 SB 219.14 SG 223.27
SC 272.26 OC 295.40 EE 316.13
TP 341.38 WP 389.26 YT 399.34
SD 419.3 FA 463.9 TB 513.18
WR 547.31 572.39 IL 650.1
GG 673.27 691.32 NT 701.15
707.30 708.30 ML 726.31
RH 789.21 MD 818.14 819.25
BM 836.7 TH 847.19 853.2
853.19

LOTS WP 392.17 PR 488.11
TB 520.32 SU 540.27 IL 648.33
NT 712.20

LOT'S WIFE FA 467.27

LOTUS PR 477.31

LOUD WM 56.31 PO 111.8
TF 127.37 GF 234.32 WS 250.35
CH 276.6 280.28 281.32 282.26
OC 283.3 291.3 EE 331.42
TP 338.20 BL 353.21 WP 387.29
393.8 FA 467.7 468.24
GG 667.7 675.16 681.14
LL 767.42 RH 802.42 MD 810.40

LOUDER LA 638.36 641.2

LOUDEST GG 686.1

LOUDLY MO 10.29 SP 46.2 WM 57.7
DV 148.7 FG 191.30 OC 296.7
BL 361.13 MN 367.4 PP 430.34
HD 444.3 444.9 TB 520.28
LA 632.3 641.8 641.22 644.8
644.11 644.40 GG 672.30

LOUD-MOUTHED FA 466.22

LOUDNESS MO 22.18

LOUD-PATTERNED SD 414.14

LOUD-SPEAKER MD 816.7 817.14

LOUISA DV 143.41 147.27 147.35
153.7 155.12 155.20 155.22
155.30 156.13 159.4 159.17
159.23 159.29 160.5 160.15
160.28 161.2 161.16 161.27
161.30 161.32 161.39 162.2
162.4 162.13 162.18 162.20

LOUISA (CONT.) 162.25 162.27
162.33 162.40 163.4 163.8
163.11 163.19 163.26
163.27 163.30 168.21
169.39 170.2 170.6 170.9
170.13 170.24 170.30
170.41 171.4 171.19 171.24
171.26 171.30 171.40
172.14 174.1 174.30 175.12
175.17 176.12 177.17
177.21 178.5 178.22 182.39
183.5 183.26 183.37 184.1
184.3 184.29 184.32 185.15
185.16 185.17 185.22
185.25 185.38 186.17

LOUISA, AUNTIE (SEE AUNTIE
LOUISA)

LOUISA'S DV 156.6 161.10
169.41 184.25

LOUIS-QUINZE TH 850.39 853.21

LOUIS-SEIZE MD 810.32

LOUNGE GG 687.6 OV 747.2
748.4

LOUNGED OA 24.17 33.5
SG 224.4 SC 271.6 MN 371.9

LOUNGING HT 43.31 TF 117.15
118.7 MN 368.30

LOUSEWORT SS 210.10

LOUSY CH 276.13

LOUVRE BO 588.18

LOVABLE MO 13.26 EA 81.1
86.32 DV 163.35 EE 310.18
FA 465.18

LOVE MO 10.25 11.19 12.39
14.7 17.10 18.27 20.5
20.6 20.9 22.9 OA 37.10
WM 54.16 57.40 61.11
62.21 64.17 64.32 64.41
EA 71.15 73.19 73.30
73.34 73.36 76.10 77.17
78.1 79.26 79.34 81.3
83.33 89.12 89.39 89.42
90.27 90.34 91.13 92.22
92.31 92.37 92.39 92.40
93.3 93.10 93.28 94.8
DV 148.40 154.27 154.31
155.39 156.2 156.3 156.11
156.17 164.31 181.11
181.18 185.22 185.23
SS 204.11 206.1 206.2
206.5 209.31 211.18
SB 217.35 220.4 SG 226.33
230.33 WS 246.12 248.26
259.24 259.29 259.30
259.37 260.4 260.20 266.5
CH 277.11 279.25 280.8
OC 300.5 EE 309.26 309.29
310.12 312.23 324.38
328.18 328.19 BL 348.30
355.10 355.15 364.24
MN 377.38 WP 381.5 381.9
381.20 382.28 384.20
384.21 388.23 YT 405.32

LUCKILY WS 260.26 TP 343.15
  HD 442.14 FA 468.22

LUCK'S MN 372.35

LUCKY WM 62.10 GF 238.42
  WS 245.18 252.5 MN 375.40
  PP 428.5 LL 777.24 RH 792.4
  792.5 792.7 792.13 792.16
  792.26 795.10 796.26 798.14
  798.25 798.30 804.19 804.21
  804.29

LUCRE RH 792.1 792.2

LUCY GF 241.9 SC 269.33 269.35
  270.16 271.28 272.18 272.35
  272.41 HD 442.40 443.30
  GG 678.34 678.41 679.17
  679.26 680.30 681.13 684.26
  687.39 689.22 691.19 695.14
  695.16 696.19 697.12

LUCY'S GG 679.28 679.31 680.30
  681.2 691.40

LUCYTOWN PR 497.18

LUDICROUS EA 88.15 BO 603.6
  BM 839.37 840.30

LUDICROUSLY BM 839.9 839.39

LUGGAGE WM 54.7 FA 459.36
  459.41 460.33 BO 601.25

LUGGED TH 849.41

LUGUBRIOUS WM 62.20

LUIS NT 717.7

LUIS COLMENARES NT 701.1

LUIS SOMETHING NT 706.22

LUKE GG 664.38 667.4 681.17
  683.20 688.4 688.12 688.26
  689.22 690.35 690.40 691.8
  691.12 691.14 691.24 691.30
  691.39 692.1 692.8 692.26
  692.42 693.1 693.6 693.15
  693.27 693.30 694.1 694.7
  699.19

LUKE'S FA 470.21 GG 691.26

LULL EE 330.12 330.19 330.42
  ML 729.24

LUM GF 242.39

LUMBERED OA 35.35 TF 135.1

LUMBERING DV 179.23 PR 499.15

LUMINOUS MO 18.11 SS 208.8
  WP 379.5 PR 489.3 ML 745.8

LUMINOUS-DARK WR 577.16

LUMINOUSNESS SG 228.22

LUMP DV 162.35 163.21 CH 276.4
  EE 317.28 PR 495.23 SU 531.17

LUMP (CONT.) NT 719.8 ML 733.29
  TH 845.13

LUMPISH PR 498.18

LUMPS ML 740.38 MD 812.24
  813.15 TH 849.3

LUMPY SP 45.13

LUNATIC SG 227.34 228.2 233.5

LUNCH EA 83.31 DV 140.15 142.17
  158.2 SS 201.32 202.23
  SG 228.10 PR 494.13 494.21
  TB 516.34 SU 542.16 GG 662.5
  663.17 667.32 LL 766.3 766.10
  RR 781.11 TH 848.42

LUNCHEON PR 475.6 BO 593.38
  594.9 BM 830.25

LUNCH-TIME SS 201.21

LUNGS DV 180.19 HD 450.14
  BO 592.26

LURCH TF 120.28 LA 631.5

LURCHED PO 114.9 CH 276.2
  EE 328.38

LURCHING DV 165.37 EE 324.35

LURID GF 242.19 FA 459.3
  WR 578.23 580.18

LURING EA 93.37

LURK EE 312.27

LURKED EE 306.26 TB 516.25

LURKING MN 369.11 YT 406.40
  408.33 WR 567.40 574.8
  NT 716.17 ML 731.33 740.37

LURKS BO 596.2

LUSCIOUS IL 649.9

LUSH PO 106.26 TF 118.41
  SS 197.18

LUST WS 264.18 TP 344.15
  NT 706.2 706.13 ML 731.25
  MD 816.32

LUSTED EE 306.22

LUSTFUL ML 731.30

LUSTIHOOD MO 18.41

LUSTRE PR 489.14 WR 556.6

LUSTRE-GLASSES OC 296.20

LUSTROUS OA 23.27 WM 58.36 59.5
  PO 115.3 OV 747.3 748.37
  750.27

LUSTROUS-GREY FA 460.42

LUSTS EE 311.31 JD 608.20

LUSTS (CONT.) ML 731.24

LUSTY PR 477.25

LUTHER FA 464.29 464.33

LUXEMBOURG BO 588.18

LUXURIANT EA 71.22

LUXURIATE BL 348.33

LUXURIES SS 207.16

LUXURIOUS EA 81.28 PR 508.10
  MD 825.34

LUXURIOUSLY PR 505.19
  LL 766.35

LUXURIOUSNESS PR 504.38

LUXURY DV 141.27 OC 294.36
  TP 337.18 PR 505.2 ML 726.4
  RH 800.13

LYING MO 3.4 9.1 WM 67.37
  EA 85.33 PO 100.29 110.39
  116.10 TF 126.19 132.13
  DV 139.34 161.24 175.12
  SS 197.30 206.20 210.9
  210.16 SB 214.15 SG 228.6
  GF 239.10 WS 247.3
  OC 297.17 297.35 299.10
  302.10 302.11 EE 317.9
  317.16 TP 338.11 338.30
  345.2 345.10 MN 369.38
  WP 386.26 SD 420.15
  HD 452.30 PR 489.37 490.25
  503.11 506.26 WR 546.33
  562.33 LA 645.26 ML 723.4
  723.29 730.21 742.12
  744.9 OV 748.37 759.10
  LL 768.5 770.27 772.31
  MD 815.37

LYING-CHAIR LL 766.14

LYING-IN EE 309.18

LYRIC OA 27.26

MA SD 413.13 415.7

MA' WP 388.10

MABEL HD 441.1 443.7 444.14
  445.3 445.30 445.34 446.36
  447.4 447.16

MABEL PERVIN HD 449.24

MACAROONS CH 274.28 274.32
  274.35

MACCHE SM 585.15

MACHINE DV 154.15 TP 338.19
  MN 374.32 FA 459.30
  PR 496.24 JD 617.36
  LA 631.20 631.25 632.10
  632.16 632.20 633.5
  633.8 634.7 637.6

MACHINE-BAND LA 632.36

MACHINE-GUN EE 331.5 RR 786.39

MACHINE-GUNS   EE 329.39

MACHINERY   WR 546.22

MACHINES   GF 238.20   238.22

MACKEREL   ML 735.9

MAD   MO 7.11   20.23   OA 35.27
   35.33   EA 80.18   93.35   PO 100.6
   100.35   105.21   115.34
   SB 213.28   SG 227.42   232.41
   233.3   WS 264.12   264.29
   TP 343.16   BL 347.34   YT 405.18
   HD 453.36   FA 462.38   PR 473.3
   474.9   476.23   479.26   480.9
   488.9   512.8   512.14   512.21
   512.23   JD 622.16   LA 641.1
   GG 684.38   685.6   691.30
   NT 703.34   704.10   704.11
   705.41   706.4   706.5   713.13
   713.27   LL 778.9   RH 793.7
   800.9

MADAM   WS 254.20

MADAME   BL 352.4   352.8   352.10
   352.27   BO 588.2   MD 823.12
   823.28   823.34   825.29

MADAME BOVARY   MO 6.30

MADAME'D   BO 587.10

MADAME LA DUCHESSE   MD 809.13

MADAME LA MARQUISE   MD 809.22

MADDENED   EA 75.25   EE 311.42
   TP 344.1   MN 373.26   SD 417.10
   420.40

MADDENING   BL 356.7

MADEMOISELLE VIRGINIA   MD 823.33

MADERO'S   NT 701.19

MADGE   EA 80.3

MADGE'S   EA 85.27

MADLY   OA 35.42   EA 90.1   PO 99.9
   TF 133.10   SD 416.21   HD 450.28
   RH 793.2   803.12

MADMAN   SC 269.21

MADNESS   TF 132.8   SG 231.14
   SC 272.2   SD 417.21   PR 479.20
   479.26   480.3   487.39   WR 554.37
   555.38   GG 664.22   683.26
   691.24   691.34   692.21
   NT 704.12   RH 800.33   803.6

MADONNA   BL 351.27

MAENAD   OA 24.33   EE 324.24
   324.29   IL 653.5

MA'ES   SC 271.36   WP 388.27

MAGAZINE   YT 399.12   TB 521.6
   JD 606.14   619.22

MAGDALEN   EE 304.40

MAGGIE   WP 388.10   388.27   338.39
   389.1   389.3   389.8   389.20
   389.31   390.13   390.20   390.35
   FA 470.21

MAGIC   TF 119.13   FG 195.38
   195.40   196.3   SG 224.16
   EE 314.28   316.5   PP 434.22
   IL 651.35   MD 811.37

MAGICAL   MO 20.17   20.19   WR 546.3
   559.2

MAGISTERIAL   OA 31.9

MAGNA GRAECIA   SU 533.26   539.11

MAGNANIMOUSLY   TB 527.23

MAGNETIC   MN 368.8   MD 812.21

MAGNETISM   WS 257.28   NT 703.27

MAGNETOS   IL 649.38

MAGNIFICENT   MO 4.14   19.21   19.30
   WM 63.36   MN 371.32   FA 461.5
   WR 561.30

MAHOGANY   OC 296.22   PP 433.21
   HD 441.10   GG 671.3

MAID   OA 23.1   23.13   24.3
   EA 74.27   74.29   77.38   84.9
   87.40   88.4   GF 241.15   241.38
   243.17   YT 406.3   FA 459.6
   TB 516.3   ML 726.8   RH 802.36
   MD 815.12

MAIDEN   WM 64.35   TF 123.27
   NT 713.4

MAIDENHOOD   PR 477.24

MAIDENLY   WR 567.31

MAIDENS   BM 830.33

MAIDS   YT 394.28   BM 833.24

MAIDSERVANT   GG 672.29

MAID-SERVANT   OA 23.17   PO 101.37
   TF 123.11

MAIL-STEAMER   ML 740.3

MAIMED   TF 122.26

MAIN   DV 166.32   CH 275.19
   TP 336.4   HD 447.22   BO 596.27
   599.41   NT 718.4   RH 802.19

MAINLAND   ML 729.27   732.36   733.7
   735.38   738.36

MAINSTAY   EE 308.42

MAINTAIN   DV 184.38   BL 350.39

MAINTAINED   MN 377.19   PR 480.38
   GG 688.16

MAIS OUI   MD 822.30

MAIS OUI JE TE CONTENTERAI TU
   LE VERRAS   MD 822.31

MAIZE   WR 558.41   561.8   561.16

MAIZE-FIELDS   WR 561.8

MAJOR   MN 378.19   RR 783.21

MAJORITY   DV 137.15   IL 652.22
   652.23

MAKE-UP   EE 314.12   IL 649.39
   BM 836.7

MAKINGS   WM 68.18

MALABAR   RH 803.17   803.18
   803.26   803.27   803.30
   803.33   803.38   804.14
   804.17   804.18   804.19
   804.20   804.22

MALAISE   LL 763.2

MALARIA   BM 829.15

MALARIAL   MN 373.31

MALCOLM   HD 443.4   444.1
   444.7   444.12   444.24   445.9
   445.13

MALE   MO 13.19   EA 82.14
   DV 152.31   154.1   154.15
   171.9   WS 252.25   261.1
   EE 315.6   315.11   315.12
   315.15   PR 484.25   SU 534.18
   534.39   544.34   WR 567.38
   569.16   569.18   570.10
   576.18   578.14   BO 594.6
   594.8   JD 622.20   623.34
   IL 651.35   RR 781.4
   MD 810.18   813.10   821.19
   821.21   822.37   BM 833.11

MALENESS   NT 710.10

MALEVOLENCE   ML 730.36
   LL 777.35

MALEVOLENT   YT 405.13   405.42
   407.5   SM 584.13   JD 623.15
   ML 732.21   743.32

MALEVOLENTLY   WP 385.14
   ML 730.30

MALICE   FG 187.24   TP 336.24
   344.40   WP 391.42   LA 631.16
   644.10   ML 727.39   LL 776.24
   777.37   BM 836.20

MALICIOUS   FG 188.13   SD 421.6
   LA 644.18   ML 730.37   731.32
   LL 762.3   MD 813.41

MALICIOUSLY   WP 389.9

MALIGNANCY   WR 570.27

MALIGNANTLY   LA 644.15

MALT ML 743.37

MAMA DV 143.22 152.8 152.12
184.25

MAN MO 1.4 5.21 11.7 11.31
12.22 13.18 16.40 17.26
17.40 18.24 18.26 18.38
OA 23.11 23.17 23.24 24.38
25.41 26.2 26.12 26.15 26.37
27.25 29.2 30.9 31.16 31.18
32.12 32.40 33.5 33.15 33.23
34.2 34.20 34.23 34.31 34.36
35.26 35.29 35.32 35.37
36.20 36.24 36.32 37.1 37.13
37.21 38.17 HT 39.2 39.7
39.26 39.33 40.18 42.18
42.37 43.5 SP 45.25 46.9
47.19 47.29 47.40 50.22
50.32 51.3 51.37 51.41 52.25
53.12 53.26 WM 54.18 54.28
56.6 56.7 56.18 56.21 56.34
56.36 57.37 59.2 60.12 64.17
65.16 EA 72.9 72.26 72.27
72.29 72.30 72.42 75.7 75.13
75.18 78.1 80.30 81.37 82.6
83.11 84.20 84.27 84.34 85.9
85.39 86.15 86.20 86.38
87.12 87.17 87.33 89.11
89.14 90.31 93.20 PO 96.9
96.19 96.21 97.16 98.14
98.16 98.27 98.42 99.3 99.9
99.23 99.32 100.7 100.14
100.36 102.1 103.24 103.37
107.16 109.38 110.13 110.18
110.23 111.33 111.36
TF 117.31 118.13 121.12 125.9
126.6 129.6 129.24 132.5
133.23 134.17 DV 136.24 139.1
139.3 139.24 139.39 140.8
145.7 145.10 145.25 145.33
145.34 145.37 146.23 147.10
147.39 148.7 148.10 149.3
149.21 149.28 151.23 151.28
152.42 154.20 156.3 156.17
157.28 158.33 162.14 163.31
163.39 164.10 164.16 164.26
165.2 165.12 166.5 166.34
166.36 170.15 171.39 172.29
173.3 174.5 174.27 176.26
176.30 177.32 177.33 183.12
183.30 183.35 184.1 184.15
184.33 184.39 185.2 185.22
186.5 FG 187.21 190.15 190.37
192.27 193.37 194.19 194.26
SS 198.3 198.6 198.16 199.15
200.22 201.28 201.34 205.14
207.2 208.30 208.38 210.29
211.16 SB 217.12 217.19
218.31 SG 221.1 221.5 222.27
222.33 224.38 226.13 226.18
227.18 228.3 228.5 232.27
GF 235.18 235.29 236.3 236.7
238.30 239.37 241.24
WS 245.15 249.8 250.22 250.37
251.9 252.5 253.12 254.7
254.16 254.27 255.17 255.25
255.31 256.8 256.13 260.23
SC 270.13 271.18 271.23
271.27 272.14 CH 274.24
274.32 275.3 275.7 275.12
275.16 275.42 276.20 276.28
277.20 277.31 278.26 279.7
279.33 280.3 280.5 280.10
280.32 280.35 281.6 281.30

MAN (CONT.) 281.39 OC 285.4
285.11 285.18 285.20 285.25
285.41 286.1 287.35 288.8
292.10 292.14 292.35 295.22
295.27 295.35 295.38 296.1
296.7 297.5 297.6 297.9
297.16 297.35 299.1 299.9
299.42 300.36 300.40 301.19
301.20 301.22 EE 304.28
305.22 305.25 307.41 308.5
308.41 311.35 313.34 313.38
314.41 318.7 320.10 320.17
321.33 322.28 322.30 326.18
326.35 327.5 327.15 328.29
329.4 329.10 329.34 333.9
TP 337.5 339.8 345.39
BL 347.3 347.23 348.34
349.4 350.31 354.23 357.8
357.24 357.33 358.11 358.34
358.41 359.37 360.2 360.23
360.34 361.20 362.22 362.26
363.32 363.39 363.42 364.1
364.9 364.12 364.16 364.22
365.14 MN 366.31 374.12
374.19 375.5 376.8 WP 379.32
388.4 388.8 388.18 388.29
390.38 393.13 YT 395.12 396.9
397.1 397.8 397.16 397.29
398.11 398.13 398.24 399.15
399.26 399.30 400.3 400.22
400.27 400.33 402.11 403.9
403.29 403.31 403.36 404.7
404.10 404.20 404.40 406.7
406.24 407.5 407.13 407.33
407.34 409.4 410.1 410.5
410.12 410.15 SD 411.1 411.7
411.15 411.17 412.13 412.16
412.19 412.22 413.4 413.37
416.29 417.4 417.27 417.32
417.36 417.41 418.5 418.14
418.24 418.28 418.34 419.1
419.22 419.28 419.32 419.42
420.13 420.18 420.19 420.24
420.31 420.40 421.9 421.22
421.27 421.31 421.37 422.6
422.8 422.26 422.32 422.36
422.40 423.9 423.31 424.31
424.40 426.9 PP 427.1 427.10
427.17 427.36 428.27 429.1
429.36 430.14 430.32 430.36
431.6 432.10 432.29 434.34
435.37 436.17 436.41
HD 441.31 443.5 443.24 444.19
444.32 446.28 446.32
FA 463.12 463.13 463.31
465.35 466.8 471.40 PR 473.10
473.26 474.8 475.30 478.23
478.35 479.26 479.30 480.12
480.29 480.30 482.13 482.18
485.21 491.27 492.18 493.34
495.4 503.31 503.37 504.24
505.37 505.40 510.26 510.27
511.1 511.10 511.12 511.16
511.18 511.20 511.25 511.29
511.42 512.13 512.15 512.22
512.26 TB 513.21 513.27
513.34 514.5 514.29 514.33
514.39 514.40 515.37 517.24
518.10 519.3 521.34 524.24
527.26 SU 539.8 539.12 540.6
540.19 540.40 544.14 544.33
WR 546.2 547.14 547.18 548.33
549.32 549.38 550.19 550.38
550.42 553.35 553.36 554.8
554.11 554.17 554.31 554.41

MAN (CONT.) 555.4 555.28
555.30 555.33 556.26
556.31 556.38 557.25
557.32 560.6 560.9 560.19
560.36 560.37 560.38
561.15 562.8 562.39 563.5
563.31 564.2 564.7 564.8
565.24 566.10 566.12
566.22 566.33 567.7 568.9
568.21 569.7 571.6 571.13
571.14 573.13 573.18
575.15 575.19 580.35
581.20 581.26 581.29
SM 583.16 585.7 586.28
BO 587.7 588.36 589.8
589.42 590.1 590.3 590.4
590.10 590.16 590.24
591.10 591.29 592.16 593.2
593.3 593.30 596.12 596.15
596.40 597.4 597.9 597.13
597.19 598.14 601.9 601.31
602.18 603.6 JD 605.9
605.23 605.26 605.33 607.4
608.1 608.16 608.23 609.6
609.19 609.20 611.31
611.35 613.16 614.4 614.5
614.40 615.4 616.6 616.30
617.1 617.10 617.21 617.38
618.3 618.12 618.25 618.30
618.36 619.17 620.6 620.8
620.10 621.31 621.41
622.24 622.39 623.32
624.18 625.6 625.16 625.22
625.28 626.42 627.8 627.15
627.17 627.18 627.30
628.17 628.33 628.35
629.8 629.9 629.15
LA 630.9 630.12 630.14
630.22 630.26 630.27
630.30 630.35 633.10
633.26 633.33 633.39 634.9
634.16 634.19 634.23
634.29 635.5 635.8 635.10
635.16 635.20 635.35 636.1
636.20 636.31 636.34
637.18 641.12 642.21
642.24 642.26 642.29
642.34 642.36 642.41 643.1
643.4 643.13 643.22 643.30
645.30 646.7 646.21 646.26
IL 647.3 649.42 652.13
653.16 656.2 657.23 657.30
657.32 657.35 657.40
659.37 GG 662.41 664.14
669.1 670.23 671.32 672.6
673.30 675.23 680.25
682.38 682.40 686.25
689.31 692.13 693.1 693.34
693.36 696.29 698.10 698.14
698.18 698.26 NT 706.12
706.13 706.15 706.30
706.32 707.1 708.24 710.10
710.15 710.16 710.18
710.22 711.37 713.3 713.27
713.31 714.25 715.5 716.20
716.23 717.15 717.19 719.2
719.23 ML 722.1 722.13
725.9 725.28 725.31 725.32
725.37 726.14 727.8 727.29
727.30 727.31 727.32
728.10 728.31 728.34 729.2
729.7 729.11 730.31 731.9
732.16 732.40 733.11
734.28 735.9 738.2 741.36

MAN (CONT.)   OV 748.4 748.10
   754.12   754.16   754.19
   756.17   756.18   757.16   757.28
   757.38   758.3   758.19   759.20
   LL 764.37   765.15   765.18
   765.23   765.29   771.21   771.22
   774.14   776.19   777.19   777.21
   RR 779.1   779.7   779.18   782.19
   783.20   783.23   785.36   786.22
   788.33   RH 794.26   794.28   795.4
   MD 805.17   806.24   807.38
   810.2   810.12   810.14   810.25
   812.17   813.34   814.25   814.26
   818.24   820.33   823.2   824.3
   BM 827.11   827.20   829.13
   831.14   831.33   831.40   837.13
   837.20   837.35   839.26   840.11
   842.7   TH 844.3   845.12   851.1
   853.10

MANAGE   DV 172.12   172.21
   OC 294.30   FA 459.18   TB 517.14
   SU 541.14   JD 624.13   625.2
   GG 671.20   684.16   687.39
   RH 798.37

MANAGED   OA 34.39   36.27
   PO 104.41   DV 138.31   SD 421.37
   SU 539.9   539.38   BO 590.7
   LA 631.6   ML 746.3   746.16
   OV 757.3   RH 798.38   MD 805.20
   806.4   808.26   BM 832.20

MANAGEMENT   GG 667.4

MANAGER   GF 238.28   239.6
   OC 297.1   297.8   297.13   297.19
   297.29   298.30   BM 830.16   834.4

MANAGES   BM 831.36

MANAGING   DV 140.26   140.28
   PP 431.27

MANDOLINE   SP 47.38   47.41

MAN'D   BM 842.26

MANE   WS 244.14

MANFIELD, T. BROOKS   (SEE T.
   BROOKS MANFIELD)

MANGLE   HT 43.24   43.27   43.37

MANHOOD   MO 11.23   TF 126.11
   EE 315.4   322.33   GG 682.36

MANIFEST   GG 672.17

MANIFESTATIONS   MD 808.32

MANIPULATED   BO 592.22

MANKIND   BO 603.4   NT 708.36

MANKIND'S   OV 758.16

MANLESS   BM 827.8

MANLINESS   YT 398.31   BO 587.26
   588.33

MANLY   WM 64.33   DV 164.5   166.6
   SS 198.10   WS 250.38   JD 624.21

MANLY (CONT.)   IL 651.32
   GG 696.13

MANN   OV 747.27   747.29

MANNA   SC 269.38

MANNER   MO 5.15   13.37   16.29
   OA 33.1   38.28   SP 47.21
   WM 56.3   PO 111.12   TF 131.23
   DV 140.13   147.17   153.32   154.7
   183.15   SS 202.34   203.37
   SB 218.21   WS 246.20   CH 277.31
   OC 285.14   EE 324.39   TP 337.40
   341.34   YT 396.24   PP 427.20
   PR 479.37   483.35   WR 573.25
   JD 608.23   613.19   615.35
   615.36   IL 655.40   GG 669.3
   669.21   NT 705.33   716.26
   RR 786.5   RH 790.10   MD 818.37
   820.18   TH 849.35   853.25

MANNERS   WM 67.36   DV 145.8
   SU 542.22   MD 820.15

MANNERS ROAD   FA 469.25

MANNIE   YT 398.30   398.35   408.4

MANN'S   (SEE MRS. MANN'S)

MANOEUVRES   PO 104.10

MANOR   FG 189.40

MANSERVANT   BL 359.22   GG 669.31
   674.28   RR 786.30

MAN-SERVANT   TF 128.38   129.12

MANSION   BM 827.28

MAN'S   MO 18.21   OA 25.34   26.32
   36.19   36.34   38.9   38.33
   SP 53.9   EA 87.20   87.26
   PO 97.11   97.24   102.21   102.23
   109.40   DV 141.32   142.8   148.15
   148.16   SS 209.37   210.26
   SG 226.23   WS 255.30   CH 276.32
   277.42   OC 284.32   299.36
   300.23   EE 328.10   BL 352.35
   353.17   356.19   MN 373.35
   WP 380.39   388.19   YT 397.42
   400.11   SD 416.23   421.20
   PP 427.37   430.8   432.12
   HD 454.17   FA 472.4   PR 475.30
   484.29   490.7   TB 513.28   517.40
   SU 544.12   544.16   WR 555.18
   560.13   560.16   560.22   570.39
   SM 586.18   604.33   604.34
   JD 619.28   BO 604.33   604.34
   LA 641.38   IL 657.17   GG 692.18
   OV 752.17   RR 781.28

MANSELL, FREDDIE   (SEE FREDDIE
   MANSELL)

MANTEL   WM 58.37   RR 786.16

MANTELPIECE   MO 7.3   8.13   10.37
   OA 33.1   EA 87.7   87.10
   DV 142.33   OC 288.24   HD 443.10
   456.17   RR 785.10

MANTLE   FG 189.26   SS 206.41

MANTLE (CONT.)   207.22
   WR 580.17

MANUEL   WR 550.30   551.12

MANUSCRIPT   ML 735.3

MANUSCRIPTS   LL 764.34

MANY-WINDOWED   YT 394.6

MAPS   TF 125.23   ML 738.16

MARBLE   WM 58.37   59.5
   EA 84.12   PO 102.10
   HD 443.10   448.3

MARBLE ARCH   EA 74.33

MARBLE-PLAYERS   SC 271.14

MARBLES   HT 42.11   SC 270.37
   271.4

MARCH   WM 54.13   PO 96.8
   105.25   111.11   115.22
   TF 134.32   SD 418.7
   SU 537.30   NT 717.31
   ML 745.26

MARCHBANKS   LA 642.5   642.8
   642.30   643.8   643.30   645.9
   645.38   646.11   646.16

MARCHBANKS   (SEE MR. MARCHBANKS)

MARCHED   PO 95.1   95.10
   TF 118.20   118.27   134.9
   SU 530.17   LA 631.26

MARCHING   PO 105.15   TF 118.19
   JD 609.19

MARCH OF EMPIRE   PR 481.16

MARCONI   LA 631.25

MARE   PR 485.9   489.22   490.35
   493.13   498.1   499.6   499.15
   503.6   WR 575.3

MARE'S   PR 485.12

MARGARITA   WR 550.31

MARGIN   PR 477.30

MARGUERITE   TF 118.40

MARIANNE   BO 601.15   601.21
   601.27   601.31

MARIGOLDS   OA 24.31   SS 210.4

MARININA   SU 533.15   533.18
   533.25   537.18   538.4   538.6
   538.28   539.1   539.14   539.17

MARIONETTES   NT 707.3

MARK   SS 211.7   SG 224.1
   CH 279.28   282.3   OC 287.27
   300.13   BL 347.7   WP 383.18
   FA 471.17   JD 621.6
   BM 839.34

MARKBURY   IL 648.4

MARKED   MO 6.26   EA 89.6   PO 97.4
   SB 217.41   FA 465.17

MARKET   MN 370.26   WR 547.5
   547.16   NT 721.5   ML 734.5

MARKET-DAY   TP 336.1

MARKET-PLACE   SP 47.10   GF 241.17
   CH 274.16   TP 334.17   MN 368.30
   WR 546.32   JD 610.7

MARKET-PLACES   TP 334.6

MARKETS   SS 204.29

MARKING   WR 554.3

MARKINGS   PO 115.34   WR 559.23
   578.39

MARK MORIER   GG 672.9

MARKS   DV 167.33   GF 235.22
   PR 498.9   TB 521.27   GG 694.19

MARMALADE   SG 223.5

MARNE COUNTRY   BO 593.26

MARRIAGE   HT 39.14   WM 66.16
   66.41   EA 89.7   89.8   DV 183.6
   WS 260.14   EE 305.10   306.17
   BL 359.24   YT 409.41   PR 480.24
   480.27   480.28   480.29   481.30
   481.41   482.7   485.38   486.6
   WR 546.1   547.24   547.34   548.4
   BO 587.12   JD 627.36   IL 647.31
   GG 664.19   692.15   OV 748.24
   748.28   MD 823.36   BM 829.42
   832.16   833.15

MARRIAGES   WR 546.1   JD 607.9

MARRIED   MO 11.28   14.28   SP 47.19
   51.15   WM 57.34   EA 71.14   71.15
   71.17   81.33   88.15   89.14
   PO 96.27   DV 136.23   136.28
   145.4   151.19   156.7   186.7
   186.22   SS 199.18   199.22   200.9
   200.15   200.20   205.23   210.25
   211.21   211.22   211.27   211.28
   SG 222.27   232.35   WS 244.19
   250.21   259.36   SC 267.16
   267.24   269.11   OC 289.9
   EE 305.8   309.37   313.9
   BL 350.9   355.10   WP 381.42
   382.1   384.17   YT 395.42
   SD 418.34   PP 429.26   430.4
   434.34   HD 446.32   447.10   457.3
   FA 463.11   463.20   469.23
   PR 486.2   508.29   512.26
   TB 513.6   514.7   514.8   519.17
   WR 547.22   567.22   SM 584.34
   BO 590.35   591.33   591.39
   592.14   597.9   601.5   601.9
   601.12   JD 605.17   607.27   608.1
   608.7   608.9   608.24   619.25
   626.27   629.12   IL 647.3   648.12
   659.1   GG 663.15   678.15   678.20
   678.22   678.23   680.3   693.6
   697.13   NT 705.36   718.20
   ML 738.37   OV 747.27   749.25

MARRIED (CONT.)   754.23   754.24
   LL 770.4   777.7   RR 782.35
   RH 790.2   792.17   792.19
   MD 805.11   805.16   806.12
   806.13   810.26   813.20   814.5
   814.8   814.14   824.37
   BM 827.19   829.6   829.9   832.17
   TH 844.3   844.21

MARRIES   DV 184.23

MARRIOTT   (SEE MRS. MARRIOTT)

MARROW   MD 806.33   807.12   811.10
   811.34   TH 848.20

MARROWS   FA 464.32   465.2

MARRY   MO 14.16   20.40   WM 66.15
   66.26   68.15   DV 152.12   152.28
   155.13   156.3   183.26   183.27
   183.29   183.32   184.6   184.33
   185.15   SS 208.22   SG 232.28
   OC 285.22   TP 342.41   BL 349.6
   359.31   YT 394.31   404.6   404.33
   404.38   407.2   407.21   407.28
   408.22   409.14   409.23
   PP 431.42   432.1   HD 442.16
   457.3   FA 459.7   459.13
   PR 473.24   486.2   486.7   510.2
   WR 547.23   JD 613.11   621.16
   626.33   IL 649.18   652.20
   652.26   657.6   657.8   657.11
   657.18   657.27   GG 662.9   665.34
   679.7   679.9   679.12   679.19
   679.38   681.33   NT 716.42
   LL 765.14   766.42   767.38
   773.17   775.9   777.11   MD 810.8
   812.26   813.14   814.3   822.2
   822.15   822.22   822.35   823.15
   823.20   824.10   825.32
   BM 828.38

MARRYING   DV 153.8   SC 267.2
   BL 348.42   349.2   349.3
   FA 463.12   PR 485.39   GG 679.11
   LL 766.41   773.20   MD 805.15
   806.6   813.40

MARS   PR 502.36

MARSH   EE 316.24

MARSHALL, GODFREY   (SEE GODFREY
   MARSHALL)

MARSHALLS   EE 309.8   316.7   325.3

MARSHES   EE 308.3   BO 599.6
   NT 716.2

MARSH-MARIGOLDS   ML 729.35

MARSH-POISON   EE 323.21

MARSH-VENOMOUS   EE 323.27

MARSHY   SS 204.34   OC 283.16
   EE 303.30

MARTHA   FG 190.23   194.5   YT 395.4

MARTIAL   LA 637.9   GG 663.32

MARTYRDOM   SM 584.30

MARTYRED   JD 606.31   606.39
   607.2   622.34   LA 631.15

MARVEL   PP 431.32

MARVELLING   WM 65.26

MARVELLOUS   SS 210.11
   EE 304.11   306.14   TB 517.11
   520.2   SU 530.29   WR 549.37
   JD 615.15   LA 633.40   640.8
   NT 702.9   702.13   702.25
   702.30   703.3   703.5   703.6
   703.28   703.31   712.14
   712.19   714.24   714.30
   714.31   717.13   LL 763.20
   774.15   MD 812.32   TH 848.29
   849.15   850.3   851.33   851.36
   851.38

MARVELLOUSLY   WR 580.13
   NT 709.40   LL 770.13

MARY   OA 25.25   25.27
   DV 138.35   147.27   149.37
   150.24   151.26   152.6   152.11
   152.34   153.5   153.6   153.7
   153.8   155.6   155.16   155.19
   155.20   155.24   155.29   156.6
   156.9   156.18   156.26   156.29
   157.2   158.19   158.27   158.31
   159.11   159.23   159.32
   159.34   159.39   160.8   171.15
   172.20   173.39   174.5   177.20
   183.37   184.9   184.25   185.7
   185.10   185.13   185.33   186.2
   186.3   YT 395.4

MARYANN   SD 413.31   415.7
   417.5   418.35   419.17

MARY HENRIETTA   PR 474.15

MARYLEBONE   JD 627.33   628.38

MARY'S   DV 143.13   151.22
   155.12   155.23

MASCULINE   MD 806.22   820.3
   BM 827.7

MASCULINITY   SB 218.9

MASH   OC 285.8

MASK   MO 3.38   SB 212.14
   GF 239.29   BL 350.40
   PR 508.20   WR 577.17
   JD 611.3   611.27   LL 771.27
   776.15   RR 784.21

MASKED   DV 169.25   YT 394.3

MASON   ML 725.36   726.13
   729.21   730.16   730.34
   731.37

MASONRY   LL 770.25

MASON'S   ML 731.6

MASS   MO 5.21   PO 104.28
   108.30   DV 161.26   FG 187.10
   GF 238.18   OC 286.41
   EE 326.40   327.3   TP 334.35

MASS (CONT.) SD 425.15 PR 483.12
  490.34 497.41 ML 745.38

MASSACHUSETTS TH 844.5 851.26

MASSAGE EE 323.10 WR 577.4

MASSAGED WR 577.2 NT 703.41

MASSIVE CH 278.33 BL 348.10
  354.29 360.5 HD 442.6
  PR 487.24 496.35 497.2

MASSY (SEE MR. MASSY; MRS. MASSY)

MASTER PO 97.38 97.40 98.10
  98.34 101.27 101.36 109.31
  DV 142.1 FG 189.4 189.16
  189.21 OC 291.17 291.25
  302.14 302.15 MN 366.5
  WP 388.36 YT 403.10 403.12
  HD 442.35 442.36 TB 513.31
  515.26 NT 711.5 717.18
  ML 726.19 726.20 726.23
  726.24 727.4 727.12 727.14
  728.8 728.30 728.36 729.2
  729.4 729.9 729.13 729.16
  729.17 729.21 729.25 729.29
  730.3 730.5 730.7 730.14
  730.20 730.42 731.28 731.36
  731.40 732.3 732.17 732.33
  733.26 733.29 734.26 734.30
  RR 783.34 MD 822.3 BM 834.3

MASTERED YT 403.19

MASTERFUL DV 140.23 MN 370.23
  BO 592.27

MASTERFULNESS BO 589.32

MASTER OF ARTS OF OXFORD
  DV 144.38

MASTER PAUL RH 794.15 796.30
  796.37 797.1 797.12 797.18
  797.28 802.26 804.14 804.17
  804.26

MASTERS MO 8.40 TF 127.19
  MN 366.4 YT 399.36 WR 571.19

MASTER'S PO 96.15 99.22
  WR 550.35 ML 728.32 728.37
  731.7 731.12 733.24

MASTERY BL 350.7 SD 411.29
  HD 442.36 WR 581.29

MAT LL 770.19

MATCH MO 18.6 18.18 SP 47.26
  50.29 50.35 51.27 EA 76.24
  DV 152.22 GF 236.15 WS 265.27
  SC 271.17 271.33 271.38
  FA 463.38

MATCHES HD 456.17

MATE WM 63.1 SS 197.3 OC 292.28

MATED EE 306.26

MATER DOLORATA EE 317.38 322.30

MATER DOLOROSA JD 606.33

MATERIAL DV 153.19 ML 725.5
  LL 764.25 TH 848.12 851.25

MATERIALISED RH 790.26

MATERIALISM TH 845.23 845.39
  849.29

MATERIALISTIC DV 163.34
  TH 847.24

MATERIALS GG 669.42 RH 799.15

MATERNAL DV 137.41 BL 351.23
  PP 430.11

MATERNITY OC 288.26 BL 348.34
  350.38 361.18

MATHEMATICAL DV 146.32

MATHEMATICS DV 146.3

MATILDA YT 394.28 305.1 395.3
  395.5 395.8 395.28 396.1
  396.28 396.41 398.23 398.26
  398.32 398.37 398.39 398.42
  399.5 399.29 399.37 399.39
  400.9 400.24 400.26 400.37
  401.1 401.16 401.25 403.15
  404.29 405.3 405.32 405.36
  406.27 406.34 406.35 406.37
  407.2 407.11 407.23 407.30
  407.33 407.41 408.1 408.2
  408.16 408.22 408.24 408.32
  409.29 409.37 409.41 410.6
  410.13

MATILDA, COUSIN (SEE COUSIN
  MATILDA)

MATILDA ROCKLEY YT 394.18

MATILDA'S YT 400.19 401.3

MATING SC 267.6 SU 532.7
  SM 585.31 GG 699.1

MATRIMONIAL IL 650.2

MATTER MO 13.37 OA 34.42
  SP 47.33 53.10 WM 61.41 62.2
  EA 92.26 PO 98.7 113.34
  TF 131.1 131.31 DV 145.34
  152.35 152.42 153.1 162.12
  168.26 170.15 182.18 183.22
  SS 205.14 206.11 SB 212.24
  218.21 SG 225.3 226.37 228.34
  228.39 229.24 230.7 230.17
  WS 260.6 260.8 SC 270.6 273.2
  CH 276.22 279.19 280.34
  OC 285.23 298.11 TP 334.34
  336.35 340.12 BL 355.11
  YT 409.13 SD 419.34 HD 444.38
  447.36 449.17 PR 510.3 511.41
  TB 514.13 523.5 523.13 523.40
  BO 597.13 601.17 JD 608.4
  609.21 619.12 LA 636.19
  644.27 645.15 IL 652.9 659.23
  GG 670.1 691.30 NT 711.18
  718.14 OV 756.3 LL 762.33
  771.11 771.20 RH 795.35
  MD 812.10 BM 833.33 834.4

MATTER (CONT.) TH 849.3
  849.38

MATTERED MO 1.9 DV 145.36
  GF 239.39 PR 510.3
  WR 559.36

MATTER-OF-FACT SB 217.33

MATTERS WM 61.38 SS 205.18
  EE 308.12 BL 349.31
  TB 515.42 RH 794.17

MATTHEW SM 583.15 583.22
  583.30 583.36 584.23
  584.28 585.18 586.22

MATTHEWS OC 297.1 298.38

MATTHEW'S SM 584.12

MATTRESS HT 42.20 43.20
  43.37

MATURE PP 439.38 SU 530.20
  WR 568.39 SM 584.8
  TH 844.17

MAUD SP 51.16 52.6 52.7
  52.22 53.19 53.22
  EA 91.23 91.27 PP 428.8
  434.12 434.41 435.5
  435.19 435.25 438.3

MAUD, AUNT (SEE AUNT MAUD)

MAUD'S SP 52.3

MAULED PR 504.20

MAUPASSANT PR 477.9

MAURICE BL 348.31 349.22
  349.27 349.37 350.2
  350.13 350.20 350.26
  350.33 351.17 353.6 353.7
  353.17 353.30 355.1 357.19
  357.31 357.35 357.42
  358.7 358.28 358.31 358.37
  359.3 359.14 360.10 360.16
  360.18 360.30 360.35 361.2
  361.31 361.36 362.15
  362.19 362.28 363.12
  363.18 363.21 363.25
  363.33 364.5 364.10
  364.16 364.23 364.26
  364.29 364.39 365.1 365.7
  SU 538.30 538.38 539.20
  539.28 539.36 541.4 542.34
  544.21

MAURICE PERVIN BL 349.7

MAURICE'S BL 347.10 349.41
  358.32 361.8 362.21
  SU 544.24 545.4

MAURO LL 774.22

MAUVE SU 532.21 535.33
  GG 683.10

MAYBE WM 63.5 DV 148.6
  GF 238.42 HD 451.39
  PR 487.4 487.5 487.9

MAYBE (CONT.) 488.12 491.34
    JD 626.23 GG 693.12 693.13
    NT 714.31 715.5 715.30
    MD 809.25

MAYONNAISE TH 853.29

MAY-TIME FG 187.8

MAZE SP 45.20

MAZED MO 19.10

MAZEPPA'S IL 651.8

MEA CULPA SM 585.14 585.33

MEADOW MO 22.6 22.15 22.23
    PO 95.6 FG 187.7 MN 366.33
    371.10 OV 749.30

MEADOWS MO 19.34 PO 95.10
    SC 271.29 WR 575.31 OV 750.40

MEAKIN, CISSY (SEE CISSY MEAKIN)

MEAL PO 100.38 DV 159.29
    SG 229.23 CH 279.7 EE 318.33
    BL 352.7 358.40 359.5
    YT 398.16 SU 542.30 WR 552.2
    ML 734.25 OV 748.33 LL 776.29

MEALS EA 81.14 ML 725.19 729.29
    738.38 RH 799.12 TH 850.34

MEAN MO 8.24 8.25 9.34 10.12
    20.12 EA 73.36 74.6 75.10
    75.12 75.13 78.22 82.26 90.6
    93.13 DV 184.33 SS 209.29
    SG 232.9 232.10 232.13 232.26
    232.30 232.32 WS 258.13
    258.26 258.39 CH 275.11
    OC 294.3 TP 341.29 MN 367.6
    369.34 370.32 374.34 374.36
    WP 384.34 YT 405.36 SD 412.39
    412.41 426.18 HD 445.39
    FA 470.13 PR 475.33 507.41
    508.5 511.40 512.4 TB 513.29
    514.25 522.36 526.11 527.5
    527.9 WR 571.1 JD 608.14
    609.16 613.3 613.4 613.9
    614.27 620.2 620.8 620.9
    620.14 621.14 LA 632.40
    633.35 IL 647.9 647.10 647.27
    653.11 658.1 658.24 GG 668.21
    676.34 680.18 680.35 680.36
    689.6 689.26 689.30 693.37
    695.34 NT 701.13 702.19 703.1
    705.10 718.18 LL 778.27
    RR 779.18 781.41 787.4 RH 792.1
    801.34 803.30 803.33
    MD 824.16

MEANER GF 237.36

MEANEST NT 711.15

MEANING MO 10.17 18.40 EA 87.39
    TF 131.1 EE 327.13 YT 401.21
    PP 435.16 PR 482.36 WR 571.18
    573.2 SM 584.29 JD 613.31
    NT 716.14 720.20 ML 741.37
    OV 747.37 RR 785.35 MD 816.25
    816.30 BM 841.4 TH 844.11

MEANINGFUL GF 240.14 YT 398.42
    LA 636.15 636.21

MEANINGLESS WM 60.26 EA 81.34
    DV 146.2 GF 240.13 PR 482.30*
    495.13 495.21 NT 719.17
    OV 748.8 BM 832.6

MEANLY TH 851.12

MEANNESS WP 385.12

MEANS MO 8.31 21.18 EA 94.1
    TF 128.9 DV 145.3 146.28
    184.11 CH 277.21 EE 315.18
    324.25 325.4 BL 364.28
    HD 446.39 PR 473.20 TB 514.19
    SM 584.35 JD 608.14 613.4
    LA 645.7 IL 653.18 GG 664.14
    NT 709.10 718.20 BM 827.10
    834.1 TH 845.3 852.29

MEANT WM 58.26 62.29 EA 78.7
    DV 157.23 165.22 175.28 177.8
    SS 203.24 WS 252.8 256.25
    266.4 CH 278.27 OC 290.12
    300.30 EE 314.20 YT 402.26
    PP 439.33 TB 514.27 515.39
    SU 542.16 WR 547.37 552.23
    BO 589.40 592.35 LA 643.30
    IL 652.36 654.15 GG 678.40
    NT 710.23 715.33 716.36
    OV 751.8 755.39 LL 769.4
    770.12 RR 779.20 782.32
    RH 791.42 792.23 BM 827.6
    830.31

MEANTIME OA 33.18 OC 290.25
    MD 814.9 814.14 TH 852.25

MEANWHILE OA 37.3 WM 66.32
    EA 89.2 PO 107.25 WS 250.16
    251.1 EE 305.20 MN 373.30
    SD 421.4 421.9 PP 430.20
    SU 531.7 WR 573.36 LA 636.33
    GG 676.26 694.28 OV 755.16

MEASURE CH 274.13 BL 356.5
    SU 529.18

MEASURED SD 425.28 BO 591.35

MEASUREMENT EE 332.22

MEASURING BO 592.36

MEAT HT 41.23 DV 163.5
    FG 192.11 SD 414.6 WR 565.2
    GG 680.25 689.18 NT 715.15
    ML 730.27

MEAT-PIE DV 142.17 IL 657.38

MEAT-PLATE JD 619.31

MEATS EA 92.8

MEAT-STALLS WR 546.34

MECHANICAL EA 80.10 PO 108.16
    TF 118.32 119.39 120.4
    DV 160.24 EE 330.8 330.31
    330.33 SD 413.35 PR 496.31
    499.33 ML 737.5 745.11
    OV 752.18 RH 793.36 BM 829.28

MECHANICALLY MO 4.27 EA 81.16
    82.6 PO 108.21 TF 117.25
    121.15 124.7 126.15
    DV 137.40 156.25 170.22
    170.39 SS 197.1 GF 240.5
    WS 263.42 264.26 OC 296.35
    PP 429.12 PR 500.19
    WR 557.6 GG 686.28 NT 708.7
    OV 751.14

MECHANISM EE 330.32

MEDICINE EE 319.17 PP 435.8

MEDICINE-MAN WR 559.32

MEDIOCRE NT 708.15

MEDITATING WP 391.14
    SU 538.26 IL 647.36
    ML 739.6

MEDITATION TH 846.2

MEDITATIVE GG 689.11

MEDITERRANEAN PR 477.32
    SU 539.21

MEDIUM HT 41.10 WM 55.29
    58.11 PO 96.42 DV 139.29
    SB 217.20 HD 444.22
    JD 617.1 GG 672.5 672.33
    679.12 MD 818.29

MEDIUM-SIZED LL 762.39

MEDUSA JD 628.6

MEEK SP 53.25 NT 707.6

MEEKLY MO 9.9 IL 654.28

MEET WM 69.22 EA 77.26 84.8
    PO 97.39 DV 138.12 SG 222.2
    223.11 WS 253.15 CH 278.19
    EE 329.18 BL 355.35
    MN 368.14 368.18 368.20
    369.1 WP 381.16 FA 458.12
    PR 512.13 SU 544.14 544.16
    WR 559.41 BO 592.40 600.28
    603.25 JD 606.3 606.6
    627.33 GG 697.35 697.36
    NT 711.38 718.29 ML 738.2
    OV 757.28 RR 780.38
    MD 819.21

MEETING MO 12.41 OA 32.32
    32.34 EA 85.11 PO 97.37
    DV 173.8 MN 368.36
    FA 458.10 PR 477.1 487.29
    SU 543.17 WR 552.26
    BO 588.3 JD 606.2 ML 737.10
    738.1

MEETINGS GG 697.37

MEISTER EA 86.17

MELANCHOLIC GG 667.37

MELANCHOLY YT 395.10
    FA 465.12 WR 570.8
    SM 586.19 GG 664.23 666.29
    MD 823.14 823.27

MELLOR, ETHEL   (SEE ETHEL MELLOR)

MELLOW WM 58.36 TF 123.12

MELLOW-GOLDEN BL 361.15

MELODIOUS WR 565.14

MELODRAMATIC IL 656.40

MELODRAMATICALLY IL 656.8

MELODY RR 783.15

MELT TF 131.36 PP 435.28
   HD 452.39 454.8 PR 510.39
   NT 714.6 ML 735.31 LL 766.33

MELTED TF 120.15 120.16
   FG 188.16 TP 339.5 MN 368.16
   WR 572.6 NT 703.11

MELTING TF 120.10 120.21 120.23
   TP 339.4 PP 433.41 SU 531.4
   544.5 NT 702.15 702.18

MELTS ML 735.31

MELVILLE TH 848.18 848.37

MELVILLE, ERASMUS (SEE ERASMUS
   MELVILLE)

MELVILLES TH 849.34 850.29

MELVILLES' TH 849.11

MEMBER OA 32.19 YT 394.37
   HD 447.15

MEMBERS CH 278.23 EE 325.14
   FA 469.2 RH 791.32

MEMBRANCE EE 331.10 332.17

MEMBRANE SG 228.18

MEMORIES MO 16.10 16.13
   SU 528.11 533.26 WR 567.6
   RR 779.29

MEMORY TF 130.5 131.30 131.33
   EE 329.6 329.25 332.39
   YT 402.40 403.26 HD 447.7
   448.23 BO 592.9 592.12
   GG 698.2 RR 779.33

MEN MO 5.39 6.4 8.39 13.22
   13.28 16.30 17.29 OA 31.23
   34.7 34.16 38.36 HT 39.16
   39.31 40.25 42.11 42.34
   43.30 SP 45.17 45.24 45.30
   45.35 46.1 46.12 46.33 47.2
   48.15 48.19 48.35 49.12
   49.14 49.27 50.18 52.38 53.4
   EA 83.30 PO 96.8 96.33 97.36
   100.9 107.37 107.41 109.30
   111.9 116.17 TF 119.9 119.41
   123.4 123.5 127.9 127.15
   127.32 129.7 134.37 DV 137.9
   137.19 142.20 144.29 163.40
   164.37 165.12 166.2 166.18
   166.28 167.2 178.10 FG 194.1
   SS 199.32 201.19 209.9 209.22
   209.40 SB 212.33 SG 223.18

MEN (CONT.) GF 241.16 243.16
   WS 251.32 257.9 260.19
   SC 269.1 269.13 269.18
   270.4 270.10 270.35 270.38
   271.6 271.7 271.16 271.21
   271.24 CH 275.26 280.5
   OC 286.10 286.33 291.4 296.42
   297.21 297.27 298.14 298.24
   298.38 EE 315.6 327.9 327.30
   330.40 TP 334.28 335.18
   335.27 BL 349.17 349.26
   351.14 351.41 364.36 MN 366.2
   367.22 367.33 368.38 369.10
   373.1 378.3 378.25 WP 389.32
   YT 394.16 394.31 399.23
   399.37 400.35 404.11 SD 412.4
   412.33 413.8 415.2 415.27
   418.18 418.19 419.15 419.26
   PP 427.3 427.7 428.3 432.24
   438.11 HD 441.13 441.21
   441.26 446.21 446.41 447.4
   449.15 FA 461.3 469.38
   PR 480.23 480.25 480.26
   481.38 481.42 482.7 482.20
   483.13 495.21 510.10
   TB 514.35 514.38 519.7
   SU 533.9 533.12 533.13 534.6
   WR 548.16 548.17 553.18
   553.26 553.30 553.31 553.42
   555.1 556.24 556.41 557.4
   557.29 557.35 559.19 560.13
   560.40 561.3 562.22 562.29
   563.22 563.25 563.26 563.35
   563.37 563.38 563.41 564.15
   566.5 566.6 566.7 566.12
   567.11 567.13 568.38 568.39
   568.41 569.20 569.28 570.5
   570.13 570.15 570.28 571.20
   571.22 571.35 571.36 573.38
   575.14 575.25 575.27 576.13
   576.33 578.15 578.21 579.7
   580.8 580.27 580.34 581.7
   BO 587.21 588.21 591.19
   593.20 593.27 599.37 601.35
   602.2 JD 606.29 606.42 609.31
   610.3 621.2 622.4 627.17
   LA 630.19 642.28 643.20
   IL 652.23 658.15 GG 663.31
   677.19 682.3 682.4 NT 703.18
   707.4 707.8 707.32 707.34
   708.41 709.1 710.9 710.14
   711.19 721.15 ML 724.24
   724.40 730.25 739.31 740.2
   742.6 742.20 742.31 742.38
   OV 757.6 757.19 757.33 758.14
   LL 770.6 RR 779.1 781.36
   782.38 MD 809.42 810.5 810.6
   812.1 812.3 812.10 812.11
   812.12 812.16 812.23 812.29
   812.34 813.2 813.14 BM 827.7
   827.11 827.23 830.24 842.16
   TH 853.14

MENACE EE 316.23 TP 344.31
   BO 595.33 595.36 JD 610.3
   625.15

MENACING MN 374.27 SD 415.31

MENACINGLY SD 417.19

MENAGE EE 307.38 PP 430.18

MENAGE A DEUX MD 814.16

MENAGERIE NT 705.40

MEND OC 295.2 EE 311.22
   326.10 MN 372.32

MENDED MN 371.29 PP 433.3

MENDING OC 287.33 EE 323.31

MENE MENE TEKEL UPHARSIN
   WR 569.33

MENIAL BL 347.20

MEN IN BOOKS AND MEN IN LIFE
   JD 609.30

MEN'S MO 11.35 19.2 HT 42.16
   SS 201.2 201.6 SC 270.39
   SD 411.36 WR 562.28 569.21

MEN-SERVANTS TB 513.26

MENTAL EA 81.39 82.12
   DV 150.31 BL 349.13
   GG 698.35 NT 716.31
   ML 735.25 MD 814.29 814.30

MENTALLY WR 547.35 LL 768.17
   TH 848.16

MENTION GF 240.35 MN 371.28
   SD 420.6 BO 590.20
   NT 714.19 RR 781.4 781.19

MENTIONED JD 605.15 NT 714.19
   ML 728.2 RR 780.30

MENTIONING GG 662.21
   RR 781.32

MENU BO 587.24

MEPHISTO JD 623.17

MEPHISTOPHELES JD 615.7 615.8
   615.9

MEPHISTOPHELIAN JD 622.33

MERCHANT MD 818.24 823.4

MERCHANT'S OV 758.10

MERCIFULLY FA 465.28
   BO 593.38 IL 647.14

MERCILESS MD 813.4

MERCY TF 124.13 TP 343.29
   BL 356.4 YT 403.1 PP 433.9
   JD 625.39 ML 726.6

MERE HT 42.20 WM 54.21
   PO 115.18 TF 118.32
   DV 144.30 165.36 178.9
   TP 339.10 WP 380.34
   YT 394.32 394.37 HD 448.12
   TB 514.39 BO 590.19
   GG 680.17 NT 715.39
   ML 727.38 732.29 MD 806.13
   816.2 BM 827.20 TH 845.13
   846.21

MEREDITH WM 66.4

MERELY   OA 33.13   HT 40.29
  PO 96.33   TF 127.21   DV 137.7
  138.11   FG 187.23   SS 203.41
  GF 240.38   OC 291.6   299.20
  EE 326.38   BL 356.4   MN 373.38
  YT 396.7   405.31   HD 444.25
  WR 556.27   BO 587.4   JD 613.14
  616.17   LA 633.27   GG 689.32
  NT 708.25   716.1   717.15   720.34
  ML 741.22   LL 771.25   RR 788.30
  BM 827.24   TH 848.27

MERFIN   SP 46.15

MERFIN   (SEE JOHN; MR. MERFIN)

MERGED   MD 810.33

MERRY   MO 16.37   16.38

MERSHAM   MO 1.21   2.4   5.6   5.13
  5.23   6.6   10.38   11.12   11.37
  12.12   12.23   12.30   12.40   13.5
  13.13   13.21   13.26   13.40   14.2
  14.16   14.23   14.27   14.31
  14.41   15.12   15.26   15.38   16.4
  16.8   16.23   17.9   17.12   17.23
  17.28   17.30   18.2   18.11   18.15
  18.22   18.42   19.7

MERSHAM, CYRIL   (SEE CYRIL MERSHAM)

MERSHAM'S   MO 5.12   12.27   12.34
  14.13   15.23   15.35

MESH   EA 90.1

MESMERISE   HD 448.26

MESMERISED   GG 681.33   683.8
  NT 703.26   BM 829.30

MESMERIZED   BM 838.3

MESS   TF 123.36   CH 276.10
  WP 387.12   JD 611.7   IL 652.19
  652.27   RR 786.33

MESSAGE   DV 166.15   EE 318.4
  WR 564.37   GG 672.3   679.12
  680.23   RH 804.5

MESSAGES   GG 679.10   679.14

MESSED   SP 51.40

MESSENGERS   WR 574.39

MESSES   IL 652.27

MESSINESS   NT 712.34

MESSING   BL 362.31

MESSY   LA 643.12   643.18
  IL 659.16

MESTER   HT 41.4   43.15   CH 279.11
  FA 461.41

MESTERS   SP 48.31

MESTER'S   HT 40.27

MET   MO 16.11   OA 28.18   29.34

MET (CONT.)   36.9   WM 57.37
  EA 72.33   73.2   PO 100.9
  TF 134.13   DV 137.27   139.19
  144.29   175.18   175.32
  SS 202.29   203.8   205.2   209.14
  209.19   SB 219.17   SG 231.36
  232.14   GF 242.30   WS 257.13
  260.17   OC 300.42   301.1   301.28
  BL 365.4   ML 367.41   WP 391.35
  YT 401.39   402.36   404.11
  PP 434.5   434.29   437.37   439.30
  HD 448.19   FA 464.8   465.17
  PR 484.21   493.3   495.3   506.35
  512.15   SU 543.11   WR 552.27
  555.17   555.30   BO 590.2   590.16
  JD 606.1   628.41   GG 682.38
  698.8   NT 701.1   714.13
  ML 725.42   726.10   737.22
  RR 779.11   MD 807.27   TH 844.3

METAL   SP 49.40   PO 96.2   GG 665.2
  665.25   NT 709.31   713.15
  TH 853.14

METALLIC   WM 62.35

METALS   OC 286.6

METAPHOR   TH 846.33

METHOD   MO 8.41

METTLE   MN 376.5   TB 525.39

METZ   TF 117.6

MEW   ML 740.35

MEWED   NT 717.37   ML 743.24

MEWING   SP 47.41   RR 783.7

MEXICAN   PR 482.22   483.6   483.16
  488.15   WR 548.14   NT 701.2
  704.20   709.27   711.7   712.6
  LL 763.8

MEXICANS   PR 482.30   483.3   496.9
  WR 548.15   NT 709.10

MEXICO   WR 546.7   NT 702.8   705.19
  706.9   706.10   706.18   706.32
  707.4   707.5   707.33   708.11
  708.12   709.15   709.24   716.28
  LL 763.11   763.13

MEXICO CITY   WR 566.36

MICE   PO 113.13

MIDDAY   DV 175.32   WP 379.3
  PR 495.38   SU 542.16   542.30
  WR 552.1   552.2   ML 725.19

MIDDLE   OA 31.15   HT 44.10
  PO 110.1   TF 133.23   DV 139.1
  SS 198.11   WS 255.6   SC 270.37
  CH 278.16   281.30   OC 288.25
  MN 377.8   YT 398.3   SD 413.9
  PR 475.23   483.26   BO 601.29
  IL 649.33   GG 664.15   ML 725.31
  732.42   RR 785.12

MIDDLETON   GG 668.30

MIDLANDS   TP 334.1   PP 431.32

MID-MORNING   WR 558.33

MIDNIGHT   WM 63.23   DV 174.39
  YT 401.30   TB 518.15
  SU 528.5   528.33   BO 604.22
  LA 630.2   NT 709.35
  BM 834.14

MIDST   MO 6.30   18.8   EA 81.3
  SS 206.19   TP 334.36
  YT 398.2   HD 449.29
  PR 483.11   WR 546.16
  GG 687.32   OV 750.35

MIDWAY   WM 60.29

MID-WINTER   FG 191.10

MIEL   MO 12.41   15.19

MIEN   CH 275.36   OC 284.7

MILAN   EA 78.22   88.42
  PR 476.24

MILD   SP 49.11   ML 743.40
  RR 788.14

MILDER   CH 277.19

MILDLY   EA 77.2   MN 372.11
  372.24   YT 408.12   TB 522.10
  MD 816.10   BM 833.39   833.42

MILE   WM 60.21   EA 81.7
  PO 95.24   107.4   SS 197.1
  MN 372.28   FA 460.14   470.10
  PR 481.23   WR 551.15
  IL 653.17   MD 808.9

MILE-LONG   WR 558.20

MILES   SP 47.37   EA 81.8
  DV 136.4   153.29   176.38
  FG 189.40   SC 271.32
  EE 317.42   MN 371.36
  SD 416.40   PR 481.23   482.17
  504.28   TB 513.11   519.16
  WR 547.42   550.28   IL 650.4
  ML 722.30   OV 750.35
  LL 762.21   BM 828.16

MILIEU   NT 706.26

MILITARISM   EE 327.14   327.19

MILITARY   PO 99.13   99.25
  108.18   110.39   TF 118.1
  121.38   124.38   134.6
  DV 150.39   164.28   172.32
  SG 226.18   226.26   EE 327.12

MILITARY-SEEMING   LA 637.9

MILK   MO 3.18   DV 156.38
  FG 191.16   GF 241.19
  OC 300.11   SU 530.23
  ML 743.37   744.35   746.18

MILKED   BL 347.21

MILKWORT   SS 210.10

MISCHIEVOUS WS 249.12 MN 370.11
    SM 583.13 584.7 MD 813.10
    822.29

MISCHIEVOUSLY MN 370.42 GG 665.7
    MD 806.18 826.22

MISERABLE SP 49.28 EA 79.37
    87.23 87.31 89.22 DV 137.24
    165.33 GF 242.24 WS 249.38
    259.19 BL 352.32 356.21
    FA 465.32 JD 624.28 IL 652.21
    NT 710.37 TH 852.28

MISERABLY GF 239.21 GG 675.7
    ML 737.1

MISERY WM 69.40 PO 100.27
    104.12 DV 138.1 GF 234.31
    EE 328.36 TP 339.24 BL 347.37
    348.10 365.5 PP 439.23
    GG 691.16

MISFORTUNE GG 693.7 699.38
    LL 777.24

MISGIVING DV 165.38 SB 219.2
    SU 528.15 534.17 WR 559.38
    IL 647.34 652.31 GG 664.13
    LL 776.10 MD 824.4

MISGIVINGS EE 313.19 BO 588.17

MISGUIDED DV 155.24

MISPLACED DV 177.24

MISS WM 67.18 DV 141.28 143.35
    CH 279.13 EE 319.13 BL 361.10
    WP 381.10 383.29 HD 445.27
    445.28 445.29 446.18
    LA 634.37 IL 649.1 OV 756.37
    BM 827.12

MISS ANNIE TP 337.22

MISS BERTHA CH 279.42 280.4
    280.6 282.16

MISS BIRCH SG 231.5 231.36
    232.15

MISS BUNBURY WM 57.15

MISS CLEVER IL 658.17

MISS CUMMINS PR 479.27 480.7
    480.11 480.35 480.37 480.38
    481.5 481.20 481.26 481.28
    483.29 485.14 487.37 488.12
    488.28 489.22 491.1 491.5
    491.19 491.22 491.28 491.37
    491.40 492.1 492.5 492.10
    492.13 492.15 492.25 492.30
    493.6 493.9 493.12 493.39

MISS CUMMINS'S PR 481.9 490.16*
    512.17

MISSED SP 49.18 WM 57.17
    TF 120.20 BL 352.10 MN 371.22
    YT 394.25 PR 510.31 SU 535.17
    543.39 BM 833.8

MISSHAPEN PR 482.34

MISSING EA 81.1 89.42 HD 451.14
    FA 458.17 BO 591.24 MD 812.5

MISSION EA 86.33 86.34
    TB 519.35 GG 662.33 ML 741.27
    MD 816.35

MISSIONARY WR 549.5 549.6

MISSIS HT 41.13 41.22 41.30
    41.37 42.26 43.25 SP 46.7
    SC 268.21 269.29 OC 295.23
    SD 416.18 416.24 416.26 417.6
    418.3 422.35 426.19

MISSIS'LL SC 269.38

MISS JAMES LA 633.8 633.24
    633.36 633.38 634.2 641.8
    641.17 641.25 645.27 645.41
    646.28

MISS LASKELL OV 760.4

MISS LOIS GF 238.9

MISS LOUISA DV 138.22 138.31
    143.2 143.11 143.22 143.30
    143.35 143.40 144.1 144.14
    144.22 144.28 146.13 147.21
    147.30 147.40 148.2 148.11
    148.27 148.35 148.38 149.5
    149.12 149.17 149.21 149.32
    150.13 150.22 150.33 152.25
    152.33 155.9 155.13 155.17
    155.33 156.5 158.12 158.16
    158.24 158.29 160.3 160.10
    160.39 162.9 168.1 168.10
    169.4 169.20 170.20 171.23
    171.39 172.4 172.18 175.36
    177.12 177.26 178.3 183.26
    183.27 184.42

MISS LOUISA'S DV 142.37 147.22
    148.32 158.32 169.12

MISS MARY DV 138.19 138.24
    138.30 143.3 144.1 144.25
    144.28 146.15 146.29 146.37
    147.18 150.5 150.11 150.14
    150.19 151.19 151.29 152.20
    152.25 152.27 174.3 177.13
    177.20 185.6

MISS MARY'S DV 147.6

MISS M'LEOD BM 828.4 828.9
    831.1 831.3 831.5 831.9
    832.12 834.18 836.4 836.13
    836.20 837.14 837.24 837.26
    837.30 838.6 838.17 840.17
    841.1

MISS M'LEOD'S BM 828.14 836.36

MISS PERVIN HD 445.32

MISS PRESCOTT PR 473.25

MISS ROWBOTHAM CH 278.38 279.4
    279.22 281.17 282.13

MISS STOKES MN 367.10 367.12
    367.18 367.33 368.7 368.10
    370.4 370.14 370.23 370.27

MISS STOKES (CONT.) 370.32
    370.33 370.42 371.24
    371.34 372.1 372.2 372.4
    372.7 372.8 372.9 372.18
    372.22 372.27 372.36 373.3
    373.5 373.8 373.12 373.16
    373.25 374.15 374.28
    374.35 376.35 378.1 378.18
    378.33

MISS STONE TP 335.32 335.34

MISS SYFURT WM 59.17 59.22
    59.31 60.2

MISS SYFURT'S WM 60.17

MISS URQUHART PR 480.36 486.3

MISSUS SD 413.5

MISS VARLEY WM 59.19

MISS WILMOT RH 802.24

MISS WREXALL TB 513.35 523.17
    523.18 524.6 524.19 524.24
    524.36 525.1 525.12 525.13
    525.18 525.20 525.22
    525.25 525.28 525.38 526.2
    526.10 526.13 526.22
    526.29 527.3 527.7 527.23
    527.29

MISS WREXALL'S SU 527.21

MIST MO 2.6 3.4 21.12
    CH 275.28 PP 430.28
    PR 473.31 WR 577.25
    ML 723.25 735.33 736.4

MISTAKE GF 243.28 WS 258.10
    OC 295.1 TP 339.1 339.13
    YT 402.17 402.23 409.1
    409.3 JD 611.29 LA 642.33
    IL 649.19

MISTAKEN SS 208.2 SD 416.26
    TB 526.20 IL 658.16
    OV 757.27 LL 761.2

MISTER SP 46.32

MISTLETOE MO 6.16 7.2
    TB 526.39 ML 724.29

MISTRESS OA 34.7 EA 92.22
    PO 96.30 CH 274.1 FA 459.41
    TB 516.29 SU 535.26
    NT 707.17 707.37 708.2
    710.4 710.26 710.36 713.31
    ML 738.42 MD 820.31

MISTRESSES TF 127.19

MISTRUST MO 21.30 OV 753.34

MISTRUSTED SU 534.7 534.15

MISTRUSTING TP 342.18

MISTY SG 225.12 WR 577.23
    NT 705.42

MITE DV 158.23 CH 277.5

MITE (CONT.) 277.10 EE 309.6
  PR 476.20

MITES WP 392.17

MIXED DV 181.28 FG 194.5
  CH 280.8 MN 376.21 HD 455.40
  RR 787.12 TH 844.35

MIXING PP 428.40 GG 688.7
  RH 802.37

MIXTEC INDIAN NT 701.25

MIXTURE BO 587.18 JD 623.16
  LL 763.10 773.29

M'LEOD BM 827.12

M'LEOD, LENA (SEE LENA M'LEOD)

MOAN DV 169.18 OC 297.18

MOANED DV 162.32 162.37 163.9
  172.16 OC 294.8 295.35 296.13
  EE 317.30 FA 468.32 JD 610.28

MOANING WM 69.5 OC 296.32
  298.28 298.29 MN 373.22
  BO 604.32 GG 693.32 ML 724.42

MOAT TF 118.36 119.4 119.10
  119.16 119.19 124.2 128.27

MOB EE 327.6

MOB-EMOTIONS GG 674.12

MOB-SPIRIT EE 327.30

MOCCASINS PR 506.21 506.28
  BM 827.21 827.22 833.9 833.11
  833.22 833.26 835.25 835.26
  835.28 835.30 835.31 835.32
  836.31 836.37 836.40 836.42
  837.1 837.34 837.40 838.4
  838.7 838.18 838.21 838.38
  840.6 840.15 840.22 840.27
  840.29 840.32 841.4 842.25

MOCK DV 138.27 FG 187.23
  WS 261.4 MN 369.17

MOCKED OA 25.1 EA 71.12 75.12
  88.23 WS 262.32 TB 517.36
  IL 655.42 GG 665.39 OV 756.20
  756.41 757.14 MD 819.20

MOCKERY WM 57.9 EA 76.11
  PO 100.25 YT 395.39 PR 486.40
  SU 538.16 538.29 LA 644.10
  NT 701.12 LL 764.27

MOCKING OA 28.6 EA 74.23 75.16
  77.26 PO 101.38 SG 231.34
  WS 263.36 EE 325.22 MN 378.24
  WP 381.33 YT 404.10 FA 467.29
  BO 601.33 JD 606.25 LA 637.35
  IL 648.9 GG 687.24 NT 711.23
  ML 727.26 LL 761.27 761.37
  762.2 MD 813.39

MOCKINGLY LL 769.31

MODE SC 267.24

MODELLED PR 479.36 481.7

MODERATE HT 39.26 PR 474.42
  RR 782.25

MODERATED CH 276.7

MODERATELY EE 304.29 MN 367.23
  GG 670.16 RH 799.32 MD 811.33
  823.25

MODERATION SU 542.23

MODERN EA 86.2 SS 197.29
  EE 307.5 309.25 322.7 328.25
  TB 514.15 521.6 521.7 521.9
  BO 589.13 598.13 JD 610.23
  610.25 GG 672.42 682.4 682.39
  NT 705.39 711.19 711.42
  RH 791.9 MD 809.23 811.25
  812.34 BM 827.3 TH 844.25
  846.1 853.17

MODEST TF 130.25 EE 307.42
  MN 368.32 PR 474.37 474.41
  BM 834.32

MODESTLY MO 15.34 MN 367.15
  GG 671.20 RR 783.30 BM 829.40

MODESTY MO 15.20 15.23
  TF 132.10 SC 270.4 SD 413.37

MODIFIED WM 64.39

MODULATED HT 40.24

MOEST EA 75.8 84.25 84.31 85.3
  85.4 85.24 86.5 86.25 86.34
  87.1 87.10

MOEST (SEE MR. MOEST)

MOEST'S EA 85.11

MOIST HD 448.38

MOISTENED WR 564.8

MOISTURE TF 132.9 BL 362.11
  WR 565.42 566.1 574.10

MOLE SB 214.17 214.27 214.31
  215.18 215.29 215.33 216.1
  216.14 218.32 219.28

MOLE-COLOURED WM 55.32

MOLE-HILLS MO 21.38

MOLES SB 216.21 219.12

MOLESKIN DV 168.15 SC 267.33

MOLEST ML 740.28

MOLLIFIED DV 185.30

MOLLUSC BL 365.15

MOLTEN EA 77.28 WS 254.40
  255.20 263.12 SU 529.36
  532.10 BM 836.16

MOMENTARY TF 130.19 WP 379.32

MOMENTS MO 10.38 18.9
  OA 24.3 WM 58.1 69.12
  EA 78.11 PO 101.36 111.6
  115.9 DV 141.39 180.23
  SS 199.9 199.19 207.9
  GF 240.21 WS 258.38 265.41
  OC 284.9 299.12 TP 338.21
  BL 350.24 MN 372.25
  SD 422.6 HD 450.29 452.35
  PR 478.1 494.31 502.26
  511.10 WR 562.38 564.1
  568.4 578.9 JD 606.22
  606.25 GG 673.9 688.15
  ML 742.32 LL 771.30
  RH 796.17 801.21 BM 838.20

MOMENT'S WM 58.30 PO 101.10
  EE 331.33 SD 412.21
  PP 427.30 WR 548.18 554.11
  557.16 572.4 MD 823.17
  BM 833.27

MONA LISA LL 761.37

MONASTERY RR 787.15

MONASTIC SU 540.19

MON CHER WP 392.21

MON CHERE WP 392.21

MONDAY WM 60.37 EE 329.16
  TP 337.9 MN 370.4 372.31
  YT 397.23 HD 443.37
  PR 488.23 488.27 488.31
  JD 626.5 626.9 627.31
  628.37 GG 668.26 668.33

MONET TH 844.26

MONEY HT 39.8 41.38 41.40
  42.3 42.5 SP 46.3 46.11
  46.31 46.39 50.20 50.21
  52.3 WM 62.16 EA 78.33
  TF 132.38 DV 136.12 144.27
  155.25 160.4 SC 267.8
  OC 285.42 EE 305.18 309.2
  309.17 310.33 310.37
  310.40 310.42 311.18
  311.24 315.37 315.40
  325.5 WP 381.21 381.22
  YT 396.19 400.15 401.20
  401.23 405.29 405.31
  406.25 406.26 406.31
  406.32 406.34 406.35
  406.37 406.38 407.28
  408.25 409.10 SD 420.27
  420.28 PP 427.35 429.31
  429.38 HD 446.40 447.1
  FA 462.24 471.41 PR 474.37
  477.42 478.19 478.27
  485.41 491.30 TB 519.25
  WR 547.23 BO 587.6 GG 662.4
  671.19 671.21 NT 701.15
  704.27 704.40 705.1 705.4
  705.6 705.14 716.33 720.39
  ML 725.11 729.33 731.10
  732.11 732.30 738.17
  742.13 OV 758.39 LL 762.33
  764.21 769.32 773.18
  RR 780.33 780.38 783.1
  RH 790.22 790.27 790.34
  790.35 791.5 791.6 791.10
  791.11 791.15 791.24

MONEY (CONT.) 791.38 791.40
   791.42 792.1 792.4 792.5
   792.6 792.7 796.6 797.11
   797.21 798.10 798.19 800.17
   800.18 MD 806.8 813.17 814.19
   817.40 821.11 BM 829.41
   TH 844.5 844.12

MONEYS TF 128.3

MONEY-STRAIN EE 309.19

MONGREL TB 523.22 SU 544.37

MONGREL-LOOKING PP 428.27

MONKEY DV 141.33 WP 389.24
   BM 836.6

MONKEYED ML 731.38

MONKEY-NUTS MN 371.4 374.1
   374.15 374.29 377.37 378.24

MONKEYS MN 371.2

MONKS FG 188.32

MONK'S SM 582.24 583.2

MONKSHOOD WM 54.27

MONOLITHIC BL 357.42

MONOLOGUE RR 783.19

MONOMANIA GG 666.30

MONOSYLLABLE MO 9.14

MONOSYLLABLES DV 177.41

MONOTONE SS 210.12 GG 665.25

MONOTONOUS OC 295.6 TB 518.17
   WR 569.4

MONOTONOUSLY PO 105.26 DV 156.19

MONOTONY DV 142.39 WR 550.20
   GG 685.9

MONSIEUR ARNAULT MD 818.30

MONSIEUR LE MARQUIS MD 809.13
   809.15 809.22

MONSIGNOR MAURO LL 774.18

MONSTER YT 407.31 PR 477.29

MONSTROUS WM 66.15 PR 496.31
   496.40 BO 591.18 IL 650.26
   GG 685.12 690.24 690.25

MONTEZUMA WR 550.5

MONTH OA 26.3 EA 78.17 78.38
   89.2 EE 325.11 328.5 SD 418.7
   FA 464.24 PR 474.25 480.33
   SU 541.15 IL 647.4 659.2
   BM 829.12 TH 850.8 850.40

MONTHS MO 4.10 7.22 14.9
   HT 39.16 SP 51.15 51.23

MONTHS (CONT.) WM 57.22 57.23
   61.10 65.33 EA 71.16 76.6
   76.29 79.40 81.33 93.16
   93.27 93.32 PO 97.41 99.29
   DV 144.36 SS 199.25 SG 231.37
   232.14 WS 260.17 OC 294.26
   EE 328.36 329.36 TP 336.39
   BL 347.31 YT 407.3 SD 419.18
   PP 427.28 HD 446.36 PR 474.6
   477.1 478.16 478.18 WR 548.8
   548.10 IL 649.11 GG 667.17
   ML 735.6 739.2 OV 748.24
   748.28 LL 767.14 RR 782.22
   BM 833.8 TH 851.17

MONTH'S DV 161.7

MONTHS' DV 150.16 150.17 151.19

MONTMARTRE TH 844.30

MONTREAL YT 396.32

MONUMENTS TH 848.23

MOO ML 723.27

MOOD BO 600.24

MOODS BL 348.35

MOODY JD 606.22

MOOED WP 379.34

MOON MO 3.13 WM 55.2 61.2
   62.17 EA 75.7 FG 194.37
   194.38 194.41 CH 275.27
   MN 371.32 373.11 YT 401.31
   WR 548.40 556.17 570.6 570.37
   571.6 571.8 571.10 571.12
   571.15 571.29 571.31 571.32
   571.34 572.24 572.27 572.30
   572.33 575.2 575.4 575.5
   575.10 575.11 575.12 575.15
   575.20 575.22 575.25 575.30
   575.37 LA 630.4 IL 651.1
   654.3 ML 723.29 731.19
   OV 747.4 748.18 748.22 748.39
   749.1 749.33 749.35 749.39
   749.42 750.2 750.3 750.18
   750.22 750.38 750.41 751.7
   751.17 751.23 755.23 755.25
   756.13 RR 782.38 MD 806.20
   823.37

MOON AND STARS HD 446.17

MOON-DUST OV 750.40

MOONLIGHT WM 68.23 MN 373.26
   WR 556.21 556.23 557.17
   IL 651.10 651.30 OV 748.38
   749.23 749.37 750.20 751.2
   751.19

MOONLIT OV 750.36

MOONS WM 58.39

MOOR GG 668.31 BM 835.19

MOORE, GEORGE (SEE GEORGE MOORE)

MOORISH BM 835.19

MOPE BM 836.12

MOPPED OC 297.27

MORAL DV 150.31 GG 662.37

MORALLY WR 547.37 GG 663.4

MORBID OA 33.35 BO 587.7

MOREOVER OA 35.35 38.1
   HT 39.23 EA 86.32 TF 128.1
   128.12 DV 169.11 JD 609.26
   RR 779.7

MORE-PELLUCID ML 734.16

MORIER GG 690.40 693.18

MORIER (SEE MARK; MR. MORIER)

MORLEY FA 464.6

MORLEY CHAPEL FA 464.6 464.10
   464.25 464.29 464.36

MORN SP 52.40 SM 582.23

MORNIN' HT 43.2 SC 267.31
   WP 389.14

MORNING OA 33.41 38.15 38.20
   HT 42.12 SP 45.2 52.23
   WM 61.17 EA 83.24 87.2
   88.39 PO 95.29 103.20
   103.29 104.10 106.6 107.19
   115.26 115.31 TF 132.15
   132.21 135.2 DV 138.14
   138.35 FG 188.22 190.3
   192.28 195.9 SS 197.6
   204.28 SB 217.31 SG 221.3
   221.4 222.10 223.38 223.40
   224.2 225.12 226.14 228.4
   232.2 GF 239.22 239.24
   240.12 241.28 WS 244.21
   245.19 250.6 SC 267.36
   270.11 271.7 CH 282.28
   EE 329.16 TP 335.42 336.13
   336.28 337.1 341.33
   MN 370.14 377.41 WP 385.27
   385.37 YT 397.8 400.30
   402.31 404.27 409.31
   PP 432.5 432.20 433.32
   FA 471.24 PR 488.27 488.31
   TB 518.19 SU 529.35 532.29
   543.37 543.41 WR 557.26
   558.9 BO 594.30 598.17
   JD 624.4 624.22 628.20
   628.37 LA 640.30 644.7
   IL 649.11 GG 682.33 699.18
   ML 727.5 730.19 730.38
   730.39 736.19 743.21
   744.19 744.28 744.40
   OV 753.8 753.29 758.41
   759.6 LL 765.40 RR 781.11
   788.41 RH 799.24 MD 826.8
   BM 830.18

MORNING-DROWSY WS 246.18

MORNING-ROOM YT 397.5
   GG 682.21

MORNINGS DV 136.5 147.21
   EE 306.14 TH 844.28 848.39

164

MORNING'S HD 441.8

MORNING-STILL SB 212.35

MOROSE GF 235.8 CH 274.24

MORRIS EE 312.2

MORRIS, WILLIAM (SEE WILLIAM
  MORRIS)

MORRIS-DANCE EE 305.17

MORROW MN 376.15 377.40
  SU 537.27

MORTAL SC 269.34 BL 364.30
  LA 640.21 GG 690.42 NT 708.31
  MD 817.9

MORTALLY HD 451.29

MORTIFICATION DV 137.25
  YT 397.15 LL 762.30

MORTIFIED MO 11.14 MN 372.26
  MD 806.21 819.27

MORTUARY PO 116.18

MOSTLY SS 202.7 MN 377.2
  WP 387.5 BO 589.39 NT 701.5
  708.14 RH 797.33 MD 812.1
  817.12

MOTH OA 29.33 WM 60.20 63.1
  WP 389.38 OV 747.20 747.36
  748.19 748.22

MOTHER MO 4.2 4.24 4.42
  OA 25.13 25.17 25.30 25.35
  25.40 26.4 26.24 26.30 27.12
  27.15 SP 52.2 52.6 52.9
  PO 96.24 113.34 TF 117.24
  128.3 131.22 132.37 133.34
  DV 138.4 138.15 139.37 142.8
  143.20 144.7 144.9 144.16
  148.17 148.20 148.21 148.25
  148.27 149.7 149.9 149.24
  149.39 152.11 152.23 154.34
  155.27 155.32 155.34 157.6
  157.22 157.26 157.30 157.35
  157.37 158.21 159.13 159.27
  159.40 160.11 160.34 163.27
  163.34 163.40 164.31 167.38
  168.20 169.6 169.15 169.17
  169.22 170.3 170.27 171.7
  171.34 171.38 171.40 172.2
  173.20 173.23 173.31 173.37
  174.33 174.34 175.3 175.20
  175.23 175.25 175.26 175.32
  176.32 182.39 184.9 184.24
  184.39 185.4 185.41 186.15
  FG 193.28 SS 201.36 SB 212.32
  220.6 SG 225.32 GF 237.22
  237.24 237.27 237.30 239.9
  WS 260.34 260.39 CH 277.9
  278.2 278.40 279.26 279.36
  280.15 280.19 281.20 281.36
  282.1 282.7 282.14 OC 284.23
  284.36 284.39 284.41 286.20
  287.1 287.4 287.8 287.10
  287.11 287.13 287.16 287.17
  287.18 287.30 287.33 288.2
  288.4 288.16 288.21 288.27

MOTHER (CONT.) 288.40 289.1
  289.2 289.4 289.7 289.13
  289.32 289.39 289.40 290.8
  290.10 290.18 293.30
  293.37 294.3 295.33 296.10
  296.12 296.33 296.35 298.3
  298.36 298.42 299.13 299.17
  299.19 299.27 299.38 300.3
  300.5 300.12 301.25 EE 309.25
  309.34 311.3 311.9 316.3
  316.14 316.25 316.28 316.42
  317.1 319.19 320.6 320.25
  320.32 321.36 322.17 322.23
  322.26 322.41 324.7 324.8
  324.32 325.18 TP 340.16
  WP 381.16 382.4 382.7 382.10
  383.32 383.35 384.1 385.23
  389.1 389.25 389.30 391.39
  YT 395.11 409.11 409.12
  409.13 SD 414.1 PP 427.35
  429.15 431.37 435.17 438.3
  438.13 438.19 439.3 440.11
  440.23 HD 447.7 447.28 448.5
  448.8 448.10 FA 463.2 469.23
  470.16 470.41 471.13 471.21
  471.23 472.11 PR 474.38 478.7
  TB 516.1 516.2 516.6 516.39
  524.21 524.32 SU 528.4 529.27
  529.32 534.15 WR 551.1 574.42
  BO 591.28 592.19 JD 608.25
  612.8 613.28 613.29 621.24
  624.34 IL 648.40 648.42
  GG 662.24 667.22 667.29
  668.14 669.4 669.8 672.2
  672.8 681.18 682.20 682.21
  684.42 685.10 685.33 688.4
  688.12 688.23 688.32 690.27
  695.2 695.11 695.15 695.19
  695.22 695.32 696.23 696.24
  696.25 696.26 696.28 696.29
  696.32 697.2 697.3 697.6
  697.7 697.8 699.29 699.34
  NT 701.25 ML 738.40 LL 762.42
  763.7 764.10 764.18 764.33
  765.12 765.16 765.27 765.29
  768.22 768.28 771.16 771.18
  772.13 773.18 776.5 776.24
  776.27 776.37 777.12 777.18
  778.11 RR 782.9 RH 790.14
  790.22 790.29 791.1 791.29
  791.33 791.34 791.38 792.1
  792.3 792.16 792.27 792.33
  793.24 793.30 793.33 793.39
  798.12 798.21 798.30 798.41
  799.7 799.11 799.13 799.20
  799.26 799.31 799.36 800.6
  800.13 800.34 800.40 801.11
  801.20 801.27 801.29 801.31
  801.41 802.1 802.11 802.29
  802.33 802.34 803.24 803.31
  804.2 804.6 804.11 804.18
  804.19 804.21 804.27 804.28
  804.30 804.32 MD 805.5 805.10
  805.12 805.18 805.19 805.23
  805.24 805.25 805.28 806.13
  806.16 807.8 807.9 807.17
  807.27 808.19 810.11 810.26
  811.11 811.41 812.14 812.30
  813.37 814.3 814.16 814.36
  815.37 816.15 816.16 816.40
  818.17 820.31 821.11 821.16
  822.20 822.36 824.6 824.9
  824.12 824.33 824.41 825.11
  825.12 825.13 825.29 826.21
  BM 827.12 TH 851.29 851.32

MOTHER (CONT.) 851.35 851.42
  852.33 853.2

MOTHERED GG 678.24

MOTHERHOOD EE 309.30
  RH 803.21

MOTHER-IN-LAW SP 51.15 51.19
  51.28 51.33 51.42 52.4
  52.14 52.29 53.14 53.19
  DV 159.42 OC 295.12 296.31
  301.40 FA 463.26 GG 670.4
  670.9 686.10 687.1 687.15
  687.39 MD 805.21

MOTHERLINESS CH 276.39

MOTHERLY SD 415.1 BO 591.8

MOTHER OF GOD EE 322.21

MOTHER OF JESUS WP 381.7

MOTHERS OV 747.33 753.4

MOTHER'S OA 25.38 27.22
  SP 53.26 DV 155.28 160.15
  168.5 174.18 174.30 175.1
  175.18 178.17 GF 237.22
  237.30 WS 260.39 CH 279.17
  OC 288.39 289.24 EE 324.10
  324.31 WP 383.17 383.20
  383.35 PP 428.39 FA 462.18
  GG 680.23 OV 758.17
  LL 771.11 776.19 RH 799.2
  MD 806.8 808.13 808.14
  811.9 813.41 815.5 817.16
  825.22

MOTHER SUPERIOR SM 583.4
  583.8 583.11 583.34 584.11
  584.17 585.15 585.19
  585.39 586.1 586.9 586.11
  586.20

MOTHER SUPERIOR'S SM 582.33

MOTH'S FG 194.17

MOTION SS 201.13 EE 304.19
  BL 362.26 WP 379.10 379.15
  383.23 386.7 HD 448.36
  PR 501.26 WR 572.18 578.35
  BO 593.13 594.4 RH 803.2
  MD 810.3 BM 829.28 829.36

MOTIONLESS OA 36.15 EA 73.12
  PO 103.15 TF 117.23 119.16
  122.34 129.36 133.18
  134.8 134.25 134.35
  DV 180.36 180.39 SS 201.5
  SG 227.8 227.26 231.13
  WS 249.24 264.27 265.15
  BL 353.18 WP 385.40
  SD 423.29 HD 449.40 449.42
  454.16 455.7 FA 467.24
  PR 492.14 507.9 509.18
  511.9 SU 544.2 WR 548.29
  552.3 BO 596.15 596.16
  596.19 JD 625.3 IL 650.3
  651.2 ML 744.31 745.3
  LL 771.1

MOTIONLESSNESS WR 581.25

MOVED (CONT.) HD 442.8 449.35
  450.15 450.23 TB 525.13
  SU 532.16 WR 561.6 578.11
  578.22 578.23 SM 586.1
  BO 593.14 JD 629.11 638.41
  IL 654.32 655.26 GG 685.23
  691.36 694.22 696.2 699.3
  NT 701.34 712.37 ML 733.7
  733.18 OV 749.13 753.17
  RR 789.20 MD 825.2 825.37
  BM 838.22 TH 845.35 851.1

MOVEMENT MO 2.27 3.17 15.28
  OA 23.14 23.15 25.6 29.23
  31.26 34.42 HT 43.18 WM 63.5
  EA 72.3 83.25 90.40 PO 97.13
  97.20 97.26 98.23 99.13
  TF 119.36 127.6 DV 152.28
  152.30 170.23 172.39
  FG 189.29 SS 203.18 SB 214.16
  214.34 SG 228.28 WS 252.27
  264.13 SC 267.6 OC 283.9
  284.29 EE 306.5 309.7 325.7
  TP 336.41 337.41 339.26
  342.25 344.21 BL 354.16
  MN 378.7 WP 379.25 YT 401.33
  PP 438.29 440.24 HD 442.5
  PR 501.24 502.13 SU 543.20
  SM 584.24 JD 617.37 622.16
  GG 678.13 698.30 NT 702.28
  ML 730.29

MOVEMENTS MO 13.25 18.22
  OA 24.15 EA 81.36 PO 98.15
  98.22 104.30 TF 127.29
  SG 225.6 231.14 GF 239.13
  WS 254.32 254.34 254.35
  CH 276.39 EE 304.23 BL 358.7
  MN 375.16 WP 387.7 SD 413.35
  415.16 PP 433.18 SU 543.9
  NT 712.23 MD 822.40 BM 830.4
  836.18

MOVES BO 596.39 OV 758.29

MOVIE PR 481.34

MOVIES MN 368.32

MOVING MO 3.15 SP 49.3 EA 78.10
  85.6 PO 96.5 109.38 111.32
  111.42 TF 117.3 118.22 119.9
  127.33 DV 167.16 171.31
  184.35 FG 190.5 SB 214.17
  215.9 SG 225.3 WS 251.29
  252.31 256.13 OC 287.26
  293.13 EE 324.12 325.32
  325.36 325.41 WP 389.32
  YT 407.29 SD 420.1 HD 449.12
  449.28 449.42 450.1 450.22
  FA 466.38 PR 483.20 487.16
  SU 538.1 WR 562.7 568.34
  569.9 578.4 579.20 SM 583.24
  586.27 JD 614.6 LA 639.35
  644.4 GG 673.36 673.37 684.38
  685.29 ML 741.41 OV 759.28

MOWING PO 106.14 SB 217.12

MOWING-GRASS FA 471.22

MR. ALLCOCK HT 42.14

MR. AND MRS. LINDLEY DV 138.10

MR. BARLOW BM 835.6 838.24

MR. BERRY PP 436.38

MR. BERRYMAN CH 274.34

MR. BRADLEY RR 787.20

MR. CATHCART ML 734.33

MR. CHAIRMAN OA 32.18 32.21

MR. CLEVELAND WM 56.14 57.1

MR. COLBRAN FG 187.19 187.33

MR. COUTTS SP 46.28 WM 56.5
  56.10

MR. DURANT DV 140.34 147.29
  147.35 150.33

MR. ENDERBY FA 468.1 469.34
  469.36 470.3 470.4

MR. FRITH JD 610.42* 616.33

MR. GEE TB 517.4

MR. GEE'S TB 525.33 525.41

MR. GOODALL FA 471.39

MR. GOYTE WP 388.13

MR. HORSEPOOL SC 272.20

MR. JACK GF 241.40

MR. JACKSON BM 839.23 839.25

MR. KENDAL CH 277.28

MR. LINDLEY DV 136.1 136.34
  138.36 139.4 139.7 139.27
  140.10 141.21 141.28 141.31
  142.15 142.36 144.26 146.24
  151.22 151.36 158.3 177.36
  183.17 183.32 184.2 184.29

MR. LINDLEY'S DV 144.35

MR. LIN'LEY DV 139.21

MR. MARCHBANKS LA 641.25

MR. MASSY DV 145.6 146.30 147.5
  147.22 148.3 148.9 148.12
  148.29 149.15 149.22 149.29
  150.7 150.9 150.28 151.19
  151.22 151.24 152.9 152.12
  152.27 152.36 154.35 155.18
  156.6 156.7 156.23 158.13
  158.25 159.9 159.18 159.25
  159.41 160.4 183.37 185.42

MR. MERFIN SP 46.23

MR. MOEST EA 85.29

MR. MORIER GG 670.9 674.36

MR. MORIER'S GG 675.10

MR. PERVIN BL 352.9

MR. PILBEAM SS 209.16

MR. PILKINGTON BM 839.29

MR. PINNEGAR JD 612.2 615.21

MR. RADFORD HT 39.35 43.6

MR. RIGLEY OC 291.11 293.12

MR. ROCKLEY YT 398.4 399.20
  399.22 400.33 400.40
  404.24 406.41 407.5 407.10
  408.13 408.19 409.39

MRS. ALLSOP SC 273.9

MRS. ATTENBOROUGH'S LL 761.8

MRS. BARLOW BM 831.3 832.12
  835.2 835.11 835.13 835.28
  835.35 838.20 838.27
  838.33 838.37 839.28

MRS. BATES OC 289.25 290.23
  291.16 294.19

MRS. BESANT TH 844.11

MRS. BETTS RR 787.6 787.7

MRS. BODOIN MD 805.19 805.34
  806.8 807.17 807.30 808.21
  808.24 808.30 808.34 810.9
  810.16 810.21 810.31
  810.41 811.13 811.17
  811.22 811.32 812.1 812.5
  812.25 812.31 813.15
  813.20 813.32 813.41
  815.7 815.19 815.28 815.34
  816.1 816.6 816.11 816.23
  817.9 817.25 817.32 817.35
  818.9 818.13 819.17 819.27
  820.19 820.24 822.38
  823.17 823.39 824.7 824.11
  824.14 824.20 825.37
  825.42 826.15 826.27

MRS. BODOIN'S MD 807.25
  814.41 815.11 816.30
  817.5 818.3 824.29

MRS. BRAITHWAITE WM 55.20
  55.27 56.17

MRS. CARLIN CH 275.40

MRS. COATES SG 222.17 222.21
  223.37 223.40

MRS. DRUMMOND RR 783.30
  783.33 784.8 787.39

MRS. DRUMMOND'S RR 787.37

MRS. DURANT DV 140.5 140.12
  140.32 140.40 142.21
  142.29 143.26 147.33 148.1
  148.6 148.9 148.18 148.34
  160.32 161.16 161.19 162.4
  162.10 162.16 162.18
  162.26 170.13 171.21

MRS. DURANT'S DV 142.37 160.33

MURMURING SS 211.19 CH 279.19
  OC 289.5 291.35 299.18
  SM 584.18 GG 672.23 LL 769.20
  772.11 773.41 774.4 MD 812.37

MUSCLE HD 443.2 LA 637.40
  637.41

MUSCLES OA 36.40 FG 189.42
  SC 268.41 BL 360.19 SD 422.3
  JD 618.4 RH 802.41 MD 806.31

MUSCULAR SC 268.38 BL 354.17
  PP 433.16 MD 806.9 808.30

MUSE DV 177.29 CH 279.15
  OC 295.6 HD 455.14 BO 603.41
  LA 642.8

MUSEAU HD 443.6 PR 501.21

MUSED SB 213.11 216.24
  GF 239.28 WP 393.2 393.14
  HD 445.29 FA 461.28 JD 610.27
  LA 643.21 GG 681.3 NT 706.41
  LL 775.11 MD 826.24

MUSEUMS LL 769.41 769.42
  TH 849.10

MUSH FA 471.30

MUSHROOMS GF 238.36

MUSIC SP 47.30 47.32 WM 59.9
  EA 75.27 DV 177.29 WS 252.19
  252.29 254.20 255.42 257.33
  EE 305.16 308.28 308.37
  TP 337.14 YT 395.5 395.14
  WR 568.38 LA 639.42 640.2
  640.5 IL 650.34 650.37
  GG 687.19 OV 748.3 LL 762.11
  RR 781.41 782.6 783.12
  MD 806.5

MUSICAL EA 85.14 DV 143.13
  PR 473.35 474.5 GG 675.21
  687.35 OV 747.23 LL 770.11
  RR 781.42 MD 805.17 813.38

MUSICALLY CH 277.33 BL 353.6
  353.29 PR 474.27 RR 782.3

MUSICIAN MD 806.41

MUSIC-ROOM RR 786.15

MUSIC-SHEET FA 467.27

MUSIC-STOOL GG 684.13

MUSING MO 20.14 CH 278.10
  WP 380.35 PR 476.42 JD 615.22
  IL 657.37 LL 767.2

MUSINGLY LL 766.39

MUSLIN SB 217.15 SG 222.3
  MD 823.3

MUSTARD JD 618.36

MUSTARD-COLOURED TB 521.15

MUST'A WP 388.9

MUSTN'T DV 171.23 SS 204.27
  OC 294.25 LA 634.38 BM 839.16

MUTE OA 37.15 PO 96.6 99.16
  DV 138.18 SG 226.28 GF 241.2
  TP 346.8 BL 364.20 YT 407.11
  407.19 GG 690.38 ML 735.19
  737.24 738.6 LL 763.38

MUTED WS 258.10

MUTELY OA 36.39 DV 138.26
  WS 258.36 WR 566.41

MUTTER GG 696.5 ML 746.35

MUTTERED HD 446.1 PR 510.22
  BM 841.4

MUTTERING HT 44.10 PO 114.21
  DV 139.25 CH 281.23 OC 296.41
  WR 557.2 560.10 GG 670.21

MUTTON DV 143.2 143.8 GF 240.17
  WR 565.2 GG 674.28

MUTTON-HEAD IL 658.13

MUTUAL MD 807.24 TH 844.10

MUTUALLY OV 754.5

MUY BIEN PR 510.13

MY DOLLIE PR 474.15

MY PRINCESS PR 474.16

MYRIAD TF 122.3 ML 745.35

MYRIADS SS 204.6

MYRIAD-THREADED SS 202.7

MYRIAD-VOICED ML 734.12

MYSEN SP 51.30 SC 268.19
  FA 463.28

MYSTERIES WR 549.25 549.27

MYSTERIOUS MO 19.30 TF 118.34
  119.1 OC 301.30 PR 501.7
  501.9 505.34 SU 535.20
  WR 549.37 550.15 552.23
  567.37 579.22 JD 607.28
  NT 710.21 ML 724.22 731.22
  732.20 732.30 LL 761.23
  764.36 770.33 RR 780.11
  BM 832.37

MYSTERIOUSLY MO 3.16 GF 235.5
  WR 547.34 574.11 ML 746.34

MYSTERIOUSNESS LL 777.2

MYSTERY DV 166.21 EE 315.6
  323.41 FA 471.42 PR 477.33
  BO 595.38 597.37 LA 634.1
  GG 665.22 682.7 NT 704.2
  ML 724.6 734.42 OV 749.6
  754.6 RR 780.25 781.7 782.14
  782.17 782.18 BM 832.42

MYSTIC TF 127.20 PR 482.37

MYSTIC (CONT.) 483.1
  WR 572.12 576.5 577.12
  581.19

MYSTICAL HD 448.16

MYSTICALLY MD 813.11

MYSTIFICATION RR 782.20 783.5

MYSTIFICATIONS RR 782.30

MYSTIFIED YT 408.18
  MD 823.10

NA SP 47.16

NADA-NADA NT 717.12

NAG HT 39.18

NAGGING MD 815.11

NAIL GF 243.12 BM 833.9

NAILED WM 61.32 61.35
  OC 297.5 GG 690.21
  TH 852.12

NAILS WM 69.3 69.11

NAIVE HT 39.5 WM 59.26
  EA 84.37 TF 126.29 130.32
  DV 164.33 OC 299.10
  FA 467.29 PR 476.15 486.37
  SM 583.13 585.41 BO 593.41
  IL 656.21 GG 692.19
  NT 705.29 LL 761.7

NAIVELY EA 84.7

NAIVETE WR 567.15

NAKED MO 2.19 2.42 4.19
  OA 26.14 WM 54.32 60.25
  PO 108.41 109.12 TF 134.2
  134.16 135.7 DV 154.40
  166.9 182.30 FG 191.20
  SS 197.31 WS 251.22
  SC 268.40 OC 296.38 297.17
  297.35 301.6 301.9 301.20
  TP 343.18 BL 363.33
  HD 451.19 455.13 PR 499.41
  TB 520.12 520.14 SU 529.35
  529.39 529.41 530.26
  531.24 532.27 534.9 535.2
  535.36 536.29 537.10
  537.11 538.7 539.35 540.3
  540.39 540.40 543.42
  WR 549.16 552.33 557.8
  559.15 561.14 563.29
  568.41 570.16 576.23
  578.15 580.26 580.30
  580.37 SM 585.4 BO 588.32
  JD 617.14 618.2 618.14
  LA 639.25 639.33 640.3
  IL 658.21 GG 682.40 690.13
  698.26 NT 704.4 714.2
  ML 724.15 OV 747.4 747.7
  748.39 749.33 750.18
  756.14 756.18 BM 836.28
  840.1

NAKEDLY GG 682.42 BM 837.5

NAKEDNESS TF 122.25 134.18
135.15 OC 300.33 EE 330.35
SU 532.10 542.8 WR 546.18
564.14 OV 749.38 750.21

NAKEDNESSES NT 704.5

NAKED-SEEMING GG 672.41

NAME SP 45.25 45.26 EA 75.8
87.27 DV 177.34 178.21
SS 204.18 SG 227.31 CH 280.10
EE 319.9 319.10 319.12
TP 336.23 WP 383.7 YT 401.12
SD 411.34 417.5 418.19 426.16
PP 437.20 HD 445.38 PR 475.8
TB 519.31 BO 589.23 593.36
601.6 601.8 601.10 601.11
601.12 JD 605.15 607.32
611.15 GG 673.7 695.38
NT 705.14 714.19 ML 734.33
736.20 738.10 741.18 742.15
RR 781.19 781.32 789.7
RH 793.42 794.1 794.6 801.38
803.3 MD 818.14 818.16

NAMED TP 338.5 338.6 WP 383.38

NAMES SS 204.37 SD 425.1
TB 520.33 ML 741.18 741.20
RH 794.3 MD 820.35

NAME'S MN 367.8 WP 381.32
SD 413.2 413.3 416.39 417.5
FA 469.23 JD 628.10

NANCY BO 594.28

NANKERVIS (SEE WILLIE; MRS.
NANKERVIS)

NAPE DV 149.25 173.12 SB 220.4
OC 290.19

NAPHTHA TP 337.20

NAPKIN BL 358.9 GG 677.8

NAPLES LL 769.34

NARCISSI SU 532.21 OV 753.22

NARCISSUS-FLOWER NT 712.40

NARROW TF 119.18 DV 137.16
144.32 SG 224.9 WS 244.27
SC 267.19 EE 305.29 307.22
TP 334.21 BL 351.39 MN 376.19
SD 423.25 PR 497.33 WR 561.25
ML 728.24 LL 767.7 RR 788.24

NARROWED OA 35.15 WS 254.16
SD 415.33 HD 446.9 PR 489.40

NARROWING DV 161.4 YT 398.27

NARROWLY WP 391.28 YT 399.26

NARROW-OPENED HT 41.11

NASAL GF 234.11

NASCENT WR 577.21

NASTILY OA 31.37 SD 418.42

NASTURTIUMS TF 117.10

NASTY WS 262.20 OC 284.36
EE 319.7 319.8 MN 369.33
WP 385.12 SU 535.4 IL 658.26
GG 673.27 NT 706.4

NAT GOULD RH 795.24

NATION EE 326.38

NATIONAL SC 270.10 EE 327.22

NATIONALITY EE 326.36

NATIVE EA 71.23 TF 127.5 128.12
WR 551.10

NATIVES WR 551.22 551.34 553.29

NATTY GG 676.25

NATURAL MO 12.34 HT 39.8
SP 48.33 EA 75.36 91.16
PO 97.34 98.5 DV 150.1 163.33
183.34 EE 315.2 326.37 326.41
MN 375.6 SD 412.25 PR 482.27
484.33 SU 533.10 BO 596.37
IL 650.20 GG 678.14 NT 703.27
ML 745.29 RR 781.17 MD 807.39
807.40 808.7 817.1 BM 831.10

NATURALLY MO 11.12 21.6
HT 40.22 EA 84.36 TF 127.4
DV 166.8 YT 395.9 HD 451.1
FA 463.2 TB 517.30 JD 606.41
607.8 609.31 NT 704.17
BM 830.27 833.18 839.18

NATURE EA 89.42 90.2 PO 98.22
99.36 103.21 TF 127.8 127.18
DV 137.21 EE 310.31 326.35
BL 361.30 YT 395.41 PP 437.11
HD 456.6 PR 487.38 SU 543.23
BO 601.14 LL 765.23

NATURES YT 396.8 FA 463.21
PR 482.33 WR 574.27 GG 676.6

NAUGHTY EA 72.8 NT 708.7 708.14

NAUSEA WS 264.22 EE 332.40
332.41

NAUSEATED DV 169.34

NAUSEOUS ML 739.1

NAVAJO WR 549.42

NAVEL SU 534.3 TH 846.24

NAVVY SP 50.42

NAVY DV 141.21 141.34 142.12
142.25 143.9 143.38 144.19
164.26 165.26 172.25
WS 250.36 250.37

NAY MO 7.36 9.8 10.11 14.10
SP 46.37 47.6 WM 68.29
EA 86.14 FG 193.23 195.32
195.33 196.3 196.24 SB 219.37
WS 253.6 EE 307.27 311.25
311.36 313.3 313.6 328.40

NAY (CONT.) TP 341.32 341.36
341.41 342.3 342.7 342.13
BL 355.9 MN 377.6 WP 384.36
385.18 YT 404.2 404.14
404.33 404.36 HD 453.15
FA 462.13 SU 530.32
BO 591.5 OV 754.19 756.5
757.20 758.39 RR 782.23

NAYLOR SS 198.19

NAYLOR'S SS 198.32 199.2
199.4

NEAR-BY PR 496.37

NEAR EAST MD 819.1

NEARED PR 489.32 WR 552.37

NEARER PO 95.13 107.5
TF 118.29 129.39 DV 136.20
181.10 SS 197.1 204.24
SG 227.41 228.1 GF 241.15
WS 255.3 SC 268.14
EE 331.20 332.12 332.13
TP 337.39 MN 373.19 373.20
PP 430.6 HD 447.27 450.33
PR 494.1 511.19 WR 579.21
LA 633.31 GG 698.33
ML 746.22 OV 750.25 756.13
756.18 MD 822.7 TH 845.37

NEAREST PO 114.41 HD 449.2
PR 510.29 RR 781.4

NEARING WR 551.41

NEARLY MO 2.6 9.39 SP 51.7
WM 63.7 EA 77.23 80.30
PO 109.18 114.31 DV 150.13
164.33 180.41 SS 204.26
SG 231.21 231.22 231.26
GF 242.38 TP 337.30
BL 349.33 361.36 MN 371.31
WP 384.2 PP 429.2 434.16
436.21 FA 460.3 462.38
471.28 PR 473.24 476.21
493.21 SU 543.16 WR 547.10
BO 600.26 LA 641.5
IL 647.19 652.16 GG 681.35
NT 707.32 ML 745.29
LL 764.26 771.20 RH 790.24
799.14 MD 807.24 TH 846.7

NEARNESS BL 348.18 356.35
357.5

NEAT PO 113.10 TF 125.34
WS 261.24 YT 400.9
PP 433.41 TB 515.35
518.25 JD 629.9 629.13
ML 722.28 742.9 BM 830.4

NEATLY WS 245.28 245.32
MN 371.19 YT 400.5
JD 618.27 ML 742.8

NEATLY-CUT PR 483.41

NEATNESS YT 397.18 407.37

NECESSARILY ML 722.4
MD 825.40 BM 827.11

NECESSARY EA 81.10 DV 158.21
  178.10 SB 218.41 219.1 219.7
  OC 294.37 EE 320.33 320.34
  320.35 321.30 322.6 BO 591.22
  MD 811.24 821.9 825.41
  TH 845.8

NECESSITIES DV 165.8

NECESSITY EA 87.20 WS 257.29*
  EE 312.41 332.10 PR 480.21
  503.37 TB 514.15

NECK MO 21.14 OA 24.42 25.21
  25.30 25.34 25.39 HT 41.18
  41.20 SP 51.7 WM 59.11 69.10
  69.20 69.22 69.34 70.7
  EA 79.31 PO 97.21 DV 149.25
  149.27 170.24 171.10 173.12
  SS 203.29 SB 215.5 220.4
  GF 239.26 242.37 WS 246.5
  247.13 247.14 247.19 247.23
  247.25 249.9 249.24 263.3
  263.30 263.32 SC 268.27
  CH 275.21 278.30 OC 290.19
  300.7 TP 344.34 BL 351.21
  354.30 WP 382.19 382.23
  386.23 386.26 386.32 386.40
  387.28 388.17 390.5 390.20
  391.31 392.41 YT 400.31 403.4
  408.15 SD 421.34 HD 444.12
  454.15 454.16 PR 482.28
  485.10 SU 531.20 BO 604.31
  604.33 IL 650.22 GG 673.3
  683.7 NT 707.26 720.11
  ML 736.41 739.13 OV 747.6
  RH 793.13 MD 806.23 806.26

NECKS MO 6.2 HT 42.25 WP 379.8
  FA 468.28

NECK-TIE WS 249.33 WR 551.8

NED WP 389.27

NEDNA SC 267.27 270.20

NEED MO 14.25 19.36 21.20
  21.28 HT 43.40 EA 86.21 92.40
  TF 122.19 133.2 133.7
  DV 140.12 156.37 164.41
  172.20 SS 209.21 209.23
  SG 232.38 WS 251.6 CH 279.20
  EE 307.23 322.40 BL 363.10
  MN 377.24* HD 447.21 447.23
  TB 513.34 527.9 527.30
  SU 536.10 BO 599.23 601.41
  JD 605.1 607.15 615.1
  IL 650.1 GG 663.31 663.32
  663.34 668.5 677.27 ML 727.26
  734.39 740.5 RH 801.3
  MD 813.28 821.36

NEEDED PO 105.31 TF 128.15
  DV 144.27 148.22 176.1
  SS 204.10 GF 234.8 WS 253.27
  SC 271.25 OC 291.37 EE 308.10
  FA 461.3 BO 598.19 JD 624.8
  IL 649.40 GG 671.18 OV 753.40
  754.6

NEEDING MD 806.37

NEEDLE OA 29.22

NEEDLES WR 556.6 BO 595.30

NEEDN'T MO 16.38 EA 78.5
  DV 168.25 169.2 SC 270.25
  CH 277.2 OC 285.29 289.17
  BL 361.31 363.6 MN 375.36
  WP 385.10 YT 403.31 406.21
  TB 527.23 BO 601.1 LA 644.12
  IL 653.13 GG 672.14 686.33
  686.39 OV 757.1 LL 762.1
  RH 798.8 801.27 801.31 801.35

NEEDS EA 93.23 DV 170.9
  SS 206.7 GG 677.25 MD 822.6
  TH 845.12

NEEDY DV 146.26

NE'ER-DO-WELL SP 46.28

NEGATION EE 315.18 315.19
  PR 510.1 BO 599.18

NEGATIVE EE 315.17 GG 682.2
  LL 771.25 771.28 771.32
  771.36

NEGATIVELY EE 315.31 315.32

NEGLECT GF 234.27

NEGLECTED WS 255.22 EE 307.13

NEGLIGENCE TB 524.28

NEGLIGENT OA 34.42 BL 360.24

NEGOTIATE MD 818.23 818.27

NEGOTIATED MD 818.28

NEGRO BM 835.27

NEGRO-EUNUCHS BM 835.41

NEIGHBOUR HT 39.4 SC 272.9
  GG 677.2 677.10 RR 781.5

NEIGHBOURHOOD FG 187.29
  JD 609.28 RH 790.20

NEIGHBOURING HD 442.15 448.1

NEIGHBOURS FA 471.37 OV 759.29

NEIGHBOUR'S OC 292.40

NEIGHING LA 632.24 633.4 633.28

NEITHER MO 6.1 22.13 OA 29.21
  30.11 HT 39.18 SP 52.1 52.33
  WM 60.15 63.17 DV 144.28
  183.7 FG 190.35 SG 229.22
  230.26 231.40 WS 262.36
  EE 307.35 311.5 327.20
  TP 343.24 MN 373.5 375.6
  WP 391.20 YT 405.21 SD 424.10
  425.4 PR 480.26 SU 528.17
  544.11 WR 547.35 550.37 552.7
  561.12 BO 599.22 JD 613.30
  IL 659.17 GG 662.7 674.1
  NT 714.6 714.10 714.11 717.41
  ML 723.37 724.34 OV 747.16
  757.35 758.11 759.34
  RR 779.37 782.36 788.30

NEITHER (CONT.) RH 803.41
  MD 808.4 820.30

NELSON, LORD (SEE LORD NELSON)

NEPHEW PP 427.19 427.23
  428.9 428.22 429.10 430.24
  430.33 430.38 431.2 431.28
  431.30 432.35 432.40 433.2
  435.36 436.13 437.36
  438.22 440.15 RH 794.8
  794.24 794.34 795.36 797.6

NEPITELLA SU 538.23

NERVE GG 690.13 692.36
  LL 777.16 777.31 TH 852.26

NERVE-DEAD BO 598.14

NERVELESS PO 104.6 MD 817.11

NERVE-RACKED ML 742.23

NERVES WM 58.22 PO 100.16
  100.23 BL 351.9 353.26
  MN 374.10 374.41 HD 449.13
  449.19 WR 548.7 RH 801.10
  801.24 MD 814.25 814.27
  814.28 814.34 814.41
  815.30 BM 830.12 831.23

NERVOUS MO 8.6 EA 85.17
  PO 109.29 DV 146.13 148.4
  148.31 151.24 SB 212.12
  217.17 WS 257.25 CH 274.29
  275.1 277.31 279.6
  BL 354.15 362.10 PP 438.18
  FA 461.8 SU 539.27 539.30
  540.7 WR 569.37 BO 597.21
  LA 639.12 GG 676.2 676.4
  NT 715.20 720.31 ML 736.38
  RR 786.11 RH 798.7
  MD 805.13 819.8 BM 834.25
  834.39

NERVOUSLY OA 30.10 31.19
  EA 84.30 85.6 85.39
  DV 146.7 148.30 152.2
  SB 212.15 SG 224.7 224.20
  CH 274.21 BL 356.42 357.29
  YT 398.25 PP 433.30 437.1
  438.35 HD 455.40 TB 525.2
  526.22 BO 599.28 GG 696.7
  697.4 BM 834.31

NESH WP 388.11

NESSUS MD 807.2

NEST SS 204.1 PP 434.20
  434.23 ML 722.20 MD 811.30

NESTING SM 585.17

NESTLE JD 605.28 605.29

NESTLED WM 61.6 63.16
  DV 136.2 SB 212.26
  JD 605.24 605.26 605.30

NESTLING WS 250.1 JD 608.29
  ML 723.15

NESTS SS 204.16 204.22

NESTS (CONT.) ML 723.18
  TH 848.24

NEST'S SS 204.20

NET MO 17.13 IL 651.27

NETHERMERE MO 22.19

NETHERMOST GG 674.26

NETS OV 758.29

NETTED EA 72.27 OV 747.11

NETTING FG 187.2

NETTLE SS 203.29

NETTLED DV 141.38 SS 198.25
  MN 375.10 ML 737.28

NETWORK WR 561.18 561.23

NEUTER BL 359.38

NEUTRAL EA 83.29 TF 133.37
  DV 137.24 139.1 141.13
  SG 229.7 WS 258.40 MN 370.22
  PP 433.32 HD 443.32 BO 599.25
  RR 786.42

NEUTRALISE BO 593.29

NEUTRALISED TF 134.41 EE 315.32
  BO 599.18

NEUTRALITY EA 81.10 PO 98.2
  98.26 TF 125.20 DV 178.23
  PP 432.32 BO 599.15 599.28

NEVER-ENDING MD 815.18

NEVER-STILL EE 316.27

NEVERTHELESS MO 20.25 EA 76.32
  86.24 DV 153.5 172.26 183.33
  SC 267.19 268.42 CH 276.10
  279.39 OC 288.23 EE 309.14
  314.18 BL 360.41 HD 447.37
  TB 518.5 SU 545.4 BO 587.25
  587.36 589.38 594.7 JD 628.1
  629.3 IL 647.17 652.5
  RH 790.8 BM 829.8 TH 846.12

NEW MO 10.39 HT 42.19 44.15
  WM 55.1 58.36 62.17 67.1
  EA 83.12 83.13 86.6 86.8
  TF 125.28 126.7 132.28
  DV 136.7 136.10 136.32 145.5
  153.17 154.39 156.12 164.2
  164.35 173.27 173.28 174.13
  SS 198.36 199.12 203.31 205.7
  208.18 210.12 SG 221.19
  224.40 GF 240.8 WS 260.19
  CH 275.30 EE 304.39 309.14
  309.24 328.16 331.1 331.3
  331.4 331.6 332.2 TP 339.28
  BL 355.37 364.29 MN 376.16
  WP 392.39 YT 402.40 402.41
  406.42 SD 414.16 415.9
  PP 430.18 436.29 440.2
  FA 466.16 PR 478.30 TB 525.17
  SU 536.16 WR 552.35 564.21
  BO 591.12 596.5 599.25 601.25

NEW (CONT.) JD 609.20 610.34
  614.9 617.30 627.34 LA 630.12
  630.21 634.1 637.14 638.12
  641.36 643.26 IL 648.25
  648.26 652.31 653.2 GG 681.1
  692.41 693.8 693.29 698.18
  NT 702.36 ML 725.25 725.38
  733.28 737.8 737.9 737.12
  738.23 745.19 OV 753.10
  LL 766.24 775.36 RR 779.32
  779.33 785.20 RH 791.19
  800.10 MD 808.1 810.35
  BM 836.28 837.12 840.1
  TH 851.1 851.2 851.9 851.11
  851.21 851.23

NEW-AWAKENED GG 698.17

NEW BRINSLEY OC 291.1

NEWCOMER TP 336.31 HD 444.26
  JD 609.4

NEWCOMERS WR 562.25

NEWCOMER'S WM 56.3

NEW ENGLAND PR 473.25 478.6
  TH 844.1 844.15 845.25
  845.37 848.27

NEW ENGLANDERS TH 846.27

NEWER OV 749.38

NEW-FLEDGED YT 398.30

NEW GUINEA LL 770.1

NEW HAVEN TH 844.21

NEW INN DV 178.8 180.2

NEW LONDON LANE JD 610.12 616.11

NEWLY OA 23.3 DV 136.22
  SS 203.30 BL 347.27 HD 454.37
  BO 597.23 ML 729.19 729.20

NEWLY-FALLING ML 744.30

NEWLY-TORN HD 454.38

NEW MEXICO PR 481.19 BM 827.21

NEWNESS PO 114.21 DV 136.17

NEWS MO 4.22 4.23 4.25 4.27
  4.32 DV 166.16 BL 356.36
  MN 378.37 GG 667.20 RH 794.9
  BM 838.31

NEWSPAPER SG 221.3 SC 267.29
  269.5 BL 347.17 WP 380.35
  380.42 SD 415.22 TB 519.32
  BO 588.5 JD 625.28 626.16
  RH 799.18

NEWSPAPERS BO 588.6

NEWT WM 62.15

NEWTHORPE MANOR FG 189.4

NEW YORK SU 541.26 WR 549.30
  549.31 NT 705.22 708.5
  712.2 714.16 717.20
  TH 849.40 850.28 850.40
  851.33 852.18

NEXT OA 36.4 HT 42.9 44.17
  SP 46.36 EA 78.25 PO 99.4
  105.27 DV 183.3 FG 189.13
  SS 211.9 SB 216.16 217.7
  219.16 219.27 SG 221.21
  WS 263.9 CH 277.19 278.12
  278.34 OC 292.25 301.27
  EE 320.1 321.2 321.42
  TP 337.37 MN 373.40 374.42
  WP 385.7 387.15 YT 400.29
  405.35 HD 444.2 FA 463.17
  PR 489.22 509.15 509.40
  SU 542.28 543.12 545.4
  WR 576.6 577.37 BO 604.3
  JD 624.4 IL 649.11 651.9
  653.22 GG 672.40 673.1
  674.37 680.19 680.24 696.3
  NT 720.30 ML 728.19 730.18
  LL 763.14 773.16 773.37
  RH 799.2 MD 818.11 825.31
  825.32 825.37 BM 829.8
  834.38 840.15 TH 850.23

NIBELUNG PR 477.14

NICE MO 8.12 8.15 SP 52.22
  SS 202.24 206.32 SB 218.19
  218.27 WS 246.38 261.27
  262.23 OC 285.31 285.41
  287.31 291.23 TP 338.23
  338.25 BL 358.5 MN 376.30
  PP 438.15 FA 461.25 469.30
  PR 481.42 486.7 507.30
  507.39 507.41 TB 514.35
  514.37 516.40 SM 583.20
  BO 593.1 593.41 594.5
  601.7 601.27 JD 606.17
  611.14 LA 640.40 641.42
  IL 647.18 650.12 GG 673.21
  673.23 675.12 680.42
  697.19 NT 720.8 ML 726.17
  736.23 LL 763.36 765.2
  RH 799.30 799.32 MD 808.12
  812.10 813.32 813.37
  813.40 819.30 822.21
  BM 828.19 830.23 831.34
  831.38 832.38 TH 844.34

NICE-LOOKING MN 376.33

NICELY OA 27.21 HT 41.30
  SP 46.8 SB 218.22 WS 262.14
  GG 676.25

NICER MO 19.37 SB 219.25
  IL 656.3 LL 762.37

NICEST JD 611.24 IL 652.38
  RR 780.4 MD 813.34

NICETY MO 5.18

NICHE SU 532.27

NICHES SU 529.16 WR 576.29

NIECE FA 461.32 463.15
  LL 761.18 762.7 764.15
  777.36 778.34

NOT-TO-BE-EXTERMINATED EE 313.28

NOTTS SP 47.26 50.29 50.30
  50.32 SC 271.13 271.23 271.24
  271.29

NOTWITHSTANDING SS 210.13

NOVEL DV 146.1 TB 521.7 521.9
  521.30 523.41 525.15 525.16

NOVELIST TB 524.2

NOVELS YT 395.6

NOVEMBER TP 337.8 BL 347.5
  350.34 PR 486.16 RR 783.9
  RH 799.7 BM 833.35

NOW-ABANDONED WR 551.20

NOWADAYS WS 261.3 TB 517.31
  GG 669.11 ML 728.5 OV 757.19
  MD 811.30 BM 827.1

NOWHERE WS 250.14 TP 334.37
  FA 458.15 PR 482.33 TB 521.1
  WR 546.27 548.39 553.17
  SM 585.12 BO 588.7 598.31
  599.30 JD 615.5 619.33 619.40
  GG 688.39 LL 774.9 TH 852.5

NOWT SP 48.23 48.31 CH 276.28
  277.39 WP 389.25 PP 428.6
  428.7 FA 470.30

NOW-W RH 800.18

NOW-W-W RH 800.18

NUCLEUS LL 778.36

NUDE WM 58.40 SU 539.23

NUDGE SM 585.34

NUDGING SM 585.1

NUISANCE WS 245.8

NUISANCES SB 216.20

NULL EE 316.17

NULLIFICATION PO 105.4

NULLITY BO 592.6

NUMB OA 37.18 PR 488.36 498.11
  512.1 WR 552.24 572.10 573.41
  BO 599.15 JD 623.35 GG 686.20

NUMBED MO 3.11 PR 503.22
  BO 602.11 602.12 602.25

NUMBER DV 166.15 BL 359.26
  MN 368.29 SD 419.39 FA 467.36
  BO 588.15 NT 707.12

NUMBER 4 OC 283.1

NUMBERLESS ML 722.15

NUMBERS EE 330.9

NUMBNESS WR 557.22 BO 592.3
  OV 749.34

NUMBS JD 609.9

NUMEROUS MD 818.34

NUN SS 209.32 EE 322.37
  SM 583.16 584.6

NUNS SM 583.40 NT 711.8
  LL 763.15

NUNS' SM 584.2

NUPTIALS LL 777.39

NURSE OC 294.33 EE 303.18
  309.15 309.16 316.26 316.28
  317.23 318.29 318.33 319.1
  321.27 323.14 326.3 YT 408.13
  HD 443.3 SU 528.3 537.29
  GG 666.37 666.40 ML 739.7
  RH 793.18 793.21 801.38

NURSE-COMPANION PR 479.25

NURSERY TF 123.28 123.38
  GG 666.33 RH 791.8 793.1
  799.13

NURSERY-GOVERNESS RH 801.39
  802.22

NURSES EE 329.13 PR 475.1

NURSING DV 157.3 172.10
  CH 275.34 278.34 EE 321.11
  321.24 322.3 323.11 YT 396.42

NUT WM 55.31 EA 91.2 PO 107.35
  FG 195.8 SB 213.25 GG 676.24

NUT-BROWN EE 304.23 304.24

NUTS SB 213.8 EE 305.36
  MN 376.40 378.12

NUTTALL SP 48.6 48.8 48.39
  SS 199.3

NYMPH LA 634.28 OV 755.40 758.6
  758.38 759.4 759.10 759.12
  759.21 759.31 759.38

NYMPH-LIKE LA 631.40 634.17
  635.7

NYMPHS OV 756.39

NYMPH'S LA 632.37 OV 758.13

O' BM 841.27

OAK MO 21.38 FG 190.16
  OC 283.12 EE 304.7 304.41
  305.3 PR 487.28 489.15 490.27
  501.40 TB 526.38

OAKS OA 23.28 FG 187.8
  SS 197.20 SB 213.2

OAK-SCRUB PR 486.11 501.34

OAK-WOOD PR 502.24

OATH PO 97.30

OATMEAL CH 274.19

OATS SS 209.30 FA 465.5
  PR 503.9 ML 723.1 723.26

OAT-SHEAVES ML 723.28

OAXACA LL 763.16

OBEDIENCE PO 108.16 CH 276.37
  EE 330.33

OBEDIENT DV 185.1 PR 488.28

OBEDIENTLY EA 89.30 YT 410.13
  IL 650.32

OBELISK MEMORIAL SERVICE
  GG 673.33

OBER-LEUTNANT TF 133.27

OBESE DV 184.7

OBEY OA 36.28 BL 349.31
  MN 378.9

OBEYED MO 6.14 EA 80.14
  PO 96.40 TF 121.15
  BL 352.22

OBEYING PO 108.21 GG 692.33

OBEYS DV 151.2

OBJECT TF 134.23 BL 355.35
  WR 577.12 ML 728.38
  MD 813.5 816.25

OBJECTING SB 212.16

OBJECTION JD 622.29

OBJECTIONABLE HD 450.14

OBJECTIVELY SS 203.32

OBJECTS WM 69.34 SB 214.11
  BL 355.26 WR 550.11 576.30
  MD 812.41

OBJET DE VERTU MD 820.27

OBLIGED BM 839.31

OBLITERATE TF 121.9

OBLITERATED PO 103.20
  DV 136.9 149.15 154.13
  WR 569.31 569.35 ML 743.17

OBLITERATING TF 129.26
  DV 182.39

OBLITERATION DV 173.28
  GF 240.1 WR 569.30

OBLIVION MN 378.35 TB 520.4
  GG 698.6

OBLIVIOUS TF 117.28 DV 164.21
  WS 254.36 OC 298.28
  WP 387.3 390.7 PR 473.34

OBLIVIOUS (CONT.) PR 503.27
  WR 557.19 JD 617.22 617.33
  618.39 GG 685.30

OBLONG SB 215.7 WR 561.33
  561.36

OBSCENE BO 589.36 GG 670.1
  NT 704.22 708.8 714.20 717.1
  719.5 ML 743.16

OBSCENITIES TP 335.24 NT 708.16

OBSCURE OA 24.36 PO 104.40
  DV 185.42 SS 207.21 FA 458.16
  JD 607.20 IL 652.18 RH 794.40

OBSCURED OC 300.30 LA 638.19

OBSCURELY DV 158.41 BO 596.14

OBSCURITY SG 224.12 OC 300.25
  HD 449.30 450.6 IL 653.7
  ML 744.31 OV 750.27

OBSEQUIOUSNESS BO 587.11

OBSERVANT OA 29.1 SS 198.5
  WS 256.10 LL 762.8

OBSERVE PO 112.17 WP 390.6

OBSERVED SB 215.10 SM 584.24
  BO 599.15

OBSERVER CH 276.36

OBSESSED TF 122.30 DV 154.36
  157.10 159.28 GG 691.21

OBSESSION DV 154.38 WR 578.37

OBSIDIAN WR 578.6

OBSOLETE DV 136.21 BM 827.3

OBSTACLE PR 485.41

OBSTINACY FA 470.14 PR 487.38
  SM 584.27 GG 685.20 687.4
  NT 720.27

OBSTINATE TF 122.30 124.25
  DV 148.11 151.10 156.13
  FA 462.38 463.19 WR 567.35
  SM 584.26 584.32 584.36
  GG 688.28 NT 712.37

OBSTINATE-LOOKING DV 138.23

OBSTINATELY SG 228.41 EE 307.3
  FA 466.11 466.24 PR 498.16
  RH 797.7

OBSTRUCTING LA 644.2

OBTRUDED ML 736.4

OBTRUSIVE BL 360.35 PR 498.15
  ML 743.20

OBTRUSIVELY RR 780.9

OBTUSENESS SB 212.16

OBVIOUS WP 380.42 FA 462.26
  PR 480.34 WR 546.9 550.14
  BO 587.32 IL 657.27 GG 663.8
  680.42 682.4 685.26 692.42
  RR 781.16

OBVIOUSLY PP 427.21 JD 613.7
  LA 638.34 RR 780.8

OCCASION CH 278.29 278.39
  MN 378.28 FA 469.14

OCCASIONAL MO 1.7 PO 95.2
  EE 312.28 PR 490.6 WR 551.33
  551.40 JD 610.29 ML 744.6
  LL 761.34

OCCASIONALLY SP 49.8 PO 96.29
  98.18 100.8 TF 117.1 118.42
  119.24 DV 140.31 163.30 164.3
  164.6 WS 249.35 EE 312.9
  330.2 MN 374.11 PR 489.34
  489.39 490.29 501.39
  WR 548.15 550.22 551.35
  555.12 GG 674.4 RR 779.11
  BM 835.14

OCCASIONS EA 79.39 CH 278.17
  GG 675.39

OCCUPATION LL 766.1

OCCUPATIONS MN 367.29

OCCUPIED MO 7.3 OA 24.9 EA 82.4
  86.15 86.17 PO 101.14 111.27
  TF 127.7 SS 206.21 206.35
  OC 286.23 BL 347.12 347.17
  PP 427.7 BO 599.36 600.7
  RR 780.16

OCCUPY BL 348.30 RR 780.18

OCCUR SG 222.11

OCCURRED EE 308.11 YT 406.30
  GG 690.19 LL 766.20

OCEAN GG 698.6 ML 738.19 740.17
  740.23

OCEANS ML 722.23

O'CLOCK MO 16.19 OA 24.7 30.42
  HT 42.9 SP 45.3 47.24 51.13
  52.23 WM 59.21 EA 81.8
  TF 128.18 SG 222.6 GF 234.24
  239.22 WS 244.5 256.24
  SC 268.3 OC 293.21 298.36
  TP 335.42 BL 361.36 MN 368.13
  371.9 371.31 WP 386.7
  YT 397.8 HD 456.22 PR 498.16
  507.14 JD 616.20 627.32
  IL 655.14 NT 716.19 720.15
  LL 765.33 765.42 777.3
  RR 783.16 RH 802.33 BM 834.24

OCTOBER GF 241.28 PR 486.15
  487.25 IL 650.42

OCTOPUS NT 719.7 720.8
  ML 732.31

ODD EA 84.30 EE 325.1 BL 357.26
  361.19 363.26 MN 374.13

ODD (CONT.) WP 379.29 380.2
  382.20 391.3 FA 468.4
  PR 476.37 481.8 484.23
  TB 513.6 SU 540.5 BO 594.2
  595.5 JD 613.15 614.4
  614.28 615.11 LA 631.40
  632.7 632.15 632.37 637.26
  GG 669.3 ML 726.36 733.30
  LL 764.27 RR 784.21
  RH 798.35 799.15 MD 807.35
  807.37 808.16 820.42
  BM 828.11 831.35

ODDLY EE 306.1 WP 390.18
  YT 397.13 399.26 PR 476.37
  WR 570.33 LA 632.31 637.16
  MD 809.33 824.19 BM 829.32

ODDMENTS WR 546.13

ODDS WM 66.21

ODOUR SC 268.29 BL 354.36
  FA 463.42 GG 695.39

ODYSSEY JD 610.25

OEUFS FARCIES MD 813.15

OFFENCE DV 177.38 184.20
  SU 533.28

OFFEND GG 679.31

OFFENDED YT 403.25 405.4
  IL 652.31 MD 814.42

OFFENSIVE OA 32.40 BL 349.22

OFFER MO 17.25 WM 68.16
  EA 74.4 DV 149.19 SS 201.26
  208.16 OC 292.38 EE 326.10
  YT 407.28 TB 520.10 526.42
  527.25 GG 671.8 TH 848.35
  853.2

OFFERED MO 22.8 OA 25.30 34.23
  WM 69.14 GF 242.33
  WS 254.19 258.2 OC 292.34
  294.35 TP 345.37 PP 430.40
  SU 530.14 WR 550.7 565.6
  RR 784.41 MD 817.33
  BM 830.16

OFFERING MO 17.8 DV 142.37
  WR 565.20 BO 589.28 602.2
  GG 670.42 681.27 NT 715.21
  716.42 OV 754.21 TH 850.41

OFFERS TF 127.14 RH 797.18

OFFERTORY FA 467.39

OFF-HAND MN 370.23 SD 416.24
  WR 550.13 JD 623.7

OFFICE OA 31.3 WM 62.1
  DV 166.28 167.12 SS 198.17
  YT 406.4 BO 596.13 596.18
  RH 790.25 MD 805.2 814.38
  815.9 815.31 815.40 817.28
  817.34 818.22

OFFICER PO 96.6 96.13 97.7
  97.14 97.27 97.29 98.2

OFFICER (CONT.) PO 98.6 98.24
  98.36 98.40 99.2 99.31
  99.39 100.12 100.29 100.35
  100.40 101.10 102.16 102.27
  102.34 102.36 103.10 103.28
  105.1 106.3 107.25 107.33
  108.2 108.10 108.12 108.18
  109.6 109.25 109.28 109.30
  109.33 109.42 110.15
  TF 119.29 120.4 121.10 121.17
  121.27 134.5 SG 231.11
  EE 330.12 330.32 331.29
  TP 335.23 MN 378.28 BO 593.39
  GG 663.18

OFFICERS TF 121.40 122.10
  EE 327.39

OFFICER'S PO 98.13 99.34 101.24
  101.40 102.13 102.30 105.8
  110.4

OFFICERS' PO 96.30

OFFICES DV 177.10

OFFICIAL OA 32.35 34.34
  EA 83.10 DV 172.19 TP 341.34
  343.2 MD 818.32 820.33

OFFICIALS BO 599.14 MD 821.7

OFFICIATE DV 144.37 MN 377.15

OFFICIOUSLY HT 43.31

OFF'N SC 271.40

OFFSPRING ML 722.15

OFTEN MO 7.25 20.22 OA 24.41
  WM 60.13 EA 74.4 74.8 80.13
  92.5 DV 146.41 FG 190.25
  SS 198.32 SB 215.20 CH 274.36
  EE 308.31 308.40 309.25
  309.30 319.29 TP 334.33 336.2
  WP 386.12 YT 396.29 PR 475.19
  483.4 SU 535.38 WR 546.24
  568.10 BO 594.42 GG 676.9
  NT 703.3 703.41 705.7 706.24
  716.19 ML 727.25 OV 752.25
  752.29 754.6 LL 766.11 766.24
  RR 781.6 MD 806.14 806.22
  821.30 BM 827.36 833.36

OH-H DV 161.35 IL 654.36 654.40

OH-H-H RH 800.18

OH-H-HS TP 344.16

OIL EA 82.24 DV 167.37 SU 534.1
  WR 577.2

OILCLOTH HT 43.8

OIL-PAINTINGS SG 221.8

OIL-SEED WR 552.26

OILSKIN TP 336.13 ML 743.26

OILY WM 55.30

OINTMENT CH 276.34 YT 395.23

O. K. MN 366.1

OLD MO 1.2 1.12 1.31 5.39
  6.36 7.9 7.15 7.28 11.3
  16.1 16.8 16.41 17.33 22.13
  OA 26.3 26.15 26.25 31.5
  WM 55.39 56.1 56.6 56.11
  56.18 56.33 56.36 58.5 64.33
  67.32 PO 100.34 103.8
  TF 123.13 132.24 133.22
  DV 138.36 141.14 141.35
  142.13 142.33 143.29 144.25
  144.35 145.2 147.39 149.3
  149.28 150.33 156.18 160.14
  161.20 161.28 161.35 162.1
  162.5 162.22 162.25 162.32
  162.37 163.2 163.13 163.19
  163.23 163.35 164.33 166.34
  166.36 168.12 168.24 169.8
  169.12 169.19 169.40 170.1
  170.3 170.8 171.25 172.12
  172.17 176.33 176.34 182.38
  FG 187.4 189.6 SS 201.22
  202.37 202.41 203.2 203.9
  203.11 203.19 203.42 204.12
  205.6 205.8 SB 212.24
  SG 222.22 222.30 230.5 231.16
  231.42 GF 238.28 239.5 242.1
  242.35 242.38 242.39 243.11
  WS 245.3 264.19 SC 270.36
  272.29 CH 275.32 276.28
  276.32 277.20 277.42 278.13
  278.20 278.26 279.7 280.3
  280.5 280.10 280.32 281.25
  OC 293.31 294.15 294.27
  294.39 295.6 295.10 295.17
  295.18 295.19 295.21 295.29
  295.35 296.4 296.8 296.10
  296.12 296.27 296.28 296.35
  296.41 297.17 298.32 299.8
  299.12 299.18 299.27 299.30
  300.12 EE 303.13 304.2 304.5
  304.20 304.27 304.32 304.37
  305.16 305.18 305.29 306.18
  306.22 307.29 308.5 308.28
  308.29 308.41 311.22 312.2
  314.4 314.24 314.28 314.29
  314.38 314.41 316.1 316.5
  316.9 316.19 319.12 323.27
  323.38 323.39 324.8 326.7
  328.5 TP 335.21 335.22 337.4
  340.14 340.17 341.18 345.39
  BL 347.17 348.4 348.26 348.38
  349.7 350.35 351.2 351.5
  351.20 356.28 358.25 361.20
  362.8 MN 366.15 368.24 372.36
  WP 391.39 YT 394.28 395.15
  395.28 395.36 396.11 399.17
  403.11 407.1 407.15 409.11
  SD 411.32 415.19 423.1
  PP 428.12 431.38 436.26
  436.41 437.41 438.5 HD 442.14
  446.32 FA 459.7 460.8 462.23
  463.36 464.40 469.24 471.3
  471.29 PR 473.3 473.16 474.21
  475.36 476.3 476.24 477.5
  477.6 477.13 478.8 479.5
  479.26 479.30 479.32 479.37
  482.16 482.25 490.7 498.9
  499.39 500.9 501.1 TB 516.6
  SU 529.14 538.8 538.15 538.19
  538.24 538.37 538.41 539.11
  543.5 WR 547.10 549.25 550.5
  550.6 550.27 559.32 560.4
  560.9 560.19 560.37 561.5

OLD (CONT.) 561.10 562.8
  562.31 562.35 562.39
  563.5 563.9 563.13 563.21
  563.25 563.40 564.2 564.7
  564.8 566.10 566.22 566.24
  566.33 566.34 566.35
  567.11 567.13 573.14
  573.22 576.13 578.1 578.4
  578.8 578.12 580.29 581.26
  BO 593.6 593.7 595.21
  599.4 599.8 600.12 600.15
  LA 634.26 635.28 639.2
  640.12 641.34 641.35
  643.24 643.27 IL 648.20
  648.36 651.25 652.2
  652.4 652.40 652.41 653.16
  653.20 654.23 GG 662.24
  662.41 667.29 667.30
  668.29 670.15 670.30 671.3
  672.39 672.41 676.1 676.9
  676.23 677.8 678.3 687.35
  693.28 697.6 697.17
  NT 701.28 702.36 704.36
  705.41 706.3 706.4 706.14
  709.23 709.29 715.23
  ML 723.39 724.17 724.24
  724.40 725.11 725.31
  725.32 726.15 727.28
  727.29 730.17 732.29
  733.8 733.11 733.21 733.33
  734.26 734.28 735.9 741.17
  741.18 OV 748.6 756.41
  757.32 757.36 757.41
  LL 761.21 763.6 763.8
  763.18 763.21 763.29
  764.2 765.20 769.11
  769.25 769.42 770.16
  775.24 776.3 776.5 776.8
  776.11 776.16 776.34
  777.15 777.16 RR 779.6
  RH 794.26 795.4 MD 806.30
  808.13 808.14 809.26
  810.23 810.28 812.33
  814.26 814.28 815.11
  821.23 822.22 822.30
  824.20 825.17 825.19
  BM 828.38 828.41 828.42
  829.1 830.10 830.21 830.38
  834.38 835.38 840.11
  TH 844.22 844.24 844.28
  847.31 847.39 848.5 848.6
  851.13 851.22 853.30

OLD ALDECROSS DV 160.25
  167.22

OLD BRINSLEY OC 287.11

OLD ENGLISH GENTLEMAN OA 32.13

OLDER MO 10.19 OA 30.8
  PO 97.10 DV 150.6 SS 202.13
  SB 212.9 217.23 SG 221.31
  231.22 BL 359.20 YT 403.35
  PP 429.14 429.16 PR 495.4
  WR 546.4 553.42 566.12
  576.31 GG 667.33 679.39
  LL 762.28 768.18 BM 827.27

OLDEST BL 347.3 WR 559.21
  560.36 581.20

OLD-FASHIONED MO 17.21
  DV 139.33 FA 463.21
  PR 476.20 GG 669.8 LL 764.3

OLD-FASHIONED (CONT.) BM 834.34

OLDMEADOW HD 449.3 449.20

OLD-TIMER WR 548.23

OLIVE SU 530.2 534.1 537.16

OLIVES SU 529.9 SM 582.29

OLLERTON FEAST SB 213.19

OLYMPIC RAWDON RR 784.6

OMAHA NT 705.23

O'MAKKIN' WP 389.26

OMAR KHAYYAM MO 6.28

OMELETTE OV 748.34

OMINOUS BL 350.14 WP 389.37
  389.38 PR 497.23 LL 777.2

OMINOUSLY BM 829.37 831.39

OMNIBUS BO 587.23

ONCE MO 21.41 WM 68.4 PO 97.28
  99.25 100.20 104.13 TF 120.16
  DV 143.19 145.21 150.34
  155.10 162.10 FG 193.21
  SS 201.33 211.27 SB 215.21
  SG 227.30 GF 239.19 240.8
  243.28 WS 260.5 260.28 265.15
  CH 277.3 OC 287.18 295.8
  298.7 EE 311.3 315.12 320.30
  321.24 324.20 TP 334.15
  334.23 342.4 BL 360.33
  MN 368.15 375.5 WP 379.21
  389.35 390.8 392.5 393.7
  YT 394.9 395.35 408.35
  SD 421.15 PP 436.40 HD 446.18
  447.38 448.20 FA 459.6 461.34
  464.36 464.37 PR 474.32
  475.11 476.34 479.31 485.15
  498.40 499.39 504.6 TB 519.20
  520.12 520.23 524.29 526.19
  SU 531.5 531.15 543.41
  WR 555.23 560.10 566.19
  568.14 569.33 569.36 569.39
  BO 590.15 592.7 592.31 594.31
  595.9 596.4 598.5 600.30
  JD 611.28 616.18 625.18
  625.19 LA 630.3 637.8 637.19
  IL 649.23 651.33 656.30
  GG 664.34 669.24 671.6 672.9
  677.9 679.13 686.9 696.12
  699.24 NT 701.3 701.17 701.33
  704.11 707.23 707.37 711.40
  716.23 718.5 718.30 719.1
  ML 724.13 732.27 742.30
  744.17 745.18 746.26
  OV 753.35 758.12 LL 765.38
  777.41 RR 784.20 784.23
  788.17 RH 799.37 802.15
  MD 805.10 809.35 814.5
  BM 832.11 832.21 838.9 838.12
  842.5 842.6 842.15 TH 844.22
  852.18

ONCE-COMEDY GG 680.10

ONCE-GERMAN BO 595.2

ONCE-MARRIED TB 514.4

ONCOMER BO 595.24

ONCOMING TF 119.3

ONCOMINGS JD 609.16

ONE-MAN MD 810.10 810.16

ONES PO 102.21 SS 205.8
  FA 462.26 PR 475.34 481.42
  SU 537.20 537.21 537.22
  WR 549.1 559.10 571.30 574.38
  IL 648.20 GG 673.27 NT 704.15

ONE'S MO 21.2 DV 157.26 161.11
  FG 194.12 SS 205.18 205.19
  BL 361.9 GG 682.35 LL 766.31
  778.22 778.23 RR 780.6
  TH 844.8

ONESELF WM 62.28 CH 274.36
  GG 692.28 TH 845.22 846.30

ONE-STOREY WR 546.18

ONE THOUSAND POUNDS SD 426.16

ONION MD 812.36 812.37

ONIONS PR 475.23

ONIONY JD 618.24

ONLOOKER SU 535.24

ONSLAUGHT TB 520.8

ON'T SC 271.3 WP 389.29

ONWARDS MO 6.27 PR 498.17
  WR 579.8 GG 676.11 NT 720.15

ONY SP 53.13 RR 770.19*

ON'Y SP 48.23 48.28 49.40
  52.41

OOS BO 600.27 600.28

OOZE SP 51.2 FA 468.17

OOZED PR 500.22

OPAQUE DV 171.4 JD 609.12

OPEN MO 3.31 4.3 4.19 19.20
  OA 35.36 35.41 SP 50.15
  WM 69.6 EA 74.28 82.40 93.38
  PO 104.2 109.14 109.33 113.31
  113.35 114.13 116.12
  TF 118.19 122.25 123.19
  127.27 127.28 129.14 134.11
  DV 139.4 139.14 139.34 153.4
  159.17 161.4 161.27 166.23
  167.12 171.16 FG 192.22 194.6
  195.18 SS 197.24 199.33
  199.34 200.33 204.38 209.39
  SB 215.7 216.3 SG 224.15
  224.22 224.29 224.33 225.26
  228.4 231.27 GF 235.31 239.8
  WS 245.24 249.4 264.16
  SC 268.25 CH 277.18 OC 283.14
  292.40 293.29 297.3 300.24

OPEN (CONT.) EE 332.7
  TP 342.38 343.1 345.35
  BL 351.36 MN 367.14
  WP 379.18 380.6 SD 423.17
  PP 427.6 435.38 438.20
  438.33 HD 446.26 451.13
  454.38 455.10 PR 480.5
  490.28 500.37 SU 540.29
  541.21 WR 546.24 546.25
  553.2 561.18 563.24 568.30
  575.9 575.10 575.21 576.17
  580.22 BO 592.31 JD 613.25
  627.12 LA 636.9 639.16
  639.18 IL 654.12 654.38
  GG 670.39 694.9 694.26
  NT 713.3 713.5 ML 731.1
  741.13 741.26 742.14
  OV 747.3 747.20 754.1
  755.8 LL 765.6 770.7
  770.41 772.32 RR 782.13
  787.27 788.8 788.18
  RH 793.10 MD 821.37
  BM 842.42

OPEN-AIR NT 709.27

OPENED MO 11.31 OA 23.1
  23.11 24.10 27.24 HT 44.1
  SP 45.10 WM 55.20 63.27
  69.33 70.1 EA 84.3
  PO 112.39 114.14 TF 125.30
  DV 159.12 167.36 178.14
  FG 195.11 195.22 196.20
  SS 198.40 199.12 199.40
  201.3 206.23 SG 229.18
  WS 245.26 245.36 251.37
  CH 275.23 277.26 OC 287.18
  290.28 298.4 298.32
  EE 332.23 TP 345.41
  BL 353.22 362.13 364.35
  WP 387.37 390.3 391.6
  YT 401.32 SD 415.32
  PP 434.1 HD 444.16 451.8
  FA 458.14 PR 474.17 500.42
  504.37 505.4 506.22
  SU 538.32 SM 583.25
  BO 604.29 JD 624.31 LA 630.7
  632.16 635.30 640.40
  IL 653.41 656.28 658.4
  660.2 GG 666.10 674.18
  681.15 691.5 694.24 694.32
  NT 713.2 ML 727.13 729.19
  729.20 730.42 740.39
  744.20 745.3 LL 775.39
  777.3 RR 785.38 BM 838.15

OPEN-EYED FA 468.12

OPENIN' FA 463.31

OPENING WM 67.41 PO 115.19
  DV 158.17 SS 202.40 204.35
  SG 224.36 WS 251.39 264.13
  OC 289.30 BL 353.1
  WP 379.12 386.27 387.29
  YT 402.25 FA 467.1
  SU 536.32 SM 584.5
  GG 685.12 ML 743.14
  LL 775.39

OPENLY PR 479.27 RR 780.8

OPEN-MOUTHED FA 467.26

OPEN SESAME MD 811.38

OPERA GG 664.27

OPERATION DV 156.23

OPERATOR LA 632.18

OPHELIA SM 582.7 582.32 584.25
  584.35

OPHELIA'S SM 582.2 582.6 586.7

OPINION MO 17.19 OA 32.40
  EE 319.12 320.29 FA 461.22
  JD 605.6 606.29 606.31 606.42
  607.2 607.3 BM 838.11

OPINIONS FG 187.35

OPPONENT OA 33.30 JD 612.14

OPPONENT'S OA 33.14

OPPORTUNITY YT 406.39

OPPOSE SG 230.40 YT 396.25

OPPOSED RH 801.1

OPPOSING WS 257.9

OPPOSITE MO 3.20 10.16 WM 60.31
  61.20 EA 72.20 72.25
  DV 143.36 151.7 SG 231.23
  WS 252.39 SC 268.23 OC 285.3
  BL 349.14 MN 376.22 WP 386.13
  FA 461.40 PR 495.28 501.18
  SU 543.3 544.20 WR 558.39
  568.27 569.14 573.33 576.33
  SM 582.15 BO 593.39 JD 611.21
  626.15 LA 636.14 GG 672.39
  686.14 OV 748.37 RR 788.7
  MD 808.19 812.22

OPPOSITION SS 199.32 WS 258.19
  EE 311.33 GG 686.17 686.25

OPPRESSED DV 156.27 BO 592.26

OPPRESSING SU 541.27

OPPRESSIVE OA 23.25 TH 849.1

OP'TAIRS OA 25.18

ORACLE MO 9.17

ORANGE MO 1.28 SB 213.4
  PR 495.27 499.3 500.27 506.19
  506.27 SU 531.28 531.33
  531.34 WR 559.20 566.8 578.34
  MD 811.5 TH 848.14

ORANGE-TAWNY PR 494.19

ORANGE-YELLOW WR 559.22

ORATORICAL SP 45.25

ORB WR 581.14

ORCHARD MO 3.7 SS 201.41 204.1
  PP 436.32 437.27 PR 481.27
  GG 695.20 699.28

ORCHESTRA BM 838.9

ORCHIDS WM 69.1 ML 736.11

ORDEAL CH 279.30

ORDER OA 31.17 37.33 SP 45.24
  53.1 PO 99.24 TF 129.3 134.6
  134.32 DV 172.28 SS 206.26
  EE 321.22 323.17 PR 477.28
  TB 516.34 IL 656.7 656.11
  ML 728.12 733.24 737.33

ORDERED GF 238.12 EE 327.38
  SU 533.17 ML 729.23

ORDERING DV 137.1

ORDERLY PO 95.34 96.4 96.8
  96.11 96.13 96.37 96.42
  97.17 97.37 98.26 98.30
  98.39 99.3 100.14 100.29
  100.38 101.1 101.16 101.20
  101.27 103.27 103.34 105.2
  105.31 105.34 107.22 107.32
  107.41 108.7 108.28 108.39
  109.3 109.10 109.34 110.3
  110.35 111.6 111.13

ORDERLY'S PO 102.31 102.35
  107.27 108.20 109.18 110.38

ORDERS SP 53.3 PO 96.39 98.28
  105.12 TF 118.17 DV 136.25
  EE 330.42 331.29 SD 416.3
  416.6 416.10 416.11 HD 445.19
  TB 516.33 BO 592.36 NT 721.7

ORDINARY MO 1.32 OA 37.42
  PO 103.37 DV 136.24 BL 353.41
  YT 395.30 395.31 395.32
  HD 449.31 WR 574.24 BO 588.27
  JD 613.8 GG 689.32 NT 703.12
  LL 768.23

ORE PO 115.1 WR 547.3 548.19

ORGAN FA 467.4 467.39 468.24
  LA 640.6

ORGANIC NT 711.11

ORGANIST'S DV 142.32

ORGAN-PIPES LA 640.1

ORIENTAL EE 303.34 MD 821.18
  824.11 824.35

ORIFICE WR 579.37 579.42

ORIGINAL NT 709.16

ORION MO 3.5 19.26 WM 60.32
  ML 733.25

ORMIN' FA 463.25

ORMING FA 463.27

ORNAMENT EA 81.13 87.8

ORNAMENTS SB 214.3 SG 222.12
  YT 397.12 MD 823.25

ORPHAN ML 733.11 BM 828.19

OSBORNE, BOB (SEE BOB OSBORNE)

OSCAR RH 803.34

OSCAR, UNCLE (SEE UNCLE OSCAR)

OSCAR CRESSWELL RH 794.11
  794.14 797.4 797.20 798.1
  798.5 803.37 804.4

OSSIANIC PR 473.18

OSTENTATIOUS EA 81.9

OSTENTATIOUSLY DV 157.38
  WS 246.22

OSTLER SP 48.12

OSTRICH RR 788.26

OTHERS MO 5.15 PO 111.30
  113.29 113.32 DV 164.20
  166.3 EE 311.6 311.31
  313.32 326.39 MN 370.40
  WP 382.33 383.12 SD 423.36
  PP 440.10 HD 443.19 FA 464.23
  PR 475.37 476.7* 477.11 481.33
  489.24 493.20 WR 567.10
  GG 687.30 NT 704.21 706.31
  706.40 712.42 LL 778.30
  RH 799.29

OTHER'S MO 4.15 19.23
  OA 35.40 38.24 38.35
  PO 99.19 WS 257.17
  MN 369.10 TB 525.8
  RR 782.37 RH 790.16 791.13
  798.38 MD 808.20 BM 835.42
  837.29

OTHERWISE MO 17.18 SG 222.29
  IL 647.12 GG 665.16 669.2
  ML 741.20 BM 829.15 835.39

OUGHT MO 8.36 OA 28.4
  HT 42.1 EA 87.27 87.34
  SS 207.17 TP 344.13 344.14
  BL 349.18 HD 456.23
  TB 515.7 JD 611.41
  IL 649.24 649.25 649.29
  GG 687.40 689.3 689.6
  OV 755.41 RR 781.27
  RH 792.16 801.34 801.36
  803.3 TH 850.11 851.30

OUGHTNA SP 48.20

OUGHTN'T SB 213.23 RH 794.29

OU NOUS ALLONS GG 676.22

OUR LADY FG 194.13

OUR SAVIOUR HIMSELF ML 727.20

OURSELVES FG 194.4 194.29
  GF 242.38 EE 313.22
  YT 407.42 PR 478.28
  ML 731.15

OUTBALANCED JD 605.22

OUT-BUILDING ML 725.38

OUTBUILDINGS

OUTBUILDINGS HD 449.4

OUT-BUILDINGS MO 3.16

OUTBURST PO 98.18   PP 428.38
  FA 464.17   467.2

OUTCAST MD 826.2

OUTCOME BL 357.12

OUTCOMING TP 334.20

OUTCRY TH 846.42

OUT-DISTANCED OC 283.5

OUTDOOR DV 137.32   OC 286.40

OUTDOORS WP 390.17

OUTER ML 726.10   738.18   740.5
  743.8

OUTFLOW TF 132.33

OUT-HOUSES BL 347.8   352.37
  YT 394.7

OUTLAWS FG 193.31

OUTLINE WM 59.12   DV 149.5
  PR 484.3

OUTLIVE JD 628.14

OUTLOOK MO 11.24   RR 779.32

OUTLYING ML 722.27

OUT-OF-DOORS MO 1.6   SS 197.32
  PR 478.35

OUT-OF-THE-WAY EE 305.36

OUT-PATIENTS HD 448.13

OUTPOURING MO 2.8

OUTRAGED BM 837.16

OUTRIGHT LL 761.17   MD 814.2

OUT-SHINING MN 374.13

OUTSIDE MO 4.23   10.29   19.14
  OA 34.9   SP 45.28   45.33
  EA 82.17   84.18   90.5   90.6
  PO 101.21   108.20   111.9   111.37
  113.29   113.30   TF 123.10
  DV 158.38   160.22   167.30
  167.35   172.6   174.9   SS 201.13
  SG 221.3   222.33   GF 240.4
  WS 252.22   CH 281.22   OC 288.18
  289.33   290.7   EE 325.19   330.1
  330.28   331.42   TP 335.10
  340.31   BL 347.2   349.40   351.11
  361.13   WP 385.30   YT 395.19
  401.31   SD 414.36   422.14
  422.19   422.31   422.40
  PP 438.16   HD 441.20   FA 461.36
  PR 475.23   475.26   477.7   477.38
  509.23   SU 537.28   WR 546.25
  548.27   561.31   561.39   562.11
  BO 588.11   602.39   JD 614.8

OUTSIDE (CONT.) LA 637.4   639.40
  640.33   641.31   644.36
  IL 654.22   GG 668.28   683.34
  NT 719.32   ML 728.22   742.30
  745.2   OV 748.1   748.36   749.23
  758.6   759.5   LL 765.35   776.41
  RR 784.17   RH 802.41   MD 819.30
  BM 834.25

OUTSIDER TF 131.10   BO 589.20
  MD 819.13   819.15   TH 848.35

OUTSIDERS GG 663.27

OUTSKIRTS JD 610.20

OUTSPOKENNESS WM 61.18

OUTSPREAD OV 755.7

OUTSTANDING TB 521.30

OUTSTRETCHED EE 324.16   PR 511.5
  WR 580.34   JD 618.12

OUTWARDLY PR 508.11   BO 592.8
  BM 831.27

OUTWARDS WM 63.5

OVAL LL 161.8

OVARIES MO 20.11

OVEN CH 282.4

OVER-ALL OA 23.9

OVERALLS MN 367.1   YT 394.15

OVERBEARING PO 96.23   WR 550.41
  BO 588.33   603.20

OVER-BRED MD 812.36

OVERCAME BL 347.32   351.34
  ML 745.13

OVERCOAT MO 19.7   DV 138.37
  147.1   WS 249.37   251.19
  TP 337.23   341.31   345.30
  BL 362.8   MN 373.30   SD 415.32
  417.36   422.28   423.6   425.30
  PP 439.40   HD 444.20   451.3
  SM 586.19   LA 630.15   631.26
  632.22   643.31   BM 841.9

OVERCOME MO 22.21   FG 190.10
  EE 326.23   TP 344.29   BL 364.21
  SD 419.26   WR 549.34   GG 684.30
  ML 746.10

OVERCOMES PR 482.20

OVERCROWDED WP 388.40

OVERCROWDING ML 722.18

OVER-CULTURED MD 817.18

OVERDOSE NT 717.17

OVERFLOW BO 599.6

OVERFOLDINGS DV 173.10

OVERGROWN SU 530.5

OVERHANGING BO 595.21

OVERHEAD MO 3.23   18.29
  WM 54.19   54.25   PO 112.30
  113.2   115.15   DV 161.2
  161.25   FG 193.18   194.37
  SS 200.7   EE 304.12   304.37
  330.32   HD 452.8   WR 547.40
  JD 608.26

OVERHEATED OA 33.27

OVER-HEATED IL 649.4

OVERLAPPED OA 29.34

OVERLAPPING WR 553.14

OVERLOOKING OA 32.39
  SG 221.26   BL 359.21

OVERLYING SB 216.36

OVERMASTERING SB 220.2

OVERMUCH GF 241.11

OVER-POPULATION ML 722.17

OVERPOWERING GF 241.12
  WR 573.23

OVER-RATE BO 590.17

OVERRIDING PO 106.7

OVER-RIPE SG 224.28

OVER-RUN OC 290.32

OVERSEAS GG 699.24

OVER-SENSITIVE BL 349.9

OVERSHADOWED LL 765.20

OVER-SHOES BL 352.34

OVERSIGHT MN 372.17

OVERSTRAINED WM 69.29

OVERSTRUNG GF 242.28

OVERTAKE PO 111.22

OVERTAKEN OV 758.36

OVERTHREW TF 121.7

OVERTHROW TP 344.37

OVERTONE BO 600.14   LL 767.30

OVERTOOK BO 603.4

OVERTURNED SD 421.27
  OV 754.7

OVER-WEENING BO 588.39   589.32

OVERWHELMED SM 582.11

OVERWORKED TB 524.41

OVERWROUGHT RH 800.34 MD 814.40

OVER-WROUGHT FA 461.8

OWBRIDGE'S MO 17.37

OWER OC 292.16 WP 388.9 389.24

OWING ML 738.24 RR 785.20

OWL LL 770.42 772.41

OWLISH MD 824.8 824.14

OWNED OV 749.26

OWNER RR 788.25

OXFORD MD 813.22

OXFORDSHIRE WP 382.5

OXFORDY JD 615.36

PACE CH 274.13 SM 586.21

PACED LL 777.34

PACES PO 107.39 PR 491.12

PACIFIC PR 481.17 481.18
  TH 851.8 851.10

PACK EA 78.21 80.4 PR 488.25
  MD 825.38

PACKAGE WS 265.36

PACKAGES WS 245.16 PR 494.21

PACKED WS 245.28 TP 334.35
  335.10 335.23 MN 371.15
  LA 637.7 BM 834.42 835.9
  837.27 839.36

PACKET DV 138.38 WS 245.26
  245.31 249.28

PACK-HORSE PR 488.11 488.20

PACKING-SHED YT 394.12

PADDED DV 146.6 146.26 151.28
  152.10 158.33 186.4 RR 786.12
  788.8

PADDING DV 146.42 153.36
  SS 203.16

PADDLED SB 214.31 PP 432.25

PADDLING SB 214.23 GF 234.3
  PR 478.36

PADDOCK OV 755.35 756.25
  LL 773.7

PADLOCKED OC 284.4

PADRON NT 704.31*

PADRONE SU 543.20

PAGAN SM 584.8

PAGANLY TF 126.29

PAGE-BOY NT 705.25

PAH EA 75.4 TF 135.11 SG 231.32

PAID OA 32.3 HT 39.13 41.39
  41.42 43.14 SP 45.1 45.5
  EA 89.16 DV 153.19 153.21
  SG 226.42 WS 265.39 SC 269.15
  EE 308.39 308.42 309.18
  TP 338.4 WP 389.32 FA 463.17
  PR 477.42 481.25 TB 519.27
  JD 628.33 LA 646.4 ML 728.17
  LL 764.10 770.7 RH 792.37
  799.1 MD 808.6 TH 851.26
  852.19

PAIL WP 379.22 379.25 JD 617.3
  617.9

PAILS PO 108.3 BL 347.21

PAIN MO 3.3 OA 30.33 35.21
  WM 57.13 60.8 66.18 EA 73.18
  78.10 90.22 92.19 93.8 93.11
  PO 95.22 95.31 102.4 104.32
  104.42 105.13 106.25 108.24
  111.27 112.3 112.7 113.20
  115.39 DV 161.35 161.37
  162.38 168.30 168.32 169.11
  169.16 169.18 169.32 169.41
  170.1 171.27 174.16 174.18
  174.20 179.39 181.16 181.30
  183.33 FG 189.29 190.8 195.9
  SS 198.35 210.13 SG 225.15
  231.34 GF 242.8 SC 269.22
  269.27 269.42 270.5 270.8
  271.5 272.22 CH 281.18
  EE 317.15 324.22 325.11
  331.41 332.2 332.3 332.7
  332.12 BL 350.18 350.37
  YT 400.21 404.27 408.19
  409.24 PP 440.1 HD 454.21 455.8
  455.13 456.36 PR 487.19
  503.21 508.19 SU 530.15
  544.10 SM 584.6 GG 667.33
  TH 846.3 846.5 846.7 846.11
  846.15 846.28

PAINED EA 92.14 SS 198.40
  CH 279.23 TB 524.3 JD 611.18
  IL 653.34

PAINEDLY FA 469.36

PAINFUL MO 6.13 8.37 8.38
  OA 29.21 WM 60.22 PO 104.11
  TF 133.13 GF 239.25 CH 279.30
  OC 293.20 EE 320.5 HD 454.36
  456.38 LL 772.16

PAINFULLY MO 3.9 OA 33.28 37.34
  EA 85.22 PO 104.3 CH 278.30
  BL 349.10 WP 387.20 BM 827.2

PAIN-QUENCHED EE 323.1

PAINS HD 448.6 SM 582.36

PAIN'S SC 269.36

PAINT SS 203.4 WR 573.35 577.15
  RR 779.33 BM 827.32 833.20

PAIN-TEARS PO 100.19

PAINTED FG 195.26 SS 210.18
  PR 481.37 WR 573.35 576.27
  580.27 LA 640.41 GG 693.21
  NT 705.38 MD 811.3 811.12
  BM 829.41 830.1 830.4
  831.11 TH 844.32 844.34

PAINTER PR 478.33 NT 701.4

PAINTING EE 308.36 YT 395.5

PAINTINGS LA 640.31 640.36

PAIR MO 11.3 WM 57.33 58.39
  WS 245.39 248.38 261.15
  261.28 263.38 263.41
  SC 267.34 YT 399.17
  SD 421.21 421.36 FA 472.2
  TB 522.8 523.7 LA 642.15
  IL 652.38 LL 777.9 MD 808.6
  BM 842.29 TH 844.9

PAIRS OC 292.8

PAISLEY OV 749.20

PAL TP 337.11 MN 366.10
  366.15 367.7 368.21 372.36
  IL 653.16

PALACE SM 582.33 BO 588.22

PALATABLE TB 515.23

PALAZZO TH 847.39 849.1

PALE MO 1.26 22.23 OA 24.8
  29.36 HT 44.8 SP 47.14
  49.11 WM 55.17 61.23 63.31
  PO 95.8 95.21 99.23
  102.1 105.2 105.20 106.42
  107.8 107.10 114.30 114.42
  115.30 TF 117.17 124.25
  133.29 DV 137.23 138.25
  139.1 158.7 167.14 179.35
  185.27 SS 200.38 201.4
  SG 221.32 226.39 230.24
  GF 235.24 239.28 241.2
  242.2 WS 258.20 263.42
  SC 270.17 OC 288.36 289.5
  293.31 296.15 EE 318.8
  318.9 319.3 322.9 322.42
  329.32 TP 338.14 339.32
  WP 379.5 387.20 YT 407.11
  410.4 PP 428.4 434.18
  439.21 HD 444.22 PR 481.6
  489.2 489.13 489.23 489.32
  490.8 490.25 490.41 493.28
  494.18 497.37 497.39
  498.34 501.17 501.18
  507.22 510.26 SU 532.9
  538.3 538.41 540.18 541.26
  WR 559.12 579.12 SM 583.12
  584.6 584.16 585.20
  BO 598.21 JD 622.17 622.31
  LA 631.29 NT 701.7 702.35
  712.36 ML 723.24 728.10
  732.8 740.3 740.19 740.22
  741.34 OV 759.22 LL 772.2
  772.24 RH 803.14 BM 827.30
  835.20 838.38

PALE-BLUE PO 96.1 FA 464.31
  PR 506.33 BM 842.29

PALED IL 657.5

PALE-DUSKY ML 741.34

PALE-FACED CH 275.12

PALE-GREY PR 489.3 494.35 498.9

PALELY EA 91.30 PR 496.32
  497.38

PALENESS FG 194.37

PALER SS 208.7 WP 387.22
  PR 489.20 ML 744.42 RR 784.9

PALE-SHOWING EE 308.3

PALE-SMOOTH PR 499.31

PALING WR 557.36

PALLID EE 324.22 WP 390.33
  PR 489.37 496.18 498.23
  507.10 SU 530.7 WR 579.17
  BO 593.20 595.42

PALLOR PO 115.14 TF 117.34
  YT 399.10 PR 489.19 WR 580.18
  BO 596.1 GG 698.35 ML 744.28
  744.41

PALM WS 265.29 TB 517.12
  ML 722.23

PALMS PO 110.8

PALPABLE DV 165.16 BL 347.28

PALPITATED OA 29.31

PALPITATION GF 239.11

PALTRY EA 74.7 SG 232.6

PAN MO 15.14 BL 353.16
  PR 502.11 JD 606.26 OV 755.37
  755.38 755.39 756.35 756.40
  757.1 757.2 757.11 757.12
  757.15 758.7 759.12 759.16
  759.18 759.20 759.21 759.22
  759.27

PANACEA EA 87.27

PANCHION DV 170.18 171.2

PANE DV 157.37

PANELLING GG 671.2

PANELS SG 231.1

PANES CH 280.20 BL 351.13

PANG PO 102.3 112.28 115.22
  115.23 TF 122.22 DV 180.9
  SG 230.31 BL 350.19 YT 396.28
  WR 571.3

PANGS TH 850.25

PANIC PO 114.8 EE 317.35
  TP 335.2 BL 348.3 SD 414.10
  PP 434.41 BO 594.18 594.21

PANIC (CONT.) 603.23 JD 625.21
  626.6

PANIC-LOVE BO 594.22

PANIC-STRICKEN BO 594.19 594.24

PAN-PERSON JD 607.1

PAN-PIPES LA 640.1

PANS BL 351.35 PR 501.2

PAN'S OV 759.31

PANT OA 30.34 EA 90.35

PANTED PO 102.20 103.41
  DV 161.38 162.3 SD 412.35
  PR 504.14 504.22 IL 653.9
  TH 852.15

PANTHER-LIKE ML 746.21

PANTING OA 30.21 PO 102.28
  TF 121.11 DV 176.24 FG 190.37
  GF 239.6 TP 345.25 IL 653.11

PANTRY HT 41.25 DV 163.6
  OC 296.36 296.39 297.10

PANTS DV 160.26

PAPA DV 184.32 185.14 185.22
  PR 477.5

PAPER EA 74.31 DV 142.27 160.6
  172.34 GF 236.38 WS 245.28
  246.9 248.24 248.36 CH 275.8
  281.27 OC 288.23 YT 407.18
  PP 429.30 LA 639.37 644.33

PAPERS WM 63.42 DV 138.38
  TB 524.17 GG 661.13 681.17
  681.21 LL 763.18

PAPP EE 331.4

PAR GG 685.39

PARADISE PR 494.12 GG 661.17
  NT 704.14 ML 725.10 730.39

PARAFFIN DV 139.17 ML 739.34
  743.17

PARAFFIN-BOTTLE DV 139.36

PARAFFIN-HUT DV 161.2

PARAFFIN-TIN DV 139.31

PARAGRAPH FG 187.37

PARALYSED DV 147.29 153.1
  SG 232.34 PR 510.35 WR 560.32
  IL 658.27 GG 685.4 LL 765.30

PARALYSING GG 688.25

PARALYSIS FG 187.14

PARAPET LL 766.30

PARASITE TB 526.38

PARASOL SG 224.12 LL 766.15

PARCEL JD 621.2

PARCELS DV 139.33 GF 241.20
  WP 385.14 385.15 WR 551.2

PARCHED PO 103.35 105.15
  105.18 OV 753.41

PARCHMENT FG 188.8 BM 827.31
  827.33 828.37

PARDON GG 675.14 696.21
  BM 840.19

PARDON MA MERE SM 586.25

PARENTAL EE 316.5 MD 805.26
  805.27

PARENTS OA 26.2 DV 143.36
  185.13 185.23 WP 384.28
  PP 429.28 JD 611.19
  RH 799.13 TH 847.10
  851.26 852.17

PARIS EA 71.6 73.37 90.11
  TF 132.38 133.3 PR 476.34
  477.10 477.19 WR 549.30
  549.31 BO 588.18 588.24
  592.42 602.35 GG 679.24
  NT 701.5 705.19 705.36
  706.8 MD 806.14 806.34
  826.3 826.8 BM 827.14
  TH 844.22 845.16 845.29
  845.31 845.32 845.41
  848.33 852.22

PARISH DV 136.4 138.39
  140.11 146.24 146.40
  147.20 184.35 FG 187.1
  BM 831.30 836.9

PARISHIONERS DV 138.17

PARISIAN BO 587.21

PARISIAN NIGHTS' ENTERTAINMENT
  EA 71.9

PARISIANS BO 587.26 TH 844.24

PARK EA 73.7 WS 251.20
  PP 431.4 HD 448.6 GG 668.32
  OV 748.1

PARLOUR MO 6.9 6.15 12.5
  SS 202.35 SC 269.8 269.29
  273.7 OC 296.15 296.29
  297.12 299.1 302.11
  JD 616.9

PARLOUR-MAID EA 84.3
  GF 241.9 TB 516.8

PAROXYSM PO 115.36 DV 182.38
  PR 478.5

PAROXYSMS DV 176.15

PARRIED RH 794.29

PARRYING GG 672.17

PEACE (CONT.) WR 573.26 573.26
 BO 591.32 598.7 598.8
 IL 647.16 GG 663.10 679.26
 679.27 679.32 700.8 700.10
 ML 730.31 734.26 MD 808.29

PEACEFUL TF 132.13 OC 300.16
 BL 347.23 WR 572.25 ML 725.19*

PEACEFULLY TF 123.17 GG 694.41

PEACHES FA 471.6

PEACOCK WP 383.28 386.22 388.16
 390.3 390.9 390.19

PEACOCKS WP 379.6 382.15

PEACOCK'S WP 392.40

PEAK WS 250.33

PEAKED GF 237.38 TP 335.21
 336.13 PR 495.22 SM 584.25
 BO 595.11 597.27 RR 786.14

PEAKS PO 95.21 105.19 PR 498.18

PEAL LA 645.13 RR 785.23

PEALING LA 645.13

PEALS SD 413.7

PEAR SB 212.14 EE 313.36
 SU 530.6

PEARL EA 81.1 WS 245.39 246.3
 247.32 260.32 263.38 263.41
 264.39 ML 741.29 OV 747.6

PEARL-BACKED EA 80.42

PEARL-GREY ML 741.27

PEARLS WS 246.11 248.25 248.33
 TB 526.9 GG 661.14 LL 763.24

PEARLY GG 698.15

PEARS CH 277.18 FA 465.3

PEAR-SHAPED SU 537.26

PEASANT EA 71.30 TF 123.26
 126.4 PR 475.3 SU 534.4
 535.39 542.28 542.35 543.3
 544.41

PEASANTS PR 482.22 SU 533.6
 543.32

PEASANT'S PO 97.23

PEBBLE WM 62.10 62.12 MD 817.7
 817.9 817.26

PEBBLES ML 739.31 745.30

PECK WP 389.26 FA 458.21

PECKED GF 243.8

PECKING JD 607.23

PECULIAR OA 27.36 27.37 29.20
 HT 40.23 41.12 FG 189.37
 SB 212.21 214.11 215.7
 SC 270.14 PP 438.26 439.39
 440.13 FA 462.37 PR 477.27
 480.27 482.30 486.4 486.18
 493.15 493.38 493.39 500.15
 509.5 SU 531.13 536.8 539.33
 543.8 543.19 WR 548.19 550.41
 565.25 JD 617.26 617.37
 619.26 625.9 627.5 627.18
 LA 633.1 633.11 GG 684.34
 ML 727.22 728.34 MD 820.2
 820.17 820.41 BM 838.17

PECUNIARY DV 145.34

PEDAL WP 388.14

PEDESTALS WM 58.42

PEEL PR 475.22 475.24 475.28

PEELS PR 475.23

PEEN SC 269.35 269.40 271.36
 272.26

PEEN'S SC 270.27 272.6

PEEP SG 225.1 SU 541.16
 WR 552.24 IL 653.42 ML 723.18

PEEPED FG 194.42 WS 245.35
 SC 273.7 LL 767.6

PEEPING PO 114.2 DV 161.12
 WP 387.17 FA 469.2 MD 812.37

PEEP-SHOW DV 161.14

PEER LA 633.9 GG 661.9 RH 793.3

PEERED FG 192.5 CH 278.8
 OC 291.14 BL 362.13 SD 411.33
 SM 585.18 LA 630.13 635.31
 GG 674.3 681.16 ML 730.20
 733.33 TH 853.32

PEERING SS 210.39 WS 245.8
 CH 277.33 BL 352.26 WR 551.11
 LA 630.10 634.27 GG 670.14
 674.34 694.34 LL 775.37

PEEVISH DV 140.21

PEEVISHLY OC 293.33

PEEWIT OV 759.42

PEEWITS MO 1.15 5.7

PEG TF 125.24 WS 253.33 253.38
 TP 340.5 345.31 MN 366.32
 PR 506.18 OV 749.19

PEGGED FG 190.2 SS 206.25
 206.27

PEGGING SP 45.21

PELLUCID ML 734.15

PELT OV 758.21

PEN DV 172.34 PR 510.20
 ML 733.34

PENALTY BO 590.34

PENANCE SM 582.1

PENCIL HT 40.19 PO 98.40
 101.19 101.22 101.26
 102.14 TB 515.40

PENDANT OA 25.22

PENDANTS LL 763.23

PENDULUM EE 332.12

PENETRATE TF 119.15 HD 450.8

PENETRATED PO 98.12 TF 120.35
 129.21 WS 247.34 WR 581.4
 LL 777.42

PENETRATING MO 11.33
 SS 198.17 WS 253.16
 PP 439.39 HD 455.28
 SU 530.38 WR 579.13

PENITENT GG 687.37 687.41

PENITENTES PR 482.39

PENNIES RH 795.31

PENNILESS WP 381.22

PENNONS SS 206.19

PENNY SD 419.19 ML 735.12

PENNY-IN-THE-SLOT FA 459.26

PENSION OC 294.30

PENSIVE FA 73.34

PENT BM 836.16

PENT-HOUSE OC 296.37

PENT-UP LL 775.14

PENURY DV 144.32 HD 446.37

PENZANCE SD 411.2 414.25

PEONIES MD 811.5

PEOPLE MO 2.28 3.8 4.10
 7.8 7.31 8.32 SP 51.4
 EA 71.17 81.17 88.15
 PO 104.37 111.41 DV 136.9
 136.29 137.3 142.40 147.4
 153.26 153.31 153.33
 160.14 160.18 162.20
 170.37 176.25 177.11
 177.14 177.15 177.29
 182.24 183.8 FG 187.25
 188.3 SS 207.41 SB 212.22
 SG 223.16 GF 234.23 241.11
 241.20 WS 251.29 SC 272.14
 272.40 OC 290.6 291.1
 EE 305.40 306.29 307.41
 323.42 327.21 332.41

PEOPLE (CONT.)

PEOPLE (CONT.) TP 334.36 335.13
336.20 BL 348.18 MN 371.11
WP 382.5 YT 395.13 SD 416.40
PP 427.5 428.3 435.11 436.14
HD 448.32 449.12 449.18
FA 463.17 465.21 466.6 466.25
468.22 PR 475.7 475.16 475.17
475.29 475.36 475.39 476.1
476.5 477.39 478.4 479.2
479.14 481.34 482.24 500.11
505.27 509.28 TB 516.32
517.11 519.35 519.37 523.25
SU 530.2 532.40 533.2 533.14
536.4 WR 551.24 567.7 570.35
573.30 575.1 575.3 575.35
577.32 577.35 577.40 577.41
578.3 578.41 580.20 580.22
BO 587.17 590.36 593.42
598.21 602.36 JD 606.3 606.4
606.5 606.10 606.11 607.19
610.16 620.17 LA 630.7 638.16
640.5 641.5 GG 662.4 662.15
662.34 663.11 667.9 670.22
673.21 673.24 675.28 675.32
675.38 676.2 682.39 685.4
685.6 693.25 693.28 NT 702.36
703.1 703.18 703.24 703.25
703.34 704.29 704.31 705.39
706.19 707.8 707.31 707.41
712.8 714.10 718.9 ML 722.2
726.29 726.35 728.20 729.30
729.42 730.6 730.12 730.15
731.13 731.31 732.12 734.4
734.35 735.7 736.1 736.13
736.31 737.10 740.18
LL 761.32 777.6 778.29
RH 792.41 798.21 798.23
MD 810.40 813.1 816.26 816.27
819.17 819.18 BM 831.38 835.3
835.9 837.27 839.36 840.21
TH 844.34 845.17 846.16
848.37 849.10 849.26 851.20
853.24

PEOPLE'S EE 311.32 RR 780.34

PEP IL 648.34

PER ANNUM MD 806.4

PERCEIVE WM 68.7 PO 106.20
DV 146.39 BL 351.11 PR 498.9

PERCEIVED OA 24.17 WM 62.8
EA 72.15 PO 100.6 DV 145.40
SS 204.5 SG 224.3 WS 260.19
WR 560.1 ML 740.26

PERCEIVING PO 99.21 WS 250.36

PER CENT SP 48.21

PERCEPTIBLE EE 309.23

PERCEPTION OA 33.13 DV 145.17

PERCH FG 187.11

PERCHANCE OV 759.2

PERCHED TP 334.5 WP 387.12
PP 434.20 435.21 PR 483.37
484.2 484.11

PERCHES SS 202.2

PERCHING GG 677.16

PERCY BM 831.6 832.15 832.18
833.25 833.35 834.12 834.15
834.21 835.18 835.40 836.23
837.5 837.21 837.33 838.16
838.32 838.41 839.25 839.33
840.9 840.14 841.12 841.25

PERCY BARLOW BM 827.37 831.33

PERCY'S BM 835.27

PERDITION LA 642.26

PEREMPTORILY GF 238.12

PEREMPTORY TF 134.4 TP 335.37

PERFECT HT 39.7 TF 133.18
DV 146.18 146.19 165.27
SS 198.12 SB 213.32 WS 252.41
254.41 EE 310.25 326.26
WP 381.5 SD 417.1 FA 467.25
PR 477.31 479.12 489.7
WR 558.37 559.1 569.21 572.19
SM 584.35 585.8 BO 599.25
IL 651.5 GG 664.18 699.8
699.21 NT 706.14 712.33
ML 725.7 726.4 726.25 727.33
727.34 OV 748.38 750.21
LL 761.3 761.8 763.21 774.28
RH 794.12 MD 808.26 809.24
816.3 820.27 BM 832.21 833.30
TH 846.6 849.17 851.4

PERFECTION BO 597.9 ML 725.8
726.26

PERFECTLY WM 58.35 68.9
EA 72.12 82.41 PO 100.30
112.37 TF 134.13 DV 149.4
SS 207.26 SB 214.10 SG 228.22
228.25 EE 307.37 TP 335.25
338.12 BL 361.31 HD 446.2
PR 473.35 477.15 484.4 484.37
TB 517.17 517.18 520.2
SU 542.36 WR 572.18 BO 596.18
JD 615.15 LA 633.24 IL 649.12
649.14 652.26 655.15 657.30
657.36 657.38 657.40
GG 679.22 682.37 694.10
OV 748.39 750.16 LL 766.29
RR 786.10 MD 807.42 808.7
809.21 815.17 816.2 820.15
BM 829.17 830.6 830.7 832.35
TH 851.4 853.22

PERFECTLY-FORMED PR 483.40

PERFIDY EA 85.26

PERFORATED DV 167.3

PERFORCE EE 327.16

PERFORM DV 137.41 155.19
TB 516.16 NT 706.33 BM 834.5

PERFORMANCE TP 338.16 MN 371.18
371.23 FA 466.26 BM 840.31

PERFORMANCES TP 338.18

PERFORMED PO 98.5 GF 240.13

PERFORMED (CONT.) BM 834.13

PERFORMING SP 49.25 EE 328.17
HD 448.7 NT 718.40

PERFUME PO 106.28 SS 200.25
GG 694.24 OV 750.3
MD 820.31

PERFUMED EA 92.10 WR 573.32
MD 822.17

PERIL TP 336.6

PERILOUS SD 415.33 422.6
FA 465.7 TH 848.24

PERILOUSLY TP 338.10

PERIOD HD 447.13 MD 809.11
TH 844.20

PERIODICAL JD 619.36

PERIODICALLY EE 324.17

PERISHED SD 413.12

PERISHING TP 341.19

PERKING GG 681.10

PERKY TP 334.25 BM 831.41

PERMANENCY EE 307.30

PERMANENT WS 249.11 250.13
259.39 EE 312.32 ML 735.33

PERMANENTLY YT 394.11

PERMISSION GG 696.14

PERMITTED SU 528.2

PERPENDICULAR OA 36.13

PERPETUAL DV 144.32 HD 448.33
WR 579.5

PERPETUALLY PO 115.7

PERPLEXED MO 15.13 OC 292.27
296.16 SD 422.23 425.7

PERPLEXITY MO 9.25 SS 203.35
OC 297.30 BL 365.6
PR 511.35 LL 767.18

PERSECUTE YT 409.10

PERSEUS GG 700.2

PERSIAN JD 625.18

PERSISTED OA 25.17 DV 150.24
170.9 SB 213.32 EE 326.17
MN 376.11 YT 409.35
HD 442.42 443.35 WR 558.19
NT 710.41

PERSISTENCE WS 256.16
WR 569.26 LL 773.2

PERSISTENCY ML 736.26 737.22

PERSISTENCY (CONT.)

PERSISTENCY (CONT.) ML 746.4

PERSISTENT DV 158.14 SB 219.27
HD 447.19 447.26 PR 487.34
ML 739.27

PERSISTENTLY WS 265.34

PERSON MO 13.34 14.37 20.17
20.19 EA 80.21 80.33 PO 97.9
DV 145.41 146.14 146.31
150.35 171.12 SS 203.31
OC 293.28 TP 339.8 WP 391.19
PP 439.27 PR 475.27 TB 513.9
SU 533.39 533.40 535.24
WR 546.10 BO 597.14 JD 613.27
LA 642.2 GG 663.9 NT 716.11
719.16 ML 731.2 LL 761.18
763.1 RH 792.12 792.26
MD 807.20 815.21 817.5
BM 831.27 840.30

PERSONABLE MN 366.21

PERSONA GRATA GG 672.20

PERSONAL EA 80.35 PO 98.9 99.32
TF 127.3 DV 145.23 171.11
183.23 EE 305.14 HD 453.14
453.15 WR 569.34 574.24
574.29 577.11 JD 606.14
607.22 617.31 MD 819.8 819.23
825.39

PERSONALITY SD 417.25 NT 705.34
ML 722.9 MD 811.32

PERSONALLY PO 98.8 PR 509.14
WR 576.3 JD 626.21 NT 703.2
703.7 BM 833.40 TH 846.25

PERSON'S MN 369.34

PERSPIRATION NT 713.34

PERSPIRING LL 767.1

PERSUADE DV 152.3 SG 221.2
LL 776.37 MD 817.32 BM 832.10

PERSUADED YT 397.4 JD 616.8

PERSUASION DV 152.3

PERSUASIVELY IL 650.11

PERTH, LADY (SEE LADY PERTH)

PERTHSHIRE BL 356.23

PERTINACITY OC 286.22

PERTINENT SP 47.18 BO 602.22

PERTURBATION OA 30.25

PERTURBED OA 30.32 PO 98.13
TF 126.25

PERVADED BL 354.36 PR 500.13

PERVADING GG 698.37

PERVERSE EA 75.26 93.37
PO 100.15 DV 153.2 WS 257.2

PERVERSE (CONT.) JD 629.6
GG 664.29 MD 817.1

PERVERSELY GG 663.1 663.14

PERVERSITY MO 4.33 MD 806.25

PERVIN BL 355.24 356.29 356.37
357.29 357.32

PERVIN (SEE ISABEL, MAURICE,
JOSEPH; MR. PERVIN)

PERVINS' HD 449.3

PESSIMIST MO 7.31

PEST SB 214.21

PESTERED CH 277.39

PESTILENCE GF 235.7

PESTLE SP 45.19

PET SG 222.32 WS 259.26

PETALS SG 225.38 OC 284.34
PR 493.21 SU 544.42 OV 747.10
753.37 754.3

PETER WM 56.13 EA 84.20 85.8
TH 849.33 850.29

PETER'S EA 85.19

PETITE WP 393.4

PETRIFIED NT 709.42

PETROL PR 501.2 502.9 509.17

PETTICOAT WS 244.11

PETTICOATS WS 262.20

PETTING IL 649.23

PETTY EA 73.36 EE 327.38

PETULANT PP 438.26 JD 626.4

PETULANTLY DV 142.30 SB 212.1
PR 497.29 BO 601.20

PEW FA 468.20

PF WS 263.5

PHALLIC PR 477.33 478.4

PHASE MO 8.24 8.37 PR 478.30

PHEASANT-COOPS SS 206.20

PHENOMENA PR 474.29

PHILADELPHIA PR 480.39

PHILANTHROPY BL 363.31

PHILIP BO 588.4 588.8 589.21
589.22 589.38 589.40 589.42
590.8 590.13 590.20 591.17
591.30 591.39 592.18 592.24

PHILIP (CONT.) 592.34 592.35
592.39 593.14 594.22
600.28 601.23 601.30
601.37 602.33 603.4 603.13
603.21 603.23 603.26
603.41 604.5 604.12 604.20
604.30 604.35

PHILIP FARQUHAR BO 589.34

PHILIP'S BO 591.22 594.23
602.41

PHILOSOPHER JD 616.26

PHILOSOPHIC BO 589.9

PHILOSOPHICAL DV 145.19

PHILOSOPHY MO 16.25 NT 709.16

PHILTRE MO 2.39

PHLEGMATICALLY SG 223.26

PHOSPHORESCENCE SS 207.12

PHOSPHORESCENT LA 644.14

PHOTO MO 8.13 8.17 10.36

PHOTOGRAPH TB 519.31

PHOTOGRAPHS MO 7.2 PP 435.10

PHOTOS MO 7.6

PHRASE OA 33.9 JD 620.21
RH 791.5

PHRASES OA 33.33 HT 40.42
DV 140.3 WP 380.36 380.40
392.20

PHYSICAL EA 71.18 81.32
81.36 83.14 90.3 PO 100.2
112.36 DV 150.29 150.30
165.27 174.16 WS 257.28
SC 267.14 EE 306.19 307.40
310.4 310.5 310.12 310.14
BL 348.33 362.7 WP 390.31
PP 433.17 FA 465.34 466.15
PR 477.40 479.23 WR 548.3
568.7 BO 603.10 JD 611.32
LA 634.15 GG 683.38 683.40
NT 710.1 ML 736.39
LL 765.25 BM 841.1

PHYSICALLY EA 80.11 80.28
DV 165.23 EE 310.2
BL 350.13 359.32 FA 465.18
PR 478.35 WR 547.36 547.37
NT 703.19 710.7 718.14
MD 821.22

PHYSIOGNOMY SG 221.16

PHYSIQUE WM 65.24 EA 81.33
CH 282.18 EE 328.26
PR 476.22 482.32 WR 547.33

PIANO SP 50.36 WM 63.32
63.37 63.40 65.11 65.25
DV 138.33 SS 202.38
SG 221.10 PR 476.26

PIANO (CONT.) IL 650.32 651.21
  651.24 656.5 LL 766.2
  RR 781.42 784.8

PIANO-CANDLES WM 63.34

PIANOLA GG 682.25 682.28 687.28

PIANO-SEAT GG 684.31

PICCOLO DV 164.7 165.31

PICK SP 48.13 FG 188.15
  TP 342.1 342.13 MN 367.7
  YT 408.34 ML 732.30 RH 795.39
  MD 820.39 BM 838.3

PICKED HT 44.11 SP 46.23 TF 124.23
  124.32 DV 162.4 SS 210.38
  211.5 SB 216.22 SG 228.6
  GF 234.15 WS 244.10 257.40
  261.23 CH 281.27 OC 297.24
  TP 345.23 345.28 BL 358.15
  360.5 SD 424.3 PR 496.27
  506.28 WR 556.42 MD 809.35
  809.36 809.40 TH 848.1 848.32

PICKING EA 79.18 TF 123.29
  SB 215.4 SD 422.26 PR 498.13
  TB 522.25 SU 544.2 TH 848.33

PICKINGS ML 731.6

PICKLE MN 377.2 TB 514.20

PICKLED TB 514.20 514.23 514.26

PICKS DV 142.8 GG 680.40

PICTURE EA 81.12 TF 125.35
  FG 192.20 SG 224.16 SC 268.7
  OC 294.35 YT 400.38 PP 434.19
  435.21 PR 476.30 476.31
  494.20 SU 535.3 540.18 542.33
  NT 708.23 RR 788.38

PICTURES MO 6.17 OA 24.8
  DV 158.40 NT 705.38 LL 764.21
  770.2 MD 811.21 811.23 818.3
  BM 827.32 829.42 831.11

PICTURESQUE TF 122.1

PIE GG 680.42

PIE-BALD SP 49.10

PIECE OA 26.18 WM 64.2 EA 74.21
  74.25 82.1 PO 101.19 101.26
  107.24 109.25 109.30 113.11
  GF 238.21 WS 248.2 CH 276.3
  276.4 OC 285.26 286.17 287.26
  288.12 TP 341.8 341.10
  MN 367.19 FA 458.3 PR 498.10
  TB 525.10 SU 542.31 WR 557.12
  578.6 JD 619.17 GG 685.33
  687.32 NT 705.42 LL 777.26
  RR 779.8

PIECES MO 20.10 OA 33.14
  EA 81.1 PO 100.23 105.11
  108.27 112.23 TF 118.24
  CH 276.1 282.19 OC 291.40
  TP 345.24 BL 351.2 PR 502.18
  WR 552.25 570.39 LA 639.37

PIECES (CONT.) OV 754.42
  LL 764.20 RH 801.24 MD 817.36

PIER EA 83.14 SU 528.34

PIERCED PO 98.32

PIERCING OA 24.40 EE 331.9
  PR 497.22 WR 559.37 559.39
  560.28 LL 767.42 774.16

PIERCINGLY OC 284.18

PIETRO EA 74.15

PIG NT 711.37 ML 733.34

PIGEON-HOUSE PP 429.33

PIGEONS DV 164.14 FG 187.11
  GF 235.19 PP 429.29 430.1
  GG 661.18

PIGMENT WR 577.7 BM 827.34
  841.28

PIGMY BO 595.25

PIGS DV 164.14 FG 191.2 191.8
  191.10 BL 347.22 WR 548.1
  IL 648.21 648.34 649.6
  GG 699.41 ML 728.42 730.32

PIGTAIL NT 715.27

PIG-TROUGHS IL 652.8

PILBEAM SS 208.40

PILBEAM (SEE ARTHUR; MR. PILBEAM)

PILE PO 101.1 101.21 EE 306.36
  312.21 BL 362.17 SU 544.2
  RH 799.28

PILED MO 1.23 1.28 GF 234.20
  OC 286.12 SU 528.36 WR 558.39
  561.35

PILES RH 800.15

PILGRIM EE 308.26

PILING SU 540.4 WR 546.26

PILKINGTON (SEE MR. PILKINGTON)

PILLAR PO 101.34 EE 309.39
  310.21 312.35 320.38
  TB 514.16 514.18 WR 580.19
  BO 589.12 GG 684.20

PILLARED SS 206.16

PILLARS DV 166.13 SG 225.25
  EE 312.3 FA 465.1 465.5

PILLOW WM 64.41 EA 92.12
  DV 147.39 175.14 EE 322.42
  RH 803.41

PILLOWS DV 159.26 159.33
  PP 434.19 RR 788.12

PIN DV 180.7 FG 191.27

PINCH SC 269.14

PINCHED OA 31.19 EE 318.5
  BO 600.39

PINCHING TP 342.30

PINE PO 95.6 107.2 112.2
  112.12 SS 206.17 EE 303.8
  303.10 WP 387.22 PR 478.42
  487.27 489.19 WR 551.41
  552.4 552.32 552.33 553.15
  556.5 556.31 556.32 559.8
  559.15 565.34 575.14
  575.26 579.7 579.9
  BO 600.10 600.15 TH 852.6

PINE-NEEDLES SS 206.22

PINES EE 305.1 305.2
  BL 347.34 PR 489.15

PINEWOOD WR 576.26

PINE-WOOD MN 372.21

PING FA 461.33 LL 761.23

PINGED FA 460.26

PINING TB 516.28 IL 653.42
  ML 732.38 MD 816.6
  BM 833.20 TH 849.10

PINIONS ML 741.29

PINK MO 1.16 WM 58.18
  EA 84.12 84.13 PO 108.37
  TF 123.2 SS 200.38 210.10
  SB 213.10 214.34 214.41
  217.9 SG 225.38 WS 245.5
  OC 284.2 296.21 EE 305.42
  323.36 SD 418.21 FA 464.38
  SU 534.10 535.32 WR 546.21
  551.40 GG 670.14 670.33
  672.38 672.41 673.15
  NT 712.12 ML 728.32
  OV 753.8 753.11 RH 791.18
  MD 809.19 809.25 823.24
  BM 828.37 836.39

PINK-AND-WHITE YT 397.31
  LA 631.39

PINK-FACED NT 705.36

PINK-FLOWERING TB 521.21

PINKISH SB 215.7 PP 436.30
  WR 546.17 546.28

PINKISH-GREY PO 107.1

PINKNESS DV 167.19

PINKS DV 161.7

PINKY HD 447.42

PINKY-BROWN WR 548.12

PINKY-FADED GG 671.4

PINNACLE WR 579.33

PINNACLES TF 122.3

PINNED MO 19.13 PO 98.40
  WS 245.4 SD 421.11 421.23

PINNEGAR JD 607.32 616.42 617.5
  617.14 618.15 619.1 619.4
  619.31 619.37 622.36 623.35
  626.16 626.27 626.32 627.4
  627.20 627.26 627.35

PINNEGAR (SEE EMILY; MR. PINNEGAR,
  MRS. PINNEGAR)

PINNEGARS JD 609.32

PINNOCK'S, FREDERICK (SEE
  FREDERICK PINNOCK'S)

PINON PR 489.33

PINPOINT IL 649.32 GG 672.41

PIN-POINTS GG 675.11

PIN-PRICKS SB 216.19

PINS WR 564.4

PIPE DV 145.8 SB 219.29
  SG 222.20 227.15 227.19
  229.15 229.27 230.4 230.19
  230.22 WS 261.25 HD 443.20
  443.25 TB 517.27 517.42
  IL 650.9 650.19 ML 728.23
  LL 772.31 BM 830.2 830.5

PIPED GG 672.32 672.35

PIPES ML 729.22

PIPKIN SS 201.14

PIQUANT MD 807.36

PIQUED WS 248.4 MN 368.27
  PR 476.35 488.22

PIRATES ML 724.30 725.3

PISTON EE 330.10

PIT MO 3.36 HT 39.8 39.11
  SP 46.10 48.12 49.1 49.5
  49.19 DV 139.2 144.19 163.38
  166.1 166.22 167.20 168.16
  SS 197.31 SG 222.9 222.11
  SC 268.21 268.29 269.1 269.20
  CH 275.25 280.20 OC 287.35
  292.12 293.18 297.1 PR 502.38
  JD 620.30

PIT-BANK OC 283.19 290.36

PIT-BOOTS SC 267.35 OC 297.5
  JD 617.6

PITCH OA 30.38 WM 61.29
  SC 268.42 271.25 TP 338.18
  WP 392.24

PITCHED HT 40.23 PO 101.32
  LA 646.24

PITCHER GG 664.1

PITCHER-FLOWERS SU 536.22

PITCHING HD 450.19 WR 555.36

PIT-CLOTHES OC 295.22

PIT-DIRT DV 169.29 178.7 178.14
  OC 289.18

PITEOUS OA 36.38 WS 264.21

PITEOUSLY SC 272.31 OC 287.16

PIT-FLANNEL DV 162.22

PIT-HILL SS 197.31 JD 608.15
  610.22

PITIABLE OA 37.16 DV 158.11
  BL 363.17 ML 732.10

PITIABLY OC 293.26

PITIED OA 33.23 34.24 DV 164.22
  ML 737.17 BM 830.24

PITIFUL MO 8.23 OA 33.30
  DV 137.27 149.9 SB 214.40
  GF 234.13 WS 258.32 OC 284.37

PITIFULLY OA 36.25

PIT-MOUTH DV 175.33

PIT-POND OC 283.17

PITS SP 45.10 DV 136.6

PIT-SHAFT JD 608.20

PITTED WS 247.12

PIT-THINGS SC 267.26

PIT-TOP OC 290.35

PITY MO 8.12 OA 33.30 37.19
  EA 87.13 PO 110.31 DV 146.42
  164.9 165.7 SB 214.26
  CH 276.31 OC 301.17 EE 321.18
  FA 464.19 WR 577.34 BO 598.23
  IL 657.28 GG 688.19 ML 736.34
  MD 826.28

PITYING WM 64.41 SS 200.23

PLACE MO 6.6 10.40 10.42
  OA 36.41 SP 45.4 45.7 50.15
  WM 54.4 EA 71.20 87.17 88.21
  PO 95.30 97.35 106.5 112.11
  113.28 113.30 TF 119.7 119.15
  123.15 128.32 DV 147.22
  157.31 166.19 174.10 176.29
  177.40 FG 190.40 195.18
  SS 202.3 202.8 206.15 206.24
  207.6 SG 222.37 222.39 223.1
  223.16 225.42 GF 238.6 243.23
  WS 253.36 255.7 257.23 257.32
  OC 290.32 300.9 EE 303.31
  304.2 306.7 309.23 309.25
  316.22 323.17 323.28 323.38
  323.42 324.7 324.12 330.28
  TP 334.10 341.1 341.9
  BL 347.11 347.20 358.8 360.22
  MN 366.6 366.28 WP 382.9

PLACE (CONT.) 387.27
  YT 397.38 400.2 409.41
  PP 427.33 427.34 432.25
  436.26 436.32 439.13
  HD 449.7 FA 464.5 465.6
  PR 479.39 482.16 486.30
  486.36 488.10 490.9
  500.14 501.8 505.5 507.30
  507.39 507.41 510.28
  TB 515.7 517.10 520.10
  SU 530.4 532.3 534.30
  537.13 537.14 538.24
  538.40 541.1 WR 548.17
  552.15 552.41 556.30
  558.9 559.2 561.22
  SM 584.28 BO 587.5 587.23
  595.8 599.7 JD 606.20
  610.13 610.31 611.39
  615.29 LA 638.8 642.28
  644.37 IL 650.7 651.20
  654.30 GG 667.22 667.29
  668.28 670.1 670.35 677.9
  680.20 688.39 693.3 693.9
  698.12 NT 702.16 708.5
  709.9 713.42 715.8
  ML 724.4 725.7 727.13
  731.36 737.40 738.2 738.7
  OV 750.33 750.41 754.8
  LL 762.23 763.3 RH 790.13
  791.21 794.33 803.5
  TH 848.9 851.16 851.20

PLACED MO 12.33 17.14
  SP 49.4 EA 89.33 TF 120.7
  DV 173.9 178.18 CH 280.1
  BL 358.31 WR 578.10

PLACER PR 487.21

PLACES MO 1.32 19.20
  DV 173.10 SG 231.42
  EE 303.30 WP 385.36
  PR 497.30 SU 529.11 538.24
  544.8 WR 551.17 558.7
  BO 599.7 NT 706.28
  ML 728.41 OV 752.23
  BM 835.29

PLACID BL 361.27

PLACID-SEEMING WR 550.40

PLACING DV 151.15 PP 433.38

PLAIN DV 160.15 WS 255.22
  PR 489.5 TB 516.6
  WR 579.6 BO 599.29
  LL 762.9 762.38

PLAINLY OA 36.16 PO 108.38
  DV 169.4 LA 642.30 642.35
  IL 659.33 GG 678.35
  RH 791.19

PLAINS WR 572.25

PLAINTIVE DV 162.41 OC 298.14
  298.34 BM 836.18

PLAINTIVELY WM 67.18
  DV 171.22 GF 241.38
  OC 289.38 290.9 ML 740.35

PLAIT EA 71.29 86.10

PLAITED   GF 237.33   SD 420.14
   423.2

PLAITS   OA 36.13   DV 175.16
   PR 494.40   495.30

PLAN   WS 260.35   MD 813.13

PLANE   DV 153.6   ML 725.34
   BM 836.14

PLANET   WR 581.13   IL 651.41

PLANGENT   PR 484.35   LA 630.15
   636.17   GG 665.1   665.11

PLANK   EE 303.3   MN 371.16

PLANKED   SC 268.12   JD 618.27

PLANKS   EE 307.22   ML 725.25

PLANNING   MD 814.1

PLANS   TF 131.8   132.37   WR 550.20

PLANT   SS 206.13   SG 221.21
   WP 392.13   WR 546.23

PLANTATION   MN 376.18

PLANTED   WM 69.21   PO 102.17
   DV 136.17   SG 222.13   SD 423.20
   424.35   PP 439.24   440.12
   GG 670.31   MD 824.25

PLANTING   HD 442.2

PLANTS   OA 24.37   CH 281.2

PLASTER   DV 149.1   162.29   168.21
   OC 298.9

PLASTIC   EA 91.36

PLASTRONS   GG 665.31

PLATE   MO 5.23   5.30   GF 240.22
   OC 285.27   PP 439.15   439.16
   PR 502.18   506.3   BO 594.11
   JD 618.36   618.40   619.1
   GG 676.27

PLATES   PO 101.2   101.21
   GF 234.26   PP 439.4   HD 442.20
   FA 465.6

PLATFORM   SP 47.40   SS 199.34
   EE 330.6   FA 458.2   459.16
   WR 562.18   562.19   580.3   580.6
   JD 628.42

PLATO   JD 607.3   MD 813.25   813.27

PLATONIC   RR 781.16

PLAY   MO 4.15   16.1   19.28
   SP 47.30   47.32   50.23   WM 58.32
   59.18   59.19   DV 164.7
   SB 212.31   WS 253.1   SC 271.13
   271.23   271.29   EE 309.36
   TP 344.34   SD 412.36   412.38
   SU 531.25   IL 650.27   650.28
   656.5   GG 682.25   687.28
   NT 702.9   712.11   712.13   712.19

PLAY (CONT.)   712.32   713.18
   LL 765.26   BM 833.36   833.38
   834.13   834.14   834.23   835.38
   836.29   839.14   839.35   840.21

PLAYCROSS   MN 366.34

PLAYED   MO 7.10   16.9   22.2
   WM 59.6   59.10   65.3   TF 128.24
   DV 155.1   164.14   165.29   165.31
   OC 289.23   EE 305.24   312.1
   312.2   319.29   MN 366.30
   YT 395.14   396.16   SD 412.38
   412.39   PR 476.26   SU 534.36
   536.9   WR 574.22   IL 650.32
   659.28   GG 687.31   NT 703.28
   714.8   LL 763.38   766.2

PLAYFUL   FA 462.19   NT 712.15
   712.17   712.18

PLAYFULLY   MO 9.4   19.35   EA 93.3

PLAYGROUND   SP 45.14

PLAYING   MO 3.6   15.2   21.25
   OA 34.19   HT 42.11   SP 50.18
   50.36   EA 86.14   92.33   TF 127.2
   128.20   SS 210.30   SB 219.28
   WS 253.21   253.25   260.22
   SC 270.36   270.38   271.4
   PP 434.8   439.25   PR 492.10
   SU 536.24   JD 628.13   GG 661.17
   NT 712.16   712.21   713.32   720.1
   720.4   OV 754.3   RH 791.12
   793.1   BM 828.17   831.25   840.25

PLAYS   OA 24.16   PR 492.8

PLAYTHING   EA 92.16

PLAYTHINGS   OC 291.39

PLAY-WORLD   OC 289.36

PLAZA   WR 549.15   561.31   573.40
   577.33   577.39   578.18   578.25

PLEADED   OA 24.23   WM 68.29
   EA 73.16   73.25   74.16
   FG 196.14   MN 377.22   OV 751.11
   RR 787.31

PLEADING   MO 8.42   OA 24.19
   EA 76.10   79.29   WR 573.24
   JD 626.4

PLEAS   LL 763.9

PLEASANT   EA 84.34   PO 110.9
   DV 161.10   GF 234.10   240.10
   EE 308.16   318.36   329.39
   TP 338.24   BL 353.41   MN 366.6
   367.27   YT 394.8   409.33
   FA 459.42   467.38   BO 587.28
   591.37   NT 715.11   LL 762.23
   764.23   RR 781.5   RH 790.19
   BM 828.8   TH 849.42

PLEASANTER   GG 688.34

PLEASANTEST   RR 780.3

PLEASANT-LOOKING   MN 366.20

PLEASANTLY   TF 123.31
   DV 166.17   WS 245.29
   MN 366.3   FA 466.19
   GG 675.12

PLEASE   SP 52.26   WM 59.33
   EA 88.31   DV 172.37
   WS 262.13   CH 274.28
   TP 335.36   SD 415.25
   416.10   TB 515.17   SU 538.35
   JD 621.20   621.24   621.27
   621.28   625.42   628.26
   628.31   IL 647.7   GG 682.6
   NT 715.30   MD 806.41   816.4
   823.7   825.1   BM 837.40
   839.1   839.24   839.36

PLEASED   MO 18.22   OA 34.32
   38.18   HT 42.36   WM 54.21
   64.5   64.18   EA 86.24
   PO 107.30   107.31   110.16
   110.17   113.39   TF 128.20
   DV 166.34   167.4   SS 202.39
   SG 223.34   228.31   WS 249.10
   252.32   260.36   EE 307.37
   319.30   MN 371.39   WP 384.6
   384.27   YT 395.42   SD 411.28
   PP 439.10   PR 512.26
   JD 605.4   621.22   IL 648.26
   648.39   GG 663.23   ML 729.17
   738.14   OV 754.17   LL 766.11

PLEASES   SD 426.17   JD 621.30
   622.7   622.28   623.36

PLEASING   BL 361.19

PLEASURE   MO 20.37   OA 26.21
   34.33   WM 55.12   EA 81.32
   83.14   92.5   PO 100.8   100.20
   100.25   102.3   TF 123.21
   133.4   DV 140.36   179.6
   SB 220.9   WS 250.2   251.10
   BL 355.27   355.35   MN 367.27
   370.29   WP 388.20   PR 504.34
   TB 515.17   BO 587.3   587.22
   594.6   596.39   GG 680.17
   OV 754.4   757.5   RR 781.29
   RH 794.21   MD 811.8   817.42

PLEASURES   MD 821.22

PLEAT   EE 303.6

PLEATED   TB 521.16

PLEATINGS   TB 525.29   525.36

PLEBEIAN   YT 400.11

PLEDGE   SS 209.2   HD 454.42

PLEE   SC 271.24

PLENTY   MO 17.19   18.33
   HT 39.11   42.5   43.41
   DV 141.9   173.5   FG 189.12
   SG 224.1   EE 307.9   308.35
   MN 366.25   368.30   WP 392.27
   YT 399.22   SD 420.28
   PR 485.40   TB 521.3
   WR 548.41   BO 590.11
   NT 704.27   BM 832.3

PLIABLE   BM 832.11

PLIANT WS 252.26

PLIGHT NT 711.3

PLOD FA 459.33

PLODDED WM 60.23 PO 105.22
  108.24 108.29 WR 553.4

PLOP MD 826.18

PLOTTING MO 6.27 YT 403.14
  ML 734.13

PLOUGH DV 174.14

PLOUGHED EE 330.40 BO 593.18

PLOVERS MO 1.17

PLUCK TF 131.38 FG 194.20
  SD 425.40 426.9

PLUCKED PO 108.27 SS 207.35
  SB 212.11 212.15 SG 231.13
  MD 809.19

PLUCKING MO 4.25

PLUM SS 200.35 200.38 202.14
  GG 699.27

PLUMAGE DV 173.12 CH 274.17
  BO 595.31

PLUMB JD 617.15

PLUM-BLOSSOM GG 695.12 695.15
  695.20 697.17 698.37 699.3

PLUM-BLOSSOM-SCENTED GG 700.7

PLUME WP 385.42

PLUMED WP 385.38 387.21
  WR 578.12

PLUMP OA 24.26 HT 42.40
  DV 138.22 143.2 160.15
  TP 337.35 SU 537.10 GG 670.23
  RR 785.7

PLUMPED SB 212.7

PLUMPER YT 395.7

PLUMS WR 565.3

PLUMY PR 489.6

PLUNGED MO 3.23 TF 120.29
  DV 170.38 PR 499.12 JD 615.38
  624.6 628.23

PLUNGES TP 334.2

PLUNGING EA 78.8 PO 101.40
  108.18 RH 803.9

P. M. MN 368.15

POCKET OA 34.24 SP 49.30
  PO 101.22 TF 118.6 DV 142.8
  142.36 SB 215.16 SG 226.36
  227.12 WS 251.19 257.33

POCKET (CONT.) 257.36 258.1
  SC 270.20 TP 335.34 WP 380.31
  SD 419.16 ML 732.31 OV 751.15

POCKET-BOOK HT 40.19

POCKET-HANDKERCHIEF YT 396.18

POCKETS SP 49.31 FG 194.15
  SB 216.40 WP 388.34 390.11
  390.39 393.12 YT 400.5 400.18
  403.18 HD 456.18 LA 631.27
  632.22 634.10 643.32

PODERE SU 542.28 543.4 543.12
  543.40

POEM SS 210.14 EE 309.13
  JD 607.33 607.37 608.27
  609.25 613.38

POFMS PR 477.14 478.33
  TB 523.32 JD 607.22 619.13
  619.24

POET EA 86.16 PR 478.32
  ML 726.27

POETIC EA 86.18 PP 437.20
  SM 582.30

POETISING MO 9.40

POETRY MO 11.27 16.11 HT 41.2
  EA 87.33 PO 102.38 102.40
  SS 200.10 207.17 EE 305.24
  305.28 305.31 305.35 306.8
  JD 608.2 619.19 621.1 623.5

POIGNANCY SB 216.35 LL 774.27

POIGNANT DV 171.38 BL 364.24
  LL 774.29 MD 822.19 TH 845.36

POIGNANTLY SB 217.37

POINT MO 7.37 13.8 13.14 20.16
  OA 32.20 32.21 32.39 37.24
  WM 59.30 66.25 67.15 67.16
  68.13 EA 78.14 89.6 PO 98.19
  TF 120.27 DV 176.1 SS 206.33
  SB 212.28 WS 254.40 262.25
  WP 382.15 YT 408.35 SD 417.27
  PP 434.14 HD 445.3 PR 473.5
  473.8 476.24 BO 587.32 599.18
  599.25 JD 605.29 LA 634.38
  GG 663.5 692.14 692.16
  NT 717.23 719.40 719.41
  ML 724.33 734.18 RR 779.26
  MD 807.4 819.7

POINTED WM 63.36 DV 157.36
  167.1 173.13 SS 208.33
  SB 214.35 216.2 WS 246.35
  OC 297.13 BL 351.4 PR 494.28
  497.10 502.29 SU 538.33
  WR 553.15 556.38 BO 595.15
  LA 634.5 GG 681.16 BM 833.5
  837.41

POINTEDLY MD 826.15

POINTING OA 24.30 YT 407.17
  PR 487.16 497.21 498.6
  SU 536.30 537.27 539.14 540.3

POINTING (CONT.) WR 554.14
  BO 599.3 LA 635.22

POINTS MO 6.27 TF 122.4
  DV 154.15 180.31 FA 461.24
  TB 515.7 WR 547.27
  LL 764.34

POISE OA 29.3 LA 635.2

POISED SG 224.30 BO 595.29

POISON SS 211.6 PP 431.23
  440.26 LL 768.24 MD 807.2

POISON-BERRIES EE 316.24

POISONED NT 720.34 OV 759.9

POISONING EE 320.3 PP 431.15

POISONOUS LL 774.6

POKED GF 242.35 WS 245.10
  TP 340.34 WP 385.21
  SD 423.34 BM 841.9

POKER BL 360.6

POKING SB 216.5 SD 424.41
  IL 653.23

POKY DV 184.18 MD 817.20

POLARISED DV 176.32

POLARITY BO 599.19

POLE WR 561.1 561.3
  LA 638.13 TH 845.10 846.34

POLES WR 576.28

POLESTAR SD 411.3

POLICEMAN SD 422.15 BO 595.11
  LA 630.33 633.6 633.11
  633.19 633.23 633.31 633.37
  634.11 634.18 634.20
  634.27 634.32 634.34
  634.37 634.42 636.33
  636.38 636.40 637.15
  637.24 637.29 638.22
  638.30 638.41 639.6
  639.12 639.20 639.27
  640.6 640.16 641.14 641.28
  643.18 644.19 645.5 645.6
  645.11 645.12 645.23
  645.25 646.5 646.30

POLISH PO 96.24

POLISHED WM 63.30 70.5
  SS 202.38 SD 423.40
  GG 664.6

POLISHING YT 397.10 MD 815.15

POLITE OA 38.39 HT 39.32
  SP 51.25 WM 64.32 FA 460.2

POLITELY SG 228.11 MN 367.13
  PR 476.5 476.8 BO 601.19

POLITENESS WM 55.34 PR 476.16

POLITENESS (CONT.) GG 664.10

POLITICS MO 5.12 OA 32.39
  YT 400.36 NT 716.28

POLLINATE MO 20.10

POLLINATION SS 200.27

POLLY TP 341.32 344.4 344.16
  345.12 345.15 346.5

POLLY BIRKIN TP 340.41 341.18

POM BM 831.2 831.7 831.29

POMEGRANATE SU 534.11

POMERANIAN BM 831.41

POMPADOUR MD 809.12

POMPOUS JD 618.32

POND FG 190.39 OC 283.19
  YT 400.18 HD 449.21 449.23
  449.37 449.41 450.7 450.11
  450.16 450.23 450.35 450.37
  451.31 452.7 PR 487.11

PONDER BO 598.3 JD 612.21

PONDERED MO 8.41 EA 88.35
  SS 205.20 MN 376.3 YT 408.21
  PR 508.39

PONDERING GG 692.37 693.36

PONDEROUS PR 483.15 489.11
  496.34 497.41 WR 579.1
  SM 582.8 BO 595.32 600.18
  JD 617.6

PONDEROUSLY GG 674.6

PONDS MO 2.7

PONIES SP 49.1 49.8 PR 495.2

PONY DV 166.14 PR 478.41

POOL YT 394.8 PR 477.30 483.37
  500.1 506.23 506.24 507.9
  511.16 WR 579.28 579.30
  ML 738.21 738.28 740.16
  OV 759.40

POOLS SS 199.41 PP 432.20

POOR MO 14.34 17.3 17.33 17.39
  OA 28.13 34.12 EA 75.13 75.17
  87.3 TF 126.34 DV 137.19
  137.39 138.9 144.27 147.3
  169.40 SS 200.29 208.13 211.4
  SB 212.24 GF 234.3 CH 277.4
  279.13 OC 294.8 294.23
  EE 304.29 311.42 315.27
  321.35 322.1 322.5 322.34
  WP 384.4 384.16 384.37 386.34
  393.3 SD 420.7 PP 428.19
  430.15 431.40 FA 461.4 461.11
  461.18 461.32 463.15 464.27
  465.26 465.27 PR 473.2 476.20
  478.21 478.25 481.32
  TB 518.22 518.31 519.40

POOR (CONT.) SU 529.4 538.35
  539.12 539.28 SM 584.19
  585.39 585.40 586.3 BO 590.21
  JD 605.9 605.23 605.26
  605.33 LA 645.40 IL 652.2
  652.4 652.40 652.41 659.5
  GG 661.30 663.26 667.20
  671.23 689.22 691.24 691.31
  691.40 692.9 692.29 694.2
  694.4 695.19 NT 701.3 706.21
  719.27 720.19 OV 748.30
  LL 762.15 765.14 765.23
  767.17 767.31 767.38 768.18
  769.21 769.25 774.11 774.31
  775.3 778.26 RR 781.13 782.11
  782.39 782.42 785.20
  RH 791.32 804.34 804.35
  MD 807.15 814.33 814.40 815.4
  815.30 821.37 822.5 BM 828.3
  836.8 TH 850.26 851.28

POORER GF 241.21 FA 464.23
  GG 666.27

POP MO 7.19

POPLAR OA 25.5

POPLARS TF 117.1

POPOCATEPETL NT 716.4 717.39

POPPED SP 51.32

POPPIES OA 28.1 TF 118.23
  EE 303.35 329.23 OV 747.10

POPPY SG 221.36

POPULACE WR 580.8

POPULAR NT 707.7 MD 809.42
  BM 830.23 830.26

POPULATED FG 187.2

POPULATION DV 136.7 136.33
  137.5 137.30

PORCH MO 3.19 BM 835.3

PORCUPINE PR 486.21

PORFIRIO, DON (SEE DON PORFIRIO)

PORK-PIE FA 462.11 462.29

PORPHYRY OV 753.7

PORRIDGE ML 743.21 743.24

PORT TP 336.36 GG 677.1 677.5
  677.24 ML 729.28 RR 782.25

PORTALES WR 546.32

PORTENTOUS WS 247.34 HD 448.25
  JD 612.21 624.35 ML 741.36
  RR 784.40

PORTENTOUSNESS MD 823.18

PORTER WM 54.7 MN 366.26
  FA 458.15 459.15 BO 594.31
  598.35 598.38 600.36 601.24

PORTERS MN 378.26 PR 477.19
  BO 587.3 587.35

PORTIA IL 656.1 658.4

PORTION EE 305.10

PORTIONS DV 143.8

PORTRAIT MO 8.18 8.19
  PR 479.37

PORTS ML 729.28

PORT SAID MD 819.29

POSE MO 3.29 MD 812.9

POSED WS 250.3

POSITION MO 18.3 WM 60.18
  PO 96.27 TF 132.24
  DV 136.31 137.18 151.8
  153.23 153.39 158.4 174.9
  184.33 184.37 184.38
  SB 213.7 SG 230.5 WS 257.1
  265.15 EE 330.13 WP 391.23
  YT 402.20 PP 437.14 438.9
  439.42 PR 484.14 TB 518.10
  JD 606.9 LA 646.26 IL 651.28
  GG 663.42 RR 780.20
  RH 790.24 MD 805.2 814.24
  BM 830.29

POSITIVE WM 63.5 DV 171.41
  PR 482.40 MD 808.41 809.9
  809.10 809.11 809.17
  810.42 811.23 821.34
  821.40

POSITIVELY HD 449.32
  BO 590.24 GG 687.17

POSITIVITY BL 355.32
  MD 809.10

POSSESS EE 324.30 BL 348.8
  355.36 YT 403.10 PR 503.39
  508.10 MD 824.23 824.29

POSSESSED PO 115.29 TF 120.8
  127.26 134.30 DV 149.38
  WS 255.17 256.14 OC 299.38
  SD 420.25 PR 505.35
  MD 808.30 824.27

POSSESSES MD 808.31

POSSESSION SP 50.3 DV 181.27
  WS 257.42 260.29 BL 350.1
  YT 400.6 HD 453.3 PR 504.34
  505.34 BO 603.40 ML 738.23
  MD 825.27

POSSESSIONS EE 310.27

POSSESSIVE TP 339.18
  MD 821.33

POSSIBILITY OV 753.32

POSSIBLE EA 80.36 89.19
  PO 98.28 99.21 DV 136.15
  158.6 175.37 178.1 185.20
  185.24 SG 229.25 EE 307.28

POSSIBLE (CONT.) EE 315.21
   320.36 332.26 TP 337.15
   337.41 FA 469.40 PR 485.7
   505.21 JD 614.36 NT 715.37
   716.26 LL 766.9 769.10
   775.12 RR 780.7 MD 811.24
   BM 828.21 TH 844.35 849.38
   850.16 851.5

POSSIBLY EA 75.19 PR 492.36
   IL 652.7 657.8 657.11
   RH 800.40 800.41 BM 838.40
   TH 844.15

POST MO 7.3 OA 35.23 PO 101.36
   TF 117.21 118.6 131.22 131.23
   133.33 WS 265.36 HD 441.8
   BO 596.13 596.18 ML 735.12
   RR 784.34 RH 799.30 TH 851.39
   851.40 852.37

POST-CARD EE 319.40

POSTED EA 82.10 RH 794.9

POSTERIOR RR 788.22 788.25
   MD 819.5 824.25

POSTMAN WS 245.15 245.20
   WP 381.35

POSTURE OV 747.16

POSTURED WS 250.3

POST-WAR BO 602.8

POSY WS 246.10

POT PO 110.2 GF 241.25
   WP 389.18 ML 728.23

POTATIONS GG 688.9

POTATO TH 845.13

POTATOES OC 286.26 TP 337.21
   FA 465.3 JD 616.22 618.25

POTENCY MD 819.4

POTENT BO 603.10 603.12
   NT 708.23

POTENTIAL ML 722.22

POT-LID PO 109.23

POT-POURRI BL 354.38

POTS SP 45.12 PO 101.33

POTTERING YT 406.9

POTTERY YT 394.2 394.6 394.10
   395.21 396.2 400.32

POTTERY-HANDS YT 394.32

POTTERY HOUSE YT 394.1 395.2
   395.18 396.2 396.35 396.39

POTTERY-LASSES YT 394.14

POTTERY-YARD YT 394.4 403.11

POUCHES SP 45.18

POUF EA 71.8 75.8 JD 619.41
   620.13 LA 644.18

POULTRY GF 235.9 235.17 242.31

POUNCE TP 335.25

POUND WP 392.17

POUNDED MD 812.42 TH 851.10

POUNDING SP 45.18 SG 230.27
   WR 578.1 TH 851.9

POUNDS TF 128.4 DV 136.30
   EE 308.19 308.38 308.40
   308.41 YT 401.11 401.13
   FA 462.23 TB 520.16 JD 628.33
   ML 728.14 732.1 OV 747.30
   LL 762.31 778.35 RH 795.16
   795.19 795.32 797.14 797.24
   799.4 799.20 MD 806.4 806.37
   809.29 823.33

POUR EA 77.17 92.8 LL 776.33

POURED PO 101.40 109.14
   DV 140.5 OC 299.24 EE 331.24
   TP 341.4 PR 494.6 501.37
   TB 524.39 GG 674.29 680.13
   681.26 685.13 RR 788.27

POURING DV 139.16 CH 281.23
   TB 519.24 SU 529.33 WR 569.21
   579.25 LL 775.29

POUTING JD 615.11

POVERTY DV 141.9 141.16 145.36
   WP 384.12 HD 447.13

POVERTY-STRICKEN TH 852.36

POWDER FA 471.1 WR 563.13
   GG 683.7 ML 746.9

POWDERY OV 755.20 755.29

POWER MO 5.36 DV 152.37
   WS 249.11 CH 282.19 EE 308.9
   308.10 314.23 314.32 315.2
   315.5 315.12 315.16 315.17
   315.18 325.6 327.17 327.29
   327.30 327.34 327.36
   TP 343.36 BL 364.9 YT 406.2
   SD 411.29 425.17 HD 448.26
   452.4 452.23 453.19 PR 477.38
   477.40 485.22 503.36 503.38
   504.33 SU 528.25 528.26
   535.20 535.27 535.28 535.30
   536.3 537.13 WR 554.22 559.38
   563.40 568.2 571.13 571.21
   571.35 572.7 572.37 575.35
   581.23 581.28 BO 592.25
   JD 623.39 LA 637.20 637.36
   GG 690.39 695.28 697.26
   NT 706.12 707.7 707.30 707.41
   708.27 709.40 ML 736.35
   737.25 745.11 745.26
   LL 764.36 778.18 778.20
   778.30 RR 780.18 780.20
   MD 805.25 805.26 814.25
   816.30 821.41 821.42 822.27

POWERFUL WM 59.11 EA 82.28
   TF 118.14 129.38 DV 181.25
   SG 228.2 EE 320.17
   BL 354.17 354.24 356.4
   357.8 MN 373.20 WP 389.35
   SD 420.37 420.41 PP 427.17
   HD 448.27 453.21 FA 463.21
   PR 473.15 485.10 504.23
   507.35 TB 522.20 SU 532.30
   537.30 544.1 WR 553.42
   556.10 557.8 563.27 563.29
   567.34 568.6 568.38 569.19
   577.4 580.26 580.34
   BO 597.42 604.16 GG 678.38
   RH 803.2 803.17

POWERFULLY PO 103.13 108.29
   HD 449.15 WR 567.38 573.38

POWER-HOUSES SD 411.9

POWERLESS TF 120.16 DV 137.12
   172.7 HD 453.23 PR 478.25
   508.7 508.11 SU 542.7
   WR 556.1 GG 686.24 LL 767.1

POWERS DV 145.17

PRACTICAL EA 91.24 DV 155.20
   SB 212.18 BL 350.7 350.8
   LA 634.3

PRACTICALLY EA 94.1 PO 96.38
   FA 472.6 481.32 MD 808.13
   810.6 BM 830.8

PRACTICE TF 119.17 WP 392.26
   RR 782.7

PRACTICES WR 549.28

PRACTISED TH 846.2

PRACTISING LL 768.3

PRACTITIONER EE 318.36

PRAGUE BO 598.37

PRAISE CH 282.28

PRAM RH 791.19

PRANCE RH 802.7

PRANCING WP 390.4 NT 712.40

PRATTLE BL 348.19 MD 809.38

PRATTLING OA 24.12 BL 348.18

PRAY CH 280.14 280.28
   WP 381.7 FA 468.10
   IL 656.14

PRAYED DV 149.29 EE 322.17
   325.25

PRAYER DV 149.19 149.29
   149.34 CH 280.17 281.30
   281.35 FA 467.40 468.13
   SM 586.10

PRAYER-MEETING TP 340.35

PRAYERS   OC 290.17

PRAYING   CH 280.25   281.26
  EE 329.12   TB 516.28

PRECEDE   MO 17.24

PRECIOUS   FA 466.30   BO 596.41
  597.39   598.7   MD 806.5

PRECIPICE   WR 579.26   579.34

PRECIPITATE   JD 628.25

PRECIPITOUS   TP 334.18   PR 510.28

PRECISE   SU 542.22   MD 805.3

PRECISELY   DV 177.41   SG 227.21
  GG 686.36

PRECONCEIVED   DV 137.11

PREDOMINANT   SS 203.34

PREFER   WM 59.34   59.39   62.38
  DV 143.37   EE 311.32   WP 385.3
  JD 622.39   MD 823.5   TH 853.27

PREFERENCE   MO 20.2

PREFERRED   MO 11.28   WM 61.30
  BL 348.21   YT 395.12   HD 448.35
  GG 683.18   NT 711.42   ML 738.40
  RR 788.4   MD 810.40

PREFERRING   PP 432.39   BM 834.6

PREGNANT   SP 51.23   DV 171.17
  JD 610.11   OV 753.38

PREJUDICED   YT 398.33   398.34

PREMISES   BL 347.12   351.32
  YT 394.25   396.3   400.32

PREOCCUPIED   TB 513.18   522.7

PREPARATION   GG 680.18

PREPARATIONS   TF 119.9   133.1
  DV 158.37   159.29   YT 397.7
  409.28

PREPARE   TF 124.42   PR 488.28
  JD 628.14   ML 739.29

PREPARED   HT 39.20   SP 45.30
  SS 202.20   GF 239.19   SC 269.26
  WP 392.31   YT 397.6   400.28
  PR 478.2   WR 570.1   SM 585.18
  RR 779.38

PREPARING   TF 123.21   124.22
  133.19   135.18   EE 316.15
  PR 502.9   IL 652.39   ML 734.24

PREPOSTEROUS   MO 15.1   PR 482.10
  JD 614.13   614.14   OV 758.1

PREPOSTEROUSLY   WP 379.23

PRE-ROMAN   BO 599.34

PRESCOTT, HANNAH   (SEE HANNAH
  PRESCOTT)

PRESCOTTS   PR 474.23   474.28

PRESENCE   MO 12.18   HT 39.10
  WM 56.20   PO 97.8   98.1   105.34
  TF 118.32   121.10   123.34
  DV 157.15   177.39   181.36
  FG 188.3   SS 202.11   SG 229.20
  WS 250.25   255.18   255.20
  260.34   EE 324.2   325.25   325.38
  326.14   TP 339.11   339.14
  341.11   BL 348.1   353.12   353.29
  355.26   361.8   WP 379.17   390.28
  PP 440.10   HD 452.23   PR 473.32
  484.24   484.33   485.37   WR 568.6
  568.7   574.7   574.10   574.16
  BO 596.9   597.35   598.19   603.12
  JD 608.16   616.15   629.8
  LA 634.20   GG 672.19   685.27
  694.23   NT 710.5   OV 749.14
  MD 815.25

PRESENCES   LA 638.6

PRESENT   MO 13.4   HT 39.31
  PO 99.10   DV 153.26   WS 257.17
  260.33   EE 307.31   WP 381.15
  PP 430.25   WR 562.29   563.22
  577.28   BO 598.4   600.23
  JD 619.36   629.11   GG 679.13
  679.17   679.19   679.23   679.33
  680.12   680.36   LL 762.36
  RH 790.8   794.11   799.4
  TH 851.36

PRESENT-DAY   EA 86.16

PRESENTED   DV 165.15   179.37
  TP 345.29   WR 577.32   GG 670.21
  OV 750.38

PRESENTING   EA 84.25

PRESENTLY   MO 5.9   OA 28.39   30.12
  32.38   HT 41.3   SP 51.12
  WM 58.3   EA 73.4   TF 118.11
  DV 163.24   169.31   SS 202.20
  SG 224.6   GF 235.34   WS 249.3
  261.20   263.20   SC 271.6
  CH 278.12   BL 354.4   WP 380.1
  PP 437.7   WR 565.28   576.34
  OV 756.26

PRESENTS   PR 474.37   LL 762.36

PRESERVE   BO 593.42

PRESERVED   TF 118.41   GF 235.26
  GG 688.27   LL 761.3

PRESERVES   TB 515.1

PRESIDED   ML 730.1

PRESIDING   MD 816.3

PRESS   OA 30.35   TP 337.19
  BO 603.13   GG 662.17

PRESSED   MO 21.14   OA 28.37   35.1
  36.3   37.28   EA 91.4   PO 104.33
  109.14   109.33   110.21
  DV 156.22   157.36   161.38

PRESSED (CONT.)   170.26
  FG 190.1   195.13   WS 255.14
  CH 277.6   BL 354.14
  364.11   HD 454.10   454.18
  PR 498.38   SU 543.22
  WR 571.31   SM 586.20
  GG 684.6   686.17   689.36
  689.42   690.35   696.10
  OV 747.10   LL 772.9   RR 785.8
  788.12   BM 837.21

PRESSED-IN   NT 702.13

PRESSING   WM 66.24   EA 72.33
  91.2   91.8   PO 110.5   110.6
  110.17   TF 130.8   FG 192.1
  SD 416.33   PP 427.2   430.37
  HD 452.41   453.1   SM 586.13
  JD 615.39   ML 745.22
  RR 784.25   785.13

PRESSURE   EA 90.39   EE 307.22
  BL 363.38   MN 373.16   373.28
  BO 596.26   IL 650.17

PRESTIGE   DV 185.24   CH 278.28
  EE 314.28

PRESUMABLY   FA 461.35   462.42
  MD 806.41

PRESUME   ML 722.9

PRESUMED   IL 650.18   BM 837.8

PRESUMPTUOUS   BL 348.19

PRETENCE   GF 240.25   PP 439.9
  IL 659.22   NT 715.39

PRETEND   WS 260.38   FA 459.10
  NT 702.26   ML 737.32
  OV 758.5   MD 813.6

PRETENDANT   MO 14.17

PRETENDED   MO 6.7   DV 166.6
  SS 209.6   MN 371.25   371.26
  PP 430.10   IL 650.3
  NT 715.16   ML 731.7   746.31
  LL 777.1   TH 850.12

PRETENDING   MO 17.37   DV 176.35
  PP 439.8   OV 747.2

PRETENDS   BM 842.6

PRETTILY   SB 217.9   WS 251.27

PRETTY   SP 52.37   EA 84.13
  94.5   PO 113.12   TF 123.30
  DV 158.15   FG 188.38
  SG 221.1   225.2   GF 235.35
  241.38   242.20   WS 244.7
  250.5   250.28   252.12   260.40
  261.24   261.29   262.16
  262.18   265.32   SC 272.15
  EE 304.39   TP 337.3
  BL 363.18   MN 367.23
  YT 395.14   SD 418.40
  PR 486.29   487.14   491.24
  493.17   507.40   508.4   508.5
  512.5   TB 521.41   525.3
  SM 584.25   584.32   JD 611.39
  LA 630.3   644.36   IL 659.18

PRETTY (CONT.) GG 681.41 689.24
   LL 761.7 RR 779.24 788.22
   788.25 788.39 RH 796.36
   BM 827.36

PREVENT SP 47.1 EA 93.28
   PO 103.10 103.17 104.20
   WS 264.42 265.1 SC 272.8
   NT 717.28 LL 764.30

PREVENTED EA 90.30 PO 103.22
   EE 328.22

PREVIOUS WP 388.3 YT 407.1
   RR 785.14

PREVIOUSLY EA 82.38 HD 446.38

PRE-WAR EE 328.5 BO 600.1

PREY DV 180.37 WP 386.14
   GG 674.33

PREYED SU 529.22

PRICE ML 732.39

PRICELESS IL 657.38 TH 847.7

PRICES EA 81.14

PRICK WM 69.23 PO 106.3
   CH 282.3

PRICKED MO 6.37 9.7 PO 114.6
   LA 634.24

PRICKING PR 501.21 RR 783.10

PRICKLES SU 535.8

PRICKLY PO 95.17 SU 530.6 535.4
   GG 674.11 674.26 686.38

PRIDE OA 23.3 31.20 SP 47.39
   EA 81.32 TF 128.1 130.20
   130.31 DV 137.29 138.18 150.3
   153.34 182.12 184.10
   SS 208.11 SB 217.2 219.18
   SC 269.1 269.3 CH 278.26
   OC 300.14 EE 322.15 322.18
   322.24 TP 335.17 YT 403.17
   405.3 HD 447.15 FA 465.19
   PR 483.10 504.31 505.2
   SU 543.14 WR 554.35 BO 596.5
   LA 634.42 637.14 OV 754.3
   759.19 RR 779.4 781.29 782.16
   MD 822.37

PRIDED TP 339.11 BL 350.7
   PR 477.32 OV 752.27

PRIED WR 548.25

PRIE-DIEU TF 125.36

PRIEST WR 578.1 580.21 580.29
   580.32 580.38 LA 631.14
   LL 762.41 764.39 777.14

PRIEST-LIKE LL 764.11

PRIESTS WR 550.7 566.7 568.31
   573.34 576.13 576.23 576.31
   578.10 578.23 579.36 580.3

PRIESTS (CONT.) 580.17 580.19
   580.25 581.13 ML 724.28
   724.29 725.1

PRIG MO 8.18

PRIMARILY EA 79.27

PRIME EE 309.31 SD 411.15
   416.30 WR 580.27 JD 618.3

PRIMED OC 290.10

PRIMEVAL EE 303.31 323.42
   WR 569.27 569.35

PRIMITIVE SP 45.26 PO 99.42
   TF 127.10 128.15 EE 305.5
   307.6 314.27 PR 475.32 500.13
   SM 583.27

PRIMITIVE CHAPEL SC 271.7

PRIMITIVELY WR 576.18

PRIMITIVE METHODIST CHAPEL
   SP 45.1 45.4

PRIMROSE ML 736.5

PRIMROSES EA 71.28 79.14
   SS 200.36 200.38 SB 214.15
   OC 283.34 EE 328.32 ML 722.33
   723.16

PRINCE PR 476.3 TB 516.13
   ML 729.31

PRINCELESS PR 479.42

PRINCE OF WALES OC 291.3 291.6
   291.21 292.17

PRINCE O' WALES OC 287.15

PRINCESS PR 474.11 475.15
   475.20 475.35 475.37 476.2
   476.3 476.9 476.13 478.2
   478.20 478.26 478.37 479.4
   479.22 479.28 479.32 479.41
   480.9 480.13 480.40 480.42
   481.8 481.13 481.25 481.29
   481.35 482.1 483.28 483.40
   484.11 485.14 485.18 485.32
   487.24 488.16 488.30 488.38
   489.22 489.29 490.21 490.26
   490.35 490.38 491.16 491.18
   491.41 492.15 492.22 492.28
   492.35 493.1 493.11 493.15
   494.17 495.16 495.22 495.27
   495.34 495.40 496.19 496.41
   497.14 497.28 497.35 498.25
   498.42 499.7 499.14 499.17
   499.21 500.15 500.19 500.25
   501.5 506.26 510.24 510.34
   510.37 511.9 511.36 512.7
   512.12 512.16 512.18

PRINCESSES PR 476.7

PRINCESS'S PR 479.40 481.2
   482.9 490.10 490.15

PRINCES STREET FA 463.41

PRINCESS URQUHART PR 475.7

PRINCESSY MO 20.22

PRINCIPLE BO 599.19

PRINCIPLES WR 547.18

PRINT JD 609.26 ML 743.15

PRINTED ML 743.15

PRINTING JD 607.37

PRISCILLA EE 304.36

PRISMS BO 595.30

PRISON ML 739.4

PRISONER EE 328.34 WP 385.35
   SD 422.18* 422.21 WR 564.31
   565.17 566.3 JD 627.9
   GG 683.12

PRISONER'S SD 422.30

PRISSY'S EE 304.38

PRITHEE SP 53.7

PRIVACY WM 61.14 TF 117.32
   WS 254.30 RH 802.31
   BM 831.21 832.34

PRIVATE MO 13.33 EA 86.37
   TF 133.27 DV 145.2 153.27
   EE 328.14 MN 367.9
   WP 380.39 380.40 SD 413.14
   PR 479.20 TB 514.10 522.12
   SU 544.30 RH 795.14

PRIVATELY LL 764.21 RR 779.1

PRIVATES SD 413.9

PRIVATION WR 550.10

PRIVET YT 394.3

PRIVILEGED MO 14.37

PRIZED OA 30.27

PRIZES GG 661.5

PROBABLY MO 14.18 OA 30.39
   WM 64.15 EA 78.14 80.3
   PO 113.22 TF 126.28
   SC 271.10 OC 286.24
   EE 317.19 327.27 BL 363.28
   WP 383.13 384.36 FA 465.10
   PR 507.21 SU 543.30
   WR 565.2 BO 600.27
   JD 618.29 618.40 619.34
   IL 652.33 652.38 GG 665.19
   678.3 ML 732.6 OV 756.15
   RR 788.21 MD 821.18

PROBED MO 9.28

PROBING LL 774.21

PROBLEM EE 333.8 BO 593.3
   JD 613.14 621.15 MD 808.38

PROCEDURE   OA 30.31

PROCEED   OA 30.30   MD 806.23

PROCEEDED   SP 49.27   WM 59.29
   SB 212.18   WS 253.9   OC 288.24
   MN 369.16   369.26   RR 784.39
   786.2

PROCESSES   LL 763.6   763.9

PROCESSION   TF 134.32   DV 138.25
   WR 579.5

PROCREATIVE   SU 545.2

PROD   BL 360.6

PRODIGY   YT 395.29

PRODUCE   ML 739.21

PRODUCED   MO 9.37   SC 270.21
   MN 370.17   ML 735.30

PRODUCES   GG 688.37

PROFANE   OV 754.8

PROFESSED   BL 349.40

PROFESSION   DV 142.10   EE 305.15
   308.17   NT 715.34

PROFESSIONAL   SP 45.6   HD 453.16

PROFFER   DV 146.22

PROFILE   DV 138.21   SB 212.12

PROFIT   FG 191.10   ML 728.17

PROFITABLE   CH 274.37   YT 394.34

PROFOUND   EE 309.26   313.20   328.2
   PR 501.13   WR 560.18   576.2
   JD 607.4   ML 742.18   TH 847.40

PROFOUNDLY   DV 145.15   TB 524.8
   LA 633.26   643.35   GG 662.37

PROFUNDITY   GG 698.31

PROFUSE   SS 200.35   WS 244.14

PROFUSELY   EE 317.31

PROFUSION   WR 559.11

PROGRESS   WP 387.19   HD 450.34
   ML 736.1

PROGRESSED   NT 708.11

PROGRESSING   PP 438.1

PROJECTED   WR 561.38

PROJECTILE   PP 436.2

PROJECTING   LL 770.25

PROJECTION   WR 576.33

PROJECTS   ML 728.24   728.28

PROLETARIAT   YT 394.37

PROLIX   EE 319.23

PROLONGED   TB 524.3   MD 821.21

PROMINENT   PR 475.10   LL 761.11
   761.25

PROMISE   TF 132.29   SG 221.22
   EE 305.20   SD 422.9   BO 597.29
   JD 616.8   OV 751.38   RR 787.34
   RH 796.24   801.8   801.23   801.24
   BM 834.28

PROMISED   DV 183.26   SB 213.36
   219.17   WP 390.25   390.27
   FA 463.17   PR 486.15   BO 597.29
   IL 649.18   GG 666.3   OV 752.10
   RH 795.2   795.7

PROMISING   EA 86.39

PROMPT   RR 785.17

PROMPTED   MD 810.2

PROMPTLY   SP 50.27   FA 467.39
   TB 517.30   MD 806.18

PRONE   OC 297.35   ML 723.29

PRONOUNCE   OA 33.2

PRONOUNCED   MO 5.16   EA 85.20
   DV 143.17

PRONOUNCEMENT   DV 155.28

PRONOUNCEMENTS   DV 145.25

PRONOUNCING   EA 85.3   MD 808.35

PRONUNCIATION   FA 464.20
   MD 818.12

PROOF   TF 125.11   SD 419.2
   IL 652.9

PROPER   GF 243.11   WS 248.35
   EE 321.2   321.11   321.28
   BL 352.32   YT 399.31   SD 425.36
   425.37   FA 461.22   461.23
   PR 483.31   LL 768.32   MD 808.13
   811.2

PROPERLY   EE 319.36   GG 674.35
   MD 808.12   BM 839.18

PROPERTIED   YT 400.13

PROPERTY   YT 405.24   407.3
   PR 480.31   ML 722.12   739.20
   RR 779.9

PROPHET   NT 706.16

PROPHETS   GG 700.11

PROPITIATION   SD 420.29

PROPORTIONS   MD 810.29

PROPOSAL   DV 151.38

PROPOSE   GG 679.16

PROPOSED   DV 177.21   MN 373.41
   ML 730.5

PROPOSES   GF 236.7

PROPOSITION   JD 613.20   615.5

PROPPED   PO 109.13   CH 277.30
   YT 398.5

PROPRIETIES   WM 57.18

PROPRIETOR   SD 411.35
   PP 432.29

PROPRIETOR'S   MO 12.8

PROPS   DV 166.13

PROSPECT   GF 234.29   YT 408.23

PROSPECTIVE   FA 463.24   463.26

PROSPECTS   PO 96.26   RH 790.26

PROSTITUTE   NT 710.39

PROSTITUTE-HOUSES   DV 165.20

PROSTRATE   PO 110.20   TP 345.2
   SD 421.40   PR 511.10   511.13
   LL 774.36

PROTECT   DV 150.8   155.25
   RR 787.8   MD 813.30

PROTECTED   TF 127.14   WR 553.7
   JD 606.19

PROTECTING   CH 279.25
   JD 615.34   GG 695.23

PROTECTION   MO 17.40   18.5
   YT 396.26   PR 503.33
   RR 787.4

PROTECTIVE   EA 91.22   BO 590.40
   JD 605.7   615.34

PROTECTIVELY   PO 98.33
   DV 147.9

PROTECTOR   MD 813.29

PROTECTOR'S   OA 34.19

PROTEST   DV 143.12   WR 550.38
   OV 756.11

PROTESTANT   OA 26.22

PROTESTED   OA 25.2   SC 273.13
   WP 382.32   TB 516.27

PROTESTING   CH 276.28

PROTRUDE   PP 434.31

PROTRUDED   CH 278.30   OC 286.16

PROTRUDING   PP 434.36

PROUD   SP 47.30   EA 71.23

PROUD (CONT.) PO 107.17 107.31
  TF 123.23 123.24 127.20
  132.17 DV 138.5 138.21 142.24
  153.21 160.16 165.28 177.13
  SG 222.2 WS 251.14 EE 310.9
  HD 446.40 447.2 FA 461.1
  PR 479.37 SU 530.10 BO 589.18
  603.17 LA 643.14 GG 661.16
  680.21 700.4 NT 704.31 704.32
  RR 779.8 781.27 BM 829.6
  TH 852.3

PROUDER PO 106.7 106.9
  DV 150.29 ML 736.12

PROUDLY PO 107.26 107.36
  DV 152.7 GF 235.29 YT 405.1

PROVE SD 418.42 OV 758.42 759.7

PROVED GF 235.28 WR 560.41
  LA 643.4 GG 662.25 TH 846.35

PROVES IL 652.12

PROVIDE MO 16.41 EE 315.40
  BL 348.35 HD 442.16 FA 462.24
  MD 818.19

PROVIDED ML 734.32

PROVIDENCE WM 54.2

PROVIDING TP 336.31

PROVINCIAL BL 349.11 NT 705.22

PROVING SD 419.4

PROVISION PP 430.23

PROVOKING SM 585.5

PROWESS RR 780.40

PROWL TB 521.15

PROWLED ML 743.26

PROWLING MD 815.36

PRUDERY HT 39.4

PRUNING DV 138.12

PRURIENT TF 132.5

PRUSSIAN PO 96.23 97.14

PRUSSIANS GF 235.13

PSALM OV 754.26

PSEUDO-CONVERSATION GG 674.30

PSYCHE GG 675.41

PSYCHICALLY MO 11.28

PSYCHO-ANALYST EE 314.40

PUB TP 335.9 JD 616.3

PUBLIC MO 12.40 TF 122.6
  SS 198.31 SG 224.32 224.36

PUBLIC (CONT.) SD 420.1
  NT 706.27 OV 754.18 BM 834.5
  838.11

PUBLICAN PP 430.20 433.1 433.7
  433.10 433.20 433.25 433.32
  434.1 434.13 435.31

PUBLICAN'S HT 39.21 PP 435.3

PUBLIC-HOUSE HT 39.25 SP 50.13
  DV 162.8 177.7 OC 287.35
  288.10 PP 432.14 JD 624.3

PUBLIC-HOUSES SP 47.11

PUBLIC-SCHOOL ML 728.3

PUBLISHED TF 120.41 ML 736.3

PUBLISHING ML 735.41

PUBS FA 469.28

PUCE LL 763.25

PUCKERED SC 272.38

PUDDING SC 270.33 OC 288.7
  EE 318.9 318.25 JD 619.31
  620.16

PUDDLED BL 351.36

PUEBLO PR 481.24 489.4 495.10

PUFF TF 119.1 SB 213.7
  WS 247.29 WP 382.15 JD 613.5
  LA 640.7

PUFFED EA 76.34 YT 398.8 407.14
  HD 443.25

PUFFS LA 637.42

PUFFY MD 807.13

PUG-FACED LL 762.13

PUGILIST GG 699.37

PULL MO 18.31 20.9 OA 25.36
  SP 45.7 DV 168.12 EE 313.39
  MN 369.26 JD 617.6

PULLED SP 51.8 EA 71.28
  PO 111.31 DV 168.29 174.42
  FG 194.26 SS 206.34 210.35
  211.30 SB 213.13 SG 221.11
  221.36 GF 235.4 239.20 239.27
  TP 337.24 343.19 BL 352.34
  MD 824.21 BM 838.14

PULLING TF 127.27 DV 161.34
  168.29 168.40 SG 222.18
  WS 249.4 OC 283.13 286.40
  TP 342.30 343.9 PP 433.34
  439.24 TB 527.7 SU 535.6
  WR 564.40 LA 637.7

PULPING MO 1.29 BL 362.17

PULSATING ML 724.20

PULSE WM 69.25 69.27 EA 71.20

PULSE (CONT.) 78.12 PO 112.4
  112.14

PULSED OC 286.9

PULSES SP 48.36

PULSING WM 69.17 EE 332.35
  SU 530.28 530.29

PUMP MO 18.18 18.20
  TF 123.17

PUNCH BOWL SP 50.37

PUNCTILIOUS LL 764.4

PUNCTUALLY SC 268.1

PUNCTURE MN 372.2

PUNISHED WS 243.34

PUPIL OA 26.34 DV 172.31
  181.24

PUPILS MO 9.29

PUPILS' BM 840.38

PUPPETS NT 707.5

PUPPY-SEXUALITY MD 821.20

PURCHASED BM 827.21

PUR DICESTI MO 16.6

PURDY, NORA (SEE NORA PURDY)

PURE MO 11.27 17.16 WM 70.1
  EA 92.19 PO 106.29 114.42
  115.1 115.16 TF 126.21
  DV 138.21 149.29 149.35
  153.8 153.12 153.16
  155.21 SG 226.4 EE 312.16
  316.25 330.32 330.33
  TP 343.40 BL 355.36
  MN 371.41 BO 604.27 BM 831.11
  TH 844.25 844.27 845.38
  850.35 853.35

PURE-BLOOD NT 715.36

PURE-BLOODED EE 326.26

PURE-BRED EE 326.19 327.1
  WR 547.42

PURELY DV 153.14 EE 322.30
  BM 837.39

PURE-MOULDED JD 618.7

PURIFY CH 279.35

PURITAN FATHER JD 621.18
  623.26

PURITAN-LOOKING TH 844.4

PURLEY WM 54.9

PURPLE MO 1.13 2.13 15.17
  SP 48.9 WM 64.7 TF 122.7

PURPLE (CONT.) SS 200.38 210.10
   EE 303.13 303.34 MN 375.12

PURPLE-LIPPED ML 725.3

PURPLING SB 214.13

PURPLISH SS 206.17 LA 641.31

PURPLISH-PIGMENTED WR 577.18

PURPOSE OA 33.37 33.38 35.28
   TF 123.14 DV 154.32 163.31
   OC 297.38 YT 400.32 FA 462.32
   NT 703.22

PURPOSELESS DV 154.33

PURPOSELY GF 239.32

PURPOSES EA 89.18 TF 128.17

PURPOSIVE SB 217.34

PURR TP 334.13 BL 357.3

PURSE HT 42.10 42.17 42.22
   44.1 EA 78.36

PURSED OA 26.35

PURSING TB 523.1 RR 779.4
   782.25

PURSUE FG 191.1

PURSUED DV 152.4 RH 795.35

PURSUING DV 165.38 NT 704.23

PURSUIT PR 498.42

PUSH TP 335.4 335.26 BO 604.28

PUSHED MO 7.25 SP 45.28
   PO 104.16 110.24 110.41 111.2
   TF 117.15 118.14 SG 229.39
   230.20 CH 276.20 OC 284.40
   296.25 TP 341.2 342.19 343.20
   MN 377.12 377.28

PUSHER EE 314.19

PUSHES EE 313.30

PUSHING GF 241.16 CH 274.22
   EE 313.31 318.31 MN 367.19
   YT 397.37 PP 433.4 439.29
   HD 450.5 PR 491.24 TB 520.38
   SU 532.14 JD 615.11 619.31
   LA 631.34 GG 665.12 ML 745.21

PUSS-PUSS HT 41.13

PUTTEES EE 328.40 MN 375.9
   375.11

PUTTING MO 8.27 10.5 SP 50.33
   WM 60.19 TF 124.12 DV 157.30
   166.29 171.36 SS 203.26
   SG 223.5 223.26 CH 275.2
   276.3 OC 288.28 288.39 296.10
   EE 321.15 TP 344.28 BL 358.28
   PP 430.9 431.23 HD 445.4
   PR 484.15 LA 632.17 636.25

PUTTING (CONT.) NT 715.42 718.39
   LL 775.31 RH 795.15 795.27
   795.37 797.9 797.42

PUZZLE WM 57.27

PUZZLED MO 8.3 WM 55.42 57.1
   EA 71.24 75.3 DV 150.38
   171.41 SG 228.38 WS 259.12
   259.19 MN 377.34 PR 481.5
   WR 560.29 SM 584.2 LA 634.34
   GG 672.8 LL 778.16

PUZZLING BL 349.25 LA 643.11

PYJAMAS PR 507.8 508.3
   RH 803.12 BM 829.24 829.33

Q.E.F. WM 66.27

QUADRANGLE SS 200.34 EE 304.34

QUADRANGLES SP 45.11

QUADRILLES WS 257.33

QUAILED OC 289.31 WR 546.15
   555.18 JD 623.31

QUAINT MO 16.27 EA 85.14
   SB 218.8 PR 476.19 481.34
   ML 726.37 LL 762.23 RH 802.2
   MD 821.26 821.39

QUAKING ML 744.16

QUALIFICATIONS TH 851.42

QUALITY HT 40.23 WM 60.11
   EA 85.14 TF 127.20 129.8
   EE 314.4 325.28 YT 403.6
   407.38 PR 474.5 479.15 481.12
   482.38 TB 519.40 RR 785.19

QUALM WR 551.6 559.38 IL 652.1

QUALMS LL 769.21

QUARREL WM 57.24 GG 681.7
   NT 718.11 LL 769.30

QUARRELLED SG 231.11

QUARRELS WM 57.25

QUARRY DV 161.5 161.23
   ML 725.39

QUARRY COTTAGE DV 176.25 178.5

QUARTER DV 163.1 174.41
   OC 287.6 293.28 TP 340.33
   BL 352.28 352.29 LA 641.18
   ML 732.18

QUARTERED SD 415.10

QUARTER-PAST HT 41.8 EA 81.18

QUARTERS RR 785.32 786.11

QUASI QUASI TROPPO DELIZIOSA +
   LL 774.20

QUATTROCENTO NT 706.5

QUAVERED WS 265.5 265.17

QUAVERING DV 148.36

QUEEN WM 64.38 DV 141.22
   CH 278.21 SD 413.2
   FA 461.20 BO 591.27
   JD 607.6 607.11

QUEEN ANNE LL 762.21

QUEEN-BEE BO 589.3 591.4
   591.27 592.18

QUEEN BOADICEA JD 621.3

QUEEN ELIZABETH TB 516.23

QUEENLY EA 84.19 DV 147.23
   159.2

QUEEN OF SPADES SD 412.41

QUEEN'S DV 141.19 141.41

QUEEN STREET SP 45.29 46.1
   51.14

QUEER EA 90.21 PO 106.30
   DV 149.15 171.12 SB 217.30
   WS 249.29 249.34 263.36
   264.8 264.12 SC 268.25
   EE 324.4 BL 358.24 MN 378.7
   WP 387.6 YT 396.30 398.12
   403.6 PR 479.19 482.37
   499.2 499.33 508.10
   TB 522.20 522.30 SU 533.29
   BO 600.40 601.3 604.9
   JD 612.38 613.42 614.25
   626.3 LA 632.25 634.11
   639.34 644.4 644.14 646.24
   IL 659.36 GG 684.12
   NT 702.34 716.33 ML 729.14
   OV 756.24 LL 761.26 766.12
   771.41 773.29 776.31
   MD 822.26 BM 828.12 829.36
   835.20 837.10 837.11 838.3
   TH 848.12 852.40 853.28
   853.34

QUEERED GG 678.32

QUEEREST GG 692.17

QUE LES D'MOISELLES SONT
   BELLES + GG 676.21

QUENCHED EE 314.39 YT 402.37
   SU 544.34 JD 610.30 623.40

QUERULOUS SU 531.31

QUESTION MO 5.33 5.34 9.20
   11.14 20.34 OA 31.8
   WM 55.5 56.37 61.15
   EA 79.13 PO 100.42 102.11
   DV 152.18 155.4 177.7
   179.15 FG 187.12 SS 198.4
   SB 215.22 GF 239.30
   OC 294.14 298.35 EE 311.11
   313.24 325.40 327.7 327.25
   332.21 BL 356.6 YT 394.22
   402.25 SD 414.36 423.33
   PP 428.15 438.5 HD 454.1
   454.2 PR 505.24 WR 553.24
   560.21 574.29 BO 589.2

RACES   PO 96.29   BO 593.28   599.4
   599.9   599.18   RH 795.36   801.4

RACHEL   MD 805.29   806.34

RACHEL BODOIN   MD 805.5   816.17

RACHEL'S   MD 816.37   816.38   817.3

RACIALLY   BO 587.13

RACING   SP 52.39   PO 112.13
   PP 428.42   RH 794.9   794.13
   796.31   801.8

RACK   WS 249.23

RACKED   BL 350.35   PR 509.4   509.7
   509.9   RH 790.30

RACKET   YT 395.20

RACKING   DV 154.31   PR 509.14

RADFORD   HT 39.14   39.21   40.2
   40.12   40.21   41.6   42.26   42.33
   42.35   43.10   43.16   43.22
   43.29   43.36

RADFORD   (SEE MR. RADFORD; MRS.
   RADFORD)

RADIANCE   MO 14.6   WM 62.23
   WP 387.22

RADIANT   MO 7.6   EA 78.30   84.19
   PO 105.19   114.40   114.42
   WS 253.21   SU 532.20   532.40
   OV 753.27   LL 763.34

RADIATOR   GG 684.11

RADICAL   PR 482.35

RADIO   LA 633.7   LL 768.38

RAFT   PO 107.4

RAG   SP 46.15   SB 218.13
   CH 276.34   277.38   FA 471.20
   JD 617.26   MD 808.23

RAGE   OA 35.34   WM 70.2   EA 76.38
   77.6   77.14   78.8   87.11   88.1
   PO 98.29   TF 127.11   FG 190.7
   191.5   SG 229.35   231.31   231.32
   WS 257.7   258.30   261.25   263.18
   265.20   CH 281.27   FA 466.9
   PR 478.4   BO 589.6   591.13
   NT 719.20   LL 775.14   BM 835.29
   835.36   837.16   841.37   841.41
   842.16   TH 852.35

RAGED   EA 82.22   DV 137.25   137.30
   137.32   FA 462.31

RAGES   DV 137.32

RAGGED   DV 161.7   161.29
   FG 190.20   OC 284.1   284.33
   TP 345.16   WP 379.8   379.13

RAGGEDLY   SG 227.19

RAGGY   HT 43.8

RAGING   DV 183.1

RAGS   PO 112.29   ML 736.10

RAHAT LAKOUM   MD 818.15

RAIL   SU 528.9   LA 634.25
   MD 814.33

RAILED   WR 558.42   LA 640.13

RAILINGS   LA 634.5   639.15

RAILLERY   TB 526.1

RAILS   TP 334.33

RAILWAY   SP 48.42   DV 139.5
   153.29   158.16   160.30   160.36
   167.15   167.28   OC 283.6   283.26
   284.10   286.7   286.31   290.33
   PP 432.15   PR 477.18   BO 593.5
   593.10   599.42   GG 668.35

RAILWAY ARMS   PP 432.4

RAILWAYS   TP 334.4

RAIN   PO 98.7   FG 195.35
   EE 323.33   BL 350.35   351.12
   352.40   353.8   361.13   MN 377.42
   PP 430.28   430.30   SU 529.33
   WR 574.6   574.7   575.1   575.31
   GG 674.9   ML 723.32   723.33
   727.10   727.11   728.22   741.14
   743.26   743.40   743.41
   LL 775.29   775.33   776.41
   RR 783.10   783.17   787.35
   BM 834.18   834.25   834.37
   841.16

RAINBOW   HT 40.1   OV 755.7

RAINDROPS   OV 753.41

RAINED   ML 741.11   LL 776.22

RAINING   DV 166.33   PP 432.20

RAIN-PIPE   LL 769.8   769.9   770.24
   775.14

RAINS   WR 548.30   574.23

RAIN-WATER   ML 738.21

RAINY   BL 347.5

RAISE   TF 123.40   WP 384.18
   FA 465.22   BO 604.29

RAISED   OA 26.30   32.39   34.26
   36.21   WM 67.2   PO 102.37
   109.36   113.7   TF 121.25
   DV 143.17   SG 230.23   WS 264.12
   265.14   OC 289.31   WP 385.38
   YT 404.7   HD 449.38   PR 493.5
   WR 547.42   561.3   576.21
   NT 704.30   ML 725.38

RAISING   TF 118.19   OC 290.25
   GG 699.41   700.4

RAISON D'ETRE   PR 482.35   482.39

RAKING   YT 396.18

RALLY   GG 685.5

RAMBLE   EA 75.33

RAMBLERS   SG 225.11

RAMBLING   SG 226.20   CH 280.29

RAMPARTS   TF 119.10   121.29
   ML 743.13

RAN   WM 54.18   54.27   55.11
   55.16   63.17   64.29   68.38
   EA 73.31   PO 95.14   99.6
   101.30   102.15   106.11   109.8
   110.27   111.5   113.8   113.39
   TF 121.36   122.33   124.11
   DV 161.30   162.8   162.14
   162.33   164.25   169.31   171.8
   FG 189.23   190.42   193.12
   193.28   SS 197.20   199.38
   GF 235.35   239.8   WS 248.24
   261.17   SC 270.17   272.13
   272.28   EE 303.2   306.40
   BL 356.11   362.25   WP 379.29
   393.15   SD 416.42   421.19
   424.20   PP 431.3   436.20
   HD 451.16   FA 471.19   471.20
   PR 490.2   494.23   TB 517.9
   SU 537.33   WR 547.41   551.38
   555.10   555.11   558.31
   BO 587.3   587.10   599.30
   LA 635.28   636.9   645.34
   GG 687.19   ML 742.1
   OV 755.5

RANCH   PR 481.22   481.24
   482.14   485.9   489.5   508.28
   512.8   WR 547.41   552.12

RANCH-HOUSE   WR 551.36

RANCHO DEL CERRO GORDO
   PR 481.20   481.31

RANCOUR   ML 732.33

RANDOM   SS 197.30   MN 376.37

RANG   OA 28.38   WM 59.36
   EA 82.10   88.38   EE 332.8
   MN 378.2   378.21   PR 492.22
   510.25   511.4   511.7
   SM 583.11   IL 656.40
   NT 701.33   720.32   ML 729.16
   745.33   RR 785.15   785.22
   787.28   BM 834.26

RANGE   PO 114.41   115.10
   115.15   DV 145.18   151.4
   SD 423.20   423.21   423.35
   IL 649.1   649.2   649.4

RANGED   PO 95.7   115.30

RANGES   PO 106.42

RANGING   SS 202.3

RANK   DV 174.3

RANKED   PO 116.6   DV 151.4

RANKLED FA 466.17

RANKS TF 118.11 118.20

RAP WM 67.22

RAPED NT 711.8 711.9

RAPID FG 193.14 CH 274.29
OC 293.18 EE 331.5 SU 539.2
MD 820.25

RAPIDITY EE 331.30

RAPIDLY TF 133.26 133.38
OC 294.31 EE 306.37 SU 538.37
WR 555.42 GG 665.16 697.4
LL 776.27 BM 831.16

RAPIDLY-CHASING WM 68.38

RAPPED OC 283.24

RAPPING PO 113.3

RAPPINGS LL 767.27

RAPTURE OC 288.33 BL 355.33

RAPTUROUSLY OC 288.38

RARE MO 17.15 OA 36.1 SB 217.29
TP 339.6 BL 349.20 YT 399.34
FA 463.33 SU 538.31 JD 605.12
605.21 LA 641.32 GG 671.11
ML 737.41 738.1 LL 764.21

RAREFIED DV 146.8

RARELY MO 2.36 PO 96.14 97.17
EE 311.9 312.31 MN 374.18
PR 475.6 483.25 GG 682.35
699.25 ML 723.33 LL 762.14
RR 782.3

RARER EE 311.41

RARITY DV 181.16

RASCAL SD 417.13

RASCALLY EA 83.10

RASH MO 9.7 TP 335.18 PR 496.4

RASPBERRY DV 161.22

RASPBERRY-CANES OC 284.20

RAT YT 407.36 407.38 TH 853.5
853.28

RATE MO 9.26 17.38 WM 63.3
66.8 EA 73.40 81.27 DV 147.10
SB 219.24 SG 231.12 GF 235.12
OC 294.37 EE 311.34 GG 680.7
687.7

RAT-LIKE TH 852.40

RATS OC 289.20 290.32 TH 852.4

RAT'S TH 853.6

RAT-TA-TA-PLAN JD 609.18

RATTLE PP 432.23 PR 490.37
JD 608.12

RATTLED DV 139.3

RATTLER MN 372.3

RATTLESNAKE NT 714.31 714.33

RATTLING OA 36.19 SS 208.35
PR 506.30 TB 518.22 BO 601.22
GG 687.32

RAUCOUS ML 740.39

RAVAGING OV 752.14

RAVED SC 269.21 YT 409.37
WR 552.41

RAVENNA TH 853.20

RAVING SC 272.9 272.14
YT 404.34

RAW PO 109.1 TF 122.17
DV 136.32 GF 234.28 WS 244.21
OC 283.5 HD 449.2 PR 480.5

RAW-BONED CH 278.18 OC 291.13

RAWDON RR 779.1 779.26 779.32
780.14 780.42 781.2 781.7
781.15 781.34 781.36 781.39
781.42 782.9 782.17 783.12
783.21 783.28 783.32 783.37
784.15 784.19 784.28 785.15
785.22 785.27 785.28 785.30
785.34 785.35 785.38 786.13
786.18 786.27 786.32 786.41
787.23 787.25 787.40 788.4
788.28 789.17

RAWDON'S RR 783.20 784.8 788.7

RAWSLEY YT 403.30

RAY WR 581.26

RAYNOR, JOHN (SEE JOHN RAYNOR)

RAYS SS 203.2 SU 530.17
WR 580.42 581.3 GG 694.31
696.23 OV 753.34

RAZOR BL 356.12

RAZOR-LINE MO 18.12

REACH MO 18.29 WS 255.24
JD 609.32 GG 667.27 NT 713.29
RR 785.6 MD 806.15 TH 846.20

REACHED OA 31.25 38.5 EA 72.4
72.29 DV 169.3 171.8 180.4
FG 188.9 194.16 194.19
SS 204.19 OC 284.39 288.25
EE 324.14 BL 352.42 355.5
YT 401.38 SD 421.3 HD 442.19
455.25 PR 506.18 SU 530.35
WR 581.1 SM 582.31 JD 619.17
ML 745.27 RR 787.16 BM 838.5

REACHING EA 75.28 EE 333.2
TP 341.30 BL 355.40 SD 424.41

REACHING (CONT.) 426.10
SU 536.41 SM 583.16
TH 845.15

REACTED MO 5.14

REACTION PO 103.15 GG 676.2
676.4

REACTIONS BO 592.3 GG 676.1

READ MO 6.7 OA 27.26 32.1
HT 40.32 WM 66.3 EA 74.31
75.2 83.34 DV 140.35
164.6 165.29 176.35
FG 188.9 WS 248.27 SC 269.5
CH 280.4 281.28 BL 347.15
350.20 MN 368.42 369.1
WP 380.34 381.1 381.24
382.38 383.2 391.7 391.29
YT 395.5 PP 430.17
PR 477.8 477.10 477.13
TB 526.11 WR 569.33 577.22
JD 607.23 619.24 626.16
GG 681.39 695.41 ML 742.15
OV 747.2 LL 763.5 769.10
777.1 RH 790.16 799.25
799.26 BM 830.11 TH 846.1

READINESS DV 151.30 172.24
GG 694.32

READING MO 16.21 OA 27.28
27.35 31.14 31.31 DV 160.6
SG 221.2 WP 380.24 380.39
383.9 PR 483.30

READING-LAMP OV 749.10

READS GG 681.38

READY OA 34.1 HT 40.34
SP 46.2 53.22 TF 132.37
134.28 DV 163.3 165.15
169.13 173.7 SB 216.28
217.35 WS 249.36 252.18
257.34 SC 267.35 268.4
268.10 268.12 269.25
CH 280.3 OC 296.14
EE 321.21 329.9 TP 335.37
346.5 BL 349.41 349.42
MN 372.1 YT 394.31 407.12
PP 437.19 438.19 FA 468.21
472.8 TB 522.37 WR 581.18
BO 588.36 596.3 JD 625.1
625.5 LA 637.8 641.28
GG 672.15 NT 714.29
MD 815.23

READY-FISTED GG 699.39

REAL MO 6.24 OA 36.9
WM 57.33 EA 80.34 89.5
91.5 92.12 PO 108.31
114.19 TF 127.19 DV 147.34
152.35 154.33 164.40
171.41 173.1 SS 202.24
205.17 WS 251.10 254.32
255.30 257.22 262.9
EE 323.13 327.9 BL 347.25
350.4 350.18 364.32
MN 366.10 WP 390.40
YT 396.9 SD 425.13
HD 443.29 448.9 FA 464.7
PR 474.8 475.30 475.31

REAL (CONT.)   PR 477.31   512.16
  TB 514.13   SU 529.21   536.21
  WR 547.35   548.23   557.29
  566.29   567.18   SM 582.15
  BO 590.1   590.3   590.4   590.16
  594.6   598.38   602.15   602.16
  602.17   602.18   JD 606.2   606.4
  606.11   607.7   607.31   LA 643.15
  IL 659.19   GG 661.29   664.17
  672.42   692.29   694.2   NT 707.1
  711.11   718.41   ML 727.35   734.4
  736.18   742.28   OV 752.33
  753.33   756.10   757.16
  LL 761.28   764.24   764.26
  773.11   777.6   RR 782.14
  RH 802.1   MD 813.16   822.33
  BM 833.40   838.40   842.10
  TH 844.18   844.19   844.24
  847.24   847.33   853.33

REALER   EE 310.15

REALISATION   PO 103.21   PP 436.18
  BO 590.42

REALISE   OA 33.29   EA 79.25   80.25
  81.6   TF 132.24   SB 217.33
  EE 310.10   WP 380.29   YT 394.25
  PP 436.3   436.17   PR 509.7
  SU 543.27   WR 579.39   BO 598.2
  598.6   JD 606.16   GG 689.25
  ML 742.35   BM 840.25   TH 846.4
  846.11

REALISED   MO 3.26   SP 51.4
  EA 89.26   TF 134.27   DV 146.20
  146.32   SB 217.29   EE 307.35
  314.6   332.23   WP 380.38   387.8
  YT 402.25   PP 435.16   FA 467.10
  PR 477.40   490.10   SU 541.30
  WR 566.5   580.42   BO 588.10
  592.14   592.23   593.17   593.25
  594.19   596.1   597.5   597.6
  597.36   600.7   603.3   GG 678.34
  689.30   689.35   693.11   695.26
  697.6   ML 736.35   737.25   742.39
  742.40   745.1   LL 777.41
  MD 806.5   806.15   806.18   812.28
  816.23   821.41

REALISES   LA 646.21

REALISING   EA 80.39   SS 203.39
  BO 591.6   GG 689.38   BM 840.7
  842.15

REALITIES   PR 474.29

REALITY   MO 15.17   PO 114.19
  TF 132.14   OC 300.40   PR 474.40
  477.29   BO 590.17   602.27
  604.17

REALM   FG 193.37   GG 661.37
  ML 724.39   OV 759.5

REALMS   JD 610.24   ML 724.2

REALNESS   WS 259.39   EE 329.16

REAP   FA 466.29   466.37

REAPPEARED   PR 482.15   TB 524.35

REAR   EE 329.39   BL 347.12

REAR (CONT.)   PR 510.26
  WR 555.32   555.35   562.21
  RR 787.41

REARED   PO 114.7   BL 362.32
  SD 420.40   TB 524.24   SU 536.31
  542.26   WR 563.5   BO 598.27
  LL 767.10

REARING   OA 36.27   TB 526.12

REASON   OA 31.24   EA 92.22
  DV 153.8   155.5   SG 229.11
  230.15   233.5   WS 256.35
  OC 301.30   EE 303.8   TP 335.6
  336.9   WP 385.4   YT 402.19
  HD 452.28   PR 485.38   485.40
  486.4   JD 607.9   622.23
  NT 706.30   710.7   ML 743.6
  OV 756.38   RH 791.23   MD 805.36

REASONABLE   EA 82.18   DV 145.24
  SD 417.4   420.18   RH 801.9

REASONABLENESS   SD 419.28

REASONING   MO 8.41

REASONS   WS 258.33   IL 656.15
  656.16   MD 805.18   805.32   822.3

REASSERTED   PO 116.4

REASSUMING   OC 285.13

REASSURE   OC 292.29

REASSURED   MO 13.6   DV 157.41
  EE 319.28   MN 378.33   SU 536.37
  WR 571.3   ML 738.34   LL 770.28

REASSURING   SC 268.28

REASSURINGLY   ML 737.17

RE-AWAKENING   BL 350.19

REBEL   PR 507.36   NT 709.9
  LL 771.39   773.33

REBELLED   FA 462.20   465.36

REBOUND   FG 189.20

REBUFFED   EA 93.34

REBUKED   OA 27.28   YT 400.15
  ML 740.33   BM 840.40

REBUKING   OC 293.22

RECALL   EE 332.24   332.25

RECALLING   SC 267.6

RECAPTURE   GG 676.36

RECEDE   BO 589.13

RECEDED   GG 669.39

RECEIVE   MO 7.38   EA 72.29
  EE 331.20   BL 349.41   YT 399.6
  NT 716.13   720.26   MD 825.8

RECEIVED   OA 35.38   HT 43.22
  PO 97.5   DV 136.32   138.30
  WS 252.42   EE 305.23
  MN 368.14   YT 403.18
  HD 443.38   PR 473.22
  492.28   492.33   TB 516.21
  WR 554.7   JD 607.21   611.42

RECEIVER   LA 637.5

RECEIVERS   LA 632.17

RECEIVING   EA 72.40   PO 99.22
  MD 815.18

RECEPTION-ROOMS   MD 810.27

RECESSES   LA 631.31

RECITING   WR 580.31

RECKLESS   OA 35.13   GF 234.31
  WS 261.35   EE 325.13
  TP 334.16   PR 498.42   499.7
  NT 706.25   BM 837.12

RECKLESSLY   FA 466.11

RECKLESSNESS   OA 30.15
  SB 219.39   GF 242.10
  OC 291.27   EE 324.42
  TP 336.34   PR 486.38
  SU 534.27

RECKON   HT 43.13   43.25
  SP 46.26   DV 167.37
  SB 212.18   219.4   SG 232.16
  EE 327.11   327.18   WP 389.7
  PR 508.25

RECKONED   SB 213.19

RECLINED   YT 400.41   407.13

RECLINING   TB 521.20

RECLUSE   PR 475.4

RECOGNISE   DV 148.39   173.29
  SG 226.39   227.1   227.28
  227.35   EE 325.16   PP 434.26
  TB 521.32

RECOGNISED   MO 21.24   EA 88.15
  TF 134.22   DV 137.23
  SG 226.38   WP 379.21
  387.26   SU 543.24   WR 572.14
  MD 808.34   821.14

RECOGNISING   SS 205.16

RECOGNITION   DV 173.2
  BL 351.19   PP 432.31
  SU 544.12   LA 646.19

RECOIL   DV 155.15   EE 325.40
  BL 357.5   MD 807.17   807.24
  807.28   816.41

RECOILED   WM 55.2   DV 149.5
  EE 327.1   WP 387.1   PP 428.1
  BO 600.24   BM 832.33

RECOILING   TF 133.30

RECOLLECTION GF 239.26

RECOLLECTIONS NT 711.24

RECOMMEND GG 668.11

RECOMMENDED EE 319.24

RECONCILIATION EA 78.36
  EE 328.33 GG 687.39

RECORD MD 816.8 816.11 816.12
  816.22

RECORDS MO 4.29 FG 188.30

RECOVER EA 91.21 94.2 TF 120.39
  121.5 123.41 DV 147.16
  SG 229.21 EE 325.9 WP 389.42
  PR 509.11 BO 592.5 LL 777.30

RECOVERED PO 103.26 TF 130.12
  OC 289.35 293.4 EE 325.9
  WP 384.11 387.13 PR 512.18
  BO 591.16 591.27 GG 684.7
  ML 744.34 BM 838.8 838.12

RECOVERING WP 387.14 BO 590.6

RECOVERY EA 94.6 GF 239.14

RE-CREATED EE 304.3

RECTOR DV 136.26 SG 224.34
  224.35 224.40 231.6 BM 830.19

RECTOR'S SG 231.6 BM 830.37

RECTORY WM 58.27 64.42 67.35
  DV 137.33 153.29 156.28
  SB 213.20 SG 224.40 BM 831.6
  839.28 842.35

RECURRED BL 348.2

RED MO 1.13 6.15 9.33 OA 26.11
  29.18 31.15 35.4 35.10
  SP 49.2 WM 63.33 64.1 68.23
  69.22 EA 71.27 72.20 76.23
  PO 97.28 110.26 113.37
  TF 123.26 125.37 DV 139.5
  161.13 FG 188.15 189.15
  189.19 190.21 190.24 194.6
  194.10 194.11 194.16 194.25
  195.11 196.5 196.9 SS 197.30
  201.14 202.4 206.37 211.6
  SB 213.3 214.2 214.17 216.39
  217.21 SG 224.28 GF 238.22
  241.31 WS 248.27 249.14
  251.34 253.30 253.31 253.33
  253.38 SC 268.26 270.22
  270.24 CH 275.15 279.8 280.21
  282.6 OC 283.20 286.12 286.15
  286.35 287.28 287.31 288.13
  290.36 296.27 EE 303.34
  314.38 314.42 320.26 326.33
  329.23 331.15 TP 337.42
  342.31 BL 351.6 351.40
  MN 366.8 374.37 WP 379.30
  SD 412.3 PP 427.2 430.33
  434.4 436.10 437.29 HD 441.32
  446.24 FA 458.6 458.26 459.30
  459.36 465.4 467.20 468.23
  PR 486.11 487.28 489.14
  490.41 511.37 TB 520.31

RED (CONT.) SU 531.28 532.13
  534.13 536.22 WR 557.26
  559.20 559.22 562.25 563.4
  564.32 565.4 566.8 568.33
  568.42 569.2 570.22 574.37
  575.2 575.28 576.29 577.1
  577.7 577.15 581.4 581.25
  BO 594.3 JD 610.21 613.25
  617.15 617.33 618.1 LA 630.9
  IL 654.33 ML 728.33 OV 750.7
  750.23 750.38 752.31 753.11
  759.39 LL 766.16 RH 793.9
  BM 835.27 TH 853.13

RED-AND-BLACK FA 458.11

RED-AND-WHITE MN 371.10

RED-BRONZE WR 579.16

RED-BROWN PP 427.8 BM 831.41

REDDENED BL 351.30 ML 746.23

REDDENING WR 581.12 581.14

REDDEST SS 211.8

REDDISH PO 99.23 112.22
  DV 139.16 171.10 BL 354.28
  WR 552.29 BO 595.23 595.26
  603.18 603.31 ML 744.38

REDDISH-BROWN PO 96.15

REDDISH-GREY BO 598.27

RED-FACED DV 148.37 FA 467.8

RED-FLOWERED EE 304.18

RED-GOLD SU 536.7 WR 578.18
  GG 700.2

RED-HAIRED BO 588.25

RED-HOT DV 173.35 WS 262.34
  JD 617.33 NT 719.23 BM 837.15

RED MEN WR 575.26

REDNESS FG 192.5 194.22

RED-NOSED FA 467.22

RED-PAINTED GG 671.2

RED-ROOFED PO 107.5

RED SEAL PP 432.35

RED-TILE EA 86.8

REDUCE SC 269.2 PP 434.8

REDUCED DV 145.29 JD 607.15
  ML 724.33 732.25 MD 806.30

REDWOOD PR 478.34

RE-ECHOED OA 24.40 WM 61.20
  BL 350.22 365.3 TB 522.25
  SU 535.1 IL 648.9 GG 665.24

RE-ECHOING IL 651.5

REEDS SS 210.3 BO 600.11

REEDY WM 58.21 60.11
  OC 283.17

REEF ML 722.24

REEFER WS 250.32

REEFS JD 612.13

REEKING LL 777.35

REEL FG 190.33 194.39

REELED MO 4.27 TF 121.28
  DV 181.1

REELING WM 69.30 BO 603.5

RE-ESTABLISHING WM 57.18

REFER EE 308.11

REFERENCES ML 728.2

REFERRED MO 13.5 EE 308.10

REFERRING BO 601.34

REFINED SS 201.27 BL 354.37
  YT 395.9 WR 574.1 RR 781.42
  782.17

REFINEMENT YT 396.15
  PP 429.34 BM 833.1

REFLECTED WM 59.3 EA 71.27
  DV 183.28 SG 221.8 HD 452.1
  JD 608.28

REFLECTING PO 111.17
  SG 224.35 OC 286.14
  HD 441.14

REFLECTION BL 351.18

REFLECTIVELY SG 222.42

REFLECTOR OC 288.29

RE-FOLDING SG 231.9

REFORMER NT 706.16

REFRAIN SD 424.38 FA 460.31

REFRAINED OC 284.37 YT 394.36
  TH 847.11

REFRESHING WR 565.21 565.26

REFRESHMENT TF 128.38
  WS 255.19

REFUGE OA 28.26 TP 335.8
  ML 734.37

REFURNISHED SS 202.36

REFUSAL MN 370.31

REFUSE PR 478.18 WR 546.22
  BO 591.19

REFUSED WM 55.5 EA 79.40
PO 103.27 103.29 DV 137.5
SS 201.26 SG 232.11 GF 234.12
WS 259.32 OC 301.13 EE 314.13
327.18 327.27 YT 396.14 407.3
408.3 PR 474.28 SU 537.28
ML 730.34 OV 752.31 752.37

REFUSES SD 418.14 GG 699.32

REFUSING MO 8.38 GF 234.14
PR 498.38

REGAIN PO 98.25 105.5 PR 505.33
ML 725.10

REGAINED DV 174.27 LL 768.25
RH 803.41 BM 832.34

REGARD MO 9.28 12.28 DV 147.23
SS 203.32 YT 396.10 TB 513.5
515.7 NT 709.3 ML 731.34
LL 773.11

REGARDED DV 157.3 YT 395.37
396.4

REGARDING EA 72.6

REGARDS WP 384.28

REGIMENT PO 95.10 EE 330.26
BO 588.29 590.32 GG 663.18

REGIONS BL 354.33 WP 387.23
ML 744.11

REGISTER IL 649.32 ML 743.38

REGISTERED SG 228.27

REGISTERING GG 698.41

REGISTRAR DV 185.36 185.38
YT 409.42

REGRET MO 8.28 SC 267.2
BL 347.28

REGRETFUL ML 732.14

REGRETS ML 732.17

REGRETTABLE DV 141.29

REGRETTED DV 145.5 FA 468.40
468.41 PR 508.39 ML 729.37

REGULAR OA 36.36 GF 234.7
MN 367.17 FA 464.10 PR 495.24
501.3 RR 782.6

REGULARLY PO 95.11 YT 396.31
HD 447.5 451.13 WR 568.35

REGULATED TF 128.30

REGULATION DV 140.32

REHEARSING BM 833.36

REICHSHALLE TF 127.24

REID, BERTIE (SEE BERTIE REID)

REIGNING GG 666.12

REINED PR 497.15 WR 555.39

REINHARDT NT 711.42

REINS PR 492.21 498.39 499.14
499.21 WR 555.40

REITERATED MN 372.18 RH 797.38
800.32

REITERATION IL 656.35

REJECT EA 92.21

REJECTED MO 7.25

REJECTS OV 747.16

REJOICE CH 279.34 WP 384.10

REJOICES EA 81.37

REJOICING DV 158.13 FA 466.31

REJOINED TB 527.17

REJUVENATION EE 306.16

RELAPSE PO 106.4

RELAPSED PO 112.26 DV 151.13
WS 261.16 WR 567.6

RELATED DV 145.40 PP 436.38

RELATION PO 106.18 RR 781.29

RELATIONS DV 171.32 171.38
SD 414.37 PR 476.39 SU 541.28
MD 818.32

RELATIONSHIP PO 112.27 DV 146.4
TB 524.9

RELATIVE RH 798.41

RELATIVES DV 176.11 YT 408.29
PR 473.5 474.39 LL 765.41

RELAX PO 110.11 WS 252.20
BL 355.6

RELAXATION WR 572.31

RELAXED WM 69.13 EA 83.37 90.39
PO 104.7 107.34 EE 310.30
SD 421.35 PR 507.25 SU 535.19
WR 572.9

RELAXING WR 572.30

RELEASE WP 387.32 WR 572.11
GG 690.34

RELEASED EA 91.5 EE 307.3
HD 455.36 BO 597.23

RELEASING EA 90.38 WR 572.25

RELENT PR 505.33

RELENTLESS TB 519.8 WR 566.18
BO 593.12 JD 611.26

RELENTLESSLY HD 456.1
JD 623.32

RELENTLESSNESS TB 515.21
BO 592.10

RELEVANT DV 146.9

RELICS PP 437.3

RELIED TB 514.2

RELIEF OA 35.19 WM 56.15
EA 91.7 PO 110.7 110.8
110.37 114.23 DV 176.42
179.6 180.5 181.37
SB 213.34 SG 222.35
CH 280.14 EE 331.12
BL 348.24 360.21 HD 450.36
PR 504.22 BO 589.16 597.20
IL 650.42 GG 683.32 693.11
ML 730.41 742.36 744.14

RELIEF'S TF 120.27

RELIEVE DV 169.42

RELIEVED TF 122.5 SB 218.33
GF 234.33 OC 288.34 296.8
EE 318.23 MN 378.36
PP 439.10 PR 480.1
BO 594.1 LA 634.9 IL 659.11
ML 740.29

RELIGION DV 140.33 140.35
146.35 WR 549.13 550.7
OV 752.37

RELIGIONS WR 549.25 TH 852.9

RELIGIOUS OA 35.32 TF 126.30
128.34 CH 279.27 WR 572.36
574.27 RH 794.17 797.1

RELUCTANCE TP 335.6 WP 383.3
PP 433.17 BO 593.15

RELUCTANT MO 21.8 PP 433.19
BO 604.28

RELUCTANTLY DV 179.31
SS 198.34 RH 802.29
TH 849.31

RELY TB 513.35 513.36

REMAIN TF 126.26 TP 339.13
YT 395.13 HD 454.20
IL 649.22 LL 761.22

REMAINDER PO 101.42

REMAINED OA 29.8 WM 69.12
EA 72.41 73.32 74.12 78.10
82.19 87.40 91.41 PO 96.26
104.42 TF 124.25 134.30
DV 140.15 152.24 153.24
160.27 163.42 164.32 171.1
177.31 SS 208.36 SB 216.11
SG 223.35 224.11 226.9
GF 236.20 242.19 WS 247.19
CH 282.20 OC 292.12 299.12
EE 331.2 TP 344.6 345.9
BL 364.14 MN 370.22 373.6
WP 384.32 385.37 SD 415.20

REMAINED (CONT.) SD 423.32
  423.37 PP 434.7 438.31
  HD 448.22 451.33 453.39
  454.16 FA 459.14 PR 481.41
  492.14 492.33 TB 514.3
  BO 587.14 594.24 LA 632.35
  GG 682.1 684.36 ML 738.12
  740.8 742.3 OV 752.33
  RH 803.23 BM 837.28 TH 850.24

REMAINING SP 51.16 SB 217.26
  JD 612.32

REMAINS WM 62.1 FG 187.9
  BO 602.15 GG 671.3 NT 701.2

REMARK DV 146.9 151.20
  MN 375.38 FA 469.40 IL 649.31

REMARKABLE OA 23.19 HT 41.14
  SP 47.29 TP 336.32 LA 642.42
  NT 706.36 706.38 707.40
  MD 808.20 810.34

REMARKABLY CH 274.29

REMARKED OA 32.33 DV 160.13
  MN 377.36

REMARKS MN 377.25 GG 673.5

REMEDY DV 144.19

REMEMBER WM 56.37 60.39 60.40
  63.22 PO 114.15 TF 122.19
  DV 184.26 GF 238.37 OC 284.24
  295.14 BL 350.15 355.37
  358.20 WP 392.23 YT 403.23
  HD 456.3 456.5 FA 471.13
  471.14 471.18 471.20
  PR 475.42 512.12 BO 595.10
  JD 615.4 628.7 GG 663.30
  663.34 698.29 NT 701.14
  701.18 702.10 LL 771.3

REMEMBERED MO 7.7 WM 56.10
  EA 82.9 83.35 92.5 PO 97.38
  TF 131.22 DV 145.31 149.40
  174.41 FG 195.36 SS 203.4
  210.14 GF 235.2 239.29
  OC 296.13 EE 329.33 YT 402.6
  403.24 FA 462.28 464.31
  PR 473.9 SU 528.18 533.41
  BO 594.37 595.21 595.33 600.1
  NT 706.20 ML 737.30 RR 782.29

REMEMBERING SP 49.29 PO 103.41
  TF 131.27 FG 190.13 HD 456.6

REMEMBRANCE PO 103.27

REMINDED OA 24.15 WM 67.3
  TF 125.25 DV 153.38 SS 200.26
  SD 416.34 421.42 OV 749.2
  TH 851.31

REMINDER DV 155.5

REMINDS WM 57.14 DV 150.16

REMINISCENCE BL 360.34

REMISS NT 705.16

REMNANT MO 2.5 OA 37.24

REMNANT (CONT.) ML 732.28 732.29

REMNANTS SD 411.10 OV 748.36

REMONSTRANCE MO 6.11 OC 291.35

REMONSTRATED MO 13.11 GF 236.9
  IL 653.34 RH 801.42

REMORSE OA 36.16 36.20 37.6

REMOTE DV 177.15 WS 255.7
  MN 368.7 HD 448.15 PR 492.16
  501.42 502.1 TB 524.4
  WR 557.37 563.6 565.38 577.13
  581.23 BO 591.6 594.7 596.16
  604.15 JD 620.24 623.40
  626.41 GG 661.28 670.35
  682.31 690.39 ML 722.23
  737.18 MD 823.27 BM 827.4
  830.35

REMOTELY BL 347.27 GG 674.6

REMOTENESS GG 674.2

REMOTE-SEEMING BL 358.10

REMOVE HD 444.21 OV 757.18

REMOVED TF 129.19 131.5
  DV 172.42 177.15 SS 207.23
  BL 364.16 HD 451.17 PR 480.4
  RH 801.39 MD 826.1

REMOVING MO 5.26

RENAISSANCE PR 481.9 TH 844.20
  848.40

RENAISSANCE ENGLISH EA 86.2 86.5

RENDED FG 188.13

RENDER WM 56.2

RENDERED WM 55.42 EA 72.16
  LL 763.40

RENEWED EE 313.41 PP 433.10
  OV 759.7

RENEWING EE 314.2

RENOIR LL 770.1

RENSHAW OV 755.35 757.3 757.9
  757.14 757.22 760.4

RENSHAW (SEE EDITH, WILL;
  MRS. RENSHAW)

RENT SP 53.11 PO 109.41

RENTED RR 779.17 TH 847.38

RENTS PO 112.2

REP SS 202.37

REPAINTED RR 779.30

REPAIR EE 307.10

REPARATION OC 301.21

REPARTEE MN 368.8

RE-PASS OA 26.6

REPEAT OA 26.20 WP 391.20
  392.20 LL 777.15 MD 816.12
  823.19

REPEATED HT 43.39 WM 57.2
  60.16 62.5 EA 79.38
  TF 135.17 DV 142.40 143.31
  157.24 170.23 180.16
  FG 188.33 SS 198.26
  WS 250.30 262.39 263.42
  OC 288.19 294.39 TP 344.22
  344.26 345.4 BL 364.6
  MN 368.20 369.5 369.19
  WP 383.7 YT 401.37
  SD 412.11 424.40 HD 453.26
  PR 475.16 507.34 SU 540.30
  WR 550.40 SM 582.19
  JD 623.42 IL 653.10 655.10
  658.31 GG 672.29 675.15
  677.1 685.8 692.7
  ML 746.24 OV 749.17 RH 801.32

REPEATEDLY WM 60.17 WS 257.11
  OC 300.33 BL 358.41
  ML 728.35

REPEATING EA 85.18 WS 262.6
  PR 505.23

REPELLED WM 60.24 HD 450.15
  LL 776.19

REPELLENT EA 79.23 PR 497.2
  BO 598.30 NT 707.27*

REPELLING NT 707.31 710.8
  710.31 710.32

REPENT DV 184.27

REPENTANCE OA 37.7 LL 778.2

REPENTED BO 598.10 IL 659.34

REPLACE OC 289.3

REPLACED OA 36.41 OC 288.35
  WR 556.21

REPLACES BL 360.22

REPLACING OA 37.17 DV 162.33

REPLIES TP 335.34

REPLY MO 5.37 OA 32.15 38.7
  PO 100.41 TF 124.24
  DV 142.31 147.37 152.19
  175.4 182.15 GF 234.25
  240.20 OC 285.24 EE 303.20
  TP 335.3 MN 367.22 373.38
  HD 443.32 LA 639.20
  GG 667.26 674.22 MD 816.15

REPLYING BL 360.30 FA 470.23

REPORT CH 281.32 LL 763.12

REPORTS NT 721.9 LL 763.8

REPOSE MO 13.25 OA 23.18

REVOLUTION

REVOLUTION   GG 661.26   NT 701.18
   721.11

REVOLUTIONARIES   NT 707.14

REVOLUTIONS   NT 706.9

REVOLVE   PO 106.22

REVOLVER   RR 786.33

REVOLVING   SG 232.41

REVULSION   EA 83.18   PO 113.7
   TF 121.24   127.26   DV 155.15
   BL 364.8

RHAPSODIC   HD 453.27   NT 715.33

RHEUMATIC   ML 730.32   731.39

RHEUMATISM   HT 39.24   WM 56.16
   SS 198.34

RHINE   BO 594.30   598.35   599.5
   599.26   599.29   600.9

RHINE VALLEY   BO 599.35

RHUBARB   GG 673.37

RHYTHM   MO 3.18   TB 521.24   521.28
   SU 528.24   GG 684.2   684.7

RHYTHMIC   EA 85.15

RHYTHMICALLY   PO 106.22   TF 118.19
   WS 252.31   SD 411.6   423.8
   WR 561.13   569.11*

RIB   HT 41.21   EA 93.17   FG 194.21

RIBBED   MO 1.13   OC 283.30
   LA 634.26

RIBBONS   DV 139.28

RIBS   SM 585.2   585.23   585.34

RICE   GG 673.42

RICH   MO 15.4   WM 55.30   65.26
   69.14   EA 86.8   TF 128.2   130.33
   DV 144.5   178.32   FG 187.6
   SS 204.35   208.15   SG 221.32
   EE 304.30   307.16   TP 339.2
   BL 347.25   347.30   348.33   351.3
   355.32   355.39   359.37   361.10
   361.18   MN 373.23   FA 460.41
   PR 481.25   481.32   WR 546.8
   SM 583.31   JD 605.14   606.36
   607.8   618.24   GG 661.11   699.2
   NT 701.28   701.29   704.29   705.1
   705.3   705.21   716.35   716.36
   719.25   719.26   719.27
   ML 728.10   OV 748.30   755.11
   RH 792.6

RICHARD   EA 74.33   74.34   77.22
   77.30   77.41   79.18   79.42
   82.26   82.27   83.1   84.26
   85.21   85.28   85.30   86.7
   86.29   88.25   88.26

RICHER   DV 179.36

RICHLY   MO 8.1   WM 65.25

RICHMOND PARK   RH 796.28

RICHNESS   DV 160.20   SU 531.10

RICKETY   TP 337.32   PR 503.3

RID   DV 153.17   153.22   154.6
   SG 224.3   WS 260.14   PP 431.9
   TB 516.26   LA 634.9   GG 681.8
   NT 710.38   ML 732.36   732.40
   741.3   OV 747.31   RR 784.20
   MD 817.38   818.2

RIDDEN   PR 492.32   WR 551.15
   551.30   RH 793.7

RIDDINGS   GG 667.28   668.13
   668.28   669.28   699.17

RIDE   SP 49.13   PO 109.3
   TF 131.13   TP 334.27   334.30
   PR 478.38   491.30   491.36
   491.38   492.31   493.7   WR 550.31
   550.35   550.39   GG 696.30
   RH 793.16   794.25   804.23
   804.27

RIDES   RH 793.25   804.36

RIDGE   WM 62.22   EA 72.25
   PO 114.41   EE 305.1   PR 487.14
   487.17   487.19   487.33   495.9
   496.28   498.23

RIDGES   PR 497.17   497.36   497.37

RIDGE-TRACK   PR 497.34

RIDICULE   DV 137.28   PR 482.9
   511.39   ML 741.6

RIDICULOUS   EA 82.18   DV 159.20
   GF 234.13   CH 274.8   PR 473.8
   482.10   TB 517.13   519.18
   IL 650.21   657.36   NT 708.20
   712.13   ML 731.41   LL 773.30
   BM 840.36

RIDICULOUSLY   SU 544.35   BO 587.4
   LA 642.17   BM 839.40

RIDICULOUSNESS   LA 642.23   642.35

RIDING   PO 96.28   DV 140.26
   157.26   FG 191.3   PR 485.15
   497.8   WR 550.21   551.6   551.7
   RH 793.19   793.27   BM 830.8

RIDING-BOOTS   PR 484.7   506.20
   511.13   WR 558.18

RIDING-BREECHES   PR 483.42   494.18

RIDING-HABIT   WR 563.3

RIDING-MUSCLES   PO 96.12

RIDING-SUIT   WR 551.7

RIFLE   PO 105.13   PR 506.39

RIFLE-FIRE   EE 330.3

RIFLES   PO 106.36

RIGHT-BANK   BO 599.42

RIGHTEOUSLY   IL 652.31

RIGHTEOUSNESS   OV 752.39

RIGHT-O   BM 841.12

RIGHTS   TF 132.35   DV 151.11
   185.15   PR 503.36   503.38
   NT 706.34

RIGID   WM 68.35   69.13
   PO 97.11   103.10   103.16
   TF 121.20   121.31   123.39
   DV 138.4   152.32   153.10
   171.1   SG 227.6   OC 301.19
   SD 417.41   ML 732.19

RIGIDITY   GG 693.22

RIGIDLY   PO 116.18

RIGLEY   OC 292.9   292.19
   293.1

RIGLEY   (SEE JACK; MR. RIGLEY,
   MRS. RIGLEY)

RIGLEYS   OC 292.9

RIGLEY'S   OC 292.39

RIGOROUSLY   DV 153.38

RILED   MN 374.10

RIM   MO 16.15   SU 529.36
   ML 734.19

RIMMED   FG 189.19

RIMS   WM 69.3   FG 194.15

RING   MO 10.32   11.16   WM 56.9
   EA 72.5   DV 167.35   SG 226.30
   GF 240.22   MN 371.13
   IL 647.17   648.15   648.16
   GG 662.25   687.35   NT 712.17
   712.22   ML 728.33   OV 749.24
   749.25

RINGED   YT 403.8

RINGING   DV 173.26   173.29
   WS 248.28   BL 356.17
   GG 665.2   684.34   ML 734.6
   LL 770.11   RR 786.5

RINGS   FG 194.25   PR 484.42
   OV 749.24

RINSING   PR 501.10   BO 595.7

RIO GRANDE CANYON   PR 493.29

RIOTIN'   SP 48.17

RIPE   OA 26.25   SU 532.35
   544.39   WR 561.8

RIPEN   SU 530.19   530.37
   OV 748.9

RIPENED RR 782.10

RIPENESS TF 132.20

RIPENING MO 4.32 OC 286.41
　ML 723.26

RIPPED WS 244.11 HD 455.10

RIPPING SP 52.39 TF 122.25
　OC 287.22

RIPPLE LA 645.7

RIPPLE-RUSTLING WR 574.3

RIPPLES WR 572.19

RIPPLING LA 640.42 641.2

RISE MO 4.4 OA 36.14 SP 48.21
　TF 121.5 DV 151.32 152.41
　154.8 FG 189.15 SS 208.17
　WS 244.17 CH 278.40 281.12
　WP 386.26 SD 414.30 HD 454.6
　455.37 PR 483.19 SU 529.37
　GG 690.16 NT 711.9 711.10
　711.12 ML 740.24 BM 829.31
　836.40

RISEN OA 32.40 FG 194.28
　HD 450.32 IL 658.18 GG 689.39
　OV 749.18 BM 838.1

RISES HT 39.27 GG 695.35

RISING MO 2.15 WM 60.29
　EA 71.19 74.30 PO 101.34
　106.40 TF 122.1 129.16
　DV 142.33 FG 196.24 SB 216.36
　WS 265.23 SC 271.33 CH 278.7
　OC 295.21 EE 303.11 TP 341.30
　WP 390.14 FA 469.6 TB 517.38
　525.39 527.25 WR 552.4 552.32
　GG 684.22 687.13 690.18
　694.13 694.26 NT 709.29
　ML 723.30 741.42 OV 752.42
　MD 818.41

RISK OA 35.16 DV 143.38
　EE 321.13 TP 335.10 WP 386.19
　ML 736.41 MD 821.12

RISKS NT 713.22

RITUAL SU 532.7 JD 617.23
　617.31 617.41

RITUALISTIC JD 619.2

RIVAL MO 13.22 OA 35.17

RIVER PO 105.24 107.1 107.3
　111.10 TF 122.6 SS 199.38
　BL 359.21 MN 371.10 FA 459.42
　WR 556.12 558.36 561.14
　561.28 567.31 578.28
　SM 586.17 BO 595.4 599.12
　OV 748.32 748.40 749.31
　750.39 BM 829.26 TH 844.28
　847.42 848.12

RIVERS WR 569.21 578.16

RIVERSIDE DRIVE TH 850.1

RIVULETS GF 235.6

ROAD MO 1.1 1.11 1.23 1.26
　2.1 OA 23.25 SP 47.25 WM 60.5
　PO 95.2 95.12 105.28
　TF 118.19 118.33 121.36
　122.35 DV 136.16 139.5 160.35
　160.39 162.13 166.32 173.34
　FG 194.30 SS 198.3 198.28
　198.31 GF 234.16 234.34
　235.35 SC 270.37 272.11
　OC 286.30 290.39 EE 304.33
　330.26 330.37 331.16 TP 336.4
　MN 371.37 372.21 372.22
　373.17 376.18 377.11 378.1
　WP 379.7 379.33 380.7 385.5
　385.26 390.35 SD 411.24
　411.30 411.32 423.9 PP 429.4
　429.13 430.32 431.26 433.3
　435.41 436.22 HD 448.22
　FA 460.22 461.40 470.14
　PR 497.19 SU 533.6 WR 551.16
　561.30 JD 624.24 LA 630.34
　631.28 634.6 634.11 634.19
　643.34 IL 650.2 GG 668.31

ROADS DV 136.7 PP 432.17
　WR 566.37 BO 593.21

ROADSIDE TF 118.23

ROAM MD 815.36

ROAMING SU 531.8

ROAN WR 551.7

ROAR MO 16.34 SP 47.7 WR 578.36
　BO 600.15 RH 795.23

ROARED GF 238.14 EE 304.12
　ML 745.39

ROARING FG 193.18 GF 238.27
　TP 335.23 BL 352.37 362.9
　PP 436.11 WR 568.39 569.18

ROAST GG 674.28

ROB EA 78.6

ROBE GG 694.38 OV 757.26 759.14

ROBELESS WR 580.32 OV 759.30

ROBE-LIKE WR 568.33

ROBERT LL 761.22 761.32 761.34
　762.10 762.12 762.28 762.38
　763.17 763.34 764.1 764.3
　764.18 764.37 764.42 765.13
　765.15 765.21 765.23 765.34
　765.36 766.2 767.37 768.19
　768.27 769.14 769.24 769.25
　769.30 770.33 770.42 771.42
　774.14 774.17 774.25 774.27
　774.34 774.41 775.9 775.28
　775.33 775.35 776.6 776.17
　776.18 776.31 776.40 777.10
　778.8 778.35

ROBERT BODOIN MD 816.20 817.2

ROBERT'S LL 764.7 768.18

ROBES WR 580.4 580.18 580.25
　OV 759.29

ROBINS SS 204.22

ROBIN'S EE 304.25

ROBINSON CRUSOE IL 653.18

ROBUST EE 305.33 313.12
　313.33 PP 435.22 PR 474.20

ROBUSTNESS EE 304.21 314.10

ROCK SG 225.13 BL 355.27
　PR 483.37 483.40 484.3
　484.8 487.17 489.16 492.5
　492.16 494.29 496.38
　496.39 498.35 500.1 510.33
　510.36 SU 539.23 WR 552.4
　552.33 552.34 556.32
　558.11 558.12 558.20
　558.28 558.34 569.22
　578.32 579.24 579.26
　579.40 580.1 BO 589.12
　ML 723.13 725.14 730.33
　733.12 733.29 734.17
　734.40 738.18 738.21

ROCKED OC 296.12 HD 442.11
　PR 499.6 503.30

ROCKER OC 296.34

ROCK-FACES WP 385.31

ROCKIES PR 493.37 497.2

ROCKING DV 161.29 FG 190.5
　192.39 OC 289.13 295.35
　296.31 298.29 TP 336.7
　BL 364.13 JD 621.30

ROCKING-CHAIR OA 26.30
　OC 289.26 JD 619.3

ROCKING-HORSE RH 791.9 791.17
　793.2 793.8 793.29
　801.39 801.41 803.12
　803.28 804.36

ROCKLEY YT 394.21 394.33
　395.32

ROCKLEY (SEE EMMA, HADRIAN,
　MATILDA, TED; MR. ROCKLEY)

ROCKLEYS YT 396.23 396.27
　396.34

ROCK-MOUNTAIN WR 558.15

ROCKS WP 386.19 PR 489.41
　490.5 490.13 490.34 490.41
　494.6 500.42 506.29
　SU 533.34 537.1 543.11
　WR 551.29 556.6 556.30
　559.8 579.19 BO 603.18
　603.19 603.32 603.39
　604.11 LA 631.31 ML 722.32
　723.25 725.2 733.14 734.1
　734.15 738.30 740.11
　740.37 741.8 741.14 741.41
　744.22 745.34

ROCK-SALT

ROCK-SALT   GG 684.20

ROCKY   EE 331.23   PR 489.41   496.7
    SU 530.4   533.6   536.19
    WR 556.18   ML 722.35   733.20
    734.21   736.30

ROCKY MOUNTAINS   PR 487.25
    BM 827.18

RODE   PO 96.29   100.28   111.40
    TF 121.40   EE 317.42   PP 436.9
    PR 481.38   489.17   489.21
    490.36   493.11   493.41   494.36
    495.26   495.32   495.40   499.30
    499.34   511.25   SU 532.31
    ML 725.21   LL 761.10

ROGUE   OA 26.32   27.2

ROGUISH   MN 376.27

ROGUISHLY   OA 25.31   BL 355.7
    LL 762.6

ROGUISHNESS   GG 673.30

ROISTERING   GG 667.1

ROLE   TF 128.20   PR 479.1
    IL 659.9

ROLL   HT 43.6   43.11   EA 84.15
    WP 382.31   BO 596.8   GG 686.13
    ML 745.41   MD 818.4

ROLLED   SS 210.36   SG 224.39
    OC 293.16   EE 321.38   TP 345.33
    MN 367.14   WP 382.19   382.22
    YT 394.13   397.12   PR 494.40
    SU 531.28   BO 604.8   604.23
    JD 616.32   617.21   LA 634.30
    640.27   641.35   OV 758.26
    LL 766.37

ROLLED-UP   JD 618.21

ROLLER-TOWEL   JD 617.10

ROLLESTOUN'S   FG 189.4

ROLLING   HT 43.7   SP 49.25
    WM 54.15   SG 224.27   WS 249.3
    OC 289.17   WP 380.17   FA 468.21
    PR 510.26   LA 646.20   GG 686.6
    NT 708.30   709.1   ML 743.11
    745.24   746.36

ROLLING-STOCK   NT 708.35

ROLLIN'S MILL CROSSING   PP 432.5

ROMAN   PR 477.25   478.8   478.10

ROMAN CATHOLIC   TF 126.2

ROMAN CATHOLIC CHURCH   EE 322.22

ROMAN CATHOLIC RESCUE HOME
    TF 126.29

ROMANCE   MO 6.24   GF 236.17
    EE 305.24   307.36   308.4
    TP 335.40   335.42

ROMANCER   RH 795.20

ROMAN LAW   DV 145.1

ROMANS   EE 324.1

ROMANTIC   SS 206.30   EE 307.35
    PR 481.33

ROMANTICALLY   TB 517.16

ROMANTICISM   WR 549.35

ROME   PR 476.34   477.19

ROMERO   PR 482.13   482.16   482.21
    483.23   483.31   484.6   485.15
    485.18   485.25   486.13   487.37
    488.7   488.29   488.41   489.17
    489.20   489.26   491.2   491.11
    491.21   491.24   491.31   491.33
    491.40   492.8   492.12   492.16
    492.33   492.42   493.10   493.33
    493.34   493.38   494.12   494.22
    495.6   495.8   495.26   495.32
    495.37   495.39   495.40   496.1
    496.9   496.12   497.8   498.19
    498.34   499.1   499.12   499.16
    499.20   499.26   500.12   500.17
    500.24   500.41   501.30   504.3
    506.28   506.33   507.23   510.33
    510.36   511.4   511.15

ROMERO   (SEE SENOR, DOMINGO)

ROMERO'S   PR 483.27   490.13
    490.38   493.10   499.9   510.30
    511.17

ROMPED   MO 7.10

RONALD   LL 762.17

RONALD, UNCLE   (SEE UNCLE RONALD)

ROOF   MO 2.14   22.25   EA 72.20
    82.20   85.5   DV 139.5   167.3
    FG 189.19   SC 268.33   OC 283.33
    EE 304.4   PP 427.3   PR 500.11
    503.17   WR 558.7   562.11   562.17
    564.33   568.23   568.29   570.12
    576.24   576.26   ML 729.42
    741.13   LL 766.22   766.25
    766.29   767.4   767.8   772.29
    773.37   RR 779.3   779.15   779.16
    779.18   779.19   779.28   779.37
    780.8   780.9   782.26   782.32
    782.42   783.5   783.14   785.18
    787.11   789.18

ROOFED   ML 739.32

ROOF-RIDGE   EA 72.28

ROOFS   TF 122.2   WR 552.29   561.33
    561.38   RR 779.35

ROOK   JD 607.23

ROOST   WS 250.15   OC 283.18

ROOT   MO 16.39   PO 109.42

ROOTED   ML 735.21

ROOTS   EA 82.40   83.2   BL 348.2
    362.17   FA 465.37   OV 754.27
    TH 844.19

ROPE   SP 51.21   SS 211.12
    OC 293.19   SD 420.14   420.38
    421.7   421.15   421.17   422.41
    423.2   HD 442.8   PR 494.15
    WR 579.35   BM 831.17

ROPED   FG 192.21

ROPES   DV 141.32   SD 421.18
    421.28   421.32   422.4   425.32

ROSARY   SM 583.31

ROSE   MO 1.20   1.25   2.6   2.32
    3.4   4.7   5.39   6.13   12.15
    12.23   19.6   OA 25.4   27.41
    34.2   38.10   38.15   HT 41.3
    SP 46.11   WM 56.7   56.12
    58.2   58.37   58.41   59.22
    EA 72.18   74.23   76.22   79.37
    80.16   82.14   83.17   84.19
    84.20   86.39   PO 95.19
    107.33   108.9   TF 118.38
    119.10   120.29   123.1   130.24
    132.16   DV 139.19   139.39
    142.27   158.32   164.30
    166.12   170.9   171.11   186.3
    FG 192.18   195.34   SG 221.7
    225.24   225.35   225.39
    226.8   226.11   226.16   227.7
    227.29   227.33   229.9   229.21
    230.2   231.30   GF 235.15
    237.17   239.18   241.5   241.33
    WS 244.22   247.18   249.3
    251.20   257.37   258.36
    263.14   264.4   264.19   264.42
    CH 277.9   278.7   278.19
    279.42   OC 283.21   284.21
    286.28   288.5   289.22   290.27
    292.9   296.35   299.24   299.27
    EE 304.42   305.42   306.2
    326.28   TP 343.31   345.16
    BL 351.18   354.20   356.6
    360.35   WP 382.29   382.34
    383.23   390.13   YT 404.32
    404.34   405.25   SD 412.2
    414.41   415.28   416.8
    416.29   420.17   421.25
    425.27   PP 437.8   439.16
    440.18   HD 443.11   445.3
    450.16   450.30   450.35
    455.40   456.10   FA 461.36
    467.3   468.29   PR 492.25
    500.31   505.28   506.18
    TB 518.19   SU 530.7   532.10
    544.40   WR 555.26   572.4
    SM 582.33   583.29   BO 595.29
    602.1   JD 617.8   618.18
    624.3   LA 639.39   IL 650.32
    658.3   GG 666.12   670.8
    677.8   681.10   694.33   695.1
    695.41   696.12   ML 723.29
    730.4   730.28   738.19   746.7
    OV 749.9   755.33   LL 763.29
    763.31   764.29   766.38
    772.6   773.3   773.36
    RR 782.12   787.16   MD 824.2
    825.2   825.30   BM 837.26
    838.20   841.14

ROSEATE   WR 577.25

ROSE-BERRY   FG 194.12

ROSE-COLOURED   MO 2.3   EA 84.6
  CH 275.26

ROSE-LEAVES   OV 753.8   753.14

ROSE-PETALS   OV 753.10

ROSE-PURPLE   MN 371.19

ROSE-RED   MO 2.11   ML 732.23
  MD 810.37

ROSES   EA 84.13   TF 123.26
  SG 221.4   224.6   225.1   225.24
  225.25   225.31   225.41   226.5
  228.13   FA 464.38   GG 671.5
  NT 718.26   ML 723.21   736.11
  MD 810.38   811.5

ROSILY   WM 68.5

ROSINESS   EE 326.29

ROSY   MO 2.8   5.2   WM 55.39
  DV 158.22   WS 246.3   SD 423.29
  SU 530.34   533.39   540.14   542.8
  LA 637.39   ML 726.8

ROSY-GOLDEN   SU 536.5

ROT   EE 307.23   TB 525.11

ROTATE   TH 845.7

ROTHERHAM COLLEGE   JD 608.8

ROTTEN   SP 53.16   EA 77.1
  MN 373.29   HD 450.13   BO 593.23
  IL 659.18

ROTTEN-HEARTED   PP 427.32

ROTTENNESS   DV 165.18

ROUE   WS 252.37

ROUGE   YT 399.10

ROUGH   MO 5.19   11.37   17.30
  19.20   WM 65.17   PO 110.10
  DV 140.18   143.10   175.15
  184.14   184.40   FG 190.6   195.37
  SS 197.24   211.12   CH 276.6
  OC 283.15   EE 303.4   313.23
  327.8   TP 340.25   BL 363.41
  WP 388.29   SD 423.1   PP 430.2
  437.19   HD 449.15   449.17
  WR 551.28   JD 617.35   GG 689.25
  ML 739.8

ROUGHLY   MO 5.22   DV 184.12
  184.24   186.15   SS 201.27
  GF 238.30   WS 244.13   249.17
  CH 276.18   TP 345.18   PP 429.34
  430.10   437.18   440.3   GG 665.19

ROUGHS   OA 35.31

ROUGH-VOICED   DV 185.31

ROUNDABOUT   TP 337.29

ROUNDABOUTS   TP 337.13

ROUNDED   HD 442.3   PR 496.38

ROUND-EYED   JD 613.24

ROUNDING   OC 288.26

ROUNDISH   FA 468.13

ROUNDNESS   SU 530.28

ROUNDNESSES   ML 741.28

ROUND-ROOFED   TF 117.9

ROUND-SHOULDERED   OA 31.17

ROUSE   PO 116.19   FG 192.39
  SC 271.25   BL 360.6   WP 389.3

ROUSED   MO 16.23   OA 25.26   26.36
  29.40   33.3   WM 54.23   65.3
  PO 96.34   116.4   TF 126.12
  129.22   130.20   FG 191.24
  SS 201.8   GF 237.19   239.27
  WS 244.22   253.21   254.7
  OC 297.10   TP 342.33   WP 386.7
  YT 397.36   SD 423.12   PP 434.21
  WR 562.40   BO 604.22   613.20
  614.21   LA 633.30   NT 716.32
  LL 769.17

ROUSING   WS 254.15   262.33
  BL 361.25   MN 375.34   SU 536.15
  NT 711.30

ROUSSEAU   LL 770.2

ROUTINE   EA 82.7   DV 142.39
  170.29   GF 240.13

ROVING   TP 336.34   HD 449.21
  PR 507.21

ROW   MO 17.35   OA 25.4   GF 242.41
  243.11   SD 421.30   LA 639.2
  640.12   ML 722.28   725.22   740.5
  741.19   LL 765.2   BM 835.11
  835.36

ROW-BOAT   ML 734.21   735.10

ROW-BOATS   ML 725.23

ROWBOTHAM   (SEE EMMA, HILDA,
  LAURIE)

ROWBOTHAMS   CH 278.24

ROWED   MD 813.22

ROWING   SB 214.41   WP 386.25
  PR 496.22

ROWS   TF 117.12   DV 136.6   167.22
  SS 197.29   SB 217.4   OC 283.27
  PR 481.1   SU 528.36   536.23
  BO 593.23

ROYAL   WS 249.20   249.26   PR 473.4
  473.7   475.35   475.36   475.41
  476.12   GG 671.1   671.10

ROYALLY   ML 726.27

ROYALTY   WS 251.36

RUB   PO 96.11   BL 362.22
  HD 456.12   SU 534.1
  JD 617.18   ML 740.9

RUBBED   MO 21.13   PO 102.35
  MN 376.3   SD 423.4
  PP 433.24   HD 451.18
  WR 577.2   577.23   JD 617.32
  617.34   617.42   NT 703.40

RUBBER   DV 159.2

RUBBING   HT 44.12   EA 73.26
  DV 170.22   SB 218.33
  OC 297.30   BL 362.21

RUBBISH   SP 45.13   SS 197.9
  JD 609.12

RUBBLE   MO 2.35

RUBY   SB 216.28

RUDDIER   WR 581.4

RUDDINESS   SB 217.22   WR 556.10

RUDDY   MO 18.6   18.11
  SP 49.9   TF 123.41   DV 149.42
  SS 198.6   SG 228.31
  EE 304.20   306.16   322.35
  322.36   TP 336.14   337.25
  BL 351.40   358.12   MN 367.2
  368.2   PR 511.26   SU 532.12
  BO 596.30   GG 670.24

RUDDY-FACED   WS 245.15

RUDE   OA 28.8   PR 478.22
  478.24   478.27   BO 587.30
  598.42   ML 727.28   TH 848.22

RUDELY   JD 626.1   IL 654.19

RUDENESS   MN 370.40   PR 477.20
  478.21

RUDIMENTARY   OA 31.26

RUDOLF VALENTINO   IL 659.3
  659.8   NT 704.11

RUE   DV 141.37

RUFFLED   OA 24.38   SS 202.2
  WP 388.22   OV 751.18
  RR 786.2

RUG   EA 77.5   SS 206.36
  OC 293.16   SU 534.33   534.36
  LL 766.26   767.1   767.23
  770.9

RUGGED   PO 96.18

RUGS   WM 63.30   70.18
  SS 206.37   GG 669.13   682.27
  LL 766.14   770.18   770.21
  770.23   775.27

RUIN   GF 238.22   CH 282.20
  TB 525.3   ML 724.41

RUINED PO 96.25 GF 235.14
  239.39 241.28 242.24 243.19
  CH 277.34 SD 411.8 BO 593.21
  MD 818.40

RUINING TB 520.5 520.6

RUINS FG 187.6

RULE OA 31.23 WM 64.39 EA 75.32
  DV 147.18 SB 218.20 YT 399.15
  PR 483.3 LL 766.3 RR 780.8

RULE BRITANNIA EE 326.25

RULED DV 140.24 140.25 EE 316.4

RUMBLE MO 11.34 DV 139.9

RUMBLED DV 161.25 OC 286.5
  LA 634.31 ML 746.22

RUMBLING ML 744.29 744.37

RUMBLINGS ML 734.3

RUMINATING JD 618.41

RUMMAGED SD 420.12 PR 495.22
  OV 754.32

RUN MO 12.13 20.18 OA 25.9
  30.37 SP 49.5 WM 56.28 60.26
  EA 89.21 PO 100.16 108.16
  108.19 TF 120.36 DV 143.8
  FG 188.26 SB 214.30 SG 229.1
  GF 238.38 243.14 OC 283.18
  292.40 EE 303.18 303.20
  316.30 PR 488.37 494.32
  SU 531.22 WR 571.25 BO 594.22
  LA 637.31 GG 674.26 674.27
  685.31 NT 707.5 710.3
  OV 758.5 758.12 758.25 759.16
  759.30 759.32 RR 780.4
  RH 802.27 MD 808.37 BM 830.22
  TH 845.22 851.19

RUNABOUT BM 834.29

RUNG TF 120.42 RH 802.23

RUNGS TF 119.31

RUNLET WR 552.2

RUNNER PR 485.11

RUNNIN' PP 433.9

RUNNING MO 22.18 OA 24.13 SP 48.42
  WM 55.8 70.23 EA 73.23 76.26
  PO 110.34 112.1 113.13 113.37
  TF 117.1 119.14 121.32 122.36
  DV 143.38 148.19 148.31
  162.24 176.39 FG 189.16
  190.16 194.28 SB 214.23
  SC 271.28 272.14 OC 294.2
  EE 317.4 329.11 330.24
  MN 377.27 PP 428.35 428.36
  436.17 438.16 HD 450.4 450.40
  FA 460.27 PR 489.39 491.7
  510.31 TB 517.7 SU 528.27
  531.12 531.39 WR 551.19
  554.29 561.20 574.17 575.27
  BO 587.21 597.32 JD 617.3

RUNNING (CONT.) 617.14 LA 639.42
  NT 705.37 709.5 ML 728.12
  OV 756.33 759.17 759.37
  RH 803.35 BM 828.18 TH 848.3
  848.7

RUNS SD 411.1 PR 487.12
  OV 750.37 758.35

RUPTURE PR 509.31 BO 597.35

RURAL TP 334.9

RUSH TP 334.7 334.9 PR 496.29
  IL 651.11 654.35 GG 687.14
  OV 749.2 RH 802.14 MD 805.30
  BM 841.30

RUSHED CH 274.30 TP 343.9
  343.13 343.18 343.19 343.23
  PR 496.20 498.28 WR 559.7
  578.28 IL 651.6 654.11
  NT 713.10 LL 776.29 RH 803.22

RUSHES RH 802.17

RUSHING MO 16.33 GF 238.24
  TP 335.2 WP 387.20 PR 496.15
  509.25 WR 556.19 569.27
  574.19 574.20 GG 685.18
  ML 745.33 RH 803.1

RUSKIN MO 6.27 GF 239.17

RUSSET MD 811.42

RUSSIAN BO 587.18 NT 708.26

RUSSIANS MO 6.29

RUST GF 241.31 BO 595.34

RUSTED OV 755.11

RUSTIC JD 608.29

RUSTLE FA 467.31 468.17
  WR 579.13 LL 775.38 TH 846.41

RUSTLED EA 85.32 SS 202.16
  SM 586.15 GG 677.7 691.3

RUSTLING WR 574.15 OV 748.41

RUSTY CH 274.9 274.10 LL 767.29

RUTH JD 605.35

RUTHLESS MD 812.42

RUTS OC 293.2

RYE PO 95.5 95.12 105.25 107.7
  TF 117.4 122.36

RYE-FIELDS PO 95.10

SABBATH GF 234.26

SACK TF 121.3 SD 421.42
  WR 561.4 RR 783.7

SACK-LIKE WS 245.3 WR 578.4

SACKS CH 274.19

SACRAMENT GG 692.31

SACRAMENTS OV 754.7

SACRED MO 7.32 EA 86.37
  EE 314.30 WR 550.4 573.40
  GG 697.33 NT 719.24
  OV 754.8 BM 837.1

SACRED HEART TF 125.35

SACRED HEART CONVENT LL 763.16

SACRIFICE MO 12.38 WM 55.3
  EE 315.1 325.37 329.3
  WR 569.41 570.37 570.40
  571.1 581.27

SACRIFICES WR 550.8

SACRIFICIAL EE 323.37

SACROSANCT GG 662.20

SAD MO 16.28 18.25 22.19
  OA 26.39 28.4 FG 187.19
  194.24 WS 250.4 TP 337.17
  BL 357.25 359.40 FA 468.11
  PR 484.35 WR 564.14 577.19
  SM 582.20 584.40 JD 609.8
  GG 662.11 665.24 ML 727.37
  TH 349.7

SADDENED HD 447.31

SADDER SP 50.41

SADDLE MO 18.38 PO 104.22
  107.28 111.27 PR 491.2
  492.15 493.9 494.14 498.20
  500.36 506.40 506.41
  WR 551.11 555.14 555.23
  555.25 556.28 557.3 558.4
  558.24 559.18

SADDLE-BAGS PR 495.23
  WR 551.10 557.3 558.25

SADDLED BL 363.13 PR 495.39

SADDLE-POUCHES PR 494.21
  500.24

SADDLES PR 494.36 495.2
  495.17 499.27 500.24
  500.25

SAD-FATED LA 641.4*

SADLY MO 20.8 WM 67.39
  WR 564.13 IL 649.27 657.33
  657.37 658.2 GG 697.26
  OV 754.20 BM 829.1

SADNESS MO 8.28 WM 66.31
  SB 216.36 CH 275.29
  WR 577.20

SAFE OA 37.39 SP 47.22
  TF 121.2 125.4 125.39
  DV 143.38 155.29 155.31
  SB 218.33 SG 224.12
  GF 234.34 237.32 238.3

SAFE (CONT.) GF 238.4 239.31
  241.36 WS 259.28 TP 340.18
  MN 371.34 HD 441.2 441.5
  FA 459.31 459.32 PR 478.14
  478.21 WR 550.23 GG 683.32
  683.34 ML 724.10 726.17
  728.17 734.21 RH 797.12
  802.15 MD 821.17 TH 853.32

SAFELY EA 93.38 TF 119.37
  FA 465.23 BO 588.13 594.32
  MD 815.29

SAFER LA 631.21 631.23

SAFETY DV 154.38 166.11
  GF 239.31

SAG LL 761.9

SAGE PR 489.2

SAGGING TF 117.21 127.29

SAIL CH 274.11 TP 335.14
  ML 742.24 743.31 746.31
  746.32

SAILED SP 53.21 EA 72.23
  CH 274.15 SU 528.5 ML 729.27
  740.2 TH 844.22 852.20

SAILING SM 586.16 ML 726.34

SAILING-BOAT ML 725.21

SAILOR DV 141.19 148.21 149.16
  183.14

SAILORS LL 763.13

SAILOR'S DV 149.6 TP 336.34

SAILS WP 379.13

SAINT FG 188.19 188.23

SAINT SEBASTIAN JD 606.31 607.2

SAKE TF 120.27 SS 204.10 205.12
  EE 312.42 TP 346.3 BL 349.28
  SU 529.31 GG 672.30 OV 758.17
  RR 781.22 781.37 784.3
  TH 848.8 849.32

SAKES SD 425.23 TH 848.8

SALAD GG 676.25

SALARY TB 518.32

SALE SS 202.36

SALLIES MN 374.37

SALLOW WP 379.30 380.12 380.19
  388.1 GG 669.21

SALLOWS SS 200.25

SALLY PP 437.34

SALMON CH 278.38 FA 471.6

SALONIKA GG 678.28

SALOTTO TH 848.11 848.15

SALT EE 315.35 MN 377.1
  TB 514.16 514.18 WR 559.4

SALUTATION SU 534.27

SALUTE DV 148.37 SG 226.24
  227.7

SALUTED PO 105.2 108.9 109.4
  DV 174.4 MN 370.13 373.14
  376.26 SU 543.39

SALVATION BL 348.25 BO 594.23
  LA 642.27

SALVE DV 174.6

SAM SP 46.31 46.35 46.39 47.2
  48.16 48.25 48.29 49.5 49.20
  49.33 49.36 49.41 50.9 50.21
  50.26 50.37

SAM ADAMS WS 248.30 250.21
  251.7 251.13 251.33 253.10
  254.9 256.36 256.38 259.34
  260.17 260.28 260.36 262.12
  262.17 262.23 263.30 265.35

SAM COUTTS SP 46.25 46.34 47.1
  47.13* 47.27

SAMPLE WS 247.6 248.11 248.13

SAMPSON GF 238.5 238.9 238.28

SAMUEL TB 518.16

SAN CRISTOBAL PR 481.24 482.18
  489.38

SANCTUARY TF 125.39

SAND LA 631.32 ML 725.24
  RR 788.26

SANDALS SU 532.26 535.6
  WR 558.17 562.37

SANDPAPER EE 328.39

SANDS PR 489.3 ML 722.16

SANDWICH JD 625.23 GG 688.27
  ML 729.17

SANDWICHES ML 729.18

SANDY CH 274.24 OV 748.11

SANDY-GOLD SS 197.8

SANE GG 685.5 691.25 NT 718.5

SANE-SEEMING GG 689.3

SANG MO 16.7 16.8 TF 126.38
  DV 164.12 WS 246.39 247.24
  247.30 262.6 EE 329.27
  TP 341.20 BL 347.15 MN 372.34
  SD 418.39 419.4 FA 464.12
  464.20 465.27 466.18 466.27
  WR 578.21 GG 669.6 676.25
  677.22 BM 836.28 838.13

SANGFROID EE 303.19 317.27

SANG-FROID TP 335.22
  HD 442.33 MD 822.30*

SANGUINE WM 55.29

SANITARY JD 624.29

SANITY GG 692.21

SANK MO 4.1 OA 28.18 30.19
  WM 56.14 65.22 EA 71.33
  72.30 84.24 90.41
  DV 169.4 170.1 FG 194.26
  SS 205.21 SB 219.17
  SG 226.17 OC 283.15 300.6
  EE 312.32 MN 371.41
  SD 421.16 421.25 HD 450.12
  FA 466.39 PR 508.22
  WR 573.27 IL 657.2
  NT 703.33 ML 746.13
  LL 767.1 771.35 BM 840.42

SANSCULOTTE GG 663.39 665.32
  667.30

SANSOVINO RH 794.3 794.5

SANTA BARBARA PR 486.16

SAP SP 49.12 PO 106.27
  EE 313.28 313.29 SU 536.14

SAP-LIKE EE 313.33

SARAPE WR 557.7 559.22
  561.11 562.35 566.34

SARAPES WR 553.26 553.30
  559.20 NT 709.23

SARCASM OA 31.8 31.42
  SP 46.9 WM 58.28 61.34
  61.37 63.9 EA 77.42
  DV 158.36 SS 208.24
  CH 275.13 SD 416.42 418.40
  419.4 JD 622.1 RR 787.5

SARCASMS EA 87.39

SARCASTIC SP 46.17 MN 374.11
  SD 417.3 420.3 JD 622.10
  LL 772.18

SARCASTICALLY MO 15.6
  OA 34.39 HT 41.36 EA 76.31
  76.39 SB 213.14 YT 398.30
  HD 444.38 TB 527.19

SARCOPHAGUS WP 385.41

SARDINES FA 471.5

SARDONIC FG 189.3 BL 351.26
  PR 479.41 482.9 492.29
  TB 513.16 JD 606.27
  LA 630.16 644.4 GG 687.35

SARDONICALLY WP 381.26
  PR 479.42 LA 631.12
  RR 786.22

SASH SU 542.18 WR 564.25
  BM 835.27

SATANIC LA 631.13

SAT'DAY OC 285.38

SATIN WM 55.32 BM 842.29

SATINY GF 241.32 SU 539.33

SATIRE PO 99.15 JD 606.28

SATIRIC FG 187.21

SATIRICAL HT 41.11

SATIRICALLY MN 370.36 378.19
 RR 786.20

SATISFACTION HT 44.5 44.14
 SP 47.1 EA 81.36 PO 99.26
 TF 118.2 130.12 130.20 131.2
 132.11 DV 140.36 153.4
 165.41 WS 264.20 SC 269.4
 269.10 TP 334.13 BL 347.21
 348.33 350.3 YT 407.6 407.22
 HD 448.4 TB 519.34 LA 634.41
 NT 710.41 711.27 ML 737.34
 742.42 744.12 MD 815.16
 BM 832.31 832.32 TH 847.40
 853.31

SATISFACTIONS DV 165.38

SATISFACTORILY MD 818.30

SATISFACTORY EE 320.31 YT 408.23
 NT 706.33

SATISFIED EA 80.29 PO 110.36
 TF 131.40 132.13 DV 152.30
 164.23 SS 197.33 205.13
 WS 247.41 EE 319.38 320.13
 320.15 MN 368.34 WP 389.32
 YT 409.38 NT 714.34 OV 749.32

SATISFY MO 2.40 DV 164.5
 SS 208.25 BM 830.29

SATISFYING TH 845.22 851.34

SATURATED HD 451.17 LA 638.11

SATURDAY MO 22.28 DV 164.14
 SC 267.25 EE 320.9 TP 336.1
 MN 368.13 368.31 370.26 371.7
 374.42 FA 471.18 PR 488.18
 JD 626.8

SATURNINE CH 275.33 WP 382.21
 SU 544.22

SATYR JD 606.29 607.1 LA 630.28
 OV 757.31

SATYRS OV 757.18 757.32 758.7

SAUCE GG 674.29 689.15
 NT 719.10 RR 780.1

SAUCED RR 780.1

SAUCEPAN OC 286.29 286.36
 PP 439.3 PR 501.6 501.11
 JD 616.12 616.21

SAUCER ML 743.22

SAUNTERED TF 122.11 SG 221.21
 YT 403.17 TB 524.5 IL 651.32
 651.42

SAUNTERING TF 121.40 YT 400.3

SAUSAGES CH 274.20

SAVAGE OA 26.18 DV 167.14
 SC 270.4 EE 303.27 303.28
 307.6 323.38 WP 386.9
 PR 485.30 507.17 WR 549.12
 568.38 570.4 578.41 BO 599.33
 600.11 LA 644.1 MD 812.2

SAVAGELY WR 573.39

SAVAGES WM 67.39 WR 549.21
 549.22 550.12 550.15 578.36

SAVAGE'S WR 549.18

SAVE MO 16.20 16.36 WM 59.17
 EA 86.19 PO 104.21 105.16
 TF 120.30 DV 143.20 147.24
 167.37 180.30 FG 187.26
 SS 199.38 209.37 WS 261.28
 SC 268.24 270.35 CH 276.17
 OC 296.28 EE 306.13 322.13
 325.4 BL 353.5 MN 370.8
 PP 434.23 HD 441.18 447.3
 456.15 FA 464.22 PR 490.18
 TB 520.1 WR 548.30 559.15
 561.37 562.32 566.12 566.15
 570.16 BO 598.15 600.20
 JD 608.5 LA 630.33 631.6
 639.4 642.17 642.18 642.20
 GG 666.22 680.24 ML 734.23
 RR 781.4 MD 821.11 BM 829.39
 830.8 835.26 837.8

SAVED MO 1.6 HT 39.9 EA 76.19
 SC 267.8 269.31 EE 323.8
 FA 462.23 BO 594.22 LL 764.36
 MD 807.11 810.34 TH 846.19
 846.25 846.26

SAVING LA 642.24

SAVINGS CH 275.32 SD 420.8
 FA 463.40

SAVIOUR EE 322.13

SAWN-OFF PR 500.9

SAXON WR 553.28

SAXONS EE 303.31 307.7

SAYIN' SC 272.31 273.1
 CH 279.16

SAYINGS WS 250.29

SCALDING BL 351.35 SD 419.14

SCALES SS 204.7 CH 274.23
 BO 592.17 592.20 592.22

SCALING-LADDER TF 119.17

SCALP MD 813.9

SCALY HT 42.35

SCAMP EE 311.33 FA 467.14

SCANDAL TP 336.26 FA 471.8
 PR 474.34 JD 615.35

SCANDALISES FG 187.29

SCANDALOUS OC 288.8

SCANTY NT 701.2

SCAR PO 98.35 OC 292.11
 BL 358.13 363.16 363.18
 364.7 364.10

SCARAB ML 728.34

SCARCE OA 26.3 FG 191.19
 SB 216.17 OC 297.34
 PP 437.23

SCARCELY OA 27.15 29.31
 30.32 33.1 SP 49.3
 WM 70.14 EA 77.28 84.20
 PO 96.13 105.38 110.23
 TF 134.27 135.6 135.16
 DV 141.22 145.5 145.10
 146.13 153.26 168.37
 170.39 174.19 181.32
 FG 187.22 SB 215.9 216.34
 WS 244.5 255.6 257.10
 263.13 SC 270.7 SD 424.38
 PP 432.33 438.37 WR 566.4
 JD 607.30 IL 651.28
 GG 696.18 ML 735.19
 741.42 OV 752.18

SCARE JD 612.42

SCARED EE 318.10 PP 437.37
 PR 485.24 SM 583.7
 JD 612.41 624.16 GG 676.8

SCARF DV 147.3 SG 224.7
 SC 268.13 YT 396.17
 HD 444.20 FA 458.11
 RR 787.30

SCARGILL STREET SP 45.29
 SC 267.16

SCARLET MO 1.33 WM 63.36
 PO 96.1 107.14 107.29
 TF 119.5 DV 161.12
 FG 194.12 SS 200.38 204.6
 SG 226.6 WS 250.33
 SC 268.25 OC 283.13
 SU 532.15 534.11 534.40
 WR 551.8 564.23 564.25
 568.32 573.35 578.11
 GG 683.22 693.31

SCARLET-SHADED GF 235.31

SCARP WP 390.38

SCARRED PO 99.5 BL 364.10
 WP 388.8

SCARS BL 357.18

SCATTER SC 270.33

SCATTERED MO 19.25 OA 36.2
 PO 106.37 107.30 TF 117.18

SCATTERED (CONT.) OC 292.6
   WP 387.12 SD 411.11 412.4
   HD 452.31

SCATTERING WR 555.36

SCENE MO 1.13 TF 121.32
   DV 159.17 GF 241.12 CH 280.6
   OC 290.12 BL 362.23 YT 405.35
   FA 459.3 ML 730.2 MD 814.41
   BM 841.24

SCENERY SS 201.39

SCENES DV 165.14

SCENT MO 1.30 OA 27.37 WM 64.7
   EA 91.16 PO 105.24 DV 168.15
   SS 207.6 SB 217.9 SG 225.34
   226.4 EE 329.25 BL 351.32
   351.34 354.37 MN 373.18
   SU 529.16 WR 565.33 569.14
   JD 610.5 LA 640.9 GG 698.37
   699.3 ML 731.18 OV 747.19
   747.35 750.31 753.9 754.25*
   LL 770.41

SCENTED PO 106.26 BL 358.30

SCENTLESS WM 64.7 64.11 64.16
   SG 225.35 PR 477.24 479.34
   OV 753.37

SCENTS CH 274.20 TB 522.34

SCEPTICAL SU 528.2 JD 616.26

SCEPTICISM TH 853.35

SCHEME MD 814.15 817.2

SCHEMED BL 348.14 YT 403.12
   NT 706.42

SCHEMES MD 821.3

SCHEMING PR 506.38 MD 811.33
   814.4

SCHOLAR ML 728.3

SCHOLARSHIP SS 208.12

SCHOLASTIC PR 480.39 TH 850.15
   850.19 850.20 853.34

SCHONER PO 102.5

SCHOOL DV 163.38 CH 274.2
   OC 287.1 EE 310.28 WP 380.15
   YT 396.3 GG 661.3 667.30
   RH 790.34 800.11 BM 831.32
   835.3

SCHOOL-FELLOWS YT 396.18

SCHOOLGIRL GG 665.7 668.25
   687.37

SCHOOLGIRL'S GG 667.5

SCHOOLING MD 819.12

SCHOOLMISTRESS CH 275.6 275.11
   275.14 278.27

SCHOOLROOM BM 833.37 834.5
   834.42 835.9

SCHOOL-ROOM SP 45.26

SCHOOLTEACHER JD 608.7

SCHOOL-TEACHERS YT 394.38

SCHOPENHAUER MO 6.28

SCHWARZE BESTIE NT 715.5

SCIENTISTS WR 550.8

SCISSORS SS 203.16 203.20
   203.22 203.24 203.25 203.27

SCOFFED FA 464.23

SCOLDED SB 218.14

SCOLDING PO 113.41

SCOOP JD 614.16 614.17

SCOOPED EE 303.37

SCORCHED SB 213.2 WR 574.12

SCORE WM 65.12 WS 262.38
   EE 326.28 326.29

SCORED SS 197.12

SCORES EE 330.26

SCORN MO 9.14 11.10 OA 37.17
   EA 74.23 WS 263.12 WP 385.11

SCORNED OA 33.31 CH 279.2

SCORNFUL DV 141.38 TB 515.5
   LA 643.14 643.15

SCORNFULLY OA 33.5 33.15 33.19
   34.35 PP 428.9 BO 590.18

SCORPION NT 715.2 716.18 716.40

SCOTCH OA 32.30 HT 39.26
   BL 349.22 357.1 HD 444.33

SCOTLAND WP 381.39 PR 473.7

SCOTSMAN BL 348.39 349.4
   BO 589.21

SCOTSMEN BO 589.9

SCOTSWOMAN BL 348.39

SCOTTISH BL 347.16 357.3 359.22
   PR 473.3 473.4 BO 588.28

SCOUNDREL SD 420.5

SCRAGGY PO 95.11

SCRAMBLE CH 274.4 BO 587.37
   ML 733.20

SCRAMBLED TF 119.27 WS 244.14
   SC 269.14 PR 490.12 505.17
   SU 538.37 543.11 LL 776.35

SCRAMBLING PR 490.40 496.22
   ML 733.14

SCRAP DV 160.6 WS 246.9
   PR 496.30 WR 546.5

SCRAPE SP 53.8 BL 352.15

SCRAPER DV 167.35

SCRAPS WP 380.18 HD 442.20

SCRAT' FA 463.32

SCRATCH TP 343.25 MN 377.35
   WR 558.28

SCRATCHED HT 42.35 SS 197.8
   IL 652.37

SCRATCHED-OUT PR 497.12

SCRATCHED-UP SS 197.9

SCRATCHING SP 47.41 OC 292.8
   BO 597.16 JD 607.23

SCREAM TF 121.24 WS 264.5
   EE 306.38 306.39 307.1
   BL 348.6 PR 504.11
   WR 570.10

SCREAMED NT 713.7 ML 731.6
   RH 800.16 803.17

SCREAMING EE 307.1 316.41
   LL 777.31

SCREAMS LL 767.42

SCREEN DV 168.37 WP 385.29
   PR 496.33 WR 557.15
   JD 609.12

SCREENED DV 168.36

SCREENING GG 671.26

SCREENS WR 556.32 JD 608.12

SCREWED DV 174.36 WS 248.36

SCREWS GG 691.19

SCRIBBLED EA 82.10 TF 117.24

SCRIBBLING WS 252.5 TB 518.18

SCRIMMY GF 242.39

SCRIPT WP 380.35

SCROLL BO 596.8

SCRUB PR 487.28 489.15
   WR 551.39

SCRUBBED SP 50.14 50.15

SCRUBBING DV 158.29

SCRUBBING-BRUSH HD 447.30

SCRUFF SB 215.5

SCRUPULOUS

SCRUPULOUS DV 146.35

SCRUPULOUSLY DV 153.42 SG 226.28
YT 399.9 HD 448.2 PR 474.36
ML 743.23

SCRUTINISED WM 66.33

SCRUTINISING WP 380.28

SCRUTINY WP 387.34

SCUDDING OA 24.38

SCUFFLED PO 113.36 OC 290.31

SCULLERY DV 161.15 168.1 168.17
CH 281.22 281.36 OC 291.14
HD 456.19 456.21 JD 616.22
617.8 617.11 618.20 618.26

SCULPTURE EE 308.37

SCUM DV 136.8 MD 819.33 819.34
819.35

SCYLLAS JD 610.26

SCYTHE SB 217.12

SCYTHES PO 106.15

S'D SB 215.37 FA 462.13

SEA EA 83.13 DV 141.23 142.21
166.23 SG 221.28 221.34
225.12 225.27 228.21 228.22
WS 254.31 EE 330.36 332.34
333.1 333.8 TP 337.32
BL 356.1 SD 411.5 411.25
TB 513.16 SU 528.4 528.10
528.11 528.32 529.6 529.33
530.5 530.9 530.18 535.34
535.37 536.12 540.21
SM 582.29 GG 681.2 690.17
NT 701.24 ML 722.32 723.4
723.26 723.30 723.31 723.38
724.13 724.30 724.35 725.29
731.20 733.13 733.25 733.32
734.1 734.2 734.10 734.12
734.14 734.17 734.20 735.9
736.42 737.1 738.29 739.8
740.2 740.12 740.19 740.21
740.22 740.42 741.14 742.24
743.2 743.7 743.11 743.30
744.22 744.24 745.6 745.11
745.24 745.28 745.33 745.36
746.14 746.31 746.33 746.36
OV 755.17 755.18 755.20
MD 821.4 821.31

SEABED LA 631.31

SEA-BIRD OA 23.16

SEA-BIRDS ML 734.40 738.21
741.15 741.39

SEA-COLOURED GG 664.39

SEA-FOG ML 723.28

SEA-FOLIAGE ML 735.18

SEAFRONT MD 819.29

SEAGULL EA 72.23

SEA-GULL MO 2.26

SEAGULLS LA 639.9

SEALED PR 511.1 IL 656.37

SEA-LEVEL WR 553.11

SEA-LINE SU 529.39

SEALING DV 142.34

SEALS ML 742.36

SEAM PO 98.35

SEA-MAIDEN MO 17.13

SEAMING GF 234.19

SEA-MIST ML 738.25

SEANCE GG 670.27

SEA-PEBBLED SG 228.14

SEA-PEBBLES SG 224.18

SEARCH WS 254.38 YT 408.26
GG 670.21

SEARCHED SP 49.37 50.5
SG 227.34 WS 265.34 WP 386.15

SEARCHERS FG 192.30

SEARCHING DV 176.4 EE 325.4
TP 338.38 WP 380.11 380.21
JD 624.40 GG 696.39 ML 728.34

SEARCHINGLY LL 772.12

SEARED DV 180.9

SEAS SU 529.9 GG 662.12 699.1
ML 738.24 741.32

SEA'S SU 529.36 532.9 ML 734.19
735.5

SEA-SHELL OV 755.14 755.32

SEA-SHELLS WR 569.9

SEA-SHORE ML 722.16

SEASIDE OA 37.41 SG 221.1
RH 800.35 800.36 801.1 801.9
801.22

SEA-SIDE SG 222.39

SEASON EE 313.2 313.8 FA 465.25
GG 699.28

SEASONABLE SD 412.14 412.15

SEASONS EE 313.37

SEAT PO 107.34 111.27 DV 179.20
SG 225.19 226.5 226.17 226.25
228.6 MN 371.16 YT 407.29
SD 412.21 415.38 417.37 419.8

SEAT (CONT.) 421.10 421.25
423.27 PP 429.10 HD 442.30
FA 467.18 467.24 467.30
WR 555.37 BO 588.1
JD 616.39 IL 653.20
GG 684.17 684.40 LL 772.36
BM 835.1

SEATED CH 278.15 OC 287.14
293.38 296.35 EE 322.33
TP 337.31 BL 351.38
SD 422.40 FA 468.29
PR 492.15 494.34 507.37
WR 576.32 576.33 JD 625.4
MD 819.38 BM 835.13

SEATING BM 838.6

SEATS GF 235.4 SD 421.21
NT 712.3

SEA-TURF ML 738.20

SEAWARDS WM 61.22

SEA-WASHED ML 743.2 743.4

SEAWEED ML 735.21 740.14
740.17

SEA-WIND ML 727.6

SEBASTIAN JD 622.34

SECLUDED TF 127.4 LL 762.22

SECLUSION EE 303.27 GG 667.21

SECOND OA 28.18 HT 39.1
39.6 39.14 39.20 WM 58.9
EA 75.3 85.12 PO 110.3
TF 121.29 129.37 DV 138.22
SS 206.29 SB 217.8 217.39
218.5 WS 257.39 264.35
SC 270.12 EE 309.32 310.8
331.22 BL 348.22 348.25
348.38 349.28 352.38
YT 400.37 SD 412.20 418.25
PP 434.7 HD 442.31 446.33
455.40 FA 466.26 467.22
469.24 PR 476.15 489.13
510.27 511.6 511.25 511.30
WR 562.18 574.7 BO 601.13
LA 637.19 IL 653.24
GG 670.35 673.42 682.34
683.3 NT 713.17 ML 731.35
732.35 LL 773.1 RR 784.33
RH 796.9 803.19 804.7
MD 805.36 808.36 816.23
BM 837.16 841.31 TH 847.38

SECONDARY MO 12.2 EE 310.12
SU 535.23 535.24

SECONDED ML 730.15

SECOND-HAND MO 14.2

SECONDLY BO 587.6

SECONDS SP 50.19 TF 134.2

SECOND-SIGHT MD 821.1

SECRECY EE 306.25 BO 589.25

SELFISHNESS EA 86.13 JD 623.37

SELF-MISTRUST WM 66.31

SELF-NULLITY BO 597.17

SELF-PITY OA 37.15

SELF-PORTRAIT LA 640.39

SELF-POSSESSED WM 58.26
   YT 397.16 GG 699.40 LL 770.14
   MD 822.41

SELF-POSSESSION OA 36.5

SELF-PRESERVATION DV 177.6

SELF-RESPECT DV 164.28 183.21
   IL 651.16

SELF-RESPONSIBLE TF 129.3

SELF-STARTER IL 649.41

SELF-SUFFICIENT SS 198.12

SELF-SUPPORTING ML 728.16

SELF-SUPPRESSION SG 221.17

SELF-SURENESS DV 145.12

SELF-TORTURE PR 482.40 483.1

SELF-WILLED CH 278.20

SELL GF 235.10 YT 401.2 401.8
   LL 769.42 MD 819.29

SELLING LL 769.41 MD 819.22

SELSTON OC 283.2

SELVES PR 483.1 486.3 SU 541.32
   TH 846.19

SEMBLANCE PR 499.39

SEMI-ANGELIC BO 602.6

SEMI-CLOISTERAL BM 831.8

SEMI-CONSCIOUS WR 557.22

SEMI-DARK JD 617.11

SEMI-EROTIC EA 81.11

SEMI-FEUDAL ML 725.11

SEMI-SECRECY DV 161.1

SEMI-TRANCE WR 576.35

SEMI-TRANSPARENT DV 138.8

SEND TF 132.37 DV 162.10
   SS 208.16 208.21 WS 246.32
   248.40 BL 356.22 356.31
   WP 381.7 384.28 YT 405.20
   405.23 FA 462.38 PR 483.23
   485.25 508.38 TB 515.11
   520.17 WR 549.10 581.26
   JD 628.31 NT 707.30 ML 731.2

SEND (CONT.) 741.17 RR 787.6
   RH 798.21 801.7 801.11 801.13
   MD 824.34 BM 834.28 TH 853.7

SENDING DV 146.28 160.26 182.37
   SS 200.10 200.21 208.18
   WP 385.14 SU 530.10 JD 621.1
   GG 694.31 696.22 LL 768.38

SENIOR OA 33.16

SENNA GG 673.37

SENOR NT 719.11

SENORA NT 716.35

SENOR DOMINGO ROMERO PR 486.3

SENSATION SP 47.38 EA 82.19
   PO 95.17 110.14 TF 120.34
   SB 214.38 SC 268.25 WR 580.39
   BO 593.9 LA 637.38 638.7
   638.8

SENSATIONAL MN 371.22

SENSATIONS MO 2.34 PO 103.16
   EE 323.41 MN 376.21 YT 402.40

SENSE MO 4.8 13.37 19.23
   OA 33.10 37.18 HT 44.5
   SP 48.37 51.9 WM 54.12 55.5
   60.13 64.29 68.8 EA 72.15
   82.28 82.35 84.11 92.38
   PO 97.9 111.29 114.18
   TF 121.37 DV 146.18 146.31
   164.30 173.23 184.21
   SS 206.32 SB 212.8 217.31
   WS 249.12 258.4 259.39
   EE 306.24 306.33 307.30
   309.19 309.26 309.28
   309.37 322.27 323.19 330.16
   BL 347.31 348.42 350.37
   356.38 SD 411.29 HD 441.28
   446.40 PR 485.6 511.39
   TB 519.30 SU 533.1 WR 572.15
   BO 588.42 589.27 591.26
   591.41 592.6 597.41 599.40
   600.5 JD 612.39 615.40
   LA 637.20 GG 661.29 669.42
   677.32 677.34 683.24 686.16
   698.38 ML 726.4 LL 772.30
   RH 790.27 802.20 MD 806.12
   822.20 825.35 TH 844.24
   845.24

SENSED WP 385.35 PR 477.22
   ML 736.27

SENSELESS RH 803.19

SENSES PO 97.6 104.42 TP 343.2
   YT 405.17 WR 565.39 568.12
   568.14 572.11 574.1 BO 591.39
   JD 609.10 IL 652.17

SENSIBILITIES EE 328.27

SENSIBILITY TF 128.10 OV 748.21

SENSIBLE DV 165.27 173.20
   SG 229.4 YT 395.9 IL 655.34
   655.41

SENSIBLY MD 818.28

SENSITIVE MO 5.14 8.19
   EA 84.36 91.20 TF 127.10
   CH 276.36 279.23 EE 305.28
   310.30 BL 349.9 349.12
   FA 461.7 462.19 PR 479.25
   484.15 BO 595.20 ML 726.24
   738.3 LL 768.28

SENSITIVELY PP 428.30

SENSITIVENESS DV 164.36
   YT 403.5 FA 462.36
   PR 483.13

SENSUAL EE 322.11 HD 441.34
   PR 477.25 WR 560.30
   NT 706.2

SENSUALITY EE 322.29

SENSUOUS OA 23.8 SD 413.30

SENT WM 70.3 PO 97.23 101.5
   112.8 113.6 TF 117.26
   135.11 DV 162.7 SS 202.35
   202.42 208.9 WS 248.21
   259.33 263.37 263.41
   EE 320.38 TP 342.27
   YT 396.11 398.21 407.10
   409.28 SD 419.19 PP 432.5
   HD 452.23 FA 465.37
   PR 474.36 TB 520.17
   SU 530.17 WR 553.7
   JD 619.12 GG 667.25 677.24
   678.32 NT 707.9 708.32
   RH 804.5 BM 842.29 TH 853.9

SENTENCE NT 701.12

SENTENCES WS 262.34 LL 768.1

SENTENTIOUSLY DV 166.39

SENTENTIOUSNESS EA 75.17

SENTIENT DV 151.16

SENTIMENT CH 279.27 PP 430.8
   TB 515.22 520.35 BO 602.10
   602.12

SENTIMENTAL TF 129.15 129.19
   OC 294.36 BL 349.5
   PP 430.17 WR 548.5 BO 602.1
   GG 673.26 NT 704.12

SENTIMENTALITY MO 2.36 6.23
   DV 145.35 BO 589.10

SENTIMENTALLY SM 584.39

SENTIMENTS SU 544.41

SENTINEL BO 594.34

SEPARATE EA 78.13 80.33
   80.35 PO 115.40 115.41
   TF 118.31 DV 150.36
   SS 207.40 209.33 OC 300.28
   YT 406.36 HD 456.20
   LL 777.1

SEPARATED PO 115.38 DV 181.40

SEPARATED (CONT.) CH 278.15
  HD 441.22 ML 724.7

SEPARATENESS DV 171.6 OC 300.30

SEPARATING BO 599.9

SEPARATION WM 61.10 EA 89.5
  DV 150.37 SS 208.19 MD 805.9

SEPARATOR BL 347.22

SEPTEMBER FA 464.24 464.38
  PR 483.38 486.9 WR 548.29
  551.18

SEPTIC EE 320.2

SEQUINS RH 799.18

SERE SB 213.39 PR 494.3 494.7
  494.10 494.17 494.18

SERENE EE 330.29 BL 347.23
  356.10 PR 490.25 LL 770.32
  RH 796.10

SERENELY LL 761.10 766.29

SERF FG 189.4

SERGE TB 521.22 ML 726.41

SERGEANT TF 118.11 119.5 119.24
  121.15 121.16 SD 413.8 413.13
  513.19 413.24 415.8 415.20
  415.35 415.39 418.1 418.9
  418.24 418.26 418.29 418.37
  419.7 419.13 419.28 419.37
  420.11 420.22 421.8 421.16
  422.8 422.17 422.34 422.38

SERGEANT HUBER TF 124.1 128.25

SERGEANT'S TF 120.37 121.19

SERGEANT THOMAS SD 420.5

SERIES OA 36.34 TF 515.29

SERIOUS MO 8.2 9.19 15.8
  HT 41.1 WM 57.30 PO 110.3
  DV 163.11 168.27 WS 247.33
  OC 287.8 EE 308.12 317.25
  IL 647.19 GG 665.2 LL 766.1
  RH 794.16 794.23 796.18

SERIOUS-HEARTED SP 50.5

SERIOUSLY MO 15.15 15.28
  DV 183.5 183.33 FG 187.34
  SG 229.35 TB 519.9 525.38
  SM 582.10 BO 603.42 LA 642.16
  NT 719.38 719.39 719.40
  719.41 720.2 720.3

SERIOUSNESS MO 6.35 EE 317.29
  SM 582.10 GG 677.30

SERMON-LAPPING PP 428.8

SERPENT SU 528.12 535.7

SERPENTS MD 820.4

SERVANT PO 96.38 97.15 98.3
  99.4 99.7 100.15 100.32
  100.41 101.12 102.2 102.37
  103.33 108.14 109.13 109.31
  FG 191.4 SB 213.20 213.31
  YT 397.34 398.21 406.2 408.18
  WR 550.36 551.5 GG 669.13
  669.40 672.23 676.26
  NT 710.17 710.22 710.25
  711.26 ML 726.5 LL 776.30

SERVANTLESS HD 446.22 446.36

SERVANT-MAID YT 395.17

SERVANTS HD 446.31 TB 513.25
  SU 534.13 WR 548.14 ML 726.28
  731.4 RH 790.19 MD 812.33
  BM 827.24 829.39

SERVANT'S PO 97.7 100.18 102.15
  106.8

SERVANTS' RR 785.32 785.37
  786.11 788.17 788.19

SERVE PO 99.30 TF 127.22 132.25
  DV 140.22 141.22 141.24
  142.20 146.38 172.24 172.42
  EE 329.4 329.9 PP 440.26
  FA 470.31 WR 560.24 BO 587.8
  GG 680.19 ML 730.35 737.20
  LL 774.17

SERVED EA 80.14 PO 98.4 98.7
  TF 126.31 DV 143.4 143.7
  164.25 169.20 SG 229.14
  SC 268.23 EE 318.33 WP 384.7
  YT 407.8 BO 592.20 593.38
  GG 663.20 673.42 ML 737.19
  740.4

SERVES HT 39.27

SERVICE PO 98.20 TF 127.18
  127.19 127.21 128.33 129.9
  130.27 DV 141.41 147.23
  164.27 172.23 172.42 177.17
  CH 280.4 TP 334.28 336.30
  340.15 340.28 MN 377.14
  PP 437.5 FA 464.26 464.28
  TB 520.7 GG 692.15 NT 709.8
  RR 780.15 BM 834.15 841.19

SERVICEABLE BM 830.35

SERVICE-DOOR RR 788.8

SERVICES DV 142.37

SERVILE PP 436.40

SERVING TF 128.33 DV 141.34
  SS 205.19

SERVING-WOMAN SU 538.26

SESAME AND LILIES GF 237.18
  239.11

SETS SP 53.4 TP 336.25
  JD 620.31

SETTEE JD 616.9

SETTIN' PP 433.8

SETTING WM 69.27 SS 206.7
  SG 222.29 GF 236.33
  EE 310.38 WR 556.4
  NT 706.14 LL 764.16
  MD 811.28

SETTLE WM 66.26 DV 176.14
  179.33 TB 522.11 JD 615.21
  MD 823.33

SETTLED OA 36.36 WM 57.30
  TF 119.22 DV 178.39
  SS 199.16 199.17 210.30
  SC 268.28 TP 344.35
  WP 389.38 HD 445.24
  TB 515.24 JD 625.29
  IL 651.28 ML 729.16 739.20
  MD 826.1 826.9

SETTLEMENT WR 551.18
  MD 823.36

SETTLER OC 286.3

SETTLES WM 63.1

SETTLING MO 1.33 OC 286.6
  SM 585.38 OV 748.34
  MD 805.10

SET-UP MO 12.22 GG 663.19

SEVEN SP 49.7 51.13 WM 58.4
  TF 126.31 DV 145.33 184.15
  WS 244.5 244.27 253.34
  OC 283.2 EE 312.5 322.18
  324.24 MN 371.9 WP 382.33
  PP 430.4 FA 470.38
  PR 488.27 BO 594.29
  OV 747.27 BM 834.42

SEVEN HUNDRED AND FIFTY POUNDS
  MD 805.4

SEVEN'S TP 341.40

SEVENTEENTH-CENTURY LL 763.11

SEVENTH MD 816.22

SEVENTY THOUSAND POUNDS
  RH 804.16

SEVENTY-TWO LL 761.1 762.24

SEVERAL OA 29.30 HT 41.28
  PO 113.12 DV 165.19 182.24
  SB 215.4 WP 383.12 SD 412.4
  421.17 PP 427.3 HD 448.33
  450.6 PR 485.16 SU 539.41
  WR 552.12 562.29 LA 638.15
  NT 718.21 720.21 ML 730.25
  731.35 738.23 RR 784.22
  RH 799.19 799.20 MD 805.14
  TH 844.2 845.29 849.38

SEVERE GF 235.22 BL 351.2
  MN 374.42 SD 422.18

SEVERITY TF 126.2

SEVERN OA 24.11 24.16 25.10

SEVERN (CONT.)   OA 25.19 25.29
  25.36 25.38 26.4 26.7 26.19
  26.22 26.29 28.13 28.37
  29.2 29.5 29.22 29.39 30.19
  31.1 31.9 31.13 31.22 31.27
  32.2 32.4 32.31 32.36 32.39
  32.40 33.9 33.10 33.19
  33.22 33.26 33.32 33.36
  33.42 34.12 34.24 34.26
  34.35 34.40 35.3 35.13 35.17
  35.20 35.21 35.23 35.27
  35.31 35.36 36.8 36.17 36.26
  36.31 36.42 37.13 37.19
  37.23 37.26 37.29 38.15
  38.20 38.27 38.35 38.37
  38.40 JD 628.2 628.19

SEVERN (SEE EDWARD; MR. SEVERN)

SEVERN'S OA 38.25

SEW WS 245.6 EE 307.11

SEWING OA 29.10 29.16 30.18
  OC 289.28 289.32 290.24
  290.28 293.27

SEWING-MACHINE DV 139.33
  YT 397.17

SEX BL 359.23 HD 447.4
  WR 567.29 569.40 ML 737.3
  737.4 737.6 MD 820.31
  BM 836.16

SEX-CONSCIOUS WR 567.28

SEXLESS PR 478.11 479.16
  WR 568.6

SEXUAL TF 127.35 DV 164.37
  165.13 WR 560.30

SH OC 298.31

SHABBINESS JD 611.4

SHABBY RH 802.7 MD 817.20
  TH 850.26

SHACK PR 487.2

SHACKETY-BOOM GF 234.22

SHACKETY-SHACKETY-BOOM GF 234.22

SHADE PO 95.3 108.36 112.1
  TF 117.17 118.7 122.11 123.18
  FG 188.41 SS 197.18 SU 537.31
  540.4 NT 712.3

SHADED EE 304.7 TB 521.19

SHADING GG 672.11

SHADOW MO 1.23 14.5 18.13
  WM 55.8 PO 96.6 105.32 105.37
  106.1 106.10 107.19 108.34
  111.4 112.1 113.8 114.29
  114.30 115.16 TF 118.35
  FG 194.3 194.15 196.20
  SS 211.10 SB 212.36 214.18
  SG 224.9 224.17 224.21 225.9
  226.12 OC 286.18 287.27
  288.18 288.36 EE 303.12

SHADOW (CONT.) 312.28 322.23
  WP 387.20 YT 400.24 403.16
  HD 447.38 450.9 453.42
  FA 458.13 468.6 PR 489.14
  489.36 489.38 490.6 490.20
  490.26 497.32 499.36 500.4
  500.37 501.11 501.14 502.39
  506.23 506.26 507.10
  SU 532.32 533.35 536.33
  537.38 WR 572.34 580.41
  BO 596.22 596.33 LA 630.17
  GG 687.3 ML 723.24 734.20
  736.30 740.24 OV 751.24
  759.37

SHADOWED SS 200.3

SHADOWILY WR 559.12 ML 735.19

SHADOW-LIKE MO 1.29

SHADOWS WM 65.27 EA 81.18
  PO 106.24 TF 117.4 134.40
  OC 283.29 286.16 288.13
  TP 334.6 PR 489.4 WR 556.18
  559.13 573.42 BO 594.26
  JD 614.32 IL 647.22 OV 751.2
  LL 770.21

SHADOWY TF 123.15 DV 160.28
  EE 303.10 PR 479.39 490.1
  BO 596.4

SHADY NT 721.12

SHAFT DV 166.30 SB 216.3
  WR 580.7 580.41 581.5

SHAFTS PO 114.17 WP 380.6
  WR 579.12

SHAGGIER WR 552.32

SHAGGY FG 190.20 EE 303.15
  303.29 304.42

SHAKE TF 119.2 DV 168.21
  SS 202.15 WS 246.29 PP 435.27
  HD 447.14 WR 574.10 574.13
  579.13 JD 616.38

SHAKEN PO 103.20 DV 177.17
  WP 386.20 387.31 SD 419.33
  SU 528.8 BM 832.14 842.16

SHAKESPEARE EA 86.17

SHAKILY WM 55.41 SB 212.26
  SG 223.22

SHAKING MO 21.3 SC 270.34
  TP 337.31 344.22 YT 398.28
  SD 418.39 HD 445.13 PR 509.22
  SU 529.39 WR 574.14 578.34
  SM 584.17 JD 628.20 NT 709.37
  OV 753.23

SHAKY SB 219.10 220.1 PP 435.20

SHAL FA 462.7

SHALLOW WM 65.25 PO 95.4
  BL 348.18 348.19 PP 432.20
  HD 441.33 448.42 449.20
  BO 599.29

SHALLOWER TH 844.20

SHALLOWLY DV 155.30

SHALLOWS SS 199.40

SHALT TH 850.14

SHAMBLING JD 611.31 LA 643.33

SHAME MO 20.24 20.37
  OA 34.12 36.17 37.36
  WM 54.12 EA 87.3 PO 100.20
  TF 120.37 120.38 120.41
  121.7 121.13 121.38 122.15
  122.17 122.25 124.34
  125.13 126.9 126.10 126.12
  130.5 131.29 131.33 133.9
  DV 153.10 153.27 164.29
  165.32 165.37 GF 236.6
  236.26 WS 253.41 264.22
  265.13 CH 275.20 279.25
  281.34 OC 294.13 301.6
  302.15 EE 326.5 TP 337.38
  WP 384.16 SD 420.9 420.10
  PP 429.40 HD 455.22
  FA 461.41 467.12 IL 658.21
  GG 679.35 680.9 680.21
  OV 750.17 751.23 LL 765.28
  772.8 772.19 BM 837.14

SHAMED TF 120.39 122.23
  WR 564.14 GG 678.18

SHAMEFACEDLY PP 437.18
  LA 646.10

SHAMEFUL GG 679.35 BM 837.6

SHAMEFULLY SP 50.11

SHANNA OC 292.3 292.23
  293.10 293.13

SHAN'T OA 34.5 SP 52.8
  DV 186.14 SG 223.4
  WS 261.42 262.6 262.7
  263.27 TP 342.39 BL 364.19
  YT 398.41 409.3 SD 420.34
  PP 432.16 HD 442.40
  IL 648.32 GG 669.4
  RH 798.8 BM 840.27 841.19

SHAPE SP 47.33 EA 83.12
  TF 117.22 SG 227.8
  BL 354.12 ML 746.7 BM 841.7

SHAPED FG 193.33 LA 631.34
  MD 808.4

SHAPELESS TP 335.21

SHAPELY PO 97.22 WS 244.29
  256.18 TB 521.17 522.23

SHAPEN DV 168.13

SHAPES PO 115.14

SHAPIN' SP 46.8

SHARE SP 50.7 DV 159.4
  172.19 HD 441.16 BM 838.13

SHARED BL 350.4 YT 403.6

SHARED (CONT.) PR 480.7 NT 708.2

SHARES HT 42.3

SHARING PR 480.21 MD 806.35

SHARP MO 1.30 HT 42.7 WM 55.2
   63.8 63.15 PO 98.28 TF 119.6
   DV 149.13 179.39 180.9 180.25
   182.12 SG 221.24 GF 237.27
   242.8 WS 246.5 CH 275.15
   276.22 276.25 279.1 OC 293.18
   295.32 297.39 EE 330.3 330.8
   330.10 330.32 330.42
   TP 336.37 343.7 344.20 344.23
   346.5 BL 361.14 WP 387.34
   390.36 SD 425.35 426.4
   PP 434.9 436.27 HD 446.6
   PR 501.16 TB 518.20 WR 546.16
   JD 614.4 LA 630.31 631.1
   634.28 638.1 639.9 GG 668.30
   ML 741.1 741.9 741.40 743.29
   LL 775.1 776.34 RH 804.10
   BM 829.28 TH 853.6 853.28

SHARP, LAURA (SEE LAURA SHARP)

SHARP-EDGED PO 110.2 LL 777.28

SHARPENED BL 356.14

SHARPENING NT 704.26

SHARPER TH 852.40

SHARP-FACED BM 830.38

SHARPLY MO 21.27 OA 36.27
   WM 61.34 62.8 PO 113.5
   TF 124.9 133.36 DV 141.20
   184.32 SB 215.12 216.26
   218.14 GF 242.7 242.12
   WS 246.4 258.29 CH 276.35
   282.14 OC 289.34 293.36 298.6
   EE 324.40 MN 374.25 WP 387.27
   387.36 388.2 HD 444.16
   FA 469.26 SU 536.28 LA 631.40
   GG 691.28 BM 829.31 831.4
   839.21

SHARPNESS WP 389.20 WR 569.37
   BM 830.42

SHARP-PEAKED WR 552.4

SHARP-PLUMAGED WR 553.14

SHATTER PR 479.23 509.1

SHATTERED PO 105.10 SG 226.14
   EE 329.40 BL 356.2 PR 509.2
   SU 528.28 ML 737.7 737.38
   737.39

SHATTERING BL 348.35

SHAVE GF 240.32 MN 366.23

SHAVED BL 356.12 MN 366.22
   PR 484.38

SHAWL DV 139.29 WS 251.16
   251.25 OC 292.1 293.16 293.30
   BL 352.34 LA 635.31 636.29
   636.35 644.21 NT 709.24

SHAWL (CONT.) 709.29 OV 749.20
   750.11 750.13 750.27 751.19
   751.28 756.26 LL 763.20 763.26

SHAWLS NT 709.26

SHEAF OA 27.42 OC 288.23

SHEARS HD 447.29

SHEATHED BO 592.16

SHEAVES SS 199.33 FA 464.40
   466.32 (SEE SHE-E-EAVES)

SHED HT 42.26 44.10 DV 139.15
   FG 191.2 191.6 191.13 191.27
   194.4 SS 202.14 EE 304.34
   304.38 MN 372.30 WP 379.18
   379.36 385.21 IL 652.28
   ML 744.28 OV 747.2 753.14
   753.35 754.29

SHEDS WP 387.27 IL 648.20
   ML 722.26

SHE-E-EAVES FA 466.34

SHEEN WM 55.37 PO 115.9
   GG 683.9

SHEEP MO 3.5 PO 106.32 106.33
   CH 274.31 PP 428.39 429.25
   PR 482.19 WR 558.41 559.16
   575.34 ML 738.27 740.8 740.39
   740.41 741.3 742.1 742.17
   742.21 742.26

SHEEPISH IL 657.33

SHEEPISHLY SP 46.29 MN 369.14
   YT 398.13 SD 418.11 FA 468.23
   469.4 JD 624.22 IL 657.22
   BM 828.34

SHEEPSKIN PR 502.5 502.34

SHEER OA 24.16 PO 95.19
   OC 300.4 BL 355.29 365.6
   WR 569.24 SM 582.9 ML 746.4
   LL 767.33 BM 837.20 837.37
   TH 848.15

SHEERED DV 160.36 SS 197.33
   TP 339.16

SHEET DV 147.40 149.2 FG 190.23
   OC 302.9

SHEETS SP 45.22 EA 92.10
   SC 272.21 WR 558.20 ML 723.17
   RR 785.39 786.13 787.32
   788.12

SHEFFIELD JD 609.29 612.9
   625.23

SHE-FOX GG 675.19

SHEIKH WR 547.29

SHEIKY MD 821.29

SHELF DV 139.19 SS 207.4

SHELL EA 83.26 PO 105.36
   TF 134.29 FG 195.8
   SB 213.13 EE 331.9 331.18
   331.19 331.22 331.30
   333.15 BL 365.15 PR 494.5
   TB 522.37 SU 533.9 534.24
   534.31 WR 578.20 GG 678.31
   LL 765.17 778.1

SHELTER TF 131.25 DV 137.38
   EE 313.35 315.15 WP 379.18
   WR 556.33 557.13 557.15
   557.28 ML 725.22 LL 767.8
   MD 825.15

SHELTERS FG 195.1 WR 556.38

SHELVES DV 139.33 162.22
   162.34 PP 433.22

SHEPHERD PO 106.32 106.34
   106.35 WR 559.15

SHERRY WS 255.39

SHERWOOD FG 187.4

SHEWBURY BM 834.27

SHE-WOLF TB 522.23

SHIELD WR 558.29 MD 820.35

SHIES TP 337.15

SHIFT HT 42.16 SC 267.27
   HD 452.22 WR 564.21
   JD 612.5

SHIFTED EA 85.9 PO 112.7
   113.5 DV 152.19 160.2
   179.20 SG 226.26 231.31
   WP 392.10

SHIFTING EA 86.7 DV 178.37
   SB 214.18 BL 363.37
   MN 377.41 PP 433.29

SHIFTY TF 127.6

SHILLING HT 44.20 EE 328.8

SHILLINGS HT 39.12 39.13
   39.19 42.21 SP 46.5 46.29
   50.12 DV 138.33 OC 285.40
   SD 420.22 RH 795.7 796.27
   796.34 796.35

SHIMMER TH 844.25

SHIMMERING TF 125.40 WR 574.18

SHINE SG 225.15 WS 244.18
   SU 532.39 WR 581.5

SHINES FG 187.8 196.1

SHINGLE ML 739.31 739.36
   745.33

SHINING OA 26.10 WM 58.38
   62.23 63.33 EA 90.22
   90.28 PO 107.19 TF 131.24
   DV 167.27 181.13 FG 194.25
   196.5 MN 371.13 HD 453.36

SHINING (CONT.) HD 454.32
  PR 497.37 500.38 WR 556.11
  JD 625.9 625.11 625.17
  IL 651.2 OV 753.28 RR 787.40
  RH 791.9

SHINY DV 159.14

SHIP MO 4.8 TP 336.35 PP 431.10
  431.11 SU 528.5 529.3
  ML 734.20 742.18 742.23

SHIPMENTS TP 336.6

SHIPS ML 726.33

SHIRE HD 441.23

SHIRT HT 43.18 TF 126.20 129.27
  134.12 WS 244.25 247.26 249.4
  SC 268.2 OC 296.30 301.38
  302.1 EE 326.4 330.20
  MN 367.14 SD 418.11 PR 484.6
  484.39 510.36 511.12
  TB 521.22 SU 542.19 543.5
  WR 549.17 557.9 562.24
  JD 618.15 618.18 618.26
  ML 728.32 MD 807.2

SHIRTS TF 123.6 127.28
  EE 323.31 326.7 SD 419.9
  WR 562.29 563.28 570.16
  570.23

SHIRT-SLEEVES MO 6.2 HT 41.17
  DV 171.29 173.4 SS 210.36
  OC 290.3 EE 307.15* 325.42
  330.19 TP 343.17 BL 362.16
  SU 540.40 LA 645.26

SHIVER BO 602.42 NT 710.3
  ML 743.42 OV 749.18

SHIVERED MO 3.7 WM 61.25 66.18
  69.42 FG 192.7 OC 296.29
  PR 501.28 509.29 BO 602.33
  604.12 GG 683.42 684.8 684.19
  ML 743.19 BM 840.2

SHIVERING PR 503.31 503.40
  509.30 WR 552.18 BO 602.41

SHIVERS TP 334.11

SHOAL OV 758.29

SHOALS PO 105.20 107.2 FG 187.2
  JD 606.15

SHOCK OA 36.9 WM 58.7 PO 97.31
  TF 121.1 121.26 128.26
  DV 145.6 161.36 175.17 175.33
  WS 264.8 EE 317.23 PP 434.6
  FA 467.10 468.15 WR 566.25
  ML 728.18 742.33 742.34
  742.37

SHOCKED MO 8.30 OA 30.36
  PO 110.29 TF 133.29 DV 147.40
  177.2 SB 216.15 SG 233.13
  OC 298.33 YT 402.10 402.16
  ML 740.32

SHOCKING BL 363.17

SHOCKINGLY TB 517.22

SHOD WR 558.17 BM 841.8

SHOEMAKER MD 808.6

SHOES GF 234.4 WS 251.18 251.25
  OC 292.5 PR 481.2 TB 521.17
  526.41 LA 636.31 NT 719.33
  OV 752.36 MD 808.1 808.7
  808.8 808.13 808.14 808.20
  BM 835.42 836.31 836.32
  836.38 837.17 841.5

SHONE MO 3.12 WM 59.4 EA 84.6
  PO 115.2 DV 160.20 166.28
  166.31 167.30 179.36 FG 194.3
  194.10 SS 203.1 210.4
  SB 212.36 213.3 SG 224.15
  225.18 225.21 CH 279.38 280.8
  280.21 OC 288.29 PP 430.30
  HD 456.15 PR 490.23 498.24
  499.32 508.8 509.41 SU 532.37
  535.11 535.38 LA 632.20
  IL 653.2 GG 683.10 ML 734.22
  745.31 LL 766.8 766.12 767.24
  RR 788.9 788.18 BM 828.8

SHONNA HT 42.5 SC 271.3

SHOOK MO 8.7 WM 58.10 EA 72.5
  73.27 74.35 77.4 77.9
  PO 110.15 TF 121.1 133.26
  133.38 134.14 DV 151.27
  173.36 SS 201.24 207.34
  209.17 SB 213.6 216.29
  WS 245.32 246.4 257.36 257.37
  264.8 264.28 SC 271.35
  CH 278.11 OC 293.39 294.27
  MN 369.24 PP 427.25 437.13
  FA 465.10 469.32 PR 488.19
  491.13 SU 541.18 WR 557.33
  566.41 567.2 JD 616.3 627.24
  IL 651.4 654.9 BM 841.41

SHOOT PR 510.16 510.19 510.21
  510.22 512.24 WR 548.41

SHOOTING SU 539.32

SHOOTS TF 123.2 PP 430.9

SHOP HT 42.13 WM 55.9 DV 139.32
  140.26 142.34 161.18
  CH 274.18 275.17 TP 336.3
  FA 461.36 462.5 BO 592.36
  JD 616.1 620.32 NT 707.34

SHOP-BELL FA 461.33

SHOPPED ML 735.40

SHOPPERS MN 368.32

SHOPPING SU 533.16 JD 625.24
  MD 815.16

SHOPS TP 334.7 334.15 PP 436.12
  HD 447.24 FA 460.19 BO 595.1
  596.28

SHOP-SIGNS BO 594.41

SHORE MO 2.17

SHOREWARDS WM 54.31

SHORN TF 123.8

SHORT MO 16.37 16.38
  WM 58.14 64.33 PO 96.16
  96.17 DV 138.22 143.2
  160.15 165.12 SS 198.8
  207.8 SG 222.19 GF 236.3
  236.5 WS 244.7 SC 267.4
  268.5 OC 285.4 289.7
  297.8 EE 309.12 320.11
  321.37 TP 340.16 342.36
  BL 357.27 359.40 363.41
  MN 373.24 WP 379.23 392.3
  YT 399.15 SD 411.20 413.8
  417.38 HD 441.15 PR 481.16
  481.18 TB 518.2 522.23
  524.20 527.7 SU 536.33
  WR 567.34 569.9 573.13
  577.31 JD 617.32 IL 651.7
  GG 662.16 680.9 NT 701.6
  701.24 702.12 705.25
  709.30 713.15 715.37
  715.38 716.22 ML 723.5
  729.25 LL 773.22 RR 779.38
  787.29 788.23 RH 798.19
  MD 809.18 819.3 819.38
  823.1

SHORTAGE BO 602.33 602.34
  602.36 RH 790.27

SHORT-CROPPED PP 433.35

SHORT-CUT PP 433.5

SHORTENED ML 742.4

SHORTER MO 12.22 YT 395.7
  WR 568.19

SHORTEST WR 580.11

SHORT-FACED GG 670.22

SHORTHAND TB 518.18 518.41
  521.27 526.36

SHORTHAND-SCRIBBLING TB 521.37

SHORTISH FA 468.19 RH 804.9

SHORTLY OA 27.39 DV 145.32
  SS 206.10 208.34 YT 398.19
  PP 430.19 FA 470.9 470.20
  RR 788.28

SHOT OA 33.4 SP 47.2
  PO 104.9 TF 133.24
  EE 323.40 330.10 MN 375.8
  WP 393.1 PP 435.13
  FA 458.25 PR 487.8 510.25
  511.4 511.7 512.14 512.23
  WR 574.3 BO 595.30 602.4
  JD 606.32 LA 646.17
  GG 685.25 NT 711.6 721.15
  ML 738.12 BM 828.20 830.31

SHOTS PR 510.30 LL 776.34

SHOULDER MO 21.13 21.16
  OA 27.22 WM 62.11 DV 149.10
  FG 187.11 190.28 193.27

SHOULDER (CONT.) FG 194.40
SS 210.35 210.37 210.40
WS 254.2 254.6 255.8
266.3 EE 326.4 TP 345.15
BL 351.22 352.14 364.1
MN 375.23 378.10 378.16
SD 423.23 PP 439.18 439.20
439.34 HD 453.32 453.39
SU 535.2 536.30 538.19
WR 564.24 SM 584.18 LA 636.30
637.26 637.28 GG 682.33 683.5
683.15 685.22 696.41 697.1
NT 702.28 707.12 713.11
BM 837.36

SHOULDER-BLADES GG 671.28

SHOULDERING SU 532.14

SHOULDERS SP 47.27 WM 59.3
63.16 65.26 EA 71.23 PO 95.16
97.21 106.16 TF 118.14
DV 147.1 153.37 171.3
SS 202.4 SB 214.40 SG 222.15
WS 244.15 258.14 261.29
SC 268.28 268.31 EE 323.32
330.21 BL 354.24 MN 376.7
WP 389.35 390.40 SD 411.16
411.18 417.41 422.3 422.5
PP 428.23 HD 453.11 453.35
455.16 PR 493.5 494.41
SU 530.42 538.30 544.2
WR 553.32 553.40 559.36 561.1
561.4 561.14 564.5 567.32
BO 590.19 604.29 JD 620.20
GG 662.18 671.28 696.25 697.7
NT 707.22 OV 749.19 756.27
LL 763.35 RR 784.24 MD 808.22

SHOULDERS' OV 749.11

SHOULDNA' SC 269.30

SHOULDN'T WM 54.6 54.9 67.34
DV 142.7 SG 222.11 WS 262.23
TP 340.6 340.7 YT 403.30
408.41 408.42 SD 416.35
425.19 425.20 PP 429.3
FA 469.23 471.16 SU 544.14
IL 658.37 GG 674.12 680.14
NT 705.1 705.6 RR 783.14
RH 798.30 BM 826.15 831.36

SHOUT TF 119.6 SC 269.27 271.25
FA 467.7 LA 641.9 641.24
644.9 644.12 644.25 644.34

SHOUTED OA 25.18 35.28 SP 46.26
46.37 47.3 48.20 PO 111.34
TF 119.29 121.14 WS 251.36
SC 270.31 271.17 271.23
271.24 271.27 272.4 OC 292.22
TP 342.24 YT 406.1 SD 412.33
PP 431.5 HD 444.17 FA 460.24
PR 506.31 511.23 LA 630.35
631.19 631.22 632.6 635.5
NT 713.12

SHOUTING FG 191.24 SC 270.39
271.21 272.9 272.18 OC 298.7
WP 393.15 YT 394.26 FA 462.12
467.2 ML 734.13

SHOUTS TF 118.17

SHOVED PO 110.8 110.12 SU 530.4
LA 631.26 632.22 634.10
643.31

SHOVEL ML 744.27 745.22 746.12

SHOVELLING MO 5.21 EE 307.34

SHOVELS MO 5.21

SHOVIN' SP 45.33

SHOW MO 14.21 OA 33.12 WM 55.18
DV 161.6 185.2 SS 201.13
204.1 204.24 SB 217.36
SG 229.10 GF 242.34 WS 246.23
OC 300.25 EE 310.24 TP 345.39
MN 372.5 BO 603.29 ML 722.8
732.22 736.25 739.13
MD 806.39 BM 841.17 842.11
842.27 843.5 TH 853.17

SHOWED SP 49.4 WM 57.6 61.23
TF 119.42 DV 148.40 179.10
SS 204.15 204.22 SB 214.6
WS 245.5 SC 267.29 OC 284.20
300.1 EE 312.31 323.33 330.18
330.21 PP 436.29 436.32
HD 442.6 PR 483.2 485.21
497.27 503.3 WR 557.11
SM 582.24 JD 604.35 LA 631.9
645.42 GG 661.17 662.41 663.8
680.1 693.31 NT 707.39
ML 734.20 736.17 745.23
RR 781.27 783.35 MD 808.37
TH 853.25

SHOWER SS 210.23

SHOWER-BATH EA 81.30

SHOWERING IL 648.35

SHOWERS SM 582.21

SHOWER-SPRAY EA 82.3

SHOW-GROUND TP 337.22

SHOWILY WR 556.12

SHOWING MO 2.13 5.5 17.27
WM 63.27 PO 108.37 110.34
TF 121.22 127.28 DV 139.6
167.1 178.28 CH 282.5
WP 390.18 391.13 YT 394.12
400.20 400.31 PP 428.41 433.5
433.23 433.34 437.31
PR 485.28 WR 547.3 557.9
562.29 573.19 576.27 BO 596.8
604.23 LA 632.6 639.3
IL 647.11 655.40 GG 671.3
671.24 671.28 679.36 694.10

SHOWING-OFF FA 463.22

SHOWN PR 473.17

SHOWS OA 38.33 NT 718.23

SHOWY WS 250.24 TB 520.37
ML 736.25

SHRANK MO 6.6 21.27 HT 44.8
WM 66.18 TF 121.13 129.28

SHRANK (CONT.) DV 146.30
164.41 FG 196.17 SS 206.15
SB 212.21 SG 232.33
GF 241.10 CH 282.28
OC 289.32 290.39 296.4
BL 354.7 362.9 363.30
364.25 HD 455.28 PR 507.31
WR 551.5 551.38

SHRED TB 514.39 IL 651.16

SHREWD FG 187.19 TP 337.5
339.30 MN 368.24 PR 477.12
SU 533.23 538.15 GG 670.19
ML 726.28 726.30 727.2

SHREWDER PR 480.24

SHREWD-LOOKING MN 366.12

SHREWDLY MN 369.3 375.16
WP 380.31 SU 538.11
WR 554.34 GG 670.20

SHREWDNESS SU 533.20

SHRIEK WS 264.14 OC 295.9
EE 316.36 331.9 TP 334.32
PR 498.29 WR 552.13
RR 788.20 MD 825.4

SHRIEKED OA 24.31 25.23
YT 394.16 IL 658.10

SHRIEKING OA 24.33 SB 216.10
YT 394.26 SD 412.34

SHRILL WS 263.31 TP 345.29
SM 585.41 LA 645.13

SHRILLY OC 298.2 TP 341.27
SD 411.36 LA 640.32

SHRIMP OA 35.4 DV 147.7

SHRINK MO 3.31 3.34 10.19
17.3 WM 61.16 TF 126.27
JD 619.29

SHRINKING SP 52.15 DV 136.17
SS 202.33 SB 215.1
PP 437.14 437.16 437.37

SHRIVEL LA 643.24

SHRIVELLED HD 455.3 LA 641.35

SHRIVELLING OV 753.9 LL 778.5

SHROUD WP 385.32

SHRUBS WP 385.38 385.42
PR 489.33

SHRUGGED SG 222.15 BO 590.19
JD 620.20

SHRUNK TF 121.8 BM 832.29

SHRUNKEN GG 669.20

SHUDDER EA 87.38 DV 147.15
147.42 OC 295.41 SD 426.13
HD 451.32 452.15 NT 710.30
RR 780.10 TH 850.21

SHUDDERED OA 29.39 WM 65.7
68.35 OC 300.7 TB 520.13
WR 577.36 ML 744.21 TH 850.19

SHUDDERING DV 146.39 FG 191.20
GF 241.26 HD 451.34 PR 503.2
LA 646.24

SHUFFLE WR 565.35

SHUFFLED GF 242.14 WS 253.40
CH 281.35 HD 452.40 IL 651.28

SHUFFLING SB 214.18 OC 296.41

SHUNNED LL 776.14

SHUT MO 5.23 13.41 18.17
OA 25.3 28.35 WM 61.24 63.1
68.35 EA 73.17 81.20 82.16
91.6 91.12 PO 98.30 100.36
105.13 105.14 109.20 DV 141.1
144.1 153.9 153.10 158.6
166.18 175.13 GF 235.3
WS 255.14 CH 280.29 282.1
OC 293.32 296.2 297.33 297.39
300.18 300.25 EE 321.41
322.38 323.16 TP 340.39 346.3
BL 353.11 356.39 361.40
362.23 YT 394.11 SD 416.7
422.25 SU 530.34 WR 575.15
575.16 575.37 575.39 576.16
JD 624.3 IL 647.6 647.33
649.6 652.29 GG 686.38
NT 701.30 ML 741.29 745.10
OV 754.2 755.26 LL 764.13
777.4 RR 780.39 786.12
MD 812.16 812.19 BM 829.21

SHUT-IN WR 546.21

SHUT-OFF DV 152.24

SHUTTER PO 115.11

SHUTTERS BL 361.15 GG 699.11

SHUTTING PO 115.19 EE 322.39
SD 415.29 JD 618.10 618.19
GG 678.9

SHY MO 5.19 EA 92.5 TF 128.15
DV 146.18 172.11 182.24
SG 225.42 EE 320.22 BL 362.36
MN 368.6 YT 396.15 PP 437.12
HD 456.32 FA 466.5 466.6
SU 532.12 539.9 540.19 541.15
543.22 544.41 WR 572.38
BO 594.2 JD 625.18 LA 636.21
GG 695.8 NT 706.25 ML 726.11
LL 762.42 764.5

SHYLY TF 123.20 BL 352.12
SM 583.17 GG 665.7

SHYNESS SU 543.14 543.25
LL 763.2 764.4 765.15 765.24
773.29

SIBILANT OC 300.5

SICK MO 2.33 OA 37.13 EA 76.32
76.33 PO 95.23 103.1 103.39
105.13 112.3 112.4 TF 120.10
DV 146.23 146.25 148.10 163.9

SICK (CONT.) 170.6 170.12
171.18 FG 190.8 SG 228.23
230.8 GF 242.26 WS 265.9
265.12 SC 268.41 271.27
EE 332.9 WP 382.3 YT 399.26
400.27 400.33 403.29 403.31
403.36 403.42 404.7 404.10
406.7 407.13 407.33 PP 434.5
435.28 HD 451.32 PR 497.24
WR 565.28 BO 604.33 604.34
IL 648.13 ML 742.36 BM 842.4

SICKENED BL 354.40 WR 579.4
ML 746.9

SICKENING IL 652.27 657.39

SICKENINGLY PO 110.1

SICKLE EE 317.9 317.16

SICKLILY GF 242.11

SICKLY PO 101.35 102.40 106.28
TF 117.17 120.28 DV 147.7
147.25 SB 217.10 BO 604.38
JD 629.3

SICKNESS EA 71.19 PO 105.25
112.14 113.20 115.18 DV 174.6
CH 274.14

SIC TRANSIT MO 18.40

SICULES SU 529.14

SIDE MO 1.5 1.8 1.24 4.8 6.36
15.14 OA 33.18 HT 44.9
SP 50.19 WM 58.41 63.16
EA 81.6 84.21 91.24 94.6
PO 95.11 114.36 116.17
TF 117.11 119.10 127.35
128.27 129.27 129.37 130.28
131.26 133.26 DV 146.7 149.24
157.17 157.28 158.4 160.37
161.38 162.35 174.30
FG 187.15 187.23 193.28
194.36 SS 200.33 205.21
206.28 SB 215.6 SG 222.30
225.22 GF 234.34 236.4 241.38
243.30 243.33 WS 246.2 251.27
255.25 258.40 SC 267.18
OC 293.21 297.19 299.32
EE 304.14 304.34 333.14
TP 338.13 340.40 342.27
BL 350.7 362.9 364.13
MN 366.6 366.7 369.24 371.11
372.23 373.8 376.29 377.12
377.21 377.25 WP 387.6 387.28
388.34 YT 401.35 401.38
SD 411.8 PP 430.28 436.1
FA 460.26 461.40 462.3 464.29
464.33 PR 490.13 497.8 497.32
497.35 TB 513.2 521.23
SU 528.14 WR 548.3 553.13
563.12 571.7 571.8 571.32
579.30 BO 590.23 590.25
591.31 592.34 597.6 597.8
597.14 597.22 602.1 JD 619.10
LA 636.14 638.41 638.42
IL 650.12 GG 669.30 678.35
679.40 680.17 684.24 687.6
690.5 690.38 699.30 699.31
ML 736.31 OV 750.14 759.25
759.39 LL 772.37 RR 784.7

SIDE (CONT.) RH 803.25
MD 825.25

SIDE-AISLE FA 465.14

SIDEBOARD EA 75.30 GG 688.9

SIDED OA 33.22

SIDES DV 143.36 149.12
OC 283.20 BL 362.22
SD 421.23 HD 446.25 446.26
WR 546.20 553.13 577.3
IL 648.20 GG 691.34
TH 853.6

SIDE-SHOWS TP 337.14

SIDE-SLOPES PR 489.12

SIDESMEN BM 835.2

SIDE-STEP GG 686.34 686.36

SIDE-TABLES TH 848.32 853.21

SIDE-TRACKING NT 717.21

SIDE-TRACK NT 717.22

SIDE-TRACKS EE 308.26

SIDEWAYS PO 102.32 TF 123.40
WS 245.42 TP 338.6 343.21
MN 375.14 WP 380.8 390.15
SU 541.6 WR 553.37 555.2
GG 664.33 664.37 695.28

SIDE-WHISKERS WM 55.40
WS 251.31

SIDINGS OC 283.30 MN 366.5
368.3

SIDLE TP 334.23

SIDNEY DV 145.8

SIENA TH 848.31 853.22

SIERRA MADRE WR 546.8

SIGH WM 63.6 SG 222.34
SU 541.17 IL 650.42
LL 767.34 769.6

SIGHED WM 65.42 DV 140.41
141.1 GF 239.27 241.6
OC 286.3 289.37 292.7
BL 348.37 360.5 FA 468.34
IL 657.26 GG 672.37
LL 773.19 773.24 774.8

SIGHING OC 293.41 SU 530.15

SIGHS TP 344.17 ML 734.3

SIGHT WM 60.7 70.1 EA 72.30
PO 99.20 99.21 110.35
112.31 DV 152.26 185.3
SG 221.11 226.13 GF 238.1
WS 245.7 264.14 OC 295.3
EE 305.24 317.4 329.7
TP 337.42 344.1 345.29
BL 347.28 350.18 351.18

SIGHT (CONT.) BL 351.42 358.2
  360.9 SD 411.25 PP 435.24
  HD 442.9 449.31 456.31
  FA 458.3 TB 522.7 SU 535.39
  537.7 539.21 WR 549.5 552.28
  562.1 BO 597.34 JD 610.33
  IL 651.42 GG 670.20 ML 731.10
  740.29 LL 772.16 777.26
  MD 814.36 815.30 816.1
  BM 836.13 TH 852.27

SIGHTLESS SB 214.41 BL 347.18
  SD 417.27 WR 581.11 581.21
  BO 592.22 JD 622.32

SIGHTLESSLY JD 615.17

SIGHTS EE 303.7 330.7

SIGN FG 195.1 SB 215.21
  GF 240.24 TP 344.11 345.41
  BL 353.1 MN 370.19 SD 411.33
  PP 432.18 SU 544.12 544.19
  WR 548.30 557.11 562.7 573.18
  573.25 573.26 IL 648.2
  NT 712.39 ML 737.19 OV 749.14
  749.28 758.39 RH 801.4
  BM 838.8

SIGNAL TP 342.29 WR 580.15
  ML 740.6 746.36

SIGNALLED GG 673.13

SIGNALS TF 119.3 PR 499.33

SIGNED TF 117.30 MN 378.37
  WP 381.24 YT 396.37 RH 800.6

SIGNIFICANCE EE 310.21 PR 482.41
  GG 673.14 LL 761.27

SIGNIFICANTLY SB 219.23

SIGNIFIED GG 674.14

SIGNIFY SP 47.34 OC 292.17
  TB 514.24

SIGNORA SU 538.5 539.14

SIGNORA GIULIETTA SU 538.5

SILENCE MO 10.28 20.39 21.10
  21.14 OA 27.36 28.15 29.20
  30.10 32.2 33.35 SP 49.12
  52.5 WM 69.17 EA 71.14 76.16
  PO 95.18 100.38 110.31 115.2
  TF 119.16 121.30 121.31
  124.12 133.16 134.2 134.3
  134.29 DV 145.30 147.15
  148.11 157.32 164.34 166.25
  169.7 176.24 179.40 180.3
  181.21 182.23 182.28 185.28
  185.39 SS 197.5 198.41 199.19
  199.30 204.33 205.20 209.18
  210.32 SB 213.1 213.39 215.18
  SG 227.26 231.32 232.19
  232.34 GF 240.29 240.35
  WS 256.5 258.40 258.42 261.11
  261.16 263.25 263.35
  CH 277.27 OC 286.21 287.37
  289.13 295.12 297.27 298.24
  299.35 EE 317.38 323.23
  325.21 325.23 331.31

SILENCE (CONT.) TP 343.39 343.40
  345.23 BL 354.22 358.13
  360.39 364.36 MN 373.17
  373.19 373.22 373.24 WP 384.31
  YT 400.41 SD 414.39 419.1
  419.10 422.13 422.23 423.37
  424.29 PP 427.30 431.26
  437.35 440.23 HD 442.29
  443.38 443.41 444.14 445.23
  452.10 455.7 FA 467.25 469.21
  470.7 PR 484.17 485.23 489.21
  490.18 491.18 492.28 492.33
  501.38 502.39 503.15 509.27
  509.41 510.34 TB 518.15 524.3
  SU 533.36 536.10 537.2 539.42
  541.11 544.7 WR 551.5 552.3
  554.7 554.11 555.1 556.34
  557.3 560.18 560.26 562.42
  563.22 563.29 566.11 567.6
  568.35 569.15 571.38 572.4
  576.32 576.36 580.9 580.16
  581.14 SM 582.34 BO 596.33
  596.35 599.21 600.12
  JD 611.37 611.42 616.14 617.7
  619.2 626.26 IL 654.4 655.38
  658.11 659.25 GG 666.37
  669.32 670.37 674.32 675.4
  676.31 684.33 684.36 687.6
  688.25 688.28 691.3 694.8
  694.25 695.35 697.18 697.22
  697.23 697.25 697.35 698.23
  NT 716.18 720.40 ML 730.30
  737.19 740.34 741.2 746.20
  OV 748.20 757.10 LL 762.41
  765.24 771.1 772.36 773.6
  774.35 775.3 775.4 776.36
  776.40 RR 780.28 781.20
  787.14 RH 793.21 MD 817.14
  819.41 823.10 823.30 823.37
  BM 831.12 832.20 833.27
  834.26 841.23 841.38
  TH 849.21

SILENCED PO 113.23 DV 141.39
  155.11 SS 200.22 206.4
  OC 289.22 301.41

SILENCES GF 241.39

SILENT MO 19.10 20.33 21.21
  22.4 OA 34.10 WM 61.42 67.40
  68.22 EA 75.23 76.22 77.8
  77.19 77.23 77.39 83.16
  87.40 88.16 88.32 PO 116.16
  TF 118.34 124.40 129.33 131.5
  134.25 DV 137.13 140.4 150.14
  152.33 154.24 155.1 158.32
  167.27 168.11 170.2 171.21
  181.14 181.28 FG 190.41
  191.12 SS 199.32 206.6 208.39
  209.24 SB 213.40 214.19
  SG 223.3 223.35 224.31 229.25
  GF 242.27 WS 248.32 256.27
  256.42 259.10 CH 276.38
  OC 296.42 301.2 EE 306.23
  315.41 328.1 330.28 BL 347.33
  358.41 360.3 360.34 MN 368.11
  370.22 373.1 373.40 WP 390.6
  390.7 YT 404.23 409.38
  SD 422.27 423.13 423.31 424.6
  PP 432.13 432.23 HD 455.7
  FA 467.4 468.24 468.31 470.13
  471.39 PR 474.18 482.25
  483.16 485.35 490.1 492.13
  507.24 TB 519.14 526.10

SILENT (CONT.) SU 536.25
  541.1 541.26 541.28
  WR 551.27 551.33 551.42
  552.30 554.1 557.20 561.29
  566.25 568.6 577.40
  SM 583.32 BO 588.34 589.6
  595.41 596.25 597.20
  597.42 602.40 603.17
  603.36 603.39 604.32
  604.40 JD 619.28 627.7
  627.19 LA 634.26 IL 657.21
  GG 666.28 669.31 681.15
  686.10 688.33 695.38
  697.23 NT 701.30 703.13
  712.36 ML 727.3 734.42
  735.26 OV 747.22 748.14
  751.12 755.21 756.12
  756.23 LL 766.15 778.31
  RR 780.29 RH 791.37 795.34
  797.7 MD 824.3 BM 829.26
  830.2 830.10 830.12 831.24
  833.4 TH 847.41 848.26

SILENTLY PO 100.1 106.21
  TF 118.37 DV 146.6 159.31
  SB 214.17 WS 264.28
  EE 315.31 TP 341.4 345.37
  MN 377.34 FA 470.39
  SU 544.6 WR 550.42 557.17
  562.1 BO 598.3 598.10
  599.27 JD 617.20 GG 669.41
  685.15 RH 793.11 BM 829.36
  TH 847.32 848.22

SILK OA 24.37 29.18 DV 147.3
  GF 235.32 239.20 WS 245.3
  245.27 246.23 251.15
  251.18 251.25 EE 322.42
  PR 495.28 TB 521.16 524.32
  524.35 SM 583.31 GG 683.10
  692.5 694.38 OV 747.9
  747.37 758.20 LL 763.21
  775.25 RH 799.18 BM 831.16
  TH 848.13

SILKEN OC 290.18 GG 682.33

SILKINESS EA 91.16 GG 698.38
  699.4 699.15

SILKS DV 179.4

SILKY PO 96.3 114.27
  EE 304.26 SU 535.33
  SM 583.33 BO 595.12

SILL BO 599.21

SILLINESS LA 642.24 642.25

SILLY EA 75.39 GF 234.12
  OC 288.40 298.11 HD 457.1
  IL 650.20 659.32 LL 767.16
  MD 821.20

SILT YT 394.24

SILTING ML 744.25

SILVER HT 42.22 SP 52.13
  EA 71.27 76.23 TF 124.23
  FG 187.31 SG 221.6
  PR 484.42 SU 536.13
  WR 547.3 547.4 547.5
  547.15 547.41 559.5 574.6

SILVER (CONT.) NT 712.12
   OV 758.30 RR 784.42 MD 811.42
   BM 829.27 831.11 831.17
   834.35 835.25 835.34
   TH 844.18

SILVER-GREEN SS 200.26

SILVER-GREY PR 496.27 OV 756.25
   MD 810.38

SILVERILY WR 574.7

SILVERING MD 809.16

SILVER-LIMBED WR 559.9

SILVER-MINE WR 547.30

SILVER-MINES WR 546.8

SILVER-MUD WR 546.22

SILVER-PAWED SU 532.30

SILVER-WORKS WR 546.17 547.40
   551.27

SILVERY SU 530.9 GG 694.18
   LL 763.20 BM 829.29

SILVERY-GREY PP 430.31

SIMBITAR SP 48.18

SIMILAR TB 515.29 NT 711.3

SIMILE SP 48.34

SIMMERING MD 823.11

SIMMONS (SEE MR. SIMMONS)

SIMPERED WS 246.7

SIMPLE EA 78.1 PO 96.40
   DV 146.5 154.25 172.25 178.23
   SB 217.17 WS 246.20 SC 267.13
   BL 353.2 MN 375.38 PP 438.34
   FA 468.3 WR 566.32 JD 605.33
   606.4 606.5 606.11
   IL 659.33 ML 728.20 LL 764.25
   MD 808.7 816.16 BM 836.29
   TH 850.30

SIMPLER DV 184.35

SIMPLEST PR 474.35 JD 614.38

SIMPLICAN JD 607.20

SIMPLICITY MO 13.24 TF 126.1
   GF 235.23 GG 668.9

SIMPLY MO 19.36 OA 38.27
   WM 65.32 EA 75.15 76.37 77.2
   77.3 77.18 77.42 86.41
   PO 100.25 DV 146.4 EE 310.31
   326.1 TP 343.17 BL 349.30
   349.37 PR 476.23 491.21
   TB 513.35 517.10 517.11
   518.31 SU 536.1 SM 582.2
   BO 593.37 603.15 JD 606.39*607.35
   IL 647.25 651.6 657.14 658.27
   NT 717.42 718.39 ML 727.19

SIMPLY (CONT.) 732.1 OV 748.40
   756.33 LL 762.31 RR 780.33
   781.17 786.36 RH 800.16
   MD 806.29 808.5 808.9 813.19
   818.16 BM 835.9 TH 846.22

SIMULATED TP 338.20 TB 526.31

SIMULTANEOUSLY WR 578.14
   GG 689.28

SIN CH 279.34 FA 468.6

SIN' WP 389.5 389.16

SINCERE SS 205.38 HD 448.4
   TB 513.5

SINCERELY MO 4.34 TB 513.2
   ML 727.28

SINCERITY GG 674.20

SINEW GG 690.12

SING MO 15.32 EA 75.31 CH 282.8
   282.11 EE 313.2 FA 466.3
   WR 573.39 LA 641.2 GG 676.23
   OV 755.16 RR 782.1 BM 830.20
   832.16 838.9 838.10

SINGED WM 70.13

SINGER MO 11.34 OV 755.11

SINGERS WR 578.13

SINGHALESE RH 796.36

SINGING MO 16.16 SP 50.38
   EA 90.27 TF 129.14 129.20
   DV 164.12 SS 200.8 WS 244.25
   247.24 261.37 CH 281.38
   MN 373.19 FA 464.11 464.25
   467.6 467.11 467.35 PR 474.12
   WR 568.38 568.40 569.16
   569.18 569.27 570.5 570.14
   OV 755.29

SINGLE SP 48.41 EA 87.17
   PO 105.16 115.38 115.39
   TF 118.33 123.14 SB 217.10
   OC 283.29 EE 313.31 314.23
   HD 453.14 FA 459.14 PR 489.17
   NT 719.37 ML 724.33 742.42
   RR 787.36 MD 811.4

SINGLED FG 194.13

SINGLE-HANDED GG 663.38

SINGLE-LINE TP 334.1

SINGLENESS EA 89.13

SINGLET SC 267.33 268.32
   OC 289.26

SING-SONG EA 73.20 FG 189.3
   SD 414.2 416.33 FA 465.12
   OV 758.4

SINGULAR TF 134.18

SINISTER BL 362.32 MN 374.24

SINISTER (CONT.) WP 384.32
   387.30 389.34 PR 482.29
   506.12 WR 577.19 JD 617.27

SINISTERLY MD 826.11
   TH 848.22

SINK OA 37.4 WM 65.33
   PO 97.32 WS 254.40
   SC 269.28 WR 581.5
   GG 698.2 MD 817.9

SINKING MO 5.3 SP 49.32
   WM 70.16 OC 286.35 298.34
   HD 448.38 456.14 SU 540.14
   WR 580.1 580.41 581.14
   JD 627.40 GG 686.26 688.29
   694.26

SIP RR 782.25

SIPPED WS 255.40 OC 285.30
   285.31 WR 565.22 GG 688.25
   688.26

SIPPING HT 39.25 EA 90.28
   MN 378.8 YT 399.16
   PR 501.38

SIR OA 34.33 HT 39.29
   PO 101.1 101.5 101.8
   101.12 101.16 102.7
   102.12 102.20 102.38
   103.3 103.7 109.20
   DV 183.29 SS 198.3 SG 228.8
   SD 415.33 419.3 PP 427.10
   LA 633.15 633.37 IL 653.37
   GG 666.42 672.32 672.35
   ML 728.30 734.33 736.23
   OV 747.30 RR 783.27 783.30
   786.4 786.8 786.9 789.5
   789.8 789.11 789.16
   RH 794.16 794.20 794.22
   796.30 796.32 797.1 797.5
   797.12 797.18 797.38

SIRENS EA 87.18 JD 610.26

SIRIUS ML 734.19

SIRRAH SC 271.11

SIRS SP 52.19 52.40 53.3
   53.9

SIR WILFRED KNIPE LL 761.33
   765.41

SISTER DV 147.20 147.28
   156.8 160.5 177.18
   SB 212.7 212.25 215.17
   GF 242.12 CH 275.9 275.38
   276.35 277.8 279.3 280.22
   282.11 YT 394.19 395.7
   400.15 407.40 HD 441.6
   442.38 443.31 447.4
   TB 516.2 516.3 516.6
   524.14 524.22 SM 583.11
   583.27 584.8 584.16 584.21
   585.20 585.22 585.40
   585.42 586.8 586.14 586.23
   BO 588.3 601.21 IL 647.14
   656.4 RH 793.20

SISTERS DV 156.10 SB 219.20

SISTERS (CONT.) EE 329.27
  YT 398.21 399.2 SM 583.32
  BO 601.29

SISTER'S DV 155.10 SB 216.13
  CH 279.24 HD 445.33 SM 585.28
  IL 647.12 654.9

SITHEE HT 42.26 SP 48.12 48.13

SITS HT 39.24 TP 334.34

SITTER MD 823.38

SITTIN' OC 294.18

SITTING MO 6.8 SP 52.22
  EA 73.12 78.29 86.24
  PO 106.38 TF 125.26 DV 160.5
  161.29 177.13 SG 221.19
  GF 234.19 242.32 WS 265.37
  OC 298.29 EE 318.8 321.36
  321.37 BL 357.42 PP 429.14
  HD 455.14 FA 460.1 462.10
  PR 478.40 495.28 506.22
  SU 537.35 542.29 WR 562.30
  SM 582.6 JD 621.2 623.11
  623.20 IL 653.21 GG 684.13
  689.13 694.41 ML 738.12
  RR 786.24 RH 791.18 MD 805.21
  805.23 819.5 819.15 824.39
  BM 835.35 836.13 836.21

SITTING-ROOM WS 245.37 248.24
  TB 515.15 LA 640.22 640.24
  641.12 645.24

SITUATION MO 5.28 10.39 15.26
  OA 34.7 WM 58.30 62.30 65.1
  PO 105.7 TF 128.35 CH 279.18
  EE 325.10 SD 420.17 HD 447.18
  455.21 IL 651.36 MD 821.42

SITUATIONS DV 146.33 HD 442.36

SIX MO 14.9 SP 50.12 EA 88.38
  TF 128.18 DV 145.33 150.16
  151.19 174.41 177.25 178.6
  184.15 SS 197.7 SG 222.9
  WS 253.34 SC 270.5 OC 289.15
  294.26 EE 316.19 317.5 319.14
  319.15 322.3 BL 354.3
  MN 371.9 371.36 WP 381.39
  382.1 YT 395.29 395.36 407.3
  SD 411.3 419.18 HD 456.22
  FA 470.38 PR 478.16 478.18
  SM 584.1 585.37 IL 649.11
  GG 672.38 OV 748.24 748.28
  LL 767.13 MD 816.10 BM 834.24

SIX HUNDRED MD 805.6

SIXPENCE SP 47.5 50.25 52.16
  52.19 52.25

SIXPENCES SP 50.20

SIXPENNY WS 244.28

SIXPENNYWORTH CH 274.27

SIX-ROOMED SC 267.17 ML 733.19

SIXTEEN YT 395.28 SD 413.27
  418.7

SIXTEENTH-CENTURY TH 848.18

SIXTH SC 270.10

SIXTY OC 293.31 SU 533.18
  GG 678.4 RR 779.6 MD 808.24
  818.24 818.33 821.8 BM 827.3

SIXTY-FOUR SP 51.16

SIXTY-THREE HT 39.23

SIZE WS 245.10 OC 284.31

SIZED MN 370.9

SIZES OC 292.6

SKATING GG 685.19

SKELETON WR 580.35 JD 622.21
  LL 761.5

SKETCHED ML 729.11

SKETCHES RH 799.23

SKETCHILY EA 82.25

SKETCHING TB 525.20 RH 799.15

SKETCHY EE 307.32

SKEWBAWD SP 49.6 49.7

SKIES GG 661.27 ML 723.32
  OV 755.27

SKILFULLY MD 815.14

SKILL FA 462.22 WR 563.41

SKIMMED DV 136.7

SKIMPY DV 138.16

SKIN HT 41.21 WM 55.30 EA 73.23
  DV 149.16 163.15 171.3
  SB 216.24 WS 247.12 CH 280.22
  EE 305.22 MN 367.24 376.27
  WP 388.20 YT 402.21 403.5
  SD 421.33 423.29 PR 481.6
  508.8 TB 518.25 SU 534.1
  534.12 534.40 534.41 539.34
  WR 564.12 JD 610.13 618.4
  620.26 624.36 LA 638.32
  641.33 641.35 643.24 643.27
  GG 665.28 691.22 NT 703.37
  705.26 707.36 OV 749.37
  BM 827.30 828.38

SKINCHIN' SC 270.41

SKINFUL WM 66.1

SKINNING ML 730.26

SKINS SS 206.25 206.40 208.40
  EE 309.11 PR 495.21 WR 564.39

SKIPPED WP 379.13

SKIPPER ML 725.27 726.1 730.16

SKIPPING OV 757.30

SKIRR OC 295.9

SKIRT SB 216.27 SG 224.1
  231.10 231.13 CH 274.10
  EE 317.24 WP 379.23 383.22
  SD 414.14 PP 437.22
  FA 458.31 TB 521.16
  522.23 525.29 525.37
  WR 551.8 NT 714.15 715.9
  OV 750.12 RR 784.25 785.8

SKIRTING MN 366.17

SKIRTS OA 24.38 EA 85.32
  WS 251.30 261.23 261.31
  OC 290.22 TP 335.21
  SM 583.8 583.23 583.33
  GG 678.41 MD 806.17
  BM 831.10

SKITTISH MD 809.5 809.7

SKITTLE-BOARD SP 50.19

SKITTLES SP 50.18

SKIVVY HD 443.1

SKULKING GG 688.30

SKULL PO 96.16 BL 363.39
  JD 622.21 LL 761.5
  RR 779.22

SKULL-AND-CROSS-BONES
  PR 482.38

SKUNK PR 486.21

SKY MO 3.6 16.16 OA 26.6
  28.21 29.31 29.35 WM 54.26
  54.34 58.39 EA 72.23
  72.27 72.29 73.1 73.6
  PO 95.7 105.19 115.1
  115.2 115.8 115.11 115.31
  TF 117.2 117.5 118.24
  122.4 FG 190.12 190.21
  SB 214.14 SG 225.14
  GF 238.26 OC 283.23
  EE 312.24 312.30 330.8
  331.24 332.26 332.27
  332.29 MN 376.16 377.41
  WP 379.1 379.5 385.32
  390.33 PP 430.31 435.22
  FA 458.7 458.25 PR 489.7
  489.13 494.1 494.26 500.38
  TB 520.28 SU 538.4
  WR 552.34 556.16 565.33
  569.23 571.5 571.7 571.9
  571.11 572.23 574.19
  574.20 575.4 578.27 578.42
  580.10 580.40 BO 596.8
  598.18 599.12 JD 610.30
  LA 630.4 641.34 643.23
  ML 738.22 743.31 744.1
  745.7 746.34 OV 747.5
  748.24 753.26 754.31
  LL 766.27 767.24 775.17
  775.26

SKY-BLUE JD 626.13

SKY-HIGH FA 459.2

SKYLESS JD 624.25

SLACK   OA 23.7   HT 42.10   PO 104.6
  TF 118.16   TP 336.1   WP 387.40
  PP 433.14   HD 452.14   GG 690.16
  690.19   690.33

SLACKEN   LL 761.15

SLACKENED   MO 12.14   DV 181.6
  SG 227.10   LL 769.18

SLACKNESS   PP 433.17

SLAMMED   LA 630.32   IL 658.10

SLANEY'S, TED   (SEE TED SLANEY'S)

SLANT   SU 538.9   WR 558.11

SLANTING   EE 330.38   PR 496.23
  498.36   SU 529.1   WR 558.15
  GG 661.14

SLAP   TP 344.23   GG 689.20

SLAPPED   BM 840.37

SLAPPING   TP 342.29

SLASH   RH 793.13

SLASHED   FG 191.17   WR 552.34
  579.1

SLASHES   WR 558.8

SLATER   BM 834.38

SLATER   (SEE MR. SLATER)

SLATY   PR 506.26

SLAUGHTER   OA 36.6

SLAVE   DV 141.36   HD 448.12
  MD 819.41   TH 850.33

SLAVED   TB 513.32   518.24

SLAVE-LIKE   DV 153.40   PP 440.23

SLAVERIN'   CH 281.25

SLAVERING   CH 276.11

SLAVERY   DV 141.42   WR 547.38
  JD 621.12

SLAVES   NT 704.30

SLAVING   BM 836.9

SLAVISH   TB 520.7   520.10

SLECK   SC 269.34

SLEEK   HT 41.10   41.14   SU 540.42
  RR 779.22

SLEEKNESS   WM 55.39

SLEEP   MO 2.16   5.41   EA 78.42
  88.13   PO 104.8   105.26   107.12
  TF 125.8   126.17   126.19   128.37
  DV 156.20   181.5   FG 189.25
  192.9   192.23   192.25   193.9

SLEEP (CONT.) 193.17   SS 211.24
  GF 237.19   WS 264.24   OC 290.13
  298.6   298.7   298.17   298.35
  300.16   BL 361.9   MN 370.3
  WP 390.6   YT 402.3   409.4
  HD 442.11   452.13   PR 488.5
  502.28   509.39   WR 556.37
  BO 594.10   JD 615.29   616.6
  616.8   624.41   GG 679.37   687.40
  688.2   691.17   697.15   697.34
  697.39   697.42   698.24   698.27
  RR 779.3   779.5   779.15   779.21
  779.28   779.35   779.37   780.8
  782.26   782.32   782.42   783.5
  783.14   787.11   MD 809.41

SLEEPERS   OC 289.33

SLEEP-HEAVY   PO 105.16

SLEEPIER   MN 366.29

SLEEPILY   JD 618.17

SLEEPING   EA 80.6   DV 136.19
  WS 265.40   PR 478.37   503.31
  SU 528.22   SM 583.18   NT 717.29
  TH 848.24

SLEEPS   JD 618.7

SLEEPY   MO 19.10   WS 244.29
  JD 618.19   LL 770.34

SLEERING   HT 41.12

SLEEVE   SS 210.34   210.42
  WS 245.6   SM 584.17   IL 652.15
  NT 713.24   MD 811.12   813.3
  813.7   BM 828.33

SLEEVED   OA 23.9

SLEEVELESS   SC 267.34

SLEEVE-LINKS   ML 728.33

SLEEVES   DV 182.11   WS 245.4
  249.4   MN 367.14   YT 397.12
  FA 468.21   SM 585.17   LA 633.32

SLENDER   SP 47.14   PO 116.18
  DV 148.37   GF 235.22   EE 312.35
  MN 370.8   WP 388.4   PP 437.24
  PR 485.2   491.8   BM 829.27

SLEPT   PO 103.19   104.7   TF 126.22
  132.12   FG 192.38   SS 204.38
  SG 222.6   EE 306.34   MN 377.39
  YT 402.24   WR 557.21   564.40
  577.37   BO 594.12   604.20
  GG 690.19   NT 719.38   ML 738.41
  744.14   744.17   OV 747.25
  LL 777.33   RR 779.34   783.1
  785.17   RH 803.41

SLICES   PR 495.25

SLID   OA 25.5   PO 113.6   115.6
  DV 157.32   167.32   EE 307.3
  PP 439.40   SU 530.26   534.33
  WR 565.42   SM 583.17   IL 652.37
  RH 793.36

SLIDE   OA 36.24   PR 498.22

SLIDING   PR 499.15

SLIGHT   MO 9.25   EA 76.13
  TF 131.20   DV 147.15
  FG 187.14   SB 212.25   217.31
  219.7   WS 256.31   OC 294.13
  EE 306.6   309.19   333.13
  BL 351.19   353.41   357.2
  357.3   359.8   MN 368.1
  WP 379.29   HD 444.33
  PR 484.35   486.40   SU 528.20
  WR 553.16   556.2   SM 583.15
  BO 597.28   JD 615.18   618.34
  619.41   GG 698.41   OV 753.9
  MD 807.36   825.2   TH 851.25

SLIGHTEST   WM 65.14   PO 99.20
  DV 157.20   172.28   RR 782.36

SLIGHTLY   MO 10.10   12.29
  OA 27.24   28.6   34.41
  WM 58.4   58.42   59.10   61.6
  EA 73.18   91.41   PO 104.2
  107.25   110.10   TF 119.11
  119.20   DV 161.29   SB 217.19
  SG 225.33   226.19   227.17
  GF 235.25   WS 247.12
  CH 275.7   OC 300.24
  EE 303.17   304.26   319.14
  328.41   329.36   BL 349.21
  351.30   352.2   364.13
  MN 366.21   374.23   375.19
  376.27   376.33   378.7
  WP 380.17   388.1   388.22
  391.14   YT 401.3   SD 425.31
  425.34   PP 428.23   430.35
  432.26   439.9   439.22   440.9
  PR 475.10   476.15   476.23
  493.5   512.21   WR 569.3
  JD 606.23   614.28   618.32
  621.30   622.32   LA 632.23
  637.9   637.10   640.40
  GG 670.17   675.13   683.42
  ML 728.39   LL 761.9
  RH 793.10   MD 813.10   814.6
  823.13

SLIGHTLY-ELVISH   MD 812.8

SLIGHTLY-WASHING   EA 83.16

SLIM   PO 107.10   108.5
  DV 138.20   GF 235.32
  WS 255.29   EE 304.22
  309.6   312.6   PP 437.9
  440.21   BO 587.2   LA 635.2
  GG 670.16   673.2   BM 834.33
  841.6

SLIM-LEGGED   PO 107.35

SLINK   OC 289.20

SLIP   OA 35.3   35.7   35.20
  EA 74.31   WS 248.24   248.36
  PR 498.33   TB 524.32
  SU 539.38   RR 784.24
  MD 807.19   BM 831.16   841.6

SLIPPED   OA 25.23   EA 90.35
  TF 131.22   131.24   WS 247.23
  CH 276.13   PR 499.6
  SU 533.36   542.17   542.18
  LA 631.30   IL 650.40
  ML 746.13   LL 770.9

SLIPPED (CONT.) RH 802.35
  MD 815.26

SLIPPER JD 617.8*

SLIPPERS DV 168.16 SG 226.13
  WS 265.36 OC 289.38 IL 654.32

SLIPPERY EA 90.7 LA 631.6
  ML 724.15

SLIPPING WM 70.12 WS 254.24
  PR 497.34 498.26 WR 572.25
  ML 723.17 BM 834.19

SLIPS OC 294.27 294.28
  ML 735.19 735.20

SLIT EE 323.31 330.20 WR 563.41
  563.42

SLITHER EE 307.24

SLITHERED PR 498.13 498.37

SLITHERING TP 334.18 WP 387.19

SLITS PO 95.20 EE 326.4

SLIVING YT 405.29

S'LL HT 40.6 41.4 SP 48.28
  50.7 DV 172.12 SB 215.13
  218.25 220.6 SC 267.27 271.15
  273.16 CH 282.7 OC 293.26
  SD 412.36 PP 435.25 436.23
  FA 470.2 BM 840.16

SLOBBER SC 267.32

SLOBBERING CH 279.9

SLOG MD 814.20 814.23

SLOGGING MD 814.30

SLOPE PO 112.12 SS 197.19
  197.24 EE 305.7 307.12
  WP 386.19 390.36 HD 449.5
  449.27 PR 489.36 490.28
  493.18 493.22 495.26 496.7
  496.11 496.14 496.20 497.10
  498.23 499.13 507.22 510.9
  510.26 SU 530.3 537.35 538.42
  539.4 WR 551.23 558.23 558.30

SLOPED OC 283.34 YT 394.8
  LA 634.10

SLOPES PR 489.14 493.25 494.27
  507.10 WR 551.33 556.18
  558.42 579.6 BO 603.2
  NT 716.6

SLOPING SP 45.13 TF 119.11
  119.20 EE 304.4 305.2
  BL 354.23 HD 446.25 449.3
  WR 580.10 LA 631.32 LL 767.6

SLOPPED PP 433.21

SLOPPILY LL 776.27

SLOPS OC 291.41

SLOSH DV 176.29

SLOTHFUL DV 140.19

SLOUCHED LA 631.27

SLOUCHING HT 43.16 MN 374.21
  LA 630.9 631.1

SLOUGH GF 240.7

SLOVENLINESS WS 244.9

SLOW MO 10.24 16.35 FG 194.39
  SB 218.9 218.42 CH 274.11
  OC 283.9 287.41 EE 304.18
  309.10 322.39 323.20 325.6
  TP 338.38 BL 349.11 355.6
  360.30 362.26 MN 376.25
  378.22 WP 379.10 SD 414.34
  PP 433.17 HD 448.24 448.38
  450.34 454.7 454.13 FA 459.37
  PR 484.35 SU 532.13 536.35
  537.1 537.6 WR 558.27 558.31
  565.13 566.15 566.31
  SM 582.18 584.9 JD 609.19
  613.35 617.37 620.12 624.38
  629.1 IL 651.35 652.42
  GG 663.22 666.17 666.24 669.6
  677.13 684.4 684.37 685.7
  687.41 690.18 692.22
  NT 712.32 ML 725.18 728.36
  LL 774.41 MD 807.38 823.6
  823.27 824.18 824.29
  TH 846.41

SLOW-COACH WS 247.16 247.17

SLOWED PO 107.21 HD 448.17
  LA 635.29

SLOWER PO 102.6

SLOWLY MO 4.27 18.42 21.3
  21.19 HT 42.31 SP 52.15
  WM 65.28 66.24 EA 72.37 73.21
  75.20 85.14 88.41 PO 104.3
  104.39 106.22 107.26 110.29
  112.32 TF 119.25 120.24
  120.35 120.42 129.39
  DV 139.41 140.8 149.4 150.19
  177.32 179.21 181.26 182.18
  FG 188.9 SS 205.23 209.11
  SG 224.14 224.28 225.23
  225.29 225.40 228.20 GF 240.6
  WS 245.21 261.34 263.14 264.4
  264.10 264.15 265.27 265.34
  266.1 SC 272.17 CH 275.7
  OC 284.29 284.33 287.25
  293.40 294.5 294.7 295.10
  299.33 EE 312.20 312.26
  312.28 321.39 322.18 322.19
  323.20 TP 345.16 BL 361.16
  361.29 361.35 364.13
  MN 369.24 377.20 378.13
  378.31 WP 388.4 388.13 388.24
  389.15 390.3 391.26 YT 404.42
  405.7 406.13 407.30 SD 418.39
  423.5 425.36 HD 444.37 449.39
  449.40 449.41 450.11 450.34
  454.5 455.4 455.6 FA 468.17
  469.32 PR 488.19 493.11
  496.17 498.16 502.17 505.28
  505.36 TB 521.28 523.30 524.5
  SU 532.14 536.42 541.19

SLOWLY (CONT.) WR 558.17
  558.27 568.35 578.1
  578.22 578.34 579.5 581.3
  BO 594.3 599.1 599.5
  JD 609.9 628.42 LA 645.42
  IL 657.5 GG 686.19 690.1
  692.37 694.14 699.10
  ML 735.30 740.4 745.5
  OV 749.18 LL 765.10 777.23
  RH 791.35 MD 824.11 826.18
  TH 846.36

SLOWLY-LAPSING MO 2.21

SLOWNESS WS 246.19 BL 349.13
  IL 659.39 BM 841.26

SLOW-STEPPING CH 275.20

SLOW-THINKING LL 771.26

S'LT SC 269.23 269.23

SLUGGISH SP 49.21

SLUGGISHLY DV 139.41

SLUM ML 722.18

SLUMBER PO 104.8 116.20

SLUMBERING EE 306.30

SLUMBROUS HD 442.6

SLUMS JD 609.8

SLUNG PO 100.17 WR 560.42

SLUNK OA 37.27 OC 286.24
  RR 784.33

SLURRED RR 784.37 785.1

SLURRING MO 10.32 LA 632.9

SLUSHY JD 610.19

SLUT MD 808.17

SLUTTISH MD 807.41

SLUTTISHNESS MD 808.12

SLY HT 41.11 SP 47.5
  YT 396.6 399.1 399.32
  MD 825.17

SMACKING MO 1.22 TP 338.20

SMALL-BOYISH BO 587.36

SMALLER TF 135.2 FG 194.35
  SB 214.4 BL 363.39
  WR 562.10 GG 669.20
  ML 733.7 746.11 BM 838.28

SMALLEST SU 535.33

SMALLISH TB 524.40 RH 804.12
  BM 830.38 TH 844.4

SMALL-LOOPED SS 203.25

SMALLNESS YT 397.20 JD 611.4

SMALL-POX WS 247.13

SMART SG 221.19 WS 250.37
  EE 318.39 TB 524.34 GG 662.15
  RH 791.9

SMARTENED MN 368.28

SMART-LOOKING MN 375.39

SMASH OA 35.8 WM 70.4 EA 88.2
  DV 137.35

SMASHED EA 87.13 TF 128.27
  SC 269.41 CH 276.4 BO 593.23
  MD 812.41 813.4

SMASHING GG 676.15

SMEAR OC 290.36

SMEARED FG 195.21 OV 754.36
  755.28

SMEDLEY, TOM (SEE TOM SMEDLEY)

SMEDLEY'S FA 471.21

SMELL OA 27.32 PO 106.28 106.31
  107.37 TF 124.14 DV 139.17
  SG 229.14 WS 246.24 OC 287.32
  288.38 289.6 296.22 TP 337.20
  BL 353.2 WP 379.3 HD 450.13
  451.28 454.24 PR 502.10
  WR 565.36 572.29 JD 610.10
  616.22 624.25 LA 643.6 646.33
  GG 677.27 677.35 678.5 683.42
  694.23 697.17 ML 734.14

SMELLED TF 117.17 SB 216.41
  BL 358.29 SU 544.36 JD 617.7
  ML 742.21

SMELLING WM 55.16 PO 108.29
  WS 246.25 BL 358.34 WR 565.33
  LA 640.7

SMELLS HD 456.39

SMELT SS 202.10 BL 354.35
  HD 454.24 JD 610.23 LA 643.6
  GG 695.12

SMILE MO 4.1 5.6 OA 30.15
  34.27 WM 57.6 58.13 61.27
  65.17 EA 90.21 PO 101.25
  101.28 102.18 102.28 102.30
  102.41 DV 167.7 FG 195.12
  SS 198.40 200.12 209.7
  SG 221.37 224.42 GF 235.30
  242.18 243.17 WS 254.16
  CH 275.4 EE 319.3 324.9
  324.42 325.27 TP 336.15
  BL 351.19 351.25 355.6 358.22
  359.12 MN 378.22 WP 379.29
  YT 398.12 405.42 409.25 410.2
  PP 437.31 439.28 HD 454.4
  PR 477.26 484.22 485.28
  486.34 507.2 TB 522.15
  WR 565.6 566.13 566.15 566.19
  567.24 567.25 567.41 570.26
  570.42 571.42 573.4 575.42
  576.6 SM 583.39 584.4 584.5
  584.9 584.10 584.12 584.14
  584.22 584.27 585.2 585.4

SMILE (CONT.) 585.23 585.27
  585.35 JD 612.38 613.2 624.38
  LA 633.1 IL 658.27 658.29
  GG 685.20 NT 702.30 713.2
  715.32 ML 726.19 727.26
  LL 772.14 RR 784.20 787.12
  789.11 MD 807.37 822.32
  826.14 BM 831.35 833.7 836.34
  837.10 838.12 838.17 843.1

SMILED MO 4.25 4.26 6.26 7.6
  8.14 10.20 11.2 13.6 16.5
  18.35 19.5 19.12 OA 29.3
  30.8 31.10 33.14 34.41 38.21
  38.27 38.31 38.35 WM 54.23
  56.18 63.41 64.5 64.18 65.37
  66.3 68.3 EA 84.4 DV 160.17
  167.12 168.2 183.30 FG 195.12
  196.15 SB 218.24 219.19
  GF 242.14 WS 245.16 245.25
  245.29 247.31 250.3 251.27
  CH 276.39 277.6 277.42
  EE 318.31 319.3 MN 375.19
  375.30 378.30 WP 380.2 380.21
  382.31 SD 418.42 425.36
  PP 431.7 HD 446.10 456.29
  PR 504.37 TB 522.14 524.31
  WR 554.35 BO 600.6 602.3
  JD 622.37 LA 634.40 GG 696.40
  NT 719.25 ML 726.6 729.8
  739.14 LL 772.14 RH 796.41
  MD 824.24

SMILELESS SM 586.28

SMILES FG 187.23 CH 278.41
  278.42 PR 485.20 ML 727.22

SMILING MO 7.13 8.1 8.20 9.1
  9.15 9.22 11.12 12.12 12.24
  12.28 13.9 15.12 15.17
  OA 29.40 34.31 SP 47.28
  WM 64.10 64.24 65.28 67.16
  EA 75.42 TF 123.20 DV 150.2
  178.28 FG 188.36 SS 201.8
  203.13 GF 242.11 242.17
  WS 245.20 EE 318.30 TP 336.40
  337.25 BL 355.13 MN 370.11
  373.26 WP 381.6 381.25 383.20
  391.42 YT 399.26 TB 517.27
  WR 554.14 JD 624.37 LA 637.16
  GG 676.26 685.41 NT 713.41
  714.41 ML 726.1 726.10
  MD 824.19 BM 829.32 838.16

SMIRCHED ML 737.40

SMIRK LL 776.25

SMIRKING RH 791.19 791.20

SMITE HT 41.22 WP 389.28

SMITHERINGALE, CHRIS (SEE CHRIS
  SMITHERINGALE)

SMITHY TF 128.7

SMOCK PO 106.32

SMOKE MO 2.15 DV 140.6
  SB 219.29 SG 226.35 227.3
  227.13 229.15 GF 241.33
  WS 253.20 SC 269.10 CH 275.25
  OC 283.15 EE 330.11 TP 334.5

SMOKE (CONT.) HD 447.32
  PR 494.37 500.22 501.39
  501.41 509.16 WR 565.36
  BO 594.14 RR 784.36
  MD 823.5 823.8

SMOKED PO 106.24 SD 418.37
  LL 770.42 RR 788.30
  BM 830.12

SMOKE-GREY SU 538.29

SMOKING WM 54.15 WS 261.17
  YT 399.17 SD 415.32 418.9
  419.8 HD 441.14 WR 562.7
  578.25 ML 725.19

SMOKY OC 300.25 EE 314.29
  JD 609.8

SMOOTH OA 26.13 HT 41.11
  41.14 PO 110.42 TF 118.39
  119.11 DV 167.17 167.33
  FG 192.17 194.29 SS 207.26
  SB 217.20 SG 226.19
  WS 247.13 OC 284.8 MN 366.8
  YT 401.41 SD 423.29 423.40
  PR 490.2 WR 554.2 561.26
  562.3 562.31 JD 618.4
  LA 632.2 633.17 GG 694.25
  695.29 NT 703.42 ML 741.28
  744.26 MD 816.2

SMOOTHED WP 382.28 TB 516.11
  SU 537.11

SMOOTHING PO 98.39

SMOOTH-LIPPED ML 726.2

SMOOTHLY DV 159.1

SMOOTH-PARTED FA 463.18

SMOOTH-SKINNED JD 606.28

SMOTE ML 734.1

SMOTHERED OA 25.17 OC 296.3
  296.7 SD 416.33

SMOTHERING OA 24.39

SMOULDERED TF 126.8

SMOULDERING MO 2.29 TF 118.15
  121.22 HD 449.1 JD 629.1
  629.2

SMUDGED DV 182.3

SMUG HT 44.5 IL 650.9 650.19
  LL 762.1

SNAIL SU 533.9 534.24

SNAILS MD 818.20

SNAKE WM 61.22 EE 306.41
  307.2 323.20 324.15
  SU 536.31 536.35 536.39
  536.41 537.4 537.8 537.14
  537.17 537.18 BO 599.10
  NT 716.6 716.8 ML 723.36

SNAKE-INFESTED EE 303.30 303.37

SNAKES EE 303.19 306.33 316.31
  323.40 324.3 SU 537.20

SNAKE'S WR 555.31

SNAP MO 18.17 OA 29.22
  SB 213.25 SC 268.21 TB 527.7

SNAP-BAG DV 167.39 SC 268.13

SNAPPED OA 34.38 SB 215.27
  215.32 SG 230.19 CH 275.11
  OC 297.19 IL 650.27 LL 776.8
  776.20 777.16 RR 782.28
  783.28 TH 846.35

SNAPPING BM 831.15

SNAPPY SB 215.10

SNARES SS 206.25

SNARL BO 603.29

SNARLED PP 439.8 SM 585.14
  JD 620.9

SNARLING GF 234.11 IL 657.9

SNATCH WM 67.19 PR 490.27
  MD 818.3 BM 836.40

SNATCHED DV 162.22 FG 189.8
  CH 282.1 BL 348.12 PR 489.40

SNATCHES LA 640.2

SNATCHING OA 24.39 CH 278.41

SNATCHY WS 244.25

SNEER WM 67.8 EA 76.13 76.17
  77.37 87.26 PO 99.28
  DV 146.10 CH 280.21

SNEERED WM 67.13 EA 75.1
  WS 263.5

SNEERING EA 75.13 PO 100.10
  DV 145.39 SD 420.29 IL 658.29

SNEEZED YT 394.35 PR 489.24

SNEEZING YT 394.36

SNEINTON CHURCH GF 235.20

SNIFFED SB 213.38 MD 809.31

SNIFFING OA 37.30 WM 55.11

SNIGGERING GF 243.17

SNIRT GG 665.6 667.5 668.25
  676.38

SNOB SB 217.39

SNOBS GG 661.16

SNORT NT 709.35

SNORTING RH 793.11

SNORTS NT 719.20

SNOUT SB 215.6 216.28

SNOW PO 95.8 95.21 105.24
  114.42 115.4 115.34 DV 157.7
  158.38 160.23 160.27 160.30
  161.5 161.33 161.39 167.3
  167.11 167.13 167.15 167.24
  167.27 167.30 167.33 173.26
  173.37 174.15 176.27
  FG 188.23 188.26 193.15
  193.24 193.34 193.38 194.4
  194.5 194.10 194.16 194.18
  194.27 194.31 194.34 195.24
  SS 202.9 WP 379.1 379.9
  385.28 385.36 385.38 386.3
  386.4 386.8 386.11 386.26
  386.27 386.30 387.15 387.38
  390.34 390.37 392.31
  PR 487.12 487.32 496.37
  503.16 503.19 509.24
  SU 529.17 535.32 WR 552.35
  558.8 569.24 572.5 572.22
  572.26 572.31 574.11 574.15
  575.36 576.19 577.40 578.20
  578.28 578.31 578.41 579.6
  579.11 579.18 BO 602.29
  602.30 602.32 603.1 603.11
  603.14 JD 610.1 LA 630.1
  631.6 631.8 631.29 632.18
  632.37 634.26 635.26 635.30
  635.33 635.40 636.31 637.4
  637.42 638.1 638.19 638.20
  638.23 639.2 639.5 639.7
  639.16 639.31 639.34 639.38
  640.17 640.33 641.31
  GG 670.13 674.4 674.32
  ML 723.12 744.6 744.25 744.26
  744.30 744.31 744.33 744.38
  745.1 745.3 745.7 745.13
  745.15 745.18 745.19 745.21
  745.27 745.31 745.34 745.35
  745.38 746.2 746.6 746.9
  746.13 746.14 746.22 746.36

SNOWBALL TB 520.31

SNOW-BED WR 578.33

SNOW-DESERTED WP 393.8

SNOWDROPS DV 139.11 161.6

SNOWED ML 744.20 744.36

SNOWFLAKES DV 157.23 157.36
  161.9 FG 193.13

SNOWING DV 166.34 166.35
  FG 193.10 PR 503.16

SNOW-LIT LA 636.5

SNOW-PATCHES BO 600.21

SNOW-POWDER ML 745.5

SNOWS GG 674.3

SNOW-SLEEP MN 746.17

SNOW-WET WP 386.23

SNOW-WHITE WR 562.39 GG 665.28

SNOWY PO 105.19 DV 160.36
  161.29 WP 387.22 WR 574.9
  578.18 578.29 LA 638.6
  MD 808.28

SNUFF DV 139.24

SNUFFED BO 602.9

SNUFFING SB 214.23

SNUFFLE IL 652.33

SNUG DV 160.38

SNUGLY SC 267.22

SOAKED PO 105.25 GG 671.30

SOAKING ML 743.1

SOAP DV 170.26 170.41
  OC 299.25

SOAP-FROTH DV 170.38

SOAPY JD 617.20

SOAR BO 595.34 OV 748.29

SOARING LA 639.38

SOB EA 83.15 91.38 WS 259.7

SOBBED WS 259.14 259.27
  265.26 266.3 SD 419.16
  419.21 419.32 HD 457.5
  PR 509.22 LA 646.2 646.3

SOBBING OA 36.35 DV 181.18
  WS 264.28 SC 272.39
  EE 317.13 SD 419.25
  HD 456.41 WR 570.7
  BM 828.29

SOBBING-SINGING PR 502.42

SOBER GG 696.13

SOBERED WS 250.36

SOBERNESS WS 256.31

SOBS OA 37.29 SC 272.41

SO-CALLED BO 594.1 ML 724.17

SOCIAL DV 137.19 EE 313.35
  314.8 BL 359.37 RH 790.24

SOCIALIST NT 706.16

SOCIETY DV 137.18 137.21
  SS 208.23 EE 311.28 312.35
  313.21 325.15 PP 428.29
  PR 473.23 NT 706.29
  MD 819.14

SOCKET SP 51.8 SU 540.15
  WR 579.37

SOCKETS JD 616.32

SOCKS YT 398.5

SODA EA 75.30 GG 688.24
  RH 802.37

SODDEN TF 118.16 DV 176.38
  GF 241.32 HD 452.15 456.19

SODDENED HD 449.20 450.5

SODOM AND GOMORRAH TH 849.28

SOFA MO 4.17 5.41 EA 85.33
  86.7 90.36 DV 162.16 178.16
  OC 290.1 293.38 HD 452.20
  JD 616.17 616.41 618.10 619.6
  LA 645.26 IL 650.12 650.15
  NT 706.41 ML 727.13 727.18

SOFAS EA 84.14 IL 650.16
  TH 848.32

SOFT MO 9.4 10.21 12.37 17.32
  20.3 OA 25.6 27.4 WM 55.32
  58.39 EA 84.15 86.9 91.36
  PO 95.21 97.2 114.40 114.42
  115.33 TF 118.39 132.18
  SS 198.9 203.28 205.21
  SB 217.8 SG 222.3 222.26
  225.12 225.31 WS 245.7 252.26
  CH 279.31 OC 299.25 EE 324.14
  324.23 329.23 TP 335.41
  338.38 339.4 BL 360.7 363.37
  364.2 MN 373.28 WP 385.28
  386.40 388.14 YT 399.11
  402.26 403.12 SD 413.33
  425.14 HD 450.12 450.18
  453.33 454.23 455.26 455.28
  FA 463.33 464.37 471.29
  471.30 PR 473.11 473.26
  475.10 479.34 483.41 493.22
  494.26 501.26 505.19 TB 518.6
  523.31 SU 530.18 531.29 533.8
  536.32 WR 553.38 558.27
  561.11 561.25 565.11 570.26
  575.42 576.4 576.14 576.41
  577.5 577.9 SM 583.23 583.24
  586.13 BO 587.2 597.3 597.7
  JD 612.29 616.9 LA 634.33
  635.6 637.8 637.13 IL 651.10
  656.35 GG 664.23 670.33
  672.41 682.33 683.40 NT 704.1
  712.24 712.26 713.8 ML 734.17
  735.20 735.32 736.4 740.22
  744.27 LL 763.22 767.2 769.18
  771.11 774.7 774.16 774.20
  RR 788.22 788.42 MD 809.26
  820.1 820.2 821.32 824.12
  BM 836.18 TH 848.15

SOFT-BREATHING SD 414.1

SOFTEN CH 275.29

SOFTENED WM 64.36 MN 376.11
  WP 379.31 JD 616.13

SOFTENING GG 694.15

SOFTER EA 89.34

SOFT-FLESHED BO 587.28

SOFT-HEARTED MN 376.4 376.6

SOFTLY MO 7.16 12.21 16.13
  20.16 21.3 OA 35.6 EA 73.27

SOFTLY (CONT.) 74.29 77.38
  88.37 90.34 TF 125.33
  DV 161.16 FG 191.37 SB 214.30
  CH 278.4 OC 295.35 298.36
  TP 338.27 339.34 BL 351.3
  353.6 363.38 MN 372.25
  WP 380.22 YT 401.32 401.35
  SD 425.15 HD 443.10 455.25
  FA 466.33 PR 479.35 503.17
  WR 565.19 572.1 576.41
  SM 583.4 583.6 585.19 586.15
  586.16 IL 648.35 651.37
  656.29 GG 666.41 697.24
  697.39 NT 713.5 ML 734.34
  734.35 735.28 735.30
  OV 752.42 LL 766.39 772.6
  772.8 773.4 774.2 775.39
  RR 784.16 788.15 789.13
  RH 803.7 MD 822.11 825.20
  BM 837.29 842.36

SOFTLY-SHADED LL 775.32

SOFTLY-STARTLED BM 837.37

SOFTNESS MO 15.21 TF 130.4
  SG 225.37 WS 244.15 SD 413.29
  WR 577.5 OV 749.12

SOFT-SKINNED GG 670.14

SOFT-SPOKEN ML 725.15

SOHO MD 817.19

SOIL WM 65.14 FG 189.41
  SS 206.14 SB 214.17 EE 303.5
  306.36 307.24 BO 593.27
  ML 728.35 729.7

SOILED GF 241.42 PR 494.41

SOISSONS BO 593.36

SOIS TRISTE ET SOIS BELLE MO 16.4

SOLD DV 153.16 153.17 FG 191.10
  GF 235.18 YT 396.17 PR 482.14
  TH 852.7

SOLDIER SP 47.29 EA 73.8
  PO 97.18 97.32 98.1 98.21
  98.29 99.8 99.10 99.15 99.19
  99.41 101.29 102.6 102.20
  102.27 102.29 103.8 107.20
  107.33 109.8 109.13 109.27
  109.33 110.16 113.42
  TF 119.27 119.30 119.34
  121.15 123.16 127.40 134.16
  WS 245.15 EE 328.14 328.20
  328.25 329.4 329.10 331.14
  WP 380.37 YT 400.16 403.36
  SD 418.37 421.15 421.19
  421.36 422.5 422.15 BO 590.35
  592.15 MD 820.32

SOLDIERLY SP 47.40 SG 227.34

SOLDIERS PO 95.14 98.19 105.28
  106.21 106.39 108.3 111.32
  116.10 116.13 TF 117.15
  118.29 119.4 119.17 119.24
  119.38 121.32 121.41 127.12
  127.21 127.25 127.27 127.36
  128.18 129.14 133.27 134.7

SOLDIERS (CONT.) 134.10
  134.26 135.1 MN 367.34
  367.37 368.28 371.7
  371.15 371.37 SD 413.20
  414.9 414.20 415.5 415.19
  418.11 418.23 419.9 420.2
  420.11 420.15 420.38 421.5
  421.13 421.29 422.26
  422.29 JD 609.7 GG 662.33

SOLDIER'S PO 97.22 98.12
  99.25 103.5 105.6 108.1
  108.8 SG 227.9 YT 400.5
  GG 676.23

SOLDIERS' TF 117.10 117.12
  129.20

SOLE PO 115.27 SB 214.35
  LL 766.1

SOLEMN SP 46.22 PR 512.2
  JD 607.23

SOLEMNITY MO 14.12 CH 278.40

SOLEMNLY WS 247.8 GG 689.28
  NT 718.27

SOLICITOR SG 227.21 YT 405.22
  405.23 408.27 409.28

SOLICITOUS EA 92.3 FA 461.35

SOLICITOUSLY SG 223.20

SOLICITUDE EE 324.10 324.41
  WR 560.37 565.19 566.16
  566.21

SOLID MO 13.21 WM 58.15
  59.15 PO 109.9 114.34
  DV 171.4 SG 228.30
  TP 334.35 SD 417.40
  PR 493.21 ML 722.25 724.15
  LL 764.37 BM 835.10

SOLIDITY WM 65.26

SOLIDLY PP 439.24

SOLITARINESS PO 99.38
  DV 156.12

SOLITARY EA 72.30

SOLITUDE BL 348.17 348.21

SOLO FA 466.27 466.36

SOLOIST FA 467.9

SOLOMON JD 607.14

SOLOS FA 464.11 464.25
  464.30 466.3 467.11

SOLUTION IL 651.14

SOLVE EE 333.8

SOLVING DV 146.33

SOMBRE EA 84.6 DV 181.15
  SS 206.17 OC 286.8

SOMBRE (CONT.) EE 322.36 325.1
 WP 385.33 PR 482.38 486.39
 508.40 509.3 SU 543.1
 WR 552.30 ML 723.35 RR 784.32
 785.20

SOMEBODIES BO 588.11 588.12
 588.15 588.21

SOMEBODY MO 2.38 17.4 SP 47.16
 PO 112.28 DV 172.3 172.12
 FG 188.34 192.10 SS 201.1
 SB 215.14 215.40 GF 235.34
 242.35 242.36 242.42 WS 259.8
 CH 275.1 OC 290.5 TP 339.27
 340.4 345.35 BL 362.37
 MN 368.18 368.20 YT 399.35
 PP 440.27 FA 462.13 WR 565.15
 BO 588.8 588.14 588.19 588.20
 JD 617.28 LA 632.1 632.6
 632.14 635.38 635.41 636.4
 640.6 IL 651.22 NT 708.21
 ML 731.1 731.3 OV 757.36
 RR 782.12 782.41 MD 814.32
 821.6

SOMEBODY'S EA 88.19 DV 169.1
 JD 621.13 MD 807.23

SOMEHOW EA 90.28 PO 113.26
 DV 157.1 164.38 SB 217.31
 GF 241.10 WS 262.17 PR 487.15
 SU 539.34 JD 625.2 IL 649.7
 659.3 GG 661.23 675.4 678.4
 ML 739.17 MD 810.36 819.9
 820.12 BM 828.8 828.13
 TH 846.14

SOMEONE OA 30.35 PO 112.32
 112.36 TF 122.29 FG 193.4
 193.8 OC 286.39 PR 503.41
 508.38 WR 559.19 562.33
 571.30 LA 633.13 636.2 636.7
 636.16 638.15 641.41
 NT 705.42 706.4 711.34 716.25
 LL 767.4 767.9 774.39
 MD 820.39

SOMEONE'S WM 59.1

SOMETHING'S JD 626.23 GG 681.4

SOMETIME PO 113.32

SOMETIMES MO 3.2 WM 65.19 65.20
 65.21 EA 80.22 92.11 PO 98.29
 106.23 115.20 TF 131.12
 DV 146.8 151.11 154.7 164.39
 168.32 FG 192.7 SS 207.41
 SG 225.32 225.34 GF 238.25
 WS 257.13 257.14 261.3
 OC 289.31 299.33 EE 312.14
 314.10 320.22 323.16 325.20
 329.19 TP 336.24 343.30
 BL 347.30 347.31 347.35
 349.23 355.32 363.12 363.21
 WP 380.38 383.10 386.27
 386.35 387.5 PR 473.11 473.14
 479.21 483.4 489.24 490.21
 498.37 TB 519.32 SU 532.12
 532.13 532.14 532.18 533.33
 535.37 535.39 542.23
 WR 548.14 566.10 566.13
 567.20 568.1 568.10 570.12
 570.15 574.17 BO 588.17 589.6

SOMETIMES (CONT.) 592.26 592.27
 603.8 JD 605.16 606.34
 620.26 LA 631.41 GG 662.5
 662.6 674.33 674.38 681.37
 698.16 698.19 NT 705.30
 708.34 709.34 709.35 710.36
 712.32 ML 727.28 735.38
 739.8 740.23 742.25 742.27
 743.34 LL 761.1 761.13 761.33
 762.40 765.5 765.35 766.4
 767.40 768.9 769.30 RR 780.32
 RH 797.30 797.31 797.32
 802.12 MD 818.38 820.25
 BM 830.12 831.20 832.4 832.5
 832.23 842.6

SOMEWHAT MO 15.9 SP 50.40
 EA 85.11 DV 157.41 TP 334.25
 YT 396.9 PP 427.16 PR 494.40
 TB 521.14 524.4 BO 587.20
 GG 661.27 687.42 MD 807.13
 BM 829.22

SOMEWHEER SP 49.34

SOMEWHERE EA 71.19 76.1 89.15
 DV 178.9 WS 256.13 BL 361.22
 MN 373.42 YT 400.40 SM 585.2
 586.26 BO 591.3 JD 605.1
 606.7 612.32 620.1 620.4
 627.12 IL 655.15 GG 681.4
 684.37 685.7 688.39 NT 705.23
 ML 724.35 LL 763.39 RR 786.21
 789.20 RH 792.37 MD 807.27
 BM 835.6 835.7 TH 846.14

SOMNAMBULE OV 753.3

SON MO 5.22 SP 46.20 52.15
 DV 141.17 144.35 148.27
 148.37 149.4 149.24 168.28
 168.31 171.38 SS 201.32
 201.40 SG 231.6 CH 281.22
 OC 284.39 284.41 295.13
 WP 383.37 388.31 388.33
 388.41 YT 395.24 FA 470.26
 PR 482.16 SU 528.22 534.7
 540.34 540.37 540.39 WR 551.1
 566.33 BO 588.28 GG 682.23
 688.15 688.19 696.42 699.26
 ML 725.28 725.30 725.36
 LL 761.32 763.17 764.33
 765.12 768.17 774.25 777.21
 777.36 778.34 RH 793.41
 794.35 795.1 795.14 795.37
 796.18 796.22 798.6 798.20
 798.32 798.37 799.40 800.28
 803.11 804.34

SONATA WM 59.7

SONG MO 12.16 16.10 GF 234.21
 WS 251.5 FA 465.22 WR 578.14
 GG 676.24 676.30 OV 755.18

SONGFUL OA 25.25

SONGS MO 16.1 16.8 EA 75.33
 TF 129.15 RR 782.1

SON-IN-LAW DV 158.5 158.12
 186.14

SONNY RH 794.37 797.35

SONORA WR 548.35 550.1

SONORITY PR 484.36

SONOROUS CH 277.29 LL 770.14

SONS HT 39.13 41.8 DV 138.28
 140.24 140.28 140.33 142.5
 142.22 142.24 146.27
 163.35 163.41 SS 201.19
 GG 695.41 LL 768.28
 MD 818.41 819.1 820.9
 825.7

SON'S DV 162.23 OC 286.20
 RH 802.31 802.39

SOONER EE 320.10 BL 361.24
 JD 626.4 626.24

SOONEST MN 371.28

SOOTHE DV 169.35 WS 259.14

SOOTHED SB 212.30 SC 270.1
 BO 591.23 591.40 GG 663.4

SOOTHING GF 241.35 SU 529.18
 537.13 WR 565.30 GG 682.30
 MD 822.23

SOOTHINGLY DV 170.11 WR 571.2
 MD 822.12 BM 839.34 842.19

SOPHISTICATED JD 606.1

SOPPY DV 167.5 GG 673.27
 674.10 674.25

SORDID DV 165.20 TP 334.22
 FA 458.30 TH 850.35

SORE EE 328.41 FA 460.40
 PR 473.8 JD 610.22

SORENESS FG 190.35

SORES FG 189.27 OC 283.20

SORREL PR 485.9 489.22
 490.15 494.16 499.5

SORROW OA 26.40 YT 397.33
 FA 468.7 BM 836.32 836.38
 TH 846.4 846.5 846.8
 846.12 846.15 846.28

SORROWFUL MO 13.27 DV 182.36

SORRY MO 8.9 OA 23.34 34.35
 35.25 38.26 SP 45.33 48.16
 48.20 WM 63.23 DV 179.29
 SS 201.21 GF 236.6
 SC 271.9 271.12 EE 320.24
 BL 356.21 WP 380.4
 FA 460.35 468.33 468.41
 PR 510.38 TB 523.19
 IL 660.4 GG 675.24 RR 786.8
 MD 806.1 807.7 825.15
 BM 840.34

SORTED SB 213.25

SORTING JD 608.12

SPARK (CONT.)   PR 493.3   503.26
   SU 544.18   WR 555.31   557.33
   IL 647.34   GG 698.11   NT 716.32

SPARKLE   JD 610.31

SPARKLED   SD 418.21   PR 489.11
   LL 763.34

SPARKLING   FG 188.27   PR 484.20
   SU 529.36   WR 558.36

SPARKS   FG 189.20   SS 210.8
   GF 238.24   EE 330.17   TP 334.32
   BL 359.8   360.7   PR 501.15

SPARROWS   BO 588.21   BM 840.41

SPARSE   PR 496.8   WR 553.38   554.3
   559.34   GG 681.30   ML 723.1

SPARSELY   EA 81.17   PP 436.41

SPASM   DV 180.34   TP 339.24

SPASMODIC   SB 212.10

SPASMODICALLY   EE 323.28
   BL 358.40   SD 415.21   WR 555.35

SPASMS   OC 283.24

SPAT   HD 441.4   NT 704.21

SPATIAL   ML 724.12

SPATS   ML 724.9

SPATTER   YT 394.24

SPATTERED   JD 606.39

SPATTERING   ML 735.5

SPEAK   MO 15.34   16.26   OA 31.22
   37.42   WM 62.1   EA 83.9   86.1
   86.4   PO 99.18   102.29   105.23
   109.12   113.42   114.33
   TF 123.32   DV 148.4   151.30
   151.35   152.8   152.17   152.25
   154.24   180.35   182.28
   WS 252.34   259.11   263.3
   CH 276.24   279.9   EE 327.41
   328.9   TP 344.28   BL 360.37
   MN 372.37   376.35   WP 380.13
   387.41   YT 408.38   409.29
   SD 417.12   421.26   423.23
   423.33   PP 432.33   PR 499.22
   504.1   509.32   511.41   TB 524.42
   WR 566.39   BO 596.24   LA 639.27
   646.31   GG 666.13   670.4   672.30
   684.7   689.26   697.21   NT 704.38
   704.39   712.39   714.11   719.18
   LL 770.28   773.5   774.39
   RR 780.7   780.12   785.21   787.15
   RH 793.6   793.25   793.32   802.18
   MD 809.41   819.3   BM 836.6
   838.24   838.33   838.35
   TH 845.18

SPEAKER   CH 276.23

SPEAKING   MO 10.30   14.2   21.24
   22.13   OA 32.15   SP 52.15
   WM 58.10   TF 123.20   DV 180.11

SPEAKING (CONT.)   SS 208.39   209.4
   SG 228.29   GF 238.32   WS 263.2
   265.7   SC 269.26   CH 276.31
   OC 300.4   EE 321.33   325.22
   325.42   TP 342.1   BL 350.17
   353.17   YT 404.4   PP 435.13
   PR 473.13   488.14   TB 525.38
   526.12   SU 536.26   WR 565.15
   571.18   572.17   JD 610.3
   GG 667.7   684.27   NT 715.21
   716.22   716.25   LL 775.1
   RH 794.17   801.17   MD 820.18
   BM 835.13

SPEAKING-TUBE   LL 769.9

SPEAR   SS 210.16   EE 307.5

SPECIAL   HT 40.5   DV 153.32   157.3
   177.36   CH 278.17   278.29
   281.16   NT 712.41   720.28
   ML 726.18   726.19   727.39
   729.23   MD 818.19   BM 831.2

SPECIALLY   RR 784.29

SPECIES   GG 663.11   663.12

SPECIMEN   BO 595.12   GG 675.20
   NT 709.26

SPECIMENS   SP 49.23   DV 145.16

SPECK   GG 698.11

SPECKLED   WP 379.7   382.18
   PR 490.24   490.30   SU 536.22
   ML 744.22

SPECTACLED   DV 145.10

SPECTACLES   JD 616.24   616.36
   622.27   626.7   626.16   626.17
   627.30   GG 668.38

SPECTRAL   BO 602.40   ML 738.28

SPECTRE   PR 473.33

SPECTRES   WR 570.17

SPECULATE   EA 82.27   ML 733.2

SPECULATING   MO 9.40

SPED   EA 72.21   RH 794.32

SPEECH   MO 4.26   5.18   10.12
   16.27   WM 61.4   62.40   64.36
   DV 155.33   181.9   SS 202.27
   SB 218.20   218.21   GF 236.4
   CH 274.29   276.12   BL 357.1
   357.3   YT 395.32   399.15
   SD 425.4   PP 429.39   429.42
   437.35   FA 462.16   463.27   468.9
   WR 554.29   564.37   567.17
   JD 613.12   618.33   NT 703.4
   ML 730.7   743.16   MD 816.3
   816.16   BM 827.30

SPEECHLESS   LL 762.38   763.40
   MD 814.35   BM 836.41

SPEED   OC 283.3   WR 555.9
   SM 586.21

SPEEDILY   DV 163.39

SPEEDWELL   MN 376.19

SPELL   TF 129.36   SG 226.15
   WS 255.31   264.2   EE 306.29
   MN 375.34   SD 419.33
   PR 480.28   493.15   WR 548.10
   554.36   568.3   568.5
   BO 589.31   593.2   597.35
   JD 625.19   627.2   627.16
   NT 702.35   709.4   712.31
   MD 807.25   807.29   811.10
   812.15   812.28   BM 837.7
   837.16   837.23

SPELLBOUND   DV 180.36
   HD 448.18   WR 569.25
   MD 823.24   BM 836.24
   836.34   836.35   837.13

SPELL-BOUND   SD 420.25
   PR 476.40   MD 806.31

SPEND   HT 43.4   EA 85.25
   OC 285.35   EE 311.16
   IL 647.2   652.5

SPENDING   EA 82.25   FA 462.26
   ML 725.11   728.15   731.42

SPENDTHRIFT   MD 807.8

SPENT   MO 22.21   OA 37.8
   PO 96.28   DV 136.27   138.11
   EE 310.42   316.20   BL 350.8
   WP 386.23   386.26   YT 396.19
   PR 478.31   479.20   482.23
   WR 553.1   ML 727.42   732.3
   732.19   732.35   735.1
   735.26   RH 800.21   MD 810.5

SPHERE   BO 588.11

SPHINX   MD 806.9   806.31

SPHINXES   EA 87.18

SPHINX-LIKE   GG 687.42

'SPHYXIATED   OC 297.37

SPICY   BL 354.37   TB 515.34

SPIED   TP 336.3

SPIKED   OA 33.14

SPIKES   SM 586.12

SPILL   OC 288.23

SPILLED   PO 101.41   DV 176.23
   SU 528.9

SPILLING   EA 83.5   PR 501.24
   SU 540.10

SPIN   EE 311.6   JD 608.20
   NT 712.22   ML 735.28

SPINE   MN 377.19   ML 724.10

SPINET   PR 476.26

SPINNEY   OC 283.14

SPINNING   WM 70.4   EA 72.6
   OC 283.23   RH 796.31   MD 819.6

SPIRE   PO 114.31   HD 449.1

SPIRES   OA 25.5   TF 123.2

SPIRIT   SP 46.15   WM 54.12
   TF 118.28   121.7   DV 151.33
   179.18   183.15   SS 197.14   201.8
   203.12   205.1   206.12   WS 244.13
   255.37   266.5   EE 303.31   305.30
   308.30   316.12   323.38   325.13
   327.33   TP 334.29   FA 458.28
   PR 477.39   508.42   510.38
   SU 534.24   WR 555.18   BO 591.42
   592.12   594.40   595.33   596.36
   599.38   604.16   JD 622.21
   624.39   GG 671.35   679.31   680.6
   680.16   680.30   681.2   681.7
   686.18   686.24   689.33   690.13
   694.22   699.14   NT 701.8   710.16
   ML 723.35   725.8   730.42   735.17
   LL 767.20   775.12   MD 806.18
   TH 847.25

SPIRIT-LAMP   GG 688.8

SPIRITS   SP 47.8   50.40   DV 174.29
   FG 193.38   193.40   WS 251.20
   OC 295.1   BL 356.32   HD 451.20
   FA 468.7   PR 488.33   JD 624.7
   629.9   GG 684.27   688.38   690.5
   ML 730.28   731.32

SPIRITUAL   DV 155.22   155.24
   156.8   GG 683.38   MD 814.12

SPIRITUALISM   GG 669.11   681.40
   689.1

SPIRITUALITY   DV 155.23

SPIRITUALLY   MO 11.27   22.5
   DV 165.23

SPIT   WM 62.11

SPITE   OA 32.37   35.37   HT 39.4
   SP 51.23   WM 63.15   EA 72.13
   88.22   88.23   89.4   PO 98.25
   98.27   99.33   SS 202.39
   SB 215.38   CH 278.28   278.42
   OC 288.15   TP 342.30   WP 388.17
   392.36   YT 408.17   SD 418.17
   PP 431.7   HD 456.29   FA 463.36
   PR 508.1   WR 546.11   547.36
   BO 509.30   LA 638.14   GG 666.14
   694.18   ML 731.41   732.22   738.6
   LL 773.39   RH 791.27   799.9
   803.37   BM 830.42

SPITEFUL   MD 817.7

SPITTING   TF 124.7   LL 762.13

SPLASH   WM 54.19   GF 241.21
   FA 471.16

SPLASHED   WM 54.20   PO 108.42
   FG 189.20   YT 394.15   PR 490.12
   WR 553.8

SPLASHING   GF 238.19   PR 490.19
   499.34   499.35

SPLEEN   OA 32.7

SPLENDID   MO 2.11   19.40   OA 23.4
   SS 203.8   WS 251.2   EE 307.34
   BL 361.11   MN 367.20   PR 475.34
   TB 516.6   SU 532.40   539.31
   540.1   540.2   540.23   541.25
   WR 548.1   BO 603.35   GG 696.22
   ML 736.20   RH 791.8   MD 810.29
   810.37

SPLENDIDLY   JD 609.25

SPLENDOUR   SU 532.6   ML 732.25

SPLINTER   JD 620.27

SPLIT   PO 116.1   SC 271.21

SPLUTTER   WR 557.26

SPOIL   CH 274.36   275.1   TB 514.27
   526.24   BO 602.4

SPOILED   OC 286.25   FA 463.19
   ML 737.40

SPOILING   DV 141.27   EE 314.24

SPOILT   FA 464.12   TB 514.9
   WR 555.26   IL 652.25   MD 805.17
   806.32

SPOKE   MO 11.35   12.21   14.12
   21.21   22.11   HT 40.25   SP 52.1
   WM 60.15   63.17   EA 85.14
   DV 144.11   156.32   174.4
   FG 192.26   SS 211.22   SG 231.40
   GF 234.10   236.3   WS 251.38
   260.5   263.6   CH 275.15   276.15
   OC 298.40   300.5   TP 343.2
   BL 353.25   357.4   MN 373.5
   375.6   377.32   WP 388.13   390.11
   391.20   SD 411.22   412.24   417.8
   HD 444.32   PR 484.34   491.9
   492.39   TB 525.35   SU 544.25
   WR 553.36   555.32   560.10
   560.19   562.15   562.38   563.1
   563.16   563.21   564.2   564.3
   564.7   566.11   566.14   578.8
   579.25   BO 599.23   JD 613.40
   614.5   614.12   614.28   625.8
   LA 637.22   IL 657.9   GG 664.21
   693.19   NT 704.21   714.13
   716.23   ML 727.25   734.34
   737.17   740.33   OV 747.38
   758.11   LL 762.14   772.18
   RH 791.26   803.37   MD 816.20
   819.2   819.40   BM 833.5   835.21

SPOKEN   MO 16.26   OA 33.36
   DV 180.12   WS 262.27   CH 275.39
   WP 379.20   GG 693.32   RH 802.10
   MD 819.41   820.23   824.6

SPONGE   OA 36.31   HD 447.29

SPONGED   GF 239.18   HD 448.2

SPONGING   MO 4.42   MD 807.22

SPONTANEITY   DV 165.40   MD 812.19

SPONTANEOUS   DV 145.22
   EE 306.3   309.26   BL 348.4
   JD 606.4

SPOON   MO 4.6

SPOONFUL   EE 319.17

SPOONING   IL 651.15

SPORRAN   PR 473.17

SPORT   TP 343.11   GG 700.5
   RH 794.19   794.20   MD 805.31
   813.12

SPORTING   WS 250.32   PP 428.41
   429.21   429.29

SPORTIVE   WS 260.21

SPOT   MO 17.32   WM 54.5
   TF 119.30   121.35   WP 386.17
   PR 489.18   499.7   507.21
   LA 631.10

SPOTLESS   TB 517.7

SPOTS   SS 210.10   EE 323.33
   PR 498.30

SPOTTED   WR 562.35   566.34

SPRANG   OA 35.37   PO 109.18
   SG 221.12   GF 238.13
   WS 244.1   EE 330.10
   TP 338.29   343.8   SU 529.41
   WR 563.10   JD 628.1   LL 768.2
   769.13

SPRAWLED   MO 13.40   OA 27.30
   WM 67.37   PO 110.30
   HD 441.14   441.21   442.29
   OV 748.4

SPRAWLING   MO 5.41   7.15
   SU 536.20

SPRAY   SG 228.20

SPRAYED   ML 736.6

SPRAYS   SS 207.4   RH 800.14

SPREAD   MO 8.20   EA 84.11
   PO 95.6   107.2   TF 130.9
   DV 140.5   FG 195.31
   SS 197.16   206.36   210.2
   SB 213.7   216.4   SG 231.1
   CH 278.16   278.37   BL 350.42
   PP 430.31   FA 464.27
   PR 494.22   502.4   506.10
   509.38   SU 534.33   536.4
   542.30   WR 561.2   579.41
   JD 616.14   617.10   GG 695.42
   NT 718.38   LL 766.35
   RR 786.3   MD 806.17   810.37
   TH 845.6

SPREADING   OA 24.26   DV 167.17
   OC 296.28   SD 413.21
   HD 450.21   PR 505.13

SPREE   SP 53.3

SPRIG   OC 289.3   TP 334.26

SPRIGGED   TF 123.26

SPRIGS   SS 210.10

SPRING   HT 42.20   EA 84.17
  SS 202.10   GF 238.36   EE 328.31
  TB 515.27   520.24   520.25
  520.38   521.39   522.35   523.31
  SU 529.13   531.17   WR 575.35
  BO 591.24   602.39   LA 640.8
  GG 694.24   695.12   695.34
  695.39   696.27   NT 716.5
  ML 723.11   736.5   RH 800.9
  MD 806.38

SPRING-CLEANING   GG 677.25

SPRINGING   EA 82.17

SPRINGS   SS 197.7   TP 336.16
  RH 791.16

SPRINGY   ML 738.27   740.11

SPRINKLED   WR 565.5   573.32

SPRINKLING   EE 323.37

SPROUTED   OV 755.24

SPROUTING   WR 553.15

SPRUCE   PR 487.12   487.20   487.27
  487.41   490.24   493.26   494.2
  494.28   494.33   495.41   496.8
  496.14   496.28   496.30   496.37
  496.38   497.8   498.9   498.29
  499.11   499.36   499.40   500.7
  500.12   502.39   507.17   510.29
  WR 553.15   556.41   575.28

SPRUNG   GF 238.41   YT 395.34

SPUME   ML 734.10   745.25

SPUN   EA 82.23   TP 338.8
  BO 591.34   ML 735.30

SPUR   PO 109.42

SPURIOUSLY   LA 642.30

SPURN   EA 72.7   76.8

SPURS   EA 73.9

SPURT   MO 9.33

SPURTED   EE 314.11

SPUTTERED   EE 304.13

SPYING   LL 775.23

SQUAB   OC 291.38

SQUALOR   PR 500.13   500.14

SQUARE   SP 45.9   45.13   45.19
  EA 72.21   PO 107.6   TF 123.12
  125.23   DV 140.20   TP 341.41
  WP 390.40   391.8   YT 394.1
  SD 411.16   422.27   HD 446.24

SQUARE (CONT.)   449.21   PR 493.3
  WR 558.38   558.40   561.24
  561.32   561.34   561.40   562.2
  562.5   562.8   568.24   568.27
  570.14   SM 585.4   BO 595.8
  598.29   JD 624.34   NT 707.13
  ML 741.9   LL 766.13   MD 810.28

SQUARES   SP 45.10   SB 214.1   214.6
  MD 810.23

SQUASH   OA 35.4   MD 805.30   819.34
  819.35

SQUASHED   NT 713.39   MD 805.32
  819.36

SQUASHING   GG 676.33

SQUAT   EA 72.21   GF 234.13
  SC 269.7   269.9   OC 283.31
  BO 594.40   NT 714.40   LL 771.2
  MD 824.3   TH 846.23

SQUATTED   DV 166.10   SG 231.8
  233.10   PR 495.39   511.20
  511.36   WR 557.5   JD 617.15
  617.39   618.5

SQUATTING   EA 85.33   WR 556.41
  557.9   557.35   570.19   JD 617.25

SQUAW-BERRY   PR 499.17

SQUAWKED   GF 242.37   243.8

SQUEAKING   FG 193.19

SQUEALED   FG 191.17

SQUEALING   FG 191.22

SQUEAMISH   WR 548.2

SQUID   NT 720.7

SQUINT   IL 648.16   MD 813.28

SQUINTED   IL 656.32

SQUINTING   JD 613.15

SQUIRM   PR 499.38

SQUIRMED   TB 525.25   JD 620.40

SQUIRMING   PR 511.7   SU 540.36
  JD 619.34   LL 778.1

SQUIRREL   OA 27.22   PO 113.36
  113.40   FG 190.27   LA 631.41

SQUIRRELS   PO 114.1   PR 486.20

SQUIRTED   GF 242.36   NT 712.25

SQUIRTS   GF 242.39

STAB   PR 481.3

STABILITY   GF 238.37

STABLE   BL 352.16   352.23   352.42
  353.10   353.18   353.42   LL 765.3
  766.23   766.25

STABLED   SU 529.15

STABLES   FG 189.5   189.14
  HD 446.25   446.27   446.29
  449.4   LL 764.42   766.13
  766.16   775.19

STABLE-YARD   HD 451.8

STACCATO   SD 416.38   ML 741.8

STACK   PO 106.37

STACKED   PO 106.36

STACKS   YT 394.12

STACK-YARD   SS 202.16

STAFF   OA 32.20   PP 429.29
  ML 732.25

STAGE   WM 59.34   69.31
  GG 664.4   BM 834.5   835.12
  835.17   835.26   836.37
  836.40   837.28   837.41
  838.2   838.5

STAGEY   TB 520.37

STAGGERED   WM 60.2   TF 121.27
  CH 282.25   TP 339.22
  MN 372.24   SD 422.27
  HD 450.38   451.4   FA 458.34
  459.28   SU 535.6   ML 743.35

STAGGERING   PO 108.4   SC 272.17
  CH 282.10   TP 342.27
  WP 386.24   WR 579.39

STAGNANT   OC 283.21   HD 454.24

STAIN   MO 15.19   OV 751.25

STAINED   BO 598.30

STAINES, LORD   (SEE LORD
  STAINES)

STAINS   GG 678.1

STAIR   OA 34.37   34.39

STAIRCASE   OA 35.12   PO 101.38
  WR 562.11   562.13

STAIR-FOOT   DV 161.19
  OC 290.28

STAIR-RODS   YT 397.11   397.37

STAIRS   OA 34.30   35.13   35.15
  35.22   36.4   36.15   37.3
  37.31   PO 101.33   102.1
  TF 125.29   134.33   DV 148.19
  160.39   SG 229.17   229.38
  GF 237.23   WS 244.26
  SC 272.8   OC 286.16   298.4
  298.8   BL 354.39   YT 397.37
  398.22   PP 433.38   435.29
  436.25   HD 456.10   456.24
  FA 468.42   470.28   WR 562.17
  LA 644.2   GG 669.33
  RR 785.37

STALE   DV 168.15   FA 460.8
  JD 617.7   LL 761.36

STALED   TH 852.25

STALK   WM 69.7   DV 161.34   162.4

STALKED   FA 468.29   BM 835.18

STALKING   BM 835.22

STALKS   PO 107.10   SB 214.13

STALKY   RR 780.23

STALL   SC 269.35   ML 735.40

STALLED   BL 362.25

STALLS   MO 6.8

STAMMERED   OC 293.13   LA 646.32
  GG 691.35   RR 787.25

STAMMERING   PR 512.3

STAMP   WR 569.4

STAMPED   SD 417.20   PP 429.41
  LA 635.26

STAMPING   WR 569.3   569.20   569.27
  570.17   570.18   BM 843.6

STAN'   SC 269.39

STAND   OA 27.41   36.26   SP 49.29
  WM 64.20   PO 115.38   DV 155.8
  GF 238.27   238.36   EE 310.19
  311.33   324.31   TP 336.12
  BL 353.38   MN 367.29   370.41
  WP 380.4   SD 420.4   420.10
  PP 427.31   429.8   HD 444.31
  FA 463.8   466.5   PR 488.12
  TB 515.37   SU 529.39   WR 546.25
  558.18   BO 589.6   601.36
  JD 605.10   LA 639.8   645.34
  IL 647.26   649.23   656.42
  657.13   657.34   658.12
  GG 662.39   679.29   689.7   691.20
  NT 702.25   706.30   719.1   720.39
  ML 727.5   739.18   RR 786.35
  786.36   MD 805.18   805.19
  805.20   811.6   TH 852.26

STANDARD   DV 143.32   SG 225.25
  CH 278.23   YT 403.2

STANDARDS   GG 662.38

STAND-BACK   PR 495.24

STANDING   OA 29.2   29.8   36.26
  HT 43.30   PO 101.1   101.28
  108.9   108.33   111.25   111.41
  TF 129.36   134.12   DV 137.19
  143.25   182.6   185.1   FG 187.10
  194.15   SS 198.2   208.36   210.28
  SB 214.28   216.3   219.4   219.14
  SG 227.38   229.40   GF 236.26
  242.25   WS 256.10   264.21
  OC 291.9   291.28   296.15   297.41
  EE 304.33   321.6   BL 362.16
  365.1   MN 367.30   367.34   373.15
  WP 388.42   390.15   PP 440.11
  HD 452.13   FA 467.1   467.6
  467.9   467.11   PR 492.16

STANDING (CONT.)   SU 538.6   538.7
  538.38   539.23   WR 548.27
  574.16   575.26   576.38   578.32
  BO 595.24   596.12   596.15
  LA 634.24   636.13   IL 658.12
  RR 784.17   788.20   RH 801.20
  BM 835.3   837.27   837.38   839.23

STAND-OFFISH   MN 374.9

STANDS   SP 45.9   DV 136.18
  EE 311.27   WR 574.34   OV 759.34

STANDSTILL   TP 334.23   MN 366.37
  370.6   WR 547.4   555.27   556.24
  BO 597.25   IL 653.2

STAND-UP-MANNIKIN   BO 601.34

STAR   MO 2.2   2.12   2.18   2.41
  WM 54.29   54.32   54.34   61.2
  DV 167.19   PR 503.28   WR 565.37
  NT 703.29   ML 734.19   744.1
  OV 756.18   756.22

STARCHED   GG 672.31

STARE   GF 241.11   MN 370.40
  PP 435.38   439.19   HD 447.36
  FA 468.29   JD 613.35   619.20
  GG 673.15   689.11   NT 715.41
  RR 784.13   784.32   784.40   785.2
  785.4   785.6   785.20

STARED   PO 97.40   99.20   107.20
  115.21   116.5   116.7   TF 126.7
  DV 139.26   149.3   156.35   157.14
  SS 198.7   199.19   200.11
  SG 226.22   226.24   231.8
  OC 297.22   MN 375.15   375.18
  376.31   376.35   377.18   WP 391.4
  YT 401.3   404.7   405.17   408.30
  SD 416.17   423.24   423.29
  PP 427.37   431.26   434.18
  439.25   HD 446.5   452.38
  FA 460.11   460.20   460.21   462.1
  WR 578.42   JD 611.17   613.28
  613.29   617.33   617.42
  LA 646.28   GG 668.39   673.9
  673.13   688.14   690.37   697.5
  ML 741.4   LL 763.37   RH 792.28
  MD 823.30   BM 840.17

STARING   WM 70.14   EA 82.19   89.24
  90.33   92.28   PO 95.18   102.32
  109.31   114.5   TF 120.24
  DV 152.13   180.20   SG 228.19
  GF 241.25   SC 272.29   CH 279.9
  MN 376.27   PP 434.15   436.2
  438.38   440.1   HD 449.27   453.38
  PR 491.25   505.31   511.9   511.20
  511.36   BO 598.4   JD 620.29
  623.21   LA 644.3   646.19   646.28
  IL 651.33   GG 670.18   678.6
  678.20   684.20   684.24   689.10
  NT 715.42   716.5   ML 744.39
  LL 768.42   769.2   RH 793.9
  804.12   MD 823.39

STARK   WM 69.35   TP 334.6
  PR 493.42   496.14   SU 531.32

STARK (CONT.)   WR 546.28
  550.12   BO 588.32   593.20
  598.28   GG 661.29   ML 746.33

STARLIGHT   MO 19.14   FG 189.35

STARLINGS   JD 606.38

STARLIT   OV 749.2

STARRED   EA 71.31

STARS   MO 19.21   19.25   19.29
  22.20   WM 60.30   DV 173.26
  SS 207.10   207.16   EE 332.26
  332.27   332.28   WP 388.10
  SD 411.4   422.31   423.7
  PR 479.1   502.36   502.41
  SU 532.22   WR 552.18   570.29
  570.30   570.31   570.32
  572.17   SM 585.22   OV 754.32
  755.23   755.25   755.28
  LL 772.35   773.9

START   PO 95.22   100.18   110.25
  112.18   114.3   EE 306.37
  BL 353.21   SD 426.2
  PP 432.31   434.10   FA 472.7
  PR 488.22   488.27   494.32
  498.25   505.15   511.42
  IL 650.1   652.19   658.14
  GG 661.26   671.33   686.3
  NT 707.2   708.42   709.19
  709.20   718.30   ML 722.17
  742.25   RR 783.4   788.37
  RH 791.10   793.16   MD 817.6
  BM 840.7

STARTED   MO 3.21   OA 24.18
  27.5   29.27   SP 52.20   53.14
  WM 60.2   68.13   PO 97.29
  109.33   112.39   114.8
  TF 121.34   123.21   DV 136.6
  148.18   151.22   152.38
  155.14   186.8   FG 189.34
  193.24   SS 198.1   SB 214.20
  SG 221.27   221.37   226.12
  230.19   GF 235.34   242.37
  WS 246.16   258.27   SC 271.11
  271.14   OC 290.31   EE 316.37
  317.40   333.13   TP 338.29
  339.15   342.28   343.35   344.4
  344.24   MN 377.20   WP 390.13
  YT 402.5   SD 416.20   425.27
  426.13   PP 429.11   434.7
  435.13   FA 459.33   PR 488.25
  489.25   493.11   508.21
  TB 524.8   WR 568.37   SM 584.1
  BO 591.41   JD 613.35
  LA 638.28   642.40   646.15
  646.16   IL 648.12   649.23
  657.14   ML 723.27   OV 754.41
  LL 763.11   764.7   766.24
  773.3   773.39   777.31
  RR 784.20   784.28   785.11
  RH 790.1   795.9   796.27
  798.12   BM 827.4

STARTING   WM 70.13   PO 106.2
  DV 184.13   GF 241.23
  BL 363.35   SD 424.38
  PP 434.14   IL 649.40

STARTLE   TB 521.36

STRANGE (CONT.) DV 169.20 170.20
  171.17 171.36 173.3 173.24
  180.39 181.24 SS 202.31
  SB 214.16 214.25 219.38
  SG 222.39 224.35 226.2
  227.25 WS 255.12 CH 280.12
  OC 299.37 EE 303.28 307.1
  309.28 317.37 322.36 324.21
  324.22 TP 342.32 343.12
  344.40 345.5 345.16 BL 353.27
  361.7 364.37 365.2 YT 400.19
  403.12 407.6 407.31 410.8
  SD 413.33 413.37 417.9 420.1
  421.20 PP 435.11 HD 441.13
  451.40 452.42 453.4 454.6
  455.8 PR 474.6 476.31 477.14
  477.18 485.38 490.39 495.42
  497.23 500.13 501.19 501.26
  502.40 504.27 TB 513.13
  SU 531.30 538.24 WR 552.9
  552.13 555.2 555.21 555.34
  556.9 564.18 564.19 564.36
  565.11 565.23 569.8 569.14
  569.15 569.31 570.4 570.26
  576.2 576.4 576.13 576.16
  576.23 576.27 577.3 579.5
  579.23 580.18 SM 584.3
  BO 592.29 593.14 595.28
  595.39 596.25 604.36
  JD 608.22 609.6 609.19 615.4
  615.5 617.7 622.16 622.23
  622.31 626.41 LA 633.4 638.7
  638.37 639.25 639.28 643.10
  645.9 646.16 IL 651.18 656.41
  658.20 GG 665.3 668.8 691.26
  693.2 694.15 696.33 696.39
  NT 702.15 702.38 706.2 706.28
  715.40 721.8 ML 724.3 724.23
  730.33 731.20 731.23 731.24
  731.29 734.3 735.4 735.15
  735.18 737.21 742.40 743.32
  744.29 745.40 OV 748.19
  749.31 LL 765.19 769.28 772.5
  RR 785.31 RH 793.5 800.26
  802.12 802.38 802.42 803.17
  803.19 MD 805.26 808.30 809.2
  819.4 820.34 821.2 821.34
  821.40 BM 829.13 829.28
  836.17 TH 850.13

STRANGELY CH 275.37 OC 290.23
  TP 343.28 BL 347.23 YT 407.33
  SD 416.1 PR 475.12 489.31
  504.3 WR 553.32 564.11 569.41
  577.15 JD 625.19 GG 668.4
  668.39 696.37 NT 716.40*
  ML 724.1 LL 775.34 BM 829.12

STRANGENESS MO 6.3 19.27
  SS 202.39 BL 359.4*

STRANGER MO 6.3 7.4 12.16
  17.28 OA 38.40 HT 39.32
  EA 84.25 85.6 85.17 86.6
  86.14 86.29 86.39 CH 277.24
  OC 285.21 300.27 300.28 301.28
  EE 326.3 YT 403.23 SD 412.23
  412.26 414.8 414.13 415.4
  415.8 415.31 415.36 415.38
  417.1 FA 460.12 WR 574.16
  BO 596.30 JD 616.17 617.22
  618.9 618.31 618.34 MD 826.6
  BM 828.2

STRANGERS MO 3.39 DV 171.16

STRANGERS (CONT.) SS 204.13
  209.34 GG 670.28

STRANGEST EE 306.38 306.39

STRANGLED OA 25.15 27.7
  WM 70.10

STRANGLING OA 36.2 TP 343.15

STRAP HT 42.18 PP 433.36

STRAPPED WS 251.18

STRAPPING WP 381.40

STRASBURG BO 588.3 594.29 600.3

STRATA GG 698.1

STRAW PO 99.27 SS 202.25
  CH 274.9 MN 376.24 YT 394.12
  SU 528.16 543.5 WR 553.30
  556.10 SM 583.16 LL 770.19
  MD 814.40

STRAWBERRIES TB 524.30

STRAWS EA 82.24 EE 332.38
  332.39 TH 851.3

STRAYING YT 402.26 PR 494.24

STRAY-RUNNING WS 262.41

STREAK SS 202.5 CH 279.3
  BL 358.25

STREAKED SC 268.6

STREAKS PO 96.3

STREAM EA 82.24 PO 101.33
  FG 193.12 193.29 194.29
  194.41 SS 199.40 EE 329.25
  PR 481.22 489.39 490.12
  490.19 490.21 490.32 494.4
  494.5 494.9 494.34 495.35
  495.41 499.11 SU 535.22
  WR 551.19 552.11 558.38 559.7
  569.40 579.15 BO 595.5
  IL 648.19 651.25 OV 755.6
  759.39 LL 762.25 765.10
  RR 785.4 BM 829.29 TH 846.1

STREAM-BED EE 307.25 PR 499.28
  WR 579.15

STREAMED SU 530.28 532.20
  GG 690.32 NT 702.23

STREAMING DV 149.14 SB 217.5
  SU 530.30 WR 563.6 567.31
  568.42

STREAM-POOL WR 579.28

STREAMS WR 561.23 BO 599.6

STREAM-SIDE WR 559.1

STREET HT 43.30 WM 63.18 63.20
  70.24 EA 72.42 73.8 81.16
  TF 121.40 DV 182.23 SG 228.15
  GF 235.25 236.27 241.15

STREET (CONT.) WS 258.38
  SC 267.11 267.18 269.6
  270.13 270.35 270.38
  271.6 271.16 271.20 272.14
  273.6 CH 275.19 YT 395.20
  PP 428.25 436.21 HD 447.22
  FA 460.26 462.3 470.11
  SM 586.25 BO 593.24 594.39
  595.21 596.27 601.30
  JD 610.34 615.9 LA 630.22
  630.33 638.42 640.18
  MD 826.5 BM 831.42

STREET-CORNER MD 806.41

STREET-LAMP HD 456.15
  JD 610.34

STREETS HT 42.12 EA 84.18
  TF 122.2 DV 155.17
  GF 241.21 TP 334.22
  PP 436.7 FA 460.19
  ML 724.17 TH 844.28

STRENGTH OA 35.42 HT 39.7
  SP 47.16 PO 108.15
  TF 126.11 DV 137.22
  SG 226.17 WS 248.7 SC 270.8
  EE 310.20 315.15 325.6
  TP 343.24 343.36 344.3
  MN 371.20 YT 400.34 406.42
  HD 442.6 451.40 WR 559.37
  559.41 BO 590.5 591.10
  596.5 601.37 603.16
  JD 609.15 IL 652.26
  ML 746.12 MD 815.6
  TH 847.13

STRENUOUS PR 488.5

STRENUOUSNESS MO 6.34

STRESS PO 103.18 DV 183.1

STRESSED MD 824.31

STRETCH MO 18.30 SP 45.12
  WM 68.39 OC 301.18
  EE 304.30 BL 355.35
  LA 637.12

STRETCHED MO 1.26 3.4 18.1
  OA 32.41 WM 55.41 67.2
  EA 72.28 PO 108.40
  WS 247.8 EE 321.35
  BL 360.18 363.32 MN 366.7
  WP 386.32 386.40 387.28
  SD 422.1 HD 446.26
  WR 546.34 IL 651.26
  GG 696.20 696.21 LL 766.14

STRETCHER OC 297.4 297.19
  297.22 298.39

STRETCHES EA 73.9 PO 107.1
  WR 552.33 558.41 GG 671.6

STRETCHING MO 19.6 EE 304.40
  WP 386.26 SD 416.29
  ML 738.25 LL 765.2

STREWED EA 79.19 SS 197.27
  TB 517.11

STRICKEN FG 194.2 PR 4⁰1.9

STRICKEN (CONT.) PR 491.26

STRICT IL 658.42

STRICTLY MO 13.26

STRICTNESSES YT 396.1

STRIDE CH 274.11 FA 459.16
  PR 506.22 SU 539.2 RR 780.34

STRIDENTLY DV 157.33

STRIDES SG 228.41 WS 251.17
  RR 783.38

STRIDING MN 370.4 WP 390.37
  SU 539.2 540.13 WR 549.17

STRIFE SP 51.10 BO 597.11

STRIKE HT 39.17 39.20 SP 46.14
  50.17 51.11 52.38 53.2 53.3
  SC 268.21 269.13 270.10
  270.12 SD 417.22 PP 428.5
  HD 446.12 WR 581.27

STRIKE-MONEY SP 45.1

STRIKE-PAY HT 39.19 SP 49.30
  51.41

STRIKES MN 377.37

STRIKING WM 54.19 59.12
  JD 609.17 ML 745.38 OV 755.1
  LL 778.28

STRIKING-LOOKING MD 807.14

STRING WS 244.11 245.26
  YT 399.11 PP 435.42 439.2
  BO 602.37 RR 782.13

STRINGS NT 707.42 LL 763.24

STRIP MO 1.5 PO 111.5 111.34
  OC 283.16 HD 441.22 SU 529.10

STRIPED MN 371.10 SU 532.21

STRIPES SB 214.2 WR 552.35
  559.25

STRIPPED MO 4.40 PO 108.40
  DV 170.17 SC 268.37 OC 297.17
  299.9 TB 520.12 WR 573.14
  GG 697.28

STRIPPING JD 623.32 623.33

STRIPS PO 107.7 107.15

STRIVE TF 132.32

STRIVEN EE 311.25

STRIVING EA 75.26 EE 306.42
  313.31

STRODE MO 3.5 PO 109.4 GF 235.9
  WS 251.17 FA 459.15 PR 506.33
  511.13 SU 539.18 IL 651.4
  GG 685.11 RR 788.16

STROKE MO 18.20 OA 36.36
  EA 77.14 SU 528.25 528.26
  IL 650.21 NT 703.33 OV 758.23
  BM 842.22

STROKED WP 386.31 IL 657.35
  MD 822.13

STROKING SB 216.24 MD 807.39
  BM 842.8

STRONG MO 2.33 OA 28.36
  HT 41.18 WM 58.15 59.11 64.34
  67.3 69.7 PO 97.1 97.20
  100.32 109.22 109.37 109.38
  109.41 110.19 TF 118.14
  123.27 124.15 125.11 130.14
  DV 137.33 145.19 164.36
  SS 198.11 SB 212.27 220.2
  SG 226.34 227.16 WS 252.28
  252.31 253.22 261.11
  SC 268.27 272.2 EE 304.17
  304.20 305.32 306.26 309.11
  322.34 322.36 BL 349.11
  354.18 360.18 361.7 363.32
  363.42 MN 367.24 SD 420.1
  421.40 421.41 HD 451.36
  FA 467.33 PR 478.35 482.27
  482.28 482.31 485.3 485.29
  TB 521.15 524.39 WR 551.6
  565.31 567.37 576.17
  BO 587.17 597.20 599.31
  600.10 JD 605.1 605.21 605.32
  606.23 615.40 617.26
  LA 632.24 632.41 637.28
  637.30 637.36 638.4 638.9
  GG 683.5 691.2 696.18
  NT 703.33 OV 750.31 LL 775.40
  RH 797.27 802.20 MD 808.23
  BM 838.9 839.25

STRONG-BLOODED BL 357.16

STRONGER OA 33.8 TF 122.37
  124.14 DV 150.28 150.30
  WS 257.28 EE 312.1 313.6
  PP 439.29 HD 452.4 BO 604.19
  LA 640.35 NT 717.14 717.27
  717.28 717.29 718.8

STRONGEST EA 82.37 DV 177.6
  JD 627.17 GG 686.12

STRONG-FEATURED SM 583.2

STRONG-JAWED OA 31.18

STRONG-LIMBED EE 305.39

STRONGLY OA 27.32 TF 118.12
  132.9 WS 254.5 JD 629.8

STRONGLY-BUILT WR 553.29

STRONGLY-FEELING HD 449.18

STRONG-SKINNED GG 681.31

STROVE OC 301.39 WP 386.17
  OV 750.29

STRUCK MO 18.6 OA 35.33
  WM 54.23 EA 76.24 76.35 78.12
  90.37 FG 194.22 WS 264.6
  265.27 CH 282.8 OC 290.27

STRUCK (CONT.) EE 331.12
  TP 343.21 MN 377.11
  WP 383.22 YT 406.8 SD 423.8
  WR 555.12 555.24 555.35
  BO 590.37 LA 630.2 640.37
  646.26 IL 655.19* GG 689.15
  ML 730.30

STRUGGLE EA 93.6 PO 112.25
  DV 144.32 177.5 SB 216.17
  OC 286.21 EE 331.37
  TP 343.35 WP 386.10 386.34
  386.37 SD 420.9 421.17
  421.31 422.2 PR 504.25
  BO 592.2 599.9 GG 686.10
  LL 768.20 MD 822.21

STRUGGLED MO 4.9 OA 32.6
  36.5 36.7 EA 89.42
  PO 112.26 FG 191.29
  GF 238.15 SC 272.7
  TP 343.15 BL 350.39
  WP 386.18 387.30 SD 421.9
  423.6 PP 435.24 PR 490.5
  ML 734.38 745.15

STRUGGLES BL 360.12 WP 387.31

STRUGGLING MO 11.23 OA 35.24
  EA 89.41 PO 114.9 DV 148.25
  164.29 SB 214.33 GF 240.6
  WS 245.26 CH 280.17
  OC 286.17 BL 363.14
  WP 386.25 HD 450.28
  WR 549.24 556.17 LA 639.40
  GG 666.28 OV 750.25

STRUMS JD 609.19

STRUNG WM 60.34 DV 168.37
  169.21 WR 547.39

STRUTTING ML 741.34

STUART PR 473.9

STUBBLE SB 214.1 214.6
  217.6 219.21

STUBBORN DV 143.40 SS 199.11
  SB 217.2 219.5 GF 242.24
  WS 263.21 WP 392.38
  YT 407.11 HD 453.25
  NT 712.8

STUBBORNLY EA 74.17 78.40
  DV 142.21 143.23 156.13
  GF 234.16 OV 751.39

STUBBS' BANK BM 834.5

STUCCO LA 630.27 638.42

STUCK WS 253.38 OC 291.26
  BL 357.33 WP 388.34 390.10
  390.39 PP 433.15 HD 443.24
  443.28 FA 464.3 JD 611.5
  616.31 620.25 NT 712.29
  ML 739.5 RR 784.23
  MD 817.34

STUDENT TH 852.20

STUDENTS GG 661.7

STUDIED MO 5.29 EE 308.18
  FA 469.37 ML 738.16 LL 764.1
  RH 796.17 800.20 MD 808.40
  BM 827.15

STUDIO LA 640.30 RH 799.16
  TH 844.23

STUDY DV 183.9 FG 187.28
  GG 691.35 ML 728.9 735.1
  735.7 735.27 LL 763.11
  BM 827.14

STUDYING EE 305.17

STUFF EA 75.36 FG 194.17 194.20
  OC 295.40 EE 306.11 WR 549.29
  564.23 JD 607.31 OV 755.20

STUFFED MO 6.38 WS 258.1

STUFFY WP 388.40

STUMBLE PO 109.8

STUMBLED MO 3.7 21.37 OA 37.22
  WM 66.9 PO 114.11 114.13
  FG 190.36 OC 292.39 JD 610.37
  611.1 ML 744.33

STUMBLING PO 109.10 112.11
  OC 283.2 BO 603.5 603.21

STUMP PO 101.22 SD 411.20
  PR 500.26

STUMPY SD 413.8

STUNG MO 21.41 YT 402.8

STUNNED PO 104.25 SU 531.2
  LL 773.37 777.40

STUNTED EA 81.17 FG 194.23
  ML 736.10

STUPEFACTION PO 104.9

STUPEFIED CH 279.40 TP 346.8
  PP 431.28 PR 500.20 SM 583.1
  IL 656.17 GG 676.37

STUPEFYING PP 435.5

STUPENDOUS BO 588.30 NT 708.24

STUPID MO 2.36 EA 75.40
  PO 100.14 103.32 DV 169.15
  BL 349.24 MN 375.31 375.32
  HD 441.35 IL 650.8 NT 703.18
  712.42 MD 821.25

STUPIDITY DV 145.42 165.40
  HD 442.6

STUPIDLY OA 36.28 DV 176.5
  GF 241.25 ML 746.29

STUPOR PO 103.34 104.8
  HD 441.37 PR 500.20 500.28
  WR 547.11 GG 692.39 ML 746.23

STURDILY PO 102.17 TP 335.35

STURDY WM 58.12 FG 189.12

STURDY (CONT.) 189.13 SS 199.34
  SG 228.32 SC 268.5 OC 284.21
  EE 305.25 320.17 TP 335.41
  SM 583.29 584.20 585.21
  585.28 586.14 RH 793.38

STUTTERING JD 613.36

STYLE OA 32.11 EE 319.20 319.22
  TP 337.34 SD 417.39 ML 735.39
  RH 790.21 790.28 MD 810.33

SUAVE SD 414.31 415.1 WR 552.40
  JD 618.14 ML 731.7 BM 836.15

SUAVELY SP 46.36* SD 412.11

SUAVITY WM 59.2 LL 774.13
  776.26

SUBCONSCIOUS OA 35.16

SUBCONSCIOUSLY OA 30.37

SUBCONSCIOUSNESS PO 97.38

SUBDUED EE 324.25 SD 422.34
  424.21 WR 567.4 577.35
  NT 712.38 LL 764.38

SUBDUEDLY DV 148.16 159.20
  OC 289.23

SUBJECT MO 8.19 DV 143.18
  FG 187.35 SS 209.41 PP 432.12
  HD 442.17

SUBJECTED EA 92.15 WR 547.11

SUBJECTION PO 107.32 TF 128.15
  SD 421.41 HD 442.7

SUBJECTS TB 516.24

SUBJUGATE EE 327.37

SUBJUGATED WS 264.36

SUB-LIEUTENANT SG 231.11

SUBLIMATION SS 203.11

SUBMERGE EA 93.20

SUBMERGED TF 122.16 DV 161.24
  PR 489.14

SUBMISSION MO 3.33 DV 138.21
  158.31 WR 549.10

SUBMISSIVE MO 3.29 PO 107.19
  DV 171.1 WR 567.30

SUBMISSIVELY ML 736.32

SUBMIT EA 75.35 76.8 80.40
  DV 137.17 150.29 151.18
  174.22 GF 240.1 WS 259.33
  EE 303.25 328.22 BL 356.8
  PR 508.7 JD 607.38 621.15
  621.16 NT 707.31 MD 822.10

SUBMITTED GF 243.34 OC 302.13
  325.10 328.21 WP 386.39
  BO 597.18

SUBMITTING PO 105.4 DV 177.38
  EE 326.12

SUBORDINATE DV 151.4 183.15
  BM 827.23

SUBORDINATES BM 827.24

SUBORDINATION DV 164.27

SUBSIDED WR 571.38 BO 598.41
  ML 746.1 LL 767.22
  TH 846.38 846.41

SUBSIDING SC 272.27 PR 499.21
  JD 616.40 TH 846.36

SUB-SMILE WR 554.19

SUBSTANCE ML 740.25

SUBSTANTIAL CH 275.30
  BL 355.30 TH 852.8

SUBSTANTIATE PR 474.4

SUBSTITUTE EE 325.39
  LL 769.26

SUBSTITUTED BL 355.38

SUBSTITUTES TP 337.16

SUBTERFUGE NT 720.17

SUBTLE MO 4.33 7.6 OA 25.7
  EA 73.29 93.29 WS 254.38
  EE 310.30 328.25 TP 337.4
  WP 391.42 YT 395.36 406.33
  408.36 HD 448.8 PR 484.25
  484.37 485.22 485.36
  486.4 WR 570.41 SM 584.5
  584.9 584.10 BO 592.17
  592.20 592.24 JD 629.10
  LA 633.18 634.41 637.17
  639.24 IL 649.37 GG 697.35
  NT 712.9 ML 727.26 LL 774.3
  774.10 RR 782.18 MD 807.2
  807.39 812.15

SUBTLER EE 311.9 SU 532.25
  MD 805.28

SUBTLETY MO 5.28 MD 820.4

SUBTLY TF 129.21 EE 326.9
  327.7 WR 569.11 578.24
  LA 634.13 GG 663.41
  ML 726.7 LL 761.37

SUBURB OA 25.3 ML 739.3

SUBURBAN IL 648.14

SUBURB-PATCHES PP 436.29

SUBURBS OV 756.40

SUCCEED PR 508.36 RH 791.2
  799.22

SUCCEEDED SB 215.4 216.1
  216.32 YT 402.33 PR 512.7
  LL 776.24 RR 782.2
  MD 814.16

SUCCEEDING GF 234.2

SUCCESS TF 120.8 SS 208.19
  208.28 EE 314.14 314.21
  BL 359.38 PR 485.23 TB 515.33
  523.13 SU 539.10 BO 588.41
  JD 624.39 NT 716.27 BM 842.28

SUCCESSFUL PO 103.30 BL 359.36
  YT 408.33 JD 606.14 LL 771.24
  RH 790.32

SUCCESSFULLY EA 81.38 PO 103.27

SUCCESSION OC 299.19 LL 776.34

SUCCESSIVE RH 799.5

SUCCINCTLY DV 175.37 RR 779.27

SUCCOUR PR 485.26

SUCCULENT SB 216.41 MN 370.8

SUCCUMB WR 574.27 MD 821.41

SUCCUMBED ML 737.26

SUCCUMBS JD 609.15

SUCH-LIKE GF 235.19

SUCKED EA 80.19 SS 211.6
  SG 223.25 CH 278.8 ML 734.1
  LL 778.22 778.29

SUCKER LL 778.22

SUCKING MO 1.22 7.18 EA 80.23
  TF 127.12 FG 191.6 191.7
  191.10 CH 277.10 JD 608.21
  GG 675.6 ML 738.29

SUDDEN MO 4.1 15.35 OA 29.31
  WM 54.20 70.3 EA 73.41 92.13
  TF 122.37 DV 168.32 181.20
  SB 216.13 OC 294.24 EE 314.11
  MN 369.41 370.39 WP 389.19
  SD 415.16 417.21 HD 442.4
  454.4 FA 468.35 472.10
  PR 477.21 480.25 484.22
  486.37 491.28 503.21 WR 551.4
  568.20 BO 593.25 JD 613.36
  LA 639.33 IL 647.26 656.41
  658.16 GG 665.6 665.40 667.18
  678.13 699.18 LL 768.23
  RH 792.27 802.12 802.13

SUDDEN-LIKE SD 419.31

SUDDENLY-RELEASED BM 841.37

SUDDENLY-RISEN WM 69.6

SUDDENNESS OA 28.17 SB 212.23
  PR 507.24

SUEDE PR 485.2

SUET WM 67.32

SUFFER EA 80.4 WS 257.24
  BL 359.2 BO 592.2 GG 679.31
  ML 743.9

SUFFERANCE SG 229.31

SUFFERED WM 58.8 68.10 EA 83.20
  83.21 89.26 PO 98.36
  TF 129.35 132.8 DV 153.30
  154.27 155.9 178.3 SB 212.34
  OC 301.18 EE 322.2 BL 350.36
  359.2 360.9 363.32 YT 402.19
  402.34 HD 447.13 FA 465.19
  IL 659.38 GG 686.8 690.9
  NT 711.35 LL 771.27 RR 780.27

SUFFERING MO 16.39 WM 68.4
  69.42 EA 72.17 PO 100.17
  115.34 TF 135.16 DV 161.36
  169.41 170.16 174.35 SB 220.7
  SG 232.19 GF 239.10 242.8
  WS 245.6 256.39 SC 270.5
  BL 348.16 WP 384.14 YT 397.33
  402.35 GG 682.39

SUFFERINGS MO 2.33 EE 324.26
  RR 780.30

SUFFICE OA 32.28 SU 533.17

SUFFICIENCY SC 269.10

SUFFICIENT OA 33.8 GF 239.14
  PR 473.19 TB 520.22 BO 588.15

SUFFICIENTLY OA 28.36 WM 57.35
  EA 80.33 86.4 OC 294.14
  TP 336.31 337.6

SUFFICIENTLY-FAR RR 780.16

SUFFOCATED OA 30.19 EA 82.15
  TF 118.21 DV 180.18

SUFFOCATING PO 95.12 106.31
  109.18 OC 295.24 HD 450.28
  BO 592.6

SUFFOCATION DV 177.4 SB 217.31
  BO 592.30

SUFFOLK DV 136.23 ML 726.13

SUFFRAGE OV 747.14

SUFFUSED PR 505.2

SUFFUSION BL 355.39

SUGAR YT 402.38 GG 681.28

SUGGEST TB 514.25 517.3
  MD 818.20

SUGGESTED MO 13.4 SP 48.39
  DV 144.10 180.4 BL 357.18
  YT 397.18 PR 482.8 484.15
  TB 523.17 523.22 BO 593.40
  JD 616.1 IL 655.13 GG 683.3
  NT 709.6 LL 762.5

SUGGESTING WM 55.30

SUGGESTION EA 79.2 DV 172.28
  172.35 BL 353.41 ML 741.6
  RH 798.38 MD 810.32

SUGGESTIVE ML 739.16 LL 762.41

SUGGESTIVELY MO 16.5
  NT 720.21

SUICIDE NT 705.11

SUIT SP 46.21 TF 133.22
  DV 136.10 WS 250.38
  EE 320.11 328.24 329.2
  MN 374.30 SD 417.39
  PP 439.37 FA 465.29
  SU 538.39 540.18 GG 668.26
  683.21 NT 715.19 719.33
  ML 722.2 OV 748.4 MD 806.38
  807.1

SUITABLE TH 852.34

SUITABLY LL 763.39

SUIT-CASES FA 458.23

SUITED BO 603.32 LL 763.28

SUITORS DV 144.28

SUITS SU 541.24

SULKIEST HD 446.1

SULKILY SP 52.18 DV 144.2
  SS 199.17 199.29 OC 288.19
  MN 376.2

SULKINESS MN 374.9

SULKY DV 160.18 SS 211.2
  CH 278.41 OC 284.17
  NT 712.8 ML 726.13

SULLEN PO 98.31 100.9
  DV 169.41 GF 234.25 235.1
  WS 263.22 CH 278.41 282.11
  282.28 OC 286.20 EE 307.2
  MN 373.36 373.40 374.4
  WP 391.2 392.38 HD 447.14
  PR 486.18 BO 600.22 604.9
  ML 725.13 745.25 OV 753.30
  LL 769.13 RH 801.21

SULLEN-LOOKING HD 441.15

SULLENLY OA 31.24 EA 72.1
  88.30 PO 99.3 DV 151.9
  159.30 WS 249.2 249.21
  CH 276.27 278.2 PR 482.26
  BO 600.19 ML 746.3

SULLENNESS BO 600.24

SULPHUR BO 596.2 JD 610.10
  610.23

SUM TP 337.3 PR 473.15
  JD 607.16 LL 778.35
  RH 799.1 TH 852.8

SUMB'DY OC 293.2

SUMMAT SP 52.35 WP 388.38
  388.39

SUMMER MO 19.39 TF 132.19
  132.21 DV 161.9 164.13
  176.40 SB 217.6 EE 317.22

SUMMER (CONT.) EE 329.22
  329.31 WP 379.21 PR 480.33
  WR 574.12 579.15 ML 723.21
  733.32 746.28 LL 765.6
  RH 800.23

SUMMERS PR 478.31

SUMMERY LL 767.25

SUMMING-UP JD 605.13

SUMMIT TF 119.12 PR 493.41
  494.3 496.8 496.11 MD 808.28

SUMMITS PR 489.6 496.38 496.39

SUMMON PO 104.5 MD 814.26

SUMMONED PO 108.6 TF 118.11
  YT 408.30 WR 559.40

SUMMONS MN 369.35 WR 564.35

SUMP DV 166.31

SUMPTUOUS WR 569.6 578.18
  578.41

SUMPTUOUSLY HD 442.4 WR 578.34

SUN MO 1.33 2.1 EA 85.2
  PO 98.7 106.33 111.16 115.22
  115.27 116.1 116.12 TF 119.11
  DV 149.42 150.2 FG 188.22
  190.11 SS 202.9 204.39
  SB 217.21 EE 306.34 312.21
  WP 390.34 PR 488.35 489.1
  489.10 490.4 493.24 494.25
  495.38 498.14 498.24 499.16
  499.24 499.32 499.40 500.2
  501.12 505.9 507.13 507.18
  507.22 507.32 507.34 507.39
  508.7 508.22 509.40 510.8
  TB 513.15 515.4 522.33
  SU 528.1 528.2 529.8 529.26
  529.34 529.38 529.39 529.41
  530.5 530.15 530.17 530.20
  530.22 530.25 530.27 530.30
  530.37 530.38 531.1 531.8
  531.17 531.22 531.25 531.36
  532.6 532.27 532.30 532.31
  532.34 532.36 532.39 532.40
  532.42 533.1 533.22 533.28
  533.31 533.33 534.8 534.18
  534.19 534.23 535.11 535.22
  535.25 535.36 535.38 536.14
  536.37 537.13 537.26 537.30
  537.35 539.24 539.33 539.35
  541.20 543.10 544.27 544.35
  544.39 WR 556.4 556.31 558.4
  558.5 558.33 559.15 569.20
  570.6 570.36 571.5 571.7
  571.9 571.11 571.13 571.14
  571.15 571.22 571.28 571.35
  571.36 572.6 572.28 572.30
  572.32 572.37 574.5 574.42
  575.2 575.5 575.6 575.9
  575.13 575.15 575.18 575.19
  575.24 575.29 576.9 580.10
  580.37 580.40 581.4 581.9
  581.11 581.21 581.22 581.24
  BO 599.27 LA 641.30 GG 698.33
  ML 723.23 743.41 745.23
  745.26 745.30 746.28

SUN (CONT.) OV 753.27 753.30
  755.28 LL 764.11 766.8
  766.12 766.28 766.30 766.32
  766.35 766.37 767.24 768.31
  768.32 770.34 774.1 774.12
  775.17 TH 845.8 848.5

SUN-AND-AIR-BATH LL 766.10

SUN-BATH SU 545.3 LL 766.9
  766.21 773.38

SUNBATHS SU 535.18

SUN-BATHS SU 533.17 LL 772.28

SUNBEAMS WR 574.13

SUN-BLACKENED SU 533.7

SUN-BLAZING PO 111.40

SUN-BLINDED SU 531.9

SUN-BURNED DV 149.16

SUNBURNT TF 117.23 SU 543.15

SUN-BURNT DV 171.10

SUN-COLOURED SU 538.10

SUN-CUP EE 304.1

SUN-DARKENED SU 536.9

SUNDAY TF 127.23 128.21
  DV 136.4 138.14 177.11
  SC 267.23 OC 285.10 TP 340.20
  340.28 MN 376.15 FA 464.5
  464.24 464.27 464.28 471.5
  471.24 PR 488.20 488.25
  488.29 488.30 JD 628.20
  628.34 628.37 LL 761.34
  MD 818.7 818.8 818.10
  BM 832.13

SUN-DAZED SU 531.10

SUNDIAL OV 759.36

SUNDOWN NT 720.13 RR 782.24

SUN-DRIED WR 546.31

SUN-FADED SU 538.7

SUNFLOWERS FA 464.39 465.4

SUNG WM 59.8 FA 464.30

SUN-GLEAM WR 577.26

SUN-GLOWING SU 538.42

SUN-INFLAMED PO 109.12

SUNK TF 118.13 126.19 DV 136.6
  GF 239.23 OC 302.12 EE 306.25
  SD 421.23 HD 450.17 FA 458.12
  SU 536.41 IL 654.3

SUNKEN MO 22.6 BL 364.40
  PP 434.30 GG 692.38

SUNLESS SU 532.19

SUNLIGHT SS 210.17 SB 214.24
  EE 303.26 WR 561.6
  MD 806.39

SUNLIT PO 109.2 SG 228.22
  EE 303.12

SUNNED SU 533.8

SUNNING TP 341.11

SUNNY HT 42.12 PO 108.4
  TF 135.1 SS 211.31
  SG 224.17 225.18 225.42
  228.13 MN 366.9 376.15
  TB 518.18 SU 534.12
  WR 547.40 ML 740.1 740.9
  LL 772.28

SUNS OV 753.26

SUN'S SU 536.2

SUN-SCORCHED DV 149.26

SUNSET MO 1.17 1.27 2.11
  2.18 5.7 OA 23.27 WM 54.15
  68.23 WR 565.38

SUNSHADE SG 224.8 225.22
  226.6

SUNSHINE MO 4.31 PO 105.25
  105.33 105.37 108.33
  108.36 111.5 111.32
  111.35 111.42 112.23
  113.9 TF 117.3 118.25
  118.36 132.34 SS 210.23
  SB 213.41 SG 221.4
  GF 240.12 CH 281.4
  EE 304.17 WP 392.30
  PR 510.34 SU 534.9 534.22
  538.40 BO 594.13 LA 640.32
  640.35 IL 648.41 OV 753.17
  753.24 753.25 758.22
  759.28 759.35 LL 770.22
  770.35 773.38

SUNSTROKE PO 113.23 SG 231.37

SUN-SWEPT TF 123.15

SUNWARDS WR 574.7

SUPERB OA 28.42 WR 579.12

SUPERBLY SD 424.17

SUPERCILIOUSNESS BO 587.36

SUPERFICIAL DV 176.15
  WS 255.18 BL 351.8
  HD 445.35 MD 809.19
  TH 847.23

SUPERFICIALLY EA 83.8

SUPERFLUOUS OA 31.37

SUPER-GUEST TB 519.21

SUPERIOR DV 136.30 151.15
  156.9 172.35 174.10

SUPERIOR (CONT.) DV 183.15
  SG 229.28 229.32 GF 235.23
  WS 251.8 CH 278.25 YT 403.20
  BO 588.37 LA 641.5 641.6
  RH 790.20 BM 836.14 837.24

SUPERIORITY WM 64.34 DV 165.35
  EE 319.3 SU 543.6 LA 641.6

SUPERLATIVE MD 805.33

SUPER-MARTYRDOM SM 584.28

SUPERNATURAL PO 105.21 TP 344.3
  LL 767.26 767.27

SUPERVENES TH 845.4

SUPERVISED WR 548.13

SUPPER MO 16.22 19.1 OA 31.14
  31.29 HT 41.17 PO 100.28
  TF 129.1 DV 177.18 178.27
  SB 219.30 WS 244.32 MN 377.7
  SD 413.40 414.15 415.4
  PR 502.6 502.9 502.12 502.22
  508.25 IL 649.7 ML 729.40
  730.3 734.24

SUPPERS SD 413.16 413.22

SUPPER-TRAY GG 688.6

SUPPLE EE 304.22 306.5 306.14
  325.29 325.30 325.32 329.29

SUPPLICATION WM 59.42 60.18
  HD 453.20 SU 542.1

SUPPLIED SP 48.33 YT 394.9

SUPPLIES ML 735.12 TH 853.29

SUPPLY ML 739.34 MD 808.15

SUPPORT DV 141.14 184.11
  WS 250.16 EE 308.8 309.39
  312.3 BL 357.10 PR 477.38
  LA 634.13 634.18

SUPPORTED DV 145.37 161.40

SUPPORTING DV 171.2 WS 257.21

SUPPORTS EE 324.20 ML 725.24

SUPPOSE MO 10.18 11.8 20.5
  SP 51.32 52.30 WM 56.28 57.4
  62.5 67.39 EA 74.30 77.1
  77.40 PO 111.10 DV 143.14
  144.14 168.29 168.35 172.3
  176.5 179.31 SS 198.32 199.20
  199.31 207.39 SB 213.14
  216.31 SG 225.3 WS 248.38
  BL 357.22 361.22 361.23
  361.30 362.2 WP 381.25 393.6
  PR 502.31 505.15 TB 517.17
  518.4 522.41 523.28 527.20
  SU 541.9 542.9 544.30
  WR 549.19 JD 615.28 626.29
  LA 641.20 642.1 644.21 645.6
  IL 653.25 654.25 655.24
  656.15 GG 665.13 667.38
  669.18 678.24 685.33 688.21
  688.31 688.41 693.38 NT 705.2

SUPPOSE (CONT.) 705.6 OV 757.4
  758.17 LL 768.30 771.39
  773.33 RR 787.6 789.10
  RH 791.35 796.14 MD 807.23
  808.15 819.23 826.20

SUPPOSED PO 114.21 FG 188.34
  WP 380.15 TB 517.31 WR 550.3
  BO 596.7 JD 605.22 605.24
  IL 651.34 657.17 GG 666.8
  671.40 676.10 695.33
  NT 708.11 708.16

SUPPOSING MO 9.19 9.32 GG 688.6

SUPPRESSED PO 98.17 103.23
  SG 229.27 GF 242.28 WS 261.7
  SD 415.13 417.23 SU 540.7
  LL 776.1 MD 808.38

SUPPRESSEDLY SG 224.5

SUPPRESSING EA 76.39 PO 95.30
  DV 137.42

SUPPRESSION TF 118.5

SUPREME SD 418.40 WR 556.1
  BO 588.20 598.13 GG 692.21
  NT 720.24

SUPREMELY PR 505.26

SURCHARGED BL 354.30 SD 421.33

SURELY MO 2.38 HT 41.25
  DV 141.34 150.11 SS 207.41
  GF 236.9 237.25 EE 318.2
  PR 495.17 SU 534.30 543.19
  WR 548.38 549.25 549.26
  BO 587.16 JD 605.36 607.32
  626.4 IL 649.36 649.37 650.25
  GG 667.19 680.34 ML 727.39
  728.15 728.17 728.21 731.9
  734.6 OV 754.12 756.20
  LL 768.40 775.6 RR 789.14
  RH 801.41 MD 822.35

SURENESS PO 97.26

SURETY TF 128.34 SS 204.3
  WS 250.18 259.39 260.3
  EE 308.8 BL 356.6 LA 637.14

SURF MO 3.1 WM 54.31 ML 722.24

SURFACE MO 1.14 EE 318.3
  HD 450.10 PR 506.29 OV 752.22
  LL 761.11 763.22

SURGE IL 651.14

SURGED OC 295.24 WP 386.30
  SD 417.32

SURGERY HD 448.13 448.31 456.23

SURGES EA 83.3

SURGICAL EE 321.25

SURGING WM 54.33 EA 83.19
  PR 504.31 RH 803.12 BM 841.31

SURMISE EE 332.11

SURPASSED FA 464.16

SURPASSES GG 698.14

SURPLICES OV 757.19 757.20
  758.5

SURPRISE OA 31.32 SG 221.25
  224.31 230.31 BL 364.31
  YT 401.42 FA 468.35 468.36
  PR 481.6 508.18 GG 673.13
  LL 771.5 RR 788.11

SURPRISED OA 28.17 EA 85.8
  PO 111.15 DV 166.7
  SS 204.18 SB 212.3
  SG 227.17 WS 257.40
  TP 339.20 YT 408.34
  SD 423.17 SU 531.14
  535.8 WR 575.20 LA 637.37
  IL 655.9 NT 712.26
  RH 795.32 802.22

SURPRISING OA 34.16

SURROUNDED TF 117.13
  YT 407.7 LL 762.22

SURROUNDING PO 114.17

SURROUNDINGS MO 6.13 8.25
  PO 112.26 DV 173.30
  SS 206.11 SB 214.11
  SG 224.11 EE 308.16
  BL 354.36 355.25 HD 451.15
  WR 573.42 BO 587.20
  GG 662.9 ML 745.24
  MD 825.26

SURROUNDS BO 596.35

SURVEY SG 221.26 OC 290.4

SURVEYED HT 43.36 GF 243.16

SURVEYING MN 367.28

SURVEYS HT 39.27

SURVIVALS TH 847.26 847.27

SURVIVE GG 700.12

SURVIVED WR 546.11

SUSPECT WS 248.30

SUSPECTED GF 239.31 TB 525.40
  RR 781.33

SUSPENDED EA 72.42 TF 117.27
  134.8 DV 180.20 OC 288.28
  289.32 HD 454.16 WR 564.17
  BO 595.36 599.21

SUSPENSE OA 29.20 WM 59.1
  59.15 TF 117.28 131.14
  DV 179.38 180.28 SG 227.2
  GF 235.34 OC 288.41 290.6
  295.11 EE 331.31 TP 343.40
  BL 351.15 351.16 FA 467.25
  BO 599.37 599.40 JD 616.25
  623.11 623.12 RR 785.20
  785.24

SUSPENSION TF 133.18 EE 331.22

SUSPICION LL 768.14

SUSPICIOUS TP 335.37 WR 551.34

SUSPICIOUS-LOOKING PR 495.16

SUSPICIOUSLY SP 46.3 PP 436.35
  NT 711.31

SUSTAIN WM 67.11 WS 255.1

SUSTAINED WS 255.26 EE 313.40
  WR 552.9

SUSTAINING PR 485.26

SUSTENANCE EE 308.4

SUTTON PP 432.31 432.34 432.41
  433.1 433.4 433.10 433.22
  433.29 433.34 434.1 434.5
  435.33 436.1 436.13 438.15
  438.20 438.28 439.5 440.11

SUTTON (SEE DANIEL, JOKY)

SWADDLED SB 215.16

SWAGGER TF 118.4 BO 598.39

SWAGGERING DV 165.10

SWALED DV 163.18 163.21

SWALLOW FG 192.8 SD 419.5
  HD 442.22 PR 506.5 NT 717.30
  ML 731.10

SWALLOWED OA 31.34 GF 238.24
  OC 286.1 JD 619.18 GG 674.40
  676.29 677.1 ML 728.14

SWALLOWING OA 32.7 SG 232.29

SWALLOWS TB 515.28

SWAM SS 200.3

SWAMP ML 727.7 729.35

SWAN CH 274.16

SWAN AND SUGAR-LOAF WM 63.14

SWANS SM 586.17 OV 759.10
  MD 810.39 821.14

SWANSEA OA 35.31

SWARM PO 111.33

SWARMS PR 481.17 JD 606.15

SWARTHY HT 40.10 PO 97.2 104.33
  GF 241.16 GG 670.22 673.2
  682.2

SWATHED DV 184.8 PR 494.34
  495.1

SWAY EE 329.23 BO 591.27

SWAYED MO 2.23 WM 59.10

SWAYED (CONT.) CH 276.3
  SD 421.12 HD 450.23 SU 528.8
  540.15 WR 547.38 580.1

SWAYING EA 83.6 FG 194.34
  BL 351.11 SD 421.5 PR 474.12
  SU 534.21 WR 569.5 569.6
  569.10 573.39 578.19 579.9

SWAYS ML 735.19

SWEAR SP 53.15

SWEARING GF 242.5

SWEAT OA 35.19 PO 95.14 95.25
  96.3 107.37 DV 169.41 170.10
  FG 189.18

SWEATER PR 483.41 494.18

SWEATING MO 6.39 WM 66.1
  TF 119.46 OC 287.35 EE 318.6
  331.6

SWEAT-MARKED PO 107.40

SWEATY TF 127.30

SWEEP PO 115.14 DV 157.9
  CH 276.7 OC 293.20 PR 499.37
  TB 520.4 SM 586.27

SWEET OA 25.27 35.17 SB 215.23
  217.7 SG 221.25 WS 249.42
  250.1 EE 305.31 BL 358.37
  362.17 MN 368.5 WP 383.20
  SD 419.28 TB 517.3 WR 567.24
  IL 650.23 GG 699.14 ML 740.9
  OV 754.39 RR 782.5 BM 832.35
  836.1

SWEETEN GG 677.28

SWEETENED WR 565.23 568.9
  572.10

SWEETHEART MO 12.18 14.1 15.24
  PO 99.41 113.34 TF 122.31
  126.39 128.13 129.10
  GF 243.18

SWEETHEART'S PO 101.23

SWEETLY TH 851.11

SWEETMEAT MD 818.16

SWEETMEATS FA 459.30

SWEET-NATURED BM 832.40

SWEETNESS PR 484.23 WR 572.30
  MD 822.17

SWEETS TB 517.4

SWEET-SCENTED BL 358.17 WR 577.2

SWEET-SHOP FA 460.25

SWELL WR 578.36 NT 707.27

SWELLED BL 347.29

SWELLING MO 5.3 OA 37.34
  SP 49.12 NT 707.25
  TH 845.42

SWEPT EE 312.16 PR 493.19
  BO 590.6 590.9 LA 638.13
  ML 743.10 RR 785.6
  MD 811.10

SWERVE PR 510.29 LL 761.7

SWERVED TF 120.14 120.20
  121.28 EE 324.15

SWERVES EE 324.15 324.16

SWIFT MO 18.20 PO 113.6
  113.13 CH 279.25 TP 342.26
  WP 379.25 PP 432.31 435.32
  PR 485.11 489.39 501.24
  SU 538.8 539.27 WR 561.12
  561.28 GG 665.35

SWIFTLY OA 24.35 27.17
  36.3 WM 61.4 65.14
  EA 90.41 PO 101.36 109.24
  113.1 113.9 114.22
  TF 124.14 124.22 129.40
  133.19 134.9 FG 193.6
  193.12 SS 201.17 207.20
  SG 228.12 230.32 230.34
  GF 234.20 EE 318.5
  MN 374.27 YT 398.10
  SD 421.6 PP 435.28
  PR 492.20 SU 539.2 539.7
  541.6 WR 567.39 LA 635.28
  GG 694.31 694.36 694.37

SWIFTNESS TH 848.3

SWILLED WS 249.9

SWIM DV 177.3 WS 254.28
  HD 450.20

SWIMMER DV 177.2

SWIMMING SB 214.33 GG 698.4
  ML 742.31 742.36

SWINDLE TB 513.26 SM 582.30

SWINDLED ML 732.5 732.15

SWINDLING ML 732.6

SWINE FG 191.26 GG 699.42
  700.4 MD 812.23

SWING MO 18.38 OA 25.14
  25.18 25.20 WS 246.4
  247.21 EE 324.5 GG 687.8

SWINGING WS 247.22 EE 324.13
  332.12 TP 343.7 MN 371.37
  376.20 376.24 HD 441.23
  442.3 442.10 WR 556.9
  561.4 569.19 BO 588.31
  BM 829.26

SWINGS MO 18.32

SWIRL BL 353.27

SWIRLED ML 745.29

SWISH WM 54.19 TF 122.37

SWISHING PO 107.40

SWITCH OC 292.41

SWITCHBACKS TP 337.30

SWITCHED MO 22.3 LA 632.19
  633.5 637.6 GG 697.5 697.9
  LL 775.39 RH 803.11

SWITCHING RR 788.10

SWOLLEN OA 38.4 38.16 38.24
  WM 69.39 GF 242.18 WS 265.41
  YT 398.9 ML 730.23 OV 748.13

SWOON BL 364.15

SWOONED DV 181.3 FG 195.6
  JD 629.2 ML 742.32

SWOONING WM 69.36 FG 191.23

SWOOP OA 34.40 TF 120.29
  EE 331.22 ML 724.3

SWOOPED MO 1.35

SWOOPING ML 742.5 745.35

SWOOPS TP 334.16

SWOP SC 271.2

SWORD BO 591.29 592.15

SWORDS EE 322.18

SWORD'S MD 807.4

SWORD-SCABBARD PO 96.2

SWORE MO 19.15 SS 210.34
  GF 234.15

SWUNG OA 25.22 25.39 25.41
  SP 48.7 EA 83.18 FG 190.8
  SS 202.2 CH 276.17 OC 294.12
  EE 324.10 331.12 TP 338.9
  MN 372.23 374.39 SD 421.9
  HD 441.38 LA 630.11

SYCOCK'S SS 204.2

SYDNEY PP 427.33 431.18 431.22

SYLLABLE LL 772.34 MD 808.37

SYLLABLES MD 808.36

SYMBOL WM 63.8 CH 277.11
  EE 325.29 325.30

SYMBOLIC ML 730.28

SYMBOLICAL EA 82.26 83.1

SYMBOLISM WM 61.5 62.34

SYMBOLS WM 62.35 62.36 62.40
  67.26 SG 226.32 EE 310.39
  WR 569.32 569.35 576.23

SYMPATHETIC GF 241.38

SYMPATHETICALLY IL 656.2

SYMPATHISE MO 14.25 DV 141.4
  FA 461.3 TB 521.31 521.32

SYMPATHISED BO 587.31

SYMPATHISING MO 14.28

SYMPATHY MO 14.35 OA 37.9
  DV 141.13 163.33 182.36
  OC 292.15 EE 324.13 GG 682.38
  ML 729.14 LL 765.19 MD 817.28
  BM 841.1 TH 845.38

SYPHON MD 824.4

SYSON SS 197.1 197.3 197.14
  197.23 197.33 198.4 198.15
  198.19 198.26 198.35 199.1
  199.12 199.15 199.21 199.24
  199.28 199.31 199.35 200.5
  200.11 200.17 200.22 200.35
  201.21 201.27 201.30 201.38
  201.41 202.20 206.26 206.30
  206.41 208.37 208.41 209.6
  209.16 209.19 209.23 209.27
  209.31 210.1 210.7 210.22
  210.28 210.32 211.9 211.16
  211.22 211.32

SYSON (SEE JOHN; MR. SYSON)

SYSON'S SS 198.40

SYSTEM TF 128.30 TP 334.1

TA PP 432.28 FA 463.25

TABLE MO 3.28 4.38 5.11 5.15
  19.1 OA 29.16 31.13 32.24
  SP 45.26 52.5 WM 63.41 63.42
  EA 71.25 72.1 79.20 81.15
  PO 100.30 101.24 103.4 105.2
  108.4 TF 123.22 123.28 125.37
  DV 140.14 140.40 159.5
  SS 202.38 SG 221.5 222.30
  229.19 GF 240.18 WS 249.7
  SC 267.26 267.29 CH 275.35
  276.27 278.16 278.33 278.37
  281.27 OC 287.18 287.23
  289.22 291.40 TP 338.14
  340.26 BL 350.42 351.2 351.39
  352.17 357.38 358.15 359.6
  SD 412.3 412.20 412.21 414.8
  414.20 415.4 421.10 421.18
  421.21 421.24 421.28 423.26
  425.30 PP 437.8 437.18 439.7
  440.5 HD 441.14 442.29 444.15
  445.3 445.31 TB 521.24
  SU 542.21 542.22 BO 594.4
  JD 616.14 618.24 618.28
  620.32 624.34 GG 672.38
  673.11 674.33 674.37 675.33
  680.26 681.10 ML 739.7 739.33
  LL 763.21 763.32 776.15
  RR 785.30 MD 812.22

TABLECLOTH PO 97.29 98.39
  SS 202.15 OC 296.27

TABLE-CLOTH SG 223.29 HD 445.42

TABLES SP 50.15 ML 729.41

TABLE-WAITER TB 516.8

T'ACCUSE SD 412.39

TACIT EE 324.37 PP 430.21
  GG 662.31 TH 847.5

TACITLY YT 396.8

TACITURN DV 140.2 OC 284.29
  MN 374.4

TACKS TB 513.30

TACTFULLY PR 512.11

TACTILE BL 358.12

TA'E WP 389.29

TA'ES SP 47.20

TAFFY SP 49.15

TAIL HT 40.1 PO 107.40
  113.37 MN 378.16 HD 442.1
  442.9 442.27 443.24 445.14
  PR 490.34 WR 569.7
  SM 585.28 LA 639.28
  NT 714.32 719.7
  ML 746.4 LL 764.12

TAILED WM 66.31 PP 437.35
  NT 720.40 LL 776.10

TAILING FA 460.22

TAILLESS WP 379.7

TAILOR DV 139.42

TAILOR'S DV 139.34 MD 806.42

TAILS WP 379.16

TAKIN' SP 46.1

TALE OA 31.5 TF 131.18

TALENT GG 661.4

TALK MO 4.36 4.39 6.35 12.1
  13.32 14.2 15.30 16.24
  17.13 19.41 HT 40.19
  40.25 WM 64.22 67.25
  EA 86.28 PO 100.1 TF 131.6
  DV 146.5 164.37 166.25
  182.4 SS 210.27 SB 218.16
  218.22 218.27 SG 223.21
  229.24 GF 240.42 241.3
  EE 310.39 314.40 BL 359.6
  360.33 362.38 MN 368.9
  WP 389.30 YT 398.42
  PP 429.2 FA 471.10 471.24
  472.6 PR 481.37 WR 549.41
  566.27 JD 605.17 612.7
  620.4 IL 655.36 GG 664.26
  664.30 681.37 697.22
  NT 702.4 703.13 709.33
  709.34 709.40 710.11
  716.32 718.9 ML 726.14
  727.2 742.6 OV 747.35

TALK (CONT.) OV 748.2 748.20
   753.6 755.31 LL 770.36
   RR 781.1 RH 796.14 796.22
   801.8 BM 828.42 TH 845.19

TALKED MO 4.25 EA 86.1 TF 127.1
   DV 149.37 166.11 SG 231.27
   SC 269.20 CH 279.5 OC 295.12
   EE 305.15 319.4 BL 347.15
   361.13 WP 387.7 388.42
   YT 400.3 400.33 400.36
   SD 415.8 PP 430.2 HD 443.7
   FA 463.10 PR 481.37 SU 541.2
   WR 550.13 557.2 560.35 567.15
   JD 612.9 GG 662.8 662.15
   669.22 NT 709.32 709.33
   716.33 ML 727.19 OV 747.6
   LL 764.22 769.11 769.18
   770.15 RR 780.26 781.1 781.3
   RH 796.29 803.24 MD 813.22

TALKERS OA 33.2

TALKING MO 11.35 12.10 16.23
   SP 47.9 EA 73.39 76.27
   PO 108.38 TF 118.8 133.26
   DV 147.8 167.24 SG 222.26
   227.23 GF 239.7 CH 275.10
   OC 290.7 EE 303.16 YT 399.14
   MN 368.5 WP 389.18 YT 399.14
   400.35 403.28 SD 411.35
   PP 428.11 FA 463.34 WR 547.3
   BO 594.41 JD 613.16 613.40
   614.5 614.19 619.42 620.5
   620.28 LA 640.32 645.21
   IL 656.11 GG 664.33 664.37
   666.18 669.24 673.24 679.37
   NT 711.7 711.41 715.13 718.35
   ML 727.7 729.4 OV 747.1
   747.14 753.1 753.3 756.32
   RR 783.4 RH 796.31 TH 845.20

TALKING-MACHINES PR 474.30

TALKS PP 429.2 NT 704.34
   RH 794.7

TALL OA 23.11 SP 47.29 WM 65.16
   PO 96.9 114.16 TF 119.12
   DV 147.2 GF 235.21 SC 267.10
   CH 274.23 OC 284.7 EE 303.13
   303.35 304.21 305.1 306.14
   311.15 TP 336.16 339.31
   BL 350.42 352.27 MN 371.32
   371.38 WP 393.5 YT 305.3
   396.41 SD 411.8 411.15 413.28
   PP 437.9 FA 458.31 460.40
   467.32 PR 482.25 483.42 489.6
   SU 533.18 535.34 WR 558.40
   561.9 BO 595.27 602.31
   JD 610.39 611.2 624.34 627.31
   LA 630.6 633.6 635.33 637.15
   639.35 GG 670.22 675.18
   ML 726.40 OV 747.15 LL 771.10
   771.23 TH 844.3

TALL-BACKED JD 619.2

TALLER BL 363.35 WP 393.6

TALLISH MN 366.20

TALL-SHAFTED BL 347.33

TAM PP 437.33

TAME SB 213.16

TAME-ANIMAL LA 638.32

TAMPERING EE 308.36

TAN SU 536.6 539.35

TANG OA 23.34 PO 106.30

TANGENT IL 653.12

TANGER GF 242.32 FA 469.24

TANGLE GF 241.30 PR 490.8
   490.10 490.33 SU 539.20
   WR 564.6 GG 686.29 MD 807.39

TANGLED MO 22.24 SS 200.34
   BL 356.1 SD 421.7 HD 453.10
   PR 490.20 506.28 GG 686.34

TANGO GG 684.15

TANK LL 774.30

TANKS SU 537.36

TANNED DV 149.27 150.1 SB 213.9
   MN 374.22 SU 536.5 537.26
   538.1 539.34

TANSY PR 485.11 485.24 494.16
   494.24 494.32

TAN-TAFFLINS'LL HT 41.30

TANTRUM SU 529.6

TAP WS 244.32 HD 441.8 JD 617.4
   RR 783.20

TAPERING OC 283.21 YT 403.7

TAPESTRIED MO 6.20

TAPESTRIES MD 819.29

TAPIOCA EE 318.9

TAPPED DV 178.5 SM 583.21

TAPPING CH 274.22 SD 417.33

TAP-TAP-TAP PO 113.2

TAR GF 234.4

TARES TF 118.23

TARN PR 487.42 506.40

TARRED OC 283.19

TARTAN BL 352.34

TARTAR OA 28.7 TP 336.37

TARTLY DV 141.31 142.23

TARTS FA 471.6

TASK EA 72.31 HD 446.2 448.7
   448.15 PR 479.19

TASKS TF 132.35

TASSELS EE 328.32 FA 465.2

TASTE MO 4.31 DV 149.35
   WS 250.35 WR 565.25
   IL 654.30 OV 758.31
   MD 808.34 813.41

TASTES RH 790.36 791.3

TAT TP 345.39

TATTOOING OC 292.13

TATTY IL 655.5

TATTY'S IL 655.3

TAUGHT MO 16.9 16.16
   SS 200.27 WR 548.13
   LA 644.19 GG 692.31
   RR 781.41 782.5

TAUNT EA 90.10

TAUNTED WP 391.17 SU 538.17

TAUNTING MO 12.4

TAUT MO 12.13 FG 190.2
   SS 198.13 SC 267.6
   HD 442.10 LL 761.24

TAWNY FG 187.32 PR 498.24
   499.8

TAWNY-BROWN SD 417.26

TAXI PP 427.17 427.22
   428.5 428.24 436.4
   BO 587.23 601.24 JD 629.6
   LA 639.3 646.9 RH 791.31

TAXI-CAB PP 427.29

TAXI-CABS PP 427.2

T. BROOKS MANSFIELD DV 178.21

TCHAIKOWSKY IL 650.30 650.33

TEA MO 5.39 14.42 15.3
   SP 52.24 52.41 53.13
   53.17 53.20 53.22
   WM 54.10 56.8 56.13
   EA 71.14 83.33 84.9
   86.25 DV 160.12 CH 278.16
   OC 285.6 285.26 285.30
   286.2 286.15 286.20 287.23
   288.4 291.41 TP 340.31
   341.4 BL 351.38 352.5
   352.22 358.4 MN 371.8
   373.41 WP 388.38 390.26
   HD 456.33 FA 460.28 460.32
   460.38 462.11 463.41
   464.4 464.27 471.5 472.6
   PR 475.6 500.29 500:33
   501.35 501.36 TB 524.23
   524.29 524.39 525.8
   JD 611.9 611.20 611.34
   618.25 619.5 619.8
   IL 649.5 NT 715.18
   LL 761.33 775.28 775.29
   RR 788.41 MD 808.2 815.19

TEA (CONT.) MD 815.27 821.30

TEACH JD 608.8 TH 852.38

TEACHER RR 782.7

TEACHERS JD 608.9

TEACHINGS TH 845.42

TEA-CUPS SG 222.34 BL 351.41
WP 389.1

TEA-LEAVES GF 241.21

TEAM DV 164.15 MN 368.4 370.5
371.4 378.2

TEAPOT GF 241.22 WS 247.24
OC 291.41 TP 341.3 BL 351.7
352.2

TEAR WS 249.35 EE 331.10
BL 351.14 HD 454.38 455.14
NT 713.26 MD 817.36

TEARING TF 121.18 SC 269.19
EE 331.9 TP 343.9 PR 509.7
TB 527.27 LA 639.36 ML 743.12

TEARINGLY PO 112.16

TEARS MO 4.31 OA 30.17 37.30
WM 60.5 64.41 68.30 DV 149.13
171.27 173.36 181.17 185.26
186.22 FG 191.32 191.38
192.13 192.35 195.33 195.34
SS 202.30 SB 212.29 219.39
GF 238.13 238.14 WS 249.32
SC 272.28 272.38 272.42
OC 294.2 294.6 294.35 299.1
299.18 299.20 MN 377.27
SD 419.14 HD 454.6 454.13
454.15 455.4 455.6 455.20
FA 460.31 466.29 466.37
PR 491.29 509.20 TB 514.28
526.29 BO 597.32 598.16
LA 645.30 645.34 IL 652.28
GG 690.1 OV 755.38 755.41
BM 828.27 828.35

TEAR-STAINED WS 265.41

TEAS OC 287.17

TEASED SP 47.21 SB 218.33
EE 326.1 OV 756.17 BM 829.4

TEASERS GF 242.39

TEA-SHOP LA 644.8

TEASING TB 525.35 JD 627.5
MD 824.12 BM 829.7

TEASPOON TB 521.9

TEA-TALK MO 5.24

TEA-THINGS CH 280.2

TEA-TIME BL 351.42 HD 448.34
TB 524.14 LL 766.4 MD 814.35

TEA-TIMES MO 7.28

TEA-TRAY EA 71.25 TB 524.14

TECHNICALITIES MO 11.37

TED WS 246.29 246.33 249.31
258.28 259.23 TP 335.31

TEDDILINKS WS 244.1 244.35

TEDDY WS 247.36 248.18
IL 653.23 653.24 653.37
654.22 654.37 655.7

TEDDY-BEAR RH 791.21

TED ROCKLEY YT 395.23 396.8
396.35

TED SLANEY'S FA 470.37

TEENS SB 212.33 PR 477.8

TEETH MO 5.5 OA 26.10 27.5
WM 57.6 57.12 EA 73.17 85.7
PO 109.20 110.4 TF 121.22
DV 148.39 167.1 178.29
FG 189.10 SB 213.25 215.7
215.11 SG 230.4 WS 245.38
262.5 SC 268.26 CH 282.6
EE 329.11 WP 390.18 PP 437.31
HD 441.34 PR 485.29 509.34
509.36 WR 574.37 576.18
SM 585.5 585.13 BO 593.23
595.41 603.29 604.35 JD 626.7
628.40 LA 632.6 632.24 646.31
NT 710.27 ML 727.7 LL 761.7
RR 780.32

TELEGRAM EA 74.27 75.5 83.31
83.37 85.16 87.2 EE 321.24
MN 368.14 368.39 368.42
369.12 SM 582.2 JD 628.31
628.38

TELEGRAPH EA 72.20 83.32
ML 729.32

TELEPATHY NT 702.24

TELEPHONE LA 637.5 646.8
RH 802.21 BM 834.26

TELEPHONED GG 677.30

TELESCOPE BO 589.15

TELLED FA 470.20

TELLIN' FA 463.30

TELLING MO 7.11 DV 139.25
WS 261.39 BL 363.15 363.26
MN 368.36 YT 399.18 GG 679.9
RR 779.22 RH 799.10 MD 814.17

TELLS BL 360.8 WR 575.32
RH 792.15

TEMPER SP 52.41 WM 55.29
PO 98.17 SS 200.31 CH 282.15
EE 311.40 324.24 MN 376.5

TEMPERED EE 324.36 OV 749.20

TEMPERS IL 647.8

TEMPEST LA 638.12

TEMPLE DV 166.14 OC 292.11
SU 533.25 WR 566.7
MD 817.10 817.27

TEMPLES OA 36.33 PO 96.10
WS 249.5 264.13 264.18
BL 354.31 SD 417.38
PR 512.20 MD 809.17

TEMPORARY WM 65.15 EE 307.28
ML 735.35

TEMPT GG 671.16 672.2

TEMPTATION DV 143.28
EE 324.18 GG 671.17

TEMPTED TB 520.16 MD 806.39

TEMPTING WM 54.2

TEN MO 16.19 OA 31.3 33.41
HT 39.18 40.31 SP 45.3
WM 57.22 57.23 59.21
DV 140.14 GF 242.1
OC 292.22 293.28 295.17
298.36 EE 305.9 308.40
308.41 321.23 TP 335.42
340.34 BL 361.36 YT 397.7
SD 415.23 415.28 416.40
PP 436.23 436.36 HD 446.38
FA 459.4 464.30 464.37
PR 482.14 TB 515.25 515.39
518.2 WR 547.10 547.22
SM 584.34 BO 589.17
JD 605.6 605.10 616.10
NT 720.38 LL 765.33 769.25
777.3 RR 783.16 RH 796.26
796.35 798.3 MD 817.40
TH 847.32

TENACIOUS WR 547.14 MD 810.13

TENDED DV 155.1 BO 604.1
MD 807.13 807.41

TENDENCY BO 589.10

TENDER WM 61.27 64.34 64.41
PO 115.30 TF 123.2
WS 259.19 BL 364.5
MN 374.21 WP 388.21
PP 430.2 PR 504.38
TB 514.13 SU 532.11
LA 643.27 IL 652.4
GG 692.41 695.29 ML 727.4
TH 846.33

TENDER-LOOKING MN 367.38

TENDERLY OA 36.21 WM 63.25
SC 268.10 IL 657.38
ML 727.24

TENDERNESS MO 12.14 OA 26.33
26.37 38.21 WM 65.20
EA 75.32 87.29 89.29
PO 115.23 DV 152.29 164.9
171.11 SB 220.5 CH 278.1
MN 370.8 YT 402.26 PR 481.3
494.31 WR 570.11 GG 690.31
BM 841.34 842.40

TENDRILS TF 123.3 EE 304.24
  TH 845.6

TENENTS DV 146.34*

TENNIS BM 828.17 831.25

TENNIS-RACKET OA 23.12

TENOR MO 11.33 HT 40.23
  SP 50.37 EE 325.42 FA 464.11
  465.30

TENSE MO 10.28 EA 72.9 72.40
  PO 96.32 97.11 109.30
  DV 151.21 169.21 SG 226.9
  WS 250.18 257.35 263.4 264.35
  EE 320.19 330.8 TP 344.6
  SD 414.10 414.13 PR 510.33
  TB 527.29 SU 535.27 WR 560.26
  562.42 564.15 569.15
  JD 613.21 628.37 LL 761.16
  RH 802.10 MD 815.40 TH 848.4

TENSELY SB 218.25 TP 344.14

TEN-SHILLING RH 795.9

TENSION OA 30.34 EA 72.10
  PO 96.20 107.26 110.7
  TF 121.13 WS 257.26 OC 290.24
  EE 325.22 331.11 SD 415.17
  TB 519.14 SU 534.32 JD 624.11
  624.12 GG 682.41 687.18
  691.27 NT 717.4 ML 735.36
  740.30 OV 757.38 LL 767.23
  RR 785.13 785.14 785.19

TENSIONS SU 530.40

TENT MN 371.11 371.13

TENTATIVE BL 354.16 357.15

TENTATIVELY DV 180.38 SB 219.13
  SD 426.11 TB 517.15 LL 778.12

TEN THOUSAND TP 335.38 RH 798.3

TEN THOUSAND POUNDS YT 394.33
  394.34

TER HT 43.28 SP 47.13 47.22
  48.21 48.23 48.28 50.7 51.27
  51.36 53.13 53.15 53.16
  SS 210.26 SC 267.28 267.31
  268.9 268.35 269.39 271.15
  271.17 271.29 271.33 271.37
  CH 279.11 OC 292.23 292.24
  WP 388.25 389.21 HD 443.22
  FA 458.20 461.41 463.31
  463.32

TERM PO 99.39

TERMINUS WM 55.9 TF 122.35
  TP 334.9 334.23

TERMS MO 20.1 ML 735.41
  TH 844.26

TERRACE TF 119.28 SG 225.20
  225.41 EE 307.13 TB 513.16
  SU 529.10 531.24 WR 568.29
  577.32

TERRACED EE 307.21

TERRACES TF 118.38 EE 307.14
  SU 537.17 538.39

TERRESTRIAL GF 240.11

TERRIBLE EA 85.21 TF 130.3
  OC 297.37 302.5 EE 312.14
  313.17 324.18 326.13 328.40
  332.42 333.10 TP 344.30 345.4
  BL 347.32 348.29 WP 383.39
  HD 453.42 454.29 454.31 457.8
  PR 477.34 504.13 WR 557.36
  557.38 560.31 566.24 569.26
  573.11 581.12 BO 591.3 598.12
  GG 665.34 667.41 684.32
  685.26 NT 704.22 705.35
  707.18 LL 769.24 778.1
  RR 784.26 MD 808.25

TERRIBLY TF 126.19 EE 310.18
  317.25 YT 396.40 HD 457.5
  TB 526.2 SU 539.34 541.27
  WR 565.12 581.16 JD 606.9
  LA 642.16 IL 648.2 GG 666.9
  689.3 RH 794.16 800.20 802.22
  MD 813.1 814.24 814.30 818.40
  BM 827.16

TERRIER SD 418.1 PP 437.26
  HD 442.21

TERRIER-LIKE SD 415.19

TERRIFIC ML 743.9 TH 853.15

TERRIFIED TF 129.8 DV 175.28
  SC 270.1 EE 317.4 YT 405.17
  PP 435.1 HD 454.32 SM 583.25
  LL 768.13 778.2 MD 824.8

TERRIFYING TP 343.34 344.14
  BL 348.29 PR 497.39 WR 573.34

TERRIFYINGLY BL 353.20

TERRITORY BO 600.7

TERROR PO 115.20 TF 129.26
  DV 153.11 154.38 156.32
  175.27 FG 190.18 SG 227.37
  GF 238.19 WS 264.5 264.12
  OC 300.4 EE 312.15 TP 335.19
  343.16 TB 522.21 WR 568.4
  BO 598.13 604.27 JD 624.9
  GG 679.22 681.1 LL 767.10
  773.39

TERRORS ML 724.11

TERROR-STRUCK BL 364.20

TER'S FA 460.17

TESS OF THE D'URBERVILLES
  JD 605.34

TESTAMENT NT 720.35

TESTED BO 590.15

TESTILY CH 278.14 YT 405.9

TETE-A-TETE IL 652.6

TEXTURE EE 306.6 LL 769.38

TH' MO 12.5 HT 42.3 42.34
  43.4 44.2 SP 48.30 48.31
  49.40 51.27 SC 267.26
  267.27 267.31 268.21
  268.32 269.29 269.34
  269.35 269.36 269.40
  270.27 271.17 271.29
  271.33 271.36 271.37
  272.6 272.22 CH 277.40
  282.4 282.7 OC 291.33
  292.18 292.24 292.25
  292.30 294.19 295.28
  295.33 295.39 296.1 296.2
  296.11 297.19 297.20
  WP 388.28 389.24 PP 428.6
  429.8 431.15 431.32
  HD 445.10 FA 463.32
  469.28 469.29 471.31

THA HT 41.40 42.5 SP 53.15
  SC 267.27 267.37 269.23
  269.38 270.20 CH 277.40
  277.41 TP 339.37 340.41
  WP 388.9 388.27 HD 443.23
  FA 460.17 463.30 463.31
  470.33

THA'D HT 43.28 FA 463.23

THA'LL SP 47.22

THA'LT WP 389.3

THANK OA 29.13 31.41 37.26
  38.13 HT 41.41 WM 57.19
  66.29 EA 88.14 DV 140.10
  142.14 CH 275.14 277.29
  278.14 OC 293.12 EE 311.40
  MN 372.4 WP 388.10
  YT 397.28 SD 412.15 416.26
  PR 477.4 499.23 TB 525.1
  527.17 527.25 SU 539.16
  JD 610.15 LA 640.14 642.32
  643.17 645.11 645.18
  GG 696.23 696.24 696.26
  696.32 696.34 697.3
  MD 826.29 BM 838.6

THANKED SU 539.6 NT 716.13

THANKFUL DV 145.16 CH 279.12
  279.20 HD 450.36 FA 465.21
  IL 649.30

THANKFULLY BM 834.40

THANKING TB 527.18

THANKLESS EE 316.13

THANKS MO 12.32 18.2
  OA 38.23 TF 117.25
  MN 370.30 372.33 YT 396.28
  GG 675.21 RR 784.37 784.38
  BM 840.11

THA'RT SP 46.8 SC 270.41
  HD 443.22 FA 461.41

THA'S HT 41.40 42.5 43.4
  43.25 43.41 SP 46.31
  46.39 49.34 TP 342.6
  FA 458.20

THAT'LL WS 257.42 SC 270.33
  TP 346.1 FA 470.40

THAW DV 176.28

THAWED DV 176.27

THEATRE EA 74.33 90.17 GG 662.6
  665.27 NT 711.42 ML 735.40

THEATREFUL GG 664.41

THEATRICAL WM 63.21 TB 520.30
  520.42 RR 781.30 783.41

THEATRICALS BM 834.6

THE BLACK SHEEP EA 90.19

THEE SP 49.34 50.7 53.15
  SC 271.36 271.37 CH 280.12
  280.32 280.34 280.40 280.41
  280.42 281.1 281.7 281.10
  281.11 282.7 TP 342.2
  WP 388.27 389.22 HD 445.28
  FA 461.41 461.42 462.13
  463.29 468.6 468.8 468.10
  470.20 GG 692.15 692.31
  BM 841.12

THEE'D FA 463.23

THEER HT 42.42 SP 49.39
  SC 268.35 OC 292.16 292.34
  FA 461.41

THEER'S SP 49.5

THEIRS EE 311.15 SD 425.10

THEIRSELVES OC 291.34

THE MASTER ML 726.22 727.27
  734.33

THEME MN 370.25

THEMSELVES MO 4.42 5.1 OA 30.22
  SP 45.5 52.39 EA 86.26
  TF 134.37 DV 138.28 WS 252.29
  EE 306.27 308.34 309.9 315.5
  316.15 TP 335.17 343.36 344.2
  346.7 MN 371.16 YT 394.36
  PP 427.4 PR 475.19 482.41
  486.27 494.38 BO 598.26
  GG 693.26 NT 707.34 718.10
  ML 742.2 LL 769.20 RH 790.16
  790.20 TH 846.3 846.15 846.26
  846.37 848.2

THENCE TF 132.38

THE OCTOPUS MO 16.21

THEOSOPHY TH 846.13

THE PRINCESS PR 473.1 474.39

THEREAFTER FG 193.28

THEREAT FG 192.17

THEREFORE MO 14.16 OA 23.2
  HT 41.1 EA 74.42 DV 155.14
  158.5 CH 279.33 TP 335.40

THEREFORE (CONT.) 336.11 336.39
  337.38 BL 349.27 WP 381.1
  391.16 HD 442.15 PR 474.24
  RH 791.26 BM 827.12 834.15
  TH 844.21 853.23

THERE'LL SG 224.38 MN 375.20
  PR 487.32 WR 549.9

THERMOPYLAE TP 335.39

THE SHOES OF SHAGPUT BM 835.15

THESIS DV 145.1

THE STAG AT BAY SG 221.9

THE SWAN WM 60.11

THE THIEF OF BAGDAD MD 823.4

THE TINNERS' SD 411.34

THEY'D GF 236.14 SC 273.13
  CH 281.5 281.11 WP 385.18
  GG 674.19 TH 850.9

THEY'LL TF 124.28 DV 182.10
  WS 261.22 261.42 SC 273.11
  OC 290.11 296.14 296.34
  BM 842.30

THICK MO 6.2 13.22 OA 26.35
  27.14 31.26 31.27 35.41
  SP 49.2 49.9 WM 55.38 63.30
  PO 100.33 106.14 114.16
  DV 161.6 FG 187.10 196.22
  SS 197.10 198.8 198.13 200.37
  205.4 SG 223.5 SC 267.34
  268.41 OC 284.31 287.26
  289.26 EE 306.23 320.10
  321.38 328.25 328.39 330.13
  332.29 332.30 WP 387.40
  HD 441.33 447.40 449.33
  PR 484.38 500.12 503.27
  SU 530.7 534.11 543.16
  WR 555.11 564.22 SM 582.12
  586.13 JD 606.24 606.26 610.2
  LA 631.11 639.2 IL 652.1
  GG 677.36 NT 705.24 709.30
  713.15 OV 750.31 LL 763.20
  765.9 766.15 770.26 MD 819.42
  820.29 821.29 822.25
  BM 828.11 829.17 832.42 843.1

THICK-BLOODED EE 305.40

THICKENING PR 486.18

THICKETS PO 95.2 TF 118.42

THICK-LEGGED SD 411.20

THICKLY-BERRIED MO 6.16

THICKLY-BUILT OA 31.16

THICKNESS SS 202.40 LA 634.21

THICK-SET OA 34.19

THIEF WP 387.36 BO 604.38

THIEVES GG 690.26 690.28

THIGH PO 102.31 109.14
  BL 362.33 GG 691.9 692.19

THIGHS MO 13.21 PO 95.28
  104.32 DV 177.28 SG 226.34
  BL 354.29 SD 422.4
  HD 450.16 452.42 453.1
  SU 530.32 531.1 536.7
  539.25 GG 681.31 683.9
  689.34 695.37 696.30
  697.2 697.8 698.29
  NT 715.26 MD 819.4 819.38

THIN MO 17.14 OA 23.11
  EA 72.11 83.24 PO 96.18
  109.37 110.27 DV 138.36
  145.26 147.25 149.22
  151.23 153.36 158.7
  FG 188.23 189.28 SS 200.1
  SB 212.14 217.8 WS 245.24
  250.23 CH 274.9 277.31
  278.30 OC 298.34 EE 319.5
  324.25 324.30 329.28
  BL 356.27 357.21 357.25
  358.33 MN 371.16 WP 379.1
  388.18 YT 395.3 396.41
  397.13 397.30 399.7 403.4
  PP 427.19 439.24 439.37
  PR 491.8 499.31 508.2
  SU 532.20 533.18 WR 554.1
  BO 593.20 600.15 JD 614.42
  617.1 618.14 625.27
  626.41 627.18 LA 630.9
  631.8 631.10 IL 648.34
  GG 682.12 NT 705.27
  ML 725.42 729.9 743.20
  MD 807.35 808.22 809.19
  814.33 815.11 815.40
  821.36 822.5 825.25
  BM 829.33

THINE CH 280.34 FA 463.34

THINGS' TH 848.8

THINK MO 8.5 8.6 8.16 9.38
  10.26 14.22 19.40 20.7
  20.17 20.28 22.21 OA 23.23
  25.19 28.35 36.11 HT 40.6
  40.17 41.22 41.26 41.35
  SP 46.4 52.15 52.28 52.29
  52.36 53.1 53.10 WM 55.25
  56.41 57.7 62.10 62.19
  65.33 68.21 EA 74.19 75.4
  75.7 79.18 80.33 80.35
  86.41 88.4 90.18 PO 103.12
  106.20 TF 122.16 125.4
  133.3 133.31 DV 141.21
  141.32 144.9 150.3 156.7
  158.19 158.21 161.41
  163.15 163.26 169.38
  173.30 175.8 176.7 177.9
  177.16 179.26 184.13
  184.19 184.21 185.18
  185.29 185.32 186.6 186.11
  FG 188.37 SS 198.29 205.2
  207.1 207.32 SB 215.24
  215.37 218.6 219.35
  SG 222.28 222.37 223.4
  224.35 228.19 232.24
  232.32 232.39 GF 235.37
  236.16 236.22 239.22 241.4
  WS 250.12 252.14 254.14
  262.23 263.5 263.11
  SC 271.39 CH 274.37 277.13

THINK (CONT.) OC 285.16 285.17
  287.29 288.35 292.36
  EE 307.27 318.21 319.37
  320.28 320.30 320.33 320.34
  320.35 321.14 321.19 321.32
  328.9 BL 350.30 355.28 356.27
  362.39 362.41 363.10
  MN 366.13 368.40 372.14 373.2
  373.10 374.30 WP 380.37
  381.11 381.42 382.8 383.40
  384.4 384.13 384.37 385.1
  385.3 389.19 392.14 YT 396.29
  398.34 403.32 403.33 404.1
  404.14 405.33 406.30 406.31
  SD 416.23 419.27 424.8 424.9
  425.5 425.39 426.15 PP 430.10
  431.14 436.3 436.17 438.6
  HD 447.20 448.39 455.12
  FA 461.17 461.18 461.20
  462.13 463.26 469.8 469.22
  469.23 469.39 472.4 PR 476.10
  479.6 479.10 485.18 491.26
  491.29 492.10 499.22 503.8
  508.15 TB 517.14 517.31 518.2
  518.5 518.8 522.32 523.13
  523.18 523.25 523.30 526.34
  SU 534.25 537.28 541.13
  541.25 542.14 WR 549.9 575.39
  BO 586.4 589.8 590.27 593.15
  598.1 601.7 601.9 601.10
  JD 615.24 615.25 619.23
  625.30 LA 636.24 636.27
  641.30 IL 648.6 652.7 653.13
  654.27 658.36 GG 662.8 662.11
  662.14 663.31 663.34 664.38
  665.3 667.1 667.9 667.39
  668.5 669.12 671.18 673.32
  674.19 675.8 675.22 675.37
  677.29 677.37 679.11 680.1
  680.2 681.17 685.37 688.5
  688.35 689.1 689.39 693.12
  695.7 696.35 697.14 697.20
  NT 701.25 702.40 702.42
  704.18 704.22 704.30 704.32
  704.40 705.16 706.8 706.10
  706.35 708.4 709.37 710.2
  710.35 713.30 716.42 718.22
  718.27 719.39 ML 727.20 731.5
  732.7 743.36 OV 747.24 752.17
  756.6 LL 771.28 777.19 778.11
  RH 792.19 794.29 798.34
  799.39 800.36 801.3 801.24
  801.26 804.19 MD 806.24
  806.26 808.29 813.37 817.38
  817.39 818.2 818.21 823.28
  823.29 824.32 824.36 824.38
  826.8 826.13 826.16 BM 830.13
  831.4 833.38 834.8 834.9
  841.3 841.27 TH 846.18 851.35
  852.42 853.3

THINKIN' HT 41.37 OC 292.25

THINKING MO 9.35 11.1 11.29
  OA 29.8 37.35 EA 78.29 90.15
  PO 103.11 104.14 TF 131.26
  131.42 132.36 DV 145.42
  155.17 173.36 179.8 186.9
  SS 199.27 SB 219.25 GF 241.7
  CH 281.20 OC 288.5 BL 351.23
  358.35 360.24 WP 383.10
  383.11 387.31 YT 400.15
  404.28 SD 414.26 PP 432.13
  PR 488.14 TB 513.19 517.30
  SU 532.6 541.26 542.12

THINKING (CONT.) WR 560.23
  SM 585.29 BO 601.3 JD 620.24
  LA 643.35 GG 671.22 672.7
  673.29 673.32 686.18 692.22
  693.15 693.19 693.28 697.25
  NT 713.19 714.21 ML 742.25
  OV 756.9 LL 768.26 768.39

THINKS MO 20.19 DV 152.22
  GF 238.42 243.23 WS 248.38
  YT 399.34 399.36 399.39
  FA 461.18 JD 627.11 GG 665.37
  687.40 OV 747.18

THIN-LEGGED GF 241.16

THIN-LOOKING WP 385.31

THINLY FG 187.1 RR 788.23

THINNED FG 190.19 MN 374.23

THINNER MN 374.20

THINNESS JD 625.15

THINNING SS 203.11

THINNISH PR 483.16

THIRD MO 13.34 OA 34.9
  DV 156.26 SG 229.37 WS 245.30
  EE 315.34 319.30 328.5
  BL 348.38 MN 366.35 378.21
  YT 409.41 WR 556.33 558.24
  BO 601.14 NT 720.32 ML 725.36
  732.19 732.26 738.1 739.29
  739.30 OV 748.21 LL 764.14
  RR 780.34 785.22 RH 796.9
  803.39 BM 839.12 839.14
  TH 852.20

THIRST PO 105.22 114.20 115.4
  115.37

THIRSTINESS PO 115.27

THIRSTY PO 105.38 WR 552.9
  LL 771.37

THIRTEEN DV 138.33 147.25
  YT 396.11 GG 680.10

THIRTEENTH SM 584.42

THIRTY MO 16.41 HT 42.21
  EA 71.22 84.27 PO 95.1
  DV 164.33 CH 274.12 BL 348.26
  YT 403.38 FA 459.6 PR 479.3
  481.25 482.24 497.15 LA 643.2
  GG 681.32 NT 708.40 LL 761.2
  762.10 MD 805.15 807.35
  BM 831.29

THIRTY-EIGHT PR 479.32 BO 591.38

THIRTY-EIGHTH PR 480.33

THIRTY-FIVE HT 39.12 SU 542.37
  JD 605.29 618.3 ML 722.11
  RR 783.23 TH 847.16

THIRTY-FOUR OA 26.25 BM 832.19

THIRTY-ODD IL 648.22

THIRTY-ONE SG 231.20
  JD 607.42 MD 813.21

THIRTY-SEVEN TH 847.16

THIRTY-THREE HD 441.31
  PR 479.16 WR 547.11
  547.32 ML 734.30

THIRTY-TWO SG 231.21
  YT 403.39 FA 462.15 462.22
  LL 763.27 MD 814.7

THISTLE-DOWN EE 309.4

THISTLES SB 213.40

THITHER MO 2.40 OA 24.29
  SB 214.18 EE 323.4

THOMAS OA 31.3 31.15 31.25
  32.3 32.6 32.11 32.15
  32.38 33.2 33.6 33.17
  33.27 33.33 34.2 34.15
  34.18 34.21 34.24 34.30
  35.1 35.9 35.19 35.22
  35.25 35.30 35.34 35.41
  36.2 36.4 36.23 36.27
  37.14 37.21 38.21 38.31
  38.37

THOMAS (SEE SERGEANT THOMAS;
  MR. THOMAS, MRS. THOMAS)

THOMAS SEDGWICK SP 46.7

THOMAS'S OA 35.39 38.16

THORN MO 2.5 22.13 22.24
  EE 305.42 WP 386.8 386.21
  FA 466.16

THORNS FG 190.35 SS 204.19
  SU 534.30 534.42 535.4
  535.5

THORNY WR 551.39

THOROUGH YT 394.28 ML 732.4

THOROUGHBRED EE 328.27

THOROUGHLY MO 5.29 TF 130.17
  TP 343.10 WP 393.10
  TH 845.16

THOU WS 246.11 248.25
  CH 280.36 280.38 280.39
  281.6 281.13 EE 331.17
  331.18 FA 468.7 TH 850.14

THOUGHT MO 4.36 6.20 6.32
  7.34 9.11 9.29 9.35
  10.20 11.3 11.25 12.6
  18.35 OA 32.31 32.32
  34.12 35.3 38.30 SP 51.29
  WM 54.16 60.17 61.30
  61.36 63.24 64.2 64.14
  64.23 64.41 EA 78.21
  80.22 81.19 82.25 83.8
  89.41 PO 97.5 99.36
  103.39 104.23 107.11
  114.22 TF 131.14 131.39
  131.41 133.12 DV 142.9
  148.1 149.38 152.36 153.2

THOUGHT (CONT.) DV 156.35
157.10 161.5 161.10 167.31
170.36 171.37 174.5 174.25
178.15 181.39 FG 188.17
189.11 190.23 190.27 190.32
193.36 SS 200.19 204.29
205.29 208.29 SB 215.26
215.30 215.36 215.37 SG 222.6
222.11 223.1 232.35 232.38
GF 237.31 241.24 242.23 243.8
WS 249.1 251.6 254.12 256.30
258.9 CH 277.20 277.40 281.20
OC 284.23 294.23 295.7 298.14
EE 307.26 307.38 307.42 308.6
319.25 325.3 326.5 327.26
328.4 330.30 TP 340.18
BL 349.2 350.28 351.12 360.28
363.35 364.37 MN 366.1 366.4
368.34 375.40 377.1 378.25
WP 382.2 386.3 YT 398.38
399.5 400.12 401.27 402.9
402.39 404.15 404.34 405.31
408.42 SD 412.29 414.32
421.26 PP 427.27 429.23
431.20 437.17 HD 444.40
447.25 453.12 453.14 455.13
PR 474.9 480.28 492.2 493.32
493.35 496.42 498.4 511.19
TB 515.34 516.41 518.14
518.30 518.38 521.34 522.2
523.24 526.14 SU 528.10
528.31 531.16 537.27 544.14
WR 546.1 573.27 579.1
SM 583.19 585.1 BO 589.3
592.9 600.30 601.9 601.11
JD 605.20 607.34 607.36
613.22 615.14 619.14 619.19
622.11 624.9 624.41 LA 643.34
IL 648.7 648.38 650.19 652.11
655.16 656.3 658.26 658.31
658.38 659.19 GG 662.36
662.42 671.32 675.8 676.9
676.28 677.4 678.25 679.20
680.5 689.12 689.14 690.24
691.10 693.13 693.14
NT 701.29 703.3 704.1 706.21
707.22 708.13 708.20 708.21
709.5 709.17 709.21 710.12
710.19 714.23 714.24 718.6
ML 722.18 728.26 732.7 732.38
737.8 739.19 743.14 744.13
OV 752.11 752.19 752.42
LL 766.22 768.7 768.11 770.29
772.42 776.10 777.11 778.2
RR 780.2 788.2 788.36
RH 794.30 795.10 795.18
797.20 798.13 798.24
MD 805.10 807.33 808.27
810.21 811.22 814.11 815.36
816.4 822.19 823.2 BM 829.5
830.13 834.2 834.33 TH 844.10
846.32 846.38 847.1 848.6

THOUGHTFUL SS 206.32 YT 404.24
WR 565.7

THOUGHTFULLY SG 225.32 226.41

THOUGHTLESS BO 596.39

THOUGHTS OA 30.29 HT 40.42
EA 82.23 DV 174.21 SS 209.41
SG 232.41 OC 294.29 WP 381.11
YT 404.3 SD 413.35 FA 468.9
PR 502.33 SU 530.39 530.41

THOUGHTS (CONT.) LL 768.37
768.38 769.20 RH 804.7

THOUSAND MO 2.24 SP 48.17
DV 136.27 EE 303.36 WP 382.5
PP 429.39 PR 504.28 TB 513.11
519.12 519.16 520.16 NT 704.9
719.26 RR 778.35 RH 797.42
798.5 799.4 799.20 799.37
800.7 803.38 804.26 804.34
MD 809.29 823.33 TH 844.7
844.12

THOUSAND POUNDS RH 799.1 799.11

THOUSANDS SD 424.3 SU 533.20
NT 706.18 ML 728.13 732.1

THRASHED FA 471.39

THREAD WM 61.20 SS 199.39 200.1
PR 494.4 494.37 509.8
SU 532.32 WR 578.33 BO 591.34
OV 748.27

THREADBARE DV 158.38

THREADED WM 61.19 EA 71.29 86.9
91.17 WS 250.2 WR 578.17

THREADING PP 436.10 PR 494.9
WR 579.13

THREADS SS 210.4

THREAT WM 61.21 PO 103.40
TH 850.13

THREATENED SP 45.6 EA 83.5
FA 471.25

THREATENING DV 136.20 GF 234.30
MN 377.42 HD 446.35

THREATS OC 283.3

THREE MO 4.12 19.26 OA 24.14
26.5 34.10 38.42 WM 59.29
63.30 EA 71.15 76.29 93.27
93.32 PO 97.41 108.3 116.10
TF 126.39 131.14 DV 136.3
144.36 147.38 148.11 156.18
156.19 173.36 FG 187.3 187.5
191.15 SS 209.26 SG 231.22
GF 242.27 WS 253.33 SC 272.40
CH 277.4 OC 283.31 284.38
284.42 290.21 296.40 297.27
EE 308.19 308.38 316.27
317.20 322.24 328.3 329.39
330.39 TP 335.13 BL 359.5
359.20 MN 366.25 373.6
WP 379.7 379.12 YT 395.33
395.37 398.3 SD 415.18 418.10
419.9 PP 427.28 428.1 429.32
435.42 439.4 HD 441.6 441.13
441.21 441.30 PR 473.31
479.20 482.6 484.10 485.19
487.7 488.32 488.38 489.10
500.9 TB 514.9 518.28 519.23
WR 548.8 548.10 550.17 551.24
553.18 556.41 559.19 562.25
SM 583.32 583.40 584.2 584.4
584.5 585.10 585.36 586.5
JD 610.36 623.11 628.33
LA 630.7 IL 654.11 GG 668.30

THREE (CONT.) 678.22 678.23
679.15 689.28 692.11
699.34 NT 712.38 ML 722.27
725.22 739.33 741.30
OV 760.5 LL 763.27 763.32
764.22 765.1 765.11 765.41
RR 781.40 783.37 786.6
RH 796.25 MD 807.32 810.29
BM 831.7 837.29 839.32
TH 844.7 844.12 848.19
852.22 852.32

THREE-FOOT HT 39.27

THREE-FOURTHS EE 310.42

THREE HUNDRED RH 795.21
795.25 797.9 MD 814.4

THREE-MILE BM 834.37

THREE-PENCE GF 242.33

THREE-PULSE SD 411.5

THREE-QUARTERS MO 1.32
OA 34.42

THREE STAR PP 435.10

THREE THOUSAND WR 558.37

THREE THOUSAND DOLLARS
TH 850.4

THREE THOUSAND POUNDS
JD 607.17

THRESHED MO 6.22

THRESHING MN 374.32

THRESHOLD OA 23.13 WR 562.6
RR 784.17

THREW MO 5.5 WM 70.18
EA 76.24 PO 95.3 95.12
105.32 SS 207.37 210.36
SB 215.5 SG 221.36
WS 252.29 252.30 254.4
EE 313.16 TP 338.14 343.35
WP 391.22 SD 412.32 417.37
420.13 421.37 HD 456.18
PR 506.41 SU 532.11 532.15
WR 555.14 573.36 GG 696.20
ML 726.8 OV 755.6
MD 811.15

THRICE-DEAD WR 546.30

THRILL SP 48.26 EA 81.30
PO 100.20 TF 129.25
DV 167.26 SB 220.8 WR 556.2
557.16 560.25 BO 599.33
603.8 NT 712.10 LL 768.32
TH 845.42

THRILLED TF 133.2 WS 249.10
252.33 SD 411.28 PR 484.18
SU 540.7 BO 602.20
GG 661.18 LL 764.37
MD 811.10 811.34 814.22
824.9 BM 830.1 831.14
TH 848.37

THRILLING PR 485.27 SM 586.8
  BO 600.1 OV 749.1 753.18
  MD 805.29 810.27 TH 845.20

THRIPPENCE HT 43.33

THRIVED SU 532.5

THROAT OA 27.14 27.18 33.38
  34.31 35.41 36.18 36.28
  36.33 36.38 36.41 HT 40.23
  WM 58.15 58.18 58.22 66.7
  68.7 69.5 69.14 69.32 70.7
  EA 89.3 PO 101.12 102.29
  120.36 102.42 103.5 104.12
  105.15 105.18 108.8 109.37
  114.1 TF 126.20 DV 173.4
  179.5 FG 191.32 192.8 196.17
  SS 201.11 203.29 205.30
  211.10 SG 229.9 GF 240.15
  WS 264.5 PP 434.39 HD 453.2
  454.11 454.13 FA 458.11
  PR 504.2 SU 530.32 531.20
  WR 555.41 GG 666.23 OV 751.9
  751.18 LL 763.25 TH 844.33

THROATS SP 48.36 GG 675.2

THROATY MO 11.33 EE 325.42
  PR 474.12 BM 837.12 840.1

THROB WM 69.25 69.28 GG 683.30
  ML 731.23

THROBBED PO 112.15

THROBBING LA 637.38

THROBS WM 69.26

THROES BO 604.37

THRONG MO 3.14 DV 137.8
  SG 225.42 WS 252.1 FA 458.1
  WR 568.28 577.39 580.20
  OV 758.30

THROSTLE'S SS 204.25

THROW WM 62.10 62.12 FG 195.41
  196.3 WR 547.1 JD 605.8
  OV 759.16

THROW-BACK BL 356.3

THROWING MO 3.33 WS 244.9
  EE 312.27 MN 369.12 SD 425.30
  PR 507.27 TB 520.13 SU 532.37
  WR 570.20 BO 591.31 603.34
  JD 625.38

THROWN MO 7.32 SP 49.27
  PO 99.27 115.16 DV 145.35
  FG 188.24 SS 211.11 EE 333.14
  TP 339.21 BL 355.41 WP 393.12
  SD 421.22 HD 456.11 PR 501.35
  WR 547.21 OV 753.8 754.41
  MD 805.27 807.21

THRUST WM 59.11 60.27 PO 101.29
  110.12 TF 118.13 121.21
  DV 171.1 SS 198.11 GF 235.3
  WS 245.33 246.23 264.3
  BL 365.13 YT 396.16 GG 681.27
  OV 757.17 LL 777.41 RH 790.4

THRUSTING OA 31.17 31.37
  EA 76.41

THRUSTS FA 470.41 OV 752.27

THUD OA 30.17 35.23 HT 43.5
  WS 245.12 EE 330.4 TP 343.39
  ML 745.39

THUDDED OC 289.33 WR 578.35

THUDDING PO 110.1

THUDS GG 684.37 685.7 685.13

THUD-THUD-THUD SP 45.17

THUMB PO 98.35 98.40 99.5

THUMBS JD 609.17

THUMPED DV 139.2 OC 283.8

THUMPING WP 387.10

THUMPS LL 774.37

THUNDER OA 23.22 28.33 29.24
  29.34 PO 114.22 LA 638.21
  ML 744.29 744.37 745.41
  746.22 746.35 LL 774.36
  775.21 775.28

THUNDER-CLOUD BL 350.14

THUNDERING MO 20.23 TF 120.38

THUNDERSTRUCK LL 776.32

THURSDAY PR 488.40 NT 714.35

THUS MO 12.7 14.1 WM 61.10
  64.5 66.37 69.13 69.37
  DV 136.28 FG 194.31 OC 299.35
  TP 336.2 BL 350.8 355.27
  358.2 364.14 SD 423.31
  FA 459.33 460.19 468.11
  PR 504.19 504.29 WR 564.26
  ML 723.9 728.40 MD 820.27

THWAITE GG 661.3 661.4 661.16
  693.21

THWARTED PR 488.24 492.40

THY SP 46.30 46.39 EA 92.7
  92.8 FG 193.23 SC 269.38
  CH 280.34 282.1 WP 388.10
  FA 463.31

THYSELF HT 43.28

THYSEN HT 43.34 SP 46.12
  SC 267.28 WP 389.3

TIBLE WP 379.4 380.33 386.3
  387.16 387.25 392.33

TICK SD 421.39 BM 840.9

TICKED IL 659.26

TICKET-CARAVAN MN 371.12

TICKET-MACHINE TP 335.26

TICKETS TP 335.36 TH 850.15

TICKING OA 24.9 LL 765.3

TIDE MO 2.18 2.21 DV 174.23
  BL 355.33 NT 708.31
  ML 745.29 MD 806.20

TIDES MO 2.24 BO 589.12

TIDIED FA 470.42

TIDY DV 139.30 182.9
  OC 302.13 HD 456.28
  IL 648.25 648.26 ML 742.9
  LL 773.32 RR 785.29

TIDYING TP 345.25 346.7

TIE FA 464.31 465.29
  WR 563.4 ML 728.32

TIED HT 42.21 WS 265.35
  EE 317.12 323.14 YT 397.13
  397.31 399.7 SD 421.23
  421.42 HD 441.38 PR 483.30
  495.27 499.4 SU 538.4
  WR 551.11 567.5 GG 678.25
  ML 739.13 742.18 OV 747.31
  RR 782.13 MD 815.10

TIGER NT 703.7

TIGER'S SD 417.27 NT 703.6

TIGHT MO 4.18 WM 69.21
  PO 95.30 TF 120.6 123.27
  DV 168.38 174.16 174.36
  181.42 SB 213.13 SG 229.18
  GF 237.37 241.18 WS 247.26
  259.21 SC 267.4 CH 276.20
  TP 335.13 BL 360.36
  SD 414.42 PP 435.38
  HD 442.9 PR 490.20 503.12
  506.32 SU 534.23 WR 553.16
  JD 616.18 LL 765.22
  RR 789.10 RH 796.5
  MD 805.22 TH 845.3 846.20

TIGHTENED EA 93.14 TF 130.9
  130.16 SD 421.18

TIGHTENING EA 91.14 DV 173.20
  FG 189.39

TIGHTER OA 25.37

TIGHTNESS WS 253.18 257.26
  PR 490.1

TIGHT-PRESSED WS 263.21

TIGHT-SHUT DV 139.11

TILED OC 283.33

TILES OC 296.38 SU 531.28

TILT WM 65.41 JD 622.33
  RH 793.32

TILTED WM 61.23 PR 497.40
  SM 582.13 ML 736.24

TILTING OA 34.31 SB 218.23

TIRED (CONT.) DV 164.1 176.38
   FG 192.18 SB 212.1 212.5
   212.28 GF 240.19 242.28
   WS 255.35 255.38 261.1 265.12
   CH 274.36 WP 386.33 YT 408.7
   SD 414.9 PP 434.29 HD 444.23
   PR 478.39 485.24 494.41
   500.16 SU 530.32 WR 555.14
   560.22 560.38 560.39 564.39
   JD 605.6 627.41 IL 648.13
   NT 706.6 713.32 720.1 720.2
   ML 739.25 LL 761.22 MD 817.13
   820.5 821.23 822.5 822.8
   822.26

TIRESOME OC 294.32

TIRESOMELY IL 651.32

TISSUE EA 83.15

TIT TP 345.39

TITLES GG 662.15 662.21

TITS TB 522.17

TITTERING TP 342.21

TOAD MO 17.33 MD 819.38

TOAD'S MD 819.38 819.41

TOASTING PR 495.25 495.30

TOBACCO SG 226.41 227.18 228.8
   HD 441.4 443.26

TOBACCO-POUCH SG 227.27 228.6

TOBOGGAN PR 498.26

TODAY EA 75.34 TF 118.8
   YT 397.40 JD 625.31

TO-DAY OA 23.20 HT 41.39
   SP 46.8 WM 55.22 TF 124.37
   124.39 SB 214.21 SG 224.29
   233.2 WS 264.38 CH 279.32
   EE 304.8 MN 368.15 369.1
   WP 390.17 SU 540.33 BO 588.13
   JD 620.1 625.40 626.2 626.8
   NT 702.32 703.37 708.37
   711.20 LL 769.7 MD 814.38
   BM 827.9

TODDLE SU 534.37

TODDLED SU 531.29

TODDLER EE 316.20

TODDLING TP 341.30 SU 534.9
   534.21

TO-DO WP 389.8

TOE GF 234.15 WS 245.33 245.34

TOES SP 48.14 WS 247.15
   GG 695.42

TOGETHER MO 4.13 9.40 11.26
   17.29 19.33 21.15 21.37
   21.39 22.12 OA 29.35 34.17

TOGETHER (CONT.) SP 45.8
   WM 59.24 65.6 65.8
   68.11 EA 73.3 78.15 80.7
   80.39 PO 99.42 106.33 116.17
   TF 126.9 126.38 127.1 127.42
   132.12 132.22 DV 148.28
   173.24 181.21 182.21 182.28
   FG 192.7 195.6 SS 203.19
   209.26 GF 242.27 WS 244.14
   CH 274.36 281.31 OC 299.9
   300.33 EE 307.20 311.29
   BL 347.14 347.15 349.18
   364.26 WP 385.16 YT 400.35
   404.26 SD 423.13 PP 429.34
   430.6 HD 445.14 446.22 446.37
   FA 464.3 PR 498.27 509.37
   TB 513.10 514.5 514.9 514.17
   SU 540.4 WR 564.29 SM 585.16
   586.5 586.18 BO 589.17
   JD 621.25 624.10 LA 645.25
   IL 649.12 GG 662.5 662.12
   667.32 670.3 695.42 697.14
   NT 705.33 709.4 ML 734.41
   OV 747.11 750.37 752.9 759.26
   LL 762.20 765.12 778.8
   RH 795.13 MD 805.14 807.34
   810.26 824.21 BM 830.7 836.28
   TH 844.6

TOIL EE 311.5

TOILED ML 744.34

TOILET EA 83.27 GF 240.5 240.13

TOILS BO 599.10

TOKEN WR 578.7

TOLERABLE IL 651.28

TOLERANCE FG 187.22 BO 590.20

TOLERANT LL 762.4

TOLERATED MD 818.13

TOLERATING LL 762.5

TOLSTOI PR 477.10

TOM MO 12.5 14.27 14.30 14.40
   15.8 15.22 17.1 18.17 20.19
   SP 46.7 SB 217.20 217.35
   217.40 217.41 219.29
   BL 352.22 BM 841.12 841.16

TOMATOES FA 465.6

TOMB EE 322.31 322.33 SU 529.15
   JD 614.14 GG 675.9

TOMBSTONE BL 350.17 HD 448.23

TOM-FOOLERY WP 389.26

TOM LOMAS BM 839.26 839.28
   840.8 841.9

TOMMY-ROT WP 384.25

TOMORROW MO 20.40

TO-MORROW'S FG 191.8 TB 516.34

TO-MORROW OA 29.7 EA 78.41
   79.11 92.26 92.39
   PO 101.13 TF 124.38
   DV 172.14 177.25 182.33
   186.23 OC 290.14 EE 321.22
   TP 336.36 MN 376.13
   YT 397.22 405.20 FA 457.4
   463.1 PR 492.37 508.28
   WR 555.7 565.18 JD 614.36
   614.38 615.1 OV 760.4
   LL 767.38 BM 842.20

TOM'S MO 14.3 18.5 SB 218.21

TOM SMEDLEY SB 213.12 218.10

TOM SMEDLEY'S SB 219.24

TOM VICKERS MO 12.27 12.32
   18.40

TONE MO 12.38 13.12 13.33
   13.34 15.8 OA 25.25 28.41
   32.12 WM 67.20 EA 88.7
   PO 102.13 DV 139.21 144.11
   145.21 158.28 162.11
   177.36 182.33 SS 198.4
   201.23 203.9 204.41
   205.38 SB 219.42 GF 234.11
   242.8 243.21 WS 248.8
   256.23 CH 276.25 277.19
   OC 289.15 291.16 TP 344.8
   BL 363.26 MN 378.24
   YT 395.40 SD 420.3 420.19
   422.18 PP 428.24 439.33
   HD 446.9 TB 519.41 526.1
   SU 528.15 WR 560.11
   BO 601.28 JD 614.12 615.34
   LA 632.29 IL 654.15
   GG 695.9 OV 751.34
   RR 786.42 789.12

TONELESS EA 73.25

TONES MO 12.38 OA 24.20
   27.7 28.36 31.29 34.34
   WM 56.14 56.17 56.23
   60.42 SS 203.15 209.4
   GF 236.23 236.40 CH 276.7
   WR 555.33 556.25 557.2
   LA 633.22 GG 665.35

TONGUE OA 27.4 27.17 36.39
   WM 57.12 70.8 EA 75.21
   PO 102.35 DV 161.4
   SG 230.21 WS 262.5
   TP 336.38 BL 357.2
   WP 389.19 YT 399.15
   HD 441.4 SU 530.11 536.32
   MD 814.39

TONGUES SP 48.11

TO-NIGHT MO 22.11 26.4 32.3
   32.32 WM 54.5 57.36
   EA 92.40 TF 124.30
   DV 180.1 SS 202.22
   GF 236.41 TP 341.22 341.24
   341.25 342.3 BL 356.10
   MN 377.14 WP 381.37
   YT 402.3 SD 414.27 415.40
   417.2 419.27 420.1 420.35
   HD 446.14 FA 469.34 472.9
   472.10 WR 555.7 IL 650.28
   650.30 655.11 GG 695.5

TO-NIGHT (CONT.) GG 695.11
   696.35 697.16 NT 717.20
   OV 753.21 753.22 760.1
   RR 786.33 787.3 MD 815.35
   818.17 BM 842.27 842.35

TONSURE LA 631.10

TOOL SS 209.11

TOOLS SS 206.25

TOOT IL 653.1 656.23

TOOTED IL 655.23 656.28 658.3

TOOTH GF 243.11 TB 521.9
   LA 645.20

TOOTHACHE ML 738.36

TOP OA 34.5 SP 48.4 WM 63.15
   EA 72.19 TF 118.39 DV 156.21
   EE 319.33 330.6 BL 352.16
   SD 423.40 PP 436.25 FA 460.20
   PR 484.38 485.1 496.28 496.30
   497.18 497.20 498.33
   WR 561.35 GG 669.33 673.27
   694.9 ML 745.4 746.2 746.27
   OV 750.7 RR 779.20 779.22
   RH 801.40 BM 840.38

TOPAZ MD 823.24

TOPIC MO 12.42 RR 783.13

TOPMOST WR 568.23

TOPPING IL 648.38

TOPS PO 109.1 SU 539.4

TOQUE EA 78.30

TORCH EE 314.29 314.30 SU 529.5

TORCHES GF 234.1 235.16
   BO 594.14

TORE EA 74.28 DV 161.35
   WS 245.24 OC 284.33 289.28
   TP 344.38 NT 713.24 ML 743.16

TOREADOR NT 701.32 702.35

TORILL HALL SG 231.5

TORMENT PO 100.27 109.22
   TF 132.10 DV 180.21 SG 230.16
   230.17 EE 329.5 SU 531.37
   WR 558.14 567.2 570.9
   BM 837.14

TORMENTED PO 99.11 SS 201.8
   SG 229.13 WR 567.6 SM 582.24
   NT 714.37 RH 803.21

TORN OA 35.41 EA 80.41
   DV 163.15 FG 190.33 194.40
   SG 228.18 228.24 229.23
   WS 244.11 OC 301.8 EE 326.4
   326.8 TP 343.13 343.17 343.31
   345.10 345.23 WP 380.35

TORPID EE 323.20

TORPIDLY MO 14.23

TORRENTS GG 696.27

TORREON WR 549.39

TORSOS MO 5.2

TORTILLAS WR 556.34 556.42
   557.30 565.1

TORTOISE HT 42.30 44.11
   GG 664.5

TORTOISE-SHELL GG 664.6

TORTURE EA 90.32 TF 126.7
   131.37 DV 169.11 180.31
   180.34 FG 190.8 SG 228.36
   CH 275.20 EE 325.32 TP 346.4
   BL 347.37 PP 434.7 SU 529.24
   GG 693.42 ML 742.6

TORTURED MO 2.39 WM 60.13
   SG 230.31 EE 322.5 BL 356.2
   PP 429.40 NT 714.34 717.5
   ML 742.23 MD 814.36

TORTURES GG 679.31 NT 711.35

TORTURING DV 165.26

TOSS WS 245.18

TOSSED SP 49.16 PR 506.24
   LA 634.41 IL 651.7 ML 738.27
   RH 793.4 803.24

TOSSING OA 26.9 HT 42.25
   PR 502.14 RH 803.41 804.13

TOTAL OC 288.14

TOTALLY BL 347.9

TOTONAC WR 550.6

TOTTERED PR 498.21

TOTTERING PR 498.42 LL 776.14

TOTTERINGLY LL 775.25

TOUCH MO 12.8 17.4 OA 30.2
   38.36 WM 57.9 58.14 60.40
   64.35 67.8 EA 75.16 76.11
   86.19 92.34 TF 126.26
   DV 137.10 152.40 165.17
   FG 188.26 SB 217.41 WS 248.14
   253.28 SC 270.20 OC 299.36
   302.3 EE 303.9 305.34 311.4
   324.14 324.39 331.4 332.13
   TP 338.28 342.15 345.7
   BL 353.32 355.18 363.29 364.6
   364.7 WP 387.38 YT 396.22
   401.39 SD 416.8 PP 429.34
   440.7 HD 453.35 454.1
   FA 466.16 PR 476.12 476.37
   481.8 486.40 504.11 508.18
   509.29 TB 515.21 SU 535.32
   536.40 542.1 WR 555.29 570.33
   SM 584.6 JD 612.31 613.1
   624.1 LA 630.16 633.21 634.16
   644.10 GG 664.22 683.2 683.22
   683.26 684.19 689.41 698.30

TOUCH (CONT.) NT 704.3 709.42
   710.6 710.28 710.29 711.32
   716.26 ML 732.33 OV 748.18
   749.37 750.1 758.42 759.6
   759.8 LL 766.35 773.26
   RR 782.14 MD 808.11 809.26
   821.33 BM 828.13 841.34
   TH 848.25

TOUCHABLE GG 689.40

TOUCHED MO 17.33 WM 64.12
   EA 90.40 PO 97.15
   DV 146.42 FG 193.4 193.8
   SS 210.5 OC 296.2
   BL 355.13 355.26 358.41
   365.14 WP 379.17 386.31
   387.6 YT 399.10 402.15
   408.42 409.15 409.19
   SD 415.35 417.38 HD 448.17
   450.25 FA 471.26 PR 473.27
   474.7 SU 531.21 WR 564.9
   566.30 573.14 LA 633.32
   638.26 643.25 643.26
   GG 687.33 690.32 696.1
   NT 704.3 718.42 720.11
   ML 745.32 745.36 LL 773.32
   RR 789.13 RH 800.7 804.11
   MD 811.37 812.40 BM 827.33
   842.5

TOUCHES WS 246.5 TP 342.14
   342.17 BL 358.42 BO 590.14

TOUCHING SB 214.23 SG 225.30
   225.31 WS 254.6 257.20
   EE 310.8 BL 355.17 363.40
   WP 382.23 SD 426.11
   WR 564.12 SM 584.25
   NT 710.6 713.26 ML 728.20

TOUGH EE 305.29 313.23
   WR 547.13 547.14

TOUGH-CLAWED MD 807.9

TOURISTS PR 483.25

TOUSLED WS 244.7

TOWARD SU 531.12

TOWD FA 463.28

TOWEL DV 171.13 OC 299.25
   HD 451.18 JD 617.18 617.35
   617.37 617.38 NT 703.40

TOWELLED DV 159.14

TOWELS DV 159.4 JD 618.23

TOWER WM 54.15 EA 72.26
   73.5 EE 310.20 BL 354.19
   SD 416.1 HD 449.1 WR 569.36

TOWERED SD 417.19 PR 490.31

TOWERING SP 52.14 WR 569.31
   BM 828.5

TOWERS FA 458.7

TOWN HT 42.10 43.2 SP 47.9
   WM 63.26 EA 72.24 78.24

TOWN (CONT.) EA 78.41
  PO 113.29 TF 118.30 119.14
  121.36 121.42 122.33 132.20
  SS 211.33 GF 234.5 235.7
  235.20 237.36 WS 259.1 259.10
  263.17 EE 308.33 308.35
  321.15 321.22 321.42 TP 334.2
  334.10 334.23 MN 368.28
  370.26 371.8 371.39 WP 381.17
  YT 394.31 396.12 PP 430.38
  432.13 436.5 436.20 436.29
  HD 447.23 447.34 448.42 449.3
  449.8 FA 460.20 TB 516.10
  WR 546.30 549.15 BO 594.39
  598.21 599.1 601.26 602.38
  JD 610.21 GG 663.17 667.32
  LL 762.21 762.29 766.2
  RH 790.25 799.14 799.34
  802.17 BM 827.35 828.2 830.33
  834.38

TOWN-BRED EE 307.33

TOWNLET SP 47.39

TOWNSEND, BEN (SEE BEN TOWNSEND)

TOWNSFOLK BO 602.37

TOWNSHIP WP 387.25

TOWNSPEOPLE PP 428.30

TOY WR 562.10 BO 601.35

TOYING MO 5.31

TOYS EE 319.29 WR 570.36
  RH 791.8

TRACE OA 23.26 36.5 WM 58.13
  TF 118.3 OC 290.34 EE 310.23
  WR 551.28 SM 582.24

TRACED MO 6.26

TRACERY FG 187.11

TRACES OC 300.1 BM 827.7

TRACING OC 289.32 BL 363.40
  ML 728.5

TRACK MO 1.6 17.30 WM 60.35
  SS 197.23 SG 224.9 OC 283.13
  283.31 290.37 EE 304.42
  SU 538.9 538.37 539.17
  WR 558.32 561.25 IL 654.4
  ML 733.14 736.30 743.14

TRACKS EE 330.25 PR 486.25
  486.26 486.31 495.15

TRACT TF 117.11 FG 187.4

TRACTION-ENGINE SC 270.32 270.34

TRADE HT 42.10 TF 128.5
  GF 235.2 235.3 235.5 235.8
  235.13 MD 818.26

TRADESMEN SP 53.10 DV 138.31
  WS 250.8

TRADESMEN'S DV 137.27

TRADESPEOPLE DV 137.20 RR 789.21

TRADITION TH 844.14

TRADITIONAL OA 23.20

TRAFFIC MO 1.3 EA 72.24
  PP 429.13 436.11 NT 708.32
  ML 724.9 OV 758.32

TRAGEDIENNE EA 93.36

TRAGEDY EA 86.21 GF 241.12
  241.27 SU 533.21 JD 606.6
  OV 756.2 757.36

TRAGIC OA 37.14 GF 239.28
  WS 247.38 250.4 EE 317.37
  317.39 JD 608.31 MD 812.25

TRAGI-COMEDY NT 707.2

TRAIL TP 334.32 PR 489.10
  489.40 490.13 490.19 492.15
  493.18 495.7 496.12 497.17
  497.19 497.33 498.1 498.4
  498.13 499.39 510.11
  WR 551.16 551.28 551.29
  551.38 553.5 553.17 553.19
  554.15 555.10 555.36 566.32
  578.26 TH 845.9

TRAILED WR 551.39 579.5
  SM 586.24

TRAILING GF 234.4 OC 283.29
  HD 456.2 PR 492.21

TRAILS PR 478.39 WR 552.12

TRAIN WM 61.19 EA 78.21 83.9
  DV 139.2 157.5 157.7 158.16
  159.16 161.25 OC 285.1 286.5
  EE 321.42 MN 371.7 FA 458.34
  459.3 SM 582.7 582.14
  BO 593.36 594.4 594.9 594.30
  598.33 598.34 599.1 599.17
  599.24 599.27 600.7 600.33
  600.35 600.37 JD 609.32 625.7
  627.32 NT 717.20 717.25
  ML 745.6

TRAINED BO 589.22

TRAINING DV 165.26 HD 443.3

TRAINS OA 25.6 25.9 26.5
  SP 48.42 WM 61.26 TF 133.3
  DV 139.10 SC 271.31 PP 432.23

TRAIT BO 587.33

TRAITOR WS 249.23

TRAM WM 60.6 TF 122.33
  WS 249.19 TP 334.33 335.11
  335.23 341.16

TRAM-CAR WM 54.8 54.27
  TP 335.38 336.7 336.29 337.30

TRAMCARS PP 436.10

TRAM-CARS WM 60.35 TF 119.14
  TP 334.12

TRAM-GIRLS TP 338.40

TRAMMELLED MO 3.33 GF 240.8

TRAMONTANA SU 535.14

TRAMP PO 96.7 TF 133.20

TRAMPED PO 109.5 TF 119.30
  134.7 DV 166.27 SD 411.14
  GG 670.37

TRAMPING MO 6.4 PO 106.21
  TF 133.14 HD 441.20

TRAMPLE DV 154.29

TRAMPLED SP 49.10 PO 108.42
  DV 154.23 167.15 EE 329.40

TRAMPLING TB 526.40

TRAMS TF 121.36 TP 334.34
  335.9 335.14

TRAM-SERVICE TP 335.16 336.10

TRAM-TERMINUS WM 59.30

TRAMWAY TP 334.1 340.15

TRANCE OA 36.16 TF 122.13
  TP 344.2 YT 402.6 WR 554.23
  568.14 570.1 577.14
  JD 613.26 613.27 NT 706.2
  ML 736.15

TRANCED YT 401.17

TRANQUIL TF 132.22

TRANSACT MD 824.17

TRANSCENDENT HD 453.21
  BM 842.3

TRANSCRIBE TB 514.41

TRANSFER OA 30.28 EE 308.33

TRANSFERENCE LL 768.7 768.11

TRANSFERRED PR 480.10
  ML 732.42 MD 814.8
  BM 842.37

TRANSFIGURATION HD 453.3
  OV 752.40

TRANSFIGURED TF 127.29 130.25
  SG 225.15 GF 240.9
  OC 287.27 BL 351.27
  WR 556.10 BM 841.29

TRANSFIGURING PR 485.20

TRANSFIXED WS 264.4 FA 467.5
  PR 505.18 511.9 WR 578.38
  GG 684.36

TRANSFIXEDLY WR 580.36

TRANSFUSED DV 181.31

TRANSGRESSION WS 253.37

TRESPASSING IL 651.21

TRESSES SB 217.5

TREVORROW (SEE MR. TREVORROW)

TRIAL DV 176.27 LL 763.12

TRIALS LL 763.9 RR 780.30

TRIANGULAR OA 35.15

TRIBAL MD 820.12 820.40

TRIBE WR 550.3 550.4 MD 819.1
   819.9 820.10

TRIBES WR 549.42

TRICK EA 90.7 SD 418.31 418.32
   LL 768.7 768.14

TRICKED OA 24.28

TRICKLE PO 110.27 PR 491.8

TRICKLED SS 210.5

TRICKLING PR 494.4 ML 741.12
   OV 750.2

TRICKS EA 93.37 EE 314.37
   TP 344.35 WR 549.23

TRIED MO 5.23 20.28 OA 29.36
   EA 80.25 80.35 83.10 PO 98.28
   99.30 100.12 114.15 TF 119.19
   120.5 DV 137.28 153.8 179.27
   SS 203.4 SG 221.10 229.24
   229.39 WS 261.18 264.5
   BL 348.3 348.15 WP 386.42
   YT 402.32 408.28 SD 423.16
   PP 431.5 439.23 HD 455.41
   456.3 PR 504.1 508.34 509.3
   SM 584.12 BO 593.37 598.5
   598.39 LA 645.34 IL 659.32
   GG 675.3 NT 709.9 710.28
   714.3 714.5 716.26 716.27
   718.4 ML 739.13 LL 772.27
   777.15 RH 789.14 790.31
   MD 813.5 817.32 BM 831.23
   TH 850.30

TRIES SG 230.35 MD 819.29

TRIFLE DV 145.34 SB 217.28
   EE 319.32 JD 622.11 GG 679.8
   LL 763.19 768.35

TRIFLES PO 96.38

TRIFLING WM 61.14 SB 216.34

TRILL MN 373.23

TRILLED RH 800.16

TRILLING LA 639.42 640.2
   ML 734.7

TRIMMING MO 18.9 ML 741.32

TRIMMINGS BO 588.32

TRINITY EE 309.35 GG 690.30

TRINITY CHURCH PP 428.4

TRINKETS WS 265.28

TRIP PR 488.3 488.4 488.13
   488.29 IL 653.28 653.36
   ML 738.23

TRIPPED WS 251.16 BM 835.23

TRITE WP 380.36 380.41
   OV 756.36

TRIUMPH OA 24.41 SP 48.37
   EA 73.35 73.40 73.42 74.1
   90.25 SS 202.32 208.22
   WS 245.39 257.41 EE 326.16
   TP 343.34 HD 453.22 FA 466.10
   466.11 466.23 WR 560.25 565.8
   573.4 577.22 581.19 BO 602.7
   JD 625.5 LA 633.18 635.1
   637.39 GG 670.1 ML 736.18
   739.15

TRIUMPHANT EA 90.23 DV 152.31
   SB 219.18 EE 325.28 HD 453.3
   453.5 FA 467.2 LA 635.21
   638.33 ML 723.15 738.33
   TH 846.13

TRIUMPHANTLY BO 603.35 LA 635.3
   640.11

TRIUMPHED SS 208.15 EE 308.6
   YT 409.36 SD 422.1 BO 591.26
   MD 822.37

TRIVET RH 802.27

TRIVIAL WS 250.30 WP 380.40
   BM 831.15

T'ROAD SP 47.5

TROD TP 335.33 HD 446.1
   WR 572.19

TRODDEN SP 49.3 SB 216.39
   WR 562.3

TROLLEY WS 262.20 BO 601.25

TROLLOPS SP 53.20 WS 262.11

TROOP SP 49.1

TROOPING OC 286.33

TROPICAL WR 546.20

TROPICS GG 669.18

TROT PR 489.26 WR 558.31

TROTTED PR 489.10 489.34
   WR 551.26 556.8

TROTTER WM 68.18

TROTTING PO 107.15 HD 442.4
   WR 555.41

TROUBLE HT 40.37 WM 62.3 62.5
   62.6 EA 77.6 88.8 88.37
   91.19 PO 104.18 DV 141.5

TROUBLE (CONT.) DV 141.6
   147.14 147.34 151.12
   172.16 185.9 SS 201.37
   211.19 SB 217.26 WS 244.10
   255.17 260.1 260.30
   CH 281.16 OC 294.42 295.2
   295.3 295.18 295.19
   297.30 EE 320.25 325.3
   BL 355.29 361.28 361.31
   361.32 MN 368.17 368.18
   WP 389.27 SD 417.35 422.10
   PP 438.4 SU 535.35 WR 549.9
   BO 596.37 JD 606.1
   GG 688.18 694.40 694.42
   695.2 NT 707.20 708.3
   ML 744.35 OV 751.38
   LL 762.7 RH 802.29

TROUBLED WM 56.16 EA 82.39
   87.38 TF 129.6 DV 148.20
   171.14 177.39 SS 198.17
   203.35 211.25 SB 215.22
   219.18 219.41 WS 260.3
   BL 355.16 363.1 SD 419.23
   JD 611.12 613.30 LL 778.16
   RH 790.9 BM 841.32 842.40

TROUBLES MO 14.33 OA 26.38
   OC 293.42 PR 475.28

TROUBLESOME OA 23.30

TROUBLING PP 432.33 WR 547.1
   MD 816.13

TROUSERS OA 24.32 SP 49.37
   PO 108.17 TF 126.22 129.27
   134.12 DV 138.17 138.28
   168.15 174.42 SB 217.28
   WS 244.25 250.32 251.17
   258.1 SC 267.33 OC 284.30
   291.38 WP 388.5 YT 398.4
   400.31 408.15 SD 418.11
   PR 484.6 484.40 SU 543.5
   JD 617.21 618.18 618.22
   618.26 RR 779.25 BM 835.25
   836.26 836.33

TROUT PR 483.29 484.10
   484.20

TRUANT YT 396.16

TRUCE HT 39.2

TRUCK MN 367.28 367.30 368.1
   370.6 378.3 378.9

TRUCKS OC 283.8 283.27 286.7
   290.34 MN 366.2 366.28
   NT 708.30 708.33

TRUDGE BO 603.5

TRUDGED FA 460.4

TRUDGING FA 459.35

TRUE MO 8.35 14.23 SP 47.37
   EA 82.37 TF 134.30 DV 144.3
   160.18 182.27 SS 207.13
   210.19 SB 219.9 GF 236.17
   WS 251.4 CH 280.31
   OC 285.38 EE 305.40 313.11
   315.15 327.5 BL 347.20

TRUE (CONT.) SD 426.10 HD 454.37
  454.39 PR 485.32 505.26
  SU 534.39 535.24 BO 604.9
  JD 615.18 LA 645.27 645.29
  GG 661.17 662.27 NT 708.26
  ML 726.8 730.9 737.14 737.42
  738.3 738.5 743.9 OV 757.20
  LL 767.14 767.15 773.15
  777.18 777.19 778.4 RR 781.31
  782.3 786.10 MD 808.3 813.21
  814.17 819.37 824.10 824.12
  BM 829.19 TH 844.1 844.9
  844.17 845.25 845.40 852.6

TRULY WM 63.10 EE 310.10 326.27
  WR 550.23 BO 602.12 LA 634.1
  NT 708.27 ML 740.29

TRUMP FA 467.4

TRUMPETING MD 810.39

TRUNCHEON SS 210.16

TRUNDLE OC 285.1

TRUNK OA 34.10 34.26 PO 113.1
  113.3 113.6 114.3 114.6
  FG 190.38 FA 458.36 459.21
  462.4 SU 530.7 BO 603.13

TRUNKS MO 1.20 PO 108.40 110.42
  111.41 114.25 SS 206.17
  PR 489.42 490.5 WR 552.39
  556.5 579.8 MD 826.1 826.2

TRUST EA 76.15 FG 191.19
  GF 238.42 MN 375.25 SD 422.12
  OV 751.41 752.39

TRUSTED DV 174.9 OV 754.1

TRUSTEES PR 478.14

TRUSTFUL TF 131.24 WP 380.22

TRUSTWORTHY PR 488.42

TRUTH MO 14.12 TF 131.38
  SS 210.21 WS 247.2 OC 301.15
  YT 396.40 SD 426.7 BO 591.32
  592.17 TH 847.27

TRUTHFULLY MO 15.15 HD 452.2

TRUTHFULNESS SD 425.16

TRUTHS BO 602.22

TRY MO 16.6 OA 31.5 31.7 36.40
  EA 71.11 76.29 TF 124.27
  124.30 124.36 DV 179.21
  185.20 SB 218.25 SC 269.2
  269.36 EE 302.2 308.29 315.20
  315.21 315.24 320.24
  TP 335.26 BL 355.36 PP 434.26
  PR 476.1 476.10 508.37
  TB 523.15 BO 598.1 JD 608.2
  IL 646.7 647.4 649.39
  GG 662.40 684.15 687.40
  NT 711.28 714.27 714.33
  LL 761.31 772.20 772.22
  772.23 MD 808.39 812.16
  BM 840.12

TRYING MO 7.21 15.19 EA 73.26
  73.31 77.8 81.29 PO 111.24
  112.6 TF 117.21 119.21 121.9
  DV 147.22 158.3 169.21 169.24
  SS 199.27 SB 216.6 SG 221.2
  GF 242.14 WS 252.40 CH 274.36
  274.37 OC 289.3 299.22
  EE 319.39 TP 336.19 BL 364.28
  YT 397.3 PP 433.40 439.18
  HD 450.22 457.1 PR 497.11
  TB 526.3 WR 572.37 BO 598.4
  JD 620.25 IL 650.22 651.39
  GG 675.34 680.21 NT 708.21
  710.41 712.30 714.1 714.28
  718.6 LL 775.28 RR 785.6
  RH 792.24 803.28 MD 814.38

TUB EA 84.7

TUBE LL 774.32 774.40 MD 815.2

TUBES LA 632.20 637.6

TUBS PO 105.28

TUCKED GG 669.5 669.13

TUCKING OA 25.33

TUESDAYS SG 224.34

TUFT PR 489.40 WR 553.38
  LA 631.32

TUFTED DV 158.40 EE 323.35
  PR 501.21 LA 634.26

TUFTS DV 167.3 SS 197.22 200.37
  EE 303.33 323.36 PR 489.6
  489.21 489.35 WR 568.42
  569.10 ML 734.15

TUG SU 528.20

TUGGED DV 159.9

TUGGING OA 24.32

TUG-OF-WAR GG 686.41 687.1

TUILERIES TH 844.30

TULIPS YT 398.7 TB 520.31
  MD 811.5

TUMBLED FG 191.22 SS 197.27
  LL 770.21 RR 788.12

TUMBLING DV 145.27 SB 216.38
  SG 225.25 225.38 EE 318.38
  HD 456.8 SU 534.21

TU ME CONTENTERAS MD 822.32

TUMOUR DV 163.15 SM 582.9

TUNDISH DV 139.17 139.18

TUNE SP 47.35 WS 262.9
  TP 341.21 JD 609.20 IL 647.15
  GG 685.13

TUNED FA 467.39

TUNIC TF 118.6 126.16 127.29

TUNIC (CONT.) TP 343.13
  343.17 345.24 MN 369.28
  WR 564.22 569.9 577.31
  580.17 BO 603.33

TUNIC-RAGS TP 345.33

TUNICS TF 127.28 WR 569.29
  570.24

TUNIS RR 789.17

TUNNEL-LIKE SC 267.19

TURBAN LA 630.8

TURBULENT DV 140.18

TURF SS 210.9 SB 212.2 213.1
  EE 303.4 ML 723.5 738.27
  740.11 740.16 741.41 742.1
  RH 794.12

TURF COMMISSION RH 797.25

TURF-PLANTS ML 740.16

TURGID JD 610.2

TURK BM 840.12

TURKEYS WR 570.19 GG 663.12
  ML 728.42

TURKISH MD 819.22 820.32
  BM 835.25 836.26 836.33
  838.39 840.24

TURKISH-CARPET MD 819.16

TURKISH DELIGHT MD 818.16
  818.18 818.33 820.21
  822.39 822.42

TURKS MD 819.13

TURMOIL HD 446.30

TURN-DOWN SD 417.40

TURNING-POINT JD 605.30

TURNIP TH 845.13

TURNIP-PULPER BL 362.16

TURNIPS MO 1.24 1.27 1.30
  ML 726.42

TURNS MO 16.27 WM 65.8
  OV 753.24

TURQUOISE PR 490.25 WR 578.6
  BM 833.13 837.2

TURQUOISE-BLUE BM 833.12

TURRET TP 334.14

TURRETS DV 136.13

TUTOR RH 800.10 800.21

TUT-TUTTING CH 276.33

TUT-TUT-TUT EE 318.40

T'VALLEY WP 388.9

TWANG HT 41.12 SS 198.4
  SD 412.25 PP 429.40 438.26
  439.1 BM 837.12

TWEED TP 337.24 HD 444.20

TWEEDS BM 831.9

TWELVE HT 39.13 SP 46.29
  DV 145.10 SS 203.5 OC 292.6
  TB 518.1 519.27 IL 648.41
  LL 768.18 MD 806.4 TH 849.26
  849.27

TWELVE HUNDRED RH 797.8

TWELVE-MILE TP 336.22

TWELVE-MONTH OC 300.11

TWENTY MO 3.37 SP 48.21
  EA 83.10 PO 106.41 DV 136.30
  138.36 143.30 143.31 164.25
  SC 267.3 OC 289.15 291.2
  EE 305.12 BL 352.28 PP 429.16
  FA 462.23 PR 496.10 497.15
  WR 546.3 547.42 GG 678.15
  678.21 ML 723.2 733.15
  RH 795.16 795.19 795.37
  796.15 796.16 797.15 797.24
  MD 806.36 BM 827.2 827.13

TWENTY-EIGHT WM 58.13 WS 244.29
  CH 276.24 PR 482.5 TB 518.24
  GG 678.21 679.17

TWENTY-FIVE SC 270.36 PR 479.3
  482.1 IL 647.19 LL 762.21
  TH 844.9 847.15

TWENTY-FOUR SC 272.10 MD 806.2
  BM 828.25

TWENTY-NINE SS 202.12 SG 231.21

TWENTY-ONE MO 3.37 8.12
  EE 305.12 YT 397.1 PP 431.39
  IL 647.15 GG 663.16

TWENTY-SEVEN OA 30.26 DV 136.22
  144.38 HD 441.16 TH 844.9
  847.16

TWENTY-SIX MO 10.19 DV 138.33
  SG 231.20 MD 813.21

TWENTY THOUSANDS POUNDS YT 408.22

TWENTY-THREE DV 144.25 SB 212.9
  212.33 OC 285.39 MN 366.19
  PR 479.17

TWENTY-TWO SP 47.14 PO 96.42
  DV 145.35 HD 443.5 PR 473.26
  LL 768.19 BM 828.1

TWICE WM 59.8 SB 215.21
  WS 248.27 260.5 OC 289.21
  EE 329.36 SD 416.35 417.42
  PR 476.34 TB 526.6 GG 671.12
  NT 718.20 ML 740.5

TWICE-DAILY RR 782.23

TWIG WM 63.21 OC 284.37
  EE 331.15 BM 840.41

TWIGGY SS 197.20 OC 283.35
  PP 436.6

TWIG-PURPLE SS 200.2

TWIGS DV 139.6 160.31 SS 202.10
  PR 478.42 500.17 WR 556.40
  OV 748.42 750.30

TWILIGHT MO 2.8 2.42 OA 23.25
  28.1 EA 77.27 89.23 TF 129.31
  DV 167.22 GF 235.15 CH 275.24
  FA 458.19 458.25 PR 500.5
  SU 533.38 JD 609.1 609.8
  ML 742.29 742.34 MD 808.37

TWILIT ML 743.4

TWIN FA 459.1 WR 575.34

TWINED OA 26.26

TWINING MO 3.30 WM 64.31

TWINK SM 585.29

TWINKLE SU 539.17

TWINKLED MO 9.4 22.20 EA 84.7
  DV 167.22 WP 388.20 389.9
  SD 411.12 418.26 SM 585.22
  GG 672.36

TWINKLING PO 113.10 SS 197.30
  SB 214.13 216.32 YT 409.33
  410.2 PR 499.3 GG 689.16
  BM 828.11 833.28 834.11

TWINS MO 3.6 SP 46.30 46.32
  GG 666.32 667.1 667.12

TWIN-SOUL MO 18.27

TWIST OA 35.12 EA 76.2
  PO 108.25 FG 187.18 187.20
  GF 242.20 WS 257.39 CH 276.40
  PR 499.38 TB 514.31 IL 649.42
  MD 822.29 826.13 BM 833.6

TWISTED WM 60.22 EA 90.16
  PO 105.20 FG 187.16 SS 210.39
  SB 216.2 SG 221.13 GF 241.30
  WS 261.23 CH 281.1 WP 382.26
  SD 421.28 HD 441.32 TB 522.14
  WR 546.3 547.13 581.8
  LL 768.42 MD 807.37 808.17
  BM 832.26

TWISTING PO 115.35 FG 190.9
  SB 214.34 215.10 GF 238.20
  WP 390.15 PR 497.22 TB 526.22
  SM 583.30 JD 613.32 GG 678.20

TWITCH SG 229.3 OC 295.32

TWITCHED PO 99.23 100.35 110.30

TWITCHES DV 179.39

TWITCHING TF 130.19 SB 214.35

TWITCHING (CONT.) MD 818.3
  TH 853.6

TWITCHINGS PO 110.19
  DV 180.25

TWITTERING WR 572.22
  BO 588.21

TWO MO 1.28 2.22 3.13 3.36
  7.2 7.17 13.1 13.24
  OA 24.36 25.9 29.4 29.20
  29.34 31.23 31.30 32.30
  33.2 34.16 35.2 35.29
  36.8 36.12 38.36 HT 39.12
  39.30 42.27 44.1 SP 45.11
  46.30 46.32 47.37 48.42
  49.3 49.9 50.10 50.17
  50.33 51.15 WM 55.28
  58.40 60.4 60.13 60.27
  61.6 61.21 EA 71.6 71.7
  78.35 79.39 93.16 PO 97.36
  99.29 99.42 100.9 102.32
  104.37 105.23 108.3 108.37
  109.30 109.41 116.17
  TF 123.20 123.36 125.7
  125.22 126.37 130.31 131.8
  133.27 134.2 134.26 134.42
  DV 136.3 136.13 148.2
  149.12 154.32 156.10 158.1
  160.8 164.39 167.34 171.1
  172.11 173.10 173.36
  174.35 175.16 178.5
  FG 189.40 194.24 SS 197.10
  197.22 199.32 200.25
  207.41 208.39 209.9 209.22
  209.33 209.40 SB 212.20
  214.10 SG 221.30 222.41
  223.35 224.41 225.21
  228.18 231.37 232.14
  GF 239.22 243.16 WS 244.19
  247.18 248.19 251.11
  253.33 254.4 257.9 264.17
  SC 269.34 CH 274.3 274.30
  277.3 280.5 281.18
  OC 283.22 285.31 290.6
  292.8 294.40 296.20 297.3
  297.5 297.16 300.34
  EE 306.18 306.29 307.41
  310.14 316.20 317.20
  318.11 319.27 319.32
  325.20 325.21 327.9 329.36
  329.37 330.12 TP 334.20
  336.20 338.14 340.5
  BL 347.1 349.17 349.33
  351.14 358.22 358.34
  360.39 364.36 MN 366.2
  366.37 367.22 367.33
  368.13 368.28 368.32
  368.38 369.10 371.7 371.15
  371.36 373.1 373.15 378.3
  WP 389.16 YT 394.21 395.10
  396.19 400.6 400.34 404.11
  404.24 406.36 407.19
  SD 413.9 415.5 PP 427.25
  428.3 429.32 432.11 432.17
  432.24 432.37 436.14
  437.42 HD 445.23 446.21
  446.25 FA 458.23 459.28
  459.33 460.10 463.10 466.3
  467.22 469.38 470.17
  471.28 PR 474.21 479.13
  480.35 482.5 484.19 485.16
  485.41 486.1 486.3 487.8
  488.38 492.27 492.30

UNCANNILY LA 641.3 ML 724.38
  LL 772.21

UNCANNY WM 68.33 SG 228.21
  GF 240.7 BL 359.42 PR 477.14
  WR 577.23 BO 589.39 595.23
  JD 610.13 616.36 LA 638.35
  GG 669.10 681.16 683.27 685.3
  686.4 693.2 ML 724.39 731.26
  738.33 745.30 LL 767.31
  770.29 RH 798.27 800.39
  802.11 MD 813.11

UNCERTAIN PO 102.4 DV 136.16
  SG 227.21 227.33 OC 286.28
  EE 330.12 TP 339.23 PP 438.9
  HD 450.19 SU 536.36 BO 591.42
  LA 640.41 GG 699.6

UNCERTAINLY TF 125.13 128.13
  DV 180.38 SS 198.15

UNCERTAINTY WM 56.11 SB 217.42
  BL 350.37

UNCHALLENGED SD 424.11

UNCHANGED YT 409.40 HD 445.7
  PR 479.33

UNCHANGING EE 331.26 BL 355.21
  355.23 WR 577.17 SM 584.21
  JD 622.19 GG 681.28

UNCLE SS 199.2 YT 396.8 399.16
  403.28 403.35 406.17
  PP 427.15 428.38 429.6 429.11
  430.25 430.35 430.40 431.28
  431.31 432.9 432.11 432.19
  432.26 435.36 436.16 436.23
  436.36 438.10 NT 720.1
  RH 793.28 794.2 794.8 794.24
  794.27 794.35 794.41 795.6
  795.12 795.13 795.18 795.23
  795.31 795.32 795.40 796.11
  796.17 796.20 796.23 796.25
  797.8 797.11 797.17 797.26
  797.29 797.37 797.39 798.8
  798.11 798.19 798.21 798.22
  798.26 798.29 798.36 798.39
  799.39 800.30

UNCLEAN EE 329.1 OV 754.36

UNCLEANNESS ML 742.21

UNCLE OSCAR RH 791.41 793.14
  793.24 793.41 795.22 795.34
  796.28 796.41 799.5 799.35
  800.2 800.6 800.29 801.2
  801.7 801.19

UNCLE OSCAR'S RH 794.32

UNCLE RONALD LL 774.25

UNCLES PR 473.2 GG 661.24

UNCLE'S SS 199.4 YT 406.23
  PP 428.31 RH 791.30

UNCLOTHED SU 532.38 533.22
  LL 767.32

UNCOILED WP 390.19

UNCOMELY CH 274.14

UNCOMFORTABLE GF 236.31
  EE 304.10 MN 373.3 377.18
  YT 402.11 PP 430.36 HD 445.35
  IL 652.32

UNCOMFORTABLY DV 140.14
  SS 199.15 CH 278.36 MN 377.24
  WP 391.32 BO 594.11 RR 786.23

UNCOMMUNICATIVE GG 674.34

UNCOMPLAINING PO 105.22

UNCOMPROMISING BM 834.34

UNCONCERN CH 275.22

UNCONQUERABLE TF 130.20

UNCONSCIOUS MO 7.12 18.41
  PO 97.8 102.17 112.38 114.12
  TF 128.1 129.39 DV 137.15
  170.23 172.8 SB 214.28
  SG 226.24 WS 263.18 263.20
  265.2 CH 277.41 BL 364.15
  HD 450.39 451.15 PR 493.16
  508.19 WR 556.22 BO 597.1
  JD 613.27 GG 679.23 687.31
  ML 742.32 RH 803.23 BM 837.7
  841.1

UNCONSCIOUSLY MO 15.26 OA 23.15
  29.39 WS 250.9 EE 310.1
  330.18 TP 345.26 BL 355.24
  362.23 NT 713.19 BM 837.22

UNCONSCIOUSNESS WS 254.41
  PR 488.1 JD 627.19

UNCONSIDERED JD 613.37

UNCONTROLLABLE DV 176.14
  WS 262.33

UNCONTROLLABLY SC 272.39

UNCONTROLLED TF 129.5

UNCONVENTIONAL OV 748.5

UNCONVENTIONALITY OV 752.25

UNCORSETTED WM 65.24

UNCOUTH DV 169.25 MN 370.40
  372.40 OV 752.28

UNCOUTHLY SD 413.14

UNCOVERED TF 132.7 CH 278.3
  HD 455.16 WR 564.2

UNCOVERING HD 441.34 LA 632.24

UNCREATED EE 330.36

UNCRYING ML 735.20

UNCURTAINED MO 3.12 SG 224.21
  BL 351.10 GG 684.39

UNDAUNTED PR 478.38

UNDECIDED GF 237.8 JD 612.15
  RH 801.20

UNDECIDEDLY PP 427.1

UNDERFOOT OV 755.14

UNDERGARMENTS OC 291.38

UNDERGROUND DV 166.18 166.28
  166.32 167.5 SS 210.12
  YT 407.38 JD 608.22 617.7
  624.26 OV 753.18

UNDERGROWTH SS 205.4 206.15

UNDERLIES SU 533.21

UNDERLIP PO 110.4

UNDERLYING DV 167.8

UNDERMINED EA 93.29 ML 742.34

UNDERMINING EA 93.37

UNDERNEATH EA 82.29 82.31
  83.13 93.29 DV 150.6
  SD 419.24 HD 450.19 450.24
  PR 497.27 502.34 WR 557.11
  566.23 BO 594.42 GG 673.28
  678.1 ML 733.36 BM 836.20

UNDER-OFFICER DV 165.3

UNDERPAYING BO 587.7

UNDERSERVED LL 762.36 762.37

UNDERSTAND MO 10.4 10.15
  11.21 17.11 20.4 21.5
  OA 27.36 29.6 WM 62.30
  66.14 EA 80.24 80.26
  80.27 80.31 86.4 87.17
  89.38 90.8 90.24 PO 104.26
  TF 120.13 128.31 132.25
  DV 169.21 185.17 SS 205.33
  211.15 SG 223.14 225.36
  WS 258.33 261.5 OC 295.15
  EE 306.31 313.16 BL 356.35
  PP 435.6 FA 468.40 469.10
  469.12 PR 477.11 477.15
  478.3 496.2 WR 575.41
  576.28 577.5 BO 598.2
  JD 607.5 628.30 GG 664.24
  674.21 678.29 689.17
  689.22 692.15 695.25
  697.11 700.3 700.8
  NT 702.17 704.6 715.22
  716.16 719.19 LL 773.42
  776.26 778.19 RR 782.33
  MD 821.4 824.22 BM 840.22
  TH 847.25

UNDERSTANDING MO 15.21 17.6
  20.15 TF 119.8 DV 148.5
  153.37 177.1 178.32
  SS 205.34 CH 281.16
  EE 324.37 326.37 327.3
  BL 349.20 360.2 YT 404.12
  PP 429.1 PR 477.12
  WR 576.15 JD 607.4
  GG 662.29 692.23 692.41
  OV 759.42

UNDERSTANDINGS PP 430.22

UNDERSTANDS WM 62.28 62.29
   DV 148.9

UNDERSTOOD MO 5.30 10.35 14.16
   14.17 OA 24.1 EA 85.31 91.19
   92.2 DV 154.4 SG 231.41
   CH 281.17 BL 349.1 360.1
   YT 396.8 399.29 405.22
   FA 463.11 PR 477.12 WR 581.7
   BO 587.29 JD 613.26 NT 702.23
   RR 780.11 786.29 MD 820.19

UNDERTONE SB 218.1 BO 599.33
   600.12 ML 734.7

UNDERVEST JD 618.15

UNDERWEAR PR 506.19

UNDERWINGS OV 759.42

UNDERWOOD SP 50.32 OC 283.6

UNDERWORLD DV 139.11 SU 534.2
   JD 610.5 GG 668.37 MD 820.34

UNDESIROUS NT 717.42

UNDIGNIFIED MD 815.9

UNDISCOVERED PO 97.36 WR 548.12

UNDISTURBED TF 118.35

UNDO CH 281.8 SD 422.14 422.18
   422.41

UNDONE DV 146.21

UNDOUBTED DV 155.16

UNDREAMING NT 715.12

UNDRESS OA 26.1 26.16 SC 270.2
   MN 369.16

UNDRESSED OA 26.7 DV 162.25
   174.34 174.39 MN 368.38
   HD 452.32 BO 597.34

UNDRESSING DV 174.38 MN 375.5

UNDULATING PO 113.37

UNDULATION PO 113.38

UNDYING ML 724.37

UNEARTHLY WR 556.7 564.34

UNEASILY HT 41.28 PO 112.7
   DV 178.37 SG 222.14 WS 247.39
   CH 277.13 TP 342.7 342.22
   345.3 345.25 WP 392.10 392.18
   SD 414.17 PP 432.24 433.24
   HD 442.18 442.30 443.11
   TB 525.13 JD 623.27 626.15
   GG 677.36 OV 753.2 753.7
   RH 793.3 795.13 797.36

UNEASINESS PO 97.35 DV 164.41
   WP 387.18 RH 802.12

UNEASY TF 126.25 DV 148.3
   153.33 157.41 165.34
   SS 197.14 202.27 SB 219.18
   WS 261.2 261.6 EE 319.33
   TP 342.18 BL 361.17 362.30
   SD 417.15 PP 427.14 430.35
   440.18 SU 542.2 542.11
   WR 565.12 568.1 BO 598.26
   JD 611.31 GG 663.9 664.10
   675.27 689.29 700.8 NT 706.28
   ML 724.31 736.28 744.38
   LL 762.42 MD 812.11 BM 832.35
   841.24

UNEDUCATED JD 605.33 ML 735.3

UN-ELEMENTAL SU 533.4

UNEMOTIONAL YT 396.10 JD 623.34
   LA 631.17

UNENDING MO 17.22

UNENDURABLE DV 179.40 WP 379.4
   FA 459.39

UNENGAGED IL 647.14

UNENTERED ML 737.10

UNEQUAL IL 651.35

UNERRING MO 18.20

UNEVEN PP 435.41 LL 767.40
   768.8

UNEVENLY WP 386.24 LA 636.30

UNEVENTFUL SB 217.25

UNEXPECTED TF 123.31 YT 398.1
   NT 712.24 712.31 ML 742.33
   OV 752.23

UNEXPECTEDLY EE 305.4 YT 397.9

UNEXPRESSED DV 164.1

UNFAILING BL 359.25

UNFAIR SD 412.38 IL 647.28

UNFALTERING OV 748.39

UNFAMILIAR SS 202.28

UNFASTEN OC 299.4 BL 354.26
   OV 751.9

UNFASTENED TF 126.20 DV 167.29
   WS 245.4 SD 422.29 PR 494.14

UNFATHOMABLE HD 454.26 454.29

UNFERTILISED OV 748.9

UNFIT TP 334.28

UNFITTING DV 138.16

UNFLINCHING JD 612.30

UNFLINCHINGLY JD 613.41

UNFOLDED DV 142.29 SU 535.19
   SM 583.16 GG 686.38

UNFOLDING WR 565.40

UNFORGIVING BO 589.18

UNFORMED DV 173.33 SU 531.29

UNFORTUNATE EE 321.19
   WP 391.19 FA 468.32 469.9
   NT 708.34 LL 777.23 777.24
   MD 825.15

UNFORTUNATELY GF 242.18
   MD 810.14

UNFRIENDLY SB 214.11

UNFROZEN JD 610.19

UNFURLED BO 604.35

UNFURLING PO 113.39 SS 206.19
   WR 569.13 569.16 LA 632.31

UNGENTLE GF 234.14

UNGLOVE OV 749.41

UNGRAMMATICAL WR 566.32

UNHAMPERED PO 97.26

UNHAPPILY OC 298.35 WR 550.42
   JD 607.27 IL 651.42

UNHAPPINESS SB 214.22

UNHAPPY SP 50.25 DV 166.1
   SS 199.24 BL 362.40
   WP 381.25 FA 466.1
   SU 542.10 BO 601.37
   GG 680.38 695.5 BM 841.24

UNHASTENING OA 28.42

UNHEALTHY SU 533.42

UNHEARD SS 202.7 SG 226.14
   LA 638.7

UNHEARING CH 281.19

UNHEEDING SB 217.17 CH 282.17
   MN 374.12 PR 489.30

UNHESITATING SD 411.7

UNHIDDEN FG 187.17

UNHINGED PR 500.8

UNHOPED-FOR BL 364.31

UNHUNG OV 749.19

UNIDENTIFIED BM 832.31

UNIFORM PO 96.1 111.4
   TF 117.21 119.23 126.22
   134.40 TP 335.20 BO 588.31
   593.40 LA 634.21 GG 663.19

UNIFORMS TF 119.5 TP 342.36

UNIMAGINATIVE NT 718.36 720.18

UNIMPASSIONED MN 375.21

UNIMPORTANT EE 329.41

UNINHABITATED JD 610.31*

UNINHABITED LA 639.4

UNINSPIRED GG 661.3

UNINTELLIGIBLE DV 157.1

UNINTELLIGIBLY DV 146.1

UNINTERESTED MO 15.29 NT 716.31

UNINTERESTEDLY OA 28.22

UNINTERRUPTED BL 358.5

UNINVITING PP 429.32

UNION HT 41.39 42.3 SP 45.23
    46.2 46.10 46.40 EA 78.14
    SC 269.13 271.7

UNIQUE SU 532.40

UNISON WR 572.32 GG 683.41
    687.7

UNIT MO 10.13 EE 333.5
    TP 335.13

UNITE OC 301.31 FA 467.35

UNITED WS 252.27 OC 289.24
    WP 381.9

UNITED STATES PR 478.16 478.19
    WR 548.9 566.36 567.1 567.8
    NT 707.32 718.4 719.4

UNITING MO 19.30 OV 750.21

UNITY EA 81.25 89.13

UNIVERSAL MO 14.12 SP 46.39

UNIVERSE BL 356.8 ML 723.39
    724.12 MD 807.27

UNIVERSITIES TH 851.39

UNIVERSITY BO 589.21 TH 851.40

UNJUST YT 396.7

UNKEMPT EE 330.22

UNKIND EA 71.13 WS 260.18

UNKNOWING TF 124.3 OC 296.12
    HD 451.35

UNKNOWINGLY PO 108.26

UNKNOWN MO 4.30 WM 68.8
    EA 82.15 82.20 PO 111.38
    TF 125.42 129.8 DV 146.16
    165.26 173.24 173.33 174.23

UNKNOWN (CONT.) 182.21 FG 188.4
    MN 369.34 YT 402.29 WR 549.33
    GG 697.38 698.21 OV 749.7
    LL 763.7 TH 848.2

UNLACED OA 37.23

UNLATCHING LA 636.28

UNLAUGHING JD 606.22

UNLEAVENED DV 156.28 EE 324.40

UNLESS MO 13.31 WM 57.11
    PO 101.14 TF 126.32 DV 137.35
    FG 191.33 EE 313.41 TB 520.39
    WR 572.10 JD 628.26 IL 653.13
    RH 801.8 TH 849.6 849.9

UNLIGHTED OC 297.11 BL 355.22

UNLIKE HD 455.27

UNLIVING PO 97.11 WS 257.7
    CH 280.9 WR 552.3 GG 686.18

UNLIVINGNESS DV 148.12

UNLOADED MN 378.29

UNLOCK RR 787.28

UNLOCKED TP 345.37

UNLUCKY GG 665.38 665.39 666.8
    RH 792.9 792.13 792.17 792.20
    798.13

UNMANNED GG 679.36

UNMARRIED SP 51.17

UNMEANING PO 99.12

UNMOVED DV 141.8 177.28
    YT 409.38 SD 417.15 419.6

UNMOVING PO 100.36 OC 286.37
    PR 502.41 GG 685.14

UNMURMURING PR 479.1

UNNATURAL WM 65.9 65.10 69.36
    DV 178.13 EE 326.38 TP 343.36
    GG 669.3 LL 767.3 768.14

UNNATURALLY CH 275.36 PR 499.19

UNNECESSARILY ML 730.24

UNNECESSARY EA 79.13 EE 310.2
    FA 463.27 TB 514.26

UNNOTICED DV 185.42 EE 331.30

UNNOTICING JD 625.28

UNOBTRUSIVE DV 138.36

UNOPENED WR 557.4 ML 742.12

UNOPPOSED MO 1.9

UNOSTENTATIOUS GG 663.40

UNPACK TH 850.6

UNPAID DV 142.10

UNPARDONABLE EA 93.26

UNPEOPLED DV 176.22

UNPINNED EA 79.17

UNPLEASANT CH 282.5 EE 311.7
    PP 438.11 GG 669.41
    MD 819.35

UNPLEASING CH 274.21

UNPOLISHED EA 84.12

UNPREPOSSESSING GF 234.8

UNQUENCHABLE OV 749.8

UNQUENCHED EE 312.12
    YT 407.39

UNQUESTIONABLY GG 663.41

UNQUESTIONED EE 316.6

UNQUESTIONING EE 313.27
    YT 404.25

UNRAVELLED SP 51.21

UNREAL MO 2.15 EA 83.30
    PO 105.6 106.24 SS 202.13
    CH 280.8 OC 298.12
    EE 329.14 YT 399.13
    WR 549.35 567.17 BO 592.1
    GG 664.18 664.20

UNREALISED PR 509.6

UNREALITY PO 114.34

UNREASONABLE WS 261.25
    BL 349.26 356.11 364.22
    YT 407.6 GG 679.22

UNREASONING SD 413.41

UNRECEPTIVE BO 593.37

UNRECOGNISABLE PO 102.38
    YT 410.8 ML 746.27

UNREGRETTING JD 612.14

UNRELAXING DV 170.4

UNRELENTING WR 576.1
    JD 612.14

UNRELIEVED MO 6.35 PR 506.37

UNREMARKABLE BO 596.41

UNREMITTINGLY DV 146.18

UNRESOLVED WS 260.8
    PP 436.30

UNRESPONSIVE OC 302.6

UNREST MO 2.16

UNRESTRAINED WR 553.40

UNROLLED JD 618.15

UNSADDLED PR 495.33

UNSAFE OA 35.15

UNSAID WR 566.29

UNSANITARY WR 549.23

UNSATISFACTORY YT 396.20
    GG 661.28

UNSATISFIED TF 129.20 WS 260.21
    ML 746.35 RR 789.21

UNSCRUPULOUS EE 313.30 313.31
    YT 403.1 NT 706.27

UNSEEING TF 135.8 DV 138.19
    149.3 178.30 WS 254.37 263.14
    BL 355.21 WP 387.24 FA 458.9
    SM 582.19 BO 593.16 GG 690.37
    LL 769.3

UNSEEINGLY CH 278.11

UNSEEMLY DV 184.37 MD 817.1

UNSEEN EE 324.3 BL 355.35
    SD 420.13 PP 433.28 SU 533.15
    WR 572.27 572.28 JD 609.7
    ML 724.27 MD 815.27

UNSELFISH TH 846.19

UNSETTLE SC 269.3

UNSETTLING HD 445.35

UNSHEATHED EE 326.13

UNSHED PR 491.29

UNSINGED PR 493.26

UNSOLD GF 235.17

UNSOLID MD 816.36

UNSOPHISTICATED JD 607.13 607.18
    608.29

UNSPEAKABLE BL 347.16 348.17
    350.10 WR 556.20 566.29
    LL 767.10 776.1 776.15

UNSPEAKABLY LL 767.4

UNSPOILT JD 606.5 606.11 607.13

UNSPOKEN PO 100.4 PR 484.32
    TB 514.3 LL 765.19 766.34
    RH 791.4

UNSTINTED CH 275.31 HD 446.39

UNSTOPPERED PR 480.16

UNSUBDUED BO 599.34 600.10

UNSUCCESSFULLY EE 311.24*

UNSUITABLE PR 474.33 LL 766.42

UNSUNNED SU 533.4 533.41

UNSURE TF 119.35 DV 152.5
    BL 352.39 BO 591.42 JD 628.27
    RH 792.10

UNSUSPECTING MO 10.33

UNSWATHED PR 494.38

UNTHINKABLE DV 145.20

UNTHINKABLY HD 451.6

UNTHINKING PO 97.19

UNTIDINESS OA 28.38 WS 244.10
    OC 292.4

UNTIDY EA 81.1 GF 241.42
    WS 244.33 PR 494.40 MD 813.27

UNTIE FG 193.23 SD 422.9 422.11

UNTIL SP 50.38 PO 103.18
    DV 172.14 FG 189.28 190.10
    EE 315.6 PP 434.30 HD 447.10
    452.23 PR 488.26 WR 555.6
    BO 588.37 LL 761.22 766.4
    MD 819.40 823.38

UNTIMELY GG 700.11

UNTIRING MO 18.20

UNTO CH 279.33

UNTOLD WP 391.18

UNTOUCHED TF 119.7 125.36
    135.13 PR 503.35 WR 557.4
    LA 635.30 ML 733.33

UNTRAVELLED PR 480.39

UNTRODDEN ML 737.11

UNTRUSSED GG 676.28

UNTRUSTWORTHY ML 726.5

UNUSED SP 49.8 PO 116.20
    PP 437.5 LL 766.16 BM 832.39

UNUSEDNESS TF 132.6

UNUSUAL OC 288.33 BL 362.3
    FA 460.8 WR 559.3 NT 701.31

UNUTTERABLE EE 332.9

UNUTTERABLY TF 126.13

UNVARYING EA 81.23

UNVEXED SB 212.32

UNWARMED DV 138.3

UNWASHED GF 243.27 JD 617.17

UNWAVERING WR 558.28

UNWEARIEDLY WR 556.8

UNWILLING DV 148.31 WS 254.21
    BL 352.41 362.11 YT 398.12
    JD 625.21 LA 638.12
    GG 686.15

UNWILLINGLY WM 61.9 DV 140.22
    140.25 149.28 MN 378.6
    FA 468.28 JD 624.27

UNWINDING MN 375.9

UNWISELY MO 7.24

UNWORLDLY CH 279.32

UNWRAPPED PR 502.4

UNYIELDING DV 172.8 WS 264.34
    YT 408.21 BO 589.5
    JD 611.26 612.12 612.14
    625.13 625.16

UNYIELDINGLY GG 670.35

UP'ARDS SP 47.32

UP-BORNE WS 257.16

UPBRINGING DV 143.24

UPHILL WM 55.13 PO 107.36
    108.24 SS 205.3 SD 411.2
    JD 610.7 LA 634.19

UPHOLSTERED WM 58.34
    SS 202.37

UPLAND SS 197.27

UPLANDS SC 267.10 WP 386.2

UPLIFT PP 429.30 TB 519.30
    GG 688.14

UPLIFTED MO 22.30 TF 134.35
    OC 288.30 TP 337.32
    BL 360.19 FA 467.27
    WR 564.35 570.4 SM 584.13

UPLIFTING DV 173.23

UPPED GF 242.37

UPPER DV 137.1 138.6 167.10
    FG 190.24 SS 203.28
    GF 241.23 241.25 BL 353.1
    353.11 355.22 362.13
    WP 379.19 387.23 TB 514.32
    516.3 516.8 WR 562.9
    568.30 572.27 574.5 577.32
    BO 595.32 595.35 GG 670.16
    RH 802.40

UPPER-ARM WS 245.5

UPPER-MAID TB 516.32

UPPERMOST JD 605.7 605.19

UPRAISED SG 225.27

UPRIGHT DV 160.27 SC 267.5

UPRIGHT (CONT.) PR 475.29

UPROOTED JD 628.15

UP-ROSE FG 188.22 193.21

UPSET WM 57.11 DV 162.39 174.2
   184.20 SS 211.14 SB 219.40
   SG 229.6 CH 282.13 OC 294.25
   EE 311.29 SM 585.25 BM 833.42
   842.16

UPSIDE DV 170.35

UPSTAIRS OA 38.10 WM 64.29
   EA 80.4 TF 129.12 134.9
   DV 147.38 148.17 159.25
   159.32 160.5 162.25 163.20
   168.20 169.31 169.40 171.13
   171.29 SG 224.4 228.17 229.26
   GF 239.9 WS 247.10 249.42
   261.17 265.17 265.27
   SC 269.30 269.32 270.17
   270.25 271.28 272.15 OC 298.2
   EE 317.14 318.7 320.17
   TP 335.24 335.35 BL 355.20
   356.30 MN 375.3 YT 397.6
   399.5 SD 417.32 HD 451.16
   451.28 452.11 FA 462.8 470.24
   470.41 LA 640.23 640.30
   GG 669.29 669.32 681.5 681.23
   686.9 687.12 LL 765.7 776.31
   RR 786.21 788.2 788.31
   RH 802.39

UP-STREAM PR 484.10

UPTILTED OA 26.32 WM 68.35
   BL 360.4

UP-TO-DATE TH 853.18

UPTURNED MO 22.23 BM 841.32

UPWARD FG 194.16 SS 209.8
   GF 238.15

UPWARDS PO 113.25 TF 120.24
   HD 442.37 FA 465.16 PR 489.42
   490.20 490.21 493.11 496.17
   496.21 WR 579.11 580.2
   LA 631.32 OV 750.29 754.17

URCHIN SU 540.4

URGE WR 555.13 GG 679.38
   RH 803.28 TH 847.25 847.26

URGED MO 2.3 20.16 WM 62.26
   SB 216.5 GF 234.14 MN 374.25
   PR 474.26 GG 679.16 RH 800.28
   803.13

URGENTLY OA 28.30

URGING MO 10.1 16.31 DV 138.13
   RH 803.20

URQUHART (SEE COLIN, DOLLIE,
   PRINCESS; MRS. URQUHART)

USE MO 10.11 12.17 HT 41.40
   42.5 SP 51.40 WM 63.41
   EA 76.42 77.7 78.24 79.41
   PO 99.5 DV 137.6 178.17

USE (CONT.) SS 203.23 204.18
   EE 321.33 TP 339.20 WP 389.28
   FA 463.34 471.18 WR 549.14
   JD 619.39 620.11 620.15
   620.16 620.19 620.28 620.30
   620.31 LA 637.21 IL 648.6
   GG 697.32 NT 706.22 LL 775.3
   RH 791.30 MD 809.28 BM 827.23
   TH 846.29 846.30

USED MO 1.3 1.11 5.16 10.15
   10.19 16.27 21.7 WM 54.4
   55.3 56.38 57.21 63.22
   EA 80.5 84.15 86.30 PO 105.18
   TF 127.5 DV 137.26 140.34
   143.41 148.40 165.28 171.25
   178.28 FG 189.29 SS 198.32
   198.38 SG 223.10 225.9 231.2
   232.30 WS 260.10 260.11
   260.12 EE 319.4 SD 420.14
   PP 438.11 FA 471.15 WR 575.12
   BO 589.40 592.11 592.13
   594.28 595.33 596.25 601.7
   JD 611.23 612.27 613.19
   615.37 624.14 LA 638.7
   GG 693.20 NT 709.27 ML 724.23
   728.41 744.16 LL 765.3
   RR 785.33 RH 792.19 800.13
   MD 809.6 809.9 817.39 822.9
   BM 831.21 834.38 840.35
   TH 848.29 848.30

USEFUL WS 261.42 NT 706.19
   MD 810.5 821.10

USELESS DV 169.35 169.39
   YT 396.24 PR 474.17 507.36
   BM 840.30 840.32

USES PP 429.2 NT 711.16

USHER BM 838.26

USHERED DV 183.9 SM 582.32
   BM 838.25

USING EA 80.32 82.42 PO 99.15
   TF 133.4 SS 204.31 TP 341.26
   BO 589.36 NT 711.14 717.1
   RH 792.34

USTED ES SENORA WR 554.24

USUAL MO 9.35 10.37 11.7 15.15
   OA 30.12 HT 42.9 WM 62.34
   63.28 EA 87.25 92.4 TF 118.27
   DV 159.31 SB 217.32 SC 270.4
   270.13 CH 274.2 TP 339.4
   BL 350.39 358.4 MN 367.26
   370.4 371.25 378.2 SD 412.28
   PP 432.26 FA 460.6 PR 483.15
   485.12 488.4 TB 520.17 522.42
   IL 655.24 GG 671.3 NT 712.13
   719.5 719.17 720.29 ML 728.3
   LL 770.32 RR 783.9 784.10

USUALLY WS 244.23 BL 354.25
   PR 473.14 476.23 481.36
   TB 513.10 514.4 516.36 516.38
   JD 613.4 GG 662.42 681.34
   NT 703.15 RR 785.17 MD 808.32
   TH 848.42

UTMOST SM 583.34

UTTER OA 33.38 DV 145.11
   150.37 154.8 181.4
   SG 233.5 OC 299.39 300.30
   WR 556.13 JD 611.4 622.38
   GG 670.27 677.14 LL 776.29
   RR 783.27 789.5 789.12
   MD 806.25 BM 839.19
   TH 852.41

UTTERANCE EA 89.22

UTTERED MO 14.12 OA 33.32
   TP 341.10 TB 518.27

UTTERING SU 536.33 BO 590.9

UTTERLY OA 31.42 EA 72.10
   DV 154.1 172.39 180.39
   WS 249.11 254.40 OC 299.14
   300.26 302.6 EE 333.3
   BL 348.8 354.1 WP 385.40
   390.28 390.29 PR 479.5
   TB 526.37 SU 540.17 541.1
   WR 564.19 566.22 SM 586.28
   BO 599.11 603.36 JD 605.22
   NT 711.24 716.31 720.18
   ML 743.10 LL 767.31 774.8
   778.16 MD 806.21 806.32
   815.12 816.40 BM 833.2

VACANCY PO 106.4 BO 599.37

VACANT WM 63.6 PO 104.2
   CH 282.18 BO 602.9 603.2
   LA 644.3 ML 737.23

VACANTLY DV 139.27 FA 469.37
   TB 520.21 LL 769.1

VACUUM GG 691.18

VAGARIES SB 212.4

VAGUE WM 61.21 65.8 68.4
   EA 77.15 PO 105.6 WS 254.30
   CH 278.1 EE 332.11
   PR 473.27 484.32 TB 521.24
   SU 535.29 WR 549.33 552.38
   567.42 BO 588.17 JD 612.19
   618.1 LA 640.17 GG 661.22
   666.18 666.20 RR 786.41
   BM 839.2 TH 850.13

VAGUELY SP 51.9 WM 65.1
   EA 84.39 TF 117.6 DV 154.5
   157.41 177.24 GF 240.5
   OC 288.37 TP 343.6 344.18
   BL 350.13 WP 380.38
   PP 433.40 HD 441.14
   PR 473.20 500.19 WR 562.41
   BO 593.4 JD 618.16
   IL 651.42 655.27 GG 693.41
   698.32 ML 741.23 OV 748.3
   LL 777.41 RH 791.41 792.39

VAGUENESS PR 473.29

VAIN SP 50.6 EA 93.34
   BL 356.9 TB 514.31 514.34
   NT 702.8 716.30 MD 813.7
   817.34 TH 848.39

VAINLY CH 276.28 ML 738.7

VALE TB 514.28

VALEDICTION MO 7.9

VALENTINE WS 245.25 246.26
  248.11

VALENTINES WS 246.22 246.32
  264.36

VALENTINE'S WS 260.24

VALENTINO, RUDOLPH (SEE RUDOLPH
  VALENTINO)

VALERIE TH 848.10 848.15 848.38
  848.41 849.4 849.19 849.22
  849.42 850.19 850.24 850.37
  851.21 851.28 851.30 851.31
  851.40 852.6 852.10 852.30
  853.15 853.16 853.26

VALERIE'S TH 851.26 851.29
  851.34 851.42 852.17

VALET DE CHAMBRE TB 516.7

VALETED TB 516.4 517.23
  ML 726.3

VALIANTLY OA 32.6

VALISE FA 460.18

VALLEY MO 2.5 3.5 WM 60.28
  60.30 61.5 61.19 61.20
  PO 95.4 105.20 111.32 111.40
  DV 160.25 FG 193.29 SS 202.6
  SC 267.21 CH 275.23 WP 385.30
  385.35 385.40 386.1 386.3
  386.12 387.19 391.23 393.9
  PP 436.29 PR 486.11 494.3
  494.5 499.30 500.1 506.24
  506.31 507.11 WR 550.4 551.17
  551.27 551.29 552.1 552.3
  552.10 553.9 553.16 558.34
  558.35 569.22 572.5 572.35
  578.31

VALLEY-HEAD WR 561.7

VALLEYS PR 496.37 498.18
  WR 550.2 JD 610.8

VALLEY-SIDE WP 386.14 387.21

VALUABLE WS 260.32 LL 778.37
  MD 810.4 825.24 825.26
  TH 852.1

VALUE BO 587.6 JD 607.34

VALVES IL 649.38

VAN FA 459.17

VANISH MO 18.38 22.30 GF 238.41

VANISHED MO 2.1 OA 29.34
  SP 51.5 SB 216.22 SG 226.15
  MN 378.35 WR 570.6 ML 724.26
  745.32

VANITY WM 54.35 TB 514.32
  518.12 BO 590.12 JD 622.38
  NT 711.35 MD 806.22 808.5

VAN-LOADS TH 849.38

VANQUISH TP 336.41

VAPORISING SS 203.12

VAPOUR PO 110.14 TF 132.19
  DV 175.15 EE 312.20 OV 748.38
  750.2

VARIANCE SU 528.27

VARIATION WM 63.35

VARIES WM 62.19

VARIETY WM 65.33 DV 166.20

VARIETY'S MN 377.1

VARIOUS HT 42.20 DV 179.23
  SS 205.5 205.6 SG 223.37
  CH 275.8 OC 292.6 WP 387.16
  SD 423.3 WR 550.10 561.41
  IL 650.24 ML 731.16 LL 770.18
  BM 827.36

VARLEY, WINIFRED (SEE WINIFRED
  VARLEY)

VARYING SS 209.1 209.3

VASE OC 297.21 297.24

VASES OC 296.20 MD 811.4

VAST SP 50.17 DV 176.20
  SS 209.1 209.3 PR 480.5
  482.19 482.41 496.17 496.24
  497.37 501.12 SU 529.9 536.17
  WR 546.25 565.41 568.16
  BO 595.27 595.29 595.36
  595.41 599.38 603.11 ML 724.3
  745.38 BM 827.17 TH 853.12

VASTLY WS 248.17 PR 497.38
  ML 724.7

VAULTED NT 713.24

VAUNTING RR 779.4

VEER ML 724.3

VEERED WM 70.8

VEERING TP 337.13 SD 411.25
  411.28 TB 524.11

VEGETABLE TF 117.11 EE 304.40
  FA 464.32 WR 546.34

VEGETABLES DV 143.4

VEGETARIAN GG 689.18

VEGETATION EE 303.27 313.12

VEHEMENT WP 387.29

VEHEMENTLY JD 623.3

VEHICLE WR 577.13

VEIL SM 583.35 586.9 LA 638.23

VEIL (CONT.) BM 835.25 835.34

VEILED MO 9.9 WR 567.40

VEIN HT 41.21 WM 69.39
  EE 313.23 WR 548.19

VEINS EA 76.38 PO 109.8
  TF 121.12 DV 149.38
  SB 217.30 SG 229.9 231.14
  WS 247.25 250.26 261.8
  EE 323.22 BL 349.12 354.28
  354.30 WP 391.31 YT 400.20
  SD 421.34 FA 458.5 466.10
  466.21 PR 473.5 473.7
  BO 587.19 GG 698.2
  OV 754.37

VELOUR FA 458.32

VELVET WM 64.12 SB 214.40
  219.32 SG 225.31 GF 241.18
  MN 371.19 376.25 SD 423.41
  NT 705.42 ML 730.3
  LL 763.22 763.25 774.3

VELVETY HT 42.25 BL 353.25
  GG 666.25

VENERATION PR 480.42

VENETIAN OA 29.29 LL 777.27
  MD 815.15 817.17 TH 848.19
  848.30

VENGEANCE WP 391.18 GG 681.2

VENICE NT 701.1 701.9 704.34
  TH 853.20

VENISON WR 557.12

VENOM IL 658.16 NT 716.18
  MD 816.21 819.32

VENOMOUSLY LL 776.9

VENT LL 767.42

VENTRILOQUISM LL 768.3 768.7
  768.11

VENTURED MO 19.28 SP 50.25
  BL 352.35 HD 450.11
  SU 541.15 GG 694.36

VENTURING EE 314.33

VENUS WM 58.42 59.14

VERANDA WR 546.19

VERDAD NT 716.30

VERDICT JD 605.3

VERILY LL 768.33

VERMILION TH 848.14

VERMOUTH ML 729.19

VERNACULAR FA 466.22

VERONAL LL 778.33

VERSATILITY ML 729.10

VERSE OA 27.26 EA 92.5
  PO 101.23 SS 202.42 WS 248.35
  EE 305.31 GG 676.23

VERSES JD 607.34 607.36

VERSION DV 145.27

VESSEL MO 21.42 EA 83.5
  TP 336.6 PR 480.12 480.13
  480.14

VESSELS SD 411.25

VEST SC 267.34 268.31

VESTRY FA 468.42 469.1

VEXATION WM 62.6

VEXED OC 293.40 SD 425.6
  TB 525.28

VIA BO 588.3

VIBRANT WS 253.23

VIBRATE PR 504.7 BO 599.32

VIBRATING MO 11.34 TF 130.8
  HD 455.26

VIBRATION PP 439.1 BO 603.8
  GG 665.3

VICAR DV 136.1 143.1 143.7
  143.14 143.26 143.31 143.37
  144.9 144.21 148.35 151.25
  158.6 158.10 183.10 183.24
  183.28 183.30 183.36 185.29
  186.6 FG 187.13 187.28 188.7
  196.24 BM 828.3

VICARAGE WM 55.6 DV 155.9 158.1
  160.4 172.22 173.39 182.29
  183.3

VICAR'S DV 138.26 184.12
  FG 187.18

VICES EE 311.36 FA 462.25
  LL 762.4

VICIOUS SB 216.20 EE 326.20
  TB 522.24 GG 661.7

VICKERS MO 13.9 14.16 14.22
  15.27 16.7 17.18 17.21 17.36
  17.40 18.4 18.6 18.35

VICKERS (SEE TOM; MR. VICKERS)

VICTIM SD 421.17 PR 504.33
  WR 568.8 577.29 580.31
  TH 846.31

VICTIMISED WR 572.9

VICTIMISING WR 577.30

VICTOR SP 50.23

VICTORIA PP 427.1

VICTORIOUS TF 131.24

VICTORY EA 73.29 TF 132.11

VICTROLA GG 682.18 685.2 685.10
  685.14 685.31 686.1 687.19

VICTROLA'S GG 687.29

VIEW SS 199.37 SG 222.23
  HD 453.22 BO 587.32 GG 663.5
  664.36 LL 772.36

VIGOROUS OA 29.9 SP 51.21
  EA 72.11 PO 97.8 SG 221.14
  SC 268.39 EE 305.33 YT 397.20
  PP 439.38

VIGOROUS-LOOKING SC 270.14

VIGOROUSLY CH 279.1 JD 617.31

VIGOUR SD 412.32 JD 617.19

VIKING EE 303.10 GG 676.34
  676.37 676.39 677.1

VILLA SP 50.29 SC 271.13 271.29
  IL 648.14

VILLAGE PO 111.34 TF 128.7
  DV 153.29 160.14 SS 197.27
  SB 213.4 214.3 SG 223.9
  223.21 EE 317.42 330.2
  TP 335.8 MN 366.5 371.40
  372.22 SD 411.31 PP 432.10
  SU 533.16 542.15 WR 550.12
  552.28 553.7 561.32 565.32
  580.9 BO 593.22 593.24
  JD 607.27 609.32 GG 668.29

VILLAGES FG 187.3 TP 334.4
  336.27 MN 371.39 WR 549.20
  JD 607.29

VILLAIN SD 417.11 417.12 419.20

VILLAS ML 729.30

VINDICATION TF 121.37 LA 634.42
  635.2

VINDICTIVE TP 340.12 344.19
  SD 421.2 PR 482.41 MD 822.19

VINDICTIVELY SS 210.38 PR 511.2
  LA 632.34

VINE TF 123.1 OC 283.32
  SU 538.39 TH 845.6 845.9
  845.11 847.30 847.31

VINE-PROPS TH 851.2

VINES TF 118.22 123.1 SU 529.9
  OV 754.38 TH 845.11 846.34
  846.37 847.35

VINE-SUPPORT TH 847.29

VINEYARD SU 529.9 OV 754.37
  TH 847.35

VINEYARDS TF 117.4

VINNY MD 805.33 806.8
  806.11 806.12 806.13 807.6

VIOLATED TF 121.17 PR 508.41
  GG 697.33

VIOLATION DV 153.11 183.18
  SG 233.11 HD 453.16
  ML 742.6

VIOLENCE SB 212.23 WS 265.13
  PR 479.22 479.23 479.30
  GG 697.32 ML 743.9

VIOLENT TF 127.8 DV 137.42
  145.23 BL 353.27 SD 415.13
  419.25 PP 429.42 FA 461.1
  461.2 463.12 PR 477.21
  509.3 509.25 SU 543.24
  543.25 GG 700.11 NT 719.20
  ML 724.27 731.24 731.29
  RH 803.2 MD 807.17 808.25
  815.9 BM 832.28

VIOLENTLY OC 294.13 BL 362.12
  WP 387.26 SD 419.21 424.21
  PP 430.16 HD 453.18
  WR 565.29 LA 638.36
  GG 670.39

VIOLETS BL 358.15 358.21
  358.29 358.35 TB 515.2
  GG 695.36

VIOLIN WM 59.7 59.19 59.20
  59.29 60.14 TF 127.2
  YT 395.14

VIOLIN-STAND WM 63.32

VIPER BM 838.1

VIRGIN MO 15.19 15.23
  TF 127.11 128.14 132.8
  PR 476.36 479.4 490.9
  490.11 512.19 MD 821.17
  821.18 821.19

VIRGINAL PR 481.5 GG 693.24

VIRGINIA MD 805.14 805.22
  805.23 805.27 805.30
  805.35 805.36 806.2
  806.34 807.16 807.26
  807.32 807.35 809.30
  809.33 810.10 810.13
  810.22 811.8 811.15 811.16
  811.20 811.26 811.33
  811.36 812.9 812.18 812.25
  812.29 813.6 813.9 813.14
  813.24 813.29 813.35
  813.38 813.40 814.2 814.5
  814.7 814.10 814.12 814.15
  814.33 814.37 815.3 815.4
  815.10 815.26 815.29
  815.37 815.39 816.5 816.7
  816.12 816.14 816.22
  816.36 816.37 816.39
  816.42 817.6 817.12 817.15
  817.30 817.32 817.34
  817.37 817.41 818.7 818.10
  818.11 818.22 818.29
  818.30 819.16 819.20
  820.16 820.36 821.15
  821.17 821.24 822.38

VOLLEYS CH 279.6 LA 639.31
  ML 723.38 745.40

VOLTAIRE MD 809.12

VOLUME OA 27.25 BO 599.8

VOLUMES SS 202.41 TB 524.42
  SM 583.33 MD 816.16

VOLUMINOUS SM 583.8 586.22

VOLUMINOUSNESS SM 583.23

VOLUNTARY HD 449.36

VOLUNTEERED GG 682.25

VOLUPTUOUS MO 5.6 EA 81.29
  WS 250.2 254.37 BO 587.3
  587.11 587.22 587.37 591.38
  592.29 NT 710.3

VOLUPTUOUSLY MO 8.20 SM 585.31
  LL 766.37

VOLUPTUOUSNESS LA 634.17
  MD 821.21

VOLUTES MD 810.39

VOMIT WR 565.28 TH 852.24
  852.25

VON TODTNAU, KATHERINE (SEE
  KATHERINE VON TODTNAU)

VOW OV 759.14 759.15 RR 782.26
  787.10

VOYEZ VOUS BIEN + GG 676.19

VULGAR DV 137.20 138.6
  SB 218.20 WP 380.41 FA 464.1
  466.25 PR 474.2 475.34 475.40
  476.8 480.5 480.19 480.21
  481.19 481.33 WR 550.14
  JD 607.20 622.11 NT 715.16
  ML 736.1 739.3 MD 811.1
  TH 844.25

VULGARISED PR 480.22

VULGARISM MD 809.28

VULGARITY EE 329.16 PR 481.35
  IL 650.15 BM 840.30

VULNERABLE BO 595.12

WADDLED FA 459.30

WADDLING GF 234.31

WADED HD 449.39 JD 610.27

WADING SU 537.37

WAFER NT 719.24

WAFFLIN' OC 287.41

WAFTED LL 770.42

WAGE FA 471.33 JD 620.30

WAGER WP 383.12

WAGERED WM 64.4

WAGERS SP 50.20

WAGES DV 144.13 OC 294.40
  FA 471.31 TB 516.16 ML 732.25

WAGGED HD 442.27 443.24

WAGGING JD 613.16

WAGON OC 289.38 MN 377.42
  378.29 PP 432.21

WAGON-BUILDER TF 128.6

WAGON-BUILDING TF 128.7

WAGONED MN 366.35

WAGONER MN 367.3

WAGON-LIT SM 582.3

WAGONS SS 197.28 OC 283.2
  283.10 MN 366.26 366.27
  366.34

WAGTAIL SS 204.23

WAIF WR 548.2 MD 820.38 820.39

WAIL PR 492.23

WAILED DV 163.2 OC 290.9 296.8

WAILING WR 552.13

WAILS GG 692.35

WAIN MN 374.15

WAIST OA 25.32 WM 59.3 EA 73.22
  TF 130.2 DV 166.9 170.17
  GF 236.28 243.2 SC 268.37
  OC 288.39 288.42 297.17
  MN 373.9 373.13 373.16 373.27
  SU 540.15 542.18 JD 617.15
  IL 650.17

WAISTCOAT HT 43.17 SP 49.35
  49.36 DV 173.4 SG 230.23
  SC 268.14 OC 284.30 WP 390.21
  LA 645.25 MD 822.37

WAISTS MO 4.41 WR 569.3

WAIT MO 11.20 HT 41.26 WM 60.42
  DV 162.7 SB 216.38 SG 227.28
  230.1 OC 297.26 TP 334.17
  335.11 340.23 FA 459.4
  PR 486.36 494.12 494.22
  500.29 500.35 WR 574.12
  BO 599.14 599.41 JD 616.27
  628.28 LA 637.23 IL 658.6
  LL 775.22 RR 787.25 787.26
  RH 801.3 802.36 MD 818.7
  818.10 823.29 BM 839.5

WAITED MO 10.2 11.20 HT 44.6
  44.7 WM 59.32 63.19 EA 77.32
  84.39 87.41 PO 97.41 98.31
  99.2 101.2 102.2 TF 117.23

WAITED (CONT.) 120.38 129.22
  129.36 DV 139.1 139.27
  141.8 151.33 151.34 152.2
  152.32 157.33 169.42
  170.13 175.7 FG 193.39
  SS 199.15 201.9 SB 217.14
  GF 236.1 240.9 WS 245.20
  252.18 255.9 OC 284.14
  288.36 294.11 295.11
  297.27 298.18 EE 329.3
  330.19 TP 345.20 BL 357.40
  358.36 MN 375.42 377.39
  WP 390.41 HD 442.22 456.23
  FA 459.3 459.13 461.13
  461.14 461.15 PR 494.25
  508.32 TB 523.2 WR 556.27
  559.17 568.36 BO 599.17
  599.24 603.36 JD 616.17
  GG 664.21 NT 719.32
  ML 744.41 OV 753.15 753.31
  LL 772.35 772.39 773.16
  RR 785.14 MD 826.4 826.7

WAITIN' SP 52.3

WAITING MO 7.19 19.2
  OA 34.30 SP 46.14 52.23
  52.24 WM 55.6 60.26
  EA 76.8 78.24 86.28
  91.40 PO 107.23 TF 117.16
  119.40 124.24 125.6 129.25
  131.42 DV 144.35 148.3
  149.17 150.36 172.1 173.5
  173.39 180.5 FG 187.24
  SS 197.15 SG 222.4
  WS 256.16 CH 274.33
  OC 286.26 288.11 EE 318.34
  TP 334.19 336.14 341.32
  BL 353.18 MN 368.35 370.19
  373.30 WP 379.27 380.4
  HD 441.10 448.32 PR 482.36
  484.26 TB 516.27 520.22
  522.40 SU 544.2 WR 574.10
  574.33 580.3 581.7 581.17
  BO 595.41 596.3 598.20
  598.34 600.12 600.19
  600.22 600.25 602.38
  603.20 604.4 JD 614.37
  616.25 627.10 LA 634.27
  637.17 637.18 637.21
  638.22 IL 654.37 GG 664.40
  678.34 NT 709.18 ML 740.30
  LL 775.33 RR 785.14
  RH 800.36 803.39 MD 819.41
  820.38 BM 843.4

WAITING-ROOM TP 340.24 340.29
  340.34

WAITS EA 85.1 WS 254.20
  FA 461.29

WAKE MO 4.1 11.19 DV 181.5
  FG 192.23 EE 332.5 YT 409.4
  NT 713.28 BM 830.37

WAKED NT 713.28

WAKEFUL OC 298.41

WAKEFULNESS WS 262.29

WAKEN OC 295.33 296.11
  YT 402.1

WAKENED MO 15.18 HT 42.34
   EA 81.35 TF 129.13 YT 402.6
   BM 830.34

WAKES OC 290.13

WAKING EE 332.5 BL 350.14
   GG 679.15 698.36

WAKKENED HT 42.33

WALK MO 2.19 SP 47.25 WM 59.34
   59.35 59.39 60.10 EA 73.10
   PO 95.22 104.40 106.25 107.21
   TF 121.34 125.17 DV 147.12
   161.41 SS 209.29 WS 259.9
   SC 267.11 270.9 271.15 271.31
   OC 291.8 TP 336.32 338.33
   340.20 BL 352.2 MN 371.8
   371.36 372.33 373.41 376.22
   376.30 377.20 WP 384.2
   SD 416.23 HD 448.35 455.42
   PR 491.12 491.39 TB 517.25
   SU 543.18 543.21 544.27
   544.35 WR 565.18 BO 603.6
   603.24 JD 610.7 626.11 627.29
   LA 631.2 636.35 645.29 646.7
   IL 658.6 658.8 NT 702.30
   ML 736.31 740.10 741.25
   LL 765.10 RR 780.14 787.24

WALKED MO 13.29 20.20 22.5
   SP 46.24 49.9 WM 60.21 62.22
   63.11 PO 95.18 95.26 95.32
   99.42 107.35 108.25 114.13
   115.8 TF 122.11 123.14 123.19
   126.38 DV 167.23 176.37
   182.23 SS 199.40 206.22
   209.40 SB 216.36 217.15
   SG 225.23 228.12 GF 243.30
   243.33 WS 264.25 OC 293.4
   EE 321.5 TP 338.39 BL 354.15
   MN 366.30 372.9 373.14 373.17
   373.18 376.17 376.20 376.25
   376.37 377.24 377.32
   WP 384.39 YT 397.16 409.20
   SD 423.6 423.9 HD 448.17
   449.40 451.31 452.8 FA 459.34
   470.7 PR 492.4 493.17
   TB 527.28 WR 558.16 562.8
   568.41 BO 597.5 601.26 603.1
   603.41 IL 654.8 GG 694.33
   ML 722.31 722.34 738.26
   741.23 741.33 743.35
   OV 750.18 LL 773.6 RR 787.40
   MD 808.8 BM 841.2

WALKIN' SP 47.15

WALKING WM 54.31 PO 103.8 114.9
   114.10 114.22 TF 121.38
   125.25 128.1 134.41 DV 147.4
   160.24 165.14 SG 222.24
   GF 234.34 OC 283.6 291.1
   TP 337.1 MN 377.30 SU 543.41
   SM 583.22 BO 596.36 597.19
   597.23 603.33 JD 610.18
   LA 636.30 GG 695.13 695.13
   695.32 ML 740.4 OV 750.13
   760.5

WALKING-CANE SB 216.13

WALKS TP 336.28 336.30

WALKURE WM 65.12

WALL MO 10.32 OA 36.23 PO 107.6
   TF 119.21 119.34 120.7 120.30
   120.32 131.29 DV 139.7 160.37
   167.17 FG 187.9 SS 200.33
   202.40 203.3 206.28 206.38
   SG 224.14 224.16 231.23
   GF 234.32 234.33 WS 264.8
   264.16 264.25 SC 269.7
   CH 277.30 OC 301.11 EE 313.38
   TP 342.14 342.16 342.19
   BL 358.21 YT 394.2 395.21
   SD 421.22 421.26 423.2 423.10
   423.27 PP 428.4 431.4 434.19
   HD 447.37 447.40 PR 496.23
   500.25 502.8 502.30 505.31
   SU 532.16 537.16 WR 561.16
   562.18 562.31 563.26 576.33
   576.39 579.24 JD 621.4
   LA 640.17 GG 699.30 ML 745.3
   LL 770.26 770.27 MD 811.37
   BM 828.27 833.18 TH 850.12

WALLED TF 118.38 EE 313.37
   ML 745.1

WALLED-IN WR 546.18

WALLET FG 193.1 195.15

WALL-FACE TF 119.20 119.26

WALLOWING PR 481.17

WALLS OA 24.7 WM 55.16 63.29
   EA 81.13 TF 122.8 125.23
   DV 137.33 139.33 158.41
   SG 221.8 GF 234.30 241.30
   OC 288.13 EE 306.24 313.39
   WP 379.15 WR 558.34 569.22
   576.24 576.27 578.32 GG 670.7
   LL 766.16 770.20 RR 779.31
   MD 818.4

WALNUT SS 202.38

WALNUTS GG 676.34

WALT OC 292.23

WALTER DURANT DV 143.24

WALTER'S OC 285.32

WALT'S OC 294.19

WAN SS 197.17 GF 241.42
   OC 284.38 BL 359.12 WR 578.39
   579.4

WANDER WM 62.41 PR 494.15
   SU 534.1 WR 549.36 GG 700.8

WANDERED PO 104.3 SG 225.34
   EE 325.19 PR 473.20 SU 535.38
   ML 738.7

WANDERING FG 189.32 WR 549.41
   JD 610.23 BM 829.24

WANDERS NT 701.5

WANING BO 600.13

WANLY TB 524.31

WANTIN' HT 42.15 43.1

WANTING HT 42.18 EA 77.41
   DV 151.34 178.15 179.32
   SG 231.29 SD 413.16
   SU 529.31 531.14 BO 593.33
   597.40 LL 767.16 767.17
   767.18

WANTS HT 40.28 DV 185.15
   SC 267.37 TP 345.18
   BL 350.23 350.25 MN 371.1
   YT 401.12 405.29 SD 419.2
   420.7 PR 492.9 WR 573.18
   JD 621.24 626.34 IL 657.18
   GG 693.17 NT 717.9
   ML 727.34 732.40 RR 788.33
   BM 838.33 TH 845.30

WAR TF 133.25 GF 235.13
   WS 262.4 EE 305.9 326.22
   326.23 327.23 327.24
   327.25 327.28 328.5
   329.39 WP 382.2 382.11
   YT 396.33 SD 415.8
   WR 547.4 BO 590.32 591.18
   591.30 593.40 594.20
   602.3 GG 661.1 663.15
   663.16 663.31 663.35
   666.3 666.21 666.29
   674.14 678.30 687.35
   RR 783.22 RH 794.10
   MD 818.25 BM 827.25 827.27
   829.41 830.39 TH 844.2
   845.35 846.9

WARE WM 55.39

WAREHOUSE WS 250.20 250.31
   PR 480.14 TH 850.8 850.24
   850.27 852.31

WAREHOUSES DV 140.27 GF 234.29

WARILY SD 424.20 JD 618.42

WARINESS JD 618.41

WARM MO 12.28 13.10 OA 23.6
   HT 39.31 WM 55.36 63.29
   63.32 68.9 EA 75.32 78.1
   81.22 81.29 82.16 91.31
   92.7 PO 97.3 97.10 98.21
   100.41 TF 130.10 130.24
   DV 144.4 144.6 148.20
   159.4 159.27 182.6
   FG 190.22 195.10 SB 212.13
   214.17 GF 236.11 WS 251.10
   251.38 252.22 252.28
   SC 267.4 267.35 OC 286.14
   287.36 291.3 299.16 299.24
   EE 306.11 319.1 TP 337.40
   338.22 338.27 339.2
   BL 351.23 WP 379.36 386.41
   387.4 388.41 SD 425.29
   426.11 PP 434.3 435.8
   437.24 HD 451.17 452.14
   FA 462.19 PR 485.31 495.38
   503.2 504.8 504.13 505.4
   507.39 507.42 TB 520.27
   520.29 SU 530.42 531.11
   531.24 531.26 534.38

WARM (CONT.) SU 539.24 SM 583.40
  BO 597.42 600.34 LA 640.7
  640.19 640.25 641.16 641.19
  IL 652.34 654.31 GG 670.1
  675.9 676.14 682.33 686.37
  686.39 686.41 690.32 690.36
  694.3 697.40 NT 705.29 713.5
  ML 746.16 OV 753.41 LL 764.18
  766.32 RR 788.13

WARMBY (SEE EPHRAIM, JOHN)

WARM-COLOURED RR 784.10

WARMED SP 53.23 WS 253.16
  TP 338.1 FA 470.18 JD 618.16

WARMER SU 530.22 530.23
  OV 753.26

WARM-GOLD OA 29.19

WARM-HEARTED EA 86.11

WARMING FG 191.39 PR 500.26
  WR 557.29

WARM-LOOKING BL 358.32

WARMLY LL 766.12

WARMLY-LIT SD 412.1

WARM-SMELLING PP 432.22

WARMTH MO 5.5 19.39 HT 42.32
  SP 49.18 WM 65.20 EA 86.12
  TF 118.9 DV 140.37 178.10
  FG 191.15 GF 240.9 WS 244.20
  246.18 246.19 252.25 255.2
  EE 315.14 TP 338.37 BL 353.3
  PP 429.30 429.34 PR 503.32
  504.13 505.5 505.13 509.38
  WR 556.31 572.25 BO 589.28
  GG 686.19 ML 730.15

WARNED PO 103.11 SS 209.9
  SC 269.25 OC 293.1 LL 767.19

WARNING OA 24.40 EE 330.9

WARRANT SP 47.35

WAR-TIME TP 334.28 337.16
  340.32

WAR-WHOOP MN 378.2

WAR-WORK BM 828.22

WARY JD 618.29 ML 731.34

WA'SCOAT SP 49.40

WASH HT 43.28 WM 64.28 65.13
  DV 182.5 WS 244.32 249.3
  SC 268.18 270.2 CH 281.23
  OC 289.19 299.26 PR 495.35
  SU 529.6 533.36 WR 564.29
  ML 724.36 TH 850.34

WASH-DAY HT 43.27 SP 45.16

WASHED MO 4.41 17.9 SP 52.24
  WM 64.30 DV 169.19 170.8

WASHED (CONT.) 170.26 178.7
  178.19 179.9 SS 202.35
  SC 268.36 OC 299.28 299.33
  FA 468.11 470.42 PR 474.35
  502.22 WR 553.41 576.39
  576.40 JD 617.20 622.12
  ML 734.1 734.11 743.22

WASHERWOMEN BO 595.5

WASHHAND TF 125.36

WASH-HOUSES BO 595.4

WASHING MO 9.36 SP 45.15
  DV 170.5 170.18 170.27
  WS 249.8 MN 366.32 YT 397.11
  JD 617.11 617.22 617.24
  622.10 622.12

WASHINGTON MD 814.9

WASHSTAND PP 435.9

WASH-TUB SP 45.18

WASTE EA 82.1 BL 347.36
  ML 746.30 OV 755.6 757.27
  RR 785.42

WASTED PO 104.2 FG 191.5
  OC 286.25 ML 735.13 OV 757.25

WASTER EE 311.26 311.27 311.32

WASTES MO 2.16

WASTREL WR 546.5

WATCH MO 1.30 OA 23.15
  FG 189.18 SB 214.8 SG 221.6
  GF 238.6 OC 287.13 WP 387.23
  391.28 YT 401.10 401.13
  401.20 401.22 PP 428.35
  438.33 HD 441.21 456.22
  PR 510.6 SU 534.29 WR 551.13
  GG 695.28 RR 785.12 BM 830.2
  831.19

WATCH-CHAIN PP 428.28

WATCHES WR 571.17

WATCHFUL TF 124.29 TP 344.6
  YT 395.34 SD 411.14 411.28
  417.9 PP 432.39 WR 560.33
  BO 596.32 GG 674.35 ML 726.10

WATCHFULNESS PR 490.39

WATCHWORD TH 847.37

WATER MO 4.7 6.5 22.17
  OA 36.31 37.22 37.34 WM 58.38
  EA 81.29 82.5 PO 105.24
  105.28 107.1 108.3 114.11
  114.23 TF 118.36 119.16
  119.19 119.27 120.36 121.30
  125.35 128.26 131.37
  DV 166.15 166.30 167.6 170.3
  170.25 170.37 170.40 182.6
  FG 187.8 190.21 190.41 194.42
  SS 200.4 202.5 204.23 210.4
  SB 216.41 SG 225.14 GF 241.16
  241.33 WS 244.30 249.9 249.14

WATER (CONT.) 258.4 CH 280.1
  281.23 OC 297.28 299.25
  EE 307.12 312.38 312.39
  315.27 316.24 319.1
  MN 376.5 YT 398.8 400.18
  PP 432.21 HD 448.2 449.39
  449.42 450.1 450.9 450.10
  450.12 450.14 450.16
  450.21 450.25 450.28
  450.32 450.35 450.40
  451.29 454.6 454.25
  PR 481.40 484.9 487.8
  487.10 487.12 487.42
  495.35 499.26 500.2 501.6
  501.10 501.15 501.24
  501.34 501.35 502.41
  505.8 506.30 TB 525.5
  SU 529.13 WR 551.10 551.19
  552.2 552.8 554.29 556.18
  556.35 557.1 561.20 561.28
  564.29 565.5 573.36 576.40
  BO 595.7 599.30 602.40
  JD 617.3 617.9 ML 735.17
  741.12 OV 749.1 750.2
  750.35 755.27 LL 766.6
  TH 850.35

WATER-BUTT ML 741.13

WATER-COLOURS MO 6.17
  SS 203.3 GG 670.7

WATERED WR 561.20

WATER-EWERS GF 241.19

WATER-FLOWERS EE 326.33

WATER-MEADOWS BO 599.39

WATER-PIPES MD 823.8

WATERPROOF TP 336.16

WATERS MO 2.26 17.14 19.30
  CH 281.9 EE 313.10
  WP 387.20 PR 490.6
  ML 724.36 734.5 743.32

WATER'S TF 122.2 PR 501.17
  BO 595.6

WATER-TOSSED ML 740.14

WATERY WR 577.5 ML 735.18

WATMORE PP 429.5

WATTER SC 268.32

WATTLES WR 579.17

WAVE OA 26.12 HT 44.6
  SP 48.35 WS 244.17
  FA 467.37 WR 551.14

WAVED SB 216.2 SG 228.20
  WP 379.21 SU 528.33
  BO 597.28

WAVER OA 30.15

WAVERED MO 4.5 EA 73.14
  TF 128.13 BL 354.21
  SD 417.26 TB 520.20

WAVERING SD 419.9 PP 438.9
   TB 520.20 WR 558.13

WAVES MO 3.1 EA 76.4 83.15
   TP 336.7 ML 745.33

WAVING OA 23.16 SP 45.20
   WM 56.7 70.17 TF 123.2
   GF 238.26 FA 458.18 PR 490.35
   499.33 TB 522.10 LA 630.28
   RH 793.4 796.12 TH 845.5
   845.6

WAX BM 828.6 832.11

WAXED SG 226.20

WAYNE, DOCTOR (SEE DOCTOR WAYNE)

WAY-OFF WR 574.42

WAYS OA 23.35 DV 143.39 143.40
   156.12 162.20 SB 218.8
   OC 294.34 295.2 EE 305.19
   321.3 MN 377.4 YT 396.6
   ML 723.12 RR 782.8 BM 829.3
   832.19

WAYSIDE MO 1.21 HT 39.24
   SG 224.14 FA 458.8

WAYWARD EE 322.15

WAYWARDLY MO 16.28

WEAK EA 89.26 PO 103.25
   TF 131.32 DV 154.2 WS 258.3
   EE 311.37 311.39 MN 368.16
   370.19 YT 400.25 HD 448.28
   WR 571.21 BO 604.21 GG 679.3
   ML 744.33 745.13 LL 767.16
   768.12 MD 806.32 807.8

WEAKENED SC 271.5 LL 778.33

WEAKENING CH 280.30 LL 775.17

WEAKER TF 120.22

WEAK-HEADED FA 465.5

WEAKLY IL 657.2 LL 767.22

WEAKNESS WS 248.14 BL 357.8
   357.13 359.29 359.35 364.21
   BO 601.38 602.7

WEAL FG 193.27

WEALTH GF 235.6 SU 531.11
   JD 607.15 607.16 NT 701.3
   OV 753.32

WEALTHY PR 473.25 MD 814.8
   818.39

WEAPON EE 311.2 324.30 326.6

WEAPON-LIKE EE 324.38

WEAPONS SS 208.33

WEAR MO 20.35 WS 246.12 248.26
   EE 326.7 326.9 WP 389.18
   NT 705.25 709.27 ML 724.9

WEAR (CONT.) OV 757.19
   MD 808.19 814.30

WEARER WS 246.12 248.26

WEARIED OC 289.29 293.24
   BL 348.20

WEARILY WM 65.22 EA 84.29
   DV 171.35 172.13 BL 361.23
   PP 434.16 PR 495.31 WR 557.20
   SM 582.4 RR 788.35 RH 801.33

WEARINESS MO 22.4 GF 234.9
   240.8 WS 265.7 OC 300.9
   BL 347.32 359.9 WR 553.12
   554.35 556.22 560.19 578.40
   BO 595.17 GG 666.26

WEARING TF 133.22 DV 159.2
   WS 260.36 260.37 262.12
   MN 376.23 WP 379.22 388.29
   PR 476.27 483.41 TB 524.16
   SU 532.25 WR 551.7 562.23
   568.32 569.9 BO 600.15 603.32
   JD 616.24 GG 665.28 668.38
   MD 823.24

WEARISOME OA 32.16

WEARS WR 574.30 LL 761.9

WEARY MO 14.18 15.3 WM 67.3
   69.13 GF 234.3 235.17
   YT 402.17 SU 531.3 WR 553.1
   554.20 555.37 556.40 559.12
   560.21 BO 588.6 595.18 599.7
   599.9 JD 610.18 LA 630.16
   630.29 GG 666.27 671.31
   674.41 694.19 LL 761.24

WEATHER WM 62.34 BL 354.6
   362.10 MN 366.9 WP 389.15
   SD 412.14 WR 549.17 IL 653.15
   655.14 ML 726.40 729.24
   734.10 735.10 740.6 741.11
   743.40 LL 772.28

WEATHERED TP 336.15

WEATHER-REDDENED DV 172.33
   PP 433.23

WEAVE OV 757.27 758.20 758.22

WEAVING MO 9.37

WEB GF 235.4

WED SC 269.12

WEDDING DV 155.10 WS 260.25
   FA 464.5 IL 648.15 GG 679.21
   OV 749.25 LL 777.38

WEDDING-RING EA 72.4

WEDGED FA 465.14 GG 662.25

WEDLOCK HT 40.34

WEDNESDAY SP 45.2 45.16
   SC 270.12 WP 389.6 389.7
   389.17 HD 444.3 444.28 445.17
   MD 825.32

WE'D WS 243.5 255.42
   HD 445.12 PR 505.21
   IL 655.16 MD 817.38
   818.1 TH 853.3

WEE BO 587.28

WEEDING ML 726.42

WEEK MO 7.1 HT 39.12 44.17
   SP 46.36 52.17 52.26
   DV 168.26 177.4 SC 270.10
   270.12 OC 289.21 294.39
   EE 308.19 308.38 319.25
   325.10 325.11 MN 370.21
   WP 381.4 381.35 383.14
   391.33 HD 443.32 WR 554.33
   567.10 GG 664.26 680.41
   ML 740.5 OV 747.30 754.37
   LL 777.30 RR 781.41
   RH 794.4 MD 825.31

WEEK-END EE 328.39 329.5
   IL 647.2

WEEK-ENDING JD 607.17

WEEKLY TF 117.19

WEEKS HT 39.17 DV 138.11
   WS 259.36 SC 269.18 270.5
   EE 322.3 327.25 WP 381.39
   SU 532.17 WR 567.42
   BO 602.36 ML 730.38 739.4
   MD 824.39 824.42

WEEK'S PO 100.34 FA 471.31
   471.33

WEEKS' BL 348.22

WEEP OC 301.40 WP 381.10
   383.39 384.14 YT 401.27
   SM 584.19 584.29 BO 590.37
   GG 690.15 ML 739.28
   OV 759.14

WEEPETH FA 466.30

WEEPING OA 37.25 FG 195.30
   SC 272.28 OC 299.19
   LA 646.5 ML 738.22

WEEPING-WILLOW JD 628.13
   628.15

WEIGH HT 40.9* FA 460.14

WEIGHED BO 601.35

WEIGHING PR 503.19 SM 582.9

WEIGHT OA 35.1 38.11
   PO 110.19 113.8 TF 127.5
   DV 156.21 157.15 171.2
   SB 214.12 WS 244.26 245.33
   OC 299.40 EE 331.36
   BL 363.8 MN 378.31
   SD 420.37 PP 439.39
   PR 501.12 WR 574.13
   SM 582.8 BO 591.31
   IL 647.31 GG 666.2 686.18
   699.2 OV 753.5 LL 771.2

WEIGHTED PO 107.23

WEIGHTING DV 138.13 FG 187.10

WEIRD MO 1.20 SS 206.27
  FA 467.32 WR 576.38 577.16
  BO 588.26 599.2 602.8
  JD 609.20 610.3 610.5 624.26
  LA 646.1 646.26 LL 763.6
  763.9 763.42 769.42

WEIRDER FA 465.8

WEIRDEST LA 632.23

WEIRDLY LA 639.4 LL 767.35

WELCOME MO 4.11 12.17 WM 55.42
  GF 235.35 WS 251.34 OC 293.13
  FA 458.20 JD 609.24 628.31
  GG 671.12

WELCOMED FA 465.11 TH 851.27

WELCOMING WM 58.6

WELFARE EA 92.4 DV 144.12

WELL-ARRANGED MD 812.4

WELL-BALANCED MN 369.40
  GG 676.25

WELL-BEING HT 43.18 PO 100.34
  DV 154.38 WS 244.30 GG 683.24

WELL-BORN MD 815.13

WELL-BRED EE 326.37 LL 771.38

WELL-BUILT MO 3.36 WS 250.36
  254.16 TP 339.32 YT 398.11
  SD 411.15

WELL-COLOURED SD 413.39

WELL-CUT SD 417.38 PR 484.40

WELL-DOING DV 146.33

WELL-DRAWN SD 412.27 413.29

WELL-DRESSED PP 427.19 TB 517.23

WELLED SD 415.12

WELL-EDUCATED PR 479.25

WELL-FAVOURED SG 222.33
  CH 276.23

WELL-FITTING SD 417.39

WELL-FLESHED PP 427.17

WELL-GROOMED WS 250.24

WELLINGTON NEW ZEALAND PP 431.12

WELL-KNOWN OA 32.5 GG 661.8
  NT 719.32

WELL-LOOKING OA 23.9

WELL-MADE FA 458.31 PR 485.10

WELL-PRESERVED GG 670.15

WELL-SET HD 441.30

WELL-SHAPEN SD 423.39 PR 482.28

WELL-TEMPERED HD 442.35

WELL-TO-DO SC 272.12 CH 278.19
  SD 417.40 PP 430.11 OV 748.30

WELLWOOD'S SC 269.12

WELL-WORN WR 561.9

WE'N SP 48.23 48.28 CH 279.11
  279.15

WENCH WP 388.39

WENN ICH ZU MEINEM KINDE GEH +
  TF 129.17

WENTWORTH SP 45.10

WENTWORTH'S HT 39.16

WEPT DV 161.36 FG 191.25 191.37
  191.42 192.32 193.10
  GF 239.18 WS 265.20 OC 294.1
  296.12 TP 339.23 YT 396.29
  409.37 SD 419.23 LA 646.7
  ML 739.19 742.38 742.39
  OV 755.4

WEREN'T MO 17.31 OA 28.26
  LA 645.31 IL 653.12 GG 692.26
  BM 840.34

WERE-WOLF TB 522.30

WE'RE MO 12.40 12.41 16.40
  17.1 SP 48.5 WM 67.39
  DV 137.9 142.26 171.25
  GF 237.32 CH 279.12 280.3
  OC 294.9 EE 320.29 TP 335.3
  335.4 341.32 BL 352.5 358.3
  358.4 361.10 361.22 364.26
  364.27 SD 415.33 419.4
  FA 457.3 JD 620.14 IL 653.14
  654.28 GG 678.8 681.18 688.22
  690.4 ML 731.14 731.15
  RR 786.18 RH 791.32 795.6
  795.26 796.38 796.39 796.40
  797.27 797.32 BM 839.42
  TH 849.21

WERNHAM BL 347.19 360.37 362.19

WERNHAM (SEE MRS. WERNHAM)

WERNHAMS BL 347.11

WESH SC 268.19

WESHIN' SC 268.22

WESLEY, JOHN (SEE JOHN WESLEY)

WESLEYAN CHAPEL SP 46.16

WEST MO 3.6 WM 54.29 60.33
  PO 96.11 DV 136.13 167.19
  WP 385.29 PR 481.14 481.15
  487.16 496.15 496.18 497.26
  497.40 WR 546.6 556.17
  IL 651.1 TH 850.29 851.2

WEST (CONT.) 851.18 851.19

WEST CORNISH SD 411.23

WEST CROYDON WM 59.24 59.35
  59.39

WESTERN PR 497.38 498.24
  ML 738.22 BM 835.30
  TH 846.18

WESTWARDS PR 481.15

WET MO 4.9 19.22 OA 27.4
  PO 105.30 106.1 115.28
  DV 148.34 159.14 181.13
  FG 195.35 WS 249.39 259.18
  OC 284.24 299.19 TP 336.12
  336.18 BL 351.36 356.31
  362.9 SD 413.19 PP 431.4
  432.21 432.25 436.6 437.27
  438.20 HD 450.4 450.38
  452.22 453.7 453.10 454.15
  456.18 FA 465.25 SU 528.23
  BO 599.7 JD 617.17
  GG 674.11 674.25 ML 723.35
  723.36 738.22 738.26
  745.34 BM 841.20

WETTED WP 386.32

WETTING FG 191.38 195.34
  HD 454.13 SU 528.23

WE'VE MO 9.38 9.39 HT 43.1
  WM 55.25 DV 141.19
  SS 201.35 WS 256.34
  CH 274.32 TP 341.33
  BL 356.33 365.1 WP 381.38
  381.42 PP 437.36
  HD 444.28 FA 469.7
  PR 492.30 505.15 JD 625.28
  GG 667.38 688.22 690.4
  690.5 690.8 RH 795.6
  MD 817.42 BM 839.36
  TH 845.27

WHA-AT MN 369.14

WHACK WR 556.14

WHALE GG 698.42 NT 701.23
  702.32

WHALEBONE TB 521.9

WHAT'D PR 511.42

WHATEVER MO 17.19 OA 31.24
  EA 92.24 92.25 PO 103.32
  DV 155.29 161.32 168.14
  GF 240.38 WS 260.3
  SC 272.21 273.17 OC 293.34
  295.14 EE 315.25 321.30
  PR 508.29 TB 526.37
  WR 559.32 JD 609.24
  LA 643.9 ML 739.1
  RR 780.40 RH 803.16
  TH 852.9

WHATEVER'S NT 717.6

WHATIVER HT 42.42

WHAT'LL CH 275.3 OC 294.24

WHAT'LL (CONT.) YT 401.15

WHAT'RE MN 374.26

WHATSOEVER EE 308.15 SD 425.1
  PP 433.11 BO 598.9

WHAT'S MO 21.1 HT 42.4 SP 47.5
  WM 66.21 DV 141.2 168.34
  175.26 FG 188.1 SB 212.24
  215.39 218.15 SG 228.34 230.7
  230.17 GF 236.39 237.3
  WS 248.33 259.12 259.16
  SC 270.31 CH 276.22 282.10
  OC 285.20 298.11 298.26
  EE 319.9 MN 368.17 371.3
  374.29 375.7 375.24 375.39
  WP 389.26 389.27 YT 401.11
  HD 444.26 446.11 FA 469.26
  470.27 TB 515.11 519.17 524.1
  JD 621.4 LA 639.12 644.27
  645.15 IL 655.2 655.10 655.31
  655.34 655.39 657.40
  GG 663.37 672.26 673.23
  687.12 691.30 NT 718.11
  RH 793.42 795.4 795.38
  BM 841.39

WHEAT PO 114.26 SB 214.1 219.20
  SU 542.29

WHEEDLE PR 507.4

WHEEDLING SD 420.3 BM 840.31

WHEEL OA 28.23 MN 372.3 372.38
  WR 561.27 BO 601.25

WHEELED JD 613.28 ML 741.23

WHEEL-FANS JD 608.20

WHEELING MO 2.25 PO 95.35
  MN 372.1

WHEELS OA 28.24 OC 283.22
  BL 347.2 TB 513.33 BO 593.10

WHEER HT 40.8 41.39 43.41
  SP 51.24 OC 292.16 297.8
  WP 389.21 FA 462.7

WHEER'S HT 41.38 WP 388.25

WHENCE DV 176.39 OC 290.38
  YT 398.6 FA 470.28 PR 495.42
  SU 544.6

WHENEVER MO 4.11 TF 120.14
  EE 308.10 TP 339.2 JD 615.26
  NT 706.19 716.11 OV 754.6

WHEN'S LL 777.38

WHEREABOUTS OA 30.33 TP 342.5
  SD 419.11

WHEREAS PO 98.21 106.7
  DV 164.11 OC 301.4 BL 364.23
  TB 513.36 BO 593.14 GG 661.31
  663.42 683.30 ML 735.34
  LL 764.15 RR 782.17 MD 806.4
  BM 832.31

WHEREIN EA 90.3 DV 181.30

WHEREIN (CONT.) FG 191.2

WHEREON BM 833.33

WHERE'S OA 25.13 25.17
  FG 188.29 MN 376.42 377.10
  PP 432.3 HD 446.15 PR 500.33
  NT 718.30 RH 795.25 797.11

WHEREUPON SP 53.20 FG 193.42
  BO 588.38

WHEREVER FA 463.33 PR 475.5
  SU 543.21 JD 627.20 GG 681.12
  ML 739.26 RR 788.40

WHETHER SS 205.18 WS 262.11
  OC 296.24 EE 310.40 328.4
  YT 394.21 394.22 SD 417.30
  419.19 PR 507.3 TB 518.34
  518.36 SU 536.36 LA 643.2
  GG 667.4 667.24 687.30 689.18
  NT 704.13 717.8 717.9
  ML 727.30 735.29 LL 769.38

WHEW PR 512.5

WHILST OA 25.1 SP 49.36
  EA 82.20 83.8 TF 125.26
  DV 137.3 146.41 147.16 164.17
  173.39 176.13 180.25 181.3
  181.21 FG 188.7 188.24
  SG 232.41 WS 252.26 254.7
  255.40 257.8 OC 298.19
  EE 307.31 TP 337.33 BL 364.14
  MN 366.30 374.19 WP 386.30
  YT 395.6 397.5 SD 425.31
  HD 449.32 RR 787.29 BM 835.11

WHIMPERED EE 317.30 318.13

WHIMPERING DV 161.30 CH 279.37
  OC 299.13 BO 602.27

WHIMPERS DV 161.37

WHIMSEY OC 283.17

WHIMSICAL MO 16.29 17.31
  OA 34.20 TF 133.23 DV 174.29
  SB 212.9 212.19 MN 374.13
  TB 514.30 514.31 522.14
  ML 727.1 MD 813.38

WHIMSICALLY MO 11.2 WM 62.20
  TB 517.28

WHINED TF 123.16

WHIP TF 121.13 NT 704.23
  RH 793.14

WHIPPED TF 127.39

WHIPS OC 284.21

WHIRL LA 638.2 638.5 639.7
  OV 755.23

WHIRLED PP 436.8

WHIRLING FG 193.41 GF 238.25
  LA 638.3 638.6 638.23 639.8
  639.22 639.31 639.32 639.37

WHIRR EA 80.2 OC 293.19
  PP 429.11 436.9

WHISKED WS 249.7

WHISKERS WS 250.37 251.39
  CH 274.24 TH 853.6

WHISKIES GG 688.26

WHISKY EA 75.30 HD 451.20
  PR 500.29 500.33 501.37
  JD 629.13 GG 676.7 688.24
  ML 739.9 RH 802.37

WHISKY-AND-SODA MD 824.1

WHISKY-BOTTLES PP 433.22

WHISKY-DRINKER YT 395.16

WHISPER TF 122.36 PR 481.10
  GG 665.26 LL 767.30 767.41
  769.7 774.38 775.5
  RH 791.23 791.25 798.17
  BM 841.26 841.36

WHISPERED MO 10.1 OA 34.28
  EA 91.13 DV 175.3
  FG 191.35 WS 257.42
  259.23 OC 299.8 300.3
  YT 399.34 PP 435.15
  SM 586.8 BO 604.27 LL 774.9
  RH 804.14 BM 838.31

WHISPERING OA 34.32 EA 93.3
  DV 174.17 SD 414.4
  ML 740.42 OV 755.32
  LL 775.11 RH 791.10 791.16
  798.14 798.15 798.16
  799.8 BM 841.41

WHISPERINGLY LL 774.2

WHISPERS RH 798.23

WHIST WS 253.1

WHISTLE WS 244.31 OC 297.33
  HD 444.15 JD 616.20

WHISTLED FG 189.36 GF 241.7
  OC 283.26 MN 376.37
  PR 496.32 LA 638.36

WHISTLING PO 113.2 FG 189.38
  EE 331.8 331.19 MN 376.39
  HD 442.21 TB 520.28
  WR 572.23 LA 638.15 638.18
  640.32 ML 734.3

WHISTON WS 244.3 244.6
  244.24 245.10 246.15
  248.32 250.16 251.1
  251.5 251.12 251.15 252.40
  253.13 253.21 253.32
  253.36 255.22 255.28
  255.39 255.40 256.1 256.4
  256.9 256.18 256.39 257.10
  257.22 258.6 258.8 259.36
  260.6 260.26 261.1 263.39

WHISTON (SEE MR. WHISTON;
  MRS. WHISTON)

WHITE   MO 2.2   2.12   9.33   13.41
   22.30   OA 23.12   24.14   24.36
   25.9   26.13   26.26   28.32   29.2
   29.9   29.30   29.32   35.33   36.1
   37.21   SP 45.19   46.23   48.9
   49.10   WM 55.15   55.18   55.40
   58.12   58.14   58.16   58.39   59.3
   62.12   67.4   68.6   68.22   68.33
   69.1   69.3   69.7   69.14
   EA 72.23   81.22   81.28   84.13
   PO 95.2   107.5   109.35   111.17
   113.9   113.11   114.7   115.8
   115.11   115.33   116.18
   TF 118.40   122.9   123.6   125.36
   126.21   DV 138.38   141.40   143.4
   148.39   149.8   149.14   149.25
   157.31   158.17   158.39   161.5
   161.9   161.23   167.25   169.40
   170.22   171.3   171.9   173.12
   178.29   179.36   180.14
   FG 194.23   196.17   SS 197.7
   198.30   203.1   203.29   206.40
   207.4   210.31   SB 213.42   214.5
   217.7   217.15   217.32   SG 222.3
   224.7   224.18   225.39   225.40
   226.5   226.10   231.9   232.26
   232.33   GF 234.20   234.31
   WS 244.11   245.27   245.31
   245.32   247.3   247.13   248.10
   251.31   253.30   257.38   257.39
   260.5   260.25   261.10   261.19
   262.18   263.7   263.22   264.26
   SC 267.31   268.6   268.7   268.26
   270.21   272.20   CH 275.21
   275.25   275.34   276.4   276.34
   277.38   282.6   OC 284.6   286.14
   286.18   290.38   300.11   300.13
   EE 303.13   303.34   309.6   312.6
   314.33   314.36   315.13   317.23
   322.9   323.1   323.32   324.25
   326.4   326.33   330.29   TP 344.1
   BL 351.4   351.40   358.33
   MN 366.29   366.30   371.37
   376.17   378.25   WP 379.22
   385.30   386.9   387.21   387.22
   YT 403.8   409.16   SD 412.3
   PP 433.23   434.9   434.26
   HD 445.42   447.42   456.3
   FA 467.19   PR 482.18   482.24
   485.2   485.21   485.29   491.10
   496.37   506.26   507.40   508.4
   508.8   TB 520.35   521.22
   SU 529.33   530.24   530.30
   530.36   532.36   533.8   533.41
   534.6   534.41   542.30   543.5
   544.20   WR 548.16   548.17   551.8
   552.34   552.39   552.40   555.19
   555.26   555.38   557.9   558.2
   559.4   559.10   559.39   560.12
   560.13   560.16   560.20   560.22
   561.21   561.33   561.37   562.24
   562.26   562.29   563.6   563.10
   563.11   563.13   563.28   563.31
   564.2   564.21   569.1   569.38
   570.16   570.23   570.35   570.37
   570.39   571.20   571.22   571.28
   571.29   571.31   571.32   571.36
   573.30   574.11   574.37   575.3
   575.8   575.10   575.13   575.15
   575.16   575.18   575.19   575.23
   575.24   575.27   575.35   575.37
   576.18   576.39   576.41   577.6
   577.9   577.40   578.5   578.30
   SM 583.4   583.17   583.26   583.28
   583.35   585.11   586.16

WHITE (CONT.)   BO 594.10   596.4
   600.21   600.22   LA 630.3
   631.32   633.11   635.30
   639.38   640.17   640.34   645.42
   646.17   IL 648.33   GG 669.34
   670.13   670.34   671.28   674.1
   674.4   674.16   675.6   677.16
   681.15   688.14   689.15   694.11
   694.12   694.25   694.35   695.15
   695.18   696.33   NT 705.26
   707.21   707.36   709.28   709.30
   710.2   712.37   719.23   720.11
   ML 723.13   723.31   724.9   725.22
   725.25   726.39   728.29   732.22
   737.15   741.30   743.29   744.21
   744.23   744.26   745.1   745.19
   745.24   746.7   746.27   OV 747.3
   747.6   748.17   748.42   749.11
   749.33   750.12   751.23   753.10
   758.13   759.41   LL 775.31
   775.35   RR 783.32   784.25
   788.22   RH 802.35   MD 809.16
   818.36   819.42   820.4   820.29
   821.29   822.9   822.25   824.3
   825.9   BM 829.17   829.20   829.27
   832.42   835.17   835.24   835.26
   836.21   840.18   840.39

WHITE-AND-BLACK   WP 385.40

WHITE-AND-GLAZED   EA 81.20

WHITE-AND-PEARL-ENAMELLED
   TH 851.5

WHITE-BEARDED   OC 297.9

WHITE-BREASTING   MO 1.16

WHITE BULL   SP 48.3

WHITE-CLAD   OA 33.5

WHITE-FLANNELLED   OA 27.29

WHITE-HAIRED   PR 479.29   WR 564.8
   GG 670.7   BM 829.16   837.38

WHITE-HOT   MO 16.35   TF 120.13
   GF 238.20   WS 259.28   259.30
   263.12   TH 853.13

WHITENED   OA 30.12   TF 117.1
   DV 161.8   176.28   BO 602.32

WHITENESS   WM 59.15   DV 171.4
   FG 193.22   WP 385.34   385.39
   WR 558.1   569.24   ML 723.14
   744.19   744.24   746.30

WHITER   DV 160.27

WHITES   PO 110.34   DV 179.10
   SC 268.11   268.24   PR 496.11
   BO 604.24   JD 616.32

WHITE-SCRUBBED   SD 412.2

WHITE-SKINNED   EE 304.25
   BO 600.13   NT 719.28

WHITE-SOULED   NT 719.28

WHITEST   MO 17.10

WHITE-TOWERED   PO 111.35

WHITE-WASH   LA 630.14   630.21

WHITEWASHED   ML 722.29
   RR 779.29

WHITE-WASHED   DV 166.28
   WR 559.4

WHITEY   EA 84.11

WHITHER   EA 80.2   DV 160.29
   SG 228.16   EE 331.17   331.18

WHITISH   EE 330.25   JD 616.37
   GG 671.4

WHITTLE   YT 405.20   405.22
   408.28

WHITTLE   (SEE MR. WHITTLE)

WHITTLE'S   YT 406.4

WHITY-GREEN   PO 105.19   107.1
   SB 213.8

WHOA   MN 367.5   370.5   378.2

WHOAM   SC 269.23   OC 292.14
   WP 389.5   389.6

WHO'D   PR 512.14

WHOEVER   SD 416.25   GG 696.27

WHOLE   MO 4.13   17.13   SP 49.23
   WM 69.25   69.39   EA 82.38
   PO 96.34   103.15   110.20
   112.15   115.8   115.12
   TF 127.18   130.6   130.21
   134.1   DV 136.27   138.14
   154.37   155.25   161.23
   174.22   179.40   SG 226.31
   232.30   CH 275.19   280.26
   EE 323.12   325.23   325.37
   326.22   BL 347.25   347.36
   356.8   358.9   WP 385.42
   YT 394.2   407.3   SD 411.26
   419.5   PP 429.32   HD 448.27
   453.34   FA 459.3   470.15
   PR 473.7   500.21   TB 513.33
   519.41   522.35   SU 531.39
   532.7   537.13   WR 558.25
   578.31   580.8   BO 591.5
   591.8   LA 640.16   GG 683.40
   NT 707.26   717.30   ML 729.6
   742.19   OV 750.15   750.19
   750.20   LL 774.37   RH 799.37
   800.7   MD 808.41   815.8
   816.30   820.11   BM 835.26
   835.40   840.31   TH 846.25

WHOLESALE   GG 686.21

WHOLESOME   DV 143.31

WHOLLY   MO 3.34   YT 407.1

WHO'LL   JD 621.20

WHOOING   EE 329.26

WHOOP   FG 189.36

WHOOPED FG 189.41

WHOOPING TP 338.20

WHOOPING-COUGH MO 17.34

WHO'RE TP 341.22

WHO'S MO 17.32 HT 43.8 SP 48.28
  SB 215.33 WS 246.25 SC 271.17
  TP 339.34 MN 369.3 375.29
  SD 412.38 JD 621.27 LA 632.5
  GG 689.8

WHO-THE-DEVIL-ARE-YOU MD 809.3

WHY-Y PR 491.23

WI' HT 42.3 SP 47.13 50.7
  SB 218.15 219.41 WS 261.10
  262.30 SC 268.32 271.12
  CH 276.29 OC 294.20 295.4
  BL 352.20 WP 388.27 388.38
  389.15 PP 431.32 440.16
  HD 443.22 445.10 FA 469.29

WICK MO 18.10 OC 288.36

WICKED OA 27.9 FG 188.25
  EE 311.25 312.4 322.10 323.19
  325.27 BL 351.26 WR 575.23
  JD 606.32

WICKEDLY WM 57.19 MD 805.30
  822.36 826.25

WICKEDNESS CH 281.13 SU 539.18
  BO 594.1

WICKER SG 224.27 TB 521.24

WICKET OV 755.35 756.9

WIDE MO 1.2 2.6 22.5 OA 30.15
  WM 69.21 EA 76.1 92.28
  PO 95.4 DV 161.23 FG 192.22
  SS 199.26 199.37 208.31
  WS 251.38 SC 267.21 CH 275.23
  OC 283.26 EE 304.7 304.11
  305.3 BL 351.31 MN 376.24
  WP 387.24 SD 414.29 422.21
  423.22 PP 430.31 435.38
  HD 451.13 453.40 456.35
  PR 473.27 474.14 474.17
  475.10 484.7 484.40 488.36
  504.37 SU 534.16 536.36
  543.17 WR 551.25 558.35
  568.29 568.30 JD 617.25 625.9
  625.17 IL 654.38 GG 661.27
  662.16 ML 724.6 RR 780.19
  RH 793.10 BM 842.41 TH 846.25

WIDEAWAKE DV 138.37

WIDE-EYED SD 421.41

WIDELY MN 373.34

WIDENED TP 344.24 PR 505.19

WIDE-OPEN PR 473.10

WIDER PR 474.18

WIDE-STARING WS 264.17

WIDOW SP 51.16 WM 55.28 57.10
  DV 163.29 OC 295.41 ML 733.10
  733.22 734.24 734.27 734.29
  RR 781.14 BM 836.9

WIDOWED ML 738.40

WIDOWER PP 430.21 ML 725.36
  MD 818.35

WIDOW'S ML 735.2 736.16

WIDTH MO 22.26 HT 39.27
  SG 233.10

WIFE MO 13.28 13.31 14.18
  14.35 14.37 OA 31.42 32.5
  32.7 32.38 HT 39.1 39.6
  39.12 39.15 39.22 40.27 41.9
  42.35 43.9 43.14 43.17
  SP 51.14 51.20 52.1 52.16
  52.31 WM 64.38 EA 71.13 72.13
  77.39 87.41 91.32 92.21
  93.13 DV 136.25 137.25 152.6
  155.4 156.24 157.12 157.29
  184.11 184.12 SS 201.18
  SG 221.28 222.25 231.8
  WS 244.6 SC 269.25 272.27
  272.32 272.37 OC 292.40 299.3
  299.39 301.26 EE 305.25
  305.28 308.27 310.1 310.10
  317.39 322.27 327.41 328.17
  328.21 TP 337.6 BL 347.25
  348.1 349.36 349.38 349.42
  350.8 355.40 MN 366.32
  WP 384.3 384.8 384.20 388.7
  390.9 391.6 391.17 392.6
  393.6 SD 423.20 423.27
  PP 429.30 429.33 430.4 430.6
  430.9 430.12 430.18 430.20
  434.15 434.27 437.42
  PR 476.42 TB 513.3 513.13
  513.28 513.36 514.6 514.42
  515.12 515.38 516.18 516.29
  516.30 516.31 517.8 518.9
  518.14 518.30 518.35 518.36
  518.39 519.7 520.1 521.34
  521.39 522.2 522.21 522.22
  522.40 523.7 523.15 523.20
  523.26 523.29 523.35 524.1
  524.5 524.15 524.19 524.34
  524.39 525.4 525.7 525.16
  525.22 526.13 526.27 526.31
  527.5 527.12 527.17 527.25
  SU 539.21 542.29 542.38 543.6
  543.28 543.33 544.12 544.21
  WR 547.26 548.19 548.23
  548.24 SM 584.23 JD 605.5
  605.16 613.10 617.9 617.19
  617.36 618.10 620.17 620.31
  621.1 621.2 621.15 621.20
  621.23 621.30 621.36 622.16
  622.37 623.6 626.28 627.4
  627.35 GG 663.24 678.15
  678.18 678.41 679.13 679.17
  679.23 679.38 680.12 680.28
  681.1 681.7 690.27 692.18
  692.38 694.28 ML 725.28
  725.31 726.12 731.11 733.9
  733.22 OV 747.1 747.5 749.9
  750.1 750.3 750.8 754.15
  754.17 757.4 757.17 757.22
  757.34 757.42 RR 779.7 780.13
  782.32 MD 806.7 820.31
  BM 832.7 832.9 834.15 835.13

WIFE (CONT.) 835.38 838.5
  838.13 839.9 839.34 839.37
  840.2 841.14 841.25

WIFEHOOD EE 309.32

WIFE'LL HT 40.16

WIFE'S OA 37.30 SP 52.25
  EA 86.27 DV 156.39
  WS 260.19 BL 354.36
  PP 435.24 WR 547.16
  SM 583.36 BO 604.33

WILD MO 3.2 7.11 16.15
  18.32 19.34 OA 24.33
  25.11 26.8 27.2 36.17
  WM 61.39 EA 76.36 PO 98.10
  98.23 TF 120.8 123.24
  126.26 FG 187.10 190.22
  SS 206.27 206.31 209.30
  SB 213.15 SG 221.37
  GF 236.10 WS 249.1
  EE 305.1 309.8 324.22
  324.23 325.8 326.34 328.35
  328.38 TP 334.11 335.40
  338.20 343.12 343.16
  343.21 343.27 343.30
  BL 353.14 MN 371.17 373.18
  WP 383.22 386.16 387.18
  HD 452.29 453.10 PR 484.3
  486.20 487.42 488.1 494.10
  494.11 498.31 500.15
  501.29 503.37 SU 532.20
  532.21 535.7 535.9 538.23
  544.9 WR 549.1 549.12
  551.15 553.34 570.5 570.8
  572.38 578.14 579.17
  580.20 BO 589.33 596.35
  599.34 603.3 603.4
  JD 622.23 627.39 LA 631.5
  633.28 637.37 638.10
  638.18 639.8 639.17 640.2
  646.19 IL 651.13 GG 676.37
  687.23 NT 714.4 ML 723.21
  731.21 736.9 736.11 740.36
  OV 748.32 758.25 759.42
  RR 784.6 RH 796.7 MD 811.21

WILD-BLOODED JD 607.13

WILD-CAT OA 25.12

WILD-EYED RH 800.26

WILDFIRE TP 338.6

WILD-FOWL MO 22.19

WILD-GOOSE WM 67.17

WILDLY OA 24.33 PO 113.40
  FG 192.39 SG 231.30
  GF 237.39 TP 344.4
  FA 468.18 BO 604.8
  LA 642.19 IL 651.25
  RH 793.3

WILDNESS EE 303.15 PR 507.18
  SU 538.24 538.25

WILDS WR 546.8

WILFUL SB 212.25 JD 626.42

WILFULLY WM 57.13 SG 231.3
  BO 597.2 MD 811.26

WILFULNESS OA 26.12 SG 225.2

WILKIESON (SEE MRS. WILKIESON)

WILKIESONS PR 482.14 487.36
  488.2

WILLED EE 325.7 PR 504.17
  504.21 504.29 ML 736.36

WILLEY-WATER SS 199.6

WILLEY-WATER FARM SS 198.27

WILL-FORM YT 406.6

WILLIAM SD 421.36

WILLIAM, JOSEPH (SEE JOSEPH
  WILLIAM)

WILLIAM JAMES MO 6.31

WILLIAM MORRIS SS 210.14

WILLIAM SELBY GF 238.38 240.37

WILLIAM SELBY'S GF 238.40

WILLIE NANKERVIS SD 417.7

WILLIN' SP 48.25 50.8

WILLING MO 21.6 SP 50.23
  DV 183.32 SS 210.25 EE 329.4
  HD 442.30 JD 619.15 GG 663.40
  664.4 668.2 668.3 693.40
  ML 733.2 LL 766.41 MD 823.16
  823.21 823.26 824.10
  BM 828.22

WILLINGLY OA 36.42 EE 327.4

WILLINGNESS DV 172.26

WILL-LESS WR 568.8

WILLOW CH 281.9 YT 394.8 400.18
  WR 579.17 BO 599.6 IL 648.35
  651.25 652.32

WILLOWS SB 213.5 216.33
  IL 648.20

WILL-POWER PO 99.5 LL 761.20

WILL RENSHAW OV 748.22

WILLS GG 686.10 687.15

WILL SELBY GF 242.14

WILL-TO-POWER EE 314.22

WILL-TO-SUCCEED EE 314.12

WILLY HT 40.14 40.38 SC 269.13
  269.19 269.23 269.36 270.39
  271.11 272.3 272.5 272.17
  273.1 273.3

WILLY-NILLY EE 315.6

WILT WP 386.35

WILTING GG 666.30

WILTSHIRE IL 648.11 GG 699.41

WILY WR 549.9

WIN DV 157.42 EE 325.8
  ML 746.25 RH 804.15

WINCE MO 3.31 TP 344.21

WINCED WM 60.17 PO 98.42
  DV 177.42 SS 201.28 CH 279.29
  OC 285.13 302.15 TP 344.7
  WR 564.11 GG 695.6

WINCING WM 58.20 SG 230.11
  BL 349.9 SD 417.28 GG 667.10
  695.8

WIND MO 1.9 SP 45.20 TF 117.1
  119.1 122.35 FG 190.25 193.15
  194.31 194.34 194.35 SB 213.7
  SG 228.21 CH 274.30 EE 304.12
  310.24 320.37 331.21
  BL 352.36 353.9 356.19 361.13
  MN 377.41 378.5 WP 379.2
  379.11 379.14 380.5 382.16
  387.23 392.30 SD 411.4
  FA 467.31 PR 493.19 493.24
  496.15 496.23 496.31 498.2
  498.3 498.11 498.28 499.11
  499.17 499.23 509.40
  WR 556.20 568.39 568.40
  574.18 574.19 574.20 574.31
  575.8 575.32 BO 594.39 595.8
  598.17 JD 616.30 LA 638.1
  639.2 639.7 639.14 639.21
  639.30 639.37 639.39 639.42
  640.7 GG 685.31 695.17
  ML 723.37 727.8 728.22 728.25
  743.9 745.5 745.21 745.23
  745.39 745.42 746.1 746.20
  LL 766.25 MD 816.13

WINDBAG RR 783.15

WINDER HT 43.39

WINDFALL MD 806.35

WIND-FLOWERS ML 736.7

WIND-HARDENED SU 542.8

WINDING WM 68.2 SS 197.20
  199.39 200.1 OC 283.23 286.8
  PR 499.31 WR 559.6 578.20
  ML 733.14

WINDING-ENGINE OC 293.18 295.8

WINDING-ENGINES OC 287.20

WINDLESS EE 332.35 ML 744.27

WINDOW MO 3.12 4.18 OA 27.42
  29.23 29.28 29.32 29.37
  29.39 30.13 EA 72.3 72.18
  72.35 72.41 73.11 82.7
  TF 125.39 132.16 DV 157.8
  157.14 157.18 159.21
  FG 187.12 188.11 188.12

WINDOW (CONT.) 188.15 188.24
  189.16 SS 197.25 201.2
  203.27 207.21 210.18
  SG 221.1 221.36 222.1
  222.22 228.20 228.42 232.4
  GF 241.25 SC 270.12 271.27
  272.10 272.29 272.39
  CH 280.19 OC 291.15
  EE 306.39 BL 351.13
  YT 398.6 400.7 400.23
  404.9 405.11 PP 434.13
  435.4 437.8 437.27
  HD 444.8 WR 576.25
  BO 593.16 595.29 JD 627.9
  LA 639.38 641.30 643.28
  643.37 IL 652.35 ML 744.20
  745.2 LL 765.7 RR 779.23
  RH 803.8

WINDOW-BOTTOMS SS 203.1

WINDOW-DRESSING NT 716.1

WINDOW-FRAMES GF 241.29

WINDOWLESS PR 501.31
  WR 561.22 562.5

WINDOW-PANES BL 361.14

WINDOWS MO 4.39 PO 107.6
  TF 127.24 SG 221.26
  224.21 225.7 228.14
  OC 291.2 EE 304.37 306.25
  BL 351.10 358.19 WP 385.29
  386.13 LA 639.16 639.30
  644.35 GG 669.27 669.29
  684.39 699.10 ML 725.13
  LL 765.11 770.41 772.37
  MD 810.30 TH 847.42 848.11

WINDS SU 536.21 MD 805.28

WIND'S ML 735.5

WINDSWEPT TP 335.7

WINDY PR 509.25 ML 727.5

WINE MO 22.1 EA 92.8
  PO 97.28 101.41 WS 254.11
  255.40 SU 542.32 BO 594.3
  594.10 GG 674.1 674.30
  675.24 678.7 680.13
  OV 754.39 RR 779.2 786.30
  788.28

WINE-BOTTLE PO 97.23

WINE-GLASS GG 678.19

WINE-GLASSES GG 674.2

WINE-MERCHANT'S SS 208.16

WINES ML 725.14

WING OA 23.16 FG 194.17
  GG 670.40

WINGING WR 574.2

WINGLESS GG 698.9

WINGS PO 113.11 GF 238.26

WINGS (CONT.) WS 252.10
  BO 593.10 593.13 596.12
  LA 639.39 NT 712.20 712.22
  ML 741.29 741.39 742.2

WINIFRED WM 57.21 57.24 57.25
  57.32 57.36 57.41 59.7 59.10
  59.15 59.21 59.32 59.34
  59.40 60.10 60.38 64.21 65.2
  65.9 66.38 67.42 68.31 70.17
  70.20 EE 304.14 304.16 306.8
  306.38 307.33 308.7 309.14
  309.22 309.27 310.3 310.28
  310.32 310.33 310.36 310.39
  311.37 313.11 315.8 315.27
  315.34 316.22 316.38 317.5
  317.10 317.25 317.28 317.33
  317.36 318.1 318.7 318.14
  318.17 318.20 318.29 319.32
  320.9 320.10 320.39 321.9
  321.31 322.4 322.10 322.32
  322.34 323.13 323.24 324.17
  325.1 325.25 326.6 327.42
  328.16 328.31 329.3 329.9
  329.18 329.29 332.37 332.40

WINIFRED'S WM 59.29 EE 304.28
  305.3 305.6 305.21 308.31
  308.39 309.31 312.34 324.40
  329.27

WINIFRED VARLEY WM 58.5

WINK ML 746.31

WINKED LA 638.19

WINKING WS 246.8

WINNER RH 793.27 794.38 804.36

WINNIE EE 320.15 321.10 321.18
  PP 435.3 438.8

WINNIE'S EE 320.31

WINNING SG 224.42 WS 250.4
  EE 313.25 NT 707.35 RR 786.4
  RH 795.9 796.27

WINNINGLY WR 576.6

WINSOME OA 38.27 WM 59.6
  EA 91.39 SB 220.3 WS 250.7
  EE 310.8 MD 813.26 813.27
  BM 832.24

WINSOMELY EE 318.32

WINSOMENESS FA 466.14 466.15
  BM 832.39 832.41

WINTER DV 138.35 SS 202.10
  OC 287.2 FA 465.24 PR 509.25
  TB 515.18 515.27 515.29
  SU 532.19 532.21 WR 572.5
  575.36 581.13 581.15
  BO 595.17 595.32 LA 630.2
  IL 652.34 GG 683.12 ML 723.32
  734.13 742.27 743.39
  OV 754.27 LL 765.9 RH 800.12

WINTER-ACONITE ML 736.6

WINTER-CRACK OC 284.1

WINTER-DARK HD 446.25

WINTERS MO 1.13

WINTRY FG 191.2 OC 283.33
  EE 330.4 WP 379.15 HD 447.31
  448.38 450.6 WR 572.30 576.19
  BO 592.37 593.17 593.18
  594.36 599.12

WI'OUT SC 268.22

WIPE PO 106.1 OC 299.32
  BO 597.21

WIPED DV 170.10 CH 279.7
  OC 290.15 294.5 294.6
  WP 386.39 SD 419.41 HD 451.3
  LA 646.10 RR 779.35 MD 810.18
  BM 828.33

WIPING MO 5.1 DV 182.8
  FG 192.16 195.24 SS 203.6
  WS 264.26 265.11 SC 268.40
  OC 286.3 294.2

WIRE HT 43.20 WM 54.21 EA 72.28
  TF 117.13 TP 345.32 WP 385.31
  WR 547.14 BO 593.21 IL 648.21
  LL 761.19 761.23

WIRE-FENCED TF 118.18

WIRELESS LA 632.18

WIRES EA 72.20 72.21 72.26
  73.5 LA 632.17

WIRY DV 149.27 WR 546.3 547.13

WI'S SP 47.22

WISDOM JD 607.14

WISE MO 14.34 21.19 DV 164.3
  SB 212.7 EE 314.25 PR 475.12
  478.20 NT 720.1 ML 726.28
  727.2 LL 761.31 RR 780.28

WISELY GG 683.7 TH 847.11

WISER SU 532.25

WISH MO 17.31 OA 31.36 WM 62.7
  62.11 62.13 62.14 62.17
  62.19 62.20 EA 93.19
  DV 137.21 156.36 182.31
  WS 253.3 CH 281.10 MN 366.6
  WP 381.15 383.29 384.28
  SD 426.9 PP 427.34 FA 472.3
  SU 538.31 541.41 543.20
  LA 636.16 IL 658.41 GG 668.20
  684.35 688.1 OV 756.40 757.1
  LL 773.28 RH 793.19 801.3
  801.23 MD 823.15 823.20
  824.29 BM 830.27 830.30
  832.21 839.17

WISHED PO 104.19 BL 348.11
  352.39 353.42 PR 509.6 509.42
  SU 534.26 WR 567.21 SM 585.30
  JD 626.37 LA 637.31 GG 665.26
  697.39 ML 739.26 OV 749.28
  LL 765.35 MD 816.12

WISHES WM 62.15 EE 319.19
  BL 349.31 349.32 WP 383.37

WISHES (CONT.) MD 811.18
  TH 844.13

WISHING EE 332.35 BL 355.1
  PP 433.41

WISPINESS MD 808.42

WISPS DV 173.13 OC 284.34

WISPY BL 357.25

WISTFUL MO 16.29 OC 287.9
  HD 454.26 454.29 PR 486.28
  TB 515.22 SM 584.37
  JD 605.34 GG 661.14
  ML 736.27

WISTFULLY MO 20.29 GF 236.2
  CH 278.1 HD 455.38
  LL 778.12 BM 828.36
  829.4

WISTFULNESS GG 661.19
  677.13

WIT MO 5.29

WI'T CH 279.14

WITCH LL 776.3 776.17
  MD 806.30 806.31 807.8
  807.9

WITCHES MD 807.15 812.22

WITCH-FACE GG 672.42

WITCH-LIKE WM 66.16 WP 380.3
  382.35 385.25 386.4 387.40
  389.34

WITE FA 464.15

WITHAL PR 489.31 TB 514.30

WITHDRAW MO 9.28 GG 687.17

WITHDRAWAL YT 408.28
  PP 432.31

WITHDRAWING MO 7.18 CH 275.24
  EE 331.30 BL 352.33

WITHDRAWN OC 301.34 BM 832.33

WITHDREW MO 4.17 CH 276.27
  EE 322.22 BL 359.27
  PR 484.16 RR 788.27

WITHER EA 91.17 EE 323.9
  SU 530.20 OV 753.15
  LL 761.36

WITHERED EA 79.19 OC 283.12
  MN 366.15 376.27 OV 753.37
  755.9

WITHERING PO 102.18

WITHHELD WR 565.14

WITHIN OA 26.11 38.18
  WM 69.18 TF 118.26 122.14

WITHIN (CONT.)

WITHIN (CONT.) TF 124.33 126.8
  126.10 129.5 132.33 DV 137.32
  FG 193.10 195.8 SG 225.12
  WS 249.12 251.29 255.27
  OC 299.40 YT 408.21 HD 447.40
  456.8 FA 458.24 PR 504.23
  507.3 510.6 WR 547.1 552.9
  552.16 560.33 570.18 578.29
  GG 661.33 662.1 662.30 667.24
  667.26 675.8 682.42 698.18
  NT 710.8 RR 785.5 RH 801.17
  MD 806.15

WITHSTAND SG 230.28

WITNESS DV 148.31

WITNESSED SP 50.41

WITS MO 13.13 TF 126.15 133.4
  WP 380.30 MD 809.6 BM 828.28

WITTICISMS SP 50.38

WITTY WS 250.28 250.29 RR 779.9
  782.34

WIVES PR 475.27

WIVES'LL SP 53.5

WOE BL 361.20 JD 608.26

WOEBEGONE LL 767.17 TH 853.19

WOEFULLY FA 463.15 PR 503.30

WOKE PO 103.20 104.10 TF 120.35
  DV 174.41 FG 189.26 192.39
  195.9 196.19 196.22 SS 205.1
  WR 557.21 564.42 LA 645.33
  GG 678.37 ML 744.19 BM 837.30

WOLF FG 196.2 TB 523.21
  WR 570.9

WOLFISH BO 602.32

WOLF-LIKE TB 521.14 521.18
  522.20 LA 634.19

WOLVES FG 193.31 196.23

WOMAN MO 11.21 12.38 14.34
  14.42 17.10 21.17 21.18
  21.24 21.36 OA 23.4 25.26
  28.36 28.41 29.17 31.5 34.31
  37.19 HT 39.2 41.9 42.29
  42.40 SP 51.19 WM 57.37 59.16
  59.26 69.36 69.38 69.41
  69.42 EA 71.13 71.22 72.34
  73.7 74.8 78.32 86.35 87.15
  89.12 89.15 90.11 93.17
  PO 96.28 100.24 100.26 114.32
  TF 123.28 DV 136.26 139.15
  139.18 139.28 139.35 139.38
  140.17 140.24 141.6 141.36
  142.16 142.33 151.16 155.36
  161.28 161.36 162.1 162.5
  162.8 162.17 162.25 162.32
  163.9 163.20 164.42 165.11
  165.14 165.15 165.16 168.24
  169.8 169.12 169.40 170.1
  170.6 170.8 170.12 170.14
  170.16 171.18 171.25 171.42

WOMAN (CONT.) 172.12 172.17
  174.10 178.6 FG 195.32
  SS 208.36 209.7 211.14
  SB 217.27 SG 221.31 224.30
  228.12 SC 270.3 CH 274.15
  275.33 275.34 276.16
  276.23 276.31 276.38
  277.8 277.18 278.11 OC 283.6
  284.3 284.7 284.18 285.5
  285.24 285.33 285.37 286.1
  286.6 286.36 288.28 288.34
  288.41 291.13 291.24 291.28
  291.36 292.1 292.33 293.29
  293.38 294.27 294.39 295.6
  295.11 295.17 295.21 295.29
  295.35 296.4 296.8 296.10
  296.41 297.17 298.32 299.8
  299.11 299.31 EE 306.13
  310.25 BL 349.42 350.42
  352.24 356.14 357.23 MN 369.6
  374.29 374.38 376.23
  WP 379.20 380.1 387.42 388.37
  390.7 392.7 YT 403.9 SD 412.2
  412.19 412.20 412.30 412.33
  413.10 413.15 413.20 414.12
  416.37 418.4 418.12 418.19
  419.38 420.2 420.12 420.25
  420.41 421.10 421.16 421.19
  421.25 421.40 422.11 422.24
  422.28 423.33 424.32 425.18
  426.4 426.5 426.6 426.9
  PP 430.17 431.32 434.5 434.33
  435.28 436.33 436.39 437.1
  437.5 437.25 437.41 438.5
  438.40 440.14 HD 441.16
  442.14 444.5 FA 460.42 461.1
  461.3 461.7 462.2 462.12
  462.36 463.18 463.19 463.38
  467.8 467.13 467.16 467.20
  467.21 468.31 468.37 471.3
  471.9 471.35 PR 475.30 478.23
  479.2 479.3 479.5 479.24
  484.2 485.36 507.40 508.4
  TB 513.1 514.17 517.31 520.25
  521.15 521.35 524.41 527.30
  SU 533.18 533.24 538.7 538.8
  538.11 538.15 538.19 538.37
  539.11 540.39 541.33
  WR 547.12 550.19 550.30
  550.39 550.41 552.19 552.40
  554.16 555.5 555.19 555.21
  555.26 555.37 556.1 556.19
  556.35 557.39 558.1 559.29
  559.31 559.39 560.20 562.14
  563.25 563.33 566.5 569.8
  569.37 569.38 570.37 571.8
  571.11 571.15 572.28 575.8
  575.16 575.18 575.22 575.23
  575.37 577.9 577.11 SM 583.7
  583.13 583.14 583.29 584.8
  585.6 BO 587.1 587.27 587.33
  589.33 589.35 591.28 591.38
  592.19 593.1 593.3 594.5
  596.39 596.40 597.3 597.7
  597.14 602.23 602.28 JD 605.2
  605.28 605.31 607.3 607.5
  607.6 607.10 607.13 607.19
  607.42 608.2 608.9 608.31
  610.39 611.2 611.28 611.34
  611.40 612.12 612.29 613.8
  613.13 613.18 613.34 613.41
  614.6 614.8 614.29 615.20
  616.21 617.24 621.9 621.16
  621.27 621.37 622.7 622.14
  622.16 623.17 623.24 624.17

WOMAN (CONT.) 625.1 626.33
  626.37 627.31 628.6 629.11
  629.14 LA 631.42 635.30
  636.29 636.35 636.39 641.4
  643.8 643.9 643.17 644.21
  IL 648.15 649.5 652.13
  657.18 GG 670.15 670.22
  673.1 679.41 680.19 680.41
  681.27 681.32 682.38
  682.40 683.31 683.33
  686.24 688.26 690.21
  690.35 691.14 692.14
  692.33 693.6 696.23 696.33
  696.38 696.41 698.20
  698.22 698.25 698.28
  699.15 NT 701.15 701.25
  703.39 705.4 705.10
  707.15 708.23 708.26
  708.28 708.40 709.8 711.1
  711.8 711.14 711.16 711.25
  715.23 715.28 717.5 718.41
  ML 725.25 727.21 727.31
  727.32 738.2 OV 747.4
  747.8 747.14 747.25 748.21
  754.13 754.26 756.14
  757.15 759.12 759.21
  LL 761.3 761.6 761.17
  762.14 762.27 765.9 765.16
  768.15 768.33 769.11
  769.28 770.16 774.17
  774.22 776.8 776.34
  RR 779.2 779.14 779.21
  779.27 780.22 780.23
  780.25 781.5 781.21 782.23
  782.26 783.4 784.10 785.17
  787.11 RH 790.1 799.19
  MD 808.27 809.6 810.10
  810.11 810.17 813.26
  814.17 814.27 814.30
  814.42 815.40 816.19
  816.24 820.30 BM 827.5
  828.7 830.39 832.30 832.32
  832.39 836.26 836.39 837.5
  837.8 837.38 838.1 839.41
  840.6 842.12 TH 844.5

WOMAN-FOND BM 842.9

WOMANHOOD MO 11.23 OA 23.2
  WR 554.36 558.2 569.34
  569.39 GG 682.36 RR 782.10

WOMANISH GG 663.22

WOMANKIND OA 34.14

WOMANLY SS 201.3 202.11
  BL 351.28 WR 576.15
  SM 583.9 BO 591.8 602.20
  JD 605.31

WOMAN'S MO 17.23 OA 27.2
  EA 76.42 DV 161.20 162.35
  163.35 SG 221.27 222.30
  CH 274.7 EE 322.12
  MN 378.14 SD 411.36 420.8
  425.40 FA 461.39 463.36
  471.25 PR 475.31 WR 549.34
  553.22 563.2 571.32
  BO 595.38 598.2 598.7
  JD 605.9 605.24 605.27
  616.13 624.39 GG 691.8
  692.9 OV 747.38 753.14
  RR 779.33 779.37 780.9
  781.25 MD 813.28 BM 837.21

WOMAN'S (CONT.) BM 842.8

WOMAN'S BILL OA 33.3

WOMB OC 299.39 300.28 300.36
   SU 535.23 WR 568.15 LL 764.8

WOMEN MO 11.18 14.5 14.28
   14.29 15.3 15.11 18.28
   OA 29.1 29.4 30.27 33.19
   HT 39.3 39.5 40.25 43.30
   SP 45.16 45.18 45.21 52.32
   52.33 53.8 TF 122.10 123.4
   123.6 123.20 123.36 124.13
   124.31 125.7 127.1 127.4
   130.31 DV 137.7 148.2 164.11
   164.37 164.38 164.39 164.40
   167.34 SG 223.18 GF 234.18
   241.17 WS 251.30 256.1
   CH 274.3 280.9 OC 297.3
   297.16 299.37 EE 318.34
   BL 349.6 359.24 359.32
   MN 370.1 WP 384.19 YT 395.26
   395.37 400.6 407.7 407.19
   PP 430.22 437.18 438.9
   HD 446.41 449.16 FA 462.17
   462.35 463.10 PR 473.28
   475.35 480.35 TB 514.34
   514.35 514.36 518.11 519.23
   525.8 SU 533.29 538.16 541.30
   WR 551.24 562.36 568.26
   569.29 569.32 570.23 570.29
   570.30 571.28 571.30 571.31
   571.34 575.3 575.10 575.11
   575.12 575.25 576.14
   SM 585.10 585.24 585.36
   BO 589.26 595.6 JD 606.2
   607.11 608.6 621.25 627.18
   IL 658.18 658.27 GG 690.27
   693.13 698.21 698.29
   NT 703.18 704.8 704.11 704.14
   704.15 704.18 704.20 704.21
   705.21 707.4 707.5 707.6
   707.7 707.10 713.7 716.29
   718.23 719.38 ML 731.37
   OV 747.1 748.14 757.6 758.15
   LL 772.17 RR 780.4 782.38
   783.14 788.33 MD 806.22
   806.27 806.30 808.24 808.31
   810.7 812.2 812.16 812.20
   812.30 812.33 817.12 817.14
   BM 827.1 829.20 839.7

WOMEN'S SP 45.15 WR 569.22
   SM 583.23 GG 690.29 OV 758.17
   BM 827.2

WOMEN-SERVANTS TB 513.25

WON SP 50.26 TF 133.8 SG 229.30
   EE 305.28 316.2 TP 338.14
   WP 392.6 NT 709.12 ML 736.2
   RH 794.5 MD 820.6

WONDER OA 31.1 WM 55.4 57.33
   62.24 66.20 67.35 PO 114.14
   TF 130.32 DV 173.21 FG 188.32
   188.33 GF 238.15 OC 292.7
   298.33 EE 309.8 BL 361.40
   SD 425.5 425.6 PP 434.21
   438.28 FA 463.6 PR 499.9
   501.20 506.10 508.18
   TB 519.40 SU 531.2 WR 548.33
   549.29 555.23 560.33 SM 584.2
   586.7 BO 589.7 JD 613.18

WONDER (CONT.) 614.9 622.32
   623.2 625.10 LA 642.4 642.7
   643.8 GG 675.29 684.4 693.3
   695.19 ML 727.3 728.36 735.15
   OV 757.3 758.27 760.1
   RR 788.14 RH 795.34 801.30
   MD 815.34 815.35 826.15
   826.21 BM 837.38

WONDERED MO 7.4 20.38 TF 123.3
   DV 141.17 167.4 174.1 178.16
   FG 194.7 195.31 195.39
   SS 204.3 SG 225.38 226.38
   OC 291.17 EE 312.14 BL 359.2
   WP 386.11 PP 428.38 HD 444.41
   FA 466.5 PR 496.3 503.1
   510.38 SU 544.7 WR 558.19
   564.13 BO 597.12 IL 650.23
   GG 682.3 NT 708.39 709.3
   ML 741.31 741.36 RR 779.16
   TH 850.9

WONDERFUL MO 1.31 18.11 20.13
   20.17 20.19 20.22 EA 71.2
   PO 116.6 TF 122.18 DV 150.20
   173.18 176.20 SS 207.12
   210.11 EE 306.12 307.39
   312.14 315.10 322.8 BL 347.15
   356.35 SD 426.6 HD 453.35
   FA 464.28 TB 516.14 WR 548.39
   548.42 549.19 549.21 549.26
   549.28 JD 615.10 627.11
   LA 636.12 641.38 642.1 642.3
   642.22 643.14 643.22 643.24
   643.25 GG 682.32 NT 703.37
   707.40 707.41 709.24
   ML 723.19 726.9 727.19 727.20
   732.16 LL 763.17 765.8
   MD 810.37 811.40 812.21
   813.25 814.12 825.13
   BM 831.11 TH 847.17 848.30
   850.2 851.33

WONDERFULLY MO 12.37 OA 24.20
   PO 114.22 TP 338.22 BL 355.15
   356.26 356.34 PP 434.22
   BO 591.37 592.5 LL 761.3
   RR 782.2

WONDERING MO 13.42 15.35 18.25
   OA 30.26 WM 55.42 EA 89.28
   92.29 PO 97.34 TF 130.29
   DV 170.6 176.18 186.5
   SS 199.26 WS 244.22 250.8
   259.22 OC 289.13 BL 363.16
   PP 430.25 BO 589.7 595.42
   GG 686.31 696.17

WONDERINGLY LA 633.32

WONDER-LIGHT PO 114.40 WR 556.15

WONDERS SU 532.39 MD 814.13

WOOD MO 1.14 19.21 19.31
   SP 48.41 PO 99.1 108.28
   108.32 108.41 111.9 111.16
   111.28 111.31 111.41 112.3
   DV 166.13 FG 189.37 190.15
   190.34 190.39 191.1 192.25
   193.14 194.35 SS 197.1 197.5
   197.11 197.19 197.25 197.34
   200.34 204.28 204.30 204.34
   209.40 210.29 GF 241.32
   OC 286.18 286.21 EE 304.13

WOOD (CONT.) SD 424.41
   FA 467.31 PR 500.26 501.33
   503.26 507.17 SU 544.2
   WR 562.31 565.34 OV 758.6
   758.37 758.41 759.3
   TH 845.13

WOODBINE COTTAGE CH 278.25

WOODEN SP 45.19 WM 63.1
   SS 206.24 GF 238.22
   TP 338.9 340.26 PR 500.8
   502.5 WR 546.24 548.27
   561.17 564.30 JD 617.5
   618.27 623.20 625.4
   IL 648.18 649.3 655.32
   656.33 657.21 657.33
   LL 769.42 RR 779.30
   RH 791.17 801.37 803.13
   803.20

WOODEN-LEGGED DV 139.3

WOODENLY EA 73.24

WOODEN-SEEMING EE 317.25

WOOD-FENCE MO 19.32

WOOD-HEDGE SS 197.10

WOODLAND FG 187.4 187.7
   SS 200.4 SB 214.2

WOOD-PIGEONS SS 200.7

WOODRUFF SS 197.21

WOODS MO 2.14 PO 95.6 107.2
   FG 189.23 189.39 192.27
   196.19 SS 202.4 SC 267.21
   CH 275.24 EE 330.38
   MN 366.7 366.27 OV 759.30

WOOD'S PO 107.7 SS 200.32

WOODS' SS 210.2

WOOL WR 564.25 564.40

WOOLLEN WM 70.18 DV 158.17
   OC 293.30 YT 408.15
   HD 444.20 WR 560.42 561.2
   564.22

WOOLLY LA 630.23 631.21

WOR SP 51.34 SC 268.12
   CH 277.39 OC 292.25 295.39
   296.1 296.3 296.7 WP 388.8
   388.10 389.8 PP 428.6

WORD MO 6.14 8.31 12.17
   22.12 HT 44.18 SP 53.17
   WM 57.41 EA 78.36 79.5
   85.30 PO 107.38 108.14
   TF 117.30 DV 141.19 143.17
   145.11 147.6 175.32
   SG 233.6 WS 248.22 263.3
   263.32 SC 271.10 CH 274.33
   280.36 OC 294.21 EE 310.37
   314.11 TP 345.41 BL 353.17
   357.17 WP 380.16 YT 396.28
   SD 413.5 418.41 424.34
   426.2 HD 454.36 FA 460.21

WORD (CONT.) FA 470.10 471.23
   471.33 PR 502.20 508.20
   TB 526.42 SU 533.1 BO 589.36
   590.9 JD 611.33 613.30
   623.28 IL 651.16 652.6
   GG 670.38 673.19 674.42 688.3
   693.35 NT 709.12 ML 734.41
   746.24 LL 772.30 RR 784.37
   RH 798.28 799.29 MD 808.36
   BM 832.9 834.40 835.14
   TH 847.3

WORDS MO 2.32 3.25 14.23 20.16
   OA 33.10 33.25 33.37 34.32
   HT 39.32 SP 51.40 EA 75.12
   77.9 77.16 88.41 93.8
   PO 98.32 102.24 114.34
   TF 117.23 121.23 131.1
   DV 180.12 SG 226.42 231.35
   GF 235.36 239.12 WS 262.7
   262.9 CH 274.30 276.11 279.10
   279.30 OC 294.12 294.14
   EE 318.18 MN 372.8 WP 380.34
   YT 404.40 SD 419.5 PP 429.2
   FA 465.30 466.28 468.9
   PR 506.10 509.37 512.1
   TB 514.40 515.41 518.27 519.1
   520.11 521.24 524.12 525.18
   WR 559.27 560.5 563.16 576.2
   BO 598.40 603.28 IL 657.9
   GG 675.1 698.1 OV 747.37
   LL 774.1 MD 806.12 824.31
   826.11 826.18 BM 836.38

WORE MO 6.1 11.16 16.19
   OA 23.9 23.12 WM 59.13
   EA 86.8 PO 96.16 TF 123.25
   DV 147.3 168.14 179.3
   SG 222.3 224.6 226.14
   WS 245.3 250.6 BL 347.30
   350.41 SD 414.13 417.38
   PP 433.12 HD 449.10 PR 483.14
   484.42 494.17 TB 515.27
   WR 563.28 567.4 JD 626.15
   GG 670.15 OV 749.11 RR 784.13
   MD 808.13 809.24 814.24
   BM 831.9 833.10 836.1

WORK MO 19.5 OA 30.10 SP 46.8
   50.33 EA 72.27 73.4 80.21
   PO 104.3 104.41 106.15
   TF 132.27 132.32 133.11
   DV 139.34 142.23 144.34 166.8
   175.6 175.20 175.31 176.39
   FG 187.37 188.40 SS 208.29
   SG 233.13 GF 236.14 WS 249.34
   250.17 259.32 OC 290.14
   297.17 302.4 EE 306.13 307.36
   310.32 310.33 310.37 312.41
   312.42 313.5 314.8 323.16
   329.21 332.42 BL 347.20
   MN 366.9 367.25 367.27 370.20
   374.27 374.39 378.11
   SD 422.35 PP 438.14 HD 445.41
   449.8 450.41 FA 463.42
   PR 508.22 TB 515.13 515.24
   517.34 517.36 517.40 518.1
   518.26 519.28 519.39 520.5
   522.19 523.10 525.7 SU 543.40
   544.8 WR 548.3 571.9 577.29
   JD 622.2 GG 665.34 683.31
   685.28 NT 704.30 706.39
   ML 725.34 729.25 729.37
   734.29 735.26 745.9 MD 813.13
   814.17 814.20 814.21 814.27

WORK (CONT.) 814.29 814.35
   815.4 815.42 817.23 817.33
   BM 829.40 831.32 TH 846.10
   852.34

WORK-BASKET SS 203.18

WORK-BATTERED JD 618.13

WORKED OA 30.4 EA 72.30
   PO 102.29 102.36 TF 118.31
   126.37 128.7 DV 155.36 164.13
   180.20 WS 245.29 251.13
   OC 289.28 299.35 EE 303.24
   307.14 307.15 307.19 307.41
   316.35 323.23 323.28
   BL 356.28 YT 403.12 SD 422.40
   423.1 HD 441.3 450.41 451.1
   PR 490.19 491.15 496.30
   497.31 TB 515.30 SU 543.3
   WR 553.31 556.34 566.37 577.9
   JD 613.13 GG 682.27 683.29
   ML 722.10 725.40 734.28
   734.30 735.6 740.20 745.21
   746.3 LL 761.23 RR 786.37
   RH 799.16 MD 807.30 810.3
   810.5 BM 834.24 837.6

WORKER SC 267.7 FA 459.7
   IL 648.25

WORKHOUSE DV 141.7 155.31

WORKING MO 11.38 SP 50.42
   EA 75.27 PO 102.42 103.13
   109.38 TF 119.35 128.30
   DV 141.42 142.13 146.32
   162.20 166.25 176.41
   SB 217.14 SG 229.34 WS 255.19
   OC 293.25 EE 303.1 311.20
   316.33 323.32 BL 351.41
   YT 395.13 402.41 406.24
   406.26 SD 422.3 HD 449.12
   PR 482.24 496.21 496.25
   TB 515.34 516.12 523.13
   526.28 526.29 526.32 526.35
   GG 667.19 ML 725.33 732.36
   735.27 RR 783.39 MD 814.31
   BM 828.21 829.28 837.17
   TH 848.40

WORKING-CLASS PP 437.5

WORKING-MEN SP 48.38

WORKINGS PR 501.1

WORKMAN DV 146.17 171.30
   FA 459.35

WORKMAN'S SG 230.41 SD 423.39
   PP 437.42 FA 459.16

WORKMEN DV 136.8 EE 307.10
   YT 304.32 FA 459.35

WORKMEN'S TP 334.4

WORK-PEOPLE WS 251.8

WORKS FG 187.31 GF 236.11
   239.38 242.24 BL 357.22
   YT 394.4 394.9 396.31
   WR 546.18 547.7 547.24 547.25
   548.31 JD 621.41

WORK'S EE 312.42 MN 378.11

WORK-SCARRED JD 618.12

WORLD MO 9.15 OA 34.13
   HT 40.4 44.2 SP 48.30
   WM 69.7 EA 79.36 PO 104.37
   106.23 111.18 114.14
   115.8 115.13 115.15
   TF 119.33 121.38 123.10
   123.42 129.10 129.23
   132.24 132.28 134.25
   DV 137.38 146.8 153.23
   154.37 155.3 156.15 157.20
   157.25 161.3 166.16 166.19
   167.10 167.25 176.29
   SS 208.17 210.11 SG 221.34
   226.31 226.38 WS 260.2
   OC 301.27 EE 304.8 305.27
   305.29 306.32 307.8 308.23
   308.30 310.33 310.37
   312.39 313.20 314.12
   314.16 314.33 314.34
   322.14 327.11 327.18
   328.18 329.19 332.27
   332.28 332.32 332.40
   BL 347.25 348.15 349.37
   355.27 355.30 MN 367.28
   WP 380.41 385.33 PP 427.18
   HD 447.39 448.5 448.9
   448.16 450.31 451.4
   PR 474.29 475.39 477.6
   477.7 478.24 479.42 480.14
   489.36 502.37 505.27
   510.2 SU 532.38 538.41
   544.34 544.36 WR 546.25
   547.21 548.28 556.15
   558.8 558.22 563.8 570.39
   571.16 571.36 575.1 575.17
   577.42 580.22 BO 587.17
   588.9 588.10 588.13 589.13
   594.13 597.22 598.13
   602.30 603.2 603.3
   JD 605.8 605.36 606.32
   612.24 615.15 618.19 620.1
   LA 630.12 630.21 633.41
   639.4 641.33 642.4
   GG 662.32 663.9 663.26
   664.36 688.2 697.42 700.10
   NT 701.12 702.37 708.10
   719.26 ML 722.4 723.20
   723.30 723.40 724.16
   725.8 725.15 725.41 726.2
   726.10 726.16 726.18
   726.37 727.33 727.34
   728.6 730.8 730.9 734.35
   734.37 738.9 741.2 741.16
   742.4 743.8 743.10 745.30
   745.38 LL 761.18 774.29
   RR 780.19 785.31 BM 834.3
   834.7 TH 844.26 846.6
   846.12 846.18 846.25
   846.29 846.40 850.20
   853.17

WORLD-ATMOSPHERE WR 565.42

WORLDLY EE 314.35 BO 588.41

WORLDS PR 502.2 WR 574.22
   BO 589.15 JD 613.31
   ML 724.37

WORLD'S EE 313.5 LA 634.29
   GG 666.5

WORM SU 531.36 JD 605.18

WORM-EATEN NT 706.3

WORMS SU 533.5

WORMWOOD JD 605.19

WORMY NT 706.4

WORN DV 139.8 SG 224.10
  SC 270.17 BL 357.21 YT 396.42
  PR 473.17 TB 518.26 518.31
  WR 561.26 SM 584.33 GG 671.23
  671.24 OV 748.27 750.24
  755.11 MD 810.40 814.15
  814.33

WORNA CH 277.40

WORN-OUT MD 817.25

WORN'T WP 389.8

WORRIED GF 237.26 SC 269.15
  EE 303.5 IL 647.1 647.21
  648.1 648.27 GG 691.7 691.11
  BM 831.17 835.8

WORRIES IL 648.8

WORRY HT 43.14 EE 317.20
  LA 645.19 IL 647.24 RH 801.27
  801.31 801.35

WORRYING BM 835.8

WORSE MO 13.39 WM 67.14
  EA 88.28 FG 190.18 192.2
  EE 319.39 320.5 322.6 329.11
  BL 347.36 360.14 MN 372.20
  WP 383.1 YT 396.24 SD 420.20
  425.39 TB 516.1 518.35
  BO 589.2 NT 721.1 LL 764.6
  768.11 RH 799.8 BM 837.6

WORSHIP WS 259.37 WR 550.11
  GG 692.16 692.30 692.32
  693.12

WORSHIPPED PR 483.1 GG 693.12
  697.27 697.29

WORST PO 103.18 104.42
  JD 605.10 IL 647.29 657.4

WORTH MO 16.36 DV 155.38 167.37
  FG 187.35 SB 216.34 WS 265.7
  EE 308.24 MN 372.14 YT 394.34
  SD 418.19 PP 428.7 GG 671.13
  692.26 RH 791.1 797.27 800.1
  804.24 MD 806.40

WORTHS GG 666.9

WOULD-BE BM 835.23

WOULDN'T MO 11.1 HT 38.6
  WM 55.22 EA 71.5 94.8
  DV 150.25 157.5 178.16
  SB 218.32 SG 222.27 GF 240.39
  WS 262.12 OC 287.15 291.32
  292.36 294.32 295.33 300.19
  TP 345.7 BL 355.1 362.6
  WP 383.1 YT 398.14 399.20

WOULDN'T (CONT.) 399.21 SD 422.11
  PP 428.27 430.40 430.41
  FA 461.20 PR 491.29 491.31
  TB 526.8 LA 631.27 642.6
  643.24 IL 652.23 655.18
  GG 669.36 669.38 674.15
  685.16 687.23 691.29
  NT 715.16 718.29 LL 777.20
  RR 782.21 782.32 782.42
  785.34 RH 800.35 801.27
  MD 808.12 814.18 BM 828.38
  842.25

WOUND TF 118.37 DV 183.1
  SS 210.14 SG 231.3 SC 269.42
  OC 292.12 EE 319.33 WP 384.1
  389.11 PR 489.35 490.5 493.18
  WR 578.33 JD 616.18 GG 666.23

WOUNDED OA 32.36 37.16 WM 60.8
  TF 133.38 134.15 DV 137.29
  152.35 FG 191.33 192.15
  SS 210.15 OC 289.27 EE 319.5
  329.36 BL 347.14 WP 381.37
  381.40 TB 518.12 GG 667.8
  RH 794.10

WOUNDS FG 190.35

WOVE OV 757.25

WOVEN MO 9.38 MD 810.36

WRAITH ML 746.26

WRAP BL 348.3 HD 455.42
  GG 690.12 OV 756.15 LL 775.24
  777.4 RR 784.13 784.24 786.19
  787.16 BM 838.21 838.37

WRAPPED OA 36.1 DV 162.22
  BL 352.34 HD 451.3 451.19
  455.36 456.4 PR 503.12 505.12
  WR 552.17 LA 634.1 NT 703.36
  709.24 LL 775.24 RR 782.19
  BM 837.25 837.28

WRAPPER SU 532.26 533.36 534.34
  544.33

WRAPPING GF 239.21 PR 502.7
  IL 656.25

WRAPS DV 158.17

WRAPT DV 165.14

WRATH SB 216.13 216.22
  OC 289.25 BM 828.8 828.9

WRATHED FG 188.13

WREAK WP 391.18

WREATHED SD 421.12 LA 633.1

WRECK CH 282.21 YT 398.11

WRECKED WM 68.29 TF 117.18
  CH 282.18 JD 612.14 LA 644.36

WRENCH DV 169.35

WRENCHED TP 342.33

WREN'S SS 204.16

WREST PR 482.40

WRESTLE TB 522.4

WRESTLED SB 214.35 216.2

WRESTLING DV 137.27 159.6
  GG 686.10 690.6

WRETCH MO 14.9 17.33
  FG 188.17 SB 216.15

WRETCHED OA 36.39 PP 439.26
  IL 649.19 TH 850.26

WREXALL (SEE MISS WREXALL)

WRIGGLE SB 214.37 JD 616.34

WRIGGLED PR 505.4

WRIGGLING SB 216.1 WS 245.34

WRING WP 392.40 MD 806.23

WRINGER HT 42.19 43.32

WRINGING YT 397.21

WRINKLED MO 15.23 SP 51.20
  SB 216.4 OC 293.32
  WR 559.33

WRINKLES LL 761.15

WRINKLING SU 531.31

WRISTS MO 13.22 WM 69.2
  69.11 EA 91.4 PO 109.22
  109.40 110.7 TF 121.1
  DV 179.5 TP 343.31
  BL 354.28 PP 439.24
  WR 569.11 LA 637.39

WRITE MO 22.29 EA 79.12
  TF 117.21 117.29 132.37
  DV 172.22 SS 209.36
  SG 223.42 WS 252.2
  EE 319.40 WP 381.21
  384.6 PR 482.4 TB 514.41
  522.14 525.33 525.41
  SU 537.28 537.29 JD 608.2
  GG 667.24 RR 780.13
  MD 806.34 815.20

WRITER TB 520.6

WRITHE ML 744.15

WRITHED OA 33.17 SB 215.8
  CH 281.33 SM 585.2
  JD 619.6 628.9 LL 773.42
  774.11 RH 798.35 MD 805.21

WRITHING TF 121.8 EE 332.33
  WR 569.7 JD 620.33 628.5
  LA 646.25 ML 743.23 744.16

WRITING HT 40.31 EA 93.16
  PO 102.25 TF 117.19
  DV 173.9 SS 200.9 WP 385.4
  385.12 391.40 TB 514.42
  JD 621.1 ML 735.28

WRITING-SACHET EA 81.15

WRITING-TABLE MD 824.36

WRITS RH 798.21

WRITTEN TF 117.24 DV 145.1
  TB 526.13 MD 824.35 TH 850.12

WRONG MO 17.17 OA 28.11
  WM 62.41 EA 83.12 89.40 89.41
  90.15 DV 148.32 155.37 156.9
  CH 280.36 OC 300.39 301.3
  EE 303.8 320.41 321.12 327.23
  327.26 327.27 TP 335.12
  388.19 BL 353.10 MN 368.22
  368.23 375.7 375.25 375.39
  PR 481.40 TB 513.29 526.17
  WR 548.7 BO 590.25 JD 612.34
  613.7 621.4 LA 643.2
  IL 655.35 657.32 GG 673.40
  674.9 675.25 675.26 678.1
  680.34 681.4 681.6 691.12
  691.17 693.41 695.25 696.7
  NT 707.34 717.6 ML 736.38
  LL 763.3 763.4 765.37
  RR 786.4 788.37 MD 807.41
  811.23 814.37

WRONGED EA 89.19

WROTE HT 41.2 DV 139.38 177.10
  WS 252.7 EE 320.9 BL 348.37
  349.29 YT 396.30 396.38
  SD 419.18 PR 474.36 478.33
  JD 607.26 607.33 607.37
  609.27 619.14 628.20
  GG 667.32 699.25 ML 739.21
  MD 807.22 807.27 TH 852.33

WRUNG WM 56.2 MD 806.26

WRY OA 38.31

WUNNA SP 48.5

WUST MO 17.40

WYER, DOCTOR (SEE DOCTOR WYER)

X-RAY EE 321.29

X-RAYED EE 321.4

XY MO 13.25

Y' WP 389.29

YACHT ML 725.27 729.26 730.33

YA ES BASTANTE BASTA NT 713.36

YAH BO 590.11

YALE PR 486.8 TH 850.17

YAPPED BM 831.7

YAPPING WR 565.34

YAQUIS WR 550.1

YARD MO 3.9 18.37 HT 43.38
  TF 118.18 DV 161.20 CH 275.41
  OC 283.33 284.39 286.27

YARD (CONT.) 290.31 291.28
  292.9 292.40 296.42 EE 304.33
  BL 352.36 352.38 MN 378.1
  YT 394.5 394.11 HD 441.24
  FA 471.15 SU 536.31 ML 726.14
  727.11

YARDS DV 162.9 SS 198.2 200.32
  OC 291.2 EE 304.38 SU 536.19
  539.41 LA 637.17

YARNS RH 796.31

Y'AVE SP 53.23

YAWL ML 725.23

YAWN MN 373.33

YAWNING MO 19.6

YE BL 352.13 352.20 SD 418.6
  PP 434.12 FA 465.21 ML 727.15

YEA OV 753.25 755.10 755.22

YEA-A PR 511.32

YEAR MO 9.37 WM 55.26 60.37
  63.12 63.20 EA 71.14 76.28
  86.35 PO 98.4 OV 136.27
  137.40 145.33 150.6 156.26
  SB 217.23 SG 231.26 WS 248.38
  261.27 264.39 264.40
  SC 269.12 269.19 EE 305.13
  BL 347.9 348.17 348.27 358.20
  YT 395.17 395.18 SD 415.9
  424.9 PR 474.4 478.16 478.18
  TB 514.4 WR 580.11 GG 661.11
  666.15 679.20 NT 704.16
  ML 728.7 728.19 731.35 732.19
  732.26 732.35 732.42 733.11
  LL 762.31 RH 796.33 799.20
  MD 805.4 805.6 807.5 809.32
  814.5 814.7 816.23 BM 829.16
  833.8 TH 844.7 844.12 849.9
  850.4

YEAR-LONG SU 528.24

YEARN OV 751.27

YEARNED GG 695.19 OV 751.26
  BM 828.19

YEARNING MO 8.42 EA 75.26 75.27
  79.21 90.23 SG 221.32 224.23
  WS 250.18 EE 320.11 HD 453.4
  TB 513.13 GG 661.19 NT 713.9
  ML 731.21 OV 756.21 TH 845.6

YEARNINGS ML 731.27

YEARS MO 2.22 4.12 6.33 13.29
  16.9 21.1 OA 26.25 30.8
  SP 45.9 WM 55.28 TF 126.31
  DV 138.11 138.36 143.28
  144.23 144.25 145.35 156.18
  156.19 164.27 164.33
  FG 187.13 SS 197.7 202.37
  203.5 SB 217.18 SG 222.41
  231.22 WS 244.19 251.11
  SC 270.36 CH 274.12 OC 285.21
  293.31 EE 303.37 305.9 307.23
  310.14 310.29 312.30 316.19

YEARS (CONT.) 316.20
  BL 348.26 349.33 350.9
  359.20 WP 382.1 382.33
  382.42 YT 395.27 395.36
  396.11 396.20 397.2
  SD 418.7 419.21 419.39
  425.23 PP 429.16 430.4
  HD 443.8 446.38 FA 459.6
  459.8 459.14 462.23
  464.30 464.37 PR 473.20
  473.31 474.21 474.39
  479.2 479.15 479.20 479.24
  479.32 479.41 480.11
  480.40 482.14 482.24
  496.10 497.15 TB 514.8
  514.17 SU 533.20 WR 546.3
  546.6 547.10 547.39 550.27
  SM 584.34 BO 587.12 589.17
  589.30 JD 605.6 LA 642.10
  IL 649.14 GG 667.11
  NT 701.2 704.33 706.1
  ML 724.19 736.3 OV 749.21
  752.19 LL 762.19 762.28
  763.41 764.7 765.17 768.18
  769.25 769.29 776.1
  RH 799.3 799.5 MD 805.9
  805.16 806.11 807.24
  807.33 810.36 817.40
  821.10 BM 827.5 827.26
  832.18 832.27 836.8
  842.26 TH 844.2 845.29
  847.32 847.33 847.38
  849.26 849.27 852.32

YEAR'S ML 731.40

YEARS' ML 722.13

YE GODS IL 648.17 649.16

YELL MN 378.27 WP 387.29

YELLED FG 189.9 IL 658.5
  658.8

YELLING MN 378.26 RH 796.7

YELLOW MO 3.13 OA 27.42
  29.19 30.13 SP 48.8
  WM 55.9 58.34 70.8
  DV 161.39 167.21 FG 188.9
  SS 202.2 210.3 GF 240.4
  OC 286.30 290.35 EE 303.35
  330.18 TP 339.32 WP 385.20
  YT 394.11 PP 436.10 436.32
  FA 464.39 465.4 PR 486.10
  489.11 489.12 490.23
  493.21 493.22 493.23
  494.4 494.9 494.16 507.13
  TB 520.35 521.38 523.8
  SU 537.20 537.21 537.37
  WR 556.4 559.10 559.20
  562.26 565.4 566.8 568.32
  568.33 569.1 570.22 573.34
  574.36 575.29 576.29 577.1
  577.7 577.16 578.11 580.40
  580.42 BO 603.4 JD 611.22
  611.25 LA 630.5 631.37
  632.19 640.42 IL 648.33
  648.34 648.37 657.5
  GG 670.25 672.38 678.1
  679.8 681.21 683.16 684.18
  684.31 699.26 NT 701.23
  702.12 702.14 702.32
  702.39 703.35 703.39

YELLOW (CONT.) NT 705.37 709.31
  711.37 713.15 713.39 715.2
  715.11 715.29 716.40
  ML 729.37 735.8 736.10 741.5
  741.35 OV 754.32

YELLOW-BROWN GG 673.3 673.9
  681.28 687.9

YELLOW-COLOURED TB 521.22

YELLOWER BO 602.33

YELLOW-EYED NT 714.40

YELLOW-FLOWERING SU 540.21

YELLOW-GREY BM 841.29

YELLOW-HAIRED PR 475.2

YELLOWING SB 214.13 PR 489.7
  WR 552.39 553.9 565.33
  LL 775.18

YELLOWISH TF 117.12 DV 170.10
  WP 390.33 SD 423.26 SU 532.24
  WR 578.30 BO 600.31 MD 810.41

YELLOWISH-DARK WP 385.33

YELLOW-SERE WR 558.41

YELPED LA 646.23

YELPING LA 646.16

YEOMEN EE 304.6 306.22

YEP PR 511.23 511.34

YER HT 41.26 41.41 43.15
  SP 47.19 53.16 DV 139.37
  WS 262.20 SC 272.6 272.22
  CH 278.14 WP 389.7 PP 432.28
  432.33 432.34 HD 445.27

YESTERDAY MO 13.39 DV 168.26
  SB 212.6 WP 383.36 YT 405.36
  PR 495.20 NT 701.10

YEW SG 225.20 OC 292.18
  LL 766.15 770.17 770.20

YEWS SP 48.9

YEW TREE OC 292.30

YEW-WALLED LL 766.13

YI HT 41.25 41.30 FA 470.34

YIELD OA 30.40 PO 110.18
  FG 195.17 EE 312.10 MN 376.8
  HD 454.3 BO 589.19 JD 623.23
  NT 720.6 BM 840.30 840.32

YIELDED PO 109.9 DV 181.3
  FG 194.21 WS 258.6 265.1
  PP 439.34 WR 550.42 BO 603.37

YIELDING HD 453.34 453.37
  BO 603.38

YIELDS GG 682.32

YIT OC 292.14 293.3

YO' SC 269.29

YOKE FG 191.26

YON SB 218.32

YORKSHIRE WM 58.25 58.26 61.17
  SG 222.26 JD 607.27 BM 828.3

YOU'N CH 279.12

YOUNG MO 1.4 17.29 18.38
  OA 23.17 23.24 24.3 25.15
  25.33 26.2 26.11 26.15 27.12
  27.25 32.40 33.5 33.15 33.23
  34.23 34.30 35.29 35.32
  35.37 36.19 36.32 37.21
  SP 46.15 47.14 51.14 WM 54.18
  54.28 55.28 56.7 56.18 56.20
  59.2 EA 84.20 84.27 85.9
  86.15 86.20 86.32 87.6 87.12
  88.1 PO 95.5 96.25 97.2 97.3
  97.8 97.13 97.18 97.20 97.22
  97.26 97.31 98.12 98.21
  98.29 98.38 98.42 99.15
  99.25 100.7 100.33 100.36
  101.15 101.29 102.3 102.8
  102.23 103.8 104.17 106.8
  107.20 107.33 108.1 108.3
  108.8 108.22 109.7 109.13
  109.27 109.33 109.39 110.3
  110.16 110.19 114.26 116.13
  116.20 TF 117.34 121.33
  123.28 123.30 124.41 125.9
  127.4 129.11 129.20 132.5
  133.27 134.5 DV 136.24 136.26
  136.28 144.29 144.37 145.7
  155.36 162.8 162.17 163.20
  170.14 171.42 174.27 176.26
  177.32 177.33 183.12 184.1
  184.15 184.39 FG 191.9 191.15
  191.22 SS 198.6 199.11 201.25
  201.27 201.33 204.25 209.31
  SB 212.7 212.17 213.12 214.30
  217.12 218.31 SG 221.1 221.5
  222.24 222.33 226.18
  GF 241.14 WS 244.15 244.29
  255.30 260.19 SC 269.21
  270.13 272.16 272.36
  CH 274.15 275.34 278.2 278.40
  279.24 279.36 280.15 280.19
  281.9 281.20 281.36 OC 286.38
  EE 304.16 306.29 307.41 308.1
  308.33 322.34 322.41 324.30
  TP 335.18 335.20 336.10
  336.33 BL 364.3 364.5
  MN 366.31 367.1 367.36 367.39
  368.21 373.35 374.12 374.19
  374.29 374.38 376.23
  WP 379.19 379.33 387.22
  388.19 388.29 YT 394.31
  395.37 397.1 397.8 397.16
  398.13 399.14 400.3 400.16
  400.22 402.11 403.22 403.36
  407.5 407.34 410.14 SD 413.9
  413.14 413.28 415.5 418.10
  418.23 418.37 419.9 419.15
  420.15 421.4 421.15 422.5
  422.29 PP 427.1 427.36 429.1
  429.27 430.17 430.19 432.10
  434.33 436.40 437.23
  HD 441.16 441.26 443.5 444.5
  444.19 444.32 444.37 445.5

YOUNG (CONT.) 445.27 446.3
  446.21 FA 464.33 467.13
  468.31 469.20 PR 481.38
  481.42 488.40 495.3 495.12
  511.11 511.29 TB 513.19
  513.24 513.31 514.33
  524.41 SU 536.24 537.33
  542.26 WR 548.21 548.26
  548.33 549.32 549.38
  550.19 550.38 553.36
  554.8 554.11 554.17 554.31
  554.41 555.3 555.10 555.30
  555.40 556.26 556.38
  557.32 559.18 559.27
  560.5 560.6 560.11 560.36
  560.38 560.40 562.15 563.1
  563.19 563.32 564.4 564.17
  564.27 564.42 565.24
  566.27 568.9 568.16 568.21
  570.13 570.22 573.1 573.18
  574.29 576.13 SM 583.11
  583.14 583.16 584.6 584.16
  585.20 585.40 586.8 586.23
  BO 596.40 JD 605.14 606.36
  625.17 LA 630.14 631.14
  633.6 633.11 633.19 633.39
  634.12 634.18 634.20
  634.22 634.34 637.15
  637.18 637.29 637.34
  638.21 640.16 641.4 641.12
  641.14 645.30 646.5 646.7
  646.10 646.13 646.30
  IL 647.34 653.4 653.6
  654.7 654.20 658.24 658.27
  659.37 GG 662.41 668.12
  670.22 673.1 681.27 682.4
  683.31 688.26 690.35 691.8
  691.14 692.38 694.17
  694.28 695.13 696.23
  696.38 696.41 699.27 700.1
  NT 703.31 704.38 712.27
  ML 726.30 729.2 739.10
  OV 748.7 757.33 757.34
  758.2 758.12 LL 761.31
  762.14 764.39 765.9 765.19
  766.5 768.21 770.14 777.5
  RR 782.8 786.22 RH 793.27
  794.9 794.19 795.19 795.24
  799.19 MD 805.17 806.31
  807.8 808.33 812.17 812.34
  815.40 BM 829.10 830.39
  830.41 834.33 835.39 836.9
  836.16 836.26 837.5
  TH 844.3 844.4 847.15
  849.34

YOUNGER MO 5.4 OA 34.20
  SP 49.14 WM 56.38 PO 100.9
  105.6 DV 160.7 166.34
  CH 276.35 281.19 BL 348.27
  MN 366.19 368.9 375.5
  376.8 PP 431.7 432.3
  432.36 PR 479.24 480.40
  495.5 WR 566.12 IL 647.14
  GG 693.23 694.11 MD 814.17
  BM 829.2

YOUNGER-LOOKING GG 695.15

YOUNGEST TF 125.26 DV 140.29
  143.11 SS 201.40 CH 275.12
  278.34 281.22 EE 304.35
  316.19 317.24 YT 404.16
  PP 428.39 HD 443.4

YOUNGNESS

YOUNGNESS GG 694.29

YOURS DV 182.3 WS 253.8
  CH 275.9 SD 416.26 HD 440.4
  FA 470.8 TB 524.36 524.38
  527.20 JD 628.32 628.38
  LA 645.19 GG 666.5 690.8
  NT 714.20 ML 726.18 LL 771.36
  774.30 BM 840.10

YOURSELF MO 8.36 9.31 HT 41.24
  41.27 42.1 44.19 SP 52.10
  52.28 52.30 WM 61.35 EA 76.10
  76.15 76.19 87.23 93.18
  93.24 94.7 94.9 DV 168.42
  169.2 172.16 182.19 185.10
  SG 223.38 224.2 232.1
  WS 253.4 253.8 256.22 261.31
  SC 268.18 CH 276.19 TP 345.39
  YT 404.21 SD 419.39 424.8
  424.31 424.34 425.5 425.7
  PP 438.22 HD 441.1 444.3
  444.41 TB 515.17 527.14
  527.24 SU 533.27 542.9
  BO 590.4 JD 622.40 628.15
  628.26 628.27 LA 631.4 631.17
  IL 651.38 GG 665.13 693.30
  696.28 NT 702.18 711.21
  717.26 719.41 ML 724.13
  726.22 LL 767.18 RR 787.8
  RH 792.18 MD 806.42

YOURSELVES TB 523.25

YOUTH MO 21.2 OA 23.20 23.21
  35.30 SP 47.21 EA 87.9
  PO 96.42 97.25 97.31 99.29
  99.40 100.18 100.34 102.8
  102.31 109.36 TF 117.20
  118.30 121.17 127.42 134.22
  DV 140.1 CH 281.38 282.11
  EE 305.20 306.15 MN 366.20
  372.26 375.31 WP 388.22
  YT 403.34 404.8 405.33 408.28
  PP 434.28 WR 551.25 IL 648.23
  648.40 648.42 649.5 649.11
  659.38 GG 694.21 700.2
  OV 748.8 LL 761.29 761.30
  MD 807.12 808.40

YOUTHFUL TF 117.22 118.3
  SS 203.3 MD 809.7

YOUTHFULLY MD 809.5

YOUTHS SC 270.36 271.24
  TP 335.26 MN 366.26

YOUTH'S MO 6.22 PO 97.9

YX MO 13.25

ZENITH WM 60.30

ZEST PO 98.23 ML 728.28

ZIGZAGGING PR 499.12

ZINC CH 276.34 SD 412.17
  ML 741.13

ZINC-COVERED SD 419.7

ZOLA PR 477.8 477.9 477.27

ZONE PO 107.36 108.29

ZOPILOTE NT 720.11

ZZZZ GF 234.22

PART TWO
THE SHORT NOVELS

CODE OF ABBREVIATIONS

TITLES	ABBREVIATIONS
Love among the Haystacks	LH
The Ladybird	TL
The Fox	FO
The Captain's Doll	CD
St. Mawr	SM
The Man Who Died	MD
The Virgin and the Gipsy	VG

A' LH 25.24 37.11 37.17 38.2
   38.10

'A LH 14.24

A 1 VG 51.34

ABACK SM 82.32

ABANDON CD 232.28 232.29
   SM 38.3

ABANDONED SM 59.39 155.7
   VG 4.24

ABANDONING VG 39.1

ABATE VG 73.25

ABATED SM 94.6 VG 77.21 77.27

ABATING CD 250.33 MD 190.22
   191.32

ABENDBLATT CD 219.21

ABER NEIN CD 193.39

ABEYANCE TL 92.30

ABIDING-PLACE SM 116.20

ABJECT CD 214.2 MD 198.22
   VG 61.10 63.20

ABJECTLY CD 215.38 VG 61.24
   61.25 64.17

ABLE LH 12.4 36.24 TL 59.24
   84.22 89.24 90.11 104.25
   FO 127.14 146.2 164.27
   CD 197.3 209.2 221.31 225.29
   225.30 SM 24.10 25.30 29.26
   48.21 68.19 79.20 85.36
   94.37 111.30 113.34 122.37
   VG 12.15 77.25

ABNORMAL VG 26.20 29.23 62.31

ABNORMALS VG 62.32

ABOLISH SM 71.7

ABOMINABLE VG 32.16

ABOMINATION VG 64.2

ABORIGINAL TL 45.41 50.36
   SM 18.34 63.34 135.28

ABRAHAM (SEE FATHER ABRAHAM)

ABRAHAM LINCOLN SM 9.18

ABREAST SM 23.27

ABROAD SM 127.35 VG 9.11 17.26

ABRUPTLY TL 102.15 102.18
   CD 253.34 SM 21.27 65.20
   78.37 104.25 104.26 MD 194.33

ABSENCE FO 167.15 SM 39.40

ABSENT FO 115.27 137.37
   CD 199.4 199.33 VG 40.23
   55.10

ABSENTLY FO 136.26 VG 14.20
   44.17 57.9 69.20

ABSENT-MINDED VG 57.34

ABSOLUTE TL 103.15 FO 165.30
   166.3 166.7 CD 199.4 SM 19.16
   73.30 74.10 147.2 147.5
   147.39 148.41 MD 194.15
   208.16

ABSOLUTELY LH 4.20 TL 72.6
   82.34 85.13 88.26 FO 113.24
   130.36 137.15 142.4 144.42
   150.32 168.20 173.22 174.13
   174.32 CD 196.26 199.34
   209.35 225.35 261.2 263.28
   SM 42.34 52.8 84.2 114.11
   114.13 114.32 135.27 157.5
   157.25 MD 191.22 VG 9.37 29.3
   30.30 39.25 41.34 42.39 44.9
   44.12

ABSORBED FO 135.32 136.10
   MD 178.33 197.39 198.21
   198.24 199.11 201.34 205.34
   205.41

ABSORBEDLY TL 85.42 FO 135.21
   SM 17.16 MD 198.40 VG 47.31

ABSORPTION SM 17.17 85.16
   136.40 MD 204.18

ABSTRACT LH 13.41 FO 138.6
   VG 54.30

ABSTRACTED VG 22.37 49.28 58.7

ABSTRACTEDLY TL 105.40 FO 117.1
   117.33 VG 37.15

ABSTRACTION VG 27.5

ABSURD TL 55.1 80.21 82.1

ABSURDITY TL 54.42

ABSURDLY SM 46.12 47.26

ABUNDANT FO 121.36

ABUSE SM 83.36

ABYSS FO 177.22 CD 240.9
   SM 77.19

ACCENT SM 29.37

ACCEPT FO 166.25 175.35 SM 6.37
   34.37 37.15 53.18 119.21

ACCEPTANCE SM 119.20

ACCEPTED TL 87.42 99.4 SM 5.27
   101.14 119.22 139.38
   MD 194.13 VG 4.8 6.32 10.4

ACCEPTING FO 125.3

ACCESS MD 186.24 VG 76.16

ACCESSIBLE FO 157.6 157.13
   161.23 161.26

ACCIDENT LH 13.30 15.14
   FO 166.15 SM 121.26
   VG 60.33 68.1

ACCIDENTALLY CD 220.21

ACCIDENTS SM 13.10 13.15
   82.18

ACCOMMODATE SM 144.10

ACCOMMODATED SM 109.17

ACCOMMODATING SM 96.9

ACCOMPANIED SM 51.26 93.14
   154.27 VG 50.28

ACCOMPANY FO 164.22

ACCOMPLISHED SM 142.10

ACCOMPLISHING SM 99.2

ACCORDING TL 89.27 FO 114.28
   151.29

ACCOUNT FO 116.6 CD 216.20
   SM 85.32 VG 25.33 28.36

ACCOUNTS VG 26.6

ACCUMULATED SM 75.40
   VG 72.20

ACCUMULATING SM 73.9

ACCUMULATION SM 71.9 71.26

ACCUMULATIONS SM 154.2

ACCURSED SM 58.33 MD 172.22

ACCUSATION TL 94.18

ACCUSED TL 72.17 SM 83.33

ACCUSING TL 63.30

ACCUSTOMED CD 200.11

ACH TL 53.14 53.26 CD 185.34
   186.7 215.7 215.27 245.23

ACHE LH 21.30 TL 98.28
   CD 233.21 233.23 SM 117.32
   MD 165.33

ACHED LH 33.9 TL 82.31

ACHES SM 118.10

ACHIEVABLE FO 177.13

ACHIEVE SM 156.10

ACHIEVEMENT SM 156.11

ACHIEVING FO 177.8

ACHING FO 179.10 SM 40.28
   VG 29.11

ACH SCHON 'S WAR SCHON DAS
   WASSER IST GUT CD 236.8

ACID   TL 48.35   FO 155.5
   CD 255.19   SM 4.23   34.25   35.14
   52.32   52.35   63.28   143.11
   143.31

ACKNOWLEDGE   SM 135.16

ACORNS   SM 103.22

ACQUAINTANCE   CD 202.5   MD 163.34

ACQUAINTANCES   CD 188.15   224.26
   SM 8.10   22.31   124.36   132.12

ACQUAINTED   VG 62.1

ACQUIESCE   FO 175.42

ACQUIESCED   TL 107.8

ACQUIESCENCE   FO 130.11

ACQUIESCENT   VG 81.12

ACQUIRED   CD 231.23   MD 163.1

ACRES   CD 264.31   SM 141.21

ACRID   TL 82.31   SM 143.11
   VG 12.36   30.12

ACRIDITY   TL 83.25

ACROSS-STREAM   VG 77.32

ACT   TL 43.21   89.42   90.9   90.20
   108.35   FO 131.10   165.26   167.2
   CD 192.14   SM 30.8   80.10

ACTED   SM 10.22   VG 38.21

ACTING   SM 58.37   VG 26.3

ACTION   TL 86.35   108.36   108.37
   108.39   108.41   FO 144.13
   SM 13.5   22.22   VG 48.26   61.7
   64.6   69.36

ACTIONS   SM 119.35   VG 28.8   33.30

ACTIVE   FO 121.38   SM 43.9   145.10
   VG 21.19

ACTIVELY   VG 5.42

ACTIVITIES   CD 225.10   225.12
   225.15

ACTIVITY   TL 86.34   86.35
   SM 130.24

ACTS   TL 89.42   SM 71.1

ACTUAL   TL 66.33   67.2   83.13
   CD 198.39   SM 44.19   55.16
   95.36   98.39   116.35   118.26
   VG 62.37

ACTUALITY   SM 20.34   35.11   87.1

ACTUALLY   TL 100.38   100.39
   FO 116.14   165.18   CD 215.11
   265.7   SM 27.16   30.7   105.21
   111.24   154.27   VG 5.22   8.22
   13.7   14.5   16.19   70.30

ACUTE   FO 123.27

ACUTELY   LH 4.24   FO 158.14

ADAM   SM 5.37

ADAPTABILITY   VG 65.3

ADD   FO 113.4   SM 77.26   VG 11.16

ADDED   LH 9.8   10.26   38.31
   TL 56.13   57.21   97.11
   FO 170.41   CD 202.7   227.35
   SM 20.19   46.26   48.29   54.18
   63.17   67.32   83.28   MD 175.28
   196.3   VG 47.18   67.17

ADDER   TL 59.12   63.36   65.37
   SM 68.32

ADDING   LH 9.11   FO 129.8
   VG 14.29

ADDITION   FO 127.27

ADDRESS   FO 166.24   CD 228.19

ADDRESSED   LH 11.23   MD 167.25
   194.23   199.30   VG 64.24

ADDRESSING   FO 171.28   SM 90.23

ADDS   VG 40.6

ADHERE   SM 71.38

ADJUNCT   SM 95.29

ADJUSTED   LH 36.26   VG 64.42   65.4

ADJUSTING   MD 187.10

ADMIRAL BURNS   TL 71.18

ADMIRALTY   TL 71.19

ADMIRATION   CD 229.2   SM 95.34

ADMIRE   TL 47.20   60.10   67.39
   CD 265.19   SM 15.36   47.14
   49.39

ADMIRED   SM 33.1   47.16   95.34
   111.27

ADMIRER   SM 50.26

ADMIRERS   VG 42.17

ADMIRING   CD 257.14

ADMIT   TL 66.11   CD 191.3   217.17
   SM 13.9   23.40   84.30   90.37
   90.39   99.23   155.27

ADMITTED   TL 78.42   FO 130.17
   SM 153.3   VG 27.40

ADOBE   SM 147.16   147.37   154.34

ADONIS   SM 112.38   113.28

ADOPT   SM 8.7

ADOPTION   TL 47.31

ADORABLE   TL 47.17   69.24

ADORATION   CD 226.20   226.23
   MD 176.21

ADORATION-LUST   TL 82.13
   82.16

ADORE   CD 208.31   226.20
   263.21   263.23   263.36
   265.9   VG 8.6

ADORED   CD 226.25   226.27
   226.28   263.31   SM 108.31
   MD 176.16   VG 6.11   8.9
   8.10

ADORER   VG 10.8

ADORES   CD 188.25   188.26
   204.37   VG 8.5

ADORING   CD 226.31   263.37
   VG 8.11   8.14   8.17

ADVANCE   FO 130.34   MD 180.2
   VG 27.30

ADVANCED   FO 120.2   120.12
   152.34   CD 218.2   SM 43.3
   111.7   MD 163.3   194.22
   VG 49.6   49.13

ADVANCES   SM 130.32   134.37

ADVANCING   FO 152.33   SM 58.18
   MD 167.14   VG 72.23

ADVANTAGE   LH 17.32   38.42
   TL 58.1   SM 134.32

ADVANTAGEOUSLY   SM 142.29

ADVENTURING   MD 181.19

ADVENTUROUS   SM 45.8

ADVISES   CD 188.33

AERIAL   SM 152.17

AEROPLANE   SM 31.35   102.10

AESTHETIC   TL 44.12

AFFABLE   FO 149.35

AFFAIR   FO 117.38   165.23
   166.6   CD 262.30   SM 3.6
   4.4   4.29   VG 4.31   29.5
   31.22   39.1   60.22

AFFAIRS   FO 167.8   CD 224.32
   225.6   SM 127.13   135.28
   MD 190.15   VG 13.3

AFFECTATION   TL 86.9
   CD 249.22   SM 52.29

AFFECTATIONS   CD 249.21

AFFECTED   TL 95.20   FO 152.38
   CD 216.25   224.27   249.23
   SM 97.10   97.11   VG 27.28

AFFECTION LH 20.14 TL 98.28
  CD 224.7

AFFECTIONATE LH 20.10 TL 47.2
  VG 5.28

AFFIRMATIVE TL 48.8

AFFORD TL 98.35 SM 29.24 30.5

AFOOT FO 167.40

AFRAID LH 20.19 21.6 23.31
  25.6 31.2 32.34 33.9 35.5
  TL 50.17 54.40 56.25 64.41
  70.3 70.15 82.1 83.40 91.8
  91.16 94.8 95.3 98.34 105.18
  108.6 FO 113.30 118.10 119.7
  119.9 119.23 122.33 124.6
  124.19 125.20 128.15 129.38
  137.4 151.19 164.10 165.41
  168.40 170.11 174.16 174.20
  174.24 CD 183.31 183.33
  185.31 185.33 185.37 193.37
  194.24 194.29 195.42 197.1
  197.3 199.23 204.27 206.9
  206.37 208.30 208.34 209.38
  209.40 215.32 218.29 254.9
  255.29 260.33 262.2 SM 10.7
  12.36 30.22 35.9 35.10 36.29
  39.11 44.12 51.20 53.21
  53.37 55.36 66.2 66.4 72.33
  73.14 76.19 76.27 76.30
  76.33 77.35 78.27 79.14 82.7
  88.37 91.18 114.1 116.1
  121.32 122.3 122.29 123.33
  133.3 152.16 MD 168.2 168.11
  169.35 169.37 170.1 173.24
  176.41 178.40 189.9 196.33
  202.24 203.14 VG 23.7 23.10
  26.34 27.13 45.25 61.9 64.29
  79.41

AFRESH CD 217.21 SM 154.1
  MD 184.14 VG 76.18

AFRICA CD 265.2 265.28

AFTER-DEATH TL 108.5

AFTER-DINNER SM 5.16

AFTER-LIFE TL 104.2 104.3 104.9

AFTERNOON LH 20.3 TL 60.28
  74.34 FO 127.30 131.19 143.14
  168.30 169.38 174.3 CD 193.25
  193.28 194.35 194.38 198.34
  SM 27.17 42.31 42.37 43.32
  79.10 92.4 92.18 92.27 92.29
  93.3 94.7 101.33 128.5
  MD 185.8 185.12 186.3 187.39
  VG 10.11 13.15 16.34 17.14
  31.24 32.22 36.36 45.15
  51.30 54.32 70.4 70.42 71.5

AFTERTHOUGHT SM 12.9 VG 14.29

AFTERWARDS TL 76.1 82.10 82.14
  FO 154.11 CD 263.11 SM 126.1
  152.23 158.21 MD 207.31

AGATE SM 118.33

AGATE-BROWN TL 94.18

AGE TL 82.19 FO 132.28 132.29
  132.34 162.25 162.29
  CD 226.33 232.10 SM 3.2 5.36
  17.10 43.16 64.39 79.21
  88.28 158.15 MD 174.9
  VG 34.33 34.40 35.27 53.26
  59.11 64.8 65.30 67.35 70.17

AGED SM 64.10 VG 15.33

AGEDNESS VG 15.23 31.21 67.40
  67.41

AGE-MOULDED SM 63.38

AGES TL 50.32 50.35 89.21 97.1
  FO 134.12 SM 51.29 63.37
  75.14 145.40

AGGLOMERATION CD 186.23

AGGRESSION VG 38.11

AGHAST VG 34.32

AGITATED LH 25.37 TL 80.5
  CD 210.2 VG 22.37

AGITATION MD 195.28

AGLEAM FO 116.19

AGO TL 80.27 80.28 80.31 85.17
  FO 120.9 CD 198.22 214.24
  218.36 222.2 251.33 SM 51.18
  95.4

AGONISED FO 141.35 174.27

AGONISING VG 73.3

AGONY TL 43.5 43.26 44.7 78.26
  107.22 FO 148.3 148.9 159.15
  164.11 174.35 178.7 SM 67.36
  MD 204.13 VG 14.34 66.32

AGREE TL 88.18 88.28 88.35
  95.13 FO 155.11 163.9 163.11
  CD 210.29 220.5 SM 29.29
  29.34 50.14 82.18 VG 40.8

AGREED LH 17.16 35.27 FO 113.35
  123.22 VG 53.26

AGREES SM 81.8

AHA FO 153.6 CD 211.33

AHEAD TL 92.16 FO 161.27 178.42
  CD 239.2 239.22 239.25 239.34
  240.18 244.27 247.20 253.17
  SM 59.9 60.2 60.33 63.20
  66.13 68.23 100.8 109.7
  154.37 MD 182.8 VG 19.9 21.33
  36.8 50.15

AH-H LH 10.3 10.4 11.7

AILED TL 47.12

AILS LH 14.14

AIM TL 86.31 86.41 87.26 92.31
  FO 131.5 CD 208.23

AIMING FO 144.6

AIN'T SM 61.10

AIR LH 21.30 22.9 34.21
  36.37 TL 74.35 74.37
  FO 116.18 145.35 146.34
  153.18 153.28 168.19
  173.34 CD 184.9 192.7
  208.39 227.22 230.22
  240.14 242.2 242.8 244.14
  245.32 248.27 252.23
  253.10 255.38 SM 3.18
  5.24 11.19 24.20 27.25
  27.28 27.31 30.27 64.35
  66.30 66.35 69.37 75.12
  102.4 103.1 104.11 104.17
  104.18 104.20 112.32
  146.19 147.10 150.39
  152.18 152.21 152.26
  MD 170.38 180.16 180.22
  185.7 195.31 198.13 202.31
  203.1 209.3 209.8 210.19
  VG 9.4 11.35 15.31 15.34
  29.42 30.1 30.2 34.30
  67.6

AIRS VG 26.32 39.39

AJAR TL 101.30 104.30

ALACRITY SM 138.19

A L'ANGLAISE CD 204.9

ALARM SM 39.4

ALARMED SM 68.21

ALAS TL 44.20 46.37 47.15
  55.16 82.17 82.24 82.26
  87.5 FO 126.42 CD 195.42
  229.20 SM 75.38 95.22
  MD 205.12

ALBRECHT CD 199.28

ALCHEMY SM 53.20

ALCOHOL SM 128.20 145.25

ALDECAR CHAPEL SM 62.41

ALDER CD 239.26

ALEC CD 200.5 206.8 214.10

ALERT LH 17.19 TL 83.25
  FO 122.16 124.40 127.31
  SM 9.3 11.19 14.13 14.23
  45.4 53.5 57.34 101.13
  146.19 MD 171.32 VG 37.12
  37.18 43.10 57.41 58.8

ALERTNESS SM 30.27 46.9

ALEXANDER CD 193.27 233.25
  233.31 246.1 247.35 248.1
  248.11 248.18 248.27
  248.28 252.4 252.22 253.17
  253.41 254.14 254.24
  257.18 257.21 261.39

ALEXANDER HEPBURN CD 186.34 225.26

ALEXANDRA (SEE QUEEN ALEXANDRA)

AMISS   LH 10.9   SM 39.8

AMMONITE   CD 203.14

AMOROUSLY   TL 79.36

AMOROUSNESS   MD 189.16

A'MOST   LH 17.26   33.1

AMOUNT   CD 191.28   216.24
   MD 163.14   177.7   VG 28.37

AMOUNTED   CD 217.13   224.22   251.8
   SM 76.12

AMOUNTS   TL 109.10   SM 157.12

AMPLE   CD 239.15

AMTHAUS   CD 232.3

AMTSGERICHT   CD 233.33

AMUSE   SM 29.2   132.14

AMUSED   TL 69.25   78.4   86.6
   89.31   91.9   FO 115.23   123.28
   CD 187.28   235.2   254.32
   SM 16.9   22.3   38.1   38.10
   104.22   120.35   129.19   VG 29.6

AMUSEMENT   FO 124.31   CD 258.2
   SM 38.28   VG 57.31   59.2

AMUSES   TL 66.18   VG 8.12

AMUSING   TL 50.20   90.18   90.32
   FO 123.28   CD 245.17   SM 17.22
   137.25   VG 40.2

AN'   LH 4.10   5.25   9.12   12.10
   17.27   17.37   17.38   18.35
   19.13   25.24   27.37   28.10
   28.18   29.1   29.18   30.13   30.22
   30.31   31.12   31.19   32.14
   32.20   33.1   35.37   36.23   37.3
   38.3   38.10   38.13   39.8

ANALYSED   SM 52.18

ANALYSIS   SM 30.29   30.32

ANARCHIST   VG 61.3

ANARCHY   VG 61.5   61.7

ANATOMY   SM 30.30

ANCESTOR   CD 210.20

ANCESTORS   SM 64.16

ANCHORAGE   VG 9.2

ANCIENT   FO 115.9   154.34
   SM 13.36   45.15   65.21   VG 12.29
   15.21   65.22   65.33   65.36
   80.30

ANEMONE   MD 168.24

ANEMONES   MD 166.40   209.2

ANGEL   TL 83.38   84.15

ANGELS   TL 83.40   85.34

ANGEL'S CHAIR   SM 56.41   63.6
   63.10

ANGER   LH 19.4   36.3   TL 47.24
   47.27   47.28   47.29   48.35   57.9
   57.10   63.3   63.4   63.9   63.12
   63.18   63.20   63.34   64.12
   64.16   65.12   65.24   65.25
   65.29   73.40   93.39   106.25
   FO 142.6   159.7   164.38   166.17
   167.8   CD 248.33   258.31   259.36
   SM 10.9   26.9   26.14   26.19
   34.3   58.9   72.37   73.1   74.33
   107.15   107.22   MD 186.21
   VG 45.2   54.28   58.22

ANGERED   SM 101.22

ANGLE   FO 146.19   172.15
   CD 242.24

ANGORA   SM 144.11

ANGRIER   SM 24.28

ANGRILY   LH 7.41   8.21   9.5
   CD 258.40   261.39   SM 156.35
   VG 33.41   43.5   43.19   71.23

ANGRY   LH 8.19   TL 63.10   65.30
   65.31   65.35   90.40   91.16
   106.24   106.27   FO 149.33
   150.15   CD 194.20   237.4   237.18
   243.6   262.15   SM 10.3   26.4
   26.6   41.26   41.27   41.28   41.29
   41.34   41.35   41.39   42.17
   42.18   42.19   MD 186.22
   VG 14.27   26.33   27.42   42.29
   49.2

ANGUISH   TL 48.15   58.4   107.10
   MD 166.2   179.20   188.8   188.16
   VG 27.24   28.33

ANGUISHED   FO 177.10   MD 176.21
   205.27

ANIMAL   LH 8.14   11.9   30.9
   TL 50.30   51.36   65.33
   FO 147.27   148.29   SM 11.20
   11.30   12.11   12.27   12.30
   17.19   18.17   23.36   38.25
   47.14   47.31   47.36   48.1   48.12
   48.13   48.20   48.30   49.33
   49.37   50.5   50.8   50.10   50.17
   50.19   50.27   50.28   50.38
   54.26   58.30   59.1   73.19   75.10
   75.11   76.5   80.31   93.27
   101.27   110.17   124.29   MD 166.9
   VG 24.7

ANIMALS   SM 11.25   48.30   50.2
   50.16   50.33   73.13   75.17
   75.19   144.27   145.18   VG 46.22
   49.10

ANIMAL'S   SM 19.19

ANIMOSITY   SM 152.33

ANKLE   TL 79.16   FO 119.2
   CD 234.36   SM 72.12   79.20

ANKLES   TL 103.27   103.28
   103.29   FO 152.39   CD 187.12
   MD 198.2

ANNAMARIA VON PRIELAU-CAROLATH
   CD 195.21

ANNIHILATING   SM 50.37

ANNOUNCE   VG 28.32

ANNOUNCED   TL 71.12   SM 121.1
   VG 45.14

ANNOUNCEMENT   SM 115.5

ANNOUNCING   SM 9.15

ANNOYANCE   SM 5.30   VG 32.8
   42.19

ANNOYED   VG 50.23   57.15

ANOINT   MD 204.6   204.7

ANOTHER'S   MD 175.37

ANSWER   LH 12.4   23.35   28.11
   28.14   28.27   28.29   28.40
   28.42   29.3   30.35   31.7
   35.14   TL 45.28   48.19   58.24
   63.27   64.4   95.32   103.10
   FO 114.20   117.7   124.37
   128.21   130.23   132.36
   132.40   139.40   140.3   140.24
   143.37   146.9   167.35   171.29
   171.31   CD 184.17   184.27
   187.2   196.5   212.34   218.25
   226.14   226.15   257.33
   258.23   264.41   265.26
   SM 12.40   21.34   32.15   34.29
   62.30   63.17   66.4   78.32
   89.36   91.2   98.16   107.2
   107.8   110.2   135.23
   MD 183.4   189.29   209.25
   VG 3.9   19.38   47.14   58.22
   60.36   62.23   64.16   78.20

ANSWERED   LH 6.15   8.18   23.29
   24.31   24.40   26.7   26.19
   29.30   31.8   31.29   33.2
   35.1   39.2   39.16   TL 53.1
   54.24   55.5   55.7   56.11
   57.35   59.12   60.20   62.1
   75.13   FO 117.15   123.19
   123.32   123.37   133.36
   142.34   150.38   159.9   162.8
   173.18   174.24   179.33
   CD 191.3   191.42   192.12
   192.23   212.2   212.4   220.4
   223.8   228.25   242.20
   242.40   257.29   SM 42.19
   63.19   MD 164.3   182.19
   189.26

ANSWERING   TL 53.13   79.31
   103.9   103.10   FO 131.39
   163.20   CD 187.34   SM 12.21
   98.15   119.31   135.22
   MD 178.31   190.36

ANSWERS   MD 163.24   182.7

ANTAGONISTS   FO 143.26   150.37

ANTECHAMBER SM 113.14

ANTE-ROOM TL 64.30

ANTHONY MD 188.34 189.2 189.14
  189.19 189.41

ANTHONY'S MD 188.33

ANTHROPOMORPHIC SM 54.14

ANTICIPATE TL 43.36

ANTICIPATION TL 75.28 CD 235.21
  SM 11.28

ANTI-PHILANTHROPIC TL 47.21

ANTLERS TL 58.36

ANTONY SM 96.30 96.35 97.14

ANTS SM 150.14 158.13

ANXIETY SM 15.23 51.24
  MD 194.31 209.32 210.20

ANXIOUS LH 11.15 11.31 12.11
  15.12 28.33 38.18 CD 228.24
  263.8 SM 4.10 6.38 15.26
  15.29 15.32 39.7 66.9 113.7
  115.26

ANXIOUSLY LH 13.25 14.26
  TL 53.24 CD 184.25 SM 113.1
  156.2

ANYBODY LH 30.31 TL 86.17
  FO 135.5 159.4 162.31
  CD 188.10 189.17 198.12
  204.29 224.17 224.24 224.25
  224.28 225.19 264.14 SM 12.29
  18.38 42.21 59.26 62.18
  62.23 77.3 77.4 85.23 85.24
  86.35 96.19 110.23 114.37
  159.5 VG 10.2 13.7 24.30
  30.33 36.29 44.33 51.8 60.5
  68.15

ANYBODY'S SM 33.11 VG 31.3

ANYHOW TL 80.18 FO 121.16
  125.20 125.39 142.35 146.16
  CD 195.28 198.6 200.29 210.37
  213.15 213.39 SM 5.33 14.18
  16.34 21.10 64.32 89.26
  106.4 121.35 122.18 137.1
  137.11 156.1 VG 19.2 55.21
  56.4 56.20 57.1 79.21

ANYONE LH 14.6 27.6 39.23
  TL 58.8 75.42 99.5 100.25
  102.23 FO 171.33 CD 198.4
  246.30 SM 25.25 117.2
  MD 168.13 VG 27.24 27.25
  62.26

ANYTHING LH 12.24 17.14
  TL 44.34 45.32 46.4 48.7
  53.7 53.29 66.20 67.6 68.10
  86.17 87.15 92.21 92.31
  98.35 107.19 108.19 FO 118.9
  122.6 137.1 140.41 143.6
  143.12 149.35 150.20 151.26
  152.3 153.2 156.30 158.25

ANYTHING (CONT.) 163.37 165.5
  171.36 CD 187.9 188.3 191.28
  195.11 203.4 203.25 203.37
  203.39 207.41 208.42 211.26
  212.13 218.28 222.19 224.17
  229.14 239.1 248.35 SM 6.18
  16.14 21.19 32.29 39.6 39.8
  42.3 42.18 47.21 47.22 56.17
  57.18 60.32 61.19 64.9 68.19
  70.16 74.28 80.20 84.22
  86.37 89.4 89.33 90.5 94.18
  100.17 103.5 103.30 104.32
  111.40 112.12 113.9 116.6
  117.14 118.17 120.1 122.37
  124.21 126.7 129.31 130.19
  137.36 158.22 MD 178.10 186.40
  VG 16.5 16.21 26.24 29.6
  33.10 38.6 49.31 55.19 55.29
  59.24 64.11 66.34 68.17
  74.15 80.5 81.2

ANYWAY FO 141.34 142.29 144.33
  170.35 CD 266.8 SM 12.41
  VG 80.15

ANYWHERE SM 3.22 3.33 77.33
  85.41 86.2 133.15 MD 182.5

APACHE SM 8.4

APART FO 135.27 135.31 171.2
  CD 201.19 205.6 225.32 231.17
  SM 45.34 119.11 120.1 120.28
  120.30 136.1 MD 180.34 181.30
  187.4 188.10 194.11 208.39
  210.17 210.25 VG 50.26

APATHY SM 68.39

APES CD 190.18

APHRODITE TL 77.2 77.35 104.39

APLOMB SM 4.17

APOLLO SM 140.8

APOLOGISE FO 166.21 VG 34.26
  35.22

APOLOGISED LH 13.36 FO 123.12
  VG 34.24 34.25

APOLOGY FO 166.25 VG 35.25

APOPLECTIC SM 83.7

APPARATUS CD 185.21 185.26

APPARENT MD 168.22

APPARENTLY TL 74.1 77.21
  FO 175.22 CD 188.11 219.26
  229.6 240.35 248.35 SM 25.12
  43.30 111.32 127.40 129.25
  135.37 MD 190.7 VG 20.17
  20.25 21.20 31.22 49.27
  56.32 58.5 63.15 65.16

APPARITION VG 40.26

APPEAL SM 138.32 MD 205.21

APPEALING VG 40.7

APPEAR CD 237.23 260.20
  SM 7.6 129.26

APPEARANCE LH 37.37 TL 70.13
  FO 131.17 CD 210.19 230.5
  SM 8.4 18.37 44.9 44.35
  VG 14.28 20.22 27.14
  65.14

APPEARANCES SM 6.8 135.28
  VG 29.6 39.41 65.5 65.6

APPEARED LH 23.2 38.40
  TL 69.7 FO 122.36 123.20
  155.36 CD 184.30 230.17
  235.13 246.39 SM 4.31
  23.23 29.21 30.6 38.29
  45.32 52.11 57.13 109.25
  121.5 MD 191.13 200.33
  VG 14.5 21.20 35.3 49.40
  70.25 77.33

APPEARING SM 34.7 104.5

APPEARS CD 188.14 203.22

APPEASED CD 250.21

'APPEN LH 17.28 19.40 32.42
  VG 15.38

APPETISING VG 9.20

APPETITE LH 15.35 VG 60.12

APPETITES MD 193.24

APPLE SM 105.26 111.6

APPLE-GREEN TL 70.25 73.18

APPLES FO 118.25 127.14
  SM 39.25 90.31 90.35
  111.14 111.17 153.31
  154.34

APPLE-TREES SM 38.12

APPRAISAL SM 30.29

APPRECIATE SM 84.13

APPRECIATION TL 93.36

APPREHENSIVE SM 11.28 13.8

APPROACH LH 37.21 FO 119.33
  131.24 169.23 169.40
  SM 138.35 MD 203.2
  VG 41.15

APPROACHED LH 18.24 TL 72.29
  FO 119.31 CD 225.14
  SM 43.28 99.24 MD 196.32
  VG 21.4

APPROACHING FO 169.42
  CD 229.26 250.34 MD 195.32

APPROPRIATELY VG 80.20

APPROVE TL 90.8 91.3
  VG 16.29 64.25

APPURTENANCES FO 114.1

APRICOT SM 34.8 58.23

AP-RICOT SM 58.25

APRON CD 233.27 SM 112.30
  VG 54.12

APRONS CD 233.12 238.20 252.6

APT FO 115.28

APSLEY (SEE LADY, MAJOR)

ARAB TL 48.1

ARCH FO 137.39 SM 13.31 VG 40.9
  50.33

ARCHED SM 10.3 14.34 58.5
  67.14 69.35 79.7 MD 163.4

ARCHED-NECKED SM 130.32

ARCHES SM 45.5 VG 70.8

ARCHING SM 5.17 15.7 66.38
  83.41

ARCTIC SM 127.1

AREN'T LH 19.39 28.23 37.39
  TL 78.6 78.32 FO 122.28 124.9
  124.11 134.25 138.19 141.32
  149.28 154.26 160.35 165.16
  CD 183.31 187.36 189.22
  190.16 192.41 201.29 202.14
  204.31 207.12 256.28 SM 47.4
  48.9 63.9 93.31 113.39
  121.35 121.36 122.29 122.31
  123.35 154.25 MD 203.23
  VG 17.6 55.31 62.25

ARGUING FO 142.36 143.30

ARGUMENT TL 87.23

ARGUS SM 9.3

ARGUS-EYES SM 9.3

ARIADNE TL 71.19

ARID VG 18.41

ARISTOCRACY SM 119.25 119.26

ARISTOCRAT TL 43.34 88.42 89.3
  89.4 89.22 90.4 CD 209.33
  210.11 SM 119.25

ARISTOCRATIC TL 43.16 91.2
  CD 200.12 218.33 252.11
  SM 9.19 124.19 VG 40.5

ARISTOCRATIC-DEMOCRATIC SM 8.22

ARISTOCRATS TL 89.2 CD 252.12

A RIVEDERTI SM 93.33

ARIZONA SM 7.28 20.39 21.3
  77.32 78.6 112.7 114.21
  141.19

ARM LH 6.31 6.39 8.13 22.39
  24.15 24.16 28.6 TL 94.36
  103.22 FO 116.9 117.29 140.21

ARM (CONT.) 159.18 159.31
  160.18 160.23 169.1 CD 188.35
  235.27 235.28 SM 35.3 65.12
  67.34 84.5 MD 167.30 181.17
  200.6 VG 12.2 12.9 14.10
  17.19 25.9 35.34 40.41 50.26
  72.31 73.10

ARM-CHAIR TL 100.6 100.27
  101.26 VG 4.34 12.22

ARMED MD 202.39

ARMFUL FO 133.40

ARM-HOLES VG 33.1

ARMIES TL 64.7 94.26

ARMISTICE TL 75.30

ARMOUR FO 157.2 SM 86.28 101.21

ARMPITS LH 14.5

ARMS LH 3.18 4.22 5.1 6.16
  6.20 21.32 23.24 23.25 24.11
  33.42 34.2 34.4 34.11 36.8
  TL 77.9 FO 133.42 152.34
  153.28 156.22 CD 183.11
  186.16 233.19 233.27 241.36
  242.34 252.6 SM 96.1
  MD 170.15 186.21 186.23
  186.39 188.13 206.21 VG 14.8
  21.22 22.32 31.32 31.34 33.1
  35.24 37.1 37.10 37.15 54.34
  64.31 74.39 77.10 77.14
  79.32 80.21

ARMY FO 128.2 CD 207.37 212.24
  212.28 225.2 225.6 SM 71.11
  VG 53.22

AROMA SM 146.23 151.38
  MD 168.34 203.1

AROSE FO 126.39 SM 54.17 141.30
  MD 203.1 VG 10.18

AROUSED TL 92.26 SM 35.2 74.33
  VG 3.17

ARRANGE FO 155.15 SM 117.12

ARRANGED TL 70.2 CD 185.14
  SM 56.40 MD 200.27 200.34

ARRANGEMENT FO 157.32

ARRANGEMENTS TL 68.17 SM 92.34
  122.41

ARRANGING LH 38.39 CD 221.38
  SM 44.20

ARRAS VG 51.14

ARREST SM 53.28

ARRESTED LH 6.30 FO 122.16
  130.8 159.36 CD 244.14 252.29
  SM 19.25 79.1 MD 179.1 199.32

ARRIVAL CD 216.6 216.15

ARRIVE TL 85.4 SM 114.17
  116.20

ARRIVED TL 93.5 FO 152.28
  CD 198.21 202.10 208.2
  229.14 233.4 240.38 256.3
  260.7 SM 37.4 51.23 93.13
  112.16 117.6 118.20 129.30
  154.11 VG 37.28 45.6

ARRIVING FO 178.1 VG 72.7

ARROGANCE SM 134.35 VG 8.35
  24.40

ARROWS CD 216.41

ARROYO SM 154.35 155.24

ART LH 8.42 26.24 CD 193.20
  196.4 196.24 226.41
  246.25 MD 178.30 197.18
  200.21 209.16 211.5
  VG 15.38

ARTEMIS TL 47.8

ARTHUR VG 35.28

ARTHUR BALFOUR SM 9.20 48.39

ARTHUR'S VG 5.4

ARTICLE TL 93.14

ARTICLES VG 37.20

ARTIFICIAL TL 46.36 CD 221.29
  SM 101.21 111.17 VG 31.18

ARTIFICIALLY SM 102.34 130.15

ARTILLERY VG 51.17

ARTIST SM 4.2 6.10 6.11
  18.27 42.3 53.16 53.25
  114.18 114.26 122.21

ARTISTIC CD 196.11

ARTISTICALLY SM 17.8 46.7

ARTISTS SM 3.34 122.17
  132.14

ARTIST'S CD 246.16 SM 17.5

ARYAN TL 45.42

ASCEND MD 179.22 182.25
  182.29

ASCENDED TL 78.27 SM 117.36
  118.1 MD 179.11

ASCRIBE CD 193.7

ASH LH 7.6 7.21 SM 133.40

ASHAMED LH 28.7 TL 79.1
  105.27 105.28

ASH-BLOND TL 46.35

ASHBOURNE VG 18.29

ASHES TL 47.3 MD 201.11 201.30
  VG 28.42

ASHORE SM 127.21

ASH-TREE SM 103.26

ASH-TREES SM 103.12 103.14
  103.16 103.23 103.25 103.28

ASHY TL 82.30 SM 97.5

ASIA TL 74.15 SM 69.29
  MD 188.36

ASIATIC SM 119.14

ASK LH 10.11 14.34 25.19 36.3
  TL 50.40 56.1 57.37 60.16
  60.35 61.25 61.28 63.11 64.1
  65.30 80.29 95.8 105.37
  108.38 FO 131.33 132.1 150.14
  150.40 166.21 167.14 167.33
  167.34 CD 197.39 213.31
  228.10 257.28 257.34 258.8
  SM 23.3 34.16 55.24 56.36
  102.32 106.21 115.20 MD 176.5
  182.19 208.38 VG 34.3 34.7
  35.35 38.32 42.27 45.4 63.6
  70.26

ASKANCE MD 178.28

ASKING LH 6.14 11.14 TL 44.34
  73.12 FO 158.2 CD 258.21
  SM 31.17 103.9 104.34 105.36
  106.6 MD 188.21 VG 60.17

ASLEEP TL 45.2 FO 114.41 128.13
  179.3 179.4 CD 201.28
  MD 192.34 VG 78.31 78.42

ASP SM 97.12

ASPASIAS SM 115.37

ASPASIA WEINGARTNER SM 111.4

ASPECT SM 157.2 157.3

ASPEN SM 151.33 151.34

ASPENS SM 134.14 154.39

ASPERSION VG 34.34

ASS CD 216.8 266.5 MD 163.20
  168.36 170.3 172.19 177.19
  198.15

ASSASSINATED SM 117.34

ASSEMBLED VG 10.36

ASSEMBLY VG 42.22

ASSENT LH 17.8 35.29

ASSERT SM 27.34

ASSERTED LH 17.41 22.41 SM 30.4

ASSERTING CD 251.35 SM 73.33
  134.35

ASSERTION SM 21.8 21.9
  MD 171.15 171.33 184.4
  VG 44.15

ASSERTIONS SM 42.8

ASSERTIVE CD 230.8 SM 134.25
  MD 190.6 VG 65.28

ASSERTIVELY SM 32.21

ASSERTIVENESS SM 136.31 136.35
  146.14

ASSERTS MD 180.28

ASSES MD 183.15

ASSIDUITY SM 60.11

ASSISTANCE TL 70.19

ASSOCIATE VG 63.40

ASSOCIATED VG 5.34

ASSOCIATES MD 176.37

ASSOCIATIONS SM 10.30

ASSORTMENT VG 54.5

ASSUMED TL 89.40

ASSUMES FO 177.38

ASSUMING CD 252.10 SM 33.16

ASSURANCE FO 134.31

ASSURE TL 83.32 89.33 CD 190.28
  206.40 212.10 257.36 258.41
  262.23 264.20

ASSURED SM 131.25 136.30 149.1

ASSUREDLY VG 43.42

ASTARTE TL 79.34

ASTERS SM 97.20

ASTONISHED CD 202.4

ASTONISHING LH 22.38 VG 54.2
  54.5

ASTONISHMENT TL 102.9 CD 203.23
  206.25 233.7

ASTOUNDED VG 58.36

ASTRAY TL 81.26

ASTROLOGY SM 53.20

ASTRONOMER CD 185.28

ASTRONOMICAL CD 185.26

ASTRONOMY CD 223.33

ASTUTELY VG 4.35

ASUNDER MD 188.10

ASYLUM FO 166.11 VG 63.2
  66.2 66.3

ATALANTA TL 47.8

ATE LH 15.17 15.24 15.30
  16.7 18.6 18.13 29.28
  30.1 FO 123.9 127.21
  134.23 138.28 156.27
  CD 232.40 245.33 256.32
  SM 103.22 103.27 132.34
  145.27 MD 169.9 170.31
  177.23 191.38 196.17
  201.30 201.31 VG 9.15
  9.17 9.22 47.30

ATHERTON (SEE MISS ATHERTON)

ATHLETIC VG 49.33 50.2 52.38
  54.27 54.33 55.9 58.8

ATLANTIC SM 114.14 126.33

ATMOSPHERE LH 20.5 34.36
  FO 143.25 CD 250.7 252.17
  SM 65.33 75.11 140.17
  VG 5.14 31.23

ATOMS SM 152.25

ATONEMENT MD 207.35 208.22

ATROCITIES TL 43.12

ATTACHED SM 137.35

ATTACHMENT SM 6.23 6.27

ATTACK SM 149.8 154.11
  VG 34.32

ATTACKING SM 100.32 149.11
  152.35

ATTACKS SM 100.37

ATTAINABLE FO 178.4

ATTEMPT SM 153.1 MD 184.12

ATTEMPTED SM 139.34

ATTEMPTING SM 52.16

ATTEND FO 126.14 126.17
  160.10 VG 80.36

ATTENDANT SM 17.18

ATTENDED FO 127.26 141.6
  SM 30.10 VG 38.27

ATTENDING TL 95.41 FO 121.39
  126.40 CD 187.35 SM 12.34
  VG 54.36

ATTENTION TL 52.22 85.26
  86.4 86.6 87.19 FO 117.6
  119.22 123.6 126.19 167.22
  CD 251.30 SM 149.12
  VG 12.34

ATTENTIONS FO 113.31

ATTENTIVE SM 41.3 125.41

ATTIC CD 184.41 193.23 216.28
217.16 219.39 220.8

ATTIC-ROOM CD 201.3

ATTICS CD 201.2

ATTITUDE FO 123.28 130.25
CD 201.20 232.7 257.16 SM 7.4
15.37 15.39 15.40 15.41 16.3
VG 27.11 58.26

ATTRACT CD 210.13 SM 132.15

ATTRACTED TL 91.30 CD 196.18
225.39 230.16 VG 57.35

ATTRACTION CD 232.38 SM 95.34

ATTRACTIONS CD 208.35

ATTRACTIVE LH 27.12 TL 70.6
70.7 CD 209.24 210.16 SM 3.18
16.16 16.18 16.21 16.23
22.39 66.18 158.20

ATTRACTIVE-LOOKING CD 235.11
235.33

ATTRIBUTED SM 26.25 VG 62.17

AUDIBLE LH 11.21 FO 140.14
SM 28.27 99.20 99.22

AUDIBLY FO 145.37

AUDIENCE CD 208.29 230.15

AU FAIT VG 12.40

AUGEAN SM 153.40

AUGURS TL 96.1

AUGUST FO 116.16 CD 233.25
SM 27.39 63.38 105.22 118.20
118.38

AUNT TL 61.18 CD 202.5 SM 61.15
62.16 98.2 105.3 105.39

AUNT ALICE VG 66.9

AUNT CISSIE VG 4.10 6.28 6.30
9.15 9.20 10.20 11.17 12.2
12.6 12.17 12.19 12.36 14.5
14.21 14.32 15.10 25.34 26.1
26.9 26.16 26.19 28.8 28.30
29.8 29.12 29.16 29.20 30.35
31.1 31.3 31.9 32.32 32.36
32.40 33.7 33.38 33.40 34.3
34.22 34.27 34.28 35.6 35.18
37.31 37.33 37.38 38.6 38.9
38.25 38.30 38.41 40.24
63.41 64.18 66.10 70.18
70.25 70.28 71.30 71.32 72.1
72.5 72.14 80.24

AUNT CISSIE'S VG 6.29 6.32 6.39
6.41 14.9 14.29 29.27 30.39
31.6 78.23

AUNT EMMA SM 85.28

AUNT LUCY VG 66.8

AUNT NELL VG 66.9 70.14 71.30
71.37

AUNT NELL'S VG 70.15

AURA CD 253.14 SM 99.18

AUREOLE SM 46.8

AU REVOIR SM 112.14

AUSTRALIA SM 4.35 10.20 14.9

AUSTRALIAN SM 3.35

AUSTRALIANS SM 28.6

AUSTRIA TL 61.6 84.28 92.23
95.11 CD 210.22 229.11 229.13
229.33 230.42 231.31 232.34
252.11

AUSTRIAN CD 229.34 229.35
230.32 231.5 231.30 234.1
252.9 252.12

AUSTRIANS CD 254.34 257.20

AUTHOR SM 82.33

AUTHORITIES CD 213.2 SM 25.17

AUTHORITY LH 13.31 TL 91.19
FO 134.40 159.9 SM 15.10
MD 168.6

AUTO-GARAGE CD 258.1

AUTOMATIC FO 117.11 CD 220.33
SM 50.34

AUTOMATICALLY TL 102.9 FO 128.24

AUTOMOBILE SM 75.36 93.1 112.23
VG 58.1

AUTOMOBILES SM 154.17

AUTUMN TL 44.3 72.21 SM 13.13
74.3 74.5 97.20 104.6 125.27
125.28 129.3 133.30 133.35
133.39 134.8 143.40 VG 39.31

'AVEN'T LH 29.22 29.30

AVENUES SM 68.2

AVERTED LH 39.12 TL 47.28 51.38
53.42 54.17 55.25 FO 123.2
127.22 133.13 139.2 140.23
171.29 CD 197.15 SM 12.34
13.19 75.10 101.9 101.11
VG 44.35 62.22

AVIDLY SM 78.28

AVOID SM 140.29

AVOIDED LH 39.19 TL 99.12 99.17
FO 152.26 VG 9.41

AVOIDING TL 99.25 SM 97.26

AWAITED SM 125.3

AWAKE LH 36.38 TL 51.5
FO 159.17 163.17 178.33
CD 201.30 SM 102.31
MD 165.8 VG 15.24

AWAKENING MD 166.12

AWARE LH 9.36 34.23 TL 87.17
FO 117.5 118.21 125.16
127.22 177.25 SM 18.19
18.31 32.18 32.19 33.23
38.20 68.41 74.20 127.16
159.10 MD 167.13 180.16
192.14 194.23 VG 24.15
47.39 48.1 48.13 48.18
48.20 48.32 57.36 71.10
72.19 74.1

AWESOME VG 76.28

AWE-STRUCK CD 184.14

AWFUL TL 49.15 66.35 75.22
75.26 78.37 79.13 82.12
FO 133.15 145.7 147.6
160.13 166.25 175.12
177.19 177.25 179.21
CD 195.28 213.9 214.18
216.7 216.17 220.31 220.36
220.38 242.3 243.39 256.31
265.3 SM 51.29 72.28 80.37
113.27 113.35 113.38 114.9
121.28 121.33 121.34 124.4
150.3 VG 5.21 8.29 9.9
10.20 12.34 13.9 16.1
25.26 27.23 28.7 28.9
33.41 55.38 56.8 56.35
58.38 59.11 60.32 66.28
70.12 74.10 77.30

AWFULLY TL 63.39 80.13 81.15
81.25 86.7 89.32 90.17
92.19 FO 126.11 129.6
129.11 147.20 165.33
CD 195.30 226.9 SM 8.39
16.16 39.35 41.32 66.18
82.24 113.16 113.18 113.30
VG 7.31 17.6 26.14 32.12
38.24 44.29 47.17 56.14
56.29 57.7 57.8 57.19
57.38 58.31 61.17 61.36
63.13 64.26

AWHILE SM 38.39 87.2 132.25
MD 195.37 208.28

AWKWARD TL 91.36 FO 157.27
171.16 CD 188.5

AWKWARDLY LH 38.30 FO 136.15
SM 63.40

AWKWARDNESS VG 14.14 14.33

AWNING LH 23.15

AWOKE FO 126.36 MD 165.4

AXE FO 168.34 170.28 171.19
173.17 173.28

AXED LH 17.38

AXE-SHAFT FO 172.4

AY FO 120.35 120.37 121.8
121.24 MD 204.39

AYE LH 8.33 8.38 9.6 10.41
12.6 13.26 15.38 17.27 26.18
37.1

AY QUE GOZO SM 91.24

BAA-ING TL 98.26 SM 143.18

BABBLE MD 197.9

BABIES SM 158.5

BABY LH 6.7 32.11 32.14
TL 46.26

BABY'S VG 59.5

BACCA LH 18.18 18.33

BACK-BEATING SM 148.18

BACKED SM 15.7 67.35 84.9
VG 20.41 37.9 62.12 63.18
63.28

BACKGROUND TL 93.19 FO 115.4
CD 227.28 234.24 236.37
SM 15.14 18.24 18.25 26.39
53.25 77.38 110.32 156.19
VG 55.41

BACKING SM 66.22

BACKS LH 7.36 SM 8.39

BACKWARD SM 3.13

BACKWARDS FO 148.20 172.19
CD 247.31 257.16 SM 19.23
66.31 67.8 69.36 69.38 83.1
83.3 83.12 83.34 VG 15.17
80.17

BACON LH 39.18

BAD LH 11.23 32.20 37.12
TL 50.16 59.10 61.31 76.8
99.41 FO 114.37 136.22 144.17
145.13 177.18 CD 211.32
211.34 SM 18.27 32.5 42.1
59.19 71.16 71.17 79.12
79.26 99.8 113.34 122.36
122.38 126.33 133.10 134.21
138.14 154.22 VG 3.10 25.25
31.24 58.6 79.30

BADE CD 224.4 VG 22.4

BADEANSTALT CD 237.30

BADGE SM 127.30

BADGERED LH 32.11

BADGES SM 127.26 128.9

BADLY LH 6.17 29.40 TL 49.34
70.38 81.15 SM 4.30 7.37
VG 33.6

BAD-TEMPERED SM 45.36

BAFFLED LH 3.28 FO 120.39 123.3
SM 65.19 VG 63.36

BAG VG 32.32

BAGGALEY,JIM (SEE JIM BAGGALEY)

BAGGY CD 230.5

BAGS SM 109.34

BAILEY FARM FO 113.17 113.24
114.26 115.8 123.21 137.21
144.28

BAKE SM 44.24

BAKER'S VG 14.6

BAKERY CD 238.24

BAKING-POWDER SM 56.29

BALANCE SM 138.6 MD 176.20

BALANCED TL 100.36 FO 114.18
123.1 SM 18.3

BALANCING SM 151.12 VG 17.1

BALCONIED CD 239.11

BALCONIES CD 234.18

BALCONY CD 230.18 236.38 265.32

BALD SM 40.12 96.28

BALDER CD 243.1

BALFOUR, ARTHUR (SEE ARTHUR
BALFOUR)

BALKED FO 166.36

BALKING SM 24.13

BALL TL 80.8 97.6 97.10 97.14
SM 133.2 VG 44.27

BALLS LH 33.16

BALM TL 83.15

BALSAM SM 141.12

BALUSTRADE VG 73.27

BALUSTRADED VG 17.16

BALZAC'S CD 207.10

BAN SM 15.9

BANAL SM 9.1

BAND TL 71.1 80.8 SM 35.39

BANDAGE TL 57.29

BANDAGED MD 165.10

BANDAGES MD 165.34 166.1 166.14

BANDANA CD 235.24

BANDANNA VG 20.22

BANDED MD 165.10

BAND OF HOPE SM 30.12 VG 9.38

BANDS MD 165.10 165.24

BANFORD FO 113.1 113.7
113.27 115.1 115.12 115.20
115.26 115.32 116.22 117.5
117.13 117.31 117.38
117.41 118.2 118.7 118.10
118.13 118.16 119.6 119.16
119.21 119.30 119.34
120.24 120.29 121.7 121.14
121.21 121.33 122.23
122.26 123.7 123.11 124.2
124.12 124.19 124.27
124.32 124.35 124.41 125.5
125.20 125.24 125.31
125.34 125.37 126.4 126.13
126.40 127.37 127.40
128.14 128.21 128.25
128.29 128.35 128.41 129.4
129.8 129.16 129.24 129.26
133.37 134.8 134.17 134.25
134.30 134.35 135.1 135.5
135.11 136.16 136.22
136.27 136.36 136.42
137.3 137.11 137.21 137.23
137.25 137.28 137.32 138.3
138.11 138.16 138.21
138.25 138.28 138.34
138.39 141.7 141.9 141.17
141.23 141.28 141.37
141.42 142.10 142.16
142.23 142.28 142.38
145.20 147.41 147.42
148.18 148.25 148.39
149.37 149.39 149.42
150.3 150.9 150.11 150.20
150.29 151.3 151.14 151.25
151.31 151.42 152.5 152.6
152.26 153.10 153.13
153.15 153.24 153.35
154.28 155.4 155.17 155.31
156.25 157.8 157.16 157.20
157.23 157.34 157.37
157.38 158.5 158.10 158.13
158.17 158.35 158.39 159.1
159.8 159.12 163.26 163.31
163.35 163.41 164.1 164.5
167.9 167.10 167.13 168.36
168.40 169.9 169.14 170.2
170.11 170.25 170.38
171.24 171.26 171.31 172.2
172.9 172.29 172.34 172.40
173.37 179.7 179.8

BANFORD, (SEE MISS BANFORD)

BANFORD'S FO 113.9 113.15
133.34 135.27 135.33
140.27 140.35 143.19
143.33 144.4 153.29 155.30
158.30

BANG VG 28.21

BANGLES CD 195.7 205.21

BANK FO 168.16 169.17 169.18
170.23 172.40 173.6
CD 233.32 243.13 VG 37.41
70.22

BANKRUPT CD 229.20

BANNERS SM 151.7

BANNISTER-RAIL VG 74.7

BANNISTERS VG 73.42

BANTAM TL 91.26 SM 108.36

BAPTIST SM 30.14

BAR LH 7.7 FO 172.39 VG 16.13
   47.6 47.15

BARBARIC SM 25.5

BARBARICALLY SM 25.13

BARBER SM 44.1

BARE TL 56.41 94.33 103.37
   FO 122.6 CD 211.27 233.13
   233.19 233.28 238.6 241.26
   241.36 242.34 242.35 252.6
   SM 25.5 27.6 64.5 74.7 91.13
   94.29 149.17 MD 170.25 192.35
   202.39 VG 18.5 35.24 36.14
   37.1 45.23

BARE-ARMED VG 34.31

BAREBACK LH 23.4 23.40 SM 20.30

BARED SM 26.36 VG 61.11

BARE-FACED SM 22.37 27.26 45.24
   VG 34.40 34.42 62.23

BARE-HEADED CD 247.34 MD 198.18
   VG 45.31

BARE-KNEED CD 232.5

BARELY MD 169.1 VG 45.39 72.38

BARENESS MD 170.9

BARGAIN SM 92.3 VG 38.25

BARK TL 59.12 SM 146.6

BARLOW (SEE MAJOR-GENERAL BARLOW)

BARKING FO 143.37 146.9

BARMECIDE SM 27.24

BARN FO 114.2 114.42 115.9
   117.10 118.27 134.14 146.27
   147.2 SM 143.13

BARNS TL 98.2

BARN-YARD SM 137.21

BARONESS CD 195.29 200.3 200.13
   200.18 210.18 211.2 212.36
   219.3 228.12

BARONESS'S CD 212.20

BARONESS VON PRIELAU-CAROLATH
   CD 228.11

BARONESS VON VON CD 195.26

BARONET SM 3.37 18.3 59.8

BARONET'S SM 4.37

BARREL CD 186.38 SM 30.1 30.7
   155.23

BARREN CD 199.7 249.6 SM 87.20
   90.18 97.1 97.3 MD 180.9

BARRICADE SM 64.6

BARRIER CD 223.17 SM 146.13
   146.31

BARS FO 153.27 VG 16.16

BASE TL 70.24 FO 168.28
   VG 66.29

BASE-BORN VG 61.27 64.13 64.14
   64.38

BASED TL 91.34 CD 230.41
   VG 54.29 61.6

BASES SM 147.15

BASHFULLY LH 22.25

BASHFULNESS SM 135.39

BASIL TL 48.1 56.3 68.37 68.38
   71.31 75.19 75.20 77.3 82.16
   83.32 84.29 84.41 85.8 85.11
   85.37 85.41 86.19 87.19
   88.18 88.28 68.30 89.8 89.16
   89.20 90.3 90.16 90.37 91.6
   91.12 91.20 91.30 91.34
   92.18 92.38 93.5 93.20 95.8
   96.14 96.32 97.4 97.10 97.15
   99.13 99.15 99.21 100.19
   105.1 105.7 106.18 106.24
   106.27 106.35 107.27 108.13
   108.14 108.18 109.3 109.9

BASIL'S TL 92.7

BASIN SM 142.12 145.19
   MD 191.26

BASINS SM 142.9 142.10

BASIS CD 259.2 262.19 262.29

BASKET LH 14.38 CD 183.7 185.4
   186.21 240.2 MD 198.36 199.2
   200.2 200.26 VG 46.28

BASKETS MD 199.2 199.41 200.3

BATH LH 21.34 33.1 FO 126.17
   SM 132.26 132.27

BATHE MD 189.16

BATHED CD 233.5

BATHER MD 174.33

BATHERS CD 233.3 234.31

BATH-HOUSE SM 142.13 142.15

BATHING LH 21.31 CD 237.29
   MD 189.15 VG 48.19

BATHING-HOUSE CD 235.18

BATHING-PARTY SM 31.37

BATH-ROBE CD 235.34

BATHROOM VG 37.23

BATHROOMS VG 29.36 29.41

BATHS SM 52.2

BATH-TUB SM 142.14 145.22

BAT-LIKE TL 100.2

BAT'S TL 100.23

BATTLE FO 130.32 130.40
   131.2 131.3 158.39
   CD 192.4 253.22 SM 19.32
   25.38 25.39 26.29 96.24
   101.14 124.37 151.7
   152.21 MD 183.19 183.21
   VG 52.17

BAUBLE TL 80.26

BAVARIANS CD 226.37

BAWLED LH 8.36 CD 261.31
   VG 58.42 59.17

BAY TL 99.26 CD 240.26
   260.18 SM 11.15 12.33
   16.14 22.5 22.23 58.4
   63.21 74.18 102.35
   MD 185.27 185.29 192.13
   197.9 198.5 198.32 209.39
   VG 62.13

BAYS MD 185.17 186.1

BAZAARS VG 26.2

BEACH SM 146.34 MD 197.29

BEAD CD 255.3

BEADS SM 48.24

BEAK SM 46.2 MD 171.6

BEAKS FO 172.31

BEAKY MD 171.30

BEAM LH 26.33 TL 69.40
   SM 11.1 27.35

BEAMED FO 129.20 SM 39.29
   40.8

BEAMING SM 81.19

BEAMINGLY SM 27.34

BEAMS LH 26.36 CD 226.32

BEAN-FIELD MD 209.3

BEAN-PLANTS SM 140.36

BEANS SM 140.37 140.38

BEANS (CONT.)   SM 142.27 154.9
  MD 170.32 VG 16.23 47.16
  47.29

BEAR LH 12.12 20.18 34.13
  TL 48.40 58.39 82.10 82.12
  FO 119.24 145.15 157.17
  CD 197.3 213.16 220.26 225.10
  SM 14.39 31.23 34.4 70.17
  74.16 75.28 112.23 117.38
  117.39 151.36 152.7 MD 175.6
  201.16 209.22 VG 12.16 31.40
  62.6

BEARD LH 17.22 TL 44.40 45.39
  49.36 49.37 49.38 51.7 53.42
  58.27 59.26 FO 169.7
  CD 244.19 256.3 SM 17.11
  18.17 22.13 22.34 22.39 23.5
  23.6 23.16 23.19 46.19 119.9
  MD 167.39 181.1 190.25 193.6

BEARDED SM 18.8 MD 186.29

BEARDS SM 23.17

BEARING LH 25.1 TL 64.33
  FO 127.5 136.11 157.28
  CD 240.4 SM 7.34 140.27
  VG 9.23 38.14

BEARS SM 152.9

BEAST TL 59.35 94.12 96.2
  FO 113.29 124.8 145.7 147.8
  149.2 165.34 CD 241.24 247.21
  253.27 SM 21.2 VG 29.15 29.17

BEASTLY TL 80.30 FO 144.36
  CD 226.36 229.12 261.15
  SM 65.4 VG 8.17 34.8 35.13
  39.23 56.41 58.33 66.8 66.13

BEASTS TL 93.30 93.32 94.7
  FO 113.5

BEAT LH 9.17 26.27 27.9 27.27
  TL 47.23 74.4 74.5 74.6 74.8
  74.13 78.12 FO 117.36 147.9
  155.22 160.14 CD 200.34
  221.10 248.29 SM 115.14
  MD 186.24 192.32 198.11

BEATEN LH 28.37 TL 44.2
  FO 174.29 SM 10.23 VG 38.2
  68.26

BEATING FO 118.25 160.23
  CD 242.7 SM 19.28 MD 167.28
  186.36 VG 67.11

BEAU SM 8.30 VG 20.18

BEAU MONDE SM 8.27

BEAUTIES TL 46.21 CD 226.21

BEAUTIFUL LH 33.35 TL 46.41
  50.9 53.10 53.22 58.17 62.19
  69.27 70.30 71.32 77.34
  83.19 97.23 106.13 108.11
  FO 114.3 136.9 CD 184.1
  184.15 184.16 185.5 185.11
  185.17 193.9 193.18 193.34
  196.10 200.3 200.27 209.15

BEAUTIFUL (CONT.) 209.24 210.8
  212.8 216.36 216.37 229.7
  229.24 230.26 235.12 238.26
  243.1 253.6 SM 13.2 13.5
  16.33 16.40 22.24 39.28
  47.9 65.39 83.22 83.30 90.12
  97.31 113.3 115.6 124.12
  129.32 137.18 144.12 144.16
  147.1 150.26 155.27 155.36
  MD 175.10 188.41 191.7
  203.17 203.18 VG 3.6 21.15
  25.11 40.3 57.18

BEAUTIFULLY TL 80.21 CD 184.7

BEAUTIFULLY-BUILT TL 46.28

BEAUTIFULLY-FRINGED TL 59.35

BEAUTIFULLY-SHAPED CD 189.36

BEAUTY LH 22.18 TL 46.37 50.33
  65.21 65.22 65.24 65.26
  67.31 67.33 68.32 68.34
  77.34 81.28 83.12 83.23
  FO 147.32 149.8 CD 210.24
  229.14 SM 11.23 83.21 119.16
  124.25 128.31 145.33 146.29
  147.1 147.2 147.5 147.39
  148.21 148.41 149.9 150.28
  155.29 155.30 MD 189.16 193.2
  193.10 208.14 VG 40.38

BEAUTY-SPECIALIST SM 45.26

BEAUTY-SPOTS VG 6.18

BEAUX VG 43.20

BECAME TL 44.18 82.29 82.30
  96.17 97.8 100.15 102.28
  105.26 FO 115.16 117.5 120.35
  122.12 124.41 125.16 128.41
  142.19 165.1 176.29 176.38
  177.16 CD 197.4 197.7 207.16
  232.33 235.32 235.34 253.38
  SM 4.30 6.31 6.34 9.6 12.36
  34.11 34.20 56.20 68.3 68.41
  75.7 128.2 132.38 MD 180.29
  188.14 VG 4.9 5.41 6.31
  10.20 18.4 27.13 48.32 72.19
  77.23

BECOME LH 13.20 TL 48.8 66.39
  68.29 76.24 89.19 100.21
  107.3 FO 115.29 115.33 118.38
  120.10 171.16 177.25 178.7
  178.17 CD 198.27 SM 37.30
  53.23 104.8 112.30 112.31
  115.21 MD 177.1 VG 16.7

BECOMES TL 66.40 FO 130.37
  MD 204.15

BECOMING SM 6.4 38.3 45.17
  65.33 78.5 132.24 MD 194.23
  VG 31.30

BED LH 4.19 8.8 8.28 9.3
  26.35 29.26 TL 44.32 45.16
  51.24 56.38 99.24 100.25
  FO 114.39 125.19 128.4 138.30
  143.29 143.30 143.39 145.27
  147.35 157.41 158.9 162.7
  164.1 CD 219.23 243.26 243.32

BED (CONT.) 252.30 252.32
  SM 37.37 38.12 39.24
  72.14 73.40 85.3 97.20
  104.13 109.31 111.33
  113.1 113.28 122.11
  132.37 133.27 152.4
  MD 191.40 200.22 200.34
  VG 11.42 12.5 12.6 29.10
  29.22 30.31 30.36 75.6
  76.8 76.12 78.7 78.37
  78.40 80.37 81.10

BEDCLOTHES VG 76.38 78.31
  79.18

BED-CLOTHES SM 111.34

BEDDING MD 200.20

BED-JACKETS SM 110.40

BED-RIDDEN VG 6.3

BEDROOM LH 22.27 TL 99.26
  CD 201.4 214.28 214.30
  219.24 SM 113.13 VG 30.40

BEDROOMS TL 97.35 VG 33.26

BEDS TL 44.20 VG 70.24

BEDSIDE SM 109.38

BEDSPREAD TL 99.23

BEDSTEAD VG 78.6 78.8

BEDTIME SM 55.23

BED-TIME FO 152.6

BEE TL 61.31 61.34 61.37
  CD 245.5 VG 15.31

BEEF VG 9.11

BEEF-TEA VG 9.14

BEEHIVE VG 15.28

BEER LH 29.30 SM 29.24 29.28
  29.38 30.2 30.7 VG 54.19

BEES TL 96.33 VG 15.29
  15.34 70.6

BEETLE TL 96.34 96.39 97.6

BEE-'IVE VG 15.40

BEFALL SM 110.28

BEFOREHAND VG 28.7

BEG TL 94.1 SM 59.21 82.9

BEGET MD 182.38

BEGGAR TL 81.16 FO 118.18

BEGGED SM 126.31

BEGIN TL 71.26 82.9 89.15
  FO 119.23 124.16 135.21
  135.22 CD 191.7 192.34

BEGIN (CONT.) CD 194.16 222.31
    238.22 262.6 SM 86.1 111.24
    120.25 VG 71.36

BEGINNING LH 31.24 TL 44.11
    44.19 61.14 87.2 FO 120.30
    CD 196.29 206.13 221.25
    SM 30.22 44.26 53.17 101.41
    157.12 157.14

BEGINS CD 240.8 SM 5.37
    MD 209.27

BEGOTTEN CD 229.3

BEGUN LH 22.7 TL 47.14 64.21
    SM 31.3 52.21 125.37

BEHALF LH 32.31 TL 47.5
    SM 135.7

BEHAVE TL 89.33 CD 222.18
    SM 123.30

BEHAVED FO 166.26 SM 4.6 20.11

BEHAVIOUR FO 149.34 VG 29.27

BEHINDHAND SM 136.27

BEHOLD TL 79.4 SM 8.18 151.12
    MD 192.28 VG 3.15

BEING LH 3.1 3.5 29.41 38.25
    TL 44.2 53.19 53.20 57.38
    64.28 65.31 67.13 68.13
    68.17 70.9 71.15 73.21 82.23
    82.40 83.31 86.15 86.26
    91.22 92.23 99.6 103.4
    FO 119.22 122.39 128.15
    152.20 156.42 162.4 166.14
    166.17 167.11 173.20 176.15
    177.11 CD 191.12 196.6 208.26
    208.27 209.7 211.4 215.28
    216.30 224.14 225.32 226.18
    229.32 232.34 237.4 245.20
    252.9 254.10 SM 3.18 3.21
    4.2 6.16 7.20 12.26 25.1
    26.17 32.27 33.15 34.4 35.17
    40.1 40.23 41.4 48.17 57.29
    69.17 72.1 76.38 94.20 97.10
    101.10 105.9 105.37 112.2
    113.26 114.1 115.16 118.24
    118.30 120.2 121.10 129.12
    131.9 131.36 131.37 142.7
    149.8 153.2 154.9 MD 165.29
    165.31 168.37 177.13 177.18
    180.26 181.23 182.11 208.20
    208.23 208.31 211.22 VG 6.26
    7.17 8.9 9.7 22.32 29.2
    31.6 31.8 31.11 39.23 41.31
    45.9 52.13 66.34 66.40

BEINGS TL 86.26 86.37 88.5
    CD 199.11 223.23 SM 80.38

BELIED CD 238.12

BELIEF TL 88.21 SM 49.5 153.10
    153.12 MD 183.5 183.39
    VG 26.40 26.41 27.6 27.14

BELIEVE LH 37.9 TL 49.21 72.14
    74.29 82.21 88.42 89.32
    93.12 96.16 108.2 108.14

BELIEVE (CONT.) FO 123.30 133.31
    133.33 142.4 142.8 154.29
    160.9 162.37 162.39 163.5
    163.6 CD 198.9 203.33 205.25
    209.17 210.41 211.19 211.27
    247.1 259.14 262.30 SM 11.9
    27.15 27.16 27.30 30.40
    35.23 41.38 41.40 43.9 43.39
    48.20 49.11 56.27 62.23
    63.17 70.11 70.13 80.23
    80.30 89.13 89.14 97.11
    97.37 98.4 100.31 104.28
    104.36 104.37 105.28 105.37
    105.40 112.11 112.41 114.27
    115.31 MD 183.2 VG 17.12
    22.15 34.39 56.29 59.10
    62.21

BELIEVED TL 74.36 77.29 87.25
    88.26 107.18 FO 179.12
    SM 20.34 95.38 106.5
    MD 169.39 VG 35.1

BELIEVER MD 183.1

BELIEVES CD 218.27

BELL SM 82.25 154.23

BELL-BOY SM 128.40

BELLE-MERE SM 35.16 35.17 82.23

BELLE-MERE'S SM 83.38

BELL-FLOWERS LH 21.27

BELL-HANDLE SM 81.18

BELLIES SM 128.30 147.9

BELL-LIKE SM 90.14

BELL-MARE SM 35.18 82.28

BELLOWING FO 174.4

BELLS CD 201.12 241.3 244.35
    247.25 SM 43.3 75.2

BELLY FO 146.37 146.38 147.8
    147.29 148.23 148.30 149.24
    SM 58.32 66.34 68.36 69.33
    153.24 155.11 MD 188.13
    188.20 196.26 203.29

BELONG TL 50.36 57.18 77.39
    CD 190.40 250.7 SM 3.23 3.33
    14.11 106.7 MD 179.25
    VG 33.36

BELONGED TL 81.20 104.3 106.40
    107.6 FO 175.14 175.19
    CD 234.29 247.4 SM 90.16
    VG 22.28 28.13 33.25 65.39
    67.18 68.15

BELONGING TL 92.3 SM 11.36
    32.38 118.28

BELONGS VG 67.18

BELOVED FO 152.9 176.29 177.11
    177.12

BELT CD 189.40 189.41
    190.2 190.3

BELTED FO 114.8 120.23
    122.14

BELTS CD 185.24

BEMUSED FO 142.39 148.40
    VG 34.29 34.30

BENCH TL 65.8 FO 113.36
    SM 33.27 VG 71.35

BEND VG 71.24 72.22

BENDING LH 7.37 TL 45.16
    FO 132.6 135.30 CD 184.41
    254.29 SM 38.9 MD 168.24
    207.8 VG 14.32 24.26
    25.10

BENEATH LH 5.33 7.32
    FO 136.39 149.6 176.9
    176.12 CD 186.24 220.31
    SM 18.36 42.28 140.21
    MD 191.8 194.16 VG 21.40
    22.16 65.36 75.1 80.31

BENEFIT LH 17.37 SM 118.38
    VG 14.42

BENEVOLENT TL 47.34 SM 23.26

BENIGN TL 82.4

BENT LH 12.27 30.8 TL 103.31
    FO 122.13 133.15 134.23
    147.13 151.4 CD 184.11
    186.17 189.2 231.25
    SM 45.27 71.2 MD 172.12
    189.36 191.9 198.1 198.21
    198.24 VG 45.33 50.25

BEREAVEMENT MD 188.8

BERGHEIL CD 241.38 241.39
    242.34 252.17 253.23

BERLIN CD 194.16

BERRIES TL 74.22 74.23
    CD 240.42 SM 152.6 152.8

BERRYMAN, CAPTAIN (SEE
    CAPTAIN BERRYMAN)

BESEECHING TL 89.12 89.13

BESIDE LH 6.1 12.20 15.29
    24.9 26.33 TL 50.37
    95.17 98.14 103.17 106.19
    FO 131.22 179.1 CD 183.8
    204.24 245.21 260.32
    261.12 SM 42.37 45.14
    60.21 63.1 63.24 65.12
    72.14 107.32 134.33 136.24
    141.39 MD 167.5 190.27
    207.1 VG 43.38

BESIDES TL 48.37 FO 120.39
    128.2 129.15 162.18
    SM 16.24 46.26 48.10
    79.39 VG 6.4 41.23 57.17

BEST LH 33.14 TL 43.27 48.15
61.13 84.33 84.35 94.15
FO 115.25 CD 216.26 219.15
229.29 SM 15.40 27.33 30.40
44.33 64.31 64.39 103.15
103.22 105.13 110.1 113.8
137.28 MD 164.23 169.33
179.31 189.23 201.39 VG 39.35
39.37 40.28 40.34 60.25
62.42

BESTOWED MD 191.28

BET LH 36.7 CD 202.39

BETRAY TL 107.41 SM 71.13
MD 174.23 210.21

BETRAYAL SM 70.39 MD 174.25

BETRAYED SM 38.25 53.27 71.21
MD 173.10 210.22 VG 4.23

BETRAYING SM 71.2

BETRAYS SM 11.19

BETTER LH 4.1 6.42 8.30 10.20
11.7 11.30 13.20 19.34 20.27
29.1 33.20 38.31 TL 48.18
48.19 48.21 49.18 49.21
49.22 52.5 52.12 52.15 52.17
54.12 54.19 62.22 63.9 63.35
65.10 65.14 65.18 65.19
65.20 65.30 FO 124.17
125.18 161.3 173.25 179.26
CD 190.11 191.7 200.15 209.30
212.30 212.31 212.36 217.9
218.8 226.12 233.16 254.40
SM 5.39 6.18 32.11 33.6
35.22 46.25 46.33 59.20
64.26 65.8 70.28 73.17 81.27
84.36 89.25 91.21 92.5 106.3
106.6 109.20 109.29 110.11
110.21 113.31 115.11 116.27
120.12 120.27 130.30 137.1
138.14 141.28 150.4 158.6
158.17 158.18 MD 173.8 174.18
VG 17.30 23.18 32.33 32.40
33.12 55.39 58.29 68.14 76.8
79.28

BETTER-NATURED CD 193.36

BEVERIDGE (SEE COUNTESS, EARL,
LADY, LORD BEVERIDGE)

BEVERIDGE HOUSE TL 46.6

BEWARE SM 124.24 MD 189.9

BEWILDERED LH 33.38 SM 129.30
158.12

BEWILDERMENT FO 148.4 CD 236.29

BEWITCHED TL 101.6 103.3
CD 201.36

BIARRITZ CD 214.28 SM 3.29

BIBELOTS CD 223.22 227.19

BICYCLE LH 25.6 25.11 26.30
29.3 30.9 FO 126.41 168.10

BICYCLE (CONT.) 169.41 170.7
170.22 VG 45.14 45.38 46.7
46.38 47.19 51.37 51.40
68.12

BICYCLED VG 10.26

BICYCLES LH 20.37

BICYCLING VG 62.3

BID TL 102.16 MD 194.39
VG 50.24

BIDDING CD 217.5

BIG LH 4.37 7.18 14.37 16.13
23.10 26.35 28.32 33.26 34.5
TL 56.39 70.4 78.20 91.6
93.5 98.14 99.23 100.7
101.26 101.28 FO 114.14
114.21 115.13 120.23 127.16
135.42 136.32 143.34 148.28
149.9 149.17 149.38 154.13
161.37 164.33 168.19 174.14
CD 192.33 194.2 205.22 216.27
216.28 223.2 230.8 230.12
231.16 232.12 234.25 235.2
238.30 239.8 240.31 241.6
244.26 244.33 247.25 248.31
253.9 257.8 257.12 260.1
260.7 260.9 SM 3.14 7.16
7.17 11.18 12.8 15.21 22.5
28.14 28.29 37.35 38.5 39.20
39.29 42.38 43.1 45.2 58.5
58.10 59.1 74.24 78.11
102.24 111.9 132.28 135.33
135.35 142.2 142.26 144.35
154.23 155.12 158.37
MD 189.14 209.30 VG 3.23 10.1
10.32 16.38 17.2 19.22 20.21
21.6 24.37 30.13 30.14 30.29
32.28 49.28 51.1 51.10 51.11
53.30 53.32 65.36 78.6

BIG BERTHAS TL 64.6

BIG-EYED CD 237.7 VG 59.13

BIGGER TL 49.24 FO 114.1
CD 244.37 249.34 249.36
249.38 249.39 249.40 251.36
255.15 SM 63.14 157.29 157.30
157.32 157.34 158.7 158.38

BIGNESS CD 230.40

BIKES VG 8.28

BILBERRIES CD 240.42

BILBERRY SM 60.13 66.13

BILBERRY-PICKERS SM 60.9

BILE TL 62.36 VG 31.6

BILL LH 10.40 14.31 15.33
15.42 16.5 17.34 20.6

BILLETED FO 128.3

BILLIARDS TL 66.13 99.14

BILLS SM 128.18

BIN LH 38.2 SM 87.24

BINGHAM, LADY (SEE LADY
BINGHAM)

BIRD LH 7.23 TL 44.11 57.39
71.7 100.36 FO 123.9
141.37 141.38 173.4
CD 222.23 222.24 222.25
223.35 225.23 SM 99.16
134.12 134.13 MD 163.33
167.27 167.34 171.2 171.28
171.29 171.38 172.12
178.26 178.29 181.40
182.40 183.2 183.24 183.32
186.9 VG 31.1 47.37 50.34
54.24 54.26

BIRD-LIKE TL 44.30 VG 46.8
57.32 62.35

BIRDS SM 118.34 134.17
MD 178.30 183.22 183.26

BIRD'S MD 171.9 171.27
172.3 VG 58.12

BIRRED VG 25.14

BIRTH TL 99.2 FO 123.20
SM 86.4

BIRTH-CRY CD 244.31

BIRTHDAY TL 50.20 60.1

BISCUIT SM 40.4

BISHOPS-CROSIER CD 244.36

BIT LH 8.29 8.38 9.7 11.28
13.26 14.29 15.29 17.24
17.25 17.36 18.3 18.17
18.41 19.8 19.19 19.27
30.16 32.35 38.6 39.16
TL 49.4 50.18 54.5 71.1
71.6 71.13 71.15 71.16
71.30 72.4 72.42 73.2
78.38 80.1 80.7 88.29
90.37 94.36 105.8 106.31
FO 121.19 123.41 126.32
129.8 154.13 157.39 161.10
168.32 171.41 172.34
CD 188.10 190.24 206.17
207.25 207.33 212.9 226.20
239.34 242.8 250.39 251.41
SM 8.30 9.4 9.28 9.30
10.39 11.32 13.11 24.20
24.32 25.33 29.20 37.10
38.30 50.10 53.1 58.15
65.28 67.33 68.36 70.17
80.2 87.18 92.5 99.1
103.36 115.13 126.3 129.30
130.37 131.25 131.26
138.26 147.23 157.41
158.20 MD 164.24 171.39
188.22 VG 8.23 9.13 17.12
20.17 21.9 21.37 21.38
24.42 25.1 25.5 25.29
25.31 28.18 35.8 40.4
40.22 41.36 42.3 42.5
42.13 46.36 53.9 58.25

BITCH VG 44.38

BITE   FO 149.6 149.7 SM 10.5
  10.6 77.3 MD 180.21

BITES   MD 180.18

BITING   FO 138.3 CD 216.40
  241.15 SM 7.3

BITS   LH 38.40 TL 65.41 67.12
  98.22 FO 148.1 CD 215.9
  SM 52.29 MD 164.23 VG 47.29
  52.4 68.23

BITTEN   FO 167.5 CD 244.30

BITTER   LH 10.13 31.35 33.31
  TL 48.7 48.28 62.39 83.15
  93.1 FO 158.40 159.27
  CD 190.13 230.2 230.9 230.13
  232.15 MD 203.35

BITTER-ACID   SM 57.19

BITTERER   TL 93.3

BITTER-INDIFFERENT   CD 231.1

BITTERLY   LH 36.2 36.6 36.15
  TL 44.18 64.5 FO 145.20
  154.28 159.41 179.6 CD 186.33
  190.26 192.30 204.12 259.11
  MD 166.14 175.5 VG 74.32

BITTERNESS   LH 18.26 35.12
  TL 47.27 108.16 CD 190.14
  255.23 SM 38.17 120.39
  MD 176.27

BITTERS   FO 168.9

BLACK   LH 3.4 4.26 8.20 21.28
  22.16 23.16 24.37 26.38
  27.26 29.11 29.34 30.37
  36.31 TL 44.39 45.7 45.8
  45.12 45.17 45.24 45.39
  46.30 49.38 50.8 51.7 51.10
  51.11 51.15 51.32 51.36 52.2
  52.32 53.38 54.13 55.37
  58.27 58.28 58.29 59.2 63.6
  67.41 68.29 73.13 74.22
  79.17 81.10 83.6 83.19 84.2
  84.4 86.21 92.24 94.3 94.33
  98.14 100.28 101.27 101.32
  101.39 FO 113.22 117.10
  119.14 134.6 136.10 136.32
  143.23 146.2 146.19 148.24
  148.28 148.37 156.40 169.5
  174.14 174.26 175.41
  CD 183.25 184.12 187.7 187.19
  187.27 189.7 189.35 189.38
  190.5 190.7 192.33 193.9
  195.5 201.22 202.25 214.36
  214.39 216.35 230.24 233.38
  238.15 238.16 238.37 239.13
  239.14 240.14 240.42 241.10
  244.4 244.33 247.17 247.41
  251.9 251.35 252.1 253.7
  256.3 SM 7.33 8.20 11.18
  12.8 13.26 16.3 17.11 17.32
  17.35 22.12 22.13 28.21
  32.20 33.27 35.37 35.38
  35.39 38.23 38.24 38.33 45.4
  45.5 45.20 45.21 46.8 58.35
  63.21 68.29 69.22 83.41 84.1
  130.41 131.29 135.34 148.10

BLACK (CONT.) 150.14 158.12
  MD 167.18 167.21 167.39
  167.40 168.7 170.13 171.12
  190.25 193.4 193.6 197.28
  VG 7.7 9.31 14.12 19.17
  19.21 19.35 20.20 20.40
  21.24 21.25 23.25 24.16
  24.39 30.15 38.10 43.10
  43.16 46.17 47.31 49.42
  53.31 56.6 70.13 72.30
  74.2 76.15 77.4 78.13

BLACK-AND-WHITE   CD 235.13 238.2
  238.36 239.15 MD 186.16

BLACK-BEARDED   SM 20.13 22.5

BLACK-BLUE   CD 244.40

BLACK-BORDERED   SM 28.21

BLACK-BROWED   TL 94.19 MD 163.17

BLACK-CAP   CD 222.24 222.30
  222.34 222.39 223.13

BLACKENED   CD 248.34

BLACK-EYED   VG 46.15

BLACK-GLINTED   FO 148.31

BLACK-HAIRED   VG 21.22

BLACKISH   SM 147.25 MD 187.38

BLACK-LOOKING   VG 71.24

BLACKLY   FO 146.18 CD 251.4
  251.6

BLACKNESS   LH 30.41 31.1
  TL 83.11 101.17 CD 240.15
  VG 25.16

BLACK-PURPLE   CD 247.14

BLACK ROCKS   VG 45.11

BLACK-WET   LH 28.36

BLADE   SM 14.35 MD 199.20

BLADES   LH 7.32

BLAME   CD 206.36 223.28
  SM 138.33

BLAMELESS   VG 64.8

BLANCHED   VG 46.36

BLANCHING   TL 73.36

BLAND   VG 57.14

BLANDLY   VG 40.3

BLANDNESS   VG 31.41

BLANK   FO 118.23 125.36 141.30
  CD 192.3 198.23 202.25 202.35
  203.31 209.35 221.4 244.2
  SM 21.14 21.15 21.22 32.35
  100.27 112.10 115.26 129.14

BLANK (CONT.) 129.19 131.18
  137.27 149.15 VG 10.39
  10.41 11.1 11.3 13.30
  49.37 50.9 64.28

BLANKET   LH 29.5 35.42 38.24
  FO 160.24 VG 24.22

BLANKETING   SM 127.4

BLANKLY   CD 257.39 VG 74.37

BLANKNESS   SM 20.19 76.25

BLAST   VG 3.15 34.13

BLASTING   VG 18.23

BLATANT   SM 45.9 VG 44.24

BLATANTLY   SM 130.19

BLAZE   SM 15.31 MD 207.9
  VG 50.6 50.12 50.14 70.6

BLAZING   LH 4.21 SM 16.6
  147.28 MD 207.12

BLEACHED   LH 7.36 CD 242.37
  SM 152.31

BLEAK   VG 3.25

BLEAT   TL 98.25

BLEATING   SM 143.25

BLEED   FO 175.26

BLEEDING   CD 224.8 230.30
  256.17

BLESS   LH 15.38 CD 190.23

BLESSED   TL 73.38 SM 116.20
  140.22 MD 205.11

BLESSING   LH 11.32 VG 25.12

BLEW   LH 7.8 26.40 30.36
  31.16 TL 63.17 FO 114.13
  168.38 CD 205.33 SM 13.24
  MD 209.1 VG 48.1 75.38
  76.27

BLEWBURY   FO 167.41 168.1

BLIND   FO 165.18 174.34
  SM 36.8 104.9 145.31
  145.32 146.9 146.14
  MD 187.5 187.7 196.14
  VG 6.2 12.1 73.37 74.6
  74.16

BLINDED   MD 180.35

BLINDER   VG 6.1

BLINDING   LH 8.21 SM 118.9
  148.17

BLINDINGLY   LH 3.3

BLINDLY   FO 178.27 MD 207.2

BLINDNESS SM 145.32 VG 65.20

BLINK SM 74.31

BLISS TL 107.20 MD 189.38
  196.14

BLITHE VG 61.35 65.7

BLITHELY LH 19.20 22.41

BLITHENESS VG 6.8 39.29

BLOCK LH 9.21

BLOCKED CD 253.11

BLOCKING SM 154.36

BLOCKS CD 252.31

BLOND TL 58.14 CD 233.6 233.7
  SM 33.15 52.14 66.13 113.15
  129.7 MD 190.29 199.9
  VG 49.28 51.40 52.36

BLONDE LH 13.5 TL 77.2

BLOOD TL 47.15 47.23 47.35
  47.36 61.16 67.22 81.39
  99.11 99.37 103.14 103.19
  FO 132.25 149.7 149.25 155.11
  155.35 158.30 163.13 174.6
  174.9 CD 209.7 209.9 209.15
  SM 6.23 27.13 63.35 67.9
  68.6 70.28 77.23 96.33
  106.37 144.26 154.11
  MD 180.12 186.9 186.25 187.34
  205.24 VG 28.25 34.5 34.34
  62.21 62.29 62.30

BLOOD-RED FO 117.36

BLOODSHOT SM 15.22 36.22 57.15

BLOOD-SISTER TL 106.5

BLOOD-STAINED VG 76.35 79.23

BLOOD-WARMTH TL 99.7

BLOOM SM 79.17 MD 194.1 VG 5.12

BLOOMED VG 4.28 5.1

BLOOMING TL 70.9 SM 83.30

BLOOMS SM 133.39

BLOSSOM TL 65.26 CD 222.27
  MD 207.24 209.4 209.16
  VG 39.38

BLOSSOMED VG 13.11

BLOSSOMING VG 48.10

BLOSSOMLESS SM 146.4

BLOSSOMS CD 185.22

BLOTCHES LH 33.8 33.11

BLOTS TL 59.41

BLOTTED LH 30.42 SM 148.9

BLOUSES FO 155.30

BLOW LH 31.6 FO 173.39 SM 28.8
  109.26 121.2 VG 30.8 39.32

BLOW-FLAME CD 255.3

BLOWING LH 24.8 TL 102.40
  FO 137.2 CD 237.18 244.35
  256.36 SM 133.31 134.2
  MD 179.4 186.31 VG 54.30

BLOWN CD 261.22 SM 150.37
  VG 27.2 31.22

BLOWS FO 168.35 173.33 VG 3.14

BLUBBERING FO 174.17

BLUE LH 4.3 4.30 7.30 7.35
  13.7 TL 56.31 56.40 59.40
  69.25 71.1 72.24 76.6 78.4
  80.2 80.7 FO 120.16 128.8
  142.25 143.22 152.32 155.37
  170.6 177.24 177.41 178.1
  178.6 CD 185.8 233.14 233.26
  234.1 235.33 236.6 236.16
  236.36 237.24 240.3 240.31
  241.3 242.28 248.29 253.1
  253.2 253.39 254.38 255.1
  255.3 255.19 255.21 255.37
  255.38 SM 3.14 15.22 18.14
  38.31 52.15 57.14 60.14
  63.38 65.18 74.2 74.8 111.2
  119.9 126.12 126.13 126.39
  126.40 127.18 128.25 128.35
  141.12 141.18 146.35 146.38
  147.8 147.14 148.13 148.17
  151.3 MD 170.25 171.12 173.13
  173.35 175.33 186.9 187.27
  192.11 193.34 193.41 195.8
  197.23 198.34 VG 12.25 31.29
  32.23 32.42 34.31 35.35
  41.23 49.7 49.29 74.6

BLUEBELL SM 150.27

BLUE-GREEN LH 33.8 TL 69.9
  69.10 CD 200.33

BLUE-GREY SM 154.38

BLUE JAYS SM 150.5 151.26

BLUE-LEAVED SM 151.1

BLUELY VG 17.17

BLUE-PURPLE CD 245.1 SM 152.2

BLUE-STOCKING TL 44.31

BLUEY CD 247.40

BLUEY-GREEN FO 156.19 CD 253.37

BLUEY-WHITE CD 247.23

BLUFF CD 243.10 243.16 SM 15.37
  75.6

BLUISH SM 57.9 146.36 VG 31.34

BLUNDERED LH 6.11

BLUNT CD 252.27 253.11

BLURRED LH 20.6

BLURTED LH 38.8 TL 48.34
  88.19 CD 190.34 222.3
  231.10

BLURTING TL 90.12

BLUSH FO 151.5

BLUSHED LH 16.22 FO 157.6
  VG 22.7

BLUSHING LH 7.12 FO 156.16
  156.32 VG 22.19

BLUSTERY VG 76.31

BOARD FO 129.23 149.19
  149.31 CD 246.9 SM 132.16

BOARDED FO 146.41

BOARDS FO 147.5

BOAT FO 176.3 CD 207.38
  207.39 207.42 208.1
  208.3 230.23 234.17
  235.31 235.36 235.40
  236.1 236.26 237.16
  237.36 265.22 265.31
  266.10 SM 123.38 124.7
  125.10 125.32 MD 185.25
  197.7 203.3 203.10 210.32
  210.41 211.7 211.10
  211.24 VG 7.32

BOAT-HOUSE CD 234.28 234.29
  234.33 235.6 236.30 237.37

BOATMAN CD 235.31 236.1
  236.35

BOATS FO 172.25 CD 263.14
  MD 185.26

BOB VG 14.1 20.5 21.4 21.34
  24.34 24.41 25.3 74.5
  80.22 81.7

BOBBED FO 141.19 168.38
  CD 205.22 SM 42.29 45.14
  121.9 VG 7.29 37.5

BOB FRAMLEY VG 13.15 78.22
  81.3

BODICE VG 30.15

BODICES CD 238.19

BODIES CD 233.18 SM 103.2
  103.35 MD 166.34 197.27
  205.4 VG 4.16 64.9

BODILESS SM 27.22

BODILY MD 166.20 179.2
  VG 45.21

BODY LH 4.5 8.20 TL 53.41 54.6
  55.23 69.27 75.5 84.11
  FO 148.15 159.20 174.7
  CD 255.6 SM 14.21 14.30 15.8
  16.6 18.11 18.12 53.28 75.9
  94.24 94.25 96.2 107.18
  107.29 107.34 108.11 108.15
  108.17 108.21 108.22 109.3
  109.5 112.16 116.36 117.39
  125.1 125.14 125.18 145.9
  MD 164.34 165.6 169.21 169.24
  172.20 175.16 177.25 177.30
  177.33 177.35 177.37 177.41
  178.2 178.3 178.6 178.7
  178.16 178.34 181.21 182.3
  183.30 187.6 187.13 188.14
  188.23 189.17 196.15 198.38
  205.1 205.29 206.17 VG 7.8
  12.12 23.32 23.36 29.29
  41.27 44.27 48.3 48.29 58.8
  68.13 68.42 69.7 69.12 75.26
  76.5 77.9 77.17 77.21 78.12
  80.6

BODYLESSLY MD 205.7

BOG VG 64.39

BOGORIK, PRINCE (SEE PRINCE
  BOGORIK)

BOHEMIAN TL 45.3 57.17 81.6

BOIL LH 38.39 FO 158.30

BOILED SM 134.24 VG 9.16

BOILING FO 133.39 SM 138.15
  138.18

BOIS DE BOULOGNE SM 8.29

BOLD LH 11.4 CD 195.19 SM 14.4
  18.14 45.7 84.2 VG 8.40 21.9
  21.10 21.12 22.23 23.31
  24.40 30.29 44.26 52.21

BOLDLY FO 122.39 VG 23.3 53.18

BOLDNESS VG 52.9 68.21

BOLEHILL VG 17.41

BOLSHEVISM SM 70.24 70.25

BOLT VG 16.13

BOLTING SM 26.36 VG 74.6

BOMB SM 66.22 149.28

BOMB-CLOCK SM 26.12

BOMBS SM 26.6

BOND FO 155.7 SM 6.21

BONDS TL 54.4

BOND STREETY VG 55.4

BONE FO 177.17 SM 124.15

BONES LH 11.30 TL 70.32
  CD 255.31 SM 34.21 53.7

BONES (CONT.) 152.30 152.32
  153.23

BONFIRE SM 31.39

BONNET TL 61.32 61.34

BONNETS TL 61.40

BONSALL HEAD VG 13.26 13.28
  13.37 14.37 41.20

BOOK TL 44.36 99.40 105.39
  FO 135.26 135.31 136.28
  137.33 157.42 158.7 CD 264.33
  SM 38.13 VG 15.2 32.39

BOOKISH VG 3.18

BOOK-JACKET SM 131.12

BOOKS TL 99.19 VG 78.6

BOOM SM 28.25 84.4

BOOMERANG FO 144.14

BOOT LH 9.18 FO 114.24 SM 65.11

BOOTED SM 57.16

BOOTS LH 12.14 28.37 TL 64.9
  64.10 FO 119.2 134.3 145.32
  154.13 157.3 CD 218.5 238.7
  241.37 242.35 242.39 243.5
  252.8 254.16 256.4 256.6
  SM 8.19 119.12 136.2 VG 16.37
  17.20 20.21 23.25

BORAX CD 255.2

BORDER LH 31.22 TL 47.14 100.39
  SM 28.1

BORDER-LINE CD 250.4

BORDERS SM 11.36

BORE TL 67.2 SM 18.27 123.2
  VG 4.42 8.7 8.17 16.26 56.8

BORED TL 73.32 86.7 FO 137.23
  137.25 SM 38.3 38.26 111.19
  VG 8.26 24.32 58.6 66.32

BOREDOM SM 135.20 138.5

BORING VG 7.31

BORN TL 46.26 47.6 89.2 89.24
  98.27 CD 221.5 221.7 221.14
  SM 22.21 31.6 76.12 MD 189.25
  VG 61.20 61.21 62.39 67.22
  71.9

BORNE SM 69.17 VG 80.21

BORN-FREE VG 61.27

BORROW SM 44.17

BORROWED FO 127.15 VG 26.13
  26.18

BOSOM LH 5.25 33.30 34.15 36.9

BOSOM (CONT.) FO 155.21
  SM 9.14 VG 12.30 69.10

BOSS LH 17.37 18.1 SM 34.30
  35.14 35.21 73.16 88.12
  130.33 131.6 155.14

BOSS' SM 130.32 131.28

BOSSED FO 144.35

BOSSINESS SM 35.1

BOSSY TL 91.8 FO 145.9

BOSTON SM 94.31 94.35

BOSWELL, JOE (SEE JOE BOSWELL)

BOTHER LH 30.13 30.19 31.32
  31.33 FO 129.9 134.38
  145.4 153.33 153.36
  CD 191.36 202.18 SM 42.25
  VG 20.11 28.6 31.33
  33.41 57.6

BOTHERED LH 38.18 FO 129.7

BOTTLE FO 131.6 152.7 158.11
  158.12 SM 40.30 127.36

BOTTOM LH 3.12 6.7 8.24
  8.29 8.33 10.1 21.20
  21.22 21.39 37.33 37.36
  TL 60.4 FO 169.38 CD 238.18
  240.13 241.11 263.28
  SM 26.10 109.12

BOTTOMLESS FO 177.27 177.29
  177.34 177.42 SM 52.40

BOTTOMLESS PIT FO 153.5

BOUDOIR CD 214.20 SM 112.41

BOUGH TL 63.42 69.10
  FO 173.38 SM 111.6
  MD 167.18 VG 23.28

BOUGHS FO 116.32 VG 20.33

BOUGHT TL 60.26 CD 227.37
  229.9 246.29 SM 20.9
  45.25 52.12 100.40 154.13
  154.16 MD 181.2 VG 14.4

BOULDERS CD 241.22 244.17
  SM 64.1

BOULEVARD SM 127.22

BOUNCING SM 59.4 144.36
  150.14

BOUNCY SM 131.25

BOUND TL 91.32 95.12
  FO 126.33 170.33 CD 193.12
  212.2 217.17 SM 5.22
  20.22 70.31 112.22
  VG 77.36

BOUNDING VG 72.17 72.29

BOUNDS VG 3.2

BOURGEOIS   CD 230.5   VG 49.26
   52.8   53.4

BOW   LH 35.32   TL 45.36   84.3
   97.28   CD 195.12   238.17
   SM 39.22   83.41   95.21   VG 77.28

BOWED   LH 7.35   13.16   17.18
   34.25   TL 75.16   85.16
   CD 184.36   215.1   SM 23.31
   81.24   99.1

BOWELS   FO 174.11   174.40
   SM 71.24   130.28   144.23
   MD 176.8   179.34

BOWING   LH 13.27   27.27   TL 105.12
   CD 195.22   SM 22.31   95.23
   MD 208.21

BOWL   CD 243.20   SM 33.27   33.29
   33.33   34.14   101.40   110.33
   110.35   110.36   113.6   118.34
   VG 38.26   45.30   50.26

BOW-LEGGED   SM 17.9   38.30

BOWLER   FO 169.5

BOWLS   TL 76.18

BOX   LH 29.2   29.4   29.23   30.7
   31.10   31.14   38.38   FO 148.4
   SM 11.13   57.33   85.40   87.30
   124.10   VG 26.10

BOXES   TL 62.26   62.29

BOY   LH 11.27   TL 44.5   45.4   45.8
   FO 121.4   122.34   129.10   137.35
   138.1   139.18   142.15   143.6
   144.36   145.21   146.38   147.7
   147.13   147.24   149.33   150.1
   151.10   151.20   151.32   153.10
   153.40   154.8   154.33   156.36
   157.16   157.25   157.39   158.6
   158.36   159.2   159.18   159.21
   159.35   159.41   160.18   164.4
   164.12   166.32   167.37   167.42
   168.2   171.1   171.37   172.3
   173.41   174.5   174.16   174.20
   174.21   178.15   178.38   179.1
   CD 208.32   211.33   212.1   222.23
   222.28   222.34   224.37   234.36
   235.8   SM 11.23   16.33   22.38
   31.7   44.13   90.24   105.39
   114.21   121.31   MD 186.20
   186.36   186.41   200.5   VG 6.13

BOYISH   FO 120.30   CD 231.14

BOY-NAME   SM 52.26

BOYS   TL 43.6   49.6   93.1
   FO 170.1   CD 222.29   SM 47.19
   47.21   50.18   131.4   VG 17.29
   21.36   57.2   57.7   78.18

BOY'S   FO 128.28   164.21   165.2
   MD 187.6

BOYS'   VG 7.39

BRACE   LH 7.42

BRACED   LH 4.23   7.35

BRACES   CD 214.22   VG 75.20

BRACKEN   SM 60.4   VG 18.4   23.29

BRACKET   CD 185.25

BRAGGADOCIO   LH 17.21

BRAGGED   LH 17.33

BRAIN   TL 78.21   FO 117.21   122.4
   166.2   CD 220.24   SM 35.15

BRAKE   VG 19.41

BRAKES   VG 19.31   48.37

BRANCH   FO 173.5

BRANCHED   VG 18.1

BRANCHES   FO 163.14

BRANDED   MD 202.9

BRANDY   LH 10.35   10.38   11.13
   SM 40.30   40.31   68.18   72.4

BRASS   CD 227.26   SM 145.15   149.2
   VG 38.1   46.31   47.25   68.25
   78.6   78.8

BRASSEY'S   TL 72.1

BRASSWORK   VG 68.23

BRATS   VG 71.8

BRAVE   SM 50.20   51.8   74.38
   75.23   75.27   153.30   MD 163.3
   171.7

BRAVELY   VG 9.23   36.33

BRAVER   VG 68.41   68.42   69.7
   69.12   80.6

BRAWLING   VG 17.37

BRAZENING   VG 62.34

BRAZIER   MD 188.2   195.22   200.27
   202.41

BREACH   TL 98.39   99.2   SM 157.38
   158.11

BREAD   LH 15.1   18.10   19.12   20.1
   29.23   29.27   30.2   FO 122.3
   122.5   122.30   123.11   129.8
   138.26   138.28   141.10   141.16
   142.37   156.28   CD 238.24
   238.25   238.26   238.27   246.1
   247.12   SM 45.39   45.40   80.3
   101.5   101.8   104.40   106.37
   107.1   MD 169.5   169.9   169.27
   171.39   177.11   191.37   200.26
   201.31   210.2   VG 54.14   65.2
   67.37

BREADTH   FO 173.10   VG 6.14

BREAK   TL 68.23   CD 192.35   255.30

BREAK (CONT.)   258.22   SM 13.8
   13.9   70.20   70.30   70.31
   70.36   71.16   71.23   71.29
   103.40   115.24   MD 164.36
   VG 16.13   33.5   33.22   33.33
   63.33   64.26   69.23

BREAKAGE   CD 186.25

BREAKFAST   LH 38.13   38.39
   FO 127.7   127.19   141.5
   149.19   153.20   SM 31.2
   56.28

BREAKING   LH 34.10   36.36
   FO 167.3   CD 212.18   264.30
   SM 29.18   139.35   VG 22.21
   34.38   48.15   71.23

BREAKS   FO 157.19   SM 71.17
   140.10

BREAST   LH 12.21   14.8   33.37
   TL 49.19   52.2   68.31   69.18
   74.30   78.1   78.12   95.23
   96.11   105.14   107.21
   FO 134.1   160.8   174.36
   CD 193.9   207.28   217.32
   231.9   231.16   234.6   234.37
   SM 75.14   75.15   MD 165.35
   203.33   206.20   207.27
   VG 20.6   34.15   64.30   74.40
   76.17   78.41

BREASTS   FO 155.21   155.24
   155.27   155.30   155.31
   155.33   155.34   MD 177.25
   207.17

BREATH   LH 11.11   14.9   21.12
   22.28   27.28   33.16   TL 57.2
   69.4   FO 133.20   144.4
   CD 193.31   236.9   252.16
   261.22   SM 93.11   133.40
   144.33   145.24   MD 166.11
   203.27   206.32   VG 11.34
   76.16

BREATHE   LH 22.28   34.37
   TL 101.13   SM 50.31   93.1
   93.10   104.15   104.16
   VG 44.33

BREATHED   LH 33.41   TL 43.21
   101.12   CD 247.41   255.17
   255.22   257.38   SM 75.13
   75.40   VG 42.15

BREATHING   LH 23.23   TL 101.10
   101.12   CD 242.29   SM 104.17

BREATHLESS   LH 23.1   CD 189.20
   209.34   MD 206.29

BREATHS   TL 101.13   CD 242.10
   242.30   SM 19.33   145.24

BRED   SM 13.20   75.20   90.35
   VG 7.10

BREDON   LH 36.14   36.15

BREECHES   FO 114.8   136.20
   153.7   157.1   CD 243.4
   SM 119.8

BURST (CONT.) SM 51.30 128.34
  148.12 149.28 VG 3.7 26.19
  40.23 80.34

BURSTING VG 77.16 80.28

BURSTS SM 144.28

BURY SM 71.31 85.29 86.15
  111.26

BUS TL 60.25 CD 260.7 260.17

BUSH LH 6.3 22.20 CD 243.28
  244.16 SM 17.37 18.16
  MD 173.37

BUSHES LH 7.1 FO 154.32 169.19
  CD 241.31 244.18 MD 167.4
  173.33 176.9 178.35 179.23

BUSHY SM 144.35 MD 200.22
  VG 36.17

BUSIED VG 67.5

BUSILY LH 15.32 FO 114.32
  CD 185.40

BUSINESS LH 10.14 TL 71.28
  71.32 FO 127.25 135.33 136.5
  150.17 152.24 161.34 165.15
  167.33 CD 190.40 226.23
  232.11 241.39 262.26 SM 18.26
  57.23 70.27 96.26 112.13
  116.12 135.5 MD 174.12
  VG 31.2

BUST LH 16.5

BUSTLING SM 143.26

BUSTLINGLY CD 186.10

BUSTS CD 230.3

BUSY TL 98.19 FO 117.32 121.37
  122.9 126.39 131.23 149.39
  168.14 CD 225.12 SM 33.21
  38.9 124.36 VG 46.23

BUTTER LH 17.9 17.10 29.25
  29.27 30.2 FO 122.4 123.14
  SM 44.23 45.39 VG 65.2 67.38

BUTTERED SM 45.39

BUTTERFLIES SM 4.26 60.3

BUTTERING VG 4.17

BUTTOCKS FO 116.35

BUTTONED FO 136.2 155.25 155.27
  157.2 CD 209.26 238.41

BUTTON-HOLE CD 214.38

BUTTONS LH 29.11 TL 61.4

BUY FO 126.41 126.42 CD 195.31
  195.40 246.19 SM 9.22 13.38
  14.11 16.19 16.21 17.20
  25.25 93.24 131.38

BUYER CD 196.17

BUYING CD 200.14 246.30
  SM 17.23 89.22

BUYS MD 177.11

BUZZ CD 252.4 SM 102.10
  MD 200.7

BUZZARD TL 58.35

BUZZING TL 61.37

BYGONE SM 45.3 45.7

BY-LANES SM 111.22

BY-PRODUCT TL 87.27

BY-PRODUCTS TL 87.28

BY-WORDS VG 10.21

CA' LH 26.14

CABBAGE CD 248.16 VG 9.11

CABBAGES CD 256.21

CABIN SM 115.40 125.35 126.31
  141.30 142.2 143.1 143.3
  145.35 145.36 149.32

CABINET TL 43.20 FO 115.5
  CD 227.25 227.30

CABINS SM 141.2 141.11 142.6
  142.21 145.14 145.21 152.1
  155.6 156.3

CACKLE FO 146.28

CACKLING FO 172.27

CACTUS CD 185.21 216.30 218.2
  SM 109.3 151.19

CACTUSES SM 78.7

CAESAR CD 215.39 215.40 218.11
  SM 96.28 96.32 97.14
  MD 188.34 189.1 190.1

CAESAR, JULIUS (SEE JULIUS
  CAESAR)

CAFE STEPHANIE CD 226.38

CAGE CD 221.39 221.40 222.24
  222.37 222.39 222.40 223.14
  223.15 223.21 223.35

CAJOLING FO 139.36 SM 39.12
  VG 21.39

CAKE LH 19.19 TL 62.14
  MD 181.33 VG 14.4 14.20 14.24
  14.29 15.12 67.37

CAKED LH 33.34

CAKES SM 56.28 107.1 MD 177.23
  VG 14.5 14.31

CALCULATE FO 130.10 SM 21.22

CALCULATING SM 116.6

CALF FO 113.30 CD 257.12

CALIFORNIA SM 77.31 77.33

CALINE LH 34.3

CALL LH 16.10 TL 63.13
  81.23 88.3 89.35 101.1
  101.24 102.1 102.13
  FO 117.7 154.8 CD 183.31
  195.28 197.39 208.11
  209.33 217.24 220.25
  228.20 228.28 263.25
  SM 24.7 47.39 48.7 48.13
  56.3 61.8 79.11 100.1
  102.39 103.14 103.17
  116.15 124.5 142.35 154.31
  156.37 159.19 MD 180.27
  VG 20.40 29.3 71.30

CALLED LH 7.13 8.32 37.30
  TL 43.15 53.11 77.3 101.33
  102.11 102.30 FO 122.35
  124.36 147.38 152.11
  167.25 169.32 CD 203.23
  206.3 209.39 218.16 219.6
  235.17 235.19 SM 5.22
  16.14 24.34 35.17 40.18
  46.33 52.26 56.41 57.10
  58.38 59.13 60.37 64.1
  66.18 90.15 90.27 98.30
  105.39 109.38 150.27
  150.30 154.29 MD 167.23
  171.39 178.39 183.16
  VG 4.15 4.40 10.13 15.7
  15.36 16.5 17.27 18.13
  23.21 25.17 26.4 26.10
  32.27 47.13 48.35 50.12
  51.39 52.2 53.16 53.22
  70.26 71.32 79.26

CALLERS CD 209.10

CALLIN' LH 9.1

CALLING LH 6.8 TL 101.2
  101.3 FO 114.19 117.5
  117.31 133.34 140.27
  140.42 147.16 CD 183.15
  184.25 219.2 234.33
  236.26 254.33 SM 90.15
  91.27 117.22 128.40
  MD 163.27 167.4 198.15
  VG 30.27 50.34

CALLOUS CD 208.17 SM 145.41

CALLOUS-LOOKING LH 19.2

CALLS SM 82.23 MD 209.21
  210.13

CALM LH 34.24 FO 124.14
  128.5 SM 24.35 MD 193.11
  210.30 VG 22.20 33.10
  35.23 44.15 57.38 64.12
  77.2 77.5

CALMLY SM 81.2 VG 25.4
  57.40 59.37 79.30

CALMNESS VG 79.34

CALYX FO 177.29

CAMBRIDGE TL 75.35

CAMEL SM 49.31

CAMISOLE CD 219.27

CAMP FO 164.33 166.32 167.18
  168.11 SM 89.1 VG 20.37 29.32
  47.33 69.23 71.1 71.5 81.8

CAMPAIGN VG 50.4

CAMPER VG 50.2

CAMP-FIRE VG 49.5

CANADA LH 35.10 35.28 FO 121.9
  121.10 123.23 144.41 150.42
  151.7 151.13 152.17 160.40
  164.27 166.7 178.41 179.26

CANADIAN FO 173.26

CANDLE LH 27.8 FO 138.39 138.40
  158.13 VG 12.3

CANDLES LH 23.19

CANDLESTICK VG 38.1 38.16 38.25
  38.31 38.41

CANDOUR TL 105.4 MD 193.11
  VG 42.11 42.16 59.10

CANE VG 36.38

CA NE CHANGE JAMAIS SM 132.19

CANNA LH 26.14

CANNON TL 94.27

CANNY SM 4.8 VG 49.25

CANOE SM 86.36

CANS SM 154.5

CANST SM 128.1

CANTEEN FO 167.20 SM 138.24

CANTER SM 21.39

CANVAS SM 114.28

CANVASSED VG 26.1

CANYON SM 78.15 134.19 142.3
  142.5 143.34 147.21 147.26
  152.1 152.12 156.4

CANYON-PASSAGE SM 147.23

CANYONS SM 142.23

CAP TL 51.17 FO 114.9 116.9
  135.29 CD 214.20 227.7 227.8
  227.9 234.32 234.35 SM 38.32
  VG 7.6 13.18 19.19 19.34
  20.21 32.28 33.36 36.34

CAP (CONT.) 37.11 38.3 65.27
  70.13 74.2

CAPABILITY SM 9.3

CAPABLE CD 240.9 VG 38.19

CAPE CD 204.22 SM 93.3 93.4
  110.5

CAPE-FRILLED CD 248.9

CAPE-WRAP CD 183.25

CAPITAL FO 123.36 SM 4.1

CAPO DI MONTE VG 54.4

CAPRI SM 4.4 4.29

CAPS SM 29.20

CAPTAIN FO 167.17 167.18 167.19
  167.20 167.23 167.25 167.26
  167.27 167.36 167.38 168.2
  168.5 168.8 168.9 CD 196.8
  197.6 214.13 219.39 224.5
  224.38 225.34 227.32 229.9
  229.22 232.37 233.4 234.12
  234.29 235.37 236.2 236.20
  236.24 237.13 241.39
  SM 125.33 125.39 126.31

CAPTAIN BERRYMAN FO 167.23

CAPTAIN HEPBURN CD 185.13 185.39
  197.41 218.16 218.22 236.33

CAPTAIN MAYNE REID FO 135.26

CAPTAINS MD 188.33

CAPTAIN'S CD 193.24

CAR TL 44.13 98.35 108.13
  CD 238.35 238.41 239.4 239.21
  239.23 239.25 239.33 240.4
  240.12 260.19 260.35 260.40
  261.5 261.11 261.14 261.20
  261.37 263.4 SM 9.12 16.30
  35.28 92.2 112.29 134.19
  134.33 136.25 139.19 141.7
  141.10 154.36 156.17 VG 8.27
  13.27 13.31 16.8 16.24 17.31
  17.40 18.12 18.31 19.4 19.24
  19.32 25.8 25.10 25.17 45.6
  48.36 48.38 49.14 49.23
  50.10 54.38 58.3 62.3 80.21
  81.7

CARAVAN VG 21.1 21.7 21.21
  22.2 23.11 23.20 23.22 24.2
  24.21 24.26 29.33 46.6 46.21
  47.3 47.20 48.16 48.40 52.1
  52.7 60.20 71.13

CARAVANS VG 20.29 20.32 20.34
  20.39 41.26 41.29 71.7

CARDBOARD SM 27.10 112.1

CARD-ROOM TL 87.3

CARDS VG 51.7

CARE LH 15.12 17.9 36.21
  TL 47.2 54.26 104.35
  FO 124.3 163.8 CD 187.32
  187.33 191.29 191.33
  194.18 216.2 250.39
  SM 10.2 36.30 44.19 47.40
  51.39 61.23 62.37 70.11
  77.1 81.17 93.8 95.27
  117.25 119.23 149.22
  149.24 158.21 MD 180.27
  VG 20.7 22.5 31.9 54.37
  56.3 56.36 57.42 61.1
  79.21

CARED TL 46.36 CD 224.13
  SM 10.28 22.15 22.16
  47.17 94.17 95.29 95.32
  95.39 124.27

CARED-FOR TL 69.7

CAREER SM 114.26 114.33
  114.39 115.15 VG 58.13

CAREFUL FO 130.20 130.26
  CD 210.39 262.36 SM 36.6
  37.16 138.30

CAREFULLY LH 6.14 TL 80.22
  84.8 FO 143.40 CD 196.17
  211.1 SM 32.24 35.35 73.22
  80.41 140.29 VG 39.8
  50.16 54.34

CAREFULLY-BARBERED VG 53.31

CARELESS LH 3.26 11.4
  CD 230.7 VG 6.8

CARELESSLY FO 122.2 VG 33.4

CARELESSNESS CD 230.41 231.6
  231.23

CARES TL 104.35 CD 188.10
  MD 180.28 VG 55.24

CARESS CD 192.8 MD 189.13
  189.35

CARESSED LH 13.17 13.27
  CD 218.5 MD 207.1

CARESSES LH 22.9

CARESSIVE VG 38.37

CARGO CD 240.7 SM 124.7

CARGO-BOAT SM 125.4

CARLTON SM 27.18

CARNATIONS CD 209.14

CARPENTER'S FO 113.36

CARPENTRY FO 113.13

CARPET TL 100.5 SM 119.7
  VG 79.23

CARPETED TL 100.4

CARRIAGE FO 164.40 CD 210.8

CENTURIES   SM 29.10   68.2   86.31

CENTURY   SM 45.9

CENTURY-DEEP   SM 154.4

CERBERUS   TL 62.15

CEREMONIOUSLY   SM 81.24

CEREMONY   SM 81.21   VG 11.42

CERTAIN   TL 47.9   48.35   50.33
   51.33   66.23   66.27   82.2   86.37
   89.11   93.24   95.29   FO 154.27
   161.23   CD 185.6   207.6   216.37
   218.17   219.27   232.21   232.35
   242.24   258.3   SM 6.3   7.31
   16.35   32.33   32.40   37.39   44.5
   45.9   51.10   51.37   58.9   65.17
   86.24   119.10   119.11   129.24
   134.16   136.30   138.8   140.17
   152.27   MD 163.21   166.36
   176.14   198.3   198.4   201.5
   VG 4.5   9.30   11.11   21.13   39.1
   63.6   65.8   67.23   67.24   71.4
   77.5

CERTAINLY   TL 90.3   97.16
   FO 113.20   151.2   CD 205.12
   205.17   215.32   217.2   217.40
   217.41   252.13   255.30   258.27
   258.28   SM 5.12   16.40   24.4
   34.12   34.13   35.23   43.39   52.5
   64.10   79.24   82.20   83.25
   84.11   96.34   155.40   VG 11.12
   40.38   59.40   59.41

CERTAINTY   FO 152.36   SM 149.30

CEZANNE   SM 5.8

CHAFED   FO 179.17   MD 204.10
   204.14   204.24   205.40   206.17

CHAFFING   LH 7.24

CHAFING   SM 116.22

CHAGRIN   FO 113.33   SM 6.36   38.18
   MD 171.2   171.38   VG 16.18

CHAGRINED   SM 94.4

CHAIN   CD 197.23   VG 9.1

CHAINS   CD 207.30

CHAIR   TL 52.36   87.13   102.39
   105.32   FO 136.16   136.20
   142.25   142.40   156.18   157.42
   158.14   158.18   CD 183.7   186.39
   187.10   190.10   197.14   213.18
   219.29   219.33   231.17   245.17
   245.25   247.32   SM 44.9   44.16
   46.20   46.27   64.2   121.16
   VG 14.8   15.17   43.42   75.9

CHAIRS   CD 234.24   SM 118.35
   119.6   VG 14.2   54.1

CHAIR-SPRING   SM 83.18

CHALLENGE   FO 162.7   SM 32.30
   92.7   151.27   MD 164.1   171.7

CHALLENGE (CONT.)   171.23
   VG 22.29   43.25

CHALLENGED   FO 134.17   CD 190.42
   203.39   211.20

CHAMBER   MD 187.32   187.41   194.22

CHAMOIS-BRUSH   CD 238.8   238.10

CHAMPAGNE   SM 127.36   128.1
   VG 54.20

CHAMPION   VG 57.39

CHANCE   LH 11.35   FO 146.14
   CD 263.25   SM 70.18   VG 52.19

CHANGE   LH 17.14   TL 107.29
   FO 164.37   CD 189.41   SM 46.38
   96.40   105.15   MD 209.13

CHANGED   TL 106.20   107.28   108.20
   108.22   FO 129.4   CD 199.27
   207.34   244.10   SM 39.18   73.41
   132.11   MD 167.36   209.4
   VG 17.40   27.27

CHANGELESS   CD 189.36

CHANGELESS-SEEMING   CD 189.31

CHANGES   TL 102.2   FO 127.11
   CD 204.14   224.11

CHANGING   TL 45.25   107.35
   FO 120.38   CD 202.19   217.33
   218.3   245.31

CHANNEL   SM 126.10   126.13
   VG 7.32

CHAOS   SM 20.17   26.38   70.1
   125.31   VG 32.25   76.29

CHAP   TL 77.31

CHAPEL   VG 25.39

CHAPEL-FOLKS   SM 104.37

CHAPELS   SM 30.14

CHARACTER   FO 129.34   SM 25.26
   72.22   VG 6.16   6.17

CHARACTERISTIC   SM 18.21   20.20
   VG 59.6

CHARACTERS   CD 186.31

CHARADE   SM 3.19

CHARCOAL   MD 200.28

CHARGE   LH 7.6   CD 195.37   SM 5.20
   93.29   143.3   144.38   153.20
   VG 26.4   27.31

CHARGED   CD 233.9

CHARGES   LH 10.21

CHARLEMAGNE   TL 96.33

CHARLES   VG 52.37   60.9   60.19
   60.21   60.24

CHARLES V   CD 210.23

CHARM   TL 72.36   98.16
   CD 216.3   216.5   216.9
   216.20   216.21   216.22
   216.39   217.6   217.8
   217.9   217.35   217.36
   218.7   SM 3.23   26.13

CHARMED   FO 129.26

CHARMING   FO 124.37   CD 195.10
   205.23   206.2   206.20   209.8
   209.13   210.12   SM 3.10
   10.9   26.12   28.40

CHARMS   SM 33.2

CHASTITY   MD 179.16

CHAT   CD 220.3

CHATTED   TL 59.37   FO 117.14

CHATTER   CD 205.32   213.10
   SM 150.7   MD 200.8

CHATTERING   TL 74.11   CD 221.39
   VG 75.27   77.3   77.6

CHATTING   SM 20.32

CHAUFFEUR   VG 15.1

CHAUFFEURS   SM 136.27

CHEAP   FO 154.5   CD 228.28
   230.27   SM 91.17   131.19
   157.20   157.21   159.19

CHEAPLY   FO 154.23   154.24
   154.25

CHEAPNESS   SM 159.11

CHECK   TL 105.21   VG 38.3

CHEEK   LH 14.16   TL 76.30
   83.27   FO 118.10   140.26
   155.18   CD 190.20   192.5
   205.23   SM 33.7   81.5   113.18
   114.31   MD 192.2   192.34
   VG 22.24   46.35

CHEEK-BONES   LH 13.9   FO 121.3
   SM 21.34   32.30   33.18
   34.23

CHEEKS   TL 46.34   78.19
   FO 117.3   120.17   129.3
   135.14   164.36   165.7
   SM 7.34   MD 193.4   VG 23.35
   49.30

CHEEKY   FO 154.9   SM 33.7

CHEER   TL 96.32

CHEERFUL   SM 113.32   113.37
   129.8   131.19

CHEERFULLY   FO 114.41

CHEERFULLY (CONT.) SM 129.18

CHEERFULNESS SM 129.13

CHEERING CD 237.25 VG 39.31

CHEERY-O SM 27.12 VG 43.36

CHEESE LH 15.1 17.9 18.10
    19.13 20.2 29.24 29.27
    FO 138.27 CD 245.33 247.12
    SM 101.5 101.8 142.31
    MD 200.26

CHEESE-MAKING SM 144.2

CHEESES SM 143.38 144.4

CHEF D'OEUVRE CD 193.32

CHENILLE VG 39.36

CHEQUE CD 219.5 SM 94.1

CHEQUER TL 98.15

CHERISH CD 265.5 265.11

CHERISHED CD 265.18 SM 150.10

CHESS TL 66.13

CHEST LH 27.25 TL 46.1 49.34
    FO 163.15 CD 216.39 242.8
    242.11 242.34 SM 26.41 84.10
    VG 50.2 54.28

CHESTER SM 31.35

CHESTERFIELD LH 32.9

CHESTNUT TL 72.25 72.27 72.42
    73.19 SM 8.25 59.6

CHESTNUTS TL 72.23 72.28 72.34
    74.9 74.18 SM 44.23

CHESTS SM 128.9

CHETIF SM 99.1

CHEW CD 249.27

CHEWED CD 233.1

CHEWING FO 135.8

CHIC CD 214.20 SM 35.38 VG 8.33

CHICAGO SM 128.21

CHICKEN LH 16.3 TL 51.20
    FO 146.27 SM 64.14

CHICKEN-COOP VG 58.38

CHICKENS FO 113.4 113.21 139.31
    146.34 149.9 149.26 SM 149.19
    149.24

CHIEF CD 208.27 224.5 SM 115.28
    VG 4.34 10.12

CHIEFLY SM 79.19 129.15 130.2

CHIEFLY (CONT.) 142.34

CHIEFS TL 90.23

CHIEMGAU CD 231.37

CHIFFON FO 155.30

CHILD LH 7.4 TL 50.6 57.37
    80.14 80.20 81.27 81.29
    81.33 FO 134.1 174.28 174.34
    178.30 179.31 CD 210.10 223.1
    SM 47.25 62.15 86.6 139.25
    MD 180.41 189.6 196.40 209.22
    210.23 VG 21.22 22.32 23.23
    23.27 30.12 44.13 49.16 53.7

CHILDHOOD TL 99.29 99.35 SM 5.4

CHILDHOOD'S SM 10.30

CHILDISH LH 7.5 19.5 FO 127.20
    CD 197.7 SM 48.23 106.2
    129.25 129.26 136.40 137.5
    139.17 MD 168.1 196.4
    VG 31.34 49.24 66.16

CHILDISHLY LH 16.4 SM 129.8
    VG 46.10

CHILDISHNESS SM 104.28 137.2

CHILDLIKE VG 38.18 48.17 51.1

CHILDREN TL 44.28 55.8 55.15
    56.6 96.22 102.29 102.33
    CD 186.8 190.36 208.32 224.33
    231.29 240.1 240.3 SM 20.33
    24.22 29.21 36.13 61.40 62.3
    62.10 104.27 141.38 VG 4.7
    4.24 5.14 5.23 5.26 20.39
    25.28 28.21 28.22 35.16
    45.31 46.14 46.16 46.22
    46.24 47.28 47.35 51.39 52.2
    52.3 52.31 53.25 61.41 70.39

CHILDREN'S LH 11.23 VG 5.29

CHILD'S TL 53.26 CD 222.9

CHILL LH 36.32 CD 238.1
    MD 166.27 167.1 190.20 192.8
    202.11 VG 9.3

CHILLED SM 65.28 VG 17.31

CHILLY CD 247.37 260.21

CHIMING SM 28.26

CHIMNEY VG 24.20 74.24 74.25
    75.5

CHIMNEY-FLUE VG 74.32

CHIMNEY-POT FO 143.8

CHIMNEYS TL 73.41 SM 101.38
    VG 17.17 36.9

CHIN LH 4.28 17.23 TL 47.9
    54.1 95.5 FO 116.26 117.25
    128.7 133.17 134.26 147.30
    149.34 CD 190.19 192.16 218.6

CHIN (CONT.) SM 17.8 67.10
    VG 20.24

CHINA SM 155.33 VG 54.18

CHINAWOMAN CD 206.6

CHINESE TL 76.41 77.1 79.10
    CD 190.18 SM 119.15
    VG 11.3

CHINK MD 165.37

CHINKS MD 166.3 166.6

CHINS VG 65.22

CHINTZ CD 233.26

CHIP VG 23.29 67.25

CHIPMUNKS SM 150.4

CHIPPING VG 67.27

CHIPS VG 20.36

CHIRPY VG 25.18

CHIT-CHAT CD 228.29

CHIVALRIC CD 232.28

CHOCK MD 198.10 198.11

CHOCOLATE VG 11.17 32.32

CHOCOLATES VG 11.18

CHOICE TL 43.13 89.19 90.9
    90.20 CD 212.37 218.6
    SM 94.23 MD 211.20

CHOIR VG 7.38 9.37

CHOIRS VG 7.39

CHOKED LH 33.28 VG 78.4

CHOKING CD 219.31 SM 151.6

CHOLERA CD 232.16

CHOMESBURY SM 37.18

CHOOSE TL 89.16 89.24 90.5
    90.24 VG 64.7 64.20

CHOPPED FO 119.12 148.1

CHOPS FO 168.24 MD 167.32

CHORUS CD 235.29

CHORUSED VG 20.9

CHOSE TL 76.16 82.2 90.5
    90.22 CD 218.7

CHOSEN TL 90.4 90.6 SM 73.22

CHREESTMAS LH 16.41

CHRISTIANIZED SM 127.6

CHRISTIANS VG 21.29

CHRISTMAS TL 58.11 83.5
  FO 155.12 163.10 164.26
  166.29 175.10 SM 14.17

CHRYSANTHEMUMS FO 153.15 153.16

CHUBBED FO 158.21

CHUBBY FO 164.35

CHUCKLED LH 5.12 5.18 6.40
  CD 237.16

CHUCKLING LH 4.19

CHUMP FO 166.8

CHUNK LH 18.5

CHUNKS FO 122.3 123.10

CHURCH LH 4.34 TL 98.4 98.14
  CD 239.13 SM 28.14 28.27 29.3
  43.2 98.7 VG 9.41 17.32
  25.35 29.34 41.7

CHURCHYARD FO 144.7 SM 28.13
  37.26 37.28 81.30 84.29 85.7
  86.10

CIDER SM 29.36

CIGAR TL 94.6 CD 231.12

CIGAR-CASE TL 94.4

CIGARETTE CD 206.5 259.32
  SM 38.4 45.31 VG 52.37 52.40

CINEMA TL 84.15

CINEMATOGRAPH SM 130.22

CIRCLE TL 85.22 90.29 90.30
  FO 139.39 SM 100.13 146.29
  146.33 MD 200.13

CIRCLING SM 67.2 146.12 148.27

CIRCUIT TL 91.38

CIRCUMSTANCE SM 41.8 96.9 96.10
  MD 171.34 183.40 VG 12.39

CIRCUMSTANCES SM 30.9 112.32
  149.21 VG 65.13 67.12

CIRCUMSTANTIAL SM 41.9

CIRCUMSTANTIALLY SM 41.6 41.7

CIRCUMVENT FO 116.3

CISSIE VG 6.33 6.35 33.36
  35.28 40.37

CISTERN FO 127.16

CITIES SM 3.20 MD 184.6

CITIZEN SM 7.30 MD 193.19

CITY TL 44.27 CD 217.7 SM 5.21

CITY (CONT.) 5.29 22.27 71.8
  128.17 128.20 MD 166.38
  167.10 181.28 VG 3.29 10.11
  10.22 41.8

CIVILIAN CD 227.9

CIVILIZATION SM 90.19 126.21
  128.33 135.18 142.22 153.28
  153.29 153.37

CIVILIZED SM 130.16

CLAIM TL 104.22 SM 102.12
  MD 179.2 181.38

CLAIMING TL 107.14

CLAIMS MD 173.4

CLAMBERED LH 23.11 24.42
  CD 235.10 VG 73.39 78.23

CLAMOROUS FO 163.8

CLAMPED TL 101.8

CLAN VG 67.19

CLANDESTINE VG 64.20

CLANGING TL 67.30

CLANGOUR MD 164.33

CLAP LH 28.16 VG 61.29

CLAPPERS SM 154.23

CLARIDGE'S SM 27.17

CLARITY SM 147.40

CLASH LH 7.32

CLASP LH 33.41 FO 125.14
  VG 77.11

CLASPED LH 33.11 33.37
  CD 197.16 SM 80.21 91.23

CLASPING FO 124.40 CD 209.35
  VG 37.14 46.39

CLASS CD 229.27 230.39 SM 32.38
  MD 192.41 VG 57.38

CLASSES TL 99.4 99.8 FO 113.13
  SM 28.37

CLASS-HATRED CD 240.8

CLASSICAL SM 111.9

CLASSICAL GODS SM 111.11

CLATTER LH 21.4 25.31 31.11

CLAWED VG 72.40 73.16 74.7

CLAWING VG 73.34

CLAWS TL 97.11 CD 255.39

CLAY LH 18.21 MD 168.30

CLEAN LH 15.18 TL 48.12
  57.6 FO 166.8 CD 254.42
  SM 11.16 13.2 22.37
  47.21 50.18 53.6 104.21
  125.32 125.33 132.25
  MD 181.29 198.22 VG 22.12
  28.24 46.17 46.18 47.23
  47.25 64.7

CLEAN-CLIPPED SM 46.10

CLEAN-CUT VG 67.14

CLEANED FO 117.33 134.3
  MD 200.1

CLEANER SM 153.38

CLEANEST SM 150.33

CLEANING FO 166.32 MD 198.39
  VG 58.2

CLEANNESS LH 18.28 SM 48.11

CLEANSE SM 71.33 154.2
  154.4

CLEAN-SHAVEN CD 185.8
  SM 11.12

CLEAR LH 8.22 9.23 TL 93.41
  106.3 FO 121.35 128.38
  134.27 135.13 136.24
  136.38 138.3 150.21
  164.17 172.12 172.18
  173.29 CD 184.12 201.15
  222.8 235.40 SM 24.15
  25.33 31.29 36.36 42.13
  90.14 101.37 103.35 126.12
  128.27 138.36 141.37
  147.22 MD 180.22 203.15
  211.4 VG 13.6 32.33 32.40
  33.40 34.26 45.23 57.24
  58.29 63.36 65.25 69.15

CLEARED LH 3.2 SM 152.21
  MD 165.28

CLEARING LH 8.28 FO 118.27
  142.41 SM 109.34 140.35
  140.40 141.3 141.15 141.34
  142.26 142.27 142.28
  145.35 150.29 155.3
  MD 187.25 187.37

CLEARLY CD 258.35 VG 4.26

CLEAVAGE CD 224.14 224.15
  224.19 241.14

CLEAVE SM 7.17

CLEAVED LH 13.13

CLEAVING SM 102.24

CLEFT CD 224.16 241.9 242.22
  243.11 SM 151.39 152.1
  MD 211.3 VG 18.4

CLEFTS CD 238.41 SM 63.4
  94.11 144.7

CLEMATIS CD 230.24 234.20

CLENCHED LH 4.22 8.9 27.25
  SM 151.30 MD 192.37 VG 75.39
  77.19

CLENCHING VG 76.32

CLEOPATRA SM 96.25 97.11

CLEVER TL 71.16 71.25 91.1
  CD 197.22 208.37 221.9 246.26
  SM 7.5 7.10 47.15 47.16 48.8
  48.9 48.15 49.10 49.12 50.15
  94.32 94.36 95.17 135.15
  VG 4.16 11.10 51.26 51.27

CLEVERLY SM 24.33 32.24

CLEVERNESS FO 131.10 SM 48.11
  49.1

CLICKING SM 49.10

CLIFF FO 179.28 CD 247.28
  VG 72.27

CLIFF-CLIMB CD 248.37

CLIFFS FO 178.39 VG 7.33 8.31

CLIMATE SM 81.8 81.10

CLIMB LH 3.14 12.12 FO 153.27
  CD 218.18 253.41 SM 134.20
  VG 17.40 71.37

CLIMBED LH 7.6 7.18 25.4
  FO 170.23 172.36 CD 236.4
  241.8 241.33 247.29 247.35
  261.13 SM 60.12 140.32 140.39
  143.18 156.3 MD 168.18 191.29
  192.17 VG 4.33 45.24 46.21
  71.15 78.10 78.22 79.1

CLIMBING FO 118.25 153.27
  CD 235.5 235.25 242.2 242.21
  243.1 245.11 251.22 SM 63.2
  VG 18.4 74.17

CLINCHED LH 32.16

CLING CD 255.31

CLINGING FO 120.25 CD 228.38
  244.18 254.26 SM 84.6 VG 73.8
  73.41 75.24

CLINK FO 154.39 CD 244.14

CLIP SM 45.27

CLIPPED SM 9.7 46.17 144.15

CLIPPING SM 45.27

CLIPPINGS VG 32.23

CLOAK CD 235.35 MD 186.28
  186.31 203.32

CLOCK CD 186.18 238.29

CLOCKWORK SM 52.21

CLODS MD 172.32

CLOGGED MD 202.10

CLOSE LH 7.36 17.29 23.30
  24.26 33.14 34.3 TL 43.19
  45.40 101.31 FO 136.20 155.25
  179.15 CD 190.8 233.39 235.26
  244.19 SM 3.26 7.23 20.27
  55.29 57.9 90.29 129.24
  MD 181.33 182.9 195.30 202.32
  VG 17.22 19.25 36.39

CLOSE-CUT CD 184.8

CLOSED TL 45.36 52.1 55.25
  57.16 78.30 95.40 101.34
  103.27 FO 160.21 CD 185.32
  185.34 186.42 191.31 245.11
  247.24 258.12 SM 68.17 79.6
  92.15 MD 165.39 166.1 168.35
  202.33 207.37 VG 11.38 12.11
  21.2 48.39 54.38 76.33

CLOSE-FITTING TL 83.20 CD 184.6
  197.27

CLOSELY LH 17.18 25.2 CD 199.3
  228.38 SM 42.5 78.23 81.7
  88.1 129.31

CLOSENESS SM 94.19

CLOSER LH 23.25 SM 55.37 68.31

CLOSES TL 66.2 FO 113.25

CLOSING TL 84.16 CD 184.23
  220.6 SM 146.35 MD 179.34
  VG 75.40 79.18

CLOT TL 58.40 SM 126.5

CLOTH LH 14.38 15.16 15.18
  21.40 24.24 24.35 24.42 25.6
  25.25 25.31 25.38 28.36
  37.20 37.22 37.24 38.3
  TL 84.10 SM 110.41 MD 165.24
  181.3 VG 24.3

CLOTHES TL 61.1 71.16 FO 144.11
  CD 195.4 201.6 222.40 SM 4.19
  5.19 21.6 52.9 103.32
  VG 75.6 79.22

CLOTHING SM 18.6 21.9 52.12
  VG 79.19

CLOTS LH 21.24

CLOUD LH 23.15 24.14 TL 58.41
  FO 152.14 164.37 179.1
  CD 205.32 211.15 216.37 238.1
  253.13 256.36 SM 25.35 26.32
  65.25 66.7 100.38 101.39
  148.4 148.10 148.12 MD 175.12
  182.28 197.13 VG 40.1

CLOUDED FO 128.8

CLOUDING VG 51.30

CLOUDS TL 59.39 CD 237.13
  237.24 237.25 242.27 247.41
  248.5 SM 125.38 126.11 128.34
  133.37 MD 203.1 VG 76.30

CLOUDY SM 26.32 125.23

CLOVER SM 115.7

CLOVER-LIKE SM 151.6

CLOVES SM 44.25

CLUB SM 50.24 106.7

CLUBBED TL 87.14

CLUCKED MD 170.15

CLUCKING MD 171.36 171.37

CLUE CD 209.38 SM 135.25
  MD 188.24 204.2 VG 6.20
  42.42

CLUMP TL 73.9

CLUMPS SM 141.5 151.2

CLUMSILY LH 6.41

CLUMSY LH 4.15 22.31
  SM 138.39 MD 169.34

CLUNG LH 23.26 23.39 23.40
  TL 103.29 VG 73.24

CLUSTER LH 23.20 FO 130.4
  CD 254.8 VG 36.23 47.29

CLUSTERED FO 169.20 CD 205.22
  235.26 239.13

CLUSTERING CD 239.15 SM 42.28
  VG 36.7

CLUSTERS SM 9.26 45.14

CLUTCH SM 127.3 VG 67.1

CLUTCHED SM 67.1 VG 78.32

CLUTCHES CD 214.4

CLUTCHING CD 236.39 MD 179.14
  VG 37.1 78.39 78.41

COACH-HOUSE SM 87.22

COAL LH 4.16 SM 31.10

COALS SM 74.5

COAL-SMOKE SM 102.5

COARSE SM 119.12

COARSENESS CD 230.14

COAST SM 126.14 MD 185.14
  185.30 185.32 185.34
  188.39 190.33 191.21
  192.8 193.31 211.14

COASTS SM 126.20

COAT LH 19.27 TL 51.16 51.18
  52.1 FO 114.8 120.23
  122.14 134.34 148.22

COAT (CONT.) 152.29 155.25
 168.37 CD 183.22 189.41
 229.30 232.13 238.33 240.31
 248.31 254.28 255.8 VG 24.2
 38.4 40.25 49.6 49.9 49.13
 49.16 49.40 51.32 53.14

COAT-BOTTOMS CD 232.19

COATS CD 229.28 SM 85.6 127.26
 VG 8.32 43.2

COAXED LH 19.8

COAXING FO 158.29

COAXINGLY MD 167.4

COBBLED SM 17.29

COBBLE-STONES SM 58.31

COBWEBBY VG 41.3

COBWEBS VG 39.28

COCK FO 159.2 SM 108.36
 MD 163.21 164.12 164.19
 167.16 167.18 167.21 167.24
 167.27 167.30 167.33 168.38
 170.16 170.41 171.4 171.13
 171.26 171.35 171.39 172.29
 177.16 178.25 178.27 178.31
 179.30 180.13 181.9 181.11
 181.18 182.6 182.39 183.21
 183.26 183.27 183.28 VG 56.2
 56.6

COCK-CROWS MD 164.28

COCKEREL MD 164.1

COCKING CD 210.32

COCKLING FO 172.25

COCKS MD 163.24 163.27 164.2
 181.21

COCK'S MD 183.18

COCK-SPARROW SM 109.6

COCKTAILS SM 127.35

COCKY FO 154.21 CD 238.10

COCOTTE SM 136.8

CODNOR VG 18.28 18.31

CODNOR GATE VG 68.7

COFFEE LH 38.38 39.18 CD 252.5
 SM 55.13 VG 47.31 47.39 47.41
 48.1 54.15 54.21

COFFEE-CUP SM 52.25 VG 48.4

COFFIN FO 147.42 148.1 148.2
 157.21 SM 85.9 85.14 85.19
 85.28 85.41

COFFIN-LIKE VG 73.35

COGITATING FO 152.15

COHESION SM 94.19 94.22

COHORTS CD 229.1

COIL FO 130.33

COILED LH 4.42 11.40 38.26
 TL 70.23

COILING LH 11.6 MD 211.23

COILS TL 63.3

COLD LH 10.36 12.30 13.11
 14.39 15.37 28.28 29.8 34.10
 34.20 34.38 37.38 39.15
 TL 49.10 51.15 63.33 75.6
 76.6 78.2 99.11 FO 131.20
 134.2 134.25 134.28 142.14
 144.1 145.10 146.34 157.37
 158.40 163.19 168.30 169.38
 170.19 CD 194.27 204.12
 204.32 213.27 234.12 237.17
 238.41 240.11 240.14 242.2
 244.33 248.6 248.13 SM 15.26
 22.1 22.32 34.3 46.23 46.30
 66.8 81.10 87.29 88.37 96.33
 100.29 100.30 103.1 107.16
 108.32 125.23 125.24 133.37
 146.4 146.26 152.7 155.29
 155.30 MD 165.5 165.9 165.10
 165.23 165.25 165.29 165.31
 165.35 168.10 169.23 185.1
 189.18 191.12 192.3 195.31
 198.34 200.8 206.4 206.32
 208.18 VG 9.11 24.20 27.2
 30.12 31.34 37.15 46.12
 46.36 46.38 46.42 49.14
 49.24 54.16 58.17 62.31
 62.32 64.38 75.7 75.25 75.38
 76.23 76.31

COLD-BLOODED SM 126.35

COLDER SM 70.4

COLDLY LH 14.24 17.42 32.38
 37.13 FO 170.38 CD 213.35
 227.38 237.11 241.3 242.40
 SM 18.2 44.5 108.24 108.28
 MD 193.22 VG 26.24 34.33
 66.17

COLDNESS TL 78.33 78.40
 SM 151.35 MD 207.36

COLD-RACKED VG 75.15

COLDS VG 11.30

COLLAPSE MD 172.4 VG 65.9 78.3

COLLAPSED LH 7.12 TL 107.24
 CD 221.28 229.32 SM 87.19
 VG 80.32

COLLAR TL 51.16 CD 215.1
 VG 24.11 61.23 61.29 63.36

COLLARS VG 8.32 17.18

COLLECT FO 132.11 CD 260.8

COLLECTED CD 231.36

COLLECTING FO 128.2
 CD 260.16 SM 33.33

COLLIERY LH 4.32 23.20

COLLYPOSY SM 110.2

COLONEL TL 50.25 CD 187.39
 188.33 192.21

COLONIAL SM 18.18 18.24
 29.1

COLONIES SM 18.22 18.33

COLORADO SM 77.32 147.30

COLOUR LH 10.35 21.26
 TL 46.35 46.42 97.30
 FO 120.38 138.13 141.12
 148.22 156.8 CD 185.3
 235.34 244.38 244.41
 245.20 253.1 253.37
 254.42 255.19 SM 10.12
 12.7 17.1 17.4 42.38
 80.15 80.35 MD 163.26
 VG 39.36

COLOURED TL 46.31 CD 183.7
 193.19 207.30 253.38
 SM 39.24 131.12 MD 171.18
 VG 19.1 19.2

COLOURFUL SM 113.3

COLOURING SM 45.15

COLOURLESS SM 82.10 MD 170.14

COLOURLESSLY SM 82.6

COLOURS SM 57.25

COLTS SM 35.18

COLUMBINES SM 150.23

COLUMN CD 228.29 SM 146.2
 146.4 146.11

COLUMNS SM 9.32 148.3

COMA MD 170.29 192.6

COMB MD 167.22

COMBED FO 135.29

COMBUSTION TL 87.22

COMELY LH 18.26

COMFORT SM 28.15 44.34
 VG 9.5 64.32 67.22

COMFORTABLE LH 35.20 TL 99.19
 FO 122.28 CD 206.16
 SM 99.35 100.1 113.39
 113.40 116.28 132.25
 VG 9.6 43.38

COMFORTABLY CD 248.7 257.7
 VG 58.23 78.7

COMFORTING   FO 145.22

COMIC   VG 16.31   59.7

COMICAL   TL 50.10

COMIN'   LH 28.24

COMMAND   LH 25.34   27.16   TL 89.25
    VG 48.23

COMMANDED   SM 34.4   51.8   VG 75.21
    76.8

COMMANDMENT   MD 195.33

COMMANDS   CD 262.36

COMMERCIAL   SM 132.28

COMMIN'   LH 10.32   37.13   37.15
    37.26   37.30   37.39

COMMISSION   CD 213.14   VG 53.22

COMMIT   TL 95.37   FO 178.24
    179.24   SM 5.6

COMMITTED   TL 43.12   96.4
    FO 167.1   CD 215.33   215.34

COMMITTING   SM 96.9

COMMODITY   SM 50.39

COMMON   LH 5.33   5.35   TL 87.29
    94.8   FO 166.4   CD 230.10
    SM 17.39   21.10   33.8   53.26
    85.31   MD 183.27   198.30
    VG 41.36   51.20   53.24   55.19
    55.20   55.23   55.29   55.31   60.9
    70.17

COMMONER   TL 46.8

COMMONPLACE   SM 15.2   48.32   48.35
    48.38   48.39   53.34

COMMOTION   FO 146.28   147.10
    CD 225.13   SM 70.16

COMMUNED   MD 180.39

COMMUNICATION   SM 42.40

COMMUNION   TL 66.10   SM 99.13

COMPANIONS   FO 136.19

COMPANY   LH 18.13   FO 122.32
    CD 209.23   241.42   SM 10.39
    25.22   113.23   VG 12.38   13.40
    14.13   16.35   49.11   76.40

COMPARATIVE   SM 42.37   113.40
    VG 53.20

COMPARATIVELY   TL 46.12   65.9
    SM 144.16   VG 9.32

COMPARE   SM 24.4

COMPARED   FO 127.9   SM 129.9
    MD 172.17   VG 66.26

COMPASSION   MD 166.36   169.32
    172.40   180.41   197.15

COMPASSIONATE   MD 169.31

COMPEL   CD 251.9   SM 94.38
    MD 179.40

COMPELLED   MD 179.40   184.13

COMPENSATION   SM 80.29

COMPETENT   SM 93.28   112.35
    155.25

COMPLACENCY   FO 143.27   VG 12.31

COMPLACENT   VG 12.28

COMPLACENTLY   LH 8.27   CD 195.9
    MD 172.2

COMPLAIN   TL 57.36   65.11

COMPLAINING   FO 169.36

COMPLAINT   TL 77.37

COMPLETE   LH 34.17   TL 91.38
    102.16   FO 166.20   CD 184.18
    SM 18.10   27.31   29.17   38.17
    77.26   84.31   85.16   109.21
    129.14   135.37   137.26
    MD 165.31   VG 5.39   20.5   48.20

COMPLETELY   TL 86.3   CD 199.33
    211.5   216.22   SM 3.3   3.15
    8.34   38.5   82.14   82.32   99.22
    MD 203.20   VG 42.18

COMPLEXION   TL 46.33   46.35
    FO 143.3   SM 8.32   39.20   121.7

COMPLEXIONS   SM 128.2

COMPLEXITY   MD 183.33

COMPLICATED   CD 199.2   259.18
    SM 49.9   96.20   VG 40.9   55.28
    65.18

COMPLICITY   VG 28.40

COMPLIMENTED   SM 111.3

COMPLIMENTS   SM 44.15

COMPOSED   TL 48.36   SM 10.13

COMPOSITION   CD 208.31   SM 17.4

COMPOSURE   FO 143.2

COMPREHENSIBLE   SM 54.6

COMPREHENSIVE   TL 88.11

COMPRESSED   VG 65.30

COMPROMISED   CD 199.9

COMPROMISING   CD 199.8

COMPULSION   TL 79.6   MD 176.39
    179.38   180.1   183.40   183.41

COMPULSION (CONT.)   184.5
    184.7   184.10   184.13

COMPULSIVE   MD 172.15

COMRADES   MD 188.33

COMTE, MONSIEUR LE   (SEE
    MONSIEUR LE COMTE)

CONCATENATION   SM 110.26

CONCAVE   SM 20.41   102.18

CONCEALED   SM 125.36

CONCEIT   CD 265.19   SM 5.10
    109.13   VG 20.25   27.4

CONCEITED   TL 50.31   50.32
    SM 8.21   90.22   VG 21.24
    22.27

CONCEIVE   FO 177.36   CD 208.9
    VG 29.31

CONCEIVED   SM 86.4   151.21
    MD 209.14

CONCENTRATED   LH 27.6
    TL 87.19   FO 146.36

CONCENTRATION   TL 100.26
    SM 131.27   MD 186.10

CONCEPTION   TL 88.39   VG 52.17
    64.42

CONCERN   LH 28.28   29.8   33.13

CONCERNED   TL 86.4   FO 125.31
    125.32   129.18   CD 261.28
    SM 133.8   155.29   157.23
    VG 22.32

CONCERNING   LH 12.11   16.24
    FO 120.40

CONCERT   VG 11.17

CONCILIATORY   LH 9.6   TL 91.6

CONCLUDED   FO 128.35   132.31
    SM 39.18   96.7

CONCLUSION   CD 213.38   250.30
    251.20   SM 85.22

CONCOCTING   VG 58.1

CONCRETE   LH 27.2   SM 145.19

CONCUSSION   SM 102.19

CONDEMNATION   TL 47.31   93.11
    SM 45.34   74.21

CONDEMNED   CD 221.2   SM 13.20

CONDENSED   SM 63.28

CONDESCENDING   SM 27.7   122.27

CONDESCENSION   VG 38.5   42.27

CONDITION   LH 8.15   FO 127.12

CONDITIONS   TL 83.34   FO 114.36
   SM 131.26

CONDUCTED   VG 9.39

CONDUCTOR   CD 260.3   260.16
   260.34

CONES   SM 146.7   VG 50.11   50.14
   50.16

CONFESS   LH 11.24   FO 138.23
   SM 12.29   152.15

CONFESSED   FO 138.27   CD 211.22
   SM 149.39   152.15   VG 30.33

CONFIDENCE   TL 44.38   SM 48.2

CONFIDENT   FO 114.11   CD 251.13
   SM 148.41   VG 8.34

CONFIDENTIAL   SM 83.28

CONFIRM   VG 64.32

CONFIRMED   VG 64.33

CONFLICT   SM 25.1   150.40

CONFUSED   LH 19.27   TL 51.39
   105.35   FO 125.28   158.38
   160.24   SM 100.30   VG 5.42
   22.19   28.29   81.8

CONFUSEDLY   FO 116.31   CD 199.38

CONFUSING   CD 259.17

CONFUSION   LH 20.19   20.29
   MD 180.35

CONGEALED   SM 107.15   109.11

CONGENIAL   CD 216.32

CONGRATULATE   TL 84.20   84.22

CONJURE   FO 122.6

CONJURED   SM 27.24   27.28   27.32
   MD 176.28

CONNECT   TL 96.41   VG 55.34   55.36

CONNECTED   CD 224.7   SM 116.13
   VG 55.37

CONNECTION   CD 224.34   MD 179.25
   VG 6.22   55.8   55.25   69.11

CONNECTIONS   TL 54.4

CONNECTS   VG 49.32

CONNEXION   SM 42.7   61.37   108.29

CONNUBIAL   CD 215.10

CONQUER   SM 96.17   96.36
   MD 176.15

CONQUERED   SM 95.36   142.8   142.22

CONQUEROR   SM 37.4

CONSCIENCE   TL 71.10   SM 15.24

CONSCIENTIOUSLY   VG 31.17

CONSCIOUS   TL 103.42   FO 118.19
   CD 224.14   SM 95.31   152.17
   MD 169.1   VG 6.26   41.21   43.8
   70.31   72.38

CONSCIOUSLY   FO 116.14

CONSCIOUSNESS   TL 45.30   68.21
   68.26   85.4   86.2   87.16   99.2
   99.3   FO 116.24   125.7   128.22
   128.23   128.40   167.16   178.28
   SM 12.11   15.13   42.40   75.17
   97.9   125.27   130.18   130.25
   MD 165.17   169.15   177.31
   193.24   194.11   205.36   206.11
   206.15   206.41   VG 41.9   44.5
   55.11   77.15

CONSENT   TL 92.41

CONSENTED   LH 36.25   SM 28.4

CONSEQUENCES   CD 214.13

CONSERVATISM   VG 61.6   61.10

CONSERVATIVE   VG 61.3

CONSIDER   TL 67.38   80.18
   FO 116.42   124.3   178.34
   CD 203.10   258.28   SM 50.26
   64.31   92.32

CONSIDERABLY   CD 250.34

CONSIDERATE   LH 34.33   SM 73.4

CONSIDERATION   SM 73.5   VG 39.42

CONSIDERED   LH 35.23   FO 135.1
   135.3   CD 251.7   SM 52.17
   VG 28.17

CONSIDERING   CD 196.23   SM 159.19
   VG 62.1

CONSIDERS   FO 135.4

CONSOLATION   TL 91.40   CD 222.4
   SM 97.3

CONSOLE   CD 222.1   VG 35.34

CONSOLED   SM 94.35

CONSOLINGLY   LH 14.20

CONSPIRATORS   SM 73.29

CONSPIRE   SM 73.30

CONSTANT   FO 116.10   119.22
   VG 41.6

CONSTANTLY   LH 39.21

CONSTRICTED   FO 146.10

CONSTRUCTIVE   TL 86.35

CONSULT   SM 133.28

CONSULTED   SM 80.16

CONSUME   VG 15.32

CONSUMED   SM 36.7   VG 51.28
   66.21

CONSUMING   MD 207.28   VG 12.34

CONSUMMATE   MD 208.32

CONSUMMATION   FO 155.14

CONSUMPTION   TL 47.25
   SM 85.20

CONTACT   LH 5.22   TL 78.26
   78.27   86.14   86.16   86.18
   86.25   86.31   86.36   86.37
   86.38   86.42   87.25   87.26
   87.32   87.35   88.6   99.5
   103.3   107.16   CD 217.18
   SM 7.23   77.39   78.2   101.13
   109.4   MD 184.12   194.12
   202.9   208.33   208.37   209.6

CONTACTS   MD 184.16

CONTAGION   SM 5.23   VG 28.2

CONTAIN   TL 89.37

CONTAINED   SM 27.10   VG 26.10

CONTAINING   CD 228.31
   SM 14.35   85.32   93.9
   MD 200.26

CONTAMINATED   VG 63.41

CONTEMPLATIVE   SM 6.38

CONTEMPLATIVELY   LH 30.1

CONTEMPT   LH 31.35   TL 73.15
   93.38   FO 159.7   SM 5.11
   7.4   34.4   88.35   88.38
   89.10   96.13   96.38   100.10
   120.35   136.7   VG 5.28
   28.16   30.26   61.26   61.29
   63.35   64.12

CONTEMPTUOUS   LH 37.28
   FO 117.27   SM 77.6   96.3
   108.23

CONTEMPTUOUSLY   LH 18.38
   VG 38.12

CONTENDING   SM 153.24

CONTENT   TL 43.21   FO 114.3
   119.15   SM 6.10   43.10
   43.13   60.29

CONTENTED   TL 98.25

CONTEST   SM 82.22

CONTINUAL   TL 57.38   CD 192.2

CONTINUALLY   SM 7.14
   VG 11.17

CONTINUE   TL 43.10   70.20

CONTINUED   LH 9.11   FO 121.31
124.36   125.23   CD 210.37
211.26   262.17   SM 124.28
156.37   MD 198.39   VG 11.40
31.24

CONTINUING   SM 46.35   76.27

CONTINUOUS   FO 118.39   119.5
SM 42.6   VG 58.18

CONTOUR   SM 119.10

CONTOURS   LH 19.5

CONTRACTED   TL 75.33   SM 55.34

CONTRADICTED   TL 107.18   FO 137.39

CONTRADICTING   TL 107.19

CONTRADICTORY   VG 79.35

CONTRARY   CD 202.33

CONTRAST   CD 186.30   187.21
228.33   SM 17.23   MD 193.5

CONTRASTED   LH 34.13

CONTRASTING   LH 19.5

CONTRIVANCE   FO 149.41

CONTRIVED   VG 5.22

CONTROL   TL 95.1   CD 264.31
SM 24.29   VG 35.10   76.37

CONTROLLED   MD 190.15   VG 61.7

CONTROVERSIALIST   VG 3.16

CONVALESCENCE   SM 7.38

CONVENIENCES   SM 52.5

CONVENT   CD 207.9   208.33   224.36
SM 4.33

CONVENTION   TL 102.36   VG 6.31

CONVENTIONAL   VG 8.38

CONVENTS   SM 157.33

CONVENTY   SM 157.40

CONVERSATION   TL 96.32   CD 219.7
SM 123.4   VG 12.41   60.31

CONVERSATIONALLY   SM 82.27

CONVERSE   LH 22.8   SM 8.41

CONVERTED   VG 78.34

CONVEY   SM 89.11

CONVEYED   CD 213.17

CONVICTION   CD 211.4   SM 132.3

CONVINCED   CD 189.29   SM 157.7
158.24

CONVINCING   VG 40.2

CONVULSED   LH 5.12   12.19
FO 152.19   174.37   SM 67.19

CONVULSION   CD 225.34   SM 67.7
VG 29.8   77.8

CONVULSIONS   FO 174.7   VG 62.36

CONVULSIVE   LH 33.15

CONVULSIVELY   LH 4.8   29.15
TL 68.30   SM 80.21

COOING   MD 171.40

COOK   SM 90.33   VG 77.33   78.10
80.10

COOKED   SM 103.30   VG 47.4

COOKING   VG 45.34   46.10

COOL   LH 11.28   21.32   FO 118.9
CD 257.17   SM 59.23   74.2
104.11   MD 168.20   170.38
189.11   189.18   VG 34.42

COOLING   LH 21.18

COOLLY   LH 13.23   SM 58.28
VG 34.36   59.19

COOLNESS   LH 15.25   SM 74.1
MD 210.19

COOP   LH 23.8

COOPED   CD 221.12

COOPS   FO 113.37

COPE   SM 25.30   124.33   149.21
155.26   VG 66.30

COPPER   CD 253.2   SM 145.41
VG 38.1   38.2   38.26   45.30
45.36   46.31   50.26   67.8   67.11
68.10   68.18   68.23   70.38

COPPER-LIKE   FO 116.17

COPPER-SULPHATE   CD 255.1

CORD   MD 164.8   164.10   164.36
171.8   171.34   171.38

CORDIALITY   SM 51.37

CORDUROY   CD 243.4

CORE   LH 34.17   SM 69.29   149.29
MD 203.19   208.2   VG 26.40
27.22   27.23

CORKSCREWING   SM 128.30

CORN   TL 69.36   FO 126.29
SM 60.17   64.5

CORNELIAN   SM 151.36

CORNER   LH 3.12   8.29   8.33
8.36   8.39   9.4   10.12
14.25   21.42   26.9   TL 76.30
FO 115.23   119.37   122.37
123.34   125.2   125.6   125.12
125.17   133.41   143.13
146.26   160.26   160.36
169.20   169.26   169.38
170.23   CD 232.42   234.21
SM 19.15   33.28   37.35
58.19   85.7   98.30   121.37
128.23   146.35   MD 163.14
170.17   190.23   194.6   198.9
VG 11.14   36.31   54.10
73.22   73.25   75.34   77.30

CORNERED   VG 61.32   61.33

CORNERS   SM 36.34

CORNFIELDS   SM 101.37

CORNFLOWERS   SM 113.5

CORNICE   VG 73.26

CORNISH   FO 123.20   132.32
167.24   167.38

CORNISHMEN   SM 63.36

CORNWALL   FO 175.11

CORPORAL   FO 128.3

CORPSE   SM 30.30   59.40   153.11
153.13   MD 204.37   204.41
205.1   205.2   205.8

CORPSES   FO 176.8   SM 30.31
71.32

CORPUS   SM 145.5

CORPUS DELICTI   SM 118.17

CORRABACH   SM 35.29   36.31
36.38   37.5   37.16   88.18
91.35   91.38   93.20   109.33
109.35   110.13   111.31
115.17

CORRABACH HALL   SM 28.6   37.8
37.20   89.34   92.18   109.29
115.7

CORRAL   SM 141.11   142.2
142.28   143.9   143.27
143.35   155.8

CORRECT   CD 197.31   233.14
SM 20.24

CORRECTED   CD 258.11

CORRECTNESS   CD 231.7   SM 81.37

CORRESPONDENCE   CD 218.20
SM 5.2   87.14

CORRIDOR   TL 97.34   99.40
100.3   100.8   100.19   101.25
101.27   CD 201.1

CORROSIVE   TL 63.40   SM 89.10

CORRUGATED LH 25.7 26.36
  SM 29.5

CORRUPT SM 30.18

COSILY VG 17.7

COSMETICS TL 67.35

COST CD 238.26 SM 16.25 142.24
  144.18 153.29 VG 48.29

COSTLY MD 169.21

COSTS FO 137.13 SM 104.40

COSTUME CD 232.6 233.11 233.13
  252.10

COSY LH 23.16 TL 97.26
  FO 135.42 SM 29.32 143.9

COTTAGE LH 21.8 23.19 FO 143.8
  146.7 CD 239.18 SM 27.41
  28.12 29.5 59.17 101.38
  MD 163.6 163.10 168.30
  VG 53.19 53.36 54.10 58.1
  62.10 68.9

COTTAGES LH 23.17 SM 29.4 29.7
  29.27 59.16 154.35 VG 18.1

COTTON FO 136.15 CD 187.24
  233.11 233.26 252.6 SM 129.17

COTTON-MILLS VG 3.24

COTTONWOOD SM 151.32

COTTONWOOD-TREE SM 147.19 155.23

COTTONWOOD-TREES SM 147.36

COUCH TL 102.19 102.21 103.17
  103.18 FO 122.41 CD 214.30
  MD 201.30 202.38 204.9
  VG 31.28 32.28

COUE SM 132.3

COUGH VG 76.18

COUGHED VG 74.9 74.36

COUGHING VG 74.2 74.32 75.14

COULDNA LH 22.42 37.3

COULDN'T LH 7.23 27.15 30.6
  35.7 TL 50.14 77.29 FO 144.5
  144.9 148.6 150.27 CD 191.12
  195.11 196.26 199.5 205.34
  207.41 208.15 208.16 210.27
  220.28 221.27 244.11 259.14
  261.25 SM 4.31 4.32 5.1 10.2
  13.1 26.15 26.27 47.2 56.19
  98.21 107.18 112.23 113.10
  113.22 113.26 135.23 135.29
  136.9 136.10 138.32 149.22
  149.24 156.36 VG 16.19 31.8
  35.9 43.6 56.38 57.3

COUNSEL VG 24.31

COUNT TL 51.3 53.4 56.4 59.24

COUNT (CONT.) 68.13 69.16 69.21
  69.30 70.17 75.19 81.6 83.17
  83.25 83.35 83.39 84.18
  84.24 84.31 84.35 85.3 85.8
  85.12 85.16 85.24 85.27
  85.41 86.9 86.20 86.42 87.12
  87.16 87.24 88.3 88.14 88.20
  88.38 89.4 89.21 89.23 89.31
  89.32 89.35 90.17 90.19
  90.33 90.36 90.38 91.1 91.7
  91.12 91.17 91.31 91.35 92.2
  92.14 92.19 92.22 92.39 93.4
  93.21 93.24 93.27 93.30
  93.32 93.37 94.2 94.4 94.6
  94.13 94.19 94.34 95.8 95.37
  96.16 96.22 96.35 97.14
  97.17 99.9 99.14 99.21 100.9
  101.1 102.6 102.7 102.34
  105.22 105.30 106.40 107.31
  108.15 108.19 108.22 108.29
  108.37 109.2 109.7 CD 203.10
  203.18 203.21 SM 135.10
  156.27

COUNT DIONYS TL 45.1 45.15
  49.32 50.7 50.18 50.26 51.37
  52.17 53.9 62.18 64.18 64.26
  65.42 69.5 72.17 72.22 75.15
  82.33 83.28 94.24 97.21

COUNT DIONYS PSANEK TL 81.4
  83.29

COUNTED CD 232.41 SM 135.14

COUNTENANCE SM 135.2 MD 167.36

COUNTERACT VG 40.15

COUNTER-MOVE SM 92.16

COUNTERPART SM 135.17 135.20

COUNTESS CD 195.28 196.12
  200.13 200.19 218.34 229.3
  234.3

COUNTESS BEVERIDGE TL 44.10
  97.21

COUNTESS HANNELE CD 184.32
  186.13 205.10 205.25 205.27
  205.28 206.1 228.36

COUNTESS OF WITTON SM 110.30

COUNTESS VON RASSENTLOW CD 195.26

COUNTESS ZU CD 205.23 205.24

COUNTESS ZU RASSENTLOW CD 193.14
  229.5

COUNTIES VG 19.1

COUNTING FO 144.18

COUNT JOHANN DIONYS PSANEK
  TL 45.3 50.27

COUNTLESS SM 153.30

COUNT PSANEK TL 83.2 93.22
  93.35 93.41

COUNTRY LH 4.29 4.31 5.32
  TL 45.6 85.32 98.7 102.25
  FO 115.36 CD 250.6 SM 8.14
  11.8 28.7 28.11 28.21
  30.4 33.2 36.5 63.16
  77.37 78.20 86.9 92.26
  92.31 92.33 93.7 94.11
  95.37 97.29 98.23 98.35
  102.11 103.13 115.32
  116.18 116.23 128.5 129.33
  130.5 134.24 145.3 145.7
  VG 3.20 9.29 45.13 50.38

COUNTRYMEN TL 93.31 CD 212.4
  SM 127.34

COUNTRYSIDE LH 9.16 SM 59.39

COUNTRY-SIDE SM 125.25

COUNTRY'S LH 17.7

COUNTS SM 48.20 79.2

COUNT'S TL 52.39 68.25
  68.41 70.22 84.1 86.30
  91.2 100.2 100.24

COUPLE FO 150.29 CD 207.14
  SM 3.11 8.15 26.6 60.9
  72.7 73.39 101.2 110.39
  127.24 127.33 140.40
  149.25 VG 53.29 54.42

COUPLES TL 62.27 VG 62.24
  62.27

COURAGE LH 11.36 36.3
  TL 82.42 CD 183.31 SM 73.23
  73.24 73.25 73.27 77.21
  131.15 MD 169.29 203.17
  203.18 VG 43.36 47.18
  61.33

COURSE LH 27.9 27.21
  TL 46.18 49.22 56.7 66.30
  68.37 81.2 82.33 84.15
  85.5 85.30 87.31 88.6
  88.10 89.37 90.17 92.14
  92.19 98.33 99.9 100.11
  108.41 FO 126.3 129.14
  140.1 144.6 150.24 152.3
  152.24 154.13 156.10
  156.12 162.21 CD 188.29
  190.15 190.35 196.22
  196.24 196.28 198.1
  206.35 207.5 208.1 209.27
  209.29 209.37 210.1 210.4
  210.25 211.19 211.25
  211.35 211.38 212.35
  213.13 213.32 214.14
  214.26 219.11 229.1
  229.32 230.36 231.3 231.26
  232.1 232.15 239.41 243.29
  246.27 251.1 257.14 257.25
  261.7 SM 3.24 4.40 5.2
  30.34 40.2 80.12 93.26
  121.33 123.4 127.16 132.30
  142.39 143.36 VG 4.7
  4.13 7.15 10.6 10.34
  16.24 27.41 28.13 32.6
  34.7 34.35 34.37 37.38
  40.3 40.5 42.26 49.22
  64.6

COURT SM 94.38 VG 6.6

COURTEOUS FO 124.37 129.5
  129.27 171.22 CD 209.8
  SM 155.17

COURTEOUSLY FO 134.33 171.40

COURTESY TL 87.3 FO 126.8
  134.28 135.11

COURTIER-LIKE SM 4.16

COURTING LH 20.33 VG 43.33
  43.34

COURT OF KING ARTHUR SM 111.22

COURTSHIP SM 94.36

COURTYARD MD 163.7

COURT-YARD SM 37.34

COVE MD 210.7 210.30

COVER LH 24.28 31.10 FO 122.38
  145.41 148.5 SM 34.26 120.33

COVERED LH 14.38 FO 159.13
  159.26 SM 15.26 81.34 85.8
  MD 192.38 VG 7.16 37.21

COVERING LH 38.26 CD 211.28
  253.14 SM 66.7 MD 187.5
  197.33

COVERLET FO 148.16

COVERS MD 200.24

COVERT VG 30.19

COW FO 113.5 CD 239.28

COW-BELLS CD 244.13

COWBOY SM 131.2

COWBOYS SM 130.38 130.40

COWED MD 187.13 VG 61.20 61.21
  62.39 63.25

COWERED MD 170.17

COW-SHED FO 114.2

COYNESS CD 183.24

COYOTES SM 143.33

CRABS CD 254.39

CRACK FO 173.26 CD 255.2 255.4
  255.20 SM 78.15 147.25
  MD 192.32 VG 11.12 42.40

CRACKED SM 154.23 VG 9.25 9.27
  12.27

CRACKING TL 74.32 74.37
  VG 74.13

CRACKLING TL 74.37

CRACKS TL 74.39 98.23 CD 255.16
  255.38

CRADLE CD 244.28

CRAFT CD 237.15

CRANBERRIES CD 241.1

CRANE CD 200.33 MD 163.23

CRANED FO 169.39 170.3
  MD 181.19

CRANING MD 167.31

CRANNY TL 83.21

CRAPE FO 156.4 156.19 156.37

CRASH FO 147.6 174.34 CD 222.20
  234.40 SM 33.30 58.30 66.33
  MD 166.8 VG 74.19

CRASHED CD 239.25

CRASHING CD 239.22

CRAVE SM 78.31

CRAVED SM 74.10

CRAVES SM 159.9

CRAVING SM 116.17

CRAWK FO 146.28

CRAWKING FO 147.11

CRAWL LH 18.34 SM 73.15 83.4

CRAWLED VG 80.39

CRAZED VG 74.23 74.27

CRAZILY MD 167.31

CRAZY SM 44.29 60.27 VG 14.21

CREAKED FO 144.1 SM 45.33 45.36

CREAKING FO 169.17

CREAM LH 22.14 CD 205.30
  SM 81.34 84.38

CREAMY LH 6.3 FO 143.2 155.18

CREAMY-GREY VG 17.21

CREASED SM 78.21 VG 49.30

CREATED SM 153.2

CREATION SM 71.6 71.12 71.21
  71.27 75.21 152.36 153.34

CREATIONS CD 228.36

CREATIVE TL 97.9 CD 229.2
  SM 71.40

CREATIVELY SM 71.38

CREATURE TL 52.4 FO 115.5
  125.11 125.13 142.11
  153.2 167.6 176.30
  CD 200.3 208.37 209.11
  211.29 221.6 245.21
  SM 16.18 25.15 36.33 46.3
  58.9 73.2 73.6 74.18 76.7
  79.40 99.17 146.25 150.9
  MD 171.30 VG 4.29 10.14
  15.37 31.10

CREATURES LH 21.38 FO 117.10
  CD 221.11 SM 12.18 69.18
  69.19 75.20 MD 171.15
  VG 7.29

CREDIT VG 28.38

CREED TL 47.31

CREEP SM 33.18

CREEPING FO 146.37 153.12
  154.35 158.24 168.31
  CD 238.14 VG 6.36 62.24
  76.26

CREPE SM 35.36

CREPT LH 21.8 27.26 TL 97.1
  FO 144.2 145.27 145.29
  SM 16.15 MD 166.13 210.32
  210.39 210.40 VG 27.36
  29.23 64.23 76.11

CREST LH 23.14 TL 61.19
  81.21 81.22 96.32 97.29
  CD 218.21 248.13 250.33
  SM 60.5 149.34 MD 171.29
  191.33

CRESTED SM 151.27 MD 185.22

CRESTS FO 117.35 CD 255.20
  SM 141.17 146.38 MD 171.16

CREVICE FO 177.24

CREVICES CD 255.21

CREW VG 56.2 56.6

CRICK LH 35.18 35.34

CRIED LH 8.42 11.17 12.34
  12.39 13.1 14.11 14.15
  22.28 23.36 24.1 24.30
  37.9 TL 76.8 85.11 96.22
  FO 118.2 118.8 118.10
  119.38 119.41 133.18
  138.10 138.12 138.18
  138.21 139.9 140.29 142.4
  148.16 150.39 151.31 152.5
  156.13 156.32 157.15
  158.26 158.35 159.16
  159.39 169.31 170.11
  171.31 171.32 172.14
  172.29 173.15 174.18
  CD 193.32 211.3 211.9
  228.5 234.36 234.38
  234.42 236.22 236.26
  242.10 242.34 244.9 244.22
  245.23 246.6 246.11 246.18
  249.38 249.41 250.1 258.36
  259.15 259.40 261.19

CRIED (CONT.) CD 261.35 262.1
  264.23 265.7 265.33 266.2
  266.4 SM 14.23 48.22 52.24
  52.28 52.33 53.39 54.11
  54.32 57.16 58.3 66.24 67.28
  78.9 100.20 108.1 108.7
  155.46 MD 179.13 179.19
  183.11 202.28 VG 8.6 8.13
  8.24 13.41 15.3 15.5
  17.6 18.14 20.8 20.10 20.12
  21.33 22.1 22.36 22.42 23.17
  25.21 30.41 31.33 32.1 32.14
  33.7 33.41 34.20 50.19 50.22
  51.35 51.42 52.37 55.36
  56.13 57.28 58.32 58.35
  58.40 59.36 59.41 60.9 63.13
  68.40 75.11 75.17 76.1 80.24
  81.6

CRIMINAL LH 12.17 VG 63.4 63.6
  64.37

CRIMINAL-LUNACY VG 63.2

CRIMINALS TL 43.11

CRIMPED VG 24.39

CRINGE SM 65.4

CRINGED VG 64.35

CRINGING SM 50.6 MD 187.13

CRINKLE SM 11.28

CRISP LH 10.36 FO 114.13 120.23
  134.6 136.9

CRISPED LH 13.6

CRISPLY LH 10.17

CRITICISE TL 90.7 90.34 90.40

CRITICISED TL 91.22

CRITICISING TL 90.11

CRITICISM SM 30.28 30.32
  VG 16.25

CRITICIZING SM 50.36

CROCHETING SM 50.13

CROCHETTED FO 136.15 143.28

CROCHETTING FO 136.8 136.21
  137.36 138.8

CROCHET-WORK FO 119.20

CROCUS MD 196.13

CROCUSES TL 56.32 98.21 VG 70.5
  70.23

CROCUS-LIKE MD 196.14

CRONE VG 71.2

CROON TL 99.34

CROONING TL 99.28

CROPPED SM 63.33

CROPPING SM 73.7 VG 36.19

CROQUET TL 65.8 66.13

CROSS TL 100.39 101.34
  CD 208.20 261.10 SM 84.29
  101.6 133.11 156.12 VG 17.42
  66.15

CROSSED TL 58.4 FO 136.20
  163.30 179.12 CD 187.11
  SM 8.23 126.33 MD 209.25
  VG 37.7

CROSSER SM 24.8

CROSSES VG 3.23

CROSS-EYED SM 43.33

CROSSHILL VG 18.29

CROSSING LH 4.36 38.12 TL 98.13
  FO 152.30 SM 102.8 121.37
  126.23 VG 36.5

CROSSLY FO 138.15 140.28
  CD 254.37 VG 33.16

CROSSNESS CD 243.9

CROSSROADS FO 168.11

CROSSWORD VG 10.37 11.10 11.40

CROSSWORD PUZZLE VG 15.2

CROUCH FO 173.39

CROUCHED LH 24.2 25.32 39.11
  FO 146.18 146.19 147.4 156.35
  163.25 MD 166.15 176.8 177.24
  186.36 206.35 207.9 VG 46.19
  49.20

CROUCHING LH 23.30 FO 163.28
  SM 19.16 33.31 145.36
  MD 166.9 177.30 186.6 198.36
  206.41 207.4

CROW MD 163.26 165.1

CROWD TL 48.40 SM 22.40 96.34
  VG 43.24

CROWDED LH 22.2 TL 44.22 51.13
  CD 229.19 232.40 260.14
  SM 24.13 143.10 VG 17.31 54.8

CROWDING SM 146.26

CROWDS CD 233.5

CROWED MD 164.27 165.1 170.41
  178.31

CROWING MD 163.24 164.3 167.16
  171.33 183.18

CROWN TL 61.23 VG 68.36

CROWNED SM 57.1

CROWNING TL 97.30

CROWS VG 66.10

CRUCIFIED FO 149.32

CRUDE FO 134.40 155.33
  SM 32.40 130.15 138.39
  141.16 145.40 146.26
  152.34 154.3 VG 20.34

CRUDELY SM 146.25

CRUDENESS SM 94.14

CRUEL TL 93.15 SM 52.17
  65.33 74.14 75.23 77.17
  77.18 79.31 80.19 90.15
  112.11 152.32 MD 175.16

CRUELLY TL 91.5 FO 133.22
  SM 66.38 VG 23.3 23.8

CRUEL-SEEMING VG 22.8

CRUELTY SM 41.2 79.30 80.20
  90.17 90.18 90.19 90.21
  134.16 MD 204.11 204.12
  204.13

CRUMBLING LH 6.3 VG 51.29

CRUMPLED TL 71.13 CD 194.41
  195.1 207.31 SM 60.16
  67.20 68.34 81.30

CRUSHED SM 13.14 68.35 69.39
  72.12 VG 17.10 27.35 73.9

CRUSTED CD 253.29

CRY LH 7.3 10.3 11.8 11.42
  29.19 TL 82.14 108.7
  FO 119.34 133.18 140.32
  140.35 141.3 159.21 159.22
  166.18 173.37 174.2 174.28
  174.29 175.1 CD 219.31
  SM 14.14 63.26 85.38 96.36
  118.2 MD 171.1 171.3
  173.17 186.20 203.29
  205.36 VG 14.13 48.37
  78.34 79.37 80.25

CRYING FO 143.19 CD 240.1
  244.31 255.9 SM 64.33
  MD 205.28 VG 22.14 49.4

CRYSTAL CD 253.2 255.2
  SM 110.33 143.29 151.19

CRYSTALLISED VG 30.37

CRYSTALLISING VG 65.8

CRYSTALLIZED SM 154.32

CRYSTALS SM 147.18

CUBE SM 147.18

CUBS TL 58.38 66.4

CUB'S FO 152.15

CUE VG 4.18

DAISY　CD 241.7

DAISY-SHAPED　TL 54.25

DALES　VG 18.18　19.8

DALLIED　CD 226.34

DAM　VG 80.32　80.34

DAMAGE　TL 46.25　FO 159.4
　CD 259.25　SM 144.30

DAMAGED　VG 29.24

DAMASCUS　MD 194.29

DAMMED　TL 47.11

DAMN　SM 36.23

DAMNED　TL 99.9

DAMNING　SM 74.21

DAMP　LH 38.35　TL 56.33
　FO 168.30　CD 241.22　SM 63.1
　87.37　112.5　VG 16.37　17.34
　36.3

DAMPNESS　VG 17.36

DAMSONS　FO 118.26

DANCE　FO 135.37　SM 27.27　66.17
　VG 10.12　42.21　42.26　43.36

DANCE-BUSINESS　SM 27.29

DANCED　VG 70.1

DANCER　TL 50.29　VG 43.13

DANCERS　VG 43.11

DANCES　VG 10.10

DANCING　SM 24.20　24.26　24.40
　27.17　27.22　36.11　36.12
　36.15　106.10　VG 41.8　42.41

DANCING-FLOOR　VG 43.21

DANDY　TL 50.28　SM 37.10
　MD 163.22　VG 23.24

DANGER　LH 5.38　7.11　CD 212.1
　SM 110.28　VG 5.35　5.37　7.19
　30.18

DANGERLESS　SM 50.41

DANGEROUS　LH 9.24　37.20
　TL 88.40　88.41　91.19
　FO 114.23　176.11　CD 202.40
　210.28　211.39　231.27　250.10
　SM 7.17　11.20　12.11　15.26
　19.39　21.32　25.17　26.31　27.2
　50.39　75.29　80.13　80.15
　131.5　MD 183.4　VG 5.33　5.38
　13.33　28.14　66.5

DANGEROUSLY　SM 10.17

DANGLED　VG 16.15

DANGLING　TL 83.24　FO 147.30
　CD 230.25　VG 17.18

DANISH　VG 53.34

DANK　VG 9.4

DAPHNE　TL 46.18　47.6　47.8
　47.17　48.23　48.29　48.34　49.6
　49.8　49.23　49.24　49.29　49.41
　50.7　50.11　50.26　50.33　50.38
　51.7　51.15　51.21　51.33　51.35
　52.38　53.20　53.40　54.35
　55.18　55.39　56.33　57.3　59.29
　59.36　71.13　71.17　71.24　72.3
　72.8　72.13　75.38　75.42　76.4
　76.14　76.32　76.35　77.8　77.17
　77.28　78.6　79.27　80.25　83.19
　84.26　85.8　85.27　85.35　86.1
　87.4　87.20　88.19　88.28　90.12
　90.33　90.38　91.3　91.12　91.31
　91.38　93.24　94.31　95.14
　95.41　96.36　97.11　99.16
　99.22　99.39　100.41　101.38
　102.3　102.6　104.33　105.2
　105.30　106.16　106.33　108.14

DAPHNE, LADY　(SEE LADY DAPHNE)

DAPHNE'S　TL 48.7　49.10　76.24
　98.27　102.37

DAPPER　TL 50.10　VG 38.2

DAPPERNESS　TL 59.28

DARE　TL 94.7　CD 193.35　SM 19.7
　124.23　MD 196.19　196.21
　VG 27.15　80.3　80.12

DARED　TL 44.12　64.40　78.24
　79.1　FO 133.1　CD 220.29
　SM 15.11　17.27　66.2　MD 196.20
　VG 22.25　43.19　65.42

DARE-DEVIL　TL 47.14　47.18

DARE-DEVILS　TL 47.19　47.35

DAREN'T　SM 10.5　10.6　84.30

DARING　LH 10.6　CD 217.11

DARK　LH 5.19　5.23　23.2　24.14
　24.36　25.11　26.36　TL 45.40
　50.1　50.12　53.33　54.16　55.34
　57.8　57.27　59.30　59.35　60.22
　63.14　67.12　67.14　67.17
　67.22　67.27　67.33　69.12
　72.36　74.29　74.35　75.6　81.10
　82.36　83.5　83.19　84.1　84.4
　84.9　84.14　85.26　86.4　86.22
　86.30　87.4　87.13　87.14　88.24
　93.6　93.10　93.19　93.39　95.16
　95.26　97.25　99.10　100.5
　102.20　102.34　102.37　102.39
　103.1　103.5　103.8　103.17
　103.30　103.39　104.12　104.17
　104.19　104.21　107.6　107.16
　107.20　107.26　107.31　FO 114.13
　114.14　114.21　115.24　117.2
　117.22　117.35　119.1　119.14
　122.15　122.22　128.12　129.36
　130.4　130.14　131.21　134.37
　135.23　135.35　137.40　138.7

DARK (CONT.)　139.33　146.3
　146.11　146.19　146.26
　149.17　149.25　153.13
　154.35　155.20　160.26
　160.37　164.33　173.37
　175.28　CD 184.8　184.9
　184.12　186.23　187.6
　187.26　188.1　188.34
　188.37　189.34　191.17
　194.2　198.21　201.16　216.38
　227.11　227.13　234.23　235.2
　235.11　235.26　236.31
　236.36　237.25　237.33　238.1
　238.19　238.20　240.34
　240.39　241.18　242.5　244.18
　244.33　244.40　247.25
　247.26　247.40　248.5　248.9
　249.2　249.19　249.30　249.31
　250.7　250.10　250.13　251.36
　253.7　255.28　257.5　263.12
　SM 7.32　9.26　11.15　12.7
　14.33　15.14　15.31　20.17
　20.35　21.16　23.34　25.5
　26.31　26.33　26.34　28.13
　31.40　38.22　38.36　57.7
　58.5　59.23　61.32　68.2
　77.35　78.17　78.20　87.36
　90.11　97.2　99.7　101.38
　102.13　102.19　135.33
　135.35　136.5　137.8　137.27
　143.24　143.28　146.19
　151.6　151.27　151.30　154.40
　MD 165.36　165.37　165.38
　170.3　175.20　185.21　186.6
　186.17　186.29　187.34
　187.40　189.30　190.23
　190.39　191.22　191.31
　191.33　193.3　194.17　194.19
　195.30　198.12　199.25
　202.27　205.35　206.25
　211.15　VG 3.5　9.30　10.31
　17.35　17.37　18.19　18.39
　19.33　19.36　20.1　20.4
　20.20　21.9　22.3　22.7
　22.12　22.27　23.35　24.16
　24.37　25.24　30.5　30.7
　36.14　36.18　37.40　38.3
　38.7　40.17　48.19　48.20
　70.24　71.14　76.31

DARK AGES　TL 90.18

DARK-BLOND　CD 185.5

DARK-BLUE　TL 59.25　84.8
　FO 152.29　CD 185.18　235.7
　244.40　SM 151.16

DARK-BROWN　VG 40.25

DARK-COLOURED　SM 34.35

DARK-EDGED-PATTERNED　SM 147.9

DARKEN　LH 21.25

DARKENED　TL 103.7　SM 92.9

DARKENING　LH 23.15

DARKER　TL 67.22　SM 22.12
　27.2

DARK-EYED　CD 183.22　235.19
　235.24　251.18　252.18

DEAD (CONT.) MD 165.13 165.19
  165.29 165.30 165.35 166.8
  166.23 168.3 168.22 169.10
  169.19 169.22 170.19 174.5
  174.12 175.17 176.13 176.29
  177.40 179.15 186.40 186.41
  187.8 187.19 188.9 188.10
  199.31 205.4 205.13 VG 7.25
  30.7 49.10 53.20 60.26 62.33
  66.29

DEADENED SM 112.6

DEADLIEST SM 157.31

DEADLOCK CD 213.8

DEADLOCKED VG 67.39

DEAD-LOOKING SM 67.21

DEADLY TL 65.40 105.20 SM 24.12
  25.31 31.28 49.27 82.39
  87.38 88.34 88.39 89.8 92.33
  101.15 113.41 114.1 127.12
  150.38

DEADNESS SM 25.34 25.35 49.22
  49.23 112.13 VG 62.31

DEAD-NETTLE SM 150.21

DEAD-WHITE MD 167.37 167.38

DEA-ED LH 10.5 10.33

DEAF FO 170.13 VG 13.21

DEAFENING VG 72.20

DEAL TL 68.21 CD 200.1 230.9
  264.9 SM 26.16 32.17 54.3
  77.8 131.7 142.25 VG 6.33
  65.2

DEALINGS SM 140.4

DEAN SM 28.20 28.29 28.39 29.9
  29.16 29.34 31.1 31.11 53.24
  54.1 54.11 54.18 54.31 79.13
  79.25 79.35 80.2 80.25 81.33
  81.40 82.8 82.12 82.19 82.23
  82.31 82.39 83.7 83.14 83.38
  84.4 84.7 84.17 84.20 84.26
  84.29 89.31

DEANE SM 13.11

DEAN'S SM 82.21 83.25

DEAN VYNER SM 48.38 49.12 51.15
  53.15 79.10 83.11 83.37 88.8
  91.40

DEAR TL 44.27 48.5 48.18 48.24
  48.32 48.42 49.18 50.7 50.21
  50.32 58.21 65.37 65.40
  68.34 71.17 71.22 71.31
  71.33 72.2 72.11 105.37
  106.4 106.6 106.36 FO 136.22
  137.3 138.24 165.14 176.19
  CD 186.5 205.13 205.16 205.41
  206.8 206.11 206.16 212.1
  214.13 215.6 215.17 215.32
  217.2 217.22 217.40 218.22

DEAR (CONT.) 218.34 225.34
  229.2 SM 5.3 5.26 9.38 10.19
  15.18 16.26 16.32 16.33
  16.40 23.29 25.25 30.39
  31.7 35.4 50.38 57.10
  66.4 72.15 72.26 81.32
  93.33 109.24 110.2 110.7
  110.9 110.22 110.26 110.29
  110.36 111.20 112.14 112.15
  112.26 112.27 113.31 114.3
  114.10 115.19 116.1 116.3
  116.7 117.21 117.32 120.34
  149.39 MD 177.16 178.29
  211.21 VG 8.2 64.24 81.16

DEAREST SM 16.29 92.25 93.22
  117.30 120.36 VG 53.37

DEARS CD 252.20

DEATH LH 30.41 32.20 34.19
  TL 43.6 44.5 45.25 52.24
  52.28 52.29 63.20 64.10
  75.21 75.37 76.9 78.24 78.25
  88.2 88.13 89.27 100.39
  101.42 102.4 104.19 108.3
  109.7 FO 147.9 147.19 158.41
  172.2 173.9 178.14 178.31
  CD 218.8 240.22 SM 18.15
  20.20 25.34 51.14 71.7 85.24
  85.25 85.27 85.33 86.1 86.17
  86.19 97.1 97.2 97.3 97.16
  97.18 97.33 125.12 126.8
  MD 167.39 169.24 170.34 171.7
  172.16 174.7 174.19 175.4
  175.17 175.23 176.21 176.24
  177.21 182.18 184.1 184.14
  195.18 196.10 196.16 196.20
  196.21 197.20 202.25 203.18
  203.36 203.38 203.41 204.5
  204.20 204.22 205.6 205.13
  205.37 205.38 206.14 206.40
  207.3 209.34 VG 11.33 25.25
  61.31

DEATH-GRIPPING VG 75.29

DEATH-HOUR MD 204.14

DEATHLESS MD 171.19

DEATHLY TL 78.18 SM 78.8
  MD 168.9

DEATH-PALE TL 105.16

DEATH'S TL 76.2

DEATH-WOUND MD 203.28

DEBACLE SM 7.25 128.3

DEBASED LH 18.6

DEBASING SM 144.37

DEBONAIR LH 3.26 VG 24.8 40.22

DEBRIS CD 252.30 253.29 SM 7.26
  VG 77.29 78.14

DEBT SM 141.36 141.37 VG 28.37

DEBTS VG 27.32

DECADENCE CD 231.34

DECANTER CD 230.17

DECAY SM 94.25

DECAYING SM 94.29 128.7

DECEIVE CD 211.33 SM 137.33
  VG 51.8

DECEIVED CD 205.39 211.18
  SM 41.37

DECEMBER FO 145.35 168.30

DECENCY'S SM 9.23

DECENT TL 92.39 VG 8.3 57.8
  62.25 62.27

DECENTLY SM 111.26

DECIDE FO 178.34 SM 92.36
  133.22

DECIDED LH 21.34 TL 60.26
  106.40 FO 114.33 173.9
  CD 208.1 213.8 224.35
  225.2 250.19 SM 8.15 12.5
  30.1 37.15 95.4 137.31
  MD 180.39 VG 3.12 3.26
  18.30 58.17

DECIDEDLY TL 73.27 VG 28.15

DECIPHERED TL 80.9

DECISION TL 94.16 SM 124.19
  133.19 133.21

DECISIVE SM 9.40

DECISIVELY SM 138.21

DECK SM 126.1 127.12

DECLARED SM 52.3

DECLINE VG 72.3

DECLINED SM 154.6

DECOMPOSING SM 59.40

DECOMPOSITION TL 97.13
  97.17

DECORATIONS VG 6.15 6.21

DECREE TL 62.27

DEDUCTED VG 28.37

DEEMED CD 219.10

DEEP LH 9.24 22.28 23.33
  26.35 27.22 27.34 33.13
  33.41 TL 44.17 52.18
  53.30 53.33 68.5 79.32
  79.40 86.21 103.10 107.8
  107.30 FO 116.2 116.5
  119.2 136.37 141.12
  145.9 145.22 149.7 155.22
  156.8 158.1 160.11 167.2

DEEP (CONT.) CD 210.10 230.20
  234.41 237.38 239.2 240.8
  247.21 254.13 SM 12.10 26.41
  30.6 57.40 59.18 63.4 94.10
  134.19 136.33 143.7 144.7
  154.35 159.6 159.9 159.10
  MD 165.14 167.12 173.14
  205.22 205.29 207.22 211.3
  VG 9.29 10.15 20.28 20.33
  37.25 44.25 61.21 74.38
  74.42 78.7

DEEPENING VG 24.19

DEEPER TL 74.40 98.25 FO 143.33
  CD 255.20 263.30 SM 41.8
  130.25 158.8 159.10 MD 169.14
  169.15 183.32 193.2

DEEPEST TL 107.11

DEEP-FLUSHED FO 141.39

DEEP-FOLDED MD 207.6

DEEP-FURRED CD 252.34

DEEP-GRAVEN CD 189.34

DEEP-HEDGED LH 4.33

DEEPLY LH 5.38 19.18 20.11
  35.9 CD 190.20 216.13 225.20
  SM 127.15

DEEPS VG 18.20

DEER FO 130.29 130.31 130.32
  130.38 130.41 130.42 131.1
  131.9 SM 37.29 50.28 VG 16.33
  16.38 17.10 17.13 17.21
  45.17

DEFEATED SM 95.9 95.10 95.11
  153.30

DEFEATEDNESS SM 140.26

DEFECTS VG 6.19

DEFENCE LH 13.15

DEFENCELESS SM 18.25 151.8

DEFENCES FO 178.17 SM 18.32

DEFEND SM 83.25 83.29 83.30

DEFENSIVE TL 93.20 SM 156.35

DEFERENCE TL 75.35

DEFIANCE FO 154.26 MD 164.4
  164.28 VG 50.39 50.42

DEFIANT MD 171.23 VG 30.20
  50.34

DEFIANTLY CD 190.22 SM 22.40

DEFICIENCIES VG 6.19

DEFICIENCY SM 18.36

DEFILE VG 28.26

DEFILED VG 27.38

DEFILEMENT VG 29.11

DEFILING VG 28.26

DEFINE SM 7.23

DEFINITE LH 10.27 36.32
  SM 30.17 32.3 117.10 133.33
  157.37

DEFINITELY CD 188.40 SM 26.9
  33.16 158.35 VG 5.42 44.40

DEFINITIONS SM 80.12

DEFLOWERED VG 27.35

DEFTLY VG 54.34

DEFY TL 92.42

DEGAGE VG 39.39

DEGENERATE SM 50.27

DEGENERATED CD 206.30 VG 9.5

DEGRADATION LH 33.32 VG 4.26

DEGRADE TL 92.31

DEGRADED VG 5.20 27.10

DEGRADING TL 92.27 VG 27.22

DEGREE TL 86.32 CD 205.8
  SM 73.24 VG 53.18

DEGREES TL 91.27 100.33

DEJECTED SM 76.29 78.1

DEJECTEDLY MD 168.31

DELIBERATE TL 75.34 77.14
  CD 227.29 SM 127.39

DELIBERATELY LH 34.8 38.27
  TL 64.9 FO 116.4 SM 15.38
  69.24 115.35

DELICACY TL 95.18 FO 155.32

DELICATE TL 43.25 46.33 66.1
  74.37 87.9 95.20 101.10
  101.12 104.38 FO 113.7 115.26
  135.15 137.38 138.13 141.19
  141.28 148.24 163.32 165.38
  176.4 CD 187.15 217.31 221.6
  231.39 SM 118.33 119.6 133.37
  134.4 134.8 140.9 140.11
  MD 188.19 193.11 VG 24.6
  28.17 45.39

DELICATE-BREASTED CD 218.10

DELICATE-FOOTED CD 242.6

DELICATELY LH 3.7 33.18
  TL 44.32 FO 171.38 176.3
  CD 184.5 213.20 VG 19.38
  55.17

DELICIOUS LH 22.10

DELICIOUSLY LH 21.32

DELIGHT LH 5.8 TL 101.13
  FO 126.10 SM 45.32
  MD 205.10 208.19

DELIGHTED LH 21.36 TL 101.14
  FO 124.21 124.29 SM 51.40
  MD 210.4

DELIGHTFUL CD 195.10 195.11
  195.41 196.12 205.28
  209.13 SM 10.10

DELIGHTFULLY SM 31.6

DELIGHTING MD 208.20

DELINQUENCY VG 28.32

DELINQUENT VG 4.18 31.10

DELIRIOUS TL 44.25

DELIVER LH 8.10 SM 5.19
  39.38

DELIVERED SM 25.31 39.33

DELIVERING TL 84.15

DELUDED CD 259.10

DEMAND FO 123.39 MD 204.4

DEMANDED SM 34.24 109.26

DEMANDING SM 109.26

DEMENTED VG 29.23

DEMOCRACY TL 90.1 SM 18.33

DEMOCRATIC TL 92.12 93.17
  SM 5.9 9.18 18.21

DEMON FO 115.11 SM 7.1
  14.37 44.29

DEMONISH SM 14.28 30.20
  65.16 145.39 VG 15.30

DEMONS SM 24.27 26.37 26.38

DEMONSTRATION FO 114.25

DEN MD 210.34

DENIED MD 175.6 VG 56.2 56.4

DENIES MD 183.6

DENSE LH 31.1 34.36
  SM 143.18 MD 175.10

DENY TL 87.40 87.41 VG 56.3

DEPART SM 71.32 MD 209.35

DEPARTED LH 19.23 20.38
  SM 6.1 25.31 116.36
  MD 191.29 VG 15.13 47.41

DEPARTMENT CD 232.11

DEPARTURE FO 157.31 SM 38.7
  93.12 MD 209.7

DEPEND SM 119.38

DEPENDABLE VG 5.31

DEPENDANTS TL 98.37

DEPENDED SM 129.27 134.30

DEPENDENT CD 212.27 SM 49.32

DEPENDS FO 151.17 167.31
  CD 197.32 SM 81.6

DEPORT CD 194.12

DEPOSITED FO 115.22

DEPOSITING VG 54.39

DEPOSITS SM 154.5

DEPRAVED VG 34.37 35.14

DEPRAVITIES VG 62.14 62.17

DEPRAVITY VG 62.34 62.38 62.40

DEPRESSED SM 126.17 129.20

DEPRESSING SM 126.19

DEPRESSION SM 68.33 VG 66.6

DEPTH SM 114.25 118.18 VG 80.4

DEPTHS TL 68.4 69.12 106.41
  CD 254.13 255.4 255.19
  SM 26.4 143.21 MD 189.30
  189.38 207.12

DE RIGUEUR CD 204.26

DERISION CD 203.19 SM 34.36

DERISIVE CD 261.33 SM 89.6

DERIVED SM 137.34

DER REGEN WIRD ES LANG DAUERN
  CD 248.22

DESCEND LH 37.25

DESCENDANT TL 96.40

DESCENDED LH 37.33 TL 44.15
  CD 256.3 263.5 SM 102.13
  VG 52.7

DESCENDING CD 243.22 SM 11.29

DESCENT CD 252.31

DESCRIBED CD 229.29

DESCRIPTION VG 55.2

DESERT CD 243.35 247.17 256.15
  SM 71.37 78.14 78.22 133.36
  133.39 134.9 140.16 140.20

DESERT (CONT.) 141.16 141.18
  142.16 146.32 146.33 147.11
  147.13 147.18 147.24 147.33
  148.1 148.4 148.11 151.19
  154.32

DESERT-AND-MOUNTAIN SM 134.15

DESERTED LH 21.17 VG 81.8

DESERTS TL 48.11 SM 20.39

DESERVED VG 4.26

DESERVES VG 81.4

DESIRABLE MD 165.30

DESIRE TL 78.2 106.2 106.7
  FO 123.2 153.10 CD 189.12
  216.41 253.42 254.16 263.30
  SM 77.34 94.15 137.40 138.1
  MD 169.8 169.10 169.11 170.12
  170.27 171.15 171.17 171.22
  177.26 178.9 182.4 182.10
  197.16 201.39 202.3 206.38
  207.20 207.28 VG 30.30 30.31
  38.21 60.5 68.20

DESIRED MD 177.28 VG 59.33

DESIRELESS MD 169.14

DESIRES SM 118.31

DESOLATE FO 119.6 CD 243.19
  243.36 253.4

DESOLATED CD 245.30

DESPAIR LH 27.32 TL 48.13
  FO 113.29 142.7 SM 3.7 7.8
  45.29 76.15 77.21 77.22
  77.26

DESPAIRING SM 56.4

DESPAIRINGLY LH 27.35

DESPAIRS SM 79.3

DESPERATE TL 44.22 47.13
  CD 229.20 MD 186.41 204.4

DESPERATELY SM 92.24

DESPERATION SM 18.28 46.21

DESPICABLE SM 47.32 VG 4.25
  4.30

DESPISE FO 145.7 SM 8.34 34.38
  108.12 VG 30.22 43.22

DESPISED CD 240.7 SM 33.1 96.6
  96.13 108.13 108.19 108.20
  VG 28.12 43.21 65.17

DESPISING SM 108.10 VG 43.24

DESPONDENT FO 115.33

DESTINIES MD 202.12 202.18

DESTINY TL 62.27 89.6 FO 157.12

DESTINY (CONT.) 166.38
  178.14 178.15 CD 216.35
  226.19 SM 20.22 20.23
  119.21 119.22 MD 163.22
  172.14 172.16 172.17
  174.32 199.21 209.36
  VG 60.34

DESTROY TL 63.18 74.42
  SM 71.13 71.25 71.27
  80.31

DESTROYED TL 47.24 SM 95.5
  150.10 VG 28.33 29.30

DESTROYING SM 71.38 71.39

DESTROYS SM 71.6 71.34

DESTRUCTIBLE SM 95.6

DESTRUCTION TL 73.36 73.37
  73.38 SM 26.14

DESTRUCTIVE TL 86.36 SM 6.28
  95.4 120.29

DESULTORILY FO 157.31

DETACHED SM 25.12 134.25
  VG 65.11

DETACHEDNESS SM 119.20

DETACHING VG 39.41

DETACHMENT VG 57.34

DETAIL VG 15.22 15.26

DETAILED VG 55.2

DETAILS TL 47.41 CD 228.25
  SM 121.40

DETAIN MD 195.40

DETAINED FO 160.1 CD 206.19

DETECT SM 15.20 102.3

DETECTED SM 137.7 137.9

DETERIORATING CD 206.26

DETERMINATION TL 43.4 47.33

DETERMINED LH 32.30 TL 43.3
  43.27 64.20 64.28 69.4
  92.34 FO 116.41 116.42
  168.20 MD 172.17 199.24
  VG 9.40 10.27 43.38

DETERMINES FO 130.38

DETEST VG 65.19

DETESTABLE CD 242.12 242.31
  SM 4.15

DETESTED FO 152.36 VG 57.22

DETHRONED VG 4.35

DEUCE-TAKE-IT VG 7.30

DEVASTATING CD 230.29 SM 81.37

DEVASTATION MD 172.36

DEVELOPED SM 112.22

DEVELOPING VG 26.35

DEVICES SM 16.2

DEVIL TL 55.23 55.26 55.28
   55.30 73.37 81.13 FO 143.11
   143.17 CD 227.1 227.19 227.22
   227.28 SM 24.9 36.18 58.2
   63.15 63.17 151.21 VG 27.32

DEVILISH FO 152.35

DEVILS CD 217.35 SM 64.25

DEVIL'S CHAIR SM 51.33 57.1
   63.7 64.38

DEVISING SM 44.21

DEVOID SM 25.5 136.9

DEVOTE CD 214.10

DEVOTED CD 215.12

DEVOTEDLY VG 41.12

DEVOTING SM 139.15

DEVOUR SM 110.7

DEVOURING VG 72.34

DEW MD 208.10

DEWY CD 240.41

DIALECT TL 44.25 44.29 99.35

DIAMONDS SM 13.23 VG 49.21

DICTATE SM 108.37

DICTIONARY SM 111.9

DIDNA LH 3.32 4.14 4.15 4.41
   5.3

DIE LH 10.42 TL 43.4 44.6
   45.42 50.17 52.16 52.24 53.8
   55.24 63.19 75.20 79.11
   81.35 81.39 82.37 100.39
   102.31 104.17 104.28
   FO 163.16 CD 203.32 222.36
   222.38 222.39 232.32 256.34
   SM 50.36 64.11 85.27 86.17
   88.26 96.30 96.35 96.37 97.1
   97.3 97.21 103.36 103.38
   104.3 113.29 114.36 133.12
   133.15 133.22 133.24 MD 173.2
   180.1 VG 16.20 44.16 47.38
   65.40 75.7 75.12 75.13 77.7
   77.9

DIED LH 32.15 TL 43.5 44.1
   108.29 FO 113.16 113.30
   120.36 167.13 168.18 175.31
   176.8 CD 222.33 223.19 232.31
   250.27 261.25 SM 4.36 54.27

DIED (CONT.) 85.20 94.34
   MD 166.19 166.28 167.7
   167.38 167.40 168.27 168.28
   170.10 171.4 171.10 171.20
   171.21 171.24 171.28 172.11
   172.24 172.31 172.41 173.1
   173.7 173.9 174.26 176.34
   177.20 178.8 178.11 178.15
   178.22 178.28 179.15 180.16
   181.12 181.13 181.15 181.26
   182.5 182.37 183.8 183.21
   183.23 183.27 183.28 189.40
   191.29 191.36 193.32 196.16
   197.25 198.6 198.29 198.39
   199.18 200.7 200.11 200.16
   200.33 200.36 201.29 202.10
   202.33 205.27 206.23 209.33
   210.38 211.2 211.10 211.17
   VG 4.19 60.26

DIES FO 133.10 SM 50.10 85.24
   111.41 118.32 142.36

DIFFERENCE TL 75.36 89.41
   108.27 FO 114.35 121.31
   121.33 126.1 156.30 CD 204.34
   SM 47.13 48.33 76.38 105.18
   134.27 MD 203.12 203.14

DIFFERENT LH 27.4 TL 65.5 69.1
   76.32 76.33 78.23 105.2
   105.23 107.3 108.23 108.26
   FO 149.16 157.1 162.32 166.3
   CD 203.7 220.9 222.9 240.5
   250.7 SM 15.32 31.18 32.8
   38.26 59.30 59.33 59.35
   136.36 136.39 137.1 MD 175.24
   203.13 203.14 203.16 203.18
   204.22 204.23 VG 3.29 40.11
   59.13 59.23 59.29 59.30 60.2

DIFFERENTLY FO 152.23 SM 43.21
   157.16

DIFFICULT TL 53.7 109.6
   FO 116.2 176.27 176.29
   CD 234.8 254.25 SM 7.23 20.21
   54.1 55.6 135.39 144.4
   VG 45.20 58.31

DIFFICULTIES MD 197.38

DIFFICULTY LH 22.36 FO 141.16
   SM 88.15 93.8 MD 169.26

DIFFIDENCE TL 78.8 CD 184.10
   251.23 SM 32.23 45.13

DIFFIDENT TL 75.34 SM 7.34

DIFFUSED SM 12.12

DIG SM 36.23

DIGESTION FO 114.31

DIGGING FO 118.26

DIGNIFIED TL 92.32 92.34
   VG 3.32

DIGNITY VG 34.30

DILAPIDATED FO 127.18 SM 155.7

DILATE TL 68.29

DILATED TL 69.12 74.26
   105.34 FO 120.22 122.1
   146.1 155.19 CD 201.42
   202.25 253.21 SM 69.36
   MD 201.15

DILEMMA CD 191.3 VG 18.30

DILIGENTLY VG 68.24

DILLY-DALLYING TL 48.12

DIM LH 22.26 23.23 TL 101.28
   FO 115.37 120.2 122.19
   128.40 140.11 164.10
   CD 193.5 199.29 242.26
   SM 125.29 134.8 MD 167.12
   202.38 206.11 206.12
   207.31 VG 42.24

DIMINISH MD 172.5

DIMINISHED CD 242.27
   MD 170.41 171.8 VG 4.32
   68.21 71.40

DIM-LIT MD 202.34

DIMLY FO 132.35 SM 13.35
   75.39 MD 167.10 VG 28.23
   41.3 64.4 64.5 75.27

DIMLY-LIGHTED FO 134.8

DIMMED LH 21.27

DIMMER MD 206.19

DIMNESS FO 138.6 140.11

DIMPLES VG 59.2 59.7

DIN VG 19.33

DINED SM 5.8

DINGILY VG 4.12

DINING VG 40.27

DINING-ROOM FO 149.37 159.5
   159.28 SM 132.35 VG 10.31
   10.33 73.33

DINNER LH 14.30 14.38 15.6
   19.3 28.1 28.11 38.9
   TL 94.22 CD 198.20 204.39
   219.26 230.17 SM 53.14
   53.33 109.16 VG 10.37
   39.26 40.36 46.10 46.13
   47.4

DINNER-GONG VG 40.19

DINNER-JACKET CD 214.27

DINNERS SM 6.14

DINNER-TIME FO 143.11
   CD 186.18

DINNINGTON VG 13.25

DIO BENEDETTO SM 96.19

DIONYS TL 59.19 83.13 87.33
  88.9 96.15 96.18 97.31 99.26
  102.8 107.5 107.36

DIONYS, JOHANN (SEE JOHANN
  DIONYS)

DIONYSOS TL 69.29

DIP SM 60.7 VG 47.26

DIPLOMATIC SM 51.37

DIPPED MD 191.37 197.32 201.31
  201.37

DIPPING LH 21.2 SM 144.15

DIRE CD 213.17

DIRECT TL 55.34 60.40 73.13
  96.2 FO 171.28 CD 189.9
  SM 76.22 88.21 VG 69.11

DIRECTED VG 52.22

DIRECTING SM 71.3

DIRECTION LH 33.7 FO 116.39
  172.4 173.11 175.34 SM 59.5
  157.35

DIRECTLY LH 31.19 39.4 VG 72.6

DIRECTNESS LH 18.29 TL 67.18

DIRT CD 253.29 SM 33.13 140.29
  MD 163.14

DIRT-LIKE SM 140.28

DIRTY LH 17.36 32.42 FO 156.13
  SM 18.7 30.26 143.7 143.23
  MD 163.7 163.22 172.27 181.29
  VG 46.1 59.40

DISADVANTAGE LH 27.19

DISAGREEABLE FO 157.39 CD 226.37

DISAGREEABLY VG 45.6

DISAPPEAR FO 122.42 MD 187.16
  199.14 199.32

DISAPPEARANCE VG 81.13

DISAPPEARED FO 126.14 CD 198.26
  246.39 SM 35.26 106.14
  MD 199.17 VG 29.21 36.15
  76.38

DISAPPEARING SM 104.5

DISAPPOINT LH 15.39 SM 65.27

DISAPPOINTED LH 12.25 TL 70.2
  MD 174.15 VG 39.17 79.17

DISAPPOINTMENT MD 206.32

DISAPPROVE TL 90.8 VG 4.37
  12.28 64.5 64.15

DISAPPROVED SM 45.37

DISAPPROVING SM 110.16

DISASTER TL 48.12 SM 139.35
  MD 200.13

DISASTERS SM 73.33

DISASTROUS CD 214.13

DISBELIEVE FO 132.15

DISBELIEVED FO 115.1

DISCARDED MD 176.27

DISCERNIBLE CD 193.5 VG 38.33
  45.39

DISCHARGE CD 212.24 SM 152.19

DISCLOSE MD 182.15

DISCOMFORT FO 119.9 SM 34.22

DISCONNECTED SM 42.8 VG 59.2

DISCONSOLATELY FO 133.37

DISCONTENT TL 62.24 74.7 87.8
  87.21 FO 179.2

DISCONTENTED VG 10.30

DISCOVER MD 168.4 203.25

DISCOVERED LH 22.8 SM 119.2

DISCRETION VG 43.3

DISCRIMINATIONS SM 7.12

DISDAINFULLY VG 56.11

DISEASE LH 4.6

DISFIGURE SM 72.7

DISFIGURED SM 79.39

DISGRACEFUL SM 123.24 VG 35.16

DISGUISED SM 89.1 VG 37.24

DISGUST TL 52.20 55.38 58.4
  62.24 63.1 CD 224.25 224.27
  225.8 225.15 MD 168.5 VG 9.24

DISGUSTED LH 18.7 FO 114.4
  CD 227.3 SM 85.18 VG 55.30

DISGUSTEDLY VG 56.20

DISGUSTING SM 5.15 60.11
  MD 193.25 VG 56.22

DISH LH 14.39 VG 54.13 54.16

DISHEARTENED LH 20.22 SM 4.39

DISHEARTENING FO 115.15

DISHES VG 9.13 54.34 57.40

DISHEVEL CD 253.16

DISHEVELLED LH 3.8

DISHONEST VG 23.31

DISHONESTY VG 27.34

DISILLUSION CD 217.23 217.26
  217.27 217.30 217.35
  217.38 252.16 SM 138.37
  MD 166.20 166.29 167.12
  168.29 169.12 169.14
  175.20 176.7 179.34
  VG 67.17

DISILLUSIONED SM 45.16
  MD 176.13

DISILLUSIONMENT LH 33.31

DISINTEGRATED VG 7.17

DISINTEGRATION SM 73.31
  144.32

DISJOINTED LH 15.14

DISLIKE TL 91.10 FO 155.5
  SM 40.15 91.18 158.4
  VG 33.24 43.1 68.22

DISLIKED TL 69.21 88.24
  FO 155.4 MD 183.4 VG 4.5

DISLOCATED VG 73.10

DISMAL FO 119.15

DISMANTLED VG 20.32

DISMAY LH 29.20 SM 9.13
  MD 205.27

DISMISS FO 130.27

DISMISSED MD 200.35

DISMOUNTED SM 67.27

DISMOUNTING SM 102.15

DISOBEDIENT LH 13.39

DISOBEY CD 191.26

DISOBEYED VG 16.27

DISPASSIONATELY SM 81.7

DISPERSE VG 66.29

DISPLAY SM 25.7

DISPLAYED VG 3.31

DISPLEASE TL 60.9

DISPLEASED TL 58.22

DISPOSE TL 89.27

DISPOSSESSED SM 20.18

DISPROPORTIONATE MD 163.13

DISQUIETUDE MD 168.37

DISREGARD LH 27.14

DISREGARDED LH 27.13

DISREPUTABLE VG 4.23

DISSATISFACTION TL 83.25

DISSEMINATED SM 75.12

DISSIPATE TL 63.19

DISSOLVE TL 99.31

DISSOLVED LH 30.42 TL 103.20
    VG 68.22

DISSOLVING SM 125.29

DISTANCE LH 8.4 23.22 23.33
    31.26 TL 45.28 60.30 98.15
    103.14 103.21 FO 115.37
    116.22 122.20 133.5 143.36
    152.41 154.34 168.34 171.17
    171.37 177.41 178.1 CD 184.33
    185.24 206.6 220.11 253.12
    SM 20.38 25.10 32.23 38.22
    39.13 66.14 68.5 75.4 94.21
    98.22 101.4 102.1 104.4
    105.16 107.23 146.32 146.37
    146.38 147.34 148.31 148.35
    148.40 157.27 MD 179.1
    VG 8.18 11.19 18.37 21.23
    24.23 45.18

DISTANCES SM 129.18

DISTANT FO 117.15 119.25 126.39
    CD 197.29 211.42 SM 60.9
    98.19 100.27 100.29 100.34
    107.9 108.28 MD 163.26
    VG 26.42 44.15

DISTANTLY SM 100.38

DISTASTE CD 217.19 SM 107.23
    VG 66.3 69.17

DISTASTEFUL TL 60.13 61.2

DISTINCT LH 10.38 FO 125.10
    125.38 CD 235.16 SM 60.18
    147.19 VG 5.29

DISTINCTION TL 91.13

DISTINCTIONS SM 7.13

DISTINCTLY LH 3.15 20.17
    FO 119.30 123.4 131.32
    CD 192.14

DISTINGUISHED FO 126.8 VG 3.16
    43.41

DISTRACT SM 65.32

DISTRACTED SM 68.7 68.12
    VG 29.25

DISTRAUGHT TL 47.10 VG 26.27
    63.29

DISTRESS LH 26.8 CD 188.1
    198.12 SM 114.22 MD 206.9
    VG 28.4

DISTRESSED TL 76.34 102.36
    FO 164.14

DISTRESSING TL 50.2

DISTRICT CD 231.37 232.3

DISTURB TL 54.36 105.19
    CD 219.2 MD 193.20

DISTURBED TL 105.18 FO 119.9
    CD 201.11 SM 125.38 MD 193.28

DISUSED VG 20.30

D'IT FO 171.6

DITCH FO 118.27 153.11 169.17
    SM 142.4

DITCH-CHANNEL SM 144.6

DIVED SM 123.1

DIVERSE SM 73.26

DIVERSION CD 232.9

DIVERTING CD 228.34

DIVESTED SM 46.37

DIVIDED FO 125.6 SM 16.35
    107.14

DIVIDING VG 18.35

DIVINE TL 79.20 SM 54.32

DIVINED FO 164.13 SM 136.29
    MD 191.1

DIVING SM 128.28

DIVORCE VG 51.5

DIVORCEE VG 54.23

DIVORCING VG 50.39

DIZZY CD 203.23

DOCILE VG 6.9

DOCK LH 6.18 6.20

DOCTOR SM 79.22 111.30 VG 16.6

DOCTORS TL 47.25 VG 31.16

DODGE FO 131.10

DODGED CD 195.15

DOE VG 17.1 45.18

DOESNA LH 16.5

DOFFING SM 39.22

DOG LH 9.22 CD 257.12 257.25

DOG (CONT.) 257.37 260.11
    260.12 260.19 SM 10.4
    10.16 VG 21.2 30.26 42.32
    62.26

DOGCART SM 87.28 87.35

DOG-FOX FO 148.21

DOGGEDLY LH 12.14 25.14
    31.36

DOGGISH VG 26.34

DOG-KENNEL VG 74.36

DOG-LIKE VG 43.23 61.12

DOGS TL 98.30 FO 143.36
    146.7 146.8 146.11 SM 50.7
    50.20 50.21 96.34 VG 30.27
    50.31

DOG-STAR MD 208.7

DOIN' LH 12.5

DOING LH 10.11 12.30 24.10
    TL 65.13 76.17 87.38
    90.25 94.2 96.11 105.5
    109.8 FO 123.26 134.11
    134.13 144.26 165.27
    171.21 CD 183.9 183.34
    235.1 254.40 265.2 SM 15.12
    24.36 39.17 79.15 118.15
    155.40 VG 41.16 41.17
    53.35 55.4 57.41

DOINGS SM 30.26 VG 41.41

DOLL CD 183.8 183.12 183.22
    184.4 184.11 184.37 186.14
    186.20 187.5 187.9 187.19
    187.26 188.35 193.27
    197.35 198.32 199.6 209.41
    210.4 211.20 211.21 213.21
    213.37 213.42 218.12
    218.13 218.14 218.24 219.1
    219.4 219.13 226.40 227.34
    227.36 227.39 228.23
    228.32 228.36 229.3 246.33
    249.5 250.29 259.8 259.21
    259.23 259.24 259.38
    263.38 263.40 264.5 264.6
    264.8 264.9 264.11 264.12

DOLLAR SM 128.18

DOLLARS SM 114.14

DOLLS CD 193.18 193.20 196.3
    196.7 196.18 196.21 196.35
    200.26 204.21 209.41 228.6

DOLOROSA, MATER (SEE MATER
    DOLOROSA)

DOMAIN MD 180.24

DOMESTIC TL 62.30 71.17
    SM 73.13 118.30

DOMESTICATED SM 50.6 73.6
    VG 30.27

DOMINATED FO 118.22

DOMINATION SM 6.25

DOMINEERING SM 32.36 65.5

DOMINOES SM 29.31

DOMPLATZ CD 204.20

DONE LH 3.32 10.14 17.26 26.8
  TL 46.24 47.16 48.12 94.34
  FO 152.42 165.41 171.25
  171.26 CD 212.19 218.9 219.11
  220.22 221.15 223.21 261.16
  264.7 264.31 SM 23.8 36.39
  44.12 46.31 71.30 76.37
  76.40 79.37 80.27 86.38
  87.25 100.9 114.29 131.16
  157.15 MD 173.39 174.11
  VG 4.6 7.1 14.19 26.26 27.41
  54.6 59.26 63.4

DONKEY MD 163.15

DONKEY'S MD 164.11

DOOM TL 99.5 FO 166.37 166.38
  CD 237.34 SM 15.17 MD 168.17
  172.16 175.15 202.13

DOOMED TL 72.20 101.19
  CD 232.37 SM 4.40 47.7

DOOR TL 76.3 100.14 100.21
  100.27 101.4 101.25 101.26
  101.30 101.34 101.36 102.6
  102.7 102.13 102.15 102.41
  104.29 FO 117.12 119.32
  119.33 119.34 134.5 138.14
  143.39 143.41 144.3 145.35
  146.41 147.3 154.40 155.37
  159.11 159.15 159.30 160.21
  CD 183.14 183.22 183.23
  184.23 184.24 184.28 185.40
  186.10 186.42 194.35 220.2
  220.6 228.21 238.24 260.9
  260.30 261.4 SM 11.14 45.30
  121.3 138.21 145.16 MD 168.35
  169.16 170.4 177.2 187.14
  188.1 190.19 198.5 199.37
  200.7 200.9 202.30 202.31
  202.33 207.37 VG 20.39 21.2
  24.26 29.12 29.13 29.21
  37.29 37.40 38.12 48.39 68.9
  73.30 73.33 74.18 75.30
  75.40 76.26 76.34 77.34
  79.26

DOORS FO 113.37 135.40
  CD 234.21 260.31 SM 37.35
  38.5 112.40 VG 16.17 70.11

DOOR-STEP SM 87.24

DOORWAY TL 46.13 101.29
  FO 120.12 122.36 155.39 156.1
  159.24 167.22 167.38
  CD 184.30 SM 11.17 45.31
  57.13 121.5 126.30 147.5
  MD 168.35 194.17 198.16
  VG 30.40 38.28

DOORWAYS SM 140.5

DORT WO DU NICHT BIST CD 196.28

DOST LH 7.41 8.16 9.12

DOTING VG 6.11

DOTS LH 3.15 TL 70.26

DOTTED CD 243.33 244.23

DOTTING SM 147.18

DOUBLE VG 38.19 38.26 65.23

DOUBLE-BREASTED VG 20.19 38.3

DOUBLED LH 14.8

DOUBT LH 28.8 FO 146.16
  CD 205.5 210.1 258.33
  SM 23.31 25.25 51.38 158.14
  MD 200.39 VG 4.25 35.23

DOUBTED CD 260.13 SM 26.25

DOUBTFUL TL 90.14 FO 171.37

DOUBTFULLY TL 73.5 VG 17.12

DOUBTLESS VG 67.27

DOUR VG 9.33

DOVE TL 58.36 63.41 SM 150.25

DOVER VG 7.33

DOVES MD 189.8

DOWNCAST LH 26.30

DOWNFALL SM 128.22

DOWNHILL FO 146.17 153.8 172.24
  CD 241.36

DOWN-HILL LH 4.37 21.2 23.38
  VG 36.33 36.35

DOWN-SLOPE SM 145.35

DOWNSTAIRS TL 99.40 100.12
  FO 127.1 145.31 158.14
  SM 81.36 112.40 VG 10.30
  40.19

DOWNWARD TL 52.6 VG 19.7

DOWNWARDS TL 76.31 79.39
  FO 122.18 148.35 172.26
  CD 183.11 241.27 243.23
  243.25 255.28 256.2 257.3
  SM 65.9 141.15 MD 168.24
  VG 54.41

DOZE VG 32.27

DOZEN TL 76.12 91.37 CD 226.12
  SM 80.32 VG 44.31 59.40

DOZY FO 114.29

DRAB CD 240.18 260.8 SM 85.29

DRAG MD 165.23 VG 8.28

DRAGGED SM 55.37 VG 13.39
  72.36 73.14

DRAGGING LH 25.25 VG 20.11
  72.41

DRAGGLED VG 41.1

DRAGON SM 153.31

DRAINS SM 157.4

DRAMATIC VG 30.39

DRANK LH 15.30 FO 123.1
  138.28 157.7 CD 245.33
  SM 94.34 128.23 144.9
  MD 201.32 VG 54.19

DRAPED TL 87.4

DRAPERY TL 83.11 87.4

DRAUGHT VG 11.32 11.34

DRAW LH 18.33 28.5 TL 53.31
  58.9 FO 131.36 140.25
  CD 265.27 SM 70.28 130.4
  VG 7.33

DRAWER CD 194.23 196.9
  197.5 VG 80.2

DRAWERS CD 238.6 VG 79.19

DRAWING LH 8.31 TL 95.42
  FO 140.29 CD 245.17 246.4
  SM 13.21 MD 191.12 VG 42.21

DRAWING-ROOM TL 43.34 46.15
  77.4 SM 28.16 55.13 81.14
  118.27 VG 10.32

DRAWING-ROOMS SM 7.18

DRAWINGS VG 11.15

DRAWL LH 12.13 SM 4.20 17.41
  81.13

DRAWLED TL 75.15 VG 35.5

DRAWLING TL 75.34 SM 9.39

DRAWN LH 18.27 29.11
  TL 45.12 47.26 69.10
  FO 135.40 155.5 155.6
  158.32 174.11 CD 192.9
  234.23 244.24 SM 35.8
  96.28 127.24 MD 185.26
  VG 19.25

DRAW-PUMP FO 127.15

DRAWS TL 88.5

DREAD FO 161.27 SM 67.22
  97.1 97.5 152.16 MD 183.41
  VG 27.23

DREADED FO 119.4 119.5

DREADFUL TL 68.7 84.39
  FO 162.19 CD 214.30 219.19
  220.29 223.7 229.28

DREADFUL (CONT.) SM 79.21 VG 4.1

DREADING MD 184.15

DREAM TL 82.33 FO 147.40 157.19
  159.20 CD 198.38 SM 10.32
  125.27 125.29 130.26
  MD 176.22 191.10 192.14
  193.25 201.16 202.29 204.18
  VG 37.5 39.14 47.38 73.12

DREAM-DESPAIR FO 148.10

DREAMED TL 69.31 FO 126.24
  136.9 147.40 CD 210.17
  SM 86.9 VG 42.9 68.38

DREAM-FOX FO 127.24

DREAM-FRUSTRATION FO 148.9

DREAMILY SM 19.19

DREAMING TL 63.42 FO 157.22
  171.34 CD 215.35

DREAM-OBJECT MD 204.19

DREAMS CD 207.23 MD 188.4

DREAM-VOICE TL 99.35

DREAMY SM 134.17 VG 70.10

DREARILY LH 29.26

DREARINESS TL 44.22 CD 263.15

DREARY LH 26.33 26.36 TL 51.13
  87.7 101.42 SM 50.37 140.24
  VG 9.10 10.32 36.17 64.21
  64.28

DREARY-HARDENED LH 29.19

DRENCHED LH 36.29

DRESDEN TL 44.27 66.34 81.6
  SM 26.13

DRESS LH 6.27 22.38 36.26
  TL 52.2 54.16 76.11 76.16
  94.33 FO 149.40 156.4 156.7
  156.11 156.15 156.18 157.13
  157.28 CD 185.4 195.4 197.28
  197.31 210.12 214.23 233.26
  233.29 238.5 SM 13.22 43.4
  117.40 VG 24.3 24.12 31.27
  31.29 32.20 32.42 34.32
  35.34 37.24 39.26 41.24
  75.28

DRESSED TL 59.24 76.15 84.8
  FO 145.29 156.3 CD 183.24
  SM 35.35 57.7 83.9 112.29
  VG 49.6 79.11 79.19 79.27

DRESSES FO 155.31 CD 233.11
  238.19 SM 52.11 VG 6.18 31.37
  40.33

DRESSING TL 76.17 CD 183.9
  219.26 SM 36.6 MD 186.8
  VG 40.14

DRESSING-ROOM CD 219.30 SM 80.40

DRESSING-TABLE TL 105.31

DRESSY TL 81.11

DREW LH 21.26 33.23 37.37
  TL 69.18 76.29 FO 126.32
  133.6 140.19 152.25 159.24
  160.21 164.40 165.3 CD 190.19
  236.12 260.29 SM 19.33 67.39
  74.23 102.23 112.29 MD 170.37
  179.23 187.10 207.27 VG 43.19
  50.11 54.32 68.36

DRIED LH 22.8 CD 201.7 MD 169.5
  200.26

DRIED-UP SM 140.36

DRIER VG 76.34

DRIFT TL 70.33 SM 143.19

DRIFTED TL 73.18 CD 186.39
  225.6 SM 3.28 13.24

DRIFTING FO 142.14 142.28
  142.34 CD 235.31 265.31
  SM 6.10 6.11 32.21 38.18
  136.38

DRILLING TL 98.12

DRINK LH 29.29 CD 231.4 240.38
  256.35 SM 29.27 40.6
  MD 169.10 201.11

DRINKING LH 39.17 CD 252.5
  SM 27.21 57.24 68.32 127.41
  VG 47.41

DRINKING-CUP MD 200.25

DRINKING-HALL SM 5.10

DRIP LH 27.24 FO 119.17 143.33

DRIPPED LH 28.37 CD 195.6

DRIPPING CD 247.20 247.36
  MD 191.27 VG 18.3 73.40

DRIVE SM 109.33 156.17 VG 36.2
  70.5 71.31

DRIVEN LH 29.13 33.32 TL 57.39
  CD 191.19 SM 80.12 143.23
  154.10 154.28 MD 165.32
  167.12 178.9 VG 3.24 14.21
  19.9 36.33

DRIVER CD 238.34 239.28 239.42
  240.10 260.32 260.34 261.2
  261.5 261.13 261.37 SM 127.28
  136.25 VG 13.33 13.34 13.35
  19.28 37.5

DRIVING SM 23.28 32.2 134.21
  VG 49.14

DRIZZLE SM 126.8

DROOP TL 76.39 96.9 FO 175.26

DROOPED FO 170.28

DROOPING LH 28.35 36.17
  MD 167.1

DROP LH 8.23 32.23 37.3
  CD 200.15 SM 73.11 MD 168.1
  VG 19.8 29.5 30.41

DROPPED LH 6.39 11.32 24.30
  TL 45.31 FO 128.32 128.33
  128.36 132.42 133.13 170.8
  179.34 CD 191.16 257.5
  SM 58.33 89.27 111.1
  VG 31.2 31.4

DROPPING FO 122.14 122.21
  155.38 CD 243.7 244.13
  SM 8.33 11.40 38.34 52.40
  73.8 141.32 VG 12.24

DROPPINGS CD 248.26 248.28

DROPS LH 8.20 24.35 27.24
  CD 201.13 257.4 SM 127.9
  150.31 150.33 MD 186.9

DROVE LH 15.7 33.10 TL 46.5
  56.34 60.28 91.24 SM 15.33
  26.20 94.22 110.10 127.22
  134.4 136.24 139.19 140.35
  155.3 VG 34.28 35.7 54.39

DROWNED VG 79.40

DROWNING SM 69.30

DRUG SM 10.22 149.22
  VG 30.32

DRUGGED SM 154.21

DRUMMED LH 27.22

DRUMMING LH 24.35

DRUNK FO 124.34 167.8
  SM 127.28

DRY LH 28.24 37.22 TL 97.6
  97.10 FO 141.16 169.17
  174.30 174.33 CD 219.28
  SM 14.17 30.4 76.15 101.8
  107.9 129.17 141.7 144.5
  150.41 MD 167.15 174.3
  185.19 197.6 201.31 210.8
  VG 17.9 18.10 23.29 72.41
  75.42

DRYAD SM 84.32

DRYING SM 143.38

DRYLY FO 162.25 SM 98.14
  103.7 156.33

DRYNESS SM 94.29 VG 76.6

DRY-STONE VG 18.6 36.23

DUBIOUS LH 16.28

DUBIOUSLY TL 67.20

DU BIST WIRKLICH BOS CD 194.9

DUCAL   VG 17.16

DUCHESSES   VG 39.26

DUCK   FO 127.26

DUCKED   SM 13.25

DUCKING   LH 4.39   FO 172.39
  VG 81.17

DUCK-POND   FO 118.27

DUCKS   FO 113.23   113.32   116.20
  127.12   147.11   172.22   172.23
  VG 14.1

DUE   LH 21.33   FO 167.15   SM 27.38

DUEL   SM 31.30

DUET   SM 31.30

DUG   VG 60.30   60.33

DUKE   VG 17.24

DULL   TL 48.7   51.17   51.22   90.40
  FO 119.25   135.16   156.4
  CD 252.27   253.8   SM 49.27
  MD 163.15   VG 16.1   18.22   18.34
  41.1   45.36   73.5

DULL-GOLD-THREADED   TL 83.20

DULLY   LH 7.38   8.24   TL 51.37
  SM 68.35

DUMB   LH 5.31   SM 100.36   131.24
  VG 35.19   58.28

DUMBLY   VG 15.8

DUN   MD 198.1   199.9

DUNG   TL 97.6   97.10

DUNNA   LH 18.16

DUNNING   TL 48.11

DUNNO   LH 12.9   39.4

DUPLICITY   SM 53.29   VG 30.11

DURANCE   VG 9.17

DURING   LH 24.24   33.32   TL 43.28
  43.29   92.27   FO 119.13   127.25
  CD 207.5   207.16   210.42
  SM 7.21   MD 192.3   VG 14.11
  35.18

DUSK   FO 119.12   130.1   131.31
  132.41   153.17   154.33   MD 180.4
  182.15

DUSKINESS   SM 30.16

DUSKY   CD 237.7   SM 124.38
  MD 190.29   193.8   199.40
  VG 30.16

DUSKY-BLACK   TL 84.5

DUSKY-BLOND   MD 191.9

DUST   LH 22.15   TL 67.12   67.14
  SM 59.14   94.30   129.18   130.8
  148.3   148.5   MD 187.21

DUST-CLOTH   SM 46.21   46.26

DUST-COAT   CD 248.11

DUSTED   LH 22.14

DUSTER-BROOMS   VG 36.37

DUST-SHEET   SM 44.10   44.16   44.40

DUTIES   VG 9.41

DUTIFULLY   SM 3.8   109.37

DUTY   TL 89.4   FO 161.15
  CD 195.32   195.32   195.37
  198.19   224.33   SM 35.24   131.34
  131.39   136.22

DWELLING-PLACE   MD 200.28

DWINDLED   LH 34.35   FO 125.14
  SM 154.6

DYING   LH 32.21   TL 50.22   50.29
  85.31   105.32   FO 132.20   179.4
  CD 196.41   SM 35.30   44.15
  50.40   51.1   112.39

DYNAMIC   TL 86.36   86.37   86.38
  SM 95.24   95.30

DYNAMITE   SM 22.1

DYNAMO   SM 95.20   96.2

D'YOU   VG 50.5

'E   LH 11.34   17.37   17.38   17.41
  27.35

EAGER   LH 22.23   FO 135.22
  SM 104.22   MD 195.15

EAGERLY   LH 39.19   FO 172.30
  SM 75.5

EAGERNESS   MD 195.35

EAGLE   SM 8.31

EAGLE-LIKE   SM 147.6   MD 189.2

EAGLES   SM 147.7

EAGLE-SHADOWS   SM 134.12

EAR   LH 5.20   TL 54.2   69.35
  100.1   FO 140.26   CD 184.21
  SM 113.28   VG 46.37

EAR-FLAPS   CD 239.29

EARL   TL 44.13   92.36   93.5   93.28
  93.34   94.3   94.14   94.18   97.21
  98.8

EARL BEVERIDGE   TL 46.10   92.23

EARLDOM   TL 47.14

EARLY   LH 39.2   TL 97.37
  99.24   FO 115.41   119.23
  127.22   131.20   CD 237.28
  237.31   244.28   257.9
  SM 53.14   57.3   57.6   74.5
  94.40   116.15   143.40   148.6
  VG 29.9   48.8   54.6   70.16
  70.27   70.29

EARN   SM 107.29

EARNED   FO 127.29   CD 186.15

EARNEST   SM 21.33   MD 204.28

EARNESTLY   TL 44.41   SM 82.31

EARNESTNESS   CD 225.11
  MD 197.17

EARNING   SM 104.38

EAR-RINGS   CD 205.22   VG 21.6

EARS   LH 38.26   TL 51.16
  51.36   95.40   FO 143.31
  145.26   149.4   CD 183.26
  196.2   200.1   206.24   207.3
  209.25   220.17   238.42
  239.29   240.11   SM 8.41
  11.16   12.34   13.18   14.29
  19.14   26.35   45.24   46.8
  46.13   46.28   47.27   53.35
  54.8   74.24   144.35   155.12
  MD 183.18   VG 8.33   11.15
  17.2   17.18   21.7   24.13
  30.14   34.39

EARTH   LH 26.32   TL 53.33
  56.33   70.11   80.35   97.10
  103.8   107.19   FO 166.39
  173.35   CD 241.11   241.18
  244.30   244.38   253.38
  SM 20.41   37.2   53.7   67.13
  69.1   69.30   71.31   74.8
  84.12   85.10   94.12   99.4
  129.5   148.14   149.27   149.28
  149.34   150.34   153.10
  MD 166.17   166.18   172.32
  172.33   172.38   173.2   173.4
  176.38   180.32   181.37
  186.40   208.21   VG 42.33
  68.15

EARTHEN   MD 164.15   168.33
  VG 54.40

EARTH-LAVENDER   CD 247.9

EARTHLY   SM 148.34   VG 39.42

EARTH'S   CD 241.13   252.37
  SM 150.37

EARTHY   MD 172.33

EASE   LH 13.30

EASIER   CD 200.18   SM 93.30
  VG 16.16

EASILY   TL 48.40   74.36

EASILY (CONT.) FO 117.14 126.1
    141.7 161.3 161.5 CD 211.18
    236.3 247.26 257.5 SM 18.28
    55.4 96.6 99.23 VG 28.16

EASING VG 70.32

EAST TL 46.25 75.21 83.33
    99.26 SM 131.2 140.19 141.24
    MD 193.20 194.29

EAST AFRICA CD 264.29

EASTWOOD VG 53.28 57.37 59.1
    59.14 61.14

EASTWOOD (SEE MAJOR, EX-MAJOR,
    MR., MRS., MR. AND MRS.)

EASTWOODS VG 53.16 55.14 57.21
    60.37 63.8 63.38 66.25 70.36

EASY LH 20.16 30.22 35.37
    37.25 TL 69.24 69.27 83.32
    FO 114.11 176.28 176.29
    CD 219.4 256.7 262.28
    SM 16.10 30.17 70.12 72.20
    97.3 98.33 130.15 132.11
    144.10

EAT LH 18.3 19.40 29.22 29.42
    30.5 30.6 TL 72.30 82.32
    FO 141.29 144.12 153.19
    CD 245.4 256.25 SM 90.33
    101.4 101.8 103.18 103.26
    103.30 111.15 MD 169.7 183.25
    201.11 205.2 VG 47.10 47.13
    67.37

EATEN FO 124.34 SM 13.3 153.23
    MD 191.38 210.2

EATING LH 15.32 39.18 TL 72.34
    FO 135.9 CD 247.12 SM 27.21
    27.24 101.5 VG 9.21 41.33
    47.29

EAVES MD 187.30

EBONY VG 54.1

ECHO CD 199.37

ECHOED LH 24.19 25.37 SM 82.13

ECHOES SM 27.1 64.34

ECLAT VG 3.8

ECONOMY SM 4.12

ECSTASISED TL 82.4

ECSTASY TL 68.39 81.42 82.7
    82.16 CD 252.39 253.23 253.26
    SM 91.26 151.22 MD 188.19

ECSTATIC TL 105.9 105.20

'E'D LH 17.38

EDDY EDWARDS SM 79.39

EDELWEISS CD 241.38

EDGE LH 9.31 TL 59.6 FO 115.10
    117.1 117.29 129.42 138.1
    138.6 142.2 145.41 147.1
    CD 234.23 241.15 247.39
    254.41 SM 24.17 102.17 102.33
    121.15 143.32 MD 185.28
    198.24 198.37 199.8 204.9
    VG 71.29 75.18

EDGED CD 240.20

EDGES SM 99.8 125.27 125.29
    147.15 MD 168.23

EDGING SM 3.15 13.27 36.15

EDUCATED TL 44.26 44.28

EDUCATION SM 8.1 99.2

EDWARD, KING (SEE KING EDWARD)

EDWARDS SM 67.2 113.14

EDWARDS (SEE EDDY, FRED,
    FREDERICK, MR. GRIFFITH, SIR
    EDWARD)

EDWARD'S SM 72.7

EERIE LH 32.5

EFFECT TL 68.17 86.14 FO 118.39
    127.11 CD 206.27 SM 6.19 64.7
    97.13 97.14 VG 40.15

EFFECTIVE TL 83.14

EFFEMINATE VG 43.3

EFFICIENCY FO 124.6 SM 45.10
    45.19

EFFICIENT FO 124.4

EFFICIENTLY SM 45.27

EFFIGY CD 249.6

EFFLUENCE VG 48.19

EFFORT LH 24.7 TL 108.39
    FO 117.6 121.42 177.10 178.26
    178.32 CD 242.2 243.9
    SM 10.14 116.38 125.8 132.14
    141.21 153.22 VG 75.39

EFFORTLESS VG 39.10

EFFORTS TL 47.5 FO 178.2 178.3
    SM 4.13 153.31 153.32
    VG 76.12

EFFULGENCE CD 226.32

EFFUSIVE SM 81.25

EGG CD 228.33 229.10 246.13
    SM 79.26 155.29 155.30
    MD 171.37

EGGS FO 114.6 CD 245.33
    MD 163.12 200.27 201.12
    201.30

EGGSHELL SM 115.13

EGO SM 145.30 146.26
    MD 184.5 VG 7.16

EGOISTIC SM 147.4 MD 184.8

EGYPT TL 88.8 MD 185.3
    187.28 188.32 190.8 190.12
    191.5

EGYPTIAN TL 96.40 103.25

EGYPTIANS TL 97.7

EGYPTOLOGIST TL 97.19

EH LH 10.14 11.27 12.27
    15.22 16.9 16.19 17.5
    19.31 FO 121.31 168.1
    171.6 171.7 171.9 171.12
    171.35 SM 11.33 82.38
    132.1 VG 10.41 11.5 46.5
    47.4 50.13 51.19

EIGHT LH 20.36 CD 202.8
    238.31

EIGHTEEN CD 202.30 225.39
    SM 85.20

EIGHTEENTH SM 45.9 VG 54.7

EIGHTEENTH-CENTURY SM 45.7
    81.20 84.1

EIGHT-TEN FO 150.7

EIGHT THOUSAND SM 143.6

EIGHTY VG 7.11

EIN SCHONER MENSCH VG 51.18

EITHER TL 71.29 90.8
    FO 154.26 165.36 CD 200.27
    208.18 212.39 SM 3.32
    54.18 85.39 105.25 115.21
    115.22 129.12 131.22
    133.25 158.24 159.8
    MD 178.9 VG 16.3 16.30
    18.5 18.8

EJACULATED FO 135.3

ELABORATE FO 115.5 SM 129.34

ELAN SM 26.21 26.23 36.32

ELATE FO 129.37 163.31

ELBOW LH 9.22 12.35
    FO 156.21

ELBOWED LH 9.2

ELBOWS LH 23.25 FO 128.6
    VG 31.41 42.41

ELDER LH 4.27 5.37 6.2 6.42
    8.5 22.20 38.20 CD 202.6
    235.27 VG 6.25 52.3

ELDER-FLOWER LH 6.5

END (CONT.) SM 118.20 157.13
  157.15 MD 164.10 164.13 172.3
  174.1 187.34 204.41 206.16
  VG 36.20 37.7 47.15 63.6
  75.34 79.15 80.19

ENDED TL 95.9 FO 178.11
  CD 240.26 SM 10.21 25.19
  63.29

ENDERLEYS SM 27.20

ENDING LH 5.4 CD 252.29 253.34
  SM 60.40 74.4 138.12

ENDLESS CD 233.21 233.23
  SM 27.21 MD 191.9 205.23

ENDLESSLY TL 59.39

ENDS LH 8.3 TL 90.15 FO 156.2
  177.33 CD 195.5 224.8 261.23
  SM 16.28 46.7 76.7 MD 170.8
  174.28 174.29

END-TIPS MD 163.5

ENDURANCE SM 117.37 VG 67.15

ENDURE SM 115.20 117.2 VG 64.2

ENDURED VG 66.23

ENDURES VG 67.16

ENDURING TL 104.2 VG 65.39

ENEMIES TL 43.11 43.13 53.5
  SM 31.28 88.40 89.1 VG 42.17

ENEMY TL 43.11 43.27 44.9 51.2
  51.23 64.27 92.25 SM 21.23
  100.32

ENERGETIC TL 84.8 SM 38.29
  142.39

ENERGY LH 22.30 TL 45.10 47.11
  47.12 SM 7.2 7.20 57.16
  117.2 125.14 125.18 131.8
  131.15 131.32 144.28 145.7
  145.13 145.25 145.31 150.12
  153.38 MD 198.23

ENGAGED LH 39.24 CD 232.33
  VG 41.34 41.37 41.39 42.8
  42.32 44.7 44.30

ENGAGEMENT FO 151.24 CD 229.6

ENGAGEMENTS SM 10.32

ENGINE SM 115.8 134.24 138.15
  138.19 138.23 VG 18.21 25.14

ENGINEER CD 208.37 VG 50.37
  52.33

ENGINES SM 125.36

ENGLAND LH 16.37 16.40 TL 43.15
  44.1 46.9 56.25 56.29 62.28
  62.29 62.32 74.13 74.14
  82.36 92.32 93.2 98.11
  FO 146.10 146.22 179.11

ENGLAND (CONT.) CD 186.8 189.12
  195.31 204.17 204.18 204.36
  213.15 224.32 SM 63.34 63.35
  65.22 103.21 114.13 124.14
  129.28 131.20 131.21 131.22
  133.1 VG 18.40

ENGLISH LH 5.34 11.22 13.17
  TL 43.19 44.33 57.17 60.34
  64.38 69.37 77.2 93.5 98.19
  FO 146.13 CD 185.29 186.1
  187.22 194.10 194.26 194.28
  194.39 195.13 195.35 196.6
  197.26 199.11 199.41 200.17
  208.42 212.5 221.19 221.21
  221.22 224.36 228.37 239.18
  SM 6.3 7.10 9.4 24.5 29.18
  37.28 53.24 65.25 74.11 81.8
  82.24 90.29 94.13 102.4
  116.39 VG 8.35

ENGLISHMAN TL 62.30 69.24 84.19
  93.25 SM 28.36

ENGLISHMAN'S SM 18.30

ENGLISHMEN CD 197.18 SM 9.8
  31.15 31.18 52.14 63.36
  115.37

ENIGMATIC FO 162.35 SM 55.21

ENJOY CD 237.32 SM 26.21 40.1
  51.14 65.35 85.17 85.18
  92.31

ENJOYABLE SM 69.10 69.11

ENJOYED SM 33.17 MD 180.25
  VG 45.9 65.25 67.26

ENJOYING TL 72.42 FO 143.27
  SM 26.17 26.24 50.37 65.33
  65.36* 66.1 105.9 111.20

ENJOYMENT SM 27.34

ENLIGHTENED LH 20.33

ENMESHED MD 201.34

ENORMOUS LH 29.10 TL 70.18
  CD 252.26 VG 10.1

ENORMOUS-LOOKING CD 240.18

ENORMOUSLY FO 173.32

ENOUGH LH 9.5 11.42 12.38
  32.37 37.1 TL 59.10 68.25
  71.10 73.26 82.12 91.30 92.2
  96.8 96.26 99.24 FO 113.35
  114.4 114.40 121.24 132.23
  132.27 137.20 137.31 141.7
  150.30 154.14 161.9 161.10
  163.37 CD 194.30 207.12
  207.19 209.37 214.32 223.31
  256.20 259.19 264.8 SM 77.27
  80.19 86.38 87.15 87.16
  93.12 94.37 107.3 116.9
  144.12 158.4 158.41 MD 202.9
  VG 11.31 22.41 25.3 30.42
  59.6 62.25 74.11 75.4 77.9

ENQUIRE CD 228.19 SM 79.9

ENQUIRED TL 85.3 96.25
  SM 121.40

ENQUIRY TL 84.36

EN ROUTE SM 94.17

ENSHRINED VG 4.20

ENSLAVED VG 67.2

ENSUED VG 63.33

ENTANGLE CD 225.15

ENTANGLED CD 198.36 199.4
  MD 191.10

ENTANGLEMENT MD 183.39

ENTANGLEMENTS MD 183.33

ENTER TL 92.25 95.38
  FO 161.28 CD 205.9
  SM 135.10 145.29

ENTERED LH 25.13 27.27
  FO 117.21 130.6 155.40
  163.27 CD 184.36 186.41
  194.41 SM 53.4 102.14
  106.11 118.14 126.10
  157.33 MD 168.33 187.40
  VG 9.3 24.17 31.14 74.30

ENTERING SM 8.35 VG 25.8

ENTERPRISE FO 113.21

ENTERPRISES SM 153.28

ENTERTAIN TL 92.20

ENTERTAINED SM 7.5

ENTERTAINING CD 228.32
  VG 13.13

ENTHRONED VG 14.35

ENTHUSIASM TL 91.35 MD 176.11

ENTICINGLY CD 257.38

ENTIRELY LH 20.10 TL 92.7
  SM 21.38 27.9 119.33
  132.5 VG 16.12 29.5 61.2
  66.31

ENTITY SM 99.5

ENTRAILS TL 96.2

ENTRANCE SM 109.9 MD 200.32
  VG 15.29

ENTRANCED VG 48.11

ENTRY TL 68.23

ENUNCIATION SM 124.19

ENVELOPE FO 150.12 CD 218.21

ENVELOPED   TL 103.34   FO 119.5
  SM 69.20

ENVIRONMENT   SM 142.8

ENVY   SM 130.13   VG 60.6

EPHESUS   MD 188.32

EPICUREANISM   CD 230.12   230.35

EPIDERMIS   CD 254.13

EPISCOPALIAN   SM 30.14

EQUAL   CD 252.1   252.2   MD 205.39

EQUALITY   TL 89.40

EQUALLY   VG 35.40

EQUINE   SM 19.12   19.37   20.6

EQUIVALENT   CD 213.40

EQUIVOCAL   TL 84.14   CD 246.11

ER   CD 205.14   206.11   206.13
  213.33

'ER   LH 5.20   6.40   19.41   38.9

ERA   SM 70.40

'ER'D   LH 5.3

ERADICATES   SM 91.1

'ERE   LH 15.33   27.35

ERECT   LH 10.6   34.16   TL 103.24
  103.30   FO 140.29   CD 184.30
  236.12   239.2   253.9   SM 5.18
  34.1   46.2   155.10   MD 185.12
  VG 36.10   73.41

ERECTED   SM 141.30   146.4

ERECTION   LH 25.7   CD 214.25

ERMINE   TL 58.34   CD 195.4

ERNST   TL 53.16

ERRAND   CD 215.22

'ER'S   LH 15.33

ERUPT   SM 10.15

ERUPTION   SM 10.8

'E'S   LH 28.25

ESCAPADE   LH 39.23   SM 74.20

ESCAPE   FO 131.1   CD 197.12
  206.40   SM 26.28   57.15   69.32
  135.19   137.13   156.11
  MD 197.21

ESCAPED   FO 151.41   CD 225.22
  SM 52.41   57.19   MD 167.23
  167.30   167.33   170.16   171.4
  181.9   186.17   186.19   192.24

ESCAPED (CONT.)   VG 77.34   80.40

ESCAPES   TL 54.42

ESCORTED   TL 93.5   VG 40.41

ESKIMO   TL 59.4

ESOTERIC   SM 53.19

ESPECIALLY   TL 73.33   FO 154.17
  CD 210.16   246.13   247.25
  SM 28.36   51.26   52.13   61.12
  64.31   95.7   95.28   152.16
  156.26   MD 168.5   203.28   204.20
  VG 6.6   7.14   45.3   58.37   70.4

ESSAYIST   VG 3.16

ESSENCE   MD 211.21

ESSENTIAL   SM 101.19   MD 205.25

ESSENTIALLY   CD 224.30

ESTABLISHED   TL 88.8   FO 118.39
  SM 6.15   MD 209.6   210.3   210.12
  VG 52.17

ESTABLISHMENT   VG 67.13

ESTATE   MD 190.15

ESTATES   SM 116.13

ETC.   TL 93.15   SM 9.35   63.26

ETCHINGS   SM 53.16   53.19

ETERNAL   TL 74.30   103.38
  CD 231.17   241.14   241.33   244.5
  245.35   263.40   SM 45.31   140.3
  140.4   MD 188.21   VG 14.4

ETERNALLY   TL 107.26   CD 251.26

ETERNITY   TL 101.40   108.30
  108.34   108.40   109.9   SM 36.36
  119.23   MD 178.8

EUNUCH   SM 90.18   90.19

EUNUCHS   SM 90.20

EUROPE   TL 49.24   74.15   95.12
  96.4   SM 3.38   4.40   54.17
  94.16   94.19   94.23   94.40   95.1
  116.19   130.30   132.38   140.19

EUROPEAN   SM 3.32   94.16

EVANESCENT   MD 171.18

EVANGELINE HEPBURN   CD 219.18

EVASIVELY   SM 63.19   88.24

EVE   MD 175.13

EVENING   LH 21.18   34.34   TL 99.18
  FO 113.13   115.2   116.1   116.8
  117.39   119.13   119.18   119.26
  134.32   135.19   139.7   139.13
  143.16   143.28   149.37   152.25
  157.27   157.34   166.16   171.11

EVENING (CONT.)   CD 192.35
  198.18   214.23   216.6
  219.20   260.20   263.12
  263.15   SM 15.19   27.18
  29.27   93.37   94.7   115.18
  126.37   143.23   146.17
  MD 167.6   170.29   172.7
  180.18   182.2   186.8   199.20
  VG 10.36   51.30

EVENINGS   FO 119.1   CD 217.16
  217.29   SM 29.24   29.38

EVENT   FO 113.31   CD 214.33

EVENTS   SM 119.24

EVENTUALLY   SM 142.33

EVER-AMIABLE   CD 257.26

EVERGREEN   MD 185.15   187.38

EVERLASTING   TL 107.31
  FO 157.14   157.36   167.38
  174.38   CD 240.33   245.36
  245.38   SM 14.33   152.28
  MD 171.25   VG 14.4

EVER-WIDENING   TL 90.30

EVERYBODY   LH 10.24   10.26
  15.19   16.6   19.24   20.20
  TL 63.24   95.4   98.30
  FO 149.39   155.8   CD 261.10
  SM 4.28   9.3   21.41   27.37
  30.8   41.21   42.24   57.2
  57.30   66.8   69.11   69.25
  83.36   96.18   97.27   105.4
  105.8   105.18   115.23   131.39
  132.29   VG 6.32   11.42   12.35
  12.37   12.39   14.8   22.5
  27.1   32.16   33.5   39.22

EVERYBODY'S   SM 30.9   VG 53.6

EVERY-DAY   TL 103.4

EVERYONE   LH 15.4   20.22
  TL 49.15   SM 121.13

EVERYWHERE   LH 30.38   TL 72.6
  102.39   FO 147.10   CD 194.31
  233.18   233.20   SM 3.21
  23.30   143.27   MD 171.11
  183.40

EVIDENT   LH 13.10   TL 51.34
  52.34   85.36   CD 196.16
  SM 32.37   57.20

EVIDENTLY   LH 4.23   FO 143.19
  153.25   CD 242.33   246.5

EVIL   FO 115.8   163.29   SM 5.36
  68.40   68.41   69.4   69.8
  69.14   69.18   69.23   69.28
  69.29   69.35   69.37   69.39
  69.41   70.7   70.22   70.24
  70.31   70.34   71.3   71.17
  71.18   71.19   71.37   72.2
  72.16   72.27   72.30   72.36
  80.19   80.20   VG 4.22   4.39
  5.20

EVIL ONE   TL 56.16

EVOLVED   SM 118.30

EWES   TL 98.26

EXACTING   FO 114.5

EXACTITUDE   SM 44.28

EXACTLY   LH 19.37   TL 77.26   85.11
91.1   109.3   FO 123.25   173.6
CD 184.2   184.18   188.32   192.21
201.39   208.12   210.23   222.11
226.19   248.25   SM 3.17   12.17
12.27   12.32   39.32   44.22
55.10   57.4   86.11   99.31   99.33
109.22   120.36   130.22   VG 66.3

EXAGGERATED   TL 75.35   SM 36.13
120.1

EXALTED   CD 249.26

EXALTER   MD 176.17   176.30

EXAMINE   TL 73.14

EXAMINED   FO 117.32   127.8

EXAMINING   TL 80.25   SM 95.3

EXAMPLE   TL 74.10   SM 48.39   55.3

EXASPERATED   FO 115.40   CD 186.19
SM 5.34   36.13   58.16

EXASPERATING   VG 11.16   12.42

EXASPERATION   SM 5.34   48.22
MD 201.5   VG 11.22

EXCEEDINGLY   LH 20.4   36.16

EXCELLENT   TL 73.1

EXCEPT   LH 4.21   TL 88.31   103.9
FO 118.17   137.1   153.15   173.36
173.41   177.36   CD 197.27
218.28   223.21   223.30   224.34
226.16   231.30   245.25   SM 3.26
4.22   14.15   21.12   22.16   57.18
62.24   78.32   80.8   86.12   86.13
86.14   105.4   115.26   131.22
132.19   134.28   158.22   MD 197.2
VG 20.1

EXCEPTIONAL   CD 245.26

EXCESS   MD 174.40   175.3

EXCESSIVE   MD 175.3   175.5   175.10

EXCHANGE   TL 68.18

EXCHANGED   SM 88.6   88.10

EXCITED   LH 5.5   7.9   21.6   22.42
24.10   TL 78.2   FO 172.32
172.38   CD 242.4   252.17   256.10
SM 63.25   138.11

EXCITEDLY   FO 172.27   CD 245.22
SM 106.10   MD 181.19

EXCITEMENT   LH 23.42   24.2   26.8
TL 51.5   75.29   76.22   106.2
FO 129.37   CD 253.22   253.23
SM 26.24   85.1   94.28   102.29
136.16

EXCITING   TL 66.38   CD 264.29
SM 15.21

EXCLAIMED   LH 15.33   16.36   17.19
17.40   20.30   25.24   25.26
26.17   28.3   35.5   36.39   38.1
39.1   TL 89.20   FO 125.22
141.31   141.40   163.12   CD 246.2
VG 40.24

EXCLAMATION   FO 138.9   CD 196.5
SM 37.13

EXCLUDED   VG 37.35

EXCLUDING   SM 99.14

EXCLUSIVE   TL 88.12   FO 155.8

EXCURSION   CD 237.10   SM 56.40
57.20

EXCUSE   CD 196.30   258.21
SM 80.34   MD 203.36   VG 13.20

EXCUSES   SM 44.34

EXECUTE   MD 181.36

EXECUTED   TL 99.38   MD 181.35

EXERCISE   VG 9.27

EXERT   FO 175.37   175.38   175.39
175.41

EXERTED   FO 175.40

EXERTION   LH 8.12   CD 241.34

EXHALATIONS   SM 147.14

EXHALING   CD 253.13

EXHAUSTING   SM 6.19   6.33

EXHAUSTION   TL 52.8   SM 75.31

EXHAUSTS   SM 118.11

EXHIBITION   CD 254.32

EXHILARATED   SM 129.6

EXILE   CD 231.26   231.28   232.26

EXIST   CD 198.41   203.29   217.24
SM 41.18   41.19   64.29   65.17
135.30   148.29   MD 171.22
VG 42.23

EXISTED   CD 217.23   SM 38.20
VG 42.36   64.1

EXISTENCE   TL 85.7   FO 156.27
SM 41.14   41.17   71.10   71.14
118.40   127.14   127.16
MD 171.20   VG 29.34   31.12

EXISTING   LH 31.1   SM 44.34
131.9   MD 171.23

EXISTS   VG 66.40

EX-MAJOR EASTWOOD   VG 63.11

EXONERATED   CD 209.20

EXOTIC   TL 46.33   87.8   95.21

EXPANDED   SM 53.31

EXPANDING   SM 20.41

EXPANSION   MD 189.36

EXPECT   LH 27.37   27.41
TL 64.40   84.30   89.8
FO 128.24   142.22   150.17
156.10   CD 188.21   202.37
207.12   SM 39.32   108.26
108.31   135.16   156.10
MD 189.24   VG 7.38   17.25
42.30   63.40   65.2

EXPECTANT   LH 3.29

EXPECTANTLY   LH 21.13

EXPECTATION   LH 7.31   MD 175.24

EXPECTED   LH 24.3   28.1
TL 77.8   FO 114.29   116.40
CD 188.8   209.27   SM 8.26
110.9   116.20   132.31   140.34
MD 196.36   VG 36.25   42.31
65.14

EXPECTING   TL 70.1   FO 113.29
170.25   171.13   CD 209.26
VG 70.10

EXPECTS   CD 202.39

EXPEL   CD 194.12

EXPENSE   SM 71.28   80.28
MD 187.36

EXPENSIVE   CD 196.19   233.12
SM 17.24   VG 20.23   49.19
50.1

EXPERIENCE   TL 75.22   CD 217.26
VG 12.13

EXPERIENCED   VG 7.20   50.2

EXPERIENCES   LH 5.19   SM 4.17
25.36

EXPERIMENTS   CD 264.32

EXPIRED   LH 39.25

EXPIRING   SM 154.39

EXPLAIN   LH 10.23

EXPLAINED   CD 196.15   VG 51.3

EXPLANATION   CD 207.41

EYESIGHT SM 42.2 42.4

FABRE TL 97.5

FACE LH 3.28 4.23 5.18 6.36
10.25 12.32 13.7 13.28 18.25
19.5 21.32 31.23 33.21 33.22
33.25 34.11 TL 44.37 44.40
44.42 45.9 45.12 45.38 45.41
46.32 50.12 50.32 51.6 51.35
51.38 53.38 53.42 54.17
54.21 54.38 55.25 56.11
56.15 56.19 56.27 56.30 57.2
58.5 58.22 59.21 62.25 62.38
63.1 64.32 65.19 65.28 68.6
69.7 74.2 74.7 74.35 76.25
76.37 77.2 77.6 77.41 78.18
78.36 78.37 79.14 81.42 82.4
83.7 83.9 83.21 83.22 84.1
84.5 84.12 84.16 85.26 86.5
86.30 87.2 87.8 87.12 87.13
87.18 89.28 92.29 93.6 94.21
95.16 95.39 96.3 96.10
103.27 103.29 104.7 104.8
104.37 105.15 105.35 106.13
107.5 FO 114.12 120.15 122.19
123.33 124.13 124.21 124.30
124.40 126.6 126.34 127.21
127.32 128.17 128.31 128.33
128.37 128.39 129.1 129.20
132.4 132.42 134.6 134.19
134.21 135.14 136.30 138.2
138.5 138.13 139.3 139.11
139.21 139.38 140.16 140.23
140.26 141.13 141.20 141.39
141.42 142.26 142.40 143.7
143.12 143.23 143.27 144.11
144.14 148.17 148.28 150.2
150.15 151.5 151.39 152.15
155.19 155.37 155.41 157.17
158.8 158.20 158.27 158.31
158.33 159.14 159.26 163.31
163.33 164.36 164.41 164.42
165.6 169.6 170.8 170.16
170.19 170.32 170.41 171.38
174.14 174.36 175.29 178.23
CD 184.7 184.23 185.6 185.9
186.41 187.21 187.33 187.42
189.18 189.24 189.29 189.32
189.33 189.39 191.23 192.16
194.36 195.1 197.8 197.14
201.41 207.30 212.17 217.3
220.6 220.9 230.2 232.14
239.2 240.21 240.40 244.2
244.10 247.20 247.28 248.40
249.2 249.19 249.30 250.3
251.32 258.2 258.12 258.31
259.31 SM 12.34 13.19 18.4
18.7 20.17 21.12 21.40 22.4
24.28 25.2 25.9 27.6 30.21
31.8 34.28 34.31 34.32 40.39
45.14 45.25 47.2 51.36 53.32
53.38 55.18 55.29 59.23
62.33 65.20 67.1 67.8 67.9
67.15 67.16 67.21 67.32
67.39 68.5 68.10 68.23 68.37
70.4 70.5 72.6 72.29 75.9
76.24 77.16 78.38 81.26
83.19 84.1 84.6 84.8 86.22
87.36 88.3 88.30 88.35 89.6
91.22 92.9 92.16 99.3 100.27
101.9 106.18 106.25 107.9
109.10 109.14 111.7 112.10
112.11 113.16 115.3 115.25
115.32 121.2 122.20 127.12

FACE (CONT.) 131.18 154.30
157.27 MD 165.9 165.24 167.31
167.35 167.37 167.38 168.38
169.4 175.10 175.20 186.25
186.38 188.7 190.28 191.1
192.41 193.12 195.38 196.2
203.22 203.37 206.36 207.7
207.14 207.25 VG 12.23 15.18
15.19 19.33 20.2 20.3 21.18
21.19 22.6 22.26 23.3 23.15
23.34 24.13 24.37 26.28
26.33 27.3 27.15 27.18 29.13
29.15 32.15 32.21 37.12
38.13 38.22 39.29 39.32
40.17 42.24 43.15 43.28
44.35 44.39 45.39 48.5 48.6
51.33 52.8 59.3 59.5 59.6
59.34 59.38 61.19 62.19
62.22 62.35 63.29 64.11
65.35 68.14 69.9 74.6 74.10
74.21 74.22 74.26 74.40 75.9
75.10 75.17 77.2 77.3 79.17
79.33 79.36 79.42

FACED LH 6.38 TL 85.13 CD 238.7
247.32 248.39 SM 62.7 145.35
MD 185.3 204.4

FACES SM 91.13 128.10 VG 7.29
20.16 54.3 73.20 78.35

FACING LH 3.1 22.40 FO 133.19
159.2 174.25 CD 236.2 244.5
247.31 254.8 SM 87.23 141.3
MD 166.9 185.2 185.20
VG 36.16 71.26

FACINGS SM 110.41

FACT TL 67.13 68.16 85.22
FO 152.26 157.28 161.40
175.39 CD 187.39 188.17
221.34 226.21 227.39 230.8
261.28 262.38 SM 42.9 49.11
84.30 86.5 86.13 97.32 98.38
101.10 118.24 129.8 129.10
137.26 142.25 MD 165.15
VG 7.5 8.36 8.41 9.21 10.4
10.20 31.4 31.7 53.23 81.12

FACTORIES SM 102.21

FACTORY TL 64.8 64.10 73.41
SM 102.3

FACTS FO 165.26 CD 244.5 264.32
VG 65.4

FADE TL 99.30 CD 188.42

FADED LH 21.28 TL 97.31 99.20
100.4 100.7 FO 141.20
SM 119.9

FADING FO 168.33 SM 126.4

FAERY CD 223.11

FAGGOTS LH 39.11

FAIL TL 108.2 SM 54.7 156.6
MD 203.21

FAILED FO 116.29 176.25 176.26
SM 3.5 130.36 MD 170.27

FAILING FO 165.4 VG 4.9

FAILURE TL 46.37 FO 174.27
176.30 177.8 177.11 177.15
SM 3.23 4.20 53.18

FAINT LH 4.30 TL 58.25
63.32 74.36 76.5 78.15
80.7 102.41 FO 117.2
125.10 133.5 133.18
140.35 175.30 CD 186.25
220.9 237.19 237.21 258.1
SM 34.27 34.35 54.23
67.34 81.24 83.40 88.2
88.34 89.16 120.35 122.26
155.19 MD 190.38 191.23
192.19 195.14 198.13
203.1 206.9 210.39
VG 45.27 76.30

FAINTED CD 219.36 VG 72.28
80.20

FAINTEST CD 230.21 SM 10.28

FAINTING SM 68.18 VG 74.4

FAINTLY LH 9.46 12.4 33.6
TL 58.26 FO 164.19
CD 201.41 242.37 SM 22.3
91.10 MD 197.38 VG 69.22

FAIR LH 23.20 33.35 TL 46.33
83.21 FO 120.17 135.28
CD 185.5 247.32 252.7
SM 8.38 33.3 59.11 63.23
63.29 64.15 64.27 64.30
65.9 66.16 70.10 91.20
124.24 MD 192.11 194.5
VG 16.21 22.15 25.25
81.18

FAIR-HAIRED SM 33.3

FAIRIES SM 103.14

FAIRISH TL 84.28 FO 120.15

FAIRISH-ORANGE MD 198.38

FAIRLY LH 36.32 FO 166.9
CD 227.13 234.28 239.37
257.2 VG 17.9

FAIRY CD 221.1 221.11 222.12
244.35

FAIRY-STORY SM 27.23

FAITH LH 35.32 39.27
TL 70.13 88.21 FO 177.15
CD 203.8

FAITHFUL CD 206.42 SM 41.16
135.3 VG 63.42

FAKED SM 99.10

FALL LH 9.33 25.18 25.20
26.3 31.11 37.2 37.4
FO 119.3 128.12 130.31
146.24 165.39 168.29
168.40 172.9 172.12 172.18
177.34 178.1 CD 209.22
212.2 220.29 226.11 SM 5.13

FEET (CONT.) MD 194.36 204.24
   204.26 204.30 206.35 VG 17.31
   23.24 70.14 70.21 72.32
   73.13 73.17 74.38

FELICITY LH 27.1

FELINE CD 242.5

FELL LH 3.33 8.20 9.4 33.18
   33.38 33.40 FO 117.30 118.20
   146.27 171.2 CD 185.1 187.15
   219.29 220.21 231.28 234.39
   261.37 261.38 SM 5.23 45.20
   55.10 63.23 67.33 87.26
   102.24 103.18 129.21 139.2
   141.36 148.16 149.20 149.27
   MD 164.14 165.25 166.1 166.15
   167.27 172.4 173.27 193.29
   194.6 197.27 VG 25.16 35.11
   43.27 48.5 63.36

FELLOW LH 3.26 4.2 17.21
   TL 55.19 67.40 69.22 92.3
   98.42 FO 167.28 170.15 SM 8.2
   13.12 17.10 17.16 17.39
   33.12 41.29 44.14 70.18
   78.18 99.25 100.10 139.1
   139.21 155.17 MD 191.18
   192.23 VG 8.3 8.17 43.14
   43.39 51.11 59.35 59.40

FELLOW-MEN CD 224.15

FELLOW-OFFICERS TL 59.33

FELLOW-PRISONERS TL 59.32

FELLOWS FO 165.29 CD 233.5
   237.30 254.38 SM 44.4 79.25
   VG 8.6 55.23 55.29 55.31

FELT LH 4.4 8.19 8.22 13.13
   13.31 20.12 20.15 22.9 23.29
   24.17 26.28 27.7 27.29 28.27
   29.38 31.1 32.39 33.16 34.15
   34.23 34.30 35.4 36.1 37.28
   TL 44.5 44.18 45.37 50.37
   51.27 51.42 59.40 64.31 68.5
   69.5 69.14 70.29 70.34 73.14
   73.22 78.24 78.37 79.11
   79.32 82.13 82.37 87.30
   93.24 94.3 94.18 96.10 98.40
   99.29 101.7 101.10 103.6
   103.22 103.27 103.28 103.37
   104.2 104.3 104.36 106.5
   FO 117.23 118.40 119.9 123.4
   126.22 126.27 127.28 128.10
   129.40 132.3 132.18 132.37
   134.5 136.17 140.39 145.27
   146.10 146.13 146.30 146.33
   149.1 152.38 155.5 155.6
   157.8 157.9 157.11 157.29
   157.39 160.10 164.7 164.8
   164.10 164.14 164.19 166.35
   166.37 167.2 167.39 175.33
   175.37 176.21 CD 191.42
   198.30 199.13 199.24 203.12
   203.23 204.2 209.19 209.20
   209.21 211.18 220.36 221.5
   222.35 225.16 225.19 229.22
   231.26 231.40 232.24 244.6
   246.37 250.9 250.22 250.38
   251.7 251.28 251.41 256.16
   256.33 SM 6.28 6.29 13.7

FELT (CONT.) SM 14.17 14.33
   15.2 15.9 16.27 17.39
   22.28 25.32 25.37 26.23
   26.35 31.27 31.38 37.33
   38.16 41.2 51.37 62.12
   69.28 75.10 75.15 76.6 80.19
   82.15 85.2 86.31 87.17 89.11
   94.12 94.15 95.13 96.39
   97.19 109.10 113.22 116.34
   117.38 118.36 124.33 124.40
   125.36 125.39 126.10 126.34
   129.36 134.34 136.28 140.13
   140.16 140.18 142.7 142.21
   145.28 149.1 152.11 MD 166.35
   168.20 175.21 177.29 183.3
   189.15 194.15 195.28 195.31
   203.40 204.4 205.28 206.4
   206.27 206.32 207.9 207.17
   VG 7.25 14.22 17.11 21.26
   21.39 24.19 30.10 30.38
   41.25 41.38 41.42 42.5 56.1
   61.15 64.28 68.14 70.9 70.42
   73.3 73.5 76.20

FEMALE TL 59.13 82.22 82.28
   FO 179.20 CD 214.4 214.5
   SM 83.28 84.6 135.16 135.20
   135.39 137.22 145.31
   MD 175.11 203.6 203.12 VG 7.9
   30.26 40.14

FEMALES CD 226.38 MD 183.29

FEMININE LH 5.29 27.5 CD 193.19
   208.28

FEMININITY SM 9.16

FENCE LH 7.7 FO 146.1 146.12
   153.26 168.16 169.12 169.13
   169.19 169.24 170.22 172.13
   172.14 172.15 172.16 172.26
   172.36 172.40 173.41 174.5
   174.15 174.18 174.21 SM 7.1
   90.23 107.15 141.11 141.31
   145.14 146.31 151.29 VG 7.23
   18.9

FENCED-IN SM 142.12

FENCES FO 113.25 SM 90.11
   VG 19.7 45.26

FENCE-SIDE FO 145.37

FERN MD 191.26

FEROCIOUS CD 241.14

FEROCIOUSLY VG 75.22

FEROCITY LH 13.15 CD 251.36
   VG 74.26

FERRETY LH 17.22

FERRY SM 128.24

FERTILE CD 228.36

FERVENTLY LH 34.18 SM 113.18

FESTIVAL SM 113.5

FETCH LH 4.16 10.36 10.37

FETCH (CONT.) 35.37 VG 11.21
   47.25 80.2

FETCHED LH 14.37 VG 3.28
   37.19 47.28 80.41

FETTER VG 16.13

FEUDAL TL 89.1 89.21

FEVER SM 144.26 MD 179.35

FEW LH 14.13 15.27 23.16
   24.35 30.36 38.33
   TL 78.16 89.1 FO 118.7
   127.13 129.10 146.18
   153.9 165.41 168.24
   CD 186.1 217.29 222.32
   227.25 232.20 240.2 240.41
   241.1 254.18 254.20 264.31
   SM 7.6 19.24 23.23 29.6
   60.35 62.24 63.36 65.30
   66.29 75.8 78.7 114.14
   117.11 121.5 122.7 122.8
   122.17 141.2 141.38 145.20
   147.37 MD 163.13 181.22
   187.33 188.1 VG 16.26
   17.13 22.39 32.38 50.14
   69.34 70.21 71.38 72.13

FEWER SM 122.9

FEYTHER LH 4.16 9.39 9.40

FIASCO SM 25.19 115.15

FIBRE FO 140.32 SM 117.33
   VG 75.25

FIBRES MD 201.22

FIBRILS FO 176.4

FIDELITY VG 4.36

FIDGETED VG 23.9

FIDGETING VG 14.2

FIDGETS CD 215.18

FIDGETTY FO 136.17

FIELD LH 3.9 3.12 4.36
   6.1 6.4 10.1 10.2 10.41
   15.34 21.22 21.23 21.42
   22.26 22.32 24.3 27.14
   36.28 TL 97.7 FO 115.10
   115.23 130.7 169.20
   SM 59.17 74.15 92.2 101.1
   101.26 141.3 145.36 146.11
   150.40 MD 168.1 172.37
   VG 19.4

FIELDS LH 3.1 15.2 15.10
   15.24 TL 62.33 98.15
   FO 113.23 115.36 126.26
   135.23 143.8 143.10
   SM 74.40 90.9 102.6
   106.28 125.28 147.36
   VG 18.35 18.38 36.24

FIENDISH SM 30.37 113.22

FIERCE LH 12.35 TL 82.23

FIERCE (CONT.) TL 82.24 SM 20.3
  147.4 150.36 152.19 155.9
  MD 172.15

FIERCELY LH 5.28 MD 201.10
  VG 25.14

FIERCENESS LH 13.16 SM 150.22
  MD 164.25

FIERY SM 16.3 27.14 144.14
  MD 163.26

FIERY-EYED VG 34.21

FIESTA SM 132.13

FIFTEEN TL 60.34 SM 56.16 56.18
  VG 26.10

FIFTEEN HUNDRED KRONEN CD 233.10

FIFTY LH 14.35 CD 194.42 229.26
  231.29 240.35 SM 8.33 21.40
  128.8 143.37 VG 6.36

FIFTY-FIVE TL 93.11

FIFTY-FOUR VG 12.8 12.13

FIFTY-ONE SM 94.26 96.40

FIGHT LH 6.25 13.14 FO 144.38
  CD 217.38 217.41 229.12
  229.13 SM 24.32 71.35 71.37
  77.12 77.20 145.17 148.38
  MD 187.2 201.7 VG 61.31

FIGHTING FO 159.2 SM 25.8 64.24
  120.32 144.21 153.36

FIGHTS FO 130.42 178.31 SM 72.2

FIGS MD 169.5 200.26

FIG-TREE MD 163.8 170.9 170.25
  171.14 180.9 180.11

FIG-TREES MD 163.5

FIGURE LH 6.29 7.4 10.1 18.23
  TL 51.33 52.35 83.18 102.8
  FO 129.35 135.32 136.10
  152.29 152.33 159.25 169.40
  170.4 CD 195.2 201.21 217.42
  227.6 227.8 227.12 228.37
  235.12 SM 12.4 12.5 15.14
  16.37 31.12 59.23 MD 194.19
  VG 4.9 43.13 47.39 50.1
  68.25

FIGURED TL 86.27 86.28

FIGURES LH 9.42 FO 154.35
  SM 9.33 26.13 60.10 119.15
  VG 71.40

FIGURINE VG 54.11

FIGURINES VG 54.4

FILE SM 63.31 MD 199.13
  VG 16.13

FILET CD 227.27 227.31

FILL LH 18.12 18.18 TL 79.33
  FO 124.35 158.11 CD 206.1
  249.27 SM 52.6 67.4 81.32
  MD 174.2

FILLED LH 9.37 18.21 21.20
  TL 47.2 96.12 98.32 CD 250.12
  252.37 SM 144.14 MD 166.20
  166.29 VG 49.34 64.41

FILLING FO 133.42 SM 129.14
  MD 185.13 VG 70.7

FILLS SM 118.10

FILM-HEROES SM 131.6

FILM-PSYCHOLOGY SM 131.3

FILMS SM 131.2

FILM-SETTING SM 131.31

FILTER SM 42.35

FILTERED LH 21.21

FILTH TL 92.33 SM 153.40

FILTHILY VG 29.25

FILTHY VG 79.24

FINAL LH 10.20 FO 159.35
  CD 250.19 257.31 SM 22.19
  97.5 115.5 MD 163.34 188.24
  VG 27.11 53.18

FINALITY FO 176.39 SM 9.40
  46.30

FINALLY TL 82.21 FO 161.26
  161.28 SM 80.9 134.38
  MD 181.36 VG 7.24 18.30 54.5
  63.37

FINANCES FO 115.24

FIND LH 12.24 12.26 27.41 31.2
  32.23 33.23 38.29 TL 47.21
  47.22 65.38 70.39 71.37 72.5
  84.28 99.40 104.25 109.5
  FO 116.40 116.41 117.1 121.28
  123.25 125.23 126.1 127.38
  145.14 148.10 148.12 148.16
  161.3 161.5 CD 185.37 185.39
  200.18 204.12 228.9 246.15
  249.18 261.8 SM 8.27 54.4
  80.29 82.21 114.32 123.32
  124.1 127.29 MD 188.12 189.11
  197.16 VG 8.14 15.22 28.5

FINDING LH 21.6 TL 72.23 88.23
  SM 123.33 123.38

FINDS TL 58.34 59.13 63.36
  SM 148.36 VG 16.17

FINED VG 28.41

FINE-DRAWN SM 7.12 7.13

FINE-LOOKING SM 80.31

FINELY LH 3.4 18.25 TL 73.3

FINELY (CONT.) CD 232.9
  SM 13.19 22.40

FINELY-BUILT TL 47.1

FINELY-FORMED VG 53.29

FINENESS SM 119.10

FINER CD 229.35 MD 193.11

FINERY CD 194.41

FINE-SHAPED VG 64.30

FINEST TL 59.15

FINGER TL 61.21 61.29 70.34
  76.29 FO 165.34 CD 190.19
  195.20 195.23 211.24
  SM 61.31 61.33 VG 49.35

FINGER-ENDS CD 254.27 256.17

FINGERNAILS CD 255.31

FINGER-PRINTS SM 87.38

FINGERS LH 14.17 29.38
  31.17 33.18 33.26
  TL 73.20 79.41 79.42
  81.32 81.35 FO 136.23
  138.3 141.28 142.38 148.34
  163.30 CD 186.38 195.8
  197.15 207.3 254.30
  SM 38.10 63.3 VG 18.19
  22.9 47.30

FINGER'S TL 62.6

FINGER-TIPS LH 33.19 33.22
  TL 103.22 103.25 MD 174.28
  207.32

FINICKINESS SM 7.11

FINICKY SM 7.18

FINISH LH 15.13 TL 64.22
  99.23 FO 172.3 CD 261.17
  261.21 261.23 263.7
  SM 122.41 VG 63.2

FINISHED LH 3.10 TL 64.39
  80.36 80.37 92.9 92.40
  99.6 101.5 FO 118.28
  131.3 CD 184.18 184.19
  194.27 225.24 225.25
  SM 3.28 46.5 46.27 95.2
  132.14 142.17 MD 165.39
  174.1 174.19 177.17 182.10
  VG 18.5

FINISHING VG 7.28 41.24

FIORITA SM 109.39

FIR FO 168.15 CD 240.16

FIR-CONES VG 50.5 51.28

FIRE LH 38.37 39.14 39.17
  TL 46.15 48.27 67.2 67.4
  67.5 67.10 67.12 67.16
  67.22 67.32 67.42 68.4

FIRE (CONT.) TL 69.26 74.27
  75.22 75.24 75.26 78.15
  78.33 78.41 91.39 99.11
  105.32 105.40 FO 116.6 116.38
  118.2 119.12 119.22 119.24
  119.28 125.9 126.34 131.19
  131.26 132.37 136.4 138.35
  138.41 140.39 142.41 148.2
  149.39 152.13 153.12 154.27
  156.35 158.1 163.14 163.26
  CD 196.19 210.38 SM 12.8
  14.21 15.8 26.33 26.34 49.26
  78.13 96.29 102.2 103.30
  103.34 103.36 103.37 104.1
  104.3 104.6 104.9 134.3
  139.11 139.14 140.4 140.8
  140.15 140.27 143.31 148.13
  149.26 MD 172.30 201.37
  207.13 VG 10.33 10.34 11.31
  13.18 20.6 30.8 30.9 33.16
  45.34 46.3 46.9 46.24 47.6
  47.7 47.27 47.29 48.4 48.42
  49.13 49.20 49.38 50.3 50.17
  50.21 51.28 52.8 53.2 53.5
  53.6 66.11 70.14 70.18 71.1
  71.11 77.4

FIRE-CENTRE SM 150.37

FIRE-COLOUR SM 150.33

FIRED TL 45.10

FIRE-LIGHT FO 130.2

FIRE-MOUTHS SM 142.35 143.17

FIRE-PLACE FO 135.36 VG 74.30

FIRE-RAIN SM 150.34

FIRE-RED SM 150.31 150.35

FIRE-ROSES VG 51.29

FIRES SM 37.9

FIRE-SCREEN FO 115.4

FIRE-WORSHIPPERS TL 57.18

FIREY FO 148.16

FIRING FO 131.6 155.11 168.22

FIRM LH 10.29 14.8 34.17
  FO 156.23 159.31 VG 30.17

FIRMAMENT MD 182.28

FIRMLY SM 79.5 VG 4.35 11.37

FIRMNESS SM 22.41

FIR-NEEDLES SM 158.13

FIRST LH 3.30 5.22 6.23 18.42
  22.37 24.42 34.9 TL 43.28
  62.17 76.11 80.37 90.13
  97.14 100.29 106.3 FO 113.30
  130.39 137.19 139.34 148.18
  151.7 151.9 151.21 152.30
  157.41 174.30 176.28 CD 187.8
  188.39 206.36 208.34 213.31
  216.29 220.42 221.8 229.25

FIRST (CONT.) 229.31 230.10
  232.16 236.38 237.36 240.38
  240.39 243.18 243.36 244.27
  250.25 254.6 SM 20.10 22.26
  24.3 25.19 25.34 31.32 36.4
  37.30 38.40 45.35 51.41
  53.10 62.26 63.26 72.13
  74.5 84.38 86.23 89.7 93.10
  94.34 116.41 149.20 MD 170.8
  181.20 181.39 187.6 190.36
  193.12 193.14 196.13 196.31
  202.34 VG 12.14 12.37 20.28
  35.18 35.36 36.22 40.39
  54.22 61.31 70.6 72.32 73.34
  77.21 79.6

FIRST-CLASS SM 125.24 128.39

FIRST PRINCIPLE TL 97.7

FISH TL 58.42 CD 199.12 235.25
  SM 67.12 MD 198.25 198.35
  198.40 199.39 200.2 VG 42.4

FISHES CD 235.40 SM 69.7 69.19
  VG 15.8

FISHING CD 252.36

FISH-LIKE SM 69.35

FIST MD 186.24 VG 18.33

FISTS LH 4.22 SM 151.30

FIT TL 48.30 64.42 71.20
  FO 166.12 SM 6.11 109.33
  115.11 131.38

FITFULLY LH 29.7 TL 44.25

FITS CD 221.10 VG 71.3

FITTED TL 65.1 CD 187.13 232.10

FIVE TL 46.3 94.22 FO 120.9
  158.5 168.25 CD 204.37 205.41
  205.42 206.4 228.27 SM 11.39
  25.7 111.29 126.21 142.39
  143.37 VG 31.19 47.36 52.34
  67.33 72.6 80.29

FIVE HUNDRED SM 142.33 143.11
  144.11 145.22

FIXED TL 47.30 47.33 84.18
  86.5 FO 123.6 146.23 146.32
  151.24 164.38 165.1 165.6
  166.37 167.7 167.14 CD 189.34
  190.17 201.23 218.5 227.11
  227.13 231.32 SM 27.11 36.28
  50.34 68.9 114.39 117.23
  127.39 143.4 VG 21.36 39.9
  51.10

FIXEDLY FO 165.3

FIXING CD 188.37

FIXITY FO 142.16

FIXTURE SM 45.33

FIZZED TL 92.10

FLABBY VG 79.1

FLAG LH 4.32 TL 43.25
  MD 172.4

FLAGGED SM 37.34

FLAGSTONES SM 87.27

FLAIR SM 123.35

FLAKES SM 45.20

FLAKY-RIBBED SM 145.41

FLAMBOYANT MD 163.33 VG 54.1

FLAME TL 52.22 67.4 84.10
  98.22 99.10 103.23 103.24
  103.34 103.39 FO 128.31
  170.19 CD 207.1 208.41
  249.19 249.31 SM 36.27
  50.29 75.24 75.25 75.26
  75.29 MD 178.26 193.13
  196.11 196.12 203.19
  VG 27.1 27.2 27.9 50.18

FLAMES TL 69.28 CD 210.39
  SM 53.4 MD 170.8

FLAME-TIP MD 193.16

FLAME-TONGUES MD 171.13

FLAMINESS MD 172.28

FLAMING SM 12.13 142.36

FLAMY MD 176.16

FLANK SM 141.13

FLANKS CD 239.22 242.3
  VG 17.4

FLANNEL TL 60.26 60.27

FLANNELS SM 34.8

FLAPPED CD 229.30 VG 44.37

FLAPS CD 240.11

FLARE LH 23.21 SM 120.13
  146.18

FLARES VG 6.37 6.41

FLASH FO 115.32 173.32
  CD 242.13

FLASHED LH 19.10 37.31
  FO 147.27 CD 259.36
  SM 10.41 56.38 58.27 66.35

FLASHES CD 251.40 VG 32.15

FLASHING FO 173.33 CD 236.5
  239.22 VG 32.14

FLASH-LIGHT FO 147.26

FLAT TL 46.6 46.14 52.2
  60.31 FO 149.31 CD 243.19
  243.36 246.4 254.7

FLAT (CONT.) SM 65.23 65.24
  74.8 130.22 130.24 MD 171.26
  185.29 198.36 199.2 199.41
  VG 78.13

FLATLY FO 140.3

FLAT-STEPPING SM 32.29

FLATTENED FO 120.15

FLATTER SM 135.24

FLATTERED CD 250.21 250.31
  VG 44.32 64.16

FLATTERING CD 264.1

FLAW SM 6.7

FLAWED TL 82.18

FLEA CD 256.26

FLEAS FO 149.29 149.30
  CD 256.23

FLED LH 14.34 22.38 SM 36.16
  45.32 128.3 MD 211.9 VG 78.15

FLEECE FO 147.29 SM 153.32

FLEECINESS LH 22.13

FLEETING SM 3.30 VG 42.35

FLEETNESS LH 22.38

FLENA SM 35.34

FLESH TL 45.11 58.26 65.1
  CD 199.12 209.7 209.9 209.15
  233.6 233.20 233.21 244.30
  254.12 SM 106.36 109.27 136.5
  MD 175.39 176.31 182.33
  182.34 195.32 201.31 204.15
  205.7 205.22 210.38 211.21
  VG 12.34 27.38 28.1 28.17
  28.24 43.12

FLEW FO 126.40 131.26 CD 184.23
  232.19 SM 34.31 36.32
  VG 35.15 37.23 78.32

FLEXIBLE CD 220.10 VG 23.38
  38.9 39.10

FLICKER FO 114.21 SM 62.33 89.6
  MD 167.25 176.1 VG 15.24

FLICKERED TL 65.28 SM 81.26
  MD 191.34

FLICKERING CD 261.23 SM 75.24
  134.17

FLIES FO 144.14 SM 143.40

FLIGHT FO 127.12 131.8
  SM 101.17 VG 3.32 48.9

FLING MD 202.41 VG 66.7 67.30
  67.34

FLINGING SM 46.27 MD 171.11

FLINTS FARM SM 91.40 93.7
  109.36

FLIPPING CD 237.6

FLIRT CD 206.38 VG 58.9

FLIRTATION SM 27.21

FLIRTATIOUS SM 122.28

FLIRTATIOUSNESS SM 113.25

FLIRTED CD 232.4 SM 3.11 32.39

FLIRTING CD 265.17 SM 52.23

FLIRTY SM 125.40 VG 16.25

FLITTING LH 22.23

FLOAT LH 14.37 20.38 SM 147.13
  VG 74.5

FLOATED SM 3.38

FLOATING CD 237.24 SM 124.4
  147.15 147.37 VG 39.42

FLOAT-LIKE VG 74.10

FLOCK FO 114.22 SM 154.6

FLOG ICH ZU DIR TL 80.12

FLOG' ICH ZU DIR TL 71.5

FLOOD FO 176.4 176.12 CD 252.29
  SM 13.36 58.35 69.21
  MD 171.16 189.35 VG 72.34
  72.38 77.27 80.28

FLOODED CD 232.40 SM 76.2 76.10
  MD 185.5

FLOODING MD 189.19 189.39

FLOOR LH 17.32 26.31 TL 44.21
  FO 135.35 CD 217.33 219.25
  SM 46.8 MD 164.16 200.20
  VG 20.35 23.29 32.24 33.5
  47.29 75.1 75.30 78.12 78.26

FLOORS VG 75.36

FLORA SM 51.29 52.3 52.24
  52.28 52.32 58.38 64.37
  64.39 65.38 66.14 67.23
  67.28 67.34 68.12 72.24
  88.18 90.37 93.24 93.37
  94.4 109.25 110.13 110.21
  110.35 111.31 112.29 113.1
  113.8 113.20 113.31 114.1
  115.9

FLORA MANBY SM 35.30 37.11
  51.26 64.32 90.18 91.19
  93.13 96.15

FLORAS SM 115.36

FLORA'S SM 51.27 112.41 113.29

FLORECITA SM 109.39

FLORIDLY SM 4.7

FLORIN VG 52.4

FLOUNCED VG 21.8

FLOUNCING VG 32.3 32.5

FLOURISH FO 114.26 143.25
  SM 45.19

FLOURISHED CD 183.10 VG 4.39
  37.41

FLOURISHING CD 241.10
  VG 32.42

FLOW TL 67.16 CD 224.12
  SM 16.3 95.30 137.36
  142.6 154.7 VG 5.32
  66.35 69.10

FLOWED TL 47.15 103.19

FLOWER TL 46.36 54.39 57.9
  57.21 58.11 75.6 77.32
  83.10 83.21 87.9 94.37
  95.21 FO 177.23 177.28
  177.29 CD 218.1 SM 4.26
  109.37 141.33 150.26
  150.27 150.29 150.36
  151.8 151.13 MD 169.25
  187.37 189.10 189.17
  189.24 189.37 189.39
  190.33 194.1 195.38
  208.14 VG 44.36 48.7
  48.8 59.34

FLOWER-BEDS VG 36.3

FLOWER-BUD TL 104.41

FLOWERED CD 214.19 214.21

FLOWER-FLESH CD 247.39

FLOWER-GARDEN SM 153.17

FLOWERING SM 151.24

FLOWER-LIKE VG 43.28

FLOWERS LH 6.3 6.9 22.2
  22.11 TL 54.25 54.26
  54.30 57.11 57.14 76.18
  FO 153.19 153.21 CD 216.30
  230.24 244.32 245.4 245.6
  245.32 247.24 247.27
  247.37 253.6 256.33
  SM 30.24 37.38 42.36
  42.39 57.6 65.31 85.9
  110.37 119.17 140.11 141.5
  141.7 150.18 151.2 151.18
  151.19 MD 207.26

FLOWERY CD 233.11

FLOWING TL 67.17 69.40
  86.21 107.26 107.32
  SM 35.37 143.39 150.17
  MD 211.22 VG 31.7

FLOWN CD 225.23 SM 125.1

FLOWS TL 69.40 SM 63.35

FLU   FO 127.42

FLUENT   VG 10.23

FLUFF   CD 192.6

FLUGLEIN   TL 80.14

FLUID   SM 95.15   144.15   148.13
  149.26   152.19

FLUNG   LH 3.4   7.38   7.39   8.11
  8.17   24.4   26.40   FO 173.40
  CD 257.4   VG 53.13

FLURRY   TL 71.14

FLUSH   LH 9.33   TL 58.12   FO 117.2
  141.35   SM 65.19

FLUSHED   LH 5.5   16.4   TL 93.39
  FO 138.13   141.12   141.35   169.1
  170.4   171.38   CD 190.20
  SM 34.31   37.11   51.24   107.20
  MD 197.19

FLUSHING   FO 156.8

FLUSTERED   VG 37.5

FLUTING   MD 188.8

FLUTTER   FO 115.14   CD 208.41
  232.14   SM 23.30   MD 167.27
  186.33

FLUTTERED   TL 44.32   45.1
  CD 232.8   239.1   MD 181.18
  VG 38.11

FLUTTERING   CD 221.38   222.29
  261.19

FLUTY   TL 102.1

FLY   TL 71.9   80.15   CD 248.6
  SM 11.27   35.10   MD 164.5
  VG 44.39

FLYING   FO 113.27   127.27   173.4
  CD 232.13   SM 31.34   103.16
  VG 34.12

FLYING-FISHES   SM 127.9   128.34

FOAL   CD 239.23   239.31

FOALS   SM 32.9

FOAM   TL 77.3   77.33   CD 241.17
  247.20   MD 171.16

FOAMING   CD 239.10

FOAM-TIPS   MD 171.12

FOCUSED   TL 78.5   78.22   86.5
  SM 20.37

FODDER   MD 163.19

FOE   LH 19.37

FOILED   FO 175.20

FOLD   TL 98.24   MD 188.13

FOLDED   TL 80.22   FO 148.12
  CD 208.39   237.17   SM 60.16
  63.3   97.22   116.25   155.11
  MD 166.24   200.4   200.6   200.24

FOLDING   LH 31.22   34.1   38.23
  MD 206.21   VG 11.8

FOLDS   SM 60.16   64.3   147.24
  MD 200.1   206.23   208.9

FOLK   LH 22.5

FOLKS   SM 63.14   98.9

FOLLOW   LH 31.33   TL 90.6   91.34
  92.18   100.31   FO 117.37
  SM 40.17   59.3   108.34
  MD 180.19   209.16   VG 64.6

FOLLOWED   LH 9.30   11.12   19.30
  25.1   TL 87.23   92.7   100.32
  FO 154.33   CD 258.22   SM 8.23
  11.12   42.26   76.24   110.5
  131.28   150.29   MD 166.39
  168.19   173.35   192.16   195.13
  195.35   198.17   202.30   VG 12.2
  24.1   48.28   49.7   53.13   54.16

FOLLOWERS   MD 175.23

FOLLOWING   TL 51.3   109.1
  CD 236.31   245.15   SM 20.24
  42.30   59.5   59.10

FOND   FO 165.33   CD 203.1   SM 6.20
  111.28

FONDLE   SM 107.26

FONDNESS   VG 6.12

FOOD   FO 114.27   114.33   114.37
  126.41   126.42   134.24   135.6
  135.9   141.42   144.12   168.13
  172.33   CD 232.41   233.2   238.23
  SM 27.24   81.10   100.40   101.25
  103.30   MD 164.23   164.31   169.8
  169.10   171.31   VG 9.9   9.19
  9.21   12.19   24.21

FOOL   LH 8.16   8.42   9.1   9.12
  TL 94.3   FO 142.13   144.12
  144.21   144.27   145.1   161.32
  161.36   165.17   165.21   165.30
  166.17   166.21   CD 198.35   214.6
  215.15   262.40   263.1   SM 58.3
  66.24   66.30   70.5   70.19   98.7
  98.8   98.11   98.14   98.17   98.23
  104.32   137.10   137.40   156.24
  156.25   156.39   157.22   VG 37.26

FOOLERY   SM 157.24

FOOLING   CD 210.35   SM 158.19

FOOLISH   TL 53.27   66.13   FO 177.8
  CD 196.27   249.6   251.34
  SM 39.20   138.12

FOOLISHLY   TL 53.22   53.23

FOOLS   FO 160.35   160.39

FOOLS (CONT.)   SM 129.38

FOOT   LH 4.33   5.6   12.17
  15.10   21.41   37.36
  FO 139.17   139.38   144.30
  148.27   173.41   177.39
  CD 234.37   235.8   260.32
  SM 7.13   44.37   58.18   79.19
  89.28   139.21   140.33
  MD 196.31   198.6   198.27
  199.17   VG 10.26   19.14
  29.33   37.3   48.31   48.33
  71.17   78.13   80.20

FOOTBALL   CD 238.6

FOOT-BOY   CD 239.40

FOOTHOLD   LH 9.4

FOOT-HOLD   CD 254.28   VG 72.37

FOOTING   LH 9.28   9.29
  CD 255.42   SM 134.39
  VG 73.11

FOOTMAN   TL 72.8

FOOT-PASSENGERS   SM 36.16

FOOTSTEP   FO 119.30

FOOTSTEPS   FO 119.33

FOOT-TRACKS   SM 66.11

FOOTWORN   SM 63.40

FORAGING   FO 114.32

FORBADE   SM 15.2   15.3

FORBID   SM 23.37

FORBIDDEN   VG 35.21

FORCE   FO 173.9   CD 250.14
  SM 24.30   53.29   58.21
  69.28   78.25   81.15   83.4
  95.4   95.15   95.24   95.25
  MD 205.28   VG 21.39   55.12

FORCED   TL 52.22   69.18
  FO 122.39   154.18   154.21
  SM 120.29   VG 43.1   65.34

FORCING   CD 241.13   VG 74.26

FORD   SM 130.41

FORDED   SM 154.36

FORDS   SM 129.16

FORE-ARM   CD 187.19   190.6

FOREARMS   CD 193.9

FOREBODING   MD 164.19

FOREFEET   SM 58.32   67.13
  67.16

FOREFINGER   VG 22.12

FOREGROUND SM 53.26 146.31
  156.20

FOREHEAD TL 77.10 81.10
  FO 118.29 120.16 SM 38.34
  MD 167.41 169.19 VG 65.36

FOREIGN LH 5.40 6.6 7.9 10.4
  10.34 13.42 27.4 36.40
  CD 199.27 SM 3.20 VG 21.13

FOREIGN-SOUNDING LH 13.17

FORELOCK LH 23.9 VG 20.12

FOREMOST LH 11.38 MD 181.39

FORESEEING MD 197.38

FOREST FO 130.30 CD 221.7
  SM 13.11

FOREVER TL 90.5 FO 176.3 178.1
  CD 244.8 MD 167.6 169.37
  181.39 211.19 VG 5.33 7.8
  66.41

FOR EVER-UNYIELDING VG 67.6

FORGAVE CD 251.38

FORGED MD 164.21

FORGET TL 43.8 54.8 54.9 56.19
  72.15 98.29 100.10 104.27
  107.39 FO 118.17 164.16
  166.22 CD 191.37 191.38
  191.40 206.8 206.11 SM 19.29
  72.27 MD 172.8 VG 66.31 71.33

FORGETFULNESS TL 100.34

FORGETS CD 214.8

FORGETTING LH 6.12 TL 85.42
  FO 156.28

FORGING CD 239.25

FORGIVE TL 61.25 62.35 70.13
  79.5 106.10 MD 203.30 VG 7.2
  28.22

FORGIVEN VG 5.8 5.9

FORGIVENESS VG 7.1

FORGOT TL 43.26 51.2 55.39
  FO 125.5 134.34 143.24 160.15
  CD 223.3 SM 93.20 MD 189.7
  204.8 VG 66.25

FORGOTTEN TL 53.15 53.31 77.30
  77.38 FO 156.26 CD 198.25
  206.10 234.6 VG 44.5

FORK LH 3.32 4.28 7.31 8.24
  8.35 8.39 9.17 VG 46.15

FORKFUL LH 8.15 8.17

FORKFULS LH 7.26 8.7

FORK-HANDLE LH 9.15

FORKS LH 7.17 15.18

FORLORN FO 165.4

FORLORNNESS CD 227.22

FORM LH 27.29 32.8 34.17
  TL 86.34 87.37 108.42
  FO 156.37 173.31 SM 10.13
  MD 178.2 201.35 VG 25.38

FORMED LH 7.7 TL 45.20 VG 65.8

FORMER SM 73.37

FORMS TL 87.36 87.39

FORMULA SM 30.39

FORRESTER SM 110.10

FORSAKE LH 36.2

FORSAKEN LH 21.42

FORTHCOMING CD 226.16 SM 115.37

FORTIES SM 94.40

FORTNIGHT LH 15.8 TL 44.4 83.5
  92.22 FO 131.18 SM 4.33
  122.10 130.14 134.8 139.28

FORTNIGHT'S TL 92.39

FORTUNATE CD 229.8

FORTUNATELY SM 109.17

FORTUNE TL 46.10 CD 207.20
  SM 16.29 104.39 VG 21.15
  22.13 41.42 55.16

FORTUNES LH 35.16 VG 19.42
  21.28

FORTY TL 49.41 70.19 CD 225.24
  226.33 264.15 SM 47.28 131.7
  VG 4.10 4.12 70.18

FORTY-FIVE SM 39.19

FORTY-ONE CD 202.8 SM 47.28

FORTY-SEVEN VG 3.31

FORWARD LH 3.14 6.13 9.17 15.5
  17.23 32.18 33.17 TL 45.16
  56.5 77.9 78.31 80.4 83.17
  87.12 93.23 95.30 103.31
  FO 120.20 121.2 121.25 125.25
  127.2 133.16 135.30 147.9
  149.6 152.39 155.38 168.3
  170.34 172.29 174.21
  CD 184.11 207.17 207.21
  227.10 227.12 236.4 239.7
  240.4 SM 11.25 19.14 52.30
  66.29 67.2 68.14 75.33 82.9
  83.28 84.5 MD 164.38 166.4
  167.28 167.31 171.5 188.7
  202.35 203.3 VG 19.15 21.18
  24.27 52.3

FORWARD-BULGING VG 7.7

FORWARDED TL 47.42

FORWARD-LEANING CD 238.21

FORWARD-LOOKING TL 87.19

FORWARD-PRESSING SM 75.29

FORWARD-REACHING FO 127.31

FORWARDS SM 97.27 VG 77.27

FORWARD-SWAYING MD 203.7

FOUGHT SM 24.24 32.3 95.8
  148.39 MD 164.8 183.26
  188.33

FOUL VG 5.27 29.41

FOUND LH 16.37 27.37 36.26
  38.3 TL 43.30 49.29 60.28
  62.18 64.26 72.38 73.32
  73.35 73.39 73.42 81.19
  102.21 107.23 FO 151.26
  CD 196.26 202.11 218.20
  220.7 223.40 226.36 229.22
  231.38 238.24 242.39
  246.16 255.41 SM 17.39
  35.34 54.1 75.18 79.5
  85.4 95.2 95.6 95.22
  109.9 109.23 112.4 126.20
  132.13 141.25 148.33
  157.34 MD 183.29 188.22
  188.23 190.12 193.22
  196.29 210.7 VG 3.13 43.23
  45.20 67.20 68.36 77.37
  78.12 80.30 80.36

FOUNDATIONS SM 107.8

FOUNDATION-STONE CD 196.6

FOUNDED SM 41.10

FOUNTAIN SM 53.6 54.25
  142.12 145.21

FOUNTAINS MD 181.33

FOUR LH 15.2 31.40 32.3
  33.32 39.17 TL 91.27
  FO 119.3 121.9 171.8
  172.23 CD 196.7 204.35
  205.41 218.36 254.30
  255.40 261.3 SM 19.23
  58.4 137.30 MD 187.19
  187.27 VG 10.30 21.34
  21.35 22.40 27.31 73.22

FOUR-FIFTHS FO 115.30

FOURS CD 255.7

FOURTH TL 50.26

FOWL FO 146.41 147.3
  CD 199.12

FOWLS FO 113.32 113.35 114.1
  114.18 114.26 114.38 115.7
  115.41 116.19 116.22 117.8
  123.29 124.18 124.23
  124.27 126.40 127.11

FOWLS (CONT.) FO 146.42 147.10
  SM 8.12 MD 163.19

FOX FO 115.11 115.19 115.40
  116.25 117.19 117.37 117.40
  118.19 118.22 118.32 118.36
  121.1 121.4 124.42 125.8
  126.28 126.33 128.13 136.12
  136.33 137.41 138.23 139.11
  139.12 139.14 139.26 139.35
  140.5 140.17 143.36 146.13
  146.14 146.20 146.37 146.40
  147.4 147.8 147.12 147.18
  147.33 148.13 148.14 148.19
  148.41 149.9 SM 63.25

FOXES TL 59.11 FO 115.17 146.21

FOXGLOVES SM 42.38 60.1 94.12

FOX-HUNTING SM 91.14

FOX'S FO 136.9 149.31

FOX-SKIN FO 148.10 166.23

FOXY FO 147.14

FRACTURED SM 121.39

FRAGILITY SM 147.14

FRAGMENTS TL 63.17 73.2
  MD 188.9 188.11 VG 67.27
  67.28

FRAGRANCE LH 21.12 22.15
  TL 43.22

FRAIL TL 44.8 44.30 93.13
  100.24 FO 137.33 141.18
  152.35 CD 214.19 214.21
  SM 137.38 MD 166.5 188.8
  188.20 VG 23.15 26.42

FRAILTY FO 155.32

FRAME TL 47.7 83.9

FRAMLEY VG 22.25 78.18 80.22

FRAMLEY (SEE ELLA, LOTTIE)

FRAMLEYS VG 8.5 9.42

FRAMLEYS' VG 70.35 80.35

FRANCE FO 121.11 126.16
  CD 231.23 SM 3.27 7.22 7.31
  126.14

FRANCESCA TL 104.13

FRANKNESS TL 86.9

FRANTIC FO 159.16 VG 29.19

FRANTICALLY LH 11.39 31.3
  SM 65.37 66.38 MD 164.15

FRAULEIN LH 6.8 10.37 11.8
  11.17 11.21 12.19 12.34
  12.39 14.34 16.2 16.9 19.32
  23.11 25.21 37.21 CD 200.21

FRAULEIN VON PRIELAU-CAROLATH
  CD 200.19

FREAK MD 163.22

FRECKLED LH 13.10

FRECKLES TL 79.41

FRED SM 52.23 66.19 66.20
  VG 11.11

FRED, UNCLE (SEE UNCLE FRED)

FRED EDWARDS SM 52.13

FREDERICK EDWARDS SM 51.27

FRED'S SM 52.37

FREE LH 20.16 TL 62.40 85.33
  90.20 90.21 90.24 90.26
  106.32 FO 129.32 151.25
  175.17 CD 207.37 212.41
  220.42 221.16 225.2 225.6
  SM 18.29 77.27 80.8 102.5
  129.26 MD 165.28 178.18
  190.16 193.19 VG 8.36 10.15
  16.11 29.2 74.9

FREE-BORN VG 61.28 64.13

FREED SM 73.12 73.14 MD 164.12

FREEDOM CD 223.36 223.39 223.40
  SM 73.11 73.14 73.18 93.11

FREELY TL 98.36

FREEMASONRY VG 53.5

FREE-MASONS TL 66.25

FREEZE TL 78.3

FRENCH SM 44.33 136.8 136.26
  VG 10.23 31.29

FRENCHMAN SM 7.32

FRENZIED SM 72.38 145.25
  MD 187.6

FRENZIES SM 76.3

FRENZY LH 33.30 CD 222.42
  243.25 245.29 SM 58.12 58.20
  58.22 145.32 MD 187.5
  VG 31.20 74.16

FRESH LH 21.41 38.24 TL 73.7
  FO 120.17 127.2 CD 187.20
  226.1 226.10 226.28 SM 33.2
  39.19 45.6 45.15 52.12 87.36
  104.16 104.20 121.7 MD 204.16
  208.2 VG 7.29 9.9 11.23
  11.34 14.5 24.13 29.42 30.1
  43.36

FRESH-FACED VG 8.34 21.29

FRET TL 104.36 SM 60.31
  MD 180.26

FRETFUL TL 82.14 82.29 99.42

FRETFUL (CONT.) 100.16
  FO 142.6 153.29

FRETFULLY TL 56.11 100.17
  FO 134.12 138.34 140.27
  153.35 157.16

FRETFULNESS FO 155.32

FRETTING FO 177.1 VG 80.12

FRICTION SM 137.13 VG 7.22
  66.19

FRICTIONAL FO 148.32

FRIDAY FO 150.21 SM 109.32
  VG 41.15 41.16 41.19
  70.4 70.15 70.19

FRIDAYS VG 38.39 46.33

FRIEND TL 43.19 49.29
  FO 118.7 CD 183.32 193.17
  194.19 207.13 212.20
  213.31 219.6 219.16
  228.2 236.33 SM 5.4
  MD 177.6

FRIENDLY LH 39.16 FO 114.25
  157.34 SM 21.36 21.37

FRIENDS TL 65.25 65.29
  65.31 65.32 65.36
  FO 115.25 153.25 CD 198.39
  199.10 199.26 199.28
  202.30 206.14 224.26
  265.32 SM 6.14 59.2
  88.8 92.25 93.35 122.17
  MD 177.15 VG 7.34 10.10
  10.29 12.33 15.13 61.13
  69.39

FRIEND'S FO 128.17

FRIENDSHIP SM 6.32 139.28
  VG 64.20

FRIENDSHIPS TL 44.27

FRIEZE MD 187.30 VG 20.20

FRIGHT FO 131.34

FRIGHTEN FO 139.24 145.39
  172.1 CD 193.37

FRIGHTENED TL 51.35 52.9
  52.34 57.40 76.5 77.20
  79.31 106.38 FO 138.21
  139.23 147.19 149.27
  155.19 155.20 163.23
  166.9 CD 189.30 189.32
  197.7 222.10 236.22
  239.32 242.8 254.15
  254.32 254.33 255.35
  256.9 SM 19.25 86.25
  103.28 103.29 149.26
  149.28 MD 170.18 170.21
  170.30 187.5 VG 62.18
  79.3

FRIGHTENING TL 66.24
  FO 163.28 CD 229.11 253.2
  SM 58.6 147.32 VG 21.17

FRIGHTENING (CONT.) VG 76.24

FRIGHTENS CD 193.38 SM 49.22

FRIGHTFUL CD 265.2

FRIGHTFULLY TL 90.32 SM 17.24
  66.1 138.22 VG 31.35 55.4
  55.15 55.28 61.2

FRINGE FO 174.5 SM 135.34

FRINGED MD 191.26

FRINGES MD 194.1 VG 46.17

FRITTERS MD 183.16

FROCK TL 46.30 FO 158.41
  CD 254.38 SM 39.23 VG 32.9
  32.19 54.12

FROCK-COAT CD 229.29

FROCKS CD 252.6 VG 39.35

FROG CD 244.35

FRONT LH 21.3 23.1 23.11 23.18
  25.9 TL 69.6 70.41 76.20
  97.33 FO 119.13 169.3
  CD 191.22 192.3 208.21 238.13
  238.34 239.35 243.16 257.38
  259.31 260.5 260.32 SM 24.14
  24.33 46.6 61.28 128.27
  134.33 138.17 138.23 139.4
  145.37 MD 167.26 187.27
  VG 15.28 25.38 36.34 48.29
  62.18 78.4

FRONTIER CD 232.16

FRONTING VG 7.21

FROST SM 143.30 MD 189.19
  VG 45.5 45.16

FROSTY FO 143.34 145.35
  VG 45.12

FROWN VG 50.24

FROWNED LH 6.18

FROZE TL 91.27 SM 143.14 VG 5.37

FROZEN FO 145.27 SM 143.22
  143.25 VG 45.10 59.7 60.31
  63.3 63.30 63.33

FRUIT VG 48.2 71.25

FRUIT-JUICE CD 245.20

FRUIT-TREES SM 37.37

FRUSTRATION TL 47.24 47.26
  SM 53.31

FUEL FO 168.23 SM 49.30

FULFIL TL 89.6 108.40

FULFILLED CD 215.25 MD 180.7
  181.13 208.37 209.5 209.7

FULFILLING FO 174.10

FULFILMENT SM 75.22 139.16

FULL LH 3.26 12.20 13.5 13.16
  22.18 22.30 23.20 25.2 33.38
  36.6 TL 44.21 46.42 50.30
  56.39 62.36 69.29 71.37
  74.22 77.8 107.26 107.32
  FO 116.16 116.19 123.8 124.42
  146.2 148.23 148.32 148.34
  152.34 165.6 CD 187.16 201.18
  201.37 211.3 214.24 219.9
  229.2 229.23 230.20 236.7
  238.19 239.22 241.35 242.22
  244.39 258.30 260.40 SM 5.13
  5.14 5.17 7.2 13.26 15.31
  28.7 31.25 38.5 49.34 54.4
  54.40 71.28 75.9 82.16 84.1
  101.17 102.8 103.33 104.10
  105.2 105.3 106.1 107.24
  109.25 111.32 128.17 136.3
  138.25 145.30 150.12
  MD 164.33 165.7 165.9 166.11
  166.20 183.2 200.28 201.18
  204.16 205.10 206.40 207.39
  208.2 208.4 208.9 208.11
  209.17 VG 3.5 7.25 16.23
  21.24 23.30 24.35 34.13 48.7
  48.8 70.6 70.7 71.19 72.12
  77.4 80.33

FULL-BOTTOM CD 229.28

FULL-GROWN SM 121.32

FULLNESS CD 230.28

FULL-OPEN TL 58.11

FULL-OPENED VG 48.10

FULL-SKIRTED CD 229.29

FULL-THROATED LH 26.19

FULLY LH 17.17 FO 125.4
  CD 257.30 SM 112.38 MD 172.7
  174.14 VG 38.33

FULNESS MD 207.4 208.16

FUMBLED LH 28.30 CD 197.23

FUMBLING LH 35.42 VG 32.32

FUMBLINGLY LH 24.32

FUME LH 33.7 CD 186.24 256.36
  SM 130.9 133.36

FUMED CD 248.5

FUMILY TL 60.30

FUMING CD 247.41 SM 116.21

FUN FO 162.34 162.37 162.38
  162.40 SM 27.11 27.36 40.17
  51.34 52.22 VG 55.6

FUNCTIONARY VG 10.40 11.2 11.3
  11.7

FUNCTIONS VG 9.39

FUND CD 231.38 VG 26.8

FUNERAL FO 157.16 157.18
  SM 37.29 37.30 85.5 85.7
  85.33 86.23 VG 80.37
  81.14

FUNERALS SM 28.17

FUNGOID VG 66.29

FUNGUS VG 65.21

FUNNY TL 62.8 81.22 91.21
  FO 127.18 CD 198.34 204.22
  238.15 SM 10.26 91.12
  107.11 112.10 112.17
  VG 6.24 53.36

FUR LH 4.26 12.37 FO 147.32
  147.33 148.34 149.25
  CD 247.23 SM 47.36 152.8
  VG 8.32 17.18 24.11 49.6
  49.7 53.14

FURIOUS FO 152.21 CD 229.14
  239.35

FURIOUSLY LH 7.12

FURNACE SM 102.3

FURNACES SM 102.2 102.21

FURNISHED VG 53.36

FURNISHINGS SM 119.13

FURNITURE TL 99.19 100.5
  CD 185.19 221.2 222.41
  223.4 223.22 SM 36.20
  118.37 VG 9.8 33.24 41.5
  53.38

FURROW TL 98.13

FURROWED CD 252.39

FURROWS TL 97.41

FURS TL 51.24 52.1 54.15
  83.6 83.11 83.19 CD 223.4

FURTHER TL 52.39 108.39
  FO 129.40 166.22 SM 75.25
  93.25 138.27 152.36 153.2
  MD 165.27 196.20

FURTIVE LH 26.37 SM 136.12
  136.35 137.6 VG 3.5 4.5

FURTIVELY LH 12.18 TL 47.29

FURTIVENESS SM 136.10

FURY LH 23.37 FO 152.20
  159.7 166.34 CD 248.41
  SM 24.28 35.13 35.19 36.6
  36.7 MD 201.5 VG 10.28
  34.19

FUSE VG 14.23

FUSED CD 254.42 255.1 255.2
  SM 94.20

FUSES   CD 255.2

FUSING   CD 253.13

FUSS   CD 231.36   SM 28.9   124.37
  VG 33.13   39.25   57.2

FUSSING   VG 33.17   34.1

FUSSY   VG 31.35

FUTILITY   SM 38.17   38.19

FUTURE   LH 35.26   TL 91.3   96.1
  103.41   104.1   104.4   FO 150.13
  155.15   CD 192.31   192.32
  192.33   192.37   192.41   219.14
  SM 4.10   VG 58.10   58.18

FUTURISITC   SM 113.15

FUZZY   CD 204.23

GABLE   FO 154.38

GABLES   FO 169.27

GAD   LH 31.38

GAILLARDIAS   SM 113.5

GAILY   CD 207.11   MD 181.18
  193.36

GAITERS   SM 38.31   119.8

GALLANT   SM 15.34   52.18   VG 40.31
  65.16

GALLANTLY   FO 113.21   VG 18.31

GALLANTRY   VG 16.25

GALLONS   VG 80.27

GALLOP   SM 24.16   36.35   36.36

GALLOPED   SM 36.30

GALLOPING   SM 20.30

GALVESTON TEXAS   SM 123.38

GAME   FO 144.7   SM 3.19   31.26
  52.36   70.15   70.17   70.39
  71.15   92.10   98.25   122.13
  VG 65.12   68.41   69.38

GAMECOCK   MD 163.2

GAMEKEEPER   TL 98.41

GAMEKEEPERS   SM 72.23

GAMINE   SM 4.18

GAOL   CD 215.34

GAP   LH 3.11   6.8   17.20   18.24
  20.38   FO 168.28   VG 76.28

GAPING   CD 215.16   MD 179.33
  VG 77.30

GARAGE   CD 240.27   260.4   260.29

GARDEN   LH 6.1   6.4   6.26
  TL 60.29   65.6   97.39   98.16
  98.21   FO 160.22   160.38   169.28
  CD 223.32   234.22   234.25
  234.28   235.13   236.38   266.2
  SM 28.25   35.7   37.24   37.36
  38.8   40.12   40.16   40.23   40.25
  42.24   42.32   45.36   112.40
  145.17   MD 168.19   172.21
  173.10   173.11   177.5   178.33
  180.3   185.29   186.20   198.15
  VG 70.10   70.21   71.19   71.25
  71.27   71.29   71.39   72.35
  72.39

GARDENER   TL 98.31   SM 45.33
  VG 15.36   36.3   71.28   72.11
  72.18   77.33   77.38   78.16

GARDENING   SM 37.39

GARDENS   TL 54.31   SM 59.17   128.6
  VG 39.38

GARGOYLE   CD 189.30   192.17   218.5

GARMENT   MD 207.16   VG 75.19

GARMENTS   VG 54.3

GAS   SM 91.16   144.34   VG 10.33

GASPED   LH 14.10

GASPING   VG 42.4

GATE   LH 21.3   25.4   FO 146.38
  169.21   169.26   169.39   170.8
  172.37   172.39   SM 36.10   63.23
  74.17   76.16   76.18   76.28
  76.34   92.2   102.14   102.16
  102.23   102.27   140.33   140.35
  VG 36.2   36.4   37.9   37.13
  37.22   39.7   54.39   67.5   77.37

GATES   CD 239.39   240.6   SM 21.31
  102.15   VG 17.33

GATEWAY   FO 146.24   146.33   146.35
  SM 147.21   147.22   MD 199.1

GATHER   FO 130.33   MD 188.13

GATHERED   LH 15.15   21.29   22.14
  TL 45.18   75.5   FO 131.14
  146.36   CD 214.24   256.33
  SM 42.9   152.2   MD 176.34   200.1
  200.6   206.2   VG 26.5

GATHERING   LH 13.33   TL 69.36
  72.34   82.42   FO 117.10
  SM 33.32   92.21   MD 197.7
  205.41

GATHERS   LH 32.12

GAUDY   LH 31.22   CD 233.12
  SM 51.24

GAUL   CD 228.39

GAUNT   TL 78.18   82.39   83.18
  85.38   86.5

GAY   CD 195.41   SM 98.10

GAZE   FO 114.23   128.42
  SM 17.5   84.9   VG 19.20
  35.37

GAZED   TL 105.39   FO 141.38
  174.26   175.3   CD 204.2
  244.3   SM 22.40   86.22
  91.25   123.1   155.22
  VG 13.23   24.39   37.15
  38.40   43.20   49.18   58.14
  59.20   74.37   77.4   78.5
  79.14

GAZING   CD 188.34   227.10
  SM 74.36   84.8   VG 19.18
  37.13   42.22

GEAR   SM 91.16   91.17   VG 17.40

GEESE   SM 8.12

GELD   SM 88.27   88.32   110.23

GELDING   SM 8.20   88.33

GELDINGS   SM 90.35

GENEALOGY   TL 96.38

GENERAL   TL 43.14   96.17
  SM 74.20

GENERALLY   SM 71.30

GENERATION   TL 43.33   SM 43.20
  45.3   96.6   96.11   96.22
  157.33   VG 16.17   65.4

GENERATIONS   LH 15.4   SM 76.1
  118.29   VG 15.35

GENEROSITY   TL 93.9   VG 29.4

GENEROUS   TL 108.1   108.2
  FO 115.26   SM 73.14   76.7
  VG 29.1   29.3

GENEROUSLY   TL 69.34   69.35

GENIAL   VG 12.38

GENIALLY   VG 35.4   35.32

GENIUS   CD 193.32   229.2

GENTIAN   CD 244.38

GENTIANS   CD 247.10

GENTILES   MD 182.27

GENTLE   LH 39.20   TL 47.34
  58.21   58.37   FO 171.28
  CD 221.1   SM 120.28   120.31
  MD 177.1   177.35   209.12

GENTLEMAN   CD 183.10   184.10
  193.30   197.19   197.39
  217.10   227.32   248.21
  SM 11.36   12.2   28.30   99.28
  99.31   125.33

GENTLEMEN   TL 44.35   CD 232.5

GENTLEMEN (CONT.) CD 256.5
  SM 31.23 VG 21.11 21.31

GENTLENESS FO 145.23 MD 169.33
  169.34

GENTLY LH 12.5 33.18 TL 76.33
  102.13 FO 125.29 130.28
  133.12 140.20 144.2 160.19
  163.22 164.19 174.11
  CD 190.19 211.28 SM 13.29
  146.12 MD 169.35 177.29
  201.23 205.17

GENUINE TL 43.23 67.16 93.14
  SM 27.35 53.26

GEOFFREY LH 3.35 4.2 4.8 4.14
  4.25 4.35 4.40 4.42 5.5
  5.17 5.37 6.4 6.12 6.24
  6.36 6.39 6.41 7.25 7.30
  7.38 8.4 8.10 8.13 8.18
  8.25 8.35 8.39 9.1 9.3 9.9
  9.27 9.28 9.32 10.2 10.19
  10.25 10.42 11.9 11.14 11.36
  12.6 12.11 12.17 12.31 13.16
  14.31 19.11 19.15 19.17
  19.22 19.36 20.3 20.6 20.14
  20.20 20.26 25.5 25.8 25.13
  25.31 25.38 26.26 26.40 28.3
  28.20 30.38 32.17 33.37
  34.10 34.14 34.21 35.3 36.28
  37.18 37.28 37.42 38.2 38.7
  38.16 38.19 38.33 38.34 38.37
  39.1 39.13 39.21 39.27

GEOFFREY'S LH 4.12 5.23 9.18
  9.30 12.8 27.25

GEOFFREY WOOKEY LH 34.31

GEORG TL 53.17

GEORGIAN SM 28.12 29.3 90.8

GERANIUMS CD 234.19 234.20

GERMAN LH 5.15 6.8 6.15 11.24
  26.19 39.22 TL 44.33 45.27
  51.26 57.17 CD 183.19 184.27
  196.29 198.39 198.40 199.10
  199.25 199.28 200.22 206.32
  209.32 210.25

GERMANICUS CD 215.40

GERMANS CD 233.8

GERMANY TL 61.6 74.14 92.9
  95.11 CD 225.5 229.13 231.23
  231.32 264.2 SM 71.16 71.17

GERONIMO TRUJILLO SM 7.26

GERRY VG 67.36

GERRY SOMERCOTES VG 8.5 10.7

GESTICULATING VG 72.21

GESTURE LH 12.35 17.11 TL 45.35
  FO 127.33 173.8 CD 231.10
  231.23 252.10 255.24
  MD 169.29 VG 19.36 28.15

GESTURES TL 44.37 VG 25.7

GETS LH 19.41 CD 204.27 205.1
  SM 42.9 42.10 48.6 122.1
  138.22

GETTING LH 7.29 8.12 11.7
  14.29 19.26 19.34 39.22
  TL 52.12 56.25 65.14 83.4
  FO 131.20 CD 198.35 254.28
  254.29 261.10 SM 17.27 24.8
  40.34 54.8 67.11 98.9 113.34
  114.24 124.36 131.16 132.23
  138.18 141.14 MD 178.19
  191.31 203.15 VG 9.26 12.5
  12.26 12.29 16.36 39.20 42.8
  44.7 46.4

GETTING-ON-FOR LH 20.23

GET-UP VG 49.19

GEWGAWS VG 40.28

GHASTLY LH 34.22 FO 176.40
  177.16 177.25 177.33 CD 214.6
  242.38 262.30 265.13 SM 27.12
  67.14 67.15 71.11 71.36
  VG 26.20 73.11 73.20

GHOST TL 45.18 78.29 97.32
  SM 21.33 118.27 MD 164.2
  186.16 203.38 VG 14.32 80.22

GHOST-CENTRED SM 151.9

GHOSTLIKE SM 67.38

GHOSTLY SM 118.26 118.27 118.35
  148.5 151.13 151.34 MD 176.33

GHOSTS SM 68.1 VG 78.24 80.23

GHOST-WHITE SM 141.32 148.8

GHOUL SM 70.38

GIANTS TL 98.7

GIE LH 17.28 38.13

GIFT TL 81.17 SM 25.27
  MD 177.36

GILDED MD 191.7

GILLS CD 255.16 255.18 255.20
  255.37

GIMLET SM 124.13

GIMLETS SM 123.2

GIN FO 168.9

GINGERLY CD 254.14 254.17
  254.24 SM 87.34 VG 79.14

GIPSIES VG 21.10 25.16 29.41
  41.26 41.42 43.22 70.2 70.37
  81.8

GIPSY SM 3.21 VG 19.17 19.32
  20.1 20.15 20.23 20.24 20.40
  21.1 21.5 21.35 22.7 22.11

GIPSY (CONT.) 22.22 22.27
  22.31 23.7 23.21 23.27
  24.15 24.18 24.23 24.35
  29.32 30.4 30.14 30.28
  30.34 30.36 37.37 37.40
  40.15 41.14 42.36 43.10
  43.22 45.29 46.11 46.35
  48.13 48.39 50.7 50.9
  50.12 50.15 50.25 50.29
  51.10 51.14 51.16 51.20
  52.1 52.7 52.42 53.6
  53.9 53.12 55.10 55.15
  55.16 55.42 56.3 59.16
  59.17 59.21 59.40 60.14
  60.25 64.31 66.31 66.36
  67.21 67.35 68.1 68.8
  68.38 69.16 70.31 71.1
  71.5 71.9 72.17 72.20
  72.29 72.36 72.40 73.30
  74.1 74.9 74.22 74.32
  74.36 77.10 77.36 78.17
  78.27 79.5 79.6 79.21
  79.35 80.14 80.38 80.40
  81.4

GIPSY'S VG 25.9 25.11 43.15
  52.21 70.40 73.4 80.6

GIRDLE TL 46.32 MD 206.3
  206.33

GIRDLED MD 188.20 202.39

GIRL LH 6.42 7.20 10.3
  10.34 12.42 13.23 13.27
  14.1 16.6 23.12 23.27
  23.39 24.7 25.37 29.13
  36.40 39.22 TL 46.28 47.1
  49.8 59.29 72.6 76.34
  77.26 81.18 105.24 108.23
  FO 120.21 161.5 165.30
  CD 207.6 208.32 224.35
  227.38 227.41 228.24 235.1
  235.19 235.24 235.28
  237.7 257.12 257.15 262.7
  SM 5.4 65.1 85.20 85.28
  85.41 86.14 86.24 86.27
  90.37 91.1 101.25 107.20
  121.7 MD 186.23 186.36
  187.15 188.40 189.1 195.40
  196.10 196.12 196.13
  VG 4.20 6.7 6.25 13.11
  27.29 29.27 55.24 56.38
  62.18 63.18

GIRLHOOD TL 52.18 SM 7.14

GIRLS LH 5.33 5.35 27.5
  TL 96.28 FO 113.1 113.17
  113.30 113.35 114.4 116.3
  119.4 119.11 119.18 119.29
  120.41 123.25 124.15
  124.30 127.18 127.25
  127.28 127.34 161.8 161.9
  168.1 169.33 171.12 171.15
  CD 225.39 226.10 SM 8.38
  28.9 47.5 52.11 59.10
  64.32 65.36 70.8 123.27
  157.33 MD 199.4 200.33
  VG 3.2 3.12 3.29 4.7
  5.23 5.26 7.6 7.24 8.32
  9.7 9.22 9.36 10.27 12.1
  12.32 12.42 15.10 15.14
  16.37 17.3 17.18 18.14
  20.9 20.28 21.12 21.14

GIRLS (CONT.) VG 21.34 22.18
  26.2 26.7 34.5 37.34 39.34
  40.19 44.32 80.35

GIRLS' VG 7.27

GIRL'S LH 7.4 FO 156.12

GIRL-SLAVES MD 200.31

GIRLS' FRIENDLIES VG 9.38

GIRLS' FRIENDLY VG 8.1

GIVEN LH 13.30 18.5 TL 54.13
  69.35 100.38 CD 215.37
  SM 45.38 112.39 MD 185.33
  189.26 202.29

GIVES LH 28.41 FO 174.29
  CD 203.2 210.9 SM 44.8 47.18
  61.11 91.21 104.19 104.20
  118.5 123.14 124.24

GIVING LH 13.18 TL 81.39
  FO 138.8 168.24 170.20
  CD 226.32 241.38 SM 36.23
  74.30 93.25 121.38 133.34
  MD 169.34 175.5 176.2 179.17
  VG 14.39 23.15 23.27

GLACIER CD 229.19 237.11 237.17
  239.3 240.19 243.38 247.7
  247.22 247.39 249.12 249.15
  250.35 252.26 252.33 253.5
  253.14 253.26 253.28 253.33
  253.41 254.17 256.19 256.23
  257.1 257.4

GLACIER HOTEL CD 244.26

GLACIER-PAW CD 248.37

GLACIER-PEAKS CD 230.22

GLACIERS CD 256.22 256.24

GLAD LH 3.29 10.19 11.1 13.31
  17.10 18.4 31.8 38.21
  TL 45.22 52.12 52.13 52.14
  65.33 73.17 77.11 77.13
  81.25 84.20 85.33 93.41
  FO 137.32 174.41 175.6 175.20
  176.42 177.3 178.9 CD 189.18
  249.5 253.19 253.21 256.27
  256.29 SM 21.29 38.15 42.23
  53.11 61.10 62.39 65.39
  91.21 95.8 111.20 111.29
  112.16 124.34 153.4 153.5
  155.25 MD 174.9 174.10 176.36
  196.6 204.2 VG 35.32 35.33

GLADE SM 59.37

GLADLY SM 84.22 MD 208.34

GLAMOROUS VG 5.31

GLAMOUR TL 98.11 CD 218.3 218.7
  253.26 SM 128.37 VG 5.35 5.36

GLANCE TL 76.41 FO 117.26
  CD 220.30 229.31 SM 3.14 7.30
  17.6 72.10 MD 171.26 175.21
  189.11 198.20 198.26 VG 50.6

GLANCE (CONT.) 71.16

GLANCED LH 4.3 8.14 18.42
  34.23 TL 77.6 79.10 87.10
  FO 116.33 122.41 143.3 143.5
  CD 187.1 187.20 189.39 220.8
  SM 15.22 33.24 34.2 59.22
  60.33 61.12 101.26 122.18
  MD 166.33 171.26 175.19
  193.35 194.31 196.34 199.17
  VG 51.9 66.14

GLANCES FO 124.38 SM 74.30 88.6
  88.10 135.33

GLANCING LH 12.18 TL 67.10
  83.17 94.40 FO 114.42 136.18
  138.4 157.42 164.4 CD 184.40
  SM 58.5 58.12 67.22 74.24
  76.30 MD 171.31 VG 68.19
  69.22 72.13

GLARE LH 3.9 33.7 SM 58.20
  102.1 VG 38.35

GLARED VG 25.19 73.23 74.23
  74.26

GLARING VG 58.36

GLARINGLY VG 43.20

GLASS TL 58.28 58.29 97.30
  FO 138.28 CD 228.32 231.12
  SM 29.24 29.27 29.36 29.38
  30.3 40.3 40.18 40.29 84.35
  MD 170.24 170.26 VG 25.35
  54.6 78.32

GLASSES VG 54.20

GLAUCOUS TL 46.42 SM 34.32

GLEAM LH 31.4 FO 129.3 CD 185.6
  201.21 SM 34.3 46.30 102.25
  119.11 MD 181.24 VG 70.11

GLEAMED SM 21.17 MD 175.33
  176.2

GLEAMING FO 129.1 SM 15.6 15.15
  15.16

GLEAMS CD 253.38 253.39
  MD 182.6

GLEE LH 14.11

GLIB SM 41.30 70.7

GLIBLY SM 41.25 42.19 70.7

GLIDED CD 261.14

GLIMMER SM 88.34 MD 211.15

GLIMPSE SM 68.28

GLINT LH 25.12 FO 127.23
  SM 7.36 11.19 20.16 32.31
  33.18 33.37 34.28 40.40
  42.15 77.17 80.36 VG 68.22
  74.8

GLINTED TL 58.12 58.28 SM 65.23

GLINTING SM 21.22

GLISTEN FO 121.2 SM 17.16
  MD 193.9

GLISTENED CD 201.21 201.41
  SM 146.15 MD 177.9

GLISTENING LH 7.18 FO 120.18
  CD 235.7 241.4

GLITTER LH 26.38 TL 98.18
  FO 129.3 SM 146.16

GLITTERED LH 30.9 CD 230.27
  SM 13.23 VG 49.21

GLITTERING LH 7.31 SM 60.4
  68.35 143.29 146.16

GLOAMING MD 183.8

GLOATED LH 26.42

GLOATING FO 141.41 CD 248.38

GLOBE TL 97.8

GLOOM TL 44.14 FO 119.10
  CD 240.32 257.9 SM 120.39
  VG 16.34 17.14 24.20 59.1

GLOOMY MD 164.19 VG 9.30
  18.6 32.22

GLORIA CD 226.32

GLORIED MD 185.21

GLORIOUS SM 17.13 MD 176.32

GLORIOUS WAR SM 29.24

GLORY TL 82.29 MD 182.30

GLOSS SM 13.33

GLOSSY LH 29.38 CD 187.27
  189.34 189.35 SM 66.15
  MD 172.6

GLOSSY-MANED SM 130.33

GLOVES CD 195.8 SM 44.41
  46.37 VG 44.37 46.40 49.7

GLOW LH 3.5 22.16 TL 74.2
  79.33 84.10 87.2 FO 119.28
  135.14 140.10 CD 217.6
  SM 78.17 MD 172.30 186.3
  189.15 190.10 195.14
  197.8 197.24 201.15 201.18
  201.36 206.34 207.16
  VG 5.32 76.15

GLOWED FO 122.1 CD 248.34
  SM 14.30 78.19

GLOWING LH 17.13 TL 72.26
  87.11 FO 117.28 170.32
  CD 249.2 249.30 250.38
  SM 12.33 14.34 26.34
  MD 171.15 189.4 203.22

GNASHING TL 63.20 FO 167.3

GOOSE   FO 174.1   VG 58.14

GORE   SM 154.41

GORGEOUS   SM 39.22   96.35
  VG 10.12

GORGEOUSNESS   CD 245.2

GORMIN   LH 29.20

GORSE   FO 145.41   154.32
  CD 222.26   222.27

GORSE-SHAGGY   FO 168.17

GOSPEL   MD 179.26

GOSSAMER   CD 192.13   VG 39.32

GOSSAMER-STRAYING   VG 65.7

GOSSIP   FO 123.8

GOSSIPING   VG 70.18

GOTHIC   CD 186.31

GOVERNESS   LH 5.40   11.23

GOVERNESSES   LH 13.42   CD 200.22
  200.23

GOVERNING   CD 230.39

GOVERNMENT   SM 3.36   34.12   34.20

GOVERNMENTAL   CD 232.11

GOVERNOR   CD 232.2

GOWN   MD 195.16

GOWNS   SM 7.6

GRABBED   VG 14.20

GRACE   VG 67.7

GRACEFUL   FO 114.9   129.35
  SM 22.2

GRACIOUS   CD 212.7   SM 28.41
  83.40   MD 191.5   VG 40.24

GRADUALLY   TL 100.30   CD 230.5
  SM 19.20   25.40   MD 206.2   206.3
  VG 7.6   77.20

GRAFIN ZU RASSENTLOW   CD 228.5

GRAIN   TL 87.16   SM 129.39
  MD 163.18   164.7   208.13   208.14

GRAINS   MD 188.2

GRAND   LH 27.20   FO 176.22   176.28
  CD 231.22   253.27   SM 3.5   8.31
  MD 197.26

GRAND-DUKE   CD 193.16

GRANDER   TL 77.33

GRANDEUR   TL 79.34   CD 239.16

GRANDFATHER   FO 113.15   120.9
  120.27   121.6   123.22

GRAND GESTE   CD 230.6   231.7

GRANDIOSE   SM 148.23

GRAND MONDE   SM 8.27

GRANDMOTHER   TL 96.23   SM 61.7

GRANGE   VG 10.1

GRANITE   SM 63.33

GRANNY   VG 4.8   4.14   5.26   6.9
  6.24   6.39   8.3   9.13   9.18
  10.35   10.38   10.42   11.24
  11.41   12.4   12.8   12.17   12.33
  12.37   13.7   13.10   13.18   13.19
  13.22   13.28   13.39   13.42
  14.15   14.35   14.41   15.9   15.16
  16.18   16.19   25.26   29.41
  30.23   31.27   32.27   33.19
  33.23   33.29   33.34   34.9   34.35
  34.40   35.1   35.5   35.19   39.22
  40.33   40.38   57.21   63.40
  63.42   64.18   65.19   65.40
  65.42   66.4   66.10   66.26   70.12
  71.33   71.38   72.5   73.32   74.5
  79.40

GRANNY'S   VG 6.27   7.25   11.21
  16.3   31.20   33.9   34.34   62.22
  64.8   78.7   80.36   81.14

GRANT   TL 87.40   SM 124.23

GRANTED   CD 251.2   SM 16.22
  MD 202.4

GRANTHAM   (SEE MARQUIS OF
  GRANTHAM)

GRAPE-LIKE   SM 45.14

GRAPES   SM 9.27   113.6

GRAPE-SHOT   SM 5.20

GRASP   LH 28.7   FO 160.7   177.24
  SM 54.16   MD 178.10

GRASPED   LH 14.7

GRASPING   MD 177.34

GRASS   LH 21.2   24.4   25.13   29.36
  36.30   FO 116.2   116.6   116.18
  139.14   169.42   174.35
  CD 243.14   247.13   247.17
  247.37   253.9   SM 66.12   129.17
  151.11   VG 16.38   17.7   17.10
  17.15   17.20   18.6   18.9   19.5
  36.4   36.32   37.18   70.24

GRASS-BANKED   VG 72.39

GRASSED   FO 169.28

GRASSES   CD 240.40   VG 20.36

GRASSHOPPER   CD 203.13

GRASSHOPPERS   SM 101.24

GRASSY   FO 154.31   169.22
  SM 38.10

GRATE   FO 135.40

GRATEFUL   TL 57.41   SM 118.7
  138.2   VG 69.11

GRATEFULLY   FO 126.12

GRATIFICATION   FO 126.16

GRATIFIED   CD 256.11   SM 41.37
  65.40

GRATITUDE   SM 4.14

GRAVE   LH 19.17   TL 54.31
  FO 124.37   125.32   157.10
  SM 85.8   85.34   VG 5.37
  79.42

GRAVELY   LH 24.20   38.30   39.21
  FO 137.24   137.26   137.29
  167.30

GRAVES   SM 86.29

GRAVESIDE   SM 28.20

GRAVESTONES   SM 28.16   92.21

GRAVEYARD   SM 87.10

GRAVITY   LH 38.28   TL 84.27
  FO 157.10

GRAVY   VG 58.14

GRAY   SM 88.38   MD 167.20
  179.3   185.27   186.28   191.13
  193.6   193.7   194.3   194.35
  199.7   202.16   203.40   208.23

GRAY-HAIRED   MD 198.16   199.15
  199.35

GRAZING   SM 141.1

GREASEWOOD   SM 133.38   154.33

GREASLEY   LH 15.5

GREATCOAT   VG 49.7

GREATER   TL 63.1   64.40   89.12
  89.13   89.19   89.26   FO 115.8
  CD 217.27   SM 43.11   48.14
  77.22   79.2   79.3   102.26
  119.26   MD 174.24   176.18
  177.41   178.5   178.17   178.24
  178.33   194.10   195.17
  195.19   200.12   200.13   201.8
  201.16   202.19

GREATEST   TL 101.20   CD 223.40
  259.25   SM 39.30   43.14
  95.18   MD 202.3

GREAT GOAT PAN   SM 53.38

GREAT GOD   SM 54.7   54.13
  54.38   54.39

GREAT GOD PAN   SM 53.38   54.2

GREATLY   TL 69.35

GREAT-ROOFED   TL 98.1

GREED   CD 245.7   MD 176.2   177.35
   178.3   VG 15.25

GREEDILY   LH 18.6   MD 171.41

GREEDY   CD 205.40   MD 178.1   178.6
   178.9   VG 29.17

GREEK   SM 19.34   19.35   MD 194.24
   194.25   203.9   205.26

GREEKS   SM 54.14   54.17

GREEN   LH 3.2   6.21   TL 60.5   66.2
   67.29   70.35   97.31   FO 115.4
   116.15   135.36   156.4   156.36
   169.40   CD 195.6   229.18   234.21
   234.24   238.8   253.38   SM 21.39
   22.25   39.25   57.8   60.13   66.13
   103.15   111.2   118.33   128.17
   128.18   128.20   147.36   151.6
   MD 163.19   168.20   170.8   170.26
   171.13   180.5   180.11   180.12
   194.4   199.26   208.7   209.16
   VG 6.37   6.41   14.22   14.33
   18.34   21.8   23.36   24.12   26.11
   26.19   30.16   38.3   39.35   45.31
   68.13   70.24   71.6   74.36

GREEN-AND-BLACK   VG 20.20

GREEN-BLUE   TL 46.42   47.28   58.10
   76.40   82.3   104.40

GREEN-GOLD   SM 17.14

GREENHALGH'S   LH 32.9   35.25

GREEN-HEAPED   MD 199.34

GREENISH   VG 77.2

GREENNESS   MD 167.3   167.21

GREEN-WHITE   VG 74.21

GREENY   CD 253.3

GREETED   SM 51.36   MD 182.14

GREETING   LH 6.28   6.32   CD 232.20
   241.38   243.6

GRENFEL   (SEE HENRY, MR., WILLIAM)

GREW   LH 20.5   27.23   28.7
   TL 51.33   51.36   FO 169.17
   177.2   CD 238.39   241.31
   SM 24.28   150.28   152.9
   MD 163.21   180.13   191.20
   206.19   VG 5.41   6.1   12.18
   37.41   73.8

GREY   LH 3.13   3.27   22.1   22.4
   26.33   36.18   TL 70.6   98.3
   98.17   FO 137.34   141.20   148.22
   148.24   CD 187.7   198.5   214.37
   237.20   238.7   243.20   244.17
   247.41   252.22   252.32   253.3
   253.16   255.15   257.9   263.12
   263.14   SM 5.17   6.17   7.7   7.8

GREY (CONT.)   8.20   8.31   10.41
   21.32   28.19   30.19   45.4   47.11
   47.25   55.13   59.34   60.2   60.19
   65.10   65.21   66.8   82.25   83.29
   84.2   91.39   125.23   126.7
   126.35   126.36   133.39   149.10
   150.6   150.37   VG 3.4   7.32
   8.31   8.32   9.25   18.12   18.38
   18.39   20.34   23.28   24.11
   36.18   46.2   49.42   54.14

GREY-AND-WHITE   VG 19.26

GREY-DEAD   CD 253.13

GREYER   VG 12.18

GREY-FACED   VG 4.12   9.14

GREY-GREEN   VG 29.13   29.19

GREYISH   FO 117.26   SM 151.11

GREYNESS   SM 127.3

GREYS   SM 63.21

GRIEF   TL 47.6   107.8   SM 75.13
   76.2   76.4   76.5   76.7   76.10
   MD 203.35   VG 3.32   81.11

GRIEFS   SM 79.2

GRIEVE   TL 104.35

GRIM   FO 149.15   SM 48.27   51.11
   77.15   77.20   128.11   146.1
   153.14   MD 164.30   VG 16.32
   36.8   37.8

GRIMACE   LH 16.38   TL 49.11
   SM 76.24

GRIMACING   TL 66.39

GRIMLY   LH 31.29   MD 164.35

GRIMNESS   SM 7.15   7.17

GRIN   CD 189.31   SM 54.23   56.5
   84.31   89.16

GRIND   LH 19.31

GRINDING   SM 50.34   105.40
   VG 39.12

GRINDSTONE   MD 198.14

GRINNED   SM 127.31

GRINNING   LH 13.5   CD 232.20
   237.11   SM 84.31

GRIP   FO 159.18   CD 254.19   254.30
   VG 73.4   77.14

GRIPPED   LH 24.4   27.30   33.29
   34.6   FO 160.1   VG 14.8   76.4

GRIPPING   LH 28.8

GRISELDA   CD 262.38   262.40

GRISLY   SM 92.21   MD 203.41

GRIT   SM 131.16

GRIZZLE   FO 174.28

GROAN   FO 121.21

GROANED   LH 10.40   CD 192.15

GROOM   TL 98.31   SM 8.17   9.13
   13.14   16.38   17.6   17.9
   18.16   19.24   19.29   20.13
   21.18   22.34   22.39   35.10
   43.28   58.17   61.29   80.1
   83.3   93.14   98.39   108.36
   110.26   122.22   123.7

GROOMED   VG 24.16

GROOMING   SM 17.11

GROOMS   SM 10.29   10.35   20.24
   22.31   23.2   32.16   110.26
   VG 51.34

GROOM'S   SM 21.6   45.4

GROOVE   MD 187.34

GROOVED   MD 191.32

GROPED   TL 79.42

GROPING   LH 31.9

GROSS   SM 119.12   VG 12.31

GROTESQUELY   CD 189.35   VG 47.2

GROUND   LH 15.17   TL 60.31
   92.38   FO 115.34   168.26
   169.35   170.29   171.20
   SM 24.37   53.8   59.18   66.38
   67.11   72.28   72.39   83.3
   101.18   103.19   154.34
   MD 166.15   209.2   VG 45.13
   45.29   47.9   78.12   79.12

GROUNDED   SM 41.13

GROUNDS   FO 165.27   165.31
   SM 37.25   52.17

GROUP   LH 12.18   FO 167.28
   172.27   CD 228.32   SM 28.21
   29.7   66.6   MD 200.6
   VG 21.23

GROUPED   CD 255.21   SM 20.32

GROUPS   SM 56.41   VG 16.33
   17.22

GROVE   FO 145.42   CD 247.14
   MD 185.14   200.17   VG 36.14

GROVELLING   LH 9.4   SM 157.3

GROVES   SM 66.12

GROW   TL 64.12   64.16   FO 146.2
   CD 247.16   256.21   SM 103.8
   110.1   120.31

GROWING   TL 84.2   98.25
   CD 187.7   SM 38.26   41.32

GROWING (CONT.) SM 83.7 99.8
   MD 167.39 206.11 210.23
   VG 5.41 20.36

GROWL VG 21.4

GROWLED LH 5.17

GROWLING FO 165.10

GROWN LH 5.36 24.14 36.17
   FO 156.5 CD 247.16 SM 8.25
   49.29 118.18 143.36 MD 170.20
   172.7

GROWS CD 256.21 MD 203.11

GRUBBY VG 28.19

GRUDGE TL 74.17 74.21 92.4

GRUESOME CD 252.24 252.31
   260.21 SM 28.23 131.5 VG 67.1
   67.39

GRUFF LH 27.34

GRUSS GOTT CD 242.41

GUARD LH 15.11 TL 44.16 69.19
   FO 115.42 SM 101.13 106.23
   134.26 146.12 146.22 VG 12.36

GUARDED SM 73.23

GUARDEDLY TL 54.15

GUARDIAN SM 145.38 145.39

GUARDING SM 109.3 134.25

GUESS FO 137.20 141.24

GUESSED VG 70.28

GUEST TL 61.11 92.20 CD 206.19
   MD 170.34

GUESTS SM 81.20

GUIDE CD 256.3 256.11 256.19
   SM 57.4 86.33

GUIDE-TRACK CD 254.1

GUILT VG 27.20

GUILTY CD 206.37 209.6 211.18
   SM 67.38 VG 13.5

GUINEA VG 28.39 28.42

GUINEAS CD 213.26 213.39 213.42

GUITAR CD 230.24

GULF LH 30.37 TL 99.3 FO 177.26
   177.29 177.42 CD 240.13
   241.20 241.30 248.39
   SM 128.35

GULF OF MEXICO SM 128.25

GULFS CD 255.18

GULLEY CD 241.35

GULLIES MD 186.1

GULLS FO 179.1

GULLY MD 191.19

GUM SM 146.5

GUN TL 57.30 FO 116.9 116.37
   117.19 117.29 117.33 117.37
   119.37 120.24 121.23 129.30
   129.42 130.31 139.14 143.11
   143.15 144.24 144.25 145.33
   145.34 146.5 146.26 146.31
   146.39 147.6 166.15 SM 106.40

GUN-METAL SM 9.24

GUNPOWDER SM 106.39

GUNS TL 57.38 96.14 FO 115.17
   115.42 127.26 CD 185.24

GUSHED SM 71.24

GUSHING SM 16.5

GUST VG 5.26

GUSTO LH 18.9 SM 70.32

GUSTS TL 102.40

GUTEN TAG CD 242.40

GUTS SM 105.41 VG 15.40

GUTTER CD 240.21 SM 75.34

GUTTERING SM 75.30

HA LH 11.18 13.40 TL 48.9
   CD 249.3 249.5

HA' LH 5.4 10.14 11.33 11.34
   28.16 36.19 VG 41.41

HABIT TL 94.8 99.27 SM 8.19
   98.26

HABITAT SM 137.22

HABITUAL SM 51.21

HACKING FO 168.25

HACKNEY SM 13.2

HADES TL 104.12 108.4

HADN'T LH 8.31 13.20 19.34
   TL 97.16 106.7 FO 121.9
   179.17 CD 186.19 210.13
   210.17 217.12 SM 23.15 47.4
   55.12 115.6 125.17 138.14

HA'E LH 4.9

HAEMORRHAGE SM 70.29

HAG VG 46.21

HAGGARD TL 44.24 76.26

HAGGARD-EYED VG 15.14

HA HA HA CD 183.35

HAIL SM 133.32 146.7 148.14

HAIR LH 13.5 16.23 18.27
   29.11 33.18 33.19 33.40
   38.25 38.40 TL 46.34
   46.35 51.8 51.36 53.38
   53.42 57.26 57.28 57.30
   58.12 58.27 59.26 61.37
   69.28 76.15 81.10 84.2
   89.31 94.34 103.28 103.31
   105.41 FO 114.13 116.9
   118.29 120.15 120.23
   120.31 122.15 134.6 134.7
   135.15 135.28 136.10
   137.33 138.4 141.19 142.35
   142.39 149.4 157.6 162.11
   168.38 169.15 170.17
   173.7 CD 185.5 187.7
   187.15 187.27 188.36
   189.35 190.7 193.10 195.9
   214.26 214.36 235.24
   235.38 241.10 241.31
   242.37 243.3 SM 7.7 7.33
   8.20 8.38 9.26 17.11
   17.32 17.35 18.5 18.17
   32.20 38.23 38.25 38.33
   39.1 42.29 43.36 44.10
   44.12 45.5 45.14 45.20
   45.25 46.6 46.12 46.40
   47.9 47.11 47.13 47.18
   47.20 47.24 47.35 87.36
   119.9 121.9 136.3 151.11
   MD 170.13 181.1 190.29
   193.4 196.35 204.27 VG 3.4
   3.34 7.7 7.30 12.25 24.16
   24.39 28.42 30.15 32.30
   32.39 43.27 46.2 46.36
   47.34 48.5 53.31 65.27
   74.2 74.3 74.10 75.10
   76.6 76.15 78.40 79.20
   79.25

HAIRLESS SM 21.13

HAIR-RAISING SM 150.19

HAIRS TL 45.39 FO 120.18
   121.2 129.3 CD 187.19

HAIR'S TL 70.6 FO 173.10
   VG 6.14

HAIR-SCISSORS SM 44.17

HAIRY CD 190.6 193.9 241.4
   244.37

HALF LH 17.28 19.32 23.34
   29.20 32.34 32.42 35.39
   39.8 TL 43.16 52.10 63.42
   75.38 75.41 76.3 76.10
   83.13 99.33 FO 116.10
   117.27 118.20 118.21
   118.23 122.18 154.14
   171.29 CD 187.34 189.35
   193.5 219.35 226.12 236.9
   251.33 254.37 255.5
   SM 12.6 29.12 35.4 54.14
   55.18 57.30 110.9 153.35
   156.38 158.1 159.14
   MD 186.7 210.15 VG 29.23
   29.24 29.29 31.25 34.32
   44.31 59.40 62.22 64.4

HALF (CONT.) VG 66.29 68.36
   70.10 70.32

HALF-ARTICULATE FO 133.9

HALF-ASHAMED TL 93.18

HALF-AUDIBLE VG 46.2

HALF-AVERTED FO 120.25 132.42

HALF-BITTERLY MD 191.11

HALF-BOTTLE SM 127.37

HALF-BREED SM 7.29 21.8 34.34
   41.22 88.14

HALF-CONDESCENDING VG 49.10

HALF-CONSCIOUSNESS MD 167.14

HALF-CREATED SM 152.34

HALF-CROWNS VG 24.41

HALF-DAY VG 31.36 70.20

HALF-DEPRAVED VG 34.9

HALF-DIVORCED VG 61.13

HALF-DROPPED SM 86.22

HALF-DRUNKEN SM 156.39

HALF-EUROPEAN SM 94.30

HALF-FORGOTTEN CD 231.12

HALF-FRENZIED SM 144.28

HALF-FRIEND SM 132.39

HALF-FRIGHTENED CD 189.18

HALF-GROWN VG 17.2

HALF-HAUGHTY TL 93.18

HALF-HEARTED CD 192.10

HALF-HESITANT VG 49.11

HALF-HIDDEN FO 129.33

HALF-HOLIDAY VG 45.5

HALF-HOUR MD 189.3

HALF-HUMOROUS SM 90.36

HALF-INDIAN SM 20.12 136.19

HALF-INVISIBLE FO 125.16

HALF-IRONIC FO 139.11

HALF-IRONICAL FO 123.42

HALF-ISLAND MD 191.25

HALF-LIGHT CD 220.10

HALF-LIT LH 29.35

HALF-MADE VG 32.19 34.31

HALF-MOCKING FO 129.29

HALF-MUSING FO 118.20

HALF-PAST CD 204.35 204.36
   204.38

HALF-REVEALED SM 12.11

HALF-SAD FO 123.42

HALF-SAVAGE SM 135.16

HALF-SECRETIVE SM 135.35

HALF-SEEING MD 171.27

HALF-SERVANT SM 132.39

HALF-SMILING TL 84.18

HALF-SNEERING VG 22.29 25.12

HALF-SORDID SM 153.33

HALF-SPENT SM 102.8

HALF-SUBMERGED LH 3.23

HALF-TOUCH CD 192.5

HALF-TRANCE TL 63.7

HALF-WAY LH 3.3 CD 241.19
   SM 18.39 19.4 20.5 110.8

HALF-WITTED SM 44.8

HALIFAX VG 60.10

HALL TL 76.19 77.4 CD 218.18
   SM 132.28 VG 73.30 73.33 74.4

HALLO CD 265.33

HALLOOING CD 265.32

HALLS CD 239.17

HALTER LH 23.10

HAM SM 44.25 VG 54.13

HAMLET VG 18.38

HAMMER TL 74.4 74.5 74.30
   74.39 VG 45.35 49.2 67.11
   71.2

HAMMERED VG 46.20

HAMMERING SM 154.23 VG 45.30
   45.38 46.8 50.7 50.22 50.23
   70.38

HAMMOCK CD 234.26 SM 43.10
   43.31

HAMPERS CD 248.16

HAMPSHIRE SM 125.25

HAMS SM 69.34 MD 197.28

HAND LH 4.32 6.28 6.29
   6.31 6.37 6.41 17.27
   20.1 22.12 29.37 31.3
   33.21 33.23 33.24 TL 49.9
   49.10 62.19 64.34 70.27
   71.30 73.4 75.14 75.16
   77.41 78.11 78.14 79.30
   82.4 82.6 85.41 88.26
   93.23 100.8 102.13 102.19
   103.31 106.36 106.37
   106.39 FO 113.34 120.20
   120.24 126.31 130.8 133.12
   135.32 139.1 140.10
   140.16 142.2 148.31 148.33
   148.35 148.38 148.41
   149.23 151.16 152.22
   155.21 160.7 160.30 168.15
   170.42 171.18 175.27
   176.39 CD 184.37 186.12
   187.18 187.26 189.40
   190.4 190.6 190.19 192.4
   192.8 192.16 197.25 201.27
   207.26 214.29 218.6 218.33
   227.6 227.7 227.18 227.26
   231.10 231.22 231.26
   232.27 234.5 254.37 255.16
   SM 11.26 11.29 13.23 13.29
   13.34 19.11 19.25 23.6
   42.26 59.40 61.32 78.10
   83.8 84.3 84.5 84.7 93.17
   95.16 95.26 95.35 96.39
   109.27 113.18 113.30
   117.39 MD 166.21 167.34
   177.7 185.23 190.16 192.37
   192.39 195.2 195.3 199.33
   204.10 204.11 205.33
   206.37 VG 6.28 7.25 12.30
   13.22 17.11 17.37 18.18
   19.36 21.16 22.4 22.8
   22.12 22.33 23.24 24.41
   25.10 30.23 37.42 47.40
   59.16 73.4 73.13 73.14
   74.7 74.14 75.31 76.40
   79.10

HAND-BARROW CD 248.15

HANDED CD 187.24 197.6 246.7
   266.13 VG 28.36

HANDFUL TL 54.25 CD 257.3
   SM 154.9 VG 50.11 68.37

HANDING SM 24.40 81.25

HANDIWORK SM 46.1

HANDKERCHIEF LH 7.2 7.10
   CD 213.20 256.34 VG 19.22
   20.22

HANDKERCHIEFS SM 28.22

HANDLE LH 8.40 FO 149.23
   SM 11.23 11.31 12.3
   VG 27.33

HANDLED SM 13.6 32.24

HANDLING TL 73.19 SM 130.12

HAND-PAINTED FO 135.38

HANDS LH 7.8 14.4 15.3
   21.31 23.41 27.30 32.36

HANDS (CONT.) LH 33.5 33.11
  33.17 39.11 39.14 TL 43.30
  57.27 57.28 57.31 57.32
  70.33 72.28 74.4 79.38 79.41
  81.34 81.35 81.37 83.30 89.5
  89.7 89.12 89.27 103.28
  107.40 FO 124.39 128.6 129.20
  129.31 131.38 134.8 136.14
  146.31 149.22 159.14 160.31
  161.21 163.15 171.1 174.36
  174.42 178.35 CD 183.8 184.38
  191.11 191.12 191.20 191.22
  191.24 191.26 191.31 205.7
  205.18 207.27 208.40 209.35
  212.15 212.16 215.19 215.27
  236.14 236.40 238.13 258.13
  SM 67.9 67.12 68.5 80.21
  83.5 91.23 93.28 96.1 101.5
  120.11 155.12 MD 165.11
  165.22 165.33 166.5 169.18
  170.32 173.15 174.24 187.3
  188.12 192.28 194.36 196.4
  196.21 201.27 205.15 211.12
  VG 11.8 11.14 16.14 30.17
  32.39 37.2 37.10 45.20 46.9
  46.11 46.19 46.37 46.39
  47.21 47.22 48.16 49.5 49.20
  49.39 73.34

HANDSOME LH 3.25 5.1 16.13
  TL 47.32 67.39 70.14 93.5
  FO 148.21 CD 184.11 184.42
  185.7 197.31 197.37 232.9
  235.12 237.9 237.30 238.35
  239.20 SM 3.12 4.4 7.7 10.3
  11.15 12.4 12.5 15.34 16.36
  18.3 18.36 27.26 34.7 45.7
  79.17 144.12 VG 3.5 19.17
  20.24 21.8 22.26 38.9 49.41
  51.18 51.22 54.24 62.19

HANDSOMELY LH 8.8 SM 11.17

HANDSOME-MOVING SM 22.10

HANDSOMENESS VG 65.16

HANDY LH 32.21

HANG LH 10.23 TL 74.22 CD 187.4
  246.23 SM 12.29 VG 8.7 30.41
  31.31 56.25

HANGED SM 71.23

HANGING FO 130.8 CD 240.40
  250.35 SM 24.37 45.14 58.31
  66.30 117.2 150.31 150.33
  151.24 152.3 MD 209.12
  VG 73.17

HANKY VG 80.1

HANNELE CD 183.1 183.6 183.16
  183.21 183.29 183.33 184.1
  184.3 184.17 184.20 184.28
  184.35 185.3 185.30 185.34
  186.3 186.4 186.8 186.13
  188.24 190.34 190.39 191.11
  193.16 193.22 193.28 193.33
  193.36 194.1 194.18 194.29
  194.34 195.15 195.25 195.36
  195.38 196.15 196.37 196.38
  197.5 197.20 197.30 197.34
  197.37 197.41 198.9 198.18

HANNELE (CONT.) 198.21 198.24
  200.33 201.2 201.5 201.9
  202.14 202.17 202.28 202.35
  203.11 204.17 204.23 205.9
  205.31 206.3 206.13 206.24
  206.28 206.31 206.34 207.3
  208.11 208.27 209.25 209.34
  209.35 210.21 210.30 210.35
  210.42 211.3 211.9 211.22
  211.30 212.15 212.22
  212.30 212.34 212.38
  212.42 213.3 213.18 213.26
  213.29 213.34 213.38 214.1
  214.14 214.18 214.31 215.10
  215.27 219.20 219.22 220.1
  220.32 221.4 221.15 221.32
  221.42 222.21 223.7 223.20
  223.24 223.26 223.37 224.2
  224.23 225.8 225.19 226.14
  226.18 228.17 230.16 230.37
  231.1 231.38 232.24 232.31
  233.25 235.17 235.30 235.37
  236.3 236.12 236.18 236.38
  237.10 237.14 237.37 238.32
  239.32 240.31 240.38 241.18
  241.42 242.41 243.10 243.15
  245.8 245.23 246.10 247.35
  248.2 248.11 248.27 248.30
  250.30 252.4 252.38 253.17
  254.31 255.35 255.39 256.8
  256.18 257.1 257.4 257.25
  260.12 260.22 260.30 261.2
  261.4 261.12 261.19 262.36
  262.42 263.8 263.20 264.19
  265.7 265.13 265.38 266.4

HANNELE'S CD 200.1 203.5 204.21
  214.12 216.23 220.17 235.22
  236.33 239.1 265.31

HANOVER LH 16.25

HAPPEN LH 18.18 TL 86.27 89.2
  FO 146.40 155.16 CD 194.31
  198.7 202.23 SM 5.22 13.16
  43.25 47.23 105.33 MD 168.14
  VG 34.38

HAPPENED LH 11.33 TL 46.5 68.20
  77.11 77.13 77.27 77.29
  92.37 106.42 FO 155.13 164.39
  CD 194.17 215.42 219.19
  220.15 220.16 224.18 SM 69.27
  80.20 82.38 86.5 145.6
  149.24 MD 198.8 VG 8.22 35.14
  62.4

HAPPENING TL 85.21 86.23
  FO 173.36 SM 27.17 VG 29.31
  57.36

HAPPENINGS SM 30.27

HAPPENS TL 86.24 91.33 FO 131.9
  151.30 SM 42.3 VG 33.31

HAPPIER CD 256.33 SM 115.9

HAPPILY SM 44.18

HAPPINESS FO 145.19 176.20
  176.37 177.13 177.18 177.19
  177.23 177.31 177.37 178.4
  178.11 CD 214.11 SM 26.23
  27.11 MD 196.5

HAPPY LH 20.13 TL 56.5 65.32
  73.12 73.13 73.16 73.21
  84.21 109.1 109.5
  FO 122.31 175.16 176.30
  176.41 177.1 177.6 177.11
  177.13 CD 196.30 208.22
  208.24 215.3 220.23 220.39
  220.40 223.31 226.25
  244.27 245.29 256.16
  SM 8.39 12.10 26.5 113.7
  114.36 132.40

HAPSBURG TL 89.23 92.10

HARBOUR SM 127.19 VG 8.40

HARD LH 19.1 23.40 28.8
  28.32 29.13 33.12 34.6
  34.13 36.7 TL 53.42 75.18
  78.5 78.22 98.28 104.41
  FO 168.27 171.27 171.39
  CD 199.41 200.9 200.12
  226.19 241.9 SM 12.25
  13.30 16.10 20.15 24.9
  39.24 42.38 73.18 74.36
  89.19 103.2 106.15 131.4
  136.3 143.30 146.9
  MD 163.8 163.18 175.16
  177.34 190.1 194.16 VG 9.6
  10.6 10.42 11.12 11.24
  22.8 22.12 23.19 23.31
  23.33 24.31 29.35 30.20
  36.23 45.5 63.33 65.10
  67.11 76.23

HARD-CLOTH FO 157.1

HARDEN TL 82.19 CD 192.22

HARDENED LH 33.33 VG 38.35
  52.22

HARDER CD 197.2 SM 147.15
  MD 196.22

HARDEST LH 9.27

HARD-LOOKING TL 94.19

HARDLY LH 4.24 TL 75.29 77.6
  91.37 FO 137.8 140.14
  143.16 170.21 CD 198.26
  203.28 204.1 205.4 206.29
  207.34 208.20 SM 16.24
  21.13 24.29 85.23 85.24
  87.14 94.26 117.6 117.39
  122.37 123.30 125.34
  127.14 135.14 135.15
  146.20 MD 166.10 VG 22.37
  34.39 63.17 64.36 81.2

HARD-NATURED VG 71.25

HARDNESS VG 9.34 23.15 65.8

HARDU HARDU HOR' AUF CD 234.39

HARE FO 131.16 VG 54.16 58.1

HAREBELLS CD 241.3 244.33
  247.25 253.7 SM 60.14
  65.31 151.17

HAREM SM 43.22 MD 164.26

HARK TL 74.33

HARM TL 86.12 FO 152.42
 CD 202.33 212.20 259.23
 SM 58.14 58.15 79.37
 MD 169.37 210.28 VG 13.7

HARMFUL TL 68.36

HARMLESS VG 16.6

HARMONY SM 29.19

HARNESS LH 26.35

HARP FO 162.29

HARRY FO 124.36 SM 52.25 52.26
 52.27 58.38 67.25 67.26
 67.29 93.21 109.28 113.32

HARRYING VG 66.40

HARSH-LONELY SM 151.39

HARSHLY TL 74.8 SM 136.32
 VG 48.35 71.17

HART VG 16.39

HARVEST LH 5.29 15.5 15.8
 15.13 24.25 SM 113.4

HARVESTERS SM 101.6 101.23

HARVEY SM 29.39

HASN'T FO 142.18 162.22 172.1
 CD 208.17 211.8 211.16 212.10
 225.24 SM 28.38 89.4 124.15
 VG 39.16

HAS RUN TL 47.41

HAST MD 183.29 209.14

HASTE FO 113.28 SM 127.37
 129.18 148.5

HASTEN MD 182.8

HASTENED CD 248.7 SM 65.29
 85.12 MD 177.1 179.5

HASTENING CD 247.31 260.30
 SM 148.5 MD 182.10

HASTILY LH 31.16 TL 56.17 56.34
 76.16 CD 201.33 SM 79.37
 82.19 106.24

HASTY TL 63.31 FO 155.14
 CD 200.35 217.15

HAT LH 6.27 6.31 8.26 18.28
 28.34 29.9 29.11 TL 83.21
 FO 120.20 127.32 134.5 134.6
 152.30 168.37 169.5 CD 183.25
 195.5 204.23 233.27 233.31
 233.37 236.21 238.42 248.8
 SM 8.20 35.38 38.32 39.22
 43.4 45.2 81.29 81.33 84.33
 84.37 84.38 85.10 119.4
 MD 186.28 190.23 190.24 192.1
 193.33 195.2 196.35 VG 24.12

HAT (CONT.) 47.33 48.41 49.1

HATBOX SM 119.3

HATCHET CD 224.6

HATE LH 5.5 TL 43.14 53.17
 53.18 55.30 62.38 74.23
 74.25 83.14 88.6 FO 144.25
 165.34 CD 210.27 242.20
 249.20 249.24 249.25 249.28
 249.29 SM 34.36 45.23 49.1
 62.14 115.2 119.40 120.36
 158.3 VG 5.24 5.26 6.41 7.21
 7.39 8.6 8.21 8.24 13.9
 16.21 26.19 27.24 30.3 30.37
 44.32 44.33 55.37 56.12
 58.20 62.11 63.30 65.24

HATED LH 11.2 13.11 19.32
 TL 47.19 56.12 69.2 83.32
 92.2 FO 179.13 CD 192.26
 227.15 240.7 241.28 242.1
 242.7 SM 5.21 24.29 35.17
 35.19 57.20 59.8 94.4 126.22
 126.35 MD 170.40 VG 6.24 6.28
 9.21 10.17 11.39 12.17 29.37
 30.11 65.23 65.32

HATEFUL TL 85.38 FO 144.36
 SM 155.16 VG 72.5

HATES SM 80.30 115.27

HATH MD 182.40

HATLESS LH 38.40

HATRED TL 92.26 SM 41.5 41.10
 41.13 80.37 115.1 152.36
 VG 29.18 30.12 61.19 65.24

HATS CD 238.8 238.10 238.15
 241.38 SM 119.2 VG 8.33

HAT'S GEREGNET WIE WAR DAS WETTER
 WARST+ CD 266.1

HAUGHTILY TL 60.23 CD 258.10
 MD 178.28

HAUGHTINESS TL 93.7 CD 210.26

HAUGHTY TL 59.30 60.15 91.16
 93.7 CD 211.42 232.21 250.10

HAULING SM 59.38

HAUNCHES SM 66.15

HAUNTED LH 22.12 SM 15.5 19.10
 72.35 78.17 MD 202.5 VG 27.19

HAUTEUR CD 232.22

HAVANA SM 114.20 127.8 127.19
 127.23 128.3 128.17 128.22

HAVEN'T LH 14.28 18.32 32.18
 35.17 FO 124.23 151.9 154.7
 160.6 167.34 CD 191.5 211.19
 211.20 222.1 249.3 257.29
 SM 12.29 46.5 46.27 105.6
 122.37 125.14 141.8 157.10
 VG 33.10 43.37 55.31 55.34

HAVEN'T (CONT.) 56.9

HAWK TL 74.12 SM 97.23

HAWKING VG 67.8

HAWKS SM 151.29

HAWTHORN FO 154.35

HAY LH 3.2 3.15 3.22 4.20
 5.14 5.29 7.17 7.30 7.33
 7.40 8.3 8.5 8.11 9.3
 10.7 11.33 12.19 15.5
 15.10 17.29 24.25 24.37
 25.17 26.35 26.41 29.26
 30.10 31.26 37.23 38.40
 FO 128.2 CD 237.19

HAY-MAKERS LH 3.15

HAYSTACK LH 17.31

HAZE LH 4.31 SM 60.19 134.9

HEAD LH 4.38 11.37 12.20
 12.31 14.4 16.3 16.12
 17.18 20.28 21.37 21.41
 23.42 30.1 30.8 33.37
 35.32 37.27 TL 53.26
 53.41 54.27 59.6 61.8
 71.36 80.17 85.9 88.14
 95.18 105.12 105.39
 FO 120.20 120.26 120.31
 120.42 121.2 123.2 125.25
 127.2 128.11 128.22 128.32
 128.33 128.36 132.5 133.13
 135.29 139.2 139.16 143.21
 145.26 145.28 148.13
 148.37 148.41 150.1 151.4
 155.38 165.28 168.3 168.37
 170.3 170.29 170.34 171.19
 174.6 CD 183.6 183.10
 189.2 189.36 190.8 191.16
 209.12 210.11 210.32 211.7
 215.1 216.33 222.32 227.10
 227.12 233.39 234.1 234.32
 236.2 236.14 237.20 238.32
 241.5 242.35 247.19 SM 5.7
 11.16 13.25 14.23 14.30
 14.41 18.9 18.12 19.13
 19.21 26.37 26.41 32.21
 38.2 38.23 38.33 44.4
 45.28 46.3 46.10 50.24
 53.3 53.5 66.36 67.13
 67.37 68.22 68.34 69.36
 75.1 75.3 75.8 79.13
 81.24 81.34 83.3 85.11
 88.29 89.27 90.11 90.12
 105.28 106.32 106.35
 155.37 MD 163.30 164.1
 165.39 171.6 181.3 181.19
 188.12 188.22 189.30
 189.36 191.9 197.23 198.1
 199.7 199.9 199.15 200.24
 VG 11.20 16.39 17.29 18.7
 18.16 19.15 19.27 21.6
 21.41 32.42 37.17 45.34
 50.26 56.11 69.19 69.28
 70.29 70.39 71.11 71.16
 72.30 73.9 74.2 75.19
 76.6 76.35 77.1

HEADLAND MD 198.33 199.14

HEADLIGHTS VG 25.19

HEADS TL 91.15 FO 119.29
  CD 241.37 SM 18.13 19.37
  104.33 MD 197.29 199.2
  199.27 200.4 VG 10.6 20.40

HEADWAY SM 114.12

HEAL CD 211.28 MD 180.40 197.20

HEALED MD 173.30 174.18 175.38
  179.33 180.25 180.29

HEALER MD 182.40

HEALING TL 51.2 MD 179.36
  196.11 196.14 204.25

HEALTH FO 121.36 176.19 SM 8.32
  95.13 97.32

HEALTH'S FO 113.10

HEALTHY SM 12.13 145.10

HEANOR VG 13.42

HEAP LH 4.30 11.32 12.19
  FO 173.41 CD 192.36 MD 199.41
  VG 77.29 79.22

HEAPED SM 65.25 71.20 MD 200.3
  VG 20.36

HEAPED-UP SM 128.33 VG 65.22

HEAP-LIKE MD 166.34

HEAPS VG 25.27 25.28

HEAR LH 9.12 9.35 22.37 25.27
  31.8 TL 45.35 48.3 51.31
  53.23 53.28 55.21 56.15
  66.21 67.2 72.33 74.38 76.23
  78.15 91.22 91.23 98.24
  98.37 100.26 100.29 102.23
  103.2 FO 116.23 129.28 137.20
  137.26 137.32 143.29 143.31
  143.32 143.38 143.40 145.21
  151.3 151.9 153.22 153.25
  171.23 CD 196.3 198.7 199.19
  206.35 215.2 263.8 SM 19.1
  19.30 27.1 49.9 74.40 81.33
  102.38 103.20 111.31 113.23
  121.25 122.6 MD 171.35 208.20
  VG 19.34 19.42 21.15 22.1
  22.5 61.13 70.28

HEARD LH 8.24 9.33 10.3 10.8
  10.11 10.19 11.10 11.14
  14.22 25.15 25.19 25.38
  25.39 30.39 33.6 36.37 37.3
  TL 44.28 54.11 66.6 71.19
  74.36 75.32 76.19 99.39
  100.2 107.23 FO 116.22 119.30
  119.32 121.9 121.27 126.24
  132.3 137.19 140.27 143.36
  146.6 147.22 151.7 153.28
  154.39 155.2 169.39 170.18
  170.37 170.39 173.23 173.36
  CD 184.25 186.40 187.4 189.40
  195.17 196.3 198.22 198.39
  199.23 199.26 199.36 201.9
  201.10 201.12 201.14 204.3

HEARD (CONT.) 209.19 216.34
  219.30 220.12 229.5 234.4
  236.9 264.8 SM 28.28 66.32
  66.33 91.27 116.2 MD 164.19
  169.1 171.22 174.14 175.9
  182.12 186.20 195.21 200.7
  201.21 205.19 210.31 210.33
  VG 11.25 17.27 28.10 30.42
  32.31 34.39 37.25 38.40
  40.20 45.27 48.37 49.4 50.36
  52.6 60.37 64.4 71.30 72.9
  72.16 72.28 73.28

HEARED LH 13.22

HEARING LH 6.35 FO 136.12
  CD 188.16 222.14 VG 10.42
  11.24 64.4 70.14

HEARS TL 74.32 VG 23.12

HEART LH 5.23 9.16 12.8 27.25
  27.27 38.21 TL 43.1 43.3
  43.32 44.26 45.38 47.2 49.28
  55.23 58.10 69.41 74.3 74.4
  74.25 74.29 75.33 78.3 78.12
  82.19 95.22 96.10 106.1
  107.21 108.7 108.9 FO 116.40
  117.36 131.7 147.41 153.11
  155.22 159.20 159.40 159.41
  160.1 160.3 160.5 160.6
  160.8 160.11 160.23 163.4
  163.8 165.23 173.8 173.12
  174.40 CD 189.6 216.40 230.26
  241.28 245.30 254.39 SM 14.16
  15.10 68.16 96.36 106.27
  112.10 114.39 141.9 141.22
  156.13 156.15 MD 175.40
  188.12 188.22 192.32 203.19
  207.23 209.33 VG 4.20 4.27
  5.7 7.8 12.11 14.23 19.16
  25.35 26.39 26.40 27.16
  29.34 30.3 30.6 30.37 47.37
  65.8 67.10 67.20 68.41 77.16
  81.10

HEART-BEAT TL 74.41

HEART-BREAKING CD 208.6
  SM 134.21

HEARTH FO 156.35 MD 168.39

HEARTILY LH 17.4 MD 164.18

HEARTLESSLY VG 21.19

HEARTS TL 108.7 108.9 CD 226.11
  241.28 SM 120.30 157.10
  VG 9.3

HEART'S VG 27.22 27.23

HEARTY LH 7.14 7.24

HEAT LH 3.18 4.31 8.12 15.26
  21.17 FO 135.16 SM 13.32
  36.27 72.39 81.10 104.19
  120.5 MD 189.29 VG 47.8

HEATED CD 185.18

HEATH MD 191.40 200.20 200.22

HEATHEN SM 105.39

HEATHER CD 222.26 SM 60.12
  63.32 66.12 66.23 67.1
  68.28

HEATHER-AND-BILBERRY-COVERED
  SM 28.2

HEATHER-COVERED SM 94.10

HEATHS MD 191.20

HEATH-TIPS MD 200.22

HEATS SM 138.23

HEAVE SM 126.10 VG 34.15
  74.4

HEAVED LH 33.38 SM 67.18
  VG 73.29 74.14 75.1

HEAVEN TL 70.11 71.22 83.37
  83.38 FO 116.23 144.16
  166.39 CD 213.12 214.18
  214.22 216.13 216.16
  216.21 226.40 255.34
  SM 23.37 53.12 71.22
  102.24 105.38 113.40
  131.23 148.14 151.30
  MD 176.32 182.28 182.36
  186.21 VG 4.40 7.1 18.34
  34.15 54.1 77.25

HEAVENS LH 21.26 CD 218.14
  259.23 SM 40.11 67.21
  149.31 VG 31.1 42.33

HEAVEN'S SM 5.24 131.30

HEAVILY LH 8.11 9.11 14.7
  26.27 27.28 SM 20.2 38.34
  78.24 85.5 94.34 MD 198.35
  VG 72.36

HEAVILY-JEWELLED CD 207.26

HEAVILY-LINED VG 49.40

HEAVINESS TL 82.11 FO 157.12
  161.23 SM 25.3

HEAVING TL 105.14 CD 255.27
  MD 186.10

HEAVY LH 4.2 4.15 21.15
  24.24 34.2 TL 46.34 46.40
  52.7 53.33 58.12 70.23
  70.26 70.27 76.38 88.29
  93.6 98.5 FO 114.29 119.1
  119.25 120.2 120.19 132.34
  134.1 160.11 CD 193.11
  197.16 205.38 218.32
  233.22 238.2 238.19 238.20
  238.21 239.40 242.38
  263.14 SM 37.1 63.38
  78.20 83.14 126.33 126.36
  134.1 148.16 152.8
  MD 165.23 165.25 VG 9.26
  18.34 21.39

HEAVY-LIDDED SM 7.8 45.3

HECTORING SM 107.5

HE'D LH 11.33 FO 139.29

HE'D (CONT.) FO 144.30 144.41
  154.21 CD 208.15 208.16
  226.12 SM 17.4 18.1 18.38
  33.4 33.6 42.21 45.25
  50.30 50.31 50.33 50.39
  76.40 78.36 89.14 112.11
  113.10 116.5 123.22 124.21
  VG 57.30

HEDGE LH 3.4 3.6 3.12 6.2 6.7
  15.16 18.24 21.1 21.10 21.15
  21.20 21.21 21.28 25.8 29.34
  36.29 FO 154.33 154.34
  VG 36.21

HEDGED SM 146.23

HEDGED-AND-FENCED SM 90.29

HEDGEROWS TL 98.11

HEDGES LH 36.17 TL 62.33 74.21
  97.41 98.17 98.18 98.20
  FO 135.23 146.13 SM 59.18
  VG 68.3

HEDGE-TOPS LH 3.20

HEED FO 167.9

HEEDING TL 55.38 VG 20.25 22.37

HEEDLESS MD 199.28 VG 42.11
  42.16

HEEL CD 254.19 255.8

HEELLESS CD 237.6

HEELS TL 92.37 FO 115.14 148.20
  165.28 CD 209.12 214.35
  215.14 232.4 237.7 239.22
  255.41 SM 131.28 VG 64.37

HEIFER FO 113.24 113.26 113.28

HEIFERS FO 113.23 123.29 124.27

HEIGHT TL 82.25 CD 220.29 239.6
  242.21 MD 186.1 VG 24.36
  25.10

HEIGHTS CD 252.35 SM 146.14
  VG 5.13 5.16

HEISS CD 236.11

HELD LH 5.32 6.28 23.41 27.11
  34.3 TL 46.31 73.3 75.14
  82.5 92.29 100.8 FO 116.24
  116.34 123.1 123.2 140.21
  140.36 144.4 151.16 160.31
  161.21 161.27 173.12 173.23
  179.25 CD 187.18 188.35
  197.15 230.38 252.39 253.9
  SM 6.21 36.27 61.32 66.39
  85.10 101.39 132.20 154.21
  MD 164.10 177.7 178.29 186.23
  190.29 203.31 VG 6.3 6.39
  22.8 51.41 64.30 73.10 73.15
  74.8 77.10 77.19

HELL TL 70.11 104.13 FO 166.39
  SM 36.5 105.4 VG 26.16

HE'LL TL 71.20 83.4 FO 118.15
  144.16 144.20 144.26 144.27
  144.41 145.7 SM 46.36 57.37
  79.36

HELLEBORE TL 83.10

HELLISH VG 6.41

HELLO LH 38.29 39.2 FO 119.36
  119.40 CD 186.42 201.28
  SM 74.23 121.10

HELLOA LH 15.33

HELMET CD 190.8

HELP LH 14.6 14.36 18.12 18.16
  24.41 25.5 35.26 38.2
  TL 49.4 49.7 58.6 59.32 74.3
  76.11 81.30 81.37 90.11
  FO 129.23 153.6 153.30 164.31
  169.36 CD 191.12 200.15
  204.28 208.22 208.42 215.2
  230.6 231.42 SM 17.25 26.15
  54.18 65.8 90.4 90.5 90.23
  113.26 122.4 138.32 MD 204.17
  VG 20.42 33.35 75.17

HELPED TL 95.37 FO 115.23
  129.29 133.42 SM 96.22
  MD 178.21 VG 9.37 14.28

HELPING LH 20.6 TL 49.7

HELPLESS LH 20.20 FO 132.33
  141.40 160.15 170.31 170.32
  174.32 CD 191.11 191.42
  225.15 SM 94.24 109.31
  MD 177.17 177.18 VG 15.11
  27.19 28.31

HELPLESSLY TL 101.24 FO 133.9

HELPLESSNESS TL 44.22 FO 175.3

HELPS TL 109.9

HELTER-SKELTER SM 150.5

HEM VG 75.14

HEN FO 114.20 SM 155.32
  MD 164.24 171.36 172.9

HENCE TL 92.36 SM 6.13 30.34

HENCEFORTH TL 75.18 90.9 92.12
  MD 179.38

HENCEFORWARD MD 174.35

HENRY LH 10.17 10.36 10.38
  11.28 12.9 12.22 12.31 12.36
  14.24 14.30 15.31 16.12
  17.14 17.19 17.29 17.42 18.7
  19.26 19.34 20.25 20.33
  FO 124.36 128.35 134.14
  138.21 138.27 138.35 139.22
  142.40 143.1 147.18 148.19
  148.39 149.8 150.4 152.12
  152.14 152.29 158.19 165.14
  167.21 167.29 168.10 170.8
  170.11 170.17 170.42 171.15
  172.17 172.21 172.42 SM 47.34

HENRY, SIR (SEE SIR HENRY)

HENRY GRENFEL FO 124.35

HENRY'S FO 157.31 SM 93.1
  155.28

HENS FO 115.12 MD 163.12
  163.23 163.31 163.34
  164.16 164.32 170.15
  171.41 182.2 182.7
  183.20 183.31

HEPBURN CD 237.10 237.32
  238.23 238.26 238.31
  238.33 238.41 239.39
  240.6 240.39 241.18
  241.28 242.39 243.9 244.27
  244.41 252.37 260.12
  260.20 260.31 261.4 261.12
  261.17

HEPBURN (SEE EVANGELINE, MRS.)

HEPBURN'S CD 237.36

HERALDIC TL 96.35

HERALD'S SM 150.24

HERBAGE MD 167.1

HERB HONEYSUCKLE SM 150.30

HERD CD 239.20

HERDS SM 37.29

HEREDITARY TL 89.3 89.22

HERE'S SM 94.1

HERMETIC TL 57.31

HERO CD 254.40 264.6
  SM 37.6 112.25 113.4

HEROES SM 19.36

HEROIC TL 50.12 58.2 SM 37.6
  77.27

HEROICALLY VG 20.14 80.18

HEROINE TL 84.15 CD 208.26
  208.27 208.31 208.38

HEROINES CD 257.16

HEROISM SM 77.22

HERRING CD 199.12

HERR REGIERUNGSRAT VON POLDI
  CD 229.6

HERS LH 33.23 TL 63.6 69.40
  107.30 CD 262.41 SM 8.10
  60.30 61.36 99.6 107.5
  124.13 MD 187.7 VG 23.19
  25.18 31.41 77.21

HESITANT SM 121.8

HESITATE CD 232.33 VG 38.15

HESITATED LH 22.15 FO 127.42
  CD 228.24 232.39 258.19
  SM 44.11 46.24 56.1 92.15
  98.5 106.25 134.18

HESITATING FO 155.39 MD 194.18

HESITATION FO 162.12 CD 254.14
  SM 46.18 MD 177.39 191.2

HESPERIDES SM 153.31

H. G. WELLS' SM 65.2

HIBERNATING VG 15.23

HICCUPING LH 11.13

HID LH 20.28 SM 14.22 14.39
  53.13 63.1 153.10 153.18
  MD 169.4 186.15 VG 6.20 15.19
  54.28

HIDDEN LH 5.18 TL 51.7 58.39
  FO 125.4 125.5 128.33 150.2
  CD 196.9 230.22 SM 54.23
  54.37 55.1 56.19 56.24
  129.11 139.14 140.15
  MD 186.25 189.30 199.28 207.1
  VG 19.8 20.37 24.25 56.4
  72.11

HIDE LH 10.7 FO 128.32 163.33
  SM 53.14 MD 168.12 207.18

HIDEOUS CD 241.27 243.11 257.8
  SM 72.39

HIDES TL 66.3

HIDING TL 77.11 MD 181.3 202.40
  206.35 207.7 VG 39.3

HIER CD 183.4

HIGH LH 3.4 3.19 3.24 4.33
  8.10 8.42 12.2 15.9 22.21
  25.5 TL 59.5 99.35 FO 119.2
  124.23 127.14 127.27 154.17
  169.13 169.23 169.31 178.39
  CD 186.26 201.7 216.27 220.26
  222.13 232.4 241.35 242.2
  242.8 242.13 242.29 247.20
  256.19 SM 8.2 21.34 32.19
  32.30 36.25 60.15 64.7 76.15
  80.36 90.28 102.9 132.16
  134.7 135.38 136.2 146.30
  151.34 154.37 MD 168.36
  174.31 175.2 185.26 185.28
  194.3 198.19 211.14 VG 12.24
  18.33 20.34 41.20 47.25
  50.33 71.29 76.30

HIGH-BONED SM 20.17 21.12 22.4

HIGH-BRED SM 12.27

HIGHBROW SM 9.19

HIGH-BROWED CD 245.16

HIGH-DRESSED CD 214.26

HIGHER TL 85.4 85.5 85.6
  CD 241.25 SM 63.13 63.15

HIGHER (CONT.) 73.24 90.8
  152.38 153.2 MD 180.5 185.33
  VG 28.14 65.41

HIGHEST CD 190.16 265.14

HIGH-LEGGED SM 129.15

HIGHLY LH 24.10 CD 228.34
  SM 95.31 VG 40.30

HIGH-PITCHED LH 12.13 TL 99.34

HIGH-ROAD CD 239.8 VG 77.35

HIGHWAY LH 23.17 SM 106.10

HILL LH 3.3 3.14 4.33 21.8
  23.14 23.16 23.17 23.40
  FO 146.7 154.36 SM 59.38
  63.32 100.34 MD 182.8 192.30
  193.29 VG 36.14 37.10 45.22
  74.34 79.16

HILLS LH 36.30 TL 54.29
  FO 115.37 CD 238.4 255.14
  SM 28.3 57.2 60.8 60.15 63.3
  63.25 64.5 64.20 64.22 64.35
  65.24 94.10 97.25 102.22
  141.13 144.36 149.2 MD 166.39
  185.13 192.9 200.14 209.11
  VG 8.30 9.29 18.18 45.10
  53.19 53.35

HILLSIDE LH 3.1 7.19 9.42

HILL-SIDE LH 22.26

HILLSIDES VG 36.18

HILL-SUMMIT VG 18.10

HIND SM 24.31 58.11

HINDER TL 84.9 CD 260.31

HINDQUARTERS CD 257.26 SM 90.13

HINT CD 209.31 209.32 219.14
  SM 26.30 VG 38.11 40.11

HIP FO 114.18 139.1 148.28
  MD 205.24

HIPPOLYTUS SM 19.36

HIPPOPOTAMUSES SM 150.15

HIPS FO 131.38 157.2 CD 234.33
  SM 18.4 MD 186.41 198.37
  VG 20.19 23.38 42.41 43.2
  43.10 43.12

HIRE FO 123.37 168.10

HIRED CD 234.17 SM 20.9 154.28
  VG 53.36

HISS LH 7.15 SM 124.11 124.18

HISSED TL 74.25 VG 29.15

HISSELF LH 11.34

HISSING FO 135.41 SM 146.6

HISSING (CONT.) VG 63.26
  74.6

HISTORY LH 16.24 TL 65.41
  FO 177.31 CD 231.37 231.41
  232.25 SM 63.29 65.2
  111.21

HIT LH 23.38 TL 74.26 74.30
  74.31 FO 169.10 169.11
  172.9 172.11 173.16 SM 6.7
  146.8 VG 44.26

HITCH FO 153.31 MD 164.14
  172.3

HITCHED VG 43.40

HITHER FO 117.4

HITS TL 74.31

HITTING FO 169.34 VG 26.32

HITTING-IN CD 255.8

HIVEFUL VG 15.32

HM LH 17.8 17.10 31.30
  FO 171.6 171.12 SM 10.21
  10.22

HMM SM 19.5

HM MM CD 211.6

HOARSE CD 243.35 244.31
  VG 37.25 52.5 73.36

HOARSELY VG 34.20 52.2

HOARY LH 22.16 34.35

HOAX FO 150.41 150.42

HOBBLING VG 47.32

HOBBY SM 142.19

HOCK SM 127.36

HODDEN MD 191.13

HOHENZOLLERN TL 89.22 92.9

HOLD LH 24.6 28.22 37.34
  TL 54.41 89.5 104.13
  FO 123.41 154.17 CD 193.31
  217.21 238.31 253.25
  SM 18.31 71.33 83.1 83.2
  86.29 103.2 105.6 110.22
  141.26 150.41 MD 172.34
  195.2 201.28 VG 12.41
  22.18 29.4 64.31 76.12

HOLDER CD 206.5

HOLDING LH 7.4 14.4 23.13
  28.31 33.8 33.24 37.33
  TL 77.40 93.23 95.28
  FO 125.25 147.24 147.27
  158.7 159.30 CD 186.17
  187.25 257.15 259.31
  SM 14.18 32.25 46.1 78.20
  99.26 113.17 MD 190.24

HOLDING (CONT.) MD 210.41
  VG 16.39 22.31 23.24 35.24
  50.29 76.4 80.19

HOLDS SM 158.35

HOLE FO 134.14 CD 217.7 233.15
  SM 65.21 MD 165.5 173.14

HOLES TL 59.11 CD 233.1
  SM 129.22 137.6 MD 204.11

HOLIDAY CD 237.28 238.5 245.35
  245.36 245.38 261.15 263.16
  VG 31.25

HOLIEST SM 116.2

HOLINESS SM 140.17 140.18

HOLLIES FO 145.42

HOLLIN' LH 8.16

HOLLOW LH 28.31 FO 115.36
  CD 231.32 248.13 250.33
  252.24 255.13 SM 6.18 18.35
  60.18 62.41 64.4 135.19
  MD 171.38 187.33 191.1 193.1
  193.4 194.2 198.10 198.12
  200.29

HOLLOWED MD 188.18

HOLLOWS FO 168.31 CD 199.37
  252.37 SM 141.32 142.34
  MD 170.14

HOLLOW-SOUNDING CD 240.32

HOLLY LH 36.36 37.18

HOLLY-BERRIES FO 156.1

HOLLY-BUSH SM 103.6

HOLY SM 139.11

HOMAGE MD 195.5 VG 4.36

HOME LH 15.2 16.26 20.31
  TL 43.32 55.13 70.1 74.41
  84.21 91.24 94.27 98.27
  100.42 FO 114.3 125.33 126.16
  130.1 131.4 131.8 134.23
  153.26 154.41 157.14
  CD 188.33 190.36 190.40
  205.35 207.18 207.22 207.34
  207.36 207.37 208.2 209.4
  212.31 235.20 235.38 260.1
  SM 3.22 10.10 14.22 21.26
  25.15 37.20 51.23 51.34 61.8
  61.10 61.14 61.17 61.40
  61.41 62.10 66.9 105.41
  133.12 133.13 145.13 152.12
  153.6 MD 163.10 163.16 170.30
  172.19 178.12 195.24 196.37
  197.11 208.1 VG 5.30 5.33
  7.24 10.19 31.19 31.24 54.39
  61.40 70.41 71.1 71.5 71.6
  71.7 71.9 80.22 80.36

HOME-COMING TL 82.9

HOMELY SM 132.26 VG 10.32 78.23

HOMESPUN MD 186.28

HOMESTEAD FO 115.9 117.8 154.37
  168.36 SM 141.20 141.29
  141.36

HONEST LH 29.12 SM 144.39
  VG 51.1 61.37 62.5

HONESTLY SM 16.30 16.32

HONESTY SM 156.36 VG 51.2 61.38
  61.42

HONEY TL 69.29

HONEYED SM 157.30

HONEYMOON TL 69.32 CD 214.34
  VG 50.32

HONEYSUCKLE, HERB (SEE HERB
  HONEYSUCKLE)

HONKED VG 19.25

HONOUR TL 64.40 87.38 93.26
  95.25 CD 262.34 262.40 263.17
  263.33 263.36 265.29 VG 40.28
  40.36

HONOURABLE TL 64.41

HONOURABLE LAURA RIDLEY SM 121.1

HONOURED CD 262.39 264.17
  264.24 VG 40.30

HONOURING CD 264.38 265.1

HONOURS CD 263.28 263.29

HOOD SM 138.15

HOOFS LH 21.4 SM 19.23 53.7
  58.31 66.34 69.33 69.37

HOOTING LH 14.22

HOPE LH 24.34 TL 48.5 48.8
  51.26 70.2 70.12 78.39 80.18
  84.22 85.30 90.38 94.29 95.7
  108.32 108.33 FO 115.35
  115.39 134.30 138.19 141.14
  152.41 152.42 153.1 163.40
  163.42 CD 195.39 204.6 204.32
  248.3 SM 17.23 34.18 79.20
  84.18 110.5 110.28 153.10
  154.26 MD 178.17 178.19
  188.38 206.30 VG 13.33 24.32
  44.34 53.8 61.42 81.17

HOPED LH 11.3 TL 46.22 48.13
  48.14 48.16 FO 155.10 155.15
  155.16 155.18 155.19 155.20
  164.26 CD 214.18 216.16 234.3

HOPELESS CD 200.30 244.15
  SM 78.1 145.4 155.19

HOPELESSNESS CD 230.36 230.40
  230.41 SM 78.2 155.26

HOPES SM 79.3 VG 81.20

HOPING TL 48.10 FO 137.27
  SM 156.11 VG 37.24

HORIZON FO 146.25 179.29
  CD 242.27 SM 146.39
  148.12 159.15

HORIZONS MD 206.10

HORIZONTAL LH 7.7 FO 169.22
  169.40 VG 47.6

HORLICKS VG 11.21 11.41

HORN TL 100.7 CD 239.42
  VG 19.13 19.25 19.31

HORNS SM 143.8 152.31
  VG 17.1

HORRIBLE TL 101.42 FO 148.7
  177.22 177.29 CD 194.15
  217.42 241.40 242.12
  243.13 253.24 SM 35.10
  66.32 79.38 122.11 149.38
  VG 12.24 28.1 31.20 55.36
  66.4 72.35 75.29 76.22
  76.29

HORRIBLY FO 174.15 CD 232.30
  VG 73.16

HORRID TL 68.27 CD 246.28
  SM 26.38 113.26 VG 5.11
  17.7

HORRIFIED TL 79.31 SM 35.11

HORRIFYING SM 9.4 69.31

HORROR TL 51.23 FO 174.6
  SM 67.8 67.22 70.3 70.4
  70.7 71.10 119.3 127.2
  128.32 146.24 MD 164.16
  VG 26.11 62.37 72.22 72.28
  78.5 79.21

HORRORS VG 63.22 63.23

HORSE LH 4.38 15.26 15.28
  20.38 21.14 23.3 23.26
  23.32 23.35 27.14
  CD 239.28 SM 3.14 9.22
  9.38 10.15 11.8 11.15
  11.27 12.10 12.19 12.27
  12.33 13.18 13.21 14.28
  14.34 15.1 15.5 15.25
  15.32 16.3 16.7 16.14
  16.29 16.39 17.6 17.12
  17.17 17.20 17.24 17.40
  19.12 20.3 20.14 20.28
  22.5 22.18 22.20 23.1
  23.20 23.22 23.39 24.29
  25.4 25.8 25.9 25.14
  25.24 31.40 32.2 32.5
  32.11 35.30 35.32 36.2
  36.11 36.28 36.37 37.6
  37.8 37.12 48.15 49.37
  55.3 55.34 57.28 58.1
  58.29 58.36 62.5 62.7
  62.21 66.27 66.31 66.34
  67.3 67.7 67.31 67.35
  68.3 68.21 68.26 69.34
  70.1 70.33 73.4 75.21
  75.28 75.33 75.36 75.38

HORSE (CONT.)   SM 76.2   76.9
76.12   76.19   76.39   77.8
77.9   77.10   79.24   80.4   80.7
80.19   80.23   80.26   82.12
83.12   83.14   89.24   91.7   91.8
93.4   93.17   102.28   102.33
106.9   108.33   108.35   111.19
117.17   121.29   122.25   123.15
123.20   123.28   123.36   123.39
124.27   130.12   VG 19.38   19.40
20.26   20.34   23.27   24.22
36.32   36.35   37.3   37.18   39.11
39.12   45.33   55.16   72.10
77.38   78.28   80.41

HORSEBACK   TL 54.28   SM 51.28
56.40   93.34

HORSE-BLANKET   SM 87.30

HORSE-DEALER'S   LH 32.9

HORSEMAN   SM 9.15

HORSEMEN   SM 8.37

HORSE-RAKING   LH 20.4

HORSE-RUG   LH 29.2

HORSES   LH 21.15   23.2   TL 98.12
CD 239.20   SM 8.11   8.15   8.41
10.28   12.40   14.8   16.24   16.36
19.35   21.20   21.28   24.12   28.2
32.7   32.8   32.24   57.23   57.24
57.31   60.3   60.11   62.13   63.20
63.39   65.30   76.33   82.26
82.29   101.2   112.7   121.37
123.23   129.34   141.1   144.30
149.25   152.30   156.17   VG 51.14
51.34   59.18   60.25

HORSE'S   SM 11.26   13.35   14.21
26.37   75.40   VG 45.32

HORSE-SHAPE   SM 21.1

HORSE-SHELTER   VG 70.39

HORSEWOMAN   SM 9.13   9.15

HORSEWOMEN   SM 8.37

HORSEY   LH 17.21

HORSY   SM 10.36   21.11   99.1

HOSE   CD 233.14

HOSPITABLE   FO 126.41

HOSPITAL   TL 44.8   44.15   46.3
51.4   51.21   54.7   56.34   59.39
CD 207.6   SM 44.13   47.19

HOSSES   LH 14.31

HOST   MD 173.7

HOSTESS   TL 94.23   CD 213.19
213.35   SM 7.9

HOSTESS'   SM 9.2

HOSTILE   LH 20.15   SM 44.5   44.11

HOSTILE (CONT.)   MD 198.31
VG 66.41

HOSTILITY   LH 19.25   CD 242.1
SM 12.12   115.33   MD 194.16
VG 67.18   67.39

HOSTS   TL 95.25   MD 184.7

HOT   LH 3.21   20.4   20.21   29.38
32.37   TL 57.6   99.10   FO 114.27
114.33   134.10   135.18   142.6
142.25   146.33   152.7   160.7
163.4   163.8   169.1   170.19
170.21   CD 204.13   204.31
222.26   237.12   238.25   248.28
252.5   252.28   253.36   SM 13.33
19.33   35.14   36.26   37.7   37.10
65.19   78.8   100.30   101.33
107.20   127.18   129.4   130.9
132.27   133.31   133.34   138.23
143.11   143.13   148.15
MD 170.11   177.24   182.1   209.10
VG 10.34   18.2   32.13   45.21
48.1   48.6   54.11

HOT-BLOODED   SM 146.3

HOTEL   CD 202.11   202.19   202.28
205.8   214.28   219.25   229.22
237.37   240.25   241.21   244.26
248.17   249.14   250.37   252.4
256.15   256.32   257.8   260.5
260.9   260.30   261.4   263.13
SM 6.16   23.35   47.2   106.13
109.15   116.40   125.21   127.31
128.39   132.26   VG 10.12   41.8

HOTEL D'ANGLETERRE   SM 127.32
128.23

HOTELS   CD 230.27   233.9   233.18
243.29   247.11   252.14
SM 128.15

HOT-HOUSE   TL 46.36   87.9   94.37
95.17   95.20

HOT-WATER   FO 158.12

HOUND   VG 21.3   21.27

HOUNDS   SM 63.26

HOUR   LH 21.33   22.27   39.8
TL 48.25   75.38   75.41   76.3
76.10   CD 251.33   SM 29.27
93.12   119.18   147.39   MD 165.3
173.3   201.13   201.20   207.28
208.29

HOUR-GLASS   SM 97.7

HOURS   LH 22.27   TL 55.37   98.6
101.16   FO 114.29   115.18
135.21   171.7   CD 198.22
SM 97.8   101.3   111.29
MD 196.24   VG 58.7   60.28

HOURS'   FO 167.15   167.32
CD 219.10

HOUSE   LH 7.2   TL 45.6   61.8
61.11   70.10   75.10   91.39
92.25   93.27   96.20   97.22   98.1

HOUSE (CONT.)   100.20
FO 126.26   126.39   127.17
129.15   133.35   136.13
136.34   144.10   144.17
153.12   160.37   169.27
CD 190.35   218.16   222.41
224.39   225.1   226.31   237.8
239.42   243.36   260.9
SM 6.2   6.13   7.14   10.25
10.32   28.12   29.3   29.4
35.27   37.25   37.34   42.27
45.33   73.1   74.3   87.8
87.9   90.8   105.29   112.21
117.22   118.22   118.41
125.6   126.7   131.38   142.9
145.38   153.6   MD 168.12
170.3   170.29   173.26
175.32   176.1   176.36
176.41   179.29   193.39
196.39   200.36   210.16
VG 3.21   3.30   4.10   4.11
4.33   6.3   9.7   12.19   12.33
16.6   17.16   17.20   24.17
29.33   30.5   33.22   33.35
34.8   35.13   35.14   36.2
36.16   36.20   37.8   37.22
53.34   54.37   54.41   66.4
66.8   66.13   66.36   71.15
71.27   72.37   72.40   73.29
73.42   74.12   74.20   74.34
74.41   75.1   75.12   75.35
76.23   77.27   77.36   78.2
78.17   78.24   78.29   79.12
79.15   79.28   80.9

HOUSE-BRED   SM 80.37

HOUSED   FO 114.1

HOUSE-DOG   VG 43.26   43.31

HOUSE-DOGS   VG 43.35

HOUSEHOLD   SM 45.38   109.31
VG 53.36   66.20   67.40

HOUSE-INBRED   SM 80.38

HOUSEKEEPER   TL 72.7   SM 118.23
121.1

HOUSEKEEPING   CD 264.38   265.2

HOUSEMAID   LH 32.10   VG 37.28
78.10

HOUSE-MAID   LH 39.23

HOUSEMAID'S   VG 70.20

HOUSE OF LORDS   TL 43.20

HOUSE-PARTY   SM 52.10

HOUSE-PLACES   CD 243.33

HOUSES   TL 62.29   62.32
FO 128.3   146.22   CD 186.23
221.2   239.11   239.15   239.16
SM 142.6   147.17   147.37
VG 10.3   29.36   36.23

HOUSE-SHOES   FO 119.19

HOUSEWORK   VG 53.35   55.4

HOVERED   TL 87.17

HOVERING   LH 26.39   SM 67.23
   113.1   MD 173.12

HOWARDS   TL 48.24

HOWLED   CD 201.15   SM 143.34
   MD 206.1

HOWLING   TL 67.42   92.28   FO 167.3
   MD 205.29

HOW'S   SM 113.18

HUBBUB   SM 102.25

HUDDLE   MD 172.5

HUDDLED   TL 51.15   101.27
   FO 174.18   CD 236.36

HUG   FO 153.20

HUGE   LH 34.34   TL 100.28
   FO 154.34   156.28   CD 185.1
   185.20   204.24   205.21   233.7
   239.10   240.17   240.25   241.30
   241.37   252.7   252.29   253.13
   254.7   255.6   255.16   257.12
   257.37   260.8   261.5   MD 199.25
   VG 17.16   58.14   76.21

HUGER   SM 153.14

HUGGED   SM 135.36   MD 187.1   192.5

HUGGING   SM 88.4

HULKING   LH 4.2

HULLABALOO   FO 146.15

HULLO   LH 17.19   TL 77.8

HUM   MD 185.7

HUMAN   TL 43.10   54.32   86.37
   88.5   102.36   103.4   FO 177.11
   CD 189.9   203.14   209.22   223.23
   224.8   225.32   230.33   231.40
   240.7   240.9   254.10   SM 12.25
   14.40   20.5   30.33   30.35   47.38
   48.33   50.21   50.27   50.38   73.3
   74.20   74.21   75.16   80.38
   87.19   102.12   102.25   117.38
   119.27   139.33   153.6   154.24
   MD 194.11   VG 16.35   64.39
   65.38

HUMANITARIANISM   SM 90.17

HUMANITY   TL 43.9   54.6   93.13
   MD 168.5   168.6   VG 64.40

HUMANIZED   SM 102.11

HUMANS   MD 164.13

HUMBLE   SM 50.6   53.25   108.26
   136.34   MD 177.25   177.30
   VG 22.29

HUMBLY   LH 28.26   31.8   35.38
   SM 108.31

HUMILIATE   TL 92.31

HUMILIATED   VG 27.35

HUMILIATING   VG 28.16

HUMILIATION   SM 139.35   MD 177.18

HUMILITY   TL 82.19   82.20
   SM 135.32   135.37   MD 192.19

HUMMED   CD 211.6   MD 190.21
   VG 11.16   39.38   56.23

HUMMING   MD 176.3   190.21   201.21

HUMMING-BIRDS   SM 151.24

HUMMOCK-MOUNDS   SM 134.10

HUMMOCKS   SM 146.36

HUMOROUS   VG 61.1   61.5

HUMOROUSLY   VG 28.41

HUMOUR   FO 162.26   SM 113.33

HUMP   SM 49.31

HUMP-BACKED   VG 6.23

HUMPED   MD 186.14   191.6   198.33

HUNCHED   LH 30.10

HUNDRED   TL 61.40   CD 228.27
   SM 127.24   143.37

HUNDRED AND SIXTY   SM 141.21

HUNDRED PER CENT   SM 21.30

HUNDREDS   TL 89.1   CD 241.1

HUNG   LH 28.37   TL 76.4   105.42
   FO 127.32   140.21   141.20
   148.19   164.38   CD 185.24   190.2
   196.19   215.38   227.27   241.3
   241.19   247.26   248.38   SM 38.12
   126.28   142.15   VG 17.42   21.30
   35.35   37.42   43.2   47.6   71.25
   71.27

HUNGARIAN   CD 245.9   245.34

HUNGARY   TL 55.12   55.15   96.19
   96.23   CD 232.16

HUNGRY   SM 101.9

HUNK   LH 19.12

HUNTED   FO 148.8   SM 52.35   63.24

HUNTER   TL 102.28   FO 130.41
   131.12   SM 52.31

HUNTERS   SM 123.24

HUNTING   FO 130.35   130.38
   CD 260.2   SM 63.24   113.24

HUNT'S HILL   LH 35.36

HUNTSMAN   FO 131.11   173.3

HUP   SM 127.30

HURRIED   TL 64.22   94.35
   101.24   CD 256.10   SM 80.40
   116.14   MD 194.28

HURRIEDLY   TL 79.8   80.4
   94.38   SM 46.26   121.3

HURRY   LH 13.29   13.33   18.40
   TL 93.17   FO 133.38
   CD 206.17   248.4   SM 73.1
   148.17

HURRYING   FO 134.8   CD 248.15
   257.3   MD 168.19   VG 45.16

HURST PLACE   TL 44.16   48.32
   49.30   50.39   60.28   64.26

HURT   LH 6.14   10.24   12.29
   13.15   28.8   35.13   TL 45.23
   57.29   108.1   FO 132.16
   145.17   162.28   165.34
   CD 202.32   259.24   SM 42.11
   86.20   100.36   100.38   103.9
   104.9   107.13   117.37   120.26
   153.9   155.39   158.36
   MD 165.7   165.9   166.17
   201.17   203.30   204.30
   207.33   209.28   VG 29.27
   29.28   29.29   52.40   76.19

HURTS   TL 50.6   SM 42.10
   86.20   144.32

HUSBAND   LH 28.1   28.18   31.28
   31.36   TL 44.13   46.25
   47.17   47.18   48.17   50.42
   56.2   58.19   68.17   68.39
   69.23   69.30   69.31   69.36
   69.37   69.42   70.21   70.28
   70.36   72.15   75.19   75.29
   82.16   82.39   83.6   83.28
   85.13   85.20   85.38   87.11
   87.15   87.25   88.26   88.29
   91.32   92.4   99.7   100.18
   100.42   102.32   106.18
   107.42   FO 169.32   CD 204.27
   204.34   204.36   204.39
   205.39   206.41   207.14
   208.14   209.3   210.28   210.40
   212.23   213.14   213.24   214.3
   214.4   214.6   215.12   215.30
   216.12   216.19   217.19
   217.28   217.39   218.8   218.10
   219.30   247.33   248.9   262.40
   263.2   263.38   SM 6.34   19.2
   31.13   34.33   51.27   79.14
   80.16   83.23   91.6   94.32
   137.41   149.18   VG 3.4   21.20
   22.42   49.23   53.26   54.22
   66.27

HUSBANDS   TL 90.35   CD 215.7
   215.8

HUSBAND'S   TL 68.40   71.13
   86.2   SM 35.3

HUSH   VG 4.19   4.27   5.10

HUSHED   CD 199.42   SM 110.1

HUSHED (CONT.) SM 112.34 113.29
    VG 42.38

HUT LH 26.28 26.31 26.34 38.23
    38.37

HUTS FO 167.18

HYDE PARK TL 46.7 SM 121.37

HYDE PARK CORNER SM 9.11 21.29

HYPERSENSITIVE LH 19.37 TL 69.17

HYPNOTIC SM 123.11 123.12

HYPNOTIZES SM 123.15

HYPOCRITE VG 29.16

HYPOTHETICAL CD 199.13

HYSTERIA FO 133.18

HYSTERICAL CD 197.11

HYSTERICS VG 29.20 80.23

I' LH 38.10

ICE LH 33.13 FO 145.10
    CD 244.14 244.29 244.30
    244.34 244.36 244.42 247.22
    249.27 252.27 252.30 252.34
    252.35 252.39 253.3 253.10
    253.11 253.28 253.33 253.34
    253.35 254.2 254.5 254.9
    254.11 254.13 254.15 254.18
    254.25 254.27 254.41 254.42
    255.6 255.12 255.13 255.14
    255.16 255.17 255.22 255.25
    255.27 255.32 255.36 255.39
    256.5 256.10 256.12 256.17
    256.25 SM 133.32 148.15
    VG 41.33 50.21

ICE-BEAR TL 66.3 CD 252.34

ICE-BEARS TL 58.37

ICEBERGS SM 147.27

ICE-BITTER CD 248.41

ICE-BLACK CD 248.5

ICE-CAULDRON CD 247.42

ICE-CHINK CD 253.8

ICE-CREAM SM 136.17 136.41

ICE-CREAMS SM 44.21

ICED SM 40.31

ICE-DARK SM 151.17

ICE-METALLIC CD 253.7

ICE-RAINS CD 249.32

ICE-ROOTS CD 243.22 243.23

ICE-SLOPE CD 254.4 254.21

ICE-THREADS FO 149.4

ICE-WATER CD 239.4 240.33
    SM 128.40

ICE-WORLD CD 256.12

ICH BIN KLEIN MEIN HERZ IST REIN
    LH 5.10

ICILY CD 247.42

ICY TL 54.40 75.37 FO 173.23
    CD 245.8 247.25 VG 34.17 58.2
    73.3

I'D LH 10.14 20.30 TL 65.3
    71.9 77.30 77.38 FO 125.18
    125.24 145.8 153.19 153.20
    153.21 161.1 CD 209.30 249.26
    262.42 SM 24.5 33.6 37.14
    92.5 109.20 113.31 121.19
    VG 68.31

IDEA LH 11.40 TL 68.26 83.13
    90.18 FO 130.12 130.21 150.40
    151.31 167.14 167.19
    CD 202.35 210.3 SM 50.3 62.37
    78.22 123.19 136.19 156.7
    157.1 VG 41.22 41.30 61.41
    67.16

IDEAL CD 207.14 SM 71.4 71.7
    71.11 142.19

IDEALISTIC TL 85.38 SM 127.6

IDEALIZED SM 116.18

IDEAS TL 105.26

IDENTIFIED FO 124.42

IDENTITY TL 87.16

IDIOT CD 215.16 VG 6.23 37.27

IDOL MD 203.33 204.1 VG 12.34

IDOLS SM 105.38

IGNOBILITY SM 76.1

IGNOBLE SM 75.18 76.8

IGNOMINY VG 7.19

IGNORANCE SM 41.36

IGNORED LH 18.31 TL 87.5
    SM 30.13 82.14 101.19
    VG 69.17

IGNORING SM 151.30

ILL TL 43.16 44.12 46.27 47.25
    49.34 49.41 50.6 56.8 56.9
    56.13 56.17 70.37 82.9 82.29
    FO 135.17 CD 220.26 SM 4.31
    6.29 29.8 110.38 115.21
    125.16 VG 3.14

I'LL LH 10.41 15.42 20.28
    28.25 30.16 35.21 36.22
    36.24 TL 62.16 81.16 83.3

I'LL (CONT.) FO 134.36
    138.37 139.5 142.4 152.8
    158.11 158.23 159.5
    CD 189.41 198.16 228.20
    264.17 265.28 265.36
    SM 8.8 44.10 44.17 46.22
    51.41 68.20 72.24 85.19
    91.8 92.38 92.39 116.8
    124.23 138.22 156.12
    VG 23.19 23.20 24.34
    57.29 64.15 64.22 75.11

ILL-BRED-SEEMING CD 230.8

ILLEGAL VG 62.40

ILLNESSES FO 114.5

ILL-STARRED VG 30.33

ILLUMINED SM 94.30

ILLUSION FO 178.4 CD 217.25
    217.27 217.29 217.31
    217.34 218.7 SM 47.6
    99.9 137.18 150.10 158.16
    158.18

ILLUSIONS VG 65.9

ILL-WILL CD 213.11

'IM LH 16.5

IMAGE CD 197.25 VG 55.41

IMAGERY VG 42.25

IMAGES SM 132.33 VG 43.9

IMAGINATION CD 199.5 199.16
    209.1 SM 64.7 131.9
    VG 70.34

IMAGINATIVE LH 27.1

IMAGINE TL 57.24 97.3
    FO 144.34 154.5 154.23
    162.17 162.18 CD 195.11
    199.5 208.5 214.19 220.25
    249.8 253.8 SM 18.7
    29.12 31.12 31.16 54.13
    85.19 90.32 108.36 121.10
    VG 35.39 52.13

IMAGINED LH 30.41 TL 106.6
    SM 137.7 137.8 VG 11.23
    42.34

IMAGINING SM 137.7

IMBECILE TL 79.13 SM 104.24
    157.35 157.41 158.40

IMBECILITY CD 203.11

IMBIBING SM 127.39

IMITATE SM 112.4

IMITATED SM 61.13 MD 171.36

IMITATES SM 113.12

IMITATION SM 155.33 155.37

IMMACULATE   MD 186.4

IMMEDIATE   FO 173.33   CD 232.3
  240.33   SM 148.38

IMMEDIATELY   LH 34.25   TL 66.8
  FO 174.2   CD 184.27   220.2
  240.29   243.2   254.22   SM 31.32
  34.11   92.39   127.21   142.5
  VG 13.5   13.10   15.28   25.15
  27.26   36.6   36.15

IMMENSE   LH 14.39   24.24
  CD 223.33   239.6   252.36   252.39
  254.13   SM 58.21   67.3

IMMENSELY   SM 9.36   135.24

IMMERSED   TL 99.13   FO 135.28
  136.5   SM 69.22   VG 66.21

IMMINENT   VG 34.4

IMMOBILE   TL 57.2   57.4   SM 45.28
  155.13

IMMORAL   VG 30.20

IMMORTAL   TL 81.30   81.34   81.36
  VG 28.14

IMMORTALITY   MD 180.25   180.31

IMMOVABLE   SM 25.2

IMPACT   LH 7.42

IMPARTED   CD 252.16

IMPARTING   MD 192.25

IMPASSIVE   SM 68.10   89.8   107.16
  134.23   134.24   VG 15.17

IMPATIENCE   TL 100.16   100.20
  FO 179.9   VG 41.12

IMPATIENT   LH 8.34   11.10
  VG 33.13

IMPATIENTLY   SM 48.6   100.8
  101.32   106.41

IMPELLED   FO 129.40

IMPERATIVE   TL 102.2

IMPERCEPTIBLE   SM 69.15

IMPERCEPTIBLY   FO 132.12

IMPERIAL   TL 92.12

IMPERIALIST   CD 229.34

IMPERIOUSLY   SM 79.7   VG 19.26

IMPERIOUSNESS   CD 250.13

IMPERISHABLE   VG 5.6

IMPERSONAL   FO 120.41   129.31
  SM 18.40   25.3   VG 29.18

IMPERTINENCE   FO 142.9   CD 258.42

IMPERTINENT   TL 69.22   SM 122.19
  122.27   138.28

IMPERTURBABLE   VG 22.22

IMPERVIOUS   SM 81.38

IMPERVIOUSNESS   SM 101.21

IMPLACABLE   VG 15.15   15.19

IMPLICATE   TL 66.22   VG 63.21

IMPLICATED   CD 216.14   SM 98.24

IMPLIED   VG 29.38

IMPLORE   MD 190.26

IMPLY   FO 173.19

IMPORTANCE   CD 190.16   225.7
  SM 112.24   133.2   134.29

IMPORTANT   CD 190.21   190.23
  190.24   190.26   190.28   190.30
  190.33   198.33   230.38   SM 34.12
  114.18   116.12   123.27   VG 4.14
  41.5   41.7   41.10

IMPORTUNATE   TL 48.10

IMPOSED   FO 128.15

IMPOSSIBILITY   FO 166.7

IMPOSSIBLE   TL 85.18   85.21
  101.37   FO 142.5   165.16   166.5
  173.22   CD 188.1   203.9   207.6
  220.15   SM 23.13   44.7   90.31
  VG 10.29   42.10   42.39   44.9
  44.13

IMPOTENCE   SM 70.5

IMPOTENT   VG 30.38

IMPRESSED   SM 22.8   28.39   48.25
  48.29   131.26   VG 69.3

IMPRESSION   LH 18.28   TL 93.17
  FO 139.16   139.24   SM 131.10
  133.34

IMPRESSIVE   SM 64.3   137.25

IMPRISONED   TL 83.24   SM 51.21

IMPRISONMENT   MD 166.2

IMPROPER   FO 125.29   157.30

IMPROVE   SM 43.11   123.22

IMPUDENCE   FO 118.18   CD 265.19

IMPUDENT   LH 18.1   TL 69.21   98.42
  FO 116.33   135.12   154.9   154.18
  SM 109.21   VG 21.24   25.18

IMPULSE   LH 5.6   33.10   MD 195.9
  VG 58.29

IMPULSIVE   CD 200.7   210.9   226.1
  226.10   231.14

IMPULSIVELY   SM 100.20

INABILITY   MD 168.1

INACCESSIBILITY   SM 98.32

INACCESSIBLE   SM 61.38   99.26
  100.28   VG 5.12   5.16   52.16

INACTION   TL 108.42

INADEQUACY   MD 190.7

INARTICULATE   MD 207.2

INAUDIBLE   TL 100.24   100.25
  SM 74.11   99.21   99.23   99.26

INBORN   SM 75.26

INBRED   SM 29.9

INCALCULABLE   CD 191.13
  SM 89.2   MD 165.16

INCANDESCENT   TL 82.25

INCANTATION   MD 186.11

INCAPABLE   SM 137.36

INCARNATION   SM 79.30

INCENSE   MD 188.2   195.21
  203.1

INCENSED   LH 19.18   37.11

INCIDENT   CD 207.35   VG 41.15

INCIDENTALLY   CD 264.39

INCIPIENT   SM 56.38   94.25

INCLINE   FO 147.3   147.4
  SM 140.39

INCLINED   SM 136.34   157.35

INCLUDED   FO 124.38

INCLUDING   VG 6.32   74.35

INCOME   CD 207.19   212.26
  224.38   SM 4.37

INCOMPETENCE   SM 136.7

INCOMPETENT   SM 139.12   139.17

INCOMPREHENSIBLE   TL 78.33
  FO 149.2   CD 189.29   251.26
  251.31   251.34   251.40
  SM 84.2

INCOMPREHENSION   SM 129.14

INCONGRUOUSLY   CD 227.20

INCONSEQUENTIAL   CD 251.35
  SM 107.11

INCONSIDERATE   VG 14.22   31.5

INCONSPICUOUS   MD 199.18

INCONVENIENT SM 52.1

INCREASE SM 143.37

INCREASING VG 48.35

INCREDULITY CD 203.5 203.31

INCREDULOUS FO 160.5

INCURABLE TL 54.9

INDECENCY TL 92.28

INDECENT VG 12.26 62.27

INDECIPHERABLY SM 81.39

INDECISIVELY LH 21.8

INDEED LH 24.36 TL 65.19 85.10
   91.11 92.41 FO 114.4 114.40
   130.11 152.5 161.12 CD 190.28
   197.22 200.9 206.32 208.36
   213.27 259.3 262.23 SM 4.24
   21.33 28.27 80.33 133.15
   VG 9.39 11.36 16.7 42.24
   77.9

INDEFINABLE FO 125.10

INDELICATE TL 61.28 CD 213.33

INDEPENDENCE CD 224.39

INDEPENDENT LH 36.1 FO 178.24
   178.36 179.22 CD 212.30

INDES CD 226.22

INDESTRUCTIBLE FO 176.13 SM 95.7

INDETERMINATE SM 17.10

INDIAN SM 7.36 8.2 20.16 20.18
   21.13 32.30 40.40 77.24
   77.26 79.1 135.5 135.31
   135.34 136.4 136.11 136.19
   155.10 155.13

INDIANS SM 132.13 132.41 140.25
   154.30

INDICATED VG 19.8

INDIFFERENCE FO 114.11 123.42
   CD 200.30 230.41 231.6 231.24
   SM 22.19 25.1 145.9 145.41
   154.37 154.41 MD 168.9 175.21
   176.14 176.18 190.30 VG 19.20
   20.5 80.14

INDIFFERENT CD 230.9 SM 38.6
   MD 168.7

INDIFFERENTLY SM 133.4

INDIGNANT LH 19.12 26.12 37.7
   FO 118.18 CD 211.4 250.5
   VG 30.40 34.33 42.36 59.36

INDIGNANTLY LH 22.28 26.24
   FO 152.5

INDIGNATION CD 251.3 258.39

INDIGNATION (CONT.) MD 164.13
   VG 54.22 54.26

INDIGO MD 185.22

INDISCERNIBLE CD 192.8

INDISCREET CD 197.40

INDISCRETIONS CD 214.22

INDISPENSABLE CD 214.34

INDIVIDUAL TL 43.19 CD 216.12
   227.17 SM 69.24 71.32

INDIVIDUALS SM 70.23

INDOLENCE SM 43.1

INDOMITABLE TL 58.13 MD 207.12

INDOOR VG 29.36

INDOORS FO 117.13 117.32 131.22
   154.41 155.42 156.16 159.36
   163.25 CD 248.12 SM 46.38
   90.7 MD 181.22 VG 8.39 38.31
   70.12 70.29 72.5 72.15

INDULGENT VG 6.12

INDULGENTLY LH 12.40

INDUSTRIAL CD 217.7

INDUSTRIALISM VG 9.31

INEFFECTUAL FO 168.35 CD 249.30
   249.32

INEFFECTUALLY VG 71.34

INEFFICACIOUS LH 3.22

INEFFICIENCY TL 83.26

INEFFICIENT TL 83.40

INERT MD 166.34 170.15 186.38
   187.2 VG 9.26 16.15

INERTIA SM 140.28 145.9
   MD 176.38 VG 15.20

INEVITABLE FO 130.23 CD 214.31
   214.34 MD 169.30

INEVITABLY TL 86.33 FO 129.40
   177.26 177.34

IN EXCELSIS TL 82.24

INEXCUSABLE VG 9.12

INEXHAUSTIBLE CD 231.39 SM 90.34

INFALLIBLE TL 107.11

INFATUATION SM 96.4

INFERIOR FO 143.22 CD 216.9
   216.12 217.3

INFERIORITY VG 26.40

INFERIORS SM 33.1

INFERNAL TL 70.7 96.14
   CD 261.15 SM 30.35

INFINITE LH 23.33 TL 87.36
   103.8 SM 107.13 107.14
   MD 183.36 194.7

INFINITELY LH 12.10

INFLAMED LH 4.5 5.21
   SM 42.2

INFLICT MD 184.12

INFLUENCE TL 43.18 43.28
   64.31 FO 120.13 CD 198.31
   SM 54.3 144.22 145.24

INFLUENCES SM 119.26 152.10

INFLUENZA FO 125.21

INFORMATION TL 47.40
   CD 226.16 231.38

INFORMED SM 5.3

INFORMING SM 35.21

INFURIATED VG 27.10

INGENUOUSLY SM 129.7 129.8

INGRATIATING TL 98.42 SM 4.13

INHABIT SM 99.6

INHABITANT SM 98.36

INHABITING LH 22.5

INHERIT SM 77.21 MD 181.37

INHERITANCE TL 104.2

INHERITED SM 77.21

INHUMAN TL 102.3 SM 14.30

INITIAL TL 61.18 61.20

INITIATE TL 66.29

INITIATED TL 66.27 66.28

INITIATION TL 79.22

INJURE LH 35.15 SM 70.18
   70.19

INJURED FO 153.37 153.38
   153.39 153.40 153.42
   SM 13.14 72.5 VG 5.7

INJURES SM 42.2

INJURY SM 109.5

INJUSTICE MD 204.13

INK TL 92.24

INK-STAND CD 227.31

INK-TRAY   CD 227.26

INKY   TL 54.13

INLAID   VG 53.39

INLAND   MD 185.1   186.19   191.32

INLET   TL 70.25

INMATE   VG 29.40

INMOST   TL 109.1   CD 263.10

INN   CD 240.25   SM 51.31   101.34
   109.17   MD 183.15   183.19
   183.22

INNER   FO 116.11   120.12   155.37
   174.9   SM 11.15   72.30   87.24
   88.39   139.37   140.8   149.11
   151.9   153.13   MD 163.7   168.35
   187.40   194.17   195.13   202.16
   206.26   206.28

INNERLY   TL 108.1   SM 31.38

INNOCENCE   VG 63.24

INNOCENTLY   LH 16.11   SM 25.29
   VG 44.4   68.18

INNS   SM 97.30

INNUMERABLE   TL 62.33   FO 146.22
   CD 243.27   243.34   SM 56.15

IN PERPETUUM   VG 5.1

INQUIRE   VG 8.2

INQUIRING   TL 79.9

INQUISITIVE   SM 8.21

INQUISITIVELY   SM 122.18

INQUISITIVENESS   VG 31.21

INSANE   FO 167.2   VG 6.38   72.33
   75.9   75.33

INSANITY   FO 167.12   178.8

INSATIABLE   FO 127.9   129.32
   CD 241.12   SM 30.23   VG 15.25

INSCRUTABLE   CD 251.32   SM 6.21
   40.39

INSCRUTABLY   CD 187.26

INSECT   LH 4.37   TL 62.9   96.35
   97.4

INSECT-HOUSES   SM 147.18

INSECTS   CD 253.17

INSECURE   LH 9.29

INSENTIENCE   SM 109.11

INSIDE-OUT   TL 67.31   67.41   68.10
   68.25

INSIDE-TURNING   TL 67.18

INSIDIOUS   CD 216.31

INSIDIOUSLY   FO 141.1

INSIGNIFICANCE   SM 96.12

INSIGNIFICANT   CD 198.27   253.15
   SM 65.24   VG 4.32

INSINCERITY   CD 217.40

INSINUATE   VG 38.13

INSINUATING   SM 55.30   VG 23.13
   43.25

INSINUATION   SM 22.11   VG 30.30
   38.34

INSINUATIONS   VG 62.16

INSIPID   VG 43.20

INSIST   SM 17.23   108.22

INSISTED   LH 26.24   FO 140.33
   CD 191.4   191.34   192.25   225.9
   248.4   251.4   251.6   SM 36.12
   36.20   41.21   VG 16.36   45.3
   59.9   59.32   78.18

INSISTENCE   FO 132.34

INSISTENCY   FO 140.37

INSISTENT   FO 133.4

INSISTENTLY   SM 28.28

INSISTING   MD 174.16

IN SITU   CD 231.28

INSOLENCE   LH 19.36   19.37
   MD 191.17   192.19   VG 20.5

INSOLENT   LH 13.39   VG 19.20
   52.23

INSOLENTLY   MD 191.14

INSOMNIA   MD 183.41

INSOUCIANCE   VG 14.28   65.7

INSOUCIANT   VG 56.33   59.10   61.19

INSPECTION   CD 196.15

INSPIRATION   SM 92.21

INSPIRED   TL 44.37   SM 5.7

INSTABILITY   VG 5.37

INSTALLED   VG 54.10

INSTANCE   TL 43.26   67.1   CD 214.9
   217.10   221.18   VG 55.14

INSTANT   LH 22.35   24.9   FO 126.32
   SM 21.19   141.9   141.10
   MD 187.4   VG 72.32

INSTANTANEOUS   CD 224.27

INSTANTLY   CD 199.23   199.24
   220.27   SM 39.4   76.24
   VG 42.36   49.32

INSTEAD   LH 21.34   27.15
   38.25   TL 46.5   FO 175.25
   177.3   CD 223.34   226.3
   SM 50.33   51.9   54.26
   96.14   111.26   158.1
   MD 171.22   VG 30.38   44.25

INSTEP   LH 33.12   TL 79.16

INSTINCT   FO 135.24   SM 127.2
   VG 61.22

INSTINCTIVE   TL 93.9

INSTINCTIVELY   LH 13.13
   CD 231.3   SM 21.23   23.6

INSTRUCTIVE   CD 228.34

INSULT   TL 48.10   CD 264.15
   SM 35.15   89.12   109.4
   115.21   138.39   VG 7.19

INSULTED   TL 61.10   FO 143.18
   CD 264.15   SM 109.11

INSULTING   FO 142.24   142.28

INTACT   TL 105.25   SM 70.27

INTAGLIO   SM 111.5

INTELLECTUAL   SM 94.36

INTELLIGENCE   FO 117.12
   CD 231.39   SM 48.2   137.26
   137.31   145.25

INTELLIGENT   FO 167.4   SM 47.21
   VG 35.40

INTELLIGENTLY   FO 118.21

INTEND   TL 105.37   CD 210.38
   211.10   218.24   257.30
   258.22   SM 34.29   111.36
   VG 39.5   63.2

INTENDED   TL 64.24   92.36
   CD 193.27   VG 45.2

INTENDING   FO 113.2

INTENSE   LH 7.27   22.30
   TL 87.11   92.4   100.9   108.37
   FO 136.5   173.42   CD 245.1
   255.1   255.19   SM 45.34
   95.29   150.12   152.17
   MD 195.29   VG 3.32

INTENSELY   LH 8.1   30.38
   TL 88.25   FO 165.4
   SM 31.37   38.23   73.19
   78.24   149.18   VG 54.23
   70.42

INTENSER   CD 255.19

INTENSIFIED   TL 75.26   82.27

INTENSIFIED (CONT.) TL 82.40
84.7 SM 34.25 84.32

INTENSIFYING SM 145.30

INTENSITY CD 241.16 SM 14.13
MD 206.18

INTENT TL 102.11 FO 138.3 165.1
SM 17.36 32.3 32.34 MD 187.3
198.4 199.29

INTENTION FO 130.17 149.36
CD 219.11 257.31

INTENTIONS CD 209.38 219.14

INTENTLY LH 36.38 TL 78.18
SM 84.8

INTENTNESS FO 138.7

INTERCHANGED SM 21.1

INTER-COMMUNICATION LH 20.16

INTERCOURSE LH 20.11

INTEREST LH 5.40 TL 66.29 67.19
FO 123.9 CD 186.35 227.41
SM 30.25 123.20 127.13 131.35
131.36 138.16 145.8 145.10
MD 192.40 VG 13.1 13.3 27.31
28.37

INTERESTED SM 154.25 MD 187.23
VG 21.27 52.30 57.41 68.40

INTERESTEDLY FO 121.29

INTERESTING TL 90.32 CD 219.7
228.35 232.7 232.8

INTERFERE SM 34.17 34.18 45.22
MD 172.35 172.41 173.3

INTERFERED SM 30.7

INTERFERENCE MD 174.7 174.11

INTERFOLDED MD 207.22

INTERIOR TL 97.25 97.26
VG 30.12 54.8

INTERLUDE SM 40.15 VG 30.40

INTERMITTENT CD 242.28 MD 202.21

INTERNAL SM 70.29

INTERNED TL 64.27 81.14

INTERPOSED VG 59.37

INTERPRETATION SM 138.34

INTERRUPTED LH 20.12 TL 60.30
84.26 FO 124.3 SM 84.4
MD 204.29

INTERRUPTION MD 192.15

INTERVALS TL 100.6 SM 122.38
146.14 146.30 VG 5.22 46.20

INTERVENING TL 97.28 SM 53.7

INTIMACIES SM 139.33

INTIMACY TL 69.32 69.33 98.38
SM 49.17 118.9 118.10 129.20
129.22 132.35 139.2 139.34
VG 52.23 60.37

INTIMATE LH 25.34 SM 49.16
49.18 53.11 129.8 139.28
VG 38.37

INTIMATELY CD 184.38 SM 134.31

INTIMIDATED SM 37.33

INTOLERABLE FO 140.36 CD 240.29
VG 10.15

INTONATION TL 44.33 75.36 84.36
FO 143.24 CD 252.11

INTOXICATION SM 145.32

INTRICATE MD 207.23

INTRIGUED TL 92.19 SM 8.6
157.32

INTRIGUING VG 52.35 57.39

INTRINSIC MD 184.6 VG 41.28

INTRODUCE TL 83.29

INTRUDER FO 143.22

INTRUDING CD 236.1 VG 48.32

INTRUSION LH 25.6 CD 235.32

INTUITIVE SM 49.12

INVADING CD 232.16 SM 145.9
145.17

INVALID LH 12.28 16.1 SM 53.15
79.16

INVALID'S SM 79.29 79.33 110.39

INVARIABLE CD 196.5

INVARIABLY CD 192.12 206.21
MD 193.22 VG 10.37 14.41

INVEIGLED SM 139.33

INVENTED CD 222.3 VG 11.40

INVENTS SM 75.35

INVERTED SM 67.3 101.40

INVESTED TL 66.35

INVESTIGATION VG 57.42

INVESTMENT SM 131.35

INVESTOR FO 113.8

INVIDIOUS SM 140.25 145.2
153.14

INVIDIOUSNESS SM 145.27

INVIOLABLE SM 139.37

INVIOLATE MD 192.33

INVISIBILITY TL 68.33
FO 131.15

INVISIBLE TL 67.4 67.32
68.4 99.10 103.11 103.20
FO 123.3 129.1 131.3
152.36 CD 248.38 SM 12.7
33.17 34.1 34.22 40.39
69.16 70.29 99.20 102.20
119.26 141.34 144.21
147.26 149.8 150.31
151.10 151.12 152.25
MD 164.27 171.12 171.17
185.2 185.6 189.31 199.31
208.9 208.24 209.38

INVISIBLY TL 57.3 FO 117.24
132.6

INVITATION SM 37.15

INVITE CD 214.5

INVITED SM 109.29

INVITING FO 117.27 SM 111.14

INVOLUNTARILY FO 128.32
138.10

INWARD SM 70.38 79.8 125.30
153.37 MD 188.18 188.27
190.7 VG 4.11

INWARDLY SM 65.35 71.2
130.39 131.5 MD 196.19
VG 5.24 35.31 65.10

INWOOD (SEE MRS. INWOOD)

IPHIGENIA SM 112.37

IRELAND CD 207.13 SM 121.17

IRIS TL 69.10 76.12

IRISH TL 43.16 CD 208.41
208.42 211.18 221.11
221.21 221.22

IRON LH 25.7 26.36 FO 152.38
155.31 155.33 176.11
CD 191.21 SM 29.5 87.28
96.28 149.3 155.23
VG 21.39 47.6 47.8 47.15

IRON-FOUNDRY LH 23.22

IRONIC LH 12.9 12.30
CD 195.12

IRONICAL SM 104.31 VG 59.6

IRONICALLY LH 15.36 CD 261.27
SM 87.1

IRONY FO 114.12 114.16
SM 4.23 52.32 53.31 63.28

IRREGULAR TL 62.34

IRRELEVANCY CD 193.4

IRRELIGIOUS SM 127.6

IRRESISTIBLY FO 155.6 SM 69.23

IRRESPONSIBLE SM 54.10

IRREVOCABLE MD 194.13

IRRIGATED SM 142.27

IRRITABLE FO 115.29 SM 57.14
   58.7 VG 6.26 10.19 31.13
   32.12 66.6 66.19 72.7

IRRITABLY LH 30.20 FO 138.3
   SM 85.15 VG 11.15

IRRITANT SM 10.22 144.34

IRRITATED SM 58.25 98.31 149.18
   VG 43.39 44.28 45.1

IRRITATING LH 8.38 SM 4.21
   58.22 58.36 VG 31.41 41.13

IRRITATINGLY VG 33.39

IRRITATION CD 211.9 SM 137.12
   VG 10.16

ISIS TL 79.20 79.34 81.33
   MD 185.8 188.5 188.25 190.12
   190.13 190.18 193.39 195.5
   195.9 195.17 195.19 195.21
   195.23 195.37 195.40 196.3
   196.6 196.10 197.35 199.5
   200.29 200.35 201.8 201.14
   201.35 203.25 204.28 205.18
   207.38 208.25 208.28 211.6

ISIS, LADY (SEE LADY OF ISIS)

ISIS BEREAVED MD 188.5

ISIS IN SEARCH MD 188.6 190.36
   196.27 197.12

ISLAND TL 62.34 MD 210.15

ISLANDS SM 128.26

ISLE OF WIGHT SM 126.1 126.3

ISLINGTON FO 113.10 113.13

ISOLATE TL 99.33

ISOLATED LH 20.16 TL 99.1
   FO 136.5 CD 244.13 SM 29.11
   29.15 98.26 146.13

ISOLATION CD 225.35 227.23
   SM 63.1 VG 53.21 54.31

ISSUE TL 89.6 FO 167.1 SM 151.8
   MD 176.19

IST NIEMAND D'RIN ALS CHRIST ALLEIN
   LH 5.11

ITALIAN TL 50.1 SM 139.29

ITALIANS SM 4.7

ITALY SM 133.9 VG 54.2

ITHYPHALLIC SM 146.3

IT'LL LH 18.12 FO 149.21
   CD 264.19

IVORY MD 191.7 198.2

JA CD 236.18

JA-A CD 183.2 183.17

JA-A ICH KOM-MM CD 235.22

JABLONOWSKY, PAULA (SEE PAULA
   JABLONOWSKY)

JACK FO 170.1 170.5

JACKET LH 28.21 28.35 28.36
   29.9 TL 67.14 CD 233.15

JACKETS CD 233.13 238.7

JACK HORNER SM 98.30

JA DA BIN ICH JA 'S WAR
   WUNDERSCHON CD 265.33

JADE TL 70.25 CD 253.39

JADE-GREEN VG 24.35

JAM FO 122.5 122.30 141.10
   SM 152.13 VG 19.41

JAMAIS JAMAIS VOYEZ-VOUS CD 186.7

JAMMED FO 151.18

JANETTE LEROY SM 47.4 47.24

JANGLED VG 29.30

JANUARY MD 186.2 194.5

JAPAN TL 95.36

JAPANESE CD 227.25

JAR CD 228.32

JASMINE MD 193.27

JAUNT VG 16.22

JAUNTY SM 65.18

JAW MD 168.1 VG 65.31 65.32
   65.33

JAWOHL CD 260.39 260.41

JAWS VG 11.18 15.30 26.16

JAY VG 50.34

JEALOUS LH 19.42 26.29
   CD 209.18 224.1 224.3
   SM 20.12

JEALOUSLY CD 221.32

JEALOUSY CD 209.17 MD 209.40

JEER TL 44.11 CD 263.11
   SM 99.24 99.25

JEERED TL 43.33 SM 76.23
   VG 63.5

JEERING FO 150.18 170.41
   173.15 CD 242.15 SM 100.6

JELLY SM 103.35

JEPHSONS SM 29.9

JERK CD 256.1 SM 19.22
   VG 37.17

JERKED FO 142.33 CD 195.23

JERKY SM 150.5

JERSEY VG 23.26 23.36 43.9
   45.31 51.12 68.14 71.6
   75.14 75.16 75.18

JERSEY-COAT CD 248.12

JERSEYS VG 49.41

JERUSALEM MD 163.1

JESUS SM 117.35 150.2

JET CD 187.27 SM 145.21

JETS MD 170.26 180.11

JETZE HARDU HOR' AUF NEIN
   JETZT RUHIG CD 235.4

JEWEL CD 218.15 SM 129.37

JEWELLED CD 197.16 208.39

JEWELLERY CD 195.7

JEWELS TL 68.12 68.27 104.40
   CD 197.8 207.30 214.26
   222.41 SM 7.7 53.8

JEWESS VG 49.16 49.18 49.26
   49.36 50.19 50.22 50.28
   50.32 51.18 51.23 51.26
   51.35 51.39 52.4 52.8
   52.31 52.37 53.4 53.14
   53.17 53.25 53.30 53.37
   54.12 54.20 54.22 54.29
   55.9 57.28 58.5 58.25
   58.32 58.36 58.40 58.42
   59.9 59.13 59.17 59.20
   59.32 59.36 59.42 60.8
   63.11 66.26

JEWESS'S VG 49.27 51.1 58.21

JEWS CD 229.23 239.40 252.8
   252.9 252.15 257.11
   257.19 SM 9.9

JILL FO 136.26 139.5 139.37
   140.29 141.3 141.14 145.17
   147.38 152.10 158.4 159.16
   159.33 160.15 162.12
   164.10 164.11 164.15

KIND (CONT.) CD 209.10 213.30
  213.32 216.2 229.28 230.35
  SM 18.28 39.39 40.37 41.21
  41.23 42.21 42.22 46.24
  86.16 90.20 116.30 120.21
  131.13 157.24 157.41
  MD 164.20 167.14 170.29 172.4
  193.2 VG 15.1 23.41 37.5
  44.28 57.19

KINDEST FO 166.28

KINDLE SM 103.40

KINDLED VG 30.3

KINDLINESS FO 126.18

KINDLING LH 38.11

KINDLY FO 157.35 MD 207.38
  VG 7.4 50.20

KINDNESS LH 32.41 TL 43.3 94.5
  CD 205.3 SM 15.35 26.1 51.21
  84.15 MD 204.12

KINDS TL 87.32 SM 94.38
  MD 193.15

KING TL 102.30 108.4 MD 169.22
  182.17 VG 59.37 60.6

KING CHARLES'S HEAD VG 14.40
  16.29

KINGDOM MD 183.29

KING EDWARD SM 54.5

KING-GOD TL 103.25

KINGS TL 90.22 SM 75.21

KINSHIP LH 19.16

KIPLING'S SM 145.2

KISS LH 6.24 23.31 27.20 34.9
  TL 75.12 75.16 FO 140.26
  140.31 163.21 163.23
  CD 192.18 SM 18.15 71.13
  95.16 95.26 95.35 96.39
  MD 173.27

KISSED LH 27.10 34.26 TL 64.34
  77.10 79.15 79.16 79.23
  106.38 FO 140.20 140.22
  140.26 140.30 163.22
  CD 184.37 193.5 231.22 231.25
  232.27 MD 205.5 205.6 VG 12.1

KISSES LH 7.8 CD 193.5 SM 71.21
  71.36

KISSING LH 5.20 24.11 TL 78.11
  CD 193.8

KIT FO 120.2 121.21 166.32

KITCHEN FO 119.19 119.32 121.27
  121.37 122.25 133.41 134.9
  138.39 142.37 145.31 148.2
  154.39 154.40 159.30 SM 33.30
  35.6 45.31 45.40 145.16

KITCHEN (CONT.) 149.4 VG 10.30
  33.26 54.32 58.2 71.24 71.27
  71.29 78.11

KITCHENS SM 145.16

KITTEN VG 44.39

KITTEN'S CD 192.6

KNACK VG 70.32

KNAPSACK CD 238.23 242.35
  242.38 243.5 247.8 252.22
  259.5 259.6

KNAPSACKS CD 241.37

KNEADED SM 106.37

KNEE LH 34.2 FO 139.2 157.2
  170.28 CD 183.9 184.4
  VG 43.40 46.37

KNEEL TL 79.19

KNEELED LH 12.22 21.31
  CD 208.21

KNEELING LH 12.20 TL 81.37
  CD 214.39

KNEES LH 4.39 23.41 24.5
  TL 80.24 106.19 FO 122.38
  124.40 125.15 135.27 135.31
  136.1 136.20 146.26 146.31
  158.7 CD 187.11 201.19 214.35
  215.14 215.31 226.24 231.17
  233.13 233.19 238.7 251.17
  259.16 SM 136.31 MD 165.34
  197.7 VG 20.17 21.26 24.3
  64.40 73.19

KNELT TL 79.15

KNEW LH 12.1 24.10 TL 44.16
  51.30 66.34 68.33 77.38
  79.18 79.19 79.20 79.21 82.1
  82.11 85.17 86.1 96.18 98.34
  100.34 101.17 105.14 107.10
  107.16 108.24 FO 114.31
  116.27 116.28 116.29 117.24
  117.25 126.28 130.21 144.22
  146.20 146.39 146.40 148.11
  150.28 156.22 156.30 161.28
  162.27 165.11 167.4 167.15
  167.16 170.22 174.8 175.5
  175.20 175.39 176.25 179.9
  179.24 CD 189.9 198.1 199.23
  206.41 209.8 209.31 209.41
  210.13 211.18 211.24 211.25
  211.37 220.2 221.39 222.36
  224.5 224.12 224.13 226.12
  227.39 233.2 237.9 258.23
  260.14 261.25 SM 6.18 6.20
  7.28 7.35 10.23 12.2 18.22
  20.7 20.8 24.36 25.18 26.1
  26.22 27.9 28.15 28.36 33.20
  40.30 44.15 44.22 44.37
  44.38 45.38 47.2 47.23 53.9
  54.28 57.4 75.1 75.7 76.11
  76.12 76.14 84.29 86.8 89.1
  89.3 90.24 94.4 97.29 97.30
  99.13 99.27 101.23 105.35
  110.23 112.6 112.28 113.32

KNEW (CONT.) 121.28 125.37
  126.17 129.39 130.1 132.30
  136.28 136.31 136.33
  137.11 138.36 152.26
  153.7 MD 163.25 164.19
  164.34 165.8 165.12 169.33
  173.22 175.40 177.26 178.2
  178.4 178.5 178.38 183.14
  187.35 201.6 201.26 207.4
  207.30 209.13 209.35 210.6
  210.18 211.2 VG 3.2 3.11
  5.16 6.14 6.30 15.10
  18.16 24.14 24.18 27.23
  27.25 30.35 34.42 43.32
  44.33 57.24 57.30 66.17
  67.7 68.14 68.15 71.4
  81.9 81.13

KNICKERBOCKERS CD 245.16
  247.33

KNIFE LH 31.12 FO 141.28
  SM 90.25 MD 187.19

KNIGHTED VG 16.6

KNIT LH 7.28

KNITS SM 49.9

KNITTED TL 74.7 CD 195.4
  248.12 SM 48.36 VG 40.25
  49.41

KNITTING LH 6.16 SM 49.4
  50.13 106.31

KNIVES LH 15.18 SM 79.31

KNOCK LH 7.41 12.35 SM 50.24
  MD 210.31

KNOCKED LH 11.17 12.1
  25.24 31.9 SM 72.6

KNOCKING SM 53.22

KNOCKS SM 79.13

KNOLL CD 239.13 239.42

KNOT LH 38.26 FO 120.23
  122.15 CD 236.14 SM 63.33

KNOTTED FO 120.23

KNOW LH 4.7 4.17 10.25
  12.33 16.21 17.6 20.35
  28.29 31.18 31.34 33.3
  TL 45.15 48.38 49.5 49.14
  49.42 50.7 50.24 55.8
  55.12 56.13 57.11 57.12
  57.29 57.31 57.40 59.13
  61.34 62.8 63.18 63.25
  64.14 64.35 66.16 66.27
  67.10 67.13 67.15 67.40
  70.12 71.25 71.28 72.18
  73.29 75.2 75.7 75.8
  75.23 76.14 76.15 76.17
  79.4 82.2 84.32 87.34
  90.22 90.25 91.25 95.35
  96.21 96.23 96.26 96.38
  96.39 97.5 103.12 105.10
  106.30 106.32 108.7 108.25
  108.29 108.34 108.38

KNOW (CONT.) FO 118.40 120.7
  120.32 120.34 120.36
  121.6 121.16 123.37
  124.11 126.20 126.23 127.40
  128.14 129.1 132.21 132.24
  132.26 133.23 133.27 133.28
  133.30 133.33 135.9 138.18
  139.15 139.42 141.1 141.8
  141.23 142.27 144.17 144.18
  144.19 144.25 144.28 144.30
  145.1 145.18 147.31 149.22
  150.19 150.20 150.24 150.34
  151.35 152.18 152.21 154.1
  154.2 154.8 154.10 159.19
  159.31 161.5 161.15 161.32
  161.39 161.40 161.42 162.3
  162.4 162.27 162.29 165.19
  165.24 165.28 165.33 166.5
  166.6 166.14 166.24 167.34
  178.10 178.19 178.34 178.42
  CD 183.29 185.31 185.32
  185.36 186.5 188.8 188.10
  188.17 188.23 188.39 189.2
  189.3 189.16 190.32 191.5
  191.8 191.39 193.26 193.38
  194.30 195.34 196.21 196.25
  196.27 196.41 197.17 197.18
  197.19 197.32 198.8 198.29
  202.1 202.33 202.41 203.2
  204.33 205.26 205.36 205.37
  205.38 206.22 206.38 207.5
  207.9 207.10 208.16 208.40
  208.41 209.1 211.14 211.35
  212.24 212.31 213.22 214.6
  214.33 215.41 218.30 220.1
  220.37 221.3 221.8 221.19
  221.26 221.40 222.1 222.25
  222.31 223.15 223.29 223.30
  224.9 224.10 227.37 227.38
  228.3 228.7 228.10 228.15
  246.20 256.27 257.33 257.35
  259.33 262.21 262.42 263.42
  265.2 SM 3.2 3.15 7.39 9.17
  10.39 11.23 11.31 12.17
  12.28 12.32 14.5 14.10 14.37
  16.23 16.26 22.38 23.15
  23.33 25.37 28.31 28.41 30.8
  30.9 30.39 31.22 31.27 38.21
  39.11 39.16 41.27 41.28
  41.29 41.34 41.35 42.3 42.20
  43.15 44.12 47.30 48.4 48.13
  49.35 50.7 50.8 50.14 50.15
  51.12 54.35 55.35 56.18
  56.34 61.11 62.9 62.10 62.28
  62.32 62.40 64.30 65.15
  67.27 69.8 72.21 72.32 74.36
  77.10 78.15 78.34 79.22
  79.36 80.13 81.2 82.22 82.33
  84.16 85.22 85.40 86.21 87.2
  87.17 88.5 88.17 88.24 89.13
  89.40 91.3 91.4 91.15 92.31
  93.19 93.38 102.35 103.15
  103.37 104.31 104.35 104.36
  104.39 105.10 105.21 106.2
  106.33 107.39 108.2 108.17
  109.38 110.19 110.22 112.12
  113.8 113.12 113.21 114.6
  114.27 115.15 117.30 117.32
  118.18 120.4 123.20 124.33
  126.2 128.14 132.31 135.15
  138.7 140.2 149.29 157.1
  157.15 157.17 157.25 157.32
  157.40 158.9 158.10 158.23
  158.26 158.35 158.37
  MD 168.13 173.27 173.31 174.6

KNOW (CONT.) 174.17 174.18
  174.25 174.26 176.4
  182.5 182.15 182.24
  182.27 183.10 189.29 193.19
  195.26 204.19 204.20 205.38
  206.14 208.40 209.27 210.36
  VG 4.1 7.36 7.38 8.4 8.5
  8.10 8.23 11.39 12.38 25.29
  27.24 28.5 29.33 31.39 32.2
  32.6 32.12 32.18 34.7 35.17
  35.26 38.38 39.4 39.24 39.33
  41.42 43.39 44.2 44.7 51.26
  55.20 55.23 56.9 56.13 56.17
  57.27 58.40 59.8 59.22 59.29
  60.17 60.35 61.15 61.17
  61.29 61.36 61.41 62.1 62.20
  62.26 62.42 63.38 63.39 69.5
  71.13 80.10 81.4

KNOWED LH 6.40

KNOWIN' LH 19.40

KNOWING LH 10.26 15.40 28.20
  TL 48.28 52.38 54.20 103.16
  107.22 FO 116.38 117.20
  117.23 121.13 128.10 139.30
  163.15 CD 209.27 227.35
  234.13 255.36 SM 55.4 56.5
  59.35 69.6 119.31 135.33
  136.36 MD 178.8 179.1 VG 55.6
  63.8 63.17 78.39

KNOWINGNESS SM 4.18

KNOWLEDGE LH 10.28 19.41
  TL 66.35 66.41 83.23 95.26
  CD 218.11 SM 4.18 44.28 90.32
  90.34 138.36 MD 164.20
  VG 63.35

KNOWN LH 22.18 27.7 TL 45.4
  70.11 77.30 105.24 108.26
  FO 113.1 137.8 144.42
  CD 188.16 198.1 205.3 212.28
  262.7 SM 19.36 25.26 28.8
  108.39 115.7 118.28 136.27
  MD 176.6 176.18 177.28 182.13
  182.20 189.1 197.5 VG 9.36
  80.40

KNOWS LH 3.35 26.14 38.9
  TL 50.23 65.38 FO 116.23
  146.25 165.37 165.38
  CD 213.13 215.21 255.34
  SM 17.40 43.25 49.13 56.31
  93.36 115.26 122.32 124.1
  MD 189.37 209.26 VG 34.15
  54.1

KNUCKLES VG 18.18

KRONEN CD 238.26

KUCK DE LEUT DIE DA BLEIBEN
  CD 236.16

LABELLED TL 93.14 SM 115.40

LABELS SM 118.36

LABORATORY SM 31.4

LABORIOUSLY FO 136.21 137.36
  143.28

LABOUR LH 3.18 8.10 TL 70.18

LABOURER LH 10.9 10.32 11.12
  11.33 12.22 35.20
  FO 144.36 SM 53.25 VG 36.28

LABOURERS LH 15.8 TL 98.12
  SM 29.6 29.23 29.38 30.2

LABOURING VG 71.41

LACE TL 83.7 83.20 CD 213.20
  227.27 227.31 VG 7.6 65.27
  70.13

LACERATIONS MD 169.18

LACK LH 5.39 SM 6.35 18.25
  48.34 131.27

LACKED SM 134.29

LACKING SM 16.1 16.2

LACKS CD 200.8

LACONIC TL 52.18 FO 118.6
  125.42 CD 261.2 SM 45.3

LACONICALLY FO 123.37 138.22
  141.34 170.26

LACQUER CD 227.25 SM 13.32
  17.14 17.15

LAD LH 4.18 6.40 12.3 20.28
  FO 129.11 146.17 CD 234.41

LADDER LH 12.14 12.17 24.32
  25.1 25.3 25.17 25.22
  26.41 36.20 36.35 37.19
  37.24 37.33 37.36 38.3
  38.5 39.8 CD 249.39
  SM 150.37 VG 78.22 78.26
  78.35 78.38 79.1 80.3
  80.13 80.17 80.20

LADDERS VG 77.26 78.2 78.19

LADDER'S LH 37.1 VG 80.19

LADIES TL 67.39 CD 232.4
  SM 31.19 83.30 131.2
  VG 3.33 4.4 19.42 21.11
  21.31 21.35 40.36

LADIES' LH 16.30

LADS LH 6.1 15.7 SM 106.2
  106.5

LAD'S LH 12.20 36.39

LADY TL 51.32 52.41 76.8
  76.22 76.33 CD 194.36
  194.41 195.17 196.11
  196.16 197.36 197.38
  198.14 207.33 208.25
  209.34 210.32 210.35
  211.29 213.24 213.41
  214.19 215.4 215.13
  215.25 215.30 215.33
  216.13 216.19 217.19
  217.28 217.39 218.9 218.10
  218.12 227.39 228.2 247.31

LARGE (CONT.) CD 193.24 195.4
   201.11 218.33 231.9 231.29
   233.29 234.28 236.5 246.8
   253.7 SM 14.27 17.1 18.14
   21.1 30.1 57.14 93.3
   MD 175.33 VG 11.31 26.37
   49.15 49.24 70.16

LARGELY TL 93.23 FO 123.9
   127.21

LARGER CD 196.20

LAS CHIVAS SM 154.29 159.16

LASHES LH 8.20 TL 45.8 50.8
   50.34 84.4 FO 122.22 170.6
   171.15 VG 21.24 49.29

LASLOW SM 114.36

LASS LH 12.37 13.2 23.8

LAST LH 3.19 4.9 5.19 8.25
   8.26 18.16 24.8 26.26 28.21
   32.2 33.32 33.41 38.8 38.31
   39.7 TL 43.29 45.34 45.35
   56.24 57.40 64.39 72.21
   75.11 76.35 77.11 82.37
   82.42 89.15 89.18 89.25
   92.27 107.4 107.38 FO 117.5
   118.26 124.41 125.8 125.14
   131.5 131.23 138.35 139.13
   146.21 147.13 157.38 158.9
   159.25 161.32 162.9 163.35
   165.35 165.36 174.26 174.27
   176.36 178.8 178.18 178.36
   179.15 179.17 CD 187.28 206.1
   210.39 213.15 217.1 222.38
   226.14 231.22 239.26 240.19
   240.24 248.22 248.27 252.23
   252.25 253.6 255.38 260.17
   260.22 261.10 SM 13.13 14.2
   25.31 30.35 39.7 46.8 50.10
   56.4 59.9 63.31 63.35 64.34
   70.35 70.40 71.22 71.29
   72.17 73.15 77.22 82.37
   86.39 88.18 89.21 91.9 95.8
   96.10 97.5 97.22 97.24
   107.10 118.37 118.38 125.3
   133.18 134.2 138.36 140.30
   140.33 141.21 153.3 MD 165.36
   176.35 177.40 183.34 188.23
   190.18 192.11 198.38 202.20
   207.28 209.11 VG 15.1 15.7
   24.26 48.20 63.34 70.5 78.1
   78.19 80.33

LASTED LH 15.8 SM 64.12 145.33
   VG 70.11

LATCH FO 143.41 154.40

LATCHED MD 202.31

LATE LH 22.22 TL 44.3 72.21
   74.34 104.34 FO 114.40 115.15
   130.2 168.30 CD 187.36 187.37
   201.9 202.19 205.1 220.1
   230.3 232.30 SM 54.5 74.20
   86.30 101.36 151.38 VG 54.7

LATELY SM 122.35

LATENCY TL 68.26

LATENT SM 22.7 140.17 140.18
   140.27

LATER TL 72.4 104.29 FO 114.42
   149.31 155.15 159.22 SM 23.23
   132.37 147.28 150.35 151.3
   MD 175.38 178.18 VG 30.39
   52.15 80.30

LATEST FO 135.37 CD 228.31
   VG 16.31 61.13

LATHAM (SEE MR. LATHAM)

LATTER FO 159.9 CD 197.6
   SM 7.21 73.35 93.23 156.35
   VG 31.27 54.9

LATTER-DAY SM 76.1

LATTICE SM 43.23

LAUDABLE SM 131.35

LAUGH LH 5.4 6.15 7.14 22.42
   25.30 28.15 31.37 36.8
   TL 62.7 65.28 74.35 108.11
   FO 123.17 123.33 124.30
   129.28 129.39 139.21 139.27
   139.32 140.4 151.6 170.21
   CD 185.41 190.34 196.42
   197.11 204.30 204.33 205.2
   207.2 207.11 207.24 208.19
   209.2 209.34 231.4 234.41
   SM 16.17 85.36 85.37 112.27
   138.12 VG 66.16

LAUGHED LH 6.38 7.9 7.22 7.24
   13.18 14.3 14.14 14.15 15.38
   16.1 16.6 16.7 16.12 16.22
   17.3 17.4 17.12 17.34 22.11
   22.25 23.30 26.2 26.19 26.25
   TL 59.36 65.33 65.40 66.7
   67.37 68.6 72.36 72.37 73.28
   84.13 97.3 108.10 FO 123.16
   124.14 124.26 137.7 137.14
   137.17 139.26 140.6 162.41
   165.9 CD 195.3 196.42 197.10
   197.33 204.29 207.1 230.42
   234.36 234.40 249.22 249.36
   256.27 264.22 MD 164.18
   175.27 189.14 196.1 211.18
   VG 40.29

LAUGHING LH 21.39 22.13 24.1
   24.11 TL 65.15 98.42 FO 124.2
   137.18 139.22 151.39 163.3
   CD 185.41 233.30 233.35
   234.30 SM 19.8 MD 183.12
   VG 19.33 20.1

LAUGHING-SNAKE CD 245.2

LAUGHTER LH 16.16 22.40
   TL 63.38 91.20 FO 124.14
   124.22 124.29 140.18
   CD 203.19 203.32 261.36
   VG 29.25

LAUGHTER'S SM 85.38

LAUNCH VG 15.31

LAUNCHED LH 3.14 VG 15.34

LAUNDRY TL 60.32

LAUNDRY-ROOM CD 201.6

LAURA SM 121.15 121.28
   122.35 123.1 124.8 124.18
   124.28 124.34

LAURA RIDLEY SM 121.4 124.11

LAUREL MD 178.35 VG 36.21

LAURELS MD 166.32 173.12
   173.17 VG 70.25

LAUSANNE VG 7.28

LAVA SM 107.16

LAVENDER-COLOURED TL 100.4

LAW TL 59.18 62.40 62.41
   109.3 109.6 CD 204.29
   SM 80.17 94.34 MD 202.7
   VG 67.1

LAW-ABIDING VG 22.30

LAWN TL 97.40 SM 37.8

LAWNS SM 37.28

LAWYER SM 94.32 116.38
   154.12

LAY LH 3.1 4.31 6.1 13.12
   25.23 TL 44.9 44.39 53.41
   54.2 54.5 55.25 55.35
   55.37 57.1 72.25 109.3
   FO 114.6 126.36 131.21
   135.29 148.6 CD 185.26
   230.20 238.2 252.23 258.13
   SM 42.32 59.40 60.15 67.20
   68.34 73.39 125.35 125.37
   126.25 139.36 143.6
   MD 165.21 165.29 165.35
   166.31 169.13 170.7 170.11
   170.15 171.24 177.13
   177.20 180.3 181.37 184.7
   184.10 186.25 186.38 187.7
   187.19 196.21 201.29
   201.32 208.30 210.30
   VG 12.12 29.32 30.3 79.22

LAYER SM 6.3 154.5

LAYERS SM 46.7 139.32 139.36

LAYING TL 72.31 109.6
   FO 133.12 CD 204.29 SM 84.5

LAZY SM 32.22 37.41 VG 70.9

LEAD LH 23.33 SM 36.38
   140.12 MD 192.29 210.34
   VG 6.1 8.8

LEADED TL 97.37

LEADEN CD 201.20

LEADER LH 38.34

LEADERS TL 43.20 89.16 89.39

LEADING   LH 6.35 23.9 SM 82.26

LEAD-MINES   VG 18.36

LEAF   LH 6.18 6.20 6.21
   CD 255.24 SM 128.17 128.18
   MD 170.26

LEAFLESS   SM 141.33

LEAGUE   FO 151.42

LEAN   FO 114.30 SM 131.7

LEANED   LH 3.31 4.28 14.7 33.29
   TL 78.14 FO 164.39 170.22
   CD 257.16 MD 165.40 166.4
   166.5 VG 38.28 77.27

LEANING   LH 8.39 9.15 9.28
   15.31 23.41 33.17 TL 78.30
   95.30 FO 121.25 154.38 169.16
   172.15 173.2 SM 52.30 82.9
   83.28 84.5 148.4 MD 199.3

LEANS   MD 189.13 208.12

LEAP   FO 128.11 153.11

LEAPED   LH 27.25 FO 132.37
   CD 237.16 240.4 SM 128.27
   MD 164.38 VG 29.22

LEAPING   FO 130.2 130.3
   MD 167.20 167.27

LEAPS   FO 116.32

LEAPT   FO 174.5

LEARN   TL 79.22 79.27 CD 221.21
   SM 157.31 MD 179.27 VG 35.10
   63.22

LEARNED   TL 84.38 94.11
   FO 113.12 SM 42.34 120.28
   MD 163.23 VG 67.32 78.1

LEARNING   SM 28.30

LEASED   SM 6.2

LEASH   CD 257.15

LEAST   LH 10.20 TL 48.39 53.9
   62.5 71.21 96.14 FO 161.42
   CD 203.29 205.40 211.24
   252.14 SM 6.5 15.36 16.23
   18.11 22.36 43.33 48.34
   52.36 95.23 97.22 111.6
   111.23 116.22 118.6 118.9
   122.5 127.13 130.28 130.29
   132.11 MD 182.6 183.29 201.17
   VG 29.42 34.9 52.29 65.14
   78.13

LEATHER   LH 9.18 CD 238.6
   SM 38.31 119.8 MD 191.37

LEATHERN   CD 233.14 233.16

LEATHERY   VG 28.18

LEAVES   LH 13.35 25.13 TL 72.25
   73.19 FO 152.32 CD 217.7

LEAVES (CONT.)   230.25 SM 22.25
   42.35 87.27 99.8 103.3 113.7
   118.5 128.20 151.33 MD 163.5
   170.8 180.11 180.38 209.16

LEAVING   TL 64.34 82.36 103.7
   FO 127.29 164.22 CD 258.25
   SM 4.37 14.26 27.38 80.35
   106.11 108.34 111.37 113.33
   117.14 123.15 145.4 145.9
   MD 206.34 VG 20.39 61.40
   70.33 75.36 78.28

LEBANON   MD 185.2 188.37 188.39

LECTURED   VG 28.3

LED   FO 119.32 169.21 172.23
   CD 254.24 SM 59.1 131.4 149.3
   MD 187.31 191.18 192.30
   VG 20.26 37.17 77.38

LEDGE   CD 200.39 201.10 241.8
   241.19 MD 166.21 VG 15.28

LEER   SM 6.17 30.19 56.33

LEFT-HAND   TL 76.30

LEG   CD 187.12 187.25 SM 20.27
   MD 164.14 164.20 164.33
   170.17 171.9 171.38 172.29
   177.18 179.30 180.14 181.10
   VG 73.14 78.8

LEGHORN   FO 115.15

LEGHORNS   FO 113.22

LEGIBLE   TL 51.11

LEGIONS   SM 68.1

LEGS   LH 18.31 TL 47.7 FO 122.14
   131.27 140.13 156.39 157.4
   157.5 CD 184.16 191.15 197.34
   197.37 216.38 228.39 231.19
   232.18 235.12 235.39 236.5
   236.15 254.30 SM 24.31 45.34
   54.20 56.33 58.11 96.34 99.1
   124.12 136.1 MD 165.10 166.19
   170.13 199.26 199.27 VG 21.22
   24.4 24.6 24.27 43.41 50.26
   53.14 66.11 73.30 73.35

LEICESTERSHIRE   TL 45.6

LEMON   SM 40.29

LEMONADE   SM 40.31 41.3

LENGTH   LH 35.9 37.39 TL 63.28
   FO 143.10 CD 201.41 222.22
   224.2 227.27 228.25 232.35
   SM 64.1 91.11 154.7 158.15
   MD 191.13 VG 48.4 48.15

LENT   MD 205.30 205.31

LEO   VG 17.40 18.13 18.24 19.13
   19.25 19.31 19.37 19.41 20.6
   20.10 20.14 21.4 21.33 21.41
   22.16 25.15 41.31 41.36
   42.31 43.12 43.35 44.6 44.37
   45.6 67.36 70.1

LEOPARD   SM 50.29 91.39

LEO'S   VG 13.27 17.27 44.26

LEO WETHERELL   VG 13.16 15.22

LEPROUS   VG 27.38

LEROY, JANETTE   (SEE JANETTE
   LEROY)

LES HALLES   SM 5.36

LESS   TL 53.13 FO 115.24
   137.13 177.3 CD 190.26
   192.36 192.37 249.40
   249.42 255.11 SM 56.26
   109.30 121.18 131.25
   134.34 136.28 136.29
   157.36 VG 65.38 76.35

LESSER   SM 53.8 MD 176.19
   193.24

LEST   LH 31.6 TL 101.20
   105.18 107.19 107.28
   FO 119.7 173.23 SM 35.10
   127.26 MD 166.36 196.33
   VG 27.24

LETS   SM 106.4

LET'S   LH 22.33 35.41
   TL 77.21 77.22 FO 133.38
   150.3 SM 30.39 37.11
   133.9 VG 20.8 39.26
   39.27

LET'S-BE-HAPPY   SM 27.10

LETTER   TL 55.6 56.3 70.15
   81.25 FO 165.13 166.32
   CD 188.17 218.19 218.23
   218.32 247.2 SM 112.15
   112.17 116.16 116.25
   116.33 117.8 117.25 117.28
   MD 165.21 VG 64.28 81.14

LETTER-CLIP   CD 186.27

LETTERS   TL 69.39 FO 149.39
   150.23 CD 186.28 188.14
   218.17 218.19 218.21
   SM 109.23

LETTER-WRITING   FO 149.42

LETTING   TL 93.16 FO 142.27
   154.8 CD 211.28 SM 102.15
   MD 163.5

LETTUCE   SM 37.41

LETTUCES   SM 38.2

LEVEL   FO 138.5 144.39
   CD 239.37 243.12 251.22
   252.23 254.6 255.10
   255.39 SM 62.36 129.3
   MD 167.20 168.18 VG 20.4
   22.26 43.16 45.24 72.41

LEVELLED   SM 9.24

LEVER   CD 250.37

LEWD   LH 19.42

LEWIS   SM 17.9   17.16   17.30
17.31   18.2   18.16   18.34   18.39
20.5   20.9   20.10   22.7   22.10
22.12   22.27   22.32   23.3   23.6
23.18   28.10   32.6   32.8   32.13
35.34   36.1   36.3   38.29   38.41
39.8   39.10   39.15   40.9   40.26
43.27   43.29   43.32   44.39
45.28   46.2   47.26   49.11   49.16
51.3   57.3   57.28   57.32   58.31
58.40   59.5   59.15   59.22   59.26
60.21   63.6   63.39   67.11   67.21
67.36   67.39   76.6   87.23   88.29
88.31   88.34   89.17   89.18
89.27   89.32   89.36   90.2   90.4
91.30   91.33   91.38   92.12
92.17   92.20   92.27   92.35   93.4
93.35   94.9   94.17   97.35   99.12
99.14   99.18   100.16   101.2
102.14   102.27   106.14   106.20
108.4   109.19   110.5   110.8
110.27   112.17   116.25   117.5
117.11   117.23   119.5   120.34
120.38   121.3   121.4   122.19
122.24   122.26   122.39   126.28
127.15   130.13   130.31   131.26
132.8

LEWIS   (SEE MR., MORGAN)

LEWIS'   SM 19.30

LIAR   LH 37.4   VG 29.15   29.16

LIBERTY   SM 17.27   35.21

LIBIDO   SM 113.38

LICKED   VG 58.4

LICKING   FO 150.12

LID   FO 160.27

LIDDED   LH 13.7

LIDS   TL 46.40   76.39   SM 86.22

LIE   LH 31.19   31.25   37.4
TL 57.3   FO 146.42   151.16
CD 208.16   SM 42.35   43.10
MD 170.5   170.36   VG 16.19   17.7
17.8   30.31   34.41   35.1   76.8

LIEF   LH 10.19

LIES   LH 37.6   37.9   37.14
TL 58.38   58.39   75.8   SM 17.37

LIFE   LH 11.40   13.6   16.32   16.35
16.36   16.37   20.19   27.3   29.14
33.31   TL 43.22   47.4   47.34
50.30   54.4   54.32   55.34   66.33
69.40   73.34   75.6   75.8   75.9
77.35   84.10   85.5   85.23   87.40
89.26   90.13   90.29   91.34
98.32   99.10   101.9   101.13
104.1   104.4   104.8   104.9
104.10   104.15   106.4   107.9
108.6   108.38   109.7   FO 113.34
114.6   135.16   152.2   161.2
161.7   161.8   161.10   161.16
162.10   164.34   165.35   165.36

LIFE (CONT.)   167.13   174.9   175.6
175.7   175.26   176.31   176.36
177.21   178.35   179.17   179.19
179.20   CD 185.7   188.16   197.18
197.19   198.39   203.3   203.22
208.22   208.24   208.28   212.11
212.18   215.3   217.30   218.6
220.42   221.9   221.12   221.13
221.27   222.4   223.21   223.23
223.30   225.24   225.25   229.24
233.9   255.24   257.15   262.8
SM 7.16   8.3   9.16   10.31   12.26
13.32   13.33   14.18   15.32
26.23   29.18   36.33   37.1   37.3
37.30   43.21   47.8   47.10   47.18
49.19   49.20   49.23   49.31
49.34   49.38   51.7   51.13   53.24
53.26   61.21   62.12   64.17
65.34   66.16   70.25   70.27
71.10   71.19   71.26   71.27
71.28   71.35   71.38   72.12
79.39   85.2   87.13   87.14   87.19
96.25   96.26   96.32   96.40
97.10   98.39   103.10   104.9
105.30   115.8   116.41   117.1
118.13   118.14   120.24   122.12
126.4   128.32   130.20   130.28
131.4   133.3   136.20   137.12
137.14   137.37   138.4   138.5
148.28   150.12   150.17   150.18
152.29   152.37   152.38   153.1
153.2   153.25   156.15   156.37
157.1   157.3   157.4   158.29
MD 164.35   168.22   169.9   169.13
169.28   170.24   171.3   171.7
171.10   171.26   171.29   171.32
171.33   171.35   172.8   172.13
172.14   172.15   172.17   172.18
172.36   173.25   174.3   174.13
174.21   174.22   176.6   177.12
177.17   177.20   177.21   177.38
177.41   178.1   178.6   178.26
178.33   178.34   179.17   179.27
181.30   182.1   182.6   182.13
182.14   183.2   188.15   193.3
193.11   193.16   193.24   194.8
194.9   194.10   196.22   200.10
200.12   200.13   201.7   203.16
203.18   204.5   204.16   204.22
205.14   205.28   205.34   207.5
207.17   208.2   209.22   209.39
211.19   VG 4.16   5.32   6.29
6.35   8.41   9.33   10.28   12.14
13.1   13.3   15.25   16.17   26.41
27.4   27.15   28.27   29.39   30.13
30.36   31.11   43.7   49.33   54.27
58.20   58.32   60.3   60.5   61.8
65.2   66.19   66.22   69.38   77.4
77.32

LIFE-FLOW   SM 111.41

LIFE-IMPETUS   TL 86.35

LIFELESSNESS   CD 255.25

LIFELIKE   SM 111.14

LIFELONG   SM 10.9

LIFE-LONG   CD 214.11

LIFE'S   SM 63.29   VG 58.31   60.32

LIFE-SMOOTH   SM 19.11

LIFE-SPIRIT   CD 230.29

LIFT   LH 10.25   TL 81.36
FO 143.41   169.35   CD 183.6
SM 19.21   69.7   MD 164.40
165.38   172.34   VG 71.11

LIFTED   LH 3.24   4.39   9.22
14.3   TL 52.20   57.27
83.8   FO 117.20   119.29
128.8   128.37   137.39
138.7   139.3   167.6   169.2
170.30   174.36   CD 186.41
189.6   192.16   205.20   207.26
SM 10.4   19.25   27.6   34.29
46.2   53.3   53.5   74.40
75.8   78.10   155.12
MD 165.22   165.23   169.27
172.31   172.33   186.39
188.7   188.17   190.39   199.15
207.25   VG 11.20   21.24
50.26   56.11   60.15   61.11
73.34   81.8

LIFTING   LH 3.19   7.38   33.21
FO 122.22   CD 211.24
SM 13.22   19.38   46.6   58.27
155.37   MD 195.1   197.9
VG 17.4   19.29   66.10   70.38

LIFTS   MD 189.36

LIGATURES   CD 224.6

LIGHT   LH 7.32   7.35   8.2   8.26
13.4   21.29   23.21   25.4
25.9   25.11   26.30   26.40
28.31   28.33   29.6   30.36
30.40   31.5   31.17   31.21
33.8   34.33   34.37   37.22
TL 67.9   67.11   67.17   78.3
78.4   78.5   78.22   89.28
100.13   101.6   101.7   101.10
101.25   101.35   102.41
104.31   107.6   FO 116.16
116.19   120.2   122.18   122.19
122.37   128.27   128.37
130.3   138.5   139.39   140.11
146.24   147.34   154.38
154.40   170.19   CD 184.42
186.24   187.15   189.15
189.24   190.3   198.22   201.37
230.27   233.31   237.24
237.38   241.16   242.22
248.12   263.13   SM 14.35
20.40   21.1   21.16   38.4
46.23   60.17   75.31   94.8
102.10   113.6   124.37   147.38
148.19   MD 164.37   165.38
166.3   166.6   166.8   166.9
185.12   193.29   201.33
202.22   202.38   207.26
VG 19.9   19.29   31.19   36.34
46.8

LIGHTED   FO 119.12   160.37
CD 259.32   SM 147.34
MD 187.41

LIGHTER   LH 27.23

LIGHT-FOOT   VG 17.4

LIGHTING   FO 138.39   SM 147.33

LIGHTLY LH 23.13 33.10 TL 66.2
  SM 24.37 24.39 VG 50.16

LIGHTNING FO 131.26 140.30
  SM 19.23 144.31 148.11 149.25
  149.32 149.35 149.38 152.30

LIGHTNING-CONDUCTOR SM 12.35

LIGHTNING-LIKE VG 15.30

LIGHTS LH 22.5 23.17 23.20
  23.23 23.32 TL 75.4 CD 230.27
  263.12 265.26 SM 27.30 102.7
  102.8 102.20 146.15 VG 25.15

LIKED LH 10.24 35.15 TL 50.18
  70.21 70.27 88.25 98.5
  FO 138.27 CD 208.8 217.25
  225.12 231.5 244.28 251.39
  SM 9.35 9.36 40.23 40.30
  41.4 41.7 44.26 44.27 50.19
  62.18 62.23 62.26 70.10
  99.30 103.14 103.21 MD 189.22
  VG 6.13 10.5 12.38 16.12
  16.23 26.3 28.32 30.13 30.16
  30.18 30.19 41.37 44.39
  65.18 67.14 67.15 67.17
  67.22 67.24

LIKELY FO 149.13 155.12
  SM 88.36 108.1 MD 181.33
  VG 8.21 56.20 79.12

LIKENESS CD 188.36

LIKES LH 14.18 CD 188.26 188.29
  205.40 SM 47.35 105.13 155.34

LIKEWISE CD 201.36

LIKING TL 62.21 SM 41.9 41.11

LILAC VG 39.36

LILAC-COLOURED TL 76.12

LILAC-VEINED TL 76.39

LILIES SM 141.33

LILY TL 75.5 75.7

LIMB VG 74.33

LIMBER LH 22.36 TL 81.33
  VG 21.22 37.18

LIMBO MD 164.3 164.28

LIMBS FO 116.17 132.37 CD 233.8
  233.17 237.31 SM 95.13 95.14
  MD 166.35 188.22 189.4 189.16
  202.2 202.3 207.14 VG 25.8
  29.11 29.29 30.3 30.37 47.42
  48.19

LIME LH 21.5 21.10 VG 68.8

LIME-TREE SM 22.26

LIMIT FO 176.33 SM 115.12
  145.22 145.23 VG 7.35

LIMITATION SM 54.16 137.29

LIMITATIONS SM 137.30 137.35

LIMITED FO 113.31 CD 216.8
  216.9 216.12 SM 146.25
  MD 169.28 194.25

LIMITS FO 177.7 SM 137.31
  MD 164.22 174.24 174.27

LIMP SM 72.12 79.22

LIMPING SM 80.32

LINE TL 51.10 FO 148.4 156.19
  172.23 SM 28.31 50.26 77.16
  81.12 112.18 VG 19.35 38.10

LINEN TL 61.23 FO 155.25
  CD 233.15 SM 30.26 57.8
  MD 166.14 166.23 166.26
  166.33 167.35 168.33 169.21
  186.33 198.2 198.10 198.23
  199.41 200.3 207.15

LINERS SM 124.4

LINES TL 45.9 57.6 71.2
  CD 189.34 216.36 SM 14.29
  19.13 66.37 VG 22.11 23.34
  68.13

LING SM 60.13 65.30

LINGER SM 104.34

LINGERED CD 189.24 260.26 261.4
  SM 42.40 82.36 VG 20.2 36.26

LINGERING FO 140.25 CD 231.8
  258.7 SM 94.11 MD 209.12
  VG 72.12

LINGERS SM 63.35

LION SM 65.14

LIONESS SM 49.37

LION-LIKE CD 239.36

LIONS VG 5.38 72.24

LIP LH 9.22 FO 169.2 170.30
  SM 10.4 23.41 27.6 34.29
  58.27 67.33 VG 61.11

LIPLESS VG 65.31

LIPS LH 5.1 9.32 10.35 34.7
  34.8 34.16 TL 45.20 49.27
  50.14 57.15 76.20 78.10
  94.37 FO 133.32 148.36 168.4
  CD 184.39 196.34 221.23 222.8
  223.10 SM 34.35 56.13 80.41
  81.7 113.30 VG 38.10 38.34
  39.41 43.16

LIQUEURS SM 127.38

LIQUID LH 15.25 SM 11.30

LISTEN TL 67.25 74.34 100.15
  100.21 104.16 FO 117.14
  CD 216.33 SM 46.25 56.7 56.10
  56.15 86.18 103.3 103.8

LISTEN (CONT.) 115.19
  MD 210.32 VG 69.1 69.8
  69.12 71.20 71.21

LISTENED LH 9.37 11.14
  30.38 36.38 TL 100.28
  101.5 101.32 FO 143.35
  143.36 144.4 CD 199.41
  202.36 SM 86.7 90.36
  91.10 106.41 MD 206.9

LISTENER FO 155.1

LISTENING LH 9.33 21.13
  TL 90.38 100.11 FO 119.16
  119.24 119.31 121.40
  135.24 136.18 136.33
  137.41 146.5 158.14
  CD 199.19 220.32 222.9
  222.10 252.12 SM 13.18
  39.12 74.29 75.3 102.38
  MD 164.1 VG 22.14

LISTLESSLY LH 29.28

LISTLESSNESS SM 116.37

LIT LH 6.38 18.15 21.9
  26.31 29.3 FO 158.13
  CD 205.33 SM 102.34
  MD 209.2 VG 53.2

LITERALLY VG 11.18

LITHE VG 50.26 77.17

LITTER MD 191.20 VG 32.34

LITTERED VG 32.23

LITTLENESS CD 230.13
  MD 202.14

LIVE LH 22.5 39.26 TL 52.26
  52.27 54.40 55.30 62.27
  74.38 104.24 104.27 109.4
  FO 115.21 115.38 120.4
  120.6 120.8 141.7 144.9
  144.20 144.29 145.19
  146.34 153.40 163.41
  165.37 174.10 CD 192.31
  196.27 215.3 221.2 225.26
  242.32 256.23 263.22
  SM 41.15 49.29 49.33 51.12
  51.15 64.22 65.3 73.30
  78.36 79.41 80.1 95.31
  95.32 103.38 120.23 129.13
  134.31 142.37 148.35
  156.31 157.16 157.18
  MD 169.12 171.2 174.27
  175.32 176.1 179.40 182.23
  186.9 204.2 205.5 205.14
  205.16 210.17 210.23
  VG 29.32 34.1 40.36 51.36
  58.3 61.40 65.1 65.40
  75.13 81.20

LIVED LH 21.38 TL 99.24
  104.1 FO 120.9 120.27
  120.34 175.14 176.7 176.9
  SM 12.11 19.35 27.16
  32.16 64.20 85.26 94.27
  97.6 99.21 137.39 139.27
  143.3 147.8 148.26 148.28
  154.8 156.31 MD 163.6

LIVED (CONT.) MD 188.31 190.14
  VG 4.12 10.30 11.18 30.5
  53.20 69.39

LIVELIHOOD CD 212.9

LIVELY FO 137.27 137.31
  CD 228.39

LIVER-COLOURED VG 21.3

LIVES TL 55.32 89.5 89.7 89.12
  98.39 107.9 FO 120.3 165.37
  SM 49.31 50.1 85.23 129.11
  153.29 VG 5.17 7.26 9.1
  12.40 16.7 16.14 22.16

LIVID LH 34.20 TL 78.20 83.27
  FO 166.35 CD 201.13 241.25
  241.26 241.29 242.4 242.23
  SM 144.22 154.38 154.39
  MD 169.17 VG 34.18 74.40
  75.24

LIVING LH 5.39 TL 67.21 70.32
  89.11 104.40 FO 113.4 113.15
  115.1 115.20 123.30 149.7
  CD 186.14 192.7 200.10 241.10
  246.14 253.26 SM 26.39 29.8
  29.10 38.18 38.23 49.30 50.7
  71.3 71.33 73.25 73.31 75.2
  76.8 95.39 100.36 103.20
  104.38 129.10 131.13 131.19
  131.31 132.29 141.37 145.10
  146.13 148.25 148.30 150.1
  MD 175.3 193.13 206.22 206.33
  207.7 207.22 210.3 VG 3.18
  23.36 53.34 66.41

LIVING-ROOM VG 10.32 10.34

LIZARD SM 67.17

LIZZIE VG 80.10

LO MD 179.26 207.21 207.38
  VG 3.15

LOAD LH 3.17 3.19 4.37 6.35
  7.15 7.19 7.25 8.32 15.15
  15.29 20.6

LOADED LH 3.13

LOADS LH 14.32 MD 199.31

LOAF CD 238.25

LOATHE VG 55.29

LOATHED LH 19.36 CD 241.29
  VG 29.35 66.21

LOATHING VG 26.21 66.21 66.22

LOBSTER SM 127.35

LOCAL CD 232.2

LOCATING SM 63.25

LOCK SM 108.18

LOCKED TL 87.22 CD 198.21
  198.23 SM 125.5 VG 73.13

LOCKING MD 190.19

LOCOMOTIVE SM 75.36

LOCUSTS CD 232.41

LOFTILY VG 42.22

LOFTINESS CD 249.24 VG 4.27

LOFTY CD 217.16

LOG FO 131.23 146.25 149.39
  152.38 CD 239.5 SM 141.30
  142.2 142.15 143.13 155.6
  VG 47.28 47.30 47.40

LOGIC CD 251.27

LOGICAL SM 42.6 42.7

LOGS FO 131.19 131.21 131.26
  131.29 133.36 133.40 133.42
  134.3 135.39 136.4

LOIN-CLOTH CD 234.32

LOIN-RAG MD 187.10

LOINS CD 191.16 235.8 236.7
  MD 188.27 195.39 207.10
  207.13 VG 39.10

LOITERED CD 238.12

LOLL CD 243.38

LOLLING CD 241.7

LONDON LH 17.2 TL 44.9 60.30
  CD 207.38 SM 3.29 7.18 8.14
  20.35 21.4 27.38 53.22
  110.40 112.19 114.4 114.17
  114.35 116.15 116.38 116.40
  117.9 117.11 118.22 121.18
  124.35 126.7

LONE VG 5.17

LONELIER VG 43.34

LONELINESS LH 33.33 SM 140.8
  MD 166.28 181.14 186.4
  VG 63.31

LONELY LH 10.30 11.41 26.27
  TL 63.42 FO 119.14 CD 216.27
  227.17 SM 10.40 40.27 73.18
  151.39 MD 179.32 VG 9.16 9.33
  24.25 43.25 43.33 67.7

LONG-COATED VG 71.36

LONG-CUBICAL SM 147.37

LONG-DISTANCE SM 102.36

LONG-EARED CD 244.24

LONGED LH 11.39 19.36 SM 97.21

LONGER TL 53.15 70.3 78.4
  85.31 90.8 96.39 FO 123.41
  125.11 157.9 CD 202.16 222.39
  229.1 232.41 237.27 SM 24.28

LONGER (CONT.) 29.23 70.37
  93.1 122.4 132.5 137.39
  MD 164.21 171.21 172.41
  174.29 207.33

LONGEST CD 243.8

LONG-FACED TL 71.15 VG 21.9

LONGING LH 10.7

LONGISH FO 171.6

LONG-LEGGED FO 136.1
  SM 129.33 130.32 131.28

LONG-SLEEVED FO 155.41

LONG-SNOUTED SM 152.7

LONG-STRIDING VG 24.4

LOOKING-GLASS VG 33.32

LOOK-OUT FO 144.21

LOOKS LH 13.15 17.34 39.20
  TL 59.6 70.16 87.10
  FO 122.42 152.37 CD 216.1
  216.2 245.23 257.23
  SM 45.24 52.24 81.30
  124.17 124.20

LOOM SM 5.37 21.1

LOOMED TL 51.24 51.34
  FO 122.20 SM 15.13 19.40
  VG 41.15

LOOMING TL 51.33 52.34
  FO 163.32 CD 255.15
  SM 14.41 27.14 28.13
  31.39 44.39

LOOPED TL 83.8

LOOPHOLE SM 82.21

LOOPS CD 240.23

LOOSE LH 3.23 8.38 14.24
  15.29 TL 46.31 54.5 74.11
  FO 114.9 120.20 132.17
  134.6 139.2 139.17 139.38
  151.16 166.1 CD 192.34
  229.26 231.29 236.39
  237.13 SM 11.13 24.10
  24.11 58.21 69.28 73.12
  146.30 MD 165.11 192.39
  VG 19.20 19.29 19.36

LOOSE-BALANCED FO 114.9

LOOSE-BODIED VG 19.17

LOOSELY TL 72.3 FO 170.29
  171.19 SM 17.10 MD 192.37
  VG 20.15 36.35

LOOSENED SM 87.35

LOPED VG 23.38

LOPING VG 21.10

LOQUACIOUS SM 11.25 132.24

LOQUACITY SM 107.9 109.1

LORD TL 53.4 93.26 94.1
  CD 243.15 SM 23.37 VG 3.19

LORD BEVERIDGE TL 92.40 93.4
  93.32 93.36 93.39 94.7 95.13
  97.5

LORDLY VG 24.9 25.31 26.32

LORDS TL 89.26 90.27 CD 252.13
  252.14

LORDSHIP LH 13.18 SM 23.38
  25.20

LORD ST MAWR SM 23.37

LORGNETTE CD 197.23 197.25

LORRY VG 36.27

LOSE TL 107.20 FO 142.13 142.15
  173.11 173.24 SM 97.17 108.1
  115.17 144.29 MD 183.24
  VG 68.41

LOSES TL 86.14 SM 153.37

LOSING TL 91.16 FO 115.34
  115.35 CD 227.20 SM 96.29

LOSS SM 25.32

LOSSES FO 115.20 123.28

LOST LH 9.4 30.41 TL 54.13
  57.37 58.6 72.14 72.16 80.1
  80.25 80.31 82.28 84.40
  95.11 95.12 95.14 95.32
  FO 122.2 132.19 133.37 142.18
  CD 221.27 223.11 238.9 238.28
  243.30 SM 21.14 61.31 97.15
  127.27 134.7 134.16 143.21
  MD 164.32 195.27 203.27
  VG 6.35 9.33 41.26 42.2 65.9
  79.37

LOST-SOUL CD 238.12

LOT LH 8.26 TL 92.33 FO 165.24
  CD 195.7 210.21 233.2 263.33
  SM 49.39 127.19 141.29
  VG 16.25 33.17 34.1 57.22

LOTS SM 27.35 48.8 48.9 51.34
  52.21 135.11 VG 57.1

LOTTIE VG 13.15 22.7 22.19

LOTTIE FRAMLEY VG 21.29 22.4

LOTTIE'S VG 22.6

LOTUS MD 188.25 189.28 189.34
  190.2 190.11 208.1

LOTUS-BUD MD 187.28

LOTUS-FLOWERS MD 187.29

LOU SM 4.33 4.38 5.9 5.31

LOU (CONT.) 5.33 5.35 5.39
  6.2 6.6 6.19 9.11 9.22
  9.24 9.36 10.24 11.21 11.27
  11.34 11.38 12.5 12.23
  13.7 15.18 16.29 16.32
  17.20 17.38 19.1 19.24 20.10
  21.35 22.1 22.30 22.35 23.27
  23.34 24.1 24.11 25.24 25.29
  25.32 28.10 28.23 28.36
  28.40 30.6 30.22 31.5 31.9
  31.14 31.25 31.38 32.16
  32.37 33.26 33.31 33.35 34.7
  34.33 35.25 37.17 38.7 39.23
  40.3 40.10 40.18 40.30 41.11
  41.21 42.31 45.11 46.38 48.6
  48.22 48.36 51.18 51.29
  52.16 52.41 53.21 53.32 54.8
  54.21 54.36 55.33 57.5 57.24
  57.34 58.7 58.37 59.3 59.10
  64.8 64.11 64.16 64.28 65.28
  65.30 66.2 66.7 66.14 66.25
  66.32 67.27 68.11 68.19
  68.23 68.25 68.37 72.4 72.14
  75.39 76.34 77.5 77.16 79.9
  79.15 79.19 79:23 79.27
  79.33 80.6 80.11 80.15 80.22
  80.35 81.2 81.4 81.17 83.24
  84.24 84.31 85.2 85.15 85.18
  86.7 86.25 86.31 87.1 87.8
  87.28 87.35 88.27 89.17
  89.29 89.39 90.27 91.10
  91.28 91.33 91.36 92.15
  92.24 92.30 92.38 93.18
  93.34 114.10 115.29 115.41
  118.20 119.19 119.28 120.16
  120.20 121.2 121.4 121.6
  121.13 121.27 122.5 122.15
  122.24 122.34 122.35 122.39
  123.10 123.34 124.17 124.21
  124.25 124.33 124.39 125.39
  126.17 126.31 126.34 127.21
  127.32 128.12 128.37 129.6
  129.19 130.14 130.16 130.37
  131.18 131.35 132.2 132.18
  132.20 132.38 133.3 133.7
  133.28 134.4 134.18 134.27
  134.33 136.24 137.10 137.38
  138.20 141.9 154.11 155.1
  155.35 155.39 156.1 156.32
  156.37 157.38 158.10 159.18

LOUD FO 119.34 146.28 174.2
  CD 234.40 236.22 245.3
  SM 21.11 66.32 82.34 MD 165.1
  183.18 VG 11.16 78.20

LOUDLY CD 261.25 VG 33.39

LOUDLY-BARKING FO 146.21

LOUD-MOUTHED LH 5.34

LOUISE SM 5.24 21.37 22.33
  23.12 30.15 37.27 37.33 43.5
  43.8 44.16 44.17 44.31 45.22
  47.11 47.26 47.37 48.3 48.19
  48.34 49.3 49.14 49.28 50.14
  50.23 55.23 55.38 56.1 56.6
  56.7 56.15 56.36 62.24 81.19
  85.17 85.22 85.37 86.11
  86.18 86.35 90.39 91.19
  91.23 92.12 92.14 92.32
  125.17 132.5 133.11 133.18
  155.15 155.25 155.40 157.7

LOUISE'S SM 44.27

LOUISIANA SM 3.24 8.22 9.6
  44.22 61.7 94.28

LOULINA SM 16.12 93.22
  110.20 114.22

LOUNGE TL 97.33

LOUNGING CD 227.17 227.24

LOU'S SM 4.17 8.13 34.2
  34.21 35.34 39.4 51.25
  81.26 88.20 90.36 91.27
  92.9 96.4 116.25 124.20
  124.36 127.2 127.16 136.6

LOUTH, LADY (SEE LADY LOUTH)

LOUTS LH 5.31

LOU WITT SM 3.1

LOVABLE FO 155.29

LOVE LH 5.22 27.12 34.9
  TL 43.10 43.11 43.23 49.14
  63.11 63.12 63.21 63.23
  67.25 67.27 68.34 68.36
  68.37 68.40 68.41 70.16
  70.29 70.30 70.31 70.40
  75.26 79.8 79.26 80.19
  82.10 85.5 85.6 87.35
  87.36 87.37 87.38 87.41
  87.42 88.1 88.3 88.4 88.7
  88.8 88.11 88.12 88.13
  88.17 88.30 88.31 89.16
  89.36 89.38 89.40 89.41
  89.42 90.1 90.15 93.13
  95.24 105.9 105.11 105.20
  105.27 105.30 106.25
  106.30 106.31 106.32
  107.30 107.31 108.35
  108.36 108.39 FO 129.22
  130.23 161.22 161.24
  165.24 165.25 165.28
  166.5 166.16 171.35 175.32
  175.36 175.37 175.38
  175.39 175.40 175.42 176.1
  176.17 177.16 178.11
  CD 191.12 194.5 202.38
  204.9 204.31 209.12
  209.23 210.17 212.3
  214.16 215.12 215.16
  215.35 222.12 225.37 226.4
  226.6 226.8 226.12 226.19
  231.28 250.18 250.20
  250.23 250.24 250.28
  250.38 250.40 250.42 251.2
  251.5 251.6 251.7 251.11
  251.14 251.17 251.18 252.1
  252.2 256.18 258.25 258.26
  259.2 259.7 259.14 259.17
  259.19 259.20 259.34
  261.26 261.29 261.31
  261.42 262.11 262.13
  262.18 262.19 262.29
  262.33 262.39 263.19
  263.22 263.24 263.26
  263.31 263.32 263.34
  264.13 264.14 264.16
  264.17 264.20 264.21
  265.5 265.7 265.10 265.39
  SM 3.5 4.4 4.29 5.13

LUST-LOVE VG 62.39

LUSTROUS LH 22.4 CD 245.1
  MD 167.22 180.13 VG 56.6

LUSTY CD 237.34

LUXURIANTLY SM 28.22

LUXURIATED FO 126.19 SM 9.37

LUXURIOUS SM 36.40

LUXURIOUSLY CD 190.10 VG 30.35

LUXUS CD 260.19 260.29

LYDIA LH 34.29 39.13 39.21
  39.27

LYING LH 6.12 12.18 26.32
  TL 44.7 44.21 49.6 58.24
  FO 115.10 CD 203.11 242.25
  252.34 SM 66.39 104.13 113.27
  125.36 127.29 146.8 147.37
  MD 192.37 VG 29.10 32.24
  62.20 62.28 62.30 81.10

LYSIPPUS MD 210.34

MABEL SM 33.6

MACHINE TL 95.1 SM 87.12 87.19
  138.17

MACHINE-DRILLED TL 64.7

MACHINE-GUN VG 49.3

MACHINES SM 27.11 75.35

MACKINTOSH SM 85.6

MAD LH 10.29 26.28 TL 61.41
  62.4 FO 133.18 CD 185.41
  222.29 240.33 249.33 250.15
  258.32 SM 15.33 40.36 42.10
  42.17 72.38 94.22 103.23
  MD 184.1 184.4 184.8 VG 31.9

MADAM SM 92.19 MD 190.25 194.25

MADELEINE MD 173.21 173.24
  173.29 173.38 174.8 174.20
  175.4 176.37 177.8 178.37
  179.5

MADMAN LH 27.22 TL 69.22
  CD 250.16

MADNESS TL 62.2 FO 136.14
  151.27 166.40 CD 233.9 251.37
  VG 3.8

MAGAZINE VG 11.20 28.33

MAGAZINES TL 69.8 SM 38.13

MAGGOTS SM 30.24

MAGIC TL 97.29 CD 192.7 217.12
  217.13 217.14 217.17 217.18
  217.22 217.29 218.7 SM 102.29
  126.15 126.16 126.20 147.35

MAGICAL TL 97.24

MAGNANIMITY FO 115.28

MAGNET CD 191.21

MAGNIFICENCE MD 206.40

MAGNIFICENT CD 233.6 233.17
  236.15 MD 185.13 207.10
  207.12 VG 50.1

MAGNIFICENTLY TL 59.40 CD 239.9

MAHOMET SM 19.6

MAID TL 60.16 60.40 61.3 70.18
  71.12 72.5 76.7 76.16 76.22
  76.27 76.29 100.18 105.41
  CD 218.17 219.37 220.22
  SM 10.36 33.4 33.32 35.34
  57.8 91.27 117.1 118.21
  118.23 MD 189.12 VG 14.3
  37.30 37.37 44.16 44.21

MAIDEN LH 36.4 TL 53.12
  CD 243.3 MD 197.16 211.5

MAIDENHAIR MD 191.26

MAIDENLY TL 105.23 CD 252.7

MAIDENLY-NECKED CD 252.19

MAIDENS CD 241.36 252.6 254.23

MAIDS CD 199.40 219.35 SM 32.34
  32.39 33.2 34.16 35.20 35.23
  43.18 44.32 45.31 MD 200.23
  VG 9.40 56.31 56.41

MAID'S VG 78.9

MAID-SERVANT CD 235.13 VG 9.22
  53.21

MAID-SERVANTS VG 10.31

MAIMED SM 153.9

MAIN CD 193.14 253.5

MAINSPRING SM 26.20

MAINTAIN SM 73.25

MAIZE SM 129.39 130.1 130.3

MAJESTY MD 193.3 VG 12.24 34.14
  34.33

MAJOR TL 83.18 84.17 84.34
  85.25 85.28 86.12 86.32 87.1
  87.34 89.10 89.30 96.16
  96.35 108.32 CD 207.16
  VG 51.32 53.20 54.14 54.19
  54.21 54.24 54.33 55.4 59.37
  60.4

MAJOR APSLEY TL 76.10 76.22
  83.29 84.20 92.20

MAJOR EASTWOOD VG 51.6 52.34

MAJOR EASTWOOD'S VG 52.10 59.19

MAJOR-GENERAL CD 188.15

MAJOR-GENERAL BARLOW CD 219.6

MAJOR'S TL 83.27 VG 51.17

MAKER VG 63.5

MAKER'S TL 60.13

MALAGA CD 200.5

MALE TL 45.10 58.39
  FO 157.12 179.19 CD 215.29
  227.22 SM 5.37 46.24 75.4
  80.20 91.9 91.14 91.15
  91.17 101.21 109.13 135.9
  135.16 135.23 135.29 136.5
  136.6 137.4 137.17
  MD 171.37 172.3 188.28
  189.16 203.14 VG 22.27
  38.14 50.31

MALEFACTOR MD 192.24 193.19
  194.32 210.35

MALENESS MD 189.24

MALEVOLENCE SM 34.3 73.6
  76.4 144.20 144.37 145.3

MALEVOLENT SM 5.37 144.33

MALICE CD 213.16 SM 58.22

MALICIOUS CD 263.42 SM 74.32

MALIGNANT FO 136.29

MAM SM 23.7 23.10 23.13
  23.14 43.38 44.4 46.34
  59.21 59.24 60.24 60.28
  60.34 60.41 61.2 61.4
  61.6 61.18 61.20 61.27
  61.29 61.41 62.2 62.4
  63.11 88.36 97.39 98.13
  99.2 100.18 100.21 100.24
  105.24 105.36 106.31
  106.36 106.40 107.3 107.6
  107.18 107.21 117.8 117.10
  117.17 117.20 122.22
  122.30

MAMMA VG 28.10 55.15

MAMMAS SM 8.40

MAMMIES SM 9.6

MAN LH 3.30 6.10 7.18 13.11
  16.13 17.31 17.41 18.1
  18.4 18.13 18.30 18.34
  19.7 19.10 19.14 19.23
  19.35 20.18 21.5 23.39
  24.6 28.32 38.15
  TL 44.39 45.8 46.9 49.39
  50.10 51.27 63.2 66.35
  66.39 70.4 71.22 74.9
  74.24 74.31 74.40 75.1
  79.35 81.10 82.7 82.30
  84.18 84.38 85.11 85.27
  85.39 86.5 86.27 87.10
  87.11 88.34 89.3 89.23
  89.41 90.2 91.25 93.6

MAN (CONT.) TL 93.8 93.18
  99.8 99.36 99.37 103.23
  107.5 109.1 FO 113.14 113.16
  113.30 114.10 120.11 120.34
  124.1 144.23 150.30 157.9
  157.11 162.14 162.18 162.20
  169.5 169.11 170.1 170.5
  170.12 170.18 170.36 170.40
  171.4 171.14 171.34 172.14
  172.20 174.15 174.17 177.5
  177.6 179.19 179.22 CD 184.30
  184.36 185.7 185.12 185.14
  187.5 191.12 193.4 193.34
  194.5 197.2 200.31 203.24
  204.4 204.37 205.40 206.29
  207.35 208.34 209.24 210.15
  212.30 214.1 214.6 214.21
  215.11 225.24 225.26 226.4
  227.13 229.8 234.17 237.9
  240.2 240.4 240.34 245.16
  247.11 248.15 248.26 254.22
  256.11 258.8 258.21 263.9
  264.4 264.30 SM 5.37 10.36
  11.12 11.35 13.9 13.17 14.1
  14.7 15.33 17.7 17.21 18.23
  20.15 20.30 23.21 24.4 27.19
  28.29 28.30 34.6 39.19 40.38
  41.23 42.22 43.35 44.11
  45.23 45.24 46.20 46.40
  47.15 47.16 47.26 47.32
  47.36 48.3 48.15 48.16 48.17
  48.20 48.21 48.30 49.6 49.15
  49.16 50.7 50.28 52.31 52.39
  53.17 54.14 54.20 55.7 55.8
  55.11 55.16 55.38 55.40
  56.10 56.17 56.21 56.22
  56.30 59.11 61.12 63.23
  63.29 64.15 64.27 64.30 65.9
  66.13 66.17 67.8 68.3 68.4
  70.10 70.18 71.25 75.22
  75.33 75.35 75.37 77.6 79.17
  80.8 83.21 84.22 88.18 89.21
  92.4 92.6 95.14 95.16 95.23
  95.31 95.33 95.35 98.29
  98.38 105.25 106.3 170.32
  107.41 108.2 108.14 108.31
  113.15 115.4 117.40 120.6
  120.9 120.21 121.30 121.32
  123.1 123.5 123.29 123.32
  125.40 127.34 127.38 128.36
  129.28 130.10 130.11 131.7
  135.2 135.8 135.13 135.15
  137.35 138.33 140.1 140.2
  140.37 144.18 144.21 144.24
  145.5 148.28 151.31 152.35
  153.15 153.35 154.1 155.16
  156.39 158.19 158.24 MD 165.4
  166.8 166.30 167.25 167.35
  167.37 167.41 168.2 168.17
  168.31 168.33 168.38 170.4
  170.10 170.19 170.22 170.30
  171.3 171.9 171.19 171.24
  171.28 171.39 172.11 172.24
  172.30 172.38 172.40 172.41
  173.1 173.5 173.6 173.8
  173.16 174.8 176.13 176.21
  176.30 176.34 177.19 178.15
  178.22 178.28 178.29 178.32
  179.15 180.16 180.18 180.41
  181.12 181.26 182.37 182.38
  183.5 183.7 183.21 183.22
  183.23 183.26 183.28 184.7
  186.29 189.26 189.28 191.10
  191.29 191.36 192.21 192.24
  193.8 193.13 193.32 194.19

MAN (CONT.) 194.23 195.20
  195.22 197.25 198.6 198.18
  198.28 198.36 199.18 199.29
  199.36 200.7 200.11 200.16
  200.32 200.36 200.38 201.29
  202.32 206.1 206.6 206.27
  208.6 209.6 210.11 210.38
  211.1 211.9 211.12 211.17
  VG 3.2 4.12 4.25 4.30 5.6
  10.23 13.22 19.9 19.11
  19.14 19.16 19.38 20.15
  20.17 20.40 20.41 21.20
  22.22 22.31 22.34 23.21
  24.15 25.24 29.3 30.5
  30.7 30.28 36.33 36.34 37.30
  37.32 37.33 37.36 38.2 38.18
  38.27 38.33 39.4 39.13 42.33
  42.40 45.29 45.37 46.2 46.19
  46.25 47.30 49.7 49.28 49.32
  50.10 50.16 50.20 50.25
  50.28 51.12 51.13 51.18
  51.34 51.40 52.15 52.36
  53.32 55.16 56.14 56.39
  57.19 58.13 58.26 59.12
  59.30 60.9 60.25 60.27 63.11
  63.14 69.15 69.17 70.38
  70.42 71.2 71.6 73.17 73.19
  73.27 78.10 78.38

MANAGE LH 18.17 FO 153.33

MANAGED FO 157.37 168.10
  CD 260.13 262.40 SM 36.38
  93.8 VG 38.13 66.14

MANAGEMENT SM 5.32

MANBY SM 52.11 59.10 65.36
  66.6 70.8

MANBY (SEE FLORA, MISS FLORA)

MANBYS SM 28.5 28.6 31.33
  115.8

MANBYS' SM 72.23

MANFULLY FO 153.27

MANHOOD TL 57.37 SM 145.4
  MD 189.4 207.9

MANIA MD 184.6

MANIACAL VG 29.15

MANIFESTED SM 127.13

MANIPULATED CD 205.33

MANKIND SM 69.5 70.33 70.35
  70.37 71.7 71.11 96.10

MANKIND'S SM 69.5 73.29

MANLY FO 117.15 CD 215.28 240.3
  SM 52.37 MD 190.6 VG 22.17

MANNER LH 4.15 TL 52.18 77.14
  FO 127.4 143.20 CD 211.32
  SM 18.39 28.29 68.15 81.20
  82.10 89.8 121.8 131.9
  VG 27.26 38.4

MANNERISM VG 52.26

MANNERS TL 93.35 FO 143.12
  SM 4.15 51.20 VG 7.30

MANNIKIN CD 183.8 183.10

MAN-NURSE TL 52.37

MANOEUVRE LH 7.3

MANOR TL 98.16 CD 238.36
  SM 8.9

MAN'S LH 27.27 TL 73.41
  93.8 FO 114.12 119.35
  119.39 129.35 157.9 179.22
  CD 185.22 186.6 245.36
  245.38 SM 13.7 23.16
  45.20 47.11 68.16 102.30
  105.2 106.1 128.32 135.18
  136.26 136.16 136.22
  137.21 141.21 145.23
  152.36 153.1 153.23
  VG 38.12

MANSION TL 97.23 MD 207.23

MANTILLA CD 200.7

MANTILLAS CD 200.6

MANTLE CD 248.10 MD 166.27
  173.35 181.3 186.34 190.27
  191.8 191.12 192.35 193.33
  195.1 197.7 198.17 199.5
  202.38 207.41

MANTLE-HEM MD 202.23

MANTLEPIECE TL 78.14 79.30

MANTLES LH 22.6 MD 166.32

MAN-TO-MAN SM 18.21 18.25

MANURED VG 19.4

MANY-HEADED VG 57.25

MAPLE-TREE SM 33.28 37.35

MAPS SM 93.2

MAQUEREAU VG 61.14 61.15

MARBLE MD 188.6

MARCH TL 59.23 59.38
  FO 113.2 113.8 113.12
  113.25 113.27 113.36 114.7
  114.27 115.1 115.3 115.12
  115.27 115.30 115.33 116.4
  116.8 116.21 117.14 118.6
  118.12 118.19 119.2 119.8
  119.11 119.15 119.19
  119.31 119.37 119.41 120.4
  120.13 120.22 121.1 121.22
  121.26 121.37 122.19
  122.36 123.10 123.13
  123.30 123.37 123.42
  124.11 124.17 124.25
  124.30 124.33 124.38
  125.11 125.38 126.14
  126.20 126.24 127.14
  127.21 128.6 128.10 128.19
  128.21 128.26 128.39

MARCH (CONT.) FO 128.42 129.18
129.34 130.7 130.22 131.13
131.16 131.22 131.28 132.3
133.42 134.5 134.19 135.3
135.8 136.7 136.19 136.26
136.29 136.32 137.2 137.6
137.8 137.35 138.7 138.13
138.18 138.22 138.26 138.33
138.39 138.40 140.11 140.29
140.39 141.10 141.33 141.34
141.39 142.35 142.41 143.25
144.15 145.3 145.13 147.28
147.40 147.41 148.3 148.27
148.40 149.36 149.40 151.4
151.15 151.32 152.6 152.8
152.11 152.16 153.7 153.14
153.23 153.27 153.38 153.42
154.3 154.7 154.14 154.24
155.5 155.33 156.3 156.27
156.32 157.18 157.24 157.26
157.36 158.2 158.9 158.11
158.14 158.26 158.38 159.2
159.9 159.15 159.24 160.1
163.32 164.4 164.5 164.22
164.27 168.14 168.20 168.34
168.42 169.13 169.34 170.3
170.27 171.17 171.23 171.28
171.32 171.36 172.4 174.2
174.13 174.18 174.21 177.20
178.5 179.8 179.11 CD 247.1
SM 90.22 VG 68.2 69.34

MARCH (SEE ELLEN, MISS)

MARCHED SM 29.35 81.36
MD 164.12 VG 11.37

MARCHING CD 243.1

MARCHIONESSES VG 39.40

MARCH'S FO 114.21 114.24 124.5
125.42 128.9 134.37 135.38
136.40 143.33 145.22 147.16
147.38 153.31 159.18 167.9

MARE LH 21.14 23.8 23.10 23.38
24.3 24.8 CD 239.21 239.30
SM 10.24 10.34 11.3 82.25
83.29 121.31 130.33 131.29

MARES SM 12.41 32.1 74.40

MARGARINE FO 122.3 122.5 123.11
156.28

MARGERY LH 13.21

MARIENKAFER TL 96.33

MARIGOLD SM 17.13

MARIPOSA SM 141.33

MARIPOSA LILY SM 151.9 151.14

MARK SM 79.24 80.29 VG 35.8

MARKET TL 92.15 FO 152.27

MARKET-TOWN FO 164.23

MARKS TL 80.7 CD 184.10 213.40
228.27 MD 194.32 VG 14.12

MAROONED SM 58.34

MARQUIS OF GRANTHAM VG 18.27

MARRIAGE TL 90.36 FO 155.14
CD 232.31 232.34 262.18
262.29 262.33 262.34 263.18
265.5 265.41 266.8 SM 6.1
6.31 6.32 8.13 114.2 117.32
117.40 120.21 120.25 139.30
VG 7.20 67.35

MARRIAGES SM 119.41

MARRIED LH 17.3 17.5 31.39
32.9 35.7 35.18 35.20
TL 46.8 46.23 47.17 56.1
61.17 90.39 102.28 FO 141.27
141.32 150.25 150.27 150.29
151.28 154.12 164.7 175.10
175.21 177.5 CD 202.31 211.40
212.11 214.32 226.3 232.30
SM 3.9 3.10 31.30 47.29
115.34 VG 4.41 5.5 8.13
12.14 50.36 53.27 55.5 58.34
58.35 61.18

MARROW SM 52.39 153.23

MARRY LH 14.35 TL 61.16 106.41
FO 113.12 130.6 130.23 132.2
132.39 133.3 133.23 144.8
144.26 150.32 150.40 152.16
155.11 160.33 160.42 161.7
161.11 161.38 163.9 163.38
164.25 165.28 165.32 166.19
CD 232.24 257.21 257.30
257.40 257.41 258.6 258.8
258.21 259.1 259.3 SM 31.7
106.22 106.27 108.11 117.26
119.20 134.38 MD 190.10
VG 8.11 8.15 22.39 25.27
51.5 57.3 57.12 57.19 60.20
60.21 67.31

MARRYING FO 140.2 CD 232.36
SM 5.3 62.19 120.6 120.8
135.6 139.39 VG 5.4 57.6
57.10

MARS CD 193.11

MARSH TL 102.28

MARSHALL PLACE SM 109.23

MARSHES TL 54.29

MARSHY LH 21.23

MARTIN CD 184.29 185.13 185.38
185.40 186.10 198.40 199.28
217.10

MARTINGALE SM 36.21

MARVELLOUS TL 69.32 71.30 79.29
80.40 85.15 FO 115.4 149.5
CD 193.34 223.2 256.31
SM 10.13 16.40 17.4 35.31
36.32 109.5 110.31 110.39
113.2 115.32 128.31 136.25
MD 180.33 207.20

MARY-BEETLE TL 60.4 96.34

MARY IN THE MIRROR VG 26.5
26.15

MARY-MARY-QUITE-CONTRARY
VG 45.9

MASCULINE TL 59.27

MASCULINITY CD 227.21

MASHED VG 9.12

MASK CD 189.33 251.33
SM 109.14 154.31 157.28
VG 15.19 29.19 59.7

MASK-LIKE CD 189.39

MASONRY VG 77.29

MASQUERADING SM 71.4

MASS LH 7.17 7.31 8.41
TL 90.19 FO 174.6 CD 254.27
SM 71.32 VG 70.23

MASSED TL 97.40

MASSES TL 89.25 89.33
CD 232.5

MASSIVE LH 3.6 7.39 TL 100.5
CD 238.19 241.30 SM 31.12
90.12 144.11 MD 199.4

MASSIVE-SLIPPERY SM 127.10

MASSY CD 253.4

MASTER TL 95.30 104.9
104.14 FO 117.24 130.16
144.31 144.34 CD 251.19
SM 3.15 15.17 32.38
70.6 70.37 73.15 122.24
122.31 153.15 MD 163.9
167.23 168.12 169.7 169.41
172.20 173.40 176.16
176.28 177.10 178.13 181.5
183.11 193.38 VG 66.42

MASTERED SM 3.16

MASTERFUL LH 26.3 CD 250.14

MASTERING TL 95.31

MASTERPIECE CD 193.33 229.3
229.4

MASTERS TL 90.27 SM 50.22
51.6 73.14

MASTIFF VG 43.35 44.39

MAT FO 134.4 MD 168.39
170.6

MATCH LH 28.38 31.13 31.16
31.21 31.23 TL 46.23
SM 9.28 95.12

MATCH-BOX LH 33.6

MATCHES LH 28.31

MATCHLESS   SM 86.26

MATE   LH 13.13   TL 58.34   63.36
  65.40   69.2   SM 137.41   140.1
  VG 43.26

MATED   LH 13.14

MATER   VG 4.15   4.32   5.23   5.25
  5.28   5.42   6.5   6.14   6.18
  6.29   6.30   6.40   7.4   7.14
  9.28   10.39   11.1   12.21   14.7
  34.25   35.22   37.34   40.35
  40.40   80.25

MATER DOLOROSA   TL 43.33

MATERIAL   CD 231.36   VG 31.29

MATERIALS   CD 185.21

MATERNAL   VG 34.34

MATERNITY   MD 209.31

MATER'S   VG 5.3

MATES   TL 58.37   58.38   59.11

MATRIX   SM 20.2

MATRON   TL 44.20   46.4   56.38
  60.35   62.17   SM 9.4

MATRONS   CD 207.7

MATTED   VG 78.40   79.20

MATTER   LH 33.28   TL 48.38   48.39
  60.24   68.16   73.23   75.9   85.22
  88.5   91.6   104.20   FO 113.25
  118.24   125.39   128.5   130.12
  130.13   132.28   157.32   161.39
  166.26   169.13   CD 187.39
  188.28   190.13   190.14   192.38
  203.25   203.29   203.30   221.33
  226.21   237.3   255.42   263.10
  264.4   SM 10.41   15.12   19.17
  22.17   43.26   48.34   49.10
  68.11   73.12   80.17   81.9   90.40
  94.21   94.22   95.3   100.38
  101.10   104.7   104.8   113.21
  114.37   125.21   156.2   157.19
  MD 204.21   VG 8.36   8.41   26.25
  33.35   39.21

MATTERED   CD 223.32

MATTER-OF-FACT   FO 149.15

MATTERS   LH 6.41   TL 66.20   66.21
  92.18   CD 192.29   192.37   192.38
  203.22   203.28   SM 49.6   53.20
  75.26   112.8   114.26   157.18
  159.5

MATURE   CD 235.12

MAURICE   LH 3.25   4.3   4.7   4.19
  5.4   5.12   5.18   5.26   5.37
  6.22   6.23   6.33   6.35   6.38
  6.40   7.3   7.9   7.12   7.26   7.33
  7.41   8.1   8.7   8.11   8.16   8.19
  8.28   8.32   8.34   8.42   9.2   9.4
  9.11   9.13   9.20   9.21   9.25

MAURICE (CONT.)   9.27   9.29   10.19
  10.22   10.24   10.42   11.4   11.13
  11.25   12.1   12.3   12.18   12.26
  12.29   12.37   12.40   13.2   13.12
  13.16   13.26   14.1   14.27   14.33
  15.31   15.35   15.36   15.39
  15.40   16.4   16.7   16.21   16.22
  19.20   19.29   20.3   20.8   20.13
  20.28   20.32   20.36   20.38   21.9
  21.16   21.31   23.11   23.40   24.3
  24.9   24.16   25.19   25.22   25.34
  25.39   26.6   26.10   26.13   26.29
  27.8   27.12   27.16   29.21   36.18
  36.23   36.38   37.13   37.18
  37.28   38.7   38.11   38.14   38.16
  38.29   38.34   39.3   39.10   39.13
  39.19   39.25

MAURICE'S   LH 5.8   8.14   9.16
  15.14   27.1

MAUVE   SM 74.5   119.6

MAYBE   TL 59.21   SM 32.6   54.15
  62.19   62.35   89.37   98.20
  125.20   129.38   VG 81.18

MAYFAIR   SM 23.35   117.21

MAYONNAISE   SM 39.34   115.13

MAYST   MD 197.16

MAZE   VG 45.25

MAZY   VG 39.28

MEADOW   FO 152.30   152.34   153.26
  169.26   172.25

MEADOWS   FO 168.17   169.18   169.22
  VG 36.17

MEADOW-SWEET   LH 21.23   21.29
  22.11

MEAGRE   CD 218.20   MD 169.28

MEAL   LH 15.17   18.15   FO 121.37
  122.2   SM 132.36   MD 186.8
  201.12   VG 9.17   10.2   12.22
  37.35   41.1

MEAL-BIN   CD 233.1

MEALS   VG 9.9   12.29

MEAL-TIME   SM 132.36

MEAN   LH 16.5   18.34   28.26   37.10
  37.12   37.14   TL 50.34   57.13
  65.14   65.20   67.6   67.35   74.13
  84.37   84.42   88.32   88.33
  89.15   89.18   90.26   90.28
  91.12   94.9   95.10   FO 125.41
  127.36   132.14   132.15   133.19
  133.22   133.29   138.17   138.20
  138.21   139.42   140.1   141.14
  150.16   161.13   161.14   161.15
  161.35   162.38   162.39   CD 188.4
  188.9   189.19   189.21   190.25
  191.27   203.37   207.10   212.19
  221.9   223.37   250.16   262.11
  SM 15.8   23.38   52.28   54.25
  55.35   56.25   64.26   69.41

MEAN (CONT.)   72.30   72.31
  72.35   73.15   74.38   77.13
  82.10   90.17   103.13   106.24
  106.26   106.32   107.4   107.21
  107.24   108.7   114.22   114.24
  115.26   124.21   124.22
  124.23   158.22   MD 184.16
  VG 34.7   39.23   39.24   42.8
  49.31   59.8   63.8   63.10
  63.38   69.4

MEANING   LH 13.33   TL 93.36
  93.41   CD 193.7   220.18
  SM 88.1   92.7   130.19   131.34
  139.10   154.31   158.24
  VG 38.19   44.23   63.31

MEANINGFUL   VG 44.23

MEANINGLESS   CD 251.32
  SM 130.16

MEANINGLESSNESS   CD 193.6
  SM 136.39

MEANLY   SM 72.31   72.32

MEANNESS   CD 230.13   SM 72.31
  74.37   101.29   MD 190.7
  202.14

MEANS   TL 59.8   59.13   73.29
  86.42   FO 166.6   CD 196.30
  203.39   207.9   226.6   228.24
  259.4   264.13   SM 30.32
  48.14   52.30   71.26   78.29
  107.2   110.17   113.33   118.17
  158.18   MD 175.4   VG 25.24
  25.25   25.26   32.36   71.21

MEANT   TL 54.20   63.33   68.33
  68.37   97.13   FO 138.18
  161.42   162.27   CD 190.32
  202.18   226.6   226.9   SM 7.24
  21.33   26.1   36.19   83.35
  84.37   88.27   112.28   130.17
  144.8   MD 166.11   166.18
  VG 32.2   34.35   61.4   66.17
  67.33   67.34   67.36   71.5
  79.5

MEANTIME   SM 27.39

MEANWHILE   LH 26.42   27.22
  34.19   FO 117.29   123.7
  CD 184.40   251.20   SM 3.38
  26.8   35.34   136.21
  MD 176.34   VG 11.14   11.38
  21.20   37.25

MEASURE   LH 12.4   CD 223.25
  259.39

MEASUREMENT   TL 60.35

MEASUREMENTS   TL 60.33

MEAT   FO 157.37   CD 248.17
  VG 9.17   47.29

MEATS   VG 54.16

MECHANIC   CD 260.36

MECHANICAL   TL 108.41   SM 131.32

MECHANICALLY LH 7.37 8.13 29.10

MEDAL VG 81.4

MEDDLE SM 91.8

MEDICINES VG 31.16

MEDITATIVE VG 59.34

MEDITERRANEAN MD 185.15

MEDIUM TL 91.41

MEDLEY CD 207.29

MEDUSA SM 21.40

MEEK TL 105.23

MEET TL 54.18 81.7 99.5
  FO 135.13 CD 207.38 207.42
  208.3 208.4 234.3 244.25
  265.37 SM 4.40 18.38 19.4
  20.4 47.10 MD 168.1 182.3
  VG 55.1 62.2

MEETING LH 10.20 38.36 SM 30.10
  30.12

MEGALOMANIA CD 250.8 251.37

MELANCHOLY CD 244.15 SM 13.17

MELBOURNE SM 3.36 4.36

MELLOW FO 116.1

MELODIOUS FO 120.5 CD 187.28
  189.28 191.31 191.41

MELODY CD 199.26

MELT TL 57.21 CD 251.33
  SM 27.31 112.10

MELTED CD 189.7 252.28 SM 14.26
  34.14 34.21 148.8

MELTING SM 40.16 133.34 143.28

MEMBER TL 66.23 CD 230.11

MEMBRANE SM 75.2

MEMORIAL VG 25.36 25.37

MEMORIES TL 64.1

MEMORIZE SM 66.19

MEMORY LH 5.5 TL 66.3 FO 126.39
  MD 165.19 203.34

MEN LH 5.36 7.35 7.42 8.9
  11.9 15.30 16.15 18.15 18.42
  19.32 20.37 TL 43.12 43.17
  43.21 44.21 44.24 44.34
  48.32 49.6 49.29 51.23 52.38
  59.7 73.33 83.24 83.30 86.38
  87.3 87.5 87.21 89.1 89.5
  89.6 89.11 89.13 89.15 89.19
  89.25 89.42 90.19 90.24
  90.40 91.4 91.6 91.7 91.15
  91.33 91.36 91.41 92.35

MEN (CONT.) 93.30 94.7 FO 128.3
  130.25 171.1 CD 193.10 198.40
  199.10 199.11 199.25 199.34
  206.27 206.32 206.39 207.13
  208.36 211.40 212.12 212.26
  213.4 213.6 217.10 229.27
  233.6 233.12 233.13 233.20
  237.29 237.34 238.5 238.12
  241.37 251.2 257.11 257.13
  257.14 260.10 SM 7.22 7.23
  15.41 22.12 22.37 23.17
  27.26 29.12 29.31 32.18
  34.33 40.24 43.23 47.16 48.7
  48.8 48.9 48.24 49.3 49.10
  49.21 49.23 49.28 50.3 50.9
  50.12 50.15 50.16 50.17 50.41
  51.7 51.10 56.2 56.28 61.40
  62.11 65.5 72.5 75.16 75.19
  75.23 75.27 75.30 76.14
  82.19 87.26 87.39 88.6 88.10
  88.38 88.39 88.40 91.12
  91.18 94.36 94.38 95.7 95.11
  95.40 96.5 96.12 96.33 101.1
  108.10 108.13 108.30 109.12
  113.1 120.26 120.30 124.30
  126.35 130.22 136.26 139.13
  139.18 140.4 140.9 144.27
  144.31 144.39 145.6 145.29
  153.27 153.30 156.5 156.24
  156.26 157.2 157.8 157.21
  158.1 158.3 158.4 158.7
  158.14 158.34 158.38 159.8
  MD 173.30 175.12 175.14
  178.20 179.35 179.38 181.6
  182.11 184.1 184.8 184.11
  189.21 189.26 190.5 192.40
  193.14 195.19 196.9 VG 3.18
  6.4 7.10 7.33 9.41 10.5
  22.30 23.40 24.23 25.36
  30.25 40.21 40.31 41.11
  43.22 43.31 50.30 51.9 51.20
  55.35 55.36 55.38 55.40
  77.25 78.1 78.26

MENACE CD 213.4 213.6 SM 15.16
  16.6 66.16 80.26 152.25
  MD 193.37 VG 21.18

MENACED VG 63.18

MENACING SM 151.40 MD 194.21

MENAGE SM 7.4

MENDING FO 149.40

MEN-FOLK VG 4.17

MEN'S LH 9.42 SM 29.30 45.25
  48.37 49.26

MENSERVANTS SM 112.33

MEN-SLAVES MD 200.34

MENTAL SM 95.18 95.19

MENTION SM 49.3 VG 6.22

MENTIONED FO 117.38 CD 211.20
  SM 89.4 VG 14.16 29.39

MEPHISTOPHELIAN SM 18.14

MERCHANT SM 123.38

MERCIFUL CD 214.22 SM 149.30

MERCI MON CHER SM 137.20
  137.23

MERCY SM 18.26 33.11 111.34
  VG 15.13

MERE CD 254.3 SM 35.1 42.38
  48.19 48.30 66.12 69.2
  71.9 95.29 97.20 101.21
  129.12 139.5 VG 61.4
  66.15 67.23

MERELY LH 27.13 34.32
  TL 79.35 91.41 FO 113.34
  119.16 SM 16.27 27.28 88.3
  100.31 110.21 VG 35.26
  43.12 56.22 60.12

MEREST FO 131.42 VG 38.11

MERIONETH SM 61.2 61.4

MERITS SM 18.23

MERRILY SM 87.37

MERRIMENT SM 109.1

MERRINESS SM 107.11

MERRITON SM 92.27 92.29
  92.34 106.16 109.19
  112.15 117.7 117.18

MESA SM 139.20

MESA-SIDES SM 147.24

MESH TL 62.34

MESMERISED VG 10.14 22.38

MESMERISM FO 130.40

MESS TL 84.28 SM 70.25
  139.25 143.27 MD 163.19
  170.31 VG 32.33

MESSAGE TL 50.42 CD 206.9
  SM 37.19 37.22 39.3 39.6
  39.33 39.39 84.3 VG 13.37
  14.38 16.3 16.28 69.33

MESSED SM 120.12 140.5

MESSIAH MD 176.11

MESSING SM 158.27

MET LH 33.24 34.7 34.9
  37.42 39.13 TL 55.34
  FO 116.27 126.23 161.6
  172.42 CD 204.20 208.7
  226.10 233.25 236.20
  SM 3.35 4.3 7.24 41.22
  47.37 60.30 61.36 63.19
  88.20 95.15 100.29 107.5
  128.8 MD 197.3 209.9
  VG 20.4 22.34 23.32 64.41
  68.1

METAL LH 9.18 26.33 31.4
  TL 57.6

METALLIC   CD 260.35   SM 153.40
  VG 24.35   45.28

METAMORPHOSE   VG 43.31

METAPHORICAL   SM 95.36

METAPHYSICAL   SM 95.36

METEOROLOGICAL   CD 212.33

METHOD   CD 258.34

METHODIST   SM 98.6

METHYLATED   SM 82.15

MEWS   SM 10.24   10.33   10.34
  16.38   117.13   124.8

MEXICAN   SM 7.27   77.25   134.6
  135.4   135.31   142.18   142.31
  143.3   143.5   143.12   154.8
  155.16   155.19

MEXICANS   SM 132.13   132.41
  140.24   141.39   142.29   142.35
  144.38   145.1   147.17   153.20

MEZEREON   TL 56.33   VG 70.8

MICE   CD 233.1

MICHAELMAS   SM 74.6   141.4   151.4
  155.3

MID-AFTERNOON   SM 126.12

MID-BLUE   CD 235.34

MIDDAY   VG 6.2

MID-DAY   VG 12.21

MIDDLE   LH 8.7   TL 76.17   77.5
  99.32   FO 130.7   147.28   159.12
  159.26   CD 231.32   SM 15.28
  44.40   53.25   112.25   119.22
  146.37   149.23   MD 174.9   211.22
MIDDLE-AGED   CD 245.15   247.33
  MD 176.13

MIDDLE AGES   TL 86.40

MIDDLE-CLASS   CD 194.38   229.31
  240.7   VG 9.5

MIDGE   MD 180.18

MIDGES   MD 180.19

MIDNIGHT   CD 230.19

MIDST   TL 95.29   100.3   CD 229.17
  250.5   SM 14.27   73.25
  MD 181.14   181.16   185.16

MIDWAY   LH 15.36

MIGHTN'T   LH 30.29

MIGHTY   LH 18.40   SM 61.10

MILD   FO 142.23   SM 82.14   VG 32.8
  44.9

MILDLY   VG 16.39

MILE   LH 35.35   CD 252.25
  SM 29.12   97.25   142.5

MILE END   SM 29.7   29.11

MILE-ENDERS   SM 29.8

MILES   LH 15.2   FO 136.11   164.23
  168.11   SM 29.13   31.33   35.33
  36.37   52.1   57.2   65.29   74.8
  78.14   97.28   106.16   142.3
  143.5   147.17   147.20   VG 8.3
  9.31   80.29

MILESTONE   FO 178.18

MILIEU   VG 3.29

MILITARY   CD 184.31   184.36
  185.24

MILK   TL 69.29   73.1   FO 138.28
  CD 252.5

MILK-FLOAT   LH 15.6

MILKY   MD 200.15

MILL   LH 35.34   SM 63.1   MD 198.16
  VG 5.3   73.3

MILL-BOARD   SM 111.39

MILLICENT   TL 71.27   76.8   76.33

MILLING   MD 198.14

MILLION   SM 71.8   154.23

MILLIONS   SM 64.16

MILL-OWNERS   VG 10.8

MILL-RACE   VG 74.35

MILLS   VG 36.8

MINCING   CD 186.11   SM 9.7
  VG 52.26

MIND   LH 8.18   9.1   9.10   12.16
  14.34   25.33   25.39   26.1
  TL 47.19   48.32   51.26   53.32
  54.10   55.40   68.13   68.16
  68.21   80.29   87.27   87.35   95.8
  108.41   FO 115.31   116.11
  118.31   121.20   121.26   122.29
  124.32   124.33   125.38   127.11
  130.9   130.28   134.35   135.2
  139.30   145.1   149.29   152.19
  159.21   165.6   165.15   166.41
  167.8   167.10   167.11   167.14
  173.12   173.15   CD 189.4   189.42
  191.6   191.34   192.23   197.13
  202.9   202.41   204.26   204.39
  205.42   207.41   208.34   208.35
  208.38   211.21   214.12   223.5
  225.18   226.4   228.22   237.3
  246.31   246.32   250.25   250.26
  250.27   251.34   256.31   263.41
  264.7   SM 22.35   35.6   41.24
  41.25   43.11   47.14   47.15
  47.31   47.34   48.4   48.7   48.11

MIND (CONT.)   48.34   48.38
  49.2   49.6   49.8   49.11
  49.13   50.26   52.25   54.16
  56.29   60.26   61.24   62.31
  79.25   92.12   93.19   93.30
  95.21   95.22   95.23   95.25
  104.35   105.2   105.11   106.1
  106.8   110.29   111.40   113.41
  119.33   132.21   140.29
  149.16   158.30   MD 176.27
  VG 13.6   15.24   20.13   22.10
  30.11   35.14   41.3   44.3
  44.17   44.20   50.5   50.12
  53.9   56.40   57.30   62.13
  62.16   79.6

MINDED   CD 206.41   VG 12.32
  57.23

MINDING   LH 14.31

MINDLESS   CD 191.25

MINDLESSNESS   FO 117.3

MINDS   TL 50.22   50.29
  FO 157.33   SM 48.33   48.37
  50.11   50.12   51.8   105.3
  105.5   105.12   109.36
  VG 64.9   77.23

MINERAL   SM 59.38

MINERS   SM 29.18

MINES   SM 102.21

MINE'S   LH 34.31

MINGLE   CD 199.38   MD 177.31
  178.7

MINGLED   VG 5.29

MINGLING   VG 76.32

MINISTERS   SM 98.8

MINISTRATIONS   MD 193.28

MINNIE   LH 26.15   26.17

MINOR   SM 73.31

MINORITY   SM 113.35

MINTY   CD 245.4

MINUTE   LH 13.14   23.8
  28.30   30.25   TL 71.14
  72.1   76.23   80.36   FO 138.32
  139.4   139.35   140.9   146.42
  147.26   158.17   158.25
  158.31   158.36   159.37
  160.28   162.2   162.36   167.29
  CD 192.28   192.30   209.12
  210.9   211.16   220.6   220.22
  223.5   231.36   236.30   237.4
  263.38   264.5   SM 62.6   91.37
  103.36   MD 172.13   187.7
  VG 15.21   15.24   32.35   46.5
  47.20   78.25   79.29

MINUTES   LH 30.30   37.35
  FO 168.26   CD 186.37   204.37

MONEY LH 35.37 36.1 TL 46.9
46.24 FO 113.9 136.41 137.4
150.31 164.29 164.30 177.9
CD 223.31 231.30 232.41
246.34 251.6 SM 5.13 5.14
31.7 44.3 53.18 89.41 90.1
93.27 104.40 105.2 105.5
131.33 131.37 134.28 134.30
134.32 135.11 136.15 142.25
MD 175.28 175.29 177.6 177.8
177.9 177.32 178.13 178.18
179.7 179.10 181.7 181.11
181.23 181.24 VG 25.28 25.30
26.23 26.26 26.37 27.30
27.33 27.38 27.40 28.6 28.30
29.1 29.2 29.4 38.41 58.21
61.40 63.12

MONEY-BOX VG 26.7

MONGREL TL 92.28 VG 26.38 61.6

MONGRELS TL 92.29 93.2

MONK CD 263.23

MONKEY TL 50.19 59.29 FO 156.33
CD 221.10

MONKEYS CD 190.18

MONKSHOOD CD 244.38 244.39
244.40 244.41 245.2 SM 57.6

MONOTONOUS TL 49.28 51.42 63.7

MONOTONOUSLY LH 7.38

MONSIEUR LE COMTE TL 69.19

MONSTER CD 253.31 257.17

MONSTROUS SM 121.36 VG 60.22

MONTE CARLO SM 8.29 126.18

MONTGOMERY SM 60.38

MONTH LH 13.35 32.3 TL 68.18
80.27 80.28 FO 144.5
CD 188.39 188.41 SM 28.4
VG 27.31

MONTHS LH 32.11 32.15 TL 80.27
80.28 80.31 FO 115.35 118.24
118.37 119.1 CD 204.39
SM 3.10 11.39 VG 9.22 10.7
53.17

MONTH'S LH 39.25 VG 61.18

MONTHS' LH 35.11 CD 212.25

MONUMENT VG 25.38

MOOD TL 102.35 CD 251.28
SM 76.22

MOODS SM 15.20 VG 66.6

MOON LH 21.25 21.27 TL 57.32
68.38 79.33 101.37 102.17
FO 117.30 117.34 CD 200.38
201.11 201.30 201.36 203.28
203.29 203.41 220.28 220.31

MOON (CONT.) 223.34 223.37
223.38 224.1 264.33 264.40
SM 101.40 102.37 103.29
103.33 103.34 104.2 104.10
104.17 104.19 104.20 VG 76.30

MOON AND STARS SM 29.33 29.35
89.21

MOON-BOY SM 104.8

MOON-FIERCE TL 82.26

MOONLIGHT LH 6.24 22.1
CD 201.18 201.21 SM 31.37
104.21

MOON-MOTHER TL 77.35

MOONSHINE TL 68.36

MOON-WHITE SM 151.2

MOOR CD 222.15 SM 64.6

MOORED MD 203.3

MOOR-LIKE SM 57.1 60.17

MOORS SM 60.6 63.2 VG 53.19
53.35

MOP SM 17.11 17.32 38.35 39.1
45.4 VG 53.31

MORAL VG 28.28 54.23

MORALITY VG 28.25 30.22 54.27
54.30

MORALLY TL 96.5 96.6 CD 206.29

MORALS CD 219.8

MORASS SM 76.8 VG 78.12

MORBID LH 5.39 11.41 SM 30.25

MORBIDLY LH 4.4

MOREOVER LH 5.31 FO 113.14
135.39 155.28 CD 260.15
SM 138.3 142.30

MORGAN LEWIS SM 103.4 116.32

MORNING LH 15.7 21.35 29.18
30.29 34.33 38.35 TL 44.15
48.4 56.31 56.32 59.39
101.16 104.32 107.38
FO 114.28 124.7 126.38 127.22
127.26 141.5 148.18 150.6
157.31 164.22 166.41
CD 192.34 219.27 237.12
237.18 237.31 266.15 SM 8.16
9.33 9.34 11.1 17.30 22.25
23.24 24.18 25.20 39.26
39.27 51.23 57.3 57.6 57.36
59.16 60.9 60.16 68.36 84.18
85.4 92.1 97.8 97.31 97.34
106.17 131.40 133.37 134.4
146.20 147.32 147.40 148.7
154.27 MD 164.36 165.4 167.6
170.7 170.39 178.32 179.3
183.17 192.8 193.34 194.5

MORNING (CONT.) 195.31 206.6
209.9

MORNINGS LH 34.20 FO 115.41

MORNING'S FO 167.7

MOROCCO SM 5.25

MORSEL MD 171.41 172.1

MORTAL TL 81.31 CD 222.12
SM 109.4 VG 41.4

MORTALITY TL 82.22

MORTALLY CD 250.29

MORTIFICATION CD 259.36

MORTIFIED LH 5.38

MOSS LH 32.13

MOSTLY TL 44.35 SM 4.5 50.16
56.3 59.28 63.14 122.32
143.4

MOTH LH 27.7

MOTH-DUST SM 151.10

MOTHER LH 5.30 5.32 5.33
10.21 13.22 14.36 TL 46.16
46.17 47.2 47.3 47.20
47.39 48.18 48.24 48.29
49.9 49.28 51.25 52.41
53.6 54.3 57.4 61.7
61.18 71.38 81.14 100.41
FO 132.23 132.27 166.28
CD 208.30 262.6 SM 3.26
4.31 5.26 7.28 7.40 9.34
17.25 21.35 22.35 24.1
25.27 25.29 25.38 26.2
27.8 27.40 28.23 31.14
35.25 43.7 43.21 43.22
43.32 44.32 45.13 45.18
47.20 47.40 48.6 48.37
49.8 49.11 49.17 49.25
49.26 49.30 49.33 49.35
49.36 50.1 50.5 50.12
50.21 50.25 50.35 50.40
51.2 51.14 51.18 55.25
55.31 55.33 55.39 56.2
56.12 56.26 56.35 59.3
64.8 66.7 73.39 81.1
81.14 81.22 84.24 84.28
84.36 85.4 85.15 85.18
85.35 86.8 86.26 86.31
86.34 90.27 90.37 91.3
91.12 91.18 93.34 93.38
94.3 109.24 110.9 110.27
111.20 112.14 112.15 114.4
114.6 114.18 114.27 114.37
115.21 115.38 116.2 117.30
119.32 120.2 120.20 120.23
121.21 123.38 125.13
125.15 125.23 127.32
128.13 128.23 128.39
130.14 131.24 132.4 132.7
132.34 133.7 133.9 133.16
133.20 134.40 154.15
154.16 154.19 154.25
155.2 155.27 155.39 156.9
156.11 156.16 156.21
156.26 156.32 156.40

MOTHER (CONT.) SM 157.14
  157.24 157.37 157.40 158.23
  158.31 159.11 MD 178.38
  179.19 190.15 195.20 197.34
  199.7 199.12 199.22 200.39
  201.6 201.26 201.28 209.24
  VG 3.13 3.28 5.31 28.12
  28.13 28.18 31.10 52.31
  63.27 64.1 70.16 79.38

MOTHERHOOD SM 86.10 86.12

MOTHER HUBBARD SM 149.17

MOTHER-IN-LAW SM 23.26

MOTHER-LOVE VG 6.19

MOTHERLY VG 65.29

MOTHERLY-SEEMING VG 15.16

MOTHER OF HORUS MD 188.5

MOTHER-OF-PEARL TL 71.35
  VG 53.39

MOTHER'S TL 47.31 61.7 SM 9.23
  20.21 30.10 30.23 34.38 73.1
  80.40 85.30 119.19 123.19
  MD 196.39 VG 80.11

MOTH-STILL SM 151.9

MOTION FO 179.34 CD 207.26
  233.23 238.22 SM 36.34 69.14
  128.28 128.35 MD 171.30
  187.13 197.39 VG 48.29

MOTIONLESS TL 45.38 103.21
  103.30 FO 173.30 174.14
  CD 201.20 201.23 244.4 255.14
  SM 68.5 101.37 141.16 151.30
  MD 210.41 VG 17.14 45.19
  75.38

MOTIONLESSNESS CD 247.27

MOTIONS CD 215.38

MOTIVES SM 30.30

MOTOR SM 31.33 31.35 VG 51.36

MOTOR-BUS CD 260.3

MOTOR-CAR CD 238.30 239.19
  240.15 240.20 240.23 257.6
  257.11 260.28 262.25 SM 91.17
  93.13 127.22 136.40 140.32
  154.28 VG 19.19 36.27 48.33
  52.25 57.39 79.16

MOTOR-CARS CD 244.25 SM 9.10
  75.35 91.15 127.24 128.8
  129.15 130.41 136.17 140.24
  VG 10.11

MOTORED SM 73.38 97.29 128.5
  132.9

MOTOR-HORN VG 17.27

MOTORING VG 14.37

MOTORISTS SM 109.18

MOTOR-LORRIES CD 222.15

MOTOR-OMNIBUS CD 238.30 240.17

MOTTLED VG 15.18 34.13 37.15
  46.11 46.37

MOUE SM 88.8

MOULD LH 34.14 TL 57.5
  CD 191.15 VG 30.32

MOULDED TL 97.27

MOULDY SM 65.4

MOUND MD 192.30 VG 76.39 76.40

MOUNDS SM 65.25 148.2

MOUNT LH 23.12 SM 58.1 58.39

MOUNTAIN CD 238.21 239.34 241.3
  241.9 242.14 242.36 245.32
  247.27 252.19 SM 19.7 65.13
  139.21 141.13 142.4 142.34
  143.16 144.26 147.30 147.33
  148.9 149.6 151.18 152.3

MOUNTAIN-BELL CD 241.4 244.37

MOUNTAIN-BUCK CD 238.11

MOUNTAIN LION SM 143.32

MOUNTAINS TL 73.23 73.30
  FO 130.34 160.41 CD 237.17
  237.21 237.29 237.33 238.40
  241.40 249.11 249.15 249.18
  249.22 249.34 249.36 249.41
  251.37 SM 78.10 78.20 133.36
  134.5 134.7 134.13 140.16
  140.20 140.33 141.18 141.19
  141.24 142.17 144.34 145.23
  146.36 146.38 147.12 147.14
  147.22 147.27 147.40 149.11
  151.35 152.32 153.14 154.36
  154.38 159.14 MD 188.37

MOUNTAIN'S SM 143.31

MOUNTAIN-SIDE CD 239.7 243.7
  SM 141.31 144.7 146.34

MOUNTAIN-TOP CD 252.27

MOUNTAIN-TOPPER CD 242.32

MOUNTAIN-TOPS CD 249.25 249.27

MOUNTEBANK TL 88.38

MOUNTED LH 20.37 25.2 CD 185.25
  245.19 254.2 255.5 SM 25.11
  36.8 59.4 68.23 93.4 130.6

MOUNTING CD 216.39 SM 102.16

MOURN MD 205.11

MOURNED MD 205.12

MOURNERS SM 28.21 37.29 85.6

MOURNFULLY FO 146.3

MOUSE SM 50.30

MOUSTACHE LH 4.26 12.36
  TL 51.10 FO 156.5 CD 184.8
  SM 7.33 39.21 39.29 52.15
  77.17 VG 3.5 9.25 19.21
  19.35 38.10

MOUSTACHED SM 18.8

MOUSTACHES SM 91.13

MOUSY SM 135.38

MOUTH LH 4.4 4.26 5.6
  29.20 33.22 34.6 34.8
  34.12 38.37 TL 47.26 49.11
  51.10 54.41 54.42 59.1
  62.37 63.37 70.5 76.30
  78.20 89.29 FO 114.15
  116.13 116.38 118.30
  121.41 122.22 123.2 124.31
  126.35 128.13 128.39
  133.16 136.8 137.36 137.38
  140.31 143.3 143.17 143.24
  149.33 151.6 156.4 156.9
  163.22 174.33 CD 189.16
  193.8 216.23 217.20 230.2
  231.11 238.40 239.9 239.12
  SM 11.5 18.15 79.6 104.16
  120.39 156.4 MD 173.14
  191.39 VG 11.19 15.21
  15.24 29.20 50.30 51.12
  58.11 60.4 60.11 65.28
  65.29 73.35 74.7

MOUTHFUL MD 191.27

MOUTHFULS FO 156.28 156.31

MOUTHING VG 15.9

MOUTHS SM 142.37 VG 77.30

MOVE LH 6.11 9.35 22.7
  24.12 TL 53.41 78.33
  103.14 103.18 FO 156.39
  159.19 173.14 173.21
  CD 187.1 212.40 223.29
  SM 68.9 92.22 92.24 136.9
  MD 165.12 165.27 170.12
  170.19 184.2 199.21
  VG 17.30 45.38 69.28
  69.36 69.37 72.20

MOVED LH 4.24 7.37 20.11
  23.26 34.12 TL 94.38
  FO 122.19 126.27 129.2
  174.39 CD 191.15 SM 3.24
  18.28 19.22 19.39 20.16
  22.23 28.1 33.18 42.15
  57.39 62.21 74.26 78.40
  87.34 120.20 130.26
  MD 165.22 165.26 210.6
  VG 18.24 25.4 28.16 37.10

MOVEMENT TL 78.13 SM 53.29
  83.8 105.14 MD 165.15
  187.17 211.7 VG 18.40
  52.38

MOVEMENTS FO 114.11 CD 184.42
  187.3 245.13 SM 32.28

MUSED (CONT.) TL 63.33 70.41
   CD 202.10 212.16

MUSEUM FO 142.11 SM 91.9 118.36

MUSIC FO 135.37 VG 42.20

MUSICAL TL 78.7 CD 200.30 215.2

MUSING LH 3.34 14.36 FO 116.10
   117.33 118.23 121.27
   CD 208.25 SM 38.15 42.33
   MD 197.13 VG 43.29 58.7 70.31

MUSINGS MD 191.9

MUSLIN SM 52.11

MUSTARD VG 54.15

MUSTN'T LH 35.5 TL 52.26 53.18
   CD 237.4 SM 119.34 156.12
   VG 63.38

MUTE FO 134.19 174.38 CD 215.40
   SM 107.9 VG 62.22

MUTED SM 25.36 VG 63.3

MUTENESS TL 95.29

MUTILATED SM 89.14

MUTTERED LH 12.33 37.41
   FO 170.12 170.40 171.34
   SM 45.35 VG 47.5 47.14

MUTTERING FO 170.13 170.36

MUTTON VG 9.11 47.16

MUZZLE FO 117.25 148.42

MUZZLES SM 19.39

MYRIAD SM 71.36 73.29

MYRTLE MD 173.36 176.8 178.35
   200.21

MYSTERIES MD 203.7

MYSTERIOUS TL 83.7 96.41
   CD 262.23 SM 14.21 59.38
   69.18 69.28 70.22 75.25
   95.29 96.24 96.26 144.20
   152.33 MD 201.37 VG 48.2 48.8
   57.42 67.15

MYSTERIOUS-LOOKING TL 76.40

MYSTERIOUSLY SM 150.30 MD 164.3
   VG 56.5

MYSTERY TL 79.28 82.28
   CD 193.10 217.32 218.2 238.27
   SM 48.14 48.16 48.17 49.20
   50.22 54.37 97.2 97.4 97.23
   98.38 99.18 140.8 158.25
   MD 188.29 190.13 190.14
   201.18

MYSTIC CD 253.22 SM 131.33
   131.39 140.1

MYSTICAL SM 78.19

MYSTIFIED CD 190.25 SM 12.23

MYSTIFY SM 99.11

NAGGING VG 32.12 34.1

NAIGHT LH 38.2

NAIL-BOOTS CD 254.38

NAILED LH 12.14 TL 99.42
   FO 149.31

NAILS CD 256.6 MD 204.11

NAIVE TL 74.2 81.29 89.32
   CD 210.8 SM 41.36 MD 204.17
   VG 8.34 24.9 38.18 58.26

NAIVELY CD 203.10 SM 82.17
   MD 203.23 VG 40.27

NAIVETE FO 125.33 SM 104.22
   VG 58.15 63.24

NAKED FO 116.17 CD 190.6 233.17
   233.18 234.31 235.27 237.7
   237.8 237.20 237.34 239.33
   241.11 241.29 242.24 243.13
   243.18 248.41 253.10 254.21
   255.27 SM 11.16 14.29 19.37
   26.37 53.3 54.27 66.37
   129.36 141.33 151.13 156.38
   MD 166.32 186.7 186.22 187.7
   197.27 198.3 198.37 199.25
   199.26 200.6 202.8 202.9
   203.15 203.32 205.19 209.22
   210.39 VG 9.16 18.12 18.33
   18.37 19.4 30.29 30.30 31.41
   33.1 38.21 49.30 59.5 68.20
   75.31 75.41 78.41

NAKED-LOOKING CD 187.18

NAKEDLY MD 171.10 202.25

NAKEDNESS MD 204.8 VG 78.33

NAME LH 16.14 16.17 16.19
   16.20 26.16 34.28 36.4
   TL 50.15 50.24 50.27 53.10
   53.15 53.20 60.13 FO 114.20
   124.35 CD 186.32 197.39 206.2
   209.31 228.3 SM 8.8 11.34
   16.16 131.30 159.20 MD 208.38
   208.39 210.1 VG 4.42 6.29
   14.19 81.22

NAMED LH 13.3 TL 82.18 VG 50.37

NAMELESS SM 142.24

NAMES TL 53.14 53.17 FO 164.24
   CD 195.28

NAP VG 32.29

NAPE TL 53.39 SM 42.28 VG 24.16

NAPLES SM 4.28

NARCISSUS MD 186.13 186.32
   193.35 208.21 208.24 209.1

NARROW TL 46.13 88.12 97.35
   CD 239.19 SM 63.31 66.11
   139.20 144.6 144.14 149.3
   MD 166.1 166.4 178.34
   183.5 200.32 VG 9.29 18.19
   19.13 36.9 74.30

NASTILY SM 34.29

NASTURTIUMS SM 145.17

NASTY FO 152.40 152.41 153.1
   153.2 CD 188.3 207.31
   SM 10.16

NASTY-MINDED SM 90.19

NATION LH 15.32 SM 7.30

NATIONS SM 69.6 69.21

NATIVE TL 93.39 SM 116.18
   134.29

NATTY LH 29.14 VG 19.40

NATURAL LH 27.42 TL 51.19
   65.41 FO 121.7 126.18
   CD 187.22 214.15 221.28
   231.21 SM 51.7 71.20
   72.1 73.32 128.32 129.35
   137.37 148.22 MD 167.3
   167.5 169.30 VG 61.21 71.8

NATURALLY TL 61.10 82.30
   CD 254.10 SM 7.19 80.7
   VG 7.16 7.18

NATURE LH 33.33 TL 47.10
   58.14 89.4 93.10 FO 124.17
   124.19 124.20 155.1
   CD 210.9 221.3 223.17
   223.18 229.33 263.29
   SM 41.13 70.20 95.4 120.6
   124.27 154.3 159.10
   VG 61.27 71.3

NATURES TL 47.37

NAUGHTY SM 111.6 111.16

NAUSEA TL 51.6 MD 165.14
   165.22 167.12 168.29
   169.13 176.7 184.11 184.14

NAUSEATE SM 157.2

NAVAJO SM 20.16 20.22

NAVAJO INDIAN SM 7.27

NAVEL MD 188.19 196.25

NAVRE CD 244.16

NAY LH 12.37 13.2 20.28
   20.32 30.17 37.5 TL 43.10
   85.37 FO 179.23 CD 215.10
   217.34 217.35 229.34
   SM 98.5 151.23 MD 174.37
   176.5

NEARED LH 9.14 SM 127.8

NEARER LH 10.1 TL 106.5

NEARER (CONT.) TL 106.26
  FO 116.18 126.29 SM 13.22
  13.27 19.22 59.22 63.7 67.39
  132.17 MD 176.17 208.35
  210.40 VG 18.26 73.14

NEAREST CD 212.20

NEARING VG 8.31

NEARLY TL 93.31 99.25 FO 139.14
  147.19 166.23 CD 248.37
  SM 36.35 69.24 MD 165.32
  VG 7.26 12.11 13.2 13.6 31.9
  35.36 36.1 60.25 70.7 73.15

NEARNESS SM 148.40

NEAT LH 29.14 38.28 VG 38.2

NEATLY SM 119.2 MD 200.27

NECESSARY TL 94.17 CD 214.15
  225.35 264.32

NECESSITY FO 174.9 SM 78.4
  MD 171.2 175.12 VG 57.24

NECK LH 8.22 33.30 TL 53.40
  61.21 FO 133.16 140.20 140.22
  173.39 174.6 CD 207.27 264.30
  SM 13.31 13.35 19.20 42.28
  45.24 46.13 46.17 46.21 58.4
  66.37 69.35 82.26 90.13
  MD 163.4 163.24 170.14 186.30
  192.16 199.10 210.28 VG 19.23
  20.22 21.18 22.24 24.16
  61.30 63.37 65.21

NECK-BAND TL 60.34

NECKLESS VG 65.23

NECKS CD 252.7 VG 61.23

NECKTIE SM 4.6

NECKTIES SM 23.18

NECTARINES SM 113.6

NEED TL 48.9 107.36 107.37
  108.35 109.1 FO 125.1 125.6
  129.24 159.3 175.38 CD 185.12
  192.1 225.19 256.29 266.9
  SM 81.8 91.7 124.14 137.37
  138.26 MD 175.5 175.10 179.10
  179.35 206.7 VG 64.19 71.21

NEEDED LH 10.30 TL 47.18 108.34
  FO 119.22 CD 246.34 SM 56.20
  78.2 112.30 135.30 136.10
  VG 10.23 26.23 27.14 54.37

NEEDING LH 34.18

NEEDLE TL 60.5 70.24 FO 128.28
  151.16 CD 226.5 SM 31.17

NEEDLE-LADY TL 72.11

NEEDLES TL 71.36 71.37
  FO 168.19 SM 49.10 146.6
  146.15 146.17

NEEDLE'S EYE SM 65.7 65.21

NEEDLE-WOMAN TL 71.34

NEEDN'T LH 18.37 18.40 TL 48.25
  FO 137.6 CD 218.29 266.8
  SM 57.21 65.35 130.4 156.1
  VG 33.17 55.22

NEEDS CD 185.15 197.34 204.15
  209.16 SM 12.28 12.31 138.24
  159.8 MD 206.7

NEGATION SM 69.2

NEGATIVE SM 41.17

NEGLECT VG 6.6

NEGLIGENCE LH 6.32

NEGLIGENTLY LH 6.29 CD 236.18

NEGLIGIBLE VG 3.13 41.15

NEGOTIATING LH 37.19

NEGRO SM 9.5 62.36

NEGROES SM 7.15 61.8 61.13
  62.24 62.27 62.37

NEGROID TL 73.28

NEGRO PULLMAN-BOY SM 24.6

NEIGH SM 79.31

NEIGHBOUR MD 183.6

NEIGHBOURING FO 113.26 146.7

NEIGHBOURS SM 28.5 MD 184.2

NEIGHED SM 26.41 75.1

NEIGHING SM 90.13

NEIN CD 261.1

NEIN KEIN REGEN WUNDERSCHON JA
  ER WAR GA+ CD 266.3

NEIN NEIN DIES IST KEIN LANGER
  REGEN CD 248.24

NEIN NEIN HARDU CD 234.38

NEITHER LH 4.14 20.9 TL 48.28
  55.35 57.17 59.32 103.18
  FO 113.19 124.27 CD 192.14
  199.12 224.17 224.24 225.10
  263.23 SM 6.10 6.20 6.37
  20.29 31.28 42.33 44.35 64.3
  97.14 105.38 116.5 126.6
  141.6 156.32 159.4 MD 167.8
  167.9 174.37 VG 21.34 55.33
  56.26 57.5

NELL FO 136.31

NELLIE FO 118.11 122.35 124.32
  125.37 128.18 129.8 135.5
  137.12 138.12 138.19 138.30
  140.34 141.27 141.32 142.4

NELLIE (CONT.) 144.8 144.26
  144.32 145.6 145.15 145.19
  150.16 150.25 150.34 151.3
  151.14 151.26 152.7 158.25
  158.35 159.6 164.1 171.31

NELLIE'S FO 170.15 171.26

NE PLUS ULTRA SM 147.5

NERVE TL 69.17 SM 40.28
  115.17

NERVES TL 47.23 47.30 69.26
  82.31 FO 131.27 131.37
  132.10 134.32 138.24
  138.30 SM 4.30 6.22 6.28
  7.11 18.27 24.23 37.3
  42.1 50.35 124.20 VG 29.30
  31.19 35.10 35.17 35.26
  35.27

NERVE-WORN TL 46.39 68.40
  FO 115.32

NERVE-WRACKING CD 262.25

NERVOUS LH 3.29 TL 44.37
  52.8 94.35 101.20
  FO 115.26 SM 6.23 8.33
  12.14 23.25 24.19 33.3
  33.17 36.5 135.11 137.12
  VG 11.22 26.21 68.29
  78.3

NERVOUS-LOOKING SM 20.36

NERVOUSLY TL 77.5 CD 197.8
  209.35 SM 8.5 33.24 48.36
  VG 23.4 31.31 46.39

NERVOUSNESS SM 36.7 VG 22.7

NERVY FO 138.19 141.9 169.8

NEST TL 59.5 SM 146.6

NESTLED LH 35.3

NESTLING VG 16.33

NET TL 62.34 62.35 MD 190.29
  200.1 200.4 210.35

NETS MD 197.9 197.29 198.22

NETTING FO 146.13

NETTLE VG 4.39 5.11 5.21
  5.27

NETTLED LH 6.17 FO 134.30
  SM 114.8 MD 196.35 VG 42.13

NETTLE-FLOWER SM 151.3

NETWORK FO 146.12 VG 18.34
  19.6

NEUROTIC TL 99.42

NEUTER CD 240.10

NEUTRAL SM 19.29 107.6
  107.12

NOISE (CONT.) FO 146.12 157.7
  CD 186.25 219.31 234.7
  SM 90.16 154.17 VG 14.14
  18.21 45.27 71.22 72.10
  72.33 74.13 74.41 76.21

NOISELESS VG 67.14

NOISELESSLY LH 16.12 18.24
  33.40

NOISES LH 11.26 FO 174.17
  CD 221.26 VG 32.31 76.24

NOISILY FO 134.4

NOLI ME TANGERE SM 117.35
  MD 194.13 195.33

NOLI ME TANGERE HOMO SM 117.40

NO-MAN'S-LAND SM 142.34

NOMENCLATURE VG 5.1

NON LH 5.17 6.40 9.12 30.17

NONCHALANCE FO 163.7 SM 39.7
  VG 25.19

NONCHALANT FO 149.30 156.13
  172.8 VG 38.42

NONCHALANTLY FO 151.11 MD 164.26

NONCONFORMISTS VG 25.37

NONE TL 55.7 67.35 FO 115.24
  157.33 166.39 167.10 176.40
  CD 193.7 197.26 212.20 223.23
  226.16 227.20 SM 44.15 89.3
  100.7 104.37 126.6 134.28
  135.5 150.21 VG 4.30 15.39
  40.16

NONENTITIES SM 96.20

NONENTITY SM 27.31 27.32 99.4

NON-HUMAN SM 14.36 61.37

NON-PHALLIC SM 146.2

NONSENSE TL 92.1 FO 116.38
  132.22 165.24 CD 212.27
  225.33 SM 51.1 89.25 106.2
  150.2 VG 44.12

NO-O LH 10.34

NOON SM 148.1 VG 12.21

NOOSE MD 180.27

NORMAL CD 203.15

NORMATON VG 51.36

NORTH TL 58.37 91.28 FO 127.16
  SM 127.7 132.11 VG 3.20 9.32
  18.20 45.13 50.38 54.30
  69.29 71.14 76.13

NORTHERN TL 69.29 SM 127.5
  148.2 VG 36.7

NORTH SEA TL 59.3

NORTHWARDS SM 147.31

NOSE TL 45.41 51.6 52.20 58.26
  62.24 84.5 93.33 93.38
  FO 123.18 137.17 137.38
  139.28 140.4 147.5 149.5
  157.7 165.7 165.9 167.6
  CD 186.34 213.20 213.24 230.2
  240.11 248.33 259.32 SM 5.31
  8.22 10.3 22.14 30.17 66.37
  124.38 VG 8.7 8.25 9.23
  19.21 23.34 31.12 40.6 43.15
  43.27 49.15 56.11 56.15
  58.34 65.28 65.34

NOSES FO 115.12

NOSING VG 63.10

NOSTALGIA SM 10.26 78.18

NOSTRILS TL 57.3 SM 67.15
  MD 170.39

NOT-BELONGING CD 227.23

NOTE TL 75.37 FO 143.33
  CD 200.30 218.25 SM 93.21
  VG 4.3 5.22 15.4 64.5 64.24

NOTHING LH 4.20 17.42 26.37
  27.2 28.13 29.22 29.42 32.25
  36.34 TL 43.30 43.31 45.26
  47.24 55.3 55.5 55.38 56.20
  58.32 61.2 65.11 65.30 66.24
  70.37 74.4 86.26 96.19 99.32
  101.31 102.40 103.8 107.14
  107.36 107.40 FO 115.39
  122.30 123.8 123.31 127.29
  132.30 132.34 138.15 143.32
  144.25 146.30 148.27 149.14
  152.42 153.21 157.34 165.5
  165.11 166.34 166.35 170.4
  170.39 171.26 172.33 175.23
  175.34 177.38 CD 191.18
  191.27 192.10 192.27 192.28
  192.38 193.1 193.2 193.3
  194.31 198.33 199.4 199.6
  203.12 203.39 209.22 209.31
  209.32 210.30 215.3 221.17
  223.24 223.25 227.18 231.31
  232.10 248.11 249.17 252.2
  256.21 259.24 260.6 263.18
  263.34 264.18 264.20 264.29
  SM 4.35 7.40 9.22 14.2 22.15
  22.16 26.1 26.22 27.33 30.35
  33.7 37.1 39.14 40.2 42.34
  43.10 47.14 54.11 56.31
  56.32 58.36 60.21 61.23
  63.13 70.11 70.13 71.30
  75.25 77.4 79.36 86.35 89.11
  93.32 96.17 96.18 97.10
  97.13 99.3 100.7 101.7 104.3
  105.25 107.2 108.8 110.10
  111.9 111.17 111.39 119.27
  120.18 127.40 128.4 129.9
  129.11 130.17 130.21 130.24
  135.9 137.39 139.31 140.34
  150.25 151.10 152.15 152.16
  MD 163.25 170.22 170.31
  172.26 173.15 174.23 174.36
  174.38 180.22 180.33 184.4
  187.18 207.3 208.3 208.38

NOTHING (CONT.) 210.37
  VG 8.16 9.9 9.15 9.19
  12.42 16.10 16.24 16.27
  25.23 27.7 30.21 35.5
  35.17 39.20 41.5 41.6
  41.10 41.18 42.18 42.33
  48.29 49.37 54.35 58.38
  60.10 66.12 66.19 66.33
  70.2 71.16 76.20 76.38

NOTHINGNESS TL 79.12
  FO 176.36 177.22 177.34
  CD 202.26 SM 96.21 97.21
  126.5 151.13 MD 184.9

NOTICE LH 7.3 8.34 39.25
  TL 72.12 84.19 87.6 105.38
  FO 116.12 131.24 143.1
  166.22 168.26 CD 188.12
  195.38 219.10 222.6 233.35
  233.37 SM 45.38 53.9
  101.24 107.38 109.20

NOTICEABLE LH 22.2 TL 59.27
  SM 146.21

NOTICED LH 17.27 22.4
  TL 51.35 75.29 105.1
  FO 114.28 122.8 127.12
  CD 190.5 206.13 SM 54.15

NOTICES SM 86.5 86.14

NOTICING CD 186.30 190.14

NOTION SM 10.28 VG 61.38

NOTIONS LH 11.37

NOTORIOUS VG 51.3

NOT-THINKING CD 191.17

NOTTINGHAM LH 4.30 15.9

NOT-VERY-NICE CD 227.27

NOVEL SM 133.5

NOVEL-COVERS CD 257.16

NOVELS CD 257.15 SM 154.22

NOVEMBER TL 44.15 FO 119.2
  130.2 SM 128.16 153.5

NOWADAYS CD 193.15 222.14
  SM 111.17 111.38 120.27
  121.35

NOWHERE TL 103.36 FO 121.14
  CD 212.9 SM 3.22 MD 166.38
  VG 19.3

NOWT LH 3.35 7.13 12.26
  12.33 14.14 19.39 38.22

NUDGING LH 9.10

NUISANCE VG 16.20

NUIT BLANCHE TL 107.27

NULL SM 87.14

NULLITY SM 87.13 MD 165.29
  165.31 VG 65.17

NULLUS CD 199.1

NUMB SM 27.13 117.3 MD 165.5
  165.8 165.25 VG 27.21 63.9
  63.30 79.17

NUMBED VG 29.24 29.29 30.3
  63.3

NUMBEDLY VG 76.5

NUMBER TL 60.34 SM 142.13
  MD 183.20

NUMBERS FO 113.21

NUMBING SM 25.40 26.3

NUMB-LOOKING CD 258.13

NUMBNESS SM 25.35 26.26 149.22
  VG 29.11

NUMEROUS FO 127.13

NUNS SM 158.4

NURSE TL 54.34 72.7 SM 44.14
  73.38 87.11 111.9 112.31
  112.41 113.13

NURSED SM 7.38

NURSES TL 59.32 SM 20.33

NURSING SM 7.22 17.8

NURSING-HOME SM 4.34

NUT TL 72.30 73.2 VG 11.12
  42.40

NUTS TL 73.4 SM 103.16

NYMPHS SM 54.10 111.14

O' LH 11.34 17.36 17.37 18.3
  19.11 19.12 19.19 31.15
  38.10 VG 19.37

OAK TL 100.6 101.26 FO 143.42
  146.4 176.13

OAK-BOUGH SM 13.13

OAK-LEAVES SM 102.41

OAKS FO 146.6 MD 185.15 187.38
  VG 16.34

OAK-SCRUB SM 151.11 151.17
  154.40

OAK-TREES SM 103.22 103.24

OAK-WOODS SM 94.11

OAR CD 233.23

OARS MD 200.5 210.31 210.41
  211.11

OATS SM 80.3 101.1 VG 23.28

OBDT. VG 81.20

OBEDIENCE TL 88.21 88.31 88.32
  88.33 CD 263.17 263.33

OBEDIENT SM 116.31

OBEDIENTLY LH 19.35 FO 160.29
  VG 48.42 75.18

OBEISANCE MD 192.18 195.16

OBESE VG 65.20

OBESITY VG 12.29

OBEY TL 90.10 106.35 107.42
  CD 262.34 263.36 265.29

OBEYED LH 38.34 FO 159.30
  CD 262.39 262.41 264.17
  264.24

OBEYING CD 264.38 265.1

OBEYS CD 263.29

OBJECT FO 153.13 SM 101.15
  132.32 148.38 VG 6.40

OBJECTIVELY FO 143.9

OBJECTS CD 185.2 193.19
  VG 37.42

OBLIGATIONS SM 116.39

OBLIGED CD 219.3

OBLIGES SM 75.27

OBLITERATED TL 93.16 FO 126.21

OBLIVION MD 166.16

OBNOXIOUS FO 114.19

OBNOXITY VG 16.7

OBSCENE CD 241.29 VG 64.36
  65.37

OBSCURE TL 102.8 FO 123.34

OBSCURELY LH 22.6

OBSCURITY TL 92.11

OBSERVANT FO 116.11

OBSERVATIONS CD 264.32

OBSERVATORIES CD 212.32

OBSERVE CD 200.37

OBSESSED VG 75.23

OBSESSION TL 83.16 100.15

OBSTINACY FO 158.21 SM 74.32
  76.4

OBSTINATE TL 55.18 FO 114.6
  143.14 158.8 178.32
  CD 194.34 SM 74.21 VG 9.4^
  32.21

OBSTINATELY LH 19.24
  FO 114.38 179.25 CD 258.29

OBTAIN VG 7.1

OBTAINED TL 92.21

OBTRUSIVE TL 51.24

OBTUSE SM 138.33

OBTUSENESS SM 138.1 138.2
  138.8

OBVIOUS TL 92.8 SM 7.10
  25.12 130.19

OBVIOUSLY CD 258.24

OCCASION FO 144.24 SM 80.18
  VG 40.28

OCCASIONAL CD 241.6

OCCASIONALLY CD 218.16 232.6
  SM 7.3 157.33

OCCASIONS FO 137.10

OCCUPANTS VG 19.19 19.24

OCCUPATION CD 208.28

OCCUPIED TL 68.16 SM 102.12

OCCUPY FO 164.18 SM 138.4

OCCUPYING MD 185.29

OCCUR LH 17.16

OCCURRED LH 21.37 FO 157.3
  CD 224.15 SM 23.15 89.29

OCEAN SM 69.3 69.6 69.16
  69.17 126.35 MD 172.14

O'CLOCK LH 20.36 22.20
  TL 100.16 FO 114.39 114.42
  119.3 121.38 138.26 157.36
  168.10 CD 219.22 238.34
  245.5

OCTAVIUS MD 188.38

OCTOBER CD 201.36

ODD TL 51.18 62.13 81.17
  96.31 FO 114.17 115.6
  115.27 116.13 118.30
  121.21 129.39 131.17
  136.8 137.30 158.37 161.18
  CD 187.34 190.24 195.1
  195.12 196.33 204.22
  231.15 SM 3.17 4.23 7.26
  46.35 54.9 65.3 84.32
  87.39 108.38 108.39 119.24
  VG 34.31 39.40 44.14 49.37
  53.38 57.31 58.14

ODDLY   SM 17.38   64.29   87.25
  VG 49.18

ODDS   LH 19.16

ODIOUS   CD 259.9

ODOUR   FO 125.8   125.10   MD 191.23

OFFENCE   TL 94.2   CD 203.20
  208.29   SM 100.16   VG 34.35

OFFEND   MD 189.10

OFFENDED   TL 91.8   91.18   93.40
  FO 135.11   162.31   CD 250.28
  250.29   SM 41.33   100.22   110.38
  VG 34.30

OFFENDING   LH 8.36

OFFER   LH 32.40   TL 104.5
  CD 252.3   264.20   SM 16.12

OFFERED   LH 30.2   TL 104.10
  FO 152.2   CD 193.26   SM 51.13
  MD 179.9   204.12   204.41
  VG 40.41   46.32   52.41

OFFERING   TL 81.38   94.4   MD 189.9
  VG 14.25   41.38

OFFERS   MD 189.38

OFF-HAND   VG 24.9   44.7   68.29

OFFICE   CD 229.32   SM 37.18   39.2

OFFICE-CHAIR   CD 245.18

OFFICER   TL 107.14   CD 184.4
  184.10   193.30   194.10   199.11
  228.38   VG 55.9   57.31   57.38

OFFICERS   TL 44.35   64.27   83.24
  FO 167.21   167.28   CD 194.26
  194.28   197.26   206.33

OFFICERS'   FO 167.20

OFFICIAL   CD 188.11   SM 3.36
  34.21

OFFICIAL'S   SM 34.12

OFFICIATING   SM 28.20

OFFICIOUS   SM 25.10

OFTEN   LH 24.6   34.39   TL 58.35
  59.15   68.25   91.33   99.15
  FO 135.22   137.20   152.9   156.23
  CD 193.24   196.32   206.13
  206.40   222.6   SM 32.39   131.5
  MD 163.15   VG 10.5   17.36   36.27
  46.30   62.7

OFTENER   CD 227.14

OH-H   FO 144.10   CD 261.27
  SM 155.36

OIL   MD 201.31   204.24   205.32
  205.41   206.17

OILED   MD 210.39

OIL-FLAME   MD 187.41

OIL-JAR   MD 199.3   200.25

OIL'S   LH 31.15

OINTMENT   MD 204.9   204.27

OLD   LH 4.34   13.4   28.34   31.16
  31.41   32.15   33.36   TL 43.16
  44.1   46.21   49.29   49.40   50.32
  50.35   61.12   62.23   64.31
  66.23   88.8   97.7   98.16   98.30
  99.28   100.28   107.24   FO 113.15
  113.16   113.20   113.30   114.2
  118.6   118.30   118.31   120.34
  123.21   127.18   132.23   132.26
  134.5   143.42   144.23   145.42
  147.1   147.6   152.32   154.37
  162.11   162.13   162.14   162.15
  162.18   162.20   162.25   162.29
  163.6   169.8   169.11   170.1
  170.5   170.12   170.18   170.36
  171.4   171.14   171.34   172.14
  172.20   174.15   174.17   175.31
  CD 190.3   194.42   196.2   209.15
  219.6   227.25   229.17   230.12
  230.20   230.34   230.42   231.34
  232.4   232.12   233.7   233.10
  233.15   236.39   238.35   239.8
  240.34   245.20   248.15   SM 5.8
  5.32   5.37   6.2   9.5   10.36
  11.38   19.34   19.35   23.30   28.7
  29.4   30.15   31.1   31.15   37.28
  45.32   45.37   47.26   49.4   49.8
  49.30   49.39   54.2   54.4   54.6
  54.34   55.9   56.41   60.11   60.22
  62.41   63.35   64.8   64.9   64.24
  71.39   81.40   82.25   83.29
  87.11   97.6   101.14   101.15
  102.34   103.11   109.39   111.22
  117.21   119.2   119.3   119.6
  119.14   119.15   125.25   128.7
  129.20   136.5   139.11   151.15
  153.33   153.39   155.10   155.12
  155.32   156.23   MD 168.5   175.13
  176.18   179.20   183.8   184.11
  184.14   189.22   189.26   198.24
  198.36   198.37   198.39   199.38
  200.2   200.19   204.8   VG 3.3
  3.23   3.28   3.30   4.16   4.34
  5.26   6.13   7.8   7.25   7.34   8.2
  8.28   8.29   9.40   11.8   11.12
  11.32   11.36   12.1   12.5   12.34
  12.36   12.42   13.9   14.8   14.40
  15.16   15.18   15.27   16.19
  16.20   17.22   17.42   18.35
  20.11   20.24   22.35   25.24
  27.27   30.25   33.38   34.14
  34.15   34.42   35.9   35.11   35.25
  37.26   42.31   44.16   44.20
  45.33   46.1   46.11   46.13   46.17
  46.20   47.2   47.5   47.14   48.24
  48.34   52.2   52.6   52.16   52.19
  53.4   53.33   54.4   56.31   56.38
  56.41   64.8   65.20   65.26   65.28
  65.29   65.37   65.39   66.30   67.9
  67.40   67.42   68.38   69.32
  70.12   71.2   74.7   78.13   78.27
  80.10   80.11   80.24   80.40

OLDER   LH 4.2   32.3   TL 77.23
  FO 130.13   130.15   CD 202.6

OLDER (CONT.)   210.15   SM 3.10
  20.2   45.12   64.9   86.31
  121.6   VG 6.1   11.27   61.39
  63.12   67.32

OLDEST   SM 5.5   VG 46.21

OLD-FASHIONED   TL 43.34
  CD 208.35   VG 7.6

OLD-MAID'S   SM 10.41   11.5

OLDNESS   VG 15.23

OLD-ROMAN   CD 232.14

OLIVE   MD 167.15   168.18
  168.20   180.4

OLIVE-REFUSE   MD 198.13

OLIVES   MD 163.9   166.40
  167.19   185.24   185.33
  196.38   198.14

OLIVE-TREES   MD 185.10   194.3

OMINOUSLY   SM 43.6   VG 34.3
  71.18

OMNIBUS   CD 240.38   260.1   260.14

ON N'EST PAS MIEUX ICI   SM 128.13

ONCE   LH 13.32   24.24   TL 46.16
  64.31   65.3   70.7   70.8
  76.13   81.6   101.38   103.7
  105.1   107.28   FO 114.15
  116.1   116.4   133.40   143.15
  145.30   146.27   167.39
  172.38   179.26   CD 186.33
  198.1   198.7   204.38   210.2
  212.11   219.4   224.36   225.8
  226.24   227.32   227.39
  231.12   237.26   262.29
  SM 4.38   9.5   9.21   10.8
  12.5   14.7   19.28   35.17
  36.11   37.2   37.14   41.37
  42.31   44.6   50.12   52.18
  54.13   57.22   57.38   60.5
  68.17   73.2   97.15   99.15
  106.23   111.3   111.18   114.32
  125.19   127.11   127.17
  127.22   128.24   MD 169.39
  187.41   188.1   188.2   189.25
  191.39   204.26   209.34
  VG 3.24   4.40   10.4   18.15
  20.8   32.15   32.41   33.2
  37.35   37.38   39.12   45.37
  62.4   64.32   65.37   66.6
  66.36   68.40

ONE-HALF   SM 137.26

ONES   TL 66.32   76.12   SM 49.12
  54.35   71.37   MD 189.22
  VG 15.8   16.2   17.3   17.5
  62.27

ONE'S   TL 48.10   86.14   97.12
  FO 149.22   CD 199.15   224.10
  256.6   SM 3.3   130.29   145.25
  VG 33.16   39.29   65.2   67.30

ONESELF   TL 62.42   97.29
  CD 203.28   SM 26.24   96.9

ONESELF (CONT.) SM 112.1

ONION-BED SM 38.8

ONIONS SM 38.10 38.27

ONLOOKER MD 186.27

ONLOOKERS SM 24.22

ON N'EST PAS MIEUX ICI SM 128.13

ONRUSH MD 166.9

ONWARD SM 75.27

ONWARD-PUSHING SM 144.25

ONWARD-STRUGGLE SM 152.36

OOZING SM 146.5

OPALESCENCE TL 58.29

OPEN LH 12.21 26.31 29.20
  TL 51.11 52.1 54.12 54.41
  55.37 57.9 63.42 69.12 98.19
  101.4 FO 113.36 135.37 143.41
  146.24 146.33 154.40 156.4
  168.16 169.2 179.35 CD 187.7
  201.27 202.26 209.25 219.32
  231.16 234.22 238.25 238.40
  239.39 241.11 242.22 243.4
  249.1 253.10 255.20 SM 11.17
  17.12 23.28 28.2 54.41 55.7
  55.15 56.27 60.8 93.6 97.2
  102.18 105.28 113.28 129.33
  145.7 146.8 147.22 150.35
  MD 165.7 165.38 171.25 176.9
  185.20 187.29 187.32 189.12
  189.24 190.2 195.35 197.8
  210.11 VG 11.23 11.26 15.21
  15.24 16.16 20.39 24.11
  49.14 49.23 70.6 79.32

OPENED LH 24.42 34.8 TL 45.7
  45.34 57.8 58.33 85.22
  100.21 102.8 102.32 105.18
  FO 119.34 143.16 143.24
  CD 183.22 184.27 238.40 240.6
  SM 11.13 68.16 102.27 140.34
  MD 165.36 167.26 170.20
  170.23 VG 24.26 29.12 29.19
  29.21 37.22 37.31 73.30
  73.35 76.27 79.19

OPEN-EYED LH 34.24

OPEN-HEARTED CD 200.7

OPENING TL 58.30 FO 117.41
  147.15 172.30 SM 37.35 102.15
  112.40 VG 29.13

OPENLY LH 39.24 SM 70.19 149.39
  VG 67.1

OPENNESS MD 208.10

OPENS TL 67.29 MD 189.36

OPERA CD 235.35

OPERA-CLOAK CD 236.36

OPERATION VG 12.20

OPERATOR'S SM 126.30

OPINION TL 87.37 93.35
  FO 124.17 124.23 CD 213.7
  SM 49.28 123.27 136.14 137.4
  156.31 156.32 VG 6.13

OPPORTUNITY SM 72.32 89.2

OPPOSE MD 201.1 201.4 201.6

OPPOSING LH 9.27 TL 91.39

OPPOSITE LH 25.8 FO 156.2
  176.16 CD 229.19 230.23 239.5
  242.23 MD 198.33 199.24 206.3
  206.15 VG 71.37

OPPOSITION TL 87.13 VG 67.16

OPPRESSIVE FO 119.14

ORACULAR VG 22.21

ORANGE CD 245.20 SM 17.1
  MD 163.4 167.18 167.21 171.13

ORANGE-RED SM 146.18

ORBS SM 147.10

ORCHARD SM 105.26 111.13
  MD 167.15

ORCHARDS SM 154.34

ORDEAL TL 84.40 85.2 CD 253.22

ORDER TL 71.31 90.26 SM 25.14
  66.27 71.4 75.22 80.27 99.10
  MD 175.17 VG 32.30

ORDERED TL 44.13 CD 196.38
  211.21 211.22 211.24
  SM 112.33

ORDERING SM 44.27

ORDERS CD 262.37 SM 117.10
  VG 16.27

ORDINARILY LH 8.5

ORDINARY LH 20.11 27.5
  CD 221.35 SM 15.2 26.7

ORESTES SM 112.37

ORGANIC SM 94.23

ORGANICALLY SM 26.5 34.34

ORGANIZED SM 29.30

ORIENTAL TL 100.7 SM 42.38
  119.13 119.16

ORIENTALS FO 178.23

ORIGIN TL 86.34 97.12

ORIGINAL TL 67.10 FO 137.3
  CD 197.35 221.1

ORNAMENTAL VG 70.24

ORNAMENTS TL 46.32

ORPEN SM 114.36

OSIRIS MD 188.10 188.28
  195.28 195.41 197.18
  203.23 208.4 208.5 208.40
  209.30

OSPREY CD 195.6

OSTENTATIOUS TL 75.6

OSTENTATIOUSNESS SM 32.40

OTHERS LH 15.32 17.32 18.7
  TL 44.6 47.6 48.16 49.4
  49.7 88.35 99.27 SM 10.7
  68.22 103.28 MD 174.28
  178.10 VG 10.8 22.13 23.17
  24.9 24.19 72.6

OTHER'S FO 137.14 SM 4.30
  63.13 VG 73.20

OTHERWISE TL 46.32 49.23
  79.1 FO 121.5 CD 225.29
  265.30 SM 19.7 109.18
  139.24 147.26 VG 79.24

OTHER-WORLD MD 199.11

OTTER MD 187.30

OTTO CD 199.28

OUGHT TL 46.17 46.18 77.36
  106.21 FO 114.31 144.13
  144.37 145.39 151.28
  175.33 175.37 179.6 179.7
  CD 189.16 221.19 221.20
  223.28 SM 58.26 72.34
  79.29 79.41 80.14 85.35
  114.17 114.30 125.40
  140.6 VG 10.9 10.16 39.22
  49.22 56.9 81.6

OUGHTN'T CD 257.33 VG 59.39

OUNCE SM 125.14 125.18

OUR LADY TL 96.34

OURS SM 27.3 121.30

OURSELVES TL 48.37 FO 123.38
  124.4 124.12 126.2 129.15
  144.38 CD 205.26 264.36
  SM 50.2 65.33 80.28 133.17
  VG 39.26

OUTBURSTS MD 163.28

OUTCAST VG 22.30

OUTDOOR FO 114.7

OUTER FO 140.35 SM 27.15
  139.36 147.28 MD 190.19
  194.22 202.6 VG 5.11 7.22

OUTERMOST MD 185.19

OUT-HOUSE   FO 115.22

OUTLAW   TL 59.13

OUTLAWS   TL 59.15

OUTLET   TL 47.22   FO 126.18

OUTLINE   SM 114.16   MD 191.33

OUTLINED   VG 23.36

OUTLIVED   MD 174.6

OUT-OF-DATE   TL 44.11

OUT-OF-DOORS   FO 155.42

OUTPOST   SM 152.6

OUTPOURING   TL 82.12   FO 167.9

OUTRAGED   VG 54.29

OUTRAGEOUS   VG 34.8

OUTRAGEOUSLY   SM 52.23   VG 10.19

OUTRIGHT   LH 14.16   FO 129.39

OUTSIDE   LH 27.24   34.22   38.31
   TL 52.22   62.40   62.41   70.22
   97.29   102.17   102.40   FO 119.14
   119.17   126.25   127.6   134.4
   134.29   135.41   139.39   143.34
   144.3   145.21   159.32   160.13
   160.17   160.21   160.24
   CD 186.22   192.27   200.39
   201.10   201.14   201.17   223.16
   223.21   223.23   231.31   247.12
   SM 7.1   20.32   26.13   57.40
   70.25   87.26   113.2   139.32
   139.41   145.16   150.24   154.18
   MD 165.18   165.31   169.1   170.25
   192.4   VG 7.18   40.13   44.27
   67.5   67.12

OUTSIDENESS   VG 67.6

OUTSIDER   TL 69.23   CD 211.24
   SM 3.21   150.9

OUTSIDERS   SM 29.7   VG 66.12

OUTSKIRTS   MD 183.7   VG 66.40

OUTSPOKEN   FO 153.23

OUTSTRETCHED   SM 134.13   VG 25.9

OUTWARD   SM 70.38   71.1

OUTWARDLY   SM 149.38   VG 65.9
   65.12

OUTWARDS   FO 173.40

OUTWATCHING   SM 147.12

OVAL   VG 68.25

OVEN   FO 134.9

OVERALL   SM 44.41   46.37

OVER-AWEING   SM 15.13

OVERBEARING   TL 93.9   CD 212.10
   251.9   SM 32.36   VG 24.14   32.16

OVERCAME   CD 193.4

OVERCOAT   FO 145.32   169.5   172.21
   CD 187.3

OVERCOATS   CD 185.24

OVERCOME   CD 244.6   SM 68.38
   77.37   153.32   153.36   MD 165.21

OVERCOMING   SM 26.26

OVER-CONTROLLED   SM 34.34

OVERCROWDED   SM 52.4

OVERHANGING   TL 52.35   SM 17.34
   VG 17.39

OVERHEAD   FO 127.13   CD 238.1
   SM 22.25   147.8   148.13
   MD 170.39

OVERHUNG   CD 240.27   240.28

OVER-KIND   SM 51.24

OVERLAPPING   MD 172.13

OVERLEAPS   VG 67.41

OVERLOOKING   SM 90.29   MD 185.32
   198.7

OVERNIGHT   SM 37.15

OVER-POWERING   VG 48.28

OVERSEER   MD 187.22   198.19
   198.26   199.30   210.33

OVER-SWEET   LH 21.12

OVERTAKES   FO 130.37

OVERTONE   SM 9.40

OVERTOOK   LH 22.39   MD 182.11

OVERTURNED   MD 172.37

OVERVISIBLE   SM 55.8

OVERWEENING   MD 171.32

OVERWHELMED   SM 52.8   58.35
   VG 27.9

OVERWHELMING   SM 135.26   MD 203.34

OVERWROUGHT   VG 39.19

OVER-WROUGHT   LH 12.16

OWE   MD 175.29

OWER   LH 7.41

OWL   FO 146.3

OWNED   MD 186.26

OWNER   SM 10.34

OWNERS   SM 131.36

OWNERS'   SM 131.35

OWNING   SM 104.41

OXFORD   SM 10.1

OXFORDSHIRE   SM 92.26   116.36

OXFORD STREET   TL 60.25   71.32

OX-SKIN   MD 200.23

PACE   FO 153.8   VG 19.12   19.27

PACED   SM 155.21

PACES   VG 72.13

PACIFICATION   SM 139.16

PACK   VG 19.10   20.38

PACKAGE   CD 246.4

PACKAGES   FO 153.28

PACKED   CD 229.11   247.8
   260.16   SM 125.5

PACKING   SM 109.34

PACK-RAT   SM 149.15   155.9

PACK-RATS   SM 144.2   144.35
   150.14

PACKS   SM 146.27   VG 70.41

PACK-TRAIN   MD 181.28

PACT   SM 135.6

PADDINGTON   SM 121.11

PADDLING   TL 98.30

PADDOCK   SM 32.1

PADRES   SM 144.12

PAGAN   MD 194.16   VG 21.30

PAGE   FO 136.3

PAID   FO 152.41   CD 238.31
   SM 93.26   138.3   153.22
   159.16   VG 26.6   28.30

PAIN   LH 5.13   11.27   33.30
   TL 44.29   46.24   51.6   52.21
   95.16   95.27   95.39   95.40
   105.17   FO 114.16   126.35
   126.36   128.13   133.5   133.10
   168.4   179.38   SM 67.33
   79.18   MD 166.18   166.19
   195.10   195.33   197.6   202.14
   203.34   204.8   205.35

PAINED   FO 163.2   SM 100.30

PAINFUL   VG 55.11   70.32

PAINFULLY   LH 34.21   MD 168.18

PAINLESS   SM 79.36

PAINS   FO 177.2   SM 119.1

PAINT   FO 115.3   SM 4.5   5.7
   17.22   42.12   114.28

PAINTED   CD 185.20   213.34   213.35
   246.8   SM 28.19   MD 185.5
   187.26   188.6   190.28   VG 54.5

PAINTER   SM 10.11   122.36

PAINTING   CD 246.26   SM 111.13
   111.39   122.35

PAINTINGS   SM 26.12   134.13

PAINT-PRIAPUS   SM 112.13

PAINTS   SM 54.32

PAIR   TL 92.6   FO 160.35   160.39
   CD 243.6   SM 6.26   20.24   44.41
   45.1

PAIRS   SM 44.36

PALACES   SM 124.5   124.6

PALAIS DE DANSE   VG 10.12

PALAVERING   CD 258.37

PALE   LH 12.18   13.10   13.12
   28.34   29.6   37.36   TL 44.36
   79.34   79.41   86.5   97.38   102.8
   105.11   FO 120.22   122.12   134.7
   134.20   136.33   137.37   146.32
   148.28   166.33   168.4   174.38
   CD 185.17   187.42   199.29
   233.39   235.6   239.4   244.17
   246.10   248.32   253.39   254.42
   255.21   SM 20.39   60.30   63.33
   66.34   78.21   88.37   89.32   94.8
   101.38   102.18   108.32   118.33
   134.9   145.40   146.38   MD 165.37
   170.39   190.29   190.33   192.11
   192.37   193.41   196.13   VG 4.10
   24.12   26.42   39.19   39.36
   54.25   63.3   67.22

PALE-AND-FAWN   VG 24.5

PALE-BLUE   TL 71.6   FO 169.7
   171.14   CD 241.5   244.34
   SM 68.36

PALE-COLOURED   SM 78.6

PALED   FO 168.5

PALE-EYED   VG 53.32   55.9

PALE-GOLD   SM 67.3   69.33

PALE-GREEN   VG 24.3

PALE-GREY   TL 97.37   CD 253.12
   SM 17.35   18.20   22.14   39.1
   46.23   61.36   119.30

PALE-LAVENDER   CD 244.37

PALERMO   SM 3.28

PALETTE   SM 111.35

PALE-WARM   SM 140.20

PALLETS   TL 44.21

PALLID   LH 21.27   TL 46.34   87.11
   93.17   SM 20.41   109.10   146.5
   MD 179.3   199.38

PALLOR   LH 34.36   38.12

PALLY   VG 10.13

PALM   LH 28.32   33.24   TL 73.4
   MD 192.39   204.10   204.14
   205.33   VG 22.8   22.11   30.18
   68.26

PALM-BREADTH   MD 180.5

PALMS   MD 198.23

PALM-TREES   SM 128.8

PALPITATING   TL 54.5

PALPITATION   VG 12.12

PALTRY   SM 48.25

PAMPERED   VG 6.25

PAN   SM 54.13   54.20   54.36   54.38
   54.39   55.1   55.3   55.7   55.9
   55.11   55.12   55.16   55.27
   55.40   56.10   56.12   56.19
   56.24   56.25   56.31   56.32
   56.35   102.34   MD 197.30
   VG 47.7

PANACEA   SM 85.39

PANAMA   CD 233.31   SM 43.4

PANCAKE   SM 56.4   56.6

PANELLED   TL 97.25   97.26
   SM 28.19

PANES   TL 97.28

PANIC   LH 9.38   35.4   FO 113.31
   SM 36.19   58.22   67.15   67.17
   MD 205.36   206.1

PANS   VG 39.7   39.8

PAN'S   SM 53.32

PANTED   LH 8.16   8.25   SM 83.20
   83.25

PANTHEIST   SM 54.30

PANTING   LH 10.8   22.39   27.30
   CD 235.11   236.13   SM 4.39
   MD 203.33

PANTOMINE   SM 29.2

PAOLO   TL 104.13

PAPA   CD 240.1

PAPAS   SM 8.39

PAPER   TL 71.1   71.6   71.13
   80.2   80.7   80.8   80.22
   CD 218.32   219.22   232.41
   246.5   SM 116.24   VG 81.16

PAPERS   CD 232.5   232.13
   SM 124.37

PAPPLE   VG 36.11   70.6   77.26
   80.33

PAPPLE HIGHDALE   VG 80.29

PAPPLEWICK   VG 3.18   7.31   8.24
   9.32   36.23   36.26   51.24
   71.41   78.1

PARADED   CD 233.11

PARADISE   CD 215.34   SM 148.32
   148.34   153.10   VG 31.1
   39.38

PARALYSED   TL 44.4   FO 160.14
   SM 35.13   VG 74.19

PARALYSING   SM 25.40

PARALYSIS   VG 29.24

PARAPHERNALIA   CD 256.4
   SM 57.23   135.18

PARASITE   SM 71.9

PARASITIC   LH 18.6   19.35
   VG 31.21

PARASOL   CD 233.26

PARCEL   SM 97.24

PARCELS   FO 152.34   153.6
   153.14   153.30

PARDON   TL 55.17   63.31   94.1
   105.37   SM 59.21   82.9
   103.9

PARENTS   VG 16.11

PARIAH   VG 21.30   22.29   67.20

PARIAH'S   VG 23.31

PARIS   LH 16.27   16.37   17.2
   SM 3.28   4.34   5.7   5.21
   8.4   47.1   52.12   53.22
   126.16   126.19

PARISH   VG 9.37   11.20   13.24
   25.36   28.33   29.34

PARK   TL 46.7   72.23   98.3
   99.15   SM 8.16   8.37   9.11
   12.1   12.4   16.31   16.37
   17.2   23.29   24.18   37.29
   VG 16.32   17.32   45.17

PARK LANE SM 9.12

PARLOUR SM 29.33

PARNASSUS CD 247.37 253.9

PAROXYSM VG 15.11

PAROXYSMS VG 74.1

PARSONS SM 98.8

PART LH 20.15 25.1 31.10 33.33
TL 46.1 46.38 81.21 84.5
98.32 106.29 FO 149.34 178.14
CD 187.14 208.27 214.15
214.34 223.17 223.18 232.38
243.32 SM 5.11 7.21 23.10
23.16 23.19 43.11 50.30 65.6
83.6 101.19 115.39 135.8
139.29 148.6 MD 186.3 208.12
VG 26.4 38.12 54.18 56.3
56.4 56.5 65.12 71.3 75.1

PARTED CD 187.27 232.6 SM 38.33

PARTICIPATE SM 130.36

PARTICLES SM 94.24

PARTICULAR TL 87.31 FO 143.13
CD 226.4

PARTICULARLY LH 22.12 FO 120.21
129.34 CD 198.37 202.29
230.37 253.6 SM 7.31 136.26
MD 192.40 VG 8.26 42.42 58.37

PARTIES VG 10.10 69.39

PARTING CD 188.36 MD 171.6

PARTLY LH 38.26 FO 149.14
149.15 VG 51.3 64.16

PARTNER FO 150.26

PARTRIDGES SM 50.32

PARTS MD 169.30

PARTY CD 215.9 SM 63.39 65.29
VG 14.1 18.8 29.10 39.35
41.7 41.24 41.30 78.20

PARVENU CD 230.11 SM 28.32

PASS LH 10.21 10.26 34.16
TL 86.11 86.37 100.35
FO 137.12 178.27 CD 250.36
SM 7.30 93.7 97.3 97.20
102.15 103.5 104.11 105.23
126.2 MD 168.31 168.32 200.9
200.31

PASSAGE FO 143.42 CD 239.17
SM 113.2 113.8 126.36
VG 34.27 79.14

PASSED LH 21.3 25.15 TL 44.16
85.39 102.11 FO 114.38 115.19
118.21 118.37 119.1 148.22
148.31 148.32 148.35 149.24
158.17 CD 205.32 225.5 232.39
241.2 243.6 247.10 247.14

PASSED (CONT.) SM 21.4 62.41
74.2 75.15 85.1 97.4 124.35
153.7 MD 166.36 167.10 168.35
170.28 180.21 181.28 198.4
199.36 204.33 206.2 VG 23.30
45.26 77.24

PASSENGERS CD 260.9 260.16
261.3 261.7 261.8

PASSES SM 97.20

PASSING LH 3.11 TL 58.41 92.8
CD 255.26 SM 40.13 103.4
125.26 126.7 126.26 MD 187.40
VG 37.7 48.36 70.23

PASSING-BELL SM 28.26

PASSION LH 3.30 7.28 TL 46.24
47.21 74.41 87.1 98.37
FO 163.16 CD 215.29 251.35
251.39 252.1 SM 6.24 91.24
120.29 145.28 145.30 147.4
MD 187.6 197.14 207.3 207.27
VG 3.6 27.9

PASSIONAL CD 224.11

PASSIONATE LH 10.33 TL 93.8
93.10 CD 250.13 SM 13.20
15.31 71.40 MD 209.41

PASSIONATELY LH 37.7

PASSIONLESS SM 146.2

PASSIONS MD 183.40

PASSIVE TL 58.13 91.41
FO 125.13 175.42 SM 40.41
MD 186.26

PAST LH 35.36 TL 107.4 FO 158.5
CD 192.42 216.17 238.35
238.37 238.39 239.8 240.20
240.24 243.36 248.7 254.39
261.13 SM 21.28 36.31 57.30
59.16 60.1 70.35 75.23 87.27
96.40 102.28 111.25 111.26
125.25 127.18 128.7 140.32
141.7 143.25 146.11 154.33
MD 166.31 166.40 174.1 174.37
183.39 209.2 VG 5.13 17.32
18.1 18.3 23.38 36.4 36.21
68.7 71.19 72.6 72.42 77.36

PASTE TL 45.11

PASTRY SM 106.38 107.1

PASTURE FO 113.27 SM 64.6

PATCH VG 18.38

PATCHED SM 141.2

PATCHES TL 60.31 SM 60.13 60.17

PATCHY MD 163.23

PATENT FO 156.40 VG 44.24 44.26

PATER VG 12.15

PATER'S VG 12.9

PATH LH 6.4 7.1 7.5
FO 160.22 CD 240.34 240.40
260.5 SM 38.12 39.21 40.12
40.20 43.28 102.6
MD 163.10 191.6 VG 72.17
72.40 72.41

PATHETIC TL 47.3 VG 42.25

PATHETICALLY LH 11.27 12.41

PATHOS CD 214.9

PATHS TL 98.21

PATIENCE CD 205.3 MD 194.7
194.21 199.20

PATIENT CD 262.38 MD 178.8
VG 38.27

PATIENTLY LH 37.35

PATRIOTS TL 92.28

PATRONAGE MD 191.28

PATRONIZED SM 53.20

PATRONIZINGLY SM 98.12

PATTERING FO 114.18

PATTERN SM 30.17 49.4 49.9

PATTER-PATTER SM 143.14

PATTING CD 257.14

PATTY FO 114.24

PAULA LH 15.34 16.18 19.27
21.33 21.35 22.24 23.36
23.41 24.5 24.8 24.26
27.4 38.36 38.39 39.5
39.10 39.15 39.18

PAULA JABLONOWSKY LH 13.3
16.14

PAULA'S LH 24.15

PAUPER CD 193.16

PAUSE LH 30.8 TL 48.22 48.28
FO 121.13 125.36 156.1
159.1 CD 202.13 202.16
202.24 203.31 210.34
210.42 212.22 220.14 221.30
223.27 228.18 231.4 246.36
246.40 247.4 262.26
SM 86.40 88.10 110.15
113.41 157.7 157.37 158.11
VG 34.11 34.16 60.31 63.9

PAUSED TL 54.35 60.20
CD 220.4 SM 13.34 14.7
104.30 122.25 VG 24.8
76.16

PAUSING TL 98.18 SM 150.7

PAVEMENT CD 219.25

PAW FO 131.42 CD 192.6 247.40
  250.35 254.7 SM 65.13 139.25

PAWS TL 73.20 93.2 FO 147.9
  147.30 CD 252.33 252.35
  252.39 VG 30.17

PAY TL 44.8 FO 129.22 137.6
  137.10 153.1 CD 195.32
  SM 94.38 104.41 131.34 153.21
  153.22 156.27 VG 24.34 26.18
  27.29 27.32 28.39 38.42

PAYING FO 137.14

PAYS SM 107.31

PEACE TL 70.10 75.1 88.41
  92.13 92.16 92.40 100.34
  107.25 FO 114.40 125.2 125.4
  145.1 145.18 179.3 179.4
  CD 245.27 SM 43.9 69.25 72.3
  132.20 140.13 MD 194.15
  194.16 208.19 209.31 210.13
  210.23 VG 32.29

PEACEFUL FO 124.41 164.9
  CD 245.24 SM 43.1 43.7

PEACOCK TL 98.18

PEAK VG 37.11

PEAKED FO 175.29 CD 238.34
  VG 16.9 26.28 28.29 29.11

PEAKS LH 36.31 CD 252.25

PEALING SM 28.26

PEAR FO 152.31 152.37 154.37
  CD 239.8

PEAR-BLOOM MD 209.11

PEARL SM 129.38 129.39 130.1

PEARL-COLOURED VG 40.1

PEARL-LIKE TL 68.34

PEARLS CD 196.2 214.26 SM 97.12
  130.2

PEAS CD 248.16

PEASANT CD 185.19 233.11 238.14
  239.11 239.16 MF 163.1 163.6
  163.15 163.29 163.32 164.17
  165.2 167.20 167.23 167.28
  167.29 167.33 167.36 168.8
  168.16 168.19 168.30 168.34
  168.37 169.2 169.7 169.16
  170.2 170.18 170.30 172.19
  172.27 172.37 172.40 173.5
  173.6 178.12 178.15 178.18
  178.21 178.25 181.4 181.7
  181.11 181.22 181.23

PEASANT-LOOKING CD 243.30

PEASANTS CD 232.42 233.21 238.4
  SM 142.31 MD 170.33 176.37
  177.14

PEASANT'S MD 163.17 164.6
  164.18 176.35 177.8 179.29

PEBBLE MD 197.29

PECCADILLOES CD 209.20

PECK CD 222.30 222.37

PECKED FO 114.24

PECKING VG 19.3

PECULIAR LH 3.29 5.8 22.42
  25.34 TL 75.11 CD 188.37
  199.15 199.26 199.39 234.6
  SM 5.30 32.31 34.1 34.22
  43.33 51.21 56.19 77.20 84.3
  95.24 98.32 123.8 124.25
  134.34 150.16 MD 175.35
  VG 22.28 23.34 24.24 32.8
  52.8 52.17 57.33 61.38 64.12
  67.17

PECULIARITY SM 37.24

PECULIARLY LH 13.7 20.13 22.10
  VG 5.38 21.25

PEEL TL 73.7

PEELED TL 72.30

PEEPED CD 183.23 205.34
  MD 173.13 187.9

PEEPING TL 100.9 100.23
  SM 147.32 MD 170.18 VG 20.39
  51.39

PEERED LH 25.22 FO 176.2
  CD 197.25 SM 17.34 VG 22.11
  31.42 77.1 77.2

PEERING LH 31.23 37.18 FO 146.1
  CD 201.18 201.34 SM 17.36
  138.25 146.39 VG 12.25 74.3
  80.18

PEG FO 127.32 149.19

PEGS CD 185.23 187.4

PELLUCID FO 128.42 134.27
  CD 253.42

PENALTY LH 11.1

PENCIL TL 70.42 80.7 CD 186.31
  186.35

PENDULOUS VG 12.23 15.18

PENETRABLE MD 203.20 207.6
  207.22

PENETRATE CD 241.17 260.3
  SM 139.34

PENETRATED FO 131.37 SM 139.34

PENETRATES SM 158.25

PENETRATING FO 122.42 128.28
  135.18 VG 44.25

PENETRATINGLY SM 17.8

PENETRATION MD 189.39

PENINSULA MD 186.14 186.30
  191.6 191.30 192.16
  193.30 196.28 198.28
  198.30 199.10 199.33
  210.28 211.16

PENNILESS VG 3.1 52.33

PENNY FO 136.31 136.36
  CD 196.23 SM 16.12 30.3

PENSIONS FO 162.25

PENSIVE VG 56.32

PENSIVELY VG 59.16

PENT-ROOF MD 164.11

PEONIES SM 37.38

PEOPLE TL 48.37 50.1 50.31
  62.27 94.22 97.22 99.30
  FO 121.16 144.39 155.2
  164.25 165.24 169.25
  172.27 CD 185.29 200.17
  200.18 205.25 209.10
  220.34 221.35 224.7 224.13
  224.31 225.9 225.11 225.32
  232.10 232.22 232.41
  236.17 238.30 238.31
  240.8 241.40 249.25 253.15
  254.2 254.8 255.40 260.37
  SM 3.34 5.12 5.16 7.5 7.11
  8.23 8.26 20.32 22.17
  22.28 27.9 29.5 30.25
  30.29 50.37 51.15 53.37
  57.37 59.29 62.14 62.22
  62.40 64.20 64.22 66.5
  69.8 69.38 70.7 71.1
  77.21 80.3 80.36 81.10
  83.36 84.34 85.12 90.5
  103.2 103.12 103.13 103.18
  103.19 103.21 103.24
  103.33 103.38 103.39 104.2
  104.4 104.7 104.9 104.10
  104.13 104.20 104.38
  104.41 105.7 105.8 105.12
  113.36 114.30 114.34 115.2
  115.16 115.20 115.25
  115.36 116.3 116.4 119.21
  119.24 120.36 121.17
  121.34 121.36 122.7 122.9
  122.10 122.18 124.1 124.5
  129.7 129.25 156.13 156.15
  157.9 157.23 158.38
  MD 179.32 194.9 194.12
  200.10 VG 11.27 16.22
  16.25 19.6 20.5 24.40
  25.32 30.2 30.6 33.17
  33.29 34.1 34.3 34.8 35.13
  41.8 43.8 52.40 55.2
  55.13 55.14 56.38 56.41
  57.26 60.17 61.4 62.25
  63.10 64.7 64.8 65.1
  65.15

PEOPLE'S TL 61.1 CD 214.22
  231.24 SM 30.29 105.3 105.5
  106.3 106.6 106.36 VG 13.3
  15.25 31.8 31.11

PER   SM 30.2

PERCEIVED   TL 68.4   CD 245.13

PER CENT   VG 27.31

PERCENTAGE   VG 27.32

PERCH   FO 146.27   VG 33.12

PERCHED   FO 168.28   CD 206.5
    248.36   255.36   VG 32.26   33.4
    36.7   36.34   65.27   78.38

PERCHING   SM 22.40   VG 78.8

PERENNIAL   SM 74.3

PERFECT   TL 44.33   57.7   59.27
    81.27   FO 138.6   177.11
    CD 184.4   184.9   190.7   208.14
    208.19   208.20   208.33   212.27
    215.15   222.42   SM 8.19   17.3
    22.23   31.19   31.20   44.34
    44.35   82.3   108.16   115.23
    124.12   124.15   128.28   140.7
    147.40   148.23   148.40   149.34
    150.32   MD 206.26   206.28
    VG 12.14   31.1   40.7   48.2
    48.17   54.12   66.1   76.29   78.23

PERFECTED   TL 100.36   SM 129.33
    MD 208.37

PERFECTLY   LH 36.37   TL 46.35
    71.30   FO 114.3   138.4   156.19
    173.1   173.13   CD 187.27   195.10
    195.40   195.41   196.3   196.10
    196.11   200.3   200.6   201.31
    201.35   205.28   206.16   207.17
    207.21   208.36   209.11   215.6
    215.30   SM 18.8   18.12   19.3
    19.9   20.11   33.22   52.3   52.23
    124.29   132.40   VG 5.29   8.10
    12.28   28.6   40.4   40.7   41.14
    41.37   46.18   56.35   57.6   58.16
    66.8   79.34

PERFORCE   FO 136.27

PERFORM   TL 90.20   CD 221.8
    MD 190.18

PERFORMANCE   FO 161.25

PERFORMED   LH 36.27   TL 90.8
    CD 215.25   221.9

PERFORMING   SM 71.1   MD 186.11

PERFUME   TL 95.20   CD 208.39
    MD 166.15   208.13   208.15   209.3
    210.40   211.20   VG 69.10

PERFUMED   MD 166.26   170.13
    187.41   195.30   202.32

PERFUMES   MD 168.34   169.20
    169.24

PERIL   VG 78.39

PERILOUS   FO 155.26

PERILOUSLY   VG 32.26

PERIOD   CD 221.5

PERISH   TL 82.38   SM 47.7   103.39
    VG 5.40

PERKILY   VG 16.8

PERKING-UP   CD 238.11

PERKY   FO 123.9

PERMANENCE   SM 146.1

PERMANENT   SM 32.30   85.11

PERMANENTLY   FO 118.39

PERMISSION   TL 92.22

PERMITS   SM 124.37   MD 190.35

PERMITTED   FO 115.17   SM 150.9

PERPETUAL   FO 173.8   SM 27.27

PERPETUALLY   CD 226.5   SM 18.6

PERPLEXED   SM 17.38

PERPLEXITY   MD 205.27   VG 64.12

PERSECUTING   SM 35.20

PERSISTED   FO 132.25   133.22
    SM 41.30   VG 32.40   63.23

PERSISTENCE   TL 58.14

PERSISTENT   VG 31.20

PERSISTENTLY   FO 152.33

PERSON   TL 82.18   88.34   CD 198.38
    213.15   216.8   216.10   219.9
    SM 62.26   VG 4.14   16.7   64.41
    80.9

PERSONAL   LH 22.17   TL 55.17
    96.17   SM 25.6   30.27   30.32
    54.11   79.2   98.25   98.27
    MD 176.19   177.37   177.38
    178.16   178.34

PERSONALITIES   SM 30.27   30.28
    30.31

PERSONALLY   TL 84.37   FO 155.3
    CD 261.34   261.35   SM 39.5
    117.3

PERSONS   CD 216.11   219.9
    SM 119.24

PERSON'S   SM 47.24

PERSPIRING   LH 8.11   SM 37.5

PERSPIRINGLY   MD 167.34

PERSUADE   CD 213.13   SM 53.23

PERSUADED   SM 113.28

PERSUADING   VG 39.34

PERTINACIOUSLY   FO 116.40

PERTINENTLY   FO 151.37

PERTURBED   LH 20.35   MD 176.26

PERVADING   SM 76.5

PERVERSE   TL 49.22   SM 50.6
    VG 23.14

PERVERSITY   SM 24.27   VG 23.14

PEST   SM 143.40

PET   LH 37.27

PETALLED   MD 208.15

PETALS   TL 58.11   MD 208.3
    209.4

PETER   VG 56.1

PETRIFIED   FO 174.13   SM 83.24
    VG 75.31

PETTY   CD 232.2   259.41

PETULANCE   VG 66.15

PETULANT   TL 82.15

PETULANTLY   FO 150.39

PEW   SM 29.3

PHALLIC   SM 135.23   135.29

PHANTASM   SM 21.3   130.26
    130.27

PHANTASMAGORIC   SM 19.40

PHANTASMAL   SM 130.38

PHANTOM   SM 128.26

PHARAOHS   TL 96.41

PHARISEE   SM 117.28

PHASE   CD 225.25

PHEASANT-TRIMMING   CD 248.8

PHENOMENA   MD 181.40

PHENOMENAL   MD 180.34   180.37
    181.13   181.20   181.29
    183.33

PHENOMENON   CD 203.13   MD 183.5

PHILANDERING   SM 94.40   120.29

PHILANTHROPY   TL 47.6

PHILIPS   SM 89.21   93.20

PHILISTINE   VG 67.29

PHILOSOPHER   MD 189.25

PHILOSOPHIC   SM 86.8   VG 7.37

PINKISH   TL 105.42   SM 102.1
  110.40

PINKY   TL 54.25   SM 60.12

PINNED   TL 62.34   SM 83.12   83.34

PINO   SM 78.11

PINON   SM 78.12

PINON-TREES   SM 139.20

PINOVETES   SM 78.11

PIN-POPPET   TL 71.33

PINS   TL 71.37

PINZGAU   CD 231.37

PINZGAU VALLEY   CD 237.26   239.3

PIOUS   VG 3.9   4.10

PIPE   LH 18.21   19.24   SM 155.23
  VG 21.21   49.8   49.34   50.30
  51.12   57.40   58.6   58.11   59.2
  60.4   60.7   60.11   60.13

PIPED   SM 142.5   VG 25.18

PIPES   LH 18.15   CD 185.23
  SM 149.3

PIQUANT   TL 97.4

PIQUANT-LOOKING   SM 44.21

PIQUED   TL 89.30   FO 129.35
  CD 251.30   SM 19.8   44.6   66.6
  110.15   130.31   VG 57.37

PISTACHIO   VG 41.33

PISTOL   SM 9.14   9.24   132.20

PISTOL-SHOT   SM 55.32

PIT   LH 14.23   FO 177.27   177.30
  178.2   SM 52.40

PITCH   LH 6.13   8.10   FO 131.4
  SM 77.4

PITCH-BLACK   LH 32.4   TL 52.39

PITCH-DARK   LH 31.9

PITCHED   LH 8.7   SM 73.23
  VG 67.39   73.26

PITCHING   LH 11.37   VG 71.32

PITH   SM 145.4

PITHED   SM 145.2   145.7

PITIED   LH 16.8   TL 47.4

PITIFUL   LH 26.10   32.35   VG 76.6

PITIFULLY   LH 34.14

PITS   VG 23.28

PITTSBURGH   SM 128.21

PITY   TL 43.3   FO 118.13   118.14
  145.12   CD 225.21   248.31
  SM 15.29   29.29   124.14
  MD 181.32   VG 55.38   72.3   72.4

PIVOT   VG 7.15

PLACE   LH 8.3   31.20   35.22   35.27
  36.35   TL 44.23   59.9   63.42
  70.7   83.31   104.23   FO 113.14
  115.14   121.31   124.1   125.23
  127.18   127.38   130.5   131.2
  131.18   141.6   144.35   144.40
  149.25   150.25   150.29   151.26
  159.39   160.41   164.26
  CD 198.35   201.8   206.36   215.11
  218.17   229.24   241.11   244.17
  247.17   255.13   260.42   SM 4.11
  5.15   5.24   8.3   8.9   10.27
  31.36   42.31   47.2   64.1   65.11
  74.1   93.1   96.14   111.12
  116.10   120.24   128.36   129.37
  140.22   140.30   141.7   141.9
  141.19   144.38   145.39   150.3
  152.34   152.35   153.21   154.8
  155.15   MD 165.16   165.18
  180.21   182.1   191.22   199.12
  200.32   206.4   VG 14.10   18.16
  33.14   43.17   44.25   66.23
  70.33   71.4   79.23   81.15

PLACED   LH 7.27   7.34   8.5   33.10
  FO 131.38   SM 156.22   VG 22.3
  28.39

PLACES   CD 243.29   243.30   244.39
  247.17   SM 14.9   63.34   102.36
  104.11   147.25   MD 191.21
  205.29

PLACING   LH 3.18   VG 50.16

PLAIN   TL 52.2   FO 156.21   165.26

PLAIN-LOOKING   LH 38.27

PLAINLY   FO 130.22   CD 211.41

PLAINTIVE   FO 142.6   142.14
  142.28   142.32   143.32   153.31
  SM 35.4   135.32   135.38   136.11
  MD 205.20

PLAINTIVELY   LH 26.6   FO 152.6
  SM 84.25   VG 52.37

PLAIT   TL 105.42

PLAITED   TL 105.41   VG 24.12

PLAN   SM 109.32   110.14

PLANE   TL 85.6   SM 20.1

PLANES   FO 125.7

PLANET   CD 201.40   221.6

PLANGENT   FO 123.42   124.5   125.42
  CD 195.13   215.2

PLANK   CD 266.10

PLANKS   FO 144.1   SM 155.8

PLANNED   FO 175.10

PLANNING   SM 114.4

PLANS   FO 150.13   150.15
  CD 191.28

PLANT   CD 185.22   SM 142.37

PLANTATION   SM 7.14   62.27
  62.36

PLANTATIONS   SM 128.7

PLANTED   LH 4.39   9.35
  CD 194.32   231.17   SM 67.16
  VG 4.34

PLANTERS   SM 7.15

PLANTS   SM 150.41

PLASTER   SM 113.16

PLASTERED   VG 75.10

PLASTIC   MD 208.8

PLATE   LH 15.34   15.41
  TL 95.30   FO 122.31   134.23
  134.26   156.26   VG 9.16
  14.5   14.21   14.23   14.31
  68.25

PLATES   LH 15.19   VG 38.1
  47.3   47.5   75.27

PLATFORM   CD 200.36   200.39
  MD 187.31

PLATONIC   SM 6.32

PLATTER   MD 169.6

PLAY   TL 66.13   FO 161.10
  CD 206.3   SM 29.31   33.26
  122.13   135.19   VG 46.22
  65.5   65.6   69.38

PLAYBOYS   SM 158.5

PLAYED   LH 26.28   TL 99.14
  99.21   FO 135.37   CD 207.30
  SM 4.25   VG 10.37

PLAYFULLY   FO 165.10

PLAYING   LH 12.6   TL 65.8
  FO 145.14   CD 208.27
  SM 3.18   16.27   34.36   83.10
  156.23   VG 45.32   70.39

PLAYMATES   CD 207.15   208.5

PLAY-THINGS   CD 223.1   223.2

PLEADED   LH 12.10   FO 160.34
  CD 198.11   SM 68.12   84.7

PLEADING   LH 14.15   23.34
  33.19   CD 198.12   SM 68.7
  84.6

PLEASANT LH 3.33 4.24 TL 64.37
  73.10 CD 209.8 217.11 232.7
  SM 28.29 40.25 155.17
  MD 177.36

PLEASANTER SM 124.6 137.2

PLEASE TL 52.32 53.4 53.27
  54.30 54.34 60.17 60.40
  66.20 80.20 FO 128.34 130.31
  166.22 CD 194.40 196.4 198.3
  198.4 198.11 198.12 198.17
  204.26 204.27 210.10 219.13
  259.42 260.25 266.12 SM 37.18
  39.18 45.22 92.13 93.29
  97.36 105.20 109.22 121.4
  MD 177.23 VG 33.40

PLEASED LH 25.20 25.37 TL 78.2
  FO 124.34 126.15 141.25
  CD 201.8 209.20 250.31
  SM 130.12 130.34 154.14
  MD 175.30 177.32 VG 40.40

PLEASES LH 38.17

PLEASURE FO 126.6 129.14 129.21
  137.18 CD 203.2 203.3 258.2
  SM 28.18 39.38 43.14 135.13

PLEDGES CD 215.26

PLENTY FO 151.40 172.17
  CD 205.41 SM 35.6 VG 22.41
  41.11

PLODDED MD 199.22

PLOTTED MD 210.6

PLOUGH AND HARROW FO 128.1

PLOUGHED LH 7.17

PLOUGHSHARE MD 172.35

PLOVERS CD 222.14

PLUCK FO 177.28

PLUCKED TL 75.5

PLUMB SM 146.7

PLUMBAGO CD 201.22

PLUMBING SM 142.23

PLUM-BLOSSOM MD 209.1

PLUMP TL 70.3

PLUNGE FO 177.27

PLUNGED LH 23.38 29.33 SM 82.15

PLUNGES LH 27.28

PLUNGING CD 239.31 SM 24.41
  75.27 VG 72.36

PLUS CA CHANGE SM 132.18

PLUS CA CHANGE PLUS C'EST LA MEME
  CHOSE SM 128.12

PLYMOUTHS FO 113.22

PNEUMONIA TL 49.19 VG 60.26
  75.13

POACHED CD 228.33 229.10 246.13
  246.14

POCKET LH 20.2 28.30 FO 147.26
  CD 227.6 227.7 227.18 233.33
  SM 5.14 31.16 VG 68.36

POCKET-BOOK TL 80.23

POCKETS TL 72.29 CD 191.11
  191.20 205.7 205.18 215.19
  238.13

POCK-MARKED SM 143.12

POETIC TL 63.39 VG 9.34

POETRY TL 77.3 99.14

POIGNANCY MD 207.19

POINT LH 9.17 FO 177.9
  CD 188.32 203.5 203.7 203.15
  203.34 213.7 258.35 258.36
  258.37 258.41 259.1 259.4
  259.12 SM 31.26 81.6 95.10
  107.32 130.4 141.22 MD 178.27
  VG 58.12 58.24 77.15

POINTED LH 17.23 22.32 TL 52.20
  73.3 FO 128.27 147.30
  CD 195.19 SM 53.35 MD 190.25
  191.25 193.6 199.33 VG 46.15

POINTEDLY FO 148.40

POINTING SM 9.14 60.36 63.6
  MD 195.4 196.37

POINTS TL 50.19 CD 209.13
  210.16 243.23 SM 130.4

POISE VG 74.27

POISED LH 7.8 SM 45.1 73.20
  90.12

POISON TL 63.36 65.38 66.1
  FO 179.14 CD 245.2 SM 71.4
  114.7 157.31 VG 61.16

POISON-BITES SM 71.36

POISON-GAS TL 64.6

POISONOUS CD 253.2 VG 14.33
  57.25 61.22

POISONOUSLY SM 131.22

POISON-WEED SM 144.19

POKE SM 51.40

POKED CD 234.37 MD 199.3

POKER SM 42.39

POKING SM 143.8

POKY SM 30.13

POLE LH 13.3 CD 226.5
  256.4 256.7 SM 69.30

POLE-CAT TL 58.35 58.37
  65.38

POLES FO 169.24

POLICE SM 25.11

POLICEMAN SM 21.28 VG 78.18
  78.30 78.33 79.1 79.8
  79.9 79.25 79.41 80.3
  80.8 80.18

POLICEMAN'S SM 71.18

POLICEMEN SM 25.10 127.29

POLISH LH 15.42

POLISHED SM 16.10 146.16
  MD 183.30 VG 23.25

POLITE TL 45.19 45.36 84.36
  85.39 FO 143.12 143.24
  149.35 SM 82.10 125.40

POLITELY TL 64.34 85.2
  VG 46.4

POLITENESS VG 14.24

POLITICIANS TL 46.9 MD 190.6

POLITICS TL 43.19

POLO SM 113.24

POLYANTHUS TL 98.21

POLYPS MD 198.25

POMMEL LH 3.31 4.28
  FO 171.19

POMP MD 180.15

POND FO 116.20 118.1
  SM 105.32

PONDERED FO 125.22 CD 250.15
  MD 175.5 VG 55.41

PONDERING CD 202.27 214.1
  250.15 256.14 MD 195.27
  VG 69.9

PONDEROUS VG 71.20

PONDS TL 97.40

PONIES SM 8.39

PONY FO 147.12

POOL CD 185.3 SM 68.33
  145.20 145.21 MD 198.12
  199.40 VG 47.26

POOLS LH 33.26 FO 174.15

POOO FO 149.21

POWERLESSNESS   SM 15.28   15.30
15.33

POWERS   TL 82.28   SM 95.18   95.19
119.26   123.9   123.12   123.32

POWLA   LH 26.14

PRACTICABLE   SM 89.30

PRACTICAL   FO 123.27   SM 68.14
VG 10.22

PRACTICALLY   TL 45.21   FO 157.34
170.40   CD 214.33   SM 126.22
155.7   VG 44.30   81.12

PRAGUE   TL 66.34

PRAISE   SM 142.30   MD 195.19

PRANCED   MD 164.21   164.25

PRANCING   CD 249.25   SM 39.21
MD 164.12

PRAY   CD 259.29   264.28   SM 157.29

PRAYED   VG 6.33   6.42   12.14

PRAYER   MD 207.21

PRAYER-MEETING   SM 30.10

PRAYERS   LH 5.15   SM 97.38   98.7

PRAYING   VG 15.12

PREACHED   MD 181.32

PREACHING   MD 181.35

PRECAUTIONS   FO 164.21

PRECINCTS   MD 167.11   190.34
199.35

PRECIOUS   TL 72.12   80.14
SM 100.5   MD 204.27   VG 26.3
27.1   67.34

PRECIPICE   FO 177.26

PRECIPICES   CD 243.21

PRECIPITOUSLY   CD 255.33

PRECISE   CD 184.32

PRECISION   LH 18.29

PREDATIVE   SM 135.9   VG 21.12
37.12   67.7

PREENED   VG 57.37

PREENING   VG 40.22

PREFER   LH 6.23   CD 256.20
SM 16.30   121.18

PREFERENCE   SM 82.23

PREFERRED   CD 193.22   SM 5.35
94.13

PREFERRING   FO 129.28

PREFERS   SM 43.31

PREGNANT   TL 96.37   CD 203.35
203.36

PREHISTORIC   TL 92.3   SM 19.39
21.2

PREJUDICE   CD 252.15   SM 52.16

PRELATE   VG 70.12

PREMONITION   SM 121.29   MD 165.14

PREOCCUPATION   MD 194.28

PREOCCUPIED   VG 40.12

PREPARATION   SM 145.19

PREPARATIONS   SM 73.9

PREPARED   LH 9.1   FO 122.2
CD 225.1   SM 8.34   18.9   20.8
92.16   112.38   142.11   VG 54.15

PREPARING   FO 121.37   126.39
127.6   CD 224.18   SM 90.25
112.36   VG 20.26

PREPOSSESSING   CD 229.25

PREPOSTEROUSLY   FO 144.1

PRESENCE   LH 5.30   18.14   19.28
24.36   32.33   TL 51.34   85.37
91.35   102.37   102.42   103.9
FO 121.26   124.42   135.18   164.9
165.4   CD 191.14   199.13   199.25
216.27   216.32   217.18   252.18
SM 22.28   31.15   32.19   33.20
33.23   MD 176.41   179.32
VG 5.34   67.14

PRESENCES   SM 20.1   74.12   139.8
139.9

PRESENT   FO 116.14   CD 190.38
195.31   198.7   199.32   230.40
SM 22.17   76.21   84.27   110.18
111.27   146.21   VG 5.13   6.5
41.27

PRESENTABLE   SM 18.6

PRESENTED   CD 234.11   VG 12.37

PRESENTLY   LH 7.17   15.33   33.7
34.4   SM 38.29   MD 169.4

PRESERVE   SM 71.35   91.8
MD 192.33

PRESERVES   SM 152.14

PRE-SEXUAL   SM 146.3   146.24

PRESIDE   SM 81.21

PRESIDED   VG 12.22

PRESS   TL 92.29   95.22   FO 152.3
175.18   CD 256.7   SM 70.23

PRESS (CONT.)   113.30
VG 65.35

PRESSED   LH 5.13   23.25   24.2
34.15   36.8   TL 87.12
FO 116.26   136.23   160.7
163.15   CD 186.16   234.5
SM 98.18   MD 206.22   VG 30.17
65.26   65.35

PRESSES   CD 185.19

PRESSING   LH 23.25   33.30
TL 70.24   95.5   103.28
SM 98.16   MD 167.2   VG 8.18
12.30   20.24   49.34   65.31
65.33   74.39

PRESSURE   TL 101.7   101.8
101.11

PRESTIGE   VG 67.23   67.24

PRESUMABLY   FO 127.15

PRESUME   SM 82.5   82.6

PRESUMED   SM 137.16

PRESUMPTION   SM 70.6

PRESUPPOSES   SM 30.30   30.31
30.32

PRETENCE   SM 118.9   118.11

PRETEND   FO 116.38   SM 86.37
111.15

PRETENDED   CD 257.19   SM 4.26
74.39   VG 4.37   12.27   21.26

PRETENDING   VG 11.15

PRETENTIOUS   CD 216.11   216.12

PRETTILY   CD 186.1   SM 38.2

PRETTINESS   CD 194.37   194.41

PRETTY   LH 19.1   38.25   38.28
TL 79.3   CD 195.3   196.1
207.27   207.29   211.8   212.5
SM 3.17   4.19   9.25   32.34
33.2   44.20   48.5   VG 19.42
27.34   40.17   52.20

PRETTY-PRETTY   SM 10.9

PREVARICATION   VG 62.23

PREVENT   TL 53.27   58.8
CD 246.30   SM 74.35   VG 42.13

PREVENTED   FO 115.7   VG 70.3

PREVIOUSLY   MD 181.14

PREY   FO 149.7   CD 241.24
SM 130.29

PREYING   LH 19.38   SM 144.23

PRIAPUS   SM 111.5   111.7   111.8
111.13   111.34

PRICE   CD 213.26   213.39   VG 21.37

PRICELESS   SM 31.1   31.8

PRICKED   FO 149.4   SM 11.16   74.24

PRICKING   CD 238.37   SM 47.27

PRIDE   FO 154.16   CD 250.21
   SM 41.37   100.28   MD 163.32
   VG 22.29   26.41   26.42   27.36
   29.24   30.20

PRIED   MD 196.17

PRIEST   TL 82.40

PRIESTESS   SM 112.36   MD 186.19
   187.17   187.22   193.1   194.28
   195.25   202.37   206.18   211.16

PRIESTESS'S   MD 196.4   204.17
   205.41

PRIESTLY   TL 82.7

PRIESTS   MD 174.31   175.2

PRIM   SM 82.26

PRIME   FO 148.21

PRIMEVAL   CD 244.15   SM 146.24

PRIMITIVE   TL 50.12

PRIMMED   FO 121.41

PRIMROSE   TL 48.4   48.25   71.14
   71.15   CD 244.39

PRIMROSES   VG 68.3

PRINCE BOGORIK   TL 96.21

PRINCE OF WALES   SM 96.16

PRINCIPAL   FO 113.8

PRINCIPALLY   CD 224.22

PRINCIPLE   TL 97.9   97.13   97.16
   SM 4.9   69.18   71.40

PRIPPY, SIR   (SEE SIR PRIPPY)

PRISON   TL 83.36   85.34   SM 22.28
   22.29   VG 16.13   16.16

PRISONER   TL 51.1   56.25   56.28
   61.1   61.26   68.14   75.1   85.28
   85.31   86.15   86.29   94.11
   104.26   107.14   MD 178.26

PRISONERS   TL 43.27   47.41   48.1
   65.8

PRISTINE   MD 193.31

PRIVACIES   SM 30.26

PRIVATE   LH 11.21   FO 128.2
   CD 216.15   216.16   SM 135.8
   VG 6.34   10.22

PRIVATELY   VG 57.23

PRIVILEGED   TL 44.10   VG 31.11

PRIVILEGES   SM 136.15   136.21

PRIZING   MD 165.38

PROBABILITY   SM 5.6

PROBABLY   TL 55.12   60.38   81.13
   84.30   94.20   96.23   FO 142.22
   142.31   147.37   162.27
   CD 202.15   214.27   216.15
   251.14   251.15   257.35   264.19
   SM 5.3   55.8   58.23   77.24
   102.2   123.14   123.22   158.28
   MD 198.18   VG 8.21   44.31   49.16
   49.26   54.6   56.26   56.30   56.38

PROBLEM   SM 79.8   VG 42.42   56.23
   56.25   56.27

PROCEEDED   FO 118.17   132.39
   VG 11.9   34.21

PROCEEDS   VG 26.5

PROCESSES   FO 114.30   115.5

PROCESSION   MD 199.13

PROCURE   FO 157.38

PRODUCED   VG 14.41

PRODUCING   FO 132.25

PRODUCTION   SM 71.19   71.20

PROFANE   MD 210.5

PROFIT   SM 144.5

PROFITEERS   CD 216.10

PROFOUND   FO 131.2   CD 231.24
   SM 94.13

PROFOUNDLY   LH 27.3   CD 225.20
   VG 4.4   11.8

PROGNATHOUS   VG 65.34

PROGRESS   FO 153.22

PROGRESSING   SM 24.26

PROHIBITION   SM 128.1

PROJECTION   FO 131.8

PROMINENT   SM 15.21   VG 42.41
   43.1   50.2

PROMISCUITIES   SM 138.38

PROMISCUOUS   SM 137.20

PROMISE   LH 36.25   CD 198.14
   265.28   265.40   SM 41.41   42.16
   100.20   100.22   VG 69.34

PROMISED   TL 48.24   FO 141.1
   164.16   166.8   CD 208.21

PROMISES   CD 215.26

PROMPTLY   VG 80.4

PRONE   VG 30.31

PRONOUNCE   SM 81.38

PRONOUNCED   LH 16.21   SM 58.25
   132.2

PROOF   VG 66.5

PROPELLED   SM 83.19

PROPER   LH 15.20   FO 156.15
   CD 214.23   263.17   263.19
   263.26   SM 37.25   98.7

PROPERLY   TL 50.24   FO 119.4
   CD 252.12   262.12

PROPERTY   SM 105.1   MD 188.39
   198.9   199.37   209.40   210.1
   VG 64.19

PROPHET   MD 182.30

PROPOSE   VG 42.31   42.32

PROPOSED   SM 5.26

PROPPED   LH 15.29   CD 209.25

PROPRIETY   FO 125.27

PROSAICALLY   SM 110.4

PROSERPINE   TL 81.35

PROSPECTORS   SM 141.38

PROSPERITY   SM 128.18   VG 25.11

PROSPEROUS   SM 9.8

PROSTITUTE   TL 82.38   82.39
   SM 139.5   MD 204.34

PROSTITUTION   VG 60.23

PROSTRATE   SM 67.24   67.33
   VG 81.12

PROTECT   CD 212.12   SM 72.2
   86.32

PROTECTING   VG 17.20

PROTECTINGLY   SM 65.12   65.14

PROTECTION   CD 219.8

PROTECTIVE   TL 46.20   VG 57.19

PROTECTIVELY   SM 86.34

PROTECTS   SM 118.6   MD 202.7

PROTEST   CD 207.26   211.9

PROTESTED   LH 20.32   35.13
   38.15   SM 10.1

PROTRUDING   VG 12.23   78.14

PROTUBERANT   VG 9.19

PROUD   LH 5.32   15.19   TL 47.32
   59.35   64.33   92.31   96.36
   FO 159.8   CD 238.8   238.10
   SM 22.23   50.7   149.19
   MD 163.11   VG 22.27   38.5

PROUDLY   TL 93.27   CD 236.37
   SM 75.4

PROVED   TL 88.40

PROVIDED   FO 114.27   SM 138.3

PROVISION   VG 5.9

PROVISIONS   CD 244.25

PROVOCATIVE   LH 5.26

PROWLED   FO 145.41   SM 127.12
   VG 70.18

PROWLING   FO 119.8   135.24   147.1
   SM 152.17

PRUNING   SM 44.26

PRUSSIC   SM 63.28

PSALM   MD 181.34

PSANEK   TL 59.13   59.17   59.18
   59.19   60.19   89.23

PSANEKS   TL 61.39   96.39

PSEUDO-HANDSOME   SM 70.34   70.38

PSYCHES   SM 30.33

PSYCHIC   CD 203.13   SM 31.3   123.8
   123.10   123.32   137.35

PSYCHOLOGIST   SM 30.37   30.38

PSYCHOLOGISTS   SM 15.39

PSYCHOLOGY   SM 30.30   30.36

PUBLIC   TL 92.29   92.30   92.33
   CD 263.16   SM 25.17   30.8   80.26
   80.28   156.38   MD 174.21
   VG 64.19

PUBLICITY   SM 9.37

PUBLISH   VG 28.34

PUCKERED   SM 147.24

PUCKERING   FO 121.41

PUDDING   LH 15.1

PUDDINGS   VG 9.12

PUDDLES   SM 93.6

PUEBLO   SM 155.11

PUERILE   VG 65.3

PUFF   MD 195.1

PUFFING   CD 206.6   SM 133.38
   150.38

PUFFY   SM 134.2

PULL   TL 73.23   SM 24.15   36.38
   83.1   83.2   VG 19.30   19.41

PULLED   LH 37.24   TL 51.16   51.17
   73.30   80.6   FO 122.10   125.15
   144.39   179.35   CD 183.25
   201.27   219.37   227.7   227.8
   237.15   238.42   266.16   SM 22.31
   23.11   24.25   36.14   66.26
   66.31   68.26   82.27   83.11
   83.34   104.26   MD 163.30   211.12
   VG 8.33   19.38   37.13   37.20
   44.31   46.6   48.38   67.29   73.7
   73.16   75.14   75.18   75.28

PULLING   LH 19.26   29.4   TL 72.28
   FO 162.32   SM 4.6   24.20   24.26
   46.20   66.38   VG 18.20   32.42
   49.7   49.8

PULLMAN   SM 129.1   132.10

PULLS   TL 73.33   SM 134.21

PULPIT   SM 64.38

PUMP   SM 57.25

PUNCTUATED   VG 37.26

PUNISH   SM 104.13

PUNTO DI MILANO   CD 209.15   214.20

PUPIL   TL 68.29   69.12   SM 20.37
   26.32

PUPILS   SM 21.16

PUPPET   CD 183.34   186.40   187.25
   194.7   194.22   197.15   199.7

PUPPETS   CD 186.15

PUPPY   FO 137.17   139.27   165.9

PUPPY'S   FO 170.20

PURCHASERS   CD 193.25

PURE   LH 5.34   21.19   32.40
   TL 43.22   75.26   82.12   82.20
   83.10   106.8   106.25   FO 148.24
   173.13   173.30   CD 209.39
   237.21   238.25   242.24   253.33
   253.35   254.4   254.9   254.11
   254.13   254.18   254.42   SM 17.13
   22.37   30.37   35.2   50.28   86.24
   114.7   141.27   146.35   147.2
   147.10   150.31   157.38
   MD 165.38   176.31   180.30   186.5
   191.40   194.5   196.24   197.25
   VG 4.20   4.27   4.28   4.36   4.42
   23.34   24.16   27.5   65.24

PURE-BRED   SM 129.31

PURELY   TL 77.2   SM 69.37   131.9
   MD 180.38   VG 48.20

PUREST   SM 150.32

PURITY   MD 176.12   VG 23.35
   23.36

PURPLE   LH 21.27   CD 234.20
   SM 35.36   83.7   141.4
   141.14   148.1   155.4
   MD 166.40   189.33   189.34
   VG 74.6   74.7

PURPLE-DARK   CD 244.34

PURPLISH   TL 56.41   VG 17.17

PURPOSE   CD 258.8   258.10
   SM 88.39   101.40

PURPOSES   SM 12.39   18.9

PURR   CD 199.22   260.29

PURSE   VG 51.41   52.5

PURSED   FO 116.37   118.29
   128.13   133.32   136.8   137.36
   137.38   143.3   148.36
   CD 196.34   230.2   231.11
   VG 15.30

PURSE-LIKE   VG 15.33

PURSING   VG 39.41

PURSUIT   LH 6.9

PUSH   LH 9.2   9.23   TL 60.5
   CD 235.9   MD 165.24   187.4
   VG 34.21

PUSH-BIKE   VG 8.30

PUSHED   LH 8.39   TL 53.39
   FO 116.9   118.28   134.7
   CD 186.10   248.13   MD 187.3
   188.1   211.11   VG 32.39
   34.22   54.33   73.24   74.9
   75.23

PUSHING   TL 79.39   FO 142.35
   170.17   CD 185.40   SM 156.2
   MD 165.33   205.17   VG 17.18
   29.13   34.18   76.31

PUTHER   SM 102.7

PUTRIDITY   VG 30.13

PUTS   FO 154.22   VG 8.16

PUTTEES   FO 114.8   120.23
   157.3

PUTTING   LH 33.14   TL 72.29
   102.19   FO 132.11   134.18
   CD 186.21   198.31   225.38
   236.14   246.1   262.21
   SM 13.3   80.41   85.29
   108.24   108.32   131.16
   VG 38.7   48.25   54.12   66.38

PUZZLE   TL 105.7   CD 251.25

PUZZLED   LH 6.18   TL 52.40
   105.9   105.20   105.25   105.26

PUZZLED (CONT.)   FO 126.20   128.41
  161.41   164.14   VG 5.42   11.40
  42.23   64.11

PUZZLES   VG 10.38   11.11

PYJAMAS   SM 57.13

QUACKING   FO 172.31

QUAILED   MD 168.8

QUAINT   TL 91.25   SM 3.18   4.17
  9.27   118.30

QUALITIES   SM 124.26   VG 26.35

QUALITY   LH 27.5   TL 63.40   105.25
  FO 135.17   SM 119.23   136.11
  VG 61.28

QUARK-QUARKING   FO 147.11

QUARREL   LH 20.8   VG 65.1

QUARRIES   VG 68.8

QUARRY   FO 130.39   131.7   131.13
  SM 29.10   VG 18.23   20.30   20.41
  24.25   25.16   41.20   41.25
  41.28   46.7   46.18   48.38   70.38
  81.7

QUARTER   TL 48.25   FO 147.39
  SM 77.24

QUARTER-PAST   LH 22.22

QUARTERS   SM 117.21

QUEEN   TL 69.1   104.13   CD 231.26
  231.27   231.28   232.26   SM 95.16

QUEEN ALEXANDRA   SM 23.30

QUEENLY   VG 35.23

QUEEN MOTHER   SM 23.29

QUEEN VICTORIA   SM 23.15

QUEER   LH 31.22   TL 45.40   52.6
  55.18   96.33   97.38   101.6
  FO 134.38   135.24   136.29
  139.11   139.27   140.4   140.32
  147.30   149.17   151.5   152.1
  153.31   163.26   164.18   164.35
  169.2   170.40   172.42   CD 185.29
  185.41   217.11   217.42   218.10
  219.30   221.11   244.2   SM 3.19
  5.9   30.19   30.20   46.24   50.18
  78.19   111.12   120.39   125.15
  126.32   130.15   130.38   144.28
  MD 171.30   171.35   201.15
  VG 14.39   23.15   34.4   39.30
  53.29   59.6   68.25

QUENCH   VG 27.1

QUENCHED   VG 52.20

QUERIED   TL 85.12

QUEST   VG 15.26

QUESTION   LH 12.13   TL 53.13
  95.33   105.37   106.14   106.15
  107.1   FO 116.13   124.35   139.40
  139.42   140.1   140.3   140.24
  151.38   CD 190.15   190.29
  202.40   203.17   215.23   225.38
  250.19   257.28   258.25   SM 14.28
  14.34   14.36   15.15   16.6   23.3
  55.30   55.32   59.25   74.37
  98.26   108.30   135.22   148.30
  MD 183.35   190.36   VG 41.9
  44.10   52.21

QUESTIONED   LH 16.24   TL 106.10

QUESTIONING   TL 63.14   SM 11.18
  15.1   15.6

QUESTIONS   FO 123.26   VG 32.8

QUICK   LH 4.40   21.4   TL 75.9
  FO 115.19   123.17   123.32
  125.40   127.9   129.29   137.18
  139.27   140.30   140.31
  CD 184.21   184.32   184.36   185.6
  187.3   199.39   199.41   200.1
  231.9   238.21   SM 9.29   15.20
  17.9   18.39   21.18   49.24   49.25
  49.26   51.8   74.30   101.27
  136.25   138.16   139.7   142.38
  MD 168.7   168.15   187.6   193.12
  195.28   VG 37.17   43.10

QUICKENED   LH 9.16

QUICKLY   LH 4.4   7.7   25.29   33.23
  TL 56.13   65.20   94.26   101.14
  FO 123.9   128.32   137.17   155.12
  156.34   CD 195.16   217.23   244.2
  253.17   254.29   257.2   266.16
  SM 15.23   17.29   34.32   35.8
  59.3   103.5   106.23   MD 179.23
  186.40   192.30   211.10   VG 4.17
  9.18   18.24   20.29   35.1   37.10
  37.11   63.1   75.26   79.18

QUIEN SABE   SM 138.28

QUIESCENCE   TL 107.4   107.25

QUIESCENT   SM 135.37

QUIET   LH 5.34   17.7   17.8   38.18
  TL 58.2   70.10   88.24   95.24
  96.14   104.42   105.25   107.14
  FO 131.28   135.19   143.34
  157.11   157.33   CD 187.3   203.7
  220.8   235.5   235.32   236.24
  246.37   247.2   SM 6.15   11.21
  11.27   11.31   21.20   23.35
  24.30   32.7   32.8   32.18   32.28
  76.20   154.19   MD 177.36
  VG 38.4   38.7   46.22   67.14

QUIETER   TL 104.33   108.28
  CD 261.40   262.27

QUIETLY   LH 13.2   13.36   35.12
  TL 70.9   106.34   FO 145.29
  179.33   CD 186.42   197.5   201.28
  212.12   219.11   246.34   263.14
  265.30   SM 22.11   32.21   57.33
  58.17   59.10   76.22   76.34
  124.35   MD 169.41   VG 25.4
  45.32   47.13   50.3   53.2   57.40

QUIETLY (CONT.)   67.5   67.8

QUIETNESS   FO 157.10   SM 11.19

QUILT   VG 76.39

QUIT   SM 116.27   119.29

QUIVER   LH 34.37   FO 132.10

QUIVERED   LH 29.17   FO 148.33
  MD 187.7   201.22   VG 30.28

QUIVERING   TL 96.1   FO 174.7
  175.31   SM 15.25   59.1
  MD 164.25   186.26   205.32
  206.29

QUIZZICALLY   SM 48.18   64.28

QUOTATION-MARKS   SM 91.13

RABBIT   TL 70.5   FO 127.26
  130.8   143.15   169.4   170.31
  SM 42.29

RABBIT-PIE   LH 14.39   15.37
  18.5   19.11

RABBITS   CD 261.9

RABBLE   TL 93.17

RACE   TL 47.13   50.35   92.3
  CD 199.34   206.37   229.27
  242.6   SM 75.16   MD 179.37
  VG 52.9   52.16   65.39
  66.40   73.3

RACED   LH 22.35

RACE-MISERY   SM 20.18   76.25

RACES   TL 50.37

RACHEL, MISS   (SEE MISS RACHEL)

RACHEL FANNIERE   SM 47.3   47.9

RACHEL WITT   SM 102.23   102.40
  103.7   103.11   104.23

RACILY   CD 232.23

RACING   LH 10.1

RACKED   FO 122.4

RACKING   CD 265.1

RACKS   SM 143.38

RACY   CD 231.6

RADIANCE   CD 237.24   MD 185.4

RADIANT   LH 3.8   14.19
  MD 200.15

RADISHES   SM 103.32

RAG   SM 155.16

RAGE   FO 143.23   153.11   166.35
  166.40   CD 259.28   SM 35.9

RAGE (CONT.) SM 58.34 152.20
  MD 186.24 VG 6.37 14.22 15.11
  15.36 19.41 27.9 28.31 63.30

RAGED SM 152.22

RAGES SM 34.33

RAGGED LH 21.28 SM 14.20 146.13
  146.30

RAGGEDLY TL 98.23

RAGGLE-TAGGLE VG 43.21

RAGING CD 239.3 SM 150.40
  MD 172.17 180.34

RAGS VG 35.32 35.33

RAIGHT LH 14.11 26.13 37.11
  37.17

RAIL CD 236.4 SM 20.32 24.14
  126.28

RAILING SM 24.21

RAILLERY SM 108.23

RAILWAY FO 119.27 SM 29.12
  59.37 117.24 125.22 126.21

RAILWAY-CARRIAGE FO 115.22

RAIN LH 24.17 24.19 24.29
  24.35 26.26 26.28 27.22
  28.24 28.35 28.36 30.37
  30.39 30.40 38.10 FO 130.2
  CD 248.1 248.6 248.13 248.22
  248.28 248.29 248.36 248.41
  250.12 250.32 250.36 250.40
  251.21 252.21 257.3 SM 66.10
  85.10 87.22 87.26 90.9 90.12
  93.5 94.6 94.7 125.38 126.2
  126.37 127.4 127.5 134.1
  148.10 MD 179.4 208.18 208.20
  208.23 208.27 VG 45.1 54.39

RAINBOW FO 177.40 177.42

RAINBOWS TL 57.13 SM 84.1

RAINDROPS LH 25.12 25.31 26.38

RAINED CD 237.22 MD 208.7

RAINING LH 30.25 34.22 SM 85.5
  125.31 VG 16.2 41.23

RAINS MD 174.2 VG 68.2

RAINY SM 126.8

RAISE TL 72.16 SM 112.7

RAISED LH 12.31 FO 127.3
  CD 205.8 SM 12.39 48.26 67.37
  154.9 MD 186.21 VG 28.6 31.41

RAISES SM 30.35

RAISING FO 113.5 SM 129.18
  130.8

RAISON D'ETRE FO 178.26

RAKE LH 6.12

RAKISH SM 9.30 VG 38.3

RAMBLING SM 152.8

RAMPANT CD 241.12

RAMPARTS LH 4.21

RAN LH 3.4 6.42 10.41 15.9
  33.15 TL 78.19 FO 116.33
  121.10 126.30 168.16 174.5
  CD 232.11 236.30 238.38
  261.39 SM 24.39 59.37 143.34
  MD 171.41 174.40 183.22
  185.28 85.34 197.29 198.8
  VG 17.34 18.12 19.4 79.36

RANCH SM 78.16 91.25 94.33
  112.7 123.20 123.21 129.2
  130.14 131.34 133.29 134.5
  141.1 141.20 142.1 142.15
  142.18 142.25 143.1 143.4
  143.6 144.27 145.13 145.28
  148.32 150.11 152.27 153.4
  153.8 153.19 154.6 154.13
  154.16 154.19 154.25 154.29
  155.4 158.33

RANCH-MAN SM 130.6

RANCOROUS SM 18.29

RANDOM LH 8.11 8.26

RANG LH 9.18 TL 76.7 CD 205.18
  MD 171.7 205.36 VG 40.20
  67.11

RANGE FO 131.5 149.3 SM 131.24
  MD 164.27

RANGED VG 21.2

RANK SM 127.23 VG 5.11 5.20
  26.35

RANKLED FO 167.10

RANKLING TL 48.17 FO 167.11
  CD 216.41

RAPACITY SM 153.24 MD 189.2

RAPID FO 132.32 132.40 170.12
  CD 231.4 SM 69.41 MD 198.20
  VG 45.35 46.8 49.2 65.3

RAPIDLY TL 49.27 63.26 102.6
  102.11 102.22 FO 119.31 122.2
  132.31 174.33 SM 106.11
  108.33 130.23 MD 191.30
  VG 19.15 46.20 48.35 64.42

RAPIDS SM 86.36

RAPT FO 116.13 118.21 MD 176.12
  176.32 196.23 199.23 203.5

RAPTURE MD 176.3 176.28 188.16
  202.28 203.6

RAPTUROUS MD 176.20

RARE TL 87.8 SM 62.33 73.22
  MD 189.28 189.31 189.34

RARELY TL 60.8 FO 135.19
  CD 203.21 SM 38.32

RASH SM 117.30

RASPBERRIES CD 240.41
  SM 151.39 152.1 152.3
  152.11

RASSENTLOW CD 205.25

RAT FO 146.30 SM 137.19
  137.21 155.18 VG 61.32
  61.33 62.13

RAT-DIRT SM 152.28

RATE LH 25.36 CD 247.7

RAT-HOLES SM 137.8

RATIONAL VG 51.2

RAT-LIKE SM 136.6 136.12
  140.26 149.10

RATS FO 134.15 SM 137.22
  144.2 155.26

RAT'S VG 63.30

RATTLE FO 119.26 SM 87.20
  VG 33.4

RATTLED SM 87.14 87.20
  102.10 VG 37.4

RATTLING LH 33.6 SM 87.13
  87.15 87.18 91.17 129.16
  130.23 VG 72.10 74.13
  75.27 75.39

RATTY CD 205.1 SM 157.3

RAVED VG 73.42

RAVELLED SM 96.20

RAVINE CD 240.13 261.14
  MD 192.31

RAVINES SM 142.23

RAVING TL 62.3 CD 252.32

RAW LH 38.35 FO 131.20
  135.42 SM 12.20 12.21
  12.23 19.31 19.32
  VG 24.20

RAW-WOOD CD 235.6

RAY MD 189.11

RAYS MD 188.27 189.34
  189.37 VG 27.36

REACH LH 8.17 FO 127.14
  146.32 170.34 177.23

REACH (CONT.) FO 177.27 CD 253.6
  SM 100.35 128.37 139.24
  MD 172.1 174.28 VG 43.25

REACHED LH 22.12 FO 159.30
  174.22 176.32 176.36 176.37
  CD 201.27 235.25 248.9 251.21
  SM 31.26 VG 11.17

REACHING FO 168.3 170.42 176.31
  176.40 CD 203.5 219.29 220.23
  252.35 SM 19.13 VG 21.17

REACTED SM 4.30

REACTION VG 44.28

READ TL 48.34 55.35 66.14
  70.15 83.25 95.42 96.1 99.21
  FO 115.2 119.23 135.20 135.21
  136.16 136.27 166.32
  CD 199.14 219.20 SM 15.39
  29.31 38.14 43.11 65.1
  116.16 126.25 133.6 138.32
  154.22 VG 11.15 22.20 22.33
  32.39 51.27

READER FO 135.20

READILY FO 129.29

READING LH 15.30 15.32
  FO 135.33 136.6 SM 42.33

READING-LAMP CD 183.7 185.1

READING-ROOM SM 29.30

READS CD 185.28 185.29

READY LH 13.14 37.41 39.8
  TL 79.36 FO 122.42 126.5
  130.37 151.13 158.10 158.13
  166.23 168.29 173.28
  CD 186.11 226.11 251.2 252.2
  SM 51.32 57.8 57.30 58.11
  73.11 81.3 95.21 112.21
  117.23 125.3 125.10 127.24
  136.13 143.1 VG 10.39 12.38
  40.23

READY-MADE SM 114.17

REAL TL 43.20 67.10 67.32
  86.41 87.26 87.28 99.5 102.1
  105.13 FO 164.34 165.33
  179.29 CD 193.35 198.32
  198.40 199.11 199.33 207.14
  208.5 211.9 212.29 214.9
  217.25 217.31 227.13 230.13
  230.34 230.42 SM 7.23 7.29
  8.27 15.35 16.4 16.5 21.3
  23.38 27.33 37.31 38.35 49.6
  49.8 49.11 49.15 50.27 71.5
  73.18 78.11 86.19 92.7 95.31
  99.5 111.16 111.18 111.25
  119.34 122.17 124.27 125.8
  131.20 131.22 131.23 133.32
  135.12 135.20 136.39 146.17
  150.21 155.14 158.34 VG 5.30
  60.14 60.19 69.36

REALISATION FO 178.7 CD 214.33

REALISE TL 70.10 FO 165.21

REALISE (CONT.) CD 225.30 230.5
  230.11 MD 206.14 VG 28.23

REALISED LH 11.1 28.6 TL 54.3
  101.9 FO 161.22 161.31 163.18
  175.12 175.21 176.42
  CD 261.28 261.41 MD 177.40
  VG 42.35 81.22

REALITY TL 86.14 86.16 CD 199.1
  199.24 199.35 SM 10.33 129.27
  130.18 130.23 MD 176.27
  188.23 205.9

REALIZATION SM 140.14

REALIZE SM 12.30 26.9 42.23

REALIZED SM 12.12 12.36 15.41
  19.33 26.19 34.37 51.19
  75.39 76.2 99.16 112.2
  114.38 114.41 138.13 138.29
  140.27

REALIZING SM 51.20

REALM SM 118.39

REAPPEAR SM 143.21

REAPPEARED LH 7.4 SM 5.6 8.13
  VG 23.22

REAPPEARING SM 44.30

REAR FO 113.3 SM 24.15 58.11
  66.28 71.8

REARED LH 3.24 24.32 36.35
  SM 24.24 26.40 36.9 36.19
  67.13 72.29

REARING SM 24.38 24.41 25.8
  69.4 72.38 77.6

REARS SM 77.5

REASON LH 15.12 35.32 TL 60.23
  69.34 92.21 94.32 FO 148.42
  CD 188.24 230.29 251.27
  258.11 258.15 258.23 SM 12.41
  14.12 96.3 117.24 148.22
  148.23 VG 26.24 39.19 39.25
  44.22 61.24 72.34

REASONABLE CD 262.35

REASONED SM 58.15

REASONS FO 151.40 MD 190.10

RE-ASSEMBLED MD 188.14

REASSURED LH 22.17 36.9

REASSURING FO 138.37

REASSURINGLY SM 39.8

REBEL VG 16.10

REBELLION SM 46.24

REBELLIOUSLY CD 190.29 192.15

REBELS SM 115.10 VG 16.8

RE-BIRTH MD 173.6

RE-BORN MD 189.28 190.3
  194.10 194.14

REBUFF LH 32.40

RECEIVE LH 8.10 TL 64.30
  93.4 FO 173.39 SM 111.3

RECEIVED LH 7.25 TL 50.42
  81.25 105.21 FO 165.13
  SM 37.21 125.32 VG 3.18
  3.26 47.38 54.8 81.14

RECEIVER TL 76.4

RECEIVING TL 93.26 SM 139.15

RECEPTIVE FO 176.5

RECESS FO 124.39 CD 237.17
  VG 20.28

RECKLESS TL 47.10 47.21
  47.35 93.37 FO 153.32
  CD 230.36 SM 75.23

RECKLESSLY SM 128.19

RECKLESSNESS SM 129.24

RECKON CD 199.31

RECKONING TL 105.21 SM 100.11
  100.12

RECKONS LH 32.7

RECLINING MD 201.29

RECOGNISE TL 45.22 CD 207.34

RECOGNISED TL 49.36 FO 170.3

RECOGNITION TL 45.18 52.19

RECOGNIZE SM 135.29

RECOGNIZED SM 7.29 18.34
  18.35

RECOGNIZES SM 72.1

RECOIL TL 88.7 CD 199.31
  MD 178.1 180.1 VG 62.18

RECOILED TL 82.17 FO 119.30
  119.37 128.10 SM 76.3
  VG 27.1 27.25

RECOILING VG 27.26

RECOLLECTION LH 5.12 VG 5.30

RECONNOITRE VG 77.33

RECOVER LH 14.33 FO 120.30
  SM 137.15 MD 166.16

RECOVERED LH 12.4 FO 121.26
  SM 6.29

RECOVERING   TL 54.11   FO 121.7

RECREATION   SM 59.17

RECTOR   VG 3.27   3.31   4.5   4.13
  4.18   4.23   6.11   6.22   7.19
  9.24   10.37   11.10   11.37   12.2
  12.27   16.28   26.22   26.33
  28.21   28.30   28.36   31.4   31.26
  35.3   37.34   38.31   40.29   40.40
  51.24   57.21   57.23   60.37
  61.19   61.24   63.18   79.16
  79.32   80.16   80.35   81.7

RECTORATE   VG 3.19

RECTOR'S   VG 4.19   4.27   4.36
  4.42   10.31   61.16   65.16   67.23
  70.19   78.5   79.37

RECTORY   VG 3.21   3.27   4.34   9.3
  9.42   10.29   25.33   29.35   29.37
  30.1   30.12   30.22   30.37   31.14
  36.11   36.13   36.16   37.8   66.21
  67.4   71.39   80.29

RECURRED   FO 118.33

RECURRING   FO 118.40   MD 205.26

RED   LH 4.26   7.10   7.18   17.22
  23.21   TL 52.8   60.29   67.5
  67.32   74.23   74.29   76.12
  FO 117.8   119.21   119.27   135.35
  136.2   136.14   140.10   142.19
  143.7   143.8   143.19   144.11
  169.1   169.29   170.9   170.32
  CD 185.4   199.12   218.1   233.27
  234.19   234.32   245.9   245.18
  245.19   247.13   SM 14.30   35.37
  42.38   54.8   67.9   74.5   78.15
  80.41   110.33   113.11   129.5
  129.16   130.7   138.17   148.2
  150.24   150.36   150.38   151.4
  MD 167.22   VG 19.22   24.38
  46.11   50.17   53.3   76.19

RED-BLOTCHED   VG 65.21

RED-BRICK   TL 62.26   SM 28.12

REDDENED   TL 46.39   47.29   54.21
  FO 141.18   141.30   163.27
  VG 46.37   49.35   65.26

REDDENING   TL 76.20

REDDISH   TL 100.7   FO 147.29
  CD 210.7   239.21   SM 154.40
  VG 12.23   15.18   76.15

RED-FACED   FO 143.6   144.36

RED-FLUSHED   MD 180.16

RED-GOLD   SM 11.29   12.7   13.33

RED-HOT-POKER   SM 42.36

RED LION   VG 77.39   78.28   80.41

RED MAN'S   SM 20.23

RED-ORANGE   SM 17.14

RE-ECHOED   LH 9.41   10.39
  SM 55.11   VG 18.21

REED   VG 36.37   37.20

REEDS   TL 58.27   CD 238.39

REEDY   SM 68.32

REELED   SM 67.8   MD 165.40   173.22
  VG 73.26

REELING   VG 73.31

RE-EVOKED   MD 204.8

REFINED   FO 135.42

REFLECT   SM 132.32

REFLECTING   CD 210.35   SM 88.2

REFLECTION   SM 134.11

REFLECTIVE   VG 59.1

REFLECTIVELY   LH 9.8

REFLEX   VG 26.33

REFRACTION   TL 67.11

REFRAIN   MD 204.25   VG 41.6

REFRESHMENT   MD 172.32

REFUGE   SM 114.2

REFUGEE   CD 193.15   193.16   209.32

REFUSAL   TL 45.29   FO 114.6
  VG 16.27

REFUSE   FO 167.30   SM 115.13
  154.2   154.5   VG 74.35   75.34

REFUSED   FO 113.24   114.38
  CD 212.34   241.39   SM 9.8   37.16
  101.16   109.28   122.13   125.38
  133.26   VG 26.24   45.7   66.38

REFUSING   SM 8.7   108.28

REFUTING   SM 100.31

REGAINED   FO 143.2   MD 164.17

REGARD   LH 20.13   27.15   27.16
  SM 119.34

REGARDED   LH 18.7   CD 203.14

REGARDING   TL 43.23

REGARDS   FO 166.28   SM 116.30
  119.34

REGATTA-CANAL   SM 8.36

REGIERUNGSRAT   CD 232.2

REGIMENT   TL 50.25   FO 131.12
  CD 184.5   SM 59.11   VG 51.17
  52.10   59.19

REGION   SM 105.23   MD 169.22
  169.23

REGIONS   CD 243.12

REGISTERED   VG 23.33

REGISTRAR   FO 164.24

REGRETTABLE   TL 108.27

REGRETTED   SM 100.9

REGULAR   LH 17.35   VG 53.22

REHEARSAL   TL 71.17

REHEARSE   TL 71.18

REIGN   TL 89.36

REIGNED   VG 10.35

REIN   SM 36.28   102.23

REINED   SM 23.1   62.5   100.15

REINFORCEMENT   CD 204.15

REINING   SM 69.40

REINS   FO 178.35   SM 58.34
  66.26   66.39   67.1   67.6
  67.11   83.2   83.4   83.13
  VG 19.29   39.11

REITERATED   CD 207.33   SM 64.39
  VG 35.33   44.13   79.29

REJECTED   TL 90.7

RELAPSE   TL 103.5

RELAPSED   SM 138.29

RELATION   TL 66.33   CD 229.28
  SM 3.26   6.35

RELATIONS   LH 35.17   SM 140.9

RELATIONSHIP   CD 225.31

RELATIONSHIPS   CD 224.8
  SM 14.40

RELATIVES   TL 55.15   SM 85.21
  VG 66.4

RELAX   TL 69.11

RELAXATION   TL 69.15   FO 132.4
  SM 73.21

RELAXED   LH 28.9   TL 82.28
  FO 125.2   125.14   132.17
  SM 11.30   MD 209.41

RELAXING   SM 138.30

RELEASE   TL 63.19   SM 116.39
  MD 210.19

RELEASED   VG 30.36

RELENT SM 74.22

RELENTED SM 110.39

RELENTLESS CD 230.14 SM 31.31
  125.7 153.14 VG 15.20 30.17

RELENTLESSLY VG 65.33

RELENTLESSNESS VG 67.17

RELIEF FO 113.33 115.31
  CD 223.33 SM 39.9 69.20 78.3
  89.12 137.11 137.24 137.27
  152.22 MD 177.13 VG 77.15
  79.26 80.23

RELIEVE FO 159.23

RELIEVED LH 12.10 20.8 38.21
  SM 52.20 65.40 MD 172.27
  VG 43.6

RELIGION SM 98.2 98.3 105.4
  158.1 158.38

RELIGIOUS SM 98.2

RELIGIOUSLY TL 79.35

RELINQUISH MD 201.8

RELISH MD 196.18

RELUCTANCE VG 69.35

RELUCTANT FO 128.15 SM 32.28

RELUCTANTLY CD 228.26 SM 55.33
  VG 21.30

RELY CD 219.5

REMAIN FO 125.4 CD 231.18
  SM 43.26 71.19 116.31 139.23
  MD 172.33 205.13 VG 65.13

REMAINED LH 6.30 9.32 9.34
  18.5 19.23 21.26 23.31
  TL 63.27 78.30 87.17 95.29
  FO 128.33 128.36 131.17
  158.14 171.29 CD 189.2 201.23
  202.24 SM 25.32 74.31
  MD 168.29 VG 19.17 27.35
  31.23 42.30 65.12 65.13

REMAINING LH 29.23 TL 92.32
  SM 77.24

REMAINS TL 65.35 SM 71.34
  MD 163.18

REMARKED FO 127.15 CD 245.26
  SM 64.14

REMARKS CD 202.36 SM 7.3 85.34
  86.1 86.3 86.15

REMEDY FO 115.16

REMEMBER TL 49.23 49.32 50.21
  51.37 53.11 62.16 65.37
  65.39 65.41 66.14 66.17
  72.10 72.11 80.17 81.8 81.12
  104.23 107.39 FO 157.26 165.8

REMEMBER (CONT.) CD 195.27
  198.27 200.4 222.19
  SM 23.18 110.7 121.33 131.21
  VG 11.27 14.18 26.30 64.6
  81.2

REMEMBERED LH 22.3 TL 44.6
  51.29 FO 126.38 127.10 145.39
  SM 127.14 136.4 140.23
  MD 182.13 VG 51.33 80.5

REMIND TL 72.31

REMINDED FO 127.23 149.1
  CD 230.34

REMINDS SM 109.39

REMINISCENCES SM 63.30 VG 13.11

REMNANT VG 53.33

REMONSTRATED LH 26.11 30.19
  CD 234.37 SM 45.18

REMOTE TL 50.11 104.32 107.5
  FO 143.7 143.20 CD 186.26
  216.31 250.2 SM 18.2 59.34
  60.30 120.40 140.9 MD 169.23
  190.39 197.14 VG 42.30 68.21

REMOTELY FO 143.9

REMOTENESS TL 45.24 FO 142.23
  143.14

REMOVE SM 93.29 118.39

REMOVED TL 64.26 101.7 101.9
  FO 115.10 CD 212.1 213.1
  213.5

RENEWED MD 178.26

RENOIR SM 5.8

RENTED SM 154.8 VG 53.18

REPAIRING FO 168.41

REPAY SM 14.10

REPEATED LH 6.20 12.29 13.33
  14.19 17.25 26.1 26.13 34.30
  36.15 38.14 TL 53.21 56.21
  103.35 FO 129.11 139.22
  151.38 174.20 CD 187.31 189.3
  189.27 190.14 192.30 220.38
  236.29 258.10 SM 11.35 59.25
  98.3 VG 52.28

REPEATEDLY VG 41.9

REPELLED TL 91.31 MD 192.23
  VG 63.24

REPELLENT SM 107.26 107.27
  139.5 MD 193.22

REPENT FO 163.41

REPENTED VG 13.10

REPLENISHED MD 190.18

REPLY LH 9.21 18.12 37.35
  37.40 38.22 38.30 TL 45.17
  108.15 FO 128.36 CD 192.1
  266.4

REPLYING TL 93.34

REPORT SM 34.17

REPOSING SM 138.31

REPRESENT CD 226.19

REPRESENTED LH 5.30 CD 231.1
  SM 96.15

REPRESSION TL 93.11

REPRIMAND LH 13.21 SM 34.38

REPRIMANDED SM 34.5

REPROACH CD 194.2 224.17
  249.5 VG 58.36

REPROACHFUL LH 12.34 VG 40.4
  40.6 49.25 53.30

REPTILES VG 65.41

REPUBLICAN CD 229.33

REPUDIATION TL 93.12

REPUGNANCE SM 94.13 VG 29.35

REPULSION SM 152.28
  MD 184.15 VG 9.23 64.41

REPULSIVE TL 72.38 CD 242.39
  SM 80.38 MD 166.35 193.23
  VG 9.10 64.34

REPULSIVENESS VG 29.37

REQUEST SM 37.21

REQUESTED SM 25.16

REQUESTS TL 44.35

RESCUE FO 153.10 CD 214.4

RESCUED SM 138.5

RESEMBLANCE CD 230.3

RESENT SM 53.9 111.25

RESENTED LH 18.20 FO 135.34
  135.42 SM 32.36 53.10
  MD 165.15 VG 10.28

RESENTFUL TL 48.19 100.20
  CD 201.29 VG 49.18 50.33
  53.30

RESENTMENT LH 36.6 CD 236.1
  SM 12.12 18.29 43.37
  46.35 VG 50.42

RESERVE FO 125.11 CD 200.8
  210.25 232.21 SM 44.5

RESERVED LH 39.16 TL 64.33

RESERVES   TL 59.31   VG 40.1

RESERVOIR   VG 80.29   80.31

RESIGN   CD 213.14

RESIGNATION   VG 14.33   74.40
   76.32   77.5

RESIGNED   VG 53.22

RESINOUS   SM 146.4

RESISTANCE   LH 9.28   27.32
   FO 174.27   SM 41.1   144.24

RESISTANT   TL 91.36   104.40
   FO 176.13   SM 146.22

RESISTED   CD 192.39

RESOLUTENESS   MD 168.10   169.14
   171.10   171.25   176.14

RESOLUTION   LH 34.13   MD 167.12

RESOLUTIONS   SM 79.3

RESONANCE   TL 77.15   VG 45.28

RESONANT   TL 49.27   72.39

RESORTS   CD 229.7

RESOUNDED   FO 168.35

RESOUNDING   SM 27.1

RESPECT   TL 44.17   44.18
   FO 154.10   SM 15.21   28.34
   28.35   28.37   85.30   95.18
   107.19   107.20   107.40   108.1
   108.2   108.18   135.30

RESPECTFUL   TL 98.33

RESPECTING   MD 189.19

RESPECTIVELY   VG 3.3

RESPLENDENT   TL 82.27   CD 201.37
   MD 163.4

RESPOND   SM 53.10   MD 169.33

RESPONDED   VG 56.5

RESPONDING   SM 81.33

RESPONSE   SM 19.20   VG 49.36

RESPONSIBILITY   TL 88.21   89.14
   FO 157.10   157.14   176.18
   176.27   177.20   177.38   179.23
   SM 73.18   80.26   86.32   VG 33.30

RESPONSIBLE   TL 91.14   FO 149.10
   161.30   166.10   176.18   176.21
   176.23   SM 35.25   VG 31.15

RESPONSIVELY   VG 58.5

REST   LH 3.16   9.7   18.22   18.31
   31.20   TL 70.33   88.32   FO 150.1
   166.27   178.38   CD 191.30   257.5

REST (CONT.)   262.26   263.23
   SM 9.2   94.21   101.3   125.22
   MD 168.13   169.41   176.38
   190.34   VG 26.12   44.10   54.15

RESTAURANT   CD 243.29   252.5
   257.8

RESTED   LH 37.20   TL 51.32
   FO 171.19   CD 250.19   SM 13.34
   67.15   95.33   110.30

RESTFUL   LH 30.9

RESTING   FO 170.29   MD 165.29
   VG 31.27

RESTLESS   LH 23.32   TL 51.5
   CD 186.16   198.18   SM 45.30
   141.23

RESTLESSLY   LH 21.17   23.26   23.35
   CD 186.39

RESTLESSNESS   CD 191.18   SM 116.19

RESTORE   SM 79.20

RESTRAINED   SM 5.2

RESULT   LH 4.12   TL 88.5   SM 29.9
   120.21   133.28   VG 60.38   78.20

RESULTS   TL 86.33   SM 34.15

RESUMED   CD 190.9   196.34   201.34
   208.31   208.40   209.37   220.14
   248.26   SM 158.11   VG 14.15

RESUMING   MD 209.40   VG 75.29

RESURRECTED   VG 60.26   60.27

RESURRECTION   MD 211.19

RETAINER   SM 132.40

RETALIATION   CD 258.34

RETICENCE   SM 13.7

RETIRE   TL 100.17

RETIRED   FO 115.21   MD 188.39
   VG 22.19

RETIRING   FO 117.9

RETORTED   LH 3.35   4.14   FO 139.8
   173.27   SM 43.7

RETRACED   MD 173.9

RETREAT   CD 200.35   SM 26.40
   71.37

RETREATED   FO 164.35   SM 40.11
   42.31

RETREATING   FO 164.35

RETROGRESSION   TL 90.18

RETURN   LH 24.23   TL 68.18   84.21
   101.40   CD 219.5   256.9

RETURN (CONT.)   SM 69.41
   135.1   MD 165.21   173.2
   177.36   179.3   181.6

RETURNED   LH 11.12   36.26
   39.10   TL 51.32   85.20
   92.14   FO 136.28   137.33
   150.11   CD 191.20   219.34
   258.5   SM 28.6   51.35
   98.25   128.24   MD 165.20
   VG 38.41   43.35   47.27
   50.10   52.36   55.11

RETURNING   CD 191.21   198.19
   VG 68.10

REUNION   TL 56.5

REVEALED   SM 7.3   147.25
   MD 182.24

REVELATION   TL 69.33

REVELATIONS   CD 209.26

REVELLED   SM 149.9

REVENGE   TL 47.37   CD 259.37
   259.41   SM 110.19

REVENGED   MD 210.2

REVENGEFUL   VG 65.11

REVENGEFULNESS   VG 65.15

REVERBERATING   FO 147.6

REVERENCE   CD 231.41   SM 29.21
   124.25   MD 177.35   VG 4.38
   64.7

REVERSE   TL 65.3   67.23   67.26
   68.37

REVERSED   SM 69.37

REVIVE   TL 61.13

REVIVED   VG 77.22

REVOKED   LH 11.2

REVOLT   VG 66.26

REVOLVING   SM 79.8

REVULSION   MD 166.4   176.6
   VG 3.8   27.36   55.37   66.24

REWARD   FO 166.38   MD 178.19

REWARDS   MD 178.17

RHAPSODY   CD 196.15

RHEUMATICS   FO 169.36

RHINE   SM 127.41

RHUBARB   SM 37.38

RHYTHM   MD 203.8

RHYTHMICALLY   MD 205.40

RIBBON CD 238.16 238.17

RIBBONS FO 177.17

RIBS LH 12.21 TL 46.2 SM 72.11

RICE LH 15.1

RICH FO 146.33 CD 229.23 236.6
236.7 244.41 SM 3.25 4.1
4.27 28.6 28.34 28.35 31.9
57.25 99.28 99.30 MD 169.20
180.10 VG 22.40 24.21 49.26

RICHES SM 28.37

RICH-GREEN MD 167.1

RICHLY TL 107.35

RICHLY-COLOURED VG 54.3

RICKETY LH 18.39 FO 169.23
SM 141.11 155.8

RICKS TL 98.1

RICO SM 3.6 3.8 3.12 3.35
3.37 4.4 4.25 4.34 4.40
5.11 5.20 5.26 5.31 6.2 6.4
6.8 6.19 6.37 7.5 8.18 9.11
9.38 9.40 10.6 10.15 10.19
10.31 14.39 15.18 15.33
16.26 16.31 16.35 17.5 17.26
18.3 18.18 19.1 19.21 20.7
20.8 23.23 23.31 23.33 23.40
24.8 24.11 24.24 24.34 24.36
24.40 25.8 25.15 25.22 25.27
25.31 25.38 26.1 26.4 27.5
27.38 28.4 28.8 28.10 29.1
30.6 30.38 31.1 31.8 31.21
31.28 31.32 34.7 34.20 34.24
34.27 35.8 35.26 36.3 36.10
36.13 36.21 36.23 36.27
36.35 36.37 37.4 37.15 38.16
38.19 40.27 47.28 50.17
51.19 51.20 52.19 52.26
52.36 53.20 53.39 54.32
57.10 57.12 57.21 57.40 58.3
58.7 58.13 58.18 58.25 58.33
58.40 59.4 59.6 59.9 64.19
64.24 64.37 65.40 66.14
66.18 66.24 66.29 66.30
66.39 67.20 67.24 67.30
68.12 68.16 70.10 72.11
72.12 72.17 73.4 73.5 73.28
73.29 73.38 73.39 80.6 80.32
87.10 87.12 90.19 96.4 96.5
96.14 96.19 109.38 110.11
110.19 110.23 110.26 110.29
110.35 111.12 111.30 111.32
111.37 111.39 112.23 112.26
112.37 113.12 113.27 113.39
114.5 114.6 114.8 114.10
114.30 114.35 115.6 115.17
115.19 115.22 115.41 118.8
118.15 121.24 121.40 125.6
126.6 130.39 136.37 136.39
137.1 139.30 155.30 159.4

RICO'S SM 12.6 15.3 18.35
19.34 24.28 26.9 34.11 34.29
34.31 35.1 38.7 52.29 67.12
70.5 80.23 113.3 113.14
115.15

RID TL 63.16 SM 80.4 93.27
110.21 121.30

RIDDANCE LH 28.14

RIDDEN SM 36.4 70.33 70.37

RIDE LH 23.3 FO 168.12 171.6
CD 264.39 SM 8.15 9.23 10.2
10.19 12.1 12.3 13.5 16.31
17.2 23.24 23.26 25.16 35.29
35.33 36.36 36.40 37.7 43.5
44.1 51.33 57.17 57.18 60.21
77.10 92.18 92.27 92.29
92.31 97.32 101.36 109.7
111.20 121.34 121.35 123.25
138.22 139.3 MD 181.40
VG 45.14

RIDER FO 170.8 SM 69.39 70.1
70.6 70.34

RIDERS SM 20.31 22.24 60.33
62.7 121.39

RIDES SM 23.20 93.20

RIDGE SM 139.20 159.14

RIDGED CD 255.17 255.21

RIDGE-TOPS FO 143.35

RIDGING CD 255.37

RIDICULE FO 130.27 CD 249.41
258.2 258.31 SM 33.37 113.34

RIDICULOUS TL 93.8 FO 130.12
158.40 CD 200.13 203.32
254.31 SM 40.13 40.14
VG 29.26 42.33

RIDICULOUSLY CD 254.30 SM 137.17

RIDING LH 23.39 TL 54.28
SM 8.20 10.2 20.30 23.35
28.3 36.21 57.19 57.28 59.13
66.11 68.23 70.35 102.6
106.17 111.21 VG 46.38

RIDING-BOOTS SM 35.38 63.40

RIDING-BREECHES SM 35.36 38.31

RIDING-SKIRT SM 57.8

RIDLEY (SEE HONOURABLE LAURA,
LAURA)

RIFLES FO 121.24

RIFT CD 254.41

RIFTED VG 12.30

RIGHT LH 6.28 6.31 8.33 9.6
14.10 14.27 14.28 18.20
23.18 23.27 26.11 29.9 30.21
30.25 31.25 37.1 37.32
TL 51.21 53.3 69.41 75.39
76.2 76.35 78.6 82.4 89.41
90.2 90.5 90.7 90.40 94.20
98.2 106.14 106.15 107.11
FO 117.35 117.40 129.18

RIGHT (CONT.) 134.39 134.41
141.3 141.41 148.11 149.23
164.17 166.23 166.25
173.26 CD 188.20 194.25
195.39 204.11 220.37
223.35 224.37 227.26
238.18 239.35 241.6 244.25
256.19 264.8 SM 7.35 11.2
11.4 13.27 17.33 18.38
19.18 33.12 38.35 39.14
39.31 39.33 40.21 40.35
45.22 57.37 57.38 61.30
63.5 63.16 77.18 83.34
87.33 103.4 119.21 122.40
124.1 135.8 136.9 142.15
158.14 159.6 MD 180.20
181.1 181.3 183.6 205.33
206.21 VG 8.10 21.41
27.41 31.35 32.35 33.11
34.39 37.31 38.36 41.35
45.27 46.5 58.16 59.35
64.15 64.22 68.35 69.13
69.31 71.34 74.29 75.6
75.8 76.1 76.2 76.38
76.42 79.27 79.34 81.16

RIGHTED CD 261.38 261.39

RIGHTEOUSNESS TL 44.12

RIGHTS LH 17.36 30.30
SM 73.3 119.33

RIGID SM 146.9 MD 165.9
VG 77.19

RIM CD 251.21 MD 197.32
208.8

RIMS TL 46.39 54.21
MD 202.17

RING LH 25.18 TL 46.4 74.27
76.1 76.11 85.23 85.28
CD 194.35 202.40 205.16
SM 111.4 141.15 VG 66.9
66.10 74.8

RINGING CD 204.38 SM 132.3
MD 164.4 171.22 183.18
VG 45.35

RINGS TL 53.21 CD 197.16
205.21 VG 30.14

RIO GRANDE SM 147.26

RIOT TL 55.14 CD 228.14

RIOTOUS TL 47.14

RIP SM 10.8

RIPPED SM 144.30

RIPPLE SM 20.41 37.1

RIPPLED VG 77.18

RIPPLING SM 128.25

RISE TL 82.25 FO 129.36
163.27 175.32 CD 220.8
231.18 SM 20.29 59.36
71.7 71.26 72.37 133.26

RISE (CONT.) SM 148.7 MD 178.21
  199.13 207.10 VG 17.2 74.34
  76.1

RISEN TL 78.24 101.38 FO 154.35
  CD 201.11 241.35 SM 69.3
  MD 168.3 169.11 170.3 175.8
  175.17 175.24 176.11 176.21
  176.29 176.30 177.40 178.5
  178.23 178.30 181.36 182.3
  182.22 182.24 182.33 182.34
  189.40 190.17 195.39 197.5
  202.8 207.11 208.4 VG 76.14

RISES MD 178.3 189.32 189.35

RISING LH 19.26 21.7 TL 53.34
  98.14 FO 142.35 176.6
  CD 259.36 265.21 SM 64.6 69.6
  69.23 75.24 80.15 80.35
  143.11 143.40 146.2 146.30
  146.36 147.19 MD 171.5 185.29
  187.28 VG 32.41 38.26 46.24
  73.38 76.23

RISKED MD 178.19

RISKY CD 199.8

RITES TL 66.28

RITUAL MD 190.18 203.2

RITUALISTIC SM 17.18

RIVAL VG 6.7

RIVALS VG 6.6

RIVER TL 107.26 107.32 CD 239.3
  239.4 239.10 239.36 240.13
  240.28 243.35 252.32 260.5
  SM 86.37 MD 206.23 VG 17.15
  17.34 35.40 36.29 70.10
  70.22 70.27 71.17 71.23
  72.12 72.23

RIVER-BANK VG 36.16

RIVER-BED CD 239.27

RIVER PAPPLE VG 3.22

RIVERS CD 243.22 SM 148.13
  149.26

RIVIERA SM 126.18

RIVULETS CD 253.32

ROAD LH 4.33 15.9 25.5 32.23
  32.27 32.29 FO 126.23 168.12
  169.23 CD 185.34 222.13
  238.38 239.22 239.24 239.34
  239.37 240.26 240.36 241.8
  241.19 243.10 244.23 244.32
  245.10 245.12 247.27 258.14
  261.5 262.27 SM 36.21 36.25
  36.35 57.40 58.38 58.39 59.1
  59.5 68.33 93.36 108.34
  127.29 132.16 134.21 134.22
  138.14 MD 166.36 166.39
  167.19 185.34 190.32 194.30
  194.40 VG 3.23 3.24 13.33
  16.33 16.34 17.27 18.1 18.9

ROAD (CONT.) 18.31 19.13 19.39
  20.26 20.29 20.35 35.37 36.5
  36.15 36.21 36.26 36.31
  41.20 47.24 68.9 70.39 71.15
  71.41 72.10 72.13

ROAD-END CD 260.18

ROADS CD 222.15 SM 97.26 110.5
  111.23 VG 16.1

ROADSIDE CD 247.10

ROAD-SIDE VG 20.31

ROAD-TRACK CD 243.35

ROADWAY LH 21.4

ROAMED FO 126.26

ROAMING SM 128.19 137.19

ROAN VG 19.39 20.26 23.27
  36.32 39.12

ROAR TL 91.20 VG 72.19 73.28
  73.29

ROARED LH 9.39 CD 235.21 241.12
  241.31 VG 11.34

ROARING FO 167.2 CD 239.3
  240.28 VG 37.26 72.24 72.27
  76.27

ROARS LH 16.16

ROAST VG 9.11

ROBBED MD 203.40 VG 38.22

ROBE MD 173.35 185.9 188.8
  188.20

ROBIN LH 21.28

ROBUST FO 113.12 153.32
  SM 31.18

ROCK TL 54.39 58.39 FO 132.19
  CD 222.26 237.21 240.20
  240.21 240.24 240.40 241.10
  241.26 241.30 242.4 242.7
  242.24 243.14 243.20 243.33
  244.29 245.3 245.31 247.23
  252.31 252.33 253.16 256.15
  SM 14.22 65.21 126.15 146.37
  154.38 154.39 MD 165.6 166.1
  166.5 166.13 166.16 178.36
  186.30 186.38 187.20 191.19
  191.26 192.16 193.17 199.10
  200.19 200.20 207.5 207.6
  210.32 211.3 211.8 VG 17.36
  17.37 20.34 23.28 36.18 65.8

ROCKED CD 243.19

ROCKETS SM 24.24

ROCK-FACE CD 243.38 247.36
  MD 173.12

ROCK-FASTNESSES SM 144.22

ROCK-FLOWERS MD 194.2

ROCKIES SM 141.22 142.16

ROCKING LH 4.38 CD 244.28
  MD 164.25 172.11

ROCKS TL 59.7 FO 179.27
  CD 242.26 243.1 243.27
  244.17 244.32 253.5
  254.1 SM 56.41 63.5 63.7
  63.37 65.7 104.12 147.8
  147.20 MD 168.23 185.19
  186.6 186.32 187.11 192.13
  193.36 194.2 196.17 198.27
  199.24 210.8 211.9 VG 68.3
  71.18

ROCKS' CD 241.15

ROCK-WALLS CD 240.16

ROCKY CD 252.30 MD 166.25
  166.30 191.6

ROCKY MOUNTAINS SM 144.23

ROCOCO VG 53.38 54.11

RODE LH 3.19 7.15 SM 13.11
  20.10 20.26 22.10 22.17
  23.24 25.11 25.15 59.36
  60.1 60.35 66.6 68.37
  94.6 97.25 100.8 109.14
  110.27 111.28 148.15
  MD 186.18

ROE VG 16.33

ROGUISH CD 183.23

ROLE SM 33.16 140.3

ROLL TL 47.27 97.16
  FO 119.20 SM 85.32 93.9

ROLLED TL 63.6 FO 156.24
  CD 260.8 260.17 SM 64.2
  106.38 128.26 VG 7.11
  43.9 70.22

ROLLED-DOWN CD 243.33

ROLLING LH 21.1 32.12
  TL 97.6 97.8 97.14
  CD 237.31 237.35 245.14
  SM 36.22 57.14 60.8 68.41
  105.31 128.29 133.1 148.7
  155.37 VG 65.22 70.6

ROMAN CD 230.4 230.34 231.34
  SM 111.22 MD 190.6 193.5
  198.18 210.33 210.40
  VG 80.30

ROMANCE CD 205.29 208.26
  208.28 231.11

ROMANCES CD 257.20

ROMAN-LOOKING MD 199.30

ROMANOV TL 92.11

ROMANS TL 98.8 98.9 CD 233.7

ROMANS (CONT.) MD 172.22 210.21

ROMANTIC SM 110.4

ROME SM 3.30 3.33 3.35 4.3
  4.27 MD 188.32 188.36 190.8

ROOF TL 97.36 97.38 98.11
  CD 193.24 200.36 200.39 201.5
  201.14 201.21 201.39 202.25
  204.8 218.1 SM 105.29 155.11
  MD 163.15 169.3 176.40 187.29
  VG 18.40 18.41 67.26

ROOF-PLANKS SM 155.9

ROOFS TL 98.13 CD 186.23 186.24
  239.10 241.21 243.31 247.16
  SM 60.20 141.2

ROOK VG 50.34

ROOKS TL 62.20 VG 19.2

ROOST FO 117.9

ROOSTER MD 163.11 163.22 163.33
  183.19 183.23

ROOT TL 75.7 75.8 SM 90.40
  91.1 95.34 MD 211.23

ROOTLESSNESS SM 136.38

ROOTS LH 16.22 TL 65.15 65.16
  FO 157.6 176.10 SM 130.17

ROPED VG 78.19

ROPES CD 256.4

ROSE LH 3.8 6.36 7.31 18.39
  19.29 19.35 23.16 36.9 36.29
  TL 43.22 44.8 46.16 58.11
  68.8 78.13 82.6 101.24 102.3
  102.4 FO 117.17 117.30 138.13
  140.12 141.2 142.3 145.29
  156.8 156.34 158.21 158.32
  158.39 163.4 163.20 CD 189.40
  191.9 201.16 213.18 214.38
  231.22 234.23 241.25 247.5
  247.37 252.32 254.4 260.2
  265.22 SM 24.28 46.20 58.9
  83.18 101.32 101.38 113.11
  121.3 122.39 127.37 145.41
  146.13 159.13 MD 164.40
  165.33 173.9 180.5 187.21
  190.23 193.29 197.32 199.38
  199.40 200.16 202.11 203.19
  206.32 207.23 207.24 208.9
  208.12 208.18 VG 12.21 14.8
  17.17 20.34 24.36 36.16
  37.38 41.9 42.29 47.9 48.23
  71.11

ROSE-ARABESQUE SM 110.41

ROSEBUD SM 64.14

ROSE-COLOUR SM 151.20

ROSE-COLOURED TL 99.20

ROSE-JEWEL SM 151.38

ROSE-RED SM 152.4

ROSES TL 76.11 CD 233.27
  SM 37.38 57.12 110.31 110.33
  110.34 113.5 146.9 151.15
  151.19 MD 193.27 211.21
  VG 24.38 50.18

ROSE-TREES SM 44.26

ROSY CD 226.19

ROSY-BLUE SM 150.26

ROSY-FACED FO 169.28

ROTE TL 94.9

ROTONDE SM 5.8

ROTTED TL 81.13

ROTTEN LH 31.15 CD 253.36

ROTTENNESS SM 71.14 71.26 71.29
  140.12

ROTTEN ROW SM 8.35

ROUGE TL 76.26 VG 39.37

ROUGH LH 23.40 FO 116.18 148.1
  152.33 SM 36.8 119.12 129.37
  130.12 130.15

ROUGHER MD 200.21

ROUGHISHNESS MD 168.22

ROUGHNESS FO 123.11 VG 38.11

ROUGH-SEEMING CD 231.11

ROUNDED LH 7.37 FO 127.3
  CD 212.6 212.10 243.10 254.25

ROUNDISH FO 120.15 127.32
  SM 118.34

ROUNDNESSES SM 63.38

ROUND-PUPILLED FO 172.42

ROUSE SM 136.12 154.1

ROUSED LH 3.30 TL 48.29
  SM 80.37 116.38 156.6
  MD 163.27 167.15 177.23
  188.15 190.17 193.14 VG 32.27
  34.6 75.3 77.22

ROUSING LH 27.5 MD 164.37

ROVER VG 30.25 37.26 42.32

ROVER'S VG 74.36

ROVING SM 132.40

ROW CD 234.17 265.36 SM 8.23
  9.33 20.10 20.31 21.39 22.30
  24.12 24.32 25.7 25.16
  121.34 VG 28.23 34.4

ROWED CD 233.21 236.35 237.13

ROWED (CONT.) MD 211.17

ROWING CD 233.22 235.31
  263.14 265.24

ROWS LH 6.30 TL 62.26 98.7
  SM 130.41 VG 78.6

ROYAL CD 245.1 MD 186.2

ROYAL ACADEMY SM 114.34

ROYALLY VG 53.13

ROYALTY TL 92.12

RUB VG 75.11 75.12 75.21
  75.26 76.3 76.5 76.8
  76.12

RUBBED LH 6.20 FO 129.20
  134.4 CD 213.24 VG 31.20
  76.15 76.17 79.10

RUBBER SM 110.5

RUBBING VG 75.30 76.5 76.35

RUBBISH-HEAP SM 97.24 105.31

RUDDERLESS SM 78.27 VG 9.1

RUDDY LH 18.26 FO 116.5
  120.14 120.17 121.3
  134.21 135.15 138.5
  148.15 155.37 158.32
  163.31 164.35 165.6
  SM 15.8 17.19 MD 197.28

RUDDY-BODIED MD 198.21

RUDDY-FACED TL 98.42

RUDE TL 62.10 FO 134.41
  135.1 135.3 135.4
  CD 226.37 SM 4.14 115.16
  134.12 VG 10.19

RUDELY VG 33.21

RUDENESS VG 39.2 66.15

RUFFIAN SM 11.32

RUFFLED TL 51.19 FO 172.25
  SM 99.7 MD 164.21

RUFFLING CD 237.16 MD 171.5

RUG LH 29.2 30.23 TL 100.7
  FO 135.35 159.5 159.28

RUGS CD 247.32 SM 119.14

RUINED FO 144.42 CD 239.8
  SM 4.6 63.1

RUINS VG 18.36

RULE FO 114.28 135.20
  SM 96.38 126.22

RULES SM 70.15

RULING TL 62.30

RUM LH 16.19 SM 44.25

RUMBLE MD 198.13

RUMINATED CD 211.14

RUMMAGED LH 29.4

RUMOUR TL 47.42 CD 229.5

RUMOURS CD 188.17

RUMPLED CD 242.38 243.4

RUMPS FO 172.38

RUMPUS VG 25.33

RUN LH 6.7 11.12 16.26 22.32
  22.33 23.36 28.18 TL 80.35
  FO 121.40 123.23 144.41
  153.12 CD 236.19 251.5 262.30
  SM 73.13 119.35 121.19 138.26
  139.21 144.14 158.2 MD 174.2
  175.3 VG 58.39 62.27 72.31

RUNG LH 12.15 37.19 37.36
  CD 205.13

RUNNEL SM 142.4 MD 167.5

RUNNELS SM 144.7

RUNNETH SM 81.34

RUNNING LH 9.42 TL 67.6
  FO 153.9 169.19 172.25 175.2
  CD 253.32 261.6 265.37
  SM 50.32 52.1 67.9 69.15
  126.13 128.27 142.8 142.10
  148.13 149.1 150.36 158.1
  MD 167.19 185.22 207.13
  VG 28.31 72.9 72.18 78.27

RUPTURE CD 224.21 VG 77.9

RUPTURED TL 78.13

RUSE LH 4.13

RUSH TL 103.26 103.39 CD 240.33
  245.28 SM 24.24 49.31 58.29
  151.3 151.4

RUSHED CD 197.17 219.35 239.33
  240.1 240.15 241.24 253.30
  SM 67.23 67.34 148.19
  VG 48.36 70.7

RUSHES SM 134.20

RUSHING CD 219.21 239.10 243.23
  243.24 244.31 256.15 261.19
  SM 67.2 VG 74.35 78.19

RUSKS VG 9.14

RUSSET-BROWN CD 184.13

RUSSIA SM 71.16 71.18

RUSSIAN VG 16.37 17.19

RUSSIAN CZAR SM 9.19

RUSTLE LH 22.38 25.38

RUSTLED TL 72.27

RUSTLING SM 97.4

RUSTY TL 51.27

RUTTED FO 169.22

SABLE TL 51.18 VG 49.6 49.16

SACK FO 120.19 VG 50.10

SACRAMENT TL 79.27 79.36

SACRED TL 81.33 89.4 89.14
  90.9 90.20 SM 140.22 140.31
  157.20 159.9 MD 198.30
  VG 4.20

SACREDNESS TL 88.39

SACRIFICE TL 81.38 SM 20.8
  80.31 MD 186.11 207.3 VG 6.32

SACRIFICED TL 96.2 MD 189.8
  VG 6.29

SACROSANCT CD 194.11

SAD TL 46.20 50.12 75.8
  FO 121.29 SM 77.17 106.30
  112.11 MD 178.15 VG 17.23

SAD-CLANGING CD 234.4

SADDENED TL 46.5

SADDEST TL 46.38

SADDLE LH 15.31 23.6 23.7
  TL 90.27 FO 168.12 SM 20.27
  20.29 21.27 43.29 43.31 53.1
  57.39 59.3 63.32 66.25 93.15
  106.19

SADDLED SM 36.1 57.31

SADDLE-HORSE SM 13.4

SADDLES SM 129.34

SADISTIC VG 62.37

SADLY TL 88.15 106.14 106.18
  MD 174.4

SADNESS TL 66.9 CD 190.18 218.4
  SM 75.10 75.40 76.3

SAD-SOUNDING CD 199.42

SAFE LH 11.39 26.21 30.26
  TL 71.22 84.21 91.18 94.17
  FO 138.35 138.37 164.8 164.19
  166.16 CD 188.29 188.31
  200.38 206.42 209.16 256.13
  SM 7.18 25.10 65.11 72.22
  89.23 112.16 114.1 137.32
  MD 168.37 172.26 VG 29.7
  67.26 79.4 79.11

SAFELY LH 39.22 FO 178.12
  SM 66.9 129.30 MD 167.30

SAFELY (CONT.) VG 5.40

SAFETY SM 25.17 73.30
  137.33 MD 177.16

SAFFRON MD 191.8 197.7
  199.5 202.37

SAGELY VG 35.33 56.28

SAGGING VG 80.4 80.17

SAIL LH 35.28 SM 114.19
  123.37 125.4 125.10
  MD 200.6 VG 39.26

SAILED CD 232.12 SM 8.36
  36.31 111.32 127.18
  VG 40.21 44.35

SAILING SM 23.27 127.10

SAILOR LH 18.28 28.34

SAINTS VG 54.2

SAINTSBURY SM 13.39

SAINTSBURY (SEE MR. SAINTSBURY)

SAKE FO 113.10 157.15 164.3
  168.6 CD 186.29 200.11
  220.40 237.1 SM 5.24 9.23
  16.27 132.6 VG 63.12

SALAD-BOWL SM 132.34

SALADS SM 44.20

SALE CD 193.27 196.39 213.28
  SM 133.29

SALESMEN SM 44.29

SALISBURY PLAIN FO 164.33
  171.3

SALLOW TL 44.40 49.42 51.9

SALMON-COLOURED SM 65.19

SALONIKA FO 121.12

SALT LH 29.25 CD 209.17
  216.24 SM 83.9 154.30
  MD 200.26

SALTY CD 230.33 231.6 232.22

SALUTE SM 85.11

SALUTED TL 44.16

SALUTING CD 233.38

SALVATION SM 71.11 MD 172.39
  174.20 174.32 174.39
  175.3 175.11

SALVE MD 179.33

SALZBURG CD 228.14 229.14

SAMSON VG 67.29

SAN ANTONIO SM 129.1 132.9

SANCTITY VG 28.24

SANCTUARIES SM 139.37

SANCTUARY MD 190.19

SAND SM 78.7 MD 210.8

SANDALS MD 191.7 192.1 193.32

SANDAL-STRAPS MD 192.38

SANE TL 62.2 62.3 FO 166.14
166.16

SANG CD 235.22 235.29 SM 113.10
VG 16.31 36.29

SANGFROID CD 237.8

SANITATION VG 29.36

SANITY CD 252.16

SANK LH 7.16 TL 74.24 FO 174.35
SM 101.36 143.13 VG 47.37
64.40

SANTA FE SM 132.11 132.13
132.25 133.14 140.25 154.12

SANTANDER SM 126.14

SAP TL 69.29 SM 90.34 146.5
MD 209.17

SAPIENTLY CD 211.6

SAPPED SM 65.34

SAPPHIRE CD 253.39

SARCASM FO 154.15 SM 19.8 29.16
81.38 83.15 107.24 MD 175.9

SARCASTIC TL 89.10 FO 172.20
SM 88.21 118.18 VG 9.27

SARCASTICALLY FO 136.36 157.23
CD 193.3 264.19

SARDINE FO 156.26

SARDONIC FO 114.15 130.27 151.6
152.1 161.18 CD 252.18
SM 7.15 7.34 76.24 77.15
78.37 88.20 VG 30.26

SARDONICALLY LH 12.36 SM 6.15
48.26 76.19 127.31

SATAN VG 11.40

SATIRE TL 71.34 72.12 FO 114.23
CD 227.29

SATIRIC TL 55.31 FO 170.16
170.36 CD 194.1

SATIRICAL FO 114.21 169.33

SATIRICALLY LH 19.17

SATIRIZED SM 21.7

SATISFACTION LH 8.14 TL 108.32
CD 251.4 SM 31.13 41.30 42.15
46.14 51.11 73.2 73.35 77.20
116.16

SATISFACTORY SM 39.38 124.29

SATISFIED LH 36.10 CD 264.11

SATISFY FO 176.26 SM 136.10

SATURDAY FO 117.40 SM 117.22

SATURDAYS SM 44.1

SATURNINE TL 82.1 SM 9.13

SATYR SM 55.9

SATYRS SM 54.3 54.4 54.6

SAUCE CD 208.5

SAUCEPAN VG 38.1

SAUCER SM 81.31

SAUCY MD 163.33

SAUNTERED CD 260.22 VG 35.33

SAUNTERING FO 148.39

SAUSAGE CD 245.33

SAVAGE FO 130.26 CD 233.8
239.38 242.3 246.37 SM 5.11
63.35 94.15 135.19 136.36
138.34 142.16 142.23 150.13
151.38 153.24 153.39 155.37

SAVAGELY SM 150.2 MD 183.26

SAVAGENESS CD 242.5 VG 75.22

SAVAGER CD 247.3

SAVAGERY SM 153.33 153.35

SAVAGE'S SM 21.9

SAVE LH 18.26 30.39 35.16
39.23 TL 82.15 96.19
FO 164.12 164.37 166.41
CD 185.19 214.22 221.27
231.19 SM 20.20 25.11 60.9
71.9 71.28 93.24 94.41
130.19 159.8 MD 169.12 172.38
173.2 179.27 183.22 185.11
VG 73.38 80.10

SAVED FO 164.29 MD 164.24
174.19 174.31 175.2 175.13
179.36 183.37 VG 28.6

SAVES TL 109.7 SM 159.11

SAVING SM 71.10 MD 171.41

SAVIOUR MD 174.11 176.29

SAVOURY VG 9.14

SAWED FO 119.13 131.21

SAWING FO 131.19 131.23
131.26 134.13

SAXE VG 54.4

SAXON TL 44.25 44.28

SAXONY TL 51.31

SAYINGS CD 251.26

SAYWELL VG 66.26 67.39

SAYWELL (SEE MR., MRS.,
MRS. ARTHUR)

SAYWELLS VG 28.13 28.18
28.19 28.25 64.13 66.20

SCALE SM 96.5

SCANDAL TL 92.41 92.42
CD 219.12 VG 3.2

SCANTY VG 12.26

SCAR TL 70.4 70.16 76.29
77.7 78.19 78.21 79.9
83.27 SM 149.34 MD 195.3
195.4 204.16 205.22 205.40
206.3

SCARAB TL 70.26 97.4 97.8

SCARABEUS TL 96.40

SCARCE FO 114.37 168.22
MD 177.9

SCARCELY LH 22.37 34.37
FO 130.17 SM 94.10 144.8
VG 38.33

SCARED TL 74.28 FO 120.1
CD 186.12 252.38 SM 130.37
VG 61.8

SCARF CD 185.5 238.33 239.1
261.23 VG 30.15 53.13

SCARLET LH 29.5 FO 142.26
CD 185.22 216.30 SM 33.33
34.31 42.36 150.23 150.33
151.7 MD 168.24

SCARRED MD 166.32 167.8
168.18

SCARS MD 167.41 173.5 181.4
192.39 204.7 207.32

SCATHED FO 140.40

SCATTERED CD 244.17 SM 34.13
MD 188.10 VG 17.22

SCATTERING MD 209.11

SCENE TL 71.17 FO 174.40
CD 214.31 214.33 215.10
215.12 253.24 VG 26.20

SCENES CD 210.40 SM 70.14 113.4

SCENT LH 3.22 21.11 21.30
CD 216.29 237.19 SM 22.26
57.6 102.3 143.33 150.21
MD 169.20 VG 50.18 70.8

SCENTED CD 245.4 245.6

SCENTING CD 245.32

SCHEME TL 90.37 91.2 FO 167.5

SCHEMING FO 167.1

SCHIEBERS CD 216.10

SCHLOSS CD 238.36

SCHOOL LH 16.30 CD 224.36
SM 3.27 3.28 47.6 95.17
105.41 VG 7.24 7.27

SCHOOL-GIRLISH VG 8.35

SCHOOLMASTER SM 141.23 141.28

SCHOOLS SM 8.2

SCIENCE-MANOEUVRED TL 64.7

SCIENTIFIC CD 185.21

SCISSORS SM 45.1 VG 32.24 32.37

SCOLD SM 150.7

SCOLDING FO 153.23 VG 39.20

SCONE CD 204.31

SCONES FO 134.9 CD 204.31

SCOOP SM 114.14

SCOPE CD 231.40 SM 119.35
135.10

SCORCHED CD 206.40

SCORE LH 32.19 FO 123.29
SM 82.8 82.11 VG 52.18

SCORESBY VG 51.36 53.19 62.10

SCORING VG 52.19

SCORN LH 19.21 FO 124.15 132.22

SCORNFUL LH 34.16 SM 8.22

SCORNFULLY MD 191.28

SCOTCH FO 168.15 CD 183.12
222.12 SM 113.12

SCOTCHES LH 7.16

SCOTLAND TL 44.14 64.24
SM 27.38 79.13 121.20 121.22

SCOTTISH CD 184.5 185.31 189.28
197.27 228.37

SCOUNDREL VG 5.10

SCRAMBLE CD 254.6 260.10
SM 65.6

SCRAMBLED SM 25.9 63.39
VG 18.15

SCRAMBLING FO 174.15 CD 240.23
254.39

SCRAMBLINGLY CD 254.24

SCRAP TL 80.22

SCRAPE LH 8.24

SCRAPER FO 134.4

SCRAPPILY VG 16.31

SCRAPS MD 171.31

SCRATCH SM 33.6

SCRATCHED LH 30.1 MD 170.16

SCRATCHING FO 114.32

SCREAM TL 98.18 SM 33.24 33.30
66.32 VG 19.31 29.20 72.28
73.36 78.32

SCREAMED LH 37.23 CD 239.23
261.23 261.27 261.30 261.32
VG 71.34 72.31 73.21

SCREAMING FO 117.7 CD 239.31

SCREECH CD 261.14

SCREECHING SM 67.24

SCREEN TL 66.3 67.29 69.11
FO 163.33 CD 195.15 197.24
197.25 MD 173.11 178.35

SCREENED LH 7.1

SCREW TL 71.36

SCREWED LH 38.25 FO 116.13
118.30 123.2 139.11 SM 129.21

SCREWED-UP TL 80.2 80.8

SCREWS FO 166.1 SM 129.20

SCRIBE SM 117.27

SCRIP MD 192.34 193.33

SCRUB SM 17.16

SCRUBBY SM 18.7

SCRUPLES SM 73.16

SCRUPULOUS VG 59.3

SCRUTINISED LH 7.19

SCRUTINY TL 84.18

SCUFFLED MD 164.15

SCUFFLING FO 147.11

SCUM TL 92.37

SCUTTLED MD 187.14

SCUTTLING CD 256.9 261.11

SCYTHE LH 6.7

S'D LH 28.14

SEA TL 58.40 58.41 FO 172.25
175.12 175.28 176.5 178.10
178.40 SM 3.4 31.36 38.18
60.3 69.19 126.11 126.22
127.14 127.18 128.15
128.34 147.28 148.7
MD 171.17 174.33 185.4
185.6 185.10 185.13
185.20 185.21 185.32 186.4
186.10 186.17 192.10
193.41 196.18 197.26
198.20 198.32 199.6 199.20
199.37 199.39 200.15
203.11 208.7 208.20 208.23
210.8 210.40 211.1
VG 22.34 74.14 75.33

SEA-GREEN VG 54.2

SEA-HAWK TL 59.5

SEAL MD 196.26

SEA-LEVEL CD 242.32

SEALING-WAX CD 186.28

SEAL-SKIN TL 51.15

SEAM SM 149.33

SEAMED SM 150.1

SEARCH TL 73.34 FO 177.31
MD 188.9 188.17 188.21
190.14 195.17 196.26
197.25 VG 20.4 78.18

SEARCHED TL 72.6 VG 52.8
68.24

SEARCHING LH 28.10 TL 60.22
88.22 96.3 FO 123.6
SM 15.23 VG 21.19 23.3
38.7 58.19 68.39

SEARCHINGLY SM 62.30 100.25

SEARED FO 126.35 126.37
SM 99.8

SEAS FO 179.12 179.26
SM 107.13 VG 8.41

SEA'S FO 179.29 MD 199.7
208.8

SEASON SM 27.37 114.23
128.16

SEASONS MD 210.25

SEAT LH 30.13 TL 79.40 94.10
CD 233.16 257.10 259.5
260.33 261.12 263.7

SEAT (CONT.) SM 63.15 66.26
  87.32 134.33 138.13 138.20
  139.4 VG 34.12 70.21

SEATED LH 17.32 23.11 TL 48.27
  77.40 87.2 103.24 105.32
  FO 136.19 CD 202.24 214.29
  239.41 247.31 255.36 261.3
  SM 67.16 83.9 87.35 MD 198.27
  VG 19.18 45.29

SEATING TL 94.13

SEATS TL 97.38 CD 234.25 260.10
  260.32

SEAWEEDS FO 176.2

SECOND TL 64.21 70.9 FO 119.33
  156.1 CD 189.9 211.19 237.19
  240.38 247.11 SM 34.2 36.2
  114.36 MD 201.13 201.20
  208.29 VG 19.23 20.4 24.21
  32.25 33.3 38.20 68.1

SECONDARY TL 87.16

SECOND'S VG 34.11

SECRECY TL 66.9 VG 24.24

SECRET TL 66.10 66.19 66.23
  66.35 66.41 69.1 98.20
  FO 129.38 130.18 141.22 155.7
  155.9 155.26 CD 241.10 251.4
  253.30 SM 6.36 11.41 16.15
  27.5 32.27 71.17 123.3
  152.12 MD 210.8 VG 5.25 23.10
  40.14 40.18 44.25 48.28 61.6
  62.40 79.36

SECRETARY VG 10.23

SECRETIVE SM 136.6

SECRETIVENESS SM 140.26

SECRETLY FO 130.34 136.18
  SM 70.19 71.12 136.14 137.16
  149.30 MD 186.14 VG 4.5 6.24
  47.14 61.7 64.16 67.13

SECRETS TL 66.28 66.31

SECTIONS SM 115.8

SECURED VG 5.3

SEDIMENT CD 238.3

SEDUCED SM 112.32

SEED LH 17.39 CD 222.30 222.37
  MD 205.25 211.18

SEED-PEARLS CD 205.22

SEEDS SM 103.17 103.26

SEEDY LH 17.20

SEEING LH 6.10 10.21 39.1
  TL 46.16 55.37 FO 117.11
  120.30 157.1 CD 205.8 227.1
  229.14 255.27 SM 5.39 15.15

SEEING (CONT.) 55.27 68.1 76.31
  90.22 105.1 134.27 149.17
  MD 167.9 170.19 171.25
  VG 14.13

SEEK MD 172.34 175.17 191.14
  210.1

SEEKING LH 34.7 SM 88.1
  MD 188.19 VG 7.8

SEEKS CD 219.15

SEEMING TL 58.25 78.30
  FO 174.38 CD 244.34 SM 99.6

SEEMINGLY SM 64.6

SEEMLY CD 183.12

SEEMS TL 49.39 57.39 71.21
  84.28 85.20 86.33 86.36
  87.34 87.40 88.4 88.30 88.35
  FO 165.16 165.26 165.31 166.2
  166.5 166.19 166.23 CD 191.39
  203.32 218.27 219.8 220.15
  258.20 SM 22.33 23.20 30.17
  48.10 48.14 48.16 48.23
  48.31 79.15 79.30 93.23
  110.11 120.26 158.1 VG 29.39

SEES LH 3.31 4.17 FO 165.2
  SM 54.30 54.41 76.7

SEETHE MD 181.38 181.40

SEETHED VG 47.7

SEETHING CD 239.4 SM 150.40
  152.37 152.38

SEIZED FO 142.36 159.36
  MD 164.31 186.23 211.10
  VG 75.18 75.26

SEIZING SM 113.29 VG 72.31

SELECTION CD 196.21

SELF LH 27.42 TL 107.25
  CD 230.42 SM 15.3 100.13
  100.30 118.39 MD 180.28
  180.29 VG 40.14 69.16

SELF-ASSERTION SM 73.21

SELF-ASSURED FO 154.22

SELF-CONSCIOUS TL 104.39
  SM 112.24 130.39 131.6

SELF-CONSCIOUSLY TL 85.9
  FO 139.17 SM 23.24 130.41

SELF-CONSCIOUSNESS LH 4.6 11.41
  TL 79.24 100.1 SM 130.38

SELF-CONTAINED FO 134.21
  SM 137.38

SELF-CONTROLLED SM 15.34

SELF-DEDICATE MD 198.1

SELF-DEFENCE CD 208.6 SM 73.20

SELF-DISCIPLINED SM 73.19

SELF-ESTEEM SM 135.24

SELF-IMPORTANCE MD 174.22

SELFISH TL 93.14 FO 145.10
  VG 28.14 29.15 29.16

SELFISHLY TL 84.38

SELFISHNESS VG 5.20 5.35
  5.38 28.34 28.35

SELF-LOVE VG 5.5

SELF-OPINIONATED SM 139.17

SELF-PERSUASION SM 53.26

SELF-PRESERVATION SM 73.20

SELF-RESPECT FO 142.13 142.15

SELF-RIGHTEOUSNESS VG 4.6

SELF-SACRIFICE SM 71.1 75.31

SELF-SAME VG 6.33

SELF-SANCTIFICATION VG 5.15

SELF-SATISFACTION TL 83.23
  SM 128.10

SELF-SATISFIED SM 94.35
  134.25

SELF-WILL VG 65.38

SELL CD 200.26 225.1 249.7
  SM 11.37 12.37 25.24 30.2
  88.15 89.7 134.6 144.4
  VG 66.37

SELLING SM 88.12 89.5 110.20
  120.7 VG 37.30 37.32 46.29
  46.30

SELVES VG 69.16 69.17

SEMI-ABSTRACTION FO 128.17

SEMI-CASUAL VG 66.27

SEMI-COMA VG 32.27 65.41

SEMI-CONSCIOUS FO 133.10
  VG 76.11 77.3 77.12 77.23

SEMI-CRIMINAL VG 62.32

SEMI-DREAM FO 136.12

SEMI-HIDDEN TL 93.19

SEMI-TRANSLUCENT TL 70.25
  CD 253.3

SEND LH 4.16 TL 76.11
  FO 167.36 CD 213.30 213.32
  218.12 218.36 219.4 219.9
  SM 37.19 40.19 84.23 91.31
  91.34 91.38 MD 197.33
  VG 13.37 15.4 64.5

SEX (CONT.) LH 145.30 157.19
  157.20 159.9 159.11 VG 6.36
  29.29 30.20 55.18 55.27
  55.32 55.34 55.39 56.8

SEXLESS SM 146.9

SEXUAL TL 106.29 SM 6.23 136.7
  137.4 137.8 137.17 137.19
  137.21 138.9 138.32 138.38
  VG 55.26 55.30

SEXUALLY CD 251.12

SHABBINESS TL 84.9

SHABBY TL 43.34 94.35 99.19
  99.20 CD 245.21 245.25
  MD 163.2 163.12 164.16 164.32
  VG 9.8

SHADE LH 6.10 FO 122.17
  SM 57.40 60.4 65.25 MD 172.5

SHADED FO 122.17

SHADOW LH 3.4 15.23 25.10
  25.12 36.31 TL 58.40 59.33
  59.34 59.36 59.41 62.25
  93.16 FO 116.5 123.5 125.1
  125.6 146.35 146.37 147.4
  175.15 CD 187.16 210.1 234.25
  237.27 237.35 237.38 238.2
  240.22 247.38 SM 8.24 11.29
  17.19 22.3 28.27 28.28 57.26
  58.32 65.23 65.24 65.26
  65.27 102.33 113.5 126.5
  134.11 140.20 140.21 146.35
  MD 172.17 179.3 185.24 187.38
  189.18 192.8 197.8 198.33
  198.34 198.35 198.41 199.7
  199.39 200.14 200.16 202.41
  203.40 209.25 VG 47.40 47.42
  48.14

SHADOWLY SM 126.2

SHADOWS LH 21.3 SM 57.7 92.7
  143.34 146.2 VG 57.17

SHADOWY FO 122.20 140.12 176.5
  SM 151.40

SHADY LH 15.25

SHAFT SM 87.34 VG 20.17 45.30

SHAFTS LH 15.28 26.32 FO 116.17
  SM 13.4

SHAGGY LH 7.20 SM 143.19 149.37
  VG 72.23

SHAKE TL 98.22 VG 39.15 41.12

SHAKEN FO 159.27 CD 239.30
  SM 67.40 VG 47.34

SHAKILY LH 26.19 CD 197.33
  254.17

SHAKIN' LH 32.20

SHAKING LH 13.6 SM 106.31 152.8
  VG 76.3 76.11

SHAKY LH 25.2 26.7

SHALLOT, LADY (SEE LADY OF
  SHALLOT)

SHALLOW LH 4.21 CD 243.18
  243.19 243.26 252.25 SM 20.40
  147.29 147.38

SHALLOWER TL 44.18 VG 18.4

SHALT MD 183.25

SHAME LH 15.39 33.31 TL 58.4
  82.11 SM 108.6 108.9 118.8
  MD 188.35 205.3 VG 40.34
  56.42 64.2

SHAMEFACED LH 15.40

SHAMEFUL CD 259.35 VG 27.7 27.8

SHANK MD 164.9

SHAN'T LH 25.36 30.33 TL 78.42
  FO 140.3 152.12 164.16
  CD 195.32 263.22 265.9
  SM 39.36 89.34 103.5 104.32
  MD 168.15 VG 13.41 32.9 34.26
  44.33 71.33

SHANTY SM 129.12

SHAPE LH 17.14 27.26 32.8
  TL 89.5 CD 252.9 SM 7.26
  44.27 59.20

SHAPELY SM 96.1

SHAPES LH 23.2 26.39 SM 130.22

SHARE LH 25.2 CD 224.28 224.29
  MD 170.24

SHARED CD 223.32

SHARING CD 225.9

SHARP LH 9.36 TL 63.14 92.5
  FO 119.38 120.17 120.40
  120.41 124.29 136.4 143.13
  148.35 151.5 158.37 174.23
  CD 220.17 223.14 241.13 257.3
  260.35 SM 5.31 11.18 30.16
  63.3 121.12 124.13 148.11
  152.8 MD 166.11 171.29 178.27
  189.37 VG 18.37 33.9 72.10

SHARPEN SM 90.25

SHARPENING CD 186.34

SHARPER FO 120.18

SHARP-EYED FO 129.31 SM 152.7

SHARP-FACED CD 260.34

SHARPLY LH 9.19 TL 75.13
  FO 115.34 137.17 156.3 171.31
  CD 209.29 209.34 VG 19.13
  19.27

SHARPNESS FO 121.7 CD 255.42

SHARP-PATTERNED VG 49.41

SHARP-RAYED SM 155.4

SHATTER SM 29.18 VG 16.14
  16.16

SHATTERED TL 47.30 47.37
  SM 148.15 MD 176.26

SHATTERING SM 6.33 7.2 7.9
  51.14 VG 51.29

SHAVE SM 23.4 23.7

SHAVED CD 219.35 SM 44.13
  47.20

SHAVEN TL 49.38 59.26

SHAVING CD 219.34

SHAWL TL 100.28 101.27
  101.32 101.39 FO 169.29
  SM 87.36 88.4 135.12
  135.36 VG 21.6

SHAWLED SM 135.31

SHE-ADDER TL 66.1

SHEARS SM 46.2 46.17

SHEATH SM 9.25 118.6 118.7
  MD 208.3 VG 43.28

SHE-BEAR TL 58.38

SHED LH 15.11 24.22 25.7
  25.13 26.31 27.23 27.26
  31.9 38.10 FO 113.37
  114.30 131.23 134.16
  146.19 148.20 160.26
  160.38 168.16 168.41
  169.10 169.11 169.20
  169.26 172.10 172.11
  172.16 MD 163.12 177.19
  181.22 183.17

SHEDDING LH 28.33 SM 128.18

SHEELING VG 21.37

SHEEN LH 22.4 SM 17.13

SHEEP VG 18.39

SHEEPISHLY LH 16.7 19.30

SHEER LH 5.39 TL 43.5
  FO 131.8 CD 203.16 241.9
  241.27 242.23 SM 145.37
  150.35 151.22 MD 193.2
  VG 17.36 65.24

SHEERED LH 7.15 25.11

SHEERING LH 25.16 CD 229.18
  MD 194.2

SHEET SM 116.24 MD 166.26

SHEETS TL 71.29 VG 78.32
  78.41

SHE-FOX FO 158.23

SHEKELS SM 109.27

SHELF FO 135.27

SHELL LH 11.6 TL 63.3 63.17
  SM 125.6 155.19 VG 41.27

SHELL-FISH MD 196.17

SHELLS TL 57.39 64.6

SHELL-SHOCK SM 20.19

SHELL-SHOCKED SM 7.37

SHELTER LH 38.31 FO 164.9
  SM 137.30 137.32 148.18
  MD 190.25 191.4 191.14 191.36
  210.7 VG 9.28 20.33 23.28
  45.32

SHELTERED MD 173.25

SHELTERING SM 21.28

SHELTERS SM 137.30

SHELVES VG 54.4 78.5

SHE-POLE-CAT TL 65.39

SHERRY SM 84.35

SHE-WHO-WAS-CYNTHIA VG 5.2 5.11
  5.21 5.24 6.8 6.21 26.36
  27.20 28.20 28.27 33.25 34.5
  61.25 62.15 62.35

SHIED SM 66.21 68.25

SHIELDED CD 265.16

SHIES SM 105.27

SHIFT LH 9.20 9.27 SM 80.26

SHIFTLESS SM 7.16

SHIFTY MD 168.8

SHILLING FO 137.12 VG 21.41
  25.3 51.41 52.4 68.35

SHILLINGS VG 26.11

SHIMMER SM 17.14 20.39

SHINE TL 56.24 56.26 56.27
  56.29 56.30 CD 189.15
  MD 189.32 207.34

SHINES VG 17.26

SHINGLE CD 241.21 MD 185.26
  185.28 192.13 198.19 198.34
  199.4 199.23 199.28 199.37

SHINING FO 137.18 155.38 158.19
  CD 228.5 233.39 256.16
  SM 48.39 145.15 VG 38.1 77.25

SHIP LH 4.38 CD 232.35 232.37
  SM 126.14 126.32 128.27

SHIP (CONT.) 128.29 132.38
  MD 195.15 VG 8.31

SHIPPED TL 84.24 92.14 92.23

SHIPPING SM 127.20

SHIPS SM 23.27 126.36

SHIRES TL 97.41 VG 18.41

SHIRT LH 12.20 TL 60.12 60.33
  60.34 60.37 61.15 61.32
  62.17 64.21 64.24 64.39
  71.24 71.25 80.32 80.33
  80.36 81.24 SM 34.9 35.36
  38.32 58.23 68.6 119.9
  VG 75.24

SHIRT-BREAST CD 243.3

SHIRT-CUFFS FO 136.2

SHIRT-NECK SM 68.15

SHIRTS LH 7.36 TL 60.13 61.14
  61.17 62.5 70.17 70.20 71.29
  71.32 71.33

SHIRT-SLEEVES FO 127.1 131.24
  134.17 134.22 134.25 135.30

SHIRT-TUNIC MD 167.20

SHIVER LH 28.27 MD 167.17

SHIVERED LH 29.15 36.32
  TL 68.39 75.28 79.7

SHIVERIN' LH 32.19

SHIVERING LH 30.11 TL 74.37
  VG 26.21 76.37 76.39 76.40
  76.41 77.7

SHIVERY FO 174.28

SH'LL FO 168.41

SHOAL VG 15.8

SHOCK LH 27.29 TL 78.38
  CD 220.34 SM 58.34 MD 206.38
  206.39 VG 64.1 75.25 77.13
  77.21

SHOCKED CD 228.39 229.1

SHOCKS CD 204.28

SHOD SM 22.41

SHODDY SM 8.30

SHOE CD 186.14 SM 44.34

SHOEMAKING SM 44.28

SHOES LH 30.22 TL 64.9 64.10
  FO 154.12 156.40 CD 187.13
  190.5 190.9 SM 44.28 44.29
  44.31 44.33 44.36 MD 181.2

SHOE-SOLES SM 132.30 132.32

SHONE LH 3.2 26.30 26.34
  26.37 29.6 FO 116.17
  126.6 CD 189.24 241.35
  MD 170.25 199.6 199.20
  207.14 VG 70.30

SHOOK LH 8.40 37.27 TL 54.27
  60.37 83.30 88.14
  FO 159.14 171.1 CD 196.2
  236.40 SM 102.19 106.35
  VG 5.24 70.29 73.29 73.42
  76.23

SHOOT TL 58.42 FO 115.17
  119.41 139.18 145.38
  145.39 SM 32.11 72.19
  72.23 80.14 80.24 81.1
  88.5 88.25 89.15 101.16
  155.18 VG 43.17

SHOOTING FO 130.30 SM 32.13
  105.21 VG 44.26

SHOOTING-JACKET VG 20.19

SHOP TL 60.13 81.19
  CD 205.27 226.40 226.41
  227.2 227.5 227.33
  SM 100.40

SHOPKEEPER LH 16.25

SHOPS CD 229.21 238.4
  SM 36.17

SHORE FO 178.9 179.12
  CD 263.14 MD 174.34 194.3
  196.7 198.7

SHORES MD 190.13

SHORN SM 9.7

SHORT LH 17.27 25.30 28.15
  31.37 36.7 TL 52.19 55.36
  57.27 58.26 72.28 90.29
  107.36 FO 131.21 153.8
  156.39 169.8 169.24 172.21
  CD 203.1 232.35 233.13
  233.29 238.6 SM 22.14
  45.18 107.2 139.2
  MD 171.29 199.24 VG 7.7
  36.1 47.28 73.32

SHORTHAND VG 10.24

SHORTLY CD 248.2 264.22

SHORT-SIGHTED MD 177.34

SHOT TL 53.16 54.6 59.18
  FO 118.13 127.26 141.37
  147.18 147.23 174.1
  CD 228.14 SM 72.13 72.16
  72.20 72.34 72.37 73.2
  73.35 79.35

SHOULDER TL 78.28 78.29
  94.37 FO 116.33 116.37
  117.27 122.11 133.13
  139.20 140.16 146.39
  169.29 169.37 CD 214.29
  255.36 SM 11.26 13.30
  17.15 19.12 59.20 59.22
  MD 165.24 200.2 206.38

SHOULDER (CONT.) VG 31.42 36.22
38.40 53.13 76.4

SHOULDERS LH 7.34 7.37 7.39
14.7 23.42 TL 46.29 53.26
94.34 95.18 FO 114.10 120.19
127.3 151.15 159.14 159.26
CD 184.6 235.27 235.28 235.39
248.29 250.40 SM 32.19 135.21
136.30 139.19 155.37
MD 165.28 187.2 198.38 199.26
200.5 VG 19.29 60.15 65.22

SHOULDER-SACK CD 246.1

SHOULDN'T LH 28.24 36.19
TL 104.31 FO 132.39 142.8
142.22 150.23 160.41 160.42
CD 205.2 209.3 210.33 259.22
SM 58.7 78.30 123.8 VG 8.21
27.41 57.5 58.17 60.17 62.5
67.30

SHOUT LH 25.27 26.21 CD 221.25

SHOUTED LH 7.11 9.5 12.16
CD 240.13 261.21 261.28
SM 157.26 MD 177.17 VG 13.25
34.13 78.35

SHOUTING CD 234.30 261.34
SM 108.9 VG 72.16

SHOUTS VG 79.31

SHOVED LH 8.40 FO 157.6
CD 238.13 VG 33.25 34.27

SHOVIN' LH 9.24

SHOVING CD 233.32 VG 8.29

SHOW LH 38.41 CD 194.23 210.3
214.8 214.16 234.9 SM 5.11
23.18 26.25 51.41 85.30
90.33 124.26 131.33 156.38
MD 189.40 189.41 191.3 204.7
VG 38.31 56.3

SHOWED LH 3.15 27.19 36.32
37.22 TL 63.32 71.26 FO 152.9
156.22 CD 209.41 211.17
SM 20.37 65.10 120.39 131.8
155.11 MD 188.20 VG 6.34
26.39 67.4

SHOWER SM 150.34

SHOWERED MD 164.28

SHOWERING SM 128.21

SHOWIER VG 28.15

SHOWING LH 4.27 6.16 14.3
TL 52.1 68.6 72.37 73.28
FO 123.17 CD 196.1 210.4
SM 11.5 44.23 58.32 60.19
68.36 74.6 128.30 147.27
158.5 VG 9.24 19.34 20.40
24.3 24.11 54.33 59.3 62.18
74.8

SHOWING-OFF VG 26.4

SHOWN CD 198.33

SHOWS SM 130.3 MD 208.10 210.29
VG 26.2

SHRANK LH 24.38 38.36 TL 68.30
78.25 FO 122.40 161.25
CD 224.25 261.2 SM 6.27 6.33
30.22 52.32 67.40 MD 175.36
187.13 VG 27.38

SHREWD FO 117.22 129.39 SM 4.8
114.30 150.8 VG 22.20 38.7

SHREWDLY TL 64.4 FO 130.6
167.39 CD 210.32 SM 14.1
130.36 VG 21.32 21.36

SHREWDNESS SM 15.35 VG 49.25

SHREWISH FO 137.38 137.39
149.16

SHREWSBURY SM 28.11 29.13 44.2

SHRIEK LH 9.36 FO 174.3

SHRILL LH 11.19 FO 141.2
MD 163.24 167.16 VG 35.30

SHRINE MD 194.18 195.13 195.30
196.23 202.30

SHRINK LH 11.3 11.5 SM 47.34

SHRINKING FO 120.25 CD 260.38

SHRIVEL CD 234.1

SHRIVELLING SM 85.9

SHROPSHIRE SM 27.41 28.4 121.25

SHROUD MD 166.33 167.26 168.2

SHRUBBERY SM 37.28

SHRUBS CD 244.19

SHRUG VG 33.13

SHRUGGED SM 135.21

SHRUNK MD 189.2

SHUDDER FO 174.30 VG 11.32

SHUDDERED LH 11.10 TL 54.20
102.20 CD 216.18 226.8 253.25
SM 79.38 VG 11.36 49.22 74.13

SHUDDERING FO 135.41 174.32
VG 49.13 73.39 73.41 74.39
75.14 75.15 75.25 75.41
76.16 77.11 77.12 77.18
77.20

SHUFFLED SM 135.40

SHUFFLING SM 135.32

SHUT LH 23.18 TL 44.39 54.41
57.1 58.25 62.37 95.40
102.15 105.16 FO 114.41
117.12 134.5 135.40 149.33

SHUT (CONT.) 152.15 155.8
155.29 CD 223.17 238.4
SM 8.6 63.3 65.2 79.6
90.31 126.24 128.15 133.26
MD 167.30 170.4 170.40
188.1 199.14 202.31
VG 8.39 29.20 31.3 34.13
35.6 35.16 38.12 39.22
39.23 65.28

SHUT-IN SM 143.10 MD 163.11

SHUTTING LH 34.12 SM 102.15
138.20 MD 208.2 VG 66.11

SHUT-UP SM 127.11

SHY LH 5.28 34.30 FO 114.15
131.25 149.15 157.27
SM 33.15 36.29 121.7
VG 40.23 43.31

SHYLOCK SM 109.26

SHYLY FO 139.2 VG 51.11

SHYNESS LH 16.8 CD 258.3
MD 194.31

SIAM VG 11.6

SIAMESE VG 10.40 11.2 11.6

SIBERIA TL 59.4

SIBERIAN STEPPE-DOG CD 257.17

SICK LH 4.35 34.36 TL 44.4
44.9 51.23 51.27 51.34
76.37 FO 141.38 142.1
142.2 144.10 CD 225.16
241.41 256.8 SM 22.4
113.25 149.20 150.16
MD 165.25 177.13 VG 75.41

SICKENING TL 68.14 MD 164.16
VG 74.4 74.19 77.20

SICKENINGLY SM 67.18

SICKLE MD 163.20

SICKLINESS LH 34.38

SICKLY FO 146.33

SICKLY-SMELLING LH 21.24

SICKNESS TL 49.18 SM 144.20
144.32 MD 166.29 177.21
VG 73.11

SICK-ROOM LH 10.22

SIDE LH 6.12 12.22 14.8
23.25 24.32 25.8 25.17
25.23 26.3 37.42 TL 51.25
70.5 78.20 83.1 83.19
106.9 108.3 108.5
FO 127.17 132.5 136.7
147.13 154.32 154.39
159.39 160.29 178.20
CD 187.27 233.29 233.34
241.33 241.35 244.18
244.20 255.8 255.16 263.11

SINGING (CONT.) FO 136.13 136.33
   CD 236.9 SM 10.21 VG 35.39

SINGLE TL 77.37 89.24 CD 196.36
   211.16 SM 50.7 MD 174.13
   174.20 VG 9.16 44.40

SINGLED SM 129.37

SINGLY TL 51.9

SINGS MD 163.29

SING-SONG LH 10.34 CD 200.30
   SM 4.21 19.1 21.35 79.27

SINISTER CD 239.20 SM 5.23

SINK FO 168.32 178.17 CD 232.35
   SM 23.20 149.4

SINKING LH 5.39 TL 103.6
   CD 242.22 SM 102.37

SINNING SM 111.17

SIP VG 48.6

SIR FO 167.30 VG 53.1

SIR CAPTAIN CD 186.1

SIRE SM 89.26

SIR EDWARD EDWARDS' SM 31.36

SIR HENRY SM 3.37 18.1 34.20
   37.19 39.3 39.31 39.36 39.39
   40.36 41.21 43.38 76.37
   78.34 79.38 88.14 89.4 89.13
   92.4 99.29 116.27 116.31

SIR HENRY'S SM 83.5

SIR PRIPPY SM 111.16

SISTER LH 26.16 35.18 35.27
   TL 61.8 71.13 71.14 106.2
   106.4 CD 202.6 262.7 SM 6.34
   51.27 93.14 VG 3.28 56.32

SISTER-IN-LAW TL 72.9

SISTERLY FO 126.19

SISTERS CD 207.7

SISTER'S VG 32.15

SITHEE LH 36.39

SITS TL 86.13 CD 222.13
   SM 155.32

SITTING LH 15.17 15.21 18.23
   29.35 TL 46.14 60.29 62.18
   98.10 106.1 FO 125.9 136.1
   136.16 137.36 138.11 146.25
   156.2 178.39 179.1 CD 201.19
   204.8 220.7 221.4 231.17
   231.18 247.11 248.7 SM 5.18
   20.27 28.18 33.27 38.38
   39.23 42.32 72.14 85.4 87.23
   87.31 111.26 111.33 136.24
   137.38 143.31 155.10

SITTING (CONT.) MD 194.19
   196.30 199.18 VG 9.26
   9.28 11.19 12.28 20.15
   37.33 43.38 47.39 58.6
   65.20 70.12 71.10 75.8

SITTING-ROOM FO 119.11 121.39
   122.7 130.3 135.33 135.35
   149.38 163.25 CD 204.14 205.7
   SM 23.34 91.31 VG 13.17 34.29
   37.29 40.21

SITTING-ROOMS TL 97.33

SITUATION CD 227.24 SM 25.11
   MD 168.1

SITUATIONS SM 119.40 120.1

SIX FO 164.23 CD 261.3 SM 80.9
   142.39 VG 16.8 18.37 21.29
   52.34 72.8

SIXPENCE VG 68.37

SIXTY TL 61.17 FO 168.11
   SM 141.22

SIXTY KRONEN CD 240.35

SIZE LH 3.6

SKATING VG 49.33

SKEIN TL 71.1

SKELETON TL 70.32

SKETCHED SM 114.16

SKIES SM 127.3

SKI-ING VG 49.33

SKILFUL VG 57.41

SKILL SM 9.1

SKIN TL 45.40 51.9 61.22 80.39
   84.12 94.37 95.17 95.19
   FO 120.17 135.15 137.37
   148.14 149.18 149.31
   CD 184.12 185.6 189.34 210.7
   242.37 SM 11.27 45.6 104.24
   130.5 130.6 MD 180.23 180.29
   192.37 193.8 VG 59.4

SKINS CD 204.22 221.41

SKIPPING SM 143.39

SKIRT LH 28.37 FO 156.39
   CD 204.23 214.24 238.18
   248.29 VG 21.8 30.16

SKIRTED FO 146.1 157.5

SKIRTS TL 71.35 FO 122.38
   CD 238.20 VG 24.2 24.35 66.11

SKULKING VG 5.5

SKULL SM 13.12 121.39

SKULLS SM 152.31

SKUNK TL 51.16

SKY LH 4.22 21.25 23.15
   23.21 TL 56.40 59.40
   FO 117.36 145.37 173.3
   CD 186.26 201.12 201.17
   201.37 222.27 237.12
   237.13 237.18 237.24
   237.33 237.38 240.31
   241.12 241.16 242.24
   242.27 243.20 252.22
   253.14 SM 20.41 63.38
   66.8 74.8 74.9 78.11
   101.39 102.9 102.12
   102.36 104.4 105.15
   105.18 105.25 105.28
   105.30 105.33 126.12
   126.26 126.37 129.3 129.4
   134.10 140.16 148.17
   149.27 154.22 154.37
   MD 170.9 170.25 170.39
   172.34 182.31 182.32
   182.35 191.34 191.40
   200.14 VG 18.11 19.7
   51.29 52.14 52.28 68.5
   76.31

SKY-BEAR CD 252.36

SKYLINE CD 247.40

SKY-LINE SM 63.4

SKY-MORNING CD 237.27

SKY-RIDGE CD 241.26

SLAB LH 21.31

SLACK LH 6.37 15.13
   FO 151.15 170.28

SLACKEN LH 8.23

SLANT TL 47.10 CD 247.28
   247.35 248.4 VG 36.25

SLANTED FO 172.4

SLANTING TL 47.28 52.6
   76.30 CD 248.37 255.7
   VG 39.40

SLANTINGLY SM 64.7

SLAP TL 90.18

SLASHES CD 237.22 241.32
   244.29

SLATE SM 60.20 105.29

SLAVE TL 79.21 SM 62.36 73.7
   73.33 108.27 MD 186.20
   191.3 191.13 191.17 191.24
   191.28 192.18 192.25
   192.30 193.17 193.36
   193.38 194.36 198.15
   198.24 198.37 198.39
   199.15 199.38 200.2 200.5
   200.31 210.27 210.41 211.5
   211.8 VG 61.32

SLAVED FO 113.34 VG 31.17

SLOWLY (CONT.) CD 241.8 241.33
247.29 247.35 265.4 SM 23.27
34.1 58.18 59.36 67.35 69.30
74.16 76.16 80.22 81.24
82.20 92.8 93.6 102.6 102.13
124.35 140.39 144.24 145.3
145.7 154.9 MD 166.13 166.39
176.35 182.11 187.10 187.23
187.40 189.27 191.38 192.14
193.41 194.30 196.32 199.36
202.41 206.26 209.11 211.13
211.17 VG 14.9 17.40 18.20
22.13 23.26 23.38 32.19
32.29 32.38 45.19 45.24
46.21 47.2 47.36 49.33 50.9
52.38 60.34 67.4 68.7 71.12
71.36 71.40 71.41 76.4 80.17

SLUMBERS MD 164.37

SLUNG CD 247.8 MD 193.33
VG 51.32

SLUSH-TRANSLUCENT CD 253.33

SLY FO 116.2 128.10 130.21
SM 98.10 VG 4.37

SMALLER CD 240.20

SMALLEST CD 205.8

SMALLISH FO 169.7 SM 20.36
21.16 22.5

SMALLNESS TL 59.27

SMALL-PANED TL 97.24

SMART LH 24.35 TL 71.16 SM 8.19
8.20 8.21 21.6 21.7 VG 57.37

SMASH FO 147.7 CD 220.36
SM 121.38

SMASHED SM 13.12 VG 33.7 33.8
33.10 78.11 78.22 80.18

SMASHING SM 80.2 VG 78.30

SMELL TL 56.32 56.33 FO 118.33
144.10 146.33 146.34 147.14
149.21 149.26 CD 222.26
SM 30.34 57.12 78.12 78.13
101.37 102.5 102.41 103.1
123.36 143.30 MD 198.12
VG 5.20 5.21 18.2 24.21
29.40 68.4

SMELLED LH 6.4 SM 110.34 151.15
MD 169.19 209.10

SMELLY TL 93.2 VG 66.28

SMELT FO 147.14 CD 248.28
SM 117.30 VG 11.24

SMILE LH 3.29 4.27 19.18 31.24
38.11 TL 45.19 55.31 57.15
58.25 79.13 80.16 84.1 86.6
FO 128.31 129.1 136.30 139.11
143.26 156.9 157.18 170.16
170.41 171.34 175.30 175.31
CD 187.33 189.23 189.29
189.30 190.17 192.17 195.19

SMILE (CONT.) 196.1 196.33
198.5 218.5 220.9 228.1
SM 10.41 21.33 33.17 34.23
34.27 34.35 39.10 40.39
43.34 48.28 54.9 54.12
54.19 55.21 62.33 77.7
77.15 81.22 81.25 81.26
82.27 82.39 88.2 89.6 98.10
101.27 120.35 122.19 122.27
128.13 155.20 MD 167.25
190.39 VG 38.34 44.14 44.23
44.26 45.39 49.29 49.30
49.37 58.12

SMILED LH 3.33 4.12 4.25 12.37
12.40 13.2 13.23 13.26 13.34
14.9 16.4 19.17 22.29 34.25
34.32 39.13 39.21 TL 56.4
56.14 57.22 61.38 63.40 65.2
65.13 83.34 83.38 85.16
85.33 86.20 89.8 89.23 89.30
90.36 91.7 91.17 93.32 93.37
96.8 96.35 97.17 108.18
108.19 FO 125.34 130.10
130.14 146.38 164.19
CD 189.15 192.16 195.17 196.1
196.33 198.14 211.25 240.3
SM 41.22 82.26 86.7 88.3
98.11 119.40 120.16 MD 178.29
180.30 181.2 183.4 191.10
VG 21.38

SMILES TL 85.39 VG 59.38

SMILING LH 12.26 12.42 13.12
13.29 19.29 38.30 TL 57.20
59.28 73.15 83.22 85.27
88.14 89.20 94.15 FO 126.10
129.2 132.6 141.21 141.24
170.35 CD 187.26 190.16
195.25 232.14 SM 11.5 33.34
39.21 55.8 55.21 87.25 87.39
91.10 MD 197.38 204.17
VG 49.10 69.22

SMITE TL 74.26

SMOCK SM 57.9 MD 177.26

SMOKE LH 4.32 33.11 TL 94.5
SM 29.31 101.38 102.3 102.5
VG 24.21

SMOKE-COLOUR SM 150.32

SMOKED LH 18.22 39.17 VG 59.14
60.24

SMOKING LH 33.8 TL 60.30
CD 220.7 VG 17.17 20.29 21.21
36.7 57.40 59.2

SMOKY SM 126.36 VG 18.38

SMOOTH LH 28.36 TL 53.39 58.28
FO 116.34 CD 188.36 189.36
190.7 207.28 233.38 233.39
SM 9.24 52.32 70.17 77.16
MD 198.11 VG 49.30 59.3 59.4

SMOOTHED MD 186.38

SMOOTHER SM 52.35

SMOOTH-FACED SM 70.33 70.34

SMOOTHLY FO 116.34 123.7

SMOOTH-SOLED CD 254.16

SMORTO TL 49.42

SMOTE MD 185.20 197.14

SMOTHERED SM 35.19 36.6

SMUDGED TL 92.11

SNAILS VG 15.38

SNAKE TL 58.39 60.4 66.3
70.23 81.21 FO 146.38
CD 216.40 SM 19.38 30.24
68.30 70.35

SNAKE-LIKE SM 19.13

SNAP VG 15.30 61.23

SNAPDRAGON SM 150.27

SNAPPED FO 146.27 CD 261.13
MD 164.39

SNAPPING FO 143.34

SNAPS VG 76.10

SNAP-SNAP-SNAP-SNAP VG 76.10

SNARL TL 66.4 66.6 SM 116.4
VG 72.20

SNARLED SM 25.22 36.10 70.5
VG 63.20

SNARLING VG 26.34

SNATCH FO 155.13

SNATCHES SM 126.37

SNATCHING SM 46.26 VG 41.31

SNEAKING SM 90.20

SNEER LH 4.1 9.25 17.30
SM 51.22 88.15 VG 23.37
26.34 26.38 27.11 61.12

SNEERED LH 9.13 20.1
VG 22.30 32.36 61.34 61.38
62.24 62.42 63.39

SNIFF FO 146.41 VG 50.31

SNIFFED CD 208.39

SNIFFING FO 146.17 146.42

SNIPE LH 28.10

SNIPPING SM 46.7

SNOUT FO 165.7

SNOUTING CD 247.18

SNOW TL 58.12 58.40
FO 148.30 CD 230.22 237.22
241.32 242.36 244.29

SOMEBODY (CONT.) CD 212.2 225.27
  232.20 SM 9.30 23.32 31.20
  32.12 32.14 40.19 105.27
  122.16 131.14 142.30 VG 6.1
  10.23 13.9 26.37 39.17 42.27
  57.10 70.33 71.4 72.16 77.37

SOMEBODY'LL LH 20.26

SOMEBODY'S VG 20.11

SOMEHOW TL 44.37 FO 115.34
  118.22 CD 199.1 SM 129.32
  129.34 MD 197.14 VG 9.8 29.1
  56.10

SOMEONE LH 15.10 TL 78.28 82.15
  FO 119.7 159.16 SM 76.13
  VG 35.39 69.37

SOMERCOTES, GERRY (SEE GERRY
  SOMERCOTES)

SOMETIME SM 77.11

SOMETIMES LH 22.10 TL 59.6
  84.32 99.14 99.15 99.20
  99.21 100.6 FO 115.32 137.11
  179.6 CD 192.6 200.37 204.28
  209.6 230.23 241.4 241.34
  254.26 255.7 SM 4.19 4.20
  14.15 63.22 98.17 98.29 99.9
  99.14 108.13 136.34 143.19
  147.12 147.16 147.20 152.27
  158.36 158.37 MD 163.16
  164.23 198.13 VG 5.19 6.42
  7.3 22.25

SOMEWHAT LH 13.9 TL 82.31 84.6
  SM 12.23 54.5 74.19 VG 3.16
  4.32 16.18 29.28 60.38

SOMEWHERE TL 82.1 87.20 98.24
  FO 125.23 132.18 132.33
  144.41 162.4 CD 196.31 264.2
  SM 5.25 6.7 8.27 12.10 12.21
  40.24 109.8 115.30 120.23
  133.9 133.16 136.32 MD 166.7
  VG 4.3 6.34 18.26 28.19
  30.11 61.19 62.13 64.11
  66.16 73.6 76.19

SON LH 12.11 16.20 TL 46.8
  96.27 SM 3.36 3.38 7.27
  13.10 VG 78.29

SONG TL 71.2 101.41 102.25
  102.35 CD 222.12 MD 181.34

SONGS TL 99.28 99.35 VG 16.31

SON-IN-LAW SM 82.23 82.29 83.1
  83.11 83.31 83.35 155.38

SON-IN-LAW'S SM 83.4

SONNY LH 5.20

SONOROUS TL 46.20 76.24
  VG 32.10

SONS LH 15.11 VG 7.17 10.8
  11.9

SON'S LH 16.8 VG 4.38

SOONER FO 159.22 SM 109.24
  112.23 VG 12.5

SOOTHE TL 57.32 SM 35.35

SOOTHED TL 82.30 SM 36.7

SOOTHES SM 158.34

SOOTHING SM 57.34 58.40
  MD 167.33

SORCERERS TL 74.12

SORCERY TL 55.41

SORDID CD 217.7 257.8 SM 5.21
  70.1 153.35 VG 9.4 9.8 9.17

SORDIDNESS SM 150.13 153.36
  153.38 VG 9.10

SORE TL 91.33 SM 12.24
  MD 165.23 173.9 205.23

SORREL SM 10.24 10.34 11.3
  60.2 63.22

SORROW TL 45.37 46.24 47.4
  53.40 105.13

SORROWS TL 47.5

SORRY TL 45.22 45.23 45.32
  51.31 51.41 52.36 59.9 65.4
  68.14 102.23 FO 137.26 147.20
  148.26 157.39 161.11 166.1
  CD 200.9 236.41 251.41
  SM 51.30 83.14 83.16 93.34
  122.2 122.6 VG 39.24 64.27

SORTS SM 104.33 124.37 VG 57.7

SOTTO VOCE CD 266.4

SOUL LH 35.16 TL 43.15 48.10
  57.39 58.1 58.6 63.3 79.32
  82.20 82.37 86.22 86.23
  86.25 88.1 88.31 88.32 89.24
  92.24 95.42 96.3 98.5 99.32
  100.35 104.10 104.15 106.41
  107.12 107.26 107.39
  FO 115.27 116.29 126.41
  128.12 129.36 130.40 130.41
  130.42 141.38 157.11 160.14
  161.24 167.11 174.9 175.25
  179.23 CD 192.15 205.2 217.11
  221.1 221.11 230.7 251.9
  SM 13.36 39.4 45.37 71.35
  71.38 76.11 116.34 137.15
  145.9 145.10 145.27 145.34
  147.4 149.41 152.38 153.23
  157.19 158.7 158.25 MD 164.34
  173.1 176.17 177.34 195.28
  195.39 197.14 203.12 206.25
  VG 7.4 27.6 41.25 41.27
  58.23 65.19 65.29 66.34
  70.32 72.38 76.26 76.33
  81.13

SOULLESS TL 58.1 82.38

SOULS TL 92.34 CD 238.9 VG 8.2
  30.1

SOUND LH 9.36 9.41 11.8
  27.38 30.38 36.33 36.40
  TL 44.23 45.21 70.6 74.32
  78.1 94.27 95.39 99.36
  99.37 99.39 100.2 100.9
  100.23 100.24 100.29
  100.30 101.32 101.42
  102.7 102.38 103.2 105.40
  FO 119.25 132.1 132.33
  145.21 146.12 147.15 158.6
  158.30 174.4 CD 183.21
  184.22 190.24 191.41
  199.21 200.2 201.13 205.29
  231.5 242.3 242.7 242.13
  244.14 260.28 SM 10.37
  53.14 68.9 72.17 74.29·
  75.2 87.21 90.14 112.16
  135.40 MD 167.16 198.15
  206.19 VG 18.22 18.40
  45.35 48.32 48.35 49.3
  55.3 72.24 74.19

SOUNDED LH 12.25 13.41 24.35
  32.30 32.35 FO 132.16
  159.35 168.38 CD 200.31
  239.42 SM 106.30 MD 185.7
  VG 19.13

SOUNDING MD 206.10

SOUNDS TL 53.22 100.20
  FO 119.25 135.25 CD 200.13
  234.7 SM 23.13 82.24
  116.13 156.12 157.17
  MD 171.7 VG 25.28 55.36

SOUP SM 111.1

SOUR VG 9.12

SOURCE SM 6.36 50.1

SOURCES SM 96.7

SOUSED LH 21.37

SOUTH LH 3.1 SM 126.38
  127.1 128.26 MD 185.2
  VG 5.30 71.26

SOUTHAMPTON SM 125.31

SOUTHERN SM 4.20 9.39 17.41

SOUTHWARDS SM 93.6

SOUTH-WEST SM 115.31 133.30
  145.1 VG 71.26 77.30

SOVEREIGN LH 35.39

SOWED MD 211.18

SPACE TL 103.8 103.30
  103.38 FO 151.34 CD 192.28
  201.2 202.26 220.27
  220.31 233.35 SM 52.6
  52.13 102.11 MD 208.13

SPACES LH 22.6 SM 74.7
  74.13 107.14

SPACIOUS CD 185.17 SM 27.2

SPANGLED SM 141.4

SPANIARD   CD 200.4

SPANIARDS   CD 210.22

SPANISH   CD 200.8   210.18   210.19
   210.20   210.24   SM 8.8   127.28
   132.41   VG 21.10

SPANISH-AMERICAN   SM 77.25

SPANISH ARMADA   FO 172.28

SPARE   LH 18.18   TL 108.39
   FO 126.4   SM 11.9   11.11

SPARED   VG 80.25   80.26

SPARING   CD 262.35

SPARK   TL 82.37   91.19   98.3
   FO 128.11   146.36   CD 208.18
   210.37   SM 20.16   73.4   VG 30.8

SPARKING   SM 150.36

SPARKLED   SM 101.40   127.8

SPARKLING   MD 178.17   193.29
   193.36   VG 51.12

SPARKS   FO 132.7   SM 150.38   151.4
   VG 34.12

SPARSE   VG 18.36

SPASM   FO 159.13

SPASMODIC   SM 67.7

SPASMODICALLY   FO 136.7

SPASMS   SM 4.23   VG 76.37

SPATULA   FO 149.1

SPEAK   LH 27.28   34.26   TL 49.35
   50.14   52.38   58.32   63.25
   63.29   64.34   84.39   95.41
   FO 115.34   128.18   133.20
   136.25   138.15   138.16   143.24
   145.6   167.23   167.26   171.33
   CD 206.14   216.16   221.23
   259.42   SM 23.21   35.20   35.22
   91.30   103.35   107.35   107.38
   117.6   MD 168.15   173.33   176.25
   179.8   179.10   186.37   192.19
   192.22   193.21   193.38   194.25
   197.5   211.6   VG 48.23

SPEAKING   LH 11.21   21.11
   TL 44.32   45.27   51.27   56.12
   59.31   64.37   93.28   94.9
   FO 116.22   123.13   158.37
   167.29   170.13   CD 199.40
   221.19   SM 23.21   52.30   57.33
   71.30   MD 182.12

SPEAKS   TL 52.23   SM 40.36   41.24
   154.20

SPEAR-THRUST   MD 176.7

SPECIAL   CD 263.15   SM 12.30
   12.31   MD 163.26   VG 9.13

SPECIALISE   TL 87.42

SPECIALLY-LICENSED   VG 31.6

SPECIES   SM 38.26

SPECIMEN   CD 214.2   SM 82.15

SPECK   SM 90.32   102.11   MD 186.19

SPECKLED   TL 58.41   CD 253.29

SPECTACLE   TL 92.27

SPECTACLES   FO 113.7   115.13
   117.42   135.6   142.17   142.20
   173.1

SPED   LH 7.6   MD 186.17

SPEECH   LH 5.1   10.4   FO 118.6
   129.27   129.39   CD 231.6   250.3
   SM 18.40   42.7   57.34   124.18
   149.13   154.24   MD 171.35
   VG 35.18   66.15

SPEECHES   TL 85.40

SPEECHLESS   TL 103.21

SPEED   FO 172.26   CD 238.39

SPELCH   FO 169.16

SPELL   LH 23.37   31.27   TL 56.16
   95.28   101.21   103.5   FO 118.31
   118.36   125.3   CD 193.12   217.36
   218.8   SM 69.13   115.30
   MD 190.6   VG 38.22   48.15   50.8

SPELLBOUND   FO 116.28   117.11
   117.16   120.14   SM 67.28   136.40

SPELL-BOUND   CD 193.11   226.41
   VG 66.23

SPELLED   MD 190.13

SPELLING   LH 5.9

SPEND   FO 162.10   CD 208.8
   SM 16.29   28.4   158.28

SPENDING   SM 104.39

SPENT   FO 136.42   SM 118.32
   131.37   142.20   152.22
   MD 168.39   206.35   VG 26.27
   26.29   27.40

SPHERE   FO 176.23   CD 190.33
   190.34   190.36

SPHINX-LOOK   CD 244.3

SPIES   CD 194.31

SPIKY   SM 151.1   MD 187.29

SPILLED   LH 29.38   31.15   VG 9.19
   32.25

SPILLS   SM 97.8

SPIN   CD 192.13   VG 21.41

SPINACH   CD 256.32

SPINE   FO 127.4

SPINES   CD 239.14   SM 151.21

SPINNING   FO 173.34

SPINS   FO 173.5

SPIRALLING   SM 149.33

SPIRE   TL 98.4   VG 17.32

SPIRES   CD 238.37

SPIRIT   TL 43.24   44.1   63.3
   65.1   98.9   100.37   FO 117.24
   118.39   131.11   178.23
   178.25   CD 246.27   252.20
   SM 56.29   63.34   68.39
   72.36   74.37   74.38   75.20
   76.14   82.15   101.12   116.36
   125.1   139.6   144.25   144.38
   146.29   148.34   149.11
   149.23   152.34   158.32   159.1
   159.3   159.7   MD 164.34
   201.7   VG 70.36

SPIRIT-FLAME   CD 205.33

SPIRITS   SM 139.14

SPIRITUALLY   TL 92.4

SPITE   LH 19.42   TL 49.36
   51.22   FO 113.33   114.26
   122.1   154.29   157.27
   164.21   SM 4.12   4.13
   4.14   4.15   4.16   6.8   12.13
   49.29   98.38   148.24   149.36
   VG 41.19   43.33   44.30   45.16
   63.34

SPITEFUL   SM 4.12   50.41   110.3

SPITEFULLY   FO 134.25

SPITTING   SM 72.17   VG 74.13

SPLASHED-UP   SM 93.13

SPLASHING   SM 24.41   58.30
   93.5   134.1   MD 185.11

SPLEEN   TL 62.36

SPLENDID   TL 46.23   47.7
   71.20   76.1   76.2   90.37
   FO 168.22   CD 242.11
   SM 8.31   14.37   16.6   27.2
   28.3   29.1   75.1   96.30
   148.22   150.4   MD 185.3
   190.6

SPLENDIDLY   SM 8.19   114.24

SPLENDOUR   FO 148.36   SM 90.16
   MD 163.21   169.28   178.24
   183.30   189.3   197.27
   202.12   202.13   202.18
   VG 5.17

SPLIT   FO 169.24   CD 234.9
   SM 14.22

SPLITTING   MD 165.1

SPOIL   CD 242.19   SM 57.19
  VG 66.41

SPOILED   VG 6.11

SPOILING   SM 70.14   114.39   115.33

SPOILT   SM 49.2   115.35   VG 6.27
  49.18

SPOKE   LH 3.33   5.34   TL 47.9
  49.27   49.28   56.38   58.30
  76.15   77.16   107.11   FO 114.24
  132.20   132.31   134.40   143.21
  150.18   157.33   159.8   159.9
  175.29   CD 186.1   191.31   192.2
  219.1   232.23   SM 13.17   19.8
  19.19   19.24   43.39   44.5   51.25
  81.13   82.20   82.31   88.14
  120.11   135.38   MD 168.5   170.22
  177.36   193.22   198.29   VG 4.38
  19.23   21.12   42.11   46.2   50.33

SPOKEN   LH 20.9   CD 216.14   221.20
  SM 64.37

SPONGE   VG 61.39

SPONTANEOUS   SM 6.24

SPOON   FO 149.1   149.5   VG 47.30

SPOONFUL   SM 40.31

SPORT   SM 70.18   70.21   70.28
  113.20   VG 23.17   61.3

SPORTING   SM 70.15   113.37
  VG 52.19   52.33   57.8   57.20

SPORTS   VG 7.34   40.25   49.32

SPOT   LH 24.17   CD 248.25   SM 6.16
  12.21   19.31   19.32   21.18
  40.12   63.26

SPOTLESS   SM 132.27

SPOTS   TL 62.11   SM 4.5

SPOTTED   TL 96.38   FO 170.9
  SM 35.37   VG 17.4   21.3

SPOUT   CD 237.26

SPRANG   LH 9.2   14.4   27.30
  SM 19.22   141.10   MD 183.21
  211.8   VG 34.11   34.18   72.41

SPRAWLING   FO 122.11   122.41
  CD 243.30   SM 94.24

SPREAD   LH 14.38   15.16   15.20
  15.23   23.17   TL 79.38
  CD 210.38   225.14   252.34
  SM 58.4   58.11   67.13   MD 198.36
  VG 46.11   47.5   49.39

SPREADING   FO 141.10   SM 65.27
  MD 197.29   200.21   VG 49.20

SPREADS   MD 189.37   VG 48.9

SPRIG   SM 128.19

SPRIGHTLY   SM 11.12

SPRIGS   SM 65.30

SPRING   LH 21.20   33.34   35.28
  TL 45.4   59.23   62.19   81.37
  97.37   98.10   98.19   FO 164.27
  SM 19.16   26.11   64.13   67.40
  104.5   133.31   133.35   133.39
  141.27   141.29   141.34   143.38
  144.10   153.7   155.22   156.1
  MD 163.3   170.10   171.15   179.33
  191.38   196.13   200.30   209.5
  210.14   VG 15.34   39.10   45.17
  47.25   68.6   69.22   70.11

SPRING-FIRE   SM 140.18

SPRINGILY   SM 24.26   59.1

SPRINGING   TL 69.28

SPRINGY   SM 22.23

SPRINKLE   LH 23.19

SPROUT   CD 252.19

SPRUNG   SM 24.37

SPUME   CD 250.33   VG 74.6

SPUME-BUBBLES   CD 244.35

SPUR   MD 164.9

SPURRED   SM 57.16

SPURS   SM 36.24

SPURT   VG 7.2

SPURTING   MD 170.8

SPUTTER   TL 92.12

SPY   MD 173.18   194.34

SQUALID   SM 29.26   VG 5.19   29.23

SQUALOR   SM 150.16   MD 166.35

SQUARE   TL 97.27   CD 238.29
  SM 32.19   VG 17.21

SQUATTED   CD 201.18   SM 141.39
  VG 17.21

SQUATTING   SM 102.21

SQUAW   SM 135.12

SQUAWBERRY-BUSHES   SM 151.25

SQUAWK   FO 115.14   MD 164.40
  167.27

SQUEAK   SM 135.38

SQUEAKY   SM 135.32   136.11

SQUEALED   SM 24.22

SQUEEZE   VG 13.27

SQUEEZED   LH 21.40   TL 99.34

SQUIB   TL 92.10

SQUIBBING   TL 92.1

SQUINTING   SM 45.16   54.9
  64.29

SQUIRE   SM 53.24

SQUIRE   (SEE MRS. SQUIRE)

SQUIRES   SM 28.7

SQUIRM   FO 157.8

SQUIRMED   SM 9.40

SQUIRMING   CD 230.30   SM 9.41

SQUIRREL   TL 72.31   SM 150.6

SQUIRRELS   TL 74.12

SQUIRREL'S   SM 9.29

SQUIRT   TL 63.38

STABILITY   SM 94.31   VG 5.39

STABLE   SM 45.30   46.32   74.16
  123.16   153.40   VG 20.33
  77.15

STABLED   SM 101.2

STABLEMAN   LH 32.8   TL 98.31

STABLES   SM 10.26   10.29
  28.25   32.16   37.35

STACK   LH 3.5   3.10   3.14
  3.19   4.21   7.15   7.25   7.27
  7.33   8.7   8.35   9.14   9.23
  9.31   10.6   10.12   10.15
  11.38   12.2   14.30   15.17
  15.24   15.29   24.28   24.29
  24.33   25.18   25.23   25.32
  25.39   37.20   37.22   38.36

STACK-CLOTH   LH 24.20   39.8

STACKS   LH 21.17   23.9   24.13
  24.16   24.22   25.4   25.8
  25.15   30.21   30.26   30.39
  36.28   36.33   37.42

STAG   TL 58.36

STAGE   SM 111.7   111.8   112.26
  153.25   153.34

STAGED   SM 29.17

STAGES   SM 153.33

STAGGERED   LH 9.29   CD 227.14
  SM 114.31   VG 73.25

STAGGERING   LH 24.23   CD 254.20
  VG 73.26   74.16

ST. MAWR (CONT.) SM 32.13 35.29
36.1 36.4 36.8 36.32 36.40
38.7 39.11 48.12 48.17 49.1
49.18 49.24 49.32 51.3 51.4
51.23 52.41 55.4 55.33 55.35
55.36 55.41 56.12 57.32
57.36 58.1 58.8 58.15 59.6
59.19 59.26 60.2 61.24
61.25 66.15 66.21 66.28
66.35 67.12 67.22 70.3
72.10 72.13 72.27 73.7 73.27
73.32 74.15 74.23 75.20
76.31 76.35 79.27 80.11
80.22 81.1 81.15 82.12 82.13
82.34 88.5 88.27 88.32 89.5
89.14 89.22 90.3 90.6 90.10
91.21 91.34 91.38 92.3 92.5
92.13 92.18 92.28 92.35 93.5
93.16 93.24 93.35 94.1 94.17
99.15 99.19 106.9 110.14
110.27 111.36 112.7 112.19
115.3 115.24 116.29 117.9
117.12 117.15 118.15 119.28
119.37 123.30 124.8 124.10
126.29 127.15 129.30 129.36
130.31 131.28 131.38 132.8
137.18

ST. MAWR'S SM 19.35 39.14 72.36
83.3 90.22 122.24 124.26
130.3

STOAT SM 42.29

STOCK LH 29.5 FO 141.6 CD 196.7
SM 64.23 64.24 123.20
VG 34.10 53.34

STOCKINETTE CD 235.7

STOCKING TL 79.17 SM 65.10

STOCKINGS FO 156.40 CD 233.28
242.38 243.5 VG 24.6 26.30

STOCKIN'S LH 30.22

STOIC SM 86.23

STOICAL SM 131.15

STOICALLY FO 152.2 SM 129.27

STOICISM CD 230.35 SM 45.8
129.25

STOLE LH 34.4 CD 237.7 SM 65.19

STOLEN MD 168.37 172.20
VG 41.27 54.9

STOMACH SM 5.13 VG 9.19 11.8
12.22 12.30

STOMACHS CD 249.27

STONE LH 21.31 32.12 TL 59.5
60.5 68.12 68.22 68.23 68.27
70.25 70.35 98.17 CD 184.22
189.35 199.37 240.21 242.26
243.33 252.31 253.16 253.29
SM 105.27 MD 165.19 167.15
187.31 187.33 VG 3.21 3.24
3.25 9.6 9.34 15.37 15.39
18.9 18.10 18.35 18.37 18.38

STONE (CONT.) 19.5 19.6 20.36
23.29 25.19 36.5 36.8 36.28
36.32 37.4 37.8 45.26 68.9
70.7

STONE-BED CD 253.4

STONE-PINES MD 191.21

STONES LH 38.16 TL 59.2
CD 206.37 243.27 243.31 245.8
245.14 247.15 247.16 253.30
253.40 255.39 SM 64.25 68.34
105.24 105.31 121.38 125.5
129.37 MD 198.11

STONE-SLIDES CD 243.20

STONE-SPECKLED CD 252.30

STONE-TRACKED CD 243.35

STONY TL 49.11 63.33 CD 239.35
SM 100.27 154.41 VG 9.33
15.20 17.34 17.41 18.40 36.7

STOOL FO 122.31 CD 201.19
202.25 VG 46.6 46.32 47.33
48.42 71.1 71.10

STOOLS VG 22.2

STOOP LH 10.7 CD 184.6

STOOPED FO 114.13 120.19 133.40
174.42 CD 190.8 218.4 247.9
MD 207.1

STOOPING TL 72.24 FO 131.25
CD 236.4 MD 166.23 205.21
206.37 VG 24.28 53.2

STOP LH 4.9 8.21 20.26 20.28
20.30 28.19 28.30 28.41
30.33 36.23 37.41 TL 53.37
58.7 FO 126.4 128.29 128.34
134.14 134.39 144.9 144.13
144.37 CD 188.21 249.26
SM 4.35 36.10 82.16 87.15
138.14 MD 167.23 VG 32.10
32.15 50.25 76.41

STOPPED LH 25.4 38.10 FO 131.26
134.13 149.42 CD 240.17 243.6
263.4 SM 76.31 92.1 141.10
MD 199.31 VG 22.17 74.18

STOPPIN' LH 20.32

STOPPING LH 30.14 FO 139.20
CD 236.17 240.37 SM 138.18
VG 16.36

STORE TL 72.31 SM 143.4

STORED CD 232.42

STORM MD 208.18

STORMS SM 149.41

STORMY MD 171.11

STORY FO 135.28 CD 199.15
207.10 SM 16.11 78.40 VG 5.13

STOUT FO 169.5 169.28
CD 229.26 231.29 SM 127.34
VG 7.7

STOVE CD 185.18 198.22

STOVES VG 54.10 54.36

STOWED VG 39.8

STRADDLED CD 201.38 SM 144.6

STRAGGLED FO 169.18

STRAGGLING SM 63.22 65.31

STRAIGHT TL 46.29 75.40
FO 114.10 128.8 136.20
138.11 139.15 139.19
141.4 150.5 165.7
CD 189.7 207.7 216.37
247.37 260.31 261.40
265.36 SM 7.32 17.34 18.5
20.27 24.30 28.13 32.20
49.23 49.39 50.1 50.29
65.16 89.19 90.40 100.30
109.14 109.33 112.21
114.20 128.28 VG 19.21
23.34 32.28 33.37 43.15

STRAIGHTEN LH 25.33

STRAIGHTENED FO 118.28
CD 183.22 SM 17.31 VG 33.38

STRAIGHTENING FO 168.42

STRAIGHTFORWARDNESS SM 136.6

STRAIGHTWAY LH 9.25

STRAIN TL 45.30 FO 119.24
175.33 175.35 177.17
177.35 178.10 178.11
179.2 179.5 CD 220.17
SM 109.30 VG 8.29

STRAINED FO 134.7 134.20
143.31 177.21 179.30
CD 185.8 185.41 VG 76.12
77.16

STRAINING FO 179.21 SM 66.36
69.35

STRAINS FO 159.20

STRAND SM 146.37 147.13
MD 198.7

STRANDED FO 144.27 VG 50.9

STRANDS LH 21.18 CD 187.16
VG 39.32

STRANGE LH 6.6 10.3 10.34
11.8 13.4 13.30 21.9 27.4
TL 44.17 49.39 49.40
52.4 53.42 66.8 73.38
74.35 75.25 76.39 78.32
78.40 101.7 102.2 103.26
104.34 107.3 108.11
FO 114.5 114.15 115.28
117.3 120.13 129.34 130.40
132.12 134.31 135.14 149.2

STRANGE (CONT.) FO 155.18 161.30
167.37 171.37 173.37 174.4
175.30 179.30 CD 189.24
189.30 189.33 191.13 191.17
193.8 211.40 216.31 216.34
218.5 232.28 244.41 251.35
251.39 253.24 254.11 SM 4.39
6.22 19.12 27.22 27.32
28.18 30.15 47.12 47.18
48.1 55.19 55.30 58.20
61.11 61.14 64.7 69.22
69.27 69.30 75.11 75.26
82.36 82.38 82.40 90.16
95.20 102.31 104.22 116.17
129.13 129.36 131.19 144.21
145.26 145.32 145.41 146.14
146.36 152.23 152.25 153.24
MD 164.39 165.15 166.10
168.10 168.34 169.25 181.29
183.39 187.13 188.16 193.10
197.39 198.28 203.5 203.7
203.17 VG 6.36 14.19 27.5
39.28 45.2 48.19 50.31 53.38
54.1 54.5 54.24 54.28 54.30
56.6 70.22 73.32 74.5 74.13
74.26 76.21 77.17

STRANGELY LH 19.5 FO 128.38
157.8 163.32 164.8 173.34
CD 220.39 253.15 SM 19.37
66.40 83.9 92.6 98.37 116.34
MD 175.34 185.23 197.35
203.13 VG 41.16 48.34

STRANGENESS FO 167.39 VG 55.8

STRANGER LH 5.32 FO 165.30
166.3 CD 215.9 SM 70.33
109.21 MD 169.8 169.18 169.32
170.31 186.28 187.11 187.17
190.23 195.37

STRANGERS CD 232.40 SM 57.39
VG 20.25

STRANGER-YOUTH FO 131.17

STRANGEST TL 66.4 SM 4.38

STRANGLE VG 30.23

STRANGLED MD 171.34

STRANGLING TL 96.10 SM 151.5
MD 184.3

STRAPPED VG 24.22

STRAPPING CD 233.5

STRAW SM 39.22 94.17 MD 163.14
164.11

STRAWBERRIES SM 151.37

STRAY FO 139.17 142.38 151.34
CD 190.31 192.1 202.36 238.9
VG 44.10 62.26

STRAYED TL 73.9 FO 136.10
CD 214.11 245.10 SM 45.11
149.20 VG 70.9 71.16

STRAYING TL 98.32 FO 142.23
169.14 CD 190.24 191.41

STRAYING (CONT.) 192.12 199.22
234.4 VG 32.8 57.34 70.33

STREAK FO 149.25

STREAKED SM 90.11 148.10

STREAKY SM 83.19

STREAM CD 243.37 252.26 256.35
SM 22.24 63.2 65.23 86.39
112.3 126.39 143.24 152.4
154.36 MD 174.2 198.8 VG 3.23
19.2 36.4 36.13 36.16 71.18
77.28 78.2

STREAM-BEDS SM 150.23

STREAMERS CD 238.16

STREAMING FO 148.17 CD 238.17
MD 167.22 VG 73.7 73.20 79.33

STREAM-IRRIGATED SM 153.18

STREAMS CD 243.22 245.3
MD 188.27

STREET CD 183.24 186.12 219.36
227.5 SM 29.22 36.11 36.15
37.36 38.5

STREETS CD 193.15 233.18
VG 3.25 43.23

STRENGTH LH 7.39 9.35 24.5
FO 145.6 CD 249.12 SM 6.29
12.14 21.24 87.15 87.16
MD 164.38 166.3 171.18 176.9
VG 9.30 23.41

STRENUOUS FO 135.33 178.28

STRENUOUSLY LH 4.39

STRESS LH 29.13 VG 55.30

STRETCH LH 23.24 FO 178.32
CD 262.27

STRETCHED FO 126.31 176.33
176.38 178.40 CD 235.9 237.33
SM 134.9 MD 198.33 202.2

STRETCHER SM 112.37

STRETCHES SM 78.21

STRETCHING FO 115.36 CD 190.10
206.24 MD 202.2 VG 31.33

STREWING SM 152.30

STREWN CD 243.27

STRICKEN TL 44.4

STRICT VG 16.26

STRICTLY SM 34.16 68.40 99.4
137.28

STRIDE FO 153.7 CD 238.21
SM 32.29 MD 164.12 174.29
196.25 199.22

STRIDENT CD 242.13

STRIDES CD 232.20 VG 73.22

STRIDING TL 93.22 FO 117.7
153.7 153.8 CD 243.4
SM 38.41 76.18 MD 195.15

STRIKE TL 74.25 74.26 74.39
74.41 74.42 FO 173.6
CD 201.13 256.5 SM 150.34

STRIKES SM 24.2

STRIKING CD 204.35 255.41
SM 9.33 53.7

STRING FO 172.38 MD 164.14
164.34 164.39 172.1
178.25 179.30 180.14
207.15

STRINGING SM 48.23

STRINGS CD 263.13

STRINGY SM 131.8

STRIP TL 102.41 MD 187.20

STRIPED LH 3.13 29.5
CD 204.22

STRIPES SM 116.7 116.10

STRIPPING CD 211.27

STRIVE FO 177.17

STRIVING FO 176.40 177.6
177.7 MD 174.27 180.28

STRODE LH 8.8 8.35 TL 105.38
FO 142.37 153.14 CD 238.20
243.1 247.33 MD 188.7
VG 25.9

STROKE FO 132.22 160.11
SM 19.26 153.29 VG 46.8
67.11

STROKED SM 13.29 19.19
VG 22.8

STROKES LH 25.13 TL 74.5

STROKING LH 33.19 FO 132.13
SM 47.35

STROLLED CD 183.31 VG 50.28
52.7

STROLLING CD 238.5 MD 172.9
VG 72.12

STRONG LH 3.28 14.7 20.12
23.10 TL 47.7 47.9 47.37
65.15 68.6 69.27 73.10
73.11 73.28 78.2 82.12
FO 123.3 140.21 149.21
156.22 157.2 CD 235.12
241.18 SM 5.17 6.28 52.15
57.25 72.3 78.5 95.12
95.13 96.1 97.32 131.8
133.40 137.36 MD 185.1

SUFFERING   TL 49.15   52.22   75.27
105.13   FO 128.39   SM 78.18
MD 191.1   193.7   193.10

SUFFERINGS   SM 77.37

SUFFICE   VG 26.10

SUFFICIENT   CD 209.38   224.38
224.39   255.25   255.42

SUFFICIENTLY   SM 18.18

SUFFISANCE   SM 18.30   101.29

SUFFOCATE   TL 92.34

SUFFOCATING   LH 3.22

SUFFUSION   SM 94.8

SUGAR   LH 29.25   SM 40.30   44.25
84.38

SUGAR-BOX   LH 26.35

SUGGEST   CD 249.3   257.41   258.6
SM 134.37   VG 42.24   65.42

SUGGESTED   TL 73.20   97.7
CD 248.40   248.42   SM 9.30
17.36   54.9

SUGGESTING   CD 248.35   VG 24.6

SUGGESTION   TL 75.35   91.10
FO 140.18   CD 249.1   SM 135.35
VG 38.14   38.21

SUGGESTIONS   VG 11.9

SUGGESTIVE   FO 140.14   CD 191.25
VG 25.12

SUGGESTS   TL 56.32   97.5   SM 114.7

SUICIDE   TL 95.33   95.34   95.37
96.4   VG 3.33

SUIT   FO 161.3   CD 233.31   235.26

SUITABLE   TL 70.21   SM 80.29

SUIT-CASE   VG 71.38

SUITE   SM 6.15

SUITS   SM 106.3

SULK   FO 154.1

SULKIER   FO 143.23

SULKILY   LH 8.32   MD 168.16

SULKY   LH 20.7   FO 142.40   143.6
164.37

SULLEN   LH 6.37   9.15   10.7
CD 253.3   254.9   MD 168.19
187.17

SULLEN-COLOURED   CD 252.27

SULLENLY   LH 6.24   10.6   20.3

SULLENLY (CONT.)   20.15   28.5
CD 253.36

SULPHATE   CD 253.2

SULPHUR   VG 68.4

SULTAN   CD 264.25

SULTRY   SM 94.28

SUMMAT   LH 18.41   19.39   30.5

SUMMER   TL 64.23   64.36   68.9
73.10   73.11   FO 115.21   115.41
137.13   139.13   149.12   168.18
CD 229.7   230.19   232.39   233.31
252.14   252.28   253.36   SM 52.13
57.5   60.19   74.1   74.4   126.12
133.32   133.40   143.39   144.9
144.13   151.32   151.37   151.38
152.18   VG 8.31   53.18

SUMMERS   SM 142.20   144.5

SUMMER-TIME   FO 114.39

SUMMERY   SM 13.22

SUMMIT   CD 248.37   253.11   SM 53.6

SUMMONS   TL 102.4

SUMPTUOUS   SM 148.28

SUMS   VG 26.9

SUN   LH 3.24   TL 56.24   56.26
56.29   56.35   56.40   57.1   57.9
57.16   57.17   57.18   59.21
59.22   67.14   67.17   98.29
FO 117.8   168.33   CD 235.10
237.23   241.34   242.22   242.36
245.3   256.16   SM 9.37   37.8
40.13   57.30   59.16   60.4   65.26
74.9   101.36   103.31   104.19
126.38   130.9   133.34   134.1
143.13   146.8   147.28   147.32
148.2   148.9   148.15   155.9
MD 170.3   170.7   170.11   170.13
170.20   170.36   170.37   178.24
179.32   180.4   180.15   185.3
185.14   185.21   186.3   187.25
188.27   189.12   189.13   189.24
189.30   189.40   190.20   192.9
193.29   194.6   195.39   196.29
196.35   197.4   197.23   197.24
197.26   198.32   198.38   199.6
199.19   201.39   202.7   206.28
207.13   208.25   209.10   VG 5.33
17.26   45.5   45.13   45.16   45.30
47.34   50.21   69.23   70.11
70.29   70.32   71.26   72.3   76.14
77.25

SUN-ARCHED   SM 13.35

SUNBEAMS   TL 67.15

SUNBURNT   SM 7.30

SUNDAY   SM 84.18

SUNDAYS   SM 28.27   VG 7.39

SUNDAY SCHOOL   SM 30.11   30.12
105.41   VG 8.1   9.38

SUNDOWN   LH 20.36   MD 196.28
VG 76.23

SUNFLOWERS   CD 228.32   229.10
SM 74.4   74.8   129.17   130.8
133.38   151.5

SUNK   SM 96.12   159.14

SUNKEN   SM 45.28

SUNLESS   CD 240.15

SUNLIGHT   LH 3.3   3.21   7.27
20.5   SM 146.20   VG 45.18

SUNLIT   VG 79.16

SUN-LOCKED   CD 254.4

SUNNY   TL 44.14   CD 194.35
SM 97.31   97.34   MD 180.6
181.26   VG 45.12   68.2
70.5   72.4

SUNRISE   SM 57.5

SUNS   MD 189.32   190.1   201.36
201.37   207.34   209.38
209.41   210.25

SUN'S   TL 67.18   MD 180.13
197.32

SUNSET   FO 116.8   CD 217.6
VG 75.33   76.30

SUNSHINE   LH 8.27   TL 59.40
67.9   67.17   98.10   CD 233.35
235.6   242.28   245.31   252.21
SM 11.1   42.35   127.18
128.20   152.23   MD 186.2
189.19   194.7   201.39   202.1
202.3   VG 47.8   48.11

SUP   CD 264.25

SUPERANNUATED   SM 75.36   75.38

SUPERB   TL 81.28   82.18

SUPERBLY   CD 215.5   249.33

SUPERCILIOUS   FO 143.20

SUPERCILIOUSNESS   TL 63.32

SUPER-CONSCIOUS   TL 99.6

SUPERFICIALITY   SM 14.40

SUPERIOR   FO 167.29

SUPERNATURAL   TL 75.27

SUPERNATURALLY   TL 100.26
FO 167.16

SUPERSTITION   SM 103.11

SUPERSTITIONS   VG 35.12

SUPERSTITIOUS   VG 33.27 34.38

SUPERVISE   VG 31.40

SUPPER   FO 117.13 117.17 157.38

SUPPLANTED   CD 250.14

SUPPLE   SM 90.13

SUPPLICATION   MD 201.21

SUPPLY   SM 30.1

SUPPORT   LH 10.30 SM 135.1

SUPPORTING   FO 128.6 SM 68.12
  MD 187.29 VG 67.27

SUPPOSE   TL 49.26 49.38 50.35
  61.31 71.17 73.12 77.27
  78.38 83.4 94.15 108.35
  109.9 FO 118.5 118.15 118.16
  121.18 123.38 125.18 125.27
  126.13 138.22 138.42 139.15
  150.8 151.11 170.27 171.7
  172.17 172.18 CD 188.16
  189.16 189.21 190.33 190.41
  191.35 195.32 200.14 204.9
  204.37 207.24 220.12 220.23
  220.30 258.20 259.37 264.23
  264.24 SM 34.14 43.26 46.36
  47.13 47.35 48.37 76.40
  79.35 80.4 80.22 80.23 81.6
  81.19 103.11 104.35 105.21
  111.18 113.35 116.4 121.33
  122.1 122.16 122.33 123.35
  155.28 VG 8.26 8.27 17.8
  26.27 55.18 55.21 55.27
  56.40 57.29 57.30 61.34
  79.12

SUPPOSED   CD 259.7 SM 95.23
  96.38 116.12 VG 26.7 55.25
  58.33

SUPPOSING   TL 69.11 69.13
  CD 264.35 SM 23.3 55.15
  106.21 106.26 106.34

SUPPRESSION   FO 167.8

SUPREME   TL 79.37 87.35 FO 131.9
  SM 20.4 70.40

SUPREMELY   VG 48.13

SURELY   TL 45.42 55.26 62.8
  77.19 104.5 CD 212.2 216.20
  SM 19.18 31.11 72.30 80.17
  96.30 120.22 143.37 MD 164.5
  178.30 VG 53.33

SURFACE   TL 53.32 FO 176.1 176.8
  CD 234.31 235.3 252.28 253.35
  254.12 254.18 SM 69.3 70.12
  70.26 71.19 130.18 143.14
  143.25 143.29 MD 190.10
  197.10 VG 15.9 23.32

SURGE   MD 172.18 VG 73.1

SURGING   SM 146.5 MD 202.35

SURLY   LH 11.41 12.33

SURNAMES   FO 113.1

SURPRISE   LH 26.17 28.28
  FO 155.36 156.4 CD 202.10
  220.5 SM 82.36 100.25 VG 32.4
  51.23

SURPRISED   LH 22.7 FO 118.5
  121.30 125.30 155.1 155.3
  156.6 SM 10.27 46.16 106.20
  114.25 159.18

SURPRISED-LOOKING   FO 137.8

SURPRISES   SM 43.15

SURPRISINGLY   TL 85.6

SURRENDER   FO 179.25

SURROUNDED   CD 223.13 240.27

SURROUNDING   LH 20.19

SURROUNDINGS   CD 230.10 SM 116.35
  118.24 118.25

SURVEY   SM 46.1

SURVEYED   SM 46.14 156.5

SURVIVED   TL 53.36 MD 174.7

SUSCEPTIBILITY   MD 176.19

SUSPECTED   TL 85.7 SM 27.8 29.16

SUSPENDED   FO 148.29 VG 75.2

SUSPENSE   LH 10.2 FO 173.30
  SM 68.22

SUSPICION   CD 199.17 211.36
  SM 67.36

SUSPICIONS   CD 211.5

SUSPICIOUS   FO 131.16 SM 58.12
  58.13 58.20

SUSPICIOUSLY   MD 182.19

SUSSEX   SM 27.20

SWALLOW   FO 141.35 178.2
  CD 204.10 240.8

SWALLOWED   FO 141.15 149.34
  MD 169.26 VG 15.31 65.21
  76.19

SWALLOWING   VG 15.33

SWALLOWS   CD 239.17

SWAM   CD 234.35 236.3 SM 143.8

SWAMPED   TL 92.36 VG 64.40

SWAMPS   SM 94.28

SWAN   TL 102.27 102.31 FO 121.17
  125.19 127.42

SWANS   TL 102.30 FO 115.3 135.38

SWARD   LH 3.5 3.13 15.25

SWARMING   CD 241.40 SM 144.3
  152.39 VG 64.39

SWARMS   SM 72.2

SWARTHY   LH 3.28 8.22
  TL 45.11 57.1 58.29
  61.22 84.11 85.39 SM 22.14
  VG 30.13 37.12

SWARTHY-TRANSPARENT   TL 59.25
  64.32

SWATHED   SM 44.40

SWATHING-BANDS   MD 166.23

SWATHS   TL 43.7

SWAY   TL 103.34 FO 132.35
  CD 247.26 MD 174.27 177.25
  209.40 209.41

SWAYED   LH 8.41 MD 170.38
  VG 36.34 74.20

SWAYING   LH 9.3 TL 68.4
  FO 175.25 176.3 CD 237.31
  SM 66.15 MD 172.14 203.3
  203.10

SWEAT   LH 8.19 34.20
  FO 120.16 CD 243.9 253.32

SWEATER   VG 54.14

SWEATING   CD 241.34 253.31
  254.5

SWEATY   FO 120.31

SWEEP   SM 46.33

SWEEPING   CD 230.7 SM 69.7
  127.3

SWEET   LH 3.21 38.28 TL 72.25
  73.1 74.18 FO 178.13
  CD 215.31 237.18 237.19
  238.26 SM 52.4 52.24 71.34
  110.19 151.15 151.16
  MD 179.20 189.9 203.1
  209.10 VG 41.31 50.18

SWEETENED   MD 177.22

SWEETEST   SM 84.12

SWEETLY   LH 16.21 FO 136.13

SWEET-WILLIAMS   SM 37.39

SWELLED   LH 5.23

SWELLING   VG 18.9

SWEPT   LH 7.33 7.39 36.35
  TL 43.13 CD 240.12 SM 69.5
  146.33 MD 170.6 186.18
  200.20 VG 3.14 35.29
  78.17

SWERVE   FO 172.36 CD 239.6

SWERVE (CONT.) CD 239.26 239.30
241.27 261.37 261.38

SWERVING SM 36.35

SWIFT LH 8.2 13.4 25.31
FO 173.33 SM 20.3 VG 5.32
17.15 36.13

SWIFTLY LH 8.8 21.3 22.23
CD 187.1 235.2 SM 91.36
MD 202.21 VG 74.17

SWIFTLY-RUNNING CD 262.25

SWIMMER VG 57.39

SWIMMING LH 20.14 FO 116.20
CD 234.31 234.34 235.1 235.20
235.38 237.34 SM 60.3

SWIMS TL 58.40

SWINDLE CD 217.13

SWINE SM 129.38

SWING LH 23.20 SM 31.25 36.8
38.12 38.38 39.24 MD 171.20
VG 36.35

SWINGING LH 21.1 FO 127.32
169.41 CD 239.11 239.37 243.2
MD 199.9 199.23 202.20
VG 21.7 24.2 24.36 37.6

SWIRL MD 195.16

SWIRLED VG 73.34

SWIRLING MD 196.24 VG 72.33

SWISH LH 30.40

SWISHED VG 16.9

SWISHING SM 57.31 MD 177.19
202.22

SWITCH SM 115.32 138.16

SWITCHED FO 147.34 SM 117.4
VG 25.15

SWOLLEN SM 71.10 71.14
MD 187.28 VG 70.22 71.23

SWOON TL 78.30 101.23 FO 132.31

SWOON-SLEEP TL 82.2

SWOOPED FO 173.38

SWOOPING CD 238.35

SWORD SM 72.2

SWORDS TL 43.1 43.32

SWORD-THRUST TL 45.37

SWUNG LH 7.26 7.32 FO 121.21
CD 234.26 235.34 SM 11.17
MD 186.7 198.2 209.5 VG 25.8

SYMBOL TL 97.9 SM 38.19

SYMBOLIC SM 139.12

SYMBOLS SM 144.37

SYMPATHETIC SM 125.33 146.22
VG 3.33

SYMPATHETICALLY LH 17.40 32.17

SYMPATHIES SM 83.20 83.38
VG 65.9

SYMPATHISE TL 83.31 CD 209.2

SYMPATHISED VG 4.4

SYMPATHY LH 10.31 TL 87.24
88.27 CD 224.27 SM 22.8 32.25
56.23 76.2 80.29 83.23 95.30
138.8 138.9 138.31 VG 3.17

SYRIAN MD 194.26

SYSTEM VG 54.9

TA LH 9.20

TABLE LH 29.25 31.10 TL 87.12
95.29 FO 117.14 122.10 122.13
122.27 127.34 128.6 136.7
142.1 142.3 142.41 143.4
144.12 156.2 156.18 156.25
CD 185.27 186.27 234.24
247.12 VG 9.15 14.10 14.39
32.22 32.25 51.7

TABLEAU VIVANT SM 10.14

TABLETS TL 68.22 68.23

TACITLY SM 6.31

TACITURN TL 93.25 SM 8.24 9.20

TACKLE CD 254.23

TACKLED SM 142.1

TACTFULLY SM 110.13

TADPOLE CD 203.14

TAIL LH 18.31 FO 148.34 148.36
149.24 CD 200.33 217.21
238.11 SM 146.19 MD 177.19
181.18 VG 17.4

TAIL-FEATHERS MD 167.22 172.6

TAILORED SM 8.19 18.12

TAILORING SM 5.38

TAILS CD 195.5 SM 57.32 128.29
144.35

TAINTED VG 26.35

TAKING LH 7.17 20.1 30.13
31.20 TL 52.36 94.6 FO 151.1
172.21 173.28 CD 213.19
242.10 259.30 SM 73.7 79.33
84.17 118.16 123.17 123.18

TAKING (CONT.) 123.28 158.24
MD 168.33 175.16 179.17
188.40 VG 9.27 16.3 45.15
45.25 47.17 47.26 51.41
52.32 58.11 60.4 69.36

TALE VG 80.38

TALISMAN TL 72.14

TALK LH 18.14 21.36 TL 53.22
54.41 54.42 56.12 56.22
58.3 58.7 58.8 77.21
77.22 96.17 98.37 98.38
FO 119.15 124.20 125.14
129.24 165.24 CD 214.5
215.20 215.21 217.11
221.25 221.32 222.18
223.22 230.16 249.33 264.8
SM 27.21 72.26 104.32
105.35 107.1 117.14 122.7
130.23 135.15 VG 16.24
16.36 44.11 57.22 58.4
61.5 62.4

TALKED LH 6.1 TL 55.35 98.30
98.35 99.22 FO 157.31
CD 218.26 230.31 230.37
SM 63.24 MD 189.4 189.23
VG 13.12 13.13 24.23 54.21

TALKER CD 230.14

TALKING LH 5.27 12.3 14.22
TL 44.25 46.15 48.33 53.23
53.37 58.7 91.21 98.32
FO 123.7 125.5 132.21
132.24 132.26 141.15
143.30 167.21 CD 187.39
199.36 200.1 200.31 214.2
221.26 221.34 222.7 223.10
231.3 231.19 259.35 262.25
SM 9.2 18.13 27.25 35.29
58.17 82.1 104.22 126.30
132.41 MD 182.11 VG 10.5
51.9 51.16 58.24

TALKS CD 199.42 SM 56.31

TALL LH 22.6 TL 46.20 46.28
47.1 51.24 52.9 52.10
52.32 52.36 62.19 69.24
81.7 84.17 85.38 FO 145.42
163.32 173.32 CD 187.5
234.23 234.31 245.16
247.32 SM 17.3 18.3 28.12
57.7 65.11 78.12 90.8
129.7 130.8 140.32 141.12
141.34 148.3 148.4 149.31
149.32 149.34 MD 191.20
VG 7.29 8.33 8.40 21.17
22.3 34.29 36.9 43.30
44.36 51.29 54.1 80.16

TALL-BUILT SM 38.22

TALLER LH 14.6

TALONS SM 151.36

TAME SM 50.12 50.20 50.21

TAMED SM 149.5

TAMELY SM 149.3

TEMPLE (CONT.) MD 210.17
  VG 67.25 67.26 67.29

TEMPLES CD 187.7 214.37
  SM 139.11 MD 193.6 VG 23.35

TEMPT LH 15.35

TEMPTATION CD 226.27

TEMPTATIONS CD 206.38

TEMPTED CD 226.23 226.33
  SM 96.36

TEMPTING VG 49.9

TEN LH 30.30 32.15 35.35
  TL 54.7 62.2 85.17 100.16
  FO 114.42 128.3 158.5 165.32
  175.10 CD 219.22 SM 29.13
  44.36 57.2 VG 31.19 74.38

TENACIOUS FO 176.11

TENDED SM 32.20 MD 187.36
  VG 31.34

TENDENCIES FO 115.6 VG 63.6

TENDENCY FO 114.5

TENDER TL 58.21 FO 145.22
  154.26 164.10 SM 86.27 134.16
  143.17 151.6 151.32 151.33
  MD 196.10 196.12 196.15
  196.22 201.39 204.24 207.26
  207.40 209.12 VG 9.23 20.3
  31.33 38.22 43.28 46.11 48.6
  62.35 76.5

TENDERER FO 155.29

TENDERLY LH 13.34 26.7 26.11
  39.15 FO 136.34 176.4
  SM 125.7

TENDERNESS LH 34.12 TL 93.24
  FO 145.23 153.24 159.8
  SM 120.33 125.8 MD 171.40
  196.15 207.27 207.39 VG 38.8
  48.2 54.28 57.34 68.13

TENDING SM 38.23

TENDRILS LH 13.6

TENNIS SM 113.24 VG 44.27

TENSE TL 52.21 SM 11.19 13.30
  21.25 124.10 147.4

TENSELY SM 13.19

TENSION FO 152.25 178.33
  CD 220.41 SM 4.12 6.24 24.19
  26.3 26.18 26.21 26.23 73.20
  75.9 127.6 137.12 VG 31.23
  77.19

TENTACLES VG 77.18

TENTATIVELY VG 78.8

TENTS FO 167.19

TEPID SM 81.11 81.12

TER LH 3.32 4.9 9.20 9.24
  16.5 37.13 37.15 37.26 37.30
  37.39 38.5 38.17 VG 15.39

TERMINUS CD 257.6

TERMS CD 252.1 252.2

TERRACE TL 59.38 60.29 62.18
  CD 230.25 VG 72.39 72.40

TERRACES MD 185.30

TERRA-COTTA MD 199.2 200.25

TERRIBLE LH 10.2 TL 45.24 49.19
  50.5 75.24 75.25 76.6 78.23
  79.9 101.41 101.41 160.11
  160.16 173.9 173.13 176.31
  CD 207.5 208.12 215.9 220.19
  220.35 230.29 241.15 244.40
  247.26 247.40 252.35 255.13
  262.9 SM 4.32 6.17 15.1 15.6
  15.16 27.15 29.25 34.34 42.3
  47.11 48.17 67.17 67.38
  95.12 96.1 96.37 111.41
  122.25 MD 176.14 194.19
  196.16 203.20 VG 77.8

TERRIBLY TL 78.12 FO 138.10
  168.4 CD 199.32 206.26 206.30
  232.29 253.10 SM 5.7 7.11
  14.32 22.8 58.25 66.25 78.7
  93.23 96.3 153.9 157.32
  VG 8.35

TERRIFIC CD 242.35 SM 20.6
  36.36 45.19 MD 167.28
  VG 25.33

TERRIFICALLY SM 58.11 66.36

TERRIFIED CD 197.17 201.33
  MD 203.39 VG 78.24 79.1

TERRIFYING SM 16.4 46.2

TERRITORY MD 163.8

TERROR TL 51.23 101.17 101.20
  FO 136.33 CD 222.13 252.38
  255.23 SM 24.21 24.31 36.13
  36.17 86.29 86.30 MD 169.17
  169.19 187.9 203.33 206.4
  211.7 VG 29.14 76.26 79.14

TERRORS MD 169.22

TESTILY FO 138.18 SM 82.12

TETHER MD 164.22 172.3

TEWKESBURY'S, LADY (SEE LADY
  TEWKESBURY'S)

TEXAN SM 129.22 129.34 130.28
  130.33 131.29

TEXANS SM 129.7 129.30

TEXAS SM 3.25 10.30 29.14 74.7
  91.25 94.30 116.13 123.21
  129.2

TH' LH 5.20 14.24 19.11
  25.22 26.3 26.21 29.2
  31.14 31.15 32.23 37.1
  38.3 38.5 38.10 38.15
  39.8 VG 15.38 15.39

THA LH 3.31 3.32 3.35 4.7
  4.17 4.18 4.41 5.3 8.42
  9.12 14.18 16.5 17.34
  22.42 23.27 26.14 38.9
  38.17 VG 15.38 15.39

THA'D LH 3.32 4.10 38.4

THAIGH LH 9.25 38.1

THAIR LH 36.41

THA'LL LH 9.10

THANK LH 32.38 TL 52.16
  53.2 53.4 54.19 65.13
  71.22 94.6 FO 144.16
  166.13 168.8 CD 193.3
  196.33 198.16 201.33
  205.31 208.17 215.5
  223.26 227.9 240.6 243.15
  263.25 265.19 SM 39.35
  40.4 40.6 43.18 43.32
  46.30 53.12 65.8 84.16
  94.2 113.13 132.17
  MD 178.13 VG 4.40 53.1
  53.5 81.6

THANKED SM 65.2 VG 15.3

THANKFUL FO 172.1 172.7
  CD 208.14 225.20 256.10
  SM 27.37 35.8 93.27

THANKFULNESS SM 140.14

THANKING VG 79.38

THANKS TL 65.23 73.11 74.20
  84.22 SM 36.3 MD 195.6
  VG 14.27 31.36 45.8 47.17
  70.30

THA'RT LH 9.1 9.10 37.41

THATCH SM 29.5

THATCHED SM 29.4

THAW SM 143.22 VG 45.13

THAWED TL 91.29

THEATRICAL SM 148.23 VG 26.2

THE-BEST-EVER SM 27.12

THEE LH 5.15 9.10 26.14
  26.15 38.2 38.20 TL 71.9
  MD 183.24 195.19 195.23
  195.24 209.17 209.18

THEFT SM 152.14

THE GREAT GOAT PAN SM 53.39

THEIRS MD 210.5

THEMSELVES LH 7.35 9.26

THORN (CONT.) FO 167.13 174.10
  CD 264.1 264.2

THOROUGH CD 231.36

THOROUGHLY FO 124.14 SM 45.37
  66.24 126.18

THOU SM 128.1 MD 178.30 183.25
  183.29 195.19 197.16 197.18
  197.20 209.14 209.16 209.22
  209.30 211.5 211.6

THOUGHT LH 3.35 7.22 8.32 8.40
  17.18 20.34 21.18 21.36
  25.10 27.3 27.35 28.16 29.36
  TL 47.22 50.9 50.27 53.14
  66.35 68.19 68.20 68.21
  68.24 68.30 69.5 69.17 69.21
  69.25 69.27 70.9 70.20 70.28
  70.29 70.32 72.11 72.34
  73.30 75.19 77.38 82.34
  82.35 83.15 89.40 89.41 93.1
  98.40 109.7 109.9 FO 118.19
  118.41 120.27 129.41 130.4
  130.6 130.9 130.14 133.37
  134.12 136.42 139.10 139.26
  141.6 154.16 154.42 155.22
  157.13 157.20 163.28 163.29
  166.13 168.13 171.9 171.41
  173.4 176.17 179.6 CD 193.36
  196.18 196.19 200.2 200.5
  201.33 202.5 209.4 209.5
  209.7 209.30 210.14 211.23
  211.29 211.33 213.27 214.12
  214.15 214.30 215.10 215.15
  216.18 217.1 217.3 219.2
  219.33 220.9 222.2 223.16
  223.17 223.18 225.3 226.8
  226.30 236.23 241.16 250.14
  250.20 262.3 262.42 SM 7.14
  10.19 12.24 17.40 19.31
  29.13 35.11 37.27 38.11
  38.25 40.11 47.2 47.32 48.12
  50.4 51.4 51.32 58.37 61.3
  69.1 70.3 70.4 70.6 72.35
  72.38 87.10 89.23 98.1 99.9
  102.2 105.9 108.5 110.30
  113.35 114.19 118.10 121.13
  121.19 121.22 135.21 138.38
  149.39 153.18 MD 172.31 180.6
  180.17 182.20 184.9 201.8
  205.4 206.13 207.28 208.4
  208.8 VG 5.2 10.16 20.6
  26.25 27.6 27.13 28.11 29.7
  30.4 30.36 31.16 38.32 40.11
  41.14 41.19 41.40 42.14
  44.11 45.26 51.33 53.10
  58.29 60.26 61.1 62.15 62.22
  63.16 64.36 79.5 79.39

THOUGHTFUL FO 126.15 SM 40.32
  VG 31.15

THOUGHTFULLY LH 35.7

THOUGHTLESS TL 103.21

THOUGHTS LH 27.9 TL 77.4
  FO 137.4 137.14 CD 216.42
  263.10 MD 177.30 VG 61.7
  64.29

THOU'RT LH 8.16

THOUSAND TL 63.17 94.1
  SM 141.17 146.32

THOUSANDS SM 45.12 MD 205.35

THOWT LH 3.32 17.27 38.3

THRASHED MD 191.30

THREAD TL 100.31 100.33
  FO 142.6 155.7 CD 187.24
  192.33 192.36 192.39 SM 20.22
  31.17 141.27

THREADED CD 256.14 263.13

THREADING CD 253.15 VG 39.36

THREADS FO 137.34 CD 192.13
  243.26 MD 193.7

THREAT CD 213.17 SM 14.35
  VG 66.2

THREATENED LH 9.11 TL 46.37
  VG 66.1

THREATENING SM 36.26

THREATENINGLY LH 9.20

THREE LH 7.28 7.35 7.42 14.20
  23.2 TL 62.13 87.2 95.40
  99.12 99.15 99.17 102.29
  FO 120.29 120.32 121.9 167.21
  169.25 169.37 172.41 CD 196.7
  198.19 198.23 198.25 205.16
  205.40 212.25 213.26 213.39
  213.41 226.3 228.33 234.34
  235.26 235.42 237.28 237.34
  255.40 257.11 257.19 258.2
  SM 3.10 8.25 23.27 59.2
  96.34 MD 163.12 163.23 163.34
  178.36 185.26 199.13 VG 9.22
  20.32 26.15 37.20 45.31
  46.15 48.9 53.17

THREE-PETALLED SM 151.13

THREE QUARTERS SM 77.23

THREE-ROOMED SM 143.1

THREE THOUSAND CD 264.30

THREE-TOED FO 114.22

THRESHOLD CD 184.33 SM 38.4

THREW LH 4.19 4.22 16.12
  TL 52.1 FO 124.13 148.9
  CD 186.35 SM 21.24 87.30
  101.18 130.6 143.12 145.37
  MD 163.18 171.39 188.1 195.21
  VG 47.24

THRILL LH 25.26 TL 66.8
  SM 136.16 158.3

THRILLED LH 33.18 TL 66.31
  66.33 79.32 CD 242.4 244.6
  245.30 256.14 SM 52.29 94.33
  145.33 VG 10.4 53.16 77.34

THRILLING LH 23.42 TL 66.10

THRILLING (CONT.) SM 18.15
  31.37 137.5 VG 25.23

THRILLS SM 94.31

THROAT TL 46.30 52.2 54.1
  61.5 78.1 FO 135.7 155.25
  156.22 CD 193.6 201.15
  238.42 261.6 SM 34.31
  MD 186.9 188.17 VG 24.11

THROB TL 102.4

THROBBING TL 67.22 67.27
  SM 97.22

THRONE VG 6.5

THRONED VG 5.17

THRONGING MD 167.3

THROUGHOUT TL 43.26 55.36
  101.19

THROW TL 103.39 FO 158.22
  CD 192.35 206.37 SM 44.31
  44.33 MD 210.34

THROWING LH 37.24 CD 254.28
  SM 105.16 MD 171.6

THROWN LH 37.22 TL 83.20
  101.21 FO 122.18 CD 187.25
  SM 16.2 17.21 18.31 69.36
  69.38 105.18 119.18
  MD 176.20 188.11 VG 71.17

THROWS TL 73.40 SM 71.6

THRUST LH 8.41 TL 74.23
  FO 127.2 149.6 CD 241.17
  244.29 SM 31.25 MD 198.23
  VG 65.34

THRUSTING FO 120.20 121.1

THUD VG 74.12

THUDS VG 76.24

THUD-THUD FO 168.35

THUMBS VG 42.19

THUNDER SM 24.19 36.26
  134.1 152.2 152.21 152.22
  VG 74.12

THUNDERBOLT SM 36.25 VG 34.16

THUNDERING LH 21.15

THUNDERSTORMS SM 74.2 133.33

THUR LH 5.3

THURSDAY VG 45.5

THUS LH 11.40 SM 67.16
  143.21

THWART MD 201.17 201.25
  201.26

TITLE CD 200.12 SM 4.37 88.14

TITLES CD 200.15 200.25 200.28
　　SM 10.37

TOAD VG 15.27

TOAD-LIKE VG 65.36 65.38

TOADS VG 65.39

TOAD'S VG 65.31

TOAST CD 228.33

TOASTED LH 39.18

TOBACCO CD 185.23 216.29
　　VG 49.34

TO-DAY LH 14.25 TL 47.37 67.35
　　90.20 CD 205.5 205.42 208.4
　　208.13 221.14 221.18 236.24
　　236.26 236.29 237.1 249.9
　　249.10 263.37 264.3 SM 49.29
　　81.22 93.29 108.27 MD 193.27
　　VG 38.6 58.16 70.37

TO-DAYS VG 58.18

TODDLING VG 23.26 53.7

TOE TL 79.15 CD 234.39 SM 22.41
　　65.11 89.28

TOES LH 33.16 MD 171.6 174.29

TOGA MD 198.18

TOGETHER LH 7.28 16.34 23.13
　　29.36 35.36 37.38 38.23
　　TL 45.40 67.28 72.3 81.31
　　87.14 87.22 88.5 91.15 91.36
　　99.18 FO 113.2 125.15 130.33
　　131.14 144.35 151.29 161.17
　　162.13 162.15 165.35 167.5
　　CD 191.27 191.29 191.36
　　196.14 196.16 207.18 226.22
　　232.8 241.42 SM 6.21 6.26
　　50.13 99.12 124.9 129.10
　　MD 165.10 176.34 181.29
　　188.13 196.4 200.1 VG 24.23
　　35.29 47.8 50.3 53.34 55.13
　　58.25 75.27 78.19

TOILED LH 8.19 CD 254.1
　　VG 17.40

TOILET LH 36.27

TOILING FO 153.4 CD 241.19
　　MD 206.13

TOLERANCE SM 41.19

TOLL CD 240.36

TOMB SM 126.25 MD 166.21 170.4
　　172.21 173.13 178.37 180.20
　　180.26 180.27

TOMBED CD 221.12 221.13

TOM-CAT TL 67.41 CD 201.26
　　SM 47.38

TOMFOOLERY FO 130.24 130.25
　　132.9 132.14

TOMMIES CD 219.8 VG 51.21

TOMMY VG 59.18 ?4

TO-MORROW TL 71.38 82.42
　　FO 150.9 150.10 171.11 171.12
　　CD 198.9 198.10 202.15 202.21
　　219.13 236.23 236.27 236.41
　　237.2 265.25 266.7 266.14
　　SM 51.33 84.22 87.11 93.31
　　105.17 109.37 111.31 117.24
　　118.19 MD 211.24 VG 13.26
　　14.37 41.24 58.16

TO-MORROWS VG 58.18

TONE LH 3.7 5.8 5.21 10.13
　　11.21 12.9 12.33 12.34 14.15
　　19.12 22.25 23.34 25.34 26.3
　　TL 43.18 49.28 55.17 63.30
　　63.32 79.1 79.6 94.5
　　FO 125.38 134.39 140.19
　　142.23 150.18 158.3 159.16
　　159.35 169.32 171.28 173.16
　　173.19 CD 183.27 191.25
　　203.19 211.42 213.17 213.27
　　246.11 261.32 SM 9.39 39.18
　　41.31 41.36 52.18 57.20
　　79.29 79.34 82.34 120.11
　　157.30 VG 51.23

TONES LH 5.26 13.21 27.34
　　CD 199.39 226.24 258.7
　　SM 34.25 52.38 58.24 107.25
　　112.35 113.3 VG 24.23

TONG-TONG-TONG CD 244.13

TONGUE TL 51.27 CD 243.39
　　257.38 SM 114.31 154.21
　　MD 185.17 187.25 VG 57.25

TO-NIGHT LH 20.30 36.11
　　FO 135.26 136.22 138.24
　　138.30 155.16 CD 191.39
　　192.19 201.31 202.17
　　SM 105.14 VG 40.35 40.40

TOO-BECOMING TL 87.4

TOOL-BOX FO 160.27

TOOLS LH 15.11 26.32 26.35
　　VG 47.9 49.2

TOP LH 6.1 7.18 24.28 24.33
　　25.39 37.19 TL 46.31 60.5
　　70.24 81.20 92.33 FO 145.28
　　147.3 148.15 152.12 154.36
　　156.20 156.21 167.4 169.18
　　172.19 172.26 172.40 173.6
　　CD 201.1 221.22 236.13 252.35
　　253.14 254.7 SM 26.5 41.2
　　46.13 66.31 90.8 139.32
　　MD 164.40 187.29 200.22
　　VG 18.31 18.32 21.21 22.22
　　24.8 45.22 48.31 48.34 70.26
　　77.37 78.26 78.29 80.19

TOPPING SM 113.20

TOPS TL 56.41 SM 152.3
　　MD 200.14 VG 18.12

TOQUE TL 54.16

TORE LH 24.3 MD 192.13
　　VG 74.41

TORMENT LH 3.33 TL 48.9 82.11
　　FO 179.11 SM 34.10 VG 80.16

TORMENTED LH 5.36 TL 63.15
　　SM 33.19 MD 180.19 188.18

TORN MD 166.21 188.10 204.15
　　VG 73.17 78.9

TORN-OPEN VG 78.6

TORN-OUT VG 79.15

TORRENT LH 11.24

TORRENTS SM 68.13

TORTOISE LH 11.6

TORTOISES VG 65.39

TORTOISE-SHELL VG 53.39

TORTURE LH 10.26 11.14
　　TL 99.41 FO 174.39 174.40

TORTURED MD 196.9 VG 41.32
　　77.23

TOSS MD 181.39

TOSSED LH 8.25 CD 183.11

TOSSES SM 105.26

TOUCH LH 4.1 27.12 TL 44.31
　　55.31 55.38 61.2 63.32
　　70.40 77.1 78.24 78.26
　　84.6 103.18 103.22 106.21
　　106.22 FO 126.31 131.42
　　133.2 155.18 161.19
　　CD 187.8 195.8 197.2
　　203.19 209.1 211.19 221.42
　　230.33 231.40 250.6 257.27
　　SM 6.17 12.21 12.31 15.23
　　15.29 25.34 27.12 44.14
　　47.17 47.33 74.3 74.26
　　74.34 80.41 98.21 101.12
　　107.11 107.22 107.26
　　107.29 108.11 108.14
　　108.17 108.21 108.23
　　112.35 117.35 117.38
　　139.18 MD 166.18 173.29
　　173.30 175.39 176.23
　　177.37 178.23 179.37
　　182.5 184.4 188.26 195.32
　　195.34 196.8 196.9 196.10
　　196.20 196.22 201.38
　　202.24 205.10 205.15
　　207.34 208.15 208.16
　　208.20 208.23 208.25
　　208.31 208.35 209.37
　　210.3 210.5 211.19 VG 3.8
　　17.3 38.5 42.23 43.30
　　45.17 52.22

TOUCHED LH 22.13 29.18 29.37

TOUCHED (CONT.) LH 31.4 33.17
   33.25 TL 79.41 83.10 97.27
   FO 133.16 CD 184.38 186.30
   193.5 244.38 SM 29.20 62.21
   68.1 98.37 101.12 101.17
   107.34 MD 167.17 176.31
   180.41 193.5 193.12 193.14
   193.15 201.5 207.17 207.19
   207.31 VG 5.18 27.37

TOUCHES LH 22.9 CD 192.6
   SM 103.37 139.6 MD 208.10

TOUCHING LH 14.16 TL 80.13
   102.20 CD 186.28 186.39
   187.11 213.20 SM 21.14 44.4
   47.35 128.29 146.19 MD 166.17
   186.37 198.32 201.38 VG 39.11

TOUCHY SM 12.14

TOUGH TL 73.6 SM 96.28 96.32
   130.5 151.5 MD 163.8

TOUGH-NECKED SM 134.35

TOUR SM 127.25

TOUR DE FORCE CD 199.15

TOURIST CD 240.25 SM 128.19

TOURIST (SEE MR. TOURIST)

TOURISTS CD 240.18 240.37 241.2
   241.23 241.35 241.37 244.23
   245.10 245.28 252.4 254.3
   257.2 257.10 260.7 SM 127.25
   127.26 128.9 132.15 132.28
   140.24

TOURISTY CD 241.40

TOUSLING MD 171.40

TOUTE LA MEME CHOSE CD 203.41

TOW SM 8.14

TOWEL VG 47.21 75.12 75.21
   75.26 75.31 76.3 76.19 76.34

TOWELS VG 79.24

TOWER SM 43.2 MD 185.27 VG 75.5

TOWN LH 23.23 FO 152.27
   CD 186.25 194.12 208.8 211.39
   212.6 212.36 218.26 219.21
   226.36 229.18 230.21 232.3
   232.19 232.40 237.15 237.38
   238.2 238.35 SM 5.23 117.24
   118.20 121.13 132.17
   MD 166.40 VG 4.13 13.12 14.11
   31.18 70.19 72.7

TOWN-DAY CD 238.22

TOWNS SM 97.30 102.20

TOY CD 257.13

TOYS CD 195.34 195.37

TRACE TL 70.32 CD 228.29

TRACED CD 246.17 VG 18.10

TRACES SM 109.35

TRACING VG 22.11

TRACK TL 87.20 CD 253.18
   SM 6.39 24.15 63.32 66.28

TRACKS TL 101.38

TRADE LH 17.35 CD 228.25
   SM 136.13 141.36 142.29 144.4

TRADED VG 6.15

TRADER SM 142.1 142.17 142.29
   142.39 143.4 144.13 145.12
   154.7 154.12

TRADESMAN FO 113.9

TRADES-UNION SM 106.8

TRADITION TL 57.20 SM 31.20
   VG 7.13

TRADITIONS TL 61.12 61.14

TRAFFIC SM 21.21

TRAGIC VG 3.34

TRAIL TL 69.26 CD 195.6 199.39
   SM 60.11 130.7 134.18

TRAILED FO 169.23 SM 39.6 60.39
   VG 19.3 60.18 60.34

TRAILING FO 148.27 CD 214.25
   VG 27.36 59.41

TRAILS SM 129.16

TRAIN TL 64.29 FO 119.26 121.18
   150.3 150.6 152.27 164.32
   164.35 164.40 165.3 CD 226.35
   VG 10.25 18.20

TRAINED VG 54.36

TRAMP LH 17.19 18.9 18.16
   19.28 19.31 32.6 FO 143.22

TRAMPED VG 16.37

TRAMPLE SM 33.9 33.14

TRAMPLED SM 143.26

TRAMPLING SM 33.16

TRAMPS FO 119.7

TRANCE LH 15.28 TL 90.16
   FO 171.23 171.30

TRANCED TL 63.7

TRANSCENDENCE MD 207.20

TRANSCENDENT TL 82.26

TRANSFERENCE VG 3.27

TRANSFERRED CD 260.13

TRANSFERRING VG 52.33

TRANSFIGURED TL 74.2

TRANSFIXED FO 131.39
   SM 127.33 MD 167.36

TRANSFORMATION LH 34.22

TRANSFUSING VG 21.25

TRANSIENT FO 132.22 SM 112.28

TRANSITORY SM 126.32

TRANSLATE TL 71.10

TRANSLUCENCY TL 84.12
   CD 255.28

TRANSLUCENT TL 51.9 84.6
   CD 253.36 255.27 SM 151.20
   MD 180.12 191.34

TRANSPARENT TL 57.1 58.26
   61.22 62.24 SM 128.35
   MD 169.24

TRAP SM 46.4 126.24 133.26
   VG 65.28 65.32

TRAVEL SM 124.3

TRAVELLED SM 97.28 132.10
   148.12 VG 10.25

TRAVELLERS SM 132.28

TRAVELLING CD 202.20 SM 124.7
   128.28 148.3 MD 167.11
   199.11

TRAY FO 122.5 122.7 138.26
   138.32 157.36 CD 185.23
   227.31 235.14 SM 42.25
   113.25 MD 199.39

TREACHEROUS SM 72.31 72.36
   VG 52.27 52.28 56.1

TREACHERY SM 70.39

TREAD LH 25.33 VG 30.6

TREADING CD 240.39 VG 30.6

TREASURE TL 107.20 SM 100.5
   141.28

TREAT FO 154.23 154.24 154.25
   CD 265.4 SM 30.13

TREATED VG 31.5

TREATING FO 165.22

TREBLE TL 98.25

TREE LH 7.6 7.21 15.16
   15.24 20.24 21.10 36.36
   37.18 TL 56.33 72.25 98.15
   FO 146.4 152.37 154.37
   168.19 168.28 168.35

TREE (CONT.)   FO 169.16 169.25
 171.22 171.39 173.2 173.4
 173.18 173.33 CD 234.25
 243.27 244.16 SM 54.25 57.26
 71.6 101.1 101.4 103.9
 103.40 150.1 156.5 MD 180.12
 196.31 198.6 198.27 199.18
 209.16 211.23 VG 17.2 17.9
 22.16 68.26 70.8 74.37

TREE-COVERED MD 185.16

TREE-FELLING FO 173.26

TREES LH 4.35 21.5 22.6 23.18
 34.34 TL 56.41 62.19 73.9
 74.9 97.40 98.3 98.6 98.12
 FO 116.15 116.17 116.21
 117.30 117.36 118.25 135.41
 143.35 145.36 146.18 146.26
 152.31 154.35 168.15 168.17
 169.19 176.13 CD 234.20
 234.23 234.24 238.37 239.8
 239.26 239.35 240.12 240.14
 240.16 240.24 240.27 240.29
 240.34 240.40 241.10 243.12
 244.18 260.12 263.5 SM 8.37
 21.40 39.24 40.13 57.6 59.2
 60.1 60.6 60.19 71.25 78.10
 87.27 90.31 94.27 101.38
 103.2 103.8 103.9 103.20
 104.12 111.14 125.28 140.35
 143.20 146.30 150.10 150.18
 152.5 MD 168.20 173.36 185.6
 190.21 190.34 191.18 192.17
 199.14 199.16 202.17 202.21
 209.1 209.9 VG 17.15 17.22
 17.37 17.39 18.3 18.5 18.37
 36.18 71.14 71.25 72.11
 72.17 73.1 75.34

TREE-TRUNK SM 150.7

TREMBLE FO 160.32 SM 56.13
 56.36

TREMBLED LH 29.38 TL 101.20
 FO 140.21 SM 74.30 MD 202.23

TREMBLES FO 177.23

TREMBLING LH 29.6 TL 44.8
 FO 126.36 174.33 SM 33.33
 67.19 MD 205.25 VG 35.31
 74.32

TREMENDOUS LH 9.39

TREMENDOUSLY FO 124.15 SM 91.14
 114.25

TREMORS LH 33.15 FO 147.13

TREMULOUS MD 171.21 196.19
 VG 40.18

TREMULOUSLY FO 135.39 MD 196.32

TRENCHES TL 64.6

TREPIDATION LH 22.21

TRESPASS MD 179.38 203.21

TRESPASSING LH 34.35 FO 113.26

TRESTLE FO 131.22

TREWS CD 183.13 197.27 227.24

TRIAL FO 136.21 CD 210.5

TRIANGLE TL 91.34 FO 143.13

TRIBE SM 20.21 VG 22.28

TRIBES TL 90.22

TRICK CD 207.31 SM 66.28 97.16

TRICKED SM 149.3

TRICKLE LH 30.40

TRICKLED CD 253.40 VG 47.26

TRICKLES CD 253.32

TRICKLING LH 8.20 CD 241.36
 SM 141.27 155.23

TRICKS CD 221.8 221.9 221.13
 SM 12.16 95.27 98.27

TRIED LH 9.4 9.23 27.38
 TL 72.4 72.14 FO 125.11
 160.38 168.27 176.28 176.30
 CD 210.27 254.27 262.29
 SM 24.30 97.11 97.12 152.15
 MD 179.40 184.10 205.28
 VG 6.42 12.10 27.1 33.13
 41.1 48.5 64.18 75.28

TRIES LH 19.42 TL 54.8
 CD 222.17

TRIFLE CD 207.36 SM 12.20 18.14
 28.32

TRIFLES VG 34.2

TRILLED VG 33.39 35.30

TRILLING VG 38.42

TRIM TL 67.40 CD 195.2

TRIMMED SM 119.9

TRIMMING SM 44.19

TRINKETS CD 223.4

TRIP CD 261.15 SM 116.7 116.14
 138.10 VG 16.3

TRIPOD VG 47.8 47.32

TRIPPERS CD 240.18 257.10

TRIPPING SM 143.25

TRIPS SM 3.30 95.1

TRIUMPH CD 244.6 SM 56.38 71.24
 96.10 MD 164.31 171.3 171.33
 174.4 174.5 174.7 175.35
 175.36 176.2 192.25 VG 45.39

TRIUMPHANCE TL 98.23

TRIUMPHANT CD 250.39 251.20
 253.20 260.28 SM 30.19
 MD 203.41 VG 64.17

TRIUMPHANT-LOOKING VG 24.37

TRIUMPHANTLY SM 25.21
 MD 171.35 193.29

TRIVIAL LH 24.19 FO 157.32

TRIVIALITY SM 14.40

TRIXIE VG 37.27

TROD CD 217.33 MD 198.35

TRODDEN LH 26.32

TROOPED VG 13.17

TROPICAL CD 221.7

TROT SM 24.30 106.11
 VG 37.3

TROTTED LH 23.13 CD 261.9
 SM 59.22 94.9 MD 199.34
 VG 16.39 17.5

TROTTING SM 20.30 22.2
 59.16 63.31 93.5 97.25
 97.27 MD 199.25 199.28

TROUBLE TL 54.22 60.17
 FO 113.35 126.9 129.12
 129.14 167.41 168.7
 CD 188.11 190.39 194.25
 194.28 194.29 218.29
 SM 16.13 37.10 74.27
 93.25 MD 195.25 196.7
 210.10

TROUBLED FO 128.16 SM 61.38
 MD 209.32

TROUBLES TL 57.36 CD 225.27

TROUBLING FO 126.7 VG 31.16

TROUGH LH 3.23 21.19 21.21
 21.22 21.37 29.34 36.27
 SM 57.25

TROUSER CD 205.7

TROUSERS CD 184.2 184.6
 184.15 184.16 214.39
 228.38 238.6 238.13 SM 4.5
 VG 20.20 23.25 43.10 43.40
 44.6 49.42 54.14 75.23

TROUSER-SEAT CD 255.33

TROUSSEAU VG 54.19

TRUDGED CD 243.16 VG 19.15

TRUDGING VG 19.9

TRUE LH 37.5 37.8 TL 52.31
 57.4 66.39 66.40 67.4
 67.11 67.15 67.21 67.27
 74.41 77.39 79.2 84.2
 84.33 87.25 106.3 106.31

TWO (CONT.) FO 113.23 115.18
  119.11 120.41 125.7 128.6
  129.25 134.3 136.17 143.26
  143.29 143.38 144.15
  150.37 152.11 153.22 154.35
  154.41 156.2 161.16 162.13
  163.15 164.25 165.8 168.17
  169.3 169.18 169.27 169.33
  171.1 173.32 174.25 CD 184.42
  185.24 185.25 190.36 193.20
  195.7 195.18 196.8 196.25
  196.35 201.13 204.20 206.1
  206.15 208.31 212.5 218.21
  226.3 226.17 228.32 231.29
  232.7 238.32 238.41 240.39
  241.8 241.33 241.36 243.29
  243.33 244.23 245.19 245.31
  247.29 252.22 253.4 254.23
  255.9 255.38 260.10 261.7
  261.8 261.9 SM 4.26 9.33
  13.10 19.32 22.12 26.7 32.16
  32.18 34.33 35.1 37.9 44.34
  45.23 51.39 56.41 59.10 62.7
  63.21 71.17 72.11 74.40
  79.24 84.29 87.26 87.39 88.6
  88.38 88.40 90.28 91.32
  93.22 93.23 93.39 94.4
  104.30 107.10 112.31 112.33
  118.34 124.9 132.34 133.1
  133.28 135.6 141.11 142.3
  145.14 145.15 145.21 145.24
  147.19 150.15 155.6 MD 182.11
  185.17 186.7 186.35 187.31
  189.8 199.1 199.25 199.34
  199.36 200.4 VG 3.2 3.12
  3.29 8.32 9.1 10.27 10.30
  11.9 14.31 15.10 15.14 17.17
  20.29 20.39 22.2 23.22 24.23
  24.41 25.28 30.33 34.5 37.20
  40.5 40.19 47.6 50.30 51.9
  52.3 52.4 52.31 53.25 54.37
  56.25 68.35 71.35 71.40
  73.17 74.31 79.23 80.35

TWO-HANDFUL LH 5.25

TWO HUNDRED SM 128.9

TWO-LEGGED VG 29.40

TWO-PENCE FO 136.36

TWO-ROOMED SM 143.2

TWO THOUSAND SM 143.15

TYING SM 37.40 38.1

TYPE CD 210.13 210.18 SM 43.22
  VG 44.39

TYRANNY TL 88.2 88.13

TYROL CD 229.7 230.26 231.33
  239.15 252.9 SM 115.30

TYROLESE CD 229.18 232.6 233.12
  238.36

UGH VG 49.22

UGLILY FO 163.35

UGLINESS MD 193.11

UGLY LH 33.36 TL 46.14 87.6
  FO 142.26 SM 59.24 MD 193.1
  VG 3.21 9.4 25.38

ULTIMATE MD 184.1

ULTIMATELY SM 18.22 153.12

ULTIMATUM CD 194.21

UMBRELLA CD 234.5 SM 85.11

UMBRIA SM 4.34

UNABASHED FO 117.22

UNABATEABLE LH 34.16

UNABLE TL 45.30 FO 122.6 156.18
  SM 124.33 VG 76.37

UNACCESSIBLE SM 119.25

UNACCOUNTABLY VG 45.7

UNALLEVIATED LH 33.31

UNALTERABLE FO 158.21

UNAPPROACHABLE SM 109.2

UNASSUMINGLY VG 58.4

UNAWARE TL 87.15 SM 33.22
  VG 14.35 31.7 31.8 31.11

UNAWARES SM 101.27 MD 207.29

UNBALANCED VG 31.14

UNBEARABLE SM 112.32 VG 11.29

UNBEARABLY LH 20.21

UNBELIEF VG 27.11 27.16 27.22

UNBELIEVER VG 26.39 28.28 61.5

UNBELIEVERS VG 28.27

UNBELIEVING SM 54.10

UNBLINKING FO 146.32

UNBORN MD 205.19

UNBROKEN SM 21.17 MD 164.35
  206.25

UNBURIED SM 152.32

UNBUTTONED CD 190.4

UNCANNILY SM 60.17 VG 70.7
  80.33

UNCANNY TL 50.3 50.5 78.40
  96.12 100.23 102.42 SM 7.2
  14.36 15.10 22.14 46.23
  59.34 74.22 88.37 108.39
  143.31 147.30 152.10 VG 43.32
  53.33 70.23

UNCARING SM 148.28 MD 180.29

UNCERTAIN LH 34.35 FO 130.18
  152.9 CD 254.3 SM 93.38
  VG 23.24

UNCERTAINTY TL 48.16 96.12

UNCHANGED FO 164.41

UNCHANGING FO 146.23 165.7
  SM 41.5

UNCLE SM 61.15 62.16 98.2
  105.3

UNCLEAN TL 92.36 SM 5.23
  MD 164.15 VG 9.6 9.7 64.8

UNCLE FRED VG 4.11 7.35
  10.25 10.37 30.24 40.29
  40.35 40.41

UNCLOSE SM 68.15

UNCOMFORTABLE FO 119.9
  CD 226.36 SM 99.33 104.23
  119.39 VG 13.22

UNCOMFORTABLY SM 40.12 41.22
  84.9

UNCOMMUNICATIVE SM 61.37

UNCONCERNED SM 25.12 148.27

UNCONCERNEDLY CD 236.37
  SM 98.20 MD 172.9

UNCONFESSEDLY VG 56.5

UNCONNECTED VG 49.33

UNCONSCIONABLE SM 112.38

UNCONSCIOUS TL 99.4 99.7
  99.33 103.24 FO 123.6
  132.42 163.13 179.35
  CD 222.16 SM 25.39 76.5
  148.20 MD 187.3 VG 15.11
  15.18 73.37 74.16 77.23

UNCONSCIOUSLY LH 6.26 TL 82.4
  FO 118.37 128.7 SM 32.26
  68.22 101.14 MD 207.14

UNCONSCIOUSNESS FO 118.22
  CD 222.17 SM 137.29
  VG 73.39

UNCONVENTIONAL VG 8.38 61.2
  61.9

UNCOUTHLY FO 142.35

UNCOVERED TL 60.31 VG 77.1

UNCREATED SM 144.23

UNCTION SM 37.21 39.34

UNCUT TL 51.36

UND AUCH ZWEI FLUGLEIN HATT
  TL 71.4 80.11

UNDAUNTED SM 142.11

UNLOCKED MD 202.30

UNLOOSENED CD 245.7

UNLOVELY TL 79.3

UNLUCKY SM 5.21 5.22 5.29

UNMARRIED CD 211.40 MD 188.41
  VG 78.38

UNMATCHED SM 17.38 39.11

UNMENTIONABILITY VG 5.15

UNMISTAKABLE TL 44.31

UNMOVED SM 59.23 VG 58.19

UNMOVING FO 140.12

UNNATURAL TL 54.14 FO 163.28
  SM 44.20 66.32 128.32

UNNATURALLY FO 121.35 VG 71.19

UNNECESSARY CD 208.11 249.32

UNNERVED SM 66.24

UNOCCUPIED VG 42.11

UNOFFICIALLY CD 188.10

UNOPENED SM 64.14

UNPEELED FO 157.29

UNPHYSICAL MD 176.16

UNPINNED LH 29.11

UNPLEASANT TL 50.22 54.14 85.36
  CD 198.36 SM 50.16 50.17
  MD 177.27 192.25 211.11

UNPLEASANTNESS VG 39.30

UNPOPULAR SM 32.32 114.41

UNPRETENTIOUS VG 17.23

UNPUCKERED FO 122.22

UNQUENCHED TL 48.18

UNREAL TL 69.30 FO 165.19
  176.38 CD 198.37 198.38
  SM 111.38 111.40 119.36
  119.40 120.1 125.25 126.32
  130.40

UNREALISABLY FO 176.35

UNREALITIES SM 27.26

UNREALITY CD 199.25

UNREASONABLY VG 43.40

UNREASONING FO 166.35

UNRELAXING SM 73.23

UNRELENTING SM 74.31 152.39

UNRELENTING (CONT.) VG 9.35

UNREMITTING FO 123.6

UNRESTRAINED VG 3.6

UNRIPE CD 241.1

UNROLLED TL 80.8

UNROUSED MD 190.8

UNRUFFLED MD 194.1

UNRUPTURED SM 71.19

UNSATISFACTORY CD 192.10

UNSATISFIED FO 115.6

UNSAVOURY VG 15.20 66.20

UNSCRUPULOUS VG 24.14 28.15
  63.24

UNSCRUPULOUSNESS VG 51.3

UNSEEING TL 45.7 45.13
  CD 188.34 189.8 189.38
  SM 20.15 32.32 MD 199.9
  VG 12.25 48.18

UNSEEN TL 100.22 FO 155.35
  SM 17.37 50.30 50.32 139.8
  139.9 139.14 MD 164.2 173.34
  189.33 196.33 208.25 VG 52.6
  71.15

UNSENTIMENTAL CD 230.35

UNSENTIMENTALITY CD 252.17

UNSHAVEN TL 44.24 SM 18.7

UNSPEAKABLE SM 68.38 MD 166.17
  166.29 VG 62.14

UNSPEAKABLY MD 165.26

UNSPOKEN SM 22.7 25.39 78.22

UNSPREAD MD 180.11

UNSTEADY LH 4.3 MD 172.11

UNSTINTED SM 45.40

UNSUBSTANTIAL CD 199.30

UNSUITABLE VG 55.15

UNSULLIED SM 148.27

UNSURE FO 158.31

UNSURPASSED SM 20.4

UNSUSPECTED VG 80.31

UNSYMPATHETIC SM 21.20

UNTACKLE VG 20.42

UNTAMABLE SM 90.34 141.16

UNTANGLE CD 192.34

UNTANGLED CD 192.36

UNTHINKABLY FO 133.6
  CD 241.30

UNTHINKING FO 128.8

UNTIDY TL 51.18 VG 10.1

UNTIE VG 47.19

UNTIED MD 207.15

UNTIL LH 5.29 9.17 35.28
  FO 114.42 176.7 176.32
  CD 220.1 222.34 225.16
  230.19 263.4 SM 71.9 95.33
  143.13 VG 7.24 18.4 22.16
  35.21 41.32

UNTO TL 78.27 CD 255.25
  SM 117.36 118.1 MD 182.25
  195.20

UNTRUE MD 174.36

UNUSUAL SM 106.18

UNUTTERABLE SM 74.13

UNUTTERABLY SM 87.9

UNWAVERING FO 134.27

UNWEARABLE TL 60.38

UNWHOLESOME SM 29.19

UNWILLING TL 54.17 87.14
  MD 165.26 VG 72.13

UNWILLINGLY TL 52.3 FO 125.18
  131.25 CD 260.22

UNWILLINGNESS FO 152.8

UNWORTHINESS SM 75.16

UNWORTHY SM 75.18 75.19

UNWOUND SM 26.28

UNWRAPPED CD 246.7

UNYIELDING TL 43.32 SM 20.20
  41.1 VG 30.19 67.8

UNYIELDINGNESS SM 14.13

UPBRINGING FO 123.20

UP-CLIMB CD 243.8 252.23

UP-CURVING VG 71.41

UPHEAVAL SM 64.5

UPHEAVING VG 74.15

UPHILL LH 23.13 CD 254.8
  VG 3.24 39.12

UP-HILL LH 6.38 7.6 21.14

UP-HILL (CONT.) FO 169.19

UPHOLSTERED CD 245.18

UPHOLSTERY TL 54.32 79.40

UPKEEP CD 240.36

UPLAND VG 19.5 45.23

UPLIFT CD 249.24 249.25

UPLIFTED FO 158.31

UPPER LH 9.22 10.2 21.22 25.1
    36.28 TL 46.1 84.5 100.37
    FO 122.18 169.2 170.30 172.24
    CD 243.11 243.18 244.5 244.27
    245.27 247.27 251.22 SM 10.4
    23.41 27.6 28.36 34.29 58.27
    147.15 MD 167.19 VG 37.1 44.5
    74.17 75.32

UPPERMOST FO 121.42 VG 61.11

UPRAISED LH 6.31 6.37

UPRIGHTS FO 169.24

UPRISE SM 141.13

UPSET TL 51.21 76.25 FO 139.5
    168.9 SM 114.38

UPSHOT SM 30.1

UPSIDE FO 148.29

UPSLOPE CD 240.33 MD 191.32

UPSTAIRS FO 138.40 140.28 141.4
    142.39 147.15 152.11 155.17
    158.13 CD 205.7 SM 113.13
    154.15 VG 34.28 35.29 35.33
    47.32 78.9

UPTILTING SM 45.5

UP-TORN VG 75.34

UPTURNED SM 69.33

UPWARD-FLOATING SM 101.39

UPWARDLY MD 200.15

UPWARDS CD 240.23 240.24 254.1
    255.5 SM 64.3 66.36 MD 189.35
    VG 18.3 18.22 37.13 65.35

URGE MD 196.26

URGED LH 8.1 23.31

URGING CD 212.23 MD 202.36

USE LH 8.2 TL 60.7 65.31 65.35
    88.16 FO 145.11 SM 28.22
    64.33 117.31 145.2 155.28

USED LH 24.24 TL 44.17 63.21
    63.23 67.38 67.39 70.22
    78.36 FO 123.35 151.19 166.4
    176.16 CD 192.32 200.22
    200.36 203.1 204.17 209.5

USED (CONT.) 209.10 209.33
    220.27 222.6 223.12 223.14
    230.1 SM 4.22 10.19 15.29
    26.21 43.22 64.17 85.26
    86.25 91.24 103.18 104.27
    106.2 107.2 107.10 129.6
    134.23 MD 195.14 VG 29.3

USEFUL TL 64.41

USELESS FO 150.31 VG 65.1

USING LH 23.12 CD 255.7

USUAL FO 114.39 128.17 134.28
    155.39 169.14 SM 22.35 27.8
    79.6 90.10 119.8 124.10
    149.40 VG 7.28 18.30 25.24
    42.11 45.6 69.39

USUALLY LH 15.10 FO 113.1
    115.25 119.11 135.1 157.41
    CD 255.8 258.8 258.15 263.16
    SM 37.16 136.27 MD 192.38
    VG 33.30 70.15

US'UD LH 4.9

UTENSILS LH 29.25

UTMOST FO 176.33 SM 82.13

UTTER TL 44.23 77.36 CD 204.2
    SM 4.19 38.18 136.7 MD 165.31
    166.20 168.29 VG 26.39

UTTERED CD 194.20 232.15
    SM 56.4 VG 78.33

UTTERLY LH 27.3 TL 78.37 102.2
    FO 176.5 CD 243.19 SM 27.5
    45.28 81.38 136.8 MD 168.26
    170.15 177.20 211.15 VG 26.41
    30.22 42.11 55.10 59.14

VACANCY CD 191.17

VACANT FO 139.33 148.37 170.30
    175.28 CD 191.10

VAGABOND MD 190.30 191.1 191.17
    192.34 VG 77.5

VAGUE FO 134.20 135.8 136.40
    142.10 142.16 142.19 158.38
    163.1 CD 197.29 199.33 211.32
    SM 9.28 75.12 75.40 76.5
    130.40 VG 4.7 6.8 6.27 14.22
    24.31 31.5 32.4 32.31 39.29
    40.22 41.3 81.1

VAGUELY LH 32.31 FO 129.19
    134.7 136.35 151.34 153.24
    176.35 CD 188.39 189.3 197.21
    SM 14.5 31.5 38.15 38.16
    38.20 VG 24.30 38.24 38.38
    44.1 47.38 55.7 56.8 71.14

VAGUENESS FO 137.41 SM 82.14
    VG 14.27 61.35

VAIN TL 69.8 76.26 FO 132.3
    SM 9.40 10.1 67.37 76.13
    MD 202.10

VALLEY LH 9.41 21.7 36.31
    CD 238.40 239.9 239.12
    239.20 239.38 240.22 241.9
    241.34 242.22 243.11
    243.19 243.26 243.32
    244.27 245.11 245.27
    247.11 247.19 247.24
    247.30 252.25 252.30
    252.31 252.36 253.12
    253.15 257.6 SM 60.18
    60.37 64.4 101.2 118.13
    147.35 151.39 VG 17.36
    36.9 36.12

VALLEY-BED CD 245.13
    MD 209.21 210.14

VALLEYS CD 243.18 255.14
    SM 102.21 141.39 VG 9.29

VALUABLE TL 85.10 SM 123.19
    123.22 144.16 VG 54.18

VALUE SM 44.16 105.1

VALVE SM 138.25

VAN SM 36.20

VANISHED LH 7.4

VANITY CD 250.21 SM 115.27
    115.28 135.24 MD 175.2
    189.7

VANQUISH VG 26.1

VANTAGE-GROUND SM 22.18

VAPOUR CD 247.20 VG 47.8

VAPOURING CD 247.21

VARIETY TL 87.36 87.39 87.41

VARIOUS CD 185.2 185.26
    210.22 SM 32.22 62.23
    VG 37.19 37.42

VARIOUSLY MD 181.31

VARY TL 98.21

VASSALS TL 89.19 89.20 89.22

VAST LH 20.19 SM 69.27 94.29
    129.3 140.27 146.6 146.37
    147.6 147.11 147.12 147.22
    148.18 148.25 152.39
    153.39 MD 171.10 171.17
    175.20 183.33 200.15
    VG 45.25 67.1 72.20

VAULTING CD 185.2

VEERING CD 200.34

VEGETABLES VG 71.39

VEHEMENT LH 26.23

VEHEMENTLY LH 17.13

VEHICLE CD 260.8

VEIL TL 83.7 83.8 83.20
   FO 178.22 178.23 SM 112.31

VEILED LH 22.1 36.30

VEILS SM 140.11

VEINED TL 46.40 CD 247.36
   VG 18.34

VEINS LH 8.22 TL 75.37
   FO 163.14 CD 224.6 236.7
   VG 7.3 34.34

VELOURS VG 31.29

VELVET TL 98.22 CD 245.18
   245.19 247.13 VG 21.40 30.16
   63.29

VELVETY LH 21.38 FO 142.9

VENERABLE SM 54.6

VENGEANCE SM 73.8 73.10 73.34
   110.20

VENISON CD 256.32

VENOM SM 25.28

VENOMOUS FO 142.32 SM 114.7

VENOMOUSLY SM 58.27 VG 66.17

VENTRILOQUIST TL 100.23

VENTURE LH 11.37

VENTURED LH 32.17 CD 187.36

VENTURING CD 254.3

VENUS TL 77.33 79.34 MD 189.8

VERBALLY VG 61.1

VERDICT VG 4.8

VERGE SM 56.37

VERILY FO 176.20

VERMILION FO 142.19 SM 150.32

VERMIN SM 154.10

VERNACULAR CD 232.23 MD 204.1

VERSATILE CD 230.32

VERSE TL 80.9

VERSION CD 229.9

VESSEL LH 3.21

VESSELS VG 67.9

VESTAL VIRGINS SM 139.10

VEXATION SM 14.15

VEXED VG 41.18

VIA SM 3.29

VIBRATING MD 172.10 VG 29.30

VIBRATION CD 253.23 SM 6.22
   MD 172.12

VIBROFAT VG 35.27

VICAR LH 11.12 11.14 11.20
   11.23 11.31 12.20 12.24
   13.10 13.21 13.36 14.20
   TL 65.29 VG 3.3 3.15 3.27
   4.4

VICARAGE LH 5.40 6.26 16.39
   25.28 26.21 39.23 VG 3.15
   3.26 5.30 33.20

VICAR'S VG 3.1

VICE SM 80.9 VG 77.11

VICE-LIKE VG 77.14

VICIOUS TL 90.29 FO 167.6
   CD 255.28 SM 80.7 80.8 80.11
   98.26 115.33

VICIOUSLY SM 24.30 66.26 71.12

VICTIM TL 78.37 SM 109.26

VICTIMS CD 225.29

VICTORIA SM 5.5 28.8

VICTORIA, QUEEN (SEE QUEEN
   VICTORIA)

VICTORY SM 154.3 VG 67.16

VICTUAL MD 197.33

VIENNA CD 232.17 257.11 SM 3.29

VIER JAHRESZEITEN CD 202.12
   204.7 217.1

VIEW LH 4.35 TL 49.25 FO 146.13
   CD 203.7 203.15 203.34
   SM 38.5 81.6

VIGOROUS FO 127.5 SM 7.7 32.20

VIGOROUSLY SM 63.25

VIGOUR LH 3.27 SM 46.6

VILE CD 263.27 VG 59.35

VILLA CD 230.18 234.15 234.18
   234.30 265.27 265.37 SM 128.6
   MD 185.32 191.35 192.10 194.5
   196.38 199.38 201.12

VILLAGE LH 23.21 TL 98.3 98.14
   99.16 FO 121.16 125.35 125.38
   126.40 127.30 127.38 128.4
   135.20 141.15 175.11
   CD 239.11 239.12 SM 29.4
   29.18 36.11 36.15 37.36 44.1
   53.16 53.24 57.40 100.40
   109.9 142.18 143.5 147.17
   153.6 153.18 MD 182.8 183.7

VILLAGE (CONT.) VG 3.22 3.25
   9.32 17.34 17.41 36.7
   36.12 36.23 72.1

VILLAGES SM 30.15 60.23
   102.20 125.28 VG 16.32

VINDICATION SM 73.3

VINDICTIVE LH 11.19 32.30
   CD 261.14 SM 12.15 21.33
   72.10

VINEGAR TL 92.5

VINES MD 163.9

VIOLATE MD 184.5

VIOLATION SM 112.37

VIOLENCE SM 145.31 VG 77.20

VIOLENT TL 93.10 SM 144.28
   149.40

VIOLENTLY LH 37.27 VG 8.20
   75.14

VIOLET MD 189.33 204.16

VIOLET-COLOURED TL 76.16

VIOLET-DARK MD 189.39

VIOLETS TL 98.20

VIPER CD 242.9

VIRGIN LH 5.36 TL 105.24
   FO 149.15 SM 78.22 86.24
   122.20 140.6 MD 178.1
   196.26 VG 42.16 42.24
   43.30 57.33 62.35 64.12

VIRGINAL SM 86.27 VG 43.29

VIRGINITY TL 104.38 105.25
   SM 157.11 MD 178.2
   VG 40.18 48.2 48.11 48.18

VIRGINS SM 139.11 140.3

VIRILITY SM 9.16

VIRTUE SM 53.2 MD 182.40
   183.2

VIRTUES CD 226.21

VISIBILITY TL 67.13

VISIBLE TL 67.15 CD 243.28
   SM 99.20 99.22 VG 76.39

VISION FO 118.22 146.36
   CD 189.9 SM 14.25 68.40
   68.41 69.32 147.38 153.37
   VG 65.15

VISIT TL 44.8 85.36 SM 94.5
   VG 54.9

VISITED SM 4.38

VISITOR TL 46.15 CD 195.39
  197.21 198.5 202.1 236.33
  SM 9.1

VISITORS TL 59.32 VG 14.42

VISITS TL 64.23 85.34 86.8
  SM 6.14

VISTA LH 23.19

VISUAL SM 94.40 VG 43.9

VISUALLY SM 130.20

VITAL LH 22.5 CD 224.8
  SM 130.21 VG 43.17

VITALITY LH 13.6 SM 26.34

VITALLY TL 95.38

VITALS SM 130.28 130.29
  MD 206.1

VITRIOL VG 7.2

VITRIOLIC VG 14.24

VIVID FO 117.2 122.15 155.37
  CD 253.1 SM 13.31 13.33
  MD 205.3 208.6

VIVIDLY FO 126.24 SM 140.29
  MD 186.16

VIVISECTED SM 30.33

VIVISECTION SM 31.3

VOCABULARY VG 11.11

VOCIFERATED VG 34.23

VOGLEIN TL 80.13 80.15 80.20

VOICE LH 5.8 5.16 6.6 6.35
  7.11 8.30 8.37 8.42 9.6
  9.24 9.39 10.3 10.16 10.36
  11.7 11.28 12.30 21.11 25.20
  26.7 27.33 31.9 32.32 33.20
  33.28 36.39 TL 46.19 51.42
  56.15 63.7 67.30 69.26 74.24
  75.11 75.32 75.33 76.6 76.19
  76.24 77.8 77.15 78.2 78.7
  78.40 79.9 79.18 90.41 95.40
  99.34 107.16 FO 114.23 119.35
  119.38 119.39 120.1 120.14
  121.27 121.41 123.19 124.5
  125.42 129.5 129.17 131.28
  131.35 131.36 131.41 132.12
  132.16 132.25 132.32 133.6
  133.34 135.12 136.40 139.35
  139.41 140.13 140.25 140.27
  141.2 142.6 142.9 142.14
  142.28 143.33 144.4 145.22
  147.16 147.38 153.31 154.27
  158.29 158.37 159.7 163.2
  169.13 169.31 170.36 171.22
  173.16 173.19 174.23 179.38
  CD 183.14 183.18 184.25
  187.29 189.28 191.32 191.41
  192.13 197.29 199.22 199.23
  199.27 199.39 199.42 200.23
  200.24 200.30 210.10 211.4

VOICE (CONT.) 215.2 217.2
  220.18 220.32 234.4
  234.7 234.41 234.42
  235.16 235.22 236.9 236.17
  236.22 236.24 236.34 242.14
  247.2 258.16 SM 11.40 19.10
  19.29 19.31 24.34 34.11
  35.19 39.6 39.9 39.12 52.31
  74.29 76.20 82.35 84.10
  102.30 106.30 107.22 114.25
  135.39 150.1 MD 164.32 168.5
  171.1 171.33 175.9 183.9
  183.18 201.21 211.4 VG 13.27
  17.28 25.12 25.17 25.18
  32.11 33.9 34.26 38.8 38.37
  48.15 48.37 49.4 50.34 51.15
  52.5 63.26 69.1 69.8 69.12
  71.20 71.21 71.32

VOICES LH 11.15 32.4 FO 153.23
  CD 199.38 234.30 266.2
  SM 53.14 74.12 135.32
  MD 164.3 VG 7.39 40.20

VOID FO 178.2 CD 225.22
  SM 89.38 MD 168.29 VG 78.9

VOLITION FO 131.10

VOLUBILITY CD 230.32

VOLUMES SM 51.25

VOLUMINOUS VG 21.8

VOLUNTARILY TL 90.27

VON POLDI, HERR REGIERUNGSTRAT
  (SEE HERR REGIERUNGSRAT VON
  POLDI)

VON PRIELAU-CAROLATH, FRAULEIN
  (SEE FRAULEIN VON PRIELAU-
  CAROLATH)

VORACIOUS CD 252.7

VORACIOUSLY FO 123.10

VORACITY MD 164.30

VOTED VG 18.27

VOWING CD 214.10 226.24

VOYAGE SM 125.37

VOYNICH HALL TL 64.27 64.29
  68.15 72.19 81.14 81.16 83.1
  92.16 108.13

VULGAR CD 216.8 216.11 217.41
  SM 54.5 72.36 81.39 124.4
  MD 194.14 194.25 VG 4.16

VULGARITY TL 94.17 CD 217.38
  217.39 217.40

VULNERABILITY FO 161.30

VULNERABLE FO 130.14 161.23
  161.26

WADDED VG 43.12

WADDLED CD 245.21

WADED SM 141.7 VG 14.9

WADING TL 59.1

WAFFLE-IRON SM 44.24

WAFFLES SM 44.24

WAFTED MD 200.8

WAFTS LH 21.17

WAGE FO 160.40 SM 41.6
  41.12 41.15 107.29 138.3

WAGES SM 107.31

WAGGING FO 172.38 CD 257.26

WAGGLED FO 172.37

WAGON LH 3.11 3.13 15.26
  23.12 25.15

WAGONER LH 6.35

WAGONS LH 4.36 20.7

WAIL FO 159.13 MD 206.9
  206.11

WAILED FO 133.9 138.24

WAILING LH 10.4 MD 206.23

WAIST LH 23.14 23.24 23.41
  24.15 27.11 FO 160.18
  CD 197.16

WAISTCOAT FO 155.41 CD 214.27

WAISTS VG 42.41 43.1

WAIT LH 18.35 18.41 TL 57.34
  64.15 66.14 73.7 FO 147.25
  159.37 172.33 CD 183.30
  186.4 186.6 186.9 236.30
  262.26 SM 35.31 62.6 72.32
  87.2 91.37 109.7 112.19
  115.29 117.9 MD 174.22
  189.28 190.3 190.11 191.11
  201.19 201.20 208.24
  VG 24.19 53.17

WAITED LH 7.30 10.2 29.3
  30.1 35.29 37.29 TL 100.16
  100.17 100.20 101.15 101.16
  101.18 FO 119.33 130.9
  132.10 132.40 133.1 153.14
  162.8 CD 201.35 207.40
  212.15 213.38 247.13 249.3
  252.3 260.20 SM 11.13
  63.23 76.13 87.6 107.8
  129.28 159.1 159.2
  MD 168.30 190.5 193.18
  200.32 202.15 206.29
  208.26 VG 40.20 48.13

WAITING LH 3.16 6.33 21.34
  22.20 TL 75.28 75.30
  FO 122.31 139.5 139.37
  147.2 160.40 168.32 179.10
  179.25 CD 184.30 205.19

WASTED TL 46.10 FO 137.4

WASTEFUL SM 4.11

WASTING SM 145.10

WATCH TL 86.21 FO 129.31 146.16
155.39 173.42 175.17 178.19
178.21 CD 251.23 251.30
SM 5.17 9.12 26.2 71.18
103.3 139.26 147.6 155.10
MD 187.23 209.30 210.27
VG 39.4

WATCHES SM 42.29 79.1

WATCHFUL FO 133.1 135.13 158.8
SM 18.2 21.18 32.31 58.6
73.22 134.23 146.21 MD 171.32
VG 20.1

WATCHFULLY SM 146.22

WATCHFULNESS SM 18.20 21.25

WATER LH 21.20 21.32 21.40
29.32 29.37 29.39 30.40
TL 54.40 57.32 58.27 86.21
FO 118.35 119.17 176.3 176.6
176.7 176.12 CD 234.40 235.2
235.7 235.9 235.16 235.20
235.23 235.40 236.5 236.25
237.16 237.27 237.31 241.3
241.12 241.14 241.17 241.24
241.31 242.3 242.8 244.28
244.31 245.6 245.7 247.38
253.30 256.15 SM 14.9 18.30
40.18 40.29 52.1 69.14
126.40 127.8 127.10 128.27
132.27 133.11 138.24 140.37
141.8 141.27 142.3 142.4
142.6 142.9 142.10 144.5
144.8 144.19 149.1 149.2
154.7 155.22 MD 167.5 169.5
169.9 177.22 185.11 186.6
191.25 191.27 191.38 197.10
201.32 VG 3.24 5.3 15.9
17.37 23.33 47.25 69.2 69.8
69.13 70.23 71.20 72.10
72.23 72.28 72.35 73.1 73.4
73.7 73.9 73.10 73.19 73.25
73.29 73.31 73.34 73.38
73.42 74.4 74.14 74.15
74.35 74.38 75.38 76.1
76.14 76.18 76.21 80.40
81.20

WATER-CRESSES SM 112.5

WATERED SM 144.9

WATERFALLS CD 243.25 247.21

WATER-GOLD TL 58.12

WATERING SM 16.39

WATERING-PLACE CD 229.16

WATERLESS SM 152.5

WATER-LILIES FO 135.39

WATER-LOGGED CD 253.35

WATER-MEADOWS CD 239.33 239.38

WATERPROOF SM 93.3 93.9

WATERS CD 234.42 243.18 243.24
243.34 245.28 248.38 253.5
SM 126.13 149.5 VG 71.32
75.33 76.27 76.29

WATER'S CD 234.22 234.30
MD 198.24 198.37 VG 76.42

WATER-SIDE CD 229.18

WATER-TAPS SM 145.15

WATER-WAVE CD 238.16

WATERY CD 253.37 SM 135.32
136.4 VG 74.42

WATERY-SOFT SM 136.18

WATSON (SEE MR. WATSON)

WAVE FO 163.4 176.9 176.10
MD 164.38 166.3 166.8 171.29
182.1 VG 72.32

WAVE-CRESTS MD 171.11

WAVED LH 6.29 6.41 7.2 7.10
CD 186.12 232.19 254.36
VG 71.31

WAVE-FRONT VG 72.23

WAVERED VG 47.8 75.1

WAVERING CD 235.39 MD 191.33

WAVES SM 69.1 69.4 126.36
127.10 MD 191.30 192.12

WAVE-TIP MD 172.13

WAVE-WALL CD 252.29

WAVING LH 4.32 FO 176.12
VG 71.31

WAVY VG 30.15

WAXEN MD 168.38

WAXY MD 167.41 169.17 175.20

WAYS FO 162.32 CD 221.37
SM 93.19 115.2 151.31
VG 14.22 26.32 40.17

WAYWARD VG 23.14

WAYWARDNESS VG 24.32

WEAK TL 82.13 FO 128.16 173.1
173.2 CD 206.1 SM 87.17
MD 182.9 VG 7.17 64.40 65.17

WEAKENED SM 14.20

WEAKER FO 177.2

WEAKNESS VG 5.5 7.9

WEAKNESSES VG 4.17 6.14 6.20

WEALTH VG 52.32

WEALTHY SM 31.10 VG 50.37

WEANING CD 224.20

WEAPON SM 21.40

WEAPON-LIKE SM 8.32

WEAPONS CD 245.28 SM 100.34
101.15

WEAR TL 60.12 60.27 61.29
76.14 FO 156.7 156.10
CD 197.27 248.12 SM 23.17
158.36 VG 46.40

WEARIED CD 186.17 SM 117.37

WEARILY CD 199.38 MD 192.4

WEARINESS TL 45.29 52.20
SM 45.15 68.38 68.39
87.38 119.15 MD 175.19
192.4 194.35

WEARING FO 147.33 155.41
157.28 168.37 CD 190.3
214.17 233.26 SM 85.29
144.24 VG 40.25 45.31

WEARISOME SM 31.38

WEARS CD 184.3

WEARY LH 28.34 TL 45.35
FO 169.22 175.38 SM 13.35
68.19 87.9 87.10 125.1
138.36 139.12 139.13

WEASEL CD 261.9 VG 11.25

WEASELISH CD 239.29 240.2

WEATHER TL 83.5 FO 124.28
CD 204.14 204.32 237.12
256.12 SM 63.37 126.34
126.40 VG 31.24 52.27
52.28 56.1 58.2 58.7
59.4 68.2 69.22

WEB SM 104.16

WE'D SM 51.32 114.19
VG 17.30 79.28

WEDDED VG 4.21

WEDDING FO 150.17 150.19
157.22 157.25 164.26
CD 208.20 214.10 214.17
SM 5.27 VG 74.8

WEDDING-NIGHT TL 75.28

WEDGE LH 15.37 CD 241.11
241.13 241.15

WEDGED CD 241.22

WEEDING SM 38.27

WIDE (CONT.) CD 186.12 187.6
  201.19 201.26 201.30 231.40
  232.13 239.17 240.26 243.19
  243.20 243.26 257.22 SM 15.1
  15.16 20.36 60.18 67.15
  74.31 82.32 129.4 129.5
  136.1 MD 171.24 188.11 VG 8.41
  17.19 17.33 26.27 49.17
  49.42 70.6 79.32

WIDE-APART FO 169.24

WIDE-EYED TL 58.13 FO 128.19
  134.31 156.36

WIDELY FO 122.16

WIDENED TL 79.13 SM 34.35

WIDENESS FO 137.40

WIDE-OPEN CD 184.9 216.35
  259.27 MD 167.39

WIDER TL 85.23 FO 158.20 178.32
  178.41 MD 181.20

WIDE-TOPPED SM 136.1

WIDOW TL 48.11 MD 188.38 196.39
  210.1 VG 4.33 16.6 70.17

WIDOWER CD 231.29

WIDOWHOOD SM 94.35

WIDTH TL 47.9

WIELDED SM 15.10

WIELDS SM 111.34

WIFE TL 45.5 50.22 55.8 55.14
  61.9 61.17 62.1 62.30 69.34
  77.32 81.7 91.24 93.13 96.18
  96.20 104.27 105.12 106.34
  106.35 106.42 107.15 107.17
  108.10 108.26 FO 131.14
  151.18 161.13 175.19 CD 186.8
  188.14 190.29 190.30 190.31
  190.40 202.3 202.19 203.41
  205.10 206.4 206.14 214.2
  225.20 226.7 232.30 246.39
  247.11 250.26 261.25 262.8
  264.7 265.4 265.10 265.12
  265.15 265.16 265.18 SM 6.35
  10.10 15.3 31.17 61.19 61.39
  62.1 62.10 66.14 68.6 83.25
  84.29 86.13 106.27 127.34
  127.38 139.40 142.20 143.2
  145.12 MD 163.17 163.31 164.6
  164.18 169.2 169.16 VG 3.1
  3.6 3.33 4.18 38.30 46.27
  52.41 63.42 69.32 70.40

WIFE'S TL 91.35 CD 214.10 216.6
  216.15 217.5 218.32 224.39
  MD 177.9

WILD LH 10.3 11.7 11.37 13.39
  TL 47.11 47.12 75.29 100.37
  100.38 FO 113.26 125.11
  127.26 135.25 152.31 174.1
  174.3 178.39 CD 239.20 239.27
  239.30 240.41 247.17 SM 13.11

WILD (CONT.) 14.23 50.10 50.19
  73.19 73.23 73.24 73.32
  90.34 93.17 120.24 128.32
  130.8 130.9 133.38 141.22
  142.15 142.34 149.2 150.17
  150.18 151.1 151.5 151.15
  151.37 152.3 152.11 152.29
  154.3 158.36 158.39 159.1
  159.7 MD 164.39 166.32
  167.16 195.33 205.35 211.9
  VG 32.15 46.22 · 74.35 78.41

WILD-CAT LH 13.5 TL 63.41 64.3
  66.2 67.28 67.32 69.2 69.3
  69.9

WILD CAT LH 13.4 13.9 37.31
  SM 17.36

WILDER CD 239.19

WILD-EYED VG 3.34

WILDLY LH 7.2 27.8 TL 83.25
  FO 136.13 147.12 CD 183.11
  SM 69.34 130.21 VG 34.28

WILFUL MD 175.13

WILHELM TL 53.16

WILHELM, KAISER (SEE KAISER
  WILHELM II)

WILLED SM 95.16 MD 205.7

WILLIAM GRENFEL FO 120.6

WILLIAMS'S SM 109.40

WILLING FO 124.9 152.8 SM 12.31
  19.4 73.31 112.8

WILLINGLY TL 89.6

WILL-LESS VG 48.20

WILLOW CD 234.25

WILLS FO 131.2 SM 25.38 25.39
  26.29 27.11 MD 196.3

WILL-TO-POWER VG 15.16

WILLY-NILLY SM 148.36 148.37

WILT MD 197.20 209.22

WIN LH 22.41 TL 95.33 FO 177.33
  SM 153.31 153.34 154.2

WINCE LH 4.5 11.5

WINCED LH 4.8 FO 140.20
  MD 205.34 VG 64.35

WINCHESTER CD 208.32

WINCING LH 4.15 6.5 MD 166.30
  VG 28.1

WIND TL 91.28 102.39 FO 116.36
  119.11 119.26 131.1 135.41
  136.13 136.18 137.1 168.38
  169.17 CD 237.15 242.36 243.3

WIND (CONT.) 248.6 261.19
  SM 13.24 36.40 66.8 90.14
  99.8 126.11 146.6 MD 185.1
  185.11 185.23 186.17
  187.21 190.22 190.24
  191.22 191.31 192.12
  195.1 200.8 208.18 VG 3.14
  3.19 12.29 27.2 45.22
  54.31 75.38 76.22 76.27
  76.31

WIND-BELLS SM 26.41

WIND-BLOWN VG 54.3

WINDED LH 11.29 14.10

WINDER LH 16.36

WINDING CD 243.36 VG 36.6

WINDMILL TL 53.27

WINDOW TL 56.39 97.28 102.39
  FO 130.3 147.15 160.37
  164.40 CD 185.26 186.37
  200.39 201.17 201.23
  201.27 202.26 208.26
  219.24 219.29 219.32
  219.33 219.36 220.26
  226.41 227.2 227.5 234.21
  SM 32.17 65.22 84.28 85.4
  86.28 90.9 90.28 91.26
  116.34 VG 11.23 11.26
  11.37 25.35 26.3 35.37
  36.27 36.39 37.14 37.16
  39.3 58.6 66.38 74.33
  75.32 76.13 76.36 78.11
  78.22 78.30 78.39 79.31
  80.18

WINDOW-CURTAINS VG 62.12

WINDOW FUND VG 25.34 26.6
  30.34 31.22

WINDOW-LEDGE CD 220.24

WINDOW-PANE CD 201.25

WINDOWS LH 21.8 TL 97.25
  FO 154.39 CD 186.22 SM 28.16
  VG 72.42 74.31

WINDOW-SEAT TL 87.7 87.18
  97.30

WINDOW-SILL CD 219.28

WINDS CD 263.16 SM 133.35

WINDY MD 191.40 192.5

WINE TL 69.30 CD 245.9
  245.34 256.35 SM 97.12
  127.41 MD 177.1 177.22
  201.32

WINE-GLASS CD 230.18

WINE-JAR MD 199.3 200.25

WINE-REDDENED CD 232.14

WING TL 62.13 CD 215.1

WOMAN (CONT.) SM 107.30 107.33
  107.34 107.40 108.3 108.9
  108.11 108.12 108.14 108.17
  108.21 108.26 108.37 112.32
  121.5 135.12 135.30 135.34
  136.14 136.19 136.21 136.29
  136.35 137.2 137.5 139.12
  139.39 145.27 147.3 148.32
  148.35 148.39 152.9 153.3
  153.17 MD 163.17 169.2 169.4
  170.5 170.18 173.12 173.13
  175.11 176.40 177.22 177.28
  177.38 178.5 178.37 178.38
  181.22 182.3 185.8 186.12
  186.26 188.29 190.9 190.17
  190.26 191.10 192.9 192.13
  192.31 194.17 195.18 195.21
  195.27 195.35 196.15 196.23
  197.25 197.32 197.35 198.16
  198.17 198.26 198.35 199.5
  199.16 199.35 200.29 200.33
  200.35 200.37 201.8 201.24
  201.35 201.38 202.34 203.5
  203.27 204.6 204.22 204.26
  204.28 205.12 205.14 205.19
  205.25 205.32 206.13 206.33
  207.1 207.5 207.23 207.41
  208.13 208.24 208.26 208.31
  208.33 209.6 210.3 210.9
  211.20 VG 3.10 4.23 4.42 7.8
  10.3 12.1 14.40 16.20 19.10
  19.14 19.23 19.26 20.38 21.5
  21.17 21.30 21.31 21.35 22.2
  22.7 22.11 22.15 23.2 23.7
  23.13 23.21 24.1 24.37 25.13
  28.33 30.4 30.10 30.14 30.21
  30.34 31.27 34.42 35.11
  45.33 46.1 46.13 46.17 47.2
  47.5 47.14 47.31 48.24 48.34
  49.4 49.9 49.15 52.2 52.6
  55.15 61.39 61.40 63.12
  65.20 65.26 65.37 66.30
  67.21 67.37 69.15 69.32
  70.41 78.13

WOMAN-FLOW MD 196.27

WOMAN-GODHEAD TL 82.21

WOMANHOOD LH 29.13 TL 82.26

WOMAN-LIKE CD 202.39 251.1
  263.9

WOMANLY LH 38.28 TL 82.28
  FO 156.38 MD 201.36

WOMAN-MATES TL 59.15

WOMAN-PRESENCE MD 202.36

WOMAN'S LH 10.1 27.16 27.33
  FO 145.21 154.16 155.24
  155.27 156.37 157.4 157.5
  178.23 CD 183.14 196.41
  235.12 SM 47.1 75.39 96.26
  136.5 136.15 138.35 145.34
  149.41 MD 201.18 VG 24.35
  34.15 48.37

WOMB TL 107.40 MD 188.25 189.18

WOMEN LH 5.28 5.31 TL 48.27
  51.12 72.12 87.21 87.31
  90.34 FO 123.39 127.6 137.7

WOMEN (CONT.) 143.29 143.38
  145.30 145.40 152.11
  153.22 154.41 156.2
  162.13 177.36 CD 193.20
  204.20 206.36 207.23 209.9
  213.4 214.8 226.17 230.36
  233.6 233.10 233.19 234.34
  238.14 238.18 238.21 248.12
  264.9 264.16 SM 3.11 6.38
  15.41 29.20 31.22 32.32
  32.33 35.1 41.20 49.4 49.7
  50.13 90.28 91.32 94.4
  107.28 108.10 108.30 120.10
  120.13 120.26 120.30 124.9
  124.40 135.4 135.5 135.11
  135.14 135.31 139.22 157.8
  157.9 MD 172.22 178.5 178.36
  179.35 184.8 189.25 189.28
  198.9 198.22 199.40 200.3
  VG 3.10 6.17 8.1 43.22 53.3
  54.35 55.40 59.41 67.32
  70.40 71.8 71.36

WOMEN'S FO 155.4 SM 52.12

WON FO 132.38 174.32 174.41
  175.5 175.7 175.18 CD 190.35
  SM 96.25 96.26

WONDER LH 22.15 22.18 22.22
  32.31 33.39 TL 50.22 50.23
  50.29 81.13 104.42 FO 120.27
  120.40 137.41 149.9 160.10
  CD 183.28 194.2 194.39 212.5
  218.35 233.6 246.29 249.30
  249.41 250.6 255.23 SM 26.19
  46.24 47.25 50.31 50.32
  50.35 55.16 55.21 86.2
  102.29 111.38 112.8 117.31
  123.8 124.39 130.13 131.18
  138.27 MD 176.28 195.25
  196.18 198.3 207.20 207.31
  VG 11.29 17.7 17.24 41.40
  42.23 44.19

WONDERED LH 11.36 21.16 21.38
  36.34 TL 57.3 CD 210.35
  229.23 257.18 260.12
  SM 110.24 119.7 157.34
  MD 206.39 VG 60.1 71.9

WONDERFUL TL 47.3 49.12 66.2
  69.7 75.30 77.24 77.28 77.30
  81.32 81.35 85.14 85.19
  90.31 98.23 106.8 107.23
  107.28 FO 145.23 148.31
  148.32 148.35 149.3 158.28
  CD 184.7 193.29 196.10 196.12
  206.21 218.1 221.31 221.33
  221.34 223.34 226.2 242.10
  242.29 242.31 243.17 244.1
  244.7 244.8 244.33 249.11
  256.30 SM 10.12 31.5 36.39
  47.7 47.33 48.21 55.11
  118.21 118.24 MD 181.25
  195.18 201.36 VG 13.1 13.6
  13.14 18.2 60.1 60.5

WONDERFULLY FO 178.5 CD 232.29
  240.24 SM 58.24

WONDERING LH 32.24 TL 55.29
  FO 120.1 148.41 148.42 158.26
  163.24 SM 97.37 MD 167.11
  168.16 195.7

WONDERINGLY LH 34.30 SM 68.30

WONDER-NOTE FO 120.5

WONDER-STRUCK VG 72.25

WONDER-WORKER MD 176.30

WONT SM 144.29

WOOD LH 11.34 TL 105.32
  FO 115.11 115.36 117.2
  117.29 118.38 119.6 119.12
  119.22 127.27 148.2 168.39
  CD 185.20 240.26 SM 59.36
  102.13 102.24 151.29
  MD 185.5 187.26 VG 71.28

WOOD-BOX FO 148.1 148.7
  157.20

WOODCOCK FO 130.29

WOODED LH 23.16

WOOD-EDGE FO 116.15 146.6

WOODEN FO 115.9 167.18
  SM 144.7 146.9 MD 169.6
  187.27 VG 22.2 70.21

WOODLINKIN VG 17.34

WOODPECKER SM 151.28

WOOD-PIGEONS FO 127.12

WOODS FO 113.26 168.31
  168.34 171.30 VG 17.17

WOOD'S FO 129.41 SM 102.17
  102.33

WOODSIDE FO 145.42

WOOKEY (SEE GEOFFREY, MR.,
  MRS.)

WOOKEYS LH 15.3

WOOL TL 46.31 SM 45.23
  144.15 MD 186.34 198.17
  VG 24.6

WOOLLEN FO 169.29 CD 200.14
  200.26 261.5 MD 166.31
  167.20 200.24

WOOLLY CD 253.12 257.12
  257.13 257.25 257.37

WOOLS CD 193.19

WOR LH 4.9 4.10 6.40 11.32
  25.19 25.22 38.9

WORD LH 10.23 TL 44.24 50.1
  88.17 91.28 100.10 105.33
  106.12 FO 117.15 132.19
  142.27 149.21 154.12
  154.22 156.25 158.12 166.5
  CD 190.31 204.4 205.4
  207.40 208.20 208.23
  217.12 226.6 232.7 265.9
  SM 39.7 55.37 56.4 72.13

WORD (CONT.) SM 72.17 78.22
  82.37 110.9 114.7 121.36
  124.5 124.16 132.23 149.14
  MD 177.36 180.18 VG 4.38
  19.23 44.33 46.2 49.12 55.30
  78.28

WORDS LH 5.9 26.26 TL 45.20
  53.27 58.9 78.1 87.22 87.25
  88.22 88.25 91.37 93.29
  95.27 96.6 102.26 FO 142.24
  CD 190.25 191.27 191.42
  215.24 215.38 220.32 221.22
  240.2 262.21 262.28 SM 19.24
  27.25 35.14 50.13 83.10
  86.17 92.6 145.2 MD 175.40
  180.19 180.21 182.38 205.16
  VG 21.40 22.21 29.19 30.4
  76.11

WORE LH 7.35 18.27 20.5 28.35
  TL 46.30 51.18 54.15 83.6
  CD 187.12 195.7 207.28 229.27
  233.12 SM 23.17 38.31 85.6
  94.7 119.7 VG 8.32 20.18
  24.5

WORK LH 7.29 8.2 8.8 8.23
  9.11 15.13 17.33 17.36 18.2
  18.30 18.32 19.26 20.21 27.2
  32.8 TL 64.8 64.10 108.41
  FO 113.3 114.7 115.1 115.5
  115.30 123.31 129.23 129.29
  144.20 144.23 150.30 156.14
  168.14 168.27 CD 183.6 193.22
  196.23 212.33 216.9 230.37
  246.25 SM 31.3 38.1 41.15
  44.19 46.14 97.16 104.41
  116.8 131.16 MD 163.16 163.18
  178.12 204.29 VG 52.1

WORK-BASKET TL 70.42 VG 32.24

WORKED LH 7.28 7.38 8.1 9.14
  9.17 20.3 FO 113.37 119.20
  123.23 131.4 171.27 171.39
  CD 216.4 216.5 SM 3.7 7.21
  17.16 41.6 53.19 66.35 81.18
  144.39 MD 163.8 206.18
  VG 10.15 11.18

WORKERS LH 20.17

WORKING FO 126.20 131.23
  CD 216.22 SM 15.38 29.10 38.8
  40.24 41.12 42.33 69.34
  69.37 78.16 144.32 153.1
  MD 186.11 VG 10.5 31.18 71.28

WORKMAN'S FO 155.34

WORKMEN'S VG 10.3

WORK-PEOPLE TL 98.33

WORKS CD 196.4 199.15 228.35
  SM 26.11 70.31 VG 18.36

WORLD LH 4.20 19.17 20.15
  22.24 TL 49.16 49.17 49.20
  54.5 56.42 59.7 61.27 62.3
  62.21 62.23 62.26 62.31 66.5
  67.21 67.23 68.10 68.25
  68.35 69.5 74.9 74.16 74.21
  74.23 74.24 74.31 74.40 75.1

WORLD (CONT.) 77.35 88.11 92.15
  97.29 97.38 99.31 100.32
  100.35 100.42 101.3 103.6
  103.42 104.4 106.42 107.15
  FO 163.17 173.31 176.21
  176.24 177.7 177.37 CD 195.32
  202.34 208.13 213.16 216.10
  221.18 222.16 222.20 224.34
  227.20 234.9 245.36 245.37
  255.13 255.25 256.20 264.2
  SM 4.11 8.16 14.24 14.26
  19.34 19.35 20.2 20.3 20.6
  22.16 22.18 26.33 27.3 27.10
  27.16 30.31 37.2 37.6 51.3
  54.3 58.36 69.20 73.9 77.39
  78.1 85.23 90.5 91.9 95.39
  96.12 96.14 96.15 96.17
  96.23 98.39 99.6 99.7 99.17
  99.20 99.22 99.27 101.20
  101.25 101.28 102.18 102.26
  102.34 105.8 105.15 105.30
  108.8 110.32 111.11 113.36
  116.2 118.3 118.13 118.39
  126.15 126.16 129.13 130.35
  135.3 135.26 136.22 145.40
  146.3 146.24 146.25 146.40
  147.2 148.9 148.15 148.16
  148.26 149.10 151.16 151.23
  153.12 155.12 155.14 156.5
  MD 163.25 164.2 165.40 167.2
  167.3 167.5 167.8 168.25
  168.26 168.27 169.30 170.23
  180.34 180.37 181.13 181.20
  181.29 183.5 183.33 183.39
  184.15 188.11 188.32 188.40
  190.20 198.30 198.31 201.9
  202.6 208.14 210.11 VG 4.22
  4.39 5.11 5.19 7.21 10.6
  18.32 28.14 28.34 44.22
  45.23 53.24 62.25 76.28

WORLD-AGE SM 90.17

WORLD-LABORATORY SM 30.33

WORLDLY SM 15.35 31.6 VG 27.27

WORLDS SM 19.32

WORLD'S TL 107.9 SM 85.34 159.6

WORLD'S-END VG 79.7

WORM VG 4.11 27.15 27.22 27.23

WORN TL 44.11 44.37 54.21
  60.12 82.38 FO 141.20
  MD 192.41 VG 14.12

WORPSWEDE'S CD 228.35

WORPSWEDE'S, THEODOR (SEE THEODOR
  WORPSWEDE'S)

WORRIED LH 8.12 SM 32.1 40.1
  VG 35.11

WORRY FO 154.25 159.3 CD 188.20
  188.23 SM 39.36 39.40 40.2
  VG 79.3

WORRYING CD 188.21

WORSE TL 48.13 48.38 48.42
  83.34 FO 176.30 177.3 177.18

WORSE (CONT.) CD 203.12
  223.9 223.10 SM 34.6 80.7
  110.28 112.2 132.19 132.38
  VG 10.17 12.19 60.29
  62.28 62.30

WORSHIP TL 79.22 79.26 79.37
  81.29 SM 14.38 105.38

WORSHIPPED TL 79.35 SM 64.24
  VG 4.21

WORSHIPPING TL 81.30

WORST LH 19.37 TL 92.32
  CD 216.11 SM 30.39 51.6
  152.33

WORSTED CD 243.4

WORTH LH 27.18 TL 71.31
  CD 196.23 217.24 217.26
  231.31 SM 11.8 31.11
  135.22 155.19 VG 38.32

WORTHY LH 22.21

WOULD-BE VG 16.31 61.1

WOULDNA LH 5.3 11.34

WOULDN'T LH 6.34 17.9 28.16
  TL 48.38 90.11 FO 125.29
  137.25 140.8 142.34
  149.37 154.11 154.13
  161.13 161.14 169.35
  175.41 CD 201.31 207.8
  208.1 208.42 216.9
  226.33 249.28 SM 3.12
  27.30 33.35 36.14 36.34
  40.36 41.26 55.11 60.26
  102.39 155.32 156.36
  VG 5.25 8.28 24.32 26.38
  37.24 55.37 56.16 57.23
  61.1 62.27

WOUND TL 87.42 FO 175.29
  CD 243.11 247.19 SM 26.10
  26.17 26.18 65.23 134.19
  MD 179.34 184.2 184.14
  204.15 205.33 205.34
  206.20 VG 64.37

WOUNDED LH 32.39 TL 44.9
  48.2 49.34 49.41 51.1
  51.23 51.31 81.15 86.28
  103.3 FO 128.40 141.38
  175.26 SM 44.13 112.25
  MD 166.14 VG 3.12

WOUNDS TL 51.1 CD 211.27
  MD 169.17 179.33 180.25
  203.28 205.28 206.10
  206.19

WOUND-SCAR TL 79.4

WOVEN CD 243.34 MD 195.33

WRAITHLIKE SM 27.23

WRAITHS SM 27.34

WRANGLING SM 150.5

WRAP LH 30.23 TL 57.26 57.28
  57.30 105.42 FO 159.29
  CD 186.11 201.16 205.11
  213.29 236.17 236.36 236.40

WRAPPED LH 22.6 TL 100.28
  101.31 101.39 CD 201.16 246.5
  247.32 MD 166.26 166.31
  166.33 167.35 192.35 193.25
  207.41 VG 77.17

WRATH LH 22.25 TL 65.29
  CD 250.21

WRATHFUL LH 36.6

WREATH VG 5.37

WREATHS SM 85.8

WRECK SM 7.38

WRECKAGE VG 77.29 78.9

WRECKED CD 232.35

WRENCHED LH 24.6

WRESTLED VG 75.15

WRETCH FO 148.26 SM 38.40

WRETCHED CD 227.11

WRIGGLE SM 82.22

WRIGGLING SM 156.37

WRINKLED FO 165.9 CD 194.36
  212.17 VG 56.11

WRINKLEDNESS VG 15.33

WRINKLES SM 30.20

WRINKLING FO 123.17 124.31
  137.17 139.27 VG 56.15

WRIST TL 60.37 FO 126.32 158.5
  VG 73.5 73.13

WRISTS TL 61.5 FO 136.3
  SM 117.3 MD 165.33

WRITE LH 36.11 36.13 TL 55.6
  68.10 68.11 68.15 96.26
  FO 149.40 150.23 CD 186.31
  231.41 232.1 232.7 232.25
  246.41 SM 37.31 116.26 116.28
  116.38 117.28 VG 64.15 64.22

WRITER VG 51.26

WRITHE CD 217.13

WRITHED LH 5.21 SM 5.20 94.18

WRITHING LH 32.40 SM 9.41 66.35
  67.3 69.39 72.28 72.39
  VG 32.18

WRITING FO 150.11 CD 185.21
  186.36 188.14 SM 112.19

WRITING-TABLE CD 185.20 186.18

WRITING-TABLE (CONT.) CD 187.10

WRITTEN TL 96.25 SM 86.10
  116.26

WRONG TL 49.33 86.28 87.37
  88.36 90.1 106.22 FO 119.40
  119.42 166.20 169.14 173.11
  CD 192.41 221.5 221.6 229.23
  239.40 252.8 252.15 262.32
  SM 12.26 21.19 35.27 36.20
  39.6 50.18 59.5 70.1 82.8
  114.11 124.30 124.31 139.3
  MD 172.34 172.35 VG 27.40
  28.11 35.4 45.25 60.19

WRONGED MD 174.25 VG 4.2

WRONGNESS TL 93.13

WROTE TL 44.36 70.3 71.2
  CD 225.8 226.14 226.15
  SM 116.40 125.6

WRUNG TL 107.21 CD 215.27
  MD 173.15

WUFFER CD 257.19

WYANDOTTES FO 113.22

WYCH LH 14.33

WYOMING SM 77.32

YAH SM 128.1

YANKEE SM 28.32 28.33 111.21

YAP FO 124.29

YAPPING VG 37.26

YARD FO 114.19 147.24 169.6
  169.21 169.26 169.28 169.38
  170.24 172.35 172.37 CD 260.3
  260.29 SM 11.13 17.29 33.28
  44.9 44.40 45.11 57.24 57.31
  87.27 145.38 146.8 147.23
  147.34 156.23 159.6 MD 163.11
  163.23 168.36 170.5 170.6
  170.20 170.37 177.13 177.16
  179.29 183.15 183.27

YARDS LH 15.27 CD 254.20
  SM 66.29 75.8 137.20 VG 17.13

YAWNING FO 168.28 VG 26.17

YE SM 96.4 MD 182.27 183.10
  191.14

YEA MD 182.23 182.26 183.2
  183.12 204.36 209.20

YEAR LH 4.2 TL 56.24 FO 113.17
  115.19 126.42 176.19
  CD 188.25 231.35 SM 79.13
  140.38 148.6 150.41 154.40
  VG 7.28 15.34 15.35

YEARN TL 82.33

YEARNED CD 217.37

YEARNING TL 100.38 CD 225.36
  233.24 MD 196.25 208.34
  VG 71.3

YEARS LH 13.4 31.40 33.32
  TL 43.5 43.18 43.28 43.29
  43.36 46.21 61.40 62.2
  85.17 92.27 92.30
  FO 118.31 120.9 120.29
  120.32 121.10 123.21
  CD 198.2 202.6 202.8
  202.31 209.18 214.24
  232.31 264.15 SM 5.32
  11.39 45.12 56.16 56.18
  86.31 93.23 94.34 97.7
  100.26 121.6 141.23 142.11
  142.13 142.39 143.36 153.3
  MD 187.36 188.17 188.22
  188.30 VG 3.3 3.31 6.31
  7.11 12.9 12.13 22.39
  52.34 53.26 54.6 67.33

YEARS' TL 93.11

YEASTY SM 143.24

YELL VG 78.20 78.33

YELLED SM 66.30 VG 19.37
  74.21

YELLING FO 146.7 SM 67.6

YELLOW LH 26.30 29.5 TL 46.15
  56.32 72.24 72.26 74.11
  77.40 79.38 98.20 98.22
  101.28 FO 126.29 153.15
  153.16 154.38 166.33
  168.4 CD 212.17 222.27
  236.39 237.24 244.39
  SM 17.15 34.32 57.13
  65.31 67.21 68.29 69.22
  74.4 87.30 94.8 110.40
  126.37 129.3 129.16 130.8
  134.2 134.14 140.36 141.5
  143.8 143.28 150.24 151.7
  151.10 151.20 154.33
  MD 173.13 173.35 185.9
  186.12 186.34 190.27
  199.8 VG 19.22 24.22 49.41
  63.29 68.3 70.5

YELLOW-AND-DARK SM 151.27

YELLOW-AND-RED VG 20.21

YELLOW-AND-WHITE MD 193.35

YELLOW-BROWN TL 73.19

YELLOW-FLOWERED SM 133.38

YELLOW-GREEN FO 172.31

YELLOW-GREY SM 53.30

YELLOWING VG 72.3

YELLOWISH TL 45.11 CD 197.8
  SM 22.4 85.9

YELLOWISH-WHITE SM 143.24

YELLOWLY LH 25.11